The *Dictionary of North Carolina Biography*, the most comprehensive state project of its kind, provides information on some four thousand notable North Carolinians whose accomplishments and occasional misdeeds span more than four centuries. Current plans call for seven volumes to be published over a period of several years. Volume 2, D–G, includes 523 entries.

The *Dictionary* contains the first compiled biographical information for many of these individuals. Included are native North Carolinians, no matter in what area they made their contributions, and non-natives whose contributions were made in North Carolina. All persons included are deceased.

Explorers, inventors, engineers, writers, chemists, business leaders, architects, artists, musicians, colonial leaders, military figures, national and state officials, and outstanding teachers and clergymen are among those recognized. And there are the infamous—pirates, criminals, a hermit, and the man who weighed more than one thousand pounds. Averaging about eight hundred words, each sketch includes the full name of the subject, dates and places of birth and death (when known), family connections, a career description, and a bibliography. Most of the sketches are based on manuscript and contemporary printed sources that are rare or difficult to find. Some research was conducted in Europe.

William S. Powell has been working on the *Dictionary* since 1971 with the help of some seven hundred volunteer contributors.

# DICTIONARY OF NORTH CAROLINA BIOGRAPHY

EDITED BY
WILLIAM S. POWELL

VOLUME 2 D–G

# DICTIONARY OF NORTH CAROLINA BIOGRAPHY

EDITED BY
WILLIAM S. POWELL

VOLUME 2 D–G

The University of North Carolina Press
*Chapel Hill and London*

Manufactured in the United States of America

**Library of Congress Cataloging in Publication Data**

Main entry under title:

Dictionary of North Carolina biography.

Includes bibliographies.
1. North Carolina—Biography. I. Powell,
William Stevens, 1919–
CT252.D5 920'.0756 79-10106
ISBN 0-8078-1329-X

In Memory of

*James Shober Brawley*
23 November 1918–6 July 1981

*Walter Conard Gass*
25 July 1918–20 June 1982

*Herbert Richard Paschal, Jr.*
8 July 1927–2 June 1982

*Tucker Reed Littleton*
3 March 1936–13 August 1983

whose counsel I sought frequently in planning this work and whose many contributions made the *Dictionary of North Carolina Biography* more useful

# Acknowledgments

I am grateful to the North Carolina Society of the Cincinnati for a generous grant to the University of North Carolina Press to assist with the publication costs of this volume; to Jan-Michael Poff for his work in verifying and arranging many of the bibliographies appended to the sketches; to my wife, Virginia Waldrop Powell, for her careful reading of both manuscripts and proof; to Stevie Champion for her skill as a copy editor and for her interest in this work beyond the call of duty; to Matthew Hodgson, director, and to Gwen Duffey, managing editor, of the University of North Carolina Press for their continuing interest and help in many ways; and most important of all, to the many authors of biographies without whose good work this volume would never have been possible.

Volume two of the *Dictionary of North Carolina Biography*, like volume one, has been produced without grant money of any kind from the federal government. It is the product of the willing scholarly labor of numbers of people who contributed their knowledge and skill. I take great pride in our joint accomplishment and extend my hearty thanks to all who have participated in this important undertaking. We intend to persist until the series is completed.

# Dictionary of North Carolina Biography

**Dabney, Charles William** *(19 June 1855–15 June 1945)*, chemist and educator, was born at Hampden-Sydney, Va., the son of Margaretta Lavinia Morrison and Robert Lewis Dabney, conservative Presbyterian theologian, professor at Union Seminary and the University of Texas, and Stonewall Jackson's chief of staff and biographer. He earned a B.A. at Hampden-Sydney in 1873, taught private school in Buckingham County for a year, and then entered the University of Virginia. There he studied chemistry under John William Mallet, choosing that subject to be of most use in rebuilding the wasted South. He was professor at Emory and Henry College in 1877–78. After graduate studies in chemistry at Berlin under August Wilhelm von Hofmann and at Göttingen under Friedrich Wöhler and Hans Hübner, he received the Ph.D. from Göttingen in 1880.

Dabney went to North Carolina as state chemist and director of the North Carolina Agricultural Experiment Station when The University of North Carolina at Chapel Hill was the seat of these offices, taught briefly in the university, and began scientific investigations of soils, fertilizers, and crops. In 1881 the isolation of Chapel Hill led him to move the Agricultural Experiment Station to Raleigh, where he established the experimental farm. His analyses produced the first discovery of new deposits of phosphate in eastern North Carolina and of tin at Kings Mountain and lithia at Lincolnton. In 1884 he was a founder of the Association of Official Agricultural (now Analytical) Chemists. Striking a lifelong theme of his interests, Dabney was among the leaders of the Watauga Club movement to develop a state school of practical arts. With Augustus Leazar, he wrote the bill that led to the founding in 1887 of the Agricultural and Mechanic College of North Carolina at Raleigh. His desk, on which the bill had been written, was presented to the college in 1952.

In 1887 he became president of the University of Tennessee and, for a few years, director of its agricultural experiment station. As president he relaxed the rules on military dress and required attendance, replaced 80 percent of the faculty, raised admissions standards, opened the university to women (1893), and established a law department, teacher training, and industrial education. In 1894 he took a leave of absence to serve as assistant secretary of agriculture in Grover Cleveland's second administration, in part to deflect a perceived plan of Julius Sterling Morton to discontinue federal funding for land grant institutions. There he established the Bureau of Soils, the Division of Agrostology, and the Dairy Division. To answer the low supply of personnel available to the department, he recommended that the department itself train scientists. He also changed the format of the department's Annual Report to that of the Department of Agriculture Yearbook, which remains useful to farmers and others today. He promoted the establishment of a national department of science and a national university, which took form as George Washington University. Hoping to retain him in Washington, President McKinley's administration in 1896–97 created for him the nonpolitical post of director of the scientific bureaus at the Department of Agriculture. But Dabney turned it down and returned to Knoxville in 1898.

After resuming his position at the University of Tennessee, he proposed a Conference for Education in the South through the creation of the Southern Education Board, to build support for free public education. From 1901 to 1903 he directed the board's Bureau of Information and Advice on Legislation and School Organization. In 1902 he established the Summer School of the South, providing training at the university for large numbers of teachers from throughout the region. When he left Knoxville in 1904, the University of Tennessee had the largest academic department of any institution of its class in the South.

In 1904 Dabney became president of the University of Cincinnati, but only after promises from the political bosses to stay out of the school's internal affairs. At Cincinnati he established a teachers' college, a graduate school, colleges of engineering and medicine, and a nursing school; integrated the law college into the whole university structure; and created programs in home economics, physical education, and vocational education. At his retirement in 1920 he left the country's first complete municipal university a school of national rank. Dabney later organized a firm of geologists and engineers in Houston, Tex., and conducted a search for and analysis of mineral deposits in the state. He also proposed the establishment of a school of practical arts in Mexico. Meanwhile, he continued his writing on education at an increased level. His major work, *Universal Education in the South* (2 vols., Chapel Hill [1936]), recommended federal aid to education. Among other works are *History of Agricultural Education in the United States* (1900), *A Star of Hope for Mexico* (1916), and *Fighting for a New World* (1919).

Dabney held LL.D.'s from Yale, Johns Hopkins, Davidson, and Washington and Lee. For his contributions to public instruction in France he was made a Chevalier of the Legion d'Honneur and Officier de l'Instruction Publique. He was director of the U.S. government exhibits at the Cotton States and International Exhibition in Atlanta in 1895 and the Tennessee Centennial Exhibition in 1897.

On 24 Aug. 1881, he married Mary Chilton Brent of Fayette County, Ky. They had three daughters, Marguerite Lewis, Mary Moore, and Katharine Brent. He was intensely interested in genealogy, and many manuscripts and unpublished records on his ancestors are in the Dabney Papers.

For a few years before his death Dabney had a home in Montreat. He died of a coronary thrombosis in Asheville, where he had stopped on his way from his winter home in Winter Park, Fla., to Cincinnati. His grave is in Cincinnati.

SEE: *Asheville Citizen-Times*, 4 May 1952; *Biographical Dictionary of Southern Authors* (1929); *DAB*, supp. 3 (1973); Charles W. Dabney Papers (Southern Historical Collection, University of North Carolina, Chapel Hill); Raleigh *News and Observer*, 17 June 1945; *Who Was Who*, vol. 4 (1952); *Who Was Who Among North American Authors 1921–1939* (1976).

MAURICE M. BURSEY

**Daingerfield, Elliott** *(26 Mar. 1859–22 Oct. 1932),* American artist, was born in Harper's Ferry, Va., the son of Captain John Elliott Daingerfield and Matilda Wickham DeBrau Daingerfield. The family moved to Fayetteville in 1861 after President Jefferson Davis appointed the father to command the arsenal there and to serve as paymaster for Confederate troops. Despite financial reverses suffered by his family as a result of the the Civil War, Daingerfield was educated at private schools in Fayetteville and instructed by a tutor until he was twelve.

From an early age Daingerfield displayed great talent for art. According to family tradition, his older brother Archie gave him a box of watercolors for Christmas and he immediately began painting beautiful pictures. While a youth, he studied under a local china painter, Mrs. William McKay. Later, as an apprentice to a Fayetteville photographer, he learned how to take pictures and to tint them.

In 1880 Daingerfield left Fayetteville to pursue a career in New York City. Shortly after his arrival on 12 January, he was apprenticed to artist Walter Satterlee, associate member of the National Academy of Design. He became an instructor in Satterlee's still life class and studied occasionally at the Art Students' League. Also during his first year in New York, Daingerfield exhibited his work *The Monk Smelling a Bottle of Wine* at the National Academy of Design. In 1884 he left Satterlee and moved to the Holbein Studios, where he made the acquaintance of artist George Inness. The two men became good friends and Inness gave Daingerfield much advice on style and technique. In later years, Daingerfield credited Inness with having taught him the technical use of color and light, often regarded as the hallmark of his work. After Inness's death, Daingerfield wrote his friend's biography, *George Inness: The Man and His Art* (1911).

In the summer of 1886, Daingerfield traveled to Blowing Rock to recuperate from a severe case of diphtheria contracted during the previous winter. This proved to be a turning point in his artistic development as he was enchanted by the North Carolina mountains and made them the subject of many of his paintings. Also, it was the beginning of his long devotion to Blowing Rock where he maintained summer homes for the rest of his life: Windwood, his second residence, was completed in 1900; Westglow, his third, was built in 1916. Meanwhile, he continued to paint at the Holbein Studios in New York City where he came in contact with several noted artists including A. H. Wyant and Kenyon Cox. He was awarded the "point d'appui" in 1891. The following year he showed his painting *The Mothers* to members of the Salmagundi Club.

Following his second marriage in 1895, Daingerfield became interested in painting religious subjects. One year later he finished *Madonna and Child*. This use of the Madonna as a subject was an innovation in the American art world because many painters felt that the theme had been overdone by earlier artists. However, the painting proved to be an instant success and was reproduced on the cover of the 1896 Christmas issue of *The Churchman Magazine*. Earlier in the same year, Daingerfield had exhibited *Could Ye Not Watch With Me One Hour?* at the Lotos Club in New York. He went on to paint *The Child of Mary, The Holy Family*, and *The Story of the Madonna*. In 1897 he studied in Europe.

Daingerfield's religious paintings continued to attract attention. In 1901 he won the silver medal at the Buffalo Exhibition. On 14 May 1902, the National Academy of Design awarded him the Clark Prize for the best figure composition in *The Story of the Madonna*. This painting was acquired by Haley Fiske, president of the Metropolitan Life Insurance Company, who commissioned Daingerfield to execute a series of murals for the Lady Chapel of the Episcopal Church of St. Mary the Virgin at 139 West Forty-sixth Street, New York. During the next five years, Daingerfield labored on these two murals, *The Epiphany* and *The Magnificat*, often working eighteen hours a day. He was a devout communicant of St. Mary's and served on the vestry for over twenty years.

In 1908 he moved from Holbein Studios to Gainsborough Studios at 222 Central Park South, where he maintained his studios until his death. In March 1911 he displayed some of his works at R. C. and N. M. Vose Galleries in Boston—his first public exhibition.

Also during 1911 Daingerfield traveled to Arizona to see the Grand Canyon. The Santa Fe Railway provided him with a private car in hopes that his paintings would entice customers onto their trains. Two years later he returned to the West, taking his family with him. This time, he stayed at Carmel, Calif., and again visited the Grand Canyon. Among his paintings inspired by these trips were *The Grand Canyon, The Genius of the Canyon, The Sleepers*, and *Trees on the Canyon Rim*—the latter shown in 1914 at the Corcoran Gallery in Washington, D.C., as part of an exhibition of the Society of Men Who Paint The Far West. In the same year he published a biography of the artist *Ralph Albert Blakelock*. In 1918 he painted the altar picture, *The Madonna of the Hills*, for the Church of St. Mary in the Hills at Blowing Rock. This church was built by W. W. Stringfellow of Anniston, Ala., in memory of his wife.

Daingerfield and his family traveled to Europe in 1924. He painted in Italy at Capri, Ravello, and Venice. However, he suffered an embolism, which marked the end of his artistic work.

For many years Daingerfield was a lecturer on composition at the Art Students' League. He also taught at the Philadelphia School of Design for Women in 1896 and 1903. In addition to his biographies of Inness and Blakelock, he wrote articles on J. Francis Murphy, Henry W. Ranger, and Albert P. Ryder. He was honored with membership in a number of societies including the Society of American Artists (1903), the Virginia Historical Society (1903), and the National Academy of Design (1906).

Daingerfield died of a heart attack at his home in Gainsborough Studios and was buried at Cross Creek Cemetery, Fayetteville. A memorial exhibition of fifty-three of his paintings was held at Grand Central Galleries, New York, on 3–21 Apr. 1934. In 1947 the North Carolina State Art Society paid him tribute by staging an exhibit "Daingerfield and His Contemporaries." Finally, the North Carolina Museum of Art gathered over two hundred of his works for a showing in 1971.

Daingerfield was married twice: on 25 Sept. 1884 to

Roberta Strange French (daughter of Judge Robert Strange French of Wilmington), who died in childbirth in 1891; and on 30 Dec. 1895 to Anna Grainger (daughter of Leander Grainger of Louisville, Ky.), who died 15 Nov. 1939. By his second marriage, he had two daughters, Marjorie (m. Oliver Ellsworth Holmes, Louis Lundean, and Arthur Howlett) and Gwendoline (m. Joseph E. Dulaney and Worth B. Plyler).

SEE: *Elliott Daingerfield* (typescript, North Carolina Collection, University of North Carolina, Chapel Hill [autobiography]); Ernst Derendinger, "A Tribute to Elliott Daingerfield (1859–1932)," extract from *The Carolinas* (March 1933); Robert Hobbs, *Elliott Daingerfield Retrospective Exhibition* (1971); Raleigh *News and Observer*, 26 Oct. 1932; F. F. Sherman, *Landscape and Figure Painters of America* (1917).

JAMES ELLIOTT MOORE

**Dalrymple, John** *(1705–8?–13 July 1766)*, army officer, the second surviving son of Sir John Dalrymple of Cousland, second baronet, and his wife, Elizabeth Fletcher, probably was born in Edinburgh.* His great-uncle, John Dalrymple, second Viscount Stair, was created Earl of Stair; his great-grandfather was the first Viscount Stair. Both of these men were active politically in Scotland and England and both were privy councillors.

Dalrymple was an officer in the British army as early as 1733. He probably was the one of this name who served as a volunteer for five years in General Sir David Colyear's regiment of foot in the Dutch service in Flanders where he was made an ensign. Afterward Major General Thomas Wentworth, who spoke highly of him, made him a lieutenant. In June 1740 Dalrymple was in New Hanover County, N.C., where he served as a juryman; late that year and in 1741 he participated in the combined British and colonial expedition against Cartagena. He returned to North Carolina and in September 1744 bought 550 acres on the north side of Old Town Creek in New Hanover (now Brunswick) County. This represented an addition to property that he already owned, as his will made 25 Feb. 1743 mentioned extensive land including his plantation known as Spring Garden. He saw service outside the province for several years, however, and in the early 1750s was associated with Joshua Fry and Peter Jefferson, the father of Thomas, in Virginia. Fry and Jefferson were engaged in surveying and mapping the territory along the North Carolina-Virginia boundary in the west. Dalrymple served as a quartermaster officer under Fry. Colonel Fry died in 1754 and was succeeded by a young officer named George Washington; during that summer Dalrymple went to London where he arranged for the publication in 1755 of the Fry-Jefferson map. Known as the "Dalrymple" edition, it contained extensive new information about western North Carolina and the trans-Allegheny region.

Returning from London early in 1755, Dalrymple, now a captain, delivered some letters to Governor Robert Dinwiddie in Virginia. Through Dinwiddie's friendship with General Edward Braddock, commander in chief of British forces in America, he secured the appointment of Dalrymple on 17 Mar. 1755 as commander of Fort Johnston at the mouth of the Cape Fear River in North Carolina, a post Dalrymple seems to have held before his service in Virginia. After some years, Dalrymple obtained leave from the commander to visit England; while in London he secured a new commission from the king, dated 27 Oct. 1760, naming him commander of Fort Johnston. Upon returning to his post he discovered that Governor Arthur Dobbs was displeased with him for having left the province without first obtaining the governor's permission. Dalrymple informed Dobbs that he was not under the governor's authority, only under that of the commander in chief of the forces in America. In what must have been an unpleasant confrontation, the governor confined Captain Dalrymple to barracks under guard. The Board of Trade refused to consider Dalrymple's plea as it concerned military matters, so he broke arrest and left the province in 1762.

During his absence from Fort Johnston Dalrymple seems to have been aboard the *Diligence*, generally stationed in the mouth of the Cape Fear River (her home port was Plymouth, England). Admiralty orders sent to Dalrymple during this period instructed him to make observations of forests, roads, sands, sea marks, and tides wherever he was. He also was among those to whom copies of His Majesty's orders in council were sent concerning a cruise against smugglers. Occasionally Dalrymple reported to the Admiralty on defense.

Dobbs died in March 1765 and was succeeded by William Tryon who promptly sought permission to name a local man, Robert Howe, to be commander of Fort Johnston. This did not sit well in London as Howe might not always be suitably objective in matters concerning both his native province and England. By early summer 1765 Dalrymple was back in the province and, having been commissioned by the king, he was again commander of Fort Johnston. Tryon seems to have accommodated himself to the situation and, with increasing local resistance to the Stamp Act centered in the Lower Cape Fear, Tryon and Dalrymple got along together. Tryon was aware that Sir Jeffrey Amherst, then governor general of British North America, was acquainted with Dalrymple's "Military Genius" and was said to consider him to be "the best Adjutant in the Army." Surely Tryon was in no position to question Amherst's judgment. Dalrymple obeyed Tryon's orders and cooperated with the commanding officers of ships in the river off the fort during the Stamp Act troubles.

When Tryon called at Fort Johnston in February 1766, he found Captain Dalrymple sick in bed. A few weeks later, however, the captain was able to carry out certain orders of the governor. Nevertheless, Dalrymple died in the fort on 13 July.

*John Dalrymple does not appear in the printed genealogies of the family, yet in his will dated 25 Feb. 1743 (exactly three months before his father's death) he describes himself as the second lawful son to Sir John Dalrymple of Cowsland, Baronet of the Kingdom of Scotland. A manuscript family tree in Scotland indicates that the baronet's eldest son died young; his second son and heir, William, was born in 1704. The next child recorded, a daughter, was not born until 1709. Between the two names on the chart there is an X where the name of another child might have appeared. John would have been the second *surviving* son. It is interesting that John Dalrymple made his will in North Carolina in the same year that his father died in Scotland (did word of his father's illness prompt him to do this?) although he lived for twenty-three more years. One of Dalrymple's slaves in North Carolina was named Cowesland. Did the family intentionally drop him from its records?

At some time prior to February 1743 Dalrymple married Martha Watters of New Hanover County, but there is nothing to suggest that they had any children. She survived him and inherited his considerable property, which she bequeathed to her nieces and nephews in her own will of June 1768. The inventory of Captain Dalrymple's estate includes thirteen slaves, extensive livestock, a large quantity of furniture, silver, linen, jewelry, books, and musical instruments. The listing of coopers' and turpentine tools suggests that he was engaged in the naval stores industry. In the settlement of his estate, accounts were submitted for nails, hinges, locks, glass, lumber, and other materials clearly intended for a new house; his death, therefore, must have been unexpected.

SEE: ADM 72/536/19, 72/538/279, 72/723/99–101, 72/723/163 (Public Record Office, London); William P. Cumming, *The Southeast in Early Maps* (1958); New Hanover County Wills (North Carolina State Archives, Raleigh); William S. Powell, ed., *The Correspondence of William Tryon*, vol. 1 (1980); William L. Saunders, ed., *Colonial Records of North Carolina*, vols. 5–7 (1887–90); Secretary of State, Inventories and Sales of Estates, 1712–87 (North Carolina State Archives, Raleigh); *Virginia Magazine of History and Biography* 15 (July 1907), 30 (January 1922), 32 (October 1924).

WILLIAM S. POWELL

**Dalton, John Thomas** *(22 Jan. 1879–5 Jan. 1966)*, inventor, was born on a farm near Franklin Junction (now Gretna) in Pittsylvania County, Va. At a very early age he demonstrated an interest in mechanical devices, such as a sewing machine and a wheat threshing machine, which he learned about from a nearby blacksmith and from his father who was a farmer, carpenter, and operator of a planing mill and a water-powered gristmill. When he was eleven, he began attending school during the winter months but discontinued the practice several years later after completing a study of the books available in the schoolhouse where all grades were taught together. His father died while he was young and his mother soon remarried.

As a youth Dalton worked long hours in the fields, although he preferred working in the shop. Before he was eighteen he had built a wagon with black gum wheels, a hand-powered wood lathe, a corn sheller, a cider mill, and a small cradle scythe to use in helping his stepfather cut wheat. Impressed by his mechanical ability, his stepfather attempted to gain employment for both of them with the Bonsack Company of Roanoke, Va. Ironically this company, which produced machines to manufacture cigarettes, did not hire them.

While working in a general store Dalton became acquainted with a man who repaired clocks, sewing machines, and watches. They formed a partnership and began traveling to increase their clientele. Later Dalton gained valuable experience as a logger, an operator of a water-powered sawmill, a blacksmith for a copper mining firm, and a partner in a blacksmith and wheelright shop. For working on a road repair gang he was paid fifty cents for a ten-hour day. On several occasions when he needed transportation he jumped trains or hoboed, wearing two suits during the winter. He eagerly tried to learn the mining business, daringly led a crew in replacing the timbers in a caved-in mine, and was made a captain or mine foreman at the unusually young age of twenty-one. Not receiving an expected raise in pay, he quit mining to work in a blacksmith shop. In 1905 a man visiting the shop informed him that Golden Belt Manufacturing Company of Durham, N.C., would offer $100,000 to anyone who could invent a machine to insert the drawstrings in smoking tobacco bags. At that time women living near the American Tobacco Company in Durham strung the bags by hand at thirty cents per thousand. Dalton was interested in the $100,000 but lacked the necessary capital for the venture. A friend, Herman Crowell, also became interested in the project and provided $9,000 to become his partner. In Virgilina, a town that derived its name from its location on the North Carolina-Virginia border, Dalton made use of his shop to develop a crude machine to put strings in the bags. This was patented at a cost of $600.

He decided to send the machine to the Murrill and Keizer machine shop in Baltimore for refinements to obtain a greater degree of accuracy. Later he redesigned the machine, adding a device to automatically feed the bags on the stringer and an index drum or wheel to pack the bags into bundles of twenty-five after stringing. He also invented a new knotter head to eliminate the large amount of wasted thread. A second patent was secured in 1907 at a cost of $1,200.

Again in need of financial assistance, Dalton took in Dr. E. J. Tucker and R. H. Wright, Sr., as partners. They formed the Bag Stringing Machine Company with Wright as president and Dalton as vice-president. The machine was moved to a building in Durham owned by Wright and offered to Golden Belt Manufacturing Company, but it was not accepted because of imperfections in production. The machine was then shipped to the Taft-Pierce Manufacturing Company in Rhode Island for modification. After changes were made the machine was again demonstrated to representatives of Golden Belt. Again they rejected it due to the low speed of production, and the machine was sent to the Detrick and Harvey Machine Company in Baltimore for further refinement. Dalton's dream came true in 1912 when Herman Crowell finally obtained a contract from Golden Belt, which hired Dalton to supervise the machine's installation and stringing operations. He also visited the American Machine and Foundry Company in Brooklyn to oversee the construction of more machines. Six years had passed since Dalton had begun working on the stringing machine; during that time he had endured long hours of work, travel, and financial problems to make the project succeed.

After finishing his work at Golden Belt, Dalton was engaged by Wright to develop a machine to weigh tea, cut tea bags, put tea in the bags, sew the seams of the bags, and attach tags. The successful completion of this job resulted in the incorporation of the Wright-Dalton Machinery Company. Later the development of a packing machine led to the establishment of Wright-Dalton Automatic Tobacco Packing Machine Company. In 1937, after Dalton and Wright disagreed over the terms of partnership, the former gave up his share in the two companies.

Dalton rejoined Golden Belt where he was assigned the task of developing machinery to staple the tags on smoking tobacco bags. The prestapled tags tangled easily and thus interfered with packing at the Durham branch of the American Tobacco Company. While Preston Fowler, Sr., was branch manager in Durham, Dalton began working with W. H. Ogsbury, who was destined to be the next branch manager. One of Dalton's first recommendations was to provide separate tagging machines for each packer rather than having the tags attached to the bags before packing. He later invented an amazing bow tier to tie the string on the Bull Durham Smoking Tobacco bags. This machine became known locally as the "tie-boy" because it replaced the young boys who sat on top of the machines to tie the bows. The automatic "tie-boy" is still used at the Richmond branch of the American Tobacco Company.

At American Dalton developed numerous innovations. One of his major accomplishments was a turntable for getting cork-tipped cigarettes turned the same way on each side of the catcher belt after the cigarettes were made. This device made it possible to have one employee per machine catch cigarettes rather than the two workers previously required. He also built a machine to fabricate one of the cigarette-making machine parts, the tube bottom, which influenced the shaping of the cigarette. Dalton devised a mechanical calculating device for quickly solving trigonometric problems. He invented a press to compress tobacco in hogsheads before shipping to redrying plants and an automatic feeder for tobacco cutting machines, and he contributed to the development of an automatic system for feeding cut tobacco to the cigarette-making machines, a system that was of major significance to the entire tobacco industry. Another one of his products was a machine for removing the pins in pin rollers.

During World War II the federal ordnance agency became interested in reducing the labor cost of loading bandoliers with cartridges. When asked by the agency to develop an automatic loading machine, the president of the Package Machinery Company recommended that Dalton be selected for the job. As a contribution to the war effort, the American Tobacco Company donated the time of Dalton and the use of its facilities with no expectation of profit; however, the government reimbursed the company for the cost of developing the machine. A government inspector sent to examine the work was terrified when he learned that Dalton was using live ammunition in his experiments, but the results were successful.

After over nineteen years of employment with the American Tobacco Company, Dalton retired at the age of seventy-seven. Shortly before his death nine years later, Dalton offered a plan to the U.S. government to assist in gaining the initial thrust in launching a rocket in space.

Dalton was a colorful individual with mechanical ingenuity; perseverance, as evidenced by the duration of his work in developing the stringing machine; and integrity, as demonstrated by his payment of small loans made years before he sold the stringing machine. He also had great willingness to work as exemplified when he worked ten hours a day in a machine shop, then learned drafting and drew plans for a new machine after hours.

Dalton married Mary Wilborn from Halifax County, Va., on 27 Oct. 1901 at North Fork Baptist Church near Virgilina, Va.; their children were Florence, Anna Maude (Buxton), Thomas Baltimore, Virginia (Huss), John Wilborn, and twins, Maye Elizabeth (Singletary) and Macon Mitchell. He was buried in Maplewood Cemetery, Durham. A portrait of Dalton by one of his children is owned by Dr. and Mrs. W. V. Singletary of Durham.

SEE: Autobiography of John Thomas Dalton (in possession of Mrs. W. V. Singletary, Durham); *Durham Morning Herald*, 6 Jan. 1966; *Durham Sun*, 6 Jan. 1966; Nannie May Tilley, *The Bright-Tobacco Industry, 1860–1929* (1948); Washington, D.C. *Official Gazette*, 1907–50.

B. W. C. ROBERTS

**Daly, John Augustin** *(20 July 1838–7 June 1899)*, playwright and for three decades one of America's foremost theatrical producers and managers, was born in Plymouth, N.C. His father, Captain Denis Daly, in the shipping and lumber business, was born in Ireland and later sought his fortune trading along the American coast and in the West Indies. It was there he met Elizabeth Duffey, daughter of Englishman Lieutenant John Duffey. After a voyage north, they were married in New York in 1834 and eventually came to North Carolina from Norfolk, Va., in 1838. Their oldest child, Catherine, died young. After the captain died in 1841 in Ocracoke from a fever contracted at sea, the widow moved with sons Augustin and Joseph Francis (1840–1916) to Norfolk and then in 1849 to New York. There, with little formal education, Joseph rose from office boy to managing clerk and to successor in an outstanding law firm, served as justice on various benches, including the New York Supreme Court, then returned to law and literature as his brother's very active collaborator and biographer.

Augustin, too, had brief formal schooling; he entered the mercantile business as a clerk, went to night school, and chased the star glimpsed early when as a child he went to the Avon Theater and produced plays in a wood house in Norfolk. He joined New York amateur dramatic societies, such as the Murdock, Burton, and John R. Scott associations, but from the beginning it was clear that he had no interest in, nor aptitude for, acting. He was manager-director born, which the rapidity of his rise and the respect of his peers proved.

Between 1854 and 1858, Daly wrote at least four plays. In 1856 he began his career as manager by hiring a hall and offering without financial backing a variety of productions, and in 1859 he became the drama critic for the New York *Sunday Courier*. At one point during the eight years he held the latter post, he was also drama critic for four other newspapers—the *Express*, *Sun*, *Times*, and *Weekly Citizen*. He gradually resigned these jobs as he became more involved in the theater itself. His first great success was *Leah, the Forsaken*, an adaptation of a German play, first performed in Boston in December 1862 (and in New York in January 1863), with Kate Bateman as the Jewess. From that moment until his death, the art of theater was his passion.

Although the late nineteenth-century theater is often dismissed as melodramatic and imported fare, Arthur Hobson Quinn says that "Modern American drama begins with Augustin Daly." It is not simply that he wrote or adapted more than ninety plays for the stage which earns that accolade. He managed theaters—at one point three concurrently. On 17 Sept. 1879 the splendid Daly's Theater at Broadway and Thirtieth opened and for twenty years housed Daly's company, called by one contemporary "Maison de Molière." Daly gathered into a true stock company some of the finest actors and actresses of the day, among them Fanny Davenport, Sara Jewett, John Drew, James Lewis, Otis Skinner, Edwin Booth, Mrs. Gilbert, and especially Ada Rehan. Many he introduced to the American stage, and he provided training and opportunities for countless careers. He elevated the tone of the theater by exacting strict standards of artistic excellence and of discipline on and off stage.

Daly encouraged American playwrights by producing their plays and calling in print and correspondence for even better plays; of Bronson Howard's first four plays, Daly produced three—*Saratoga* (1870), *Diamonds* (1872), and *Moorcraft* (1874). He also encouraged contemporary literary figures such as Bret Harte, Mark Twain, Howells, and James to write plays for production. Daly's own plays broke new ground. Among the best or most influential were *Under the Gaslight* (1867), a "realistic" melodrama that provided the imitated last-minute rescue from the railroad track; *Horizon* (1871), an innovative western drama; and *Divorce* (1871) and *Pique* (1875), domestic dramas of manners. Adaptations were his forte, especially from French and German plays, from fiction, and even from poetry. Popular among theatergoers were *Frou-Frou* (1870) and *The Lottery of Love* (1888) from French; *Needles and Pins* (1880), *The Passing Regiment* (1881), and *Seven-Twenty-Eight* (1883) from German; *Griffith Gaunt* (1866), *Pickwick Papers* (1868), and *Man and Wife* (1870) from fiction; and Daly's version of *The Foresters* (1891) by Tennyson, who requested that Ada Rehan play Maid Marian. Particularly fine were Daly's productions of Shakespeare and English comedy, as well as classical and modern English plays.

Daly was the first to take an American company on successful tours to England, Germany, and France, or to establish a theater abroad—Daly's Theatre, which opened in Leicester Square on 12 Mar. 1893, with a cast of sixty-one and Ada Rehan as Katharina in *The Taming of the Shrew* and to an ode of welcome written by Daly's English counterpart, Sir Henry Irving.

On 9 Jan. 1869 Daly married Mary Duff, daughter of theater proprietor John A. Duff. They lived most of their lives at 214 West Twenty-fifth Street where their two sons, Leonard and Francis Augustin (Austin), were born in 1870 and 1873; both children died of diphtheria on 5 Jan. 1885. Apparently weakened by pneumonia on the voyage from America to England during a business trip, Daly died at the Hotel Continental in Paris with his wife and Ada Rehan at his side. Daly was a Roman Catholic and member of the Catholic Club. His funeral was at St. Patrick's Cathedral on 19 June 1899, and he was buried in the Daly Vault, Calvary Cemetery, New York.

Daly's nondramatic writing includes "The American Dramatist," *North American Review* (May 1886); "American Playwrights on the American Drama," *Harper's Weekly*, 2 Feb. 1889; and *Woofington, a Tribute to the Actress and the Woman* (1888, 2nd ed. 1890).

SEE: W. W. Austin and Matthew White, Jr., "A Famous American Manager: The Late Augustin Daly, His Position," *Munsey's Magazine* (August 1899); A. I. duP. Coleman, "Augustin Daly: An Appreciation," *The Critic* (August 1899); *DAB*, vol. 3 (1930); Francis Daly, *The Life of Augustin Daly* (1917); E. A. Dithmar, *Memories of Daly's Theaters* (1896), *Memories of One Theater with Passing Recollections of Many Others* (1891); Marvin Felheim, "The Career of Augustin Daly" (Ph.D. diss., Harvard, 1948), *The Theater of Augustin Daly: An Account of the Late Nineteenth Century American Stage* (1956); D. Forbes-Winslow, *Daly's: The Biography of a Theatre* (1944); John P. Jackson, "New York's 'Maison de Molière,'" *The Curio* (January–February 1888); Gustav Kobbé, "Augustin Daly and His Life-Work," *Century Magazine* (August 1899); *New York Times*, 8, 9, 11, 17, 18, 19, 20 June 1899; *New York Times Illustrated Magazine*, 18 June 1899; Arthur Hobson Quinn, *A History of the American Drama* (1964); Adelaide Louise Samson, "Augustine Daly: America's Foremost Play Producer," *Metropolitan Magazine* (August 1898); Ernest Short and Arthur Compton-Rickett, *Ring Up the Curtain* (1938); J. Rankin Towse and George Parsons Lathrop, "An American School of Dramatic Art," *Century Magazine* (June 1898); Deshler Welch, "Augustin Daly—Dramatic Dictator," *The Booklovers Magazine* (April 1904).

SUE FIELDS ROSS

**Damtoft, Walter Julius** *(11 Nov. 1890–22 Nov. 1976)*, forester and business and civic leader in western North Carolina, was born in Southport, Conn., the son of Knud Julius and Dagmas (Jacobi) Damtoft. He received a bachelor of philosophy degree from the Sheffield Scientific School of Yale University in 1910 and a master of forestry degree from Yale in 1911. From 1911 to 1917, he served as a forest examiner with the U.S. Forest Service in Colorado, Virginia, Tennessee, Alabama, Georgia, New Hampshire, and North Carolina. In 1917 he was named administrative assistant of the Pisgah National Forest.

Upon his appointment as chief forester of the Champion Fibre Company of Canton, N.C., in 1920, Damtoft became one of the nation's first full-time professional industrial foresters and the first trained forester to be employed by a pulping enterprise in the Southeast. Other positions he held with the pulp and paper company included assistant secretary, assistant secretary-treasurer, assistant division manager, assistant secretary of the general woods department, and vice-president and general manager of Hamilton Laboratories, a Champion subsidiary in Asheville. He retired in 1958. At Champion, he and President Reuben Robertson were early pioneers in adapting forest conservation, selective cutting, and reforestation practices to commercial timber operations. Through speeches, demonstrations, and articles, he urged area farmers, industries, and state officials to manage the forests so that they could continue to be used in the future.

Damtoft's civic duties were numerous. He served as a member of the board of directors, Asheville Division, Wachovia Bank and Trust Co.; trustee, Memorial Mission Hospital; director, Forest Genetics Research Foundation; codirector, Forest Products Division, Economic Stabilization Administration; director, Forest Product Division, Office of Price Stabilization; vice-chairman, North Carolina Board of Conservation and Development; industry panel member, Regional War Labor Board; and industry member, North Carolina State Labor-Management Committee. Other offices included general chairman, 1947 Southern Governors' Conference; secretary, Western North Carolina Committee for Development of the Great Smoky Mountains National Park; vice-president, Society of American Foresters; president, Southern Pulpwood Conservation Association; director, American Pulpwood Association; president, North Carolina Forestry Association; and member, American Forest Products Industries, Inc. He was chairman of the board of appeal, Asheville District Selective Service; chairman of the Canton Planning Commission; a member of the Asheville Zoning and Planning Commission and of the North Carolina Industrial Council; president of the Western Carolina Manufacturers Association and of the North Carolina Traffic League; and director of the North Carolina Citizens Committee and of the Asheville Chamber of Commerce. He also belonged to the Newcomen Society, the Yale Forest School Alumni Association, Civitan, Mountain City, Pen and Plate, and Downtown Clubs.

Damtoft was awarded an honorary doctorate of forest science by North Carolina State University in 1954 and was an honorary alumnus of the Biltmore Forestry School. In 1956 he received the Achievement Award of the North Carolina Forestry Association.

Damtoft married Keene Martin in 1917; she died the following year. In 1921 he married Dorothy Athenson of Asheville. They had two children, Anne Elizabeth Damtoft Campbell and Walter Athenson Damtoft. Damtoft was a Democrat and an Episcopalian. He was buried at Riverside Cemetery, Asheville.

SEE: *Asheville Citizen*, 13–14 Feb. 1951, 15 Nov. 1956, 19–24 Apr. 1959, 23 Nov. 1976; Champion Paper and Fibre Company (Hamilton, Ohio), *The Log*, December 1958; Elwood R. Maunder, *Voices from the South: Recollections of Four Foresters* (1977); William S. Powell, ed., *North Carolina Lives* (1962); *Who's Who in the South and Southwest* (1954, 1956).

E. KAYE LANNING

**Dancy, Frank Battle** *(4 Aug. 1860–1 July 1922)*, chemist, teacher, and businessman, was born in Tarboro, the son of William Francis and Mary Eliza Battle Dancy. He attended the schools of Mrs. William D. Pender and Frank S. Wilkinson in Tarboro before entering the Bingham School near Mebanesville, Alamance County, at the age of fourteen. Three years later he enrolled in The University of North Carolina, as a third generation student. His average grade for his four years was slightly higher than 93 percent, and he received several honors including the Latin medal in his freshman year and election as chief marshall in his junior year for the 1880 commencement exercises. He was graduated in 1881 with an A.B. and returned in the fall for further study in the field of chemistry. In February 1882, before he had completed work for the M.A. degree, he was named assistant analytical chemist to Charles W. Dabney at the newly-created Agricultural Experiment Station in Raleigh. He remained there seven years and became the chief chemist.

During this time Dancy contributed several articles to scientific journals and other publications having to do with science or agriculture. He also collaborated with Herbert B. Battle on *Chemical Conversion Tables for Use in the Analysis of Commercial Fertilizers*, published in 1885. This forty-two-page booklet was well received and brought him an unsolicited offer as professor of chemistry at Minnesota Agricultural and Mechanical College and chemist to the Minnesota Agricultural Experiment Station. Dancy declined this dual position, primarily because he wanted to remain in the North Carolina area. In 1889 he left his post at the Experiment Station to open a private laboratory. His reputation as a chemist increased considerably but his income did not, and for six months he was professor of chemistry at Peace Institute.

With the organization of the Caraleigh Phosphate and Fertilizer Works in 1891, Dancy began his business career as that company's secretary and treasurer; he subsequently was appointed general manager and, eventually, president. He also became a director of Raleigh's Commercial and Farmers' Bank. From 1894 to 1900 he lived in Norfolk, Va., first as manager of the Old Dominion Guano Company and later as a director of the Virginia-Carolina Chemical Company, which was created by the merger of the Old Dominion company and seven others. When Virginia-Carolina Chemical Company was sold to northern financiers, Dancy became manager of its Norfolk Sales Division. In 1900 he was named managing director of the company's Georgia Sales Division; in that post he directed sales operations in Georgia, Florida, Alabama, and parts of Tennessee. With headquarters in Atlanta, he became a part of Georgia's business development as a director of the Central Bank and Trust Corporation of Atlanta and other business institutions. He also was lieutenant colonel in the Georgia state troops in 1903. He served as vestryman and senior warden in the Episcopal church and as finance committee chairman for the Georgia diocesan convention. He died in Baltimore on a job with the chemical company.

Dancy was a member (later fellow) of the American Association for the Advancement of Science, served as vice-president of the Elisha Mitchell Scientific Society, held membership in the American Academy of Social and Political Science of Philadelphia, and became an associate member of the Association of Official Agricultural Chemists of Washington, D.C.

In 1887 Dancy married Elizabeth Hanrahan Grimes of Raleigh, daughter of William and Elizabeth Hanrahan Grimes. They had one daughter, Eliza Battle, and three sons, William Grimes, Frank Battle, Jr., and Bryan Grimes.

SEE: Samuel A. Ashe, ed., *Biographical History of North Carolina*, vol. 6 (1905); Frank Battle Dancy and Herbert B. Battle, *Chemical Conversion Tables for Use in the Analysis of Commercial Fertilizers* (1885); Daniel L. Grant, *Alumni History of the University of North Carolina* (1924).

MAUD THOMAS SMITH

**Dancy, John Campbell, Jr.** *(8 May 1857–13 Apr. 1920)*, editor and public official, was born in Tarboro, the son of John C. Dancy, Sr., a slave who became a freeman and, after the Civil War, was a builder and contractor and an Edgecombe County commissioner. After receiving home instruction, the younger Dancy attended the county school and worked briefly in the printing office of the *Tarboro Southerner*, where he learned to set type. In 1873 he entered Howard University in Washington, D.C. The death of his father interrupted his education; he returned to Tarboro where he taught and was principal of a school for blacks, which was attended by three hundred pupils. During a brief interlude he accepted appointment by Congressman John Adams Hyman, a black Republican from North Carolina, to a position in the Treasury Department in Washington, D.C. Resigning, he returned home again and renewed his interest in education as well as in the cause of temperance. Already active in the North Carolina Independent Order of Good Templars, he attended the international meeting of the order at Liverpool, England, in 1879, where he was elected right worthy grand marshal. He was president of the temperance convention of blacks that met in Goldsboro in 1882.

Dancy's interest in politics was growing, and in 1887 he was secretary of the State Convention of Colored Men held in Raleigh. He was also chief secretary of the state Republican conventions in 1880, 1884, 1886, 1888, and 1890. In 1892 he campaigned for congressional candidate Thomas Settle. He was elected register of deeds of Edgecombe County in 1880 and reelected in 1882 but defeated in 1884. As a delegate to national Republican conventions, he seconded the nominations of General John A. Logan for vice-president in 1884 and John Sherman for president in 1888. During campaigns he frequently worked in Virginia, West Virginia, Tennessee, Illinois, Ohio, and Indiana. In 1891 President Benjamin Harrison appointed Dancy collector of customs at the port of Wilmington—the highest paying federal appointive position in the state—and he served until the Democrats returned to power in 1893 following the election of Grover Cleveland.

While in Tarboro Dancy had been editor of the *North Carolina Sentinel*, apparently for the period 1882–85. Long active in the African Methodist Episcopal Zion Church, he was named editor of the *Star of Zion* in 1885 and moved to Salisbury for this position. He continued as editor until 1892. One of his objectives, never realized, was the union of his church and the African Methodist Episcopal Church. He was general manager of his church's centennial in New York and spoke at Carnegie Hall together with Booker T. Washington and other noted black leaders. He was a popular and effective speaker and delivered commencement addresses at various schools and colleges including Tuskegee and Livingstone.

From 1901 until 1910 Dancy served as recorder of deeds in Washington, D.C., a Republican political appointment. At various times during his life, he was also occupied with a variety of causes. In 1895 he was a commissioner for Negroes in North Carolina for the Cotton States and International Exposition in Atlanta. He was a board member of the Coleman Manufacturing Company, a black-owned textile mill in Durham, and a trustee of Livingstone College in Salisbury.

Dancy's first wife was Laura G. Coleman of Morganton by whom he had five children, two boys and three girls (two of whom died in infancy). She died in December 1890, and in March 1893 he married Florence Virginia Stevenson of Allegheny City, Pa. Their son, John C. Dancy III, was active in the Urban League and author of *Sand Against the Wind*, his memoirs, published by Wayne State University Press in 1966.

SEE: African Methodist Episcopal Zion Church, *Quarterly Review*, 1892–1912; Allen E. Burgess, "Tar Heel Blacks and the New South Dream: The Coleman Manufacturing Company, 1896–1904" (Ph.D. diss., Duke University, 1977); J. W. Hood, *One Hundred Years of the African Methodist Episcopal Zion Church* (1895); I. Garland Penn, *The Afro-American Press, and Its Editors* (1891); W. H. Quick, *Negro Stars in All Ages of the World* (1898); W. J. Simmons, *Men of Mark* (1887).

MARVIN KRIEGER

**Daniel, John Reeves Jones** *(13 Jan. 1802–22 June 1868)*, lawyer, congressman, and planter, was born near Halifax, the son of Judith Jones and Willie Daniel. He attended The University of North Carolina, from which he was graduated first in his class with an A.B. degree in 1821 and received a master's degree in 1831. He was a university trustee from 1833 to 1853. Admitted to the North Carolina bar in 1823, he practiced law in Halifax with much success. In 1831 he was elected to the House of Commons where he served until 1834. In that year he became attorney general of the state, a post he held until 1841 when he was elected to the U.S. House of Representatives from the Second District. On entering Congress he was appointed to the Committee on Roads and Canals and later to the Committee on the Territories. For several sessions he was chairman of the Committee of Claims. A supporter of states' rights and the annexation of Texas, he was one of the two signers from North Carolina of Calhoun's Southern Manifesto. He remained in the House until 1853.

Some time after retiring from Congress, Daniel moved to Louisiana. There he settled on a plantation in Caddo Parish, on the Red River a few miles south of Shreveport, and continued to practice law. His son Junius joined him in 1858 to assist in the management of his plantation. Junius, a West Point graduate, returned to North Carolina to serve in the army for the Confederacy, rising to the rank of brigadier general. He was killed in the Battle of Spottsylvania Courthouse in 1864.

Daniel had a reputation as a brilliant lawyer and an able speaker. He has been cited for his clear and discriminating mind, patient industry, and high integrity. He seems to have been generally respected and, according to his obituary, was known as "Honest John Daniel."

Daniel was married in Halifax on 5 Apr. 1825 to Martha Elizabeth Long Stith, the daughter of Colonel Basset Stith and his wife Mary Long. Martha's sister Margaret Maria Basset Stith was the wife of Daniel's first cousin, Judge Joseph John Daniel, also of Halifax. John Reeves Jones and Martha Daniel had four children: Willie Augustus (1826–58), John Napoleon (1827–52), Junius (1828–64), and Virginia Frances (1830–died in infancy). Of these, only Junius was married; he had no children. Daniel's wife Martha died in Halifax in August 1831 after a short illness. On 29 Aug. 1844 Daniel married Sarah Frances Washington Stith, the sister of his first wife. There were no children of this marriage. Mrs. Daniel died on 26 Nov. 1895 in Washington, D.C., and was buried in Raleigh.

Texts of Daniel's speeches in Congress appear in appendices to the *Congressional Globe*. Duke University's Perkins Library has two manuscript letters. There are scattered references to Daniel in the Papers of David Outlaw, located in the Southern Historical Collection of the Library of The University of North Carolina at Chapel Hill. (Outlaw and Daniel served together in both the House of Commons and Congress.)

SEE: W. C. Allen, *History of Halifax County* (1918); T. H. Benton, *Thirty Years' View*, vol. 2 (1856); Mark M. Boatner, *The Civil War Dictionary* (1959); *Congressional Directory* and *Congressional Globe* (1841–53); A. C. Gordon, "Daniel Family of Halifax, North Carolina," *Tyler's Quarterly Historical and Genealogical Magazine*, vol. 13 (March 1931); Daniel L. Grant, *Alumni History of the University of North Carolina* (1924); *Raleigh Daily Sentinel*, 14 July 1868; *Raleigh Register*, 15 Apr. 1825, 11 Aug. 1831, 3 Sept. 1844; John H. Wheeler, *Reminiscences and Memoirs of North Carolina* (1884).

LOUISE MCG. HALL

**Daniel, Joseph John** *(13 Nov. 1783–10 Feb. 1848)*, legislator and jurist, was born in Halifax County, the son of Anne Brinkley Daniel; the name of his father has not been found. Little is known of his childhood or early education. He attended The University of North Carolina in the term 1801–2 and was a member of the Philanthropic Society, but was not graduated. After leaving Chapel Hill he read law in Halifax under William R. Davie.

Daniel had a home in the town of Halifax and was elected to represent the borough in the House of Commons in 1807 and 1815; he also owned a rural home, Burnt Coat, near Heathsville, and represented the county in the House of Commons in 1812. He later represented Edgecombe County in the House of Commons in 1836–37. In 1816 he was elected a judge of superior court for a three-year term, and in 1832 he was elected to the North Carolina Supreme Court where he served until his death. For eleven of those years Daniel sat with Thomas Ruffin and William Gaston. Daniel also represented Halifax County in the Constitutional Convention of 1835. Although not regarded as an outstanding public speaker, he was thought to be a fine conversationalist, perceptive and witty. He had simple tastes and was practical in everyday affairs.

Married to Maria Stith on 1 Jan. 1822, Daniel was survived by three children: William A., Mary Long Gordon, and Lavinia Bassett Battle.

An unsigned portrait of Daniel hangs in the Philanthropic Society hall at The University of North Carolina; a copy is in the Supreme Court Building, Raleigh.

SEE: W. C. Allen, *History of Halifax County* (1918); George T. Blackburn, II, and others, *The Di and Phi Portrait Index* (1980); Walter Clark, *History of the Supreme Court of North Carolina* (1919); Margaret M. Hofmann, *Genealogical Abstracts of Wills 1758 through 1824, Halifax County, North Carolina* (1970); John H. Wheeler, *Historical Sketches of North Carolina* (1851).

JOSEPH K. L. RECKFORD

**Daniel, Junius** *(27 June 1828–13 May 1864)*, Confederate general, was born in Halifax, the son of John Reeves Jones Daniel (1802–68), attorney general of North Carolina and member of the United States Congress, and his wife, Martha Stith. He was educated at an elementary school in Halifax and at the J. M. Lovejoy Academy in Raleigh before receiving an appointment by President John Knox Polk to the U.S. Military Academy at West Point in 1846. Upon graduation in 1851, Daniel was sent to Newport, Ky., as assistant quartermaster; in the following year, he was stationed at Fort Albuquerque, N. Mex., where he remained for five years. In 1857 he resigned his commission to begin a career as a planter in Louisiana, joining his father who had moved there following his last term in Congress in 1851.

In October 1860 Daniel married Ellen Long, daughter of Colonel John J. Long of Northampton County, N.C. They had no children.

Though offered a commission by the state of Louisiana after Lincoln's call for troops in April 1860, Daniel returned to Halifax and offered his services to his native state. He was chosen colonel of the Fourth (later Fourteenth) Regiment and remained as the commanding officer until the period of enlistment expired. He was then offered command of the Forty-third and Forty-fifth regiments and the Second North Carolina Cavalry. He accepted the command of the Forty-fifth Regiment.

Daniel led four regiments from Raleigh to Goldsboro and organized them into a brigade; afterward, he organized two other brigades. In June 1862 he was ordered to Petersburg, Va., where his brigade joined General Robert E. Lee's Army of Northern Virginia before the Seven Days' Battle, though it took no active part in this battle.

He was commissioned brigadier general on 1 Sept. 1862, making him one of five men from Halifax County to serve as brigadier generals in the Confederate Army. He spent the fall of 1862 with his brigade at Drury's Bluff and subsequently served in North Carolina. After the Battle of Chancellorsville, he was transferred to General Robert E. Rodes's division of the Second Corps in Lee's army where he served with distinction in the Pennsylvania Campaign. His brigade was entrusted with the bearing of the "Corps Flag." In the Battle of Gettysburg, Daniel's brigade suffered the greatest losses of any brigade in the corps on the first day of the battle.

While leading his brigade at the "Horseshoe Bend" near Spottsylvania Court House, Va., on 12 May 1864, General Daniel was struck in the abdomen by a minie ball and died the next day. His body was taken to Halifax and buried in the old colonial cemetery, which is now a part of the Historic Site Area.

SEE: W. C. Allen, *History of Halifax County* (1918); Ezra J. Warner, *Generals In Gray* (1959).

RALPH HARDEE RIVES

**Daniel, Robert** *(d. May 1718)*, a prominent figure in the politics of both North Carolina and South Carolina, arrived in South Carolina from Barbados about April 1677 and took up warrants on 1,500 acres of land. He returned to Barbados briefly but had settled in Oyster Point, S.C. by 1679. Early in his career he became associated with the antiproprietary Goose Creek faction and was a leading participant in political agitation during Philip Ludwell's governorship in 1692. When the Lords Proprietors issued a general pardon to the agitators the following year, Daniel was one of two men excluded from its provisions. However, his social prestige in the colony remained high (he had been named a landgrave in 1691), and in December 1697 while visiting in England he was made deputy to the new Earl Craven. While revising the Fundamental Constitutions in 1698, the Proprietors consulted frequently with Daniel; later that year he returned to South Carolina with the completed revisions.

As a Proprietor's deputy Daniel was entitled to membership on South Carolina's council, in which he subsequently took an active role. Like so many of his fellow Barbadians in the colony, Daniel was a loyal supporter of the Church of England, and he led the successful opposition to appointment of a dissenter as president of the council in 1700. Two years later he participated in an expedition to Florida to fight the Spaniards and Indians and earned a solid reputation for bravery. When the high Anglican, Sir Nathaniel Johnson, became governor of Carolina in March 1703, he turned to Daniel for frequent counsel. In July Johnson sent the landgrave to North Carolina as deputy governor. Shortly after arriving in the Albemarle region, Daniel set about gathering prominent Anglicans as councillors and provincial officers. Early in 1704 the document arrived with which the deputy governor would purge the North Carolina assembly of its large number of dissenters. From England the Privy Council had ordered that all persons in places of public trust must pledge an oath of allegiance to the recent Queen Anne. Daniel required that all members of the government swear to the oath; he would not allow affirmations as had been done in the past. Because Quakers were prohibited from swearing by their religious creed, they were barred from the assembly that met late in 1704. This purged body then passed a vestry act requiring public support for the erection of Anglican churches, as well as a measure barring from the government anyone who had not sworn to the oath of allegiance.

North Carolina dissenters began seeking ways to get rid of Daniel and, with their counterparts in South Carolina and their friends in England, succeeded in pressuring Governor Johnson to remove Daniel from office early in 1705. During the following four years Daniel seems to have frequently traveled back and forth between North Carolina and South Carolina. He owned considerable property in Bath County at the time but also served in the South Carolina lower house of assembly from 1706 to 1709. In 1708 he participated briefly in the North Carolina upper house during the contest between Thomas Cary and William Glover for the presidency of that body. For reasons that are unclear, Daniel never allied with either man and withdrew to Bath where he apparently married a woman named Martha Wainwright. His first wife, Dorothy, had died earlier in South Carolina.

In 1709 Daniel deeded most of his North Carolina holdings to Martha to help her in rearing their son, John, and returned to South Carolina as his permanent residence. He lived in Charleston in 1710 and moved to the Waccamaw area the next year. During the period 1713–15 he again served in the South Carolina assembly. When in August 1712 that body was seeking a commander for its forces preparing to battle the Tuscarora in North Carolina, Daniel was offered the position, but his terms were considered too extravagant. However, he did lead troops during the Yamasee War in South Carolina in 1715.

When Governor Charles Craven left South Carolina in the spring of 1716, he named Daniel as his deputy to preside over the government. By this time Daniel was an old man close to senility, and he became embroiled in a series of petty arguments with the legislature over questions of personal privilege. He was succeeded by Governor Robert Johnson in the fall of 1717. By early May 1718 Daniel was dead. He had named his wife Martha as his executrix and had made bequests to a son- and daughter-in-law and two grandsons. He was also survived by a daughter, Martha, a noted South Carolina florist and wife of Charles Logan. She died in 1779 at the age of seventy-seven.

SEE: William Darlington, *Memorials of John Bartram and Humphrey Marshall with Notices of their Botanical Contemporaries* (1849); Deeds of Beaufort County (North Carolina State Archives, Raleigh); Caroline T. Moore and Agatha A. Simmons, eds., *Abstracts of the Wills of . . . South Carolina, 1670–1740* (1960); William S. Price, Jr., ed., *Colonial Records of North Carolina, Higher-Court Records, 1702–1708*, vol. 5 (1977); William L. Saunders, ed., *Colonial Records of North Carolina*, vol. 1 (1886); M. Eugene Sirmans, *Colonial South Carolina* (1966); Stephen B. Weeks, "Robert Daniel," C. L. Van Noppen Papers (Manuscript Department, Library, Duke University, Durham).

WILLIAM S. PRICE, JR.

**Daniel, Robert Thomas** *(10 June 1773–14 Sept. 1840)*, Baptist minister and agent for benevolent agencies, was born in Middlesex County, Va., the fifth son of Samuel and Eliza Thomas Daniel. At the close of the Revolutionary War, the family migrated to Orange County, N.C., and settled near Hillsborough. Young Daniel probably attended a local school for a short time. He was brought up in the two businesses conducted by his father, a blacksmith and cabinetmaker.

In July 1802 Daniel professed his faith and in August was baptized by Elder Isaac Hicks at Holly Springs Baptist Church, Wake County, of which he became a member. By 1803 he felt the call to begin speaking at church meetings; he was formally licensed to preach in April. Three months later he was ordained at Holly Springs by Elders Isaac Hicks, his pastor, and Nathan Gully. From that day until his death he devoted himself exclusively to the ministry, thereby expending his fortune and his health.

Throughout his career, Daniel spent most of his time traveling as an agent for various Baptist causes but he did have several brief pastorates. As one of the first missionaries of the North Carolina Baptist Benevolent Society, he organized the Raleigh First Baptist Church (presently located on Salisbury Street near the state capitol), on 8 Mar. 1812, serving as pastor in 1812–13 and again in 1822–26. During the latter period, he began sunrise services and took steps to increase the Negro membership. In 1823, one Joseph, a slave of Sherwood Haywood, was appointed to officiate for members of his race at the Lord's Supper; in the same year permission was granted for any colored minister of like faith "possessing proper credentials" to preach in the church whenever it was not being used. Success as a pastor did not affect Daniel's desire to travel, and he again resumed his missionary efforts.

On 14 Aug. 1814, Daniel helped organize Yates (now Mount Pisgah) Baptist Church in Chatham County and was its pastor until 1818 and again in 1822. He also assisted in the organization of Mount Carmel Baptist Church (1816) and Sandy Fields Baptist Church (1823), both in Orange County. From 1819 until 1820 he was pastor of Grassy Creek Baptist Church, Granville County. During his travels as agent, he preached at many churches—at May's Chapel, Chatham County; at Carthage; and at Sawmill Baptist Church in South Carolina, among others.

According to abstracts of the minutes of the Sandy Creek Baptist Association, Daniel served as a delegate to the Raleigh Baptist Association (1808, 1825), to the Pee Dee Baptist Association and the General Meeting of Correspondence, North Carolina (1815), and to the Charleston Baptist Association (1817, 1821); as a correspondent with the Baptist Board of Foreign Missions (1815, 1817); and as moderator for the Sandy Creek Baptist Association (1816, 1817, and 1822). He wrote a circular letter for the Sandy Creek Association in 1816 and another in 1822 on "The Encouragement of Itinerant Preachers." In 1823 he was present at the Sandy Creek Association as an agent for domestic missions and took up a collection of $18.73 and a gold ring.

In 1826 Daniel went to Virginia where he served the Black Creek and High Hills Baptist churches in the Virginia-Portsmouth Baptist Association; at Black Creek he took the position of a pastor who would not baptize slaveholders. In November 1827 he began to preach just across the state line in Gates County, and by February 1828 he began baptizing converts. That May he organized a church of thirty-one members at Sandy Cross. For four years (1827–30) he attended the Chowan Baptist Association as a delegate from the Virginia-Portsmouth Baptist Association.

At the first meeting of the North Carolina Baptist State Convention, held in 1830, Daniel was appointed an agent of the convention. He soon was preaching and traveling from Northampton County to Camden County in northeastern North Carolina. Daniel then removed to Tennessee and, after spending some time in itinerant work in the central part of the state, settled in Lexington. From there he moved to Paris, Tenn. In July 1837 he wrote to the *Biblical Recorder* that his health was restored and that he was able to travel and preach each day. In the fall he was elected as a delegate from Paris Baptist Church to the Western Baptist Convention of Tennessee and the Western Baptist Education Society. As a member of the committee to locate a literary institution, he persuaded the delegates to select Paris for the site; he also served on the committees assigned to secure a charter from the legislature and to appoint trustees for the institution. In August 1837 he informed the *Biblical Recorder* about the committee's determination to establish an educational institution and requested the support of other states.

In 1839 Daniel moved to Mississippi. There he issued a circular calling for a meeting to organize a Southern Home Mission Society. At the meeting, held in Columbus, he was elected as the general agent to travel in the society's behalf. He finally settled in Salem, Miss., which he regarded as home for the remainder of his life.

Daniel was a wanderer and had no continuing home base. He was easily discouraged and just as easily induced to change his place by the prospect of greater usefulness elsewhere. The revival spirit appealed to him and he was disposed to fix his residence where religious excitement prevailed. Consequently, he played a prominent role in the organization and maintenance of many religious and benevolent associations. Much of his time was occupied in these duties, and during the greater part of his life he was either a missionary or an agent of one of them. He served the North Carolina Baptist Benevolent Society, the North Carolina Baptist Society for Foreign and Domestic Missions, the Baptist Board of Foreign Missions, the American Baptist Home Mission Society, the Baptist State Conventions of Tennessee and North Carolina, the Southwestern Baptist Home Mission Society, and educational societies in Tennessee and Mississippi. When overtaken with his final illness, he was on a projected tour of Tennessee, Virginia, North Carolina, South Carolina, Alabama, and Mississippi for two of these societies.

Just before his death Daniel wrote: "During the thirty-seven years that have passed since I commenced the work of the ministry, I have travelled for the purpose of preaching the gospel about sixty thousand miles, preached upwards of five thousand sermons, and baptized more than fifteen hundred people." His doctrine was of a high Calvinistic cast, but his feelings with regard to the spread of the gospel were apostolic. He felt a peculiar anxiety that could not be confined to the narrow compass of a town, a county, or a state.

Daniel was a vigorous, graceful, and often brilliant writer. Some of his letters were printed in the *Biblical Recorder* (Raleigh) and the *Baptist Banner and Western Pioneer* (Louisville, Ky.). His circular letters, agency reports, and other writings appear in the minutes of the various associations and agencies he represented. In 1812 he published *Daniel's Selection*, a 280-page songbook (printed in Raleigh by Thomas Henderson) containing 176 hymns and 52 "Spiritual Songs." Thirty-eight of the hymns were composed by Daniel himself.

In later years Daniel suffered from dyspepsia and chronic diarrhea, which caused him to lose weight and exhausted his physical powers. In July 1840 when his health began to worsen, he went to the top of the Cumberland Mountains to take the waters, but this did not help him. He became bedridden at Solomon Hartsfield's home, "awaiting the place of final deposit"; nevertheless, he rallied enough to travel to his son's home in Paris, Tenn., where he died and was buried.

At twenty-three Daniel married Penelope Cain Flowers of Chatham County, N.C., a quiet, unassuming coworker. They had eight children, five boys and three girls, three of whom died in infancy. Mrs. Daniel was crippled and confined to her bed for several years before her death on 1 Jan. 1840, in Salem, Miss.

SEE: *Biblical Recorder* (1835–40); Charleston (S.C.) Baptist Association, *Minutes* (1822); Chowan Baptist Association, *Minutes* (1827–30); R. I. Devin, *History of Grassy Creek Baptist Church* (1880); North Carolina Baptist Society for Foreign and Domestic Missions, *Minutes* (1817–19, 1824); George Purefoy, *History of Sandy Creek Baptist Association* (1859); *Triennial Register* (1832, 1836); Virginia Baptist State Convention, *Minutes* (1834); *Wake Forest Student*, October 1905–September 1907; Western Tennessee Baptist State Convention, *Minutes* (1837).

JOHN R. WOODARD

**Daniels, Charles Cleaves** *(23 Sept. 1864–20 Mar. 1951)*, editor, lawyer, and government official, was born on Ocracoke Island where his mother had fled after Union troops wrecked the Daniels hometown of Washington. His father, Josephus Daniels, Sr., died on 28 Jan. 1865 and never saw his youngest son. His mother, Mary Cleaves Seabrook Daniels, raised Charles Cleaves and his two older brothers, Josephus, Jr., and Franklin Arthur, in Wilson. Young Daniels attended Wilson Collegiate Institute and the summer school operated by Edward Morse Nadal in Wilson. With his brother Josephus, he began the Kinston *Free Press* in April 1882. After editing the *Free Press* for three years, he returned to Wilson and edited Josephus's *Advance* while his brother worked in Raleigh. He read law in Wilson and in the early 1890s moved to Macon County to practice with George A. Jones.

In 1893 Daniels became a special agent of the U.S. General Land Office investigating frauds on public lands and Indian reservations in the Cherokee Strip, later Oklahoma. He also served briefly as county attorney for "L" county, which became Grant County, Okla.

In the late 1890s Daniels returned to Wilson to practice law; in 1898 he was elected chairman of the Democratic county committee. The following year he was chosen chief clerk of the state senate. In 1901 Governor Charles B. Aycock appointed Daniels solicitor for the Fourth Judicial District, which included Wilson County. Elected twice to the post, Daniels served as solicitor until 1913. In Wilson he also practiced law with Frederick Dudley Swindell and from 1909 to 1912 represented the Ware-Kramer Tobacco Company of Wilson in a successful suit against the American Tobacco Company under the Sherman Antitrust Act.

The U.S. attorney general named Daniels a U.S. attorney to protect the Chippewa Indians in Minnesota, and he successfully prosecuted numerous fraud cases for Indians. He again left the government in 1916 to practice law in New York City. After World War I he headed a secret bureau of anti-Jewish investigation that had been established by Henry Ford. From 1934 to 1940 he served as a special assistant to the attorney general representing the federal government in matters pertaining to Iroquois Indians.

After practicing law in New York for many years, Daniels died in Saint Luke's Hospital, New York. He was buried in Maplewood Cemetery, Wilson. Daniels married Mary Robinson of Franklin, and they had three children, Charles Cleaves, Jr., James Robinson, and Evelyn Hope.

SEE: Charles Cleaves Daniels Papers (Southern Historical Collection, University of North Carolina, Chapel Hill); Josephus Daniels, *Tar Heel Editor* (1939); Joseph L. Morrison, *Josephus Daniels, Small-d Democrat* (1966); Raleigh *News and Observer*, 21 Mar. 1951.

CHARLES W. EAGLES

**Daniels, Frank Arthur** *(9 Sept. 1858–15 Apr. 1939)*, jurist, was born in Washington, N.C., the eldest son of Josephus and Mary Cleaves Seabrook Daniels, both of families of English descent long settled in eastern North Carolina. With the coming of the Civil War, Josephus Daniels, a Whig and Union man who did not believe in slavery or secession, remained a noncombatant but worked as a skilled carpenter in the Confederate shipyards in Wilmington. Later he moved to New Bern and sent his family as refugees from the Union-occupied area to Ocracoke Island. In early January 1865, while on a mission of relief to old friends in Washington, N.C., he was wounded when a small group of Georgia troops fired on the noncombatant vessel on which he was traveling. He died in New Bern on 28 Jan. 1865.

Frank Daniels and two younger brothers, Josephus and Charles Cleaves, were reared in the Methodist tradition of the family by a strong Christian mother who supported her boys as a milliner and as postmistress in Wilson. Frank was educated in the Wilson Collegiate Institute, at The University of North Carolina (1878–79), and at the law school of Judges Robert P. Dick and John H. Dillard in Greensboro (1880). He was licensed as an attorney in the spring of 1881. In January 1882 he began to practice with Charles Brantley Aycock in Goldsboro; the partnership continued until Aycock, after serving as governor, moved to Raleigh in 1909. Daniels served in Democratic party councils and in 1899 and 1900 in the state senate. In 1910 he was unanimously nominated for judgeship of the superior court for his district, then composed of Wayne, Johnston, Wake, and Harnett counties. Elected in November 1910, he was twice reelected and served for twenty-four years. In 1934, at the age of seventy-five, he declined to seek reelection and retired to the emergency bench.

A man of austere countenance whose slim features often broke into a smile, he had stern views about justice but added warmth and humor to mercy. He held court under the system then prevailing in practically every county of the state. He was welcomed as a "Southerner of the old school" in all of them. As judge and citizen he was regarded as a dyspeptic optimist. On the bench he was sometimes tart about "conflicting decisions and poorly considered legislation." Lawyers and court officials in every county regarded him with veneration and accepted with amusement his complaints about drafts in the courtrooms and the indigestibility of food available in the county seats. The convivial Charles Aycock joked that, while Frank never joined in the social drinking of bench and bar, he amassed an array of patent medicines of high alcoholic content. In his day he was certainly the state's favorite hypochondriac, attaining, despite a life of uninterrupted fragility, the age of eighty-one.

In 1885 Daniels married Carrie Whitfield Borden of Goldsboro. Their children were Frank Borden Daniels, George Seabrook Daniels, and Mary Cleaves Daniels (m. Henry M. Stenhouse). The first Mrs. Daniels died in 1906; in 1920 he married her sister, Mary Carrow Borden, who died in 1937. The judge was buried in Willow Dale Cemetery, Goldsboro. In 1940 a portrait of Judge Daniels was unveiled in the Wayne County Superior Court in Goldsboro.

SEE: Josephus Daniels, *Tar Heel Editor* (1939); Raleigh *News and Observer*, 16, 17 Apr. 1939, 8 Feb., 7 June 1940.

JONATHAN DANIELS

**Daniels, Jonathan Worth** *(26 Apr. 1902–6 Nov. 1981)*, editor and author, was born in Raleigh to Josephus and Addie Worth Bagley Daniels. Named for his maternal grandfather, Jonathan Worth, who was governor of North Carolina, he was the third son of the owner and editor of the Raleigh *News and Observer*. After attending Centennial School in Raleigh (1908–13), he moved to Washington, D.C., with his family in 1913 when his father became secretary of the navy. After studying there at John Eaton School (1913–15) and St. Albans School (1915–18), he continued his education at The University of North Carolina. He received a B.A. in 1921 and an M.A. in English the following year. As a student in Chapel Hill, he edited *The Daily Tar Heel* and participated in the Carolina Playmakers; during the summers he worked as a reporter for his father's newspaper.

After completing his studies at the university, Daniels briefly reported for the Louisville (Ky.) *Times* before studying law at Columbia University in 1922–23. Failing out of law school, he passed the North Carolina bar examination after an intensive summer course in Chapel Hill. He never practiced law. He returned to Raleigh in 1923 as a reporter and sports editor for the *News and Observer*; from 1925 to 1928 he served as the paper's correspondent from the nation's capital. In 1930 he moved to New York City to write for *Fortune* magazine. His novel *Clash of Angels*, published in the same year, brought him a year-long Guggenheim Fellowship in creative writing that allowed him to travel and write in France, Italy, and Switzerland during 1930–31. He resumed work on the staff of *Fortune* before rejoining the *News and Observer* in 1932 as associate editor. When Josephus Daniels became ambassador to Mexico in 1933, Jonathan Daniels assumed the editorship of the family's newspaper and held the post until 1942.

During the 1930s Daniels strongly supported President Franklin D. Roosevelt's New Deal, advocated equal treatment for Negroes, defended the rights of organized labor, and, as a result, gained a reputation as a southern liberal. In *The Mind of the South*, W. J. Cash described Daniels as "sometimes waxing almost too uncritical in his eagerness to champion the underdog." While expressing his opinions on the *News and Observer*'s editorial page, he also contributed scores of articles and reviews to national magazines and wrote *A Southerner Discovers the South* (1938) and *Tar Heels: A Portrait of North Carolina* (1941). In 1940–42 his column, "A Native at Large," appeared weekly in the *Nation*.

Early in 1942 Daniels joined the war effort in Washington, D.C., as assistant director of the Office of Civilian Defense in charge of civilian mobilization. In the fall of 1942 he began special assignments for President Roosevelt, and in March 1943 the president appointed Daniels one of his six administrative assistants. His work for Roosevelt involved the Tennessee Valley Authority, wartime baseball overseas, the Rural Electrification Administration, and domestic race relations. In March 1945 Roosevelt named him his press secretary, and he continued in the position temporarily under President Harry S Truman. Daniels campaigned with Truman in 1948 and wrote a biography of the president, *The Man of Independence*, in 1950.

Daniels moved back to Raleigh in the summer of 1945 and continued his writing. His *Frontier on the Potomac* (1946) recounted his wartime impressions and experiences. He assisted his father as the *News and Observer*'s executive editor in 1947 and succeeded to the editorship after Josephus Daniels's death the next year. Under his direction the newspaper followed a liberal editorial policy. Daniels supported W. Kerr Scott's gubernatorial candidacy in 1948 and, while Democratic national committeeman (1949–52), suggested in 1949 that Governor Scott name Frank P. Graham to the seat left vacant by the death of Senator J. Melville Broughton. In 1950 Daniels endorsed Senator Graham and worked for his campaign for reelection. During the 1950s he urged the South to accept school desegregation, and in 1956 he strenuously opposed Governor Luther H. Hodges's program for the state's schools. As an editor and politician, Daniels was, according to the *Charlotte Observer*, not only "a graceful writer and tart social critic" but "also a force for progress in North Carolina," especially in race relations.

In addition to his editorials, Daniels in the postwar years wrote dozens of books and articles. *The Time Between the Wars* (1966) and *Washington Quadrille* (1968) first publicized Franklin D. Roosevelt's affair with Lucy Mercer Rutherford. His historical studies included three children's books and a biography of General Milton Littlefield in *Prince of the Carpetbaggers* (1958), an account of crusading editors in *They Will Be Heard* (1965), and *Ordeal of Ambition: Jefferson, Hamilton, Burr* (1970). *White House Witness 1942–1945* (1975) covered his work for Roosevelt.

Daniels also devoted much time to public service. He represented the United States on the United Nations Subcommission for the Prevention of Discrimination and the Protection of Minorities (1947–53), was a member of the public advisory board of the Economic Cooperation Administration and the Mutual Security Agency (1948–53), and served on the Federal Hospital Council (1948–53). He also was a member of the board of trustees of Vassar College in the 1940s and of the United States Advisory Commission on Information in the 1960s.

In the 1960s Daniels began spending increasing time at his home in Hilton Head, S.C.; in 1970 he moved there. He helped establish the Hilton Head *Island Packet* and contributed a weekly column, "Sojourner's Scrapbook," to the paper.

Daniels was a lifelong loyal Democrat. He belonged to the Episcopal Church of the Good Shepherd in Raleigh and St. Luke's Episcopal Church in Hilton Head. He was a member of Delta Kappa Epsilon, the National Press Club, the Watauga Club, and the Century Club of New York.

On 5 Sept. 1923 Daniels married Elizabeth Bridgers; they had one daughter, Elizabeth. His first wife died in December 1929. He married Lucy Billing Cathcart on 30 Apr. 1932, and they had three daughters, Lucy, Adelaide, and Mary Cleves. His second wife died in January 1979. Daniels died in Hilton Head and was buried in Six Oaks Cemetery on the island.

SEE: *Charlotte Observer*, 10 Nov. 1981; Jonathan Worth Daniels Papers (Southern Historical Collection, University of North Carolina, Chapel Hill); Charles W. Eagles, *Jonathan Daniels and Race Relations: The Evolution of a Southern Liberal* (1982); Raleigh *News and Observer*, 10 Nov. 1981.

CHARLES W. EAGLES

**Daniels, Josephus** *(18 May 1862–15 Jan. 1948)*, newspaper editor, secretary of the navy, and ambassador to Mexico, was born in Washington, N.C., the fourth of five children of Josephus and Mary Cleaves Seabrook Daniels. His great-grandfather, Thomas Daniels, had migrated to Roanoke Island from Ireland in the late eighteenth century. His father, a Whig and a Unionist before the Civil War, was a ship carpenter and worked in the Confederate shipyards at Wilmington during the war; he was killed 28 Jan. 1865 when a steamer in which he was a passenger was fired on by Confederate troops at Washington.

Josephus's mother then moved to Wilson and in December 1866 became postmistress of that community. She raised young Daniels as a devout Methodist and sent him to the Wilson Collegiate Institute, a private boarding school. He left the school in 1880 to become the local editor of the *Wilson Advance*. Two years later he purchased the paper. By 1885 he was also writing editorials for the *Kinston Free Press*, which he owned with his brother Charles, and for the *Rocky Mount Reporter* of which he was part owner. In the same year, he was president of the North Carolina Press Association.

In 1884 Daniels "conceived the idea" of practicing law while continuing in his chosen profession as editor. He entered the law school at The University of North Carolina at Chapel Hill in the summer of 1885 and passed the bar examinations in October. In the meantime, through the generosity of Julian S. Carr, a wealthy Durham industrialist, he had acquired ownership of a Raleigh weekly, a recent combination of the *State Chronicle* and the *Farmer and Mechanic*. The new weekly succeeded, and Daniels's growing reputation persuaded the legislature to appoint him state printer in 1887, 1889, 1891, and 1893. Encouraged by relative prosperity, in 1890 he converted the *State Chronicle* into a daily, a venture that failed financially two years later. He disposed of the *State Chronicle* but promptly established the weekly *North Carolinian*.

During these years, Daniels's editorial writing was influenced by his membership in the Watauga Club which he had joined in 1885, the year after the club's founding. Among the goals of this organization were the promotion of popular education and the encouragement of industry in the South. Daniels endorsed these goals in principle and supported federal aid to education and the establishment of the North Carolina College of Agriculture and Mechanic Arts (chartered in 1887 and opened in 1889). However he distrusted "big business" and fought the "tobacco trust." Like the Populists, he favored the establishment of a state railroad commission, antitrust legislation, the free coinage of silver, a graduated income tax, and the direct election of senators. He was, moreover, an early supporter of woman suffrage, of workmen's compensation laws, and of the regulation of child labor. Although he frequently supported such issues through his editorial columns, he remained a loyal Democrat throughout his career. Indeed, his partisanship in the 1880s had caused his mother to lose her job as postmistress at Wilson; and his effective campaigning in 1892 resulted a year later in Cleveland's appointing him to a post in the Department of the Interior.

For years, one of Daniels's principal rivals in the newspaper business had been the Raleigh *News and Observer*, edited by Samuel A. Ashe. In 1894, an agent of Julian Carr in collaboration with Daniels purchased that newspaper with the understanding that Daniels would be its editor. In August of the same year, Daniels began writing editorials from Washington, D.C., for the *News and Observer* and early in 1895 moved back to Raleigh to assume complete control.

Daniels returned to a state in political turmoil. In 1894 a "fusion" of Republicans and Populists had won control of the state legislature, and in 1896 a Republican, Daniel L. Russell, was elected governor. Daniels became a devoted follower of William Jennings Bryan and helped plan Bryan's strategy for obtaining the presidential nomination in 1896. Having proved his effectiveness as a party worker, Daniels in 1896 was appointed Democratic national committeeman from North Carolina, a post he retained until 1916. In North Carolina he did his best to split the Republican-Populist coalition. In the "white supremacy" campaign of 1898, the *News and Observer* emotionally warned white voters of the dangers of "Negro domination." Two years later Daniels enthusiastically backed Charles B. Aycock, a lifelong friend, for governor and supported the amendment to the state constitution that effectively disfranchised most black voters. During these years, too, Daniels led a fight against those who would deprive The University of North Carolina of state financial support and supported all measures that would control the sale of alcoholic beverages, particularly the referendum for statewide prohibition in 1908.

Under Daniels's vigorous editorship, the *News and Observer* became a success. He had taken a virtually bankrupt paper with a circulation of perhaps 2,500 in 1894, paid off its debts, bought up Julian Carr's stock in 1905, and saw the circulation steadily increase (by 1947 it had reached about 100,000). He had also founded *The North Carolina Yearbook and Business Directory* and published *The North Carolina Review*, a literary supplement, from 1909 to 1913.

In the meantime, he had become a friend and political supporter of Woodrow Wilson. Daniels succeeded in healing some of the differences between Wilson and Bryan, played an effective role in securing Wilson's nomination in 1912, and became Wilson's publicity chief in the presidential campaign. Appointed secretary of the navy, he was one of four cabinet members to serve throughout Wilson's two terms. As secretary, he demonstrated an unprecedented interest in the lot of enlisted men, providing them with schools aboard ship and in the navy yards. He upset the navy brass by banning the use of alcoholic beverages in those locations, carried out Wilson's orders in the occupation of Vera Cruz in 1914, and fought continually to protect naval oil reserves against private exploitation. In 1915 Daniels launched an enormous building program and established the Naval Consulting Board headed by Thomas A. Edison; the following year he won congressional approval for the building of a government-operated armor plate factory. During the war he also served on the Council of National Defense, the general agency supervising the war effort, as well as on the Committee on Public Information, the agency responsible for censorship and propagandizing the war effort.

In 1921 Daniels returned to Raleigh and the *News and Observer*. He had become a member of the board of trustees of The University of North Carolina in 1901 and remained an active trustee until his death. During the 1920s, he was a persistent advocate of the consolidation into one university of the three state-supported colleges at Chapel Hill, Raleigh, and Greensboro; he also championed the nomination of Frank P. Graham to succeed Harry Woodburn Chase as president of the university in 1930. In politics, he fought the Ku Klux Klan; he supported McAdoo in 1924 and Cordell Hull in 1928 for the Democratic nomination for the presidency, but on both occasions loyally endorsed the party's nominees. Despite a long-standing principle to avoid running for elective office, he probably would have accepted the nomination for governor in 1932 had he not been seriously injured in an automobile accident.

In 1932 Daniels supported Franklin D. Roosevelt first as a candidate for the Democratic nomination and then in the presidential campaign. Roosevelt had served as assistant secretary of the navy under Daniels from 1913 to 1921, and in spite of some differences each came to have sincere admiration for the other. In 1933, Roosevelt appointed Daniels ambassador to Mexico. In this post Daniels in 1934 negotiated a settlement of special claims of U.S. citizens for losses incurred during the recent Mexican revolution; over a longer period of time, he worked out terms for the expropriation by the Mexican government of foreign-owned oil properties. He otherwise comported himself to win the plaudits of Roosevelt and the affection of Mexicans of all classes.

Throughout his life Daniels was a devoted, indeed, a sentimental family man. On 2 May 1888 he married Addie Worth Bagley of Raleigh. They had six children. Two daughters died in infancy, Adelaid in 1893 at the age of one and another shortly after birth in 1911. Four sons survived: Josephus (b. 1894), Worth Bagley (b. 1899), Jonathan Worth (b. 1902), and Frank Arthur (b. 1904). His wife's increasingly crippling arthritis led to his resignation as ambassador to Mexico in 1941. They returned to Raleigh where she died in 1943. Again a full-time editor, Daniels fought for a nine-month school term and for a "good-health" program in the state. Nationally he opposed compulsory military service after the war and supported Roosevelt's renomination in 1944. On the question of civil rights, he opposed efforts on the part of southern delegates to write a white supremacy plank into the Democratic platform in 1944. He advocated fair treatment for black people, but opposed federal civil rights legislation and feared social intermingling. Although he was ashamed of the extreme racism that had inspired him in 1898 and 1900, he continued to favor what he considered to be Aycock's approach of solving racial problems through education.

Daniels wrote a number of books, including *The Fallen Hero: A Biographical Sketch of Worth Bagley, Ensign, U.S.N.* (1898); *The Navy and the Nation; War-time Addresses . . .* (1919); *Our Navy at War* (1922); *The Life of Woodrow Wilson, 1856–1924* (1924); *Tar Heel Editor* (1939); *Editor in Politics* (1941); *The Wilson Era: Years of Peace, 1910–1917* (1944); *The Wilson Era: Years of War and After, 1917–1923* (1946); *Shirt-Sleeve Diplomat* (1947); and *Roosevelt and Daniels, A Friendship in Politics* (1952).

Daniels remained vigorous until November 1947 when his health declined. Nevertheless, he went to his office regularly until 3 Jan. 1948. He died of pneumonia at his home and was buried in Oakwood Cemetery, Raleigh.

SEE: Bagley Family Papers (Southern Historical Collection, University of North Carolina, Chapel Hill); J. Leonard Bates, "Josephus Daniels and the Naval Oil Reserves," *U.S. Naval Institute Proceedings* (February 1953); E. David Cronon, "A Southern Progressive Looks at the New Deal," *Journal of Southern History* 24 (1958), "Josephus Daniels as a Reluctant Candidate," *North Carolina Historical Review* 33 (1956), *Josephus Daniels in Mexico* (1960), ed., *The Cabinet Diaries of Josephus Daniels, 1913–1921* (1963); Addie Bagley Daniels, *Recollections of a Cabinet Minister's Wife* (1945); Jonathan Daniels, *Tar Heels* (1941), *The End of Innocence* (1954); Jonathan Daniels Papers (Southern Historical Collection, University of North Carolina, Chapel Hill); Josephus Daniels Papers (Manuscript Division, Library of Congress, Washington, D.C.); Helen G. Edmonds, *The Negro and Fusion Politics in North Carolina* (1951); Joseph L. Morrison, *Josephus Daniels Says . . .: An Editor's Political Odyssey From Bryan to Wilson and F.D.R., 1894–1913* (1962), "Josephus Daniels—Simpatico," *Journal of InterAmerican Studies* 5 (1963), *Josephus Daniels: The Small-d Democrat* (1966); Joseph F. Steelman, "The Progressive Era in North Carolina, 1884–1917" (Ph.D. diss., University of North Carolina, 1955); U.S. Senate, Naval Affairs Subcommittee, *Hearings, Awarding Medals in the Naval Service* (1920), *Naval Investigation, Hearings* (1920); Daniel J. Whitener, *Prohibition in North Carolina, 1715–1945, James Sprunt Studies in History and Political Science* 27 (1946); Woodrow Wilson Papers (Manuscript Division, Library of Congress, Washington, D.C.).

RICHARD L. WATSON

**Darby, John Fletcher** *(10 Dec. 1803–11 May 1882)*, congressman and banker, was born in Person County, near Roxboro, but the names of his parents do not appear to be recorded. At the age of fifteen, he moved with his family to Missouri, probably rural Warren County, where his father engaged in farming. His education in local schools was fragmentary. In 1825 the family moved again, this time to Frankfort, Ky. There Darby began to read law and was admitted to the bar. He subsequently located in St. Louis, Mo.

Immediately active in the political life of that midwestern city, in 1835 Darby was elected its mayor at age thirty-two. Three years later he was a successful candidate for the Missouri state senate, though he continued to serve as mayor of St. Louis for three full terms through 1841.

After fifteen years in public life and practicing law, Darby was elected to Congress on the Whig ticket. He served two years in the Thirty-second session (1851–53). When he returned to St. Louis, he spent the rest of his life as a banker and was a respected financial adviser in the mid-century expansion of that area for nearly thirty years.

Darby died in his seventy-eighth year at his home near Pendleton Station in Warren County, Mo., and was buried in Calvary Cemetery, St. Louis.

SEE: *Biog. Dir. Am. Cong.* (1950); Leonidas L. Polk, *Handbook of North Carolina* (1879); *Who Was Who in America* (1967).

C. SYLVESTER GREEN

**Darden, Mills (or Miles)** *(7 Oct. 1799–23 Jan. 1857),* innkeeper and farmer, was reputed to be the heaviest human on record until the twentieth century. He was born on a farm near Rich Square in Northampton County but moved to Madison County, Tenn., about 1829. By 1840 he was living in Henderson County, Tenn.; ten years later he was operating a hotel on the square in Lexington, the seat of Henderson County. He also owned a farm in the county.

Darden's first wife, Mary, died in 1837 and was buried on his farm in the Chapel Hill community of Henderson County. The name of his second wife was given in the census as Tameria. In 1850 the household included Tameria, age thirty-eight, and seven children whose ages ranged from one to twenty-one.

Although Darden apparently refused to be weighed after moving to Tennessee, his neighbors, by testing the tension on his ox wagon springs while he was aboard and then piling on rocks for a corresponding tension, estimated his weight to be a little over 1,000 pounds. The *Guinness Book of World Records* (1977 ed.) accepts his weight as 1,020 pounds, second only to that of Robert Earl Hughes of Illinois, who died in 1958.

Darden's height was 7 feet, 6 inches; his waist measurement was 6 feet, 4 inches. The records of William Brooks indicate that he furnished 16 yards of cambric for Darden's shroud. The coffin required 156 feet of lumber, 3 pounds of nails, 4 boxes of tacks, 17 yards of flannel lining, and 44 feet of trimming ribbon. Seventeen men were required to put the body in the coffin. Darden was buried on his farm beside his first wife.

SEE: Darden documents (in possession of William L. Barry, Lexington, Ky.).

H. G. JONES

**Darden, William Abram** *(15 May 1836–2 June 1890),* farmer, politician, and Alliance leader, was born in Greene County to William Augustus and Harriet Speight Darden. He was educated in neighborhood schools before he began the study of law at Randolph-Macon College. Poor eyesight compelled him to abandon his studies in his junior year and take up farming.

In April 1861 Darden volunteered for service with the Confederacy and was elected second lieutenant under Captain R. H. Drysdale in Company A, Third North Carolina Regiment (Greene County Rifles). He represented Greene County in the Secession Convention of 1861–62. Again volunteering for Confederate service, he assisted Captain Andrew Moore to raise troops for Company F, Sixty-first North Carolina Regiment (Clingman's Brigade), of which he became second lieutenant and later captain. He was captured in the attack on Fort Harrison, Va., on 30 Sept. 1864 and imprisoned at Fort Delaware until June 1865.

When the war ended Darden returned to his farm and became active in Democratic politics. In 1884 he was elected to the North Carolina House of Representatives from Greene County and served one term. In the late 1880s he became active in the Farmers' Alliance, a farm protest organization that spread from Texas into other southern states. He served as first president of Enterprise Alliance, a subordinate order, and first president of Greene County Alliance. In 1888 he was elected the first business agent of the North Carolina Farmers' State Alliance. He declined to serve a second term but accepted appointment as district lecturer for the First and Second Congressional districts.

Darden was married twice. On 13 Aug. 1857 he married Sarah Speight Moye by whom he had three children. She died on 25 Aug. 1863. Six years later, on 26 Jan. 1869, he married Catherine Speight Adams who bore him nine children, seven of whom survived. He died from a heart attack in Gatesville, Gates County, at one o'clock, the hour scheduled for his Alliance lecture. His funeral and burial took place at his home, Speight's Bridge. He had been a member of the Methodist Episcopal church since the age of six.

SEE: Levi Branson, ed., *North Carolina Business Directory* (1878); Elias Carr Papers (Manuscript Collection, East Carolina University, Greenville); John L. Cheney, Jr., ed., *North Carolina Government, 1585–1974* (1975); Walter Clark, ed., *Histories of the Several Regiments and Battalions from North Carolina in the Great War, 1861–65* (1901); J. G. McCormick, *Personnel of the Convention of 1861* (1900); North Carolina Farmers' State Alliance, *Proceedings* (1889–91); Raleigh *Progressive Farmer*, 16 Apr. 1889 (photograph); Lala Carr Steelman, "The Role of Elias Carr in the North Carolina Farmers' Alliance," *The North Carolina Historical Review* 57 (1980).

LALA CARR STEELMAN

**Dare, Ananias** *(fl. 1587),* was one of twelve "Assistants" in the government of the Citie of Ralegh in Virginia and a member of the "Lost Colony" of 1587 that arrived at Roanoke Island in July. He was described in 1586 as a tiler and bricklayer but the next year, in a document drawn up by Sir Walter Raleigh, he was referred to as a gentleman "late of London." His wife was Eleanor White, daughter of Governor John White of the 1587 colony, and Dare's name appears third in the list of colonists. Nothing further is recorded of the members of the colony after White sailed for England on 27 August. Dare was survived in England by an illegitimate son, John Dare, to whom his property was awarded by court action in 1597. The Dare family likely resided in the Parish of St. Bride's, Fleet Street, London, although the name also appears in records of other London parishes of the sixteenth and seventeenth centuries as well as in Devon.

**Dare, Eleanor White** *(b. ca. 1565)*, a member of the "Lost Colony" of 1587, was the daughter of Governor John White of that colony. She may have been the Elinor White who married John Underwood on 17 Jan. 1580 in St. Botolph Church, Bishopgate, London, but was widowed prior to her marriage to Ananias Dare. Her name appears first in the list of women of the "Lost Colony." Her daughter, Virginia, was born less than a month after the colony landed.

**Dare, Virginia** *(b. 18 Aug. 1587)*, the first English child born in America, was the daughter of Ananias and Eleanor White Dare and granddaughter of Governor John White. Born on Roanoke Island, she was christened on 24 August by the name given by Queen Elizabeth to the new country. A terra cotta memorial to her was installed in St. Bride's Church, Fleet Street, London, after that church was restored following World War II.

SEE: Richard Hakluyt, *The Principall Navigations Voiages and Discoveries of the English Nation* (1589); Cornelius Hallem, *The Registers of St. Botolph, Bishopgate, London*, vol. 1 (1889); Paul Hulton and David B. Quinn, *The American Drawings of John White, 1577–1590*, vol. 1 (1964); William S. Powell, "Roanoke Colonists and Explorers: An Attempt at Identification," *North Carolina Historical Review* 34 (April 1957); David B. Quinn, ed., *The Roanoke Voyages*, 2 vols. (1955).

WILLIAM S. POWELL

**Dargan, Edmund Spann (or Strother)** *(15 Apr. 1805–24 Nov. 1879)*, jurist, was born in Montgomery County, near Wadesboro. His father was a Baptist minister of Irish descent. His mother, a Miss Lilly before her marriage, was the daughter of an Englishman. Dargan's father died when he was young, leaving him to support himself. A farm laborer until the age of twenty-three, he was mostly self-educated. He studied English, Latin, and Greek, and in 1828 read law in the office of Colonel Joseph Pickett in Wadesboro. In 1829 he walked from his home to Washington, Autauga County, Ala. It is said that not only was he poor, but also he was not handsome and was quite careless of his appearance. On the way to Washington a ferryman made fun of him and his journey. Dargan angrily replied, "You will yet live to see me chief justice of Alabama." He fulfilled the prediction twenty years later.

Dargan was immediately admitted to the Washington bar when he applied in 1829. He taught in a private school for three months and was elected justice of the peace for several years; at the same time, he practiced law. Finding few opportunities in the rural village of Washington, he moved to Montgomery in 1833 and opened a law office there. In 1840 he ran for the legislature but was defeated. One year later the General Assembly elected him judge of the circuit court of the Mobile district over Judge William Hale of Mobile County. Dargan immediately moved to Mobile to fill the position. Once when he went on circuit he took six shirts with him, but returned with an empty travel bag. To his surprise, he discovered he was wearing all six shirts, one over the other.

In 1842 Dargan resigned as judge and resumed his law practice. In 1844 he was elected mayor of Mobile as well as state senator, filling both offices at once. He resigned from the senate the following year to become the Democratic candidate for Congress. Dargan defeated his Whig opponent, William D. Dunn, a popular and polished politician. During the campaign the two candidates went to Washington on their stumping tour. After they spoke, a Colonel Prince, the wealthiest man in the area, headed for home with Dunn. "You are going to be beaten," remarked Prince. "How's that?" asked Dunn. "Didn't you write to me that I was the strongest man in the district? and haven't we a majority in it?" "I know that," said Prince looking around, "but here you are walking off to dinner with me, the richest man in the county, and there sits Dargan, in that crowd of one-gallus fellows, picking the ticks off his legs."

Dargan served in the House of Representatives in the Twenty-ninth Congress. His proposals during discussion of the Oregon question led to the compromise settlement that was adopted. At the end of his term in 1846 he was renominated but declined. On 16 Dec. 1847, the General Assembly elected him associate justice of the supreme court of Alabama to fill the vacancy caused by the death of Judge Goldthwaite. He became chief justice on 1 July 1849, when Justice Collier resigned. On 6 Dec. 1852 he resigned the position to resume his practice in Mobile and was not again involved in politics until 1861. In that year he was a delegate from Mobile to the convention where he voted for secession. His district elected him to the Confederate Congress in 1862. In the House, his efforts were instrumental in leading to the secretary of war's order in 1863 that, except in urgent cases, there would be no government impressment of goods held for consumption by oneself, employees, or slaves, or while being carried to market.

While serving in Congress, Dargan became the object of some derogatory remarks made by Governor Foote of Tennessee, a fellow congressman. In his rough manner, Dargan jumped up, grabbed the governor by the collar, and raised his hand as if to strike him. He was accused of raising a bowie knife to Governor Foote by E. A. Pollard, a writer, although it was later made known that he was actually still holding the pen with which he had been writing when assailed. In 1864 Dargan declined renomination to Congress and took no active part in public affairs when the war was over.

He married Roxanna Brack of Montgomery. One of their children, a son named Moro (b. 24 Mar. 1845), was a major and aide on the staff of General Clayton; after the war he was a broker in San Francisco, Calif. He died in Spokane Falls, Wash., on 6 May 1883.

Dargan's decisions on issues won him support among the learned men of his day, whereas his appearance and manner won him the favor of the rougher elements. His shoes were of the cheapest sort and he tied them with leather thongs. Before appearing in front of a jury in an important case he was careful to mar his appearance. His hair would be uncombed and his collar open, and he would untie his shoes to make them gap. Outside of court Dargan appeared dull, drowsy, and dissatisfied, but when presenting a case his face became luminous with intellectual life until he closed the argument and assumed his former expression.

Dargan was buried in the Magnolia Cemetery, Mobile, Ala.

SEE: *Biog. Dir. Am. Cong.* (1950); W. Brewer, *Alabama: Her History, Resources, War Record and Public Men* (1872); William Garret Brown, *A History of Alabama* (1900), *Reminiscences of Public Men in Alabama* (1872); *DAB*, vol. 3 (1959); Clarence Phillips Denman, *The Secession Movement in Alabama* (1933); *Dictionary of Alabama Biography* (n.d.); Walter L. Fleming, *Civil War and Reconstruction in Alabama* (1905); Leonidas L. Polk, *Handbook of North Carolina* (1879); B. F. Riley, *Makers and Romance of Alabama History* (n.d.); *The South in the Building of the Nation*, vol. 2 (1909); *Who Was Who in America* (1967).

SARAH E. HOLEMAN

**Dargan, Olive Tilford** *(11 Jan. 1869–22 Jan. 1968)*, writer, was born at Tilford Springs in Grayson County, Ky., the daughter of Elisha Francis and Rebecca Day Tilford. About 1879 her schoolteacher father moved the family to Missouri and later to Arkansas, where Olive herself began teaching at age fourteen. Three years later she won a state scholarship to study at Peabody College in Nashville, Tenn., from which she was graduated. For several years she taught school in Missouri and Texas, but wanting more education she took graduate courses at Radcliffe College in Massachusetts. After this she taught for a year in a girls' school in Nova Scotia and then took a position as private secretary to a rubber company executive in Boston. Because of failing health, she moved in 1897 to Blue Ridge, Ga., where on 2 Mar. 1898 she married Pegram Dargan, a South Carolinian whom she had met while at Radcliffe.

The young couple settled in New York City as writers, with Pegram concentrating on poetry and Olive on blank verse dramas. Mrs. Dargan's *Semiramis and Other Plays* was published in 1904, followed by *Lords and Lovers* in 1906. These dramas were well reviewed; one critic called her a "poet of exceptional genius." When her health again declined, Mrs. Dargan spent several years in England; there she published another series of plays entitled *The Mortal Gods* in 1912 and a volume of lyric verse, *Pathflower*, in 1914. It was also from England that she published her rarest volume, a serious bit of nonfiction on *The Welsh Pony* (1913), which she researched for a friend in Virginia.

After returning to New York City, Mrs. Dargan suffered a tragic blow when in 1915 her husband was lost at sea on a voyage to the West Indies. Afterward she wrote a series of sonnets in her husband's memory: *The Cycle's Rim*, dedicated "to one drowned at sea." These poems were well received by critics and for them Mrs. Dargan received the poetry award given by the Southern Society of New York. She continued to write, publishing stories and poems in such periodicals as *Scribners*, *Atlantic*, and *Bookman*, and in 1915 she moved to a farm, which her husband had bought some years earlier, near Almond, in Swain County, N.C. In 1922 she published another volume of lyric poetry, *Lute and Furrow*, and in cooperation with Frederick Peterson, a group of plays entitled *Flutter of the Gold Leaf*. A series of short stories written about her mountain neighbors was published in 1925 as *Highland Annals*. Her literary abilities were recognized in 1924, when The University of North Carolina awarded her an honorary doctor of letters degree.

In 1923 the farm home in Swain County burned, destroying many valuable manuscripts including unpublished ones. Once again, Mrs. Dargan took an extended trip to Europe, this time visiting France and Switzerland. In 1925 she returned to North Carolina and bought a home, Bluebonnet Lodge, in Asheville, where she was to remain for the rest of her life. At an age when most writers would have considered retiring, she turned to a new medium—the novel—and produced two of her most notable works: *Call Home the Heart* (1932) and *A Stone Came Rolling* (1935). Written under the pseudonym of Fielding Burke, these were "social problem" novels concerned with the poor mountain men and women who came down out of the hills to work in the textile mills of the North Carolina Piedmont. Widely reviewed, they received both high praise and severe criticism. Although such terms as "avowed radical" and "most radical of the economic novelists" were applied to her, these works did establish Mrs. Dargan as a southern writer who could not be ignored. Since then she has been mentioned in most southern literary histories and anthologies.

Most of Mrs. Dargan's works published after the 1930s were anticlimactic. In 1941 a somewhat reworked and illustrated version of *Highland Annals* was published as *From My Highest Hill*. This was followed in 1947 with a historical novel of the coal mining industry, entitled *Sons of the Stranger*. A book of poems, *The Spotted Hawk*, appeared in 1958, and another group of short stories, *Innocent Bigamy*, in 1962. Mrs. Dargan died at her home in Asheville after an active life of almost a century.

SEE: Clyde H. Cantrell and Walton R. Patrick, eds., *Southern Literature: A Bibliography of Masters' and Doctors' Theses* (1955); Stanley Kunitz, ed., *Twentieth Century Authors* (1955); Virginia Terrell Lathrop, "Olive Tilford Dargan," *North Carolina Librarian* 18 (1960); *New York Times*, 24 Jan. 1968; *North Carolina Authors* (1952); Jane and Thomas Polsky, "The Two Lives of Olive Tilford Dargan," *Southern Packet* 4 (1948); Louis O. Rubin, ed., *A Bibliographical Guide to the Study of Southern Literature* (1969); Richard Walser, ed., *North Carolina Poetry* (1951); Harry F. Warfel, ed., *North American Novelists of Today* (1951); *Who's Who in America*, vol. 6 (1914).

E. D. JOHNSON

**Darnell, William Nelson** *(27 Oct. 1830–30 Oct. 1915)*, missionary, was born in Wilkes County, probably the son of Peter Darnell, Esq., the only one of that name in the county at the time of the 1830 census. In 1834 he moved to Indiana where he attended local schools and Bedford Academy in Lawrence County. Following apprenticeship to a carpenter, he moved to Minnesota in 1854 and fought in regional Indian wars. Early in the Civil War he enlisted in the Seventh Regiment, Minnesota Volunteers. He received several changes in assignment but eventually was named a captain in the Sixty-fifth Regiment, U.S. Colored Troops. After the war he lived in Mississippi for a time and in 1867 was a missionary for the Methodist church among the freedmen. The following year he was in Missouri, also as a missionary among blacks. By 1875 he was living in Greene County, Ind.

In addition to his work as a missionary, from time to time Darnell was a schoolteacher and a farmer. He was a Methodist and a Republican. In Indiana he was a Greene County councilman for four years and represented the county in the General Assembly of 1889. He was an unsuccessful candidate for a seat in the U.S. House of Representatives. After the Civil War he was active in the Grand Army of the Republic. In 1855 he married Mary Adams and they were the parents of four children. He died in Greene County, Ind.

SEE: *Biographical Directory of the Indiana General Assembly* (1980).

WILLIAM S. POWELL

**Darr, Edward Austin** *(23 July 1889–8 Oct. 1958)*, tobacco official, was born in Baltimore, Md., the son of

William H. and Mary Coffman Darr. He was educated in the Baltimore public schools and the McDonogh School for Boys; by attending night school, he received the LL.B. degree from the University of Maryland in 1913. For several years he practiced law in Baltimore before joining a wholesale tobacco firm. He served as a Marine Corps sergeant during World War I and returned to Baltimore as president and part owner of B. L. Frey and Brothers, tobacco dealers. He joined the R. J. Reynolds Tobacco Company in 1920 as assistant secretary and was named sales manager in 1937, vice-president in 1946, and president from 1952 to 1957. At the time of his death, he was vice-chairman of the board and chairman of the executive committee.

Darr married Frances Payne in 1919 but she died in 1920. They had one son, Edward, Jr. In 1924 he married Ruth Ely, a former opera and concert singer, who died 11 Feb. 1958. They had five children: Drusilla Brewster (Mrs. Richard R. Hall), Deborah Ely (Mrs. Robert P. Sartin), Mary Ruth (Mrs. Norman Messner), David William, and Cicely Ann (Mrs. William C. Roth).

Darr was a member of the Winston-Salem Polo team in the late 1920s, a member of Winston-Salem's first boxing commission, and for ten years a member of Reynolds Park Recreation Commission. He served as chairman of the fund drive to build Ernie Shore Field baseball park and as chairman of the United Way. He also held membership in the National Planning Association, the Winston-Salem and National Sales Executives Clubs, Rotary, Twin City Club, Forsyth and Old Town Country clubs, New York Athletic Club, and the Metropolitan Club of New York. He was a member and officer of the Christian Science church, which he joined after a healing, through the church, of his sight. In addition, Darr was instrumental in starting North Carolina's driver education program for students.

In 1957, for the first time, Reynolds Tobacco Company went over the billion dollar sales mark partly as a result of the phenomenal success of the first filter-tipped cigarette made for the American market. Darr brought the idea for filter cigarettes from Switzerland in 1951 but met with opposition within the company. It was noted that "the effort was little more than perfunctory until November 1952, when Darr became Reynolds' president. He immediately threw his entire weight behind the inchoate development effort, and work proceeded with vigor." He "gave instructions to Haddon S. Kirk, . . . director . . . , in charge of manufacturing, to 'start experimenting again with filter-tip cigarettes and develop a blend.' " The new brand, Winston, sold 6.5 billion during the first nine months. Salem filter-tipped menthols followed in April 1956 with corresponding success.

SEE: "The Battle of the Filter Tips," *The National Observer*, 17 Apr. 1967; Bowman Gray, *The Strategy of Change for Business Success*, ed. by Sidney Furst and Milton Sherman (1969); Winston-Salem *Twin City Sentinel*, 8 Oct. 1958.

DEBORAH DARR SARTIN

**Darst, Thomas Campbell** *(10 Nov. 1875–1 Sept. 1948)*, Episcopal bishop, the son of Major Thomas Welch Darst and Margaret Rebecca Glendy, his second wife, was born at Fancy Hill in Pulaski County, Va. Major Darst, who died when his son was seven, was of English and Huguenot ancestry; Mrs. Darst was Scotch-Irish. Both were Presbyterians, worshipping in a church also used by Episcopalians. Young Darst attended public school in Pulaski and, after his mother's death in 1891, continued his schooling in Salem, where he lived with his sister Gillie (Mrs. David Terry Martin). He was graduated from Roanoke College in 1899 after four years of study interrupted by a two-year stint in business in West Virginia and New Jersey.

Soon afterward Darst would fulfill his mother's wish that he become a clergyman; but it was to be in the Episcopal church, into which he had recently been confirmed. He entered the Episcopal Theological Seminary, Alexandria, Va. Ordained deacon by Bishop George W. Peterkin of West Virginia in 1902 and advanced to the priesthood by Bishop Coadjutor W. L. Gravatt the next year, he was successively assistant at Christ Church, Fairmount, W. Va. (1902–3) and rector at Upperville-Middleburg-Aldie, Va. (1903–5); St. Mark's, Richmond (1905–9); St. Paul's, Newport News (1909–14); and St. James's, Richmond (1914–15). As secretary of the General Convention of the Episcopal Church held at Richmond in 1907, he demonstrated his capacity for sustained and productive labor and devotion to duty.

Darst was elected Bishop of East Carolina on 7 Oct. 1914 and consecrated in St. James's Church, Wilmington, on 6 Jan. 1915. By personality and precept he soon won the hearts of his people and guided the diocese through the difficult and demanding years of world war, prosperity, and depression. There were organizational and procedural changes and statistical growth in the diocese, but he put them in perspective with his keynote that organization cannot take the place of the Spirit of God. An earnest and effective preacher, Bishop Darst stressed the importance of missions, taking special interest in those along the Intracoastal Waterway and at the military bases. The bishop was a trustee of Thompson Orphanage, Pineland, St. Mary's Junior College, St. Augustine's College, and The University of the South. He served his church as president of the Fourth Province, member of the Field Department, first chairman of the National Commission on Evangelism (1925–34), and originator and director of the Bishops' Crusade (1926–27). He suffered an illness in 1943, retired as diocesan in 1945 but continued his ministry, and died three years later. The funeral was held at St. James's and interment at Oakdale Cemetery, Wilmington.

Bishop Darst was honored with the D.D. degree by the Virginia Seminary, The University of the South, Roanoke College, The University of North Carolina, and Duke University. He was a member of Pi Kappa Alpha, the Masons, the Knights of Pythias, Kiwanis, and the Democratic party. He took a keen interest in the work of the Roanoke Island Historical Association and in the restoration at Bath.

By his marriage on 5 Nov. 1902 to Florence Newton Wise of Alexandria, Darst had three sons: George Wise (b. 1904), Thomas Campbell, Jr. (b. 1907), and Meade Clark (b. 1910). The first Mrs. Darst died in 1914 and he married, on 26 Apr. 1916, Fannie Lauriston Hardin of Wilmington; from their union was born in 1917 Margaret Glendy, who became the wife of John Clayton Smith.

SEE: Gertrude Carraway, *Crown of Life* (1940); H. J. Darst, *The Darsts of Virginia* (1972); Diocese of East Carolina, *Journals* (scattered vols., 1914–48); *Nat. Cyc. Am. Biog.*, vol. 35 (1949); *North Carolina Biography*, vol. 3 (1941); *Stowe's Clerical Directory of the American Church* (1935); *The Mission Herald* (scattered issues, 1914–48); *The Southern Churchman*, 11 Sept. 1948; Frederick A. Turner, *Bishop Darst and East Carolina During the Last Twenty-Five Years* (1939); *The Virginia Seminary Journal*, Alumni Directory Supplement (October 1959).

LAWRENCE F. BREWSTER

**Dauge (Dozier), Peter** *(7 Dec. 1739–1 Sept. 1801)*, colonel and legislator, was born in Pasquotank County. The first of his family in America was Jacques D'Auge, who moved to Charleston, S.C., from the Province of Berry in France with a band of French Protestants in the early part of the eighteenth century. A son of the D'Auge family, Pierre, moved to Currituck County, N.C., and married Angelica Gregory. One of the large family of children born to this marriage was Peter Dauge, as the name had been anglicized. Around 1706 Peter Dauge crossed over into the Camden area where he met his bride. The interrelated Dauge, Fenner, Ferebee, Boushall, and Etheridge families mainly remained in the counties of Pasquotank and Camden, and some in the Piedmont of North Carolina.

At twenty-six, Dauge was appointed a road overseer in Camden. On 22 Apr. 1776, he was made a major in the Second Regiment of the Pasquotank militia. As second major his first task assigned by the Provincial Congress was for him and Dempsey Gregory to take the slaves belonging to the Tories Thomas McKnight, James Parker, and Robert Gilmore. McKnight's slaves were moved with dispatch in May 1777 by Dauge's regiment. On 3 May 1776, Dauge was appointed lieutenant colonel in the state militia from the district of Edenton; on 11 May 1776, he was given the rank of colonel. On 8 Aug. 1776, he was appointed lieutenant colonel of the Tenth North Carolina Regiment, Continental Line, which joined General George Washington in 1777 and fought throughout the Revolution. In November 1776 he was also appointed lieutenant colonel of the First Battalion, which was ordered to assist South Carolina.

From 1786 to 1790 Dauge was a member of the House of Commons. He and Lemuel Sawyer represented Camden and often split their votes. Dauge voted in favor of proposals to increase the jurisdiction of the justices of the peace, to prevent the sale of goods except for "hard money," and to abolish recompense for executed or outlawed slaves. Sawyer opposed all. On 20 Nov. 1787, while in the house, Dauge was added to the Committee of Claims and on 22 November he was added to the court of claims. The house on 4 Nov. 1788 appointed Dauge and others to act on as a Committee of Propositions and Grievances. On 3 November he was appointed to serve on the Committee of Privileges and Elections.

From 1790 to 1794, Dauge was a member of the state senate where his corepresentative from Camden was Lemuel Sawyer's son, Enoch. They generally voted together on important measures. On 2 Nov. 1790, Dauge was appointed to serve on "a committee to hear and report on such excuses as may be offered by members of this house who failed to give their attendence agreeable to law." Both Dauge and Enoch Sawyer were delegates to the Hillsborough and Fayetteville conventions of 1788 and 1789, respectively. In 1789 Dauge was named a trustee for the newly formed Currituck Seminary of Learning, and in 1799 he was appointed sheriff of Camden.

Dauge was granted 2,057 acres of land on which he developed a plantation. According to the census of 1790, he owned twelve slaves.

Dauge was married twice: first to Elizabeth Lamb, daughter of Thomas Lamb and Sarah Beckwith of Pasquotank; second to Margaret Sawyer Lamb, widow of Abner Lamb, of Camden. Of the first marriage there were five children, Isaac, Willoughby, Amelia (m. Ezekiel Trotman), Sophia, and Margaret. There were no children of the second marriage. Dauge died in Camden and was buried in the family cemetery at his plantation.

SEE: Walter Clark, ed., *State Records of North Carolina*, vols. 11, 18, 20, 21, 22 (1895–1907); North Carolina Society of Sons of the American Revolution, *Lineage Book of Past and Present Members of the North Carolina Society of Sons of the American Revolution* (1951); William C. Pool, "An Economic Interpretation of the Ratification of the Federal Constitution in North Carolina," *North Carolina Historical Review* 27 (1950); Jessie H. Pugh, *Three Hundred Years Along the Pasquotank* (1957); William L. Saunders, ed., *Colonial Records of North Carolina*, vol. 10 (1890).

CLAUDIA A. FRY

**Daughtridge, Elijah Longstreet** *(17 Jan. 1863–12 June 1921)*, farmer, merchant, and politician, was born in Edgecombe County near Rocky Mount, the fourth of seven children (five girls and two boys) born to William M. and Dellah Williford Daughtridge. He attended the Bingham School in Mebane during 1881 and 1882, thereafter returning home to engage in farming with his father. Although farming remained a priority throughout his life, he was also an active merchant. He was the principal owner and director of Daughtridge Supply Company, president of Planters Cotton Oil and Fertilizer Company, and a director in other corporate organizations.

After serving as lieutenant and captain in a local military company from 1896 to 1897, Daughtridge became active in politics. Beginning in 1898, when he was a member of the Township 12 Committee (Edgecombe County), Daughtridge served two years as an alderman and vice-recorder of Rocky Mount. In February 1900 he was one of eleven delegates recommended by the Edgecombe County convention for the Democratic state convention; in November of that year he was elected, along with Benjamin Shelton, to the state house of representatives. As a member of the 1901 and 1903 legislatures, he was chairman of the Agriculture Committee and served on both the Finance and Penal Institutions committees. He was also a member of the State Board of Agriculture and the board of trustees of A & M College during a portion of his legislative tenure.

During the next ten years, Daughtridge served in several organizations. In 1906 he was president of the State Fair Association and was the first to carry over a surplus for that organization. He also acted as treasurer for both the North Carolina Jamestown Commission in 1907 and the Rocky Mount Road Commission from 1907 to 1913.

Daughtridge's greatest political achievement, however, was his election as lieutenant governor of North Carolina in 1912. Running as a Democrat, he defeated Republican James R. Gaskill (also of Edgecombe County) in the general election as Locke Craige swept the gubernatorial election. In his opening speech to the state senate, Lieutenant Governor Daughtridge stressed the investment of money for the practical education of farm children as a primary directive for the new General Assembly. His policy also called for equalizing the tax burden, building better roads, improving rural conditions, and erecting a residential institution for veterans' widows. While lieutenant governor, he served as vice-president of the North Carolina Good Roads Association and as a member of the Committee on Constitutional Amendments. In addition, he was appointed by Governor Craige to the American Commission, which toured Europe in 1913 to study banking and agricultural conditions. Upon his return he became one of the leading proponents, along with John Sprunt Hill, of "rural credits" in the South and lectured and wrote extensively on the commission's findings. He was later elected a director of the Southern Commercial Congress.

In 1916 Daughtridge entered the Democratic primary for the governorship against Thomas Bickett, attorney general during the Craige administration. Labeled by his followers as a Conservative, Daughtridge battled Bickett in a campaign of historical significance—this was the first statewide primary held in North Carolina. In the June Democratic primary, Bickett garnered 63,121 votes to 34,017 for Daughtridge. Of the sixteen counties that Daughtridge won, nearly half were in the far western corner of the state, with the others spread out over eastern North Carolina. His term as lieutenant governor ended on 11 Jan. 1917.

Daughtridge married Mary W. Odom in 1883 and they became the parents of five sons—John, William, Henry, Edward, and Archie—and two daughters—Annie (m. Millard Jones) and Mary. He was a member of the Elk's Lodge of Rocky Mount, a Pythian, president of Post H of the Traveler's Protection Association, and a Methodist. He died at his home in Rocky Mount and was buried in Pineview Cemetery.

SEE: Census of Edgecombe County, 1870 (North Carolina State Archives, Raleigh); John L. Cheney, Jr., ed., *North Carolina Government, 1585–1974* (1975); *Daughtridge for Governor of North Carolina* (1916); *Greensboro Daily News*, 6 Nov. 1912; *North Carolina: Rebuilding an Ancient Commonwealth*, vol. 2 (1929); *North Carolina Senate: Character Sketches* (1917); *Progressive Farmer*, 11 Oct. 1913; Raleigh *News and Observer*, 16 Jan. 1913, 13 June 1921; J. Kelly Turner and Jonathan L. Bridgers, Jr., *History of Edgecombe County* (1920).

LINWOOD JONES

**Davenport, William Henry** *(8 May 1868–20 May 1936)*, clergyman and journalist, the son of Mack and Phillis Simmons Davenport, was born in New Bern where he attended the common school and State Normal School from 1884 to 1888. Beginning in 1888 he was a student at Livingstone College, Salisbury, from which he received the A.B. (1894), A.M. (1897), and D.D. (1906) degrees. He financed his education by working in the college printing office. Later he returned to Livingstone to edit the *Livingstone College Monthly*. From 1897 to 1900 he was a correspondent for the *Camden* (N.J.) *Daily Courier*. While in New Jersey he was involved in the building of African Methodist Episcopal Zion churches in Bayonne and Red Bank. From 1902 to 1904 he worked with the *Mobile* (Ala.) *Press* and edited the *Church Observer* while pastor of the State Street A.M.E. Zion Church. For the 1917–18 term he served as dean of Walters Institute in Warren, Ark., where he was also pastor of a church.

In the early 1920s Davenport moved to Durham to become pastor of Saint Mark's A.M.E. Zion Church; there he was again involved in the building of a new church. From 1924 until his death he was editor of the *Star of Zion*, the national periodical of the A.M.E. Zion church. He was the author of several books about the church, among them *The Anthology of Zion Methodism* (1925) and *Membership in Zion Methodism* (1936).

On 15 Jan. 1895 Davenport married Mary I. Walker, and they had one child, Lillian M. (b. 12 Jan. 1897). He married his second wife, Nena M. Ray, on 1 May 1918. In the last decade of his life, he lived in Charlotte. He died suddenly soon after being elected to his fourth term as editor of the *Star of Zion*. Politically he was an Independent.

SEE: Thomas Yenser, ed., *Who's Who in Colored America* (1944).

BRENDA MARKS EAGLES

**Daves, Graham** *(16 July 1836–27 Oct. 1902)*, antiquarian, railway agent, and Confederate officer, was born in New Bern, the fifth of six children of John Pugh Daves, a planter in that town, and Elizabeth Batchelor Graham, his third wife. An older brother was educator Edward Graham Daves. An older sister, Mary McKinlay Daves, became the second wife of future governor John W. Ellis. The father died when Graham was about two years old, but the mother survived until 9 May 1885. Young Daves's childhood and youth were passed in his hometown, where he attended the New Bern Academy. In the autumn of 1851 he was placed as a cadet at the prestigious but short-lived Maryland Military Academy, at the village of Oxford on the Eastern Shore of Maryland, where he studied under Superintendent John H. Allen for almost two years. In the autumn of 1853 he enrolled as a freshman at Trinity College, Hartford, Conn., where his brother Edward was professor of Greek. At college he pledged Iota Kappa Alpha fraternity. He was graduated in July 1857, delivering a commencement oration on "Recent Events in Mexico."

Returning to North Carolina, Daves began the study of law with Judge Richmond M. Pearson, subsequently chief justice of the state, at his Richmond Hill home in Surry County. On 1 Jan. 1859, upon election to the governorship of his brother-in-law J. W. Ellis, Daves became the governor's private secretary and remained in that position until Ellis's untimely death on 7 July 1861.

North Carolina having seceded from the Union on 20 May 1861, Daves enlisted on 11 July in the Twelfth Regiment North Carolina Infantry (volunteers), later designated the Twenty-second Regiment (state troops), commanded by Colonel J. Johnston Pettigrew, and was commissioned first lieutenant. On 24 July he was named unit adjutant and served with the outfit at Raleigh and at Richmond, Brooks Station, and especially at Evansport (now Quantico) in Virginia. On 1 Apr. 1862 he was detached and transferred to general staff duties under Major General Samuel G. French as assistant adjutant general assigned to Wilmington, Goldsboro, and Petersburg, Va., with rank as captain. On 5 Nov. 1862 he was promoted to major, remaining on active duty in Virginia until June 1863. He was then transferred to the Mississippi and Eastern Louisiana sector, where he served as assistant adjutant general of division, based near Morton, Miss., under General Joseph E. Johnston during the campaigns in that state prior and subsequent to the Confederate surrender of Vicksburg. Daves returned to North Carolina and resigned his commission for unknown reasons on 16 Nov. 1863. Reporting to the Conscription Bureau, he was enlisted as a private and assigned to the conscription office at Raleigh. There he served until 7 July 1864, when he was commissioned first lieutenant of reserves and aide-de-camp to Lieutenant General Theophilus H. Holmes, with whom he remained until March 1865. He was then temporarily transferred by Holmes to the division of Major General Robert F. Hoke, with which he saw duty until the surrender of Johnston's forces to Major General William T. Sherman near Durham on 26 Apr. 1865. His personal parole bore that date.

After the war Daves went to work at Wilmington for DeRosset & Company, general commission merchants. Subsequently he engaged in the railway business at Wilmington and, during the eighties, at Charleston, S.C., as freight agent for The Charleston Line. He retired from business in 1891 when his health deteriorated and, settling at New Bern, took up his favorite avocation, the study of the colonial, Revolutionary, and Confederate history of his native state. In its obituary the Raleigh *News and Observer* asserted that Daves had produced "many written contributions of great value" in the field of North Carolina history; and Mrs. Elvira Moffitt, state regent for the Society of the Daughters of the Revolution, affirmed in 1906 that he had "contributed many articles of historical value to the columns of various periodicals."

Despite these statements, only fourteen items from Daves's pen have been identified: four articles in the *Southern Historical Society Papers* (Richmond, Va.)—"The Battle of Averasboro'," 7 (1879), "Artillery at the Southern Arsenals," 12 (1884), "Twenty-Second North Carolina Infantry: Its History . . . ," 24 (1896), reprinted from the *Charlotte Observer*, 21 Apr. 1895, and "The Causes of the War 1861–5, and Events of Its First Year: The Events in North Carolina during the Administration of Governor J. W. Ellis," 32 (1904); a Memorial Day address at Raleigh, 10 May 1901, reprinted from the *News and Observer*, 11 May 1901; *A Sketch of the Military Career of Captain John Daves* (1892), a sixteen-page pamphlet on his paternal grandfather, who served in the Third Regiment, North Carolina Continental Infantry, during the American Revolution; three articles on the officers of the North Carolina Continental Line and of the State Cincinnati, all in *University of North Carolina Magazine* N.S. 12–13 (October 1892, May 1893, May 1894); *In Memoriam, John A. Guion, M.D., New Bern, N.C., 1816–1894* (1894?), an eight-page pamphlet; a note on Virginia Dare, *University of North Carolina Magazine* N.S. 14 (March 1895); an expansion thereof entitled *Virginia Dare* (1901), a sixteen-page pamphlet ranking as the first item in the "North Carolina Booklet" series; "Twenty-Second Regiment," in Walter Clark, ed., *Histories of the Several Regiments . . .* , vol. 2 (1901), an eighteen-page narrative dated New Bern, 9 Apr. 1901, which revised and augmented his 1896 paper; and "Enlistments for the War," *Confederate Veteran* 10 (January 1902).

In 1894 Daves succeeded his brother Edward as second president of the Roanoke Colony Memorial Association, a post he held until his death. At the ceremonies marking the dedication of a monument on the site of Fort Raleigh, 24 Nov. 1896, he delivered the principal address. He spoke again on the Roanoke Colony at the second Annual Meeting of the State Literary and Historical Association, Raleigh, 22 Oct. 1901. In the mid-1890s, for reasons of health, Daves commenced regular summer sojourns in Asheville. There he met Major Charles L. Davis, a Union veteran then in the Tenth U.S. Infantry and assigned as instructor in military tactics at the Bingham School. Daves had for some time been interested in attempting a revival of the State Society of the Cincinnati, founded at Hillsborough in 1783 but dormant since about 1800. Under his guidance and enthusiasm Major Davis (an hereditary member of the Pennsylvania Society) worked toward this goal, and their efforts were rewarded by the revival of the North Carolina Cincinnati at Raleigh in April 1896. As principal reorganizers the two men were elected the new society's first honorary members. Though genealogically ineligible for membership—his late brother Edward's right having passed to son John Collins Daves—Daves was accorded the tribute of appointment as assistant secretary of the society and in 1897 was named its vice-president. He was one of the group's delegates to the triennial meetings of the General Society of the Cincinnati held at Philadelphia in May 1896 and at Hartford in June 1902. His pioneering researches were used by Major Davis and Captain Henry H. Bellas in their volume, *A Brief History of the North Carolina Troops on the Continental Establishment . . . A Sketch of the North Carolina Society of the Cincinnati . . .* (1896).

Daves was a charter member (1893) and on the board of visitors of the state chapter, Sons of the Revolution, and a member (as of 1901) of the State Literary and Historical Association. He also belonged to the Association of Confederate Veterans and was regularly addressed as Major Daves. After his death the Virginia historian Robert A. Brock mourned (1904) the passing of "this broadly accomplished and most lovable man. He was our valued friend and correspondent for years." Marshall DeLancey Haywood declared (1907) of Daves: "He was the friendliest, most polished, and in many respects, within his sphere of life and action, the most useful gentleman of the State."

On 27 Nov. 1862, at Hillsborough, Daves married Alice Lord DeRosset (1835–2 Sept. 1897), daughter of Armand John DeRosset, M.D., of Wilmington, and Eliza Lord DeRosset. The couple had one child, a boy, who did not survive infancy. Mrs. Daves died at her father's home in Wilmington. Daves died at the Hotel Manor, Asheville, of a tubercular heart condition. Both were buried in Cedar Grove Cemetery, New Bern. Daves was an Episcopalian, but his political affiliation is unknown. The only likeness known of him is as a bearded young lieutenant in a group photograph of officers of the Twenty-second Regiment.

SEE: Alumni Archives (Trinity College Library, Hartford, Conn.); Samuel A. Ashe, ed., *Biographical History of North Carolina*, vol. 6 (1907); *Asheville Citizen*, 27 Oct. 1902; Bassett Papers (Manuscript Department, Library, Duke University, Durham); Curtis C. Carroll, *Revolution's Godchild* (1976); Walter Clark, ed., *Histories of the Several Regiments and Battalions from North Carolina in the Great War, 1861–65*, vol. 2 (1901 [photograph]), *The Papers of Walter Clark*, Aubrey L. Brooks and Hugh T. Lefler, eds., vol. 1 (1948); Confederate Records (Manuscript Division, Library of Congress, Washington, D.C.); J. C. Daves, ed., *Minutes of the North Carolina Society of the Cincinnati*, vol. 2 (1903); Hemphill Family Papers (Manuscript Department, Library, Duke University, Durham); E. E. Moffitt, "Major Graham Daves, AB.," *North Carolina Booklet* 4 (July 1906); William S. Powell, *Paradise Preserved* (1965); Raleigh *News and Observer*, 28 Oct. 1902; Ruffin Papers (Virginia Historical Society, Richmond); Saunders Papers and Fries Collection (North Carolina State Archives, Raleigh); N. J. Tolbert, ed., *Papers of John Willis Ellis*, vols. 1, 2 (1964); *Weekly Raleigh Register*, 10 Dec. 1862. Daves's personal copies of *Southern Historical Society Papers* were donated to the Maryland Historical Society.

CURTIS CARROLL DAVIS

**Daves, John** *(1748–12 Oct. 1804)*, Revolutionary War officer, was born in Virginia where his paternal ancestors had immigrated during the middle of the seventeenth century. When he was two years old, his family moved to New Bern. Residing there the rest of his life, he built—largely with his own hands—an early frame house on lower George Street that has recently been restored. In its rear yard is a huge mulberry tree, thought to be one of a number planted by Baron Christopher deGraffenried, founder of New Bern in 1710, who reportedly imported silkworms and attempted to start a silk industry.

As a soldier of the first Continental line troops,

Daves was appointed quartermaster of the Second Regiment, aided in the repulse of Lord Dunmore in December 1775 at Norfolk, Va., and helped defeat the British the next June at Sullivan's Island. Commissioned an ensign 30 Sept. 1776, he was ordered to join General George Washington's forces, with which he served bravely at Brandywine, Germantown, Valley Forge, Eutaw Springs, and Monmouth. Following duty at Morristown and in the New York highlands, he was wounded in 1779 at Stony Point. In September 1781 he was promoted to captain.

After the war Daves was a major of the North Carolina state troops. Aiding with the organization of the North Carolina Society of the Cincinnati, he was among its sixty original members. On 9 Feb. 1790 President Washington named him the first collector of customs at New Bern, where a customhouse had been opened in March. He became inspector of surveys and ports 6 Mar. 1792. Daves was a warden of Christ Episcopal Church. At his death he was buried with military and Masonic honors in Cedar Grove Cemetery, New Bern. Still standing there is a tombstone listing his chief accomplishments. During June 1893 the casket was taken to a place of honor at Guilford Court House National Military Park.

Major Daves was married twice. His first wife, Sally Bryan, died shortly, leaving an infant, Mary (1776–1840), who became the wife of James McKinlay (1751–1819), a native of Scotland and for forty years a New Bern merchant and banker. During April 1782 Daves married Mary Haynes Long Davis (1751–11 Apr. 1822), twice a widow previously. They had two daughters and two sons. Sally Eaton Daves wed, in New Bern, Morgan Jones of Maryland, but died 17 Feb. 1802 at the age of nineteen. Ann Rebecca Daves was married in New Bern to Josiah Collins of Edenton in December 1803. Thomas Haynes Daves, who married Harriet Hatch on 11 Mar. 1812, was a Craven County sheriff but moved in 1836 to Alabama where he died in 1839. John Pugh Daves (23 July 1789–21 Mar. 1838), the older son, was a planter. He married three times: on 4 Feb. 1813 to Mary Bryan Hatch, who died the next February; on 1 Feb. 1816 to Jane Reid Henry (1793–1827), sister of Louis D. Henry; and on 14 Jan. 1830 to Elizabeth Batchelor Graham (3 Aug. 1804–9 May 1885), the daughter of Edward Graham (18 Feb. 1764–22 Mar. 1833) and Elizabeth Batchelor (1772–26 Apr. 1850), who were married 16 June 1795 at New Bern.

John Pugh Daves and his wife Elizabeth were the parents of several distinguished children, including Edward Graham Daves (31 Mar. 1834–1 Aug. 1894); Major Graham Daves (16 July 1836–27 Oct. 1902); and Mary McKinlay Daves (2 Jan. 1835–23 Jan. 1916), who, on 11 Aug. 1858 at Christ Episcopal Church in New Bern, became the second wife of Governor John Willis Ellis and after his death married, on 15 Sept. 1866 at New Bern, Haines E. Nash of Petersburg, Va. When the Ladies' Memorial Association of New Bern was organized in 1866, Mrs. Nash and her mother were its first vice-president and president, respectively. The group erected and dedicated (11 May 1885) the tall Confederate monument in Cedar Grove Cemetery, New Bern. Mrs. Nash was from 1892 to 1896 the first appointed state regent of North Carolina, National Society, Daughters of the American Revolution, having joined the organization on the service of her grandfather, Captain Daves.

SEE: Samuel A. Ashe, ed., *Biographical History of North Carolina*, vol. 2 (1905); Christ Church Records (New Bern); Craven County Records (North Carolina State Archives, Raleigh); Tombstones, Cedar Grove Cemetery (New Bern).

GERTRUDE S. CARRAWAY

**Davidson, Adam Brevard** *(13 Mar. 1808–4 July 1896)*, planter and developer, a son of John ("Jacky") Davidson, Jr., and his wife Sarah Harper Brevard, was born at Rural Hill, the plantation home in Mecklenburg County built by his grandfather, Major John Davidson (d. 1832). He was given only an English education (without Latin and Greek) and hence sometimes referred to himself as a "clodhopper" in contradistinction to his three youngest brothers—one attended West Point and the other two obtained degrees in the first graduating class at Davidson College. He began life as a planter, he and his father owning together some five thousand acres and fifty or sixty slaves in the Hopewell section of Mecklenburg. When construction was begun on Davidson College in 1836, on land belonging to his cousin and uncle-in-law Major William Lee Davidson, Adam Brevard contracted for and supplied the lumber for the early buildings. All lumber was sawed at his own mills.

On 20 Apr. 1836, at Springfield in York County, S.C., Davidson married Mary Laura Springs (b. 13 Mar. 1813), a daughter of John Springs, III, who had given her every advantage. She first attended the Moravian Academy at Salem, N.C., and later the select school of Madame Sarazin in Philadelphia. She bore her husband fifteen children. Her manuscript journal (1836–43) is in the Southern Historical Collection at The University of North Carolina, Chapel Hill. An entry for 9 June 1837 reads: "We went to housekeeping. Father and Mother-in-law moved to Rural Retreat," which meant that the brick mansion house, Rural Hill, was turned over to the young couple and the older family moved to the original log house on the same plantation. Many entries in the journal refer to the family's participation in religious services at Hopewell Presbyterian Church, where Davidson was an elder from 1846 to 1875. In 1856 he was a delegate from Concord Presbytery to the General Assembly of the Presbyterian Church in New York City.

He was elected a trustee of Davidson College in 1844 and served with few intermissions until 1877. Two of his sons were educated at the Presbyterian college: Robert who died as a result of mistreatment in a northern prison during the Civil War, and Baxter who was, at his death, the largest single donor in the college's history.

Davidson was a conspicuously successful planter. He was made president of the Mecklenburg Agricultural Society some fifteen years before the war and served intermittently until the society was disbanded by the Confederate defeat. On 16 Jan. 1854 he delivered an address to the society on "Deep Ploughing." His address to the society "On the Culture of Clover" was published in the Charlotte *Western Democrat* of 12 Feb. 1861. He was interested not only in crops but also in livestock, Devon and Durham cattle, and particularly horse breeding. Advertisements appeared in the local papers of stallions available at his stables for improving blood lines of other stock raisers in Mecklenburg and neighboring counties. In addition, he was a believer in internal improvements and railroads and invested his money in many enterprises for progress. In 1847 he became one of the first directors for the Charlotte, Columbia, and Augusta Railroad and continued in that office until his death. He was also a director of the Granitesville Manufacturing Company in South Carolina.

It was well known that, as an old line Whig, Davidson was opposed to the secession of North Carolina until Lincoln's invasion of the South. Thereafter he invested heavily in Confederate bonds and three of his sons—John, Robert, and Richard—served with distinction in the Confederate Army. As a result of the war and the failure of friends whose notes he had signed, he lost over three-fourths of his considerable fortune. He became convinced that much of the South's future prosperity lay in the cities, and in 1872 he turned Rural Hill over to his son John Springs Davidson and moved to Charlotte. He invested in real estate and left a handsome property to his children. It was said that he built sixteen stores and dwelling houses in the city. His own city residence stood on the lot known as the Queens College grounds on South Tryon Street. It was demolished later to make way for Charlotte's fourth courthouse.

Mary Laura Springs Davidson died in Charlotte on 24 Oct. 1872 and was buried at Rural Hill. On 29 July 1876 Davidson married Cornelia C. Elmore (1835–1921) of Columbia, S.C. Her lineage was quite as distinguished as his, her father having been Franklin Harper Elmore who succeeded to Calhoun's seat in the U.S. Senate, and her mother a daughter of Governor John Taylor of the same state. There were no children from this union.

While a resident of Charlotte, Davidson was a consistent and generous member of the First Presbyterian Church. From 1873 to 1880 he served on the board of directors for the Theological Seminary at Columbia, S.C. He retained his interest in Davidson College and continued to support it. The "Mecklenburg Declaration of Independence," of which his grandfather Davidson was a "signer," was also a cardinal doctrine of his faith; on 8 June 1896 he gave an affidavit to the clerk of the Mecklenburg Superior Court testifying to conversations with his grandfather confirming that event and date (20 May 1775).

Before the war, according to Dr. J. B. Alexander's *History of Mecklenburg County*, "Mr. Davidson was well known not only in Mecklenburg county, but through Western North Carolina as the foremost farmer in this part of the State. . . . He was worth prior to 1865, a half million dollars." After his removal to Charlotte, he became equally outstanding as one of the builders of the New South. His obituary in the *Charlotte Daily News* (6 July 1896) states: "He was a prominent and influential factor in building and supporting the railroads and mills of this section and gave of his wealth and influence liberally to educational institutions. He was a man who has done good to all people and all things that come under his influence. He was liberal and charitable and was generous in his treatment of mankind."

All fifteen children of Adam Brevard and his first wife were born at Rural Hill: Mary Laura married the Reverend Alexander Sinclair; John Springs, the only son to have children, married Martha Caldwell and inherited Rural Hill where his descendants still live; William Lee died at seventeen; Robert A. left Davidson College for the Confederate Army and died as a result of imprisonment in the North; Richard A. and Sarah were unmarried; Jenny married Dr. J. M. Miller; Isabell married Charles G. Montgomery; Amanda, twin of Isabell, married A. J. Beall; Adam Brevard, Jr., died at seventeen; Blandie was unmarried; Leroy Springs had no issue; Julia married the Reverend Thomas H. S. Strohecker; Edward Lee Baxter married late in life and had no issue; and Fanny died in infancy.

A portrait of Adam Brevard Davidson hangs in the E. L. Baxter Davidson Faculty Room at Davidson College.

SEE: *Charlotte Observer*, 8 May 1927; *Charlotte Statesman*, 10 July 1930; *Daily Charlotte Observer*, 6 July 1896; Davidson Family Papers (Southern Historical Collection, University of North Carolina, Chapel Hill); Gail W. O'Brien, "Power and Influence in Mecklenburg County, 1850–1880," *North Carolina Historical Review* 44 (April 1977); C. L. Van Noppen Papers (Manuscript Department, Library, Duke University, Durham).

CHALMERS G. DAVIDSON

**Davidson, Alexander Caldwell** *(26 Dec. 1826–6 Nov. 1897)*, congressman and cotton planter, was born in Mecklenburg County near Charlotte. The names of his parents do not appear to be recorded. The family moved about 1830 to Marengo County, Ala. After secondary and elementary education in the local schools, he entered the University of Alabama at Tuscaloosa in 1844 at age sixteen and was graduated four years later. For several years he read law under attorneys in Mobile, but there is no record of his being admitted to the bar or of his practicing law. Instead, he acquired extensive land in Perry County, near Uniontown, Ala., and became a successful cotton planter.

Davidson's general interest in public affairs led him into a political career that occupied his major attention for a decade. He was first elected to the Alabama legislature (1880–81), then to the state senate for four years (1882–85). In 1885 he was a successful Democratic candidate for the United States Congress, where he served four years as a representative from Alabama in the Forty-ninth and Fiftieth sessions (1885–89).

Afterward he returned to Westwood, his home near Uniontown, and resumed his farming operations. He died there and was buried in the Holy Cross Cemetery of the Davidson Memorial Church, Uniontown.

SEE: *Biog. Dir. Am. Cong.* (1950); *Who Was Who in America* (1967).

C. SYLVESTER GREEN

**Davidson, Allen Turner** *(9 May 1819–24 Jan. 1905)*, lawyer, Confederate congressman, and member of the Council of State, was born in Haywood County, the son of William Mitchell, a Burke County farmer, and Betsy Vance Davidson. His grandfather was Major William Davidson, an officer in the American Revolution. Captain David Vance, also an officer in the Revolution, was his maternal grandfather. Both men fought as patriots. Young Davidson's mother was the aunt of Zebulon B. Vance. He was educated in the "old field" schools of Haywood County and at Waynesboro Academy.

At the age of twenty, Davidson began working in his father's general store. The following year he was commissioned a colonel in the state militia. Shortly thereafter he began to study law under Michael Francis. In 1843, while still a student, he was appointed clerk and master of equity for Haywood County, an office from which he resigned in the spring of 1846. On 1 Jan. 1845, he was admitted to the North Carolina bar and moved to Murphy to begin his law practice as a solicitor for Cherokee County.

In April 1860 Davidson was chosen president of the newly organized Miner's and Planter's Bank in Murphy. In October of the following year, as a Democrat, he was elected over two opponents as a member of the North Carolina Secession Convention. In June and July 1861 he served in the Provisional Congress of the Confederacy, and in 1862 he was elected to the House of Representatives of the Confederate Congress in Richmond, Va.

Davidson served his term with "quiet, but steady opposition to congressional encroachment on state or individual rights." From the outset, he allowed the Confederacy "full authority over matters of diplomacy, commerce, and transportation." He usually agreed to allow the "administration early, moderate requests, but resisted further requests for authority." However, he made no allowances for financing the Confederacy or for recruiting and maintaining an army.

He had been an "old Union" man, firmly opposed to secession. Opposing Davidson's group were the "original secessionists," those who had supported secession very early in the effort.

During his term in Congress, Davidson served on the Committee of Post Offices and Post Roads and the Committee of the Quartermaster's and Commissary Department. In 1863, he lost his seat to George W. Logan. Davidson's tact and moderation were not enough to please his constituents. Most North Carolinians, especially those in the western part of the state, were disgusted with the war. Logan, who called for peace at any cost, more nearly pleased the people in his district. After this election, although active in public affairs, Davidson never again held public office.

In 1864, North Carolina Governor Zebulon B. Vance named Davidson to the Council of State and an agent of the Commissionary Department of the State. Until the end of the war it was Davidson's duty to provide necessary goods for the widows of Confederate soldiers of western North Carolina.

Late in 1865, Davidson moved to Franklin in Macon County. Nearly four years later, early in 1869, he moved to Asheville. After this move, he rose to the top of his profession in western North Carolina and became president of the Asheville Bar Association. His record as a criminal lawyer was excellent: not one of the fifty-seven clients he defended in murder cases was executed. He retired in 1885.

Davidson married Elizabeth A. Howell in 1842; she was described as an "educated, Christian Lady who greatly assisted him in his professional and life work." They had four sons: Allen Turner, Jr., a teacher, school superintendent, and lawyer in Amarillo, Tex., who died at the age of twenty-seven; T. F., an attorney general of North Carolina; Wilbur S., a cashier of the National Bank of Beaumont, Tex.; and Robert Vance, a lawyer in Galveston, Tex. The Allens also had three daughters.

Davidson was a member of the Methodist Episcopal church, South, a Royal Arch Mason, and a stockholder in the First National Bank of Beaumont, Tex., and in the North Georgia Railroad. After his retirement, he lived with his son, T. F. Davidson of Asheville. He died in Asheville where he was buried in Riverside Cemetery.

SEE: Samuel A. Ashe, *Cyclopedia of Eminent and Representative Men of the Carolinas in the Nineteenth Century* (1892); John L. Cheney, ed., *North Carolina Government, 1585–1979* (1981); Daniel L. Grant, *Alumni History of the University of North Carolina* (1924); John Gilchrist McCormick, "Personnel of the Convention of 1861," *James Sprunt Historical Monographs* 1 (1900); Ezra J. Warner and W. Buck Yearns, *Biographical Register of the Confederate Congress* (1975).

JANIS BRIDGES JOYCE

**Davidson, John** *(15 Dec. 1735–10 Jan. 1832)*, patriot and ironmaster, was the son of Robert and Isabel Ramsay Davidson who are believed to have come from Scotland on the "Diligance of Glasgow" in January 1729. There is a tradition that they brought two servants with them when they landed in America. John was born in Middle Octoraro Settlement, Chestnut Level, Pa. His father died young and the widow migrated to the North Carolina Piedmont in the 1750s. Her second husband was Henry Hendry, a schoolmaster said to have been educated at the College of New Jersey (now Princeton University). John and his sister Mary received exceptional educational advantages from their stepfather, but John chose the trade of blacksmith for a livelihood on the frontier. There is a land grant, dated 17 Apr. 1759, for land on Coddle Creek, Anson County, N.C., to John Davidson, blacksmith; Henry Hendry is mentioned in the deed.

Davidson chose as his permanent residence a commanding hilltop about a mile east of the Catawba River near Toole's Ford in what is now Mecklenburg County. Nearby lived Samuel Wilson, a wealthy Englishman who had migrated from Virginia and settled in this area in 1750. On 2 June 1761, Davidson married Samuel Wilson's eldest daughter Violet (13 Aug. 1742–3 Dec. 1818). He built a substantial log house that lasted a hundred and twenty-odd years, and by the time of the Revolutionary War he and Violet were the parents of six children. They later had four more; the last, Benjamin, was born in 1787.

During the colonial period, Davidson served as a justice of the peace and as a member of the House of Commons for Mecklenburg County, attending the meetings of the North Carolina Assembly in New Bern in 1773. He and Representative Thomas Polk were instrumental in having a bill passed making Charlotte the permanent county seat of Mecklenburg (19 Mar. 1774). Apparently Representative Davidson saw nothing in New Bern (including the recently completed palace for Governor Tryon) to enlist his loyalty to the king. When the Whigs and their local committees took over the government in 1775, he was elected a member of the Committee of Safety for Mecklenburg County.

Mecklenburg's independence movement has been and will continue for many years to be a subject of controversy among historians. As the last surviving member of the Mecklenburg convention, Davidson's testimony is of special significance. It was given when he was ninety-five years old and living at Beaver Dam with his daughter and son-in-law, Elizabeth and Major William Lee Davidson. According to his family, his mind was still clear. He testified as follows:

"There were two men chosen from each Captain's company to meet in Charlotte to take the subject into consideration. John McKnitt Alexander and myself were chosen from one company. . . . When the members met, and were perfectly organized for business, a motion was made to declare ourselves Independent of the Crown of Great Britain, which was carried by a large majority. Then Dr. Ephraim Brevard was appointed to give us a sketch of the Declaration of Independence which he did. Then James Jack was appointed to take it on to the American Congress, then sitting in Philadelphia. . . . When Jack returned he stated that the Declaration was presented to Congress, and the reply was that they highly esteemed the patriotism of the citizens of Mecklenburg but they thought the measure to [be] premature.

"I am confident that the Declaration of Independence by the people of Mecklenburg was made publick at least twelve months before that of the Congress of the United States."

The affidavit mentions neither the exact date nor a "signing," but neither of these were matters of controversy in 1830 and it is said that Davidson called his son Benjamin, who was born 20 May 1787 (d. 25 Sept. 1829), "my Independence Boy."

At the outbreak of hostilities between the colonies and Great Britain, the North Carolina Provincial Congress organized its state militia on 9 Sept. 1775. Thomas Polk was appointed colonel for the Mecklenburg troops and Davidson was second major. These troops participated in the "Snow Campaign" against the South Carolina Tories in 1775 and in General Griffith Rutherford's expedition against the Cherokees in 1776. Major Davidson is believed to have participated in both campaigns. He then accepted a transfer from field service to the position of brigade major for the Salisbury militia, commanded first by Rutherford and after his capture at Camden, by General William Lee Davidson. He rendered service to militia and Continental troops alike. There is a "Field Return of the Southern Army under command of Major General Gates, Camp New Providence, on November 25, 1780," by Brigade Major Davidson listing over a thousand men each for state and national forces. Tradition relates that General William Lee Davidson stayed at the home of Major John Davidson while organizing his volunteer army to delay Cornwallis's crossing of the Catawba, and that he was riding a horse from the major's stables when shot on the banks of the river at Cowan's Ford on 1 Feb. 1781.

The major prospered after the war. In 1788 he built what the *Charlotte Observer* described ninety-eight years later when it burned as "the finest country residence in all this section of the State." It was undoubtedly the first notable house on the Catawba River. Davidson named his new home Rural Hill and the older log house was known as Rural Retreat. The latter, inhabited by sons and grandsons, outlasted the mansion that replaced it until it, too, went up in flames in 1898. In the census of 1790, Major John Davidson owned twenty-six slaves, an estate exceeded in Mecklenburg only by those of Colonel Thomas Polk and John Springs.

An important contribution to the economic development of North Carolina was made by Davidson in developing the iron industry in Lincoln County. In 1789 the Big Ore Bank had been granted to General Peter Forney, who sold interests to Davidson and his sons-in-law Captain Alexander Brevard and Major Joseph Graham. By 1795 the latter three had bought out Forney and were conducting a flourishing business. Davidson furnished the capital and the practical experience in working iron; Graham operated Vesuvius Furnace and Brevard Mt. Tirzah Forge. Iron became practically a medium of exchange in a region where hard money was scarce. Munitions were manufactured for the government in the War of 1812.

In the fall of 1823, in his eighty-ninth year, Davidson decided to retire from business; his wife had died five years previously. He appointed his son-in-law Major William Lee Davidson to be his trustee in selling off his property in order to give his children their inheritance. He reserved a room for himself in his mansion house at Rural Hill but apparently spent the remainder of his days at the Beaver Dam plantation of his son-in-law and daughter Elizabeth ("Betsy Lee"). This homestead, still standing, was about two miles east of the future Davidson College, which was located on land belonging to Major William Lee Davidson. Here Major John Davidson died at ninety-seven. He was taken back to Rural Hill for burial beside his wife in the place selected by himself.

John and Violet Davidson were the parents of ten children who grew to maturity: daughters Rebecca (Mrs. Alexander Brevard), Isabella (Mrs. Joseph Graham), Mary (Mrs. William McLean), Violet (Mrs. William Bain Alexander), Sarah (Mrs. Alexander Caldwell, son of Dr. David Caldwell), Margaret (Mrs. James Harris), and Elizabeth (Mrs. William Lee Davidson, II); and sons Robert, John (inherited Rural Hill), and Benjamin Wilson. All except Robert and Elizabeth left families. The most distinguished of Davidson's more than sixty grandchildren was Governor William Alexander Graham, who was said to resemble most in appearance and bearing the almost legendary grandfather of this numerous progeny.

SEE: Samuel A. Ashe, ed., *Biographical History of North Carolina*, vol. 7 (1917); Chalmers G. Davidson, *Major John Davidson of "Rural Hill" Mecklenburg County, N.C. . . .* (1943); J. G. deRoulhac Hamilton, ed., *The Papers of William Alexander Graham* (1957–61).

CHALMERS G. DAVIDSON

**Davidson, Robert** *(7 Apr. 1769–14 June 1853)*, planter, the oldest son of Major John Davidson and his wife Violet Wilson, was born on his father's Rural Retreat plantation on the Catawba River in Mecklenburg County. He was privately educated and, to judge from the few extant letters and publications, adequately so. By deed on 23 Feb. 1795, his father made him a gift of 430 acres on the Catawba River, next to his own resident plantation. This plantation, known as Holly Bend, eventually comprised 2,803 acres and was valued at $16,000 (census of 1850), the highest evaluation in Mecklenburg County.

On 1 Jan. 1801, Davidson married Margaret ("Peggy") Osborne, daughter of Colonel Adlai Osborne of Belmont plantation in Rowan (later Iredell) County. According to family tradition, the mansion house at Holly Bend was built at this time. It is one of the largest still extant in Mecklenburg County and notable for its Georgian interiors. Robert and Peggy Osborne had no children of their own but reared several nephews, notably Mrs. Davidson's nephew James W. Osborne and David Alexander Caldwell, son of Robert Davidson's sister Sarah. They were known throughout a large connection as "Uncle Robin" and "Aunt Peggy," the former for his financial acumen and the latter for her kindness of heart. An "Old School" Presbyterian, Davidson was generous to Hopewell Church and to Davidson College, both of which were heavily supported by his family. In politics, he was a Whig and he was extremely proud of his nephew, Governor William A. Graham.

In the census of 1850, Davidson is listed as the owner of 109 slaves, the only planter in Mecklenburg County to own over 100. He also owned land and slaves in Alabama. An oil portrait was painted of him, probably about 1841, by an artist named Wiseman. This portrait was taken to Alabama by his niece, Patsy Caldwell Davidson, and is now at Cedar Grove plantation near Faunsdale. In 1853, after Davidson's death, J. F. G. Mittag was sent to Alabama to make copies for his legatees. Six copies were made. There are also extant two stylized miniatures of Davidson and his wife, painted earlier than the portrait, in the possession of the family of Colonel Thomas D. Osborne of Asheville.

*The North Carolina Whig* of 6 July 1853 carried a notice of Davidson's death at Holly Bend: "Died, at his residence in this County, on the 14th ult., Mr. Robert Davidson, aged 84 years. During a life protracted beyond fourscore years, he lived so as to secure the esteem and respect of all with whom he associated. Those who knew him best will long cherish his memory as that of an honest man and a true patriot." He was buried in the family graveyard on his father's plantation at Rural Hill.

SEE: *Alabama Portraits Prior to 1870* (1969); *Charlotte News*, 4 July 1972; *Charlotte Observer*, 20 Aug. 1933; Chalmers G. Davidson, *The Plantation World Around Davidson* (1973); William A. Graham Papers (Southern Historical Collection, University of North Carolina, Chapel Hill); *North Carolina Portrait Index 1700–1860* (1963); *Raleigh Register*, 22 June 1850.

CHALMERS G. DAVIDSON

**Davidson, Theodore Fulton** *(30 Mar. 1845–11 June 1931)*, lawyer and politician, was born in Haywood County, one of eight children of Allen T. and Adeline Howell Davidson. His father, also born in Haywood County, was a lawyer and president of the Miner's and Planter's Bank at Murphy, a member of the Secession Convention of 1861, and a representative from his district in the Confederate Congress. The Davidson family was Scotch-Irish and moved to North Carolina from Pennsylvania. Theodore's great-grandfather, William Davidson—a Whig and Revolutionary War patriot—was instrumental in the formation of Buncombe County. His son, the grandfather of Theodore Fulton Davidson, settled on a farm in Haywood County after marrying the daughter of Captain David Vance, leader of Continental troops in the Revolutionary War.

Davidson began preparation for college by studying under Colonel Stephen Lee, cousin of Robert E. Lee, in Asheville. When the war broke out, he was a naval cadet at Annapolis; however, he returned to North Carolina on 16 Apr. 1861 to enlist as a private in the Buncombe Rifles, the first company organized in North Carolina west of the Blue Ridge Mountains. At age sixteen, Davidson was one of the youngest members of the Confederate Army from North Carolina. When this company, headed by W. W. McDowell, disbanded, Davidson reenlisted as sergeant major in Company C, Thirty-ninth Regiment, under Colonel David Coleman. After the Battle of Murfreesboro, he became a commissioned aide to General Robert B. Vance, commander of the military district of Western North Carolina. Later, he served as assistant adjutant general on the brigade staff successively under Colonel John B. Palmer and General James G. Martin.

When peace came in 1865, Davidson resumed his studies under Colonel Lee; at the end of the year, he commenced a three-year study of law under Judge J. L. Bailey of Asheville. In 1868 he formed a partnership with his father that lasted until the latter's retirement in 1882. From 1867 to 1868 Theodore Davidson was the solicitor for Clay County, an office that was abrogated by the new Constitution. He served as chairman of the Democratic Executive Committee of Buncombe County from 1872 to 1882; he was also chairman of the Democratic Congressional Committee for the Ninth District during the same period. In 1878 he was elected to the state senate and reelected two years later. In the legislature, he was instrumental in promoting the extension of railroad construction in North Carolina and, in 1879, was appointed director of the Western North Carolina Railroad for the state-at-large. In 1881 he was named a director of the Western North Carolina Insane Asylum.

In 1882 Davidson was appointed judge of the criminal court of Buncombe County, a post he held until his election to the state attorney general's office in 1884. He was reelected to another term as attorney general in 1888. In that position he succeeded in simplifying and improving the administration of criminal law in North Carolina. From 1891 to 1892 he also served in the state legislature, and in 1895 he was elected mayor of Asheville.

As an attorney, Davidson founded the law firm of Davidson, Bourne, & Parker and was an active member of both the North Carolina Bar Association and the American Bar Association. He served as counsel for the Wachovia Bank & Trust Company and was vice-president and counsel for the North Carolina Electric and Power Company. He also played an important role in clarifying the law of titles in North Carolina.

Affectionately called "General" by his friends, Davidson claimed he was a "pure Thomas Jefferson Southern rebel, and an unreconstructed democrat." He was a member of the Masonic Order and the Asheville Club. An Episcopal layman, he was chancellor of the western diocese of the Episcopal church. He was a trustee of St. Mary's School for Girls and a founder and trustee of Weaver College. He was also interested in history, and a number of his addresses were published. In addition, he contributed to Ashe's *Biographical History* and to Dowd's *Life of Vance*. In a pamphlet reprinted from the *Asheville Citizen* entitled "Reminiscences and Traditions of Western North Carolina," Davidson recalled historical anecdotes covering everything from the Buncombe Rifles to the Catawba grape.

On 6 Nov. 1866 Davidson married Sallie K. Alexander, who died in July 1887. On 12 Oct. 1893 he married Sally L. Carter of Raleigh. There were no children by either wife. Davidson was buried in Riverside Cemetery, Asheville.

SEE: Samuel A. Ashe, *Cyclopedia of Eminent and Representative Men of the Carolinas of the Nineteenth Century* (1892); *Greensboro Daily News*, 21 June 1931; North Carolina Bar Association, *Proceedings* 33 (1931); *North Carolina Biography*, vols. 3, 5 (1919), and vol. 2 (1929); *Prominent People of North Carolina* (1906); *The Wachovia* (July 1931 [portrait]).

DAVID CALEP WRIGHT III

**Davidson, William** *(12 Sept. 1778–16 Sept. 1857)*, congressman, was born in Charleston, S.C., but as a youth moved to Mecklenburg County, N.C., with his parents where they engaged in extensive farming. He represented Mecklenburg County in the state senate for five terms between 1813 and 1818, when he was elected as a Federalist to Congress to succeed a resigned member; he was reelected for a full term but defeated by a Democrat when he ran again. He served from 2 Dec. 1818 until 3 Mar. 1821. Returning home to Charlotte where he had moved in 1820, he served four more terms in the state senate between 1825 and 1830. While a member of the General Assembly in 1817, Davidson moved that Archibald Debow Murphey's *Report on Education* be published. The motion was approved, and the document proved to be very significant in making it possible for the state to establish a system of public schools.

Davidson's wife, Sarah, died in 1812, leaving four small children. He lived in Charlotte on the southwest corner of Trade and Tryon streets until the age of eighty when he was killed when thrown from his carriage by a runaway horse. He was survived by three children: William, who became a lawyer and served in the General Assembly; Harriet, who married Dr. D. T. Caldwell; and Sarah, who married a man named Blake. Davidson was buried in the Old Cemetery, Charlotte.

SEE: J. B. Alexander, *The History of Mecklenburg County* (1902); *Bio. Dir. Am. Cong.* (1961); Charlotte *Western Democrat*, 22 Sept. 1857; John L. Cheney, Jr., ed., *North Carolina Government, 1585–1974* (1975); William H. Hoyt, ed., *The Papers of Archibald D. Murphey*, vol. 2 (1914); *Raleigh Register*, 7 Aug. 1812.

WILLIAM S. POWELL

**Davidson, William Lee** *(ca. 1746–1 Feb. 1781)*, Revolutionary War officer, was born in Lancaster County, Pa., the son of George Davidson of County Derry, northern Ireland. When William Lee was about two years old, his father joined the migration from Pennsylvania to the Piedmont of the Carolinas and settled on Davidson's Creek in what is now southern Iredell County, N.C. George Davidson's will, probated in 1760, names as guardians for his children his "trusty and well-beloved Friends" Alexander Osborn and John Brevard, Esquires. These were the most substantial men of the Catawba River section of Rowan (later Iredell) County and they obtained classical educations for their more ambitious sons. William Lee Davidson attended Sugaw Creek Academy near Charlotte at the time when the Reverend Alexander Craighead was pastor and perhaps pedagogue.

On 10 Dec. 1767 the twenty-one-year-old Davidson gave bond of his intention to marry Mary Brevard, daughter of his guardian John Brevard. The Brevards were originally Huguenots who had fled to northern Ireland and thence to America and the North Carolina Piedmont. In many respects, they were the intellectual leaders of Centre Congregation in Rowan County though none of them became ministers. They were also ardent Whigs. At the beginning of the American Revolution John Brevard became an original member of the Salisbury District Committee of Safety, and all eight of his sons saw service as soldiers in the war. One son, Dr. Ephraim Brevard, wrote the famous Mecklenburg Resolves of May 1775.

Many years later, Davidson's Virginia friend and fellow soldier, "Light-Horse Harry" Lee, wrote of him that he was "enamoured of the profession of arms." The spring before his marriage in 1767 he had served as lieutenant in the Rowan militia regiment, which accompanied Governor William Tryon into Cherokee territory to settle a boundary dispute. Less than a decade later, Captain William Davidson was enlisting minutemen to defend the colonies against the king's government. There is evidence that Davidson was prominent in the Charlotte meetings leading to the Mecklenburg Resolves as he owned property in Charlotte. In December 1775 he served as adjutant to Colonel Griffith Rutherford and the Rowan regiment in the "Snow Campaign" against the Tories in upper South Carolina.

North Carolina added four regiments to its Continental line, as distinguished from the state militia, in the spring of 1776. Of the Fourth Regiment, Thomas Polk was made colonel; James Thackston, lieutenant colonel; and William Lee Davidson, major. The North Carolina regiments marched to Wilmington to defend that port from the expected attack by Sir Henry Clinton; when he sailed the British fleet to Charleston, S.C., instead, these troops followed down the coast and participated in the American victory there. It was soon obvious that Major Davidson was a popular officer and, as was observed later, "able to keep up discipline without disgusting the soldiery." Because of his popularity, he was detached from the idle army and sent back to his home territory to recruit.

In the fall of 1777 he marched north with his regiment to join the army of General George Washington. Whether these soldiers arrived in time to fight at Brandywine is not clear, but Davidson was certainly present at the Battle of Germantown and was promoted to lieutenant colonel of the Fifth Regiment, traditionally for gallantry in action in that battle. Then followed the harrowing winter at Valley Forge. Along with his command, Davidson suffered the freezing weather, the inadequate supplies, and the shortage of food. There was some compensation for these trials in the excellent military training given at Valley Forge by Baron von Steuben. Among the friends acquired during this icy ordeal were "Light-Horse Harry" Lee and Daniel Morgan, both to aid later in the defense of the Carolina Piedmont.

The North Carolina regiments were so depleted that they were consolidated and the supernumerary officers reassigned. Davidson returned to his home state to recruit. His commission was transferred from the Fifth to the Third Regiment and in the fall of 1778 he returned to the north. A year and a half of military duty without much action followed. When the North Carolina troops were again sent south in the autumn of 1779, Davidson asked for and received a well-deserved furlough. He reached his home in Centre Congregation in late December or early January 1780. There were six children in the family, three boys and three girls, and there was to be another son before their young father fought his final battle. By the end of Davidson's leave, his regiment was beleaguered in Charleston and he was unable to join it. The Americans surrendered to Sir Henry Clinton on 12 May 1780, and North Carolina lost practically its entire Continental line.

Left without a command, Davidson offered himself for service in the militia. The brigadier general of Salisbury District was his old comrade-in-arms, Griffith Rutherford, who appointed him second-in-command of the district, which comprised the entire western section of the state. In the battle at Colson's Mill, near the junction of Rocky River and the Pee Dee, Colonel Davidson received a severe wound in the stomach while fighting the Tories. It was said that his Continental uniform made him a conspicuous target. He won the battle but was confined at home for several months. During his convalescence, the Americans were defeated at the Battle of Camden and General Rutherford was captured. Davidson was then promoted to brigadier general of the Salisbury District in Rutherford's place. The British and Tories were infesting the Piedmont of both Carolinas. Cornwallis was determined to take over Charlotte and put an end to the local "rebellion." Davidson and the other commanders kept partisan bands deployed for many miles around. They harassed the British, attacked the Tories, and kept up the spirit of patriot resistance. Cornwallis with his greatly superior force occupied Charlotte in September 1780. Throughout his stay, his men were constantly under sniping attack from the militia. The British could obtain few provisions and get no news from outside. It was this period of the war that gave Charlotte her proud nickname of "The Hornets' Nest."

The colonels mustering their forces to attack Patrick Ferguson in the west petitioned the state for General

Davidson or Daniel Morgan to command them. Neither could be spared but the colonels won a signal victory at Kings Mountain. When Cornwallis learned of this, he despaired of success and left Charlotte for Winnsboro with the hornets in hot, but cautious pursuit. The following January, Cornwallis decided once again to invade North Carolina. This time he planned to go around Charlotte and cross the Catawba at one of the numerous fords. General Nathanael Greene, who had been sent by Washington to command the Whig army, relied on Davidson to rouse the militia and delay Cornwallis until the Americans were ready for battle. The militia had been much in the field but at the call of the young commander—Davidson was only thirty-four—they returned with their arms and horses to guard the river. Greene retired northward to Guilford Court House. Davidson stationed men at each of the fords. On the cold morning of 1 Feb. 1781, Cornwallis's army crossed at Cowan's Ford. The Whig picket at the water's edge gave the alarm and Davidson rode at the head of his troops to reinforce them. But it was too late. The British had reached the bank and the young brigadier was shot from his horse by a Tory bullet. The body was recovered late that evening and buried by torchlight the same night in Hopewell Churchyard, there being too many victorious redcoats and Tories in the vicinity to attempt to transport it back to Centre.

Although Cowan's Ford was an American defeat, the British were sufficiently delayed for General Greene to complete his "retreat" that led to the battle at Guilford Court House. The successive failures of Cornwallis culminating at Yorktown are matters of national history. The youthful brigadier had not died in vain.

After the war, Davidson's family moved to land given them for his services in what was then western North Carolina but has since become Tennessee. The county to which they moved was named "Davidson" in his memory and the county seat "Nashville" in honor of the state's other general killed in action. Davidson's widow married Robert Harris of Cabarrus County, N.C., but long outlived him. She died at the home of her daughter Pamela in Logan County, Ky., where her will was probated on 1 Mar. 1824.

Davidson's sons were George Lee, who became a militia general in Iredell County and eventually moved to Alabama; John Alexander, who migrated to Mississippi; Ephraim Brevard, who died in New Madrid, Mo.; and William Lee, born a month before his father's death, who married his cousin Betsy Lee Davidson, settled in Mecklenburg County, and gave the land on which Davidson College—named for his father—is located. The daughters were Jean, wife of Henry Green of Mississippi; Pamela, wife of George McLean of Kentucky; and Margaret, who married the Reverend Finis Ewing and is herself the subject of a small volume called *Aunt Peggy* (1876).

SEE: Chalmers G. Davidson, "General Davidson's Wallet—183 Years Later," *State Magazine* 32 (1 Feb. 1965), *Piedmont Partisan* (1951); William Lee Davidson Papers (Library, Davidson College, Davidson).

CHALMERS G. DAVIDSON

**Davie, William Richardson** *(22 June 1756–5 Nov. 1820)*, statesman, Revolutionary War officer, and founder of The University of North Carolina, was born in the parish of Egremont, County Cumberland, England. His parents, both Scottish, had established their residence below the Solway Firth some time before the arrival of their first born, William Richardson. According to family legend, his father, Archibald Davie, had established a "manufactory of damask" in Egremont and his mother, Mary Richardson, came from a substantial, cultivated family in Dumfriesshire, Scotland. Some evidence as to the position of the family in the British Isles may be inferred from the heraldic arms that his father had engraved on his wife's tomb in Old Waxhaw Presbyterian Churchyard near Lancaster, S.C.

In 1764, at the age of eight, Davie moved with his parents, a brother, and a sister to the Waxhaws near Lancaster, S.C. There they joined his maternal uncle, William Richardson, minister of the Old Waxhaw Presbyterian Meeting House, the religious mecca for the inhabitants of the entire Waxhaws. Richardson's wife was the daughter of the noted divine, the Reverend Alexander Craighead, the first Presbyterian minister with a regular pastorate in western North Carolina and the third in the colony—the Rocky River Church in Mecklenburg County. In view of these associations, it may be assumed that Davie held to the Presbyterian faith throughout his life, but there is no available evidence of this other than his burial in the Waxhaw Presbyterian Churchyard.

Young Davie finished at the College of New Jersey (later Princeton University) in October 1776 just as the American Revolution broke out, and at once he plunged into the partisan warfare of the Carolina Piedmont. So successful was he as a partisan leader that contemporaries ranked him with Francis Marion ("the Swamp Fox"), Thomas Sumter ("the Gamecock"), and Andrew Pickens. Wounded at the Battle of Stono Ferry near Charleston in June 1779, he retired to Salisbury, N.C., where he read law under Judge Spruce Macay, as did Andrew Jackson several years later. After the fall of Charleston and the arrival of Cornwallis in the Carolina Piedmont, Davie organized a company of cavalry and set out to harass the British forces. When Nathanael Greene assumed command of the Southern Army at Charlotte in December 1780, he persuaded Davie, who was at first reluctant, to give up his field leadership and serve as Greene's commissary general, charged with the onerous and almost impossible task of subsisting Greene's army during the closing year of the war.

After the war, Davie practiced law in Halifax, N.C., where he married Sarah Jones, daughter of the conservative aristocrat Allen Jones and niece of the radical, democratic aristocrat Willie Jones. Here he became part of the social and political life of eastern North Carolina with its love of sports and its interest in politics. His interest in sports—especially horse racing—led to his acquiring the famous race horse, Sir Archy, and his interest in government and politics led to his steady rise in the Federalist party.

At thirty Davie was a framer of the Constitution of the United States. He served on the Grand Committee and cast North Carolina's vote for the Great Compromise over representation in the two houses of Congress, making possible the success of the convention and the Constitution. Attendance at court in North Carolina precluded his staying to sign it. He spent the next two years, along with James Iredell, in fighting its anti-Federalist opponents led by Willie Jones. At the Fayetteville Convention in 1789, he introduced and successfully guided the bill for North Carolina's ratification of the Constitution. He also introduced the bill to charter The University of North Carolina. Chiefly responsible for its establishment, building, and endowment, the selection of its faculty, and the planning of its curriculum, he is recognized today as "the Father of the University." In recognition of his services, he was awarded the first LL.D. degree in 1811.

There followed years of constructive leadership in the General Assembly culminating in Davie's election on the Federalist ticket as governor of North Carolina in 1798. The next year President John Adams appointed him, William Vans Murray, U.S. minister at The Hague, and Chief Justice Oliver Ellsworth as ministers plenipotentiary to France to bring an end to the undeclared naval war with France following the XYZ affair. After months of tedious negotiations—some directly with Napoleon Bonaparte—they negotiated the French Convention of 1800, thus ending the war.

When he returned to North Carolina, Davie found that the political scene had changed in both state and national politics with the election of Thomas Jefferson and the Democratic-Republicans. A Federalist in a thoroughly Democratic state, his political fortunes began to decline, and he lost out in the campaign of 1803 for U.S. congressman against Willis Alston of Halifax County. Disillusioned, he retired to his South Carolina plantation, Tivoli, near Lancaster where he occupied himself with farming, horses, books, a voluminous correspondence, advice to the trustees of the university at Chapel Hill, and writing the sketches of his participation in and observations on the American Revolution. He died at his plantation, a Federalist to the end. He was buried in the Davie family burial enclosure at Old Waxhaw Presbyterian Church.

Davie was survived by three sons and three daughters: Allen Jones, who had moved to Mississippi with his wife and two sons; Hyder Ali, who lived with his wife and daughter three miles from Tivoli; Frederick William, then at school; Sarah, who married William DeSaussure, the son of Chancellor DeSaussure, and lived in Columbia; and Mary Haynes and Rebecca, who lived at Tivoli.

An active Mason, Davie was Grand Master of Masons in North Carolina from 1792 until 1798.

Several excellent portraits of Davie have been preserved, including an oil portrait copied by Charles Xavier Harris from the original executed in Paris in 1800 by John Vanderlyn. The original has been lost or destroyed but the copy, formerly owned by Preston Davie, a collateral descendant, is now at The University of North Carolina, Chapel Hill. A bust-length miniature showing him in the uniform of a brigadier general, U.S. Army, executed in Paris in 1800 by Eliza Mirabel, is in Independence Hall, Philadelphia. A pastel portrait, painted by James Sharples in America in 1799 before Davie embarked on his mission to France, is also in Independence Hall. Finally, an original physionotrace, made in Paris in 1800 by Gilles Louis Chrétian, who invented the process of making profile silhouette portraits, is owned by The University of North Carolina, Chapel Hill.

SEE: William R. Davie Papers (Southern Historical Collection, University of North Carolina, Chapel Hill); William R. Davie Papers, 1778–1817 (North Carolina State Archives, Raleigh); Blackwell P. Robinson, *The Revolutionary War Sketches of William R. Davie* (1976), *William R. Davie* (1957).

BLACKWELL P. ROBINSON

**Davies, William James.** *See* **Faduma, Orishatukeh**

**Davis, Alexander Jackson** *(24 July 1803–14 Jan. 1892),* American architect, designed a number of buildings in North Carolina between the 1830s and the Civil War, thus bringing the state into the mainstream of Romantic architecture in America. His work for the state began in the first part of his career when he was a young partner in the prestigious New York architectural firm of Town and Davis (from February 1829, with interruptions, until July 1843). The older partner, Ithiel Town (1784–1844) was an established architect and engineer, inventor of the patented Town truss used for bridges. One of these bridges, constructed in Fayetteville in 1819, made Town known in North Carolina. In 1831, after a calamitous fire in Fayetteville, Davis designed a special Town truss for the reroofing of the Presbyterian church damaged in the fire. Another fire of the same year destroyed the North Carolina capitol in Raleigh. Its replacement, designed by Town and Davis in 1832–34, is regarded as one of the finest examples of Greek Revival style in America.

During these years Davis became a friend of Robert Donaldson, a Fayetteville native and graduate of The University of North Carolina, who had moved to New York. Davis remodeled Donaldson's Manhattan house and designed several structures that Donaldson commissioned for the university and offered to his alma mater. The projects could not be executed during hard times in North Carolina, but in 1844, when the university was ready to embark on a program of campus improvements, Donaldson secured the contract for Davis. By this time the Town and Davis partnership was over and Davis was practicing alone. He designed impressive additions to Old East and Old West in 1844, a ballroom-library (now the Playmakers Theatre) in 1850, and a Presbyterian church in Chapel Hill (now destroyed) in 1848. These structures are within Romantic Classicism with elements freely adapted from various Classical sources.

Work at Chapel Hill led to commissions elsewhere in the state. Projects in Greensboro and vicinity began with Blandwood, the home of Governor John Motley Morehead. In 1844 Davis designed an addition to the governor's home in the new Italian style. A view of it was immediately published in an architectural book, which, because of its subsequent popularity, was instrumental in the dissemination of the style. Locust Grove, the home of Morehead's friend, industrialist Edwin Michael Holt, was built in 1849 in what Davis called his American style. His buildings for two girls' schools—Edgeworth Academy, operated by Morehead, and the school that is now Greensboro College—were both later destroyed by fire. Main Hall, for the school that is now Salem College, was built in 1853; it has a Doric porch in the spirit of the earlier Greek Revival.

The North Carolina Hospital for the Insane, a huge Romantic Classical structure in Raleigh, was built in 1850 (most of Davis's work was pulled down after a fire in the twentieth century). Another massive Classical structure, Chamber's Hall at Davidson College, built in 1858 but later destroyed by fire, was Davis's last work in North Carolina before the Civil War stopped construction in the South.

Davis's total work for North Carolina, including ten to fifteen unexecuted projects, was considerable. Extending through a quarter of a century and exhibiting some of his finest buildings, it is a significant chapter in the architect's life as well as the artistic life of the state.

SEE: John V. Allcott, "Architect J. A. Davis in North Carolina, His Launching at the University," *North Carolina Architect* 20 (November and December 1973); *DAB*, vol. 5 (1930).

J. V. ALLCOTT

**Davis, Champion McDowell** *(1 July 1879–28 Jan. 1975),* railroad official, was the son of Robert Burns, a captain in the Army of Northern Virginia during the Civil War, and Cornelia Nixon Davis, daughter of Nicholas N. Nixon, who established Porter's Neck plantation. He was born near Hickory and was reared on a farm in Catawba County. His family later moved to Wilmington. After receiving a public school education, he began working with the Wilmington and Weldon Railroad, which became a part of the Atlantic Coast Line Railroad Company. He entered the railway service on 1 Mar. 1893 as a messenger boy and retired on 20 June 1957 as president of the Atlantic Coast Line. In his sixty-four years on the job, Davis worked in almost every capacity the railroad had to offer. Before becoming president of the Coast Line on 14 Oct. 1942, while still an executive vice-president, he was named president of four of the Coast Line's subsidiary companies: the Savannah Union Station Company and the Charleston Union Station Company in 1941, and the Tampa Southern Railroad and the Goldsboro Union Station Company early in 1942. He served as either president, vice-president, or director of many of the Coast Line's subsidiary companies. In addition to his duties with the railroad companies, Davis was an officer of several of the Coast Line's affiliates, including terminal companies and land development companies. He was a director of Home Savings Bank, Jefferson Standard Life Insurance Company, Home Insurance Company of New York, and other businesses. He also served as director of a number of national groups such as the Association of American Railroads and the Transportation Association of America. He was director of the United States Chamber of Commerce for two consecutive terms (1949–1952) and a member of the governing board of *Nations Business.*

Davis's long career was only interrupted by the Spanish-American War in 1898. He enlisted as a private in the Second Regiment of the North Carolina Infantry and in three years served as corporal, first sergeant, and when first lieutenant as adjutant. He resigned as a captain of the North Carolina State Guard in 1901.

Although he severed all ties with the railroad company when he retired in 1957, Davis remained an active member of the Wilmington community. He was a trustee of both Wilmington College (The University of North Carolina at Wilmington) and Cape Fear Technical Institute. On 14 June 1952 the Citadel awarded him an honorary doctorate of science. He was one of the few nongraduates of this college to be so recognized. He belonged to numerous civic and social clubs, both state and national, including Cape Fear Country Club, Carolina Yacht Club, North Carolina Society of the Cincinnati, The Newcomen Society, and the New York Southern Society.

Davis was active in the Episcopal church. He was a member of St. Johns Episcopal Church in Wilmington, but his work with the church was primarily on the national level. He served as chairman of the finance department of the church's National Council from 1946 to 1952; he was a former trustee of the Protestant Episcopal Theological Seminary in Virginia and of the Episcopal Radio-Television Foundation. At the time of his death he was a director of the Episcopal Church Foundation.

Davis's altruism is probably best reflected by his establishment of the Champion McDowell Davis Charitable Foundation in 1963 and the construction of a nonprofit, nondenominational nursing home for the elderly at Porter's Neck plantation. The home was completed in 1966 and named for his mother, Cornelia Nixon Davis. He was recognized in 1965 for his philanthropy by the North Carolina General Assembly, the New Hanover County Commission, and the city of Wilmington. In 1966 he was presented a plaque from the National Woodmen of the World for his humanitarian services in establishing the nursing home. He was again commended by New Hanover County in 1968 for his work in the advancement of the county and, as a result of his efforts, was selected as the *Star-News* Newspapers' Citizen of the Year in New Hanover County for 1973.

Davis died at age ninety-five. He was cremated and his ashes spread in the flag pole area at Cornelia Nixon Davis Nursing Home. He never married.

SEE: Roy C. Cook, ed., *Atlantic Coast Line News* (scattered issues); Resolution 33, passed by the North Carolina General Assembly, 1975 Session; Wilmington *Star-News* (scattered issues); *Who's Who in the South* (1927); *Who's Who in the South and Southwest* (1950).

JUANITA ANN SHEPPARD

**Davis, Dolphin Alston** *(28 July 1802–14 Dec. 1881),* banker, educator, and local official, was born at Cool Spring Inn, Fayetteville, of English and Scottish ancestry. His father was Dolphin Davis (1759–1818), a native of Halifax County, Va., who moved to Cumberland County before 1784. In 1789 he opened a tavern called Cool Spring Inn. A soldier of the American Revolution, he had taken part in the Battle of Kings Mountain. His mother was Ann Stevenson, a daughter of one of the Scottish emigrants who went to the Cape Fear valley shortly after the Battle of Culloden in 1746. Both parents were devout people and his father was long a ruling elder of the Presbyterian church.

When his father died in 1818, Davis was hired as a clerk in the Fayetteville branch of the Bank of the United States. Although his advantages in education were limited, he had enjoyed a period of instruction in the Fayetteville Male Academy under the Reverend James L. Turner and the Reverend Colin McIver. The excellence of his style as seen in his letters and business papers shows that he made good use of his time while in school. After working seven years in the bank, he purchased a farm near Fayetteville and spent twelve years in agricultural pursuits. In 1837, he moved with his wife and two children to Salisbury to be cashier of the Salisbury branch of the Bank of Cape Fear, a position he held until after the Civil War. For several years before his removal to Salisbury he had been magistrate and financial agent of Cumberland County. He was chosen for the same position in Rowan County. His ability, accuracy, and fidelity soon won the confidence of his fellow citizens.

A year after his arrival in Salisbury, Davis was named a director of the Salisbury Female Academy and was on the building committee that in 1839 erected the school behind the Presbyterian church that came to be known as the Wren Building. In 1839 he was named a director of the Salisbury Cotton Factory that later served as a Confederate prison. Also in 1839 he was elected president of the Temperance Convention that met in the Methodist church to form a temperance society in Salisbury. He was a stockholder in the Salisbury and Taylorsville Plank Road Company, a director of the North Carolina Railroad, chairman of the Special Court, and a warden of the poor. A friend and promoter of schools and higher education, he was a founder and trustee of the Salisbury Female Seminary in 1855 and served as chairman of the board of superintendents for the Rowan County common schools from 1854 to 1866. He was also a trustee of Davidson College, from which all four of his sons were graduated.

For a man who was three times elected mayor of Salisbury (1849, 1855, 1856) and twice was chairman of the county commissioners (1868, 1869), it seems unusual that Davis had no broad political ambition nor did he enter into the hustings to any marked degree. It was because of his great financial acumen and innate honesty that he was chosen to lead the city and county government. Because of his prudence the finances of Rowan County were in good condition, and during his time in office Rowan and Salisbury were free of debt. He was considered a model businessman, and his religious, moral, and social character marked him as a leader. He was elected an elder in the First Presbyterian Church in 1839 and served in that office for forty-two years. He represented his church in the presbytery, the synod, and the general assembly. He was clerk and treasurer of the session, and for thirty years, as a trustee, he served on the executive and financial committees of Davidson College.

After the Bank of Cape Fear closed, Davis opened a private banking house, which he operated successfully until his death. Afterward his son, O. D. Davis, formed a partnership with Samuel H. Wiley; they operated the only bank in Salisbury until it was sold to the Atlantic Bank and Trust Company of Greensboro in 1926. Davis was buried in the old English Cemetery, Salisbury.

By his several marriages Davis had nine sons, two of whom became Presbyterian ministers and another a ruling elder.

SEE: Samuel A. Ashe, *Cyclopedia of Eminent and Representative Men of the Carolinas of the Nineteenth Century* (1892); *Carolina Watchman*, 2 Sept. 1837, 10 Feb. 1838, 25 Apr., 15 Nov. 1839, 8 Feb. 1849, 7 Jan., 21 Feb. 1850, 1 Feb. 1855, 29 Jan. 1856, 15, 22 Dec. 1881, 13 Aug. 1885; D. A. Davis Papers (Southern Historical Collection, University of North Carolina, Chapel Hill); Dolphin Davis, "Memorandum of My Childrens' Ages" (MS in the author's possession); Salisbury *Old North State Tri-Weekly*, 25 July 1868; Anna Morrison Wilson, "Genealogy" (typescript in Rowan Public Library, Salisbury, N.C.).

JAMES S. BRAWLEY

**Davis, Gary** *(30 Apr. 1895–5 May 1972)*, blind black street singer and minister, was born in Laurens, S.C., to a farming family and was raised by his grandmother. As a young man he joined the steady stream of rural blacks who moved into the industrial town of Greenville, S.C. By 1912 he was playing with a string band of some six or eight pieces, which included another guitarist similarly blind from birth, Willie Walker, rated by Davis as the finest guitarist he knew. About 1914 he began attending the South Carolina School for the Blind, in Cedar Springs, Spartanburg; there he taught music although he never learned to read it. In 1919 he married a woman named Mary; they separated in 1924. He spent the next two years in Asheville, N.C., where he was led by banjo player and guitarist, Arron Washington, who later lived in Albany, N.Y. In 1926 Davis arrived in Durham, moving into 410 Poplar, south of Pettigrew Street, in the area of the tobacco factories of Hayti. His mother, Belle, was living there at the time and an uncle resided on Enterprise Street.

Although Davis had played around Greenville and Spartanburg with such fine musicians as Willie Walker and Blind Simmie Dooley, it was while he was resident in Durham that his influence on other bluesmen became really marked. By his own statement he was ordained a minister in Washington, N.C., in 1933; however, his Durham County Welfare file of 21 July 1937 puts the date much later, quoting his ordination as having taken place "two months ago," which is more probable as he had been on file since December 1934. Moreover, in July 1935 he had recorded in New York under the name Blind Gary—as he was generally known—and the first two numbers of the fifteen that he recorded were secular blues. In view of his later religious "obsession," as one caseworker mentioned, it is unlikely that he would have recorded secular music at that time had he been already ordained. Present at the sessions that he attended was fellow blind guitarist from Durham, Blind Boy Fuller, whom Davis actually seconded on at least one song.

Applying for Aid to the Blind in July 1937 Davis was found to be "hopelessly blind"; his application was accepted and he continued to receive aid until he left the state in 1944. He frequently played at religious meetings, as well as in churches and barber shops and on Pettigrew Street in Durham, near the tobacco factories. Local bluesmen, who remember him playing on the street, testify that he would play blues but only the songs he had recorded. Generally, and certainly later in his career, he played only gospel songs. In July 1939 he was offered a further recording trip to New York, again for the American Record Company, where his friends Blind Boy Fuller and Blind Sonny Terry, a harmonica player recently arrived from Georgia, were recorded. Davis refused the offer as he felt he would not be paid enough. He was to play frequently with Terry when both were in New York some years later.

In December 1943 Davis married a Wake County woman by the name of Annie and moved to Raleigh; in January 1944 he left the area for good and went to New York, where he first lived in the Bronx. Apart from a short visit to Durham in February 1948, he did not return to North Carolina again, making his home at last in Jamaica, N.Y.

Davis played in the fast, finger-picked style of Greenville, S.C., which yielded other superb guitarists such as Willie Walker and Josh White. Davis's touch was clean, each note picked carefully with few elisions, and as such, he fitted entirely into the Piedmont style of East Coast bluesmen. Although Davis claimed he didn't sing blues, he certainly played them, even though he called them gospel pieces. With his harsh, angular voice and rhythmic, surprisingly melodic guitar lines, he had all the accoutrements of a bluesman, bar the lyrics. His musical importance was considerable in Durham for he taught Blind Boy Fuller much of his music, especially how to play in the key of A. Local bluesmen who knew both Fuller and Davis corroborate this and many of Davis's guitar characteristics are to be found in Fuller's playing, such as his fast, finger-picked runs and powerful base line. Fuller, in his turn, was to be the most influential bluesman in the southeastern states, and there can be few bluesmen of the late 1930s and 1940s who failed to hear his records. Much of what they heard was really Gary Davis.

Once in New York, Davis became famous as a street singer in Harlem, was accepted into the "folk" set, and, fortunately, was heavily recorded—sometimes with his old friend, Sonny Terry. He played until the day he died and even made journeys to England to appear in concerts when he was well into his seventies. His astonishingly beautiful guitar lines remained unblemished by time.

Davis had no children from his two marriages. His second wife, Annie, outlived him.

SEE: Bruce Bastin, *Crying for the Carolines* (1971); Hugh Penn Brinton, "The Negro in Durham" (Ph.D. diss., University of North Carolina, 1930); Stefan Grossman, "A Rare Interview with Rev. Gary Davis," *Sing Out!* 23 (March/April 1974); Bill Phillips, "Piedmont Country Blues," *Southern Exposure* 2 (1974).

BRUCE BASTIN

**Davis, George** *(1 Mar. 1820–23 Feb. 1896)*, lawyer, Confederate senator, and attorney general, was born on his father's plantation, Porter's Neck, in New Hanover (now Pender) County. His parents were Thomas Frederick and Sarah Isabella Eagles Davis. Among his mother's forebears were Sir John Yeamans, who in 1665 had received a grant of land near Wilmington for his family's loyalty to the Stuarts and in 1671 had become governor of South Carolina; and John Moore, governor of South Carolina in 1700. The Davis family, which reached Cape Fear via Massachusetts about 1725, was closely related to the Ashe, Lillington, Swann, and other prominent families of that region.

Davis attended W. H. Harden's school at Pittsboro and was then tutored at home. He entered The University of North Carolina at age fourteen and was valedictorian of the class of 1838. Afterward he studied law with his brother, Thomas Frederick, and was admitted to the bar at twenty. A year later he was licensed to practice throughout the state. Davis's first law office was in Wilmington, where his brilliance and eloquence quickly won him renown at the bar. His specialty was corporation law, though his reputation was almost as wide in maritime and criminal law and in equity practice.

In addition to his varied and remunerative law practice, Davis was in constant demand as speaker and lecturer. His lectures were generally historical in nature, with his chief interest being in colonial Cape Fear history. Although his papers are no longer authoritative, they corrected many errors in earlier writings and dramatized a little known period in North Carolina. For their preparation Davis consulted a wide range of primary sources and had the audacity to criticize both the style and interpretation of the premier nationalist historian, George Bancroft. Davis's biographical papers provide an insight into his respect for his superior officers. His address on former President Jefferson Davis, delivered in 1890, is particularly notable for its analysis of that beleaguered man's trials, for George Davis was one of the president's closest friends and advisers during the Confederacy.

Davis was a Whig in politics and his eulogy on the death of Henry Clay won high praise even from the Democratic Wilmington *Journal*. Though rather conservative, in national politics he favored a bank, the protective tariff, and territorial expansion; in state affairs he supported government aid to education and internal improvements. Locally he was a director of the Bank of Wilmington and a member of various literary and historical societies. In 1848 he became general counsel of the Wilmington and Weldon Railroad and remained so until it was absorbed into the Atlantic Coast Line, of which he served as general counsel until his death. Despite his public service, Davis never held elective office outside the Confederacy, though the Whig state convention of 1848 came within one vote of nominating him for governor.

When the Whig party died, Davis found no existing party acceptable. By 1860, however, he considered the ultra southern Democratic party so objectionable that he aligned with the Constitutional Union party on the grounds that the preservation of the Union preempted any sectional controversy. After Lincoln's election Davis wrote and spoke against immediate secession and urged continued search for remedies within the Union. His resolutions expressing these views, presented before a public meeting in Wilmington on 11 December, were unanimously adopted. On 26 Jan. 1861 the legislature elected him one of five delegates to the Washington Peace Conference. But he returned home with his hope of reconciliation crushed. In a speech on 2 March he castigated the constitutional amendments proposed in Washington as dishonorable and completely inimical to North Carolina's requirement of "property in slaves." He was now a secessionist, arguing that "The division must be made on the line of slavery. The State must go with the South." This startling conversion caused Davis's name to be considered for a place in the convention of May 1861 but he published a card blocking his candidacy.

Nevertheless, a caucus of secessionists strategically included Davis in their slate of nominees for the Confederate Provisional Congress, and on 18 June he was elected delegate-at-large. That September he won a seat in the Senate on the twenty-fifth ballot, but drew only a two-year term and in 1863 lost reelection to William A. Graham. In the Senate Davis was on the committees of Buildings and Finance and was chairman of the Committee on Claims. As senator he became such a strong supporter of the administration that other ex-Whigs in his delegation considered him a "camp follower of the precipitators." A fairer interpretation would be to rate him as one of North Carolina's strongest Confederate nationalists. Most of the bills that he introduced aimed to create as large and effective an army as possible. And except for his extreme conservatism in financial matters he withheld no important powers from the central government. Indeed, he was one of four senators willing to give the proposed supreme court appellate jurisdiction over state courts. On 31 Dec. 1868, the president appointed Davis attorney general.

Assuming office on 22 Jan. 1864, Davis performed the many routine duties of attorney general with dispatch and satisfaction. He wrote seventy-four opinions, most of them brief but often containing ideas of real merit. Generally he maintained a rigid compliance with the law, but frequently he had the common sense to disregard laws when necessary, particularly when they seem to have been poorly formulated. His chief service to the Confederacy, however, may have been his friendly advice to the president. Davis's kindly nature and winning personality often bridged gaps between the sensitive president and his critics. The president undoubtedly developed a genuine respect for his gracious and cosmopolitan appointee, and their relationship developed into a lasting friendship. When Lee surrendered, Davis advised the president to accept the best terms obtainable and to divide the remaining money in the Treasury with the soldiers. He accompanied the refugee government as far as Charlotte, then attempted to flee to England by way of Florida and Nassau. He was captured at Key West, however, and taken to Fort Hamilton in New York. Immediately after his parole on 2 Jan. 1866, he returned to Wilmington.

Davis was now in poverty with six motherless children. For the next few years his open criticism of Reconstruction kept him before the public, but he generally refused to seek public office, devoting most of his energies to rebuilding his law practice and to his work as railroad counsel. The few public services that he performed, therefore, were of brief duration. In 1866 he was a delegate to the Philadelphia Convention, designed to unite moderate Republicans and Democrats. On 14 Apr. 1868, before a capacity crowd in Wilmington, he excoriated the Radicals and their proposed constitution of that year. When it was approved, Davis labored for its reform and eventually saw success in 1875. Three years later Governor Vance offered Davis the chief justiceship of the state supreme court, but he declined it on the grounds that he could not live on the salary. In 1880 a group of northern financiers offered to buy the state's interest in the Western North Carolina Railroad; Governor Jarvis asked Davis and Thomas Ruffin to handle the proposition, both serving without remuneration. The legislature was divided on the advisability of sale, but on 22 March Davis "swept away all opposition" to the sale. Thereafter, with the exception of a few historical addresses, Davis attended to his law practice until his death. He died at home in Wilmington after several years of declining health and was buried with military honors in Oakdale Cemetery.

Physically, Davis was short and heavy-set. He possessed only ordinary vocal powers, but the preparation, imagination, and style of his addresses earned him an enormous reputation. By faith he was a devout Episcopalian. On 17 Nov. 1842 Davis married Mary A. Polk of Mecklenburg County, who died in 1863; on 9 May 1866 he married Monimia Fairfax of Richmond, who died in 1889. The surviving children by his first wife were Junius Davis and Mrs. George Roundtree; deceased children were Mrs. John E. Crow and Mrs. S. P. Shotter. The surviving children by his second wife were Mary Fairfax and Carry Davis.

SEE: Samuel A. Ashe, ed., *Biographical History of North Carolina*, vol. 2 (1905 [portrait]); H. G. Connor, *George Davis* (1911); Fletcher M. Green, "George Davis, North Carolina Whig and Confederate Statesman," *North Carolina Historical Review* 23 (1946); *Journal of the Confederate Congress*, vols. 1–3 (1904); *Journal of the Convention of North Carolina, 1861*; *Journal of the General Assembly, 1861, 1863*; Rembert Patrick, *Jefferson Davis and His Cabinet* (1944), *Opinions of the Confederate Attorneys General* (1950); James Sprunt, *Chronicles of the Cape Fear River* (1911); Wilmington *Messenger*, 25 Feb. 1896; W. B. Yearns, *Letters of Thomas J. Jarvis*, vol. 1 (1969).

BUCK YEARNS

**Davis, Harry Ellerbe** *(25 Aug. 1905–15 Sept. 1968)*, professor of dramatic art, distinguished himself as constructional engineer, as craftsman and lighting expert, as actor and playwright, and, especially, as stage director. What established his continuing reputation as a practical theater artist, more than anything else, was his direction of Kermit Hunter's outdoor play on the conflict between the Cherokee Indians and the white pioneers in the Great Smoky Mountains, which Davis staged and supervised from 1952 until 1967.

The son of Braxton Bragg and Ada Boland Davis, he was born in Little Mountain, S.C. When he was five years old, his family moved to Columbia, which has long boasted one of the leading community theaters in the South. Here he attended school and went on to the University of South Carolina, from which he was graduated with an A.B. degree in English literature. He played football, and he won prizes for essays. Attracted to the Town Theatre, he became involved in acting and directing, then went to Mississippi to teach for a year at the State College for Women. In 1931, when Professor Hubert Heffner left The University of North Carolina to accept a position at Northwestern University in Illinois, Professor Frederick Koch, director of the Carolina Playmakers at Chapel Hill, invited Davis to join his staff as business manager of the Playmakers and as Koch's assistant in his playwriting classes.

Unlike many academic administrators who separate their official life from their home life, Davis made the two one. He liked to have his university colleagues and his students around him; consequently the Davis residence on Mallette Street became a favorite rendezvous for everyone interested in theater. Harry Davis and his wife Ora Mae were expert cooks. In the Davis home there was always an abundance of good food as well as good conversation.

In 1939, with the help of a Rockefeller Foundation Fellowship, Davis took a year's leave of absence to do advanced study at Columbia University, from which he received an M.A. degree in 1940. In 1962 he was awarded an honorary doctorate of fine arts by Catawba College.

During World War II Davis entered the army as a private and served in England, France, and Germany, first as an interpreter in military government, then as a commissioned officer supervising education and religious activities in Upper Bavaria. For a while he helped to revise textbooks for use in postwar Germany.

Upon his return to The University of North Carolina, Davis assumed the directorship of Kermit Hunter's outdoor drama, *Unto These Hills*, and continued to administer this enterprise, summer after summer, until his death. Under his direction *Unto These Hills* developed into a distinguished drama, drawing more than a million spectators from all over the country. It opened up new fields of employment for the Indians of the area, provided funds for the education of many of the young men and women of the mountains, and benefited the economic life of several of the surrounding counties. In 1960 Davis was elected to the board of directors of the American Educational Theatre Association. He was a member of the National Theatre Conference, the Southeastern Theatre Conference, the American National Theatre and Academy, the Cherokee Historical Association, and the Administrative Board of the Institute of Outdoor Drama. From 1960 to 1963 he served on the faculty council of the university.

When Samuel Selden went to the University of California in 1959, Davis replaced him as chairman of the Department of Dramatic Art at North Carolina and held this position until he died. He was married three times, to Ora Mae Jackson, Susanne Marden, and Anne Osterhout. Two of his wives died. He was survived by his last wife, Anne. Though he had no children of his own, he was very fond of young people and wrote and produced several plays for them.

SEE: Harry Ellerbe Davis, "Academic Discipline for the Performing Artist" (typescript of address to Philological Club, Chapel Hill, 7 Feb. 1967, North Carolina Collection, University of North Carolina, Chapel Hill); "Cinderella: A Dramatization for Children in Three Acts" (mimeograph copy, North Carolina Collection, University of North Carolina, Chapel Hill); "The Roland Holt Collection," *Carolina Playbook* 9 (June 1936); *Who's Who in the South and Southwest* (1967).

SAMUEL SELDEN

**Davis, Hayne** *(2 Nov. 1868–5 Mar. 1942)*, lawyer and author, was born in Statesville to E. Hayne Davis, veteran captain of the Confederate Army, and his wife Mary Williams Pearson of Richmond Hill. He was educated at the Bingham School in Mebane, where he distinguished himself by winning medals in both Greek and Latin. He entered The University of North Carolina in 1884 and was graduated in 1888. From the university Davis went into politics and campaigned for his uncle, Governor Daniel G. Fowle. During this period he became secretary of the State Democratic Executive Committee.

When the election was over, Davis returned to Chapel Hill for the law course and received his license to practice. At this time he accepted an invitation to practice law with a distant relative, General James C. J. Williams of Knoxville, Tenn. Within a year Davis was admitted into partnership, and he handled many of the firm's cases in the Tennessee Supreme Court. He left the law firm of Williams, Henderson, and Davis in 1894 to practice in New York City. He became engaged in mining enterprises and was sent to London to investigate a company "which had been misconducting itself with European exports of the company he was connected with." It was during this trip that he became aware of European politics. He is quoted as saying, "I became convinced that the political situation of Europe could not continue, and that a union or federation of these nations, along the lines of our union of states would be the outcome." Upon his return to the United States, he began a series of articles in the New York *Independent* and in so doing convinced the editor, Hamilton Holt, of his point of view.

In the five years that followed Davis's 1903 articles, both he and Holt became known as authorities on international affairs. In part because of the articles, Congressman Richard Barthaldt persuaded the American delegation to the Inter-Parliamentary Union to invite Davis to become secretary of that body for the 1904 St. Louis Meeting. When the Inter-Parliamentary Union returned to Washington after a tour of the country, Davis, among others, convinced President Theodore Roosevelt to call a second conference at The Hague. Davis was also secretary to the 1905 and 1906 international congresses held at Brussels and London; the program formulated at these meetings was the basis of discussion at the 1907 Hague conference. While at the Inter-Parliamentary Union, he formed a friendship with Baron Estournelles de Constant that led to his appointment as secretary of the International Conciliation. Through these many different peace boards Davis was the key leader in organizing the Peace and Arbitration League. From the Hague conference came the organization of the International Court of Justice and a proposal for a permanent international congress. But hopes for a Third International Congress to be held in 1914 were shattered with the outbreak of war and this country's subsequent refusal to join the League of Nations formed through the efforts of President Wilson.

Concurrently with his work for peace Davis maintained an active Wall Street law practice, and from 1904 to 1908 he was legal adviser to the Colombian delegation. His main task was to advise Colombia on the best method of obtaining compensation for Panama. He was dropped from this position when two close associates in the delegation left Washington.

In 1913, Davis became a member of the Christian Science church and worked diligently to raise funds for that organization and to restructure the New York churches. One year later he was elected to The University of North Carolina Alpha chapter for alumni membership in the Phi Beta Kappa Society.

Davis continued to contribute articles on international questions to periodicals; many of these pieces appeared in book form, notably *Among the World's Peacekeepers* published in New York in 1907. As his law practice diminished during the twenties, he began making more frequent appearances as a lecturer. In 1932, Davis became the vice-president for world cooperation of the World Narcotics Association. He resigned from the post three years later after a dispute with the association's president. By this time he had completely retired from his law practice and spent a great deal of time lecturing at college campuses across the country.

Unmarried, Davis died in Boston, Mass., and was buried in the Chestnut Hill Cemetery, Salisbury, N.C.

SEE: Hayne Davis File (Alumni Association, University of North Carolina, Chapel Hill); Hayne Davis Papers (Southern Historical Collection, University of North Carolina, Chapel Hill); Raleigh *News and Observer*, 23 Jan. 1927; University of North Carolina General Alumni Association, *The Alumni Review* (February 1927); *Who's Who in America* (1940).

TYNDALL P. HARRIS, JR.

**Davis, James** *(21 Oct. 1721–February or March 1785)*, North Carolina's first printer, was born in Virginia. The exact location of his birth is not known, but in 1745 he was living in Williamsburg. He probably learned his trade under William Parks, who established the first press in Virginia at Williamsburg in 1736. Davis came to North Carolina in 1749 to fill the post of public printer, an office created that year by the Assembly to print a revisal of the colony's laws. He set up his print shop on Pollock Street in New Bern, later moving to Broad Street. His first job was printing currency for the province. Not until 1751 did the revisal of the laws appear. Though sometimes called "Swann's Revisal" from the name of the editor, Samuel Swann, the official title was *A Collection of all the Public Acts of Assembly, of the Province of North Carolina: Now in Force and Use.* Meanwhile, in 1749 Davis published the *Journal of the House of Burgesses*, North Carolina's earliest imprint.

Davis served as public printer for North Carolina nearly thirty-three years, during which time he printed at least a hundred titles. Most of these were of an official nature. However, he did publish other material. In 1753 he issued Clement Hall's *A Collection of Many Christian Experiences*, the first nonlegal book written by a North Carolinian published in the province; Clement Hall was rector of St. Paul's Church in Edenton. But before this, in August 1751, Davis began *The North Carolina Gazette*, North Carolina's first newspaper. Isaiah Thomas, an early historian of colonial newspapers and himself an active printer during and after the Revolutionary period, says the *Gazette* was discontinued around 1761, though no copies after 1759 have been located. In June 1764 Davis began a second newspaper, *The North-Carolina Magazine: or Universal Intelligencer.* He continued to publish it under this title until 1768 when he returned to his first title, *The North Carolina Gazette.* He suspended publication in 1778, principally because of the difficulties of publishing as a consequence of the war.

As a newspaper editor and printer, Davis produced work that compared favorably with that turned out by printers in the other colonies. His *Gazette*, issued weekly, was small, generally four pages, and contained, as did most colonial newspapers, much outside news and a minimum of local news. The circulation, never large, was restricted to the vicinity of New Bern, though advertisements appearing in the paper came from other parts of the province.

Davis began to put down roots almost as soon as he arrived in New Bern. He acquired property and in 1753 became a member of the county court, an office he held for twenty-five years. The next year he was elected sheriff of Craven County; he resigned after ten months when he was chosen to represent New Bern in the Assembly, only to be denied the seat because of dual officeholding. In 1755 he was again elected to the Assembly and continued to serve until 1760, the last year representing Craven County. In 1755 Davis was also appointed postmaster of New Bern; in October he was awarded the contract by the Assembly to carry the mail from Suffolk, Va., to Wilmington, N.C. Then, beginning in 1768, he served as justice of the peace in New Bern, remaining in that office until 1778.

As the American Revolution approached, Davis allied himself with those opposing the mother country, opening the columns of his newspaper to stories and essays favorable to the American cause. He became a member of the Council of Safety of New Bern, when that body was formed, and represented New Bern in the provincial congresses. In 1777 the Assembly chose him as one of the judges on the Admiralty Court for the port of Beaufort. He climaxed his political career by becoming a member of the Council of State in 1781.

Clearly, Davis was an active and ambitious man; but he may have been a bit overweening because of the prestige he enjoyed. Also, the many activities in which he engaged surely interfered with his work as public printer. Governor Arthur Dobbs thought so, at any rate; in 1764 he refused to approve Davis's reappointment as public printer, stating that he was negligent in his duties. The governor appointed Andrew Steuart, a printer then residing in Philadelphia. But the Assembly objected to this use of power exercised by the governor and reappointed Davis, at the same time refusing to appropriate any money for Steuart's salary. Dobbs persisted, however, and Steuart settled in Wilmington where, in September 1764, he began publishing a second *North Carolina Gazette*. It was discontinued three years later. Steuart drowned in 1769 while swimming in the Cape Fear River. Adam Boyd purchased his printing equipment and in October 1769 began the *Cape Fear Mercury*.

In the *Mercury* of 22 Sept. 1773 there appeared a confession by one Spencer Dew, who was about to be hanged for horse stealing. Dew said that he had passed counterfeit money printed by James Davis. Whether this was an attempt by certain opponents of Davis to incriminate him, or the effort of a convicted felon to embarrass prominent men, is not clear. In any event the charge had little or no effect on Davis's career. In 1774 he was reappointed public printer while continuing to serve as justice of the peace in New Bern.

In 1776, when an armed ship fitted out by North Carolinians to prey on British shipping anchored in the Neuse River off a plantation owned by Davis, the printer revealed another side to his personality. Davis complained that the crew raided his cornfields. He depicted them as drunk and rowdy idlers, "the most abandoned sett of wretches ever collected together." Others referred to the group as "healthy men all anxious to adventure." This display of temper, however, was mild compared with Davis's conduct toward a French officer who, in 1778, had persuaded the Assembly to allow him to recruit a regiment from among French settlers in New Bern. This officer enlisted a young Frenchman who was an apprentice of John Davis, ship captain and son of the printer. Captain Davis was enraged and, with his father and some twenty seamen from his ship, assailed the regiment's quarters demanding that the young recruit be released. The sergeant on duty refused. Thereupon the elder Davis abused the French officer and threatened to drive every Frenchman out of town along with any who sympathized with them. This latter threat was directed at the other justices of the peace who had earlier refused Davis's demand that the militia be called out. Davis's behavior on this occasion was not widely endorsed in New Bern. Richard Cogdell, a tavern owner and Revolutionary leader, wrote Governor Richard Caswell that "the arbitrary and scandalous behavior of [Davis] in many instances before has given the town a name . . . as every inhabitant except himself and minions would blush at." Yet, Davis still must have been respected, for in 1781 he was elected by the Assembly to the Council of State.

Shortly after arriving in New Bern in 1749, Davis married Prudence Hobbs, widow of Christopher Gregory Hobbs and daughter of William Carruthers. To them were born four sons and three daughters. James, the eldest son, was a merchant in New Bern. John, the ship captain, died while a prisoner aboard a British ship anchored in the Charleston, S.C., harbor. Of the others only Thomas is known to have followed his father's trade. Not only did he assist the elder Davis in his print shop until drafted into the army in 1778, but he also succeeded him as state printer in 1782, a position he held until 1785. In that year James Davis died in New Bern. His will was probated at the March term of court.

SEE: Clarence S. Brigham, *Bibliography of American Newspapers, 1690–1820* (1947); Walter Clark, ed., *State Records of North Carolina*, vols. 11–14 (1895–96), 22–24 (1905–7); Alonzo T. Dill, *Governor Tryon and His Palace* (1955); Robert N. Elliott, Jr., "James Davis and the Beginning of the Newspaper in North Carolina," *North Carolina Historical Review* 42 (1965); *Journal of the House of Burgesses of the Province of North Carolina, 1749* (facs., 1949); William L. Saunders, ed., *Colonial Records of North Carolina*, vols. 5–10 (1887–90); Mary L. Thornton, "Public Printing in North Carolina, 1749–1815," *North Carolina Historical Review* 21 (1944); Stephen B. Weeks, *The Press of North Carolina in the Eighteenth Century* (1891).

ROBERT N. ELLIOTT, JR.

**Davis, James Wagner** *(8 June 1886–31 May 1955),* physician, was born in Statesville, the son of Lawson Davis of Wilkes County and Delia Josephine Wagner Davis of Statesville. He studied in the public schools of Statesville until 1904, when he went to Oak Ridge Institute near Greensboro. He was graduated from The University of North Carolina Medical School at Chapel Hill in 1908 and the University of Pennsylvania School of Medicine in 1913. He did his internship at Robert Packer Hospital in Sayre, Pa.

During World War I Davis served with the American Expeditionary Forces in France and Germany. While in Germany in June 1919, he was sent on a highly confidential mission into Russia to confer with Lenin and Trotsky. He retired from the army as a colonel. Upon returning from the war in 1919 he opened Davis Hospital in Statesville. Here Davis became widely acclaimed for his surgical technique; he also pioneered in adapting scientific and technical developments for medicine. The doors of his facility were open to rich and poor alike, and scores of people were never billed for the services they received. It was the first hospital in North Carolina to use air conditioning in its operating rooms and to establish blood donor services and blood banks; it was one of the first hospitals in the United States to use glucose solution intravenously in postoperative treatment. Under his direction and that of Miss Elizabeth Hill, the Davis Hospital School of Nursing was opened in 1920 and became one of the outstanding schools of nursing in the state.

Davis took an active interest in political, civic, and religious affairs. He served as treasurer of the North Carolina Republican Committee; and, although he never ran for public office, he campaigned publicly for Republican candidates throughout the state. He was a staunch opponent of what he felt was an encroaching socialized medicine in the United States. He was a leader in the founding of WSIC radio station in Statesville and of the Davis Memorial Baptist Church in Wilkes County. Davis continued to perform surgery even during his last two years, when he battled against intestinal cancer which eventually took his life. He died in the hospital that he had erected on the grounds of his birthplace. He was married to Nancy Smith of Guilford County, and they were the parents of a son, John L.

SEE: LeGette Blythe, *James W. Davis, North Carolina Surgeon* (1956); *Mooresville Tribune*, 1 June 1955; *Statesville Daily*, 17 Dec. 1925, 1 June 1955; *Winston-Salem Journal and Sentinel*, 21 Feb. 1975.

STEVE WOOD

**Davis, Joseph Jonathan** *(13 Apr. 1828–7 Aug. 1892)*, congressman and state supreme court justice, was born in Franklin County, the tenth of eleven children of Jonathan Davis, a planter, and his wife, Mary Pomfret Butler. William Davis, his grandfather, served as a colonel in the Continental Army during the Revolution. On his father's side, he was descended from Sir Jonathan Davis, who immigrated to Virginia in 1660 and settled in what later became Hanover County, where he owned several thousand acres under royal grant. Dolan Davis, one of Sir Jonathan's brothers, who accompanied him to America, was an ancestor of Jefferson Davis, the Confederate president.

Davis studied at Louisburg Male Academy, Wake Forest College, the College of William and Mary, and The University of North Carolina, where he read law under W. H. Battle and was graduated with an LL.B. degree in 1850. Admitted to the bar that June, he began to practice in Oxford, then moved to Louisburg in 1852. An ardent Whig, Davis initially opposed secession, but accepted a commission as captain of Company G, Forty-seventh North Carolina Infantry, on 29 Mar. 1862. He saw service with the Army of Northern Virginia and in eastern North Carolina and was present at the Battle of Kinston. On 3 July 1863, although wounded in the arm and forehead and with his horse shot from under him, Davis led his company to a point "over the stone wall" on Cemetery Ridge in the Pickett-Pettigrew charge at Gettysburg. Unable to withdraw, he and the survivors of his unit were captured; he was interned at Fort Delaware and later at Johnson's Island, where he remained until the end of the war.

Returning to Louisburg, Davis resumed legal practice, this time in partnership with Charles M. Cooke, and entered politics as a Conservative. In 1866 he was elected without opposition to a term in the House of Commons, where he served on the committee that voted to reject the Fourteenth Amendment. In 1870 and 1872 he canvassed for the Democratic party, gaining notice for his stirring oratory; in 1872 he was a state elector-at-large for Horace Greeley. During this period, it was later learned, he was also a high-ranking leader in the North Carolina Ku Klux Klan.

In 1874 Davis served on the Democratic State Executive Committee. The same year he defeated J. P. H. Russ and Josiah Turner for the party's nomination to the U.S. House of Representatives from the Fourth District; in November he won election over J. H. Hendon. Serving in the Forty-fourth, Forty-fifth, and Forty-sixth congresses (1875–81), Davis established a record typical of Southern Democrats of the period, defending southern claims for war damages and extension of Mexican War pension benefits to otherwise deserving ex-Confederates; he seems to have acted as a southern spokesman against federal interference in elections procedure.

Retiring from Congress, Davis resumed private practice in Louisburg. In October 1885 an abortive convention to organize a state bar association elected him first president of that association; however, its almost immediate demise seems in no way to have been his responsibility.

In 1887 Governor Alfred M. Scales appointed Davis an associate justice of the North Carolina Supreme Court, a singular honor since Davis had not served the customary previous term on the superior court bench. He quickly confuted any critics of the appointment through his probity and devotion to duty, earning a reputation for exhaustive personal study of the legal and factual background of each case. "If he was not so profound a lawyer as some others who have graced the bench," observed Josephus Daniels, "he gave full proof of his judicial qualities and undoubtedly shortened his life by attention to duty." Elected in his own right in 1888, he remained on the bench until his death.

After the supreme court was expanded from three to five justices in 1889, Davis frequently held the swing vote between the "liberal" bloc (A. C. Avery and Walter Clark) and the more conservative Chief Justice A. S. Merrimon and Justice J. E. Shepherd. Thus in February 1892, when Davis suffered a stroke that left him partially paralyzed, the court was left divided 2-2 on a number of cases. Among these was *Wilmington and Weldon Railroad v. B. I. Allsbrook* (110 North Carolina 138), involving the state's right to tax the road's property in light of an exemption granted before the Civil War, when its operation had been unprofitable. Davis was known to favor the state in the case, but it was believed that, if he resigned due to ill health, Governor Thomas M. Holt would appoint a prorailroad justice to succeed him. Informed of the situation by Avery, Davis left his sickbed in Louisburg and traveled by closed carriage to Raleigh to cast the deciding vote; *Railroad v. Allsbrook*, upholding the state, was later regarded as a landmark in the struggle for effective railroad regulation.

Davis, an Episcopalian, died in Louisburg and was buried in Oaklawn Cemetery. Known to his contemporaries as "Honest Joe," he was celebrated for his extreme personal integrity; throughout his term on the supreme court, he allotted $1,000 of his $2,500 annual salary toward repaying a surety on a defaulted bond, a repayment he could have easily and honorably avoided. A loyal alumnus, he served on the board of trustees of The University of North Carolina from 1874 to 1891. With William A. Graham and Kemp P. Battle, he was a member of the committee that recommended a plan for the organization of the university on its reopening; in 1883 he was chairman of the visiting committee. In 1887 the university awarded him an honorary LL.D. degree.

On 21 Oct. 1852 Davis married Katherine Elizabeth Shaw of Louisburg (d. 1881). There were five children by this marriage, Mrs. Katherine McAden Davis Crenshaw, Robert Henry, Hugh Levin, Mrs. Mary Helen Davis Allen (m. James M. Allen of Louisburg), and Lily Davis, who died while still a child. In 1883 Davis married Louisa Kittrell of Oxford (d. 1899).

A number of Davis's congressional speeches were reprinted in pamphlet form by the United States Government Printing Office and were apparently widely distributed. His judicial opinions appear in 96-110 *North Carolina Reports* (1887–92). Among the more notable are *Cagle v. Parker*, 97 (on easements); *McCanless v. Flinchum*, 98 (on definition of homestead); *Troy v. Railroad*, 98 (on contributory negligence); *Michael v. Foil*, 100 (on establishing definitive North Carolina rule regarding privileged communication between lawyer and client); and *Goodman v. Sapp*, 102 (on failure of a witness to take the stand as subject of comment in trial procedure).

SEE: Samuel A. Ashe, *Cyclopedia of Eminent and Representative Men of the Carolinas of the Nineteenth Century* (1892); Kemp P. Battle, *History of the University of North Carolina* (1907–12); Fannie F. Blackwelder, "The Organization and Early Years of the North Carolina Bar Association," *North Carolina Historical Review* 34 (1957); Walter Clark, ed., *Histories of the Several Regiments and Battalions from North Carolina in the Great War, 1861–'65* (1901), "The Supreme Court of North Carolina," *The Green Bag* (October–December 1892); Josephus Daniels, *Tar Heel Editor* (1939); Edward Hill Davis, *Historical Sketches of Franklin County* (1948); Joseph Jonathan Davis, Congressional Speeches (North Carolina Collection, University of North Carolina, Chapel Hill); Joseph Jonathan Davis Papers (Cecil W. Robbins Library, Louisburg College, Louisburg, N.C.); J. G. deRoulhac Hamilton, *Reconstruction in North Carolina* (1906); "In Memory of Joseph J. Davis, Associate Justice," 111 *North Carolina Reports* (1892); Van Noppen Papers (Manuscript Department, Library, Duke University, Durham); John W. Wheeler, *Reminiscences and Memoirs of North Carolina and Eminent North Carolinians* (1916).

BENNETT L. STEELMAN

**Davis, Junius** *(17 June 1845–11 Apr. 1916)*, lawyer, was the son of George Davis, a lawyer, orator, and attorney general of the Confederate States, and Mary Adelaide Polk Davis, the daughter of General Thomas G. Polk of Mecklenburg County and granddaughter of Colonel William Polk of Raleigh. Junius Davis was born in Wilmington at the old Davis family home on Second Street. He attended schools taught by Levin Meginney and George W. Jewett until he was twelve, when he enrolled in the Bingham school at the Oaks, twelve miles southwest of Hillsborough. He studied there for four years until his education was cut short by the Civil War.

At the beginning of the war the Davis family moved to Charlotte. In 1863, at age seventeen, Junius Davis enlisted as a private in the Confederate Army, serving with Company E, Tenth North Carolina Regiment, commanded by Captain Alexander D. Moore. The battery that served with General Hoke was officially named the "Wilmington Light Artillery," but became known as "Moore's Battery" and later "Miller's Battery" when Moore resigned in 1863 and Captain John Miller took command. In 1864 the battery was ordered to Virginia and attached to a battalion commanded by Major N. S. Moseley. Davis was promoted to corporal and served in the battles of Drewry's Bluff and Bermuda Hundred, the attack on Fort Harrison, and the final days of fighting around Petersburg where he was slightly wounded in the neck the last day in the trenches. He continued on duty while his battery was part of the rear guard in the retreat to Appomattox. The Confederate soldiers drove back an advance of Sheridan's cavalry from their position about one mile from Appomattox, but later a surprise attack captured some of their guns and drove Davis and several others into the woods. The next day they were informed by an officer of McGregor's Mounted Battery that General Lee had surrendered. Unable to document the information, Davis and the two men with him proceeded to Lynchburg where they were advised to go home, subject to being recalled to active duty. Davis then attempted to reach Johnston's army but learned at Greensboro that Johnston had also surrendered. He surrendered himself to the federal provost marshal in Greensboro and was paroled.

Returning to Charlotte, Davis was hired to accompany railroad cars of cotton from Charlotte to New Bern. In the fall of 1865, at age twenty, he returned to Wilmington and worked as a clerk in the dry goods store of Weil & Rosenthal. His father, who had attempted to escape to British territory, was captured and imprisoned for several months; when paroled he returned to Wilmington and resumed his law practice. In 1867 Junius Davis resigned his clerkship to study law in his father's office and was admitted to the bar in the spring of 1868. He was associated with his father in the firm of Davis & Davis until the elder's death in 1898. Clients included the Atlantic Coast Line Railroad Company for which Davis served as division counsel, the Consolidated Railways, the Light and Power Company, and other corporations. He was president of the Wilmington Railroad Bridge Company.

Although an active Democrat, Davis never sought political office. In the riot at Wilmington in 1898 he was a member of the committee that directed events in the racially troubled town, his efforts leading to Governor Daniel L. Russell's decision that there should be no Republican opposition to the election of the citizens' candidates.

Davis presented portraits of James Iredell and Alfred Moore, justices of the United States Supreme Court, to the state supreme court on behalf of the North Carolina Society of the Sons of the Revolution of which he was a member. He was an honorary member of the North Carolina Society of the Cincinnati and a member of the Protestant Episcopal church.

History, especially that of the Cape Fear region, interested Davis. He served on the advisory board for Samuel A. Ashe's *Biographical History of North Carolina* and supplied information for some of the sketches. He also published a number of articles including one on Locke's Fundamental Constitutions and another on John Paul Jones, published first in the *South Atlantic Quarterly* and later in pamphlet form. The article, entitled "Some Facts About John Paul Jones," was thought at the time of its publication to settle the dispute over how Jones acquired his name.

On 19 Jan. 1874 Davis married Mary Orme Walker, daughter of Thomas D. and Mary Vance Walker. She died some years later, and on 6 Nov. 1893 he married Mary Walker Cowan, daughter of Colonel Robert C. Cowan of Wilmington. He had eleven children; his son, Thomas W. Davis, became an attorney and a member of the Davis law firm.

SEE: Samuel A. Ashe, ed., *Biographical History of North Carolina*, vol. 2 (1905 [portrait]); Henry Groves Connor Papers (Southern Historical Collection, University of North Carolina, Chapel Hill); Junius Davis Papers (North Carolina State Archives, Raleigh); Thomas W. Davis, *Prominent People of North Carolina* (1906), ed., North Carolina Bar Association, *Proceedings*, vol. 18 (1916); John De Berniere Hooper Papers (Southern Historical Collection, University of North Carolina, Chapel Hill); H. M. London, ed., North Carolina Bar Association, *Proceedings*, vol. 25 (1925); Louis H. Manarin, ed., *North Carolina Troops, 1861–1865*, vol. 1 (1966); Leonidas Lafayette Polk Papers (Southern Historical Collection, University of North Carolina, Chapel Hill); James Sprunt, *Chronicles of the Cape Fear River, 1660–1916* (1916).

SARAH E. HOLEMAN

**Davis, Justina** *(1745–6 Dec. 1771)*, second wife of Governor Arthur Dobbs and later wife of Abner Nash, who became governor of North Carolina after her death, was born probably in Brunswick. She is thought to have been the daughter of John Davis and his wife, Rebecca Moore, who was the granddaughter of the second Landgrave Thomas Smith and of Governor James Moore, both of South Carolina. Justina married Governor Dobbs when she was fifteen and he in his seventies. A savage lampoon, purporting to be a letter written by a North Carolinian to a friend in Maryland, indicates the ridicule and scorn aroused by this match:

"Our Old Silenus of the Envigorated age of Seventy Eight who still Damns this Province with his Baneful Influence grew stupidly Enamored with Miss Davis a Lovely Lady of sprightly fifteen of a good Family and some Fortune. After much doting parade, Young Miss (for surely parents know best) is persuaded to be a Governor's Lady altho she loved and was beloved by Dear Eighteen Y____g M____r Q____n-ce [Quince?] The day is fixed the nuptial feast provided when Lo a Discovery is made which surpasses in Villainy the Description of the most envenomed Satyrist. It is much above my power I'll humbly therefore attempt the Tale in Common Homespun phrase The catastrophe was truly Poetic Justice. When the Antedeluvian had agreed, the Old Fellow old in every human characteristic but sense and virtue sends for his Secretary a man of motly cast They form a conveyance of his whole Estate to his son (not even leaving a reversion of his Potatoe Lands near Carrick Fergus) [the Dobbs family seat in Ireland] which he enters into and Dispatches a Messenger with it to one of the Sup[r] Court Judges Its proved *secundem Legem* How was this scheme marred. Some secret power blows the matter Some friendly Sylph protects the Lady The Deed's discovered Her friends warm with indignation send for the youth, the Pensive & Dejected Lover—relate the Injury, propose immediately to consummate the marriage Hymen attends Venus & Apollo add Ringlets and ten thousand Charms to adorn the Lovely pair. Assist me some poet or assist me Dr. Betty with your Fancy They are married. The Leecher waits, 10,11,12 past, the Day wakes, Accursed jealousy takes place, his old Teeth of Enormous length that for many years despised to be clothed with Gums shake in his jaws with Rage He orders his horse to the chariot and feebly in his course would Emulate a Youthful passion he enters her parents house demands the Lady, is conducted into the apartment of Youth Love and Virtue Here I stop. for no pen can describe the Rage and Ridicule."

It is not known who "young Mr. Quince" was, nor if the young pair were indeed engaged to be married. Records indicate that Justina was a dutiful and loving wife to the aged governor. Upon his death at their home, Russellborough, near Brunswick, she wrote to her stepson in Ireland: "I have lost one of the best and tenderest of husbands."

Justina later married Abner Nash. They lived, it is thought, on King Street (now Main Street) in Halifax, where she bore him three children: Abner, who died young; Margaret, who married Thomas Haslin; and Justina, who died unmarried. Mrs. Nash died at the untimely age of twenty-six and was buried in Halifax, where her tombstone may still be read: "Mrs. Justina Nash / O. B. 6th December An Dom 1771 / in the 25th year of her age."

SEE: W. C. Allen, *History of Halifax County* (1918); Lawrence Lee, *The Lower Cape Fear in Colonial Times* (1965); Letter from Assistant Site Manager, Halifax State Historic Site, 1976; William L. Saunders, ed., *Colonial Records of North Carolina*, vol. 9 (1890); *South Carolina Historical and Genealogical Magazine*, vol. 36 (January 1936); Alfred Moore Waddell, *A Colonial Officer and His Times* (1889).

JAQUELIN DRANE NASH

**Davis, Kathryn Rachel Sarah Rebecca Speight Darden** *(24 Sept. 1905–10 Oct. 1979)*, physician and legislator, who was usually known as Rachel Darden Davis, was born at Seven Springs, Wayne County, the daughter of Herbert W. and Harriette Isler Davis. One of six children, she was reared on her father's farm and attended James Sprunt Institute in Kenansville and Mount Olive High School. She was awarded the B.S. degree at Salem College in 1926 and attended The University of North Carolina in 1927–28. After receiving the M.S. degree at Columbia University in 1928, she entered the Woman's Medical College of Pennsylvania and was awarded the M.D. degree in 1932. Following her internship and residency in Philadelphia, she served on the staff of Parrott Memorial Hospital in Kinston during 1934–57 and at the Lenoir Memorial Hospital, also in Kinston, from 1946 until shortly before her death. She also engaged in private practice specializing in obstetrics and gynecology, operated a farm, and engaged in extensive public service.

The first woman in eastern North Carolina to be elected to the state legislature, Dr. Davis represented Lenoir County in the General Assembly for three terms (1959–63). In the Assembly she spearheaded a crusade to ease adoption requirements for single persons and, single herself, adopted a daughter, Harriette Elizabeth Davis (Mrs. Hugh L. Wilde). She also supported the promotion of fertility, population, food, and cancer research in the universities of the state. She helped found Lenoir Community College and was especially active in the American Cancer Society, serving as a delegate to the International Cancer Congress in Moscow in 1972. She served on numerous state and local boards and commissions including the Water and Air Resources Board, the Commission of Correction and Detention, the Board of Dobbs Farms (chairman), Lenoir County Welfare Board, Kinston Recreation Board, and others. She was a member of and active in local, state, and national medical societies, the Business and Professional Women's Club, and a number of hereditary patriotic societies such as the United Daughters of the Confederacy, Daughters of American Colonists, Magna Charta

Dames, and Daughters of the American Revolution. Her artistic interests were expressed through service on the North Carolina Arts Council and in support of ballet in the state.

Dr. Davis, originally a member of the Baptist church in which she was a deacon and a Sunday school teacher, later became an Episcopalian. She was a Democrat and the friend of many state and national political leaders; friends reported that she was the only Democrat invited to the inauguration of Governor James E. Holshouser, Jr., a Republican.

SEE: Stephen E. Massengill, *Biographical Directory of the General Assembly of North Carolina, 1963–1978* (1979); *North Carolina Manual* (1961); Raleigh *News and Observer*, 14 Apr. 1976, 11 Oct. 1979; *Who's Who in the South and Southwest* (1969).

WILLIAM S. POWELL

**Davis, Oroondates** *(ca. 1750–81)*, lawyer, legislator, and member of the Board of War of North Carolina during the American Revolution, was born in what is now Halifax County, the sixth and youngest son of Thomas and Hastwel Davis. He was named after a fictitious Persian soldier of the fifth century B.C. who figures in the popular French romance by La Calprenède, *Cassandra* (Cotterell's translation of which ran through ten English editions between 1652 and 1737). Late in 1743 Thomas Davis moved from Virginia to North Carolina with other members of his family and began acquiring land on Looking Glass Swamp in Halifax County. By the time of his death in 1764 he owned a town lot in Halifax and approximately 9,000 acres in Halifax, Bute, and Edgecombe counties.

Young Davis was put to reading law, possibly in the office of Joseph Montfort, clerk of the Halifax County court and vice-auditor and custodian of the records of the Granville Proprietary land office. He was licensed to practice as an attorney-at-law in North Carolina by Governor Josiah Martin, and in April and May 1775 he presented his credentials preparatory to conducting business in the courts of Edgecombe and Bute counties. Upon the death of Montfort on 2 Apr. 1776, Davis briefly succeeded him in the clerkship of the Halifax County court until Benjamin McCulloch was appointed as the regular clerk at the November 1776 term.

Upon the outbreak of the American Revolution, Davis joined other members of the Halifax County squirearchy in supporting the American cause. Two of his neighbors, Willie Jones and Benjamin McCulloch, were members of the Halifax County Committee of Safety, and late in 1774 Davis was chosen clerk of the committee. Consequently, when the records of the Granville Proprietary land office (which had been surrendered earlier by Montfort to an agent of Governor Martin) were seized by the committee, the records were entrusted to Davis for safekeeping.

In 1778 Davis was elected one of the representatives of Halifax County in the General Assembly; in 1779, 1780, and 1781 he served in that body as senator from Halifax County. He faithfully attended sessions of the Assembly and was active in its service, especially as it related to the revenues of the state. His bill to extend the North Carolina–Virginia boundary was passed into law, and he was named one of the commissioners to extend the line early in 1780. While he served in the General Assembly a land office was open in Halifax County for the first time in fifteen years. Taking advantage of the new office, he immediately made entries on approximately 16,000 acres of vacant land. Presumably as custodian of the records of the Granville Proprietary, he knew where many of the vacant lands in the county lay. For reasons no longer clear, only a handful of the entries made by Davis in February 1779 ripened into grants.

At the opening of the autumn session of the 1780 General Assembly, Governor Abner Nash complained to the legislature that the executive office was crippled by a lack of councillors of state willing to perform their duties. The governor recommended that the Assembly fill vacancies in the council and appoint a body of military advisers to aid the executive. Adopting his recommendation, the legislature created a Board of War with extensive powers to raise, organize, equip, and provision the militia force of the state. This board virtually functioned as a "department of the army." Its two most senior members (Archibald Maclaine and Thomas Polk) declined to act, leaving execution of the board's duties to Alexander Martin, John Penn, and Oroondates Davis. Immediately upon the rising of the Assembly on 13 Sept. 1780, the Board of War sat. After its initial session at Hillsborough, Martin and Davis departed briefly for their homes to attend to private business that had been neglected during the General Assembly's spring and summer sessions. In their absence sole exercise of the board's powers was left in the hands of Penn until Martin assumed his duties as senior member on 9 October. Davis rejoined the board on 15 October.

Much disliked by some leaders of the state, the Board of War has frequently been described as extra-constitutional, interfering, confusing, and a nuisance. A third of a century later William R. Davie retrospectively excoriated the board and characterized Oroondates Davis as a fribble "who knew nothing but the game of Whist." One admires the neatness with which General Davie skewered a dead enemy while wondering about the justness of it. Davis frankly described himself as "having no pretensions to military knowledge," and his responsibilities on the board appear chiefly to have been those of equipping and provisioning the state's army of militia rather than planning defense strategy, ordering troop movements, and so forth. Nevertheless, his legislative experience with the revenues of the state and his earlier work with the committee to furnish the state with arms and ammunition must have stood him in good stead. Davis's candid assessment that the board would not be able to furnish suitable mounts for Davie's cherished project of a personal cavalry unit apparently earned him the general's lasting wrath.

Davis incurred Governor Nash's anger by importuning him to use the weight of his executive office to remove the state supply of salt (essential for the preservation of pork and beef rations for the army) from the control of the state's commissioners of trade and to place it at the disposal of the Board of War. "Shall the Independence of this State be endanger'd by the want of a few Thousand Bushells of Salt?" he inquired of Nash at one critical juncture, adding "If your Ideas correspond with mine Your Excellency will give the necessary directions [to release the salt]." Nash, stung by the tenor of the question and the rhetorical rider to it, retaliated by accusing Davis of using "arts or undue methods to enhance the respect due to the Board or occasion a Diminuition of that due to our first Magistrate." Within a few weeks the cause for the quarrel was removed; in January 1781 the General Assembly abolished the Board of War and replaced it with a Council Extraordinary to which Davis was not appointed.

That the Board of War operated efficiently in carrying

out many of its functions will be admitted by the objective observer. Indeed, the American success at the Battle of Kings Mountain was owing in part to its effectiveness. In acknowledging the accomplishments of the board, it is necessary to give Oroondates Davis the credit that is due him.

Davis, a member of the Anglican church, died in Halifax. He was survived by his wife Mary and their two minor daughters, Mary and Elizabeth Ann.

SEE: Board of War Proceedings and Correspondence, 1780–81; Bute County Court Minutes, 1775; Edgecombe County Court Minutes for 1774 and 1775; Granville County Deed Books A–G; Halifax County Deed Books 5–14, Will Books 1 and 3, and Entry Book, 1778–95; William L. Saunders and Walter Clark, eds., *Colonial and State Records of North Carolina* (1886–1914).

GEORGE STEVENSON

**Davis, Richmond Pearson** *(23 June 1866–17 Sept. 1937)*, career military officer and major general of artillery, was born in Statesville, the son of Hayne and Mary Williams Davis. He was graduated from the United States Military Academy in 1887, ranking sixth in his class. From 1891 to 1896 Davis taught chemistry, mineralogy, and geology at West Point. Upon promotion to captain on 2 Feb. 1901, he was transferred to the School of Submarine Defense at Fort Totten, N.Y., where he served as an instructor for two years. In 1907 Davis directed the Coastal Artillery School at Fort Monroe, Va. From 1 Sept. to 27 Dec. 1911 he was enrolled as a student officer at the Army War College in Washington, D.C.

After serving an appointment to the General Staff in Washington, Davis was promoted to the rank of brigadier general on 5 Aug. 1917. At Camp Pike, Ark., he was assigned to the 162nd Field Artillery Brigade, which he commanded in France during World War I. The 162nd Brigade participated in the Battle of Saint Mihiel and Camp de Songe. From 1918 to 1919, Davis commanded all artillery units in the U.S. Army 9th Corps. In the latter year he was ordered to Manila Bay in the Philippines where he designed and commanded coastal defenses for U.S. military bases. After a career of forty years, Davis retired from the army on 22 Dec. 1929. He died seven years later while a patient at Walter Reed Army Hospital and was buried in Arlington National Cemetery. He was survived by his wife, Bertha Marie Bouvier Davis, whom he married in 1887.

Davis contributed much to the technical development of coastal defenses using fixed artillery, and he originated a system of mines for use against submarines in harbor defenses. Camp Davis, located at Holly Ridge in south Onslow County, was named for him. The base opened in April 1941 and closed four years later, having served as a major center for antiaircraft training.

SEE: Charles Braden, *Biographical Record of the United States Military Academy*, vols. 5 and 6a (1910); William S. Powell, *The North Carolina Gazetteer* (1968); Raleigh *News and Observer*, 17 Sept. 1937; *Who Was Who in America*, vol. 1 (1943).

TIMOTHY L. HOWERTON

**Davis, Thomas** *(8 Mar. 1761–after 1790)*, printer and journalist, was one of three sons of James Davis, the colony's first printer and journalist at New Bern. Thomas was the only son to enter the printing trade. In a letter of 2 Nov. 1778 to Governor Richard Caswell, James Davis said Thomas was his "chief hand in the Office, and if he goes, I must be forced to drop the Newspaper." This suggestion of Thomas's importance to his father's *North Carolina Gazette* was affirmed by the suspension of its publication in late November 1778 about the time young Davis was drafted into the army. He returned to the New Bern area in late 1781 or early 1782 and began to make preparations to succeed his father as state printer. In a 15 Feb. 1782 letter to Governor Thomas Burke, Thomas Davis reminded Burke of a promise to arrange for a wagon to move his press to Halifax and expressed a desire to set up his equipment before the General Assembly met. On 18 May 1782 the Assembly approved his appointment as public printer.

Davis's term as public printer was beset with difficulty, largely caused by shortages of essential supplies. In September 1783 a citizen wrote to Governor Alexander Martin to complain about the lack of printed laws in the state. The letter said other printers, including one from Philadelphia, had applied for the job, and suggested that action be taken if the current state printer, Davis, did not print the laws correctly and punctually. In 1784, however, he was reappointed, relieved of some of his responsibilities for delivering the printed laws, and granted an annual salary of £500. On 20 Nov. 1784 a senate committee refused his request to be paid for expenses and labor instead of the salary. It also recommended that Charles Cist of Philadelphia be induced to come to North Carolina to take Davis's place, maintaining the laws could be printed faster and cheaper under someone other than Davis. In December 1785 the General Assembly selected the firm of Arnett and Hodge to replace Davis. When James Davis died in 1785, he left Thomas his printing office at the corner of Broad and Front streets in New Bern and some book binding material.

While engaged in state printing, Davis resumed the newspaper career that had been interrupted by the war. A letter from James Iredell to his wife in March 1784 suggested that a newspaper was being published in Halifax. Since Davis was the public printer, he was the most likely publisher. The name of the newspaper is not known, and no copies have been located. The 9 Dec. 1784 issue of *The North Carolina Gazette* at New Bern says it was printed for Thomas Davis, suggesting he may have had some affiliation with the newspaper established by his father and continued by Robert Keith. There is also some evidence that Davis published another *North Carolina Gazette* in Hillsborough in 1785 and 1786. A 27 July 1785 letter from Major Robert Fenner to Governor Caswell implied the existence of a newspaper at Hillsborough. A 16 Feb. 1786 issue of a *North Carolina Gazette* does not bear a city imprint, but the fact that most advertisements were for Hillsborough establishments has led historians to conclude that it was published in Hillsborough. A note at the bottom of the first page says it was printed by Robert Ferguson for Thomas Davis, which suggests that Davis was an absentee owner. This is the last known reference to Thomas Davis.

SEE: C. S. Brigham, *History and Bibliography of American Newspapers, 1690–1820*, vol. 2 (1947); Walter Clark, ed., *State Records of North Carolina*, vols. 15–17, 19–20, 24–25 (1898–1906); D. C. McMurtrie, *A History of Printing in the United States* (1936); Elizabeth Moore, *Records of Craven County, N.C.* (1960); M. L. Thornton, "Public Printing in North Carolina, 1749–1815," *North Carolina Historical Review* 21 (1944).

THOMAS A. BOWERS

**Davis, Thomas Frederick** *(8 Feb. 1804–2 Dec. 1871),* lawyer, Episcopal priest, and later bishop of South Carolina, was born in New Hanover County near Wilmington, the son of Thomas F. and Sarah Isabella Eagles Davis. His father was clerk of court for New Hanover County; his young brother, George, served as senator in the Confederate Congress and was appointed attorney general of the Confederate States. At the age of ten, Davis was sent to a boarding school in Chapel Hill in preparation for college. He was graduated from The University of North Carolina in 1822 and returned to Wilmington to study law.

After admittance to the bar, Davis practiced successfully for six years. In 1828, shortly after the death of his first wife, he was confirmed in the Episcopal church and proceeded to leave the legal profession for the ministry. He was ordained a deacon by Bishop Levi S. Ives on 27 Nov. 1831 and a priest on 16 Dec. 1832. He first journeyed as a missionary to the towns of Wadesboro and Pittsboro, where he held services in each on alternate Sundays. Although these congregations were a hundred miles apart, Davis succeeded in establishing Calvary Church in Wadesboro and building and consecrating St. Bartholemew's Church in Pittsboro, both in 1833. Afterward, he was called back to Wilmington to become rector of St. James Church; there he continued his missionary work in the city. At the end of three years, Davis became ill and required a year of rest. Upon regaining his health, he moved to Salisbury where he served as rector of St. Luke's Church for ten years. In addition to his growing parish, Davis worked with missionary stations and distant congregations in Lexington and Mocksville and was long active in church affairs in the state. In 1846 he accepted a call to Grace Church in Camden, S.C., thus entering the diocese of that state. He was elected bishop of South Carolina in May 1853 at the church convention held in Charleston. It was rumored that he was also being considered to fill the vacancy of bishop of North Carolina, but that convention met later in the year.

On 17 Oct. 1853 both Davis and the bishop-elect of North Carolina, Thomas Atkinson, were consecrated at St. John's Chapel in New York City with more than thirty bishops officiating. Davis took his seat as the presiding officer of the diocesan convention in February 1854. He continued his active ministry, although a nervous disorder had brought on total blindness by 1862. He worked to establish a theological seminary, was involved with the religious divisions during the Civil War, and gave early support to the founding of the University of the South, located in Sewanee, Tenn.

Davis was married twice: in 1828 to Elizabeth Fleming, by whom he had a son, Thomas Frederick Davis, Jr.; and to Ann Ivie Moore, also of Wilmington. Children of the second marriage were Ann E., Sallie, James M., John, Bruce, and Junius.

Davis remained bishop of South Carolina until his death. He was buried at Grace Church in Camden, S.C.

SEE: Thomas Frederick Davis, *A Genealogical Record of the Davis, Swann, and Cabell Families of North Carolina and Virginia* (1934); Daniel L. Grant, *Alumni History of the University of North Carolina* (1924); John Johnson, *A Sermon Commemorative of the Rt. Rev. Thomas Frederick Davis* (1872); Leonidas L. Polk, *Handbook of North Carolina* (1879); William S. Powell, "North Carolina Church History," *North Carolina Churchman* 44 (1955); Stephen B. Weeks, Scrapbook, vol. 3 (North Carolina Collection, Library, University of North Carolina); John H. Wheeler, *Reminiscences and Memoirs of North Carolina and Eminent North Carolinians* (1884).

ANNA JEANETTE BASS

**Davis, William Henry** *(22 July 1880–26 May 1960),* editor and publisher of a partisan newspaper, *The Hornet*, was born at Fork, Davie County, the son of Daniel V. Davis and Sarah Hodges. He was married to Maude Williams. After graduating from Hodges Business College, a private academy near Fork, he taught school and toured as a lecturer on contemporary topics.

In 1902, at his home in Fork, Davis began publishing *The Hornet*, according to its editor the "Hottest Democratic Paper in the United States." Considering "fire-eating politics at the national level," he competed with the Republican *Yellow Jacket*, published at Moravian Falls, N.C. To launch the paper, Davis sent out sample copies and ran an advertisement in *The Commoner*, published by William Jennings Bryan. *The Hornet* quickly attracted national attention, received help from the national headquarters of the Democratic party, and by 1914 attained a circulation of some 25,000, much of which was in California, New York, West Virginia, and Kentucky. The large circulation required Davis to build an office near his home and to stop printing the paper on his own cylinder press. In 1913, following the election of Woodrow Wilson, the post office at Fork was reestablished to facilitate the mailing of the paper; Davis was postmaster.

Initially, *The Hornet* appeared only before the November elections. From 1912 until World War II, however, it was published monthly except from 1930 to 1932. After Pearl Harbor and the United States entry into the war, the paper was suspended in an effort to discourage partisanship. When *The Hornet* was discontinued as a Democratic party newspaper, Davis continued to publish it as an organ for the Free-Thinkers of America until about 1955. Its circulation was about 10,000.

Davis was buried in the Fork Baptist Church cemetery.

SEE: *Davie County Enterprise-Record*, 2 June 1960; Martin Collection, Davie County Library, Mocksville; J. W. Wall, *History of Davie County* (1960).

JAMES W. WALL

**Davison, Wilburt Cornell** *(28 Apr. 1892–26 June 1972),* physician, teacher, and medical educator, was born in Grand Rapids, Mich., but grew up on Long Island, N.Y., the son of William L. Davison, D.D., a Methodist minister, and Mattie E. Cornell Davison. He was graduated with honors from Princeton University and awarded a Rhodes Scholarship, with which he pursued a medical education in Oxford University, England, and Johns Hopkins University, Baltimore. He became a protégé of Sir William Osler, Regius Professor of Medicine at Oxford, formerly of Johns Hopkins. Davison was one of the last students of this great medical humanist. During his Oxford years he became an "adopted" son to Sir William and Lady Grace and frequented their home at 19 Norham Gardens. It was here that he courted his wife and shared the grief of the

Oslers when Revere, their only child, at age twenty-one was mortally wounded in the Ypres salient of Flanders. This intimate personal bond between a sensitive, brilliant young man and his teacher strongly influenced Davison's later career as dean of the first four-year medical school in North Carolina.

Davison began his studies at Oxford in the late summer of 1913 and received a B.A. degree in 1915. He then entered Magdalen College as senior demy and was awarded a B.Sc. in medicine in 1916. Returning to Baltimore for clinical clerkship at Johns Hopkins, he was graduated with the M.D. degree in 1917. Further graduate work at Oxford earned him an M.A. degree in pediatrics and preventive medicine in 1919. Interspersed with his formal medical studies was voluntary duty with the American Red Cross on a typhus commission in France and Serbia (1914–15) and military duty as lieutenant to captain, medical corps, U.S. Army, Allied Expeditionary Force (1917–19).

Back at Johns Hopkins after the war, Davison progressed rapidly in the years 1919–27: from resident to instructor in pediatrics (1919–21); associate to acting pediatrician-in-charge, Johns Hopkins Hospital; and assistant dean, Johns Hopkins School of Medicine. During the same period he was editor of *The Bulletin of the Johns Hopkins Hospital*. From 1927 to 1961 he was professor of pediatrics, dean of the medical school, and, until 1954, chairman of the pediatrics department at Duke University. He was also James B. Duke professor of pediatrics (1953–61); trustee and consultant, Duke Endowment (1961–72); consultant, Womack Army Hospital, Fort Bragg (1942–62); member, advisory council, North Carolina Board of Mental Health (1962–65); vice-president, board of directors, Doris Duke Foundation (1938–72); and member, board of visitors, Davidson College (1961–72). He was awarded the D.Sc. by Wake Forest College (1932) and the LL.D. by The University of North Carolina (1944) and Duke University (1961).

Davison's professional associations were numerous. He was a past member and vice-chairman (1942–43) of the Division of Medical Sciences, National Research Council, as well as a former member of the council's Committee on Atomic Casualties; colonel, Medical Corps, AUS, retired; consultant, office of the Surgeon General, U.S. Army; and member of the advisory group, Armed Forces Medical Library, and of the Committee on Veterans Medical Problems. He was also a member of the National Health Council; executive committee, Association of American Medical Colleges; Executive Reserve, office of the assistant secretary of defense (health and medicine); medical advisory panel, Oak Ridge Institute of Nuclear Studies; council of chief medical consultants, Veterans Administration Hospitals; National Advisory Committee on Chronic Diseases and Health of the Aged; Civilian Health and Advisory Council; dean's committee, Durham Veterans Administration Hospital; medical advisory panel, North Carolina Hospital Board of Control; North Carolina Nuclear Energy Advisory Committee; North Carolina governor's working committee, Research Triangle Foundation; Advisory Committee on Health Service, American Red Cross; and editorial board, *Quarterly Review of Pediatrics*. He was a trustee of the Educational Council for Foreign Medical Graduates and a director of the Playtex Park Research Institute.

The Duke Medical Center is an enduring tribute to Davison. When he went to Durham in early 1927, there was to be an interval of nearly three years until the building program was completed for the medical school and hospital. During this period he assembled a faculty, acquired the nucleus of a medical library, and conferred with architects on structural arrangements congenial to the dual purpose of teaching students and caring for patients. With the help of Dr. Watson W. Rankin, director of the Hospital and Orphan sections of the Duke Endowment, he made a detailed study of medical practice in the state's urban and rural communities, with particular attention to adverse conditions in a physician's practice. Notably, the economic depression of the period had bankrupted the hospitals serving an impoverished populace; this impelled Davison to pioneer a solution in the form of medical care insurance. Impressed with the administrative and clerical burdens of hospital professional staffs, he later established in the Duke Medical Center training programs for hospital administrators and medical records librarians, both of which are now indispensable disciplines.

Davison was the author of over two hundred scientific and professional publications and coauthor with S. A. Waksman of a treatise on enzymes. He wrote a "shorthand" compendium on pediatric practice for medical students entitled *The Compleat Pediatrician*, published in 1934. It has gone through eight editions with translations in Italian, Japanese, and Spanish and has sold over 100,000 copies.

The philosophy of medical education espoused by Davison called for the cultivated, intellectually disciplined physician who was civic-minded and innovative. In the choice of faculty, including those requiring complex technical skills, he favored teachers with special interests; superiority was the common denominator. He was a man with deep compassion, a ready wit, and a robust sense of humor. A world traveler, he had friends in many countries; foreign colleagues and students were frequent guests in his clinics and in the Davison home.

On 2 June 1917 Davison married Atala Thayer Scudder of Glen Head, Long Island, culminating a courtship that flourished while his fiancée also was a medical student in pediatrics at Oxford. To them were born three children: William Townsend, Atala Jane Scudder Levinthal, and Alexander Thayer.

An international ecumenical symposium on "The Commonwealth of Children" was held at Duke University to honor Davison and his wife on his retirement on 5 Oct. 1961. From then until his final illness the Davisons made their mailing address their summer home in Roaring Gap, N.C. He continued his foundation work, writing, and travel until shortly before he died of leukemia in his eighty-first year. His ashes were placed behind a bronze tablet in the chapel of the medical school building that bears his name.

SEE: J. P. McGovern et al., *William Osler—The Continuing Education* (1969); *Medicine in North Carolina*, vols. 1, 2 (1972); W. R. Perkins, *The Duke Endowment* (1930).

WARNER WELLS

**Dawson (Dauson, Dosson, Dowson), Anthony** *(ca. 1643–October 1717)*, council member and general court justice, came to North Carolina in or before 1687. In a deposition made in 1695, Dawson indicated that he was born about 1643. He may have been the same Anthony Dawson who was living in Dorchester County, Md., in 1679. If so, he immigrated to Maryland in 1665 with his father, William Dawson, and married Rebecca Osborne, daughter of Henry Osborne of Calvert County, Md. However, there is no evidence in North Carolina records that Dawson had a wife or children.

Dawson settled in Perquimans Precinct, where he took up by patent the 100 acres to which he was entitled by transporting himself and one John Chapman into the colony. He acquired an additional 590 acres by purchase. Dawson, who gave his occupation as "carpenter," soon became a captain in the North Carolina militia. By January 1693/94, he was a member of the council. He probably was also a member of the Assembly, as he was elected to the council by that body. As council member he was ex officio justice of the general court, which was then composed of the council members. He held office through December 1696. He also was active in an unofficial capacity. His name frequently appears as witness to wills and other documents, as appraiser of estates, and as attorney in court actions. For several years the Perquimans Precinct court was held at his house.

In February 1697/98 an episode occurred that resulted in Dawson's banishment from North Carolina. Apparently acting in his capacity as captain of the militia, Dawson undertook to secure "as a wreck for the proprietors use" a ship of the royal navy, HMS *Swift Advice*, which had been cast ashore in Currituck Precinct. The ship had been abandoned by its commander and crew off the Virginia coast during a storm. Local inhabitants were pillaging the wreck when Dawson and others under his direction seized it for the proprietors and removed guns, sails, rigging, and other furnishings. Under pressure from the commander of the *Swift Advice*, who came from Virginia to salvage the wreck for the Crown, Dawson and his assistants were indicted and tried on charges of feloniously rifling, spoiling, and embezzling the king's ship of war. Dawson was found guilty and condemned to death by hanging, but his sentence was commuted to banishment, effective 26 May 1698.

After his exile, Dawson went to New Jersey and settled in Newton, Gloucester County, where he spent the remainder of his life. In his will he left his estate to a "cousin" (probably nephew), John Dawson, of Burlington County, N.J., whom he named sole heir and executor.

SEE: Jane Baldwin, comp. and ed., *The Maryland Calendar of Wills*, vol. 1 (1904); J. Bryan Grimes, ed., *Abstract of North Carolina Wills* (1910); J. R. B. Hathaway, ed., *North Carolina Historical and Genealogical Register*, 3 vols. (1900–1903); William Nelson, ed., *Calendar of New Jersey Wills*, vol. 1 (1901); Mattie Erma E. Parker, ed., *Colonial Records of North Carolina, Higher Court Records, 1670–1696* and *1697–1701*, vols. 2 (1968), 3 (1971); William S. Price, Jr., ed., *Colonial Records of North Carolina, Higher Court Records, 1702–1708*, vol. 4 (1974); William L. Saunders, ed., *The Colonial Records of North Carolina*, vol. 1 (1886); Gust Skordas, ed., *Early Settlers of Maryland* (1968); Ellen Goode Winslow, *History of Perquimans County* (1931). Unpublished sources in North Carolina State Archives, Raleigh: Albemarle Book of Warrants and Surveys, 1681–1706; Colonial Court Records (scattered documents re. HMS *Swift Advice*, boxes 188–89, 191–92); Perquimans County Deeds, Book A (microfilm); Perquimans Precinct Court Minutes, 1688–93, 1698–1706.

MATTIE ERMA E. PARKER

**Dawson, John** *(ca. 1690–1761 or 1762)*, member of the Assembly for Bertie and Northampton counties, justice of the court, and member of the governor's council, was born in Isle of Wight County, Va. His grandfather, William Dawson, had come to Virginia about 1621. His father, Henry Dawson, lived first in Warwick County, Va., and later in Isle of Wight. His mother was Martha (probably Shepard) of Warwick.

Dawson, the second son of his parents, came with his family to Bertie County about 1732. He first represented that county in the Assembly of 1735. After the formation of Northampton County, he continued as representative of the new county. He became justice of the peace in 1739 and later sheriff. He was a member of the commission to lay out the town of Windsor. During the Spanish alarm of 1748, he was made colonel of the Northampton Regiment. He became an associate justice of the North Carolina court in 1751. In the same year, Governor Johnston proposed his name to the Board of Trade as a member of his council; Dawson was sworn in on 28 May 1752. He remained a member of the council until his death, serving under both Governors Johnston and Dobbs.

Dawson married first Elizabeth Thomas Boddie, sister of Barnaby and Philip Thomas and widow of John Boddie (d. 1720). By Elizabeth, he had a son, Henry, and a daughter, Mary. By his second wife, Charity Alston, he had two daughters, Charity and Elizabeth, and a son, John. His second wife having been an heiress of considerable fortune, a marriage settlement was made to provide equitably for the children of the first wife and for the possible issue of the second. The family lived in Northampton County on the banks of Bridgers Creek. Dawson's will suggests a ménage of more than usual comfort, if not elegance, for that period in North Carolina. His two sons served in the North Carolina Assembly: Henry, from 1766 until his death in 1770; and John, from 1780 to 1782 and again from 1787 to 1798.

SEE: John B. Boddie, *Seventeenth Century Isle of Wight County, Virginia* (1938); Joseph A. Groves, *The Alstons and Allstons of North and South Carolina* (1901); Annie L. Jester and Martha W. Hiden, *Adventures of Purse and Person: Virginia, 1607–1625* (1964); Northampton County Will Book, vol. 1 (North Carolina State Archives, Raleigh); William L. Saunders, ed., *Colonial Records of North Carolina*, vols. 3–6 (1886–88).

JAQUELIN DRANE NASH

**Dawson, John** *(early 1730s–March 1770)*, planter and lawyer, was born in Williamsburg, Va. His father, the Reverend William Dawson, D.D., was minister of the church in Jamestown, so John was probably baptized there. William Dawson later became a member of the governor's council and king's commissary and second president of the College of William and Mary. John's mother was Mary Stith Dawson, granddaughter of William Randolph I of Turkey Island, the emigrant. His maternal uncle, the Reverend William Stith, was third president of the college. His father's younger brother, the Reverend Thomas Dawson, followed the Reverend John Blair as rector of Bruton Parish Church and was later fourth president of the college and commissary.

Young Dawson probably attended the College of William and Mary, although the records are incomplete and do not include his name. Left an orphan, he made his home with his uncle Thomas Dawson. His youthful extravagances and a tendency to run up bills he could not pay probably tried his uncle's well-known "Sweet, Engaging Temper." John was appointed "Surveyor of Albemarle in the room of Col. Joshua Fry, dec." by his uncle, President Stith, in 1754. He lived for a time with one J. Nicholas in Albemarle, and in 1755–56 spent several months in the office of Colonel Peter Jefferson to learn "practical Surveying."

A young heiress, Penelope Johnston, the orphaned daughter of Governor Gabriel Johnston of North Carolina, had been living in Williamsburg for a year or more with Governor Dinwiddie's family, sharing the instructions of the Dinwiddie tutor and absorbing the amenities of life in the governor's palace. Her elopement with young John Dawson in 1758 caused consternation, certainly on the North Carolina side of the border. But the match was a happy and auspicious one. The couple lived at Eden House, Bertie County, and had four children: Mary, who married Nathaniel Allen; Penelope, who married Tristram Lowther; William, who died unmarried; and Lucy, who evidently died young.

Dawson, who is referred to by contemporaries as "Col. Dawson," practiced law, but was chiefly busy with the management of his wife's large plantations on or near the Chowan River. Although described as a member of the Assembly and of Governor Dobbs's council, he has been confused with a contemporary of the same name. Visitors to Eden House spoke of being "highly pleased with the family," as well as "surprised at the good sense and accomplishments of Mrs. Dawson." Colonel Dawson's mansion was noted for its "splendid hospitality" and the "refined society generally assembled there."

Dawson died at Eden House and was probably buried there. His miniature by an unknown artist is owned by his descendants.

Dawson's widow, Penelope Johnston Dawson, was one of the signers of the "Edenton Tea Party" declaration, in which fifty-one ladies of the Albemarle region supported the decisions of the First Provincial Congress in North Carolina. His son, William Johnston Dawson, was a member of the Convention of 1788 and of Congress. He also was one of the commissioners to select a site for and report the plan of the city of Raleigh, giving his name to one of its streets.

SEE: Mary A. R. Goodwin, "The President's House and the Presidents of the College of William and Mary," 1975 (typescript, College of William and Mary, Williamsburg, Va.); Hayes Papers (Southern Historical Collection, University of North Carolina, Chapel Hill); Laura McMillan, *North Carolina Portrait Index* (1963); Griffith J. McRee, *Life and Correspondence of James Iredell*, 2 vols. (1857–58); *Sketches of Church History in North Carolina* (1892).

JAQUELIN DRANE NASH

**Dawson, John Gilmer** *(19 Apr. 1892–18 Jan. 1966)*, lawyer and legislator, was born in Institute Township, Lenoir County, the son of John H. and Ann Daly Dawson. His grandparents were Thomas J. Dawson and Huldah Daniels. The founder of the Dawson family was Christopher Dawson, who served as a captain in the militia and was the father of Colonel Levi Dawson of the Continental Army.

Dawson was educated in the Kinston public schools and, after working for several years as a clerk in Kinston, studied law at The University of North Carolina from 1906 to 1909. Soon after receiving his license to practice in 1908, he joined the firm of Loftin and Vassar in Kinston. L. R. Vassar later moved to Lumberton and served on the North Carolina Supreme Court. Dawson continued to practice law with the firm of Loftin and Dawson until Loftin's death. He was an active member of the Kinston bar until he died.

A lifelong member of the Democratic party, Dawson served in the General Assembly from 1919 through 1923—in his last year, as speaker of the house. He also served as chairman of the Democratic Executive Committee. In the legislature he became closely associated with Governor O. Max Gardner, and many expected that Dawson would attempt to succeed him. But Dawson did not offer himself as a gubernatorial candidate, and never again held public office, although he continued to be influential in the Democratic party.

As a lawyer, Dawson was highly respected; as a speaker, he was without peer. He was a lifelong member of the Lenoir County Bar Association, the North Carolina State Bar Association, the American Bar Association, and the American Judicature Society.

On 23 Nov. 1911 Dawson married Margaret Regina Weyher, daughter of Dr. Victor E. Weyher, a prominent Kinston physician who was born in Austria. Their children were Victor, born 27 Jan. 1916, and Ann (Mrs. Seavy Highsmith), born 1 Dec. 1919. Both Dawson and his wife were members of St. Mary's Episcopal Church, Kinston, and at times he served on the vestry. He also served on the board of trustees of The University of North Carolina (1911–53) and was a member and onetime president of the General Society of Cincinnati.

SEE: Daniel L. Grant, *Alumni History of the University of North Carolina* (1924); Talmage E. Johnson and Charles Holloman, *Kinston and Lenoir County* (1954).

ALBERT W. COWPER

**Dawson, William Johnston** *(1765–16 Jan. 1796)*, congressman, was born near Edenton in Chowan County, the son of Colonel John Dawson, member of the provincial council, and Penelope Johnston, daughter of Governor Gabriel Johnston. Dawson was reared at his maternal grandfather's estate, Eden House, in Bertie County before being sent to England for his education. Upon his return to North Carolina, he entered politics and was elected a delegate to the Hillsborough Convention of 1788. He was an ardent supporter of that unsuccessful bid to have North Carolina ratify the Constitution. In 1791 Dawson was elected to the House of Commons. During the same year, he was appointed to the committee of legislators entrusted with the selection of a permanent seat of government for the state and was influential in the final choice of Joel Lane's plantation as the future site of Raleigh.

In 1793 Dawson was appointed by the legislature to represent the Eighth Congressional District in the U.S. House of Representatives, where he served until 1795. While in Congress, he advocated going to war with Great Britain over the British destruction of American vessels; however, the United States avoided war at this time. At the end of his congressional term, Dawson settled at Eden House, by then his mother's estate, and died there while still a young man. He was buried on the plantation.

SEE: *Biog. Dir. Am. Cong.* (1950); Griffith J. McRee, ed., *Life and Correspondence of James Iredell*, 2 vols. (1857–58); John W. Moore, *History of North Carolina from the Earliest Discoveries to the Present Times* (1880).

JAMES ELLIOTT MOORE

**Day, John** *(1797–1860)*, political leader and jurist, was one of the American founders of the African republic of Liberia and for four years was chief justice of its supreme court. He was born in Halifax County, the son of free mulattos. His putative grandfather on his father's side was Ephraim Knight, a white planter of modest means and considerable education. In 1789 Knight petitioned the North Carolina General Assembly to emancipate his two young mulatto men called Alexander and Richard. The legislature granted the petition but ironically deleted the surname "Knight" and gave the young men the surname "Day." In his will, written 25 May 1789, Ephraim Knight had already provided for the emancipation of Alexander and Richard and their wives, Sabinah and Polly, "with their present and future increase."

Ephraim Knight died in Halifax County in 1800. Soon afterward, Richard Day migrated to a western county and Alexander Day moved to neighboring Warren County. Richard had been taught the trade of a carpenter and Alexander, the trade of a miller. Each of them had a son named John Day. Richard's son John became noted as a talented designer and craftsman of household furniture.

John Day, the son of Alexander, acquired a good education. He became active in the movement for the emancipation of slaves in the United States and for their repatriation to what is now Liberia. The African colony, which began under American auspices in 1820, became in 1847 the independent republic of Liberia with a constitution and governmental structure modeled after the United States. Day's political statesmanship and keen intelligence earned for him the highest respect, confidence, and trust not only of his compatriots in Liberia but also of influential American and British officials. He was a member of the convention in 1846 that declared independence, and he was a signer of the constitution. In 1856 he became the second chief justice and held that office until his death in the autumn of 1860.

SEE: *A Brief History of the Supreme Court of Liberia* (1956); Walter L. Clark, ed., *State Records of North Carolina*, vol. 25 (1906); Legislative Papers, North Carolina General Assembly (North Carolina State Archives, Raleigh); Public manuscript records for Halifax and Warren counties (North Carolina State Archives, Raleigh); Nathaniel R. Richardson, *Liberia's Past and Present* (1959); *Wilson Ledger*, 5 Feb. 1861.

CHARLES R. HOLLOMAN

**Day, Thomas** *(ca. 1801–ca. 1861)*, cabinetmaker, was the son of Morning S. Day (b. ca. 1766 in Virginia), but his father is unknown. Thomas Day married Aquilla Wilson (b. ca. 1806) of Halifax County, Va., in Halifax on 7 Jan. 1830. Their children were Mary Ann (b. ca. 1831), Devereaux (b. ca. 1833), Thomas, Jr. (b. ca. 1837), and possibly another daughter A. [Aquilla?] (b. ca. 1835). All children were presumably born in Milton, where Day lived from about 1823 until 1861. A free black, Day's place of birth is listed in census records as Virginia and, judging from his age as listed in those records, his date of birth was 1801. Much information concerning Day is based on oral history and tradition. According to various reports, he was born on a farm outside Milton, he was born in Virginia, he was Portuguese, he was born in the West Indies, or he was born in Guilford County. Because Milton is on the Virginia border and the census lists Day's and his mother's place of birth as Virginia, it is likely that he was born near Milton, in either Halifax County or Pittsylvania County, Va.

On 27 Nov. 1851 Day wrote his daughter: "I am perfectly satisfied as regards Milton—I came here to stay four years & am here 7 times four I love the place no better nor worse than [the] first day I came into it." It can be inferred from this that Day arrived in Milton about 1823. He was certainly there in 1827 when he appeared in the tax records as a property owner. In the same year he advertised in the 1 Mar. 1827 *Milton Gazette & Roanoke Advertiser*: "Thomas Day, Cabinet Maker, returns his thanks for the patronage he has received, and wishes to inform his friends and the public that he has on hand, and intends keeping, a handsome supply of mahogany, walnut, and stained furniture, the most fashionable and common bedsteads, &c. which he would be glad to sell very low. All orders in his line, in repairing, varnishing &c., will be thankfully received and punctually attended to."

When Day arrived in Milton he may have already trained as a cabinetmaker, though he would have been only twenty-two. Within four years he had funds sufficient to purchase property and go into business for himself. Among the stories involving his childhood and training as a cabinetmaker, one tradition maintains that he showed marked ability as a child, copying to scale pieces of furniture that he saw in homes he visited with his parents. It is possible that he spent his first few years in Milton in the shop of someone else. There were a number of other Milton cabinetmakers or carpenters with whom he could have been apprenticed, but by January 1827, when he placed the newspaper advertisement, Day already had a shop, customers, and available stock.

In 1830, when Day crossed the border from North Carolina into Virginia, married Aquilla Wilson, also a free black, and attempted to return with her to Milton, he was prohibited from doing so by North Carolina law, which in 1827 had halted the immigration of free blacks into the state. Day ultimately appealed to the General Assembly, and late in 1830 a special act was passed to allow his wife to enter the state. In a petition to the legislature on his behalf, some sixty-one white citizens of the area supported the special act for Day, noting that he was "a free man of colour, an inhabitant of this town, cabinet maker by trade, a first rate workman, a remarkably sober, steady and industrious man, a high-minded, good and valuable citizen, possessing a handsome property in this town." Attached to the petition was a letter from R. M. Saunders, a former speaker of the North Carolina House of Commons and member of Congress, who in 1828 had been elected attorney general of North Carolina. Saunders wrote "I have known Thomas Day . . . for several years and am free to say that I consider him a free man of color, of very fair character—an excellent mechanic, industrious, honest and sober in his habits—and in the event of any disturbance amongst the Blacks, I should rely with confidence upon a disclosure from him—as he is the owner of slaves as well as of real estate."

Day was indeed in the unusual position of the pre-Civil War free black who not only owned slaves, but who also trained white apprentices in his cabinetmaker's shop. He also sat on the main floor of the predominantly white Milton Presbyterian Church in a front bench, one of the pews that he had carved for the church, built about 1837. He and his wife were accepted into full membership in 1841. Over the years Day purchased as his residence and place of business—he added a brick addition to contain his workshops—one of the most important structures in Milton, the Union or Yellow Tavern. He became a major stockholder in the local branch of the North Carolina Bank and purchased additional land outside the town.

The cabinetmaker sent his children to Wilbraham Academy (now Wesleyan University) in Connecticut. At least one daughter studied music in Salem, where she boarded with a Moravian family. She is said to have studied later in England. Day himself was certainly well educated, writing literate letters to his children and clients and sometimes evoking philosophical arguments or quoting from classical writers.

Day suffered financial reverses in 1858, but was able to recover and remain in business with the assistance of his business associate Dabney Terry, a white housebuilder and contractor in Milton. Day disappeared from public records in 1861, though his shop was operated by his son, Thomas, Jr., for at least ten more years. Day is believed to have been buried on his farm outside Milton where a grave is marked by a cairn.

What is most unusual about Day, a free black in the pre-Civil War South, is not that he established himself as a cabinetmaker at a relatively early age, but that for almost forty years he maintained his business, producing furniture and architectural detail for a number of important clients. His work seems never to have been out of favor, nor to have been lost at any period. Over the years articles about Day or his work regularly appeared in newspapers of the Virginia and North Carolina Piedmont, especially in Caswell County where Milton is located. Here both his cabinetwork and architectural interiors have been pointed to with pride. Houses with mantels by Tom Day, as he is known locally, are well known, and Day interiors appear in many area houses built during the county's boom era between 1830 and 1860, when bright leaf tobacco culture brought great wealth to the county. Many of these houses also contain furniture produced by Day.

Among Day's clients were Attorney General Saunders (later minister to Spain) and Governor David Settle Reid (later a senator from Rockingham County). According to tradition, Day carved furniture for the North Carolina governor's mansion but it was rejected because of its cost. He did raffle furniture in Raleigh, possibly the pieces carved for the governor's mansion. During the 1840s he worked on the interiors of the two society halls at The University of North Carolina, entering into correspondence about the work with D. L. Swain, then university president. He carved furniture and interiors for the Milton Presbyterian Church and the Milton Baptist Church and for a large number of other important as well as quite ordinary clients. A surprising number of bills, letters, diary entries, and other documents concerning his production of furniture and architectural detail survive, many still with the objects to which they relate. Some of his architectural work—including the William Long house in 1856—was accomplished in partnership with Dabney Terry, the Milton builder who came to Day's financial rescue in 1858.

No signature has yet been discovered on any piece of furniture or on the architectural detail that Day produced. His earliest work seems to have been simple, academic, and pure. Some of his Gothic Revival output was more innovative and expressive than the earlier work, but it was with Greek Revival and Italianate architectural detail and Empire style furniture that he reached his stride. Such output is bold, sometimes expressing African themes or Afro-American impressions of classical themes, sometimes closely approximating the work of Belter and other well-known cabinetmakers of the mid-nineteenth century. He frequently used three-dimensional motifs, evidently in an awareness of the changing aspects that light and shadow allowed with such work.

Much of Day's work seems to have been produced for a given space within a dwelling or public building, though he also carried prefinished stock in his shop and had catalogues of his own designs from which clients could choose. At least two volumes of his designs survived until 1928, when they were destroyed in a house fire in Raleigh.

Examples of Day's work have recently been included in a number of exhibitions at well-known museums, as well as in several publications on black artisans. The only special collection of his work is in the North Carolina Museum of History in Raleigh, although the Greensboro Historical Museum also owns a number of Day pieces. The Yellow Tavern, the cabinetmaker's home in Milton, is on the National Register of Historic Places and is a National Registered Landmark to honor the cabinetmaker and his important work in pre-Civil War America.

SEE: Rodney Barfield, *Thomas Day, Cabinet Maker* (1975); David C. Driskell, *Two Centuries of Black American Art* (1976); Ruth Little-Stokes, *An Inventory of Historic Architecture, Caswell County, North Carolina* (1979); William S. Powell, *When the Past Refused to Die* (1977).

TONY P. WRENN

**Deane, Charles Bennett** *(1 Nov. 1898–25 Nov. 1969),* lawyer and congressman, was born in Anson County, the youngest son of John Leaird and Florence Boyette Deane. The elder Deane was employed as a tenant farmer in Ansonville Township until shortly after the turn of the century, when he accepted employment with Pee Dee Mills and moved his family to Mill Village No. 2, Rockingham. Upon completion of grammar school at Pee Dee Academy, young Deane joined his father as a mill hand. Convinced, however, that he should further his education, Deane attended Trinity Park Preparatory School in Durham from 1918 to 1920 and was graduated from the law school of Wake Forest College in 1923. He was awarded the honorary doctor of humanities degree by Wake Forest in 1961.

Deane spent three years as a practicing attorney in Rockingham before being elected register of deeds for Richmond County in 1926; he retained the latter post until 1934. Returning to his private law practice, he spent considerable time in Washington, D.C., in the succeeding years as the compiler of the United States Congressional Directory (1935–39) and as an attorney for the Wage and Hour Division of the Department of Labor (1938–39). In 1940 he purchased an insurance business in Rockingham and for six years was engaged in administrative law and general insurance.

Though he had waged unsuccessful campaigns in 1938 and 1940 to represent North Carolina's Eighth Congressional District, Deane was victorious in his third bid to capture this seat in 1946. He then served five successive terms in the House of Representatives before he was defeated for reelection in 1956. Retirement from national politics found him spending the last thirteen years of his life in Rockingham, devoting his time and energies to the practice of law and to a multitude of civic and religious pursuits.

It was Deane's service on the House Appropriations Committee for National Defense that made him acutely aware of America's role in the ideological battle with world communism. He urged the ethical absolutes of moral rearmament—a movement with which he was closely allied—as the strategy for waging and winning this ideological warfare. It was his application of these same moral absolutes in personal decisions that dictated his refusal to sign the Declaration of Constitutional Principles (the so-called "Southern Manifesto") of 11 Mar. 1956—a document pledging its signers to the use of "every lawful means" to resist what they considered the usurpation of power by the federal judiciary in public school desegregation. Deane's subsequent defeat for reelection, in what was generally considered a "safe" district, is attributable to this refusal. In a later comment to his pastor, he said: "I do not have to remain in Washington but I do have to live with myself. I shall not sign my name to any document which will make any man anywhere a second-class citizen."

On 15 Oct. 1927 Deane married Agnes Walker Cree. To their union were born three children: Betty Cree (Mrs. Richard B. Sherman), Agnes Carol (Mrs. T. J. F. Becker), and Charles Bennett, Jr.

Deane was a Democrat and a Mason. He was also a prominent churchman within the Baptist denomination, serving in important positions of leadership locally, in the Baptist State Convention of North Carolina, and in the Southern Baptist Convention.

SEE: Baptist State Convention of North Carolina, *Annual* (1969); Charles Bennett Deane Papers (Ethel Crittenden Collection, Wake Forest University, Winston-Salem); First Baptist Church of Rockingham, "Charles Bennett Deane—1898–1969"; William S. Powell, ed., *North Carolina Lives* (1962); Raleigh *News and Observer*, 25 June 1950.

R. HARGUS TAYLOR

**Deberry, Edmund** *(14 Aug. 1781 [1787?]–12 Dec. 1859)*, planter, businessman, and congressman, was born near Mt. Gilead, Montgomery County. The birthdate is disputed although his tombstone indicates 1781. He was descended from French Huguenots (De Berry) who first settled in Bertie County. His father, Henry (1758–1818), and mother, Sarah ("Sally") Edmund Deberry, moved to Montgomery County from Bertie before the American Revolution and operated a gristmill and forge on Clark's Creek near Mt. Gilead. The father served in the Revolutionary War, was once sheriff, and for several terms represented Montgomery in the General Assembly. Edmund had two brothers, John and Benjamin.

Deberry received his education at home and at an early age became a successful farmer, businessman, and real estate owner. He was active in the Masonic Order and Sons of Temperance. Elected to the state senate in 1806, he served thirteen terms until 1828. While in the Assembly he was active in the movement for internal improvements. A supporter of John Quincy Adams, he was an elector on the National Republican presidential ticket of 1828.

Congressman John Culpepper declined to run for reelection from the Fayetteville district in 1829, announcing his support of Deberry for the seat he would vacate. John Cameron, editor of the pro-Jackson *North Carolina Journal*, declared in opposition to Deberry. In the heated campaign, Cameron accused his opponent of making large sums of money constructing public buildings while a member of the state senate. The contest was close, Deberry winning by barely two hundred votes. In the next three elections Deberry was opposed by Democrat Lauchlin Bethune. Bethune ousted Deberry by thirty-seven ballots in 1831, Deberry won by exactly the same margin two years later, and Bethune was defeated finally in 1835. Deberry continued to represent the Fayetteville district until March 1845, when he was not a candidate.

After he left Congress Deberry organized the Swift Island Manufacturing Company. He proposed to produce silk, hemp, wool, and iron. Although other business concerns kept him busy, he did not lose interest in politics. In 1849 his partisans persuaded him to return to Congress for one last term. During his political career Deberry was a staunch National Republican or Whig and believed in active government. In Congress he served on committees to monitor government expenditures and on the Agriculture Committee, of which he was chairman for several sessions.

In 1812 Deberry married Temperance ("Tempie") Lightfoot (1774–1871) of Virginia. They had eight children: Henry Winslow, Ann ("Nancy"), Lemuel, Gaston, Edmund, Jr., Mary, Sallie, and Betsy. The congressman and his wife were buried in the family graveyard on their old plantation in Pee Dee Township. The home, near Wadesville, is identified by an historical highway marker.

SEE: *Biog. Dir. Am. Cong.* (1971); *Charlotte Observer*, 10 Nov. 1950; Edmund Deberry Papers (Southern Historical Collection, University of North Carolina, Chapel Hill); H. D. Pegg, "The Whig Party in North Carolina, 1834–1861" (Ph.D. diss., University of North Carolina, 1932); *Rockingham Post-Dispatch*, 24 Oct. 1951.

DANIEL M. MCFARLAND

**Debnam, Waldman Eras** *(31 Dec. 1897–15 Feb. 1968)*, radio commentator, author, and Raleigh city councilman, was born in Snow Hill, son of Joseph Eppe and Birdice Speight Debnam. For some time his father was a public school teacher and superintendent of schools in the Snow Hill area where in 1902 he started a weekly newspaper, *The Standard Laconic*. After her husband's death, Birdice Speight Debnam took over *The Laconic* at the age of sixty-five and continued to publish it until she was eighty-two.

In 1915 Debnam entered Mars Hill preparatory school and in 1917 attended The University of North Carolina. At the university he was an active member of the Philanthropic Literary Society and the ROTC program. He returned to Snow Hill in 1918 and worked on *The Standard Laconic* until about 1922, afterward becoming a reporter for *The Danville Register*, *The Washington* (D.C.) *Herald*, and *The Virginian-Pilot-Ledger Dispatch* in Norfolk. While with *The Virginian-Pilot*, he had a radio program in Norfolk and Richmond with a series called "The Tales of Ole Virginia."

After leaving *The Virginian-Pilot*, Debnam started his own paper, *The Norfolk News Index*, which he operated for two years. Later he was employed by radio station WRVA in Richmond and in 1941 joined radio station WPTF in Raleigh. During World War II he served as WPTF's Pacific correspondent. Before leaving the station, he wrote *Weep No More, My Lady*, an answer to Mrs. Eleanor Roosevelt's criticisms of the South in the early 1950s. The book sold over 500,000 copies.

While living in Raleigh, Debnam was elected to the city council in 1953 and reelected in 1954. He resigned his seat in 1955 as increased sales of his latest booklet, *Then My Old Kentucky Home, Good Night!*, took more of his time. In 1956 he lost a close race with Harold Cooley for Fourth District congressman in the Democratic primary. In the same year Debnam entered television, joining the Greenville station WNCT-TV where he did a popular morning show; in 1963 he moved to WITN-TV in Washington, N.C. There he became vice-president in charge of news and public affairs, continuing in the post until his death at the age of seventy.

In 1924 Debnam married the former Stella Glass and they were the parents of William S. and Betty Glass Debnam. William S. Debnam is an orthodontist in Portsmouth, Va. Betty Debnam, now of Raleigh, is the editor of *The Minipage*, a children's newspaper used by over three hundred larger papers throughout the country. Debnam was buried at Greenwood Cemetery, Greenville.

SEE: Mrs. W. E. Debnam, interview, 18 Sept. 1977, Raleigh; Raleigh *News and Observer*, 21 July 1955, 16 Feb. 1968; University of North Carolina student annual, *Yackety Yack*, 1917.

JAMES F. HARPER

**DeBow, John** *(ca. 1745–8 Sept. 1783)*, Presbyterian minister and chaplain in the American Revolution, was born in either Monmouth or Hunterdon County, N.J. He was a descendant of migrants from Amsterdam, Holland, who changed their surname from deBoog to DeBow after arriving in America about 1649. In 1753 his parents, Solomon and Hannah DeBow, moved from New Jersey to a farm on Hyco Creek in present Caswell County, N.C. When the father died in 1767, he left a respectable estate to his wife and nine children: John, Frederick, Benjamin, Hannah, Jane, Ann, Mary, Sarah, and Elizabeth.

Aided by his patrimony, DeBow was able to enroll in the College of New Jersey (now Princeton University) where he was graduated in 1772. Having elected to become a Presbyterian minister, DeBow was licensed under the Synod of New York and Philadelphia and for a short time was assigned to the New Jersey churches of Oxford and Mount Bethel. On 17 May 1775, the Synod sent him to North Carolina to supply vacancies there. This work brought him to Orange County, where in February 1776 he promptly joined Colonel John Butler's militia as chaplain and accompanied it on the expedition to the Battle of Moore's Creek Bridge. Later the same year, the Provincial Congress of North Carolina awarded him fifteen pounds and ten shillings for his services.

On 22 May 1776, DeBow was fully ordained into the Gospel ministry by the New Brunswick Presbytery and accepted a call to become the official pastor of the Hawfields and Eno churches in North Carolina. By this transfer, he became a member of the Presbytery of Orange and devoted as much time as he could spare from his official duties to minister to the congregations at New Hope, Little River, Stony Creek, and other places where no resident pastors were available. Like most of his Presbyterian colleagues, DeBow conducted a school; with unusual foresight, he petitioned the General Assembly for financial aid in its operation until a state university was established. The latter event, he concluded, was inevitable.

The lengthy journeys on horseback, regardless of weather, that were necessary to serve a territory so widespread made rigorous physical demands on the clergyman, but he kept apace of his duties and his ministry proved influential. William Hodge was so inspired by DeBow that he joined the Hawfields church and determined to become the first son of that congregation to enter the ministry. However, his dismay at the sudden death of the pastor caused him to abandon his plans, and they were only revived successfully many years later under the influence of James MacGready.

The date is unknown of DeBow's marriage to Lucy Rice, to whom the clergyman gave the name of "Liney" in his will. She was the sister of John Rice, perhaps best known as the founder of Memphis, Tenn. The only known children of the couple were two sons, Solomon and Stephen. The Hawfields minister owned a respectable estate and his concern for his family is evident in provisions set forth in his will for the education of his sons. DeBow's sister, Jane, married Archibald Murphey and became the mother of Archibald DeBow Murphey. Another sister married Jacob Lake, who followed his brother-in-law as pastor of the Hawfields and Eno churches.

DeBow was only thirty-eight when he died of smallpox, contracted while nursing soldiers who fought in the closing days of the Revolutionary War. His grave was the first in the new cemetery at Hawfields, the church having been moved from its original location to where it now stands in Alamance County. None of his sermons nor any portrait of DeBow have been found. He is remembered for his untiring efforts to serve a large area of North Carolina as a Christian minister, for his promotion of public education in the state, and for his patriotism in the American Revolution.

SEE: William H. Foote, *Sketches of North Carolina, Historical and Biographical* (1848); William H. Hoyt, *The Papers of Archibald DeBow Murphey*, 2 vols. (1914); *Princeton University Biographical Catalogue*, 1746–1916 (Library, Princeton University, Princeton, N.J.); Records of Orange County, North Carolina (Offices of the Register of Deeds and the Clerk of the Court, Orange County Courthouse, Hillsborough); Herbert S. Turner, *Church in the Old Fields* (1962).

DURWARD T. STOKES

**Decrow, Sarah Moore Delano** *(ca. 1750–1795)*, the first woman postmaster in the United States after the adoption of the Constitution, was born almost unnoted and died in obscurity. No portrait of her was ever painted; none of her private correspondence is extant. Almost the only authentic sources of information about her are court records, and it is from them that the course of her life and character may be determined. It is thought that she was the daughter of John Moore and Mary Ratlif, and that her birthplace was in Perquimans County. In 1767 she married Ichabod Delano and soon became the mother of two children, Mary and Robert Delano. Ichabod Delano died in 1774; she served as executrix of his will and inherited land from him. In 1775 she married Robert Decrow; to this union were born two children, Sarah and Elizabeth Decrow. Robert Decrow, a man of substance, owned many acres in Perquimans County and, with her assistance, kept an ordinary until his death in 1784.

Articulate and contentious, the widow became a controversial figure. As either plaintiff or defendant, she was in and out of the courtroom for years. In October 1787, with James Iredell as her attorney, she haled Hinchea Gilliam into court on a charge of slander:

"Hinchea Gilliam late of Perquimans County Innholder was attached to answer Sarah Decrow of a plea of Trespass . . . the said Sarah is a Chaste, pious, Virtuous and faithfull Citizen of this State. . . . Nevertheless the said Hinchea not ignorant of the premises but contriving and maliciously intending the good name & credit of the said Sarah to injure and take away did on the twentieth of August in the year of our Lord one thousand seven hundred and eighty six and at divers other times . . . speak, pronounce, publish & declare 'Sarah Decrow (meaning the now plaintiff) is a Whore and I can prove that Nat Williams . . . keeps her (meaning the said Sarah and that she lived in a state of Fornication & adultery with the said Nathaniel Williams in open violation of every Law Human & divine) and I will Indict her (meaning the said Sarah the now plaintiff) for it (meaning the Infamous & hurtfull Crimes of adultery and Fornication)' by reason of the speaking of which false, scandalous, malicious and opprobrious words . . . the said Sarah was in a great measure deprived of the benefits & comforts resulting from Society."

In the settlement of the case, made 14 Oct. 1788, she agreed "to dismiss the suit being an action of slander at her instance agt him for calling her a whore and for saying Nath Williams Senr had improper connections with her the said Mrs. Decrowe—upon the Condition of the said Hinchea making a proper apology & recanting the truth of such suggestions—the said Hinchea doth therefore deny his having used any such words to the best of his knowledge, swears that if he did use them, it was not with any intention of injuring the said Sarah."

On 15 Apr. 1789, Mrs. Decrow obtained a license to keep "an Ordinary, or Victualing house, at Hertford," promising not to "suffer unlawful gaming . . . nor on the Sabbath Day to suffer any person to tipple or drink more than is necessary." She failed to keep her promise, and on 27 April the sheriff of Perquimans County was "commanded to take the body of Sarah Decrowe Inn holder in your County . . . and her safely keep . . . so that you may have her . . . at the Court-house in Hertford on the second Monday in July next." In the words of the bill of indictment, "Sarah Decrow . . . on the 14th day of January . . . and a long time before that day and year and continually since that time with Force and Arms at the Dwelling House . . . did keep a Public Ordinary and did sell and continue to sell Victuals and Spiritous Liquors in small Measures to all persons calling for the Same. Contrary to the Act of the Assembly in that case made and provided to the great Injury of the Revinue of the Government and against the Peace and Dignity of the State." The final disposition of the case is not known. In 1791 she brought into court Dr. Ebenezer Belnap, a former lodger who was in debt to her twenty-one pounds and fourteen shillings. He absconded, but she was compensated by a court order to attach enough of the Belnap possessions to pay her.

The first mention of her in a federal document was in 1790, when she appeared in the first census of the United States as the head of a family of "three white females" and the owner of nine slaves. Meanwhile—the date is unrecorded—a post office was established in Hertford. On 27 Sept. 1792 she was commissioned postmaster, thus becoming the third woman postmaster in the United States and the first after the adoption of the Constitution. She submitted her first accounts to Postmaster General Thomas Pickering on 20 Mar. 1793. During the same year, feeling she had not been paid enough for her services, she threatened to resign. Assured on 25 Aug. 1793 that she was "entitled to 40% which is the highest rate of compensation the Postmaster General is authorized to allow any of his deputies," she continued in the office until the end of her life. She was succeeded by Thomas McNider on 9 Apr. 1795.

Mrs. Decrow died that year and was buried near Hertford in the Decrow Cemetery, the exact location of which is no longer known. Her will was probated in May 1795, and her chattels were sold at a public auction on the twenty-first and twenty-second of that month. The Account of Sales of the Estate, a three-page, closely-written document, reveals that she was wealthy. Even after death she was controversial. A legal paper dated 12 Aug. 1798 shows that John Skinner, the only surviving executor of her estate, was still having difficulty with the settlement.

SEE: Gertrude E. Enders to Esther Evans, letter, 1964; J. R. B. Hathaway, ed., *North Carolina Historical and Genealogical Register*, vol. 3 (April 1903); Postmaster General Letter Book (Manuscript Division, Library of Congress, Washington, D.C.); 1790 Census; Jane F. Smith to Esther Evans, letter, 1964; Ellen G. Winslow, *History of Perquimans County* (1931).

ESTHER EVANS

**Deems, Charles Force** *(4 Dec. 1820–18 Nov. 1893)*, clergyman, educator, and author, is best known for his connection with the Church of the Strangers in New York City during the late nineteenth century and for his friendship with Cornelius Vanderbilt that resulted in the establishment of Vanderbilt University in Nashville, Tenn. However, his quarter of a century in North Carolina, from 1840 until 1865, left an enduring mark on the state.

He was born in Baltimore, Md., the son of George W. and Mary Roberts Deems. His mother was the daughter of Zachary Roberts, a Methodist minister, and his father, of Dutch ancestry whose ancestral name was De Heems, became a local Methodist preacher; in 1859 he was admitted to the North Carolina Conference of the Methodist Episcopal Church, South, and was sent to Topsail. Both parents were extremely pious, and the son showed early evidence of a religious bent. After his mother died, he went to live with a maiden aunt in order to study law at Dickinson College, a Methodist institution in Carlisle, Pa. Before his graduation in 1839, his religious bent had turned him to the ministry; afterward he taught school and preached in New York City, where he met his future wife, Annie Disoway, daughter of a prominent hardware merchant there.

Deems joined the New Jersey Conference of the Methodist Episcopal Church and was sent to Asbury Circuit. He soon exchanged his work there for the general agency of the American Bible Society in North Carolina, a state that had always had an appeal for him. In 1840 he began his new job in Caswell and Iredell counties and before long found himself in demand as the "boy preacher"; in 1841 he had his conference membership transferred to North Carolina.

In 1842 former Governor David L. Swain, president of The University of North Carolina, prevailed upon Deems to join the university in order to get a Methodist on the faculty. Deems served as professor of humanistic studies for five years. Shortly after he accepted the post, he went back to New Jersey and married Annie Disoway on 30 June 1843. In 1848 he left the university to take the position of professor of natural sciences at Randolph-Macon College, a school supported jointly by the Virginia and North Carolina conferences of the Methodist Episcopal Church, South, located at that time in Boydton, Va., just across the Virginia line north of Raleigh. He remained there only one year, resigning with the intention of going into the itinerancy. However, he was soon back in educational work as president of Greensboro Female College, putting in order the affairs of one of the oldest women's colleges in the United States which he found at a low ebb. He remained there from 1850 until 1854, when he again resigned to enter the itinerancy. From then until he left North Carolina in 1865, he busied himself with preaching in the eastern part of the state; for four years, he also served as presiding elder of the Wilmington District.

Meanwhile, Deems's interest in education continued. In 1852, while president of Greensboro Female College, he had purchased the Sylva Grove School property in Davidson County, where Thomasville later developed, renamed it Glenn Anna, and supervised it as a preparatory school for Greensboro College under the auspices of the North Carolina Conference. Late in 1858 the citizens of Wilson built a school for boys and girls and presented it to Deems, who organized and supervised it as St. Augustin's Institute, a nondenominational school. He also was instrumental in the conference's move to take over Normal College in Randolph County and served as chairman of its board of trustees; later he was chairman of the board of trustees of Olin High School, another Methodist institution, in Iredell County.

While Deems was at Randolph-Macon, a feud developed between him and William A. Smith, president of the college. Their personal disagreement was to have a tremendous impact on the development of Methodism in North Carolina. Essentially, each man thought that the other was trying to thwart his ambitions, Smith to become a bishop and Deems to become president of Randolph-Macon. For years their conflict rocked the Virginia and North Carolina conferences, with Smith preferring charges of immorality (lying) and slander against Deems in the North Carolina Conference in 1854 and Deems retaliating with like charges against Smith in the Virginia Conference the next year. Both men were exonerated by their own conferences, but opinions became polarized, with most of the North Carolinians taking the part of Deems and most of the Virginians siding with Smith. As a result, the North Carolina Conference established the *North Carolina Christian Advocate* and withdrew its support from the *Richmond Christian Advocate*, which had been outspoken in its support of Smith. Also it adopted Braxton Craven's Normal College in Randolph County as its college and gradually withdrew support from Randolph-Macon. Deems, as chairman of the board of trustees, renamed Braxton Craven's school Trinity College. Out of his personal problems had grown a successful movement of independence by the North Carolina Methodists from the overlordship of Virginia.

When the Civil War broke out, Deems opposed secession but supported the Confederacy; his oldest son, Theodore Disoway, lost his life leading a charge at Gettysburg. During the war he deserted Trinity College and threw his support behind Olin High School in Iredell County. In that move he did not receive the support that he received in his conflict with Smith; when Trinity College reopened after the war, he went in 1865 to New York to establish a religious and literary newspaper, *The Watchman*. The periodical was of short duration. In 1866 Deems began the ministerial work that developed into the Church of the Strangers, meeting first in one of the chapels of the University of the City of New York and then in a chapel given to him by Cornelius Vanderbilt. That was his main work until his death. For some time he received appointments to New York from the North Carolina Conference, but in 1875 he was located by that conference and ended his connections with it. That did not mean the end of his connections with North Carolina. In 1877 he was back in the state to receive an honorary LL.D. degree from The University of North Carolina. He had already been awarded a D.D. degree by Randolph-Macon in 1853.

Deems was a prolific writer and publisher. As early as 1840 he published a book of poems and a biography of Adam Clark. His best known works, *Life of Jesus* and *Scotch Verdict in re Evolution*, were both from his later years in New York.

He died and was buried in New York City, leaving two sons and two daughters. The sons, the Reverend Edward M. Deems, Ph.D., a Presbyterian minister, and Francis M. Deems, Ph.D., published a life of their father containing entries from his journal and an autobiography covering his earlier years.

SEE: *Autobiography of Charles Force Deems and Memoir* (1897); Nora Chaffin, *Trinity College* (1950); North Carolina Conference of the Methodist Episcopal Church, South, Journals (Manuscript Department, Library, Duke University, Durham); C. L. Van Noppen Papers (Manuscript Department, Library, Duke University, Durham).

HOMER M. KEEVER

**Delany, Henry Beard** *(5 Feb. 1858–14 Apr. 1928)*, was the first black man to become an Episcopal bishop in North Carolina and only the second in the United States; he was also an educator. He was born in St. Mary's, Ga., the son of Thomas Delany, a ship's and house carpenter and Methodist preacher, and Sarah Louisa Delany. During his early childhood the family moved to Fernandina, Fla., where he worked on his father's farm, learned bricklaying and plastering, and attended a school supported by the Freedmen's Bureau and taught by northern missionaries. He studied theology and music, both vocal and instrumental, as well as elementary subjects. Enrolling in 1881 at St. Augustine's School (now College) in Raleigh, he continued his theological studies and was graduated from the academic course in 1885. He remained at his alma mater as a member of the faculty until 1908, teaching religion, music, and in the normal department; he was also chaplain, vice-principal (1889–1908), and supervisor of building projects. Along with his students, he participated in the actual construction of several buildings at the college, notably the chapel (1896), the 1898 library (later part of Taylor Hall), and the former St. Agnes Hospital (1909). These buildings were partially constructed of stone quarried on the campus. The chapel contains a plaque dedicated to him, not only in recognition of his service to the college but also of his career in the Protestant Episcopal church in which he became a communicant while at St. Augustine's.

On 7 June 1889 Delany was ordained a deacon in Raleigh's St. Ambrose Episcopal Church, where he continued to assist in services and where he was ordained a priest three years later on 2 May 1892. For the Diocese of North Carolina he was a member of the Commission for Work among Colored People from 1889 to 1904, visiting congregations in several counties and assisting in organizing schools for Negroes. He also made monthly visits to prisoners in the county workhouse. In 1908 he was named archdeacon for Negro work in the diocese, necessitating his resignation from St. Augustine's faculty; but the family continued to live on the campus, where Mrs. Delany was teacher and matron. Shaw University awarded him an honorary D.D. degree in 1911.

On 15 May 1918 Delany was unanimously elected

suffragan bishop in charge of Negro work in the Diocese of North Carolina. At that time the only other Negro suffragan bishop in America was the Right Reverend E. Thomas Demby, who served Arkansas and other southwestern states and who was consecrated in the same year as Delany. In his first report to the diocese Delany stated: "On Thursday, the 21st of November, 1918, in St. Augustine's Chapel, on the campus of St. Augustine's School, I was consecrated Suffragan Bishop of the Diocese of North Carolina for Negro Work. At the instance of my election an agreement was made, through our Diocesan that I should also assist the Bishops of East Carolina and South Carolina with their Negro Work." Bishop Joseph B. Cheshire, who presided at his consecration during a conference of church workers among Negroes being held in Raleigh, described Delany's work among North Carolina Negroes as one of the major influences leading to the improvement of Negro life in the South.

Delany continued as bishop until six months before he died at his home on the campus. His funeral was conducted by Bishop E. A. Penick in St. Augustine's Chapel, and he was buried in Mount Hope Cemetery, Raleigh. A memorial published by the diocese noted his steady rise "to a position of eminence in which he had won not only the esteem of his white colleagues throughout the country but also their love," as well as "his congeniality and the uniform gentleness and sweetness of his disposition." Years later the editor of the *North Carolina Churchman*, the Reverend I. Harding Hughes, recalled him as "a man I so admired—gentle, humble, big hearted, and dedicated."

On 6 Oct. 1886 Delany married Nannie James Logan of Danville, Va., who had enrolled in St. Augustine's in 1877 and remained after graduation as teacher of cooking and domestic science; she was named matron in 1888. A plaque in Delany Residence Hall, built in 1929, indicates that the building was named in recognition of her fifty years' association with the school. She died 1 June 1956 and was buried beside her husband. Their ten children, all born at St. Augustine's, became teachers, doctors, dentists, and attorneys. They include Julia (Mrs. Cecil Bourne), Laura E. (Mrs. Edward Murrell), and Sarah R. Delany, teachers, Henry T. Delany, Jr., and Bessie Delany, dentists, all of Mt. Vernon, N.Y.; Hubert T. Delany, judge of the New York Domestic Relations Court, Lucius L. Delany, attorney, William Manross Delany, and Samuel R. Delany, undertaker, all of New York; and Lemuel T. Delany, a surgeon in Raleigh until his death in 1956.

SEE: A. B. Caldwell, ed., *History of the American Negro*, North Carolina ed., vol. 4 (1921); Cecil D. Halliburton, *A History of St. Augustine's College* (1937); Protestant Episcopal Church, Diocese of North Carolina, *Journal* (1892, 1897, 1918, 1919, 1928), and Diocese of East Carolina, *Journal* (1928); Raleigh *News and Observer*, 16–17 Apr. 1928; *Raleigh Times*, 22 Nov. 1918, 17 Apr. 1928; Elizabeth Davis Reid, ed., *Raleigh Magazine*, Wake County Bicentennial ed. (December 1971); St. Augustine's College, Record (scattered issues).

ELIZABETH DAVIS REID

**deMille, Cecil Blount** *(12 Aug. 1881–21 Jan. 1959)*, motion picture producer, was born in Ashfield, Mass., the second son of Henry Churchill deMille, playwright and partner of David Belasco, and Matilda Beatrice Samuel, teacher and later founder of the De Mille Play Company and screenwriter. His older brother William C. deMille was a playwright, motion picture director, and professor of drama at the University of Southern California. His first American ancestor, Anthony deMille, arrived in New Amsterdam in 1658 from Amsterdam, Holland; his son Pieter became mayor of New Amsterdam. Another ancestor, William Blount of North Carolina, was a signer of the Constitution.

Cecil B. deMille spent his boyhood in Washington, N.C., New York City, and Echo Lake and Pompton, N.J. He was educated at a private school in Pompton, the Pennsylvania Military Academy, Chester, Pa., and the American Academy of Dramatic Arts, New York. In his early career he was a playwright and stage producer, one of the organizers of the Standard Opera Company, and an associate of his mother in the De Mille Play Company. In 1913 he was a founder, with Samuel Goldwyn and Jesse L. Lasky, of the Jesse L. Lasky Feature Play Company for which he was director general; the company merged in 1918 to become Famous Players-Lasky, and in 1927 to become Paramount Pictures Corp. In 1924 he established DeMille Pictures Corp. and in 1928 joined Metro-Goldwyn-Mayer as producer-director. He returned to Paramount as independent producer in 1932.

In the next forty-three years (1913–56), Cecil B. deMille produced some seventy pictures, beginning with *The Squaw Man* in 1913. Others of note were *Carmen* and *Joan the Woman*, both starring the metropolitan soprano, Geraldine Farrar. Later came *The Ten Commandments*, *The Volga Boatman*, *The King of Kings*, *Dynamite* (his first sound film), *The Sign of the Cross*, *Cleopatra*, *The Crusaders*, *The Plainsman*, *The Buccaneer*, *Union Pacific*, *The Story of Dr. Wassell*, *Samson and Delilah*, *The Greatest Show on Earth*, and finally a second *Ten Commandments*.

He was producer of the Lux Radio Theatre of the Air from 1 June 1936 to 22 Jan. 1945, when he was dropped rather than pay a one-dollar political assessment levied by the American Federation of Radio Artists. In addition, he was founder of Mercury Aviation Company, one of the first American airlines to carry air freight and passengers commercially on regularly scheduled runs; vice-president and chairman of motion picture loans for Commercial National Trust and Savings Bank of Los Angeles, which was purchased by the Bank of Italy and later became the Bank of America; and president of the DeMille Foundation for Political Freedom, which was dissolved after his death.

In August 1902 deMille married Constance Adams, daughter of Judge Frederick Adams of East Orange, N.J. They had a daughter Cecilia Hoyt (Mrs. Joseph Harper) and an adopted daughter and two sons.

Cecil B. deMille was a Republican and an Episcopalian. He died in Hollywood, Calif., and was buried in the family plot in Hollywood Cemetery.

SEE: *Charlotte Observer*, 21 Dec. 1941; *DAB*, Supplement, vol. 6 (1980); Cecil B. deMille, *Autobiography* (1959); Charles Higham, *Cecil B. DeMille* (1937); *New York Times*, 22, 24, 28 Jan. 1959; *Washington Daily News*, 21 Jan. 1959; *Who Was Who in America*, vol. 3 (1960).

LOUISE L. PITMAN

**deMille, Henry Churchill** *(17 Sept. 1853–10 Feb. 1893)*, playwright, was the son of William Edward and Margaret Blount Hoyt deMille, both of Washington, N.C., where young deMille was born. During the Civil War his father joined the Confederate Army and the family refugeed to Greenville. He rapidly learned the difficulties and inconveniences of life in wartime, including early education under his own mother. When peace came the family returned home, but under straitened economic conditions for them and the community. In 1867 deMille made a trip to New York to visit his grandfather, Thomas Arnold deMille, who persuaded the boy's parents to let him stay in the North. That September, at age fourteen, he entered Adelphi Academy, in Brooklyn, which was to become a strong motivating force in his life.

In 1871 deMille entered Columbia College from which he received the A.B. and A.M. degrees. Following graduation in 1875, he taught at Lockwood's Academy, then at Columbia Grammar School. A devout member of the Episcopal church, he was a lay reader at St. Stephen's, Brooklyn. In 1878 he was accepted as a candidate for Holy Orders in the Diocese of Long Island, though he was never ordained. Instead, he turned to the theater. His first assignment was as a playreader on the staff of the Madison Square Theatre. Through Daniel Frohman, the stage manager, he met David Belasco, with whom he developed a close friendship. They became partners after production of *The Main Line* (written in collaboration with Charles Barnard) at the Lyceum Theatre on 18 Sept. 1886.

By this time deMille had acquired a summer home at Echo Lake, N.J., where for the next five years Belasco practically became a member of the family. The first of their collaborations was *The Wife*, produced at the Lyceum on 1 Nov. 1887. This was followed by *Lord Chumley*, produced 21 Aug. 1888, written especially for E. H. Sothern to give that actor a character somewhat like the Lord Dundreary his father had made famous, and *The Charity Ball*, produced 19 Nov. 1889. They were among the most popular plays of the period and acted for several successive seasons throughout the country under the management of Daniel Frohman, at whose Lyceum Theatre they had first been produced. The two productions gave deMille a national reputation.

Because he saw life mainly in terms of the theater, deMille's plays were artificial in structure, written in the conventional manner of the society drama of the day, with alternate layers of intrigue/drama force and comedy. Except for occasional performances by local stock companies their popularity did not continue beyond the early years of the twentieth century. The last of the Belasco-deMille productions, *Men and Women*, opened on 21 Oct. 1890 and ran until the end of March 1891. DeMille had come to feel that his and Belasco's professional interests no longer coincided, though their friendship continued. DeMille was becoming more interested in social and economic problems, reflected in his last play *The Lost Paradise*, produced first in Chicago on 17 Aug. 1891. He was greatly influenced by the philosophy of his friend, Henry George, the noted "Single-Taxer." He started work on *The Promised Land*, but it was never finished.

In 1876 deMille married Matilda Beatrice Samuel in St. Luke's Church, Brooklyn. Of their three children, a daughter died in early childhood and two sons, William C. and Cecil B. deMille, reached positions of prominence in the motion picture world. DeMille was an Episcopalian and a Democrat. He died suddenly of typhoid fever at his home in Pompton, N.J. Some years later his ashes were interred in the grave of his mother in Washington, N.C.

SEE: *DAB*, vol. 5 (1930); Personal recollections of the late William C. deMille and Elizabeth deMille Pitman.

LOUISE L. PITMAN

**deMille, William Churchill** *(25 July 1878–5 Mar. 1955)*, playwright, the son of playwright Henry Churchill and Matilda Beatrice Samuel deMille, was born in Washington, N.C. He spent most of his boyhood in New York City and at Echo Lake, N.J., until 1891 when he moved with his family to Pompton, N.J. He well remembered that in the late eighties the family lived at 119 Waverly Place, New York, in an apartment directly opposite that of David Belasco, with whom his father collaborated. In those years, he and his young brother Cecil were students at the Horace Mann School, which was then on University Place. From 1891 to 1893 both attended a private school in Pompton and from then on the Henry C. deMille School for Girls, established by their mother, also in Pompton.

In the summer of 1895, his mother took William with her on a trip to Europe and left him for a year's study at Freiburg, in Baden, Germany. When he returned to America, he entered Columbia College at the age of eighteen. He was graduated from Columbia in 1900 and from the American Academy of Dramatic Arts in 1901. He took postgraduate courses for two years in Columbia University, where he concentrated on history and literature of the drama under Professor Brander Matthews, known affectionately as "Brandy" by his students. Beginning in 1902 he taught in his mother's school at Pompton, as well as in the American Academy of Dramatic Arts in New York, while continuing his stage training.

DeMille was a playwright, actor, and producer combined. In 1901 he produced his first dramatic sketch, *A Mixed Foursome*, at the Educational Alliance in New York. Both he and his brother Cecil were in the cast. The same year he also wrote and produced a longer dramatic work, *The Forest Ring*, a play for children. It was written in collaboration with Charles Barnard, who had also been his father's collaborator in *The Main Line*, and produced in the Children's Theater at Carnegie Lyceum, New York, with the author in the cast.

Until 1913 deMille wrote various other plays, sketches, and magazine articles. His best-known plays are probably *Strongheart*, produced in 1905; *Classmates*, written with Margaret Turnbull three years later; and *The Warrens of Virginia* and *The Woman*, produced by David Belasco in 1909 and 1911. Among his most familiar vaudeville sketches were *In 1999*, *Food*, *Poor Old Jim*, *The Squealer*, *The Martyrs*, and *The Deceivers*.

In 1914 deMille went to the West Coast to make motion pictures with his brother, Cecil B. deMille. In Hollywood they were associated with the Jesse L. Lasky Feature Play Company, which later merged with the Famous Players and then became Paramount. For twenty years William deMille was busily engaged in motion pictures, as writer, director, and producer. During that period he directed nearly sixty films, in addition to the many he wrote but did not personally produce. He also wrote many magazine and newspaper articles, largely dealing with motion picture production as a growing art. In those years deMille was connected with Paramount, Metro-Goldwyn-Mayer, and Pathé; he made films on both coasts. He was one of the first to believe in the new talking picture when it first appeared, and personally produced the second all-talking picture made by Paramount. For three years in the late 1920s he was president of the Academy of Motion Picture Arts and Sciences.

Outside the world of drama, deMille was interested in sports and politics. An athlete during his college years, he was a member of the varsity track team for three years and as a senior represented Columbia in the International Fencing Contests. For many years he played tennis—he was a member of the West Side Tennis Club in New York and one of the founders of the Los Angeles Tennis Club. During his Hollywood period deMille was active politically as a believer in Henry George's theory of the single tax; consequently, in some circles he was considered somewhat of a radical. His late father had been one of George's early disciples and so the two families became friends.

In March 1903 deMille married Anna George, youngest daughter of Henry George; they were divorced in 1927. In August 1928, in Albuquerque, N.Mex., he married Clara Strousse, who under her professional name of Clara Beranger had been associated with him in the production of motion pictures. From his first wife, deMille had two children: Agnes, the well-known choreographer, and Margaret.

DeMille spent his last years as head of the drama department, which he founded, at the University of Southern California. He died at his home in Playa del Rey, Calif., and was buried in the family plot in Hollywood Cemetery.

SEE: William C. deMille, *Hollywood Saga* (1939); *New York Times*, 6, 9 Mar. 1955; Raleigh *News and Observer*, 12 Feb. 1937, 5 Mar. 1955; *Who Was Who in America*, vol. 3 (1960).

LOUISE L. PITMAN

**Denman, Charles** *(d. 24 Apr. 1739)*, merchant, assemblyman, and local official, was living in Perquimans Precinct by April 1716 when he purchased 100 acres of land there. In addition to his mercantile business, he often bought land that he soon afterward sold. A grand jury list of 26 Oct. 1725 refers to him as Captain Charles Denman. As clerk of court of Albemarle and Perquimans counties at various times between 1728 and 1734, he was witness to wills, executor of estates, and involved in cases at law, primarily to collect money. For a number of years he was also treasurer of Perquimans Precinct. Between 1723 and 1735 (except for the session of 1727), he served in the Assembly where he was active on the committee that prepared replies to addresses of the governor. Several times he was chosen by the Assembly to deliver messages to the Council; in 1731 he delivered one maintaining that the Carolina Charter of 1663 denied the right of legislative bodies other than the colonial Assembly to levy taxes, and asking that officers' fees be regulated by the Assembly. At one session he was chairman of the Resolutions Committee and made its report.

Denman served on the grand jury several times and once wrote the report for the foreman who apparently could not write. In April 1731, as a member of the provincial grand jury, he signed an address to the king expressing gratitude that North Carolina had become a royal province. As an assemblyman he was also active in efforts to regulate the payment of quitrents and in inspecting and settling accounts. He apparently was a member of the Church of England, for in 1731 he was a vestryman in Perquimans parish.

Denman's first wife was named Sarah; they were the parents of Ann (b. 5 Feb. 1713), who married a Moore, Christopher (b. 30 Sept. 1717), and Sarah (b. 2 Oct. 1719). On 24 Mar. 1737 he married Rebecca Jones (widow, successively, of Joseph Sutton and Francis Toms), but they apparently had no children. His recent death was announced in the Assembly on 2 Mar. 1740. His widow was asked to pay his unsettled accounts as treasurer in February 1740.

SEE: John L. Cheney, Jr., ed., *North Carolina Government, 1585–1974* (1975); Bryan Grimes, *Abstract of North Carolina Wills* (1910); J. R. B. Hathaway, ed., *North Carolina Historical and Genealogical Register* 3 (July 1903); William S. Price, Jr., ed., *Colonial Records of North Carolina*, vol. 5, *Higher-Court Minutes, 1709–1723* ([1977]); William L. Saunders, ed., *Colonial Records of North Carolina*, vols. 2–4 (1886); Mrs. Watson Winslow, *History of Perquimans County* (1931).

WILLIAM S. POWELL

**Denny, Emery Byrd** *(23 Nov. 1892–24 Apr. 1973)*, lawyer and North Carolina Supreme Court justice, was born on a farm near Pilot Mountain in Surry County, the son of the Reverend Gabriel and Sarah Delphina Stone Denny. After attending the public schools of Surry County, he studied at Gilliam's Academy from 1910 to 1914 and at The University of North Carolina School of Law from September 1916 to December 1917, when he joined the aviation section of the Signal Corps, U.S. Army. During World War I he held the ranks of private, corporal, sergeant, and master electrician. He returned to the university's law school from June to August 1919. The honorary degree of LL.D. was conferred upon him by The University of North Carolina in 1946 and by Wake Forest College in 1947.

On 27 Dec. 1922 Denny married Bessie Brandt Brown, daughter of Jeremiah Moses and Catherine Clementine Krider Brown of Salisbury. They were the parents of four children: Emery B., Jr., Betty Brown (Mrs. Lenoir G. Shook), Sarah Catherine (Mrs. Bailey P. Williamson), and Jean Stone (Mrs. Wallace Ashley, Jr.).

Admitted to the bar in 1919, Denny practiced law as a member of the firm of Denny and Gaston from 1919 to 1921, was associated with Mangum and Denny from 1921 to 1930, and practiced alone from 1930 to 1942. He served as attorney for Gaston County from 1927 to 1942 and for the North Carolina Railroad from 1937 to 1938, and was mayor of Gastonia from 1929 to 1937. He also served as president and director of the Ranlo Manufacturing Company from 1936 to 1941 and as a trustee of The University of North Carolina from 1941 to 1943. During the General Assembly of 1941 he was special counsel to Governor J. Melville Broughton. On 3 Feb. 1942 he was appointed associate justice of the North Carolina Supreme Court by Governor Broughton to succeed the late Associate Justice Heriot Clarkson. After completing the unexpired term, he was elected to a full eight-year term on 3 Nov. 1942; he was reelected on 7 Nov. 1950 and again on 4 Nov. 1958. On 9 Mar. 1962, he was appointed chief justice of the North Carolina Supreme Court by Governor Terry Sanford to succeed Chief Justice J. Wallace Winborne, who retired. In November 1962 he was elected to serve out the unexpired term of Chief Justice Winborne. He retired on 5 Feb. 1966 and qualified as an emergency justice of the supreme court, a position he held until his death.

Denny served as chairman of the North Carolina Judicial Council from 1956 until his appointment as chief justice. He also was a trustee of the North Carolina Baptist Hospital, Winston-Salem; of the Baptist State Convention of North Carolina; and (except for one year, from 1950 until his death) of the Southeastern Baptist Theological Seminary, Wake Forest, where he also served as a member of the executive committee and chairman of the board of trustees. In 1968 he was appointed chairman of the State Constitution Study Commission by Governor Dan K. Moore. In addition, he belonged to Phi Delta Phi legal fraternity; Holland Memorial Lodge 668, Ancient Free and Accepted Masons;

Gastonia Chapter No. 66, Royal Arch Masons; Gastonia Commandery No. 28, Knights Templar; and St. Titus Conclave No. 72, Red Cross of Constantine. He was grand historian, grand steward, and grand deacon of the Grand Lodge of North Carolina A.F. and A.M.; judge advocate of the Grand Lodge (1965–71); and member of the Board of General Purposes (1967–73). He was chief adept of the North Carolina College Societas Rosicruciana In Civitatibus Foederatis. He held membership in the Watauga Club, Raleigh Executives Club, and the Newcomen Society in North America. A Democrat, he served as chairman of the Gaston County Board of Elections (1924–26), chairman of the Gaston County Democratic Executive Committee (1926–28), and chairman of the State Democratic Executive Committee (1940–42).

A teacher of a men's Bible class for twenty-eight years, Justice Denny was a member of Hayes Barton Baptist Church, Raleigh, where he had served on the board of deacons and as its chairman. He died in Raleigh and was buried in Oakwood Cemetery.

SEE: John L. Cheney, Jr., ed., *North Carolina Government, 1585–1974* (1975); Family papers (in possession of the author); William S. Powell, ed., *North Carolina Lives* (1962); Charles H. Stone, *The Stones of Surry* (1955).

BESSIE B. DENNY

**Denny, George Vernon, Jr.** *(29 Aug. 1899–11 Nov. 1959)*, educator and radio commentator, was born in Washington, N.C., the son of George Vernon and Carrie Ricks Cobb Denny. After attending the public schools of Washington and Bingham Military Academy, Asheville, he entered The University of North Carolina in 1918; he was graduated in 1922 with a B.S. degree in commerce. While a student at the university, Denny was active in the Carolina Playmakers, which was organized his freshman year by Professor Frederick H. Koch. He was given a role in one of its first productions, *When Witches Ride* by Elizabeth Lay, and in his junior year was made its business manager at a salary of fifty dollars a month. He was also a member of the Pi Kappa Phi fraternity and the Dialectic Society. Following graduation he was employed as director of the Bureau of Lectures and Entertainment in the university's Extension Division. In 1924 Professor Koch appointed him business manager of the Carolina Playmakers and instructor in play production. In that capacity he handled the Playmakers' publicity and booked its tours throughout the state.

In 1926 Denny left North Carolina and went to New York where he hoped to make a career of acting. After two years of going, as he said, from "flop to flop" in the theater world and a brief stint as manager of a small lecture bureau, he gladly accepted an offer from Columbia University to direct the extension work of its Institute of Arts and Sciences. For the most part his job consisted of engaging lecturers on a large variety of subjects for the Institute's adult education program. Hearing of his successful work at Columbia, the League for Political Education, headquartered at Town Hall on Forty-third Street, employed him as its associate director in 1930. Since 1894 the league had presented lecturers of all political creeds to speak on various aspects of public affairs. In 1937 Denny was made director and changed the name of the organization to Town Hall, Incorporated. In addition to scheduling lectures, short courses, and discussion groups and concerts, he edited *The Town Crier*, the league's official publication.

In considering how he could broaden the scope of Town Hall's concept of providing open discussions of vital and controversial issues of the day, Denny conceived the idea of using the medium of radio to bring this kind of program into American homes. After he had conferred with John Royal, vice-president in charge of programs for the National Broadcasting Company, Royal committed NBC to pay all expenses for six experimental and uncensored programs, beginning on 30 May 1935. Thus was born America's Town Meeting of the Air. The subject of the first program was "Which Way America—Fascism, Communism, Socialism, or Democracy?" discussed by Lawrence Dennis, A. J. Muste, Norman Thomas, and Raymond Moley. Following the initial broadcast, Town Hall received over 3,000 letters commenting favorably on the program. At the conclusion of the six broadcasts NBC agreed to carry the program as a regular weekly feature on Thursday night. As moderator of the Town Hall program, Denny opened each meeting by ringing the town crier's bell and giving the folksy greeting, "Good evening, neighbors." He conducted the programs as nearly as possible on the model of an old-fashioned New England town meeting, adding a touch of well-planned showmanship. The timely topics he chose for discussion frequently provoked heated exchanges between the speakers and the audience. The town meeting, in his opinion, "played a part in the founding of this country, and will continue to play a part in preserving the principles upon which the nation rests." Denny frequently asserted that free speech was "the most powerful and at the same time the most dangerous thing in the world," and that it meant "the right to advocate the wrong as well as the right."

Following several years of successful production, Denny decided to take America's Town Meeting of the Air on tour. In the first coast-to-coast tour in 1941, the program originated in five different cities. The tour idea proved to be popular and was expanded to include more cities. In May 1942 the Junior Town Meeting League was formed to encourage the use of the town meeting idea in high schools. Not content to spread the gospel of the town meeting concept in his own country only, Denny planned a world tour in 1949. With the cooperation of leaders in business, labor, agriculture, and the professions, forty representatives of these groups participated in the discussions presented during a two-month tour of fourteen cities in Europe, the Near East, and the Orient.

On the occasion of the fifteenth anniversary of the founding of America's Town Meeting of the Air, Denny declared that "we rededicate ourselves to the high purposes for which this institution was founded and we invite our fellow Americans and freedom-loving peoples everywhere to join us in our search for wise and just solutions to the serious problems before us." He believed that many of the world's problems could be solved through "a program of education" embodying the principles of the Town Hall ideal. After seven years as associate director of the League for Political Education and fifteen years as president of Town Hall, Incorporated, he resigned in 1952. During the presidential campaign of that year, Denny commented on the news five nights a week over a Los Angeles radio station. In 1956 he was made vice-president of Eisenhower's "People to People Program," established to promote friendship and understanding among people throughout the world. The year before his death he took a group of thirty-two American leaders through seven South American countries where he conducted his now famous "Town Meeting" programs.

Denny received the LL.D. degree from Temple University in 1940 and from Ithaca College in 1951. He was an Episcopalian and a Democrat.

On 12 June 1924 Denny married Mary Traill Yellott, fellow student and actor at The University of North Carolina. They had three children: Mildred Nelson (Mrs. James Davidson), George Vernon Denny III, and Mary Virginia (Mrs. Donald Horton). The marriage ended in divorce in 1943. On 2 Apr. 1944 he married Jeanne Sarasy. He died and was buried in West Cornwall, Conn.

SEE: *Asheville Citizen*, 25 Dec. 1957, 12 Nov. 1959; *Chapel Hill Weekly*, 8 July 1955; *Current Biography* (1940, 1950); *Freedom's Bell Rings Round the World* (1949); *New York Times*, 12 Nov. 1959; Raleigh *News and Observer*, 8 Dec. 1946; Walter Spearman, *The Carolina Playmakers, The First Fifty Years* (1970); Town Hall, Inc., *Good Evening Neighbors!* (1950); S. J. Woolf, "The Umpire of the Town Meeting," *New York Times Magazine*, 6 June 1943.

LAWRENCE F. LONDON

**Denson, Claudius Baker** *(29 Sept. 1837–15 Jan. 1903)*, soldier, educator, and public speaker, was born in Suffolk, Va., the son of Josiah Armistead (1814–1907) of Suffolk and Mary Baker Denson, daughter of the Reverend Daniel Baker, also of Suffolk. In 1624 Denson's ancestor, Thomas Jordan, had come from Dorsetshire, England, to settle in Nansemond County, Va. Denson entered the Virginia Collegiate and Military Institute at Portsmouth in 1853. There he became commandant of the corps of cadets and later a member of the faculty. In 1858 he founded and became principal of the first military school in North Carolina, situated at Franklin, six miles east of Faison in Duplin County. It was known as the Franklin Military Institute. Associated with him there was Professor Richard Washington Millard, a native of Clinton.

In 1861 the approach of war brought immediate, drastic changes at the military school. Among the first troops to offer their services to the governor of North Carolina was a company composed largely of the students of Franklin Military Institute. Organized at Faison on 16 Apr. 1861 and called the "Confederate Greys," this company elected C. B. Denson, captain; R. P. James, first lieutenant; L. T. Hicks, second lieutenant; and L. W. Hodges, third lieutenant. It went into camp on the Franklin Institute grounds, was quickly recruited to full strength from young volunteers of the surrounding area, and was drilled in a regular course of military tactics. Except for the flintlock muskets of the school, all uniforms and other clothing, food, camp equipment, and military supplies were made or financed directly by the company's members, families, and patriotic friends. Two weeks after its organization the company was ordered to active duty at Fort Johnston, Smithville (now Southport), N.C., to aid in defense of the essential port of Wilmington. The Confederate Greys of the North Carolina Volunteers made an enviable record for itself during the war; after reorganization it was known as Company E of the Twentieth Regiment.

In 1862 Denson was transferred to staff duty; subsequently, in view of his knowledge of mathematics and engineering, he was commissioned a lieutenant in the Second Engineer Troops. Stationed first at Wrightsville, he later took part in arduous preparations and fighting as the tide of war advanced up the Cape Fear valley. Many years later, he was to write for Walter Clark's *Histories* of the North Carolina Regiments (1901) the article on the Engineer Corps of the Army of the Confederacy. Captain Denson never surrendered to the Union flag. Just before the war ended he, with his corps, was ordered to South Carolina to await further orders. Those orders never came.

Immediately after the war, Denson opened the Pittsboro Scientific Academy at the seat of Chatham County. It succeeded the well-known Pittsborough Academy, which had been established under authority of an Act of the General Assembly ratified in January 1787 and where many citizens of later prominence in the state received their education.

In 1887 Denson, at fifty years of age, moved to Raleigh where for ten years he was coprincipal, with Professor Hugh Morson, of the Raleigh Male Academy. At that time the school's average attendance was one hundred pupils. Required courses were orthography, penmanship, English composition, and declamation; other subjects included English, Latin, Greek, French, and German languages and literature, bookkeeping and mathematics, and the natural sciences. The Raleigh Male Academy was located one block from the new governor's mansion. Its students marched as a body in the parade at Raleigh's Centennial Celebration in 1892, each wearing the city colors and a white silk badge bearing Raleigh's emblem, the oak tree. A member of the board of managers of the Centennial Celebration and chairman of two of its subcommittees, Denson played an active part in the planning and presentation of the elaborate four-day program.

In all Captain Denson, as he continued to be called, was a teacher of young North Carolinians for forty years. He was a president of the North Carolina Teachers' Assembly. During the last fourteen years of his life he was secretary of the State Board of Public Charities, which supervised the state's charitable and penal institutions. One of his main interests was an effort to establish a reformatory for young criminals in North Carolina. To this end he prepared bills and appeared before legislative committees to urge their passage. Such an institution, the Stonewall Jackson Training School at Concord, was opened six years after Denson's death. He was on the commission for selecting the site and plans for the Western Insane Asylum of North Carolina, now the Broughton Hospital, at Morganton. For almost twenty-five years he was treasurer and assistant secretary of the North Carolina State Agricultural Society; its major function was to organize and present a program of importance to commercial and community life in North Carolina—the State Fair held annually in Raleigh. For nine years he was secretary of the North Carolina Confederate Veterans Association. In 1889 this group cited the need of a home for helpless, disabled veterans, raised funds by subscription, and opened a suitable building at Polk and East streets in Raleigh at a rental of $12.50 a month. It was soon full to overflowing, and on 16 Feb. 1891 the legislature passed an act leading to the state-financed Soldiers' Home on New Bern Avenue.

An eloquent speaker, Denson was invited to make commemorative addresses on many public occasions.

At St. Bartholomew's Episcopal Church in Pittsboro on 4 Jan. 1863, Denson married Margaret Matilda Cowan, daughter of Thomas and Mary Ashe London Cowan. The bride's parents, originally from their plantation at Old Town on the Cape Fear near Wilmington, had refugeed to the little village of Pittsboro in 1862. Of this union, Denson was survived by four sons: Thomas Cowan, Lee Armistead (m. Jane Saunders), Eugene Grissom (m. Julia McInnis), and Claude Baker (m. Gertrude Satterfield); and three daughters: Sarah Cowan, Mary Ashe Baker, and Kate Whiting (m. Richard Beverly Raney of Raleigh). Kate, at age twenty-two, designed and painted the flag of the city of Raleigh, which was borne by the cruiser USS *Raleigh* after its memorable service in the Spanish-American War; it was also used during World War I.

Denson died in Raleigh at the age of sixty-five. Funeral services were held at Christ Church, Raleigh, of which he had long been a communicant. Burial was in the family plot at St. Bartholomew's Church, Pittsboro.

SEE: Board of Public Charities of North Carolina, *Annual Report, 1909* (1910); *Centennial Celebration of Raleigh, N.C., 1792–1892* (1893); C. B. Denson, "The Corps of Engineers and Engineer Troops," *Histories of the Several Regiments and Battalions from North Carolina in the Great War, 1861–'65*, ed. Walter Clark, vol. 4 (1901); Sarah Cowan Denson, "Family Tree," 1938 (in possession of R. B. Raney, M.D., Chapel Hill); Wade Hadley and others, eds., *Chatham County, 1771–1971* (1971); Faison W. and Pearl C. McGowen, eds., *Flashes of Duplin's History and Government* (1971); J. B. Oliver and others, *History of Company E, 20th North Carolina Regiment, 1861–'65, Confederate Greys* (1905); Raleigh *News and Observer*, 16 Jan. 1903; *Raleigh Times*, 20 Feb. 1969; Charles L. Raper, *The Church and Private Schools of North Carolina* (1898); Royal G. Shannonhouse, ed., *St. Bartholomew's Parish, Pittsboro, North Carolina, 1833–1933* (1933); Charles L. Smith, *The History of Education in North Carolina* (1888).

R. BEVERLY RANEY, JR.

**De Rosset (DeRosett), Armand John** *(17 Nov. 1767–1 Apr. 1859)*, physician, was born in Wilmington, the son of Moses John and Mary Ivy De Rosset and grandson of Armand John De Rosset. His father died when De Rosset was an infant, but he was affectionately reared by his stepfather, Adam Boyd, who also served as his efficient teacher at home. Well equipped with a rudimentary education, the youth continued his studies at a school in Hillsborough before enrolling at Nassau Hall (now Princeton University), from which he was graduated in 1787. He then completed his medical education at the University of Pennsylvania, where he was privileged to number Benjamin Franklin and Dr. Benjamin Rush among his acquaintances. At age twenty-three he returned to Wilmington and began to practice medicine, adding to the record begun by his forebears and continued later by his descendants as a physician and respected citizen.

De Rosset married Mary Fullerton, whose father was John Fullerton, a nephew of the Scottish philosopher David Hume, and whose mother was Elizabeth Toomer Fullerton. The couple had three daughters who died in infancy, and one son, Moses John De Rosset, born 11 Feb. 1796. The following year Mrs. De Rosset died, and on 1 Aug. 1799 Armand John married her sister, Catherine Fullerton. The children of the second marriage were Catherine G., Elizabeth Ann, Magdalen Mary, Mary Jane, Armand John, and two sons who died in infancy.

On 10 Oct. 1814 De Rosset was commissioned a surgeon in the Third Regiment of the North Carolina Militia, which was his only military service. For many years he served as a justice of the peace. He was not a frivolous man and organized the Nine-Penny Whist Club more to provide occasions on which the members could enjoy congenial discussions than to play cards. Members of his family had always served as wardens, vestrymen, lay readers, and treasurers of Saint James's Church—both while it was Anglican and later when it became a part of the Protestant Episcopal church—and he was active in all of its affairs. He assisted in the founding of the Bible Society in Wilmington in 1816, serving as vice-president and later as president. An affluent citizen, De Rosset was a director of the Bank of Cape Fear for thirty-seven years. He also invested $10,000 in The Rockfish Company and a similar sum in the road that became the Wilmington and Weldon Railroad.

A contemporary described De Rosset as "short in stature, being not over five feet four inches, with light blue eyes and ruddy complexion; not handsome, though a benign expression lent a pleasing and attractive appearance to his countenance." He was buried in Saint James's Churchyard, Wilmington.

SEE: "Autobiographical Sketch by Dr. Armand John De Rosset, in 1847," *James Sprunt Historical Monograph* 4 (1903); De Rosset Family Papers, Group 1 (Southern Historical Collection, University of North Carolina, Chapel Hill); Catherine De Rosset Meares, *Annals of the De Rosset Family* (1906); New Hanover County wills (New Hanover County courthouse, Wilmington); Durward T. Stokes, "Adam Boyd, Publisher, Preacher, and Patriot," *North Carolina Historical Review* 49 (1972).

DURWARD T. STOKES

**De Rosset, Lewis Henry** *(ca. 1724–22 Feb. 1786)*, planter and colonial officer, was the son of Armand J. and Madeline De Rosset. His father was a Swiss-educated physician who immigrated to North Carolina about 1736. By 1741 the De Rossets were residing in Wilmington. Lewis initially pursued a mercantile career but, like many colonial figures, he also had agricultural interests and referred to himself as a planter in a letter written in 1759. As was the case with his brother, Moses John, who was mayor of Wilmington during the critical period of the Stamp Act crisis, Lewis was active in politics. He was sheriff of New Hanover County in 1748, justice of the peace in 1751, and Assembly representative from Wilmington in 1751–52. Early in 1753 he was elevated to the royal council, but he did not begin active service there until after the arrival of Governor Arthur Dobbs in October 1754. From that time until the final executive session in June 1775, he was a regular participant in council meetings.

De Rosset was closely allied with Governor Dobbs and consistently supported his programs. In return, the chief executive rewarded the faithful councillor. De Rosset was appointed judge of the southern court of oyer and terminer in the summer of 1757 and replaced John Rutherfurd as receiver general later that year. He would hold that lucrative position until Rutherfurd was reinstated three years later by order of the Privy Council.

In addition to a house in Wilmington, De Rosset owned a plantation called Red Banks eight miles northeast of the town. He possessed 31 slaves and not less than 3,000 acres of land. Married to the former Margaret Walker of Wilmington, the couple had no children. During the campaign against the Regulators in 1771, De Rosset served as a lieutenant general. He had previously been a colonel of the Johnston County militia as early as 1754.

On 30 Apr. 1779 De Rosset fled Wilmington for the loyalist sanctuary of New York with as many possessions as he could carry. However, his ship was captured by an American privateer and taken to New London, Conn. De Rosset was stripped of all his goods and sent to New York in June under a flag of truce. When Sir Henry Clinton sailed to attack Charleston late in 1779, De Rosset accompanied him after offering to lend his considerable knowledge of the area. Clinton made De Rosset chief commissary of prisoners in Charleston, a post that he held until evacuation of the city by British troops at the close of the war. De Rosset then went to London and in July 1783 claimed losses of £10,000 sterling on his confiscated North Carolina property. He further told the Loyalist Claims Commission that when revolutionaries had ordered him to sign the oath of allegiance in Wilmington in 1779, he refused to do so and had been banished for it. Supporting letters from governors William Tryon and Josiah Martin attested to De Rosset's years of loyalty and service. On 22 Feb. 1786 De Rosset died in London with little compensation for his great losses in North Carolina.

SEE: Kemp P. Battle, ed., *Letters and Documents Relating to the Early History of the Lower Cape Fear* (1903); De Rosset Family Papers (Southern Historical Collection, University of North Carolina, Chapel Hill); Donald R. Lennon and Ida Brooks Kellam, *The Wilmington Town Book* (1973); Loyalist claims (transcripts, North Carolina State Archives, Raleigh); William S. Price, Jr., " 'Men of Good Estates': Wealth Among North Carolina's Royal Councillors," *North Carolina Historical Review* 49 (1972); William L. Saunders, ed., *Colonial Records of North Carolina*, vols. 5–10 (1887–90).

WILLIAM S. PRICE, JR.

**De Rosset, Moses John** *(27 Dec. 1726–1767)*, physician, was the son of Armand John De Rosset, a French Huguenot physician, and his Swiss-born wife. The couple left France after their first children, Gabrielle and Lewis Henry, were born and visited London, where Moses John was born. Within the decade, the De Rossets arrived in Wilmington, N.C., where the doctor established himself as a medical practitioner and influential citizen. Medicine appealed to his descendants as a profession to the extent that there was a De Rosset physician in Wilmington until 1881. Nothing is known of the early years of Moses John until he was sent on a sea voyage to prevent a marriage of which his parents disapproved. Unfortunately, he was captured by either Spanish or Algerian privateers and confined for two years, after which the chastened youth returned to North Carolina and applied himself to the study of medicine. He then followed in his father's footsteps as a physician and influential citizen of Wilmington.

On 7 Jan. 1754, De Rosset was commissioned captain in the North Carolina regiment commanded by Colonel James Innes and served in this command during the French and Indian War. For many years he was one of the justices for New Hanover County and served on the governing board for Wilmington; in January 1766 he was elected mayor of the port city. Although his brother, Lewis Henry, was a prominent loyalist who was finally exiled, the mayor was a staunch patriot and a leader in the resistance to the hated Stamp Act, although he wrote conciliatory letters to Governor William Tryon after the affair was settled. Moses John De Rosset was also a devout Anglican and a faithful member of St. James's Church, which his father had helped to found. In 1759 he married Mary Ivy, whose sister, Ann, married James Moore. The De Rossets had two children, Magdalene Mary and Armand John. De Rosset was buried in St. James's Churchyard. He left a comfortable estate to his widow, who for several years used the knowledge gleaned from her husband's medical practice to minister to the physical needs of those around her. In May 1774 she married Adam Boyd; after the American Revolution failing health prevented her from accompanying him to his clerical post in Georgia, and she made her home with her daughter, Mrs. Henry Toomer, until her death in 1798.

SEE: Deeds of New Hanover County (New Hanover County Courthouse, Wilmington); De Rosset Family Papers, Group 1 (Southern Historical Collection, University of North Carolina, Chapel Hill); Catherine De Rosset Meares, *Annals of the De Rosset Family* (1906); William L. Saunders, ed., *Colonial Records of North Carolina*, vols. 4, 5, 7 (1886–88); Durward T. Stokes, "Adam Boyd, Publisher, Preacher, and Patriot," *North Carolina Historical Review* 49 (1972).

DURWARD T. STOKES

**De Rosset, Moses John** *(4 July 1838–1 May 1881)*, physician, teacher, and editor, was born in Pittsboro but his parents made their home in Wilmington. His father, Dr. Armand John De Rosset (1807–1897), and grandfather, Dr. Armand John De Rosset (1767–1859), were distinguished physicians in Wilmington; his mother was Eliza Jane Lord. In 1854 he was sent to Geneva, Switzerland, to study at Diedrich's Academy. He returned to the United States in 1857, and in the following year entered the medical department of the University of New York under the private tutelage of Dr. Gunning S. Bedford; he was graduated in 1860. The same year he was appointed a resident physician at Bellevue Hospital in New York City.

At the outbreak of the Civil War, De Rosset entered the Second Medical Division of the Confederate Army where he served as an assistant surgeon of artillery under General "Stonewall" Jackson's command. In 1863 he was made a full surgeon and was placed in charge of General Hospital Number 4, the officers' hospital in Richmond. He was later appointed inspector of hospitals for the Department of Henrico.

In 1865 De Rosset moved to Baltimore where he was appointed an adjunct professor of chemistry in the Medical Department and a professor of chemistry in the Dental College at the University of Maryland. He served as secretary of the Maryland Academy of Science in 1868. Leaving Baltimore in 1873, De Rosset moved his practice in diseases of the eye and ear to Wilmington. There he was instrumental in establishing the *North Carolina Medical Journal*, the publication of the North Carolina Medical Society, and served as an associate editor from 1878 until his death. In 1878 he moved to New York City where he was appointed consulting ophthalmic and aural surgeon at St. Elizabeth's Hospital. He left New York in 1879 to start a practice in San Antonio, Tex., but returned to New York within a few months. In October 1880 he suffered a paralytic stroke; he died in New York the following year at the age of forty-three.

De Rosset was known for his teaching ability and his success as a practitioner. He was the author of several papers on ophthalmology, otology, and physiology of vision and audition which were published in various medical journals. His most notable publication was a translation of *Bouchardat's Annuaire*, entitled *Annual Abstract of Therapeutics, Materia Medica, Pharmacy and Toxicology for 1867 by A. Bouchardat*. On 13 Oct. 1863 he married Adelaide Savage Meares of Wilmington; they had nine children: Kathryn Davis, Edward Meares, Armand

John, John Lord, Eliza Jane, Adelaide Savage, Graham Daves, Addis Emmet, and May Ivie. He was buried in Oakdale Cemetery, Wilmington.

SEE: *DAB*, vol. 3 (1959); De Rosset Family Papers (Southern Historical Collection, University of North Carolina, Chapel Hill); *North Carolina Medical Journal* 2 (1878), 4 (1879), 6 (1880), 7 (1881); Leonidas L. Polk, *Handbook of North Carolina* (1879); Ludlow P. Strong, *List of Direct Descendants of the de Rosset Family* (1948).

J. MARSHALL BULLOCK

**De Rosset, William Lord** *(27 Oct. 1832–14 Aug. 1910)*, soldier and businessman, was the eldest son and second of eleven children of Dr. Armand John De Rosset III and Eliza Jane Lord. The De Rosset family originated in France from which the founder of the Wilmington branch, Lewis Henry De Rosset, fled after the revocation of the Edict of Nantes. Four succeeding generations including William Lord De Rosset's father, all physicians, resided in Wilmington and were prominent civic leaders.

Born in Wilmington, De Rosset was educated successively at St. Timothy's Hall in Catonsville, Md.; St. James College near Hagerstown, Md.; and The University of North Carolina, which he left in 1851 at the end of his first term as a junior. Apparently he preferred active endeavors to the more passive pursuits of scholarly study. Upon leaving college he became an apprentice in the Lawrence Machine Shops, Lawrence, Mass., in an attempt to become a machinist and mechanical engineer. When the New England climate proved too severe for his delicate health, he returned to Wilmington where he helped to establish the Clarendon Iron Works. In 1860 he became a member of the commission house of De Rosset and Brown, organized by his father and John Potts Brown in 1839.

De Rosset was particularly interested in the military, however; he considered it his most gratifying and successful undertaking and the one of which he was proudest. Joining the Wilmington Light Infantry in 1854, he was given the rank of lieutenant and then captain in 1856. Governor John W. Ellis ordered the company into service in April 1861. On 6 May 1861 De Rosset was appointed major and assigned to the Third North Carolina Regiment. He was promoted to lieutenant colonel in 1862, saw action in the Richmond area, and succeeded to the command of the regiment as colonel upon the death of his brother-in-law, Colonel Gaston Meares. De Rosset came back to North Carolina in the summer of 1862 to enlist new recruits but returned to Virginia to serve throughout the autumn campaign. At Antietam he received such a serious wound in the lower part of his body that he was pronounced dead on the battlefield and the newspapers prematurely published his obituary. Permanently disabled by the injury, he reluctantly resigned his commission in July 1863 after which he assisted his father in blockade-running. In January 1865 President Jefferson Davis appointed De Rosset colonel in the Invalid Corps, P.A.C.S. He surrendered with General Joseph E. Johnston's army in April 1865.

After the war De Rosset and his father organized De Rosset & Company, a continuation of their prewar commission trade. In 1881 the younger De Rosset joined the Navassa Guano Company as superintendent of agencies. He became secretary and treasurer of the organization, positions that he held until poor health forced him to resign just before his death.

De Rosset was particularly active in community affairs. When the surviving commissioned officers in the Third North Carolina Regiment organized the Third North Carolina Infantry Association in 1865, De Rosset as senior officer was made president for life. He was president of the Cape Fear Agricultural Association in 1870, president of the Chamber of Commerce in 1872, master of the Orient Lodge of Masons in 1886, and alderman of Wilmington for many years. He served as commander of the Cape Fear Camp Confederate Veterans and major general of the North Carolina Division of the United Confederate Veterans. He was also a vestryman and senior warden of St. James's Episcopal Church, a member of the standing committee of the Diocese of North Carolina and East Carolina, and treasurer of the Diocese of East Carolina.

On 12 Dec. 1854 De Rosset married Caroline Horatia Nelson; after her death on 10 Nov. 1861, he wed Elizabeth Simpson Nash on 10 June 1863. By the first marriage there were two children, Annie and William Lord, Jr.; by the second, six children, Armand John, Mary, Henry Nash, Kate, Frederick Nash, and Anita. De Rosset died at his home in Wilmington after an extended illness of several months. After a military funeral he was buried in Oakdale Cemetery, Wilmington. An excellent picture of William Lord De Rosset accompanied his obituary in the Wilmington *Morning Star*.

SEE: W. L. De Rosset, ed. and comp., *Pictorial and Historical New Hanover County and Wilmington, North Carolina, 1723–1938* (1938); L. P. Strong, *List of Direct Descendants of the de Rosset Family* (1948); Autobiographical sketch by W. L. De Rosset and biography of W. L. De Rosset in the manuscripts of Charles Van Noppen (Manuscripts Division, Library, Duke University); the Wilmington *Morning Star*, 16 Aug. 1910.

ALAN D. WATSON

**de Roulhac.** *See* **Roulhac.**

**Devereux, John** *(11 Mar. 1761–1 July 1844)*, merchant, planter, and influential citizen of New Bern and Raleigh, was born in County Wexford, Ireland. According to family sources Devereux, a younger son, was sent to St. Omar in France to prepare for the Roman Catholic priesthood. He rejected that profession while still quite young, but he remained a Roman Catholic throughout his life. He apparently obtained a commission in the British navy sometime before the American Revolution and saw action with the royal navy in that war and elsewhere, eventually attaining the rank of lieutenant. Several years later, however, Devereux resigned his commission and settled in Charleston, S.C., where he joined a "Mr. Fitzsimmons" as partner in a shipping and trading firm.

During one business trip on board a company ship in the late 1780s, Devereux was shipwrecked off Cape Hatteras and forced to remain in North Carolina while determining the company's losses. During this period he visited New Bern where he decided to settle and where he met his future wife, Frances Pollock (18 Mar. 1771–3 June 1849), whom he married in 1790. She was the daughter of Thomas and Eunice Edwards Pollock, the granddaughter of theologian Jonathan Edwards, and the great-granddaughter of Governor Thomas Pollock. Through her father's estate she eventually inherited eight plantations plus "7500 milled Spanish pieces of eight." This wealth, coupled with the capital accumulated by Devereux, firmly established them in the upper economic level of the state.

Devereux continued in the mercantile business with two partners, Stephen M. Chester and Robert V. Orme, trading between New York, Charleston, and the West Indies. He also managed his wife's estate and purchased land and slaves himself in Craven and Wake counties. His success in business was widely recognized by his contemporaries, one description by Stephen Miller stating that "His wealth and dignified character had a sensible influence on society, and in business circles his name was similar to that of Rothschild in Europe." Devereux apparently studied law as well because he bequeathed his law library to his only surviving son, Thomas Pollock Devereux. His other son, George Pollock Devereux, died in 1837 after a short illness; his only daughter, Frances Ann Devereux, married Leonidas Polk, the Episcopal bishop and Confederate general, and lived in Louisiana.

In addition to his business enterprises, Devereux supported various educational institutions in North Carolina—among them The University of North Carolina and the Griffin Free School for "indigent Scholars," New Bern, where he was a trustee. He also insisted on good educations for both of his sons, sending them to Yale for their degrees and legal training. Frances Devereux, who supported several charitable institutions with her own money, was one of the founders of the First Presbyterian Church in New Bern. Her will enumerated a long list of institutions and people to whom she bequeathed money.

When Thomas Pollock Devereux moved to Raleigh to live while serving as a federal district attorney and as clerk for the state supreme court in the 1820s, John and Frances Devereux accompanied him, purchasing a two-acre lot near the present Peace College. John Devereux later added other city property to his holdings, and sold portions of it to the Raleigh and Gaston Railroad in an effort to promote its success. He continued his interest in the New Bern business but left its immediate control to his son, George.

Devereux died in Raleigh and was buried in the family plot at the City Cemetery. He directed that his Raleigh house and property be left to his wife. The proceeds from the sale of his New Bern house and business property were ordered combined with the remainder of his North Carolina estate, except for one hundred slaves bequeathed to Frances Devereux Polk, all of which was to be divided between his son Thomas and his grandson and namesake, John Devereux. The estate amounted to approximately $800,000 due to the inclusion of his wife's Pollock property, which they jointly agreed should descend to their heirs. Frances Devereux continued to live in Raleigh until her death; she was buried next to her husband in the City Cemetery.

SEE: Kemp P. Battle, *History of the University of North Carolina*, vol. 1 (1907); Charles L. Coon, *The Beginnings of Public Education in North Carolina, A Documentary History, 1790–1840*, vol. 1 (1908); John Devereux Account Book (Southern Historical Collection, University of North Carolina, Chapel Hill); John Devereux Papers (North Carolina State Archives, Raleigh); Margaret Devereux, *Plantation Sketches* (1906); Margaret Engelhard and Katherine Devereux Mackay, "Hinsdale Genealogy" (unpublished typescript, North Carolina State Archives, Raleigh); *First Census of the U.S. 1790* (1908); Stephen F. Miller, *Recollections of Newbern Fifty Years Ago* (1873); North Carolina Wills, Wake County (North Carolina State Archives, Raleigh); Pollock-Devereux Papers (North Carolina State Archives, Raleigh); *Raleigh Register*, 13 May 1830, 4 July 1844, 6 June 1849.

TERRELL L. ARMISTEAD

**Devereux, John, Jr.** *(17 Dec. 1820–10 Apr. 1893)*, planter and chief quartermaster for North Carolina during the Civil War, was born in Raleigh, the only surviving son of Thomas Pollock (17 Nov. 1793–7 Mar. 1869) and Catherine Ann Bayard Johnson Devereux (1796–18 July 1836). His mother was from Connecticut; his father, the son of John and Frances Pollock Devereux, was a native North Carolinian who resided at his plantation, Conneconara, in Halifax County. Thomas P. Devereux had practiced law and served as reporter for the state supreme court (1826–39) before he decided to concentrate on farming. John Devereux had six sisters, Frances, Elizabeth, Catherine Ann, Mary Bayard, Honoria, and Sophia Chester, among whom Mary Bayard (Mrs. William J. Clarke) became a noted North Carolina poet and writer. Little else is known about Devereux's early life except that he and his sisters received extensive educations during adolescence.

Devereux, whose "predominate trait was a genuine love of books," was graduated from Yale with distinction in 1840. Returning to North Carolina, he briefly practiced law and helped manage his family's extensive Devereux-Pollock estates. In 1842 he married Margaret Mordecai (19 Oct. 1824–10 Mar. 1910), the daughter of Moses and Ann Lane Mordecai of Raleigh, after which he relied on farming as his major source of income. His plantation, Runiroi Meadows on the Roanoke River in Bertie County, had belonged formerly to John Devereux, Sr., the grandfather after whom John Devereux, Jr., was named. It then passed to his father, Thomas P. Devereux, who sold it to John Devereux in 1846. The elder Devereux also left his grandson a sizable inheritance in 1844, independent of that which descended to his own son. This inheritance enabled the Devereux to live at Runiroi during the winter and in Raleigh during the summer season. From her mother Margaret Devereux had inherited an old Lane family home in Raleigh, Wills Forest, which became the favorite residence of the Devereux family. The Devereux attended Christ Church in Raleigh, and John Devereux served as a trustee for the Griffin Free School both before and after it was moved from New Bern to Raleigh.

The seemingly stable and prosperous life of John Devereux, Jr., became, by the 1850s, increasingly mired in debt. His farming partnership with his father and their joint and individual ownership of over fifteen hundred slaves left little cash for other expenditures unless crops were consistently good. The 1850s were lean years in crop production, however, and Devereux grew increasingly concerned about the fact that both he and his father had to "live by borrowing." The advent of the Civil War multiplied these problems and led to the financial ruin of the family.

Upon North Carolina's secession, Devereux considered raising his own volunteer infantry company or joining his brother-in-law's (Patrick M. Edmondston, who married Catherine Ann Devereux) volunteer cavalry troop. Instead, he accepted a commission as assistant commissary of subsistence with the rank of captain in May 1861. His competent performance that summer earned him a promotion to chief quartermaster with the rank of major in September 1861, although he personally felt that the Commissary Department was "reaping the fruits of political favoritism" and that "the whole concern Confederate and State is going or rather has already gone to the dogs."

As chief quartermaster, Devereux was responsible for supplying North Carolina troops with numerous provisions, clothing, and food. He also hoped to meet the needs of private citizens as much as possible. His agents canvassed North Carolina and other southern states for goods, and contracts were established with factories and private citizens to manufacture a variety of items. One of the most time-consuming and important areas Devereux managed was the state's blockade-running business, which brought goods from the West Indies into Wilmington in exchange for cotton. The state's blockade-running account required floating loans, buying cotton, procuring ships for transportation, and other details; it eventually totaled over $12 million and was a resounding success. The proficiency of the Quartermaster Department's work was reflected in the quantity of goods and food flowing not only to North Carolina's troops and citizens, but also to the armies in Virginia and Tennessee. It prompted the Confederate government in 1863 to offer Devereux the post of tithing collector for the state, due to his "first-rate business qualifications." Devereux declined the post, however.

When the state's Confederate government collapsed, Devereux served as a member of the Raleigh delegation sent to General Sherman to arrange terms for the city. This was his final act as the state's chief quartermaster. After the war he lived quietly in Raleigh with his family and struggled to keep ahead of debts incurred before, during, and after the war. These problems, compounded by the loss of capital invested in slaves and his inability to profitably operate his plantations thereafter, forced him to seek work within the city. He opened a small insurance company and worked briefly as clerk to the superintendent of public instruction, but this failed to produce the required income. Equally troublesome was the bankruptcy in 1868 of his father, whose debts totaled over $257,000. John Devereux had to pay these along with his own; this required him to sell most of the land that had been in his family since the early 1700s. Upon his death, his wife Margaret was obliged to sell Wills Forest as well as its surrounding 150 acres to meet the remaining demands on his estate.

The Devereux's private lives after the war were not entirely happy either. Their six daughters—Annie Lane, Katherine (Mrs. J. J. Mackay), Ellen (Mrs. John Hinsdale), Margaret (Mrs. Samuel Ashe), Mary Livingstone (Mrs. Arthur Winslow), and Laura—all remained deeply attached to their parents. But the two sons—Thomas Pollock and John Devereux—were disappointments. Thomas, a lawyer and the eldest son, joined the Republican party "which was a disgrace to the family," whereas John, who was "bad through and through," eventually left the state and moved to Oklahoma.

Devereux died in Raleigh after a long illness and was buried in Oakwood Cemetery. His wife continued to live in Raleigh in a house on North Person Street until her death.

SEE: *Business Directory of the City of Raleigh, North Carolina, 1887* (North Carolina State Archives, Raleigh); Walter Clark, *Histories of the Several Regiments and Battalions from North Carolina in the Great War 1861–'65*, vol. 1 (1901 [portrait]), "The Raising, Organization and Equipment of North Carolina Troops During the Civil War," *The North Carolina Booklet* 19 (1919); John Devereux letter, August 1859 (in possession of Mrs. Graham Barden, New Bern); John Devereux Papers (North Carolina State Archives, Raleigh); Margaret Devereux, *Plantation Sketches* (1906); Catherine Ann Devereux Edmondston Diaries (North Carolina State Archives, Raleigh); Eighth Census of the United States, 1860, Slave Schedules, Bertie, Halifax, and Wake counties (North Carolina State Archives, Raleigh); Margaret Engelhard and Katherine Devereux Mackay, "Hinsdale Genealogy" (unpublished typescript, North Carolina State Archives, Raleigh); Daniel H. Hill, *Bethel to Sharpsburg*, vol. 1 (1926); Hugh T. Lefler and Albert R. Newsome, *The History of a Southern State, North Carolina* (1973); George Mordecai Papers (Southern Historical Collection, University of North Carolina, Chapel Hill); North Carolina deeds, marriage records, and wills, Wake County (North Carolina State Archives, Raleigh); James W. Patton, "Serious Reading in Halifax County, 1860–1865," *North Carolina Historical Review* 42 (1965); Pollock-Devereux Papers (North Carolina State Archives, Raleigh); Quartermaster Letterbooks, Adjutant-General's Records (North Carolina State Archives, Raleigh); Raleigh *Daily Standard*, 4 Nov. 1863; Raleigh *News and Observer*, 12 Apr. 1893; *Raleigh Register*, 13 May 1830, 27 May 1842, 4 July 1844, 6 June 1849; Seventh Census of the United States, 1850, Slave Schedules, Bertie, Halifax, and Wake counties (North Carolina State Archives, Raleigh); Wake County Church Records, Christ Church Minutes, 1860–79 (North Carolina State Archives, Raleigh); James G. Wilson and John Fiske, eds., *Appleton's Cyclopaedia of American Biography*, vol. 2 (1887).

TERRELL L. ARMISTEAD

**Devereux, Thomas Pollock** *(17 Nov. 1793–7 Mar. 1869)*, lawyer and planter, was born at New Bern, the oldest of the three children of John (1761–1844) and Frances Pollock Devereux (1771–1849). John Devereux, a native of Ireland, was a former lieutenant in the British navy. Shipwrecked off the North Carolina coast near New Bern, he had remained in that city where he continued the mercantile business he had previously entered in Charleston, S.C.; he became the owner of a fleet of ships that traded between Boston, Mass., and Barbados. Frances Pollock Devereux, a native of New Bern, was a daughter of Eunice Edwards Pollock (1743–1822), the seventh daughter and eighth child of theologian Jonathan Edwards (1703–58), and of Thomas Pollock III (d. 1777), grandson of Thomas Pollock of Balgra (1654–1722), a native of Glasgow, Scotland, who came to North Carolina about 1700 and twice (1712–14 and 1722) served as acting governor of proprietary North Carolina. Thomas Pollock Devereux's sister, Frances, was the wife of Leonidas Polk (1806–64), Episcopal bishop of Louisiana and lieutenant general in the Confederate Army. Through the second marriage (1800) of his grandmother, Eunice Edwards, to a Mr. Hunt, Devereux was a half-cousin of Thomas Pollock Burgwyn.

In 1813 Devereux was graduated from Yale College, where he was a schoolmate of George E. Badger (1795–1866), later a prominent North Carolina lawyer and politician, and Elisha Mitchell (1793–1857), who would become a distinguished professor of mathematics and science in The University of North Carolina. Both men became Devereux's lifelong friends. Devereux chose the law as his profession but for some years did not actively seek clients because he already had a competent fortune. Business reverses, however, eventually compelled him to devote his full energies to the duties of the bar. He soon attained both a large practice and a reputation for unusual legal ability, especially in equity cases. He was appointed U.S. attorney for the District of North

Carolina and served competently in that position for many years. In 1826 he became joint reporter with George E. Badger of the North Carolina Supreme Court and soon was made the sole occupant of the post following Badger's resignation. Devereux produced four volumes of law and two volumes of equity reports. In 1834 he obtained the assistance of William Horn Battle in reporting the court's decisions.

Devereux was influential in persuading William Gaston in 1833 to accept an appointment to the state supreme court. Though convinced of the continued need for the court, which had been created in 1818, he was aware that it was unpopular throughout the state. Devereux believed that it could be saved from abolition by the legislature only if a lawyer of Gaston's ability and prestige could be secured to fill the vacancy created by the death of Chief Justice John Louis Taylor in 1829.

Upon the death of his uncle, George Pollock (1772–1839), Devereux inherited the care and management of a large family estate, consisting mostly of several plantations and some fifteen hundred slaves. These duties forced him to abandon the legal profession, and he spent the remainder of his life in agricultural pursuits and such public service as he could render as justice of the peace and as a presiding justice of the county court of Halifax.

Devereux was married twice. His first wife, Catherine Ann Johnson of Connecticut, was a lineal descendant of Samuel Johnson (1696–1772), the first president of Kings College, New York City, and his son, William Samuel Johnson (1727–1819), the first president of Columbia University, the successor institution of Kings College. She was also related to the Bayard, Livingston, and other Knickerbocker families. Following Catherine Ann's death on 18 July 1836, Devereux married a Miss Maitland of New York who outlived him. The father of a numerous progeny, he was survived by one son and seven daughters as well as several grandchildren. His son John, an 1840 graduate of Yale College who served as North Carolina quartermaster during the Civil War, married Margaret Mordecai (1824–1910), a daughter of Moses Mordecai, a prominent Raleigh attorney. They were the parents of Thomas Pollock Devereux II, who served as a courier in the Confederate Army of Northern Virginia (1863–65) and whose letters to his parents and his sister (now in the State Archives in Raleigh) give detailed descriptions of army life and of the battles in which he participated.

Devereux's daughter Frances was the wife of Henry W. Miller, Wake County lawyer and Whig leader, whom she married on 15 June 1837. Catherine Ann, her mother's namesake, who married Patrick M. Edmondston of South Carolina, kept a diary of her experiences as a North Carolina planter's wife during the Civil War; it reveals her to have been a well-educated, widely read woman of penetrating intelligence who was fond of playing chess with her father, the resident of a neighboring plantation. Another daughter, Mary Bayard Devereux Clarke, was a novelist and poet of note.

In his seventy-sixth year Devereux died at his plantation, Conneconara, on the Roanoke River in Halifax County. His remains were taken to Raleigh and interred in the City Cemetery. In politics he was a Whig. Although a staunch Unionist prior to the state's secession in 1861, he loyally supported the Confederate cause during the Civil War. Postwar emancipation deprived him of slave property valued at $750,000. From early life he was a communicant of the Episcopal church, though both his mother and his maternal grandmother were charter members of the First Presbyterian Church in New Bern and his mother gave money for the first Presbyterian manse in Raleigh. Apparently no portrait of Devereux exists. Portraits of his parents, his uncle, George Pollock, and his daughter-in-law, Margaret Mordecai Devereux, are reproduced in the *North Carolina Portrait Index, 1700–1860* (1963).

SEE: George Edmund Badger Papers, John Devereux Account Book, Margaret Mordecai Devereux Papers, Thomas Pollock Devereux Papers, William Gaston Papers (Southern Historical Collection, University of North Carolina, Chapel Hill); Beth G. Crabtree and James W. Patton, eds., *"Journal of a Secesh Lady": The Diary of Catherine Ann Devereux Edmondston, 1860–1866* (1979); Edward Jones Hale Papers, Charles E. Johnston Collection, John Devereux Papers, Thomas Pollock Devereux Letter Book, Pollock Papers, Pollock-Devereux Papers (North Carolina State Archives, Raleigh); James W. Patton, "Serious Reading in Halifax County, 1860–65," *North Carolina Historical Review* 42 (1965); Raleigh *Daily Standard*, 10, 11 Mar. 1866; L. C. Vass, *History of the Presbyterian Church in New Bern, N.C. . . .* (1886).

W. CONARD GASS

**Deweese, John Thomas** *(4 June 1835–4 July 1906)*, Union soldier and North Carolina congressman, was one of the most remarkable men who scrambled to prominence in North Carolina as a result of the Civil War and Reconstruction. His career was characterized by political opportunism and amoral conduct. A native of Van Buren, Crawford County, Ark., Deweese received his first formal education from his mother. Subsequently, he read law and was admitted to the Kentucky bar. In 1856 he opened a practice in Henderson County, remaining there only a short time before moving to Denver, Colo. In 1860 he settled in Pike County, Ind.

In politics Deweese was an old-line Whig, who, upon the demise of the Whig party as a national institution, became an ardent Republican. Early in the Civil War (6 July 1861) he entered Federal service as second lieutenant, Company E, Twenty-fourth Regiment, Indiana Volunteer Infantry. In February 1862 he resigned, but that August he became a captain, and later a lieutenant colonel, in the Fourth Indiana Cavalry. He was honorably discharged in March 1864. In July 1866, when the army was reorganized, he was appointed second lieutenant in the Eighth Regiment, United States Infantry, which was assigned to North Carolina. A rabid political partisan, Deweese soon embraced Radical Republicanism, became active in North Carolina politics, and attacked President Johnson with reckless abandon. At one time he served as judge of provost court for thirty-two eastern North Carolina counties, with Raleigh as his seat. He resigned from the army (under considerable pressure because of his extreme political views) only to be appointed to the lucrative position of commissioner in bankruptcy for North Carolina. There he distinguished himself by charging—and pocketing—exorbitant fees, while urging economically distressed men to apply for bankruptcy with the false assurance that the government would collect all debts owed to them by others. But this post only whetted Deweese's ambitions. In the spring of 1868, when North Carolina had complied with the Congressional Reconstruction acts, he was elected to represent the Fourth District in the Fortieth Congress despite considerable opposition from within his own party. In the regular elections of 1868 he bought the withdrawal from candidacy of

James T. Harris and the support of John A. Hyman, popular Fourth District blacks. Thus, in a time of Conservative impotence, he assured his election to the Forty-first Congress.

In November 1868 Deweese characterized himself as "a Radical Republican" of the Stevens-Butler stripe who believed "Holden & Brownlow the only men who understood how to reconstruct the Gvt in the South & handle Rebels & make treason odious." His actions in Congress were consistent with this avowed philosophy. He sometimes waved the "bloody shirt" and engaged in extravagant and provocative rhetoric. On one occasion when discussing the removal of political disabilities from a North Carolinian whom he did not know, he expressed a willingness to accommodate "deserving men" but concluded: "I do not want to see the gate thrown open so that all these rebels whose hands are red with the blood of my fellow-soldiers shall be brought in." Whereas he opposed the unrestricted right of southern governors to declare martial law, Deweese argued vigorously that arms should be made available to "loyal" men in the South. Claiming that the former rebels were well-armed, he viewed opposition to providing arms to Union men as a Democratic plot to undermine the newly reconstructed state governments and to disperse "us carpet-baggers." He threw down the gauntlet to Conservative Southerners, warning: "Now, I say to them, come on whenever you feel disposed to do so. Stretch forth your traitorous hands and touch one fold of the old flag, and the representatives of four million men, who, although black in skin, are yet white and loyal in heart, will throw themselves as a bulwark between you and these loyal governments, and you will live only in the sad memories of past events. . . . I think it is about time . . . that we ceased consulting these rebels. They grow worse the more we endeavor to coax and please them. The only thing they fear or respect is the mailed hand of power."

Deweese's congressional career ended abruptly on 28 Feb. 1870, when he resigned his seat without explanation. The reasons soon became clear as the House Committee on Military Affairs reported that he had accepted a $500 bribe in return for recommending a cadet for admission to the Naval Academy. The committee declared him "unworthy of a seat in the House of Representatives," indicating that it would have recommended expulsion had he not already resigned. The beleaguered former congressman pleaded ignorance of wrongdoing, indicated that he had merely accommodated a friend, and denied that the money—which had been returned—was a factor. He complained: "Hundreds have done the same thing before and will do it again."

Deweese did not return to North Carolina but took up residence in Cleveland, Ohio. There he practiced law and invested an ill-gained fortune in real estate. By 1876 he had become a Democrat, even serving as a delegate to that party's national convention. During the ensuing campaign, *The Cleveland Plain Dealer* published a sensational Deweese letter recounting the political and fiscal chicanery practiced by himself and other Republicans during the early years of Reconstruction. The *Raleigh Daily Sentinel* gave wide circulation to his allegations, causing deep consternation and chagrin among North Carolina Republicans in a crucial election year. Deweese's own cynicism and moral obtuseness were revealed when he explained his North Carolina career as follows: "I was compelled to pay money for any favor I ever received from the republican party. Their offices appeared to be in the market for sale and I purchased them, like any other doubtful stock on which speculation is made. I know of no friend of mine who had any favor from either his party or its leaders he did not pay for." The nature of Reconstruction politics implied in these remarks provides a sad commentary on the motives and actions of at least some American leaders in a time of grave national crisis.

Deweese died in Washington, D.C., and was buried in Arlington National Cemetery.

SEE: *Biog. Dir. Am. Cong.* (1971); *Congressional Globe* (1868–70); J. G. deR. Hamilton, *Reconstruction in North Carolina* (1906); Charles Lanman Papers (Southern Historical Collection, University of North Carolina, Chapel Hill); *Raleigh Daily Sentinel*, 27 Mar., 16 Apr. 1868, 18 Aug., 2 Sept. 1876; *Raleigh Register*, 4 Mar. 1868.

MAX R. WILLIAMS

**Dewey, Charles** *(28 Nov. 1798–20 Oct. 1880)*, banker, was born in New Bern, the son of John Dewey, who was born 29 Apr. 1767 at Stonington, Conn., and died 22 May 1830 at New Bern. John Dewey, an architect, built the Masonic Temple and Theater in New Bern. Young Dewey's mother was Mary Mitchell Dewey, a native of Elizabeth, N.J., who died in 1839 at the age of sixty-seven.

Virtually nothing is known about Dewey's early life. He began his career in 1820 as a clerk with the New Bern branch of the State Bank of North Carolina. His work was recognized in a tangible way in 1826 when he was appointed cashier of the Fayetteville branch of the same bank. The following year he was elected cashier of "the mother bank" in Raleigh, succeeding William Henry Haywood. On 7 May 1828, one Hu Campbell wrote to Dewey attesting to his integrity, his pleasing personality, and the accuracy of his work. In Raleigh Dewey served as cashier of the Bank of North Carolina and its successor, the Bank of the State of North Carolina. After the Civil War, when that bank was closed, he was elected cashier and later president of the Raleigh National Bank, a position he held at the time of his death. Thus for sixty years he was affiliated with a bank, rising from clerk to president.

Dewey continued working in his later years. Writing to a niece in October 1872, his wife observed that her husband was "so busy all the time in the Bank—has not had recreation this year except those summer drives—We rode until it was too cool for an open carriage, and I only go for the good sweet air, and care not to be shut up, but for old folks we are wonderfully well thus far." Five years later, in a letter of 12 Apr. 1877 to a nephew, Dewey referred to the good health that he and his wife enjoyed.

Dewey was married three times. His first wife was Catherine M. Hall of New Bern; a marriage bond was signed 30 Jan. 1822. His second wife, Ann Letitia Webber, was born in New Bern, 6 Jan. 1803, and died in Raleigh, 17 Nov. 1835; the date of their marriage is not known. On 5 Jan. 1837 he married Juliana ("Julia") Ann Haylander, a native of Philadelphia who moved to Raleigh at an early age; she was born 12 Jan. 1804 and died 21 May 1886, surviving her husband by six years. Four children survived Charles Dewey. One of his sons, Thomas W., married Bessie Lacy, daughter of Dr. Drury Lacy, pastor of Raleigh's First Presbyterian Church. Dewey was a faithful member of the same church for over fifty years, serving as longtime superintendent of its Sunday school and as a ruling elder. In 1837 he presented the church with two communion plates.

Although he owned a few slaves and a moderate

amount of property, Dewey never accumulated vast wealth. He left a house and lot in Charlotte to Anna Maria Dewey, wife of his son Frank H., who resided there. Bonds, notes, stocks, and other property were willed to his wife and his daughters Mary Ann and Rachel D. Wilder. He and his wife resided on Cabarrus Street in Raleigh.

Because the First Presbyterian Church was undergoing repairs, Dewey's funeral was conducted at Raleigh's First Baptist Church. He was buried in Oakwood Cemetery.

SEE: D. L. Corbitt, ed., "Letters from Hugh Luckey, Raleigh Hatter, 1843," *North Carolina Historical Review* 25 (1948); Dewey family record book (in possession of Mrs. Rita C. Dewey, Goldsboro); Charles Dewey Papers (Southern Historical Collection, University of North Carolina, Chapel Hill); Marriage bonds for Craven and Wake counties (North Carolina State Archives, Raleigh); Tombstones, Oakwood Cemetery (Raleigh); Raleigh *News and Observer*, 21 Oct. 1880, 22 May 1886; *Raleigh Register*, 24 Nov. 1835; Records of First Presbyterian Church, Raleigh (North Carolina State Archives, Raleigh); Tax lists for Wake County and Wills of Charles and Julia A. Dewey (North Carolina State Archives, Raleigh).

MEMORY F. MITCHELL

**Dick, Robert Paine** *(5 Oct. 1823–12 Sept. 1898)*, jurist and Union leader, was born in Greensboro, the second son of John McClintock and Parthenia P. Williamson Dick. His father was a state superior court judge for twenty years, and his mother came from a prominent Person County family. After attending local schools, Dick received his college preparatory training at the Caldwell Institute and entered the sophomore class of The University of North Carolina, from which he was graduated with distinction in 1843. Choosing law for his professional career, he studied under his father and George C. Mendenhall; in 1845 he began to practice at Wentworth, the seat of Rockingham County.

In 1848 Dick moved to Greensboro. Four years later he began his political career as a delegate to the Democratic National Convention in Baltimore. An energetic Franklin Pierce supporter, he was named U.S. district attorney by Pierce in 1853 and retained the post until 1861. In 1860 he strongly endorsed the candidacy of Stephen A. Douglas at the Democratic conventions at Charleston and Baltimore, refusing to join other state delegates who left the national party or supported the candidacy of John C. Breckinridge. In fact, upon his return to the state, Dick secured the nomination of a Douglas electoral ticket and campaigned tirelessly though unsuccessfully for Douglas's election as the best way to preserve the Union and prevent the secession of southern states.

When actual fighting began in the Civil War, Dick joined with other Union men in the state in voting for an ordinance of secession in the 1861 state convention, although he was never an active supporter of the Confederate cause. By 1862 he supported the Conservative ticket of Zebulon B. Vance, and after Vance's gubernatorial victory he was elected to the Council of State by the legislature. In 1864, recognizing the futility of further resistance to the Union forces, Dick joined the "peace movement" led by W. W. Holden and was elected to the state senate on that platform.

For his loyal Unionist support, Dick was one of twelve North Carolinians summoned by President Andrew Johnson in May 1865 to discuss with him the best mode of restoring the state government to the Union. From this meeting came the presidential decision to appoint W. W. Holden as provisional governor of the state, and the formation of a close political alliance and friendship between Holden and Dick that would last the remainder of their lives. Dick was tendered and accepted the office of U.S. district judge, but resigned when he found himself unable to take the "ironclad" oath of loyalty, having served in the state legislature during the time of the Confederacy. He also declined a Holden appointment as a provisional judge, although he did serve as one of the leaders at the 1865–66 constitutional convention. By 1866 he was one of the leading advocates of the Howard or Fourteenth Amendment, and he strongly supported Holden in his efforts to have the state rejoin the Union under the terms of the amendment. He also participated in the formation of the Republican party in the state and campaigned tirelessly for its successful 1868 victory. In April 1868 he was elected a justice of the North Carolina Supreme Court and held that position until 1872, when he was appointed a federal district judge by President Grant. He served in this capacity with great distinction but was forced to resign in 1898 because of poor health.

As associate justice of the state supreme court Dick helped mold and direct the new mode of legal pleading and procedure introduced by the 1868 constitution, as well as deciding the many difficult questions arising out of the new system of jurisprudence. As judge of the district court he was recognized for his kindly temper in administrating the internal revenue laws of the United States. Also, for many years Dick and John H. Dillard conducted a private law school in Greensboro which was noted for the outstanding legal training given to its many young students.

Judge Dick was acclaimed for his scholarship in history and biblical literature, and for many years he was an ardent advocate of temperance reform. He was a faithful member and a ruling elder of the First Presbyterian Church in Greensboro. He died of Bright's disease and was buried in Green Hill Cemetery, Greensboro. In 1848 he had married Mary Eloise Adams of Pittsylvania County, Va., and from this union there were five children: George A., Samuel W., Mrs. R. M. Douglas, Mrs. W. E. Stone, and Mrs. Emma D. Williams.

SEE: Samuel A. Ashe, *Cyclopedia of Eminent and Representative Men of the Carolinas of the Nineteenth Century*, vol. 2 (1892); B. D. Caldwell, *Founders and Builders of Greensboro* (1925); *DAB*, vol. 5 (1932); Jerome Dowd, *Sketches of Prominent Living North Carolinians* (1888); Daniel L. Grant, *Alumni History of the University of North Carolina* (1924); John H. Wheeler, *Reminiscences and Memoirs of North Carolina and Eminent North Carolinians* (1884).

HORACE W. RAPER

**Dickins, Asbury** *(29 July 1780–30 Oct. 1861)*, bookseller, publisher, and government career man, was born in Halifax County, the son of John and Elizabeth Yancey Dickins. John Dickins played an important part in the formation and early growth of the Methodist Episcopal church in the United States, and served appointments as a minister in North Carolina in the 1780s. In 1789 he assisted with the organization of the Methodist Book Concern and became the church's first book agent, moving his family to Philadelphia where he set up publishing offices. When his father died in 1798, Asbury

Dickins, then eighteen years old, and his mother carried on the publishing business for some months under considerable financial strain. In 1800 they moved the book shop to 25 North Second Street in Philadelphia. Late that year Dickins and John Dennie began to publish *The Port Folio*, a political and literary weekly that compared favorably with the best magazines in England.

In his early years Dickins failed to follow in the religious footsteps of his parents, causing great concern to his mother and her contemporaries, particularly Bishop Francis Asbury, for whom he was named. In 1801 he became involved in some incident serious enough to make him leave the country. He fled to England, where he married Lillias Arnot, a Scottish woman of noble descent. For a number of years he was chancellor of the U.S. consulate in London. Through connections of his mother's family he returned to the United States to serve as a clerk in the Treasury Department under Secretary William H. Crawford from 1816 to 1833. From 1833 to 1836 he was chief clerk in the State Department, and in 1836 he was elected secretary of the U.S. Senate, an office he held until the advent of the Lincoln administration.

Dickins and his wife were the parents of nine children. A son, Francis Asbury Dickins, in 1839 married Margaret Randolph, daughter of Thomas Mann Randolph of Tuckahoe, Goochland County, Va.

Asbury Dickins died in Washington, D.C.

SEE: Nolan B. Harmon, ed., *The Encyclopedia of World Methodism* (1974); Ruth K. Nuermberger, "Asbury Dickins (1780–1861): A Career in Government Service," *North Carolina Historical Review* 24 (1947 [portrait]); James P. Pilkington, *The Methodist Publishing House, A History*, vol. 1 (1968).

LOUISE L. QUEEN

**Dickins, John** *(24 Aug. 1747–27 Sept. 1798)*, Methodist clergyman and pioneer book agent, was born to John and Elizabeth Aston Dickins in London. Educated there and, according to tradition, at Eton, he became "well acquainted with Latin and Greek and well skilled in mathematical science." Before 1774 he came to America, was converted in Virginia, and in 1777 became a traveling preacher. His first appointment was to North Carolina when in 1780 he was sent to the Roanoke Circuit, a part of which was in North Carolina. He bought 215 acres in the vicinity of Halifax County and made his home on Fishing Creek. There he prepared one of the earliest plans for a Methodist school in America. The funds for its establishment were donated by Gabriel Long and Mr. Bustion—the first money ever given for a Methodist education in this country. About 1793 a Cokesbury school was founded on the Yadkin River in Davie County, but it had a short life.

In 1783 Francis Asbury persuaded Dickins to go to New York and reenter the itinerant ranks. The following year, while a member of the Christmas Conference in Baltimore (24 Dec. 1784–2 Jan. 1785), Dickins gave the name to the newly organized body, "The Methodist-Episcopal Church," and was elected to deacon's orders. In 1785 he was appointed to Bertie Circuit, N.C., and in 1786, doubtless while living in his own home near Halifax, he prepared the first *Discipline* of the Methodist Episcopal church in its present form. (By 1968 the *Discipline* had grown to 596 pages.)

In 1786 Dickins returned to New York where he was ordained an elder, stationed at John Street Methodist Church, and became the first book agent or superintendent of the Methodist Book Concern, now the Methodist Publishing House with branches across the nation. The date 1789 in the colophon of the Methodist Publishing House signifies the year in which Dickins was officially designated book steward and began issuing books for the Methodist Episcopal church with his name in the imprint. Philip Cox may have been appointed steward before Dickins; if so, Dickins was soon his superior. As book steward, Dickins published 14,000 copies of books and pamphlets, including *Spiritual Catechism*, *Christian Perfection* by Thomas á Kempis, a pocket hymn book of 300 pages, the *Arminian Magazine* (of which he was also editor, 1789–90), Baxter's *Saints' Everlasting Rest*, and the *Methodist Discipline*. Other agents of the early period were Ezekiel Cooper, Joshua Soule, Nathan Bangs, and John Emory.

Dickins married Elizabeth Yancey and they were parents of six children. Asbury, their son, became secretary of the U.S. Senate; Dr. Samuel Baker, a son-in-law, was named professor of *materia medica* at the University of Maryland in 1809. In Philadelphia, Dickins and daughters Betsy and Elizabeth contracted yellow fever; he died suddenly and was interred in the churchyard of Old St. George's Church (now United Methodist). Dickins's portrait, painted by Charles Hargens, is based on a small woodcut identified for many years as the likeness of Dickins; it is in the possession of the Methodist Publishing House, Nashville, Tenn.

SEE: Gordon P. Baker, ed., *Those Incredible Methodists* (1972); Grady L. E. Carroll, *Francis Asbury in North Carolina* (1965); Elmer T. Clark, *Methodism in Western North Carolina* (1966); Albert W. Cliffe, *The Glory of Our Methodist Heritage* (1957); Paul Neff Garber, *The Romance of American Methodism* (1931); John O. Gross, *The Beginnings of American Methodism* (1961); James P. Pilkington, *The Methodist Publishing House: A History*, vol. 1 (1968 [portrait]); Louise Stahl, *Lest We Forget* (n.d.); William W. Sweet, *Methodism in American History* (1933).

GRADY L. E. CARROLL

**Dickins, Samuel** *(ca. 1775–22 July 1840)*, surveyor and congressman, was born in Person County near Roxboro, the son of Robert and Mary Dickins. His father was the younger son of a family belonging to a mercantile firm in London, "Granville and Dickins," and became a partner in its American operation in Norfolk, Va. Robert Dickins served in the Revolutionary Army as a colonel and married Mary Brown, daughter of an Englishman of Norfolk or Petersburg, Va. They settled in Caswell (later Person) County, N.C.

Samuel Dickins was the fourth of his parents' eight children, three sons and five daughters. He may have attended Solomon Lea's Boy's Academy at Leasburg, N.C. He married Jane Vaughn of Mecklenburg County, Va. His name appears in records of Person County as early as 6 Jan. 1799 when he served as bondsman for the marriage of James Paine to Polly Williams, and on 26 July 1808 when he witnessed the will of William Tapp of Person County. His father was a landowner and wealthy citizen of Person County; in his will he left to Samuel his silver watch "which was purchased of John Stout and has his name in the face of her." Robert Dickins ordered his land sold at public auction, leaving the bulk of his wealth to his son Jesse. He appointed his sons Samuel and William executors of his estate in 1804.

From 1813 to 1815 and again in 1818 Samuel Dickins was a member of the North Carolina House of Commons, where he served on the House Finance Committee and on a joint committee to inquire into the advisability of increasing the banking capital of the state. He was elected to the Fourteenth Congress of the United States to fill the vacancy caused by the death of Richard Stanford in April 1816. He served in the House of Representatives from 2 Dec. 1816 to 3 Mar. 1817.

Dickins had nine children by his first wife, who died four or five years after the family moved in 1820 to Madison County, Tenn., to what was then called the Chickasaw Purchase. He established himself as an efficient surveyor and locator of land in western Tennessee and in 1821 was appointed by Archibald D. Murphey and Joseph H. Bryan to locate and sell the Tennessee land claims of The University of North Carolina. His partner was Dr. Thomas Hunt; their firm, "Hunt & Dickins," employed numerous young men to help with the work. Dickins was compensated for his services with the usual 16⅔ percent of the value of lands surveyed. For selling, collecting, and paying he received 6 percent and later 10 percent, all payable in land. In an 1823 meeting of the university's board of trustees it was noted that he had sold 25,000 acres of land, something over the amount specified. His actions were approved and commended and other sales were authorized from time to time.

On 2 Aug. 1831, Dickins married Frances H. Burton of Williamsborough in Granville County, the sister of Governor Hutchins G. Burton; they had no children. He died in Madison County, Tenn., and was buried beside his first wife, the spot having been designated by him for that purpose when he first moved to Tennessee.

SEE: Kemp P. Battle, *History of the University of North Carolina, 1789–1868*, vol. 1 (1907); *Biog. Dir. Am. Cong.* (1950); Carrie Broughton, ed., *Marriage and Death Notices in the Raleigh Register and North Carolina State Gazette* (1968); Mary W. B. Hicks, *A History of the Dickins Family of Panola County, Mississippi* (1860); Virginia R. Lyle, ed., *Person County Patchwork* (1971); J. G. deRoulhac Hamilton, ed., *The Papers of Thomas Ruffin*, vol. 1 (1918).

SARAH E. HOLEMAN

**Dickinson, Matthew** *(11 Sept. 1780–17 Sept. 1809)*, teacher, son of Noah and Hannah Dickinson, was born in Somers, Conn. He entered Yale College in September 1800 and was graduated in 1804. In October of that year he traveled to Louisburg, N.C., to serve as the first preceptor of Franklin Academy, which had been chartered in 1787 and again in 1802. He was well received by the people of Franklin County and the surrounding area. Governor James Turner invited him to dinner with the British consul, a federal court judge, and others.

Dickinson organized instruction at the academy on two levels. In addition to the basic courses of reading, writing, arithmetic, geography, belles lettres, rhetoric, and English grammar, he offered such advanced studies as Latin, Greek, Hebrew, French, Italian, algebra, trigonometry, geometry, metaphysics, surveying, navigation, and astronomy. An average of between seventy and ninety students attended the academy during his tenure as preceptor. Perhaps because of his success, David H. Mayhew, a graduate of Williams College, was secured in 1807 to assist Dickinson.

Academia did not monopolize Dickinson's time, however; he read law under Alexander Falconer, who lived about nine miles north of Louisburg in an area known as the Glebe. He also was a competent businessman. Although he arrived in Louisburg with few possessions, by 1809 he had acquired an estate valued at between $6,000 and $10,000. This was accumulated through land and slave speculations and by lending money.

In 1808 Dickinson resigned his position at the academy to begin a career in law. He practiced briefly in Louisburg and Franklin County, but died the following year as a result of "bilious fever" contracted during a trip to the eastern part of the state. He never married. He was buried in a family cemetery eight miles north of Louisburg near what is today U.S. Highway 401.

SEE: Charles L. Coon, *North Carolina Schools and Academies 1790–1840: A Documentary History* (1915); Franklin B. Dexter, *Yale Biographies and Annals*, vol. 5 (1911); Matthew Dickinson Papers (Manuscript Department, Library, Duke University, Durham); Michael R. Hill, "Historical Research Report: The Person Place of Louisburg, North Carolina" (North Carolina State Archives, Raleigh); Raleigh *Minerva*, 21 Sept. 1809; *Raleigh Register*, 21 Sept. 1809; Cecil W. Robbins, "Matthew Dickinson: He Laid the Foundation," *Louisburg College Alumni Bulletin* 35 (1976); Miriam L. Russell, "A History of Louisburg College 1787–1958" (M.A. thesis, Appalachian State Teacher's College, 1959).

MAURY YORK

**Dickinson, Platt Ketcham** *(19 Sept. 1794–12 May 1867)*, the founder of a profitable lumber business in Wilmington and a lifetime director of the Wilmington and Weldon Railroad, was born in New England and migrated to Wilmington when he was twenty-one, first residing at the boarding house of Mrs. Mary Vance, then a mecca for young emigrants from the North. A year later he complained of "want of business," stating he was of the opinion that "the harvest of this place is already gathered." Early in 1817 he wrote from Wilmington that he had "advertised the stock in trade and wish to quit the business." But three years later he was still in Wilmington for on 20 Nov. 1820 he married Jane Vance, daughter of Mrs. Mary Vance who had died the previous April. By this time he had begun his lumber business in the northern section of the town on a site along the Cape Fear River, though he still lamented that Wilmington's only contact with the country was via water or stage coach. He realized that such a transportation constraint stunted the growth and commerce of the city.

Early in the 1830s Dickinson returned to Wilmington from a trip to his native New England with great enthusiasm for the building of a railroad from Wilmington to Raleigh that would connect Wilmington with the coastal towns and the interior. This he avowed would assure the growth and prosperity of Wilmington. In time his enthusiasm ignited the imagination of others including Edward B. Dudley, who with Aaron Lazarus subscribed $30,000 for the project, and Andrew Joyner, W. D. Moseley, James Battle, Alexander Anderson, William B. Meares, James Owen, R. H. Cowan, and Thomas H. Wright. Dickinson, who subscribed $25,000 to the project, and these associates formed the first board of directors of the railroad, which was chartered in January 1834 and completed 7 Mar. 1840; he remained a director until his death.

Dickinson also inaugurated the North Carolina Railroad, and for many years served as a director of the Bank of Cape Fear. In 1850 he built a substantial brick residence at the northeast corner of Front and Chestnut streets that was enhanced by an extensive landscaped garden embellished with many rare plants and shrubs.

Dickinson's wife, Jane Vance, died 5 May 1825 and

was buried in St. James's Churchyard; she left two daughters, Mary Vance (b. 2 Sept. 1821) and Eliza (b. 3 Oct. 1823). In 1845 he married Alice Heron London (22 Feb. 1814–18 Oct. 1881), daughter of John R. and Sally London.

P. K. Dickinson, as he invariably signed himself, was a member and benefactor of St. James's Church as well as a prominent benefactor of the poor in the city. He died at his home in Wilmington and was buried in Oakdale Cemetery.

SEE: Platt K. Dickinson Papers (Southern Historical Collection, University of North Carolina, Chapel Hill); Ida B. Kellam and Elizabeth F. McCoy, *St. James Church Historical Records, 1737–1852* (1965); Richard F. Langdon Papers (Southern Historical Collection, University of North Carolina, Chapel Hill); James Sprunt, *Chronicles of the Cape Fear River, 1660–1916* (1916); Wilmington *Daily Journal*, 14 May 1867.

DOROTHY F. GRANT

**Dicks, Zacharias** *(ca. 1728–late 1809)*, pioneer, itinerant Quaker minister, and abolitionist, was born in Chester County, Pa., the son of Nathan Dicks, Sr., who had moved to Pennsylvania in 1686, and the grandson of Peter and Esther Dicks of Chester, England. In 1755 Dicks and his brothers, Peter and Nathan, were among the early settlers in the New Garden settlement (now Guilford College community) in North Carolina. They were also members of the Warrenton Friends (Quaker) Meeting in Pennsylvania. On 7 Dec. 1756, at New Garden, Zacharias married Ruth Hiatt, daughter of George and Martha Wakefield Hiatt of Rowan County. She was born "1st of 4th Mo. 1735." They had eight children: Deborah, Martha, Nathan, Esther, Lydia, Peter, Ruth, and Mary.

As a minister in the Society of Friends Dicks spent much of his time on religious visits to Quaker communities widely scattered from Georgia to New Hampshire and in the British Isles. He is believed to have visited most of the Quaker meetings in these areas. In 1761 and again in 1767, he with William Hunt, a noted Quaker minister, made the rounds of the American meetings, traveling most of the time on horseback. For nearly three years (1785–87), he visited among the Quaker meetings in England and Ireland.

In 1775 Dicks, his wife, and their children moved from the New Garden community to a 770-acre tract of land located on both sides of Cane Creek in the southern part of what is now Alamance County. Their new home was situated one mile west of Lindley's Mill and two miles west of Spring Friends meetinghouse. On 13 Sept. 1781 the sharp Battle of Lindley's Mill was fought between Tory and Whig armies within a mile of the Dicks home. Immediately after the battle the Tory army began its hurried march toward Wilmington with the Whig army in pursuit, leaving their dead and seriously wounded where they fell. Dicks said that he and his Quaker neighbors buried the dead, variously estimated at between 50 and 100. The greater task was the care of the seriously wounded, estimated at between 100 and 150. The people of the community took these soldiers into their homes and assumed complete responsibility for their care.

In his home community and on his extensive travels, Dicks was recognized as a powerful minister. He was said to possess prophetic insight and the gift of prophecy. According to tradition, he exercised this power on at least two occasions. About the time of the Declaration of Independence he told New Garden Friends that blood would flow in their meetinghouse. Five years later, on the morning before the Battle of Guilford Court House (15 Mar. 1781), the advance guards of the American and British armies fought on the grounds around the meetinghouse, which served as a temporary infirmary for those injured in the conflict. Two days later Lord Cornwallis, the British commander, sent more than seventy of those most seriously wounded in the Battle of Guilford Court House to New Garden to be attended by the Quakers. Some of them were placed in the meetinghouse. From all these wounded men much blood did flow in the New Garden meetinghouse, as Dicks had predicted. It seeped into the floor and scrubbing with soap and sand did not remove the stain.

The most noted of his prophecies of which we have any knowledge related to the migration of Friends to the Middle West. Dicks was an abolitionist and a major objective in his religious visits among Friends in America was to warn of the dangers of slavery. In 1803 this concern led him to travel through the Quaker communities in Georgia and South Carolina. Deeply shaken by the massacres accompanying the recent slave uprising in Santo Domingo, he warned Friends in those states that a similar fate awaited them if they did not leave their slave-ridden communities and migrate to free territory north of the Ohio River. Though such a migration had already begun, the dire warnings of this able minister created something close to a panic. In the rush to leave, Friends sold their lands and homes at a fraction of their true value and abandoned much personal property.

Between 1793 and 1798 Zacharias and Ruth Hiatt Dicks were members of Centre Quaker Meeting near the southern border of Guilford County. It is not known just where they lived, but his brother Peter, who belonged to the same meeting, had been active in the development of light industry on Deep River in Randolph County. After this sojourn they returned to their home on Cane Creek.

In May 1808 Dicks and his wife were caught up in the wave of migration to the area where Zacharias had been urging Friends to relocate. They settled in Clinton County, in the southeastern part of Ohio, and on 23 Sept. 1809 became members of Centre Friends Meeting. On 7 Mar. 1810 it was reported that Dicks had died a few months after reaching the new community but the exact date of his death is not known.

SEE: Floyd Dix, The Records of the Dix Family (MS, Quaker Collection, Guilford College Library, Greensboro); Errol T. Elliott, *Quakers on the American Frontier* (1969); Willard Heiss, *Abstracts of the Records of the Society of Friends in Indiana*, 6 vols. (1965–75); William W. Hinshaw, *Encyclopedia of Quaker Genealogy*, vols. 1, 5, 6 (1969); William P. Johnson, *The Hiatt-Hiett Family* (1951); Rufus M. Jones, *Later Periods of Quakerism* (1921).

ALGIE I. NEWLIN

**Dickson, James Henderson** *(December 1806–28 Sept. 1862)*, physician, was the son of James Dickson, a commission merchant of Wilmington. He was not only one of the first physicians of his day but also a man of remarkable intellect. He entered The University of North Carolina at age thirteen and was graduated with the class of 1823 at seventeen. Rapidly acquiring the fundamental truths of medicine, Dickson became a student of Dr. Armand J. de Rosset, the oldest physician in Wilmington. Later, he attended lectures at the Medical Department of Columbia College, New York, and was graduated in 1827. He began practicing in South Washington but sometime in 1827 he moved to Fayetteville, where he lived for ten years. During this period he cultivated a talent for surgery and endeavored to perform operations that seldom had been attempted before his day. In 1853 Dickson performed a direct transfusion from the arm of one sister to another, saving the latter's life. His more notable operation, however, was the subcutaneous tenotomy—the correction of a club foot deformity—on his brother, Dr. Robert D. Dickson, in 1835. This was the first tenotomy to be performed in the United States. According to the *North Carolina Medical Journal*, "Dickson operated many times with a success very little if any less than that now attained by his followers, notwithstanding the great advance made in the appliances for after-treatment." Unfortunately, no records of his cases have been preserved.

Dickson left Fayetteville in 1837 to practice medicine in New York. Four years later he returned to Wilmington at the request of his father, whose health was declining, and in 1842 entered into a copartnership with Dr. Louis J. Poission. At this time he became involved with the medical field statewide. In 1852 he joined the Medical Society of North Carolina, organized in 1849; he was elected president in 1854 and served two terms. Dickson had much influence in the formation of a State Board of Medical Examiners—the first experiment with state medical examinations—and in 1859 became its president. He also spent much time traveling and speaking before medical groups. Although his research was extensive, he found little time to publish his conclusions.

In 1845 Dickson married Margaret Owen, the daughter of General James Owen. Owen was the first president of the Wilmington and Raleigh Railroad and a member of Congress from the Cape Fear district in 1817.

Dickson was known not only as one of the leading physicians of the state, but also as one of the most public-spirited men in Wilmington. He played in the Thalian Association, served on many committees for the city, was an elder in the Presbyterian church, and helped form the Wilmington Library Association. Committees on which he served varied from managing a ball in honor of Henry Clay's visit to Wilmington in 1844 and entertaining Daniel Webster on 8 May 1847 to serving on the building committee of the First Presbyterian Church. When the church burned, Dickson organized another committee to have it rebuilt. In 1860 he and the Honorable George Davis formed a public library. Dickson purchased many books from New York and these selections formed the basis of the Wilmington Library Association. They were kept in the city hall until after the Civil War. Dickson was chosen as first president of the Library Association in 1860.

Politically Dickson was a Whig. During the political agitation that led to the Civil War, he counseled prudence and moderation, favoring the settlement of troubles in a friendly way. After secession, he was not hopeful of success because it divided the South; nevertheless, he aligned himself with the Confederacy.

On 17 Sept. 1862 Dickson reported five cases of yellow fever. After working night and day for five days, he contracted the disease himself and died eleven days after the epidemic began. He was buried in Oakdale Cemetery, Wilmington.

SEE: Kemp P. Battle, *History of the University of North Carolina, 1868–1912* (1912); Guion G. Johnson, *Ante-Bellum North Carolina* (1937); *North Carolina Medical Journal* (1879); James Sprunt, *Chronicles of the Cape Fear River, 1660–1916* (1916); Thomas F. Wood, *James Henderson Dickson* (1891).

JUANITA ANN SHEPPARD

**Dickson, John Augustus** *(4 Nov. 1795–28 Sept. 1847),* teacher, minister, and physician, was born in Charleston, S.C., the son of Samuel and Mary Neilson Dickson. Both parents were strict Presbyterians of Scottish descent who had emigrated from Belfast, Ireland, before the American Revolution. Although his father was a schoolmaster by profession, young Dickson was prepared for the sophomore class at Yale by Dr. John MacKay of Charleston. He was graduated from Yale in 1814 and taught in Charleston and Columbia before attending Andover Seminary in 1820 for a year of theological study. In 1821 he returned to South Carolina and married Mary Augusta Flinn of Charleston. After a year as professor of languages at the College of Charleston, he assumed the chair of moral philosophy at the same institution.

Dickson was ordained to the ministry on 20 Mar. 1825 by the Charleston Union Presbytery but a weakness of the lungs prevented him from accepting a pastorate. His poor health soon forced him to give up both preaching and teaching and led him to study medicine with his brother, the distinguished physician, Samuel Henry Dickson. In 1832 he retired to the highlands of western North Carolina; there he spent the rest of his life practicing medicine and engaging in the ministry and education. He lived and taught in a house he had built at the junction of Biltmore Avenue and St. Dunstan's Road in Asheville.

Dickson's Asheville College for Young Women was the first school for females in Buncombe County. A young English girl, Elizabeth Blackwell, lived in his home and taught music in his school. She decided to study medicine and received instruction from Dickson. Later through the influence of his brother Samuel, Miss Blackwell was admitted to a medical school in Geneva, N.Y., where she received the M.D. degree in 1849; she was the first woman allowed into the medical profession in this country.

Dickson assisted Dr. Elisha Mitchell in his efforts to determine the highest peak in the Black Mountain range. He was placed in charge of one of two barometers that Mitchell used in his measurements. The one in Dickson's charge was comparable to the one Mitchell took with him on his explorations into the mountains. As Mitchell was a careful and painstaking scientist, it is safe to assume that he called on the assistance of Dickson, whom he revered for his learning.

Surviving his first wife, who was the mother of his five children, Dickson married Louisa O'Hear of Charleston in 1839. He served the First Presbyterian Church of Asheville as an assistant minister from 1843 to 1845. He died in Asheville and was buried beneath the annex of the First Presbyterian Church.

Dickson published "The Mocking Bird," in blank verse, in *Microscope* 1 (1820); "Notices of the Mineralogy and Geology of Parts of South and North Carolina," *American Journal of Science and Arts* 3 (1821); and *The Essentials of Religion, Briefly Considered in Ten Discourses* (1827).

SEE: *Asheville Citizen Times*, 6 Feb. 1949; Franklin B. Dexter, *Biographical Sketches of the Graduates of Yale Col-*

*lege*, vol. 6 (1912); Dickson Family Papers (Southern Historical Collection, University of North Carolina, Chapel Hill).

WILLIAM F. MASSENGALE

**Dickson, Joseph** *(April 1745–14 Apr. 1825)*, congressman, planter, and military leader, was born in Chester County, Pa., a few miles north of Wilmington, Del. About 1755 he moved with his family to Rowan County, N.C., near Salisbury, where he continued his schooling begun in Pennsylvania. He read law, was admitted to the North Carolina bar, and practiced in Rowan County. He early assumed responsibility for the family's farm and became widely known throughout the area as a successful cotton and tobacco planter.

During the restless days prior to the American Revolution Dickson filled many positions of leadership on behalf of the colony. In 1775, at the age of thirty, he was a member of the Rowan County Committee of Safety, a group designed for negotiation as well as defense. Before the end of the year he accepted a commission as commanding captain in the Continental Army. In 1780 he served as a major of the "Lincoln County Men," a unit that distinguished itself at the Battle of Kings Mountain under the command of Colonel Charles McDowell. One year later he won praise for his bravery and military acumen in opposing the invasion of Lord Charles Cornwallis into North Carolina. For that service he was commissioned colonel; his continuing military leadership earned him the rank of brigadier general in the militia.

Having established his residence in Lincoln County, Dickson was elected clerk of the Lincoln County court, a position he held for several years until he was elected to the North Carolina Senate where he served four terms from 1788 to 1795. There he revealed a special interest in education, serving on several committees and the legislative commission that established The University of North Carolina. He was named a trustee in the William R. Davie bill to establish the university, dated 12 Nov. 1789. Subsequently he was listed in the charter of 11 Dec. 1789, and was consistently present at meetings of the trustees through 1796. In the latter year he was a member of the small Committee on Visitation.

In 1793 Dickson was reported to have "occupied property in Chatham County" that later belonged to the university. Whether he simply lived there for a time or owned the property is not clear. Further, in the university records for 7 Dec. 1796, he is listed as representing the "Morgan District" on the Committee on Visitation while someone else represented the Rowan District. There is no evidence that Dickson lived in other than Rowan and Lincoln counties until he moved to Tennessee in 1803. Following his retirement from the North Carolina senate he returned to his Lincoln County home and remained active in public affairs, especially politics. Three years later he was a successful Federalist candidate for election to the U.S. House of Representatives where he served during the Sixth session from 1799 to 1801.

Political observers have long credited Dickson with valuable yeoman service on behalf of Thomas Jefferson in his contest with Aaron Burr in 1800 for the presidency of the United States. The regular election ended in a tie: seventy-three votes each for Jefferson and Burr. That threw the election into the House of Representatives where Jefferson was finally chosen president on the thirty-sixth ballot. It was during that prolonged floor fight that Dickson raised his voice and exerted his influence on Jefferson's behalf. Aaron Burr became vice-president and served throughout Jefferson's first term.

In 1764 Dickson married Margaret McEwen, probably a resident of Rowan County. She was the daughter of James and Isabella Miller McEwen. The Dicksons had nine children: James, Elizabeth, Isabella, John, Joseph, Robert, William, Ezekial, and Margaret, all born in North Carolina.

In 1803 Dickson left North Carolina and settled in Tennessee. There he became a noted and prosperous planter in Davidson County (the part now known as Rutherford County), and continued his law practice in the town of Murfreesboro. He also was an active churchman and is credited with the organization in 1812 of the Presbyterian church in Murfreesboro. He was one of the founders of the Murfreesboro Lodge, Ancient, Free and Accepted Masons.

Politics continued to interest Dickson and in 1806 he was a successful candidate for election to the Tennessee legislature. He served two terms from 1807 to 1811; during his last term he was speaker of the house. The remaining fourteen years of his life were spent on his farm in Rutherford County, Tenn., where he died and was buried in the family cemetery on his plantation northeast of Murfreesboro.

SEE: *Biog. Dir. Am. Cong.* (1950); Walter Clark, ed., *State Records of North Carolina*, vols. 16–22, 24 (1899–1905); R. D. W. Connor, ed., *Documentary History of the University of North Carolina, 1776–1799*, 2 vols. (1953); Robert M. McBride, et al., eds., *Biographical Directory of the Tennessee General Assembly* (1975); *Who Was Who in America* (1950).

C. SYLVESTER GREEN

**Dickson, William** *(10 Jan. 1739–20 Jan. 1820)*, colonial leader, was born in Chester County, Pa., of English and Irish ancestry. His paternal grandfather, a stern English Puritan, fought with Oliver Cromwell and was rewarded with a grant of land in Ireland; upon the restoration of the Crown, he became a tenant on the same land. His father was John Dickson (1704–74), who emigrated from Ireland to Pennsylvania, thence to Maryland, and finally to North Carolina where he settled about 1740–45. The second in a family of seven sons and one daughter, his formal education, according to family tradition, was limited to about three months.

A prominent leader in the civil affairs of Duplin County, N.C., Dickson served in the militia under Colonel, later General, James Kenan, the county's military leader. He saw much service in all fights in the area, including the Battle of Rockfish, and, though wounded only once, he narrowly escaped capture or death three times. He represented Duplin County in the colonial assemblies of 1769 and 1770–71 and in the House of Commons in 1795. He also was a delegate to the provincial congresses held at New Bern, 25 Aug. 1774; Halifax, 3 Apr. 1775 and 12 Nov. 1776; and Hillsborough, 21 Aug. 1775. In 1777 he was elected clerk of court of the Court of Pleas and Quarter Sessions, a post he held until 1819, shortly before his death, for the remarkable period of forty-four years.

Dickson is probably best known as the author of the so-called "Dickson Letters." The first four, to a cousin, the Reverend Robert Dickson, a Presbyterian clergyman at Narrow Water, near Newry, Ireland, cover the years from 1784 to 1790. The fifth, and last known in existence, was to a niece, Linda Dickson, while she was visiting her older sister, Mrs. Elizabeth Johnson, in

Charleston, S.C., in 1818. Undoubtedly, there were others. He discussed political affairs with an intuitive knowledge and foresight that was remarkable. His fears of the power of the president and the central government were allayed by the early leaders selected. Of the federal Constitution he wrote that "it is formed so as to lay the foundation of one of the greatest empires now in the world." He felt, however, that the southern states would not enjoy equality with the North. "The Southern States will have their vote," he predicted, "but will not be able to carry any point against so powerful a party in cases where either general or local interest are the object." He further wrote that northern actions with regard to the slavery question had alarmed the South and, "though they did not carry their point, they [the North] seemed determined never to drop the matter until they do."

A staunch Presbyterian, Dickson was devoted to the causes of church and education, and in 1785, by act of the General Assembly, he was made a trustee of the yet-to-be-organized Grove Academy at Kenansville. In 1767 he had married Mary Williams, daughter of Joseph Williams, of Onslow County; they had nine children. One son, Dr. William Dickson, was a three-term member of Congress from Tennessee, where a county is named for him. The exact place of the elder Dickson's burial is not known, but it is highly likely that it was on his plantation on Grove Swamp, near the present community of Summerlin's Crossroads.

SEE: Samuel A. Ashe, ed., *Biographical History of North Carolina*, vol. 1 (1905); James O. Carr, "The Battle of Rockfish Creek," *James Sprunt Review* 1 (1972), and ed., *The Dickson Letters* (1901); William Dickson, "Historical Sketch of Duplin County, 1749–1810," *James Sprunt Review* 1 (1972); R. B. House, ed., "A Picture of the Last Days of the Revolutionary War in North Carolina," *North Carolina Booklet* 21 (1921–22).

CHARLES M. INGRAM

**Dillard, John Henry** *(29 Nov. 1819–14 May 1896)*, attorney, judge, and law teacher, the son of Lucy Moorman of Campbell County, Va., and James Dillard of Albemarle County, Va., who moved to North Carolina and settled on Matrimony Creek above Leaksville, was born on his father's farm in Rockingham County. He attended the Patrick Henry Academy in Virginia and Samuel Smith's school in his native county where a classmate was Thomas Ruffin. Between 1837 and 1839 he spent eighteen months at The University of North Carolina, but ill health forced him to withdraw. In 1879, however, the university conferred upon him the honorary degree of doctor of laws. He entered the law department of the College of William and Mary in 1839 and, after studying under Beverley Tucker there and receiving the degree of bachelor of laws, he was admitted to the bar in Richmond. In 1841 he opened an office in Patrick County, Va., where he practiced for five years; for a portion of that time he also was commonwealth's attorney. Returning home to Rockingham County in 1846, he soon formed a partnership with Thomas Ruffin that lasted until 1861 when the Civil War brought about its dissolution.

As a Whig Dillard was opposed to secession and did all he could to prevent it, but once that step was taken he supported the state's action. For a brief time he served as captain of Company G, Forty-fifth Regiment. Returning once again to Rockingham County, he resumed the practice of law until 1868 and was for a time county attorney and for a number of years the clerk and master in equity. Settling in Greensboro, Dillard formed a partnership with John A. Gilmer and Thomas Ruffin and in 1878 was elected an associate justice of the North Carolina Supreme Court. Because of ill health, however, he resigned in 1881 to resume his practice in Greensboro until his death.

Dillard probably made his most significant contribution as a teacher. In 1878 he and Robert P. Dick established a law school in Greensboro where they trained a great many influential lawyers.

In 1846 Dillard married Ann Isabel, daughter of Colonel Joseph Martin of Henry County, Va. They became the parents of five children: Lucy (Mrs. John T. Pannill), Thomas Ruffin, Annie (Mrs. E. F. Hall), John Henry, and Drury. After the decline of the Whig party, Dillard became a faithful Democrat. He was a member of the Presbyterian church in which he was a ruling elder and a Sunday school teacher; he was also a member of the Freemasons. Throughout his life he was described as shy and reticent; he took little part in political affairs and was uninterested in social life.

SEE: Alumni records, University of North Carolina, Chapel Hill; Van Noppen Papers (Manuscript Department, Library, Duke University, Durham).

WILLIAM S. POWELL

**Dillard, Richard** *(5 Dec. 1857–15 May 1928)*, physician and local historian, was born at Farmers Delight, his father's plantation in Nansemond County, Va. The son of Dr. Richard and Mary Louisa Beverly Cross Dillard, he was educated at The University of North Carolina where he was a student from 1875 to 1877. He then studied medicine at the University of Virginia and was graduated from the Jefferson Medical College of Philadelphia in 1879. Rutherford College in 1901 awarded him an honorary master of arts degree. He established a practice in Edenton, N.C., which continued for the remainder of his life; in 1880 he was named assistant surgeon of the U.S. Public Health Service in Edenton.

Dillard became interested in local history and during his leisure time engaged in research and writing. He contributed to various magazines and journals, including the *Magazine of American History* and the *North Carolina Booklet*, and published a number of pamphlets and booklets dealing primarily with the old Albemarle region of North Carolina. Among his earliest publications was *The Historic Tea-Party of Edenton, October 25th, 1774*, which appeared first in 1898 and was reprinted several times. *Some Legends of Eastern North Carolina* appeared in 1926. Other publications dealt with traditions and lore, Indians, reminiscences, and fiction; he also wrote "prose poems" and pieces of "poetic beauty." Governor Charles B. Aycock named him to the first North Carolina Historical Commission, and he was an active member of the Roanoke Colony Memorial Association. He held office in the North Carolina Medical Society and in the North Carolina Folklore Society. A knowledgeable botanist, he was fond of flowers and gardening and contributed to *House and Garden Magazine*.

Dillard, a Democrat and an Episcopalian, never married; he was survived by a number of nieces and nephews and his home in Edenton, Beverly Hall, continues to be occupied by a relative.

SEE: Daniel L. Grant, *Alumni History of the University of North Carolina* (1924); *North Carolina Biography*, vol. 6 (1919); *North Carolina Booklet* 6 (October 1906 [portrait]);

Bettie Freshwater Pool, *Literature in the Albemarle* (1915 [portrait]); Raleigh *News and Observer*, 16 May 1928; *Transactions of the Medical Society of North Carolina* (1929). A list of his writings appears in Mary L. Thornton, comp., *A Bibliography of North Carolina, 1589–1956* (1958).

WILLIAM S. POWELL

**Dimock, Susan** *(24 Apr. 1847–8 May 1875)*, North Carolina's first woman doctor, was born in Washington, N.C., to Henry Dimock and his wife, Mary Malvina Dimock, daughter of the sheriff of Beaufort County. Dimock, from Limington, Maine, was one of a group of young New Englanders who moved south in the 1830s and 1840s looking for adventure, and stayed to marry southern women and become solid citizens. For a few years he taught school before becoming editor of the local newspaper, *The North State Whig*. Following their marriage, the Dimocks acquired the town hotel, The Lafayette. Here their daughter, Susan, was born and spent her girlhood. Across the street lived the family doctor, Dr. Solomon Samson Satchwell. He made a pet of this little girl and sometimes took her with him when he made calls in the country. While still very young she became obsessed with the ambition to become a physician.

Susan Dimock received her elementary education at a small private school and then attended the Washington Academy where Latin became her favorite subject. A brilliant student, she amused herself by translating prescriptions in an ancient pharmacopoeia in Dr. Satchwell's collection. One month before her fifteenth birthday, Union soldiers entered Washington as conquerors and occupied the town for more than two years. Some of the officers made their headquarters at the Lafayette Hotel and the Dimocks were greatly criticized by loyal Confederates for being friendly with them. But, after all, Dimock himself was a Yankee. He lived only a few months after the occupation of Washington, however. A year and a half after his death, the Lafayette was burned to the ground in the holocaust that destroyed most of the town.

In some way Susan and her mother managed to obtain transportation to the home of Dimock's sister near Sterling, Mass., where they lived briefly. Susan attended school in Sterling for six months and then secured a job as a teacher in Hopkinton, Mass. She was then seventeen.

The opportunity to pursue a medical career arose through her close friendship with Bessie Greene, daughter of a wealthy Bostonian. Colonel Greene, Bessie's father, became interested in Susan and her desire to study medicine, an ambition rare in a young woman in the nineteenth century when there were only a few women doctors in the world. Of the two or three in the United States, one was Dr. Marie Zakrzewska, a Polish woman who had received her medical training in Germany. She had come to the United States under the sponsorship of Dr. Elizabeth Blackwell, the first woman doctor in this country. By 1862 Dr. Zakrzewska had established the New England Hospital for Women and Children in a small rented house in Boston. Through the Greenes, Susan met Dr. Zakrzewska who furnished her a list of medical books to study. Not long afterward Dr. Zakrzewska accepted Susan as a student at her hospital.

Opposition to women invading the medical field was particularly bitter. When all efforts to have Susan admitted to Harvard failed, Dr. Zakrzewska urged her to study in Europe. Colonel Greene, convinced of the rare ability and dedication of this unusual young woman, offered to finance her studies in Switzerland where women doctors were welcome. At the University of Zurich Dimock had a brilliant record and in 1871 received a medical degree with honors. Her graduating dissertation was a treatise on "The Different Forms of Puerperal Fever." Before returning to the United States, she pursued specialties in hospitals in Vienna and in Paris.

The American Medical Association, meeting in San Francisco in 1872, expounded feelingly on the dangers of entrusting life to the weak, unstable feminine intelligence. Happily North Carolina was more liberal in its attitude. At the 1872 meeting of the North Carolina Medical Society Susan Dimock was received as an honorary member of the profession—"honorary" because she was in Paris at the time and thus was not present to be examined for her license. Her credentials were submitted by her childhood friend, Dr. S. S. Satchwell of Washington, N.C. Satchwell was highly respected throughout the state and at that time was serving as secretary of the Medical Board.

In July 1872 Dr. Dimock took up duties as resident physician at the Boston hospital where she had matriculated as a student only a few years before. After three years of hard but successful work, she asked for a vacation before renewing her contract with the hospital. The directors were delighted to give her five months' leave for recreation and further study in Europe. Accompanied by her two close friends, Bessie Greene and Caroline Crane, Susan sailed from New York on 27 Apr. 1875 on the *Schiller*, considered one of the best of the great iron-rigged steam ships of the day. Two weeks later the *Schiller*, ploughing her way through an impenetrable fog, was wrecked on a granite reef off the Scilly Isles twenty-five miles off the coast of Cornwall, England. Almost all on board were lost. Friends from London identified Susan's body. Her watch had stopped at seven minutes to four so it was assumed that was the hour of her death. Most of the victims of the shipwreck were buried on St. Mary's Island. However, Colonel Greene arranged to have his daughter and her two companions, Susan and Caroline, brought home to Boston where the three were interred in Forest Hills Cemetery.

For weeks the press echoed with tributes to Susan Dimock, pioneer woman doctor. One distinguished physician went on record as saying that he had always been opposed to women doctors until he met Susan Dimock. Her intelligence, her modesty, and her devotion to her work had convinced him that he was wrong.

SEE: *A Memoir of Susan Dimock* (1875 [reminiscences and tributes]).

PAULINE WORTHY

**Dinwiddie, James** *(29 June 1837–2 July 1907)*, educator, was born in Campbell County, Va., to William Walthal Dinwiddie, who followed agricultural and mechanical pursuits, and Nancy Bryan Dinwiddie. He was the grandson of Joseph Dinwiddie, a Virginian, and the great-grandson of William Dinwiddie, first of the family in America and a soldier who fought at Kings Mountain in 1780 and at Cowpens. He was educated at Hampden-Sydney College and the University of Virginia where he earned the M.A. degree in 1861. During the Civil War he joined the University Volunteers and received promotions to lieutenant, assistant adjutant general, and captain of artillery in General "Stonewall" Jackson's corps; he was major of infantry when the war ended. A valiant soldier, he participated in engagements at Cross Keys, Port Republic, the Seven Days Fight Around Richmond, Second Manassas, First Fredericksburg, and others.

Dinwiddie began his career in education as principal of Sayre Institute, Lexington, Ky., for one year. He was professor of mathematics at Southwestern Presbyterian University, Clarksville, Tenn., for ten years and served in the same position at the University of Tennessee for five years. In 1885 he purchased the Central Female Institute at Gordonsville, Va., where he remained for five years. In 1890 he assumed the presidency of Peace Institute, Raleigh, following the administration of John Burwell and his son Robert, and served seventeen years until his health failed in 1907. The family lived on the campus. During his tenure he bought most of the stock in the institute and became its virtual owner. The institute had ten "schools": mathematics, English, history, natural science, mental and moral philosophy, languages, pedagogy, music, art, and commerce. Associated with the institute at the time were Dr. Hubert Haywood, physician; Mrs. Mary T. Fowler, matron and nurse for thirty years; Professor James T. Brawley, music; William McSwain, helper for forty years; Dr. William A. Withers; Miss Pearl Rodman; Charles Duncan McIver, later first president of Woman's College of The University of North Carolina at Greensboro; and Miss Nannie, daughter of the president. Dinwiddie's chief contribution was to make Peace "a more progressive school" and to assist in its evolution into a form recognizable today as a college. In 1922–23 the renovated chapel was named The James Dinwiddie Chapel; his portrait hangs outside.

The educator was a member of the Odd Fellows, the Masonic Order (William G. Hill Lodge, No. 218, Ancient, Free, and Accepted Masons), Royal Arch Masons, and Raleigh Commandery, No. 4, Knights Templar. He was a Whig but became a Democrat and was a member of Raleigh's First Presbyterian Church.

Dinwiddie married Betty Morton Carrington, daughter of Dr. William Carrington of Halifax County, Va. To this union were born ten children, two of whom died in infancy. At his death in San Francisco, Calif., seven children survived him: James of New York; William of San Francisco; Nannie and Jane of Raleigh; Mrs. B. W. Kilgore and Mrs. E. B. Crow of Raleigh; and Mrs. A. B. Croom of Maxton. Burial was in Raleigh's Oakwood Cemetery.

SEE: Raleigh *News and Observer*, 3 July 1907; C. L. Van Noppen Papers (Manuscript Department, Library, Duke University, Durham); Sidney A. Wilson, *Personae: The History of Peace College* (1972).

GRADY L. E. CARROLL

**Divine, John Francis** *(27 June 1830–21 Aug. 1909),* railroad builder, was the son of Michael and Eleanor Patterson Divine from Glasgow, Scotland, who settled in Baltimore, Md., when their son was four. On 15 Sept. 1851 he moved south to superintend the building of locomotives for the Wilmington and Weldon Railroad. After serving in the Confederate Army during 1861–65, he returned to the road and in 1872 was appointed general superintendent. He later became general superintendent of the entire Atlantic Coast Line system. Through his efforts, and those of Colonel R. R. Bridgers, president of the Wilmington and Weldon Railroad, B. F. Newcomer, and Henry Walters, the Coast Line system became one of the principal railroads of the South. Divine himself was recognized as one of the foremost railroad men of the region, and his advice was often sought by officials of other lines. When the city of Wilmington was without waterworks and fire protection and without funds to provide them in the 1880s, Divine, with Edwin Buruss and Edward Kidder, established the Clarendon Waterworks Company. These men invested their time and money without prospect of profit. Divine was president of the company until its sale to the city. He was also president of the Wilmington Bridge Company, which owned the only outlet by rail over the Cape Fear River. He served for some time as an alderman and was a consistent Democrat.

On 13 Apr. 1861 Divine enlisted in the Goldsboro Rifles, later known as Company A, Twenty-seventh Regiment of the North Carolina Infantry. He was ordered with his company to Fort Macon and was appointed quartermaster sergeant with the rank of captain on 15 July 1861. He was captured on 25 Apr. 1862, was exchanged in August, and was back on duty in September. He served until his discharge on 2 May 1865.

On 13 Dec. 1854, in Sussex County, Va., Divine married Augusta Elizabeth Howle, daughter of Epaphroditus Howle and Sallie Stuart. Some years after the Civil War he bought a house on Chestnut Street in Wilmington that had been constructed about the time of the American Revolution. He and his wife were the parents of William Charles (m. Hattie Pendleton), Mary Elizabeth (m. Daniel P. Foley), Sarah Augusta (m. James Dudley Horne), John Sidney (m. Vina Hinton), Morrison W. (m. Eliza McPherson), and Virginia Stella (died unmarried). James Dudley Horne of Wadesboro, who married Sarah Augusta Divine in Wilmington on 13 Jan. 1892, was born 13 Feb. 1850 on the ancestral Horne plantation in Anson County and died 17 May 1932; he was president of the First National Bank, a director of the Wade Manufacturing Company and West Knitting Mill, member of the state legislature, and owner of the J. D. Horne Company and of the Horne plantation. Their children were Elizabeth Divine Horne, Anne Baldwin Horne (m. George W. Little), Mary Virginia Horne, and Sarah Divine Horne (m. Clifton H. Sutherland).

Funeral services for Divine were conducted at Saint Thomas Catholic Church, Wilmington, of which he was a member. All engines of the Atlantic Coast Line system were draped in black for his passing.

SEE: Samuel A. Ashe, ed., *Biographical History of North Carolina*, vol. 6 (1907); John Bennett Boddie, *Southside Virginia Families*, vol. 1 (1955); Andrew J. Howell, *The Book of Wilmington* (1930); Weymouth T. Jordan, Jr., *North Carolina Troops, 1861–1865, A Roster*, vol. 8 (1980); *Wilmington Dispatch*, 22 Aug. 1909; Wilmington *Morning Star*, 21 Aug. 1909.

MARY VIRGINIA HORNE

**Dixon, Amzi Clarence** *(6 July 1854–14 June 1925),* Baptist pastor and evangelist for more than fifty years, was born in Shelby, the son of Amanda Elvira McAfee and Thomas Dixon, Jr., a pioneer preacher among the rural people of North Carolina and South Carolina. He was baptized when he was twelve years old along with ninety-seven others in a revival led by his father. Educated at the Shelby Academy from the age of six, he entered Wake Forest College in 1869. He planned to become a lawyer but, while on vacation between his junior and senior years, his father sent him to New Prospect Baptist Church to inform the congregation that due to a revival still in progress the elder Dixon could not keep the appointment. Young Dixon was invited to lead the meeting, which he did, and for two more weeks continued to attend the church daily. A classmate observed the change when Dixon returned to college and wrote in retrospect: "It was not until his last year at college that he definitely heard and heeded the call of God to preach the Gospel. But, his decision once made, he entered into his new work as he played baseball, whole-heartedly, with every power of heart, mind, soul, and body."

After his graduation from Wake Forest College Dixon spent the summer of 1874 preaching with his father. In the fall he accepted the pastorate of Mount Olive Baptist Church, Wayne County, and Bear Marsh Baptist Church, Duplin County. He was ordained at Bear Marsh in 1875. In September 1875 he enrolled at the Baptist Theological Seminary, Greenville, S.C. In the spring of 1876, he received a pressing invitation to come and preach to the Baptists in Chapel Hill that summer. His evangelistic gifts resulted in many conversions of University of North Carolina students and townspeople alike.

In 1880 Dixon resigned his pastorate in Chapel Hill and accepted a call to the Asheville First Baptist Church; on the last day of June he married Susan Mary Faison at her home near Warsaw. In 1882, at the age of twenty-eight, he was offered the presidency of his alma mater, Wake Forest College. Dixon declined the position in order to accept the pastorate of the Immanuel Baptist Church in Baltimore, Md. After serving that church and assisting measurably in the growth of Baptists in and around Baltimore, Dixon accepted the pastorate of the Hanson Place Baptist Church, Brooklyn, N.Y., where he remained from 1890 to 1901.

Dixon's work in Brooklyn was marked by evangelistic zeal, support of the temperance cause, and frequent controversy over liberal teachings, especially evolution. In 1893 he was associated for one month with D. G. Moody, preaching to the throngs that attended the Chicago World's Fair. In 1901 Dixon left Brooklyn to begin his ministry at Ruggles Street Baptist Church, Boston, Mass., which continued until October 1906 when he became pastor of the Moody Church, Chicago, Ill. He left the United States to accept the pastorate of Spurgeon's Tabernacle, London, England, where he served from 1911 until 1919 during the trying days of World War I.

For several months following his London ministry, Dixon was engaged in Bible conferences, in evangelistic meetings, and in writing and preaching in support of the Fundamentalist movement. While attending a missionary conference in China in 1922, his wife died after a brief illness. Returning to America, he accepted the pastorate of the recently organized University Baptist Church in Baltimore. To this new work he gave the closing years of his ministry from 1922 to 1925.

From his earliest days in Baltimore, Dixon had begun to appreciate the power of the printed word to amplify his spoken message. In each of his pastorates he devoted much time and thought to issuing a church paper. In Baltimore and Brooklyn it took the form of a weekly leaflet containing his sermons. *The Gospel Worker* at Immanuel Church developed into *Work and Worship*. In Brooklyn he published a weekly magazine entitled *Gospel*, which was devoted to biblical exposition and illustration. Through the last years at Hanson Place a sermon was printed every week in a new leaflet entitled *The Living Word*. In Boston, two or three sermons at a time were published monthly in booklet form. At the beginning of 1908 Dixon purchased a column in the Saturday issue of *The Chicago Daily News* as a vehicle for carrying the Gospel message to nonchurchgoers. He also wrote many books and pamphlets in support of the Gospel and Fundamentalist movements.

Dixon and his wife Mary had five children: Clarence Howard, Mary Faison, Abner Faison, Clara, and Grace. On 25 Jan. 1924, Dixon married his second wife and future biographer, Helen Cadbury Alexander, widow of Charles M. Alexander, a widely known evangelistic singer in London, England. Less than a year and a half later Dixon died at Union Memorial Hospital in Baltimore. After funeral services in the University Baptist Church he was buried at Druid Ridge, ten miles from Baltimore.

SEE: *Biblical Recorder*, 12 Aug. 1925; W. H. Brannock, "Amzi Clarence Dixon," *Encyclopedia of Southern Baptists*, vol. 1 (1958); A. C. Dixon Biography File (Baptist Historical Collection, Wake Forest University, Winston-Salem); Helen C. A. Dixon, *A. C. Dixon—A Romance of Preaching* (1931); Edward C. Starr, *A Baptist Bibliography*, vol. 6 (1959).

JOHN R. WOODARD

**Dixon, Archibald** *(2 Apr. 1802–23 Apr. 1876)*, U.S. senator and lieutenant governor of Kentucky, was born in the Red House community of Caswell County, the son of Wynne and the grandson of Henry ("Hal") Dixon, both revolutionary officers. In 1805 Wynne Dixon and his family moved to Henderson County, Ky., where Archibald spent the remainder of his life. He was educated by his mother and in the local common schools before beginning to study law at the age of twenty. In 1825 he began to practice law and it was said that because of his talent and learning he enjoyed a wide practice until 1860 when he retired. Young Dixon represented Henderson County in the lower house of the Kentucky legislature in 1830 and in 1841 and in the senate between 1836 and 1840. As a member of the Whig party he served as lieutenant governor during the period 1844–48. In 1849 he was a delegate to the convention that drew up a new constitution for the state; by a vote of 48 to 50 he failed to be elected president of the convention. As a candidate for governor in 1851 he was defeated by 850 votes, but on 30 December of that year he was elected to the U.S. Senate to fill the vacancy caused by the resignation of Henry Clay. In Congress he was the author of the Kansas-Nebraska Bill repealing the Missouri Compromise act of 1820. He served in Congress from 1 Sept. 1852 until 3 Mar. 1855 but was not a candidate for reelection, preferring to return to his law practice and to the management of his plantation.

Prior to the outbreak of the Civil War Dixon was described as "unceasing in his efforts to preserve the peace and the Union." Attending a convention of the Border States, he favored their neutrality in the hope that they might form a barrier to halt the tide of sectionalism. When this failed, he remained loyal to the Union but devoted his efforts during the war to aiding Confederate soldiers and sympathizers who were victims of arbitrary arrest. After the war he opposed Republican plans to humiliate the South. In 1863 Dixon was a delegate to the Frankfort peace convention.

In 1834 Dixon married Mrs. Elizabeth B. Pollit and they were the parents of five surviving children; in 1853 he married Sue Bullitt of Jefferson County, Ky., and they were the parents of three children. He was buried in Fernwood Cemetery, Henderson.

SEE: *Bio. Dir. Am. Cong.* (1961); *Biographical Encyclopaedia of Kentucky* (1878); Lewis Collins, *History of Kentucky*, vol. 2 (1924); Robert R. Russel, "The Issues in the Congressional Struggle Over the Kansas-Nebraska Bill, 1854," *Journal of Southern History* 29 (May 1963).

WILLIAM S. POWELL

**Dixon, Arminius Gray** *(13 Feb. 1870–12 Jan. 1962)*, minister and official in the North Carolina Annual Conference of the Methodist Protestant Church, was born in Rockingham County, the son of John F. and Elizabeth Harrison Dixon. He was educated in the local county school, was graduated from Oak Ridge Academy in 1895 and Western Maryland College in 1899, and received the doctor of divinity degree from Adrian College, Michigan, in 1919.

In 1901 he joined the North Carolina Annual Conference of the Methodist Protestant Church and began his pastoral ministry in Rocky Mount. Afterward, he served appointments in Henderson, Orange Circuit, High Point, Liberty, and Siler City. He was chosen in 1908 to be the first field secretary for the young people's work in the North Carolina Annual Conference. As national secretary of the Board of Young People's Work of his denomination from 1917 to 1922, he worked with Sunday school and Christian Endeavor leaders in thirty-three states. He served as president of the North Carolina Annual Conference of the Methodist Protestant Church from 1922 to 1927. In 1928 he was appointed superintendent of the Methodist Protestant Children's Home in High Point, where he remained until his retirement in 1941. He served as an official delegate from the North Carolina conference to six general conferences of the church. He also took an active role in the establishment of High Point College and in helping to bring about the union of the three major Methodist denominations in 1939.

Dixon conducted many revivals throughout the North Carolina conference area and is credited with influencing many men to enter the ministry. For some forty years "he was a dedicated supporter of the total program of the church and the kingdom . . . he not only supported the program, but ofttimes initiated it and led in it, and to him, the church and the kingdom were synonymous." He once wrote: "There is no position in the church of our Christ that is more important than the pastorate"; yet his own diverse talents as administrator qualified him to hold positions of leadership outside the pastorate for three-fifths of his active years of service.

In October 1902 Dixon married his college classmate, Mary Etta Watts of Baltimore, Md. In July 1904, shortly after the birth of a daughter, Mary Vista, Mary Etta Dixon died of typhoid fever in Henderson. In 1908 he married Margaret Minerva Kuhns (1867–1950), who had served as a missionary to Japan for about five years. Mrs. Dixon in 1908 became the first president of the Woman's Home Missionary Society of the North Carolina Annual Conference of the Methodist Protestant Church and led in the organization of women's societies across the state. In 1909 she was chosen to serve as the national president of the Woman's Home Missionary Society, a position she held for many years.

The Methodist Protestant Children's Home in High Point, to which Dixon was appointed superintendent in 1928, was a project of the state branch of the Woman's Home Missionary Society. The Dixons stressed the need for education beyond high school and were personally responsible for helping more than sixty young people obtain professional and college training. On many occasions, the couple took young ministers into their home until they could get started in college or in a pastorate.

Dixon died in Baltimore and was buried in the mausoleum at Guilford Memorial Park, High Point.

SEE: Mrs. Cuthbert W. Bates and Mrs. A. A. Clodfelter to Ralph Hardee Rives, letters (in possession of the author); Ruth C. Coble and Mildred L. Clodfelter, *This is Your Life—Arminius Gray Dixon* (1960); Nolan B. Harmon, ed., *Encyclopedia of World Methodism*, vol. 1 (1974); North Carolina Annual Conference of the Methodist Protestant Church, *Journal* (scattered issues, 1901–62); *North Carolina Christian Advocate*, 25 Jan. 1962; *Rocky Mount Sunday Telegram*, 24 July 1962; Western North Carolina Methodist Conference, *Journal* (1962); *Who's Who in America* (1920).

RALPH HARDEE RIVES

**Dixon, Benjamin Franklin** *(27 Mar. 1846–26 Sept. 1910)*, soldier, teacher, minister, and physician, was born in Cleveland County, the son of Thomas Dixon, a successful farmer in the county. He had one brother, Edward. When the Civil War broke out he enlisted on 25 Apr. 1861 at the age of fifteen. He was assigned to the Fourteenth North Carolina Regiment, commanded by his brother, Major Edward Dixon, who was killed at Richmond in 1862. Despite his youth, Benjamin Franklin Dixon received his commission on 9 June 1863. As a captain, he participated in such campaigns as Yorktown, Williamsburg, Seven Pines, Fredericksburg, Chancellorsville, Drury's Bluff, and the nine-month siege of Petersburg. He was captured at Five Forks on 1 Apr. 1865.

When the war ended Dixon, at age nineteen, returned to his native county and began a teaching career. Two years later he passed the examination to enter the ministry of the Methodist Episcopal church. His first charge was in Sumter, S.C., but he transferred to Monroe in the North Carolina Conference. Later he went to his old home in Shelby; here he was allowed to stay put and resume his study of medicine. In 1874 he was graduated from Charleston Medical College and practiced at Kings Mountain, where he remained for ten years.

On 7 July 1877 Dixon married Mrs. Nora Catherine Tracy Durham, widow of Plato Durham and daughter of Dr. James W. Tracy of Kings Mountain. They had a daughter, Pearl, and twin sons, Benjamin Franklin, Jr., and Wright Tracy. In 1883 Dixon was named superintendent of Oxford Orphanage. In 1890 he was elected president of Greensboro Female College by unanimous vote of the trustees; he resigned four years later and returned to Cleveland County. In the fall of 1896 he was elected to a seat in the state house of representatives.

On 8 May 1898, at the age of fifty-one, Dixon was commissioned as a major in the U.S. Army when the war with Spain erupted. His sons also joined the Second North Carolina Regiment but none saw action. The elder Dixon was discharged on 25 Nov. 1898.

Dixon was nominated by the state Democratic convention for the office of state auditor in 1900; he was elected and then reelected to a second term in 1904. He was a member of the Masons, Odd Fellows, Knights of

Pythias, and the Junior Order of United American Mechanics.

SEE: *Cyclopedia of Eminent and Representative Men of the Carolinas* (1892); D. C. Mangum, *Biographical Sketches of Members of the Legislature* (1897); *North Carolina Biography*, vol. 4 (1929); *Trinity Alumni Register* (1916); Weeks Scrapbook (North Carolina Collection, University of North Carolina, Chapel Hill) 2 and 6 [portraits].

FRANK SALTER

**Dixon, Dorsey Murdock** *(14 Oct. 1897–18 Apr. 1968),* millworker, songwriter, and country musician, was born into a family of Darlington, S.C., factory workers. His father, William McQuiller Dixon (1875–1939), was a steam engine operator in the Darlington Cotton Manufacturing Company whose seven children followed him into the mill. Dorsey left school after the fourth grade and began working in the Darlington mill when he was twelve. At an early age he showed an aptitude for music in a setting that fostered homemade music. He learned traditional and sentimental songs from his family and neighbors, who would gather at the Dixon house for music making. A local schoolteacher gave him violin lessons, and by the age of fourteen he had taught himself to play the guitar.

World War I brought Dixon a four-year respite from the textile mill while he worked as a railroad signalman for the Atlantic Coast Line in Darlington. In 1919 he was laid off by the railroad and joined the countless mill workers who traversed the Piedmont in search of jobs. During this period he was employed in a Lancaster, S.C., mill and may have worked elsewhere. Sometime around 1927 he made his way to East Rockingham in Richmond County, N.C., where he found work in the cloth room of the Aleo Mill. His parents, his sister Nancy, and his brother Howard all followed him to North Carolina.

In 1927 Dixon married Beatrice Lucele Moody, a fellow mill worker. They were the parents of four boys: Dorsey, Jr., William, Thomas, and Roger. Shortly after their marriage, Dorsey and Beatrice followed Howard Dixon to the Little Hanna Pickett Mill village in East Rockingham. During this time, Dorsey's interest in music intensified with the discovery of his talent for composition. A disastrous fire in a Cleveland, S.C., schoolhouse in 1923 had lingered in Dixon's memory, and in 1929 he expressed his reaction in a poem. His mother and his brother Howard noted that the words could be set to the popular tune, "Life's Railway to Heaven." Encouraged by their enthusiasm, Dorsey began to compose in earnest, developing a pattern he would follow all his life. His first-hand experiences were cast into poetry and set to traditional and traditionally inspired tunes. His subject matter was overwhelmingly drawn from his religious speculations on local tragedies. In spite of long working hours, Dixon would rise at five o'clock in the morning to pursue his art, and he began to play at local functions with his brother Howard.

In the early 1930s, two events played a major role in forming Dixon's musical career. The turn of the decade was a period of unrest in the Carolina textile mills. The violent 1929 strike in Gastonia fueled unrest in Rockingham, where workers went out on strike in 1931. William B. Cole, the intractable owner, shut down his second mill, the Little Hanna Pickett, in retaliation. The strike spread to the Aleo, East Rockingham's third mill, and the town became locked in a bitter dispute between owner and worker, which was only settled with the governor's intervention. Dixon turned to his mill experiences for several songs. A fragment he had learned in the Lancaster mill became "Weaver's Life." He made wry commentary on Rockingham mill conditions in "Spinning Room Blues" and "Weave Room Blues," sung with relish by the strikers. These songs led to his late rediscovery by students of occupational song.

More significant for Dixon on a personal level was the arrival in East Rockingham of the itinerant country musician, Jimmie Tarlton. A fine instrumentalist and confirmed drifter, Tarlton made several sojourns with relatives in the Little Hanna Pickett village. He so impressed the Dixon brothers that they abandoned their guitar and violin duet in 1931. Dorsey developed a unique finger-picking style, and Howard took up the Hawaiian guitar. Their new sound gained them local fame and notice by Fisher Hendley, a fellow musician and talent scout for radio station WBT in Charlotte. In 1934 the brothers became regular performers on the J. W. Fincher's Crazy Water Crystals Saturday Night Jamboree, a popular and influential program that brought the brothers wider recognition. On 12 Feb. 1936, they had their first recording session with an RCA Victor field crew in Charlotte. Over the next two years there were six more sessions in which fifty-five songs were recorded. In two of these sessions, Dorsey also recorded twelve songs with his wife Beatrice. Their commercial recordings brought the Dixons little financial return, however, and the reputation that Dorsey might have enjoyed for his compositions was thwarted by their identification with better-known artists. His songs proved popular among fellow musicians: Jimmie Tarlton had recorded "Weaver's Life" in 1932, Fisher Hendley recorded "Weave Room Blues" in 1937, and "Intoxicated Rat" was recorded by many musicians. A song Dorsey had composed on a fatal car accident in East Rockingham, which the brothers recorded in 1938 as "I Didn't Hear Anybody Pray," was recorded by Roy Acuff in 1942 as "Wreck on the Highway." It is unclear where Acuff had learned the song, but he chose to copyright it under his own name.

Although "Wreck on the Highway" quickly became a country music standard, it brought no assistance to Dixon, who had moved from Little Hanna Pickett back to the Aleo Mill and thence to the Dunean Mill in Greenville, S.C. Disheartened by the Dixon brothers' reverses, by his continued reliance on mill work, and especially by the lack of recognition for his composing ability, Dixon approached a lawyer at his family's urging. In 1946 the threat of a lawsuit in the face of the Dixon brothers' prior recording brought Acuff's partner Fred Rose from Nashville to Greenville, where an out-of-court settlement was reached. With high hopes of further settlements, the family migrated to New York City in 1947; however, a year of this pursuit, supported by work in a Union City, N.J., rayon plant, brought no success, and the Dixons returned to East Rockingham.

His hopes for a musical career lost, Dixon continued his mill work until 1951, when he and his wife moved to Baltimore with their son William. In 1953 Dorsey and Beatrice separated, and he returned alone to East Rockingham. Sustained by his religious convictions, his music played a role in services at the Church of God of Prophecy in Hamlet, N.C., where he performed with his brother Howard once again.

Dixon's songs continued to interest students of hillbilly and occupational song. John Edwards, a young Australian collector, traced Dixon through record company royalty statements and began to correspond with him. His whereabouts identified, he was visited in 1961 and 1962 by folklorists Archie Green, Ed Kahn, and Gene Earle. Their visits produced an album of Dixon's music and led to his invitation to the 1963 Newport Folk Festival. The revival of interest in his music encouraged Dixon to resume performing. During a stay in Washington in November 1963, he was asked to record his music for the Archive of Folk Song in the Library of Congress and for Piedmont Records. His performing comeback was halted in 1964, when he suffered the first of several heart attacks. Forced to decline further invitations, he retired to the care of his son, the Reverend Dorsey Dixon, Jr., in Plant City, Fla., until his death. His body was carried home to East Rockingham.

SEE: Pat Conte, *Beyond Black Smoke* (Country Turtle Records 6000 [notes]); "Dorsey Dixon: A Place in the Sun for a Real Textile Troubadour," *Textile Labor* 25 (1964); Dorsey M. Dixon Papers (Archive of Folk Song, Library of Congress, Washington, D.C.); Dorsey M. Dixon Papers (John Edwards Memorial Foundation, University of California, Los Angeles); William Dixon, Archie Green, Mrs. Ollie Melton, and W. T. Prevatte, interviews (Archive of Folk Music, University of North Carolina, Chapel Hill); Archie Green, ed., *Babies in the Mill* (Testament Records T-3901), "Dorsey Dixon: Minstrel of the Mills," *Sing Out!* 16 (1966), and "Tipple, Loom, and Rail" (Folkways Records FH 5273 [notes]); Rodney McElrea, "A Portrait of the Life and Phonograph Recordings of the Dixon Brothers," *Country News and Views* 2 (n.d.); Mike Paris, "The Dixons of South Carolina," *Old Time Music* 10 (1973).

DOUGLAS DENATALE

**Dixon, Elizabeth Delia.** *See* **Dixon-Carroll, Elizabeth Delia.**

**Dixon, Eula Louisa** *(27 Nov. 1872–21 Oct. 1921)*, leader in agriculture, local industry, school management, and community development, was born at Snow Camp where she lived most of her life. She was the daughter of Thomas Clay and Sarah Eleanor Albright Dixon and a descendant of Simon Dixon, one of the early settlers in the Cane Creek valley in the southern part of what is now Alamance County. The efforts of her Dixon ancestors to promote light industry in the Cane Creek valley produced a gristmill, the first in the valley; an iron foundry; and a textile mill for the manufacture of woolen goods established about 1886. Eula's cousin, Joseph Moore Dixon, was born and reared within sight of her home on the opposite side of Cane Creek. After graduation from Guilford College, he went to Montana and later served that state as governor and U.S. senator.

Eula Dixon's home was within a few hundred yards of Sylvan Academy, a preparatory school established by Quakers immediately after the Civil War. After completing her studies there she entered Guilford College at the age of seventeen; however, poor health prevented her from obtaining a degree.

Eula Dixon never married. She was the youngest of three sisters, one of whom married; the other was an invalid most of her adult life and remained at the Dixon home. At the death of her father in 1899, she assumed responsibility for the management of the Dixon farm and served as president of the Snow Camp Woolen Mill until it burned in 1912. Realizing the need of the people in her community for improved methods of farming, she entered the North Carolina College of Agriculture and Mechanic Arts (now North Carolina State University) at the age of thirty. She was the first woman to enroll in that institution. She returned to her home community to apply what she had learned to the Dixon farm and to use her influence to raise the standards in agriculture and cattle breeding in the community.

When Sylvan Academy was converted into Sylvan High School, the first public high school in the southern part of Alamance County, Eula Dixon became a member of its school board. Partly because of her influence an adequate building was erected for the school, quarters were provided for teachers, and school districts were consolidated to make the high school available to pupils of a wider area. One of her interests was for the school to offer courses in vocational training. For several years she coached the high school debating team; one of her teams reached the semifinals of the state interscholastic debating contest at Chapel Hill. While associated with the school she enjoyed a close rapport with teachers and pupils alike.

Following the lead of a long line of her ancestors Eula Dixon was a lifelong member of the Society of Friends (Quaker). She was a dynamic leader both in the spiritual life and work of Cane Creek Friends Meeting and in the statewide organization of Friends. She also was a leader of the temperance movement, then at the peak of its influence in that section of North Carolina. A supporter of the woman suffrage movement, she was a living demonstration of the liberated woman long before the term "women's liberation" came into use.

SEE: Cane Creek Monthly Meeting of Friends, *Minutes*; *Greensboro Daily News*, 3 Oct. 1954; Mary M. Hobbs, "In Loving Memory of Eula Dixon," *The Friends Messenger* 28 (1921); Records of Guilford College (Greensboro); George R. Ross, "Miss Dixon of Alamance," *State College News* 20 (1947).

ALGIE I. NEWLIN

**Dixon, Henry ("Hal")** *(ca. 1750–17 July 1782)*, Revolutionary War officer, was born in the part of Granville County that later became Orange and then Caswell, the son of Henry Dixon, Sr. Little is known about his life before the outbreak of the American Revolution. In 1763 he married Martha Wynne in Halifax County, Va. That Dixon had received some militia experience is clear, for when North Carolina was charged to form its first units of the Continental line in September 1775, he was commissioned captain of the First Regiment. He rose through the ranks quickly, becoming a major in July 1776 and a lieutenant colonel in May 1778 (amidst some controversy from several more senior officers). In the spring of 1778 the North Carolina legislature appointed Dixon "Inspector General over Militia," a post he held for the remainder of the war. His considerable duties involved raising militia units, equipping them for action, and coordinating their service with the Continental command. He was in close contact with Generals Jethro Sumner and Nathanael Greene in the defense of the southern states.

In June 1779 Dixon was severely wounded at Stono Ferry near Charleston, S.C., in the campaign commanded by General Benjamin Lincoln. As the war moved into North Carolina, he played a key role in raising militia to meet the British advance. In 1781 he fought in the actions at Wetzell's Mill and Guilford Court House and was wounded again at Eutaw Springs, S.C. He never recovered from the injuries and died at home the next year. Dixon left his wife and seven children and apparently the family moved west to Tennessee and Kentucky. A grandson, Archibald Dixon, succeeded Henry Clay as senator from Kentucky.

SEE: Walter Clark, ed., *State Records of North Carolina*, vols. 12–22 (1896–1907); William S. Powell, *When the Past Refused to Die, A History of Caswell County* (1977); Phillips Russell, *North Carolina in the Revolutionary War* (1965); William L. Saunders, ed., *Colonial Records of North Carolina*, vol. 10 (1890).

MARK F. MILLER

**Dixon, Howard Briten** *(19 June 1903–24 Mar. 1961)*, millworker and musician, attained recognition with his brother Dorsey as a country musician and recording artist. Born in Darlington, S.C., to William McQuiller (1875–1939) and Mary M. Braddock Dixon (1874–1939), he began work in the cotton mill there at the age of ten. In World War I, by concealing his age, he found work with his brother as a railroad signalman. In 1920, he married Mellie Barfield of Darlington; their children were Beatrice Smith, Elizabeth Pratt, Larry, Howard, Jr., Gordon, Alfred, and Hayden.

After the war, he returned to mill work, and followed his brother to East Rockingham in Richmond County, N.C. Here the brothers formed a singing partnership and enjoyed local success. Influenced by the country musician Jimmie Tarlton, Howard took up the Hawaiian guitar, and the Dixon brothers achieved a measure of success on Charlotte radio and in recordings made for RCA Victor. His instrumental ability was in demand by other musicians, and he also recorded several songs with Frank Gerald as the Rambling Duet.

When his brother moved to Greenville, S.C., Howard remained in East Rockingham to raise his growing family. A skilled loom fixer, he eventually acquired land in an area of Hamlet, N.C., which became known as Dixonville. There he was active in the Church of God of Prophecy, and with Lloyd Harris, Norman Walts, and James Collins performed gospel music as the Reaping Harvesters. Occasionally aided by his brother Dorsey, he continued to play with the group until his death from a heart attack at work. His work in religious music was carried on by his children in the Hamlet community.

SEE: Sources cited under **Dorsey Murdock Dixon**.

DOUGLAS DENATALE

**Dixon, Hugh Woody** *(3 July 1825–6 May 1901)*, manufacturer and civic leader, was born at Snow Camp, the son of Joseph and Mary Woody Dixon. His father was of the line of Thomas Dixon, an English Quaker, who came to America about 1700 and located in Bucks County, Pa. Fifty years later Thomas's son, Simon, left Pennsylvania and settled in the Cane Creek community of what is now Alamance County, N.C. The Dixons acquired a large tract of land and began various business enterprises in present-day Snow Camp. This marked the beginning of a heavy Quaker migration into the colony that continued for the next quarter of a century. Thomas Dixon, the son of Simon Dixon, died in 1827, and his two sons, Joseph and Jessie, carried on the various enterprises initiated by the family. Joseph Dixon became a famous iron caster whose foundry produced most of the castings for multiple grist and sawmills in that section of North Carolina.

When Hugh Woody Dixon was thirteen years old, he was enrolled in the New Garden Boarding School (later Guilford College) near Greensboro, but apparently did not attend more than a year. He returned to New Garden in 1841, however, and after that spent three years teaching and surveying, supposedly in Alamance County. For the next thirteen years (1844–57) he was a partner in the Unthank and Dixon Foundry, except for the twenty-four months he worked in the construction of the Gulf and Graham plank road.

On 29 Nov. 1855 Dixon married Flora Adaline Murchison of the Cane Creek community. She was not a Quaker, but probably was a Presbyterian. Dixon was challenged for violating a Quaker rule and marrying outside the denomination. His reply to the Quaker committee has often been quoted—that he had no regret for having married Miss Murchison, only that friends felt compelled to frown on the marriage. In 1857 he left Alamance County and settled in Chatham County at Ore Hill. There he was busy operating gristmills, a steam sawmill, and a foundry.

As a community leader with a Quaker background, Dixon was tested sorely during the Civil War. In spite of his antislavery position, which he expressed freely and frequently, he held his job as postmaster at Ore Hill, paid the $500 indemnity exempting Quakers from active military service, and lived through the war in a degree of peace and prosperity. He had accumulated some wealth, and in 1866 decided to return to Snow Camp where he had been a founder of Sylvan Academy, an educational force in the community for several years. In business he was also a respected leader. With his brother, Thomas, he established the Snow Camp Woolen Mill. In the community, he taught classes in adult education and Bible classes on Sunday; served as a trustee of New Garden Boarding School and its successor, Guilford College; and was active in the work of the Pleasant Hill Temperance Society after 1837, and later the Sons of Temperance.

Politically Dixon was never prominent, although he was twice named a candidate for public office over his protest but never elected. It was said of him, "Probably no member of the Quaker Church in North Carolina sacrificed more for religion, education and temperance than did Hugh W. Dixon." His life was happy and successful as he prospered in business and retained until his death a leadership position in many good causes in his community and state.

Dixon and his wife had four children of their own and an adopted son. Their daughters were Mary (Mrs. Z. H. Dixon), Roxie (Mrs. Alpheus White), Nora K. (unmarried), and a son, Joseph M. Dixon, governor and U.S. senator from Montana; their adopted son was A. H. Hinson, who later became a prominent citizen of Kansas City, Mo. His wife preceded him in death (1900), and both were buried at Snow Camp.

SEE: Samuel A. Ashe, ed., *Biographical History of North Carolina*, vol. 8 (1917); "Hugh Woody Dixon," *Guilford Collegian* 12 (1900).

C. SYLVESTER GREEN

**Dixon, Joseph** *(9 Apr. 1828–3 Mar. 1883)*, congressman, was born in rural Greene County just across the county line from the town of Farmville in Pitt County. There apparently is no record of the names of his parents nor information on his early education. It is reported that he was tutored privately but his schooling probably did not include college. As a young adult he operated a farm and a grocery store in Greene County. On 4 July 1861 he enlisted as a private in Company H, Ninth Regiment (which became the First North Carolina Cavalry); he was discharged at Kinston on 19 May 1862 by reason of "frequent attacks of inflammatory rheumatism following typhoid fever." After the Civil War, however, he served as a colonel in the state militia.

In 1864 and 1865 Dixon served as a judge of the Greene County court, although he had not been trained in law. Elected from Greene County, he served two terms (1868–69, 1869–70) in the North Carolina House of Representatives. In 1870, upon the death of the incumbent, David Heaton, he was elected to the U.S. House of Representatives as a Republican, defeating his Democratic opponent, Dr. C. J. O'Hagan, by a vote of 14,076 to 12,333. He served in the closing days of the Forty-second Congress, from 5 Dec. 1870 to 3 Mar. 1871, at the end of the first term of President Ulysses S. Grant. He did not seek election to a full term thereafter. Later that year he was appointed U.S. commissioner of claims, a post he held for two years (1871–73); he then returned to his farming interests in Greene County where he remained until his death. His only additional public activity was service as a delegate from Greene County to the North Carolina Constitutional Convention of 1875. He died eight years later, a month before his fifty-first birthday.

On 24 Dec. 1850 at Holly Grove, near Greenville, Pitt County, Dixon married Sallie A. E. Brown, daughter of Captain John S. Brown of the county. If they had children, their names are unknown, although one may have been Joseph Dixon from Fountain Hill who was a student at The University of North Carolina during 1882–84. The elder Dixon died in Pitt County near Fountain Hill, but it is not known whether he had been living there. He was buried in the Edwards Chapel Cemetery in Lenoir County.

SEE: *Bio. Dir. Am. Cong.* (1928); John L. Cheney, Jr., ed., *North Carolina Government, 1585–1974* (1975); Daniel L. Grant, *Alumni History of the University of North Carolina* (1924); Henry T. King, *Sketches of Pitt County* (1911); Louis H. Manarin, ed., *North Carolina Troops, 1861–1865, A Roster*, vol. 2 (1968); *Raleigh Register and North Carolina State Gazette*, 8 Jan. 1851; *Who Was Who in America*, vol. H (1963).

C. SYLVESTER GREEN

**Dixon, Joseph Moore** *(31 July 1867–22 May 1934)*, legislator, congressman, U.S. senator, and governor of Montana, was born at Snow Camp, Alamance County, the son of Hugh Woody and Flora A. Murchison Dixon. His father owned an iron foundry. Young Dixon attended Sylvan Academy and New Garden Boarding School near Greensboro before entering Earlham College in Richmond, Ind. He returned to North Carolina to complete his education and was graduated from Guilford College in 1889. He wanted to enter politics but he sensed little opportunity as a Quaker and a Republican in North Carolina. After working for a time in a woolen mill near his home, he moved in 1891 to Missoula County, Mont., where he began to read law in his uncle's office. He was admitted to the bar in December 1892 at the age of twenty-five and practiced for several years.

Dixon's first step toward a career in politics began when he became assistant prosecuting attorney of Missoula County in 1893, serving two years. As a Republican in the election of 1895, he won the race for prosecuting attorney, defeating his Democratic boss. In 1900 he was elected to the state house of representatives and in 1904 he was a delegate to the Republican National Convention in Chicago. Early in the new century he purchased the local daily newspaper, the *Missoulian*, which provided a springboard for further political advancement. He served a second term in the legislature and two years later was elected to the United States Congress, serving from 4 Mar. 1903 to 3 Mar. 1907. While in Congress he was active in securing larger homesteads, long- and short-haul regulation of railroads, and the opening of the Flathead and Crow Indian Reservations in Montana to settlement by non-Indians. He continually advocated federal funds for irrigation and woman suffrage.

Ultimately Dixon was a delegate-at-large to the Republican National conventions in Chicago in 1904 and 1916. In addition, he was elected to the U.S. Senate in 1906, serving from 4 Mar. 1907 to 3 Mar. 1913. An unsuccessful candidate for reelection in 1912, he was named chairman of President Theodore Roosevelt's Progressive convention the same year. He became a close friend of Roosevelt and was his campaign manager on the "Bull Moose" ticket, which split the Republican party and resulted in the first election of Woodrow Wilson to the presidency.

In 1913 Dixon resumed the practice of law, edited a Missoula newspaper, and managed a dairy farm. He returned to politics in 1920 and was elected governor of Montana, serving from 1921 to 1925. He ran as a Republican and defeated his Democratic opponent, Burton K. Wheeler, by 111,113 to 74,875. During Dixon's one term in office he brought reform to state government, including a very controversial modification in the method of taxing the state's large copper mining industry. Due to his progressive programs, he lost his bid for reelection in 1924. Four years later he was also defeated when he ran again for the U.S. Senate. During the administration of President Herbert Hoover, Dixon was acting secretary of the interior and later first assistant secretary of that department.

Dixon married Caroline M. Worden on 12 Mar. 1896; their children were Mrs. Virginia Dean, Mrs. Florence Leach, Mrs. Dorothy Allen, Mrs. Mary Jo Hills, Mrs. Betty Stearns, Frank, and Peggy. He died in Missoula and was buried in the city cemetery. Since 1958 the childhood farmhouse home at Snow Camp has been open to the public during July and August.

SEE: *Bio. Dir. Am. Cong.* (1961); Robert Sobel and John Raimo, *Biographical Directory of the Governors of the United States*, vol. 3 (1978); *Who Was Who in America*, vol. 1 (1943).

MARY BODMAN KENNER

**Dixon, Nancy Alena** *(23 Oct. 1892–16 Aug. 1973)*, folksinger, who contributed an important link in the history of American traditional music, was the oldest child of the family that produced the Dixon brothers, Dorsey and Howard. At the age of eight she began work as a spinner in the Darlington Cotton Manufacturing Company in Darlington, S.C. She was employed as a spinner for the next fifty-four years, moving with her family to East Rockingham, N.C., where she cared for her ailing parents until their death. She retired from mill work in 1954.

While a child at the Darlington mill, Nancy Dixon learned a number of songs about mill life which she kept alive in later years by singing them for nieces and nephews. Folklorists Archie Green and Gene Earle, who recorded her brother Dorsey in 1962, visited her in the Glenwood Boarding Home where she sang for them "Hard Times in Here" and the "Factory Girl." The latter song, perhaps the earliest American industrial ballad, was composed in Lowell, Mass., sometime in the 1830s and carried south by migrating mill workers. Nancy Dixon's version was almost certainly the last surviving example of an industrial song's tradition, tying twentieth-century Carolina mill workers to the earliest stages of American industrialization.

Nancy Dixon never married. Following her death in a nursing home in Sanford, she was buried in Eastside Cemetery, Rockingham.

SEE: Sources cited under **Dorsey Murdock Dixon**.

DOUGLAS DENATALE

**Dixon, Richard Dillard** *(5 Oct. 1888–26 July 1952)*, businessman, lawyer, clerk of court and superior court judge, and judge of the United States Military Tribunals, was born in Edenton, a descendant of distinguished eastern North Carolina and Virginia families. His father was Minton H. Dixon, the son of George Beverly Dixon, who moved to Edenton from Warrenton, Va. For more than a quarter of a century Minton Dixon was a leading merchant; for fifteen years he served as a justice of the peace and, from 1913 to 1918, as the first judge of the recorder's court in Chowan County. Richard Dillard Dixon's mother was Sally Dillard, the daughter of Dr. Richard Dillard, Sr., a surgeon in the Civil War, and of Mary Louisa Beverly Cross, the granddaughter of Richard Brownrigg.

Dixon's birthplace was Beverly Hall, a thirteen-room brick house erected in 1810 by Joseph and John Blount as a combined bank and living quarters for its staff. The institution prospered from its inception until 1835, when Andrew Jackson's withdrawal of federal funds from all banks necessitated its liquidation. Since that time the building has been used solely as a residence; in 1879 it was acquired by Richard Dillard, Sr., whose plantation home, Wingfield, had been burned during a Civil War skirmish. This historic house became the permanent home of Richard Dillard Dixon. As a child, he spent each summer in Nags Head and in Warrenton, Va. He received his early education at the Edenton Academy and in 1904 completed its program of study. He then attended Trinity Military School, at Chocowinity, and was graduated in 1906. The same year he entered The University of North Carolina; financial constraints caused him to withdraw in 1909 before he completed work toward a degree.

Dixon's first position was that of assistant in the Edenton graded school. At the end of the term he accepted employment with the brokerage firm of Charles Syer and Company, Norfolk, Va., beginning as a shipping clerk. He soon worked his way up to branch office manager and eventually became both sales manager and part owner of the business. He remained with the company until 1916, when his father's ill health made his return to Edenton advisable.

On 25 July 1917 Dixon volunteered for service in World War I, enlisting in New Bern as a private. He was assigned to Battery A of the 113th Field Artillery, 30th Division, then transferred to Camp Sevier, Greenville, S.C.; he was commissioned second lieutenant on 5 August and promoted to first lieutenant in February 1918. He was sent overseas and landed in Brest, France, on 20 May 1918. He participated in the St. Mihiel and Meuse-Argonne offensives, the engagements in the Troyon sector, and the Woevre offensive, opposite Metz. After the armistice, he went into Germany with the Army of Occupation and for thirty days was billeted at Colmar-Berg, Luxembourg. In February 1919 he was promoted to captain. His final station was in the Le Mans sector, where he remained until 25 Mar. 1919 when his battery was ordered home. He was honorably discharged on 15 Apr. 1919 at Camp Jackson, Columbia, S.C.

After he returned to civilian life, Dixon began to study law under state Senator Charles S. Vann of Edenton; in 1921 he continued his studies under Needham Y. Gulley at Wake Forest College. In November 1922 he was elected clerk of the superior court of Chowan County and in December was admitted to the bar. For nineteen years he served not only as clerk of superior court but also as clerk of recorder's court, judge of juvenile court, and county accountant. In 1941 he gave up his various duties to accept an appointment by Governor J. Melville Broughton as a special superior court judge, a position he held until 1945.

In 1946 Dixon went to Nuremberg, Germany, to assist in the war crime trials held under the authority of the Allied Council Law No. 10. In May 1947, at the recommendation of General Lucius D. Clay, he was appointed by President Harry S Truman to serve as an alternate to any of the tribunals. He presided over four of the trials: Case No. 1, *U.S. v. Karl Brandt et al.* (Medical Case); Case No. 2, *U.S. v. Erhard Milch* (Milch Case); Case No. 5, *U.S. v. Friedrich Flick et al.* (Flick Case); and Case No. 9, *U.S. v. Otto Ohlensdorf et al.* (Einsatzgruppen Case). He returned to the United States in 1948 and spent the remaining years of his life as an attorney in Edenton.

On 30 Apr. 1923 Dixon married Louise Manning Badham, also a member of widely known North Carolina families; they had one son, Richard Dillard Dixon, Jr. The elder Dixon was a member of St. Paul's Episcopal Church, Edenton, where he served as a vestryman at various times during a thirty-year period. In politics, he was always loyal to the Democratic party. He was a member of the Tryon Palace Commission from its organization on 6 Nov. 1945 until his death. He was also a member of Delta Kappa Epsilon, the North Carolina Literary and Historical Association, the North Carolina Society for the Preservation of Antiquities, the Edenton Chamber of Commerce, Rotary Club, and Edward G. Bond Post No. 40 of the American Legion. His primary interests were history and gardening.

He died at Beverly Hall and was buried in the churchyard of St. Paul's Episcopal Church. Two portraits, one unsigned and the other by Herr Birkman, of Nuremberg, are in the possession of his family.

SEE: Dixon's personal records of the Nuremberg trials (Southern Historical Collection, University of North Carolina, Chapel Hill); *North Carolina Biography*, vol. 4 (1928); Nuremberg War Crimes Trials, *Records of Judges*, 1945–48; Raleigh *News and Observer*, 30 Apr. 1950.

ESTHER EVANS

**Dixon, Simon** *(1728–1781)*, Quaker pioneer and miller, was born in Lancaster County, Pa. He was the grandson of William Dixon who moved to Pennsylvania from Ireland in 1638. His father, Thomas Dixon, a Pennsylvania Quaker, married Hannah Hadley on 20

Aug. 1727 at New Garden Meeting, New Castle, Del. At a public sale, Thomas bought a cradle in which a baby had died of smallpox. He brought it home on his horse, resting it in front of him. A short time later he developed smallpox and died in 1734 at age thirty. His widow was left with three small children: Simon, seven years; Rebecca, four years; and Ruth, about one year. On 13 Aug. 1742 Hannah Dixon married John Stanfield.

In the general Quaker migration from Pennsylvania into Virginia and the Carolinas, Simon Dixon—now age twenty-one—arrived in the spring of 1749 in the vicinity of Cane Creek, Orange (now Alamance) County, N.C., and unloaded his wagon on the north bank of the creek. (Today, this area is the community of Snow Camp.) He cleared some land, built a typical pioneer cabin of logs cut from the virgin forest, and planted a crop of corn. However, the primitive surroundings coupled with loneliness promoted discouragement and homesickness, causing him to return to his native Pennsylvania in the spring of 1751.

In 1752 Dixon married Elizabeth Allen. The following year, he returned to North Carolina accompanied by his wife and other settlers including two sisters and his mother, Hannah Hadley Dixon Stanfield. In 1751 he had purchased a vast tract of land from Earl Granville. Dixon's tract, combined with that of a friend, surrounded what is now Snow Camp and Cane Creek. On this land he and his family constructed a house of native stone, cutting and splitting logs by hand for flooring and doors. In 1753 he also built a rock dam across Cane Creek using a team of oxen to haul the rock. The creek provided waterpower for grinding grain in a mill that he soon built. Inside was a set of millstones brought from Pennsylvania. Known through the years as Dixon's Mill, it was repaired and partly rebuilt several times and served the community well. In 1946 the aged structure was torn down, but the millstones had been rescued earlier. At a reunion of Simon Dixon's descendants in 1925 at Cane Creek Friends Meeting, one of the millstones was placed at his gravesite as a memorial to him and his family for their contribution to the community and to the meeting.

By industry and economy Dixon accumulated a good deal of property. The countryside along Cane Creek filled fast with immigrants mostly from Pennsylvania. Their need for goods other than what they produced themselves was met when Dixon built a store. Each spring and fall he traveled by wagon to Philadelphia to replenish his stock. Entries found in his old account book indicate that he sold his goods for something above cost and carriage.

A week after the Battle of Guilford Court House, probably about 20 Mar. 1781, British troops stopped at Snow Camp and took over the Dixon house as headquarters. Dixon and his family were forced to take refuge elsewhere. Tradition emphasizes that Lord Cornwallis kept himself warm before an open fire in the Dixon home, sitting in a straight armchair. It is thought that the soldiers tried to run the gristmill; they failed because Dixon had jammed the mill wheel, making its operation impossible. According to another legend, some of Cornwallis's men, believing that Dixon possessed a money box, tortured him with red hot iron tongs to make him reveal its location. The chair and the tongs are now in the city museum of Greensboro.

The British resumed their march to Wilmington on 25 Mar. 1781. A few days later Dixon, about sixty years old, died from so-called camp fever contracted from some of the soldiers. Death came while he sat in the same armchair that was much used by Cornwallis. He was buried in the cemetery of the Cane Creek Friends Meeting, of which he had been a charter member.

Simon and Elizabeth Allen Dixon had eight children: Thomas, John, Naomi, Jesse, Simon, Solomon, Benjamin, and Elizabeth.

SEE: Simon Dixon, *Recollections of Cornwallis' Encampment at Dixon's Mill, Orange Co., 1781* (n.d.); Juanita O. Euliss, comp., *History of Snow Camp, North Carolina* (1971); *Greensboro Daily News*, 2 Nov. 1925; Wade H. Hadley et al., *Chatham County, 1771–1971* (1976); Lyndon Stuart, *A Short History of Cane Creek Monthly Meeting of the Religious Society of Friends, Snow Camp, North Carolina* (1951); Walter Whitaker, *Centennial History of Alamance County, 1849–1949* (1949).

FRANCES OSBORNE GUST

**Dixon, Thomas, Jr.** *(11 Jan. 1864–3 Apr. 1946)*, minister, writer, lecturer, lawyer, playwright, producer, director, actor, legislator, and clerk of the federal court for the eastern district of North Carolina, was born near Shelby in Cleveland County. On his father's side, he was descended from the pioneering Scotch-Irish who settled the Piedmont before the American Revolution. Dixon's ancestors and their numerous kinsmen had fought on the patriot side in the Battle of Kings Mountain. His father, Thomas Dixon, Sr., was locally eminent as a Baptist minister even as a young man. In 1848, while pursuing his ministry in York County, S.C., the elder Dixon met and married Amanda Elvira McAfee, the daughter of a well-to-do planting family. In 1854 she gave birth to Amzi Clarence, the first of five children to survive infancy and childhood. In 1861 the Dixon family joined the general American migration to the good lands of the west, themselves going to settle with relatives and friends in central Arkansas. In 1863, during the midst of the war, the small family determined to return to North Carolina. Marching with livestock, thirty-two slaves, and a covered wagon, the Dixons passed perilously through the armies bloodily contesting for possession of Atlanta. Shortly after they arrived in Cleveland County, Thomas Dixon, Jr., was born.

For a time, the family lived on a farm. Later in 1865, however, they moved into the town of Shelby where Dixon opened a store to supplement his meager income as a minister. Like so many Southerners in those difficult years of Reconstruction, the Dixons labored hard for a meager living. As a child in Shelby, Tom helped his father in the store. Also, he came to know and idolize his uncle Leroy Mangum McAfee. McAfee was graduated from The University of North Carolina in 1858, entered the Confederate Army at the opening of hostilities, and was promoted to colonel of the Forty-ninth North Carolina Regiment before he was twenty-five. When Tom knew him, McAfee was a prominent lawyer in Shelby, the leader of the Ku Klux Klan in Cleveland County, and a hero. In 1872, the Dixons moved to a farm near town. During the next four years, before moving back to Shelby, young Tom came to know hard labor in the fields.

Dixon was educated by his parents and in the Shelby Academy. In 1879 he followed his older brother Clarence to Wake Forest College. He left behind a younger brother, Frank, and two younger sisters, Elizabeth Delia and Addie May. At Wake Forest, Tom distinguished himself as a scholar, winning the highest honors attained up to that time in the Baptist school. His academic achievements earned him a scholarship to graduate school in the recently established Johns Hopkins University in Baltimore. He entered Johns Hopkins in the fall of 1883, enrolling in the famous seminar offered by Professor Herbert Baxter Adams. One of his classmates was another young Southerner, Woodrow Wilson.

In Baltimore Dixon became enamored of the stage. Within a few months, he left graduate school and moved to New York, determined to become an actor. In college he had established himself as a brilliant orator, but bitter experience finally persuaded him to abandon his efforts to enter the theater. He returned to Shelby and began to read law. In 1884 he was elected to the General Assembly and immediately sought election to the speaker's chair. Although he did not win the speakership, he proudly took his seat on the floor of the house when the 1885 legislative session began, four days before his twenty-first birthday. As a legislator he participated in shaping the first bill ever passed to pension Confederate veterans. He also joined in a movement to promote public education. After the session, he was admitted to the bar, experienced early success as a lawyer in Shelby, and on 3 Mar. 1886 married Harriet Bussey (d. 29 Dec. 1937). However, he found the practice of law frustrating. After much soul-searching, he resolved to follow his father and older brother into the ministry. Ordained, he took churches first in Goldsboro and then in Raleigh. Quickly gaining fame, he moved on to a pulpit in Boston and, after 1889, in New York. In New York, he was soon marked as an advocate of the "social gospel" because of his activities to promote political, economic, and social reform.

In 1895 Dixon left the Baptist church to become a nondenominational minister. Meanwhile, he had become a very popular lecturer, junketing throughout the country and speaking night after night on various subjects. Before long, he could claim a fee of a thousand dollars for each performance. During the late 1890s, he had also established a home in Virginia. He bought Elmington Manor, a large and beautiful antebellum estate in Gloucester County on the lower Chesapeake Bay. There he became a gentleman farmer and a very knowledgeable yachtsman while maintaining both his ministry in New York and his speaking engagements throughout the country.

In 1901 Dixon happened to attend a performance of the long-running play, *Uncle Tom's Cabin*. Incensed by what he believed to be a libel of the South, he resolved to write an answering novel. For a year he gathered material and finally took sixty days from his other interests to write *The Leopard's Spots*. The novel was a twin plea for the exclusion of the Negro from American society and for a reunion of North and South. The book was a tremendous success, selling more than a million copies.

Though never deserting his title of "Reverend," Dixon was known for the remainder of his life as a writer. *The Leopard's Spots* was soon followed by two other books, both arguing strongly and dramatically for racial segregation and reunion. In 1905 he adapted one of these for the stage; his play, *The Clansman*, was also a great success, and he proceeded to write, direct, produce, and act in others. In 1913 he agreed to allow a motion picture company headed by David W. Griffith to make the play into a film. Two years later that production was premiered as *The Birth of a Nation* and it, too, won widespread applause. Thereafter, into the 1920s, Dixon was very active in film-making. In addition to his trilogy on race, he was also writing a trilogy of novels attacking socialism. These were followed by more than a score of books. The last, *The Flaming Sword* (1939), predicted that the Communists would take over America using an easily duped Negro population as its tool.

Dixon's immediate family was an impressive one. Somehow between a stern, puritanical, and patriarchic father and an aristocratic, gentle, and romantic mother, five gifted children were marked for distinction. In 1922 four of the children were recognized in *Who's Who*. Clarence became an international figure in his church, and, if Baptists had bishops, he would surely have gained that rank. Frank, too, became a minister and much sought-after lecturer. Elizabeth Delia, with much moral and some financial support from her brother Tom, became a pioneer woman physician in North Carolina. Addie May became a writer, a public relations celebrity, and a cobiographer of Warren Gamaliel Harding.

Ever an adventurous, willful, driving person, Dixon fell upon hard times in his last days. During his life, he made and lost at least three fortunes. The money he earned from his first books he lost on the stock and cotton exchanges in the crash of 1907. His final venture in the late 1920s was a vacation resort, Wildacres, in the mountains of western North Carolina. After he had spent a vast amount of money on its development, the enterprise collapsed as speculative bubbles in land across the country began to burst before the crash of 1929. In 1937 the once affluent Tom Dixon was appointed clerk of the federal court for the eastern district of North Carolina. His health failing and a widower, he married on 20 Mar. 1939 the leading lady of one of his early films, Madelyn Donovan. Dixon lived in illness during his last years, the flashing intelligence still flickering through rising pain. He died at his home on Hillsborough Street in Raleigh.

Three children were born to Dixon's first marriage: Jordan, Louise, and Thomas Dixon III.

SEE: Raymond A. Cook, *Fire from the Flint, The Amazing Careers of Thomas Dixon* (1968); Helen A. Dixon, *A. C. Dixon, A Romance of Preaching* (1931); *Who's Who in America* (1922); J. Zebulon Wright, "Thomas Dixon: The Mind of a Southern Apologist" (Ph.D. diss., George Peabody College for Teachers, 1966).

JOEL WILLIAMSON

**Dixon-Carroll, Elizabeth Delia** *(4 Feb. 1872–16 May 1934)*, physician and director of medical services, professor of physiology and hygiene, and infirmary physician of Meredith College, Raleigh, was born in Shelby of English and Scottish ancestry. She was the daughter of Thomas Dixon, Sr., a Baptist minister in Shelby who was much respected in western North Carolina, and Amanda McAfee Dixon. One brother, Clarence, was a celebrated Baptist preacher in London, England; another, Thomas, Jr., author and lecturer, wrote *The Clansman*, the stirring Civil War story that was adapted for the motion picture *Birth of a Nation*. A sister, Addie May, was married to a Presbyterian clergyman, J. E. Thacker of Norfolk, Va.

Elizabeth Delia attended public school in Shelby; she was awarded an academic degree from Cornell University, Ithaca, N.Y. and a medical degree in 1895 from Women's Medical College (later Columbia) in New York City. That year she rated first among two hundred medical licentiates. While enjoying an adventure of world travel following graduate training, she met and became engaged to Dr. Norwood G. Carroll, a young dentist of Magnolia. They were married in about 1900 after both had begun practice in Raleigh.

When Meredith College opened on 27 Sept. 1899, Dr. Dixon-Carroll became its first physician, holding the position until her death thirty-five years later. Her course in physiology and hygiene was eagerly sought; confidante and counselor, she was dearly loved by students and faculty alike and respected by her professional colleagues. She insisted on strict preventive medical practices and took pride in the fact that during her entire tenure she never lost a patient, the deadly influenza epidemic of 1917–18 notwithstanding. From mid-fall to spring she insisted that all students wear high-topped shoes and warm underwear with sleeves to the wrists.

Public-spirited, she espoused the causes of woman suffrage and youth welfare. She advocated reform in the care of delinquent youth before the North Carolina legislature, exciting an enthusiasm reminiscent of the General Assembly's response to Dorothea Dix in the 1840s when the latter pleaded for improved treatment of the mentally ill. In 1917 the legislature enacted a bill to "establish 'The State Home and Industrial School for Girls and Women' for the reclaiming and training of delinquents, $25,000.00 having been appropriated for the purchase of grounds and the erection of buildings, and $10,000.00 annually for operating expenses." Dr. Dixon-Carroll was on its board of directors, appointed by Governor Thomas W. Bickett. Acting for the North Carolina Federation of Women's Clubs, an organization that she helped establish, she was influential in the purchase of a defunct school for boys at Samarcand in Moore County, comprising 224 acres and buildings in good repair. For favorable psychological impact, the school and farm were given the name Samarcand Manor; it was one of the first establishments of its kind in the South. Each Christmas, Meredith College students enhanced its holiday sparkle by sending Christmas stockings.

Dr. Dixon-Carroll was the first woman medical practitioner in Raleigh. She maintained private offices for many years with Dr. Bessie Evans Lane, who assisted her at Meredith College and on her death succeeded her at Meredith. In addition to her general medical practice, Dr. Dixon-Carroll practiced ophthalmology and counseled both young and older women. She was a member of the American Medical Association, the North Carolina Medical Society, and the Raleigh Academy of Medicine of which she was one-time president. She was also an honorary member of the North Carolina Dental Society, founding member and first president of the Raleigh Women's Club and the North Carolina State Federation of Women's Clubs, vice-president (1917–30) and president (1930–34) of the board of directors of Samarcand Manor, founding member and president of the Raleigh Garden Club, and a member of the Fortnightly Review Club.

She and her husband had no children. After their marriage a young nephew of Dr. Norwood Carroll, Herbert Norwood, became a frequent visitor to their hospitable and rustic log home, Nordel Hill, in the old Bloomsbury section of north Raleigh and in time was like an adopted son. He enhanced the Carrolls' pleasure in a leisurely cruise around the world when his uncle retired from dentistry in 1914. Later he was graduated with honors from the U.S. Naval Academy at Annapolis to become a career officer. Serving with distinction during World War II, he was reported missing in action when his ship was lost during the Battle of the Solomon Islands. A naval fighting ship bears his name.

Dr. Dixon-Carroll died in Rex Hospital, Raleigh, of injuries suffered in an automobile accident the previous day. The funeral service was conducted in the First Baptist Church by the Reverend Dr. J. Powell Tucker. The Reverend E. McNeill Poteat said in eulogy, "She was utterly impatient of things that cramped the human spirit." Burial was in Oakwood Cemetery. Her husband died on 5 Apr. 1942 while visiting friends in Cincinnati.

SEE: *Bulletin of the North Carolina State Board of Charities and Public Welfare*, 1918–23; Helen Harrison, "Famous Women in North Carolina" (North Carolina Collection, University of North Carolina, Chapel Hill); Mary Lynch Johnson, *A History of Meredith College* (1956); "Medical Women in North Carolina," *North Carolina Medical Journal* 2 (1950); *Medicine in North Carolina*, 2 vols. (1972); *Meredith College Quarterly Bulletin*, November 1934, November 1938; Raleigh *Biblical Recorder*, 23 May 1934; Raleigh *News and Observer*, 15 and 16 May 1934; Katharine Ripley, *Sand in My Shoes* (1931); *Samarcand Manor* (n.d.); Lou Rogers, "Dr. Delia Dixon-Carroll," *We the People of North Carolina* 1 (December 1943).

WARNER WELLS

**Doak, Frances Blount Renfrow** *(13 Oct. 1887–14 Sept. 1974)*, leader in women's organizations and in the North Carolina Democratic party, first woman radio announcer in North Carolina, and civic, religious, and political leader, was an accomplished speaker and writer who was well-known and highly respected throughout the state. She was born in Spring Hope, the daughter of Perry Van Buren and Ellen Douglas Sorsby Renfrow. Her ancestors—the Renfrows, Pridgens, Blounts, and Sorsbys—had lived in eastern North Carolina since the eighteenth century. She attended Littleton Female College, a private Methodist-related college, on a scholarship established there by General Julian S. Carr; afterward, she studied at Meredith College and Draughon's Business College in Raleigh. When Charles B. Aycock retired as governor and entered into private legal practice in Raleigh, she became his secretary and was assisting him in his campaign for the U.S. Senate at the time of his death in 1912. The following year she married Charles Glenn ("Chick") Doak, a longtime coach and professor at North Carolina State College.

Mrs. Doak became the first woman radio announcer in North Carolina in 1928 and pioneered in presenting the first hourly woman's program over radio station WPTF, where she was a staff member for three years. From 1934 to 1941 she was employed by the U.S. Department of Agriculture, serving as executive secretary in the Farm Debt Adjustment Section of the Farm Security Administration, then headed by future Governor W. Kerr Scott of North Carolina.

For many years Mrs. Doak was active in the Raleigh Woman's Club as vice-president and president; she also served on a number of committees. While chairman of the club's welfare department, she was instrumental in establishing the first day-care center for black children in Raleigh. In 1933, she was chairman of the International Relations Committee of the Federation of Women's Clubs. Later, she spoke on behalf of the Dumbarton Oaks Proposals and in favor of the formation of the United Nations organization. She was, in part, responsible for the founding of the Institute of International Relations in North Carolina, which functioned for seventeen years. In 1941 she began a ten-year stint as executive secretary to the North Carolina Federation of Women's Clubs and edited the *North Carolina Clubwoman*.

Among her civic works, Mrs. Doak helped to organize the first statewide Negro Parent-Teacher Association Congress. She took an active interest in prison reform and, for over forty years, presented an annual Christmas program at Central Prison in Raleigh, a project she started in 1910. This was the first such entertainment ever offered to the inmates of the prison. For thirty years, she was the secretary of the Wake County Cancer Society; she also served as president of the Raleigh Women's Christian Temperance Union, chairman of the United Nations' first State Children's Crusade, vice-president of the Health Publications Institute, Inc., for the U.S. Public Health Service, and board member of the Aycock Memorial Commission and of the North Carolina School for the Blind. In addition, she wrote a history of the North Carolina Federation of Women's Clubs for the period 1942–62.

Early in her life, Mrs. Doak was affiliated with the Methodist church; however, in 1927 she joined the Raleigh Monthly Meeting of Friends (Quakers), which her husband helped to organize, where she was active in peace and service work. Several times she served on the North Carolina Board of the American Friends Service Committee. Faithful to her alma mater, she took a deep interest in the work of the Littleton College Memorial Association—organized in the late 1920s following the burning of the school in 1919. She was secretary of the association for many years and assisted in establishing a Littleton College Scholarship Fund at Scarritt College in Nashville, Tenn., and a Littleton College Loan Fund at North Carolina Wesleyan College in Rocky Mount. She also assisted in compiling memorabilia connected with Littleton College which was placed in the libraries of several colleges and universities in the state.

An active member of the North Carolina Democratic party for many years, Mrs. Doak was involved in the campaigns of Governor Cameron Morrison, Congressman Harold Cooley, Governor and Senator W. Kerr Scott, Senator Frank P. Graham, and Governor Terry Sanford. She wrote the constitution for the first unit of the North Carolina Democratic Women. She was one of the founders and president of the Wake County League of Women Voters, as well as chairman of the Child Welfare and Women in Industry Committee of the state league.

Mrs. Doak was the mother of two sons and one daughter. During the thirty-three years her husband was associated with North Carolina State College, the Doak home frequently served as an "Open House" for students. At Littleton College, where she studied elocution, and in her early years in the Raleigh Woman's Club Mrs. Doak helped to present and appeared in various amateur theatrical productions including the dramas of Shakespeare. She died at the Confederate Home for Women, Fayetteville, where she had lived during her later years. Funeral services were held at the Community United Church, Raleigh, and at the New Garden Friends Meeting House, Guilford College; burial was at New Garden Friends Cemetery.

SEE: William S. Powell, ed., *North Carolina Lives* (1962); Raleigh *News and Observer*, 6 July 1941, 22 May 1951, 16 Sept. 1974.

RALPH HARDEE RIVES

**Dobbin, James Cochran** *(14 Jan. 1814–4 Aug. 1857),* legislator, congressman, and secretary of the navy under Franklin Pierce, was born in Fayetteville, the son of John Moore Dobbin and Anness Cochran. His paternal grandfather, Hugh Dobbin, was a successful merchant in the Carolinas; his maternal grandfather, James Cochran, was a prominent planter and politician from Person County. Young Dobbin was educated at the Reverend Colin McIver's academy in Fayetteville and at the Bingham School in Hillsborough. At the age of fourteen he entered The University of North Carolina, from which he was graduated with high honors in 1832. From 1832 to 1835 he read law with Robert Strange in Fayetteville and was admitted to the bar in 1835, thereafter practicing in Fayetteville and vicinity.

Although he participated in local politics, Dobbin shunned political office until he was nominated—without his knowledge—by the Democrats of his district as a candidate for Congress. Elected in 1845, he served one term in the House (1845–47) but declined to run a second time. Soon after returning to public life, he was elected to the North Carolina General Assembly. In the 1848 legislative session he gained distinction by making an impassioned speech supporting the establishment of a state hospital for the insane. Dobbin's efforts, which his contemporaries credited with saving the bill but which were contrary to the tendencies of his party, were made at the request of his dying wife. She had been befriended and nursed during her fatal illness by Dorothea Dix, who had come to North Carolina to crusade for better treatment of the insane.

In 1850 Dobbin was reelected to the General Assembly and chosen speaker of the Commons. Two years later he led the North Carolina delegation to the Democratic National Convention in Baltimore. When the convention deadlocked over the competing candidacies of James Buchanan, Lewis Cass, Stephen Douglas, and William L. Marcy, Dobbin nominated the relatively unknown Franklin Pierce. In a brief speech he led a convention stampede that selected Pierce as the party's candidate for president. In the victorious campaign that followed, Dobbin strongly supported Pierce and himself won reelection to the General Assembly. When the legislature met in 1852, he was a leading Democratic candidate to succeed the retiring Whig senator, Willie P. Mangum. However, disaffected members of his own party prevented an election, and for a time North Carolina had only one senator.

Because of Dobbin's service in gaining his nomination and election in 1852, Franklin Pierce appointed him secretary of the navy. Though unfamiliar with naval matters, Dobbin worked tirelessly as secretary and succeeded in bringing about significant reforms in that nearly moribund department. In his annual reports and recommendations he advocated an enlarged and more modern navy through the building of six steam propeller frigates and five steam sloops and through increasing naval personnel by one-third. He also sought to make the navy more vital and efficient by securing a number of reforms, including promotion by merit instead of by seniority and the establishment of an officer retirement system. In addition, he attempted to establish the navy as a permanent body of seamen and promoted the reintroduction of a naval apprentice system. During his four years in office from 1853 to 1857, his unflagging efforts to correct many of the weaknesses of the U.S. Navy helped put it on a sound footing and demonstrated the potential importance of intelligence, courage, and persistence in naval administration.

Dobbin's dedication and hard work while secretary took its toll on his health, which had never been robust. Five months after leaving office, at the age of forty-three, he died at his home and was buried in Cross Creek Cemetery, Fayetteville.

In 1838 Dobbin married Louisa Holmes of Sampson County. Before her death in 1848, their marriage produced three children: Mary Louisa Dobbin Anderson, James C., Jr., and John Holmes. Portraits of James C. Dobbin are owned by the Navy Department, Washington, D.C., and by the Philanthropic Society of The University of North Carolina, Chapel Hill.

SEE: Samuel A. Ashe, ed., *Biographical History of North Carolina*, vol. 6 (1907); James C. Dobbin Papers (North Carolina State Archives, Raleigh); Harold D. Langley, *Social Reform in the United States Navy, 1798–1862* (1967); Helen Marshall, *Dorothea Dix* (1937); Henry E. Shepherd, "James Cochran Dobbin," *The North Carolina Booklet* 16 (1916 [portrait]); Charles O. Paullin, *Paullin's History of Naval Administration, 1775–1911* (1968); Leonard D. White, *The Jacksonians: A Study in Administrative History, 1829–1861* (1954).

H. THOMAS KEARNEY, JR.

**Dobbs, Arthur** *(2 Apr. 1689–28 Mar. 1765)*, colonial governor of North Carolina, surveyor-general of Ireland, promoter of exploration for a Northwest Passage, and scholar and scientist, was a son of the Enlightenment and one of his colony's ablest executives. He was born in Ayrshire, Scotland, whither his mother had been sent for safety's sake because of political and religious unrest. His ancestral home was Castle Dobbs, County Antrim, Ireland, where he spent most of his life and where his descendants still reside. His father was Richard Dobbs, and his mother, Mary, was the daughter of Archibald Stewart of Ballintoy. The first Dobbs landed near Carrickfergus in 1599; since then the family has been prominent in that area of Northern Ireland and, before Irish independence, in Dublin. In the late seventeenth and early eighteenth centuries the Anglican Dobbses distinguished themselves in Dublin intellectual circles and became close friends of Jonathan Swift, who for a time had a residence near Castle Dobbs.

Though Dobbs's recent biographer did not discover the place and manner of his early education, and though his name does not appear on the incomplete alumni lists of the principal Scottish or English universities or of Trinity College, Dublin, it is obvious from his writings, his speeches, and his library that he received good training, perhaps beyond that possible to obtain in the grammar school at Carrickfergus near his home. Regardless of where he received his formal education, Dobbs was back in County Antrim for a year or two before he obtained a commission in the dragoons, joining his regiment in March 1711. In October 1712, after his father died, he was placed on the half pay on which he remained until he was appointed surveyor-general of Ireland almost twenty years later. In 1720 he became high sheriff of Antrim and soon after mayor of Carrickfergus. Like his immediate Dobbs ancestors, Squire Arthur in these and later political posts identified himself with the interests of Ireland at the same time that he was an imperialist. In 1727 he was returned from Carrickfergus to the Irish House of Commons, being identified with the ruling Whig party rather than Swift's Tory faction. In the 1720s he had demonstrated his scientific curiosity with reports to the London Royal Society on a Parhelion or Mock Sun (1721–22), on an Aurora Borealis (1725–26), and on an eclipse of the moon (1728–29)—all published in the society's *Transactions* (vols. 32, 34, and 36). Among his extant unpublished manuscripts of the period is an essay on coinage in Britain and Ireland in which he proposed a method of preventing frauds and abuses. The paper reflects Irish protests against a new Irish coinage authorized by the British Parliament; it also suggests early interest in a matter with which he was to be concerned in North Carolina, the issuance of a provincial coinage.

Meanwhile, Dobbs improved his estates agriculturally and developed even greater interest in local politics. Concomitant with both these interests was a third, Irish trade. The squire and MP became a champion of the rights of his fellow countrymen and of the necessity that foreign and British purchases from his homeland be increased. On the subject he wrote and published *An Essay on the Trade and Improvement of Ireland* in two parts (Dublin, 1729, 1731), both serious and significant contributions to Irish economic thought and history that anticipated the kind of encouragement he gave or tried to give North Carolina trade a full generation later. In the essay he also championed the right of the "commonalty" to own land. Here and later he insisted that parts of the empire outside Great Britain—that is, Ireland and the North American colonies—be allowed new markets for their produce.

The *Essay on Trade*, his experience in the Irish Commons, and a letter from Archbishop Hugh Boulter to Walpole brought the limited political recognition he was to enjoy the rest of his life. Before he actually met the prime minister, however, Dobbs sent him a sixty-page "Scheme to Enlarge the Colonies and Increase Commerce and Trade" aiming to advance the prosperity of the mother country and Ireland as well as of America. In the treatise he traced the growth of colonial empires, stressed the need for more settlers and settlements in America, pleaded for a just treatment of the Indian and a more vigorous missionary effort, and, as in his *Essay on Trade*, asked for the repeal of the Navigation Acts. Finally, he proposed means of forestalling the French threat in North America. His suggestions were sound politically, economically, and militarily, as events within the next generation were to prove, for he definitely anticipated the necessity for various British moves in these spheres.

Though Walpole could do little at the time to implement Dobbs's proposals, apparently the prime minister was impressed. Soon afterward, Dobbs was asked to assume control of the vast Conway estate in Ireland and to act as legal adviser and court agent for the heir who was still a minor, a rather complex task that took too much time from the MP's own public and private business. In 1733 Dobbs received some reward for his diligence, however, for he was appointed engineer and surveyor-general of Ireland, a lucrative post that was by no means a sinecure. Under his supervision the handsome new Parliament House was completed, the result one of the finest Georgian buildings in Dublin. Other public buildings were rebuilt or erected in the city also under his supervision and planning. He appears to have been an architect of considerable skill.

A few years before this major political appointment Dobbs had become interested in the Northwest Passage, partly at least concomitant with his ardor to increase British imperial trade. He made a methodical study of the subject and, as he rose to political prominence, besieged the admiralty and the Hudson's Bay Company with proposals for exploration. Though he met with indifference or hostility from the company, in 1735 he and a group of influential London merchants—including at least two who were within a few years to be his partners in the acquisition of North Carolina lands—laid their own plan of procedure before the government, attacking the company for its inertia and monopoly. Dobbs appealed to the English people, combining as motives religion, patriotism, and profit—the usual incentives to promotion. The rising tide of public opinion forced the Hudson's Bay Company to send two ships to the northwest section of Hudson Bay, but they returned without accomplishing anything, leaving everybody unsatisfied.

With the support of such powerful friends as merchant John Hanbury and First Lord of the Admiralty Sir Charles Wager (both friends and correspondents of Virginian William Byrd II), Dobbs managed to get independent action, and an expedition of two ships set out in 1742–43 under the command of Captain Christopher Middleton, an old Hudson's Bay Company employee. The results were again disappointing, for Middleton proved beyond any reasonable doubt that no passage existed in the area searched. The expedition was successful only in charting an unknown region. Dobbs refused to believe Middleton's report, which he thought suggested withheld information, thereby demonstrating the stubbornness of which he was later accused as well as his high hopes for British imperial economy, both traits actually or allegedly displayed during his colonial governorship. There was a long controversy between the seaman and the surveyor-general, in part recorded in such tracts as Middleton's *Vindication of the Conduct of Captain Middleton . . . In Answer to Certain Objections and Aspersions of Arthur Dobbs, Esq.* (1745) and Dobbs's *Remarks upon Captain Middleton's Defence* (1744) and *A Reply to Captain Middleton's Answer* (1745), among others. In the midst of the turmoil Dobbs published *An Account of the Countries Adjoining Hudson Bay in the Northwest part of America . . .* (1744), a large volume full of current inaccuracies but still indicating the author's immense knowledge of the nature and geography of Canada and its almost unknown interior. It includes an account of Joseph La France's travels from Lake Superior to Hudson Bay in 1740, a significant and detailed relation. Curiously little of the book is concerned with the Middleton controversy, though it is mentioned in the long subtitle.

A second voyage of discovery ensued in 1746, this time backed entirely by Dobbs and his friends and commanded by two bitter enemies of Middleton and the Hudson's Bay Company. Two ships were sent on the expedition: the *Dobbs Galley* and the *California*. Fairly thorough search of the bays and inlets revealed nothing, though Dobbs to his dying day continued to believe firmly in a Northwest Passage. The proof of its above-and-below-water-and-ice existence was to come centuries too late to be of importance. His insatiable interest in America and its potential is borne out further by two other unpublished essays of this period on the beaver trade and the settling of Labrador, and a published piece on the distance between Asia and America (*Transactions*, vol. 44). All are perceptive expositions of the imperial situation.

In the next several years Dobbs wrote two unpublished papers on the necessity of a union between Britain and Ireland and a third on extending trade with Labrador. He also published his observations on bees and honey manufacture (*Transactions*, vol. 46) and in other ways demonstrated the scientific observation he was to continue in America. In the same period, perhaps beginning even a little earlier, he showed his direct interest in the established colonies of America by purchasing lands in North Carolina and making plans to bring a large number of Irish, especially distressed Protestants, to settle on them. According to some historians before the end of 1735 he, other Irish gentlemen, and London merchant Henry McCulloh had purchased a tract of 60,000 acres along the Black River, though in fact Dobbs had no financial interest in the purchase. The next year McCulloh and his group (including James Huey and Murray Crymble) secured a vast area so unwieldy that within a few years they sold off considerable sections to other speculators, including Dobbs. In 1745 Dobbs and Colonel John Selwyn, a prominent court figure, purchased from the McCulloh associates 400,000 acres lying roughly in the present counties of Mecklenburg and Cabarrus. A provision required the grantee to settle one white person on every 200 acres and at the end of ten years all unsettled land was to revert to the Crown. Dobbs persuaded Mathew Rowan, a native of County Antrim and surveyor-general of the colony, to act as their agent for the grant, and by 1747 a survey had been completed. The Dobbs-Rowan correspondence reveals the former as an astute businessman who understood the possible confusion concerning and the frequent invalidity of land grants and who already had some knowledge of the people, products, and topography of the colony. With his usual vigor and enthusiasm Dobbs at once set about the planting of settlers, despite Rowan's warnings, for North Carolina was still sparsely occupied by a mixture of middle-class and vagabond or rough adventurers from neighboring colonies who might give newcomers trouble. Dobbs is frequently given credit for bringing the Scotch-Irish who stabilized the colony's society, and he did induce numbers of out-of-work Irish Presbyterians and Scottish Jacobites to settle in the province. But people of the same stock came from other sources, and German Moravians were at least as sturdy and "moral" as the Britons.

Though Governor Gabriel Johnston of North Carolina, a former professor of Oriental Languages at St. Andrews' University, Scotland, had served ably for twenty years, he had to contend with a number of problems including the bitter rivalry for representation between the older settlers in the north and the new settlers in the south. Among Johnston's opponents in Britain, hostile primarily because of fear of losing their lands, were Dobbs and his associates Crymble, Huey, and especially McCulloh. Charges were submitted through the Duke of Bedford to the Board of Trade, the latter admitting that there was clear evidence of considerable disorder and confusion in the colony, ironic enough in view of what Dobbs was to experience.

In 1748, the Ohio Company of Virginia was organized to develop lands in the western area of Virginia—partially to exclude the French, partially to extend the British Empire. Merchant Hanbury presented the petition to the Board of Trade for 500,000 acres. Besides thirteen Virginia gentleman-planters, partners or shareholders included the two future colonial governors Dobbs and Robert Dinwiddie (Virginia) and also Samuel Smith, Dobbs's personal agent in London. Dobbs's influence was considerable in the founding and development of this stock company, as the discussions noted in the bibliography below indicate. Its aims coincided almost exactly with his own as to trade, curtailment of French power in America, and territorial enlargement of the empire, among others. In 1754 he drew up and was the first signer of the company's second petition to the Board of Trade for an additional 300,000 acres. Though this and similar land companies were hardly financially more successful than the first Virginia Company of London in 1606–24, they made major contributions to American colonization, major despite feeble support from home or colonial governmental agencies. Today the Ohio Company is given considerable credit for the ultimate fate of the Ohio Valley, though the investors individually may have lost a great deal financially.

Since 1750 Dobbs had corresponded steadily with his agents or with settlers in North Carolina concerning his lands and the general and specific state of affairs there. He frequently considered visiting the province, as he wrote Rowan. He continued to be overly zealous in dispatching settlers without making proper provision for their sustenance during the early months of residence, a weakness he shared with other colonizers from the days of Roanoke and Jamestown. When Governor Johnston died, Dobbs pressed claims for the governorship for himself. Toward the end of 1752 he wrote his son Conway (his first wife had died some years earlier) that he expected the appointment before the beginning of the next year. He was officially appointed 18 Apr. 1753. While awaiting the drafting of his Instructions, Dobbs attempted to improve his estate and to persuade French Protestants or Moravians to settle on his Carolina lands. He was also active in the Irish Parliament, aligning himself with the government against the Patriot party, consistent with his belief in British imperialism and the "English interest" in Ireland. It must be repeated, on the other hand, that throughout his long life he had frequently supported causes of the Irish commonalty, Protestant or Catholic, and that he had always been concerned for the welfare and suffrage of the Irish people as equal partners in the British nation.

Before his departure from Ireland Dobbs also made arrangements for the payment in Britain of his gubernatorial salary, as he was aware of the tremendous arrears in the late Governor Johnston's income from provincial quitrents. Undoubtedly the independence this gave him personally would be later a source of irritation to the North Carolina lower house, which like those of other colonies controlled or wished to control all revenue. Meanwhile the French threat in America had grown more apparent. It was clear that the French were going to fight rather than submit to British claims to the Ohio Valley. As Dobbs arrived at the port of Hampton, Va., in late 1754, the French were already moving to drive English traders and settlers from the border territory and to erect a series of forts along the Ohio and Allegheny rivers as a bar to British expansion.

Though certain historians have alleged that Dobbs landed with a host of needy relatives and friends, the records indicate that he was accompanied by only his younger son Edward, his nephew Richard Spaight, and a few personal servants. At any rate, upon his arrival he was met by Governor Dinwiddie of Virginia. The two with Governor Horatio Sharpe of Maryland conferred at Williamsburg on the situation before Dobbs set out for his own province. He reached New Bern via Edenton and Bath on the last day of October, having been greeted on the way by his friend Mathew Rowan, the acting governor, and by James Murray, the attorney general; the latter was to become a thorn in his side during most of his decade as viceroy. Thus at sixty-six Dobbs began the most difficult task of his life.

Despite his age, the new governor commenced his administration with vigor and statesmanlike conduct. He was received with great cordiality, for all parties were weary of the necessary indecisiveness of interim governments under the two presidents of the council who succeeded Governor Johnston. Everyone knew that there were vital problems to be coped with, including the war with France, irregularities in the collection of quitrents and concomitantly the survey of lands county-by-county, the South Carolina boundary, the location of a permanent capital, the franchise for freeholders, the need for a currency or coinage, the establishment of a post, and dozens of other matters. Dobbs spoke always first in general and then in specific terms, usually surveying the whole imperial situation and then turning to the province's peculiar problems, mindful that he must obey his Instructions from the home government. Beneath the surface were the tensions between "parties" including coastal and backcountry, north and south, Granville District versus settlers on royal lands; the greed and long-accustomed semiindependence of local officials and landowners; and a reluctance to devote adequate revenues in support of troops to meet a frontier threat North Carolinians believed far removed from themselves. Many of these problems were inherited; however, the accelerated conflict with the French, Dobbs's firm conviction that what benefited the empire would benefit North Carolina and usually vice-versa, his ardor for the established church, and his justifiable suspicion of misappropriation or noncollection of royal revenues were to bring him into a collision course with his General Assembly.

At first he attempted to compromise when he found he could get defense funds from the legislature in no other way. But one compromise hurt him in reputation at least, that concerning the establishment or appointment of a local judiciary system in defiance of his Instructions. For his conscientious efforts to do his best with an impossible situation he received a severe reprimand from London authority. Thereafter, as political and war matters grew more acute he became more intransigent, for he resolved to follow his Instructions to the letter, though he was never quite capable of doing so.

Meanwhile he was most active in internal affairs. With Governor James Glen of South Carolina he attempted to settle their mutual boundary line, though not fully or finally successfully. He did plan and have built a string of blockade forts on the coast and inland for defense, employing some of his own experience as Ireland's chief engineer in drawing up his plans. He felt compelled to suspend two men and then a third from government positions on the council or other prominent places, and for several years he was engaged in acrimonious disputes with them through correspondence with the home government. Because the majority of North Carolinians were not Anglicans, he naturally encountered opposition in his efforts to secure clergy and build edifices for the established church. Apparently unjustly he was accused of attempting to make a personal profit on lands he bought (and sold for what he paid) as a location for a capital city and capitol building. Several historians have stated that his obstinacy and general irritability increased with age. This accusation is not justified based on the extant records of the legislature and Board of Trade, his personal correspondence, and other documents.

Dobbs undoubtedly (and even critics hostile on other matters agree on this) had the welfare of North Carolina at heart in all his major moves, defending the colony against attacks by the London Board of Trade and attempting, as he had in Ireland, to have a foreign trade that would increase the prosperity of the colony. His plans for a general education system and for aiding the Indians were implemented to the best of his ability, and he reiterated his interest in both many times. As representative of North Carolina at the governors' conference in Williamsburg when he landed in 1754, at another top-level meeting in Philadelphia in 1757, and at the famous Indian Treaty Conference in Augusta in 1763, he placed his colony as a political entity for the first time on a par with its neighbors. At the heart of each of his disputes with the Assembly, which generally increased with time, was the long-present and by now rapidly growing conflict between the prerogatives of the Crown as represented by the governor and those of the people embodied in the legislature. Even the highly personalized controversies with James Murray, John Rutherfurd, and John Starkey were deeply rooted in the question of prerogative, though records indicate that Dobbs had ethical as well as political authority on his side.

Dobbs's personal life in North Carolina is of considerable interest. He made Russellborough, his house and estate near Brunswick, a comfortable domicile into which he moved in 1758. Within this mansion were his hundreds of books on many subjects; especially interesting were the varied histories, chronicles of exploration, theological studies, and current belles-lettres. In the colony he wrote "An Account of North Carolina" and the much longer manuscript, now fragmentary but clearly ambitious and deeply pondered, "Essay upon the Grand Plan of Providence and Dissertations Annexed thereto." The latter is a work of speculative theology and philosophy, evidently part of an extensive treatise affording one of the recently discovered proofs that there was considerable writing on religion in the colonial South. It should be studied and edited for publication. In the correspondence of the English botanist Peter Collinson is a letter from Dobbs describing the Venus's-flytrap, a description declared by historians of science to be the first ever recorded. Thus Dobbs continued his scientific investigations or observations in the colony.

As already noted, Dobbs had as a companion in America his younger son Edward Brice Dobbs, a career army officer who served with North Carolina militia and later with the troops of General Edward Braddock. In his will the governor bequeathed to this son £1,000 and all lands and much other property held in America. Also accompanying him was his nephew Richard Spaight who, with Dobbs's son, was appointed a member of the council and who held other important posts (there was plenty of precedent for such nepotism in colonial annals). Spaight married Mary Moore, daughter of the distinguished John Moore of Craven County, and left descendants who became prominent in North Carolina history. Dobbs was seventy-three when he married his second wife Justina Davis, daughter of another eminent colonial family, thus committing, according to his detractors, the supreme folly of old age. A scurrilous mock-epistle (the original of which cannot now be located) concerning the alleged scandal connected with this marriage was printed in the *Colonial Records of North Carolina*. But Justina's letters surviving in the Dobbs Papers give every indication of genuine mutual affection in the marriage.

The governor suffered a stroke of apoplexy in 1762 while preparing to go to Britain on leave. He recovered sufficiently to carry on most of his duties until his death three years later. He died while packing his books for what he must have known would be a permanent return to Great Britain; he was buried in the uncompleted church of St. Philip near his home. There was no Anglican cleric within a hundred miles, and a justice or judge read the burial service.

The evidence that Dobbs was irascible, arbitrary, and obstinate rests almost entirely on the testimony of enemies he felt forced to make because of their ill service to the colony. Obstinacy of a kind not meant by his enemies, a determination to follow imperial instructions, is evidenced in his speeches, proclamations, and letters. But he was also a far-sighted man who realized what the British must do about the French and what his home government must allow in free trade if it was to retain its empire. As other British imperialists of his day, he had a world vision of which his own province of North Carolina, and his old home of Ireland, were integral parts. Recent opinion has very much altered the hostile nineteenth-century portraits of a petulant, senile, and tyrannical governor. Dobbs's major role in persuading the Scotch-Irish, especially from County Antrim, to make North Carolina their permanent home has often been cited. But he did more, as he was largely responsible for moving his colony from a position of inferiority to one of equality among the thirteen coastal provinces, thus assuring it a prominent place in the moves toward independence.

SEE: Samuel A. Ashe, *History of North Carolina*, vol. 1 (1925), and ed., *Biographical History of North Carolina*, vol. 3 (1906); Kenneth P. Bailey, *The Ohio Company of Virginia and the Westward Movement, 1748–1792* (1939); Walter Clark, ed., *State Records of North Carolina*, vol. 22 (1907); Desmond Clarke, *Arthur Dobbs, Esquire, 1689–1765* (1958); Peter Collinson Correspondence (Linnean Society, London, England); *DAB*, vol. 3 (1959); Richard B. Davis, "Three Poems from Colonial North America," *North Carolina Historical Review* 46 (1969); Arthur Dobbs Papers ([microfilm] Southern Historical Collection, University of North Carolina, Chapel Hill); Marvin L. M. Kay, "Provincial Taxes in North Carolina During the Administrations of Dobbs and Tryon," *North Carolina Historical Review* 42 (1965); Gertrude Kimball, *Correspondence of William Pitt*, vols. 1, 2 (1906); Lawrence Lee, *The Lower Cape Fear in Colonial Days* (1965); Hugh T. Lefler and William S. Powell, *Colonial North Carolina* (1973); John W. Moore, *History of North Carolina* (1880); A. J. Morrison, "Arthur Dobbs of Castle Dobbs and Carolina," *South Atlantic Quarterly* 16 (1917); Louis Mulkearn, ed., *George Mercer Papers Relating to the Ohio Company of Virginia* (1954); William L. Saunders, ed., *Colonial Records of North Carolina*, vols. 5–6 (1887–88); Stanley A. South, "Russelborough," *North Carolina Historical Review* 44 (1967); Robert M. Weir, "North Carolina's Reaction to the Currency Act of 1764," *North Carolina Historical Review* 40 (1963); John H. Wheeler, *Historical Sketches of North Carolina* (1851).

RICHARD BEALE DAVIS

**Dobbs, Edward Brice** *(1729–February 1803)*, colonial official, was born to Arthur and Annie Osburne Norbury Dobbs at Castle Dobbs in Carrickfergus, Ireland. Little is known about his early life, but in October 1754 he accompanied his father to North Carolina where the elder Dobbs served as royal governor from 1754 to 1765. Brice, as he was called by his contemporaries, was a professional soldier and held a captain's commission in the British army. His interest in military life found an outlet in the growing colonial hostilities with the French and the Indians. Early in 1755 he was captain of two companies of North Carolina militia going to Virginia to serve under General Edward Braddock. Although he did not play a direct part in Braddock's defeat on the Monongahela in July (his forces being held in reserve), Dobbs suffered temporary blindness after the action apparently due to contact with a poisonous weed. He remained in a defensive station in Virginia until he led his troops to New York late in 1756. Eventually commanding three companies there, he was temporarily promoted to the rank of major but returned to North Carolina in the spring of 1757 suffering from what his father described as rheumatism.

Dobbs was sworn in as a royal councillor of North Carolina on 17 May 1757. Thus the Privy Council honored father and son for their service in the war with France. The younger Dobbs attended sessions of the Council regularly until March 1759 when he left the province. Before his departure his father in October 1758 named him naval officer for the whole colony—a lucrative position in terms of fee collections. What drew him away from North Carolina was the chance to command a company of English fusiliers at Gibraltar. In reply to a letter from Governor William Tryon, which had reached him in Scotland in 1767, Brice Dobbs said he would never return to North Carolina and would willingly resign his Council seat. Before all of the necessary paperwork was processed, he was suspended from the Council for nonattendance in November 1769.

After 1770 Dobbs apparently spent most of his life in his native Carrickfergus and twice served as its mayor. He and his brother, Conway, submitted claims in excess of £11,000 for confiscation of their North Carolina property during the American Revolution, but they received only about £1,000 each in compensation.

SEE: Sir John Bernard Burke, *Burke's Irish Family Records* (1976) and *Burke's . . . Landed Gentry of Ireland* (1958); Desmond Clarke, *Arthur Dobbs, Esquire* (1957); Arthur Dobbs, Loyalist claims (North Carolina State Archives, Raleigh); William L. Saunders, ed., *Colonial Records of North Carolina*, vols. 5–7 (1887–90).

WILLIAM S. PRICE, JR.

**Dockery, Alfred** *(11 Dec. 1797–3 Dec. 1873)*, farmer, legislator, congressman, and Baptist layman, was born in Richmond County, the son of Thomas Dockery. John H. Wheeler states that the Dockery family was very large and Thomas Dockery could not afford to educate his many children. Alfred, the eldest, took care of his younger brothers and sisters "and was often heard to say that he had never attended school for three months consecutively in his life." After marrying Sallie Turner of Anson County, who bore him seven surviving children (the total number is not indicated), he settled down to the life of a small farmer, increasing his estate by hard work. He returned to this life whenever his political fortunes suffered a reversal. For reasons unknown, he acquired the nickname or title "General," despite not having served in the armed forces. This nickname is used frequently in accounts of his life and was apparently the title by which his friends and associates addressed him.

Dockery's first, very brief appearance in public life was in 1822, when—at twenty-five—he was elected to the House of Commons from Richmond County. He returned to farming after his term, but thirteen years later was a delegate to the Constitutional Convention of 1835 from his county. John W. Moore, in "Early Baptist Laymen of North Carolina," says Dockery sided with Supreme Court Justice William Gaston in favoring the abolition of the Protestant-only restriction in the state constitution. Dockery made a speech in which he declared that, despite the "persecution and proscription" of the "Romish church," he, Dockery, would "comply with . . . charity . . . and return good for this evil." A more controversial proposal was his idea that free blacks should continue to be allowed to vote, which the convention rejected. However, he joined his fellow westerners in successfully ending the disproportionate power previously wielded in state government by the eastern counties. Moore, writing in the post-Reconstruction period, took the view that if the convention had also listened to Dockery's suffrage proposal—a very moderate measure that would have given the franchise only to those blacks with $250 or more in property—the horrors of Reconstruction would have been avoided.

Dockery ran for the newly reorganized state senate in 1836 as the candidate of the new Whig party. He served six terms in the senate, taking the standard Whig positions. Throughout his political career he was convinced that the Whigs and their platform of internal improvements and general reforms were the only hope of North Carolina or the nation. In 1845 he decided to run for Congress despite his party's decision to nominate Jonathan Worth. Dockery prevailed over Worth by 900 votes. Refusing reelection in 1847, he returned to farming until he again contested for Congress against Green W. Caldwell, an avowed Secessionist. Dockery, an equally avowed Unionist, campaigned even in those parts of his district adjacent to pro-Secessionist South Carolina "at the peril of his life." He ignored this seeming danger by openly advocating, as had President Andrew Jackson in the 1830s, a show of force by Federal troops if South Carolina attempted to secede. The courageous Dockery won by 1,200 votes and served again in Congress during 1849–51.

In 1854 the declining Whigs tapped Dockery as their candidate for governor against Thomas Bragg. Wheeler states their contest was "*the* campaign of campaigns" in North Carolina history, even though he was writing eight years after the 1876 "Battle of the Giants" campaign. But Dockery failed in his gallant bid by 2,000 votes.

Sadly convinced that the Whigs were dead as a political force in the state, Dockery, along with many other Whigs, joined the American or Know-Nothing party. It is not recorded whether he supported that party's nativist policy; it is known that his primary interest was to push for his old program of internal improvements, the support of which had made him a hero in the West.

Dockery probably hated to see war come in 1861; yet, like most Southerners, he loved his region and sent his sons into the Confederate Army. One, John Morehead Dockery, "fell victim to camp disease." After the war Dockery decided to make the best of the South's defeat, a decision for which Moore (and probably others) accused him of having become excessively fond of Yankee ways. Although he did not campaign when he was nominated for governor in 1866 (against his will) and lost by a wide margin, Dockery willingly served in the postwar Reconstruction government. First he was a member of the 1865 state convention that, if President Andrew Johnson had had his way, would have ended Reconstruction in North Carolina, but whose work was tossed out by the Radical Republicans in Congress. Then he was president of the board of directors of the state penitentiary. Even though it would cost him his vote, he supported the provisions of the Fourteenth Amendment, referred to as the "Howard Amendment" in North Carolina, depriving ex-Confederates of their political rights.

There is some confusion over the date of Dockery's death, some accounts noting that he died 12 Dec. 1875. Contemporary newspapers, however, give the date as 3 Dec. 1873.

Dockery is remembered not only for his political contributions, but also for his strong support of the Baptist church and of Wake Forest College. He was a founder and trustee of the latter institution and gave it a set of blacksmith tools, among other gifts. He served as president of the Baptist State Convention for many years, and was treasurer of the North Carolina Bible Society. The Wake Forest *Student* said of him in 1906, "General Dockery was a very fine business man. In this way he was of great service to his church and the Convention. He was a good judge of men and firmly attached to what he deemed the right."

SEE: *Biog. Dir. Am. Cong.* (1961); Joseph G. deR. Hamilton, ed., *Papers of Thomas Ruffin*, vols. 1 (1918), 4 (1920); Robert C. Lawrence, *Here in Carolina* (1939); John W. Moore, "Early Baptist Laymen in North Carolina" (Scrapbook, North Carolina Collection, University of North Carolina, Chapel Hill); E. W. Sikes, J. A. Stradley, et al., eds., "The Baptist Historical Papers," *Wake Forest Student* 26 (1906); Stephen B. Weeks, Scrapbooks, 1823–73 (North Carolina Collection, University of North Carolina, Chapel Hill); John H. Wheeler, *Reminiscences and Memoirs of North Carolina and Eminent North Carolinians* (1884); *Who Was Who In America* (1963).

MICHAEL J. FAWCETT

**Dockery, Claudius** *(5 Apr. 1865–14 Jan. 1941)*, lawyer, public servant, farmer, and, briefly, historian and diplomat, was born in Mangum, Richmond County, the son of Confederate Lieutenant Colonel Oliver Hart Dockery and Sallie Dumas Dockery and the grandson of "General" Alfred Dockery. Young Claudius followed in his father's footsteps by attending The University of North Carolina, where he was president of the Dialectic Society, a member of Sigma Alpha Epsilon and Phi Delta Phi fraternities, and an editor of the *University Magazine*. Graduating in 1887, he was appointed to the faculty as instructor in Latin. During his one-year term the precocious Dockery produced a remarkable historical essay, "A Criticism of Accepted Historical Opinions of Governor Gabriel Johnston's Administration." In this perceptive document, presented to the North Carolina Historical Society in May 1888, he argued that the progress credited to the colonial governor who served from 1734 to 1752 was actually stimulated by factors beyond Johnston's control.

Dockery and his father were both Republicans. When their party regained the presidency in 1889, Benjamin Harrison appointed Oliver Dockery as consul general to Rio de Janeiro, Brazil, then ruled by King Don Pedro. Claudius was his father's deputy. The Dockerys were recalled when Democrat Grover Cleveland replaced Harrison in 1893.

After receiving a University of North Carolina law degree in 1894, the younger Dockery returned to his native Richmond County where he was register of deeds from 1894 to 1897. He was elected to the North Carolina House of Representatives in 1896; apparently he also continued to serve as state prison director under Governor Daniel L. Russell, a Republican. Dockery held the latter post until 1901, when Russell was replaced by Democrat Charles Brantley Aycock. This departure marked the end of Dockery's political career, for the Democrats under Aycock and Furnifold M. Simmons were determined to keep both blacks and Republicans "in their place." Under presidents Theodore Roosevelt and William Howard Taft, he served as U.S. marshal for the Eastern District of North Carolina—a federal appointive office. From 1912 until his death he was a member of The University of North Carolina Trustee Executive Committee; he also held membership on the building committee for the third university infirmary, Abernethy Hall. In his last years he also practiced law.

A leader of the state Republican party, Dockery served on its executive committee during the Taft administration and was a delegate to the 1920 Republican National Convention in Chicago.

On 16 Apr. 1900 Dockery married Maude May Ryder of New York. She bore him two children, Claudius, Jr., of Greensboro and Mrs. Calvin L. (Dorothy) Dickinson of Santa Rosa, Calif. Dockery was a Baptist and a member of the Odd Fellows.

SEE: Claudius Dockery, "A Criticism of Accepted Historical Opinions of Governor Johnston's Administration," *University of North Carolina Magazine* 7 (May 1888); Daniel L. Grant, *Alumni History of the University of North Carolina* (1924); John J. Parker Papers (Southern Historical Collection, University of North Carolina, Chapel Hill); Raleigh *News and Observer*, 15 Jan. 1941; Edwin Yates Webb Papers (Southern Historical Collection, University of North Carolina, Chapel Hill).

MICHAEL J. FAWCETT

**Dockery, Oliver Hart** *(12 Aug. 1830–21 Mar. 1906)*, congressman and diplomat, was born in Richmond County, the son of "General" Alfred Dockery, at that time a private citizen, and Sallie Turner Dockery. He was probably the first of his family to attend college, graduating in 1848 from The University of North Carolina where he was a member of the Dialectic Society. John H. Wheeler states that, although he was a qualified lawyer, Dockery never chose to practice. He farmed until 1858, when he was elected to the North Carolina House of Commons for one term.

Like his father, Oliver believed in the Union. He supported John Bell of Tennessee for president in 1860, as did a plurality of North Carolinians, and was an elector on the Bell ticket. With the coming of war, he entered the Confederate Army as a captain and later earned the rank of lieutenant colonel. His son Claudius was born just before the war ended.

Again in the pattern of his father, Dockery served the postwar government of North Carolina. A Republican, he was elected to fill an unexpired congressional term in 1867. He was reelected a year later but failed to win a second full term in 1870. Returning to his farm, he remained in private life until selected as a delegate to the important Constitutional Convention of 1875. This convention modified the 1868 constitution to suit the Democratic party, so it is probable that Dockery was in the minority opposing these changes.

Dockery ran for Congress again in 1882, but lost to Risdon T. Bennett. He was also an unsuccessful candidate for governor in 1888. That year Benjamin Harrison, a Republican, was elected president and subsequently appointed the former congressman consul general in Rio de Janeiro, Brazil. Dockery occupied the post until July 1893. For the remaining thirteen years of his life, he was a farmer. He died in a hospital in Baltimore, Md.

Dockery married Sallie Dumas and had at least two children: Claudius Dockery, who served with him in Brazil and was a longtime University of North Carolina trustee; and Oliver Hart Dockery, Jr., who became adjutant general of the U.S. Army, serving in Washington, D.C., in the early years of the twentieth century. His army career covered the years from 1898 to 1924 and he held the rank of lieutenant colonel.

SEE: *Biog. Dir. Am. Cong.* (1961); Jerome Dowd, *Sketches of Prominent Living North Carolinians* (1888); Daniel L. Grant, *Alumni History of the University of North Carolina* (1924); *North Carolina Biography*, vols. 2 (1919), 3 (1929); John H. Wheeler, *Reminiscences and Memoirs of North Carolina and Eminent North Carolinians* (1884).

MICHAEL J. FAWCETT

**Dockery, Thomas Pleasant** *(18 Dec. 1833–26 Feb. 1898)*, planter, civil engineer, and Confederate officer, was born probably in Montgomery County, the son of Colonel John Dockery and Ann Mask, presumably the daughter of Pleasant M. Mask. The family soon moved to Tennessee and then to Arkansas, where the elder Dockery established a plantation in Columbus County and was instrumental in the construction of the first railroad in the state. At the outbreak of the Civil War in 1861 the twenty-seven-year-old Dockery was appointed colonel of the Fifth Regiment of Arkansas state troops and with this regiment became a part of Brigadier General N. B. Pearce's brigade of Arkansas forces assembled by Brigadier General Benjamin McCulloch in the summer of that year. On 10 Aug. 1861 these troops participated in the Battle of Wilson's Creek, Mo., where Dockery's regiment played a conspicuous role. Dockery later became colonel of the Nineteenth Arkansas Regiment, which formed part of the brigade of Brigadier General William Cabell Maury's division when Major General Sterling Price's Confederate army moved east of the Mississippi River in May 1862. His regiment was present at the Battle of Iuka, Miss., on 19 Sept. 1862 but was not engaged. On 3 and 4 Oct. 1862 Dockery and his regiment took part in the bloody fighting at Corinth, Miss. Recrossing the Mississippi with Price's army, he was assigned to command a subdistrict of middle Arkansas.

In the spring of 1863, Dockery and his regiment took part in the Vicksburg Campaign as a part of Brigadier General Martin Green's brigade. On 1 May 1863 Dockery's regiment was fiercely engaged in the Battle of Port Gibson. Fifteen days later, in the Battle of Champion Hill, his regiment took part in the brilliant counterattack by Bowen's division that nearly succeeded in routing the right flank of Grant's attacking Union Army. Eventually overcome by superior numbers, however, Dockery's men, with the rest of the Confederate Army, retired into the earthwork defenses of Vicksburg and participated in the siege of that city. During the fighting Dockery's brigade commander, General Green, was killed by an enemy sharpshooter. As senior colonel Dockery succeeded to the command of the brigade, which he led through the remainder of the siege. With the rest of Bowen's division, this brigade occupied a reserve position behind the left center of the Confederate defense line. When the city capitulated on 4 July 1863, Dockery was captured and paroled.

Dockery's fine record and leadership abilities were cause for his promotion to the rank of brigadier general on 10 Aug. 1863. Serving again under Price in Arkansas, General Dockery commanded a brigade of Arkansas cavalry consisting of the Eighteenth, Nineteenth, and Twentieth Arkansas regiments and an additional battalion in the Red River Campaign. At this time he was attached to the division of Brigadier General J. F. Fagan. Thus he took part in the efforts to delay the advance of Steele's Union forces and participated in the battles of Mark's Mills and Jenkins' Ferry in late April 1864. In the fall of that year he accompanied Price's army on its ill-fated raid into Missouri. At the close of the war Dockery was paroled in Arkansas in June 1865. Afterward, his property having been taken from him, he took up the profession of civil engineering and lived for some years in Houston, Tex. He died alone in a rooming house in New York City and his body was transported to the residence of his two daughters in Natchez, Miss., for burial.

SEE: C. A. Evans, *Confederate Military History*, vol. 10 (1899); John L. Ferguson, Arkansas State Historian, correspondence with the author; *New York Times*, 27 Mar. 1898; Ezra Warner, *Generals in Gray* (1959); M. J. Wright, *General Officers of the Confederate Army* (1911).

PAUL BRANCH

**Dodd, William Edward** *(21 Oct. 1869–9 Feb. 1940)*, educator, historian, and diplomat, was born on his father's farm near Clayton, the oldest of the seven children (five boys and two girls) of John Daniel and Eveline Creech Dodd to survive infancy. Of English or Scottish origin, the Dodd ancestors of William Edward had been in America since the 1740s, when the first of the family to arrive in the New World, Daniel Dodd, settled among the Highland Scots in the Cape Fear valley. Through his mother William Edward was related to Sam and Ashley Horne, industrialists of the New South, who in the 1890s established a cotton mill at Clayton. Although better off economically than most of their neighbors, the Dodds felt the pinch of the poverty that plagued the post–Civil War South. Young William Edward worked on his father's farm, but he also studied hard enough to earn the reputation of being Clayton's most studious boy and soon exhausted the resources of Clayton's five-months-a-year free school. He then attended the Utopian Institute, a private academy at Clayton, before spending a year at Oak Ridge Military Academy in the north central area of the state. Unsuccessful in his attempt to win appointment to West Point and failing to gain admission to The University of North Carolina, he served briefly as principal of the Glen Alpine public school and then enrolled in the Virginia Agricultural and Mechanical College (now the Virginia Polytechnic Institute) at Blacksburg.

In his four and a half years at Blacksburg, Dodd studied a variety of subjects, most of which were new or nearly so to him, but he was most interested in English, history, and economics. He also discovered that he had a talent for writing and gave much time to student publications. Following his graduation in the spring of 1895, he spent the summer teaching in Clayton's public school but returned to Blacksburg as a graduate instructor in history the following autumn. After completing the M.S. degree in 1897 he combined his savings of $750 with $1,500 he borrowed from his Uncle Sam Horne, a Raleigh businessman, and on 7 June sailed from New York for Germany and the University of Leipzig to study for the Ph.D. in history. At Leipzig he was fascinated by Karl Lamprecht's lectures on German cultural history but probably was more influenced in his development as an historian by the seminar in recent German political history conducted by Erich Marcks, who also directed Dodd's dissertation. Although based on scant research, this work, entitled *Thomas Jeffersons Ruckkehr zur Politics, 1796* (1899), or *Thomas Jefferson's Return to Politics in 1796*, arrived at conclusions about the origins of the Democratic party that are still accepted as valid. In early August 1899 Dodd passed his final examination for the Ph.D. *cum laude* and soon afterwards returned to the United States. Despite the help of Josephus Daniels, influential editor of the Raleigh *News and Observer*, he found it impossible to obtain a college teaching position. Believing that professional recognition could be gained mainly by his spoken and written word, he began a program of research, lecturing, and writing, including research for a biography of Nathaniel Macon (1758–1837), political theorist and agriculturalist and for thirty-seven years a member of the United States Congress.

In the summer of 1900 Dodd accepted a one-year contract to teach and organize a department of history and economics at Randolph-Macon College, a Methodist school at Ashland, Va. Despite a heavy teaching load, he undertook to introduce into his classes the latest and best methods of studying and teaching history. Less than a month after joining the faculty in September, he organized the Randolph-Macon Historical Society for the collection and study of North Carolina and Virginia documents. He soon had a small number of junior and senior students writing essays and editing documents for *The John P. Branch Historical Papers*, a quarterly journal that Dodd launched in June 1901 and named for its financial sponsor, a wealthy Richmond banker. Although Dodd disliked Ashland, he was unable to find another position and agreed to remain at Randolph-Macon for a second year. On 24 Dec. 1901 he married Martha Johns of Wake County, N.C.

Meanwhile Dodd had begun to correspond with his fellow scholars as well as with men prominent in public life, a practice he was to continue for the rest of his life. He had also joined with John Spencer Bassett of Trinity College (now Duke University) and others in a crusade to raise the standards of history teaching in southern institutions. The publication of his *Life of Nathaniel Macon* (Spring 1903) won him national recognition as an historian and secured his position at Randolph-Macon, where he was granted tenure and his teaching load was reduced to nine hours a week. Nevertheless he remained anxious to leave Ashland. He continued to work on his *Jefferson Davis* (1907), published articles in the *American Historical Review*, the *South Atlantic Quarterly*, and other periodicals, and took an active part in Virginia politics as a progressive Democrat.

In 1908 Dodd accepted a teaching position at the University of Chicago, then the country's leading graduate school, and in January 1909 joined its excellent history department, which was eager for him to develop the study of the Old South. He rapidly settled into a productive routine of teaching and writing and was soon at work on a one-volume history of the South. Believing that he could best present his story through the analysis of individual lives of southern leaders, he determined to base his book on earlier lectures on Thomas Jefferson, John C. Calhoun, and Jefferson Davis, whom he considered the most important statesmen of the Old South. The result was his *Statesmen of the Old South* (1911), which immediately gained the approval of fellow historians. In its emphasis upon Jefferson's reliance on a political alliance of the South with the West in gaining the presidency, the book appealed especially to progressive historians. And in its argument that the antebellum period demonstrated a shift in power from Virginia's Jeffersonian liberalism to South Carolina's political conservatism and cotton capitalism it provided historians of all creeds with a still valid point of departure for the study of the Old South. The sketches of individual statesmen have fared less well.

Shortly after moving to Chicago Dodd became actively involved in Illinois and especially Chicago politics. By the end of 1910, like thousands of other Democrats, he had concluded that all hope for the success of progressivism in the United States depended on the election of Woodrow Wilson as president in 1912 and had begun to work toward that end. Highly pleased by Wilson's victory at the polls, he did not hesitate to write to the new president about policies and personnel appointments as late as April 1913. Although he could see no evidence that his advice had any influence on Wilson, he continued to have faith in the president's liberalism and redoubled his efforts to make history a tool for progressive advance.

Toward this end he decided in March 1913 to abandon his extensive book-reviewing and lecturing in order to concentrate on the preparation of a new four-volume survey of American history: Houghton Mifflin's *Riverside History of the United States*, of which he was to be editor and of which he was to write the third volume, *Expansion and Conflict, 1828–1865* (1915). Although he had drafted seven of the projected sixteen chapters by the following May, he found it impossible to work steadily on the book while carrying his usual teaching load through the spring and summer quarters. Consequently, when the summer session ended on 29 August, he left immediately for a nine-months' siege of writing in the Blue Ridge of Virginia, where he had purchased a 150-acre farm in Loudon County, three miles outside the village of Round Hill and fifteen miles west of Leesburg, an environment in which Dodd's writing prospered. Here he completed a first draft of *Conflict and Expansion*, although it was not ready for the printer until the end of 1914. The book emphasized western and southern developments of the antebellum period, focusing on sectional conflicts and the shifting political alliances that rose to power or disintegrated according to the triumph or failure of the economic groups that supported them.

Dodd found time to make known his opposition to U.S. involvement in the war that had erupted in Europe in the summer of 1914. However, he became increasingly aware of the potential threat to the United States posed by a possible German victory and neither opposed nor supported the policy of "reasonable preparedness" adopted by President Wilson following the sinking of the *Lusitania* (7 May 1915). From the moment the United States declared war against Germany (6 Apr. 1917), Dodd opposed all dissent and made evident his desire to contribute to the public information on the war. He agreed to prepare for publication by the Northern Trust Company of Chicago a series of pamphlets on prewar American foreign policy. In addition, he sent a variety of materials to George Creel's Committee on Public Information and to the National Board for Historical Services. In October 1917 he agreed to prepare a report on the problems of American foreign trade, the Far East, and the Monroe Doctrine for Colonel Edward House's American Preparatory Commission (the Inquiry) on American proposals for the peace conference at the end of the war. At his own request he was soon excused from this task. And in December 1917 he resumed work on the Yale Chronicle volume he had tried unsuccessfully to begin in 1916. This book, *The Cotton Kingdom* (1919), which dealt with the lower South from 1840 to 1860, argued that the cotton plantation had dominated antebellum southern life and analyzed that dominance.

After the war Dodd gave his unreserved support to the cause of the League of Nations, especially in lectures and in the publication of his highly propagandistic *Woodrow Wilson and His Work* (1920). Although he met with repeated defeats in political efforts to promote the cause of progressivism in the 1920s, he derived much satisfaction from his personal and professional life. He was, in fact, probably the University of Chicago's most exciting teacher at this period. Popular as a lecturer to undergraduate classes, he evoked equally enthusiastic response from his graduate seminars. With Ray Stannard Baker he edited six volumes of *The Public Papers of Woodrow Wilson* (1925–27), and in 1928 he published his *Lincoln and Lee: Comparison of the Two Greatest Leaders in the War Between the States*. In 1927 he was appointed chairman of the history department at Chicago. He resigned the position on 13 June 1932 in order to devote more time to his teaching and writing but especially to politics, mainly, it appears, because of the prospect of a Democratic presidential victory in the forthcoming November election.

Although Dodd had backed Franklin D. Roosevelt for the Democratic nomination as early as April 1932, he played only a limited role in his campaign after the nomination. For believing Roosevelt a sure winner, Dodd concentrated on postelection concerns and especially on his hope for an influential position in the new administration. Following Roosevelt's inauguration, Secretary of State Cordell Hull offered Dodd his choice of several minor diplomatic posts, all of which Dodd declined. Apparently he had given up all expectation of a significant role in the Roosevelt administration when, on 8 June 1933, the president offered him the ambassadorship to Germany; under Roosevelt's prodding Dodd accepted it within two hours' time. In Berlin Dodd worked hard but soon alienated his embassy staff by trying to live within his income and according to his Jeffersonian ideals rather than diplomatic protocol. Finding it impossible to conduct meaningful negotiations with the Nazis, who more and more dominated all aspects of German life, he increasingly limited his mission to investigating and reporting developments within Germany and evaluating their likely effects upon European and world affairs. His never-cordial relationship with the State Department deteriorated rapidly after February 1937 and he was recalled the following December.

Returning to the United States in early 1938, Dodd retired to his Round Hill farm to attempt a defense of his Berlin mission and to resume his historical writing. In the midst of his strenuous labors in Berlin he had found time to complete the first volume of a four-volume history of the Old South, which he had long planned to write. Entitled *The Old South: Struggles for Democracy* (1937), it was a study of the seventeenth-century southern colonies, which Dodd saw as the battleground of a significant struggle between democracy and absolutism. But his health failed rapidly from a combination of respiratory, nervous, and abdominal ailments, and a second volume was never completed. During 1938 he lectured widely on foreign affairs despite a throat condition that made it increasingly difficult to speak. On 24 Jan. 1939 he entered Georgetown University hospital for rest and observation of his throat ailment. Although he left the hospital on 28 February, he was never able to resume his speaking schedule. On 8 Feb. 1940 he contracted pneumonia at his Round Hill farm, where he died the following day and was buried on 10 Feb. He was survived by his two children, William Edward, Jr., and Martha Dodd (later Stern). His wife had died suddenly of heart failure on 28 May 1938. A United Press International photograph of Dodd as he appeared in early 1938, shortly after his return from Berlin, serves as the frontispiece of Robert Dallek, *Democrat and Diplomat: The Life of William E. Dodd* (1968).

SEE: William K. Boyd Papers (Manuscript Department, Library, Duke University, Durham); Gordon Craig and Felix Gilbert, eds., *The Diplomats, 1919–1939* (1953); Robert Dallek, *Democrat and Diplomat: The Life of William E. Dodd* (1968); William E. Dodd Papers (Manuscript Division, Library of Congress, Washington, D.C.); William E. Dodd Papers (Library, Randolph-Macon College, Ashland, Va.); William Henry Glasson Papers (Manuscript Division, Library, Duke University, Durham); Hugh T. Lefler, ed., "Selected William E. Dodd—Walter Clark Letters," *North Carolina Historical Review* 25 (1948); William J. Peele Papers (Southern Historical Collection, University of North Carolina, Chapel Hill); W. H. Stephenson, "A Half Century of Southern Historical Scholarship," *Journal of Southern History* 11 (1945), and *The South Lives in History* (1955); *The John P. Branch Historical Papers of Randolph-Macon College*, ed. W. A. Mabry, new series, vol. 2 (1953); Lowry P. Ware, "The Academic Career of William E. Dodd" (Ph.D. diss., University of South Carolina, 1956); Jack K. Williams, "A Bibliography of the Printed Writings of William Edward Dodd," *North Carolina Historical Review* 30 (1953).

W. CONARD GASS

**Donaldson, Henry A.** *(fl. 1807–1856)*, merchant and builder of cotton mills, appears in Edenton, Chowan County, in 1807 when he married Elizabeth McDonald whose father apparently was a merchant in that county. Donaldson, described in a wedding notice as a merchant, seems not to have been from eastern North Carolina himself; one source suggests that he was from Providence, R.I., though a search of records in that state reveals nothing about such a person. In 1812 Donaldson was clerk of the Chowan County Court, whereas in 1816, with Joel Battle, Peter Evans, and John Hogun, he began buying land around the Falls of Tar River, the present site of Rocky Mount. The next year Hogun sold his share to Battle, and in 1816 or 1817 a stone mill was constructed at the falls and expanded in 1819. By 1820 the three partners owned the entire area, and the cotton mill was in full operation. In that year they received a license to build a dam at the falls. Dissension among the partners in the early 1820s led to Donaldson's buying Evans's interest in 1821 and then, in 1828, selling his share to Battle. The Battle family continued to control the mill for a number of years. Donaldson moved to Fayetteville and opened the Fayetteville Mill on Cross Creek which he purchased from William L. McNeill. In 1830, however, he was living in Wake Forest Township, Wake County, when his family was recorded in the census as consisting of six males (presumably five sons and himself) and four females (probably his wife and three daughters); he also owned twenty-seven slaves. He is said to have used slave labor in the Fayetteville Mill. In time financial problems made it necessary for him to sell his interests in the state. In 1833 he moved to Mobile, Ala., where he reportedly attempted but failed to build a mill.

From Mobile on 19 Apr. 1841 Donaldson wrote to Calvin Jones, whom he undoubtedly had known in Wake Forest, that he was working for the state bank and had planted a scuppernong vineyard. The 1842 Mobile city directory lists him as a note clerk and note teller in the state bank, whereas the 1856 directory identifies Henry Donaldson as city treasurer (although this may have been the son of Henry A.). The 1850 census for Mobile lists a clerk of this name, his wife Eliza, and two sons, Henry and James, age twenty-four and twenty-one, respectively, all born in North Carolina.

SEE: Calvin Jones Papers (Southern Historical Collection, University of North Carolina, Chapel Hill); Fayetteville *North Carolina Journal*, 14 June 1826; Sarah M. Lemmon, ed., *The Pettigrew Papers* (1971); John A. Oates, *The Story of Fayetteville and the Upper Cape Fear* (1950); *Raleigh Register*, 9 Mar. 1807.

WILLIAM S. POWELL

**Donaldson, Robert, Jr.** *(16 Jan. 1800–18 June 1872),* banker and patron of the arts, was a native of Fayetteville and the son of Robert Donaldson, Sr., a wealthy Scottish merchant and importer who developed the largest mercantile business in the South. Young Donaldson attended The University of North Carolina where he was graduated in 1818. Returning to Fayetteville, he engaged in his first architectural venture, the Lafayette Hotel, built in preparation for the 1825 visit of General Lafayette to the town named after him. In 1828 Donaldson married Susan Gaston, daughter of the jurist William Gaston, and moved with her and with his younger brother, James, and two sisters to New York City. There he became a patron of young artists and writers of the rising Romantic movement.

The Donaldsons' Manhattan residence, an elegant location overlooking the Battery, was remodeled by Robert's friend, New York architect Alexander Jackson Davis—perhaps his first work for Donaldson—and included decoration by sculptor John Frazee. Paintings by inventor-artist Samuel F. B. Morse and C. R. Leslie and furniture by Duncan Phyfe made the home a haven for art lovers, as noted by the art historian William Dunlap.

Influenced by his friends Samuel Morse, who painted landscapes celebrating nature, and poet James Hillhouse, who advocated living in the country, Donaldson—a true Romantic—left New York City in the mid-1830s to live at Blithewood, an estate he purchased on the Hudson. Becoming a creator like his friends, he developed Blithewood into a showplace of new ideas in landscape design, building an English garden with winding roads, waterfalls, and bridges across ravines. Gatehouses, a gardener's cottage, and other structures on the estate were designed by Alexander Davis, who, Donaldson felt, was inspired by Pegasus, the winged horse of the muses. In this classical image Donaldson also saw himself, the patron: "When [Davis] mounts the Pegasus of design he may require the *restraining taste of another.*" Blithewood was featured in a popular book, *Landscape Gardening and Rural Architecture* (1841 and subsequent editions), by Andrew Jackson Downing, and thus became known to many Americans. Another Downing book, *Cottage Residences* (1842 and subsequent editions) was dedicated to Donaldson as "arbiter elegantiarum," supreme arbiter in matters of taste.

In 1852 Donaldson sold Blithewood and bought a nearby estate, Edgewater, for which Davis designed a chapel, houses, and other buildings. Whereas most of the structures at Blithewood have been destroyed, those at Edgewater remain. The estate has been purchased by a present-day North Carolinian, Richard Jenrette, who is a businessman in New York. Jenrette is collecting Donaldson's paintings, furniture, and books with the intention of turning the main house, a splendid mansion of the early nineteenth century with an addition by Davis, into a museum.

Donaldson always remained attached to his native state. To his Presbyterian church in Fayetteville he gave property for the church-sponsored school he attended as a child and the Donaldson family home as a manse. To the Presbyterians in Chapel Hill, where he went to college, he gave a design by Davis for their church building (1848), now destroyed. And to his alma mater he offered in the 1830s Davis designs for structures, unexecuted. Most importantly, however, he arranged for Davis to visit the campus in 1844 and undertake a program of architecture and landscape design. The trip led to a number of Davis commissions in the state during the following years. Also in 1844 Donaldson advised the university to plan a model farm on the campus and introduce courses in agriculture, a forward-looking idea at the time. At his death he left bequests to the university and to Presbyterian and other religious groups. But his will was contested by his children and declared invalid.

SEE: John V. Allcott, "Robert Donaldson, the First North Carolinian to Become Prominent in the Arts," *North Carolina Historical Review* 52 (1975).

J. V. ALLCOTT

**Donnell, John Robert** *(1789–15 Oct. 1864),* lawyer and superior court judge, was a native of Scotland. He was graduated with honors in 1807 from The University of North Carolina and became a prosperous lawyer at New Bern. From 1815 to 1819 he was solicitor for the New Bern judicial circuit, and from 1819 until his resignation in 1837 he was a judge of the superior court.

On 18 June 1816 at New Bern he married Margaret Elizabeth Spaight (1800–1831), daughter of Governor Richard Dobbs Spaight, Sr., and Mary Leech Spaight. After his wife's death Judge Donnell never remarried. Their son, Richard Spaight Donnell, was a congressman, state senator, and speaker of the North Carolina House of Commons. Their daughter, Mary Spaight Donnell (28 Sept. 1817–30 Apr. 1883), became the second wife of Congressman Charles Biddle Shepard on 24 Mar. 1840. One of the two Shepard daughters, Margaret Donnell Shepard (11 Jan. 1841–11 Oct. 1925), was married to Samuel Stewart Nelson (12 Nov. 1835–24 Mar. 1876). The other daughter, Mary Spaight Shepard (18 Mar. 1843–1 Jan. 1892), was the first wife of James Augustus Bryan; they were the parents of Colonel Charles Shepard Bryan.

In his *Recollections of Newbern Fifty Years Ago*, Stephen F. Miller wrote in part: "Judge Donnell was always in the habit of attending market to purchase what articles of produce he needed, and was a man of strict integrity, as well as a kind, considerate, generous neighbor.

"He was a rigid economist, and by the skillful management of the large property which he obtained by inheritance from an uncle, and by his marriage with a daughter of Gov. Spaight, he increased it probably to half a million of dollars. . . . He was a quiet, unobtrusive, upright gentleman, and used to bear with quiet equanimity the biting sarcasm which Mr. [John] Stanly was in the habit of thrusting at the court whenever it suited his policy. . . . His life was exemplary, and his abilities and integrity as a Judge secured him a spotless reputation."

Miller reported that Donnell died "at Raleigh, October 15, 1864, while a refugee from his princely house and estates, after Federal occupancy in Newbern." His "princely" brick home at New Bern, renowned for its exquisite, hand-carved woodwork, was destroyed by fire in late January 1970. His adjacent law office, with a "perfectly-proportioned" entrance, was moved to a waterfront site on Trent River near New Bern for restoration and enlargement by a collateral descendant.

A portrait of Donnell is displayed in the conference room on the second floor of the Archives and History–State Library building, Raleigh.

SEE: John L. Cheney, Jr., *North Carolina Government, 1585–1974* (1975); Daniel L. Grant, *Alumni History of the University of North Carolina* (1924); Stephen F. Miller, *Recollections of Newbern Fifty Years Ago* (1874); Records (Christ Episcopal Church, New Bern); Tombstones, Cedar Grove Cemetery (New Bern).

GERTRUDE S. CARRAWAY

**Donnell, Richard Spaight** *(20 Sept. 1820–3 June 1867)*, congressman and speaker of the North Carolina House of Commons, was the son of Judge John Robert Donnell and namesake of his grandfather, Governor Richard Dobbs Spaight, Sr. A native of New Bern, he attended New Bern Academy and Yale College and was graduated in 1839 from The University of North Carolina. Admitted to the bar the next year, he began to practice law at New Bern. As a Whig, he was elected from Craven County to Congress, serving from 1847 to 1849, but did not seek renomination.

Donnell moved to Washington, N.C., where he opened a law office and was one of the founders of the Bank of Washington in 1851. In 1855 he was one of the founders of Pamlico Bank. From Beaufort County he served in the 1858 state senate and the 1860 North Carolina House of Commons. He was a delegate to the 1861–62 state Secession Convention and then returned to the house. Upon the resignation of Robert B. Gilliam of Granville County, he was chosen speaker of the house for the 1863 session and was renamed for the 1864–65 sessions. At the second 1865–66 session he resumed his seat in the house from Beaufort County; he also attended the 1865–66 state Constitutional Convention.

Donnell died in New Bern. Over his grave in Cedar Grove Cemetery a tall monument is inscribed: "Beaufort County, his chosen home, records her gratitude for many years of distinguished services upon his honored tomb." He left no will and Mary S. Shepard administered his estate.

SEE: *Biog. Dir. Am. Cong.* (1971); John L. Cheney, Jr., *North Carolina Government, 1584–1974* (1975); Daniel L. Grant, *Alumni History of the University of North Carolina* (1924); *New Bern Republican*, 4, 6 June 1867; Tombstones, Cedar Grove Cemetery (New Bern).

GERTRUDE S. CARRAWAY

**Donnell, Robert** *(April 1784–24 May 1855)*, Presbyterian minister and evangelist, was born in Guilford County, the son of William Donnell and Mary Bell. His grandfather, Robert Donnell, of Scottish descent, had immigrated to Pennsylvania with Scotch-Irish colonists and had lived for some time in York County; from there he moved to the north bank of North Buffalo Creek in Piedmont North Carolina, where he and other members of the Nottingham Company had bought extensive tracts of land about 1850. During Donnell's childhood his parents moved to Tennessee, where his father died when Robert was fourteen. Under his mother's guidance, his primary education consisted chiefly of reading the Bible and religious books. A popular lad, he was known for his height, strength, feats of hunting and rail-splitting, and use of tools.

A camp meeting in the Cumberland revival deepened Donnell's inherited religious conviction, and in 1801 he decided to be a minister. Unable to leave farming in order to get a better education, he held prayer meetings. Under jurisdiction of the council formed in 1805 by workers in the revival, he rode circuits over a wide territory between the Cumberland and Ohio rivers and then undertook pioneer preaching in northern Alabama. He was ordained in 1813 by the independent Cumberland Presbytery, formed in 1810 as successor to the council. Helping its expansion into the Cumberland Presbyterian church, he was one of the framers of its 1814 confession. The sect attained national notice when an article he wrote with Finis Ewing in 1813 was published in Woodward's 1814 edition of Charles Buck's *Theological Dictionary*.

Continuing to study, travel, and preach, Donnell was sometimes away from home for months, working in Tennessee, Kentucky, Pennsylvania, North Carolina, and Alabama. For half a century he averaged one camp meeting a month, preaching once, twice, or more each day. His imposing personality, powerful sermons, convincing oratory, and emotional appeals often resulted in tears and shouts from his inspired listeners. Moving to Alabama, he developed a cotton farm near Athens, where he resided most of his life; but he did not neglect his profession. A number of churches, especially in Alabama, were started by him. He also gave much attention to enlarging congregations and building church edifices, as in Nashville and Memphis, Tenn. His main emphasis, however, was always on spreading Cumberland theology, and he left sound impressions of religious reality.

Throughout his career Donnell was recognized as an outstanding leader, noted particularly for his efforts at peacemaking. He was the first president of the first missionary board of his denomination, and in 1837 was moderator of its general assembly. Deeply concerned about education, principally religious education, he was instrumental in the founding of Cumberland University at Lebanon, Tenn. Attracted by its students, he became its pastor in 1846. His last years were spent at Athens, Ala. In 1852 he published a book entitled *Thoughts on Various Theological Subjects*. A portrait of him was printed in D. Lowry's 1867 *Life and Labors of Rev. Robt. Donnell*.

Donnell was married twice: in 1818 to Ann Smith, daughter of Colonel James W. Smith, who brought him considerable property; and in 1832 to Clarissa Lindley, daughter of the Reverend Jacob Lindley.

SEE: Richard Beard, *Brief Biographical Sketches* (1867); *DAB*, vol. 3 (1959); C. L. Van Noppen Papers (Manuscript Department, Library, Duke University, Durham).

GERTRUDE S. CARRAWAY

**Donner, George** *(ca. 1784–[26 Mar.?] 1847)* and **Jacob** *(ca. 1781–March or April 1847)*, western immigrants for whom the Donner Pass in the Sierra Nevada Mountains of California was named, were born in Rowan County, probably in the part that is now southern Davidson County, the sons of George Donner, of German descent. The elder Donner was listed in the 1790 census with a family composed of himself, two males under the age of sixteen, and five females; he was made a road overseer in the Flat Swamp-Lick Creek area of the county in 1794. The younger George, who in 1795 inherited some property from his uncle, Jacob Donner of

Rowan County, moved by stages from North Carolina to Kentucky (in 1818), Indiana, and Illinois (in 1828); he also spent a year in Texas. Jacob may have followed the same route, but he at least was living in Illinois by the spring of 1846. George was married three times. The name of his first wife is unknown but his second wife was a sister of the second Mrs. Jacob Donner; his third wife was Tamsen Eustis, a native of Newburyport, Mass., but a former teacher in Elizabeth City, N.C. The name of Jacob's first wife is unknown, but his second wife, Elizabeth, had been married before to a man named Hook. In 1846, when he was 62, George Donner's children by his present wife, Tamsen, were listed as Frances E., 6, Georgia, 4, and Eliza P., 3; by a former wife there were Elitha Cumi, 14, and Leanna C., 12. Jacob was the father of George, 9, Mary M., 7, Isaac, 5, Samuel, about 4, and Lewis, about 3; by her former husband, Elizabeth Hook Donner was the mother of Solomon E. Hook, 14, and William Hook, 12.

The Donners were pioneer settlers of Sangamon County, Ill., and George's farm was not far from Springfield, the county seat. Printed descriptions of California apparently set the family to thinking about a move. Advertising in a local newspaper, George offered his farm for sale in September 1845 and the following spring sought others who would join a caravan to California. Plans were well made, extensive supplies laid in, and George Donner was elected leader. On 16 Apr. 1846 George and Jacob Donner, their families, a number of other families and individuals, including servants and teamsters—around thirty-two altogether—left Springfield. Their first destination was Independence, Mo., the "jumping off place" for such expeditions. There they joined others who were going to Oregon, but the California-bound immigrants would branch off at Fort Hall, Wyo., and follow John C. Frémont's trail to the green and fertile lands of California.

All went well across the Great West even though for a part of the way the men had to blaze their own trail (which later proved useful to the Mormons moving through Utah). The trek took longer than anticipated, for the caravan had to stop a number of times to rest the livestock accompanying them as well as the horses and oxen pulling the many wagons. George Donner had three wagons loaded with trade goods and his wife had supplies that she expected to use when she opened a school. The immigrants entered the mountains along the modern boundary between Nevada and California just before the heavy winter snows were due, but they believed they had time to get through the pass. Unfortunately they were caught in the high elevations of the Sierra Nevada Mountains. Sixteen feet of snow covered their makeshift shelters and their supplies, already low, were soon exhausted. Many died. Their presence was known, however, and relief expeditions were sent out from California. The bad weather delayed the rescuers and some of the travelers unwisely set out on foot. George and Jacob Donner and George's wife, Tamsen, were among the victims. Some of the children, however, were rescued as well as some of the others. Donner descendants still live in California and have been noted citizens, particularly of the San Jose area. The mountain pass in which the group was trapped was soon named Donner Pass and a large bronze monument there now commemorates the bravery of all the pioneers who went to the West.

The Donner party has been widely discussed and studied. Several diaries and some letters that they wrote have been preserved; many of the survivors were interviewed at a later time and their story recorded. The fact that cannibalism was resorted to in those desperate days has also attracted attention.

SEE: Robert Glass Cleland, *From Wilderness to Empire* (1944); Homer Croy, *Wheels West* (1955); Rockwell D. Hunt, *California and Californians*, vol. 2 (1932); C. F. McGlashan, *History of the Donner Party, A Tragedy of the Sierra* (1947); Rowan County Minute Docket (1794–95) and Will Book E (Courthouse, Salisbury, N.C.); George R. Stewart, Jr., *Ordeal by Hunger, The Story of the Donner Party* (1936).

WILLIAM S. POWELL

**Donner, Tamsen Eustis** *(1 Nov. 1801–March or April 1847)*, western immigrant, was born in Newburyport, Mass., the daughter of William and Tamsen Eustis, respected and well-to-do members of that community. Young Tamsen was encouraged to pursue an education and finished her studies at the age of fifteen. In 1826 she accepted a position at the Elizabeth City (N.C.) Academy where she presided over the Female Department. Her marriage to her first husband, Tully B. Dozier, was announced on 31 Dec. 1829. They had two children who died of fever in infancy; Dozier died of the same cause in 1831. She then returned to Newburyport.

In 1836 she journeyed to the home of her brother in Illinois to teach his motherless children, remaining with his family for one winter before obtaining a teaching position in a school in Auburn, Ill. The following year she moved to the school at Sugar Creek where she met George Donner, whose home was near Springfield. Donner, a native of Rowan County, N.C., was a wealthy and respected man, twice widowed with young children still in the home. They were married on 24 May 1839, and in the following years Tamsen Donner bore three daughters, Frances (4 July 1840), Georgia (3 Dec. 1841), and Eliza (8 Mar. 1843).

Tamsen Donner was an intelligent woman, proficient in mathematics, geometry, and philosophy; she was fluent in French, an avid botanist, a competent painter, and a writer of prose and poetry. She is described as a small woman, five feet in height with a usual weight of ninety-six pounds, richly but quietly dressed, gracious, and charming. She and her husband were members of the German Prairie Christian Church near Springfield.

It is somewhat surprising that the Donner family chose to leave their wealth in Sangamon County, Ill., to undertake a hazardous journey by wagon to California in 1846. George was sixty-two years old; Tamsen was forty-four with three small children and two stepdaughters. In early May George, his brother, Jacob, and their families left Independence, Mo., with a sizable train and traveled west during the summer with little difficulty. Nearing the end of their journey, they were beset by bad judgment and weather and were snowed in near what is now called the Donner Pass. Nearly half of the travelers died from exposure and starvation during the winter of 1846–47. Those who survived resorted to cannibalism.

Although small in stature, Mrs. Donner remained in good health and able to care for her family. Her daughters were rescued by search parties, but she refused to leave her husband who was dying from an infected wound. She was last seen by members of the third rescue party. The fourth and last group found only one person alive in the camps. There was no trace of Tamsen Donner's body. She is presumed to have died between 26 March and 17 April 1847, approximately one year after leaving her home in Illinois.

SEE: Edwin Bryant, *What I Saw in California* (1848); *Elizabeth City Star*, 23 Sept. 1826; William A. Griffin, *Ante-Bellum Elizabeth City* (1970); C. F. McGlashan, *History of the Donner Party* (1879); *New England Historical and Genealogical Register* 32 (n.d.); *Raleigh Register*, 31 Dec. 1829; Jessy Quinn Thornton, *Oregon and California in 1848*, vols. 1, 2 (1849); Wills of Camden County, N.C., 1755–1854 (North Carolina Collection, University of North Carolina, Chapel Hill).

MARTHA NELL HARDY

**Dooley, Tom.** *See* **Dula, Thomas C.**

**Dortch, William Theophilus** *(23 Aug. 1824–21 Nov. 1889)*, legislator and Confederate senator, was born on his father's plantation near Rocky Mount, which had been in the Dortch family since 1742. His parents were William and Drusilla Bunn Whitfield Dortch. Young Dortch attended the local schools, then entered the Bingham School in Hillsborough. After completing his studies he read law in Halifax under Bartholomew F. Moore. In January 1845 Dortch became eligible to practice in his county's Court of Pleas and Quarter Sessions, and a year later was licensed to practice over the state. He opened his first law office in Nashville, but in 1848 he moved to Goldsboro, which had just become the county seat of Wayne. He soon had a large practice and in addition became county attorney. Over the next ten years he also bought land and engaged extensively in planting.

In 1852 Dortch was elected as a Democrat to the House of Commons and was reelected in 1854. During his second term he was chairman of the Judiciary Committee. He was elected to the same seat in 1858 and 1860. In the session of 1858–59 Governor Thomas Bragg attempted to secure a charter for a railroad from Greensboro to Danville that would link the North Carolina Railroad with the Richmond and Danville. Believing that such a connection would defeat the concept of a North Carolina Railroad system linking the eastern and western parts of North Carolina, Dortch was a leader in the fight that defeated the proposed charter. In 1860 he was elected speaker of the House of Commons. During the winter of 1860–61 he acted with the immediate Secessionists, but at the same time expressed such strong attachment to the Union as to discredit himself with that group. This was probably why the Whig-dominated legislature of 1861 resolved a close contest for a Confederate senatorship by turning to Dortch as a compromise appointment.

In the Confederate Senate Dortch was chairman of the Committee on Engrossment and Enrollment. He was a personal friend of Judah P. Benjamin and often acted as intermediary between him and Governor Zebulon B. Vance. In his legislative capacity Dortch supported all major programs designed to strengthen the Confederacy, though he differed from extremists in his refusal to sacrifice local interests completely. He was also North Carolina's strongest opponent in Congress to the schemes that would force Jefferson Davis to tender peace feelers to the Lincoln administration.

Dortch emerged from the Civil War almost bankrupt, much of his property destroyed and most of his library burned by Sherman's soldiers. For the next decade he labored to recoup his fortunes and eventually rebuilt his practice into the most lucrative in the state. He had similar success with his plantation. In 1875 Dortch lost a close race for a place in the state constitutional convention. From 1879 to 1885 he was a member of the state senate, serving as president in 1879 and chairman of the Judiciary Committee in 1883. He was the author of the "Dortch bill," which provided enlarged facilities for the common schools. Appointed a director of the state-owned North Carolina Railroad by Governor Vance in 1877, Dortch was one of the legislative leaders in 1880 who tried to prevent the sale of that line to a group of northern investors. He not only lost the contest but also saw defeated his amendment that would have protected North Carolina against rate discrimination by these investors. In 1881 Dortch was appointed chairman of a commission, consisting also of John Manning and John S. Henderson, to revise the North Carolina Code. This was a monumental task, as the revisal had to incorporate many fundamental changes in the law. Successfully completed after two years, the commission's work was not superceded until the revisal of 1905.

Quiet and reserved in temperament, Dortch was conservative and slow to change. His pleadings before the bar were precise, thorough, and straight to the point; his delivery was smooth and almost conversational. He was a member of the Episcopal church. Early in 1889 he suffered a stroke and died after a long illness. He was buried in Willow Dale Cemetery. Dortch's first wife was Elizabeth Pittman of Edgecombe County; their children were Corinne, Fitzhugh, Harrod Pittman, Isaac Foote, William T., Mrs. Annie B. Hill, and Mrs. Mary D. Scholfield. Dortch's second wife was Hattie Williams of Berryville, Va.; to them were born Allan W., Helen W., James Tyson, and Selene.

SEE: *Address of Hon. Henry G. Connor, Presenting the Portrait of Hon. William T. Dortch to the Supreme Court of North Carolina* (1911); Jerome Dowd, *Sketches of Prominent Living North Carolinians* (1888); Goldsboro *Headlight*, 27 Nov. 1889; *Journal of the Confederate Congress*, vols. 2–4 (1904); *Journal of the Convention of North Carolina, 1861*; *Journal of the General Assembly, 1852–55, 1858–60, 1879–85*; *North Carolina Biography*, vol. 5 (1919); Zeb Vance Walser Papers (Southern Historical Collection, University of North Carolina, Chapel Hill). Information on Dortch's Confederate senatorship is taken from scattered issues of Virginia and North Carolina newspapers, 1861–65.

BUCK YEARNS

**Doub, Peter** *(12 Mar. 1796–26 Aug. 1869)*, Methodist circuit rider and professor of biblical literature, Trinity College, was born in Stokes County, the youngest of the nine children of John Doub, German immigrant, and Mary Eve Spainhauer, born of Swiss parents who had moved to Stokes County in 1763. His father engaged in farming and tanning. Both parents became adherents of the new sect of Methodism introduced in western North Carolina in 1780, and their home served as a regular meeting place of the circuit.

Home study was a part of the weekly activities of the Doub household; the only schooling that Peter ever received outside the home was provided in the old field schools at irregular intervals over a seven- or eight-year period, totaling perhaps a year and a half. Doub, who was given strict religious training from an early age, recorded that his first personal religious "experience" occurred at a camp meeting in 1802 when he was six;

however, his conversion took place on 5 Oct. 1817 at a camp meeting in Davie County. Ten days later he joined the Methodist Episcopal church. At the fourth quarterly conference of the Yadkin circuit, he was recommended as a candidate for the ministry to the annual conference in Norfolk, Va., in 1818. His first assignment was to the Haw River circuit, with twenty-seven appointments. The next year he was sent to the Culpepper circuit in Virginia. In 1820 he was ordained as deacon and went to Bedford and Lynchburg. The following year he was back at the Haw River circuit. In 1822, the annual conference held at New Bern ordained him elder and sent him to the Raleigh circuit. In 1823 and 1824 he served the Granville circuit and in 1825, the Roanoke circuit; in 1826–29 he was superintendent of twenty-six churches in the Yadkin district. In 1830 he requested to be returned to the circuit and during the next eight years he served six circuits in North Carolina and two in Virginia.

Doub's career spanned more than a half century. He spent forty-two of those years traveling on the Methodist circuits and districts, four at stations, one as a temperance lecturer, and three as a professor. In all of this time, he was unassigned for only one year when he withdrew to regain his broken health. His life was characterized by a strict regimen of study. Much of his preaching was doctrinal as well as lengthy. In 1830 in Rockingham County, he preached one sermon for four hours and fifteen minutes. He engaged in disputes with the Calvinists defending the Arminian doctrine of free will and free grace, a belief so congruent with frontier life. One of his most significant accomplishments was in 1830, when he organized the Methodists in Greensboro to build the first church building of any denomination within the town—now the West Market Street United Methodist Church. In 1832 a school was opened across the street for the children of the members. This was the beginning of the movement that led to the establishment of Greensboro Female College (Greensboro College), chartered by the Methodist Conference on 28 Dec. 1838. In 1843, Doub was a delegate to the general conference in New York, out of which grew the separation of the southern Methodists from the general conference. As a delegate to the convention of the southern church in 1845, he suggested the name "Methodist Episcopal Church, South," which was adopted. In 1855 he was awarded the doctor of divinity degree by Normal College, soon to become Trinity College. After the age of seventy, a new career opened when he was invited to join the faculty of Trinity College as professor of biblical literature in 1867.

That Doub should end his career as a professor was a fitting climax to a life given to the Christian ministry and to education. The journey from the old field schools to a college professorship represented a lifetime of self-education and devotion to enhancing the quality of life of the early North Carolina communities. He died in Greensboro and was buried in the Methodist cemetery. In 1917 the remains of Doub and his wife were removed to Green Hill Cemetery in Greensboro.

On 19 Aug. 1821 Doub married Elizabeth Brantley of Chatham County; they had seven children. A portrait of him hangs in the library of Greensboro College. His handwritten journal and autobiography, together with personal letters, are in the Perkins Library of Duke University.

SEE: Bettie D. Caldwell, ed., *Founders and Builders of Greensboro, 1808–1908* (1925); William C. Doub Papers (Manuscript Department, Library, Duke University, Durham); M. A. Hites, "Peter Doub, 1796–1869," *Methodist History* 2 (1973); Raleigh *Enterprise*, 19 Apr. 1866, 8 Apr. 1867; *Raleigh Episcopal Methodist*, 29 Sept. 1869.

MARGARET A. HITES

**Dougherty, Blanford Barnard** *(21 Oct. 1870–27 May 1957)*, teacher, college president, state leader in public education, and influential politician, was born in Boone of Irish and English ancestry. His father, Daniel Boone Dougherty, a Confederate veteran, settled in Boone soon after the close of the Civil War and became a leader of the town and county. His mother was Ellen Bartlett, whose father was a hotel owner and a leading citizen in Jefferson and Ashe County in the 1800s.

Boone was a small, isolated mountain community when Dougherty was born and it had severely felt the effects of the recent war. He qualified as a public school teacher at age eighteen, taught several terms, and then entered Carson-Newman College, Jefferson City, Tenn., where he was graduated in 1898. That fall he enrolled at The University of North Carolina and the following year was granted a B.Ph. degree. On returning to Boone, he became superintendent of Watauga County public schools, serving about sixteen years. On 5 Sept. 1899, he and his older brother, Dauphin Disco, opened Watauga Academy, mainly for the training of public school teachers to serve the "lost provinces" of the state. He also led the fight in the state legislature to establish Appalachian Training School for teachers (now Appalachian State University). The school was chartered 18 Mar. 1903 with "Prof. B. B. Dougherty" as its head, a position he held for fifty-five years.

From early in the century, Dougherty visited counties throughout the state to study their tax systems; he became an authority in that field, and was appointed to the State Board of Equalization in 1927. Two years later, he wrote the Hancock School Bill and soon afterward was named to the state Board of Education by Governor O. Max Gardner; he served on the board for twenty-six years. In 1916 he was a member of the state textbook committee and in 1937 was chairman of the state's Committee on Salaries. From 1943 to 1950 he was on the Board of Trustees of the North Carolina Baptist Hospital, Winston-Salem. In 1946 he was named president of the Northwestern Bank, serving eleven years. In 1950, the North Carolina Citizens Association, Inc., commended him as the number-one man of the state.

A truly great day in Dougherty's life was 7 July 1949, when the county observed "Education Day" in celebration of its one hundredth anniversary and his fiftieth as an educator. The event drew noted figures from the nation's capital and from North Carolina. Those who spoke ranked him at the top in developing the state's public school system and making other worthy contributions.

Dougherty held honorary degrees from Elon College (D.Litt.) and Wake Forest College (Dr.Ed.). He was a Southern Baptist and a Democrat, and never married. His name is inscribed in the state's Education Hall of Fame. He was buried in the city cemetery in Boone.

SEE: O. Lester Brown, *Blanford Barnard Dougherty—A Man to Match His Mountains* (1963), interviews with members of the Dougherty family, and personal knowledge from an acquaintance with Dougherty extending from 1912 until his death; Ruby J. Lanier, *Blanford Barnard Dougherty, Mountain Educator* (1974).

O. LESTER BROWN

**Dougherty, Dauphin Disco** *(11 Mar. 1869–10 June 1929)*, educator, was the cofounder, with his brother Blanford Barnard Dougherty, of the educational institution that later became Appalachian State University. The oldest son of Daniel Boone and Ellen Bartlett Dougherty, he was born in Watauga County where he lived all of his life except for his school years and a seven-year period in the 1890s. He attended school briefly in Boone and at New River Academy, but most of his college preparatory work was completed at Globe Academy in neighboring Caldwell County. In the fall of 1888 he enrolled at Wake Forest College and was graduated in 1892; the majority of his courses were in the classical languages, mathematics, and physics. He then joined the faculty of Holly Springs College, a small school in Butler, Tenn., as professor of mathematics and natural science. Perhaps the most important event of his years at Holly Springs was his marriage to Lillie B. Shull in June 1897. The union proved to be a happy one and the couple had four children: Clara, Annie, Barnard, and Edwin.

In 1899 Dougherty returned to Boone to teach school. Simultaneously, he and his brother, with the encouragement of their father, began to build a school that they planned to operate under the name of Watauga Academy. It opened on 5 Sept. 1899 with four faculty members and some college level courses. The Dougherty brothers were coprincipals. Three years later they secured a grant for the school from the state legislature; it became primarily a teacher training institution and its name changed to Appalachian Training School. Dauphin Disco Dougherty was the "principal." For the last twenty-six years of his life he devoted himself almost completely to the school. At first he taught a full load, but as years passed he devoted more time to the business affairs of Appalachian. He bought the food, ran the school farms, looked after the heating plant, made the payroll, and kept the accounts. He is generally credited with establishing and building up the library of the institution, which is now named for him and displays his portrait.

Although Dougherty's schoolwork apparently left him little time for other activities, he served on the county school board from 1923 to 1929 and was superintendent of the Sunday school at the First Baptist Church of Boone from 1900 to 1914.

In 1925 Dougherty was stricken with a serious heart attack but gradually returned to his work. A second attack four years later proved fatal. He was buried in the Boone cemetery. His students remembered him as a demanding but sympathetic teacher, his employees as a benevolent supervisor. Although his achievements were considerable, they have been overshadowed by those of his almost legendary brother, who continued to administer Appalachian State until 1955.

SEE: *Asheville Citizen*, 11 June 1929; O. Lester Brown, *Blanford Barnard Dougherty—A Man to Match His Mountains* (1963); *Charlotte Observer*, 11 June 1929; Ruby J. Lanier, *Blanford Barnard Dougherty, Mountain Educator* (1974); Wake Forest College *Bulletin* (scattered issues, 1888–92).

RICHARD L. ZUBER

**Doughton, Robert Lee** *(7 Nov. 1863–1 Oct. 1954)*, farmer, banker, congressman, and Democratic party leader, was born at Laurel Springs in Alleghany County, the son of Jonathan Horton and Rebecca Jones Doughton. The family was prominent in North Carolina politics. His brother, Rufus A. Doughton, served as legislator and lieutenant governor; a nephew, J. Kemp Doughton, was speaker of the house in the 1957 General Assembly. Although educated at Laurel Springs School and Traphill Academy, Robert Doughton credited an itinerant teacher with opening his mind to the marvels of mathematics. Later in life he was awarded honorary degrees by The University of North Carolina and Catawba College.

Doughton began his career in public life as a member of the state Board of Agriculture (1903–10), of the state senate (1909–10), and of the state Prison Board (1909–11). Known for his ruggedness, frugality, and business acumen, he acquired in 1911 the majority stock of the Deposit and Savings Bank, North Wilkesboro, where he and his family often spent the winter months, and served as president until 1936. Through a merger in 1937 it became a part of The Northwestern Bank, now the state's fifth largest banking system with deposits in excess of $1 billion. After the merger he was chairman and director of the bank.

Nominated in 1910 by the Democrats of the Eighth Congressional District, Doughton defeated the Republican incumbent, Representative Charles H. Cowles. His forty-two years of service in the U.S. House of Representatives began 4 Mar. 1911 and ended with his voluntary retirement 3 Jan. 1953, a period covering the Sixty-second through the Eighty-second Congress during the administrations of seven presidents.

Known affectionately as "Farmer Bob" and "Muley Bob," Doughton was a physically large, vigorous man, six feet two inches tall and weighing 215 pounds. He found relaxation in farm work and was a farmer all of his life. As a young man and cattle raiser he drove livestock from the Blue Ridge Mountains to markets in the Piedmont. In Congress he was known to rise before daybreak to be at his office by sunup, attending to his legislative duties quietly and effectively; he was not loquacious. He rose through the ranks of the Ways and Means Committee, becoming chairman in 1933 with the ascendancy of the Democrats led by Franklin D. Roosevelt. He was a leader in preparing the far-reaching tax legislation of that era, including the formulation and passage of the Social Security Act in 1935 and later amendments.

In a letter to President Truman in 1952, Doughton observed: "I take more pride in my successful efforts on Social Security legislation than any other legislation that I have ever been responsible for or actively supported." At the time of his retirement he was credited with the authorship of more tax bills than any man in history; he had been chairman of the Ways and Means Committee longer than any previous chairman and was the first farmer to serve in that post. Described as flinty and frugal, Doughton kept the taxpayer in mind, admonishing his colleagues that "You can shear a sheep every year but you can skin him only once." Because of his financial conservatism and business judgment in the House, he was occasionally unopposed for reelection with the support of leading Republicans. Wilkes County, one of the strongholds of the Republican party, was not assigned to his district when redistricting placed Doughton in the Ninth Congressional District. He retired having never been defeated for public office.

In the late 1930s Doughton was urged to run for governor or senator. On 25 Feb. 1938 President Roosevelt, realizing the importance of the veteran congressman in the House of Representatives, urged him to remain there. In his reply of 28 February, Doughton thanked the president for his confidence and told him that he would seek reelection. Following his retirement he served two years as Democratic national committeeman and resigned from that office on 5 Aug. 1953.

Instrumental in creating the Blue Ridge Parkway, he lived to see the former Bluff Park named Doughton Park. He was also successful in his efforts to establish the Veterans Hospital in Salisbury after World War II. At age ninety, he was found dead in bed in his Laurel Springs farmhouse; death was attributed to a heart attack while he slept. Although in failing health, he had been involved in the political campaign and was preparing to appear at a rally in support of his successor, Representative Hugh Q. Alexander. Funeral services were held in the Sparta Baptist Church, with burial in the cemetery of the Laurel Springs Baptist Church where he was a longtime member and deacon. His portrait hangs in the Ways and Means Committee office, U.S. House of Representatives, Washington, D.C.

Doughton was married twice: in 1893 to Belle Boyd Greer, who died 18 Dec. 1895; and in 1898 to Mrs. Lillie Stricker Hix, who died 8 Feb. 1946. By his first wife he had a daughter, Emorie, who married Dr. B. O. Edwards of Asheville. Children of the second marriage were two sons, J. Horton and Claude Thomas, and a daughter, Reba.

SEE: *Biog. Dir. Am. Cong.* (1961); John L. Cheney, Jr., ed., *North Carolina Government, 1585–1974* (1975); *Congressional Directory* (1952); David L. Corbitt, ed., *Public Addresses, Letters and Papers of Governor William Bradley Umstead, 1953–1954* (1957); Doughton Family Papers (in possession of Mrs. Virginia P. Doughton, Raleigh); *Greensboro Daily News*, 4 Mar. 1933; Johnson J. Hayes, *The Land of Wilkes* (1962); Ina W. Van Noppen and John W. Van Noppen, *Western North Carolina Since the Civil War* (1973); *Winston-Salem Journal*, 2 Oct. 1954.

T. HARRY GATTON

**Doughton, Rufus Alexander** *(10 Jan. 1857–17 Aug. 1945)*, legislator and state official, was born in Laurel Springs in what is today Alleghany County but was before 1859 part of Ashe County. He was the son of Jonathan Horton Doughton, a farmer and sometime county commissioner for Alleghany, and Rebecca Jones Doughton, and the older brother of Robert Lee Doughton (1863–1954), congressman from North Carolina from 1911 to 1953 and for many years chairman of the House Ways and Means Committee.

Doughton was educated in the local schools and at Independence (Va.) High School. In 1879–80 he studied law at The University of North Carolina and in the fall of the latter year was licensed to practice. Settling in Sparta, the county seat of mountainous Alleghany County, the "tall and raw-boned" Doughton soon became a prominent local attorney. A Democrat, he was first elected to the North Carolina House of Representatives in 1887. Reelected many times, he subsequently served in the lower house of the General Assembly in the sessions of 1889, 1891, 1903, 1907, 1909, 1911, 1913, 1915, 1917, 1919, 1921, 1923, and 1933. In 1891 he was chosen speaker of the house and in 1892 was elected lieutenant governor, serving in that capacity from 1893 to 1897. In the Fusion-dominated General Assembly of 1897, Doughton was the nominee of the Democratic caucus for the U.S. Senate, but polled fewer votes (33) than either of his rivals, Jeter Pritchard (88), Republican, and Cyrus Thompson (43), Populist.

As a member of the house, Doughton supported enactment of the Watts Bill of 1903 banning the manufacture and sale of intoxicating beverages outside of incorporated towns and in 1907 led the house faction opposed to a controversial railroad rate bill championed by the more progressive Democrats. Especially interested in fiscal matters, he served often during his long legislative career as chairman of the house Finance Committee. As such, he was an ex officio member of the state's first budget commission in 1919. In the same year he helped to secure passage of the Revaluation Act, which introduced important reforms in the state's revenue structure.

As befitting a spokesman of the isolated mountain counties of western North Carolina, Doughton cosponsored in 1921 the landmark Doughton-Connor-Bowie Bill (Highway Act) committing the state to a bold fifty-million-dollar highway construction program financed through the sale of state bonds. Known variously as "The Grand Old Man of the West," "The Old Tiger of Alleghany," or as simply "Governor Rufe," he was generally recognized by 1921 as the most influential member of the house. Doughton "shaped" more legislation in North Carolina "than any man of his generation," declared the Raleigh *News and Observer* in 1945. Although invariably regarded as a party "regular," he was not closely identified with the leadership of the so-called "Simmons Machine," the political faction headed by Senator Furnifold M. Simmons that dominated the Democratic party in the state for much of the first third of the century.

In 1921 Governor Cameron Morrison appointed Doughton to the recently reorganized and enlarged State Highway Commission, a position he held while continuing to serve as a member of the General Assembly. Two years later, however, he relinquished his house seat to accept appointment as state commissioner of revenue. He was subsequently twice (1924, 1928) elected to the office. In 1929 Governor O. Max Gardner appointed him chairman of the State Highway Commission, a post he held until 1931.

At the close of the 1933 General Assembly, Doughton retired from active politics. In his declining years he devoted much of his time to the banking business, serving as president or on the board of directors of several banks in the northwestern section of the state. He died in Sparta at the age of eighty-eight and was buried in Shiloh Cemetery.

Doughton married Sue B. Parks of Alleghany County on 3 Jan. 1883. The couple had two children, James Kemp and Annie (Mrs. Sidney Thomas). Doughton was a Mason, a member of the Methodist church, and for fifty-six years (1889–1945) a trustee of The University of North Carolina.

SEE: Samuel A. Ashe, ed., *Biographical History of North Carolina*, vol. 4 (1906); *North Carolina Biography*, vol. 5 (1941); Raleigh *News and Observer*, 18 Aug. 1945; Capus Waynick, *North Carolina Roads and Their Builders* (1952).

NATHANIEL F. MAGRUDER

**Douglas, Robert Martin** *(28 Jan. 1849–8 Feb. 1917)*, associate justice of the North Carolina Supreme Court, was born near Douglas, Rockingham County, the son of Stephen A. Douglas of Illinois, prominent U.S. senator and Democratic presidential candidate in 1860, and Martha D. Martin. His maternal grandfather, Robert Martin, had large plantations on the Dan River and on the Pearl River in Mississippi. When Robert Douglas was four years old his mother died, leaving him and his brother Stephen A. Douglas, Jr., in the care of their grandmother, Mary Martin. After their father's marriage to Adèle Cutts, the boys lived primarily in Washington, D.C. Following the death of his father in 1861, Robert was reared by his stepmother. He became a Roman Catholic and was educated in private schools, Loyola College, and Georgetown University. From Georgetown he was awarded an A.B. in 1867, a master's degree in 1870, and an honorary doctor of laws degree in 1897.

Although his father had been a national leader in the antebellum Democratic party, Robert Douglas followed his deathbed admonition to "support the Constitution" and cast his lot with the Republican party. Upon graduation from Georgetown he went to North Carolina to oversee his property; in July 1868 Governor William W. Holden appointed him private secretary to the governor and an aide with the rank of colonel. On a visit to Washington in March 1869 Douglas called on his former neighbor and greatly admired family friend, Ulysses S. Grant, who had just become president. Intending only to offer his congratulations, young Douglas found himself with an appointment as assistant secretary to the president. After seven months, he became the president's private secretary and remained in that position for the balance of the first term. As a native southerner and trusted friend of the president, Douglas was able to reinforce Grant's moderate attitude toward the South.

In 1873 Douglas was appointed U.S. marshal in North Carolina's new Western District of the United States Circuit Court and settled in Greensboro. On 24 June 1874 he married Jessie Madeleine Dick, the daughter of Robert Paine Dick, who had been an associate justice of the state supreme court and was then a federal district judge. Law enforcement work and the influence of his father-in-law led to the study of law under Judge Dick and Judge John H. Dillard. Douglas passed the North Carolina bar in 1885, and by the next year he was serving as the standing master in chancery of the Western District of the United States Circuit Court.

Douglas was nominated for the North Carolina Supreme Court on the Republican ticket in 1896. The Republican-Populist fusion victory in that election enabled him to take his seat as an associate justice on 1 Feb. 1897. He served on the court eight years until he was defeated for reelection in 1904. His reputation as an able jurist was widespread. A contemporary, William P. Bynum, wrote that as a judge "he was noted for his learning, his fairness, his patience and his utter impartiality. His written opinions display not only a thorough comprehension of fundamental legal principles, but an ornateness of style and lucidity of expression which have never been excelled by any member of that court." The bitterness of partisan state politics, however, enmeshed him in an impeachment proceeding in 1901. The Democrats, newly returned to power in a racist campaign, feared that the Republicans on the court might try to overturn the recently passed constitutional amendment on suffrage that required a literacy test and poll tax but exempted most illiterate whites by a "grandfather clause." Consequently, they were determined to purge the court of its Republicans, David M. Furches and Robert Douglas. Articles of impeachment were drawn on a technical violation of the constitution concerning tenure of office. The 1899 Democratic legislature had attempted to oust Republicans and Populists by creating new state offices with the same duties as existing offices. The state supreme court had ruled on a number of the disputed office-holding cases, and in the case of Theophilus White the court had issued mandamuses on the state auditor and state treasurer ordering the payment of White's salary. The Democrats charged that the mandamuses violated a section of the constitution stating that in a claims suit the court could only make recommendations. Despite the fact that the impeachment proceeding was politically motivated, Locke Craig presented an impeachment resolution in the North Carolina House of Representatives in January 1901. A strong Democratic minority led by Henry G. Connor sided with the Republicans and fought the resolution, but it passed. The senate procedure began in February and the trial lasted from 14 to 28 March. The justices were acquitted on all five articles.

After leaving the supreme court in 1905, Douglas returned to Greensboro where he practiced law, wrote articles, and became involved in business and civic affairs in the community. He was an organizer of the first chamber of commerce in Greensboro, a director of the first streetcar company in the city, and a director of the Greensboro Loan and Trust Company. As a writer he contributed to the *Youth's Companion* magazine, and several of his historical addresses were published—the best known being *The Life and Times of Governor Alexander Martin* (1898). From 1906 to 1910 he served a term on the North Carolina Corporation Commission. He also was active in the Guilford Battleground Company and was a trustee of the Catholic orphanage in North Carolina.

Douglas had three sons, Robert Dick, Stephen Arnold, and Martin F., and one daughter, Madeleine. His son Robert, an attorney, was appointed attorney general of the state in 1900–1901. A portrait of Justice Douglas hangs in the North Carolina Justice Building, Raleigh.

SEE: W. P. Bynum, "Judge Robert Martin Douglas," North Carolina Bar Association, *Proceedings* 19 (1917); B. D. Caldwell, comp., *Founders and Builders of Greensboro, 1808–1908* (1925); Douglas Family File, Greensboro Public Library; R. M. Douglas, "Reminiscences of President Grant," *The Youth's Companion*, 12 Dec. 1912; *Trial of David M. Furches and Robert M. Douglas on Impeachment by the House of Representatives for High Crimes and Misdemeanors* (1901).

LINDLEY S. BUTLER

**Douglass, John Jordan** *(4 Aug. 1875–28 May 1940)*, clergyman and poet, was born in Cumnock, Lee County, the oldest of nine children of William Campbell and Josephine Tysor Douglass. His father was a successful attorney and his brother, Clyde A. (1889–1973), was a longtime counselor-at-law in Raleigh. His childhood was spent in Troy and Carthage, but the family later moved to Raleigh.

In 1892 Douglass finished his preparatory schooling in Carthage and that fall entered Wake Forest College, where he was a student for two years and distinguished himself for his work in the Literary Society and for his writing, especially poetry. In later years he often paid tribute to Dr. Benjamin Sledd, his English teacher at Wake Forest. He also studied for a short time at the Southern Baptist Theological Seminary, Louisville, Ky. In 1892 he had been licensed in the Baptist ministry by the Carthage Baptist Church and subsequently was ordained by a presbytery appointed and functioning on behalf of the Sandy Creek Baptist Association in its 1895 session. From his studies at Louisville, he went to Beaufort as pastor of the Baptist Church and then successively served Baptist churches at Clinton, Warsaw and Mt. Gilead, Wilson, and Dunn, as well as at Clio, S.C. In 1910, following his five-year ministry at Clio, he changed his denominational affiliation to Presbyterian and distinguished himself as pastor, preacher, and community leader in churches at Blenheim, S.C. (1910–18), Wadesboro, N.C. (1918–25), Jefferson City, Tenn. (1926–29), and Newton, N.C. (1930–40).

An avid reader, Douglass accumulated a formidable library and was known both for his studious care in preparing sermons and the superior quality of his delivery. He spoke clearly and forcefully in an extemporaneous fashion, without notes of any kind. His sermons were sprinkled with high imagery and multiple poetic references to buttress his careful exegesis of the Scriptures. In all communities where he ministered, he found time to be active in local affairs, particularly in matters relating to education and religion. He was a true community leader.

For more than fifty years, Douglass produced a voluminous amount of written material, both prose and poetry. Three volumes of his poems were published: *The Bells, The Quest of the Star*, and *The Gates of Dreams*. The last was a carefully selected arrangement of his poems, published by his wife the year after his death. He also published one novel, *The Girdle of the Great, or The New South*. He left three unpublished novels; those manuscripts have been lost or, in one instance, destroyed by fire. Although no definitive study of his literary production has been made, his individual poems appeared in many magazines and journals and frequently in the Raleigh *News and Observer*, some of them even boxed on the front page.

Douglass gained national publicity through a tribute in verse to President Woodrow Wilson, to which Wilson responded personally with appreciation. In 1938 Douglass read some of his poems before the Edgar Allan Poe Society in New York, and he often appeared before clubs and civic groups to lecture and read his poems. He was an active member of the North Carolina Poetry Society and the North Carolina Literary and Historical Association. In an appraisal of his poetry, G. A. Wauchope, professor of English literature at the University of South Carolina, wrote: "As a sea-poet, the author's style and treatment remind one of Allen Cunningham, a poet of a century past who excelled in ballads and songs of the free salt seas. . . . Mr. Douglass' mind is modern, but his soul is Greek. Though by profession he happens to be a Protestant clergyman by divine calling he is a son of Apollo whose magic flute has lured him into the secret haunts of nature, where he communes with the lovely nymphs and goddesses of the great outdoors."

Douglass was married first on 24 Feb. 1897 to Annie Duncan Rumley of Beaufort. They had five children: Annie (died in infancy), John Jordan, Jr., Mary Elizabeth (Mrs. Walker Hudson), Josie Tysor, and Donald Drake (died in infancy). Mrs. Douglass died 16 June 1927. In 1928 Douglass married Martha Taylor of Laurel Springs. He met her when she was a student at Carson-Newman College, Jefferson City, Tenn., where he often spoke and conducted panel discussions on poetry during his ministerial tenure in that city. They had one child, Clyde Virginia (Mrs. John M. Harper).

Douglass died at Presbyterian Hospital in Charlotte at the age of sixty-five. Memorial services were held in the Newton Presbyterian Church of which he had been pastor, and burial followed in the family plot in Oakwood Cemetery, Raleigh.

SEE: *Charlotte Observer*, 23, 25 Apr. 1923, 20 Feb. 1924; *Christian Observer*, 14 Oct. 1940 (Historical Foundation of the Presbyterian and Reformed Churches, Montreat [obit.]); John Jordan Douglass Papers (Baptist Collection, Wake Forest University, Winston-Salem); Elizabeth D. Hudson, Columbia, S.C., personal information; George Lasher, *The Ministerial Directory of the Baptist Churches in the United States of America* (1899); Raleigh *News and Observer*, 10 Dec. 1922, 22 Apr. 1923, 28 May 1940; Records of Presbyterian churches at Blenheim, S.C., Jefferson City, Tenn., and Wadesboro, N.C.

C. SYLVESTER GREEN

**Dowd, Clement** *(27 Aug. 1832–15 Apr. 1898)*, congressman, author, and lawyer, was born in Moore County, the son of Willis Dickerson Dowd, a longtime clerk and a state senator in 1860, and Ann Mariah Gaines. He was the grandson of Major Cornelius Dowd, who served Moore County as deputy and sheriff, legislator in the North Carolina House of Commons, clerk of court and register of deeds, and state senator, and of Mary Dickerson Dowd. His great-grandfather was the Tory leader, Connor Dowd, who was forced to seek exile in England for his part in aiding the Crown.

Young Dowd attended the local private schools and then became a teacher at the age of seventeen. In 1852 he entered The University of North Carolina where he obtained the A.B. degree in 1856. He returned to Carthage and for a time taught at the Carthage Male Academy; he also served on its board of trustees. On 10 Feb. 1857 he married a young widow, Lydia Josephine Person, the daughter of Dr. Samuel C. Bruce of Carthage. He was admitted to the bar in 1859 and began to practice law in Carthage. At the approach of the Civil War he joined a volunteer group, the Moore Independents, which became part of Company H, Twenty-sixth North Carolina Regiment. He first held the rank of lieutenant; following the Battle of New Bern, where his captain, William Pinkney Martin, was killed, Dowd was made a captain. In 1862 he was forced to resign because of ill health. Back home, he became a major in the home guard.

In the fall of 1866 Dowd moved his family to Charlotte. There he formed a law partnership with his old commander and former governor of the state, Zebulon B. Vance. The partnership continued for the next six years. Later he was to write Vance's official biography, *The Life of Zebulon B. Vance* (1897). Dowd served two terms as mayor of Charlotte. He was elected to Congress in 1880 and 1882. In 1885 he was appointed collector of internal revenue for the Sixth District of North Carolina, and in 1888 he was named receiver of the State National Bank at Raleigh. He was president and founder of Merchant's and Farmer's Bank and the Commercial National Bank, both of Charlotte. He was also closely connected with other members of the Dowd family who bought several local newspapers; his nephew, W. C. Dowd, owned the *Charlotte News* and *Mecklenburg Times*.

A man of wealth and influence, Dowd died at his North Tryon Street home. After services in the North Tryon Methodist Church, he was buried at Elmwood Cemetery, Charlotte. He was survived by his widow, who died in 1910, and by his children Ella, Mattie, Willis D., Jerome, Julia, Nan, and Herman.

SEE: Samuel A. Ashe, *Cyclopedia of Eminent and Representative Men of the Carolinas of the Nineteenth Century* (1892); Walter Clark, ed., *Histories of the Several Regi-*

*ments and Battalions from North Carolina in the Great War, 1861–1865*, vols. 2, 4, 5 (1901); Daniel L. Grant, *Alumni History of the University of North Carolina* (1924); M. W. Wellman, *The County of Moore, 1847–1947* (1962).

K. S. MELVIN

**Dowd, James Edward** *(10 Aug. 1899–12 Mar. 1966)*, newspaper editor and executive, was born in Charlotte, the son of William Carey and Eloise Butt Dowd. His father owned *The Charlotte News*. His ancestral line includes Connor Dowd, who settled at Deep River in Cumberland County about 1760. Young Dowd attended Charlotte public schools and Horner Military Academy and was graduated from The University of North Carolina in 1920. While at the university, he became a member of Delta Kappa Epsilon fraternity and joined the Student Army Training Corps in 1918. After working for a year as a salesman for the advertising department of *The Charlotte News*, he accepted a sales position with W. E. Thomas Real Estate. From 1924 to 1927 he was employed by the Bank of Virginia in Richmond. When his father died in 1927, he returned to Charlotte to work in the business office of *The Charlotte News*, which was published by his brother Carey. Two years later he joined editor Julian Miller in writing editorials. When Miller resigned in 1932, Dowd became editor.

Dowd hired W. J. Cash to be his associate editor. In his book, *The Mind of the South*, Cash called Dowd's editorship "one of the most lively, intelligent, and enterprising in Dixie." Cash had spent some time in Europe and Dowd let him handle most of the world news while the editor concentrated on local, state, and national news. Dowd developed a reputation for direct, candid expression and realistic analysis. His editorials, which centered around North Carolina and Charlotte, were marked by a strong desire for community improvement. He was a crusader in such areas as political corruption, slums, state mental hospitals, and bootlegging (he advocated ABC stores). In 1942 he resigned the editorship and accepted a Navy commission. He held the rank of lieutenant in the U.S. Naval Reserve and was on active duty from 1942 until 1945.

After the war Dowd became general manager of *The Charlotte News*. He was named vice-president and general manager when a group headed by Thomas L. Robinson bought the newspaper from the Dowd family in 1947. Dowd resigned in 1955 to join Knight Publishing Co. as general manager of his old rival, *The Charlotte Observer*. He was placed in charge of the entire operation except for the news department, a position he held until his death. At the time of his death, he was also vice-president, treasurer, and a member of the board of directors of Knight Publishing Co. of Charlotte, a director of Knight Newspapers Inc., treasurer of the Observer Transportation Co., and vice-president of Observer Charities Inc.

Dowd was active in many civic and professional organizations. He was founder of *The Charlotte News*' Man of the Year Award and one of the founders of the City Club (Charlotte). For several years he directed programs aimed at beautifying Charlotte. He was a director of the Charlotte Merchants Association, a director of Goodwill Industries, and a member of a commission that revised Charlotte's city charter. In addition, he was a director of both the North Carolina Press Association and the Southern Newspaper Publishers Association.

On 21 June 1930 Dowd married Elizabeth Mebane Robins of Richmond, Va. They had three children: Cornelia Jordan, Berkeley Robins, and Elizabeth Mebane.

SEE: *Charlotte News*, 12, 14 Mar. 1966; *Charlotte Observer*, 13 Mar. 1966; Daniel Lindsey Grant, *Alumni History of the University of North Carolina* (1924); William S. Powell, ed., *North Carolina Lives* (1962); *Who Was Who in America*, vol. 4, 1960–68 (1968).

PATRICIA J. MILLER

**Dowd, William Carey, Jr.** *(11 Oct. 1893–13 Aug. 1949)*, newspaper publisher and job printing executive, was born in Charlotte, the son of William Carey and Eloise Jordan Butt Dowd. William Carey Dowd, Sr., was first an executive officer of the *Charlotte Chronicle* and in 1893 purchased the *Mecklenburg Times*. Four years later he acquired *The Charlotte News* and subsequently bought and consolidated with it *The Charlotte Evening Chronicle*; he also consolidated *The Charlotte Democrat* with the *Mecklenburg Times* and in 1922 merged all of these papers with *The Charlotte News*.

It was this background of publishing and printing that marked the inherited interest of the younger Dowd. His secondary education was acquired in the public schools of Charlotte and at Bingham Military School, Mebane. He attended Wake Forest College and studied journalism at The University of North Carolina before beginning his career with *The Charlotte News*. He was first sports editor, then managing editor and business manager. When the senior Dowd died in 1927, the son succeeded him as publisher, a post he held until 1947 when the paper was sold. During those years, through a combination of good business practices and service to a wide clientele in the two Carolinas, the paper was very profitable. The job printing plant, which was not sold with *The News*, became the Dowd Press and Dowd continued as its chief executive until his death.

Dowd had a varied and impressive record of service in World War I. Trained at Camp Joseph E. Johnston, Jacksonville, Fla., he saw duty as a first lieutenant in the Quartermaster Corps in the campaigns at Rochefort, St. Mihiel, Vede Toul, Verdun, and Meuse-Argonne. Over the years, the insights into military problems and personnel gained from his experiences overseas were consistently reflected in the news and editorial coverage of *The Charlotte News*. He also maintained an active interest in the affairs of the American Legion.

Throughout his adult life, Dowd served a broad spectrum of church and civic interests. A longtime member of the First Baptist Church, Charlotte, as was his father, he was a leader in its organizations and programs. He was a charter member of the Myers Park Baptist Church and played a substantial role in making that church one of the most successful and influential of the denomination in the state, its congregation dedicated to a vast program of religious and social service to the city and the area. He served as a deacon and was especially active on the church's finance committee. In addition, he was a founder of the Charlotte Community Chest, as well as president (1934) and director (until 1938); a member of the war industries committee of the Charlotte Chamber of Commerce and influential in bringing several large businesses to Charlotte, which provided employment for several thousand people; a long-standing director of the North Carolina School for the Deaf; and founder of the Empty Stocking Fund to provide Christmas gifts for poor children. He also was active in the Good Fellows Club, the Kiwanis Club, and both City and Country clubs of Charlotte.

In the newspaper field, Dowd was a member of the

North Carolina Press Association, of which he was president and an honorary life member; the American Newspaper Publishers Association; the Southern Newspaper Publishers Association; the North Carolina Associated Press Club; and Sigma Chi journalistic fraternity. Although he was a registered and vocal Democrat, he never sought political office. He was an avid spectator sportsman although golf was his favorite recreational activity.

Dowd married Ann Garvey Rogers in Jacksonville, Fla., on 11 May 1918. She was the daughter of William Frederick Rogers of Fort Worth, Tex. They had two children, William Carey Dowd III and Marie Eloise (Mrs. Walter Bennett Latimer). He was buried in Charlotte.

SEE: *Asheville Citizen, Charlotte News, Charlotte Observer, Mecklenburg Times*, 11 Aug. 1949; William C. Dowd, Jr., Papers (Baptist Collection, Library, Wake Forest University, Winston-Salem); "In the Service of the State," *Wake Forest Student* 30 (1911); *Nat. Cyc. Am. Biog.*, vol. 38 (1952); *North Carolina Biography*, vol. 3 (1928); *Who's Who in the South* (1927).

C. SYLVESTER GREEN

**Downing, William** *(ca. 1680–1 Apr. 1739)*, colonial official, was descended from the Downing family of Isle of Wight County, Va., which had traveled in the Albemarle area as early as 1650 and moved to the area sometime after 1683. Because of this date it can be safely assumed that Downing was born while the family still resided in Virginia. He was the son of one of the three sons of Major Richard Downing, probably of William Downing, but this link has not been definitely established. His paternal grandmother was a full-blooded Cherokee, and his aunt, Nannie Downing McSwain, was a direct ancestor of American humorist Will Rogers.

The first record of this William Downing in North Carolina was on his conveyance of all his mercantile interests to a William Sharp in Chowan Precinct in 1715. He was recorded to have been living by 1717 in an area that is now part of Hertford County, near the present site of the community of Tunis, but by 1720 he was living in what is now Washington County, near the present-day town of Mackeys. According to colonial records, he was a juror for the courts of the Chowan Precinct in the session of 1720. On 24 Oct. 1724 he was named by the Assembly as an associate justice of the colony, serving first under Thomas Pollock and then under Christopher Gale. For some reason that is not explained in the records, the Assembly dismissed him as a judge on 2 May 1727.

Downing was first elected to the Assembly from the Chowan Precinct in 1725 and served until his death. Almost immediately he established himself as a maverick in the Assembly by lodging an official protest with the governor after the lower house was prorogued on the second day of the 1725 session. He soon became involved with colonial finances and was named to the Committee on Claims; by 1731 he was appointed "keeper of the box of bills" for the treasurer, Edward Moseley, and by early 1735 he was on the committee responsible for overseeing the payment of bills and issuing public credit. Later that year he was named treasurer for the northern district of the colony, the first person to hold that office for only a portion of the colony. This prompted a rather heated debate between the governor and the Assembly over which had the power to appoint the treasurer. As the Assembly's choice, Downing won and held the post until his death. On 29 Nov. 1734 he was appointed by the governor to be an associate justice of the Court of Oyer and Terminer. He was reappointed and served until 1738, when he was not returned by his own request.

Downing's residence was in Tyrrell Precinct upon its formation in 1729, but he continued to represent Chowan until 1735 when the representative districts were rearranged to include Tyrrell. In that year he became the new precinct's first representative, and he was unanimously voted to be speaker of the lower house. He was returned to the speakership by unanimous vote and with the approval of the governor until his death.

In many records he was referred to as Captain William Downing, suggesting that he was probably an officer in the militia. He was married to Dorcas Slade, and they had at least two children, William (d. 1748) and a daughter who married Thomas Lee.

SEE: John L. Cheney, Jr., *North Carolina Government, 1585–1974* (1975); Walter Clark, ed., *State Records of North Carolina*, vol. 23 (1904); Jack P. Greene, "The North Carolina Lower House and the Power to Appoint Public Treasurers, 1711–1775," *North Carolina Historical Review* 40 (1963); J. Bryan Grimes, ed., *Abstracts of North Carolina Wills* (1910); J. R. B. Hathaway, ed., *North Carolina Historical and Genealogical Register*, vols. 1 (1900), 2 (1901); Worth S. Ray, *Old Albemarle and its Absentee Landlords* (1968); William L. Saunders, ed., *Colonial Records of North Carolina*, vols. 2–4 (1886).

MARTIN REIDINGER

**Drage, Theodorus Swaine** *(ca. 1712–[October?] 1774)*, Anglican clergyman, explorer, and author, was the grandson of William Drage (1637?–1669), a medical writer of Northamptonshire, England, and the son of Theodorus and his wife, Mary Bowen Drage, who also had a son named William. The younger Theodorus is said to have been "a school Fellow of Lord Hillsboroughs," but nothing further is known of his early education except that he later noted that he was prepared as a youth for the church. William matriculated at Oxford in 1726; Theodorus Swaine was admitted at Gray's Inn, London, to study law, in 1737. The register lists him as "Drage, Theodore, of Greenwich, late of the office of Clerks of the Rolls, gent."

Drage and Arthur Dobbs, afterward governor of North Carolina, probably became acquainted through some service rendered by Drage, and Drage served as "clerk" on a voyage in 1746–47 in search of the Northwest Passage of which Dobbs was sponsor. Drage is considered to have been the author of *An Account of a Voyage for the Discovery of a North-West Passage by Hudson's Streights*, published in two volumes (London, 1748–49), and of *The Great Probability of a North-West Passage* (London, 1768), dedicated to the Earl of Hillsborough. (Drage often appears in contemporary records as Swaine Drage and sometimes, apparently, as Swaine, but Theodorus Swaine Drage beyond doubt was the "clerk" on the voyage and the books are identified as having been written by the clerk.) Dobbs became governor of North Carolina in 1754 and by 1758 Drage was living in Philadelphia as partner in the firm of Croghan & Drage, primarily selling wines and liquors. By 1768 he appears to have been studying again for the ministry; the following year he was in London where he was ordained deacon on 21 May and priest on 26 May 1769. Licensed by the Bishop of London, he prepared to sail to North Carolina. Lord Hillsborough may have arranged the position for his old schoolmate; William Tryon was then governor of North Carolina and Mrs. Tryon and Hillsborough were related. Tryon was described by Drage as being "a Family acquaintance." Benjamin Franklin was one of Drage's sponsors.

After a long passage at sea, Drage landed on the Outer Banks in November and made his way to New Bern to call on Governor Tryon. The governor promptly informed the vestry of St. Luke's Parish, Salisbury, that Drage would be assigned there for two or three months to give both the people and the priest an opportunity to determine whether the assignment might prove agreeable. If so, the governor would make the appointment permanent. Inhabitants of Rowan County had recently requested the governor to assign an Anglican priest to St. Luke's. Although Drage encountered resistance from the vestry (elected by all freeholders), he was cordially welcomed by many individuals who agreed to support him financially if the vestry failed to do so.

Within six months Drage had established twenty-six preaching stations around the county; some chapels were constructed and others planned. At the end of two years he reported that he had baptized over eight hundred persons and organized forty congregations among about seven thousand people. Nevertheless, he was operating outside the established channels as the elected vestry declined to accept him, or, indeed, to hold a formal meeting to discuss his acceptance. By withholding his salary, the vestry made Drage's position untenable, and it apparently was early in 1773 that he accepted an invitation to remove to Camden, S.C. He died there between October and December 1774. His will, drawn on 5 October that year, left his worldly goods to his "wife Hannah Swaine Drage in Philadelphia" and continued, "As what I cou'd devise to my children would be so inconsiderable and difficult to be got to their hands, I recommand them to the blessing of Almighty God." One of his children was Charles Swaine Drage who in 1759 married Hannah Boyte in Christ Church, Philadelphia.

SEE: Herma Briffault, "Biography of Theodore Swaine Drage" (Stefansson Collection, Dartmouth College Library, Hanover, N.H.); Ernest S. Dodge, *Northwest by Sea* (1961); Howard N. Eavenson, *Map Maker & Indian Traders* (1949), *Swaine and Drage* (1950); William S. Powell, *St. Luke's Episcopal Church, 1753–1953* (1953); William B. Willcox, ed., *The Papers of Benjamin Franklin*, vols. 16 (1972), 18 (1974).

WILLIAM S. POWELL

**Drake, James Perry** *(15 Sept. 1797–12 Aug. 1876)*, military officer and public official, was born in Robeson County, perhaps the son of Albriton or Silas Drake, the only men of this name recorded in the 1800 census of that county. Both had sons then under ten years of age. He removed to Kentucky in 1808 but by about 1816 was in Indiana where he served in the state militia; he was brigadier general of the Twelfth Brigade in 1825, and he served in the Black Hawk War (1832). He saw duty as a colonel in the Mexican War and afterward was civil and military governor of Matamoras as well as commander of U.S. forces in the lower Rio Grande Valley. Leaving Indiana, he lived briefly in Missouri but was back in Indiana by 1841. He removed to Tennessee in 1861 and finally to Alabama.

While in Indiana Drake held a variety of elective and appointive offices; among them were a seat in the General Assembly (1848–49), county clerk and auditor, receiver at the United States Land Office in Indianapolis and in Vincennes, director of the state bank, trustee of the deaf and dumb asylum, state treasurer, state superintendent of common schools, and commissioner from the state to the Paris Exposition in 1855. In Missouri he was a probate judge. He read law as a young man and may have practiced for a time, but otherwise he was a merchant and a farmer.

Drake married Priscilla Holmes Buell in 1831 and they were the parents of seven children. He died in Huntsville, Ala.

SEE: *Biographical Directory of the Indiana General Assembly* (1980).

WILLIAM S. POWELL

**Drane, Robert Brent** *(9 Jan. 1797 [or 1800]–14 Oct. 1862)*, Episcopal clergyman, was a native of Prince Georges County, Md., the son of Anthony and Ann Smith Drane of Wilderness Plantation. Young Drane attended Phillips Academy at Andover, Mass., and was drummer boy for the First Massachusetts Regiment during the War of 1812. It is said that he changed his given names of Lilbourne Boyd to Robert Brent while at Harvard College, from which he was graduated with distinction, receiving the A.B. in 1825 (though listed with the Class of 1824) and the M.A. "out of course" in 1841. For a time he had charge of a classical school in Salem, Mass. He studied for the Episcopal ministry and was ordained deacon on 3 May 1827 by Bishop Alexander Griswold of the Eastern Diocese, and priest by Bishop Philander Chase of Illinois in Washington, D.C.

Until 1836 Drane served at St. James's Church, Hagerstown, Md., from which he came to St. James's Church, Wilmington, N.C. Except for a brief period in 1843–44, when he took time out to assume the presidency of Shelby College, Shelbyville, Ky., he was the diligent and respected rector of Wilmington's historic parish to the day of his death from yellow fever in the war year of 1862. During his rectorship the new (and present) parish church was erected (1839–40), and the daughter churches of St. John's (1853) and St. Paul's (1858) were organized. The Reverend Dr. Drane, who had received the S.T.D. degree from The University of North Carolina in 1844, turned down several calls to churches elsewhere to remain at his post in Wilmington. A tablet to his memory was placed near the altar of St. James's Church.

Drane was married in 1828 at Salem to Augusta Endicott of Boston. They had two sons: Richard Hooker, who married Martha Wilson and lived in Maryland, and Henry Martin, who married Virginia Lloyd of North Carolina. Mrs. Drane died in 1847 and about three years later Drane married Catherine Caroline Parker of Halifax County, N.C., widow of John Hargrave of Lexington. A son, Robert Brent (1851–1939), was the only child of this marriage.

SEE: Diocese of North Carolina, *Journal* (scattered issues, 1836–62); Frederick B. Drane, correspondence with author; Harley P. Holden, correspondence with author; *One Hundredth Anniversary Commemorating the Building of St. James Church, Wilmington, N.C.* (1939); C. L. Van Noppen Papers (Manuscript Department, Library, Duke University, Durham).

LAWRENCE F. BREWSTER

**Drane, Robert Brent** *(5 Dec. 1851–31 Oct. 1939),* Episcopal clergyman, was born in Wilmington, the son of the Reverend Robert Brent Drane and Catherine Caroline Parker Hargrave. After his father's death in 1862, he was reared at Tarboro in the homes of his uncles, the Reverend Joseph Blount Cheshire and Governor Henry Toole Clark. In 1872 he was graduated with a B.A. from St. Stephen's College, Annandale, N.Y., and became a candidate for the Episcopal ministry. Upon completion of his studies at the General Theological Seminary, New York City, he was ordained deacon on 1 July 1875 by Bishop Thomas Atkinson in St. James's Church, Wilmington. He served as assistant to the rector of St. James's from 1 Aug. 1875 to 31 Oct. 1876. Ordained priest on 29 Oct. 1876 at Calvary Church, Tarboro, by Bishop Atkinson, he took charge of St. Paul's Church, Edenton, where he continued as rector until 1 Nov. 1932. In Edenton he rendered exemplary service to his congregation and community. For a number of years he ministered to the Church of St. John-the-Evangelist, Edenton's Episcopal parish for blacks, and to missions at Rockyhock and Colerain. In the Diocese of East Carolina, formed in 1883, he served as president of the convention and of the standing committee, examining chaplain, delegate to the provincial convention and to the General Convention (1890–1929), and trustee of St. Mary's College, St. Augustine's College, and The University of the South, which awarded him the D.D. degree.

A member of the Roanoke Colony Memorial Association and the North Carolina Historical Commission, Drane contributed to various periodicals including *The North Carolina Booklet*, and served as minister at the Roanoke Memorial Chapel. In addition, he had a part in the erection of the Church of St. Andrew's-by-the-Sea, Nags Head, of which he was rector from 1934 to 1939, and in the restoration of St. Thomas's Church, Bath. Horticulture, fishing, and boating were his hobbies.

Married 4 Dec. 1878 at Edenton to Maria Louisa Warren (d. 1921), daughter of Major Tristram Lowther Skinner, C.S.A., and Eliza Harwood Skinner, he was the father of seven children: Brent Skinner; Eliza Harwood, who married Cheshire Webb; Frank Parker (d. 1917); Robert, a physician in Savannah, Ga.; Frederick Blount, an Episcopal clergyman in Edenton; Katherine Parker, the wife of Bennett Perry of Henderson; and Marian, who married Frank P. Graham. Drane was buried in St. Paul's Churchyard. A portrait of him hangs in St. Paul's parish house.

SEE: Diocese of East Carolina, *Journal* (scattered issues, 1875–1939); Diocese of North Carolina, *Journal* (scattered issues, 1875–1939); Robert Brent Drane, Jr., Collection (Southern Historical Collection, University of North Carolina, Chapel Hill); N. C. Duncan, *Pictorial History of the Episcopal Church in North Carolina, 1701–1964* (1965); G. B. Holmes, *History of St. Paul's Episcopal Church, Edenton, North Carolina* (1964); William S. Powell, *Paradise Preserved* (1965); *The Mission Herald* 6 (November 1939); C. L. Van Noppen Papers (Manuscript Department, Library, Duke University, Durham).

LAWRENCE F. BREWSTER

**Drew, John** *(ca. 1719–26 July 1819),* merchant and ship owner, was born in Virginia but died in Bertie County, N.C. The son of William Drew (1682–1739) and Judith Wood, daughter of Thomas Wood of Isle of Wight County, Va., John Drew was an early inhabitant of land acquired by his father in the Roanoke River valley in northeastern North Carolina. He also seems to have owned land in Edgecombe County as well as in Surry and Nansemond counties, Virginia. The Drew family was well represented in southeastern Virginia and held great tracts in North Carolina as well. John's brother, Dolphin, represented Isle of Wight County as a burgess in 1766 and as a militia colonel in 1772. John's sons, John, Jr., and William, were quite successful in the mercantile business and law, with William serving as attorney general of North Carolina in 1815.

Drew's educational interests are vague but, according to the Harris Letters, he gave sixty-four dollars to The University of North Carolina upon subscription in 1793–94. His financial endeavors were numerous: among them, he owned stud horses, sailing ships to Barbados and London, and mercantile establishments in Halifax, Scotland Neck, and Louisburg. He also seems to have bought and sold vast tracts of land in Virginia and North Carolina. Advertisements from North Carolina newspapers offer sales of coffee, rum, sugar, molasses, and other commodities that arrived on brigs such as the *Betsy*, the *Poll Carey*, and the *Jonathan Jacocks*. Drew evidently offered young men the chance for apprenticeship in his business. Charles Harris arranged for his brother, Robert, to work under Drew, and Dolphin Samuel Pete, the son of John, Jr., died of yellow fever in St. Bartholomew aboard his grandfather's ship.

Perhaps the greatest of Drew's accomplishments was his incredible longevity. According to the obituary appearing in the *Raleigh Register*, he died a "very old and respectable inhabitant." Simple calculations reveal him to have lived eighty years after his own father's death. Moreover, Drew survived two wives, two children, and one grandchild.

Drew married Patience Brewer, daughter of Thomas Brewer of Nansemond County, Va., and after her death, Winifred, who died on Salmon Creek, Bertie County, in 1810. Four children were born to Drew, but it is not known to which wife: William, John, Dolphin, and Mary, who married Starkey Armistead of Bertie County.

SEE: John B. Boddie, *Historical Southern Families*, vol. 4 (1968); Fayetteville *North Carolina Minerva*, 9 Feb. 1799; Halifax *North Carolina Journal*, 22 Jan. 1798; Lois S. Neal, *Abstracts of Vital Records From Raleigh, North Carolina Newspapers, 1799–1819* (1979); Claiborne T. Smith, Jr., *Smith of Scotland Neck* (1976); H. M. Wagstaff, ed., "The Harris Letters," *James Sprunt Historical Publications*, vol. 14 (1916).

ERNEST RAWLS CARTER, JR.

**Drew, William** *(ca. 1770–8 May 1827),* attorney general and legislator, was probably born in Bertie County, the son of John Drew and his wife Patience Brewer. His grandfather, William Drew of Surry County, Va., acquired large tracts of land in the Roanoke River section but never lived in North Carolina. There is no information on the younger Drew's early life. In 1792 he became a member of the Royal White Hart Masonic Lodge in Halifax. He represented the borough of Halifax in the legislature in 1803, 1809, 1813, 1814, and 1816. In 1816 he was elected attorney general of the state, a position he held until November 1825.

William Drew and his father shared the enthusiasm then prevalent in the Roanoke River section for breeding and racing thoroughbred stock. *Solicitor*, bred by

John Drew of Halifax County and foaled in 1783, "won upwards of one hundred races in Virginia and North Carolina." This horse was certified in the *American Race Turf Register* by William Drew of Halifax Town in 1824. Another noted horse owned by John Drew, the imported *Silver*, was bred by the Duke of Grafton and foaled in 1789. It became the property of a Lord Sackville who sold him to Drew. Several other horses were certified by William Drew in the *Register;* this does not indicate ownership but does imply Drew was an authority on the subject.

From the records of Halifax County, it appears that William Drew acted as attorney for many of the prominent citizens of the town of Halifax. He never married and became bankrupt shortly before his death. His will, dated 8 Apr. 1827 and probated in Halifax in May of the same year, bequeathed his secretary, gold watch, and bedstead "now at Mr. Calvert's in Northampton Court House" to his friend Mrs. Mary Stith for her kindness and attention to him in his last illness. Mrs. Stith, known in her youth as "the Divine Polly Long," was the leading resident in Halifax Town at this time.

John W. Moore, in his *History of North Carolina,* said that William Drew realized the truth of Dryden's aphorism regarding the close alliance sometimes existing between a great wit and a madman. The historian went on to say that Drew's eloquence and learning were such that his eccentricities did not prevent him from being elected to positions of public trust. The reference Moore gave for this evaluation of Drew was "personal observation."

SEE: John B. Boddie, *Historical Southern Families,* vol. 4 (1968); Deeds and wills of Bertie and Halifax counties (North Carolina State Archives, Raleigh); Patrick N. Edgar, *The American Turf Register* (1833); John W. Moore, *History of North Carolina* (1880); Thomas C. Parramore, *Launching the Craft* (1975); John H. Wheeler, *Historical Sketches of North Carolina* (1851).

CLAIBORNE T. SMITH, JR.

**Drinkwater, Alpheus Walton** *(31 July 1875–23 Sept. 1962),* U.S. Coast Guard communications officer, was born near Oregon Inlet on the Outer Banks of North Carolina, the son of Edward and Josephine Etheridge Drinkwater. He was one of fourteen children—thirteen boys and a girl. His father was for many years officer-in-charge of Virginia Beach's U.S. Lifesaving Station; his mother came from a prominent Roanoke Island family. Drinkwater was a self-made man who became widely known before his death. Although often credited with transmitting the first message of the Wright Brothers' flights of 17 Dec. 1903, he actually—as he often told his intimate friends—only relayed the message. On that date he was assigned to send daily reports on a salvage operation of an early submarine, *Moccasin,* which had broken a tow line while enroute from New England to Norfolk, Va. and drifted south to fetch up on the beach in the village of Corolla. He explained that it was necessary to break in the line for telegraph communications between Kitty Hawk, near the site of the first flight, in order to send his reports of the salvage operations at Corolla. Thus all messages being transmitted from south of Corolla had to be relayed from there into Norfolk.

As a youth Drinkwater lived in Virginia Beach, where one of his first jobs was selling tickets at the railroad station for trains leaving the beach early in the morning. By 1908 he was living in Manteo. In addition to covering the U.S. Lifesaving and Weather Station lines between Hatteras and Norfolk, he also, as a telegrapher, sent messages to U.S. government facilities and to Western Union. During the 1908 experimental flights of the Wright Brothers, he became closely associated with many newsmen who had come to witness the flights that were preliminary to selling the planes to the federal government for military purposes. He transmitted press copy to many New York and other big city newspapers.

Drinkwater was one of the coastal areas' best loved personalities. His home was a meeting place for many friends ranging from local townspeople and *Lost Colony* cast members to nationally known dignitaries. As a stringer for the Associated Press, he was always quick to tip off friends on newspapers when a story would break on the coast—be it a shipwreck, hurricane, death of a prominent person, or an item on some unusual incident.

When he retired as a communications officer with the U.S. Coast Guard in 1946, Drinkwater joined the Civil Air Patrol as a communications warrant officer. He took pride in being the oldest CAP member in the United States at the time. He helped organize the Kill Devil Hills Memorial Society (now the First Flight Society); he was also a charter member of the Manteo Rotary Club and a Scottish Rite Mason of the Coinjock Lodge. Governor Terry Sanford named Drinkwater "Wreck Commissioner" following his retirement from other duties. A great sportsman and reputed to be an excellent shot, he made it a point to hunt on each opening day of the wildfowl season. He had no problem getting his limit of ducks and geese.

Drinkwater was a newsman to the end. Apparently sensing he was about to die, he asked his daughter to call Manteo newsman Aycock Brown about 2:30 A.M. on a Monday. Dorothy, a retired army nurse who lived with him, quoted her father as saying, "Tell Aycock to call the AP with my story." He died three hours later.

On 23 Aug. 1905 Drinkwater married Rosa Lee Gray of Long Point near Coinjock. They had two children, Dorothy Lee and Marguerite Lyle. He was a Democrat and a Baptist.

SEE: *Asheville Citizen-Times,* 15 Oct. 1961; Aycock Brown, interviews with Drinkwater family; *Durham Morning Herald,* 17 Oct. 1961; Elizabeth City *Daily Advance,* 30 Nov. 1948; Carl Goerch, *Characters . . . Always Characters* (1945); Manteo *Coastland Times,* scattered issues, 1908–62; Raleigh *News and Observer,* 31 Mar., 13 Aug. 1961, 25 Sept. 1962; Rocky Mount *Evening Telegram,* 12 Dec. 1958.

AYCOCK BROWN

**Dromgoole, Edward** *(1751–[before May] 1835),* pioneer Methodist circuit rider, was born in Sligo, Ireland. After hearing the preaching of Methodist missionaries, he renounced Catholicism and was ostracized by his family. He came to America in 1770 and entered the Methodist ministry in Maryland in 1772, later becoming a merchant, preacher, and planter in Virginia. He continued preaching for over sixty years until his death.

Dromgoole began to travel what was called the Frederick circuit in Maryland in January 1774. Later that year he was appointed on trial by the Philadelphia Conference to ride the Baltimore circuit, which took in part of Pennsylvania as well as Maryland. In November 1774 he was moved to "the other side of the Chesapeake Bay" to ride in part of Maryland and Delaware, where he continued until the spring of 1775. At the Philadelphia Conference that year he was sent to preach in Virginia, which had "but one Circuit, which extended from Chesterfield County . . . to the north of Petersburg, to the south of Tar-River in North Carolina, including many counties, making several hundred miles to ride once around," as he described it in a letter. In February 1776 the large circuit was divided into three—Sussex and Brunswick in Virginia and Roanoke, lying in North Carolina. Dromgoole first went "to ride over Roan Oak" in May 1776. He was in the neighborhood of Halifax, N.C., when news of the Declaration of Independence was received; at the request of "Wilie Jones, Esquire, and other distinguished patriots of the town," he read the manifesto to the congregation after finishing his sermon. It is not known whether this reading took place before the more celebrated reading of the declaration in Halifax by Cornelius Harnett on 1 Aug. 1776.

On 7 Mar. 1777 Dromgoole married Rebecca Walton, daughter of John Walton, "a respected citizen and man of much substance," of Brunswick County, Va. The Reverend Mr. Dromgoole established a plantation, Sligo (later known as Canaan), near Gholsonville in Brunswick County.

In the spring of 1778 Dromgoole attended, in Leesburg, Va., a conference at which ordination was discussed. Speaking of the North Carolina ministers there, he said, "The Circuit to the south was supplied with preachers," but he thought the absence of an older preacher to guide the young ones was felt. These young Carolina ministers were again present at the spring 1779 conference at Broken Back Church in Virginia. This time the subject of ordination split the group; Dromgoole, who opposed the laying on of hands, left the conference. He continued to preach and attempted to act as a peacemaker between the followers of old Methodism and the "newside." After he wrote to Bishop Francis Asbury in spring 1780, Asbury came to a newside-called conference and proposed a reunion of the factions. The bishop asked the newside to suspend ordinations for one year on the condition that he write to John Wesley to let him know "the situation of the Societies in America." They agreed and a foundation for reconciliation was laid. In the latter part of 1782, Dromgoole went to several counties "low down in North Carolina, and preached at Edenton, Hartford, Nixonton, Pasquetank, Camden and Currytuck and went round the great desart" (Dismal Swamp) back to Virginia. During the winter and the following spring he continued to visit small communities in North Carolina. Writing to Asbury, he said: "the last time I went round I preached twice on Roan Oak Island, to this place I went about 22 miles by water." The Baltimore Conference of May 1784 assigned Dromgoole to Bertie County for that year, but in late summer tragedy struck his family. Two of his children died, and his wife and another child became seriously ill. At this point, despite a great love for what he termed "the travelling plan," he decided to give up circuit riding to remain with his family and become a local preacher in Brunswick County, Va.

Dromgoole's connection with North Carolina continued, however. According to tradition, he was one of the twenty-two ministers who attended the 1785 conference at the home of the Reverend Green Hill in Louisburg. It was at this gathering, the first held in North Carolina, that Jesse Lee, a powerful preacher and early historian of the church, was received into the ministry. Built near Dromgoole's plantation in Brunswick County was the Olive Branch Meetinghouse, also called Branch Chapel or Dromgoole's Chapel, where he preached and where the Virginia Conference of 1803 was held.

Dromgoole was opposed to slavery. For a number of years he corresponded with former residents of his neighborhood who had moved to the new state of Ohio. He told Asbury in 1805, "a state where none of the human race are in captivity, would afford my mind more rest." Yet he never was able to break away from his possessions in Virginia. He and his wife had ten children, four of whom died young. One of his sons, Edward II (1788–1840), was a Methodist minister, physician, and planter in Brunswick County, Va. Another son, George Coke (1797–1847), was a planter, lawyer, Virginia legislator, militia general, and Democratic congressman. George attended The University of North Carolina during 1813–14, but, according to an account in the Richmond, Va., *Dispatch* at the time of his death, "was expelled on account of a Democratic speech delivered at the college against the orders of the faculty," which the story said was Federalist in sympathy. While at the university he was a member of the Philanthropic Society. He later attended the College of William and Mary and then studied law. He served three terms in Congress during 1835–37 and 1843–47 and was a participant in the famous Dugger-Dromgoole duel in 1837. A third son, Thomas, was sent to Cokesbury College in Harford County, Md.; however, he was "of an ungovernable and wicked turn, so that he could be kept there no longer."

As a young man, Dromgoole had learned the trade of weaving in Ireland and worked as a tailor's assistant in Maryland when he first came to America. The thimble that he used before the American Revolution was carefully preserved by his family. In his will, dated 2 Nov. 1833 and probated in May 1835, it is stated that he and his son Edward were partners in a mercantile business. The elder Dromgoole bequeathed several thousand dollars for the education of children in his neighborhood.

SEE: Elmer Clark, ed., *Journal and Letters of Francis Asbury*, vols. 1, 2 (1958); Bruce Cotten, "Peter Dromgoole," *The Carolina Magazine* 55 (1924); Edward Dromgoole Papers (Southern Historical Collection, University of North Carolina, Chapel Hill); George Coke Dromgoole Papers (Manuscript Department, Library, Duke University, Durham); Jesse Lee, *A Short History of the Methodists in the United States of America* (1810); Henry W. Lewis, "The Dugger-Dromgoole Duel," *North Carolina Historical Review* 34 (1957); Richmond *Dispatch*, June 1847 (scattered issues); William W. Sweet, *Religion on the American Frontier: The Methodists*, vol. 4 (1946). Apart from its holdings of Edward Dromgoole papers, the North Carolina Collection, University of North Carolina, Chapel Hill, possesses a portion of the circuit rider's library.

E. T. MALONE, JR.

**Dromgoole, Peter Pelham** *(b. 8 Feb. 1815)*, the student whose mysterious disappearance from the campus of The University of North Carolina in Chapel Hill in the spring of 1833 inspired several Tar Heel literary works and gave rise to a university secret society, was born in Halifax County of Irish ancestry. His father was Edward Dromgoole II, a Methodist minister, physician, merchant, and planter; his mother was Sarah Creese Pelham. Congressman George C. Dromgoole (1797–1847) of Virginia was his uncle. Peter's younger brother, Edward Dromgoole III (1825–95), was graduated from

The University of North Carolina with honors in 1845 and, as a representative of the Philanthropic Society, appears to have been in 1844 one of the three editors of the first volume of the *University Magazine*. Peter was the grandson of the Reverend Edward Dromgoole (1751–1835), a native of Ireland who renounced Catholicism and, after coming to America in 1770, became a Methodist minister. Peter's grandfather was a rider on the Virginia circuit in February 1776 when it was subdivided into three—Sussex, Brunswick, and "the other in Carolina, called Roan Oak." He played an important part in the early growth of Methodism in North Carolina.

Dromgoole was named for his maternal grandfather, Peter Pelham, who was for many years clerk of the court for Greensville County, Va. In 1802 Pelham removed with his family to Greene County, Ohio, where, on 28 Mar. 1810, Peter's mother married Edward Dromgoole II. The newlywed couple returned to North Carolina and resided for about nine years at The Oaks, a plantation Dromgoole owned in Halifax County at or near the present Roanoke Rapids. Sligo, the plantation home of Peter's grandfather Dromgoole, was located near Gholsonville Post Office in Brunswick County, Va., about fifteen miles above Roanoke Rapids. In 1819 Edward Dromgoole II left Halifax County and took up residence at Sligo, where Peter spent most of his childhood.

In 1832 his father sent him to the Franklin Male Academy in Louisburg, N.C., for college preparatory studies under the tutelage of headmaster John B. Bobbitt. There are several letters extant from Peter to his father written while he was a student at Louisburg. In January 1833 he was sent to Chapel Hill to attempt to gain entry as a freshman at The University of North Carolina. In a letter of 26 Jan. 1833, young Dromgoole told his father that he had failed the entrance examination but was studying under a tutor and expected to be accepted "with ease next June." The elder Dromgoole was extremely displeased by his son's rejection at the university. To add fuel to the flames of parental wrath, a letter from a faculty member to the father implied that the son was engaged in dissipating activities. In an exchange of bitterly phrased letters, Peter told his father "I have determined never more to see that parent's face whom I have treated with so little respect," and said he was sailing for Europe. He then disappeared from his Chapel Hill quarters under mysterious circumstances, leaving behind most of his possessions and owing money to at least one Chapel Hill merchant. Dr. Kemp P. Battle, in his 1907 volume of a two-part history of the university, quoted Dromgoole's roommate, John Buxton Williams of Warren County, as saying Peter Dromgoole was "a moody youth and inclined to wildness." In an October 1924 article in *The Carolina Magazine*, a University of North Carolina publication, Bruce Cotten, a Dromgoole relation, took issue with a number of statements made by Battle about the Dromgoole disappearance. Citing an 1834 letter from a Wilmington minister, Cotten maintained that in the summer of 1833 Peter Dromgoole joined the U.S. Army at Southport, then called Smithville, under the assumed name of Williams. Although unsuccessful in locating official records of the enlistment or of a subsequent military career, he was able to present evidence that much of Battle's account of the Dromgoole story was inaccurate.

Peter Dromgoole's vanishing soon became the stuff of legend. When in 1837 his uncle, the Virginia congressman George C. Dromgoole, killed a man named Daniel Dugger in a duel on the banks of the Roanoke River in Northampton County, N.C., memory of the deed soon was merged with that of Peter's disappearance. A promontory on the east side of Chapel Hill known as Point Prospect or Piney Prospect, was said to be the site of a nocturnal duel, caused by a romantic rivalry, in which young Dromgoole was killed and buried under a boulder. Dark stains on the rock are reputed to be his blood, which would not wash away with the passage of time. University students, who told many versions of the duel legend, formed in 1889 a secret chivalric society called the Order of the Gimghoul, whose members in 1926 completed construction of a gothic edifice called Hippol Castle at Piney Prospect. The legend became a uniquely North Carolina literary motif. It was used in the 1873 novel, *Sea-Gift*, by Edwin W. Fuller; in the 1881 novel, *The Heirs of St. Kilda: A Story of the Southern Past*, by John Wheeler Moore; in a long 1892 poem, "In Piney Prospect," by L. R. Hamberlin in The University of North Carolina *University Magazine*; in a 1903 short story, "Dromgoole," by Martha Fowle Wiswall in the *University Magazine*; in Cotten's 1924 article, "Peter Dromgoole: In Which Much Light Is Thrown on an Interesting Tradition"; in the story, "The Vanishing of Peter Dromgoole," in John Hardin's 1949 book, *The Devil's Tramping Ground and Other North Carolina Mystery Stories*; in a 1957 article, "The Dugger-Dromgoole Duel," by Henry W. Lewis in the *North Carolina Historical Review*; in "The Castle Amid the Pines," in Phillips Russell's 1972 book, *These Old Stone Walls*; in a February 1972 article, "Edwin W. Fuller and the Tall Tale," by E. T. Malone, Jr., in *North Carolina Folklore*; in a Summer 1976 article, "The University of North Carolina in Edwin Fuller's 1873 Novel, *Sea-Gift*," by E. T. Malone, Jr., in the *North Carolina Historical Review*; and in various unpublished manuscripts and portions of published books and monographs on other topics.

SEE: Bruce Cotten, "Peter Dromgoole," *The Carolina Magazine* 55 (1924); Henry W. Lewis, "The Dugger-Dromgoole Duel," *North Carolina Historical Review* 34 (1957); *North Carolina Biography*, vol. 2 (1941).

E. T. MALONE, JR.

**Drummond, William** *(ca. 1620?–20 Jan. 1677)*, first governor of the County of Albemarle, was born in Scotland where he apparently received a sound education. He went to Virginia about 1637 as an indentured servant of Theodore Moyes, who owned a large plantation on the Chickahominy River. By 1639 his bond had been acquired by Stephen Webb of the Lower Chippoakes area south of the James River. In 1640 he was deeply involved in what the Virginia General Court called "a most dangerous conspiracy." This appears to have been a plan by indentured servants and others in the plantations along the Chickahominy "to run out of the country." Although several persons were severely punished for their part in the conspiracy, Drummond escaped with a public flogging and an additional year of servitude.

In 1648 Drummond obtained a twenty-one-year lease of twenty-five acres of "the Governor's Land" in James City County, and a number of years later leased another two hundred acres. This property became Drummond's home plantation. At the time of his death it was reported as being "commodious . . . with mutch housing and mutch pasture ground." By the early 1650s he had married Sarah Prescott, by whom he had at least five children. He prospered as an attorney, as patentee of several thousand acres, as the owner of large herds of cattle, and apparently as a merchant or factor. By 1656 "Mr. Drummond of James City, Gentleman" was a justice of the peace and by 1658, high sheriff of James City County.

In December 1664, Drummond was commissioned the first governor of the newly formed County of Albemarle in the Province of Carolina by the Lords Proprietors of that colony. He probably was recommended for the post by his Virginia neighbor, Sir William Berkeley, royal governor of Virginia and one of the Lords Proprietors of Carolina, whose great Green Spring plantation was close to that of Drummond.

Drummond's commission and instructions reached him by late February 1665 and sometime that spring he convened the first Albemarle assembly. From the beginning, he was gravely concerned about the Proprietors' land policy, which he considered so ungenerous as to discourage settlement of Albemarle County. His task of governing and defending a colony of a few hundred people scattered along the streams that flowed into Albemarle Sound was extremely difficult. In the fall of 1666 the Tuscarora Indians attacked settlements on the Chowan River. Drummond mobilized the colony but was able to settle the Indian troubles before they erupted into a general war. His most conspicuous undertaking as governor was to negotiate with Maryland and Virginia for a cessation of all tobacco planting in the three colonies during the 1667 growing season in an effort to force up the price of tobacco. Though Albemarle endorsed the idea, Maryland eventually withdrew thereby aborting the scheme. Adding greatly to his problems was his rupture with Governor Berkeley of Virginia about 1666. Drummond rather openly charged in letters to England that Berkeley obstructed all things relating to Carolina despite his proprietorship of the colony. The real reason for the animosity that developed between the two men seems to have been an obscure squabble over land leases in the Pasbyhayes region in which they both lived on neighboring plantations.

Although the Albemarle government was permanently established under Drummond's leadership, this could not overcome his growing discontent with the proprietary land policy and his rupture with Berkeley. He undoubtedly welcomed the Proprietor's appointment of a new governor, Samuel Stephens, in October 1667. Within a short time Drummond left Albemarle and returned to his plantation just outside of Jamestown. Here he was active in business affairs while a number of brushes with Governor Berkeley kept alive the strong enmity between the two men.

Circumstances in the spring of 1677 made it possible for Drummond to give full rein to his hatred for Governor Berkeley. Indian attacks along the Virginia frontier aroused the settlers to take up arms and retaliate despite orders from Governor Berkeley not to do so. The beleaguered frontiersmen found a leader in a young and wealthy newcomer to the colony, Nathaniel Bacon, who did not hesitate to defy the governor and lead the settlers against the Indians. Infuriated by Bacon's defiance, Governor Berkeley sought to punish him for his actions but found that Bacon had become a popular hero among the colonists, a great number of whom were—for various reasons—in a rebellious mood. Berkeley sought to regain his popularity by calling for the election of a new assembly. It was probably at this point that Drummond first became involved with Bacon and assumed the role of one of his chief lieutenants. Drummond and his Jamestown friend and neighbor, Richard Lawrence, came to be viewed as "the chief Incendiarys and promoters to and for Bacons Designes; and by whose Councells all transactions were, for the greater part, managed all along on that Side." To Berkeley, Drummond was always the one "we all suppose was the original cause of this rebellion."

At the time of the June assembly Drummond and Lawrence were among Bacon's chief advisers, despite the governor's warning to the assemblymen "to beware of Two Rogues amongst us." Many of the measures associated with this assembly may originally have been expressions of Drummond's own long fermenting discontent with Berkeley and his government. Indeed, much of the limited ideological and philosophical thrust of Bacon's rebellion probably came from Drummond and Lawrence. Drummond was active throughout the rebellion both in the council and in the field. He first took up arms when Berkeley returned from Accomac to take Jamestown. When Bacon recaptured Jamestown and ordered it burned, Drummond and Lawrence set fire to their own houses to inspire the hesitant troops. It was on this occasion that Drummond dashed into the burning statehouse and saved the provincial records from the flames.

Although chosen a commissioner of Bacon's army, Drummond lost favor with his leader when he proposed that Sir Henry Chicheley be taken from prison and made governor. However, he continued to fight after Bacon's death and with Lawrence and a force of about three hundred men and boys seized the Brickhouse in New Kent on the south bank of the Pamunkey River. Unable to hold this position or gain additional recruits, the force soon dispersed, and on 14 Jan. 1677 a half-famished Drummond was captured by the Berkeleyites in Chickahominy Swamp. On 19 January Governor Berkeley came ashore at Utiemaria plantation on the York, where he met Drummond "and Complimented him with the Ironicall Sarcasm of a low Bend, saying 'Mr. Drumond! You are very welcome, I am more Glad to See you, than any man in Virginea, Mr. Drumond, you shall be hang'd in half an hour;' Who Answered 'What your honour pleases.' " On 20 Jan. 1677 Drummond was escorted by a party of horse to the home of James Bray at the Middle Plantation. Here before a court martial board, consisting of the governor and eight officers, he was charged with treason and rebellion against the king. He was found guilty and was hanged within four hours of the verdict.

SEE: Charles M. Andrews, ed., *Narratives of the Insurrections, 1675–1690* (1915); W. W. Hening, *The Statutes at Large . . .*, vol. 2 (1823); H. R. McIlwaine, ed., *Journals of the House of Burgesses of Virginia, 1659/60 . . . 1693* (1914), and ed., *Minutes of the Council and General Court of Colonial Virginia, 1622–1623, 1670–1676* (1924); John D. Neville, comp., *Bacon's Rebellion: Abstracts of Materials in the Colonial Records Project* (1976); Nell M. Nugent, ed., *Cavaliers and Pioneers*, vol. 1 (1934); William S. Powell, *Ye Countie of Albemarle* (1958); William L. Saunders, ed., *Colonial Records of North Carolina*, vol. 1 (1886); *Virginia Magazine of History and Biography* (scattered issues); Wilcomb E. Washburn, *The Governor and the Rebel: A History of Bacon's Rebellion in Virginia* (1957), and "The Humble Petition of Sarah Drummond," *William and Mary Quarterly* 13 (1956); Thomas J. Wertenbaker, *Torchbearer of the Revolution: The Story of Bacon's Rebellion and its Leader* (1940); *William and Mary Quarterly* (scattered issues).

HERBERT R. PASCHAL

**Dry, Marcus Baxter** *(23 Oct. 1871–27 Jan. 1946),* teacher and school administrator, whose career spanned over half a century, was born on a farm in Union County, the eldest of twelve children of Henry and Jane Alice Parker Dry. The family lineage was German and originally the name was Derr. Settlers came first to Pennsylvania and descendants migrated south to Cabarrus County as early as 1754. Dry's father engaged in farming and sawmilling until 1893, when he sold his interests in Union County and, with the exception of Marcus and one daughter, moved the entire family to Texas. Young Dry, who was graduated from Union Institute at the age of seventeen, began his teaching career in a clay-chinked, one-room log schoolhouse. After six years of teaching he had acquired enough money in 1893 to enter Wake Forest College where he received the master of arts degree, with valedictorian honors, in 1896. He distinguished himself in the classics, was a member of the Euzelian Literary Society, class poet, and an editor of and frequent contributor to the literary magazine, *The Wake Forest Student.*

In 1896 a new school, named Wingate in honor of former President Washington Manly Wingate of Wake Forest, was established by the Union Baptist Association. Dry was employed as the first principal. Under his guidance in the next twelve years it developed into one of the most successful boarding schools in the area and is now Wingate College. From 1905 to 1908 he also edited and published a monthly newspaper, *The Baptist Messenger.*

In 1907 North Carolina endeavored to create a new system of public high schools by offering state funds to local schools. The Cary school in Wake County, a private institution since 1870, became on 6 Apr. 1907 the state's first public high school under the new law. In 1908 Marcus Dry became principal and, drawing patronage from a wide area, soon made it one of the leading boarding schools in the state. In 1913–14 a new brick building was erected, the first of six plant additions, which immediately became an architectural model for other schools across the state. Dry pioneered in curriculum development and sought to make the school a working partner with the rural community. In 1913 he established a Farm-Life department, offering agriculture and home economics. He also pioneered in vocational training for retarded children. His "Betterment Association," forerunner of the Parent-Teacher Association, enabled him to provide hot lunches for children. A student council was instituted in 1919, followed by public school music and band in 1922, a commercial department in 1924, physical education (establishing the first rural high school gymnasium in the state) in 1925, and a teacher training department sponsored by the state Department of Education in 1922–28. Indeed, because of its progressive programs, its proximity to Raleigh, the capital, and its support by state educational agencies, Dry's school became a model for the development of North Carolina's public school system in the 1920s. Younger principals consulted him on the qualities of good principalship.

Between 1918 and 1923 Dry took an active part in promoting both the movement for school consolidation and bond issues to sustain the movement. In 1927 five other schools were consolidated with Cary and the M. B. Dry Building was constructed to accommodate them. Dry also played a leading role in the work of the North Carolina Education Association and was a member of the first state Textbook Commission. During the summer he pursued graduate study at Columbia University and elsewhere and subsequently conducted teacher institutes for the state Department of Education. In 1939 a new brick building replaced the 1913 building on the same site; at its dedication the state superintendent of public instruction noted that "Dry is the only principal in North Carolina who has worn out a schoolhouse." He retired as principal in 1942 but continued teaching until 1944.

Dry was over six feet tall, with dark eyes and hair, somewhat formal in manner and dress, but naturally genial and kind, possessing all the equanimity, patience, and dedication required of a good teacher. He was highly regarded by his students, many of whom went on to successful careers as college educators, business, and professional leaders. A bronze plaque commemorating his leadership was presented to the Cary school at a memorial service on 18 May 1947 and a portrait by Mabel Pugh hangs in the school building. In 1964 the Dry Memorial Chapel, contributed by his former Wingate students, was dedicated at Wingate College where another portrait hangs in the trustee room.

Dry was a dedicated member of the Cary Baptist Church and for over thirty years taught the Men's Bible Class, also named for him. In 1930, as a token of their affection, his school and Sunday school students gave him a trip to the Holy Land which included visits to thirteen European countries. Throughout his life he was regarded as "the first citizen" of Cary.

In 1904 Dry married Wilma Annie Perry, daughter of William Marion Perry, one of the founders of the Wingate school; they had three children, Helen, William, and Hallie. His grave is in Cary, not far from the school he served so long and so well.

SEE: Tom Byrd and Evelyn Holland, *Cary's 100th Anniversary* (1971); *Cary News,* 1 Feb. 1967; Marcus Baxter Dry, "History of Education at Cary," *North Carolina Education* 2 (February 1936); Marcus Baxter Dry Papers (in possession of William Henry Dry, Raleigh); Jasper L. Memory, interview, 21 Sept. 1976; *North Carolina Biography,* vol. 3 (1941); Raleigh *News and Observer,* 6 May 1942, 28 Jan. 1947; Wingate College, *Annual, 1946–47.*

PERCIVAL PERRY

**Dry, William, III** *(1720–3 June 1781),* Brunswick merchant, planter, and royal placeman, was born in Goose Creek, S.C. The progenitor of the Dry family in Carolina was Robert Dry who immigrated to South Carolina about 1680. His son, William Dry I, inherited the home plantation near Charles Town which he bequeathed to William Dry II. The marriage of the latter to the sister of Roger, Maurice, and Nathaniel Moore probably prompted him to join the Cape Fear enterprise initiated by the Moores in the 1720s. In 1736 he moved his family, including sixteen-year-old William Dry III, to Brunswick where the elder Dry was justice of the peace, militia captain, and prominent merchant until his death in 1740.

William Dry III, the revolutionary, stood ready to succeed his father as one of the leading citizens of the Cape Fear. Retaining the magistrate's office and militia command in the family, he first achieved provincial prominence as leader of the militia force that counterattacked and repulsed the Spanish raid on Brunswick in 1747. For his efforts he was eventually elevated to the rank of colonel. In 1754 the provincial assembly designated him one of the commissioners of Fort Johnston, which not only protected the Cape Fear but also much of Dry's property along the river from Brunswick to Wilmington. During the French and Indian War the assembly commissioned Dry to repair the fort, but he proved so dilatory that the war ended a year before the repairs were completed in 1764.

In the meantime Dry continued to serve the Cape Fear community as one of the commissioners of the roads in the southwest district of New Hanover County (1745–64) and as commissioner of pilotage for the Cape Fear River. In 1764 he was named one of the commissioners to determine the dividing line between Bladen and Brunswick counties. Eight years later he and John Rutherfurd, receiver general of the quitrents, joined representatives of South Carolina to survey an extension of the boundary between the colonies. Dry was also a communicant of the Anglican church, which he staunchly supported.

Amid these services to the colony Dry, at the rather late age of forty, evinced an interest in politics. In 1760 he became one of the charter aldermen of Wilmington and successfully stood for election to the provincial assembly from the town of Brunswick. After a brief and rather colorless career in the lower house, he was appointed to the council in 1763. When councillor John Swann died in 1761, Governor Arthur Dobbs wrote the Board of Trade to recommend Dry as a replacement. He characterized Dry as "a Gentleman of Great Worth and Fortune and zealous in Supporting his Majesty's Rights." Dry assumed his position on the council in the summer of 1764.

Dry's service to the king as councillor was antedated by his employment in the customs department as collector of the Port of Brunswick in 1761. This position brought him in conflict with the Cape Fear mobs during the Stamp Act crisis in 1765 and 1766, and those harrowing times seem to have constituted a turning point in his career. His circumstantial support of the Crown during the Stamp Act affair jeopardized his social and political standing in the colony. Thereafter, he worked assiduously to court popular favor. The transition proved relatively easy because Dry was fundamentally "a good-natured man" who made no pretense "to knowledge or understanding in anything" and lacked fixed political principles. By 1774, however, the collector had definitely emerged on the side of the popular majority when he and other councillors contradicted instructions from the Crown and exhortations from the governor by supporting assembly bills that altered the nature of the county and superior courts of the colony. The following year Dry detached himself completely from the royal cause, toasting to the success of American arms in New England and, according to a British partisan, talking "treason by the hour." In 1775 Governor Josiah Martin suspended Dry from his seat on the council, noting that Dry's unreserved support for the revolt in America probably "astonished even the foremost leaders of sedition" in the colony.

Despite Dry's protestations of support for the Americans, he did not prove to be a fervent patriot. When the legislature of the new state of North Carolina appointed him one of seven members of the Council of State, he declined to serve. No evidence exists to substantiate his active participation in the conflict with Great Britain. Basically he was a jovial planter who was more concerned with setting a fine table and entertaining guests than actively pursuing politics. Massachusetts journalist Josiah Quincy, Jr., found "Dry['s] is justly called the house of universal hospitality." Moreover, in 1776 the British literally brought the war to Dry's doorstep when they looted Brunswick and burned his elegant home, Bellfont (formerly Russellborough), which he had purchased from Governor William Tryon. Dry spent the remainder of his life on Blue Banks plantation, a 3,800-acre estate in Brunswick.

Dry married Mary Jane Rhett, maternal granddaughter of Nicholas Trott and paternal granddaughter of the notorious William Rhett of South Carolina, and "a lady of great fortune and merit" in her own right. The couple had two daughters: Rebecca, who married Thomas McGuire, attorney general of North Carolina before the American Revolution; and Sarah, who married Benjamin Smith, a future governor of North Carolina. A loving father, Dry was much aggrieved at the early death of Rebecca in 1776. He died at age sixty-one and was buried in St. Philip's churchyard in Brunswick where most of his immediate family also lie.

SEE: Walter Clark, ed., *State Records of North Carolina*, vols. 11–25 (1895–1906); William L. Saunders, ed., *Colonial Records of North Carolina*, vols. 5–10 (1887–90); Janet Schaw, *Journal of a Lady of Quality* (1923).

ALAN D. WATSON

**DuBois, John** *(ca. 1700–1768)*, landowner in North Carolina and New York, Wilmington merchant and captain of a fleet of ships, and colonial official, was probably of Huguenot stock and born either in New York or Virginia. He lived on Market Street near the court house in Wilmington. In 1754 the town governors ordered that all future surveys of Wilmington were to be made beginning at the southeast corner of DuBois's home. In 1758 he was one of the commissioners appointed to supervise the construction of St. James Church in Wilmington; two years later he was assigned the same position for the building of a prison and an office for the sheriff. The assembly also named him a commissioner to supervise the pilotage on the river. During 14–22 July 1757 one of his ships delivered ordnance to strengthen Fort Johnston, which guarded the entrance into the Cape Fear River.

DuBois probably was a man of strong opinions for he seems to have been a stern slave master and father. Respected by many of his fellow merchants, he was one of the signers of a letter from Wilmington merchants to Governor Tryon concerning the Stamp Act proceedings. Apparently Tryon had interpreted their earlier comments about the seizure of two ships by Captain Jacob Lobb as criticism, but after receiving the letter he forgave them for casting aspersions on him in connection with the proposed act.

It appears that DuBois was married several times. His will refers to a monthly clock he had given to a nephew, Caleb Grainger, because it was once owned by his third wife who was an aunt of young Caleb. The names of the first three wives have not been discovered; his fourth wife, Jean, was one of his executors and the mother of at least two of his children. During the American Revolution Mrs. Jean DuBois and a Mrs. McNeill and their families were ordered by the Council of Safety in Wilmington to leave the city within eight days of the order, dated 15 June 1776. Despite the fact that John DuBois, Jr., was a member of the safety committee, there seems to be no record that he tried to help her. But he may have had some influence with the patriot governor, who gave Mrs. DuBois permission to return to Wilmington in 1777.

Apparently John DuBois, Sr., died before 1 Mar. 1768 as Archibald Maclaine, one of the witnesses of the will, appeared that day before Governor Tryon and swore that DuBois was of sound mind when he made his will on 13 Sept. 1767. The same year DuBois had eight living children, five sons and three daughters. Three sons—Peter, Walter, and John—were of legal majority; the other two sons—Isaac and James—were minors. Their sisters were Magdalene-Margaret, Margaret, and Anna-Jean. The minor children were left in the care of DuBois's fourth wife. The three oldest sons and Mrs. DuBois, with Lewis Henry and Moses John De Rosset, were made guardians of the children and executors of the will. Peter and Walter, the oldest sons, were prosperous and so were left money rather than land by their father. John received lots in Wilmington, a plantation on Smith's Creek, guns, a sword, and a large diamond ring. DuBois bequeathed town properties to his minor children. He also gave his daughter Magdalene-Margaret her mother's two diamond rings, and his son James his windmill and land adjoining the town of Wilmington. This land, known as DuBois's mill, was fortified in December 1775. Mrs. Jean DuBois received the family home in Wilmington and an adjoining lot together with the profits from her husband's bake house. According to his will, on her death this property would go to their daughter Anna-Jean. The profits from the merchant fleet and slaves were to be supervised by the guardians and used for the care and education of the minor children.

Two sons of John DuBois gained public attention. The property of Isaac was confiscated by the state in 1784, and John, Jr. (known as Captain John DuBois), was active in the American Revolution as a major in the militia, commissioner, notary public, justice of the peace, and inspector of the polls.

SEE: Lester J. Cappon and Stella F. Duff, eds., *Virginia Gazette Index, 1738–1780* (1950); Walter Clark, ed., *State Records of North Carolina*, vols. 12, 13, 15, 17, 22–25 (1895, 1896, 1898, 1899, 1907, 1904, 1905, 1906); J. Bryan Grimes, ed., *North Carolina Wills and Inventories* (1912); William L. Saunders, ed., *Colonial Records of North Carolina*, vols. 6, 7, 8, 10 (1888, 1890).

VERNON O. STUMPF

**Duckenfield, Nathaniel** *(13 June 1746–20 Oct. 1824)*, baronet, landowner, and councillor, was the son of Nathaniel and Margaret Duckenfield of Chester, Cheshire, England. His father, who had extensive holdings in Bertie County, N.C., inherited from his cousin William Duckenfield, died in 1749 and bequeathed his land to his wife. In 1756 Margaret Duckenfield appeared in Bertie County court to petition for appointment as executrix of her husband's estate. How long she remained in North Carolina at that time, or whether her son had come with her, is not known, though she apparently settled in the colony at some point in the 1760s and married John Pearson, a lawyer. They lived on an estate called Duckenfield on Salmon Creek in Bertie County.

On 15 May 1768, young Nathaniel became the fifth Duckenfield baronet when his uncle Samuel died without issue. The following year he decided to visit his mother and his North Carolina holdings. He soon informed Governor William Tryon that he intended to settle in the province permanently. Several years later Duckenfield wrote to James Iredell that he had hoped to find a wealthy wife in the colony who could help support the financial strain of a baronetcy. In January 1771 Tryon nominated him to a place on the royal council. Although he was not seated until November, Duckenfield had created a considerable stir in the council the previous April by claiming the senior position in that body by virtue of his baronetcy. He was firmly resisted in this ploy by his fellow councillors and in November took his place as a junior member.

During 1771 the baronet courted Hannah, daughter of Samuel Johnston; early in 1772 he proposed to her but was rejected. Although Hannah would later marry James Iredell, Duckenfield and Iredell remained friends and corresponded until 1791. Duckenfield decided to return to England by the spring of 1772, convinced that he was not suited to managing a plantation (he owned over 3,600 acres of land) and that he would not make a "good match" in North Carolina. In England he purchased a coronet's commission in the Queen's Dragoons. In 1773 he resigned his council seat, stating that he would not return to North Carolina. Two years later he advanced to adjutant in his regiment but declared that he would not serve happily in revolutionary America, and he never did. In 1778 his North Carolina lands were confiscated by the state, although he had managed to deed all of his slaves to his mother after his departure from the colony. Whereas other loyalists, especially Henry Eustace McCulloh, owned more land than Duckenfield, his properties brought in more money from state sales than those of any other person except Lord Granville. His friend James Iredell attempted to prevent confiscation but was unsuccessful.

In 1783 Duckenfield married Katherine Warde, who eventually gave him four sons and a daughter. The following year he went on half pay as a captain in the Eighty-second Regiment of Foot—effectively retiring from active duty. Before his mother died at Duckenfield in December 1784, she directed that most of her property be sold and the proceeds sent to her son. The next year Sir Nathaniel was awarded £3,000 by the Loyalist Claims Commission in London for his North Carolina losses—considerably less than the £8,762 at which he had valued his holdings. Nevertheless, with this money and his wife's wealth, Duckenfield appears to have lived comfortably in England for the remainder of his life.

SEE: *Appleton's Cyclopedia of American Biography*, vol. 2 (1887); George E. Cokayne, *Complete Baronetage*, vol. 4 (1904); Nathaniel Duckenfield, loyalist claim (North Carolina State Archives, Raleigh); R. Don Higginbotham, ed., *The Papers of James Iredell*, 2 vols. (1976); Lorenzo Sabine, *Biographical Sketches of Loyalists of the American Revolution*, vol. 1 (1864); William L. Saunders, ed., *Colonial Records of North Carolina*, vols. 8–9 (1890).

WILLIAM S. PRICE, JR.

**Duckenfield, William** *(d. ca. February 1721/22)*, member of the North Carolina Council and justice of the General Court, came to the colony before June 1683 from Cheshire, England. For many generations his family had belonged to the Cheshire gentry. By May 1684 Duckenfield was a member of the Council of the colony, a position that he also held in November 1687. Surviving records do not show whether he was on the Council in the intervening years. He was again a Council member from November 1694 to September 1695. In that period he was ex officio justice of the General Court, which was then held by the Council. He appears also to have been a member of the Assembly in those years. In November 1699 and again in March 1701, he was commissioned justice of the Chowan Precinct court although the length of his service is not known.

A communicant of the Church of England, Duckenfield served on the vestry of St. Paul's parish from 1701, when the parish was established, until 1715, and at times was warden. Church services were sometimes held in his home, which was headquarters for at least two of the Anglican missionaries sent to the colony. In 1721 he donated fifty-two acres of land to the vestry of "the southwest parish" for a church building and other uses that the vestry might deem "convenient for promoting the true worship of God."

On 28 Nov. 1694 Duckenfield married Susannah Garraway Hartley, widow of Francis Hartley and daughter of John and Frances Garraway. The couple had no children so far as surviving records show. At the time of his marriage and for some years before, Duckenfield lived on Little River in Perquimans Precinct. Before 1699, however, he moved to a plantation on Salmon Creek, then in Chowan Precinct but now included in Bertie County. By patent, purchase, and marriage he acquired extensive landholdings, particularly in Chowan. Although he cultivated or leased several plantations, his transactions in land appear to have been speculative in part. He also participated in the profitable fur trade, apparently in conjunction with a mercantile business. He seems to have obtained skins and furs from small-scale traders in exchange for imported goods and to have exported furs and skins to Virginia, England, and elsewhere to pay for the goods he imported. Through his various enterprises he acquired sufficient wealth to live comfortably for his time and place. Christoph von Graffenreid reported that Governor Edward Hyde and his family "found pretty good lodgings" at Duckenfield's plantation, where they stayed for a time following their arrival in the colony. Graffenreid referred to Duckenfield as "a good old English nobleman."

Duckenfield died shortly before 27 Feb. 1721/22, when his will was proved. His wife apparently died before the date of the will, 17 May 1720, as she is not mentioned in it. Duckenfield bequeathed some furniture and an annuity of £40 to a brother, John, who lived in his home. He made lesser bequests to a cousin, Charles Barber, and a friend, Edward Moseley. His executor and principal legatee was a nephew in England, Nathaniel Duckenfield, son of his brother, Sir Robert Duckenfield.

SEE: Arthur Adams, *Cheshire Visitation Pedigrees, 1663* (1941); Albemarle County Papers, 2 vols. (1678–1714, 1715–39), and Council Minutes, Wills, Inventories, 1677–1701, and Will of William Duckenfield (North Carolina State Archives, Raleigh); Sir George J. Armytage and J. Paul Rylands, eds., *Pedigrees Made at the Visitation of Cheshire, 1613* (1909); William Betham, *The Baronetage of England* (1802); J. Bryan Grimes, ed., *Abstracts of North Carolina Wills* (1910), and *North Carolina Wills and Inventories* (1912); J. R. B. Hathaway, ed., *North Carolina Historical and Genealogical Register*, 3 vols. (1900–1903); Mattie Erma E. Parker, ed., *Colonial Records of North Carolina, Higher-Court Records, 1670–1696*, vol. 2 (1968), and *1697–1701*, vol. 3 (1971); William S. Price, Jr., ed., *Colonial Records of North Carolina, Higher-Court Records, 1702–1708*, vol. 4 (1974); William L. Saunders, ed., *Colonial Records of North Carolina*, vols. 1, 2 (1886).

MATTIE ERMA E. PARKER

**Dudley, Edward Bishop** *(15 Dec. 1789–30 Oct. 1855)*, governor, congressman, and capitalist, was born in Onslow County, near Jacksonville, the son of Christopher (1763–1828) and Margaret Snead Dudley (1764–1827). His father was a prominent planter, merchant, and shipbuilder who in 1827 was listed as the owner of ten thousand acres and eighty-seven slaves. His paternal grandparents were Bishop Dudley (1744–88), who was active in the American Revolution, and Rebecca Ward. His maternal grandfather was Robert Snead of Onslow.

Dudley represented Onslow in the House of Commons in 1811 and 1812, and in the senate in 1814. During this period he also served as an officer in the Onslow regiment that helped guard Wilmington during the War of 1812. After the war he moved to Wilmington, which he represented in the House of Commons in 1816 and 1817, and later in 1834 and 1835. In 1816 he opposed the presidential candidacy of James Monroe, and eight years later he was active in a coalition opposed to William H. Crawford and the Old Republican Virginia Dynasty. He challenged Congressman Gabriel Holmes for the Wilmington District seat in Congress, but was defeated in a close contest in August 1829. However, Holmes died a few weeks later, and in a special election Dudley easily defeated William B. Meares. One of his first votes in Congress supported a measure to reduce the pay of its members. During his single term he served on the Private Land Claims Committee. In Washington he quickly developed an aversion to Andrew Jackson and Martin Van Buren, and he refused to run for a second term on grounds that Congress was not a fit place for an honest person. In 1831 he represented his state at the National Anti-Tariff Convention; the following year he was identified with the Barbour movement to stop Van Buren's political rise.

After Dudley returned from Washington, he became a leader in the formation of the Whig party in North Carolina. He incessantly advocated constitutional reform, stronger banks, government support for railroads, public works, and education. He played a dominant role in the creation of the company that built a railroad from Wilmington to Weldon on the Roanoke River, the beginning of the Atlantic Coast Line.

North Carolina's constitutional revisions in 1835 provided for a state chief executive to be popularly elected for a two-year term. The Whigs nominated Dudley as their candidate to oppose the incumbent governor, Richard Dobbs Spaight, Jr. Dudley won by slightly more than 4,000 votes, 33,993 to 29,950. Two years later he was easily reelected over former governor John Branch with a wide margin of 14,000 votes. These years constituted the most progressive period in the antebellum history of North Carolina, and they initiated a decade of Whig control of the state government. In 1840, when Dudley completed his term, his party captured both houses of the General Assembly, elected John Motley Morehead as Dudley's successor, and won the state's electoral vote in the presidential race.

From 1841 to 1847 Dudley served a second term as president of the railroad he had helped to organize. Although there was a movement to send him to the U.S. Senate, he was never again a candidate for public office. In 1844 he was a delegate to the National Whig Convention in Baltimore. After 1847 his health began to fail, and he spent most of his time at his home beside the Cape Fear River.

In November 1815 Dudley married Elizabeth Haywood, daughter of William Henry Haywood, Sr., of Raleigh. Elizabeth was the sister of a U.S. senator and of the wife of Charles Manly, who also served as chief executive of North Carolina. The Dudleys had three boys and three girls: Christopher H., William Henry, Edward, Elizabeth Ann, Jane Frances, and Margaret. After Elizabeth died, Dudley married the widow of General John Cowan; they had no children and she survived him. He died five years before the Civil War and was buried in Oakdale Cemetery, Wilmington.

SEE: *Biog. Dir. Am. Cong.* (1971); John L. Cheney, Jr., *North Carolina Government, 1585–1974* (1975); *DAB*, vol. 5 (1930); J. G. de R. Hamilton, *Party Politics in North Carolina, 1835–1860* (1916); W. S. Hoffmann, *Andrew Jackson and North Carolina Politics* (1971); D. M. McFarland, "Rip Van Winkle: Political Evolution in North Carolina, 1815–1835" (Ph.D. diss., University of Pennsylvania, 1954); H. D. Pegg, "The Whig Party in North Carolina, 1834–1861" (Ph.D. diss., University of North Carolina, 1932); *Raleigh Register*, 5 Nov. 1855; D. W. Roberts, "Edward Bishop Dudley" (Manuscript Department, Library, Duke University, Durham).

DANIEL M. MCFARLAND

**Dudley, Guilford** *(17 Apr. 1756–3 Feb. 1833)*, Revolutionary militia officer, was born in Caroline County, Va., the son of Christopher and Elizabeth Dudley. In November 1763 his father moved to Halifax, N.C., where the younger Dudley lived until January 1785. In July 1775 he volunteered for service as a private in a company of minutemen at Halifax. He participated in the Moore's Creek Bridge campaign but was primarily engaged in gathering loyalist prisoners after the battle. Not until after the fall of Charles Town, S.C., did he return to the army. In June 1780 he enlisted as a private in the dragoons of the North Carolina militia. The North Carolina militia marched into South Carolina under General Horatio Gates, and at Camden on 16 August the American army was crushed. Dudley engaged in both the night action and the main battle the next morning. He and his unit remained on the field after the bulk of the militia fled, and they retired only when compelled to retreat by the British advance.

Following the British invasion of North Carolina in 1781, Dudley was again called to serve with the militia dragoons. During the maneuvering before and after the Battle of Guilford Court House, the dragoons were on detached duty patrolling and foraging. After the battle the remaining forces were organized at Troublesome Creek Ironworks into the First Battalion, state militia, and Dudley was appointed major on 22 March by Governor Abner Nash. On 30 March—after only eight days' service—he was commissioned a lieutenant colonel. General Greene moved into South Carolina and Dudley and the militia saw action at Hobkirk's Hill on 25 April. The day after the battle Dudley became commander of the North Carolina militia in Greene's army.

On 10 May Dudley was discharged from active duty and returned home. While journeying through his state he narrowly escaped capture by the notorious loyalist Colonel David Fanning. He lost his baggage wagon to Fanning and had to detour nearly a hundred miles out of his way to escape. At Hillsborough on 22 May he was commissioned a colonel in command of a volunteer unit to campaign against Fanning. He returned home to Halifax in July but on 2 September was recalled to command a light dragoon force sent to Virginia to scout the British army.

After the war Dudley returned to Halifax and on 23 May 1784 he married Anna Bland Eaton of Warren County, N.C. A native of Prince George County, Va., she was born on 21 Dec. 1763, the daughter of Thomas and Anna Eaton. The Dudleys had six daughters and four sons: Frances Elizabeth (b. 25 Feb. 1785), Frances Bland (b. 30 June 1786), Julia Anna Eaton (b. 16 Oct. 1788), Theodoric Bland (b. 5 May 1790), Thomas Eaton (b. 9 Aug. 1792), Elisabeth Helen (b. 18 Mar. 1794), Sarah Bland (b. 8 Sept. 1796), Guilford (b. 22 Jan. 1799), Judith Randolph (b. 24 July 1800), and Caroline (b. 28 Apr. 1802). The Dudleys lived a decade in Fayetteville and then moved to Prince Edward County, Va., in January 1796. In April 1807 they moved to Williamson County, Tenn., and settled in the town of Franklin where they remained the rest of their lives. Dudley apparently was a farmer; his ownership of slaves varied from six in 1790 to nine in 1830.

SEE: L. S. Butler, ed., *The Narrative of Col. David Fanning* (1981); Walter Clark, ed., *State Records*, vols. 17, 18 (1898–1907); John C. Dann, ed., *The Revolution Remembered: Eyewitness Accounts of the War for Independence* (1980); Pension Claim of Guilford Dudley (National Archives); United States Census, 1790, 1830.

LINDLEY S. BUTLER

**Dudley, James Benson** *(2 Nov. 1859–4 Apr. 1925)*, educator and college president, was born in Wilmington to John Bishop and Annie Hatch Dudley, slaves of Edward B. Dudley (1789–1855), governor of North Carolina from 31 Dec. 1836 to 1 Jan. 1841. Young Dudley's early education consisted of instruction in the carpentry trade given by his father and attendance at the Wilmington Normal School sponsored by the Freedman's Bureau. At that institution, he was instructed in Latin grammar by Ella Roper before traveling to Philadelphia to take classes at Fannie L. Coppin's Institute for Colored Youth, an experimental school organized to test the Negro's capability to master the higher branches of learning. He also attended Shaw University in Raleigh where he majored in elementary education. Later in his career, he was awarded a master of arts degree from Livingstone College in Salisbury and a doctorate of letters from Wilberforce University in Ohio.

After working briefly as a mechanic's apprentice, in 1880 at the age of twenty-one he became a first-grade teacher in Sampson County. The following year he accepted a position as principal of the Peabody Graded Normal School in Wilmington, a post he held for fifteen years until 1896.

On 23 Feb. 1882 Dudley married Susan Wright Sampson, a Wilmington teacher and, later, the author of the college song for the Agricultural and Mechanical College at Greensboro. They had two daughters; one died young and the other became the wife of Dr. S. B. Jones, British health officer at St. Kitts in the West Indies.

While in Wilmington, Dudley edited the *Wilmington Chronicle*, a Negro weekly newspaper, and was active in politics, serving as register of deeds for New Hanover County in 1891 and as delegate to the 1896 Republican National Convention in St. Louis. He was secretary of the board of trustees for the Agricultural and Mechanical College at Greensboro from 29 May 1895 to 27 May 1896 before succeeding John O. Crosby as president of that institution on 28 May 1896; he retained the post for twenty-nine years.

Because of his talent in winning both black and white support, Dudley was able to raise the college at Greensboro from the point of bankruptcy to a position of prestige in the state. He was particularly successful in resolving conflicts between the faculty and administration, in making the school industries self-sustaining, and in convincing not only the white legislature to appropriate funds for Negro education, but also a reluctant Negro populace to support the previously unpopular agricultural and mechanical curriculum. During his administration the number of buildings on campus was increased from 2 to 13, the student body from 58 to 476, and the faculty from 8 to 46. He also played an important role in defining the character of the school. Believing that black students could be most effectively taught by black instructors, he began the gradual transition from a predominantly white to a predominantly black faculty. Further, because he shared with Booker T. Washington an intense faith in agriculture and public service as the principal areas for Negro acceptance and progress, he sought the development of a thorough agricultural program at the Greensboro school, stressing the agricultural over the mechanical or industrial aspects of the curriculum. This devotion to agricultural training led Dudley in 1901 to discontinue the female department at the college, on the assumption that young women were not well suited to agricultural pursuits and that their presence only hampered such programs at the school.

His faith in the importance of agriculture in the Negro's life also led Dudley to establish farmers' institutes in conjunction with the Greensboro college. In 1912, with J. H. Bluford, an industrial arts instructor on the faculty, he cofounded the State Farmer's Union and Cooperative Society to encourage thrift, economy, and enterprise within the Negro race. This organization was especially concerned with helping the Negro deal with problems arising from the credit and mortgage system of the state, and in assisting Negro farmers in buying and selling products at reasonable prices. Dudley also canvassed the state in 1917 to obtain matching funds for the Smith-Hughes appropriation so that a vocational agriculture department could be created to train agriculture teachers for the state's public rural schools.

Dudley was a member of the National Teachers Association (later the National Education Association) and one of the organizers of the North Carolina Negro Teachers Association, of which he was president for six years. He was chairman of the Negro section of the Greensboro Interracial Committee and the only member of that city's Committee of Extension. Although always concerned about the necessity of fundamental justice for the Negro, Dudley counseled his race to be patient and nonresistant. During the 1898 Wilmington riot he rushed home from Greensboro, reportedly to calm the Negro population and act as mediator between black and white. On his arrival, he was met by the mayor of that city and received police protection for the duration of his visit.

Dudley also urged North Carolina's Negroes to remain loyal to the American cause during World War I and offered the Agricultural and Mechanical College campus to the federal government as a military training camp. A deeply religious man, he was a member of the Bethel African Methodist Episcopal Church, Greensboro, where he taught a Sunday school class and served as trustee. He was also a member of the Odd Fellows, the Pythians, and the Masons, serving for twenty years as foreign correspondent of the Grand Lodge of Masons.

In 1908 Governor Robert B. Glenn appointed Dudley as a delegate to the National Negro Fair Association in Mobile, Ala., and in 1920 Governor Cameron Morrison appointed him state commissioner for the National Memorial Association; in the latter capacity he was responsible for erecting a memorial in Washington, D.C., commemorating the Negro soldiers and sailors who had fought in the national wars.

Dudley died at his home in Greensboro at the age of sixty-six and was buried at Forest Cemetery, Wilmington.

SEE: A & M College, *President's Reports* (1902–10); Department of Public Instruction, *North Carolina Public Documents*, vol. 2 (1903); Warmoth T. Gibbs, *History of the North Carolina Agricultural and Technical School* (1966); Carrye Hill K. Kelley, *Profiles of Five Administrators* (1964); Nathan C. Newbold, *Five North Carolina Negro Educators* (1939); Albert W. Spruill, *Recollections from Aggieland* (1964).

KENNETH WARLICK

**Duffy, William** *(d. August 1810)*, lawyer and politician, was the son of George Duffy, an unsuccessful lawyer of New Bern. Little is known about young Duffy's early life. In 1792 he was licensed to practice law in New Bern and five years later moved to Hillsborough to establish his practice. Family problems figured prominently in his decision to relocate; Archibald DeBow Murphey, a future student of Duffy, recounted that William Duffy "was the child of misfortune, thrown upon the world without friends and without fortune." His parents separated in 1797; after settling his father's debts and affairs, he, with his mother and two sisters, hoped to start anew in Hillsborough. One sister, Elizabeth, died in 1800; the other, Mary, married Thomas Scott. The young lawyer enjoyed immediate success and in a short time had acquired the largest practice in the Orange County court. In addition, Duffy acted as counsel and land agent for the fledgling University of North Carolina. In 1802 he moved for a final time to Chatham County but retained a country home, Oakley Wood, near Fayetteville. The following year he was involved in a duel with Duncan Cameron for the hand of Rebecca Bennehan. Duffy lost both the duel and Rebecca and was severely wounded in the exchange. Nevertheless, his law practice and reputation continued to grow and in 1806 he represented Fayetteville in the General Assembly. On 21 August of the same year he married Peggy Bell, daughter of Robert Bell of Orange County. Through years of perseverance Duffy had become a gifted orator despite a speech impediment. He was recognized as one of the ablest lawyers in the state and his pupils included Archibald DeBow Murphey and future Vice-President William R. King. When Duffy died at his home in Chatham County, he was described as being "in middle age." He had no children but left a part of his meager estate to a niece, Elizabeth Sanderson.

SEE: Chatham County wills (North Carolina State Archives, Raleigh); William Duffy Papers (North Carolina State Archives, Raleigh); William Hoyt, ed., *The Papers of Archibald D. Murphey* (1914); *North Carolina Journal*, 16 Feb., 9 Mar. 1795, 7 Mar. 1796; *Raleigh Register*, 22 Sept. 1801, 25 Apr. 1803, 1 Sept. 1806, 6 Sept. 1810; John H. Wheeler, *Historical Sketches of North Carolina* (1851).

MARK F. MILLER

**Dugger, John Edward** *(19 July 1836–9 March 1888)*, teacher, was born in Brunswick County, Va., the son of Daniel Dugger, proprietor of the hotel in Lawrenceville. At a political dinner at the hotel in 1837, an argument developed between Daniel Dugger and George Coke Dromgoole, who then represented the local district in Congress. This led to a duel between the two men, fought 6 Nov. 1837 at the plantation of Thomas Goode Tucker in western Northampton County, N.C., not far from Brunswick. Dugger was fatally wounded. Writing in 1891, Stephen B. Weeks stated that Dromgoole, overcome with remorse, provided for the widow and educated the two sons, John Edward and Macon Tucker, who were infants when their father was killed. The fact that both sons were graduated from The University of North Carolina, Dromgoole's alma mater, gives credence to this claim.

On finishing at Chapel Hill with an A.B. degree in 1857, John Edward Dugger settled in the town of Warrenton where he became head of the Warrenton Male Academy. During the Civil War, he served as a captain in the Confederate Army. Returning to Warrenton in 1865, Captain Dugger, as he came to be called, reopened the academy and taught there for ten years. In 1876 he was called to head the Centennial School in Raleigh, the first public graded school in that city. Here Dugger excelled in pioneering work but found it difficult to relate to school authorities. In August 1882, he moved to Rocky Mount where he became principal of that town's first graded school, located in the old fair grounds in what is now Braswell Park. After two years he returned to his home in Warrenton and resumed his teaching duties at the Warrenton Academy.

Dugger was a trustee of The University of North Carolina from 1874 to 1883. He was described by a former student as small of stature, but graceful, well formed, and remarkably handsome. As a teacher, he was capable but a strict disciplinarian. In his relations with men, particularly school authorities, he was unnecessarily outspoken.

Dugger and his wife Anne Wilson were the parents of two sons, John and Daniel, and two daughters, Alice and Janet. Alice married Walter Grimes of Raleigh, and Janet became the wife of Edward Simpson of Enfield. Mrs. Dugger died in Warrenton in 1891.

SEE: Daniel L. Grant, *Alumni History of the University of North Carolina* (1924); Henry W. Lewis, "Dugger-Dromgoole Duel," *North Carolina Historical Review* 34 (1957); Lizzie W. Montgomery, *Sketches of Old Warrenton* (1924); *North Carolina Teacher* 2 (1884), 5 (March 1888); R. D. Trevathan, *The Life History of Demsey Trevathan and Descendants with a History of Rocky Mount 70 Years Ago* (1940); Peter Wilson, *Southern Exposure* (1927).

CLAIBORNE T. SMITH, JR.

**Dugger, Shepherd Monroe** *(26 Feb. 1854–13 Sept. 1938)*, educator, orchardist, landscape architect, mining prospector, geologist, surveyor, road engineer, lecturer, author, and "wandering Bard of the Balsams," was born in Johnson County, Tenn., one of ten children of George Washington and Elizabeth Caroline McNabb Dugger. His family was among the first settlers of the mountain region along the Tennessee–North Carolina line. When he was an infant, the Duggers settled on a farm where the town of Banner Elk now stands. There he was educated at an old field school with a two-month autumn term. Afterward he immediately began teaching on a third-grade certificate at eighteen dollars a month. In 1875–76 he attended school in Weaverville, and for the next three years the Presnel Academy at Jonesboro, Tenn. Meanwhile, he visited Mount Airy, N.C., and met the Siamese Twins, and in 1876 traveled to Philadelphia for the Centennial Exposition. For the academic year 1880–81, he was a law student at The University of North Carolina, where he was an outspoken campus prohibitionist.

In June 1881 Dugger left the university to accept an appointment as the first superintendent of schools in Watauga County. After his marriage in October 1887 to Margaret A. Calloway, he spent nearly a year in middle Tennessee on business, then returned to Banner Elk when his first son, Balsam, was five weeks old. A second son was named Clarence. By the summer of 1891 he had begun giving lectures, had built a hotel to accommodate visitors to the mountains, and was surveying a turnpike from Elk Park to Valle Crucis. His wife died in December 1891 and his third son, Shepherd Monroe, Jr., seven months later. In 1892 he attended the Teachers Institute at Boone, gave a Fourth of July lecture at Eseeola Inn, Linville, and published *The Balsam Groves of the Grandfather Mountain* (reprinted 1895, enlarged 1907, 4th ed. 1934), a romantic novel whose extravagant vocabulary charmed readers far and wide. The book, entered in a one-thousand-dollar contest sponsored by the Linville Improvement Company to promote the Grandfather Mountain area, did not win a prize but was the only entry deemed sufficiently propagandistic for publication. Fame came to Dugger in 1894 when the *Ladies' Home Journal* printed a lengthy article on the book by editor Edward W. Bok, who termed it "unique, in that it may be said to have had no predecessor and probably it will be without a successor."

After his wife's death, Dugger sold his house in Banner Elk and moved to a hillside cabin where he made a home for his two sons while they were in school. Rarely idle, he pursued his interest in mining and surveying. In 1910 he was a census taker in Macon County. In 1915 he became superintendent of roads in Avery County (afterward humorously calling himself "The Colossus of Roads"), and for the next seventeen years served intermittently as a surveyor and highway engineer. During the 1930s Dugger was a familiar figure along the mountain roads, usually traveling on foot, though occasionally he would accept a ride in an automobile. Carrying only a walking stick, he moved about, giving lectures and readings, staying overnight wherever he found himself at sunset. He died in the home of a cousin at Matney on Craborchard Creek in Watauga County, and was buried by the side of his wife in the Banner Elk cemetery.

Dugger's *The War Trails of the Blue Ridge* (1932), containing local history and childhood reminiscences, was followed by two booklets: *Romance of the Siamese Twins and Other Sketches* (1936) and his memorial *Remarkable Career of Mr. John Balsam Dugger, Written by His Father* (1938). His reputation is based on his delightfully wild and uninhibited use of the English language, as here: "My darlin' Mihilda, Mahulday, Mahighla Jane, if you'll allow me to implant upon your cavernous mouth some faint evidence of my inconsiderable ability as an osculatory artist, I'll cure your toothache."

SEE: Alumni Office Records (University of North Carolina, Chapel Hill); Leslie B. Cottingham and Carol L. Timblin, *The Bard of Ottaray: The Life, Letters and Documents of Shepherd Monroe Dugger* (1979); Leslie B. Dawson, "Shepherd Monroe Dugger: A Critical Biography" (M.A. thesis, University of North Carolina, Chapel Hill, 1973); Shepherd M. Dugger, Autobiography (MS in possession of Douglas Dugger, Tulsa, Okla.); Joint Committee of the North Carolina English Teachers Association and the North Carolina Library Association, *North Carolina Authors: A Selective Handbook* (1952); Lenoir Family Papers (Southern Historical Collection, University of North Carolina, Chapel Hill); Edmund Pearson, *Queer Books* (1928); Phillips Russell, "The Bard of Ottaray," *North Carolina Folklore* 17 (May 1969).

RICHARD WALSER

**Duke, Benjamin Newton** *(27 Apr. 1855–8 Jan. 1929)*, industrialist, the son of Washington and Artelia Roney Duke, was born in the modest farmhouse built by his father in 1852. Except for a brief period toward the end of the Civil War, when his father fought for the Confederacy and he, his sister, and his brother lived with their Roney grandparents in Alamance County, Ben Duke grew up on the family farm a few miles north of Durham in what was then Orange County. Often sickly as a child, he developed an especially close relationship with his more robust younger brother, James B. Duke. He received some improvised schooling as a child and after the war attended sessions at an academy in Durham. In 1871 he and his sister Mary enrolled for one year at the New Garden School (later Guilford College) near Greensboro.

Duke was associated with his father, brother, and sister in the home manufacture of smoking tobacco, a business that Washington Duke began soon after the Civil War ended. Ben Duke became a partner when the business, which had been moved to Durham in 1874, was formally organized as W. Duke, Sons and Company in 1878. In the subsequent rise of the company to preeminence in the tobacco industry, he played a key role, though one that was secondary to that of his brother James. When W. Duke, Sons and Company became part of the great combination known as the American Tobacco Company in 1890, he became a director and also served for some years as treasurer of the vast company.

Maintaining a home in Durham even after he acquired a mansion on New York's Fifth Avenue early in the twentieth century, Duke took the leading role in involving his family in the textile industry when he brought William E. Erwin to Durham in 1892 to launch the Erwin Mill. That enterprise, which ultimately had branches in Duke (later Erwin) and Cooleemee, grew to be one of North Carolina's major textile producers. The Dukes also invested largely in other textile plants in the state. In addition to serving for many years as the president of the Erwin Mills, Ben Duke also served as president of the Fidelity Bank and the Citizens National Bank in Durham, of the Durham and Southern Railway Company, and of other North Carolina enterprises in which the Dukes and their partner, George W. Watts, held substantial investments. As an outgrowth of the family's interests in textile manufacturing and the need for economical power, Ben and James B. Duke became interested in hydroelectric power around the turn of the century and in 1905 launched the Southern Power Company, headquartered in Charlotte. This pioneering venture, which played a major role in the rapid industrialization of the Piedmont region of the two Carolinas, later became the Duke Power Company.

Duke was an able businessman but not the business genius that his younger brother proved to be. In fact, throughout his life he was less single-minded about business than his brother and took the major role in conducting the Duke family's philanthropies from the late 1880s on. While his aged father put up the money to bring Trinity College to Durham in 1890–92, Ben Duke accepted the burdensome responsibility of sitting on the executive committee of the college's board of trustees and of saving the institution from bankruptcy after it opened in Durham. He became the primary benefactor of Trinity College and, as the main link between the Duke family and the college, the principal reliance of presidents John F. Crowell, John C. Kilgo, and William Preston Few. Keenly interested in various other institutions such as the orphan asylum at Oxford, the Methodist Conferences of North Carolina, and various schools and churches of both white and black North Carolinians, he set a large part of the philanthropic pattern that would become embodied for posterity in the Duke Endowment, established by his brother in December 1924.

During the last fifteen or so years of his life, Duke suffered from intermittent illness that gradually made him a semi-invalid. Having earlier given large portions of his wealth to his wife and children, he disbursed nearly $3 million during the last four years of his life to a large number of schools and colleges in the South, especially in the two Carolinas.

On 21 Feb. 1877 he married Sarah Pearson Angier. Their first child, George Washington Duke, died at the age of two. Two other children were born to the couple, Angier Buchanan Duke on 8 Dec. 1884 and Mary Lillian Duke on 16 Nov. 1887. In 1915 Angier Duke married Cordelia Biddle of Philadelphia and Mary Duke married Cordelia's brother, Anthony J. Drexel Biddle, Jr. The subsequent death of Angier Duke in a boating accident in 1923 was a great blow to Ben Duke during his last years. He was buried in the Memorial Chapel of the Duke University Chapel, Durham. His portraits hang in libraries on both campuses of Duke University.

SEE: Samuel A. Ashe, ed., *Biographical History of North Carolina*, vol. 3 (1905); Benjamin N. Duke Papers (Manuscript Department, Library, Duke University, Durham); R. F. Durden, *The Dukes of Durham, 1865–1929* (1975); E. W. Porter, *Trinity and Duke, 1892–1924: Foundations of Duke University* (1964).

ROBERT F. DURDEN

**Duke, James Buchanan** *(23 Dec. 1856–10 Oct. 1925)*, industrialist, the youngest of the three children of Washington and Artelia Roney Duke, was born on his father's farm located a few miles north of Durham in what was then Orange County. He received some education in an improvised school near his home, attended an academy in Durham for a while, and was sent briefly to New Garden School (later Guilford College) in 1872. Not inclined toward literary subjects, he later studied at the Eastman Business College in Poughkeepsie, N.Y., but he clearly learned most and fastest from his deep engrossment in the family's business of making and selling smoking tobacco.

Mastering every phase of the tobacco business from growing and harvesting the crop to selling the manufactured product in trips across the nation, James B. Duke became the hard-working, driving force behind the rise of W. Duke, Sons and Company to national importance in the tobacco industry in the 1880s. Soon after becoming president of the company and moving permanently to New York to supervise a branch factory there in 1884, he persuaded his partners to gamble on machine-made cigarettes, even though most of the older and larger cigarette producers insisted that the public preferred the hand-rolled variety. He negotiated a secret and favorable contract with the Bonsack Machine Company of Virginia for the use of the cigarette machine invented by James A. Bonsack. That fact plus the unceasing, hard work of Duke and his associates and the large amounts of money spent on an extensive and varied advertising campaign led to the rapid rise of the Duke firm in the late 1880s.

Interested in forming a combination of the larger cigarette manufactures almost from the time he moved to New York, Duke played a key role in organizing the

American Tobacco Company in 1890 and, at age thirty-three, became its president. In the following years, the American Tobacco Company and its various offshoots gained control not only of cigarettes but also of smoking tobacco, snuff, and practically all tobacco products except cigars. Duke provided vigorous leadership for the company's expansion, both in the United States and in various foreign markets such as Canada, Japan, and China. In a struggle to gain a larger share of the British market early in the twentieth century, he concluded an arrangement in 1902 whereby the American Tobacco Company and its affiliates relinquished all of their business in Britain and Ireland; in return, Britain's Imperial Tobacco Company agreed not to manufacture or sell tobacco in the United States or Cuba. To carry on the tobacco business outside of Britain and the United States, the British-American Tobacco Company was incorporated under the laws of Great Britain, with the Duke-led companies receiving approximately two-thirds of its stock and the Imperial Tobacco Company the remaining third.

An "Old Guard Republican" and great admirer of President William McKinley and Senator Mark Hanna, Duke had good reason to fear President Theodore Roosevelt and his "trust busting." The federal government's antitrust action against the American Tobacco Company was launched in 1907 and culminated in 1911 when the Supreme Court ordered the dissolution of the giant combination. Except for the British-American Tobacco Company, which was headquartered in London, Duke dissociated himself from the tobacco industry after 1911.

Some years before that, he, his brother Benjamin N. Duke, and their partner George W. Watts had become interested in hydroelectric power as an outgrowth of their extensive investments in the textile industry in North Carolina. In 1905 they launched the Southern Power Company, with headquarters in Charlotte, and began to pour millions of dollars into a pioneering hydroelectric industry that played a key role in the industrialization of the Piedmont region of North Carolina and South Carolina and that ultimately became the Duke Power Company. After the dissolution of the old American Tobacco Company and especially after the outbreak of World War I, James B. Duke became increasingly interested in the power company. In 1919 he acquired a home in Charlotte where he frequently lived when not at his estate near Somerville, N.J., or his mansion on Fifth Avenue in New York, which he built in 1909–10.

Around 1915 Duke and his associates also acquired two major power resources on the Saguenay River in Canada's Quebec Province. In 1923–24, William States Lee, an engineer with whom Duke had become closely associated in 1904, supervised the building at one of the power sites of what has been described as the "world's largest hydrostation" at that time. Duke and Arthur Vining Davis of the Aluminum Company of America struck an agreement about the other power site in 1925 whereby Duke exchanged it for one-ninth of the stock ($17 million worth) of the reorganized Aluminum Company of America.

Unusually close to his older brother Benjamin, James B. Duke had long encouraged him to take the chief responsibility for various philanthropic causes supported by the Duke family from about 1890 on. Around 1915, however, when Ben Duke's long illness began, James B. Duke began to engage more directly in philanthropic support for Trinity College in Durham and other causes supported by the Methodist church. About the same time he began to plan for a philanthropic foundation to serve Trinity College and other charitable institutions in the Carolinas and to be based in large part on a substantial portion of his holdings in the electric power company. Duke first informed Trinity College's President William Preston Few of those plans in 1919. Though encouraged by Few as well as by Ben Duke, James B. Duke refrained from acting on his philanthropic plans until he could win from North Carolina's Corporation Commission approval of increased rates for the power company to provide what he regarded as more adequate dividends on its stock.

In 1921 Few proposed to James B. Duke that a university be organized around Trinity College and that as a memorial to Washington Duke, whose gifts had brought Trinity College to Durham in 1892, the enlarged institution be named Duke University. Duke refused to sign the memorandum that Few submitted to him in 1921 but, nevertheless, generally approved of Few's idea. By December 1924 Duke was finally ready to sign and announce the indenture creating the Duke Endowment. Providing securities worth $40 million for the endowment (with an additional $67 million to come from his will), he specified that fifteen trustees were to distribute the annual income from the fund among educational institutions, hospitals, and orphanages in the two Carolinas and the Methodist church in North Carolina. In addition to Duke University, the other educational institutions to be supported were Davidson College, Furman University, and Johnson C. Smith University.

Duke selected the architect to design the new buildings of Duke University, Horace Trumbauer of Philadelphia, and took great pleasure in helping to choose the stone from a quarry near Hillsborough that would be used; he also participated in various decisions about the extensive new campus to be built and the rebuilding of the old Trinity campus. Before the work was barely underway, however, he became ill at his home in Newport, R.I., and then died in his New York home of what was diagnosed as pernicious anemia. He was buried in the Memorial Chapel of Duke University Chapel.

Duke married a divorcee, Mrs. Lillian McCredy, in September 1904, but the marriage was ended by his successful suit for divorce in 1906. In July 1907, he married a widow from Atlanta, Ga., Mrs. Walker P. Inman (née Nanaline Holt of Macon, Ga.). Their daughter Doris was born on 12 Nov. 1912. Portraits of Duke are in the libraries of both campuses of Duke University and in the main foyer of Duke Hospital.

SEE: Samuel A. Ashe, ed., *Biographical History of North Carolina*, vol. 3 (1905); James B. Duke Papers (Manuscript Department, Library, Duke University, Durham); R. F. Durden, *The Dukes of Durham, 1865–1929* (1975); E. W. Porter, *Trinity and Duke, 1892–1924: Foundations of Duke University* (1964); N. M. Tilley, *Bright-Tobacco Industry, 1860–1929* (1948).

ROBERT F. DURDEN

**Duke, Washington** *(20 Dec. 1820–8 May 1905)*, industrialist, the eighth of the ten children of Taylor and Dicey Jones Duke, was born on his father's farm on the Little River in what was then Orange County. Raised accustomed to hard work, Washington Duke became what his father had been: a diligent yeoman farmer who had virtually no formal education but who was well respected in a community where the great majority of people were in similar circumstances. By the 1850s,

Duke owned some three hundred acres situated about four miles north of the new village known as Durham's Depot or Station (later Durham) after the North Carolina Railroad reached there in 1854.

In 1842 Duke married Mary Caroline Clinton and the couple had two sons, Sidney Taylor (b. 1844) and Brodie Leonidas (b. 1846). After his first wife's death in 1847, he married Artelia Roney of Alamance County in 1852. A daughter, Mary Elizabeth, was born a year later followed by two sons, Benjamin Newton (b. 1855) and James Buchanan (b. 1856). In 1858 Sidney Duke died of typhoid fever. Within a short time Artelia Roney Duke also died of the same disease, and Washington Duke, with the help of his maiden sister and sisters-in-law, had the responsibility of caring for his four young children.

Outside of his family, the most important institution for Duke and the one that exerted the greatest influence on him all his life was the Methodist church. Converted at an early age in Mount Bethel Church in the village of Balltown (now Bahama), he later belonged to Mount Hebron Church, which his oldest brother, William J. Duke, had been instrumental in establishing and which was later renamed Duke's Chapel in William's honor.

Though a Democrat, Duke, like so many North Carolinians, opposed secession in 1861. Two years later, however, he was called to arms when the Confederacy in late 1863 moved to draft men up to forty-five years of age, even those with motherless children. Entering the Confederate service in April 1864, he was soon assigned to duty aboard a Confederate receiving ship in Charleston, S.C. Later in the year he was sent to join the James River squadron near Richmond, Va.; when Richmond fell to Union forces in early April 1865, he was taken prisoner. Paroled some weeks later, he was taken by ship to New Bern, N.C., and from there he walked the 130 or so miles to his home.

Whereas before the Civil War Duke was remarkably typical of the great majority of white southerners, he became distinctly atypical afterward. As soon as the Republican party formally appeared in North Carolina in 1868, he joined it, probably because he believed that the Southern Democrats had been primarily responsible for secession and the war. For the remainder of his life, he never faltered in his loyalty to the Republican party at all levels.

Economically, Duke was atypical in the decision that he made soon after the war: rather than turning back to the land for his livelihood, as did most southerners, he launched his family on the small-scale manufacture by hand of smoking tobacco made of the new bright leaf variety that was being increasingly produced in the area. Beginning as a wagon-borne peddler of the family's brand, "Pro Bono Publico," Duke became, as the business slowly prospered, a salesman who "drummed the trade" across the nation. In 1874 he moved his family and business into Durham. In 1878, when George W. Watts of Baltimore purchased a one-fifth interest in the enterprise for $14,000, the firm of W. Duke, Sons and Company was formally launched. It consisted of Washington Duke, his three sons Brodie, Ben, and James, and George Watts. The firm's subsequent growth in the 1880s to preeminence in the cigarette industry was not, however, the work of Washington Duke so much as it was that of his youngest son, James B. Duke. In 1880 when the elder Duke was sixty, he virtually retired from the tobacco business and devoted himself primarily to the affairs of his family, the Methodist church, and the Republican party.

Another aspect of Duke's atypicality in the postwar South was that he and his family began to grow rich, modestly so in the 1880s and more markedly in the next decade. Even more unusual, they began to give money regularly and systematically for various philanthropic causes, particularly but not exclusively Methodist ones, in an era when there were no income taxes to encourage such giving for the purpose of gaining tax deductions. Aided and encouraged in philanthropy by his son Ben, Washington Duke in 1890 offered to give Trinity College, the North Carolina Methodists' institution for the higher education of men, $85,000 to move from rural Randolph County to Durham. After the offer was accepted, he headed the building committee in Durham and became the foremost supporter of the college. In 1896 he offered Trinity $100,000 for endowment on the condition that women students be admitted, an offer that the college promptly accepted. In 1898 and 1900 he gave similar amounts to Trinity.

Although Trinity College headed the list of Duke's philanthropies, he also gave to many other institutions in the state—including those of black North Carolinians, with whom Washington Duke, as a Republican, had friendly ties even in the era of Jim Crow laws and black disfranchisement.

Always a taciturn, dignified man, with a dry sense of humor, Duke lived to be nearly eighty-five and in his later years was widely and affectionately referred to around Durham as the "old gentleman" and "Uncle Wash." He was buried in the Memorial Chapel of the Duke University Chapel in Durham. His portraits are in libraries on both campuses of Duke University.

SEE: Samuel A. Ashe, ed., *Biographical History of North Carolina*, vol. 3 (1905); Washington Duke Papers (Manuscript Department, Library, Duke University, Durham); R. F. Durden, *The Dukes of Durham, 1865–1929* (1975); E. W. Porter, *Trinity and Duke, 1892–1924: Foundations of Duke University* (1964); N. M. Tilley, *Bright-Tobacco Industry, 1860–1929* (1948).

ROBERT F. DURDEN

**Duke, William, Jr.** *(ca. 1720–before 26 Oct. 1793)*, planter and public official, was born in Southside, Va., where his father, William Duke, was a prominent planter. Recent research and records now available support the contention by the Duke family of Warren County, N.C., that they were descendants of the first Colonel William Byrd of Westover through his youngest daughter, Mary. The twentieth-century publication of the second William Byrd's *Secret Diary* makes clear that she was the wife of James Duke of James City County and later of Charles City County, Va. James Duke was himself a son of Colonel Henry Duke of James City County, a member of the council, and a close friend and political associate to both colonels Byrd of Westover. James Duke and his wife Mary (who later married Richard Corbett) had a number of children, among them Anne, who married Joab Mountcastle; Henry, who married Elizabeth (probably a Marston); John; Edmund, who married Jane Gresham and whose children resettled in Granville County, N.C., after 1787; Sarah, who married Charles Christian; and William, the father of the subject of this sketch.

William Duke, Sr., was the eldest son of James and Mary Byrd Duke. An early nineteenth century genealogy of the Duke family states that he was educated at Westover by his uncle, Colonel William Byrd II. It is likely that the son of James Duke referred to in Colonel Byrd's *Secret Diary* on 3 Aug. 1709, was this William.

Like several other of his siblings, William Duke, Sr., moved away from his home in the James River region and settled on Rocky Creek in Brunswick County, Va. In 1742 he deeded to his son, William Duke, Jr., 317 acres of Brunswick County land that had been granted to the senior Duke on 28 Sept. 1728. By this time William Duke, Sr., was remarried to a widow, Elizabeth Bartholomew; his first wife, Thamar Taylor, had died. His known children were by his first marriage: Samuel, the first of the family to remove to North Carolina; John, who married Mary Myrick; Thamar, who married Peter Green; Joseph, who married Mary Eppes and whose descendants became prominent settlers of Georgia and Tennessee; and William, Jr. On 11 May 1744 William Duke, Sr., and his wife Elizabeth, and William Duke, Jr., and his wife Mary, sold their lands in Brunswick County and removed to North Carolina where they settled on Possum Quarter Creek in what was then Edgecombe County—it shortly became Granville County, even later Bute County, and finally Warren County in 1779. The elder Duke acquired an estate of over six hundred acres before 1746 but soon afterward gave much of it to his children or sold part of it, retaining only about fifty acres for his own use for the remainder of his life.

William Duke, Jr., began to amass a large fortune in land and slaves. Purchase Patent plantation, as he named it, was the seat of his operations and amounted to several thousand acres. An inventory of his holdings in 1794 shows that he owned fifty-three slaves. A number of other Dukes in Warren County also had large estates.

One of the most interesting aspects of William Duke's residence in Warren County was the house he, or his father, built. Said to date from about 1750, it clearly demonstrates a high standard in domestic Georgian architecture in that section of North Carolina. According to strong, sustained, local tradition, the Duke house was similar to that of Colonel William Byrd II at Westover. On the surface, this assertion seems clearly erroneous. When the facts are more closely examined, however, there appears to be evidence to support the claim. The original house at Westover, which Colonel Byrd built in the late seventeenth or early eighteenth century, is thought to have been a story and a half in configuration. The main block of the present mansion was raised by Colonel William Byrd I after 1730. Architectural historians now believe that the large chimneys at the ends of the west dependency of the present mansion were built much earlier than the 1730 buildings, and that a story-and-a-half wooden structure stood there. An 1866 photograph of Purchase Patent clearly shows large chimneys, similar in construction to those at Westover, and a house that demonstrates a high degree of sophistication for Georgian style houses in the Carolina Piedmont at mid-century. If one adds to this the close ties of kinship between the Byrds and the Dukes, and the statements in the *Secret Diary*, which only came to light in this century, the evidence seems to point with some reliability to the design origins of the Duke house. Purchase Patent was clearly one of the most handsome houses in the region for this period.

William Duke, Jr., Samuel Duke, John Duke, and Joseph Duke—all sons of William Duke, Sr.—were listed with their father on the muster roll of Granville County in 1754. On Friday, 23 June 1775, William Duke was listed as a member of the Committee of Safety. The minutes of the committee show that William and other Dukes were active members. On 8 July 1775 William Duke, along with such notable figures as Jethro Sumner, Philemon Hawkins, Jr., James Ransom, William Alston, Green Hill, Thomas Eaton, and sundry others, designed a document that virtually endorsed the actions of the Continental Congress then sitting in Philadelphia. This was clearly treasonable to the British authorities, and places all these men in the vanguard of revolutionary activities.

William Duke, Jr., was one of the men in 1779 commissioned to measure the Bute County boundary and to divide the county in two new units to be named Franklin and Warren counties. Though he did not serve in the armed forces during the Revolution, the military pay vouchers for the Halifax District indicate that in 1781 the revolutionary government owed him £6,000, probably for supplies furnished the military. In 1779 he was appointed one of six commissioners to lay out the county seat town of Warrenton on the one hundred acres that had been purchased for the purpose. He was clearly interested in the new town and county and its educational facilities, for in 1787 he was appointed a trustee for the Warrenton Academy when it was founded. Duke was later styled "William Duke, Sr.," as his father had died in 1775 and the younger William Duke later had a grandson named William.

Duke's wife, Mary, was a daughter of Edward Green of Brunswick County, Va., who later settled in Granville County, N.C. She is thought to have been a widow when Duke married her and the mother of one daughter, Winnifred. Mary was not married before 17 June 1740 when she witnessed a deed in Brunswick County as "Mary Green." By May 1744 she was the wife of William Duke, Jr., when they, with his parents, William and Elizabeth Duke, sold their land in Brunswick County and moved to North Carolina. William and Mary Duke had five children: Green (m. Mary Parham); Thamar (m. Edward Jones); Sarah (m. Captain Thomas Christmas); Ann, called Nancy (m. Robert Jones); and Mary (m. Isaac Howze). The Green Duke plantation is the site for the Soul City project in Warren County; its handsome mansion house is now listed on the National Register of Historic Places.

Mary Green Duke survived her husband. They are said to be buried on his Purchase Patent plantation, near the town of Warrenton.

SEE: Evelyn Duke Brandenberger, *The Duke Family* (1979); Military pay vouchers, Warren County (North Carolina State Archives, Raleigh); Marion Tinling, ed., *Correspondence of the Three William Byrds of Westover, Virginia, 1684–1776*, vol. 1 (1977); Warren County Bicentennial Committee, *Bute County Committee of Safety Minutes, 1775–1776* (1977); Warren County Records, Purchase Patent and Green Duke files (Survey and Planning Unit, Archaeology and Historic Preservation Section, North Carolina State Archives, Raleigh); Thomas T. Waterman, *The Early Architecture of North Carolina* (1941), and *The Mansions of Virginia* (1946); Louis B. Wright and Marion Tinling, *The Secret Diary of William Byrd II of Westover, 1709–1712* (1941).

EVELYN DUKE BRANDENBERGER
JOHN BAXTON FLOWERS III

**Dula, Thomas C. ("Tom Dooley")** *(20 June 1844–1 May 1868)*, Confederate war veteran, convicted murderer, and folk subject, was born in Wilkes County, the son of Mary Dula. On 15 Mar. 1862 he enlisted in the Confederate Army as a private, serving in Company K, Forty-second Regiment, North Carolina Infantry. He remained a private until March 1864, when he was rated as "Drummer." Dula was hospitalized at Episcopal Church Hospital, Williamsburg, Va., on 10 Aug. 1864. He was captured at Kinston and was a prisoner of war at Point Lookout, Md., where he was released after signing the oath of allegiance on 11 June 1865.

Dula returned to Wilkes County and resumed a liaison with Ann Melton, wife of James Melton, which had begun when Dula was fifteen. Early in 1866 he began to cohabit with Laura Foster, from whom he eventually contracted syphilis which he then transmitted to Ann Melton.

On the morning of 25 May 1866, Laura Foster was seen on Stony Fork Road riding her father's mare with a bundle of clothing in her lap and headed toward the Bates Place, a lovers' rendezvous. The next morning, the mare returned to the Foster home with a broken rope dangling from its halter. A search for the missing Laura began immediately; on 18 June her body was found in a shallow grave near the Bates Place. Death was the result of a stab wound, and it was reported that she was pregnant at the time of death. The next day, Dula fled to Watauga County and then to Tennessee. He was captured and returned to Wilkes County about three weeks later.

Dula and Ann Melton were brought to trial for the murder of Laura Foster in the Fall Term, Wilkes County Superior Court; the trial was moved to Iredell County, where the cases of the defendants were severed. Dula was convicted, but the North Carolina Supreme Court reversed the conviction and returned the case to Iredell County. After several postponements, Dula was tried by a Court of Oyer and Terminer in January 1868 and was again convicted. After the decision was sustained by the supreme court, he was hung in Statesville on 1 May 1868.

Even before Dula's execution, a ballad about him and Laura Foster was being sung in Wilkes and Watauga counties to the tune of "Run, Nigger, Run, the Patter Roller's After You":

Hang down your head, Tom Dula
Hang down your head and cry;
You killed poor Laura Foster
And now you're bound to die.

SEE: Henry M. Belden and Arthur Palmer Hudson, eds., *The Frank C. Brown Collection of North Carolina Folklore*, vol. 2 (1952); Compiled Service Records of Confederate Soldiers Who Served from Organizations from the State of North Carolina (North Carolina State Archives, Raleigh); Original case records, North Carolina Supreme Court (North Carolina State Archives, Raleigh); John Foster West, *The Ballad of Tom Dula* (1971).

THORNTON W. MITCHELL

**Duncan, Samuel Edward, Jr.** *(27 Apr. 1904–10 July 1968)*, educator and college president, was born in Madisonville, Ky., the oldest of seven children of Samuel E. and Lena B. Duncan. At a time when blacks did not find it easy to obtain schooling, all of the children were educated and each became a leader in his chosen field. In 1917 the family moved to Salisbury, N.C., where Duncan completed his elementary education in the public schools. After receiving an A.B. degree from Livingstone College in Salisbury, he began teaching science in Washington High School, Reidsville, where he also served as coach from 1927 to 1930. He then attended Cornell University and was awarded an M.A. in education. From 1931 to 1937 he was principal of Dunbar High School in East Spencer; in the summer he renewed his relationship with Livingstone as a visiting instructor. He returned to Washington High School as principal in 1938.

The North Carolina Department of Public Instruction appointed Duncan state supervisor of Negro high schools in 1946. Somehow he found time to complete requirements for the Ph.D. in education at Cornell University three years later. Often during the summer he was a visiting instructor at various Negro colleges; in each instance he worked to improve the competencies of black principals and teachers.

On 1 July 1958 Duncan became the fifth president of Livingstone College, serving until his sudden death. Although dedicated to the college and its growth, he was also involved in serving people and numerous causes in the community including the improvement of race relations. He was a tireless worker at local, state, and national levels in the professional teachers' organization. While the state still had dual professional associations, he served on many committees of the North Carolina Teachers Association and finally as its president in 1964–66. When that organization began to work on a merger with the North Carolina Education Association, he was actively involved in the work of the Liaison Committee where his calm manner often helped to reconcile opposing viewpoints. He was serving on the committee at the time of his death. A life member of the National Education Association and of the National Association for the Advancement of Colored People, he also served on the North Carolina State Board of Higher Education and the Southern Regional Education Board. He was president of the North Carolina Council of Churches; vice-president of the Piedmont University Center; and a member of the U.S. Civil Rights Commission, the North Carolina State Welfare Board, the Connectional Budget Board of the A. M. E. Zion Church, and the National Conference of Christians and Jews.

Duncan's service as a college administrator was marked by a sound philosophy of education, a love for people and for learning, and a compassion for students. He was always moved by the poverty and need of a bright young student and he wanted Livingstone to be a "school where no one gets lost." Under his presidency, new buildings were erected on the campus and the faculty and student body were lifted to new academic heights. After his death the Samuel Edward Duncan Memorial Scholarship Fund was established at Livingstone College. On 26 Apr. 1974 the Board of Education of the Salisbury City Schools dedicated the Samuel E. Duncan School to his memory.

On 16 May 1933 Duncan married Ida Hauser of Salisbury; they had two children.

SEE: Samuel Edward Duncan Files (Library, Livingstone College, Salisbury); Lois V. Edinger, interviews with Ida Hauser Duncan and other members of the family.

LOIS V. EDINGER

**Dunn, John Ross** *(d. 1783)*, Salisbury lawyer and founder, was born in Ireland. According to Archibald D. Murphey, he studied to be a Roman Catholic priest but "left Ireland suddenly in consequence of some fracas" and boarded a privateer for America when he was about twenty years old. He married Mary Reid and settled on Reid's Creek, a tributary of the Yadkin River, where he worked for a time as shoemaker and schoolteacher. They had two daughters and at least one son. Susan Dunn married Lewis Beard, a son of John Lewis

Beard, and the other daughter married a Mr. Fisher. Later Dunn married Betsy Howard and Frances Petty.

Apparently Dunn began his legal career as deputy clerk of the Anson County court. When Rowan was formed from Anson in 1753, he became clerk of the Rowan County court. He was licensed to practice law in 1755 and eventually served as Crown attorney. In 1754 he was one of the two commissioners who marked the lots and streets for the new town of Salisbury. Dunn's land purchases reflect the growth of the town and of his law practice. First he attended to building a plantation base between 1758 and 1762, buying over twelve hundred acres on the middle fork of Crane Creek, a few miles from Salisbury. At this time he owned only two lots in Salisbury, but between 1770 and 1772 he bought six and one-half additional town lots. His militia record paralleled his economic and professional advancement. Dunn was adjutant in the Rowan County militia during the mid-1750s. He was a commissioner to deal with the Cherokees in 1757, and as a militia major he supplied wagons for the expedition against them in 1759–60. During the Regulator upheavals Dunn was the commanding colonel of Rowan County militia, which assisted in the defense of the Hillsborough court; he also served on the committee of officials who met with the Regulators.

Dunn represented Rowan County in the colonial Assembly in 1762 and Salisbury during 1769–71. In the latter Assembly he was a member of the committee on public claims, serving for a time as chairman. He introduced a bill for the collection of back taxes in the wake of the Regulator crisis and another for building a jail in Salisbury. Both became law. With other men from the area he was entrusted with several responsibilities under the Assembly's surveillance: to contract for building courthouses for the new counties of Guilford and Surry and for surveying their lines, for building a new Rowan courthouse, and for building a road from the frontier to Campbellton. The commissioners did not accomplish the two latter tasks.

In the years before the American Revolution Dunn figured in a controversy over the established church. An Anglican, he is said to have been responsible for bringing the Reverend Theodorus Swaine Drage to organize the established church in Rowan County. The minister started a chapel in the Jersey settlement, but in 1769 dissenters captured the vestry election and their new vestry withheld the Anglican's salary. Their action forced Drage to leave the county in 1773. During this time, Dunn was a conspicuous Anglican. Drage held services in Dunn's commodious Salisbury house, which was noted for its Christmas greenery.

In 1774 and 1775 Dunn and a wealthy English lawyer in Salisbury, Benjamin Booth Boote, came under attack by the Rowan Committee of Safety. It has been suggested that the attack was part of an attempt by a new lawyer, William Kennon, recently arrived from Wilmington, to force out the established ones. Their first brush with the Committee of Safety came as a result of a declaration bearing their names. About two years later Dunn explained the origin of the declaration. He said it had originated in late August or early September 1774 when a magistrate showed Dunn and Boote a newspaper account of a New York resolution condemning Bostonian action against the authority of Parliament. The magistrate persuaded Boote to draft a declaration of allegiance to king and Parliament. Four men signed it, and they agreed not to offer it to anyone else. The declaration got out, however, and Waightstill Avery read it to a Presbyterian congregation in Mecklenburg County. Thus it was general knowledge by the time Dunn attended the September court in Mecklenburg County.

On 23 September the Rowan Committee of Safety, with Kennon as chairman, condemned the declaration and had it displayed on the gallows and whipping post. The safety committee referred to the document as a "Protest," for its statement of allegiance to king *and* Parliament challenged the committee's resolution made at its first recorded meeting on 8 August; in it the committee had vowed its allegiance to the king alone and had accused Parliament of usurping the rights of the colonial assemblies. In his later description of the declaration, Dunn clearly implied that he and Boote had been unaware of the committee's resolution. It is conceivable that Dunn was telling the truth, for the committee did not meet again until 23 September, when they condemned the "Protest."

Although Dunn refused to participate in revolutionary elections and committees, there are indications that he used his influence to oppose Kennon's leadership and tried to curb his forwardness as the latter's star rose with the events of 1775. The Captain Jack episode publicly displayed the weakness of the conservative position and provided enough revolutionary momentum for Kennon to rid Salisbury of Dunn and Boote, its leading conservative spokesmen. While Captain James Jack was in Salisbury on his way from Charlotte to Philadelphia, Kennon had the Mecklenburg Resolves read from the courthouse. Dunn and Boote denounced the Resolves as treasonous and called for Jack's confinement, but the horseman rode away.

Soon afterwards a party of armed men from Mecklenburg County went into Rowan to seize Dunn and Boote. They acted in concert with Kennon and a few others who arranged with subterfuge to remove Dunn and Boote from Salisbury for the rendezvous with the men from Mecklenburg. The legality of the abduction was challenged by several prominent Salisbury revolutionaries. After a long debate, the Rowan Committee of Safety recorded the incident as an unofficial act not to be taken as precedent. The 1775 Provincial Congress, of which Kennon was a member, went on record as deploring the action (abduction without a hearing) as a general rule but approved it in the particular case.

The two lawyers were taken to Charles Town and were kept there for over a year. The South Carolina Provincial Congress had not requested their presence and did not know what to do with them. The congress paid part of their maintenance expenses on the promise of reimbursement from North Carolina and paroled the men within Charles Town. Enjoying his relative freedom, Dunn became intoxicated and spoke too loosely, for which he was reprimanded by the congress. Dunn and Boote returned to Salisbury early in September 1776. The North Carolina Council of Safety, meeting there, paroled Dunn to Salisbury and required £1000 bond from him but admitted Boote into citizenship on his taking the state oath.

Both lawyers accommodated themselves to the Revolution, but only Dunn's accommodation was permanent. In August 1777, two years after their removal, they were allowed to return to the bar, and Dunn became state's attorney for Rowan County as he previously had been Crown attorney. Boote continued his legal practice under the new regime until Cornwallis's presence in 1781 offered an alternative. He joined the British but was taken prisoner at Yorktown. Boote returned to England and died soon after the war.

Dunn, on the other hand, cast his lot with the county

and town he had helped to build. There are no indications of further difficulties with neighbors with whose political views he had disagreed. An appropriate, if incidental, sign of their reacceptance of him was his appointment to contract for building a new courthouse in 1778 and for repairing the old one in 1781; he shared these responsibilities with one of the men who had arranged for his abduction. Dunn's career was not politics but the practice of law—the maintenance of the courthouse, one might say—and he successfully resumed it. Perhaps it is significant that Kennon was no longer in Salisbury. Beginning in 1775 Kennon obtained several jobs as a commissary for the state government and seems to have managed them from Wilmington; he died in late 1777 or early 1778.

Dunn practiced law in Salisbury until his death. Tradition relates that he became ill while pleading a case and was carried from the courtroom. He is believed to have been buried on his land at "Dunn's Mountain," which still casts its gaze toward courthouse square.

SEE: James S. Brawley, *The Rowan Story, 1753–1953* (1953); Claim of Benjamin Booth Boote (PRO, Audit Office Papers 13:117), New Hanover County Court Minutes, Rowan County Civil and Criminal Cases, Rowan County Committee of Safety Minutes (Secretary of State's Papers), Rowan County Court Minutes, Rowan County Deed Books (microfilm) (all in North Carolina State Archives, Raleigh); Walter Clark, ed., *State Records of North Carolina*, vols. 11 (1895), 19 (1901), 22 (1907); William H. Foote, *Sketches of North Carolina . . .* (1846); Whitehead Kluttz, "Rowan's Committee of Safety," *North Carolina University Magazine* 18 (1900); Archibald D. Murphey, "Historical Memoranda," *North Carolina University Magazine* 1 (1852); Walter Murphey, *Memorial Address Commemorating the Memory of the Distinguished Members of the Rowan County Bar* (1938); William S. Powell, *St. Luke's Episcopal Church* (1953); George Raynor and Aubrey Atkinson, *Sketches of Old Rowan* (1963); Jethro Rumple, *A History of Rowan County, North Carolina* (1881); William L. Saunders, ed., *Colonial Records of North Carolina*, vols. 9, 10 (1890); John H. Wheeler, *Reminiscences and Memoirs of North Carolina . . .* (1884).

CAROLE WATTERSON TROXLER

**Dunn, Poindexter** *(3 Nov. 1834–12 Oct. 1914)*, Arkansas congressman, was born near Raleigh, the son of Grey Dunn, a prosperous planter, and his wife, Lydia Baucum Dunn. In 1837 he moved with his parents to Limestone County, Ala., where he attended the county schools. In 1854 he was graduated from Jackson College, Columbia, Tenn., and then studied law. During this period he was married and in 1856 moved to Saint Francis County, Ark. There he was elected to the state house of representatives and served from 1856 to 1861. He also was engaged in growing cotton. At the beginning of the Civil War he was elected captain of a company but did not see actual military service. After the war he completed his study of law and was admitted to the bar. He established a practice in Forrest City, Ark.

Dunn was a presidential elector on the Democratic ticket of Greeley and Brown in 1872 and of Tilden and Hendricks in 1876. As a Democrat he was elected to the Forty-sixth and the four succeeding congresses, serving from 4 Mar. 1879 until 3 Mar. 1889. He was not a candidate for renomination in 1888. Following his last term in Congress he moved to Los Angeles, Calif., where he continued to practice law until 1893. That year he was named to a special commission for the prevention of frauds on the customs revenue in New York City. In 1895 he moved to Baton Rouge, La., and engaged in railroad construction. In 1905 he finally settled in Texarkana, Bowie County, Tex., where he died and was buried in Rose Hill Cemetery. The names of his wife and children, if any, are unknown.

SEE: *Bio. Dir. Am. Cong.* (1961); J. H. Brown, ed., *Lamb's Biographical Dictionary of the United States*, vol. 2 (1900); John Hallum, *Biographical and Pictorial History of Arkansas* (1887); Little Rock *Arkansas Democrat*, 4 Apr. 1884; David Y. Thomas, *Arkansas and Its People: A History, 1541–1930*, vol. 1 (1930).

MARY BODMAN KENNER

**Dunning, Paris Chipman** *(15 Mar. 1806–10 May 1884)*, physician, lawyer, and governor of Indiana, was born in Greensboro, the son of James and Rachel North Dunning. He had two brothers, John and Thomas. After attending the Greensboro Academy he studied medicine at Transylvania University, Lexington, Ky., for a year and then studied law. He was admitted to the bar in 1833 and in the same year was elected to the house of representatives in the General Assembly of Indiana, where he had moved about 1823 following the death of his father. After serving three successive terms he was elected to the state senate for three more successive terms. He was president pro tem of the senate in 1863 and 1865. Elected lieutenant governor, he served in that office until Governor James Whitcourt resigned upon being elected to the U.S. Senate in 1848. Dunning served as governor from 27 Dec. 1848 to 5 Dec. 1849.

In addition to holding elective office, Dunning was a physician and a lawyer. From 1838 to 1841 he served on the board of trustees of Indiana State College. He was a Democrat and a delegate to the national convention of his party in 1860. In 1826 he married Sarah Alexander; they were the parents of five children: Martha, Mary, Rachel, Paris, and James. His wife died in 1863 and in 1865 he married Mrs. Ellen Lane Ashford by whom he had a son, Smith Lane. After completing the term as governor, Dunning returned to his home in Bloomington and it was there that he died. He was buried in Rose Hill Cemetery.

SEE: *Biographical Directory of the Indiana General Assembly* (1980); Robert Sobel and John Raimo, *Biographical Directory of Governors of the United States*, vol. 1 (1978).

WILLIAM S. POWELL

**Durant (Durand, Duren), Ann Marwood** *(d. 22 Jan. 1694/95)*, the first woman named as an attorney in extant records of North Carolina, came to the colony with her husband, George Durant, about 1661. Ann Marwood married Durant on 4 Jan. 1658/59 in Northumberland County, Va. Her earlier history is not known. The couple settled first in Nansemond County, Va., but in 1661 or earlier they moved southward to the area then called Roanoke, which was soon to be granted to the Carolina Proprietors and named Albemarle. There they settled on the peninsula now called Durants Neck, in present-day Perquimans County, where George Durant bought an extensive tract of land from the local Indians.

Both of the Durants contributed substantially to the newly begun colony to which they had moved, although George's political activities are better known than Ann's less conspicuous contributions. During his frequent absences on public business or in pursuit of his occupation as mariner, Ann ran their plantation, acted as attorney for her husband and for others on occasion, and provided a variety of services and commodities for neighboring settlers. Not the least of her contributions was that of providing accommodations for the numerous officials and others attending meetings of the Assembly, Council, and courts, which frequently were held at the Durant home as well as informal meetings of politicians. During the period of civil strife that characterized the age, prisoners were sometimes lodged there.

The distinction of being the first woman known to have appeared as an attorney in a North Carolina court comes from Ann Durant's appearance on 25 May 1673 as attorney for a seaman named Andrew Ball. She successfully brought suit for wages due to Ball for service on a vessel called the *Two Brothers*. That she also acted as attorney for her husband is evidenced by an extant power of attorney, dated 17 May 1675, in which George empowered Ann to bring suit and take other actions to collect debts due him or to recover property belonging to him. Unlike her appearance on behalf of Ball, Ann's actions as attorney for her husband are not recorded in the few surviving official records of the period. That she did so act, however, is indicated by the endorsement on George's letter of attorney, which shows that the document was proved and officially recorded on 9 Oct. 1677.

Surviving records also show that Ann appeared in court on her own behalf from time to time to sue for debts owed her or as defendant in suits against her. The debts at issue in such suits arose in connection with her business activities, which apparently included operation of an inn or at least a less formal provision of board and lodging. Her bills contain such items as "his accommodations," "the Trubell of my House," and "attendance in his sickness." Other services listed in her bills include making shirts and leather breeches, making coffins, and arranging funerals. Among the articles for which she sought payment were beverages (rum, cider, and "quince drink"), stockings, cloth, thread, planks, nails, and corn.

Ann Durant's business and court room activities were combined with the bearing and rearing of a large family. She had nine children: George (b. December 1659), Elizabeth (b. February 1660/61), John (b. December 1662), Mary (b. February 1665/66), Thomas (b. August 1668), Sarah (b. January 1670), Martha (b. August 1673), Perthenia (b. August 1675), and Ann (b. April 1681). The eldest child, George, died shortly before his twelfth birthday, but the others lived to adulthood. In addition to her own children, Ann reared two of her grandchildren, Ann and Elizabeth Waller, children of her daughter Elizabeth, who were orphaned in infancy or early childhood.

At least six of the Durant children married. Elizabeth's husband was Thomas Waller. Sarah married Isaac Rowden. Perthenia was married twice, first to Joseph Sutton and subsequently to John Stevens. Ann married William Bartlett. John married Sarah Cooke (rendered *Jooke* by J. R. B. Hathaway). Thomas married Elizabeth Gaskill. It is not known whether Mary and Martha were married.

Ann Durant survived her husband about a year.

SEE: John B. Boddie, *Seventeenth Century Isle of Wight County, Virginia* (1938); Durant Family Bible, 1599 (North Carolina Collection, University of North Carolina, Chapel Hill); J. Bryan Grimes, ed., *Abstracts of North Carolina Wills* (1910); J. R. B. Hathaway, ed., *North Carolina Historical and Genealogical Register*, 3 vols. (1900–1903); Mattie Erma E. Parker, ed., *Colonial Records of North Carolina, Higher-Court Records, 1670–1696*, vol. 2 (1968), and *1676–1701*, vol. 3 (1971); Perquimans County Births, Marriages, Deaths, and Flesh Marks, 1659–1739 (North Carolina State Archives, Raleigh); Wills of George and Ann Durant (North Carolina State Archives, Raleigh).

MATTIE ERMA E. PARKER

**Durant (Durand, Duren), George** *(1 Oct. 1632–ca. January 1693/94)*, leader in Culpeper's Rebellion, speaker of the assembly, and attorney general, migrated to Virginia from England before July 1658. Apparently he lived for a time in Northumberland County, Va., where he bought three hundred acres of land. In July 1658 he was a witness in the Northumberland County court. He seems to have left the county soon after his marriage the following January and to have lived for the next year or two in Nansemond County or perhaps Lower Norfolk.

For about two years after leaving Northumberland, Durant explored the Albemarle region, to which he later moved. At that time the area was part of Virginia and was known as Roanoke. It had recently begun to interest Virginians who were seeking land, and several had bought tracts from the Indians and moved into the region. In his explorations Durant was associated with Nathaniell Batts, a longtime explorer and fur trader in Roanoke, who was then living in Lower Norfolk County. In that period he also was associated with Richard Batts, a wealthy sea captain and merchant of Barbados who traded with Virginia and is thought to have been a brother of Nathaniell. As Durant was a mariner by occupation, he may have been employed in that capacity by Richard. In 1660 and 1661, however, he was devoting much time to the exploration of Roanoke, in which he may have been an employee of Nathaniell. Possibly he worked intermittently for both.

On 24 Sept. 1660 Durant and Richard Batts served as witnesses to a deed in which Kiscutanewh, king of the Yeopim Indians, sold to Nathaniell Batts all land on the southwest side of Pasquotank River from the mouth of the river to the head of New Begun Creek. The deed is the oldest for North Carolina land known to be on record. As the land conveyed was then in Norfolk County, Va., the deed was recorded there.

The following year Durant bought land in Roanoke. On 4 Aug. 1661 Cisketando, as king of the Yeopims, sold to Durant a tract on Perquimans River. On 1 Mar. 1661/62 Durant obtained a second deed, in which Kilcocanen, as king of the Yeopims, conveyed a point of land projecting into Albemarle (then Roanoke) Sound and lying between Perquimans River and Little River (then Katotine River). The second deed may have been a clarification and confirmation of the August deed, in which the description of the land was not so precise as in the later one. The land conveyed, then called Wikacome but now Durants Neck, is in present-day Perquimans County, where both deeds were recorded in 1716. They are the earliest deeds on record in North Carolina. Although the deed to Nathaniell Batts was earlier, it was recorded in Virginia, not North Carolina.

Durant probably began living on his Roanoke plantation as early as 1661, perhaps before the actual signing of a deed. In 1662 he already had built a house there and had cleared part of the land. Soon after he moved, however, complications arose regarding title to his land, which were not resolved during his lifetime.

Apparently by request, Durant, while selecting land for himself, also chose land for a fellow Virginian, George Catchmaid of Nansemond County, to whom he recommended a tract adjacent to his own. In 1662, when Catchmaid came to view the land and arrange for settling it, he informed Durant of recent changes in governmental requirements for title to land in Roanoke, which no longer could be established by purchase from the Indians but instead required a patent from the Virginia governor. On learning of the new requirements, Durant determined to go to Jamestown and take out a patent, but Catchmaid offered to handle the matter for him and Durant accepted. Instead of securing a patent in Durant's name, however, Catchmaid had Durant's land included in his own patent, thereby obtaining for himself legal title to Durant's land. Although Durant obtained from Catchmaid a paper in which Catchmaid acknowledged Durant's right and promised to have the land patented in Durant's name, Catchmaid never obtained the patent. After Catchmaid's death Durant tried to get clear title through the general court of Albemarle but the court, although recognizing Durant's right, appears not to have had competence in such a matter. An effort to obtain a patent through Timothy Biggs, who had married Catchmaid's widow, also was unsuccessful, and it was not until 1697, after Durant's death, that the title was cleared. In that year a suit was brought in the North Carolina Court of Chancery by Durant's sons, who were their father's heirs, against one Edward Catchmaid of London, who was nephew and heir to George Catchmaid. The suit resulted in a decree giving Durant's sons title to their father's land, on which the family had then lived more than thirty-five years.

Despite the trouble about his land, Durant apparently decided by 1665 that he would live permanently in Roanoke. About that time he sold his land in Northumberland County and also several headrights entitling him to additional land in Virginia. By then the Roanoke area no longer was part of Virginia but had been included in the Province of Carolina and granted by King Charles II of England to eight of his supporters, who were designated Lords Proprietors of Carolina. The Carolina Proprietors, in turn, had named the Roanoke area the County of Albemarle and had set up their own government for the colony there.

By the 1670s Durant was one of the leading inhabitants of Albemarle. Although he appears never to have held the higher offices of the colony, he was one of the ablest and most influential men in the county. By the mid-seventies he was a leader of the political party representing the interests of the original settlers, who bitterly opposed the increasingly restrictive measures imposed on the colony by the Crown and the Proprietors. In 1675 or the following year Durant went to London and presented to the Proprietors the views of his party, protesting against conditions then existing in Albemarle and warning of trouble to come. When Albemarle erupted in the so-called Culpeper's Rebellion in late 1677, Durant was one of the chief leaders of the uprising. He apparently had participated in planning the revolt, and his arrival from London as mate on a ship bringing weapons served as signal for action. Later he was a leader in restoring order under the so-called rebel government. His home became headquarters for the government, which held meetings and for a time kept prisoners there.

In the later stages of the uprising Durant and another colonist went to London as agents to present to the Proprietors the colonists' views. They apparently made an effective presentation, for in reestablishing government under their own authority the Proprietors appointed to office some of the leaders of the recent uprising.

After *de jure* government was reestablished, Durant appears to have continued to exert great influence. In 1679 he was attorney general and also served as speaker of the assembly. Some of his contemporaries claimed that he had so much influence on the acting governor, John Jenkins, that in effect he was the governor.

Durant's influence in governmental affairs ended abruptly in late 1682, when Seth Sothel, one of the Proprietors, arrived and took office as governor. Sothel instituted procedures that increased the governor's power and gave him pretexts for exploiting and abusing the colonists. Durant seems to have openly opposed Sothel from the start. On 12 March 1682/83 he was brought before the county court to answer for "an infammous Libell he Writ." Apparently he was held in prison on order from the governor either before or after his court appearance or both. The court, which the governor controlled, ordered Durant to give the governor a bond with power of attorney to confess judgment. Although Durant appealed the order, the higher court also was dominated by Sothel, so the appeal only delayed his compliance. Eventually Sothel, using the bond and warrant as pretext, forced Durant to execute a deed conveying to Sothel his plantation containing about two thousand acres. The deed was dated 20 Dec. 1687. Sothel's treatment of Durant was one of the numerous abuses that led Albemarle inhabitants to rise against the governor in 1689 and banish him. It also was one of the charges for which the London Proprietors called Sothel to account when at last they took notice of his behavior.

Durant, who identified himself as a mariner in his will and other documents, appears to have continued in that occupation after settling in Albemarle. It is likely, however, that operation of his plantation and his political activities were his chief occupations. His home appears to have been operated as an inn, and his plantation seems to have been a center for enterprises providing a variety of services and commodities for the colony. In appearance, at least, he was innkeeper and merchant as well as planter and mariner. In fact, however, the business enterprises and at times the entire plantation were operated by Durant's remarkably able wife, Ann Marwood Durant. Contrary to the custom of the time, Ann Durant conducted business in her own name instead of her husband's, and on occasion she appeared in court as attorney for her husband or others. She was the first woman known to have appeared as an attorney in a North Carolina court, which she did as early as 25 May 1673.

George Durant and Ann Marwood were married by an Anglican minister in Northumberland County, Va., 4 Jan. 1658/59. Although some writers have identified Durant with other faiths, no evidence has been found indicating that either he or Ann subscribed to any but the Anglican faith. The couple had nine children: George, Elizabeth, John, Mary, Thomas, Sarah, Martha, Perthenia, and Ann. All except George lived to adulthood. At least six of the children married. John, the elder of the two surviving sons, married Sarah Cooke, daughter of Thomas and Ann Cooke. He became a council member and a justice of the general court. Thomas, the other son, married Elizabeth Gaskill; he appears not to have entered public life. The eldest daughter, Elizabeth, married Thomas Waller. Both she and her husband died about 1687, leaving two daughters, Elizabeth and Ann, who were taken into the custody of their Durant grandparents. Of Durant's remaining daughters, Sarah married Isaac Rowden, Ann married William Bartlett, and Perthenia first married Joseph Sutton and subsequently John Stevens. Most if not all of the couples had children.

In his later years Durant appears not to have been active politically, although it is likely that his influence was felt in the actions resulting in Sothel's overthrow and in later developments. His will, dated 9 Oct. 1688, was proved 6 Feb. 1693/94. In it he named his wife, who was appointed executrix; the six children then living; a brother, John Durant, who was then living in London; and three nephews—George, Henry, and John Durant—who were sons of his brother John.

Durant's wife survived him only a year. She died 22 Jan. 1694/95. The two no doubt were buried on their plantation, but the location of their graves is now unknown. Indeed, the exact location of their house has been lost.

SEE: John B. Boddie, *Seventeenth Century Isle of Wight County, Virginia* (1938); Durant Family Bible, 1599 (North Carolina Collection, University of North Carolina, Chapel Hill); J. Bryan Grimes, ed., *North Carolina Wills and Inventories* (1912); Hugh T. Lefler and A. R. Newsome, *North Carolina: The History of a Southern State* (1973); Memory A. Lester, comp., *Old Southern Bible Records* (1974); Elizabeth McPherson, ed., "Nathaniell Batts, Landholder on Pasquotank River, 1660," *North Carolina Historical Review* 43 (1966); Nell M. Nugent, comp., *Cavaliers and Pioneers*, 2 vols. (1934, 1977); Mattie Erma E. Parker, ed., *Colonial Records of North Carolina, Higher-Court Records, 1670–1696*, vol. 2 (1968), and *1697–1701*, vol. 3 (1971); Perquimans County Births, Marriages, Deaths, and Flesh Marks, 2 vols. (1659–1739, 1701–1820), Deeds of Perquimans County, Book A (microfilm), and Will of George Durant (North Carolina State Archives, Raleigh); William L. Saunders, ed., *Colonial Records of North Carolina*, vol. 1 (1886); Ellen G. Winslow, *History of Perquimans County* (1931).

MATTIE ERMA E. PARKER

**Durant (Duren), John** *(26 Dec. 1662–January 1699/1700)*, North Carolina Council member and General Court justice, was the son of George and Ann Marwood Durant, early settlers and leaders of the colony. The younger Durant probably was born at his parents' plantation on the peninsula now called Durants Neck in Perquimans County. He was the third of nine children and the second of three sons, of whom the eldest died in childhood.

By January 1693/94 Durant was a member of the North Carolina Council and ex officio justice of the General Court. He held those offices through October 1695. Most likely he was also a member of the Assembly in that period, as he sat on the Council by vote of the Assembly. In November 1697, he again became a justice of the General Court, which was then composed of justices appointed by the Council instead of the Council members themselves. He held that appointment the remainder of his life.

Durant married Sarah Cooke (rendered *Jooke* by J. R. B. Hathaway) on 9 Apr. 1684. The bride was the daughter of Thomas and Ann Cooke of the North Carolina colony. About the time of the marriage John's father gave him a plantation in Perquimans Precinct, on which no doubt the couple settled. The children born of the marriage were George, Ann, Elizabeth, Sarah, and Mary.

After Durant died, his widow married William Stephens on 1 Jan. 1703/4.

SEE: Albemarle Book of Warrants and Surveys, 1681–1706 (North Carolina State Archives, Raleigh); Colonial Council Minutes, Wills, Inventories, 1677–1706 (North Carolina State Archives, Raleigh); Durant Family Bible, 1599 (North Carolina Collection, University of North Carolina, Chapel Hill); J. R. B. Hathaway, ed., *The North Carolina Historical and Genealogical Register*, 3 vols. (1900–1903); Mattie Erma E. Parker, ed., *Colonial Records of North Carolina, Higher-Court Records, 1670–1696*, vol. 2 (1968), and *1697–1701*, vol. 3 (1971); Perquimans County Births, Marriages, Deaths, and Flesh Marks, 2 vols. (1659–1739, 1701–1820) (North Carolina State Archives, Raleigh); William L. Saunders, ed., *Colonial Records of North Carolina*, vol. 1 (1886).

MATTIE ERMA E. PARKER

**Durham, Carl Thomas** *(28 Aug. 1892–29 Apr. 1974)*, congressman, was born in the White Cross community six miles west of Chapel Hill in the house built by his great-great-great grandfather, Matthew Durham, when he moved from New England in 1734 to settle on a plantation near the Haw River. He was the oldest of six children of Claude and Delia Ann Lloyd Durham. Young Durham attended White Cross School and the Manndale Academy at Saxapahaw, and in the summer of 1913 began work at Eubanks Drugstore in Chapel Hill. By 1916 he had sufficiently qualified himself as an apprentice in pharmacy to be admitted to The University of North Carolina as a special student in pharmacy, pursuing the course of instruction during the next two years. A popular student, he became a member of the Kappa Psi fraternity and was elected president of his pharmacy class. Toward the end of 1917 the war in Europe brought his academic career to an end; on New Year's Day 1918, he enlisted in the Navy Hospital Corps for the final period of World War I. Released from the navy the following Christmas Eve, he returned to Eubanks Drugstore as a professional pharmacist.

From an early age Durham took an active interest in community life. In 1914 he helped organize the Men's Bible Class in the Chapel Hill University Baptist Church; he also served as a deacon in the church and was a president of the Bible class. He was a member of the Chapel Hill Board of Aldermen from 1921 to 1930 and of the Chapel Hill School Board from 1924 to 1938. Serving for eight years on the Orange County Board of Commissioners, he proposed and secured in 1935 $22,000 in federal aid for a rural electrification line in the Calvander–Orange Grove area of Orange County. He was a charter member of the White Cross Junior Order of United American Mechanics and of Post Number Six of the American Legion in which he was commander. He belonged to the University Lodge, No. 408, of Masons in Chapel Hill. In 1937 Durham was elected to The University of North Carolina Board of Trustees and served for many years; in 1958 the university conferred on him the LL.D. degree.

A Democrat, Durham was a member of the North Carolina State Democratic Executive Committee and managed the congressional campaigns in Orange County for Frank Hancock of Oxford and William Umstead of Durham. In 1938 he was elected to the Seventy-sixth Congress and served twenty-two years during eleven terms. He was a member of the House Military Affairs Committee and the House Armed Services Committee and in 1945 became a charter member of the Joint Atomic Energy Commission. At the beginning of World War II, he sponsored a bill in Congress creating the U.S. Army Pharmacy Corps. In 1949 he won unanimous approval in the House for a bill to support a $161,000,000 radar network around the United States and Canada. On passage of the bill he remarked laconically: "It seems to give more protection for less money than anything else I have seen." At the end of the war Congressman Durham was appointed to the new Joint Atomic Energy Committee and later, as a senior member, served as its acting chairman. He sponsored civil defense legislation and was coauthor of a bill tightening drug laws. In 1955 he was a U.S. delegate to the Atoms for Peace conference in Geneva and in 1957 attended the first meeting of the International Atomic Energy Agency in Vienna. Durham retired from public life in 1961, at the end of the Eighty-seventh Congress. In 1964 the American Pharmaceutical Association elected him honorary president and retained his services as a special consultant.

Durham was in the forefront of polity at the beginning of the Atomic era. His longtime service in the Joint Atomic Energy Commission during three administrations afforded him a unique perspective on global accommodation to the splitting of the atom. His reaction was one of restraint in the military use of atomic power, caution in its application as a domestic energy source, and enthusiasm for international diplomacy in its control. He was a leader in the congressional battle for the civilian control of atomic energy.

On 30 Dec. 1918 Durham married Margaret Joe Whitsett of Guilford County. They had five children: Celia (Mrs. Gregg Murray), Mary Sue (Mrs. Willard Sessler of Asheville), Carl Durham, Jr., of Wilmington, Peggy (Mrs. Joe Thomas Wall of Chapel Hill), and Ann Durham Wyatt of Durham. Mrs. Durham died on 10 Jan. 1953. On 8 June 1961 Durham married Louise Ashworth Jefferson of Chapel Hill. They had between them eight children and twenty-six grandchildren.

Carl Durham died in Duke Hospital in his eighty-first year. Funeral services were held in the Chapel Hill University Baptist Church and burial followed in the churchyard of the Antioch Baptist Church in the White Cross community.

SEE: *Biog. Dir. Am. Cong.* (1961); *Chapel Hill Newspaper*, 29, 30 Apr., 1 May 1974; *Chapel Hill News Leader*, 4 May 1956, 9 June 1958; *Chapel Hill Weekly*, 12 Apr. 1946, 14 July 1950, 31 May, 6 Aug. 1957, 16 May 1960; John L. Cheney, Jr., ed., *North Carolina Government, 1585–1974* (1975); *Durham Morning Herald*, 13 May 1973; Daniel L. Grant, *Alumni History of the University of North Carolina* (1924); *Greensboro Daily News*, 16 Aug. 1950, 23 Sept., 14 Dec. 1960, 17 Apr., 9 June 1961, 21 Jan. 1962, 21 Oct. 1963; Raleigh *News and Observer*, 2, 3, 29 Nov. 1938, 29 May 1939, 21 July 1946, 14 Aug. 1955, 21 Nov. 1959, 21 Oct. 1963; "Two Stalwarts Gone From Congress," *We the People of North Carolina* 18 (October 1960); *Who's Who in the South and Southwest* (1947).

WARNER WELLS

**Durham, Columbus** *(28 Apr. 1844–14 Nov. 1895)*, Baptist minister and corresponding secretary of the North Carolina Baptist State Convention, was born in Rutherford County, the son of Esther Baxter and Micajah Durham and brother of Plato Durham, a Conservative legislator during Reconstruction. He was baptized in September 1860. At the age of seventeen, he enlisted in Company E, Twelfth Regiment, North Carolina Troops. He was wounded in the hand at Chancellorsville, Va., in 1863 and hospitalized with a gunshot wound in the leg in 1865. He was paroled at Appomattox Courthouse, Va., on 9 Apr. 1865.

After the war Durham entered Wake Forest College in 1867 and was graduated in 1871. In 1890 his alma mater awarded him an honorary doctorate of divinity. Ordained in 1871, he began his first pastorate at Goldsboro Baptist Church. Under his direction the membership more than doubled, and a pastor's study and parsonage were built. His next pastorate was at Durham First Baptist Church where he served from 1876 to 1887. It was from this church that he was called in 1888 to become the corresponding secretary of the North Carolina Baptist State Convention. During his term he played a leading role in the formation of the Baptist Orphanage (now the Baptist Children's Home) in Thomasville. He served on the orphanage's first board of trustees for a brief period prior to his death. He also was a member and president of the Wake Forest Board of Trustees (1878–95), a trustee of the Southern Baptist Theological Seminary, Louisville, Ky. (1884–85), and a vice-president of the Sunday School Board of the Southern Baptist Convention.

Durham married Lila Walters. They had three children: Walters, a Raleigh banker; Baxter, for many years state auditor of North Carolina; and Ellen, a longtime choir director at Raleigh First Baptist Church.

Durham's funeral was held at Raleigh First Baptist Church. He was buried in Oakwood Cemetery.

SEE: *Biblical Recorder*, 20 Nov. 1895, 25 Oct. 1939; *Encyclopedia of Southern Baptists*, vol. 1 (1958); Weymouth T. Jordan, comp., *North Carolina Troops, 1861–1865 . . . 11th–15th Regts.*, vol. 1 (1975); George W. Paschal, *History of Wake Forest College*, vol. 3 (1943); John R. Sampy, *Southern Baptist Theological Seminary, 1859–89* (1890).

JOHN R. WOODARD

**Durham, Plato** *(20 Sept. 1840–9 Nov. 1875)*, legislator and Conservative political leader during Reconstruction, was born at High Shoals (later Henrietta), Rutherford County, the eldest son and fourth of thirteen children of Micajah and Esther Baxter Durham. Although the family was well off by the standards of the time and place, Durham's early education was gained, in the words of his son, "at the county schools and at the plow handles." When he was about eighteen he began reading law in Rutherfordton and then continued under his uncle, John Baxter, in Knoxville, Tenn. At the outbreak of the Civil War, Durham joined a Confederate military company in Knoxville; however, he soon returned to North Carolina, enlisted in a Cleveland County company in June 1862, and quickly saw active service as part of the Army of Northern Virginia. Rising from private to captain, he was never far from the sound of battle until the guns fell silent at Appomattox. In fact, his company claimed to have fired the last shots in that battle. Durham emerged from the war with an enviable record for gallantry and with a wholehearted dedication to the "Lost Cause." His father, an enthusiastic member of the Secession Convention of 1861, enlisted in the army at an advanced age and lost his life, as did two of his other sons.

After the war Durham attended The University of North Carolina law school and was admitted to the bar at Shelby in August 1866. His legal practice soon won him distinction and financial success. On 9 Apr. 1868 he married Nora Catherine Tracy, daughter of Dr. James Wright Tracy of Kings Mountain. They had five children, Nora Catherine, Robert Lee, Stonewall Jackson, Plato Tracy, and Micajah Rush, the first and last dying in infancy.

Durham's public service began with his election to the legislature of 1866–67. In the Constitutional Convention of 1868 he emerged as a bold and articulate leader of the Conservative minority, advocating the inviolability of the state debt, the removal of political liabilities from ex-Confederates, and the barring of Negroes from holding public office or serving as guardians of white children. He was similarly an outspoken minority leader in the legislature of 1868–70. He ran for Congress in 1868 and was declared elected by a margin of eighteen votes. However, the result was set aside by General E. R. S. Canby on grounds of fraud; on a recount the seat was awarded to his Republican opponent, A. H. Jones. Durham again received the Democratic nomination in 1870 but withdrew at the last moment because of his inability to take the test oath if he was elected. Denied the nomination (which he felt rightfully to be his) in 1874, he ran as an Independent but lost to the regular Democratic nominee. For several years after 1871 he edited the weekly *Cleveland Banner* in Shelby.

Durham joined the Ku Klux Klan in late 1868 or early 1869. He regarded it as a political weapon against the Republican party, but like other upper-class members he became alarmed by its uncontrolled attacks on obscure Negroes and white Republicans. He tried unsuccessfully to curb the violence, only to become further enmeshed himself in the tangled web of conspiracy and illegality surrounding the order. He was arrested by federal authorities in 1871 but was never brought to trial. For two years his major efforts were directed to exculpating fellow Klansmen, serving them as defense counsel, raising money for their bail and reportedly to bribe jurors, and seeking executive clemency for those convicted—all at considerable personal sacrifice.

Durham's final political service was in the Constitutional Convention of 1875, where he was a leader in dismantling Radical Reconstruction; he also advocated legislative regulation of railway rates. Later that year his life was cut short by pneumonia at the age of thirty-five. He was a Methodist. The University of North Carolina owns an oil portrait of Durham; it was reproduced in the *Charlotte Observer*, 26 Mar. 1933.

SEE: Durham's testimony before congressional investigating committee, 1871, *Senate Reports*, 42nd Cong., 2nd Sess., no. 41, or *House Reports, ibid.*, no. 22, North Carolina volume; Plato Durham Papers (Southern Historical Collection, University of North Carolina, Chapel Hill); J. G. deR. Hamilton, ed., *Randolph Shotwell Papers*, 3 vols. (1929–36).

ALLEN W. TRELEASE

**Dwire, Henry Randolph** *(8 Oct. 1882–17 July 1944)*, editor and university executive, was born in Winston, the son of Henry Xenophon and Mary Hanes Dwire. His father was a deputy collector of internal revenue in Winston-Salem. Young Dwire attended elementary and secondary public schools in that city. Upon graduation in 1898, he entered Trinity College (now Duke University) where he received a bachelor of arts degree in 1902 and a master of arts degree in 1903. While an undergraduate he was a contributor to *The Archive*, the college magazine, and became its editor in his senior year. As a graduate student he served as an assistant in English under Dr. Frank C. Brown. His writings appeared in the *South Atlantic Quarterly*, also published by the college, of which he later became editor.

In the fall of 1903 Dwire was an instructor of English at Fishburne Military Academy, Waynesboro, Va. At the end of the term he resigned his post to assume the editorship of the *Winston-Salem Sentinel* (now the *Twin City Sentinel*). From 1904 to 1926 he was its chief editorial writer and policymaker and from 1918 to 1926, copublisher. Few newspapers in North Carolina accumulated as much prestige and influence as did *The Sentinel* under his leadership, and his provocative editorials were widely quoted. The Sentinel Printing Company, of which he was secretary and coowner, also published the *Western Semi-Weekly Sentinel*, which had a large and respected circulation.

Dwire's civic service to the Winston-Salem community was broad and innovative. He was chairman of the School Commission (1923–30); secretary of the board of directors, North Carolina Hospital for the Insane (1929–33); founder of the Winston-Salem Fine Arts Foundation, a successful instrument for cultural growth and promotion; member of the board of lay activities, Western North Carolina Conference of the Methodist Episcopal Church, South (1925–29); director of the North Carolina Art Society; chairman of the Winston-Salem chapter, American Red Cross (1927–29); and charter member of the Winston-Salem Rotary Club, organized in October 1915, as well as its president (1918–19) and district governor of Rotary International (1929–30). He later continued his Rotary membership in Durham, where he was active in local and district programs and a frequent speaker at local clubs and district conferences. He also belonged to Alpha Tau Omega (social), Phi Beta Kappa (scholarship), and Omicron Delta Kappa (leadership) fraternities. He was a member of the Cosmos Club in Winston-Salem, the YMCA in Winston-Salem and Durham, and the Hope Valley Country Club in Durham. In 1928 he was awarded the civic trophy for distinguished community service by the Winston-Salem Chamber of Commerce.

In 1929 Dwire was enticed from semiretirement to become director of public relations and alumni affairs for his alma mater, Duke University. In addition to the multiple duties of his office, he edited the *South Atlantic Quarterly* and *The Alumni Register* of the university. To each he gave a professional ability that endowed both with new credibility. He served for a time as a trustee of Duke and in 1941 was elected one of its vice-presidents. He also was director of the Duke University Press. Dwire was particularly loyal to the program of worship and community service of the Duke University Chapel. In 1943 Davidson College conferred on him the honorary degree of doctor of letters.

Dwire was a registered Democrat but was not active in politics. He never married. During his later years he maintained a residence in both Winston-Salem and Durham (Hotel Washington Duke). He died at Duke Hospital and was buried in Winston-Salem.

SEE: *Durham Morning Herald*, *Winston-Salem Journal*, Winston-Salem *Twin City Sentinel*, 18 July 1944; Henry R. Dwire Papers (Manuscript Department, Library, Duke University, Durham); *North Carolina Biography*, vol. 1 (1941); Office of Information, Duke University, Durham; *Who's Who in America*, vol. 23 (1945).

C. SYLVESTER GREEN

**Earl, Daniel** *(d. 1790),* Anglican clergyman, school teacher, and missionary of the Society for the Propagation of the Gospel, was born in Bandon, County Cork, Ireland, the youngest son of an Irish nobleman. Commissioned in the British army, Earl resigned in order to take holy orders on 13 Sept. 1746 after marrying the daughter of a church official. He was licensed to serve in North Carolina by the Bishop of London on 19 Sept. 1756, and arrived in the Albemarle region in 1757. There he was curate for the aging Anglican minister, Clement Hall. Upon Hall's death in 1759 he became rector of St. Paul's Parish in Edenton, where he served until his resignation in 1778.

Earl's first wife died before his departure for North Carolina; their two daughters joined him after he settled there. Soon after his arrival he married a widow, Charity Jones, of Smithfield, Va.

Earl built a plantation, Bandon, fifteen miles above Edenton on the Chowan River. A knowledgeable farmer, he showed local residents improved methods of weaving and preparing flax for the loom. He was a pioneer in the shad and herring fishing industry and was accused of devoting too much time to his herring fisheries. About the time of the Revolution, a placard appeared on his church door:

A tumble-down church
And a broken-down steeple
A herring-catching parson
And a damn set of people.

From 1759 to 1783 Earl received partial support from the Society for the Propagation of the Gospel. His annual reports to the society recount the difficulties experienced by a missionary in a large colonial parish. Earl preached at Edenton and at four chapels in Chowan County. To the society he reported his large number of baptisms, described the poor physical condition of the parish church, and pleaded for funds to establish a school. In May 1775 he reported that he had not received a shilling from his parish for nearly three years. Earl regularly complained of poor health, and in 1775 the society granted his request to move to one of the northern colonies. In a letter dated 30 Aug. 1775, he thanked the society for permission to move but said he was too weak to travel at a time when political conditions were so unsettled and when many men were under arms.

In that letter Earl indicated that he had avoided censure by never introducing "any Topic into the Pulpit except exhortations and prayers for peace, good order and a speedy reconciliation with Great Britain." Although he refused to sever his connection with the Church of England, which he believed to be of divine origin, Earl actively supported the Revolution. He presided at a revolutionary meeting in Edenton on 23 Aug. 1774, and was appointed the following year to a committee to raise funds to promote local industry.

In 1778 Earl resigned as rector of St. Paul's, and his former assistant Charles Pettigrew was elected to succeed him. He spent the remainder of his life at his country home, Bandon, where he taught classical school for boys. He was buried at Bandon.

SEE: Corporation of St. Paul's Parish, The Reverend Robert B. Drane, et al., comps. *The Religious and Historic Commemoration of the Two Hundred Years of St. Paul's Parish, Edenton, N.C.* (1901); John W. Graham, "History of St. Paul's Episcopal Church," *200th Anniversary of the Building of St. Paul's Episcopal Church, Edenton, North Carolina* (1936); Marshall D. Haywood, "Daniel Earl," *The Carolina Churchman* 4 (October 1913); Lawrence F. London, "Clergy of the Episcopal Church in 1785: N.C.," *Historical Magazine of the Protestant Episcopal Church* 20 (1951); Charles F. Pascoe, comp., *Classified Digest of the Records of the Society for the Propagation of the Gospel in Foreign Parts, 1701–1892* (1893); William L. Saunders, ed., *Colonial Records of North Carolina,* vols. 6–10 (1888–90).

GEORGE TROXLER

**Earle, John Baylis** *(23 Oct. 1766–3 Feb. 1836),* drummer boy and militiaman of Revolutionary North Carolina, planter, congressman, and longtime adjutant general of South Carolina, was born probably in Virginia as were his parents, Thomasson Prince and the frontiersman John Earle, who described himself to the Virginia House of Burgesses on 12 June 1770 as "late of the county of Frederick but now of the province of South Carolina." After pioneering settlement just below where the North Pacolet River entered Ninety-Six District (now Spartanburg County), S.C., the father established his growing household a few miles upstream in what became known as the Earle's Fort neighborhood of Rutherford (now Polk) County, N.C. From here he weathered the Revolution as a captain of Rangers, while John Baylis, the eldest son, took up the drum and before the arrival of peace blossomed into a Morgan District militiaman. The father helped site the courthouse for Rutherford County, became a justice of the peace, was named coroner, and by the turn of the century owned fifteen slaves and was called Colonel John Earle.

By 1800, as the second census shows, John Baylis Earle had become head of such a growing family of his own in Pendleton District (now Anderson County), S.C., that he must have married Sarah Taylor, eldest daughter of Major Samuel Taylor, as much as a dozen years before. Silver Glade, the Earle estate, was located near Big Beaverdam Creek, some twelve miles south of Pendleton village. From northwestern South Carolina, about to be traversed by President Jefferson's mail route from Washington to newly acquired New Orleans, Earle was elected as a representative to the Eighth Congress, 1803–5. The master of Silver Glade did a creditable job as congressman, but henceforth concentrated on farming and stock raising, diversified by travel over the state to supervise its militia affairs.

He may well have been the Adjutant General Earle whom Edward Hooker on 10 Dec. 1805 pronounced "an excellent officer," exhibiting "a handsome appearance" in contrast to the ill-kempt troops Hooker saw being directed in parade ground maneuvers. If so, Lieutenant Colonel John Baylis Earle could have been the state's adjutant general in the War of 1812. The excellent South Carolina archives of today have no records of the Adjutant General's Office earlier than 1836, but an act passed by the legislature on 13 Dec. 1815 explicitly upgraded Lieutenant Colonel Earle to brigadier general and expanded his duties to that of adjutant and inspector general.

Owner of thirty-eight slaves in 1830, a believer in states' rights, and conspicuous as a veteran of the Revolution, General Earle took a leading but much overlooked role in the convention that drafted the Nullification Ordinance of 24 Nov. 1832. When the legislature and the governor moved to implement the ordinance, it was Earle's General Orders of 20 and 21 Dec. 1832 that geared the state's emergency defense to individual volunteering rather than to unit mobilization.

Fortunately for all concerned, the immediate tariff issue was compromised. In August 1835 Governor George McDuffie, with Earle present, alluded "in a handsome and feeling manner to the long and faithful services of the Adjutant General of the State, who had assured him, that he had commenced his military career during the Revolutionary War as a drummer boy."

After death ended the general's career, his executors-sons-in-law B. F. Sloan and George Seaborn obtained the legislature's permission in December 1836 for payment of his salary for the quarter in which he died. The general's first wife predeceased him in 1815, leaving at least four sons and five daughters; his marriage to the widow Nancy Ann Douglas resulted in a sixth daughter. He is said to have been buried at Silver Glade.

SEE: Joseph E. Birnie, *The Earles and the Birnies* (1974); *Columbia* (S.C.) *Telescope-Extra*, 21 Dec. 1832; I. N. Earle, *History and Genealogy of the Earles of Secaucus* (1924); B. Elliott and M. Strobel, *The Militia System of South Carolina* (1835); Gertrude S. Hay, Harriet R. Whitaker, et al., comps., *The Roster of Soldiers of North Carolina in the American Revolution* (1932); J. F. Jameson, ed., "Diary of Edward Hooker, 1805–1808," *Ann. Rept. Am. Hist. Assn. for 1896* 1 (1897); *Journal of the People of South Carolina, Assembled at Columbia on the 19th of November, 1832, and again, on the 11th March, 1833* (1833); *Pendleton* (S.C.) *Messenger*, scattered issues through 1837; *Population Schedules*, first five national censuses (microfilm, North Carolina Collection, University of North Carolina, Chapel Hill); U.S. House of Representatives, *Journal*, 8th Cong., 1st and 2nd sess. (1826).

H. B. FANT

**Eastchurch (Esthurt), Thomas** *(d. ca. January 1677/78)*, surveyor general in the North Carolina colony and speaker of the Assembly, was commissioned governor but died without taking office. Described by the Carolina Proprietors as "a gentleman of a very good family," he was related to Thomas Clifford, lord high treasurer of England (1672–73). He may have been related to a Thomas Eastchurch of Devon who in 1628 was graduated from Queen's College, Oxford, but he probably was not that individual.

Eastchurch was in the northern Carolina colony, then called Albemarle, by October 1669, when he was surveyor general. He probably held office at that time by appointment from local officials. In 1671, however, he was appointed to the same position by the Carolina Proprietors, following a period of more than a year in which he had been in Virginia. He returned to Albemarle and assumed the post of surveyor general in December 1671 or soon afterwards.

In the fall of 1675 Eastchurch was speaker of the Albemarle Assembly and leader of the political faction then in control of that body. Aided by his followers, he ousted the acting governor, John Jenkins, and had him imprisoned on charge of "severall misdemeanors." Eastchurch, as speaker, then assumed the powers of governor and exercised them for some months, although he did not assume the title of the office he had usurped. By March 1676 his seizure of the governor's powers was challenged by Jenkins, whose followers had released him from prison by force and held an election in which Jenkins was chosen "Generalissime." For a time Eastchurch and Jenkins headed rival governments, each attempting to control the colony. In late spring or early summer, however, Eastchurch went to London to appeal to the Proprietors for support.

The struggle between Eastchurch and Jenkins had resulted chiefly from failure of the Proprietors to appoint a governor in 1674, when the term of the incumbent, Jenkins, had expired under a provision of the Fundamental Constitutions of Carolina. In the absence of a duly appointed successor, Jenkins had continued to hold office until ousted by Eastchurch. Although each contender advanced legal arguments to justify his actions, the colony in fact was without de jure government, for the Fundamental Constitutions made no provision for such an emergency as had arisen.

The constitutional crisis was exacerbated by factional feuds and personal animosities, which had long plagued Albemarle. For years the colony had been subjected to disorders and irregularities, such as disruption of the proceedings of governmental agencies, verbal and physical assaults on officials, and vindictive lawsuits on trumped up grounds against political leaders. Eastchurch had been involved in the factional feuds before September 1670, when his property was attached through lawsuits that appear to have been politically inspired. At that time Eastchurch was in Virginia, and he did not return to answer the suits against him. He remained in Virginia until some date after 11 Dec. 1671, when he wrote to the Albemarle governor, Peter Carteret, informing Carteret of his recent appointment as surveyor general by the Proprietors.

Eastchurch had aspired to the governorship of Albemarle long before his seizure of its powers in 1675. At least two years earlier he had sought the position through his influential kinsman, Lord Clifford, who approached the Proprietors on Eastchurch's behalf and obtained commitments of support from several. At that time, however, the Proprietors in London expected to relinquish their interests in the Albemarle area to their fellow Proprietor, Sir William Berkeley, then governor of Virginia. Consequently, they did not appoint a governor for the colony when the office became vacant in 1674.

Possibly the commitments some Proprietors had made on his behalf emboldened Eastchurch to seize prematurely the powers he sought. Whatever the source, his confidence was justified. When he appeared before them in 1676, the London Proprietors gave full credence to his account of affairs in Albemarle and granted his request for their support. Despite strong opposition from George Durant, who had gone to London as spokesman for the opposing faction, the Proprietors commissioned Eastchurch governor in November 1676 and appointed a council composed chiefly of his supporters.

Eastchurch did not leave London to assume office as governor until early summer 1677. He was accompanied on the voyage by one of his chief Albemarle supporters, Thomas Miller, who had joined him in London and had received commissions as member of the Council, register (or secretary) for the colony, and customs collector. In the earlier feuds, Miller, even more than Eastchurch, had aroused personal hostility among the colonists. On their way to Albemarle, which lay by the West Indies, Eastchurch and Miller stopped for a time at Nevis. There Eastchurch met a wealthy woman, whose name is not known, and married her. Wishing to extend his stay at Nevis, Eastchurch gave Miller a "commission" as president of the Albemarle Council and sent him to govern the colony until his own arrival. In so doing, Eastchurch overlooked or ignored the fact that he had not qualified as governor in Albemarle and for that reason and others lacked legal authority to appoint an acting governor. Despite the lack of validity of his appointment, Miller assumed the powers of governor on his arrival in Albemarle, using armed force to obtain and hold office. The opposition that he met initially was soon increased by illegal and oppressive measures that he and his council instituted. Plans for his overthrow were well under way by fall.

Meanwhile, Eastchurch pursued his honeymoon in Nevis. Not until December did he reach Virginia en route to Albemarle. By that time, an armed uprising against Miller, later called Culpeper's Rebellion, was in progress. Miller and members of his council had been imprisoned and their chief supporters had fled to Virginia. On hearing the news, Eastchurch decided to remain in Virginia and seek aid from the deputy governor of that colony, Herbert Jeffreys. He sent a proclamation to Albemarle, dated 22 Dec. 1677, ordering the colonists to lay down their arms and release Miller from prison. The Albemarle inhabitants responded by sending armed forces to the northern part of their colony to prevent Eastchurch from entering it. As events developed, armed forces were not needed to keep Eastchurch out of Albemarle. Soon after issuing his proclamation, Eastchurch became ill and died in Virginia.

SEE: Land Grants, III, 329 (Office of the Secretary of State, Raleigh); Mattie Erma E. Parker, "Legal Aspects of 'Culpeper's Rebellion,'" *North Carolina Historical Review* 45 (1968), and ed., *Colonial Records of North Carolina, Higher-Court Records, 1670–1696*, vol. 2 (1968); Herbert R. Paschal, "Proprietary North Carolina: A Study in Colonial Government" (Ph.D. diss., University of North Carolina, 1961); William S. Powell, ed., *Ye Countie of Albemarle in Carolina* (1958); Hugh F. Rankin, *Upheaval in Albemarle: The Story of Culpeper's Rebellion, 1675–1689* (1962); William L. Saunders, ed., *Colonial Records of North Carolina*, vol. 1 (1886).

MATTIE ERMA E. PARKER

**Eaton, John Henry** *(18 June 1790–17 Nov. 1856)*, U.S. senator, member of Andrew Jackson's cabinet, governor of the Territory of Florida, and U.S. minister to Spain, was born in Halifax County near the town of Scotland Neck, the son of John and Elizabeth Eaton. The father was a maker of chaises, coroner of the county, and representative in the Assembly—thus obviously a man of some importance in the community. The 1790 census lists the senior Eaton as holder of twelve slaves, and the manuscript record of the 1810 census reports his ownership of sixteen; in addition, he had acquired a large tract of land in middle Tennessee.

John Henry Eaton attended The University of North Carolina from 1802 to 1804, and, according to university records, was registered for those years as a sophomore and junior. In 1825, he received an honorary M.A. from the university. After he left college Eaton read law, and in 1808 or 1809 moved to Franklin, in Williamson County, Tenn., to take up residence on lands owned by his father. Here he was to meet his future wife, Myra Lewis, daughter of William Terrell Lewis, a prosperous landholder. Myra and her sister were the wards of General Andrew Jackson; thus Eaton's marriage brought not only additional wealth but also opened for him a career in politics. Quite important in his emergence to public notice was a biography of Andrew Jackson, started by John Reid but completed by Eaton. The volume was published in 1816 and, though by no standard can it be classed as good biographical writing, received sufficient publicity to warrant at least three English and two German editions.

In 1818 Eaton was appointed to the U.S. Senate to fill a vacancy caused by the resignation of George W. Campbell; at the end of the term he was elected as a Democrat. Eaton served in the Senate from September 1818 to 9 Mar. 1829, when he resigned to become secretary of war in President Jackson's cabinet. He remained in that position only until June 1831. After Mrs. Eaton's death, he had, on 1 Jan. 1829, married Margaret ("Peggy") O'Neale (or O'Neill) Timberlake, the attractive daughter of a Washington tavern keeper. This second marriage caused a rift in the cabinet, attributed largely to the cabinet wives. In 1833 Eaton sought unsuccessfully to regain his seat in the Senate; the following year Jackson appointed him governor of the Territory of Florida, and in 1836 envoy extraordinary and minister plenipotentiary to Madrid. The latter appointment he held until 1840, during which time Mrs. Eaton enjoyed great social success. Eaton broke with Jackson in 1840, when the former declined to support Van Buren for president.

Eaton lived comfortably in Washington for the remainder of his life. He was not a church member, and perhaps because of this his funeral service was conducted at the Eaton home on I Street. He was buried in Washington's Oak Hill Cemetery. The obituary in Washington's *Daily National Intelligencer* spoke warmly of him, and noted that the chief justice had announced adjournment of the Supreme Court for the afternoon of the eighteenth in order that the justices, members of the bar, and officers of the Court might attend the funeral. Eaton's second wife, who possessed considerable charm, remarried, this time to a young Italian dancing master who subsequently eloped with her granddaughter.

SEE: *Biog. Dir. Am. Cong.* (1961); Walter Clark, ed., *State Records of North Carolina*, vols. 11 (1895), 17 (1899), 20 (1902); *DAB*, vols. 5, 14 (1946); *Nat. Cyc. Am. Biog.*, vols. 5 (1894), 6 (1896); U.S. Bureau of the Census, First Census, 1790, *North Carolina* (1908), and Third Census, 1810, "Population Schedules . . . , 1810, North Carolina," (1957) (microfilm, National Archives); University of North Carolina, Chapel Hill, *Alumni Directory* (1954), and "Student Records and Faculty Reports" (1802–4) (Archives, Library, University of North Carolina); Washington *Daily National Intelligencer*, 18 Nov. 1856.

J. ISAAC COPELAND

**Eaton, John Rust** *(12 Aug. 1772–5 June 1830)*, planter and legislator, was born in Granville County, the only son of Charles Rust Eaton (1743–1822) and his wife Elizabeth, daughter of Osborne Jeffreys. Charles Eaton, the youngest son of William Eaton (d. 1759), a prominent early settler in the area, was a representative from Granville to the Provincial Congress in Halifax (4 Apr. 1776) and served during the Revolutionary War as lieutenant colonel of militia.

There are indications that John Rust Eaton was educated at the University of Pennsylvania, but the records for that institution are incomplete for students who did not graduate. Eaton was a close personal friend of William H. Winder of Baltimore who did attend the university, and Governor Benjamin Williams later corresponded with Eaton about educational facilities in Philadelphia. In 1794 Eaton read law in Richmond, Va., and in May of that year wrote his father that he would be returning home in the fall. In 1799 he was private secretary to William R. Davie, then governor of North Carolina. Entering politics, he represented Granville in the House of Commons in 1801, 1802, and 1812. As a member of the house, he has been described as active but not a leader. Like his father before him, Eaton was interested in racing and breeding horses. The most noted horse from his stable was the stallion Columbus, sired by the well-known Sir Archie.

Eaton's surviving correspondence was given to the North Carolina Historical Society not long after his death and is now in the Southern Historical Collection in Chapel Hill. Among his correspondents prominent in the state were Nathaniel Macon and Governor Benjamin Williams, who had married Eaton's first cousin. He also corresponded with William H. Winder of Maryland and General James Winchester of Tennessee. Winchester handled affairs relating to land Eaton owned on the Obion River in that state. The Eaton letters were edited by J. G. deRoulhac Hamilton and published in 1910.

On 15 Sept. 1801 Eaton married Susan Somerville, the only daughter of John Somerville of Granville County. They had seven sons and four daughters. Eaton's wife survived him by twelve years, dying in 1842 at the age of fifty-nine. They and other members of the family were buried in a private cemetery two miles east of Williamsboro. Of the sons, Charles Rust Eaton represented Granville in the House of Commons during 1835–37; his brother George was a state senator in 1844. John Somerville Eaton, the oldest son, married Sarah Burwell in 1827. When their only son, named John Rust for his grandfather, was killed in a hunting accident in 1841 at the age of thirteen, his parents turned to religion. They were the prime movers behind the establishment of an Episcopal church in the town of Henderson; the parish was named the Holy Innocents as a memorial of young Eaton's death.

SEE: John B. Boddie, *Southside Virginia Families*, vol. 1 (1955); Patrick N. Edgar, *The American Race-Turf Register* (1833); J. G. deR. Hamilton, ed., "John R. Eaton Letters," *James Sprunt Historical Monographs* 9 (1910); Letter, Lawrence F. London to Claudia Hunter (in possession of Claudia Hunter, Henderson, N.C.); Blackwell P. Robinson, *William R. Davie* (1957).

CLAIBORNE T. SMITH, JR.

**Eaton, Thomas** *(ca. 1739–June 1809)*, Revolutionary patriot, was the son of William Eaton (d. 1759) and his wife Mary Rives. He was born probably in North Carolina a short time after his father's removal there from Prince George County, Va. As an adult, Thomas Eaton lived in the county of Bute, which had been formed from the eastern portion of Granville. He represented that county in the Assembly at New Bern in 1769 and again in 1770 through 1771. In the latter year, Governor William Tryon appointed him colonel of the Bute Militia in the War of the Regulation.

Active in the Revolutionary cause from the beginning, Eaton represented Bute in the provincial council of 1775–76. He was also a member of the Council of Safety in 1776, at times serving as president pro tempore; a member of the Second Provincial Congress at New Bern in April 1775; and a member of the Third Provincial Congress held at Hillsborough later that year. In 1776 the Provincial Congress at Halifax appointed him colonel of the Bute regiment. When the congress met again at Halifax in November 1776, Eaton was a delegate. At this congress he was elected to the Council of State, the body that—with Governor Richard Caswell—ruled the state during those trying times. Eaton was reelected a councillor in 1779. After serving with the army in the field for several years, he was once more elected to the Council by the legislature in 1784.

By 1779 the theater of war had shifted to the southern colonies. On 3 March Colonel Eaton was present at the disastrous battle at Brier Creek, Ga.; on 4 November the legislature appointed him brigadier general. On 15 Mar. 1781 he and other officers vainly attempted to stop the flight of the militia at the Battle of Guilford Court House. Griffith McRae, in his biography of James Iredell, reported an anecdote about the wartime experience of General Eaton. He had a very small foot and wore a boot of unusual finish and neatness. In the patriot flight at Brier Creek, these boots were left behind. They eventually fell into the hands of Colonel John Hamilton, the former Halifax resident and Tory leader, who recognized them. Years later, at a dinner at the home of Willie Jones in Halifax, Hamilton produced the boots and passed them to the former owner. Eaton was not amused and threw them across the table at Hamilton's head.

When Bute County was divided into the counties of Franklin and Warren in 1779, the lands of Thomas Eaton, located at Eaton's Ferry on the Roanoke, fell into the eastern part of the latter county. A man of wealth, he was one of the largest slaveholders in the state at the time of the 1790 census. His will, dated 30 Apr. 1807, was probated in Warrenton at the August court of 1809. Eaton's place of burial is not known.

Eaton was married three times. About 1761 he wed Anna Bland, the daughter of Theodorick Bland of Cawsons, Prince George County, Va. Her sister Frances was successively the wife of John Randolph and St. George Tucker, and by her first husband she was the mother of John Randolph of Roanoke. Eaton and Anna Bland were the parents of one child, Anna, born in 1763, who married Guilford Dudley of Halifax County, Va., and Tennessee. Their son, Theodorick Bland Dudley, was reared by his famous relative, John Randolph, and later published the latter's letters to him under the title *Letters to a Young Relative*. After the death of Anna, Eaton in 1781 married Anne Stith, daughter of Buckner Stith of Brunswick County, Va. They had two sons, Thomas Buckner, who died young, and William, and a daughter, Harriet Bolling, who married Grandison Field of Virginia. William Eaton married Seignora, daughter of Nathaniel Macon; their son, also William, was the noted Warrenton lawyer and statesman. Eaton's third wife was Elizabeth Jones, daughter of John and Priscilla Weldon Jones. John Jones was first cousin to the brothers Allen and Willie Jones.

SEE: John B. Boddie, *Southside Virginia Families*, vol. 1 (1955), and *Virginia Historical Genealogies* (1954); Bute-Warren County wills (North Carolina State Archives, Raleigh); Stuart H. Hill, "Eaton Family" (North Carolina Collection, University of North Carolina, Chapel Hill); Northampton County wills, deeds, and estate records (North Carolina State Archives, Raleigh).

CLAIBORNE T. SMITH, JR.

**Eaton, William, Jr.** *(18 Aug. 1809–29 June 1881)*, attorney and legislator, was born at Eaton's Ferry on the Roanoke River in Warren County, the son of William Eaton and his wife Seignora Donald Macon. He was the grandson of both General Thomas Eaton and Nathaniel Macon and half-brother of Ella Reeves Eaton, later the wife of Peter Hansborough Bell. He was referred to by his contemporaries as William Eaton, Jr., to distinguish him from his father who lived to a great age, dying in 1869. Young Eaton was graduated from The University of North Carolina in 1829. He read law under Judge John Hall in Warrenton, then began to practice in that community the following year. Entering politics, he represented Warren County in the House of Commons from 1838 to 1841 and again in the sessions of 1850, 1854, and 1856. He was elected attorney general of North Carolina for the term 1851–52.

A conservative Democrat, Eaton was against secession but supported the southern cause during the Civil War. With the return of peace, President Andrew Johnson, in May 1865, summoned several prominent North Carolinians, among them William Eaton, to a conference in Washington to present his plan for the reconstruction of his native state. D. L. Swain, B. F. Moore, and Eaton objected to the plan on constitutional grounds—particularly with regard to the appointment of a provisional governor by the president—and left the meeting without taking part in the proceedings. As his last public service, Eaton represented Warren County at the constitutional convention of 1865–66. In the famous lawsuit contesting the will of James C. Johnston, Eaton was attorney for the defense and received substantial credit for the favorable outcome of the case. Always interested in his alma mater, The University of North Carolina, he served as trustee from 1838 to 1868. He died at his home in Warrenton and was buried in Fairview Cemetery.

Considered an authority on the law, Eaton wrote *A Book of Practical Forms, with Explanatory Notes and References to Authorities*, intended as a manual for the practicing lawyer in North Carolina. It was first published in Philadelphia in 1854 and highly respected at the time. A revised edition was printed in Baltimore in 1867. In 1860 Eaton wrote a memoir of his legal mentor, Judge John Hall, which was printed in the *University Magazine*. He also was the author of a sketch of George E. Badger, published posthumously in 1886. His kinsman and law student, Peter Mitchell Wilson, described Eaton as the best jury lawyer in the courts of his day and a fine flower of the old aristocratic tradition.

In 1832 Eaton married Rosa Gilmour, the daughter of William Gilmour of Petersburg, Va., and his wife Mary Parsons. They were the parents of three daughters, of whom Rosa died young. Laura married William T. Alston and Susan married Samuel Peter Arrington. There were no children by either marriage.

SEE: John L. Cheney, Jr., ed., *North Carolina Government, 1585–1974* (1975); J. G. deR. Hamilton, *Reconstruction in North Carolina* (1914); Lizzie W. Montgomery, *Sketches of Old Warrenton* (1929); Raleigh *News and Observer*, 1 July 1881; Peter M. Wilson, *Southern Exposure* (1927).

CLAIBORNE T. SMITH, JR.

**Eaton, William Clement** *(23 Feb. 1898–12 Aug. 1980)*, historian, was born in Winston, the son of Benjamin and Mary Gaston Hough Eaton. His father, born in Davie County in 1859 and educated at The University of North Carolina, was a prominent citizen of Winston and served as its mayor from 1900 to around 1914. His mother was a native of Lancaster, S.C. Eaton was one of eight children. Charles Eaton, the poet, is his brother.

At the age of fifteen, Eaton entered The University of North Carolina where he majored in English, was a member of the Golden Fleece, and was elected to Phi Beta Kappa, of which he was president. At the university he counted among his friends Thomas Wolfe, Paul Green, Luther Hodges, and Albert Coates. He received an A.B. degree in 1919, and in the following year was awarded an A.M. in history. In 1920 he entered Harvard University to continue graduate work in history and in 1929 received the Ph.D. While at Harvard he was awarded the Edwin Austin Fellowship and the Sheldon Travelling Fellowship, the latter enabling him to study at Cambridge University. In 1923–24 he was an assistant professor of American history at Whitman College in Walla Walla, Wash.

For the academic year 1929–30 Eaton was assistant professor at Clark University. Moving to Lafayette College as associate professor in 1930, he was promoted to professor in 1933 and became head of the history department, a position he held until 1946. In that year he went to the University of Kentucky as professor of history. There he was named Distinguished Professor in 1956 and Hallam Professor in 1961. He retired in 1970.

Eaton was Pitt Professor of American history at Cambridge University in 1968–69. He taught in summer sessions at City College, N.Y. (1940 and 1941), The University of North Carolina (1946), Princeton University (1948), and Columbia University (1951). He also served as visiting professor at the University of Wisconsin (1949), the University of South Carolina (1970), and Old Dominion University (1972–73). He was a Fulbright professor at the University of Manchester in 1951–52, the University of Innsbruck in 1957–58, and the Johns Hopkins Center at Bologna in 1964–65. He was a Guggenheim Fellow in 1945–46, and was awarded a Huntington Library research grant for 1955–56. He held honorary degrees from Wake Forest University, Cambridge University, and the University of Kentucky. In 1976 he was the recipient of a Distinguished Alumnus award from The University of North Carolina at Chapel Hill.

An authority on the history of the South and an acknowledged leader in his field, Eaton produced a number of major works, beginning with *Freedom of Thought in the Old South* (1940). This book, published by the Duke University Press, received the Press's Centennial Award in 1939. It was followed by *A History of the Old South* (1949), *A History of the Southern Confederacy* (1954), *Henry Clay and the Art of American Politics* (1957), *The Growth of Southern Civilization* (1961), *The Mind of the Old South* (1964), and *The Waning of the Old South Civilization, 1860–1880* (1969). *The Leaven of Democracy* (1963), which he edited, is an anthology of sources with an essay on Jacksonian democracy. *The Civilization of the Old South* (1968) edited by Albert Kirwan, is a selection from Eaton's major works and contains a useful introduction by the editor. Eaton also wrote a number of articles appearing in leading historical journals, and contributed to the *Dictionary of American History* (1976–78) and *The Encyclopedia of Southern History* (1978).

His writings have been praised for their comprehensiveness, objectivity, and judicious evaluation. But not all of his works met with unqualified praise. Fletcher Green, for instance, in reviewing *The Mind of the Old South*, wrote, "This is an excellent study, well worth reading, but it has one major weakness: each chapter stands alone, and the book lacks unity."

One scholar has described Eaton as a true gentleman and a great historian who wrote with a sure hand for interpretation. He was chosen as one of twenty-eight outstanding American historians to be interviewed for the Columbia Oral History Collection, which holds the record of that interview. The transcript of the interview is in the Columbia University Library's manuscript collection. The University of Kentucky Library has two major segments of Eaton's manuscripts.

Eaton was a Democrat and a liberal. As president of the Southern Historical Association in 1961, he led the fight to ensure that black members of the association would receive accommodations equal to those of white members. The biographical information in *Who's Who in America* concludes with his statement: "My goal of self-development is to realize the ideal of Renaissance Man in an American Culture."

He and his wife, the former Mary Elizabeth Allis, were the parents of three children: Allis (Mrs. Henry Bennett), William Clement, Jr., and Clifton Packer.

SEE: *Contemporary Authors*, 1st rev., vols. 1–4 (1962–63); *Directory of American Scholars* (1978); Fletcher Green, rev. of *The Mind of the Old South*, in *American Historical Review* 70 (1965); Albert D. Kirwan, "Introduction," *The Civilization of the Old South* (1968); *Lexington* (Ky.) *Herald*, 13 Aug. 1980; Elizabeth B. Mason and Louis M. Starr, eds., *Oral History Collection of Columbia University* (1979); *National Union Catalog of Manuscripts* (1975); *North Carolina Biography*, vol. 2 (1928); Obituary, "William Clement Eaton," *Journal of Southern History* 46 (1980); *Prominent People of North Carolina* (1906); *Who's Who in America*, 1978–79.

LOUISE MCG. HALL

**Eberhardt, Johann Ludwig** *(17 May 1758–10 Apr. 1839)*, clockmaker, the son of Johann Gottfried Eberhardt, was born in Stadtilm, Thuringia (southeast Germany). Raised in a devout Lutheran family, he was educated in a Lutheran school and confirmed by and admitted to the Lutheran church. His career as a clockmaker began at the age of fourteen when he was taught in his father's shop. In 1783 he moved to the Moravian town of Gnadau, working as the community clockmaker and locksmith. After living in several other places, including Zeist, he moved to Gnadenfeld in Silesia, where he served as master of the Single Brothers' clockmaking shop.

In November 1799 Eberhardt migrated to Salem, N.C., at the request of the Moravians there. His excessive pride, impatience with the public, and especially his frequent drunkenness caused conflicts, however, and the authorities excluded him from the Communion on several occasions. Nevertheless, he was a talented and industrious craftsman, undertaking some impressive projects while in Salem. In 1801, he added a minute hand to Salem's town clock and moved it to the gable of Home Church. Five years later he altered the clock so that it would strike the first, second, and third quarter hours. In 1805, he made a musical clock for a Quaker in Randolph County. The organ placed in its base could play one of several tunes on the hour, and it could be adjusted to repeat the songs from three to six times so that entire hymns could be sung. Eberhardt crafted many movements for tall case clocks, over thirty of which survive. He also repaired watches and clocks; in 1806 he reconditioned the Hillsborough town clock at the request of Duncan Cameron, a lawyer there. His craftsmanship was not limited to the field of horology, for he made some jewelry, silverware, and other metal objects, including five chandeliers for Home Church. He performed his work first at the Single Brothers House, then at the Christoph Vogler Shop, and finally at his house on Salt Street where he moved in 1814.

Throughout his life Eberhardt was plagued with financial difficulties. In 1835, the Congregation Diacony considered securing his house and unsold clocks to help defray his debts, but no action was taken. The next year, his salaries for caring for the town clock and ringing the noon bell were raised in an effort to help him financially. Lewis Ferdinand Eberhardt assisted his father in March 1837 by buying his house and assuming his debts, though he allowed Eberhardt to live in the house until his death.

Eberhardt married Julianna Michel on 2 June 1800. They had four children: Carolina, Lewis Ferdinand, Christian Thomas, and Carl Theodore. Eberhardt died in Salem and was buried in the Salem Moravian Graveyard.

SEE: Frank P. Albright, *Johann Ludwig Eberhardt and His Salem Clocks* (1978); Adelaide L. Fries and Minnie J. Smith, eds., *Records of the Moravians*, vols. 6–9 (1943–64).

MAURY YORK

**Eddleman (Adleman, Ettleman), Peter** *(1762–19 May 1847)*, cabinetmaker, was born probably in Rowan County of German parentage. His father, Bastian Eddleman, moved to Bucks County, Pa., from Germany in 1750; with his wife, Sarah Pratt, he moved to Rowan County in 1758 or 1759. Rowan County militia records show that Peter Eddleman joined the militia in 1777 as a substitute for his brother-in-law who had been drafted. Eddleman was a substitute in two other tours—one in 1780 at Camden, S.C., and another in 1781. During the latter tour he was in Wilmington when the news of the surrender of Cornwallis arrived. Subsequently he was discharged and returned home. For his military service he filed for and received a pension in 1831 of $31.66 per annum.

A grant to Bastian Eddleman in 1787 is the first indication that the family had moved to Lincoln County (now northeast Gaston). The Lincoln County census lists Peter Eddleman as head of a household in 1790 and his land transactions on Leeper Creek are recorded in 1791, 1802, 1817, 1818, and 1832. In 1825 he built a house on part of the land and in 1832 made a large purchase of 240 acres in the same vicinity of Leeper and Dutchman's creeks. In a tax listing of 1837 it is recorded that he owned the 240 acres but no slaves. Perhaps his land purchases were for the acquisition of timber, as farming such acreage would have required additional hands.

Eddleman's early training is unknown. The general heaviness of pieces attributed to him would indicate either his being apprenticed to a country cabinetmaker or possibly self-taught. In the diary of John Arends, a minister, there are a number of references to the Eddleman family and a specific reference of payment to Peter in 1781. The payment reference follows a list of building materials. Family tradition indicates that Peter Eddleman built furniture for the Thomas Rhyne family of Lincoln County in 1799, and that he lived in their home while constructing it. A cupboard ten feet high and six feet wide, which remains in the house today, is believed to be his work. Three additional pieces presently in North Carolina collections are attributed to Eddleman—two desks and bookcases and a corner cupboard. These pieces are similar in construction techniques, particularly in the way the drawers are paneled on all four sides rather than the usual three. Eddleman had at least one apprentice—John Henry White of Lincoln County, apprenticed in 1821.

Eddleman remained a bachelor until 1830. At age sixty-eight he married Dicia Swanson Clippard, a young widow with three small children. He and his wife had two sons, David Franklin (b. 1831) and William Peter (b. 1833). Eddleman was buried in Whitehaven (Lutheran) Churchyard near North Carolina Highway 16.

SEE: Research files (Museum of Early Southern Decorative Arts, Winston-Salem), with information drawn largely from public records of Rowan and Lincoln counties.

WHALEY W. BATSON

**Eden, Charles** *(1673–26 Mar. 1722)*, governor of North Carolina under the Lords Proprietors, was born in England of the family of West Auckland, County Durham, which later produced a governor of Maryland, Sir Robert Eden. He received his appointment as governor from Queen Anne in 1713 to succeed Edward Hyde and was sworn in before the North Carolina Provincial Council "holden at ye house of Capt. John Hecklefield in Little River" on 28 May 1714. He had been given a thousand acres of land by the Lords Proprietors. The location of this property is not known, but it may have been in Beaufort County, as he lived for a while in Bath—traditionally on the west bank of Bath Creek, near its mouth. He later sold his property, Thistleworth, to John Lovick, secretary of the Council, and in 1719 moved across the Chowan River to what was soon to become Bertie County where his plantation, Eden House, was his home until his death. He was made a landgrave of the order of Carolina nobility as provided for by the Fundamental Constitutions of the colony. He was the last person to hold this title.

A staunch member of the Church of England, Eden was made a vestryman of St. Paul's Parish soon after his arrival in the colony. He was solicitous for the welfare of the church and the spread of its work in the colony, corresponding often with the Society for the Propagation of the Gospel in London on church matters. With Governor Alexander Spotswood of Virginia he appointed a commission to settle the long-standing boundary dispute between the two colonies, but no agreement was reached during his administration. Early in 1715 Eden sent North Carolina forces to aid South Carolina in its war with the Yemassee Indians. This was a quid pro quo for South Carolina's vital military assistance four years before, when the Tuscaroras threatened the existence of North Carolina settlements.

Eden's administration is remembered best for the activities of pirates—notably Stede Bonnet and Edward Teach ("Blackbeard")—in North Carolina waters, and for the purported connivance of colonial officials with these desperadoes. Tobias Knight, secretary of the governor's council, was implicated when a letter written by him to Teach was found on the pirate's body at his death, and also by the fact that a cargo taken from a captured ship was stored by Teach in Knight's barn. In Knight's letter, mention of the governor's desire to see and talk with Teach was deemed grounds for suspicion of Eden's collusion with the pirates, but no further proof was found. Knight was acquitted by the council of the formal charges brought against him. However, North Carolina authorities were far too slow in taking steps to stop the pirate's depredations. Virginia and South Carolina had complained for some time about their shipping losses. Finally, Governor Robert Johnson of South Carolina sent an expedition to the Cape Fear River, where Stede Bonnet was apprehended, taken to Charleston, and hanged. Shortly thereafter, Governor Spotswood of Virginia sent two sloops in pursuit of Teach. Near Ocracoke Inlet he was overcome and slain on 22 Nov. 1718, thus ending the "Golden Age of Piracy" in Carolina waters.

Eden married Mrs. Penelope Golland of Mount Golland (later known as Mount Gould) on the Chowan River. He had no children of his own; Mrs. Eden had a daughter, Penelope, by her former marriage. This young lady was married four times, first to William Maule, next to John Lovick, then to George Phenney, and last to Governor Gabriel Johnston. Eden left his stepdaughter no provision in his will, probably because of a dispute in 1720 with young Penelope's then husband, William Maule, surveyor general of the colony, over fees that the governor thought were due him. Eden's chief beneficiary was his friend John Lovick, secretary of the colony. By an interesting stroke of fate, Lovick's subsequent marriage to young Penelope (then the widow Maule) made her the owner of Eden House plantation. Four generations of Penelopes, mother to daughter, lived at Eden House before it finally burned.

Eden was buried on his plantation. In 1889 his remains and those of his wife, with their gravestones, were moved to St. Paul's Churchyard, Edenton. The town of Edenton, formerly known as "the Town on Queen Anne's Creek," was renamed in the governor's honor shortly after his death. His epitaph states that he "governed the province eight years to ye greatest satisfaction of ye Lords Proprietors and ye ease and happyness of ye people. He brought ye country into a flourishing Condition and died much lamented."

SEE: Sir John Burke, *Genealogical and Heraldic History of the Peerage . . . of the British Empire* (1858); J. Bryan Grimes, ed., *North Carolina Wills and Inventories* (1912); J. R. B. Hathaway, ed., *North Carolina Historical and Genealogical Register*, 3 vols. (1900–1903); Hayes Collection (Southern Historical Collection, University of North Carolina, Chapel Hill); Hugh T. Lefler and Albert R. Newsome, *North Carolina: The History of a Southern State* (1973); Records of St. Paul's Parish (Edenton, N.C.); Charles W. Reed, *Beaufort County* (1962); William L. Saunders, ed., *Colonial Records of North Carolina*, vol. 2 (1886).

JAQUELIN DRANE NASH

**Edens, Arthur Hollis** *(14 Feb. 1901–7 Aug. 1968)*, educator and foundation executive, was born in Willow Grove, Tenn., the son of Everett C., a Methodist minister, and Barbara Ellen Jolly Edens. His education began in the public schools of Clay County, Tenn., in which he later taught. He attended the Cumberland Mountain School, Crossville, Tenn. (1921–24), earned two degrees at Emory University (B.Ph., 1930, and M.A., 1938), and studied at the University of Chicago (1941). From Harvard University he received a master's degree (1944) and a doctorate (1949)—both in public administration.

Edens's rise in the educational world was rapid: at the Cumberland Mountain School he was successively teacher (1926–27), assistant principal (1929–30), and principal (1930–37). He was associate dean of the Emory Junior College, Valdosta, Ga. (1937–42), then associate dean of the Emory undergraduate college in Atlanta (1942–44), where he became associate professor of political science (1944–47) and dean of administration (1946). In 1947 he was appointed vice-chancellor of the University System of Georgia, in 1948 associate director of the General Education Board of the Rockefeller Foundation, and in 1949 president of Duke University.

Edens became president of Duke in a time of transition when its chief builders had passed, or were passing, from the scene. Comfortable with the aims and traditions of the university, he felt that the policy of the new administration should be "one of development, not expansion," and that the existing interests of the comparatively small university should be strengthened rather than diversified. The first tasks were to provide for increased enrollments, better faculty salaries, and further development of the graduate program. Always the faculty should be "free to teach and its students to learn without intimidation or fear."

Immediate attention was given to a fund raising campaign. To the success of a revitalized Loyalty Fund was added a large matching gift from the General Education Board and a smaller one from the Carnegie Foundation. In the next five years the university invested over $6,000,000 in new construction and repairs, including a new wing of the hospital and the men's Graduate Center, which opened in the fall of 1953. In 1952 the Duke Endowment established James B. Duke professorships to reward the more distinguished scholars on the faculty. The Duke Endowment also provided $750,000 for fellowships in the Graduate School. The U.S. Public Health Service awarded Duke $1,500,000 to establish a regional center for the study of aging. In addition a Rule of Law Center was created for the study of international affairs, and the Commonwealth Center, with special attention to Canadian affairs, was established through a gift from the Carnegie Corporation.

Early in Edens's tenure he appointed Dr. Paul M. Gross, professor of chemistry and dean of the Graduate School, to be vice-president in the educational division and dean of the university. Edens, whose educational background was in the social sciences, thought it would be helpful to have a natural scientist in close association with the administration. Eventually, however, there came to be differences of opinion between the president and the dean on the best ways to promote the welfare of the university. Gross complained that the administration devoted "entirely too much time to matters of purely budgetary assignment and detail," that the need was for long-range planning and policy discussions on which the future of the university would depend. He expressed the hope that the resources of the university could be expanded until Duke was among the first ten in the nation. In his report to the trustees for 1957–58, Edens noted that a Long Range Planning Committee had been set up with Vice-President Gross, who had been relieved of his duties as dean, as chairman. The first report of the committee set as goals higher salaries, building projects, the strengthening of existing areas of the university, and the establishment of an Office of Development. Edens in his report to the trustees said, "I hope I have conveyed my own enthusiasm for the prospects ahead."

Early in 1960 rumors began to circulate in the local press that there was trouble between Edens and Gross, caused by the president's opposition to some of the features of the long range plan, which he considered too expansive and too extravagant; that there had been a proposal to make Edens chancellor, without any executive duties; and that there was to be an administrative reorganization. This news seemed to reflect the Gross view. Edens said nothing at all. He made no attempt to rally his friends, for he had resolved to resign. Although the administration of the university was in the hands of the trustees, the principal funds were controlled by the endowment trustees who were reported to be in sympathy with Gross. On 16 Feb. 1960 Edens informed the university trustees by letter that he expected to resign at the next meeting of the board, the resignation to take effect when his successor was elected. He said that the next ten years in the life of the university were "going to demand vigorous promotion and management on the part of an administrative leader who could be expected to remain at the helm" over a longer period of time than he would wish for himself. When the trustees met on 23 Mar. 1960, they accepted Edens's resignation "with reluctance." They also "demanded" that Gross resign as vice-president and as chairman of the Long Range Planning Committee. He was to remain on the faculty as William H. Pegram Professor of Chemistry, however.

Edens continued as president until 30 June 1960; his successor, Dr. Deryl Hart of the Duke medical faculty, took office 1 July 1960. The chairman of the board of trustees authorized the university to retain Edens as a consultant for ten years at a salary of $18,000 a year. With some reluctance he accepted; he understood that the funds did not come from the resources of the university itself. After an extended vacation with his family, Edens was retained by the directors of the Mary Reynolds Babcock Foundation as its first executive director. This appointment extended from 14 Aug. 1961 to 31 Aug. 1966, when he retired. In his first year the grants totaled about $1,500,000, in his last year nearly $6,000,000. The grants went to charitable enterprises and generally were related to educational programs or social institutions and not restricted geographically within the United States.

After retirement Edens moved to Decatur, Ga. From his summer home near West Jefferson, N.C., he made his last journey to the Emory Hospital where he died of cancer. He was buried in the Decatur Cemetery.

Edens received honorary degrees from Emory University, Davidson College, The University of North Carolina, Wake Forest College, Roanoke College, American University, Northwestern University, and the University of Chattanooga. He was a member of numerous boards and commissions having to do with educational affairs. He was president of the National Association of Schools and Colleges of the Methodist Church (1954), president of the National Commission on Accrediting (1954–56), and a member of the President's Commission on Education beyond the High School (1956–57). He also served two terms on the executive committee of the Southern Association of Colleges and Secondary Schools. In 1964 he became a member of the Emory board of trustees. He was a member of Phi Beta Kappa, Omicron Delta Kappa, and Sigma Chi. He was a Democrat, Methodist, Mason, and Rotarian.

At Emory Edens was an outstanding intermural football player, and his golf was above average. In making his way in the world from the mountains of East Tennessee to a university presidency he had been a lumberjack, boss of a road gang, laborer in an Akron rubber plant, night watchman, rural mail carrier, and volunteer preacher serving seven rural churches.

On 29 Dec. 1930 Edens married Mary Kathleen Bussell of Livingston, Tenn. They had one child, Mary Ann, who became the wife of Jefferson L. Wingfield, Jr.

SEE: *Atlanta Constitution*, 8 Aug. 1968; William L. Bondurant, Mary Reynolds Babcock Foundation, Winston-Salem, personal information; *Duke Alumni Register*, vols. 35–46 (1949–60); *Duke Chronicle*, 10 Feb. 1960; *Durham*

*Morning Herald*, scattered issues, February–March 1960, 8 Aug. 1968; Edens Papers and Minutes of the Board of Trustees (Manuscript Department, Library, Duke University, Durham); Raleigh *News and Observer*, 21 Jan. 1951; Report of the President, *Bulletin of Duke University*, vols. 20–33 (1949–60); *Who's Who in America*, 1968–69.

ROBERT H. WOODY

**Edgar, Patrick Nisbett** *(ca. 1770–ca. 1858)*, the first man to publish a stud book of American racehorses, was born in Dublin, Ireland, the son of Patrick Edgar. Although his name does not appear in the published list of alumni of Trinity College, Dublin, he is said to have been educated at the University of Dublin. His ungovernable temper led him, in rage, to murder his father's gardener, according to one report; he fled Ireland and made his way to America where he was employed by wealthy planters as tutor to their children. He was considered eccentric and such names as "Sir Patrick" and "Edie Ochiltree," after the character in Sir Walter Scott's novel, *The Antiquary*, came to be applied to him. Nevertheless he was respected and soon came to be recognized as an authority on blood horses and blood lines. This knowledge and his scholarship attracted the attention of Captain James J. Harrison of Diamond Grove, Brunswick County, Va., "Father of the American Turf," who selected Edgar to take over the gathering of data that led to the manuscript for *The American Race-Turf Register* by Patrick Nisbett Edgar, identified on the title page as "from Granville County, North Carolina." It was printed in 1833 in New York by Henry Mason for "Patrick N. Edgar & Co." The dedication is to Captain Harrison and signed by Edgar from Williamsboro (now Vance County). A second volume was anticipated and mentioned on the title page but was never published for lack of funds. Others offered to take over Edgar's material for publication but he refused; he was reported to have sent it to Ireland for safekeeping although it has never been found.

According to the 1850 census of Granville County, Edgar was eighty years old and living in the household of twenty-five-year-old James Currin and his wife and children, in that part of the county known as Abraham's Plains. His love of horses and riding contributed to his death from exposure after he was caught in a snowstorm riding near the plantation of one Jigget in the vicinity of St. Tammany Ferry on Roanoke River. He was buried in the family cemetery there.

Edgar's *The American Race-Turf Register* has been described as "a literary monument" and the compiler as "a personality." His book has been widely cited and is regarded as accurate and reliable but there are omissions. He has been suspected of leaving out horses belonging to men with whom he was not on good terms. The noted stallion, Sir Archie, for example, was omitted.

Apparently Edgar never married. In those census reports in which his name appears, he is always listed alone.

SEE: Elizabeth A. C. Blanchard and Manly Wade Wellman, *The Life and Times of Sir Archie* (1958); Fairfax Harrison, "The Equine F. F. V.'s," *Virginia Magazine of History and Biography* 35 (1927); John Hervey, *Racing in America, 1665–1865* (1944).

JANE WILSON

**Edgeworth, Richard** *(1764–19 Aug. 1796)*, mechanical engineer and planter, was born in Oxfordshire, England, at Black Bourton, the ancestral estate of his Hungerford grandmother. He was the oldest son of Richard Lovell Edgeworth (1744–1817) and Anna Maria Elers. His father, whose living was derived from a family estate in Edgeworthstown, Ireland, was interested in science and mechanical inventions. An admirer of the educational theories of Rousseau, Edgeworth gave his son Richard a practical rather than a classical education, one designed to make him independent and self-sufficient. In 1771 he took him to France, where the seven-year-old boy met the French philosopher. In Lyons the elder Edgeworth became involved in the engineering feat of diverting the Rhone River. Richard soon spoke French better than his English tutor, and Edgeworth became aware that his son's education was making him alarmingly independent. While in France, Richard was placed in a Jesuit school; later, in 1776, he was sent to the Charter House in London. While not a remarkable student, Richard shared his father's interests in mechanics. In 1778, at the age of thirteen, he was awarded a silver medal for "Early Mechanic Genius" by the Society for the Encouragement of Arts and Manufactures. Finally, father and son decided that a naval career might best suit Richard's temperament, and he joined the British Navy, with the encouragement of his cousin Edward Pakenham, Lord Longford, who was later killed at the Battle of New Orleans.

By 1781 Edgeworth was a midshipman on the *Monmouth*, which had seen service in the American Revolution. While aboard the *Monmouth* he participated in battles against the French off the Coromandel Coast of India, at Madras, and off Ceylon, the ship suffering heavy damages and loss of life. On 10 Feb. 1783 Edgeworth, not yet nineteen, jumped ship at Goa, thereby forfeiting his naval career as well as exhausting his father's patience. He was "lost" to his family for several years.

Edgeworth appeared in the Pee Dee area on the North Carolina-South Carolina border, having come down from Virginia, in 1786 or 1787. He became a tutor in the home of Claudius Pegues, a planter, and some time later in the homes of several gentlemen in Georgetown, S.C. In May 1788 he was married in Richmond County by John Speed, J.P., to Elizabeth Knight, daughter of a hatter. By her he had three sons, Nathaniel Lovell (1789), Achilles Sneyd (1791), and Richard (1795). Edgeworth purchased land in Anson County on the Pee Dee River, where he projected establishing a town. Having effected a reconciliation with his father, he returned to visit his family in England in 1792 and 1795. He stayed some time at a property named Ashton Bower, near Clifton, rented by two maiden stepaunts, the Misses Mary and Charlotte Sneyd. Furnished with monies and credit from his father, he bought more land in Anson and named his plantation Ashton. In projecting a town on the Pee Dee, he doubtless had his father's work at Lyons in mind. If he could make the river navigable from Georgetown, S.C., to Anson County, a town at the head of navigation should prosper. He would name the town Sneydsboro after his two stepaunts who listened so sympathetically to his plans. But Edgeworth returned from his last trip to England a very ill man, and, owing to a flood of the Pee Dee and an epidemic of equine distemper, he suffered financial reverses. He was forced to sell Ashton to pay his debts. On 7 Mar. 1796 he sold it to William Johnson with the understanding that, if a town were established on the property, it should be named Sneydsboro.

Five months later Edgeworth died in Anson; his place of burial is unknown. His will, written 23 Nov. 1792 and proved in the January Anson court 16 Jan. 1797, was subject to much misinterpretation by his descendants. The property he left his two youngest sons had been sold to pay his debts. The European property left to his oldest son was not the Edgeworthstown estate still in the possession of his father but three small properties left to him by his grandfather. Richard Lovell Edgeworth and his daughter Maria, soon to become celebrated as an author of educational treatises and popular novels, endeavored to aid the widow of Richard and his three young sons. Owing to the difficulties of communication and the legalities of disposing of the three small Irish properties, years elapsed before any substantial assistance could be made. Nathaniel Edgeworth migrated to Alabama and left descendants there and in Mississippi; Achilles moved to Fort Valley, Ga., and left descendants there and in Texas; Richard, the youngest, lived in Chesterfield County, S.C., and left descendants there, as well as in North Carolina and Virginia.

On 3 Apr. 1902 an almost wholly fictitious account of the life of Richard Edgeworth and his family appeared in the Wadesboro *Messenger and Intelligencer*. Unfortunately this article became the basis of fabrications by other journalists so that the early history of Sneedsboro, the town that came into being after Edgeworth's death, is largely apocryphal. These fictions appeared most recently in *A History of Anson County* (1977). The correspondence of Maria Edgeworth with Rachel Mordecai Lazarus perhaps gave currency to the myth that Maria and her father had established schools in North Carolina. The Mordecai School in Warrenton incorporated the educational principles advocated by the Edgeworths, and later a school in Greensboro was named the Edgeworth Female Seminary, but Richard Edgeworth was the only member of that family to come to these shores.

SEE: Harriet Jessie Butler and Harold Edgeworth Butler, *The Black Book of Edgeworthstown and Other Edgeworth Memories, 1585–1817* (1927); Desmond Clarke, *The Ingenious Mr. Edgeworth* (1965); Edgar E. MacDonald, *The American Edgeworths* (1970); *Memoirs of Richard Lovell Edgeworth, Esq., Begun by Himself and Concluded by His Daughter* (1820).

EDGAR E. MACDONALD

**Edmondston, Catherine Ann Devereux** *(10 Oct. 1823–3 Jan. 1875)*, diarist and member of the planter aristocracy of Halifax County, was one of six daughters of Thomas Pollock (17 Nov. 1793–7 Mar. 1869) and Catherine Ann Bayard Johnson Devereux (1796–18 July 1836). Her sisters included Frances Ann (Mrs. Henry W. Miller), Honoria (Mrs. Robert Cannon), Sophia Chester (Mrs. Josiah Turner, Jr.), Mary Bayard (Mrs. William J. Clarke), Elizabeth (Mrs. Thomas F. Jones), and Susan Devereux, a half sister through her father's second marriage. Her only brother was John Devereux, chief quartermaster of North Carolina during the Civil War and a planter in Bertie County.

Catherine Ann ("Kate") Devereux was an educated woman of strong character whose intelligence and prejudices surfaced repeatedly in her letters and Civil War diaries. Raised at Conneconara, her father's major plantation in Halifax County, she and her sisters were thoroughly tutored in literature, mathematics, science, and philosophy. Catherine also attended Belmont, a school near Leesburg, Va., where she finished her formal education. On 19 Feb. 1846 she married Patrick Mair Edmondston (1 Aug. 1819–19 Aug. 1871), a younger son of Charles and Mary Pratt Edmondston of Charleston, S.C. Charles Edmondston, a wealthy merchant and planter, had formed business contacts with the Devereuxs as early as 1819 through his shipping firm. This, presumably, led to the initial meeting and subsequent marriage of Patrick and Catherine.

Patrick Edmondston evinced a lifelong interest in "scientific farming" and eventually served on the executive committee and as vice-president of the Scotland Neck Agricultural Society in the late 1860s. Shortly after their marriage, however, the Edmondstons moved to Charleston where Patrick served for a time as an "aid to the governor" of South Carolina. They stayed there until 1848 when Catherine's dislike of city life, her poor health, and her father's inducement of a plantation of their own in North Carolina led them to settle permanently in Halifax County. Initially, they apparently rented from Thomas P. Devereux part of the extensive estate Devereux inherited from his mother, called Barrows, but financial reverses forced them to seek other arrangements. Devereux then offered them the Looking Glass plantation, which adjoined Conneconara, plus another tract of land that the Edmondstons called Hascosea, in final execution of a $10,000 marriage settlement he had promised them but only partially paid. These two pieces of property formed the nucleus of the Edmondstons' home life and figured prominently in Catherine's diaries.

During the 1850s the Edmondstons, who remained childless, enjoyed a calm, fairly prosperous life although crop losses caused by the frequent flooding of the Roanoke River forced them to economize occasionally. Patrick served as a county justice of the peace, joined the state militia, and helped organize the Scotland Neck Mounted Riflemen, a volunteer cavalry company. By 1860 they owned eighty-eight slaves and a 1,894-acre estate valued at $19,600.

Both Edmondstons were ardent secessionists, and once the Civil War began Patrick entered Confederate service while Catherine contributed clothing and food to the army. Her diaries provide detailed accounts of this period and also describe her passionate interest in the war and her home. She composed patriotic poems of dubious quality, scrutinized military and political figures in both the North and the South, and championed her husband's futile efforts to raise a cavalry battalion. She expressed little sympathy for those who deplored the dissolution of the Union, and she never reconciled herself to the South's defeat, bitterly recording her antagonism toward the North in a short essay she published anonymously in 1872 entitled *The Morte d'Arthur*.

Financially, the Edmondstons suffered greatly from the war. Depreciated currency and high taxes had led Thomas P. Devereux to revise the deed under which they controlled Looking Glass. The value of Hascosea and Looking Glass, when combined with Devereux's earlier payments on the marriage settlement, surpassed $10,000. The Edmondstons, therefore, had agreed to pay the difference from their yearly share of the Looking Glass profits while Devereux retained title to the land until the final payment. Devereux was not anxious to accept depreciated Confederate currency for his land, however, and he obtained the couple's grudging consent to revoke the sales bond on Looking Glass until after the war. In 1865 and 1867, various deeds noted that Edmondston then rented the Looking Glass tract from Devereux, but stated further that Devereux was indebted to the Edmondstons and that he had agreed to apply this debt, or any future ones he might owe them, toward their purchase of Looking Glass.

Unhappily for the Edmondstons, Devereux's bankruptcy in 1868 resulted in the confiscation of his entire estate for distribution to his creditors. The North Carolina Supreme Court included Looking Glass in the distribution despite persistent appeals by the Edmondstons that the land belonged to them via the 1865 and 1867 deeds. In 1872 the court agreed that Devereux, since dead, owed Edmondston over $4,000, but ruled that the debt did not constitute a legal claim to the land although Edmondston was entitled to collect the $4,000 from the proceeds of the Looking Glass sale. He died before the final verdict on his appeal. After his death his wife managed Looking Glass and Hascosea while seeking to "prevent the crust of age & isolation thickening around & over me until I become self absorbed—self contained—hateful to myself & to all with whom I come in contact." At the Looking Glass sale in December 1874, less than a month before her own death, she returned the highest bid on the land. The bid was accepted and she won the fight to retain what she had always considered to be her property.

Catherine Edmondston's will, proved 1 Mar. 1875, left her real estate, including the then unpaid-for Looking Glass tract, to her brother's son, Thomas P. Devereux, Jr., bound by certain trusts. The will also provided legacies for several of her relatives and a yearly income and lifelong residence for two of her former slaves, Owen and Dolly Richardson. The monetary legacies she bequeathed to various members of her family, totaling $7,000, proved larger than her personal estate, however, and required another case in the state's supreme court before the legacies were settled.

The Edmondstons, staunch Episcopalians, were buried in the cemetery of Trinity Church in Scotland Neck.

SEE: Deeds and wills of Halifax and Wake counties (North Carolina State Archives, Raleigh); Catherine Ann Devereux Edmondston, Diaries (North Carolina State Archives, Raleigh), Letter, 10 Sept. 1871 (in possession of Mrs. Graham Barden, New Bern), and *The Morte d'Arthur: Its Influence on the Spirit and Manners of the Nineteenth Century* (1872); *Hawkins v. Blake*, 108 *U.S. Reports* (1884); Louis H. Manarin, *North Carolina Troops, 1861–1865, A Roster*, vol. 2 (1968); 78, 81 *North Carolina Reports* (1878, 1879); North Carolina Supreme Court records (North Carolina State Archives, Raleigh); James W. Patton, "Serious Reading in Halifax County, 1860–1865," *North Carolina Historical Review* 42 (1965); United States Census, 1850, 1860 (North Carolina State Archives, Raleigh).

T. L. ARMISTEAD

**Edwards, Alonzo Clay** *(29 Sept. 1904–1 Mar. 1968)*, farmer, Sunday school superintendent, and legislator, was born in Hookerton, the son of Dr. Grandison C. Edwards, a country physician, and Katharine E. Herman, a schoolteacher and daughter of a Methodist minister. Lon, as he was known to his friends, attended school in Hookerton and Trinity College (later Duke University) in Durham. When he returned home from college in 1925, he assumed management of his father's farm and continued to operate farms around Hookerton as a life vocation. On 20 Feb. 1935, he was married to Bettie Hardy Taylor in Duke Chapel, Duke University, by his brother, R. G. L. Edwards, a Methodist minister; they had one child, Alonzo Clay Edwards, Jr.

During the depression of the 1930s Edwards was in the forefront of organized support for agriculture, which led to legislation establishing price supports and the soil bank. In this he was assisted by his friend Harold Cooley, a congressman from eastern North Carolina and chairman of the House Committee on Agriculture. As a member of various farm and business groups, Edwards made frequent trips to Washington to confer with Department of Agriculture officials, Congressman Cooley, and other congressmen and senators. In 1936 he helped organize the North Carolina Farm Bureau in Greenville, serving on the first board of directors and on the first executive committee. In 1938 he was elected representative from North Carolina to the National Farm Bureau Convention.

A lifelong Democrat, Edwards was elected representative from Greene County to the General Assembly in 1941; he was reelected through 1955, when he retired voluntarily. In the Assembly he was chairman of the House Agriculture Committee. This fourteen-year service in Raleigh had a decided influence on his life. His horizon was broadened; his circle of business, political, and agricultural friends became statewide and national; and his visits to Washington became more frequent.

In 1942, Edwards was appointed Sunday school superintendent in the Hookerton Methodist Church. A Methodist since baptism as an infant, he had become a steward in the Hookerton church in 1928; however, this Sunday school leadership role established the basis of state and national service in Methodism. He was district lay leader (1955–61); member of the World Service and Finance Committee, North Carolina Conference (1961–62); five times a delegate to the General Conference of the Methodist Church; five times a delegate to the Southeastern Jurisdictional Conference; and a member of the board and vice-president of the Methodist Foundation, Inc.

Edwards believed in soil conservation and pioneered in conservation work. In 1942, he signed the original petition for the formation of the Coastal Plains Soil Conservation District. From 1961 until his death he served as council member from North Carolina on the National Association of Soil and Water Conservation Districts. His friends in the North Carolina Farm Bureau elected him state membership chairman (1942–48), president (1949–50), and executive vice-president (1957–59). It was while he was executive vice-president that the central office of the State Farm Bureau was moved from Greensboro to Raleigh. North Carolina State University invited him to participate in various programs, including the North Carolina Agricultural Foundation, Inc., and the Agricultural Institute.

In March 1957 Edwards was elected to the board of directors of Tobacco Associates, an organization created to expand the foreign export market of tobacco—the chief money crop in many southern states. He remained on the board until his death. With other officials of Tobacco Associates he made several trips to Europe to promote foreign tobacco sales.

A Mason, a member of the Junior Order, and a man with recognized humanitarian interests, Edwards was appointed a trustee of the Junior Order United American Mechanics Children's Home in Lexington, N.C.; of the Methodist Children's Home in Raleigh; and of the Methodist Retirement Home in Durham. In addition, his legislative experience and broad interests in the public welfare resulted in his appointment to the North Carolina Advisory Budget Commission (1949–57) and to the North Carolina State Board of Education (1943–57). He was also a trustee of Louisburg College (1958–60) and The University of North Carolina (1952–61). The alumni of his alma mater, Duke University, elected him chairman of the Duke National Council (1951–52) and president of the General Alumni Association (1954–55). On 27 Aug. 1965, Governor Dan K. Moore appointed him a trustee of the North Carolina Agricultural Hall of Fame; his term, which was to end 1 Jan. 1971, was cut short by his death of a heart attack.

SEE: *Agricultural Review*, 1 Apr. 1971; "Edwards Elected to Hall of Fame," *North Carolina Farm News* 41 (July 1970); John A. Garraty, ed., *Encyclopedia of American Biography* (1974); *Goldsboro News-Argus*, 7 Mar. 1968; *Greene County Ledger*, 7, 11 Mar. 1968; Kinston *Daily Free Press*, 2–4 Mar. 1968, 21 May 1970; *North Carolina Christian Advocate*, 7 Mar. 1968; Raleigh *News and Observer*, 2–4 Mar. 1968.

HERMAN EDWARDS

**Edwards, Isaac** *(fl. 1765–January 1775)*, attorney, private secretary and aide-de-camp to Governor William Tryon, member of the First Provincial Congress of 1774, deputy auditor of the province under Governor Josiah Martin, and ardent convert to the cause of colonial American rights, was the eldest son of Colonel Nathaniel Edwards (d. 1771), burgess from Brunswick County, Va., and deputy secretary of the colony (1770), and Jane Eaton Haynes Edwards, daughter of William Eaton (d. 1759) and Mary Rives of Granville County, N.C., and widow of Anthony Haynes. Isaac Edwards was also the grandson of John Edwards (d. 1713) of Brunswick County and the brother of Mrs. Rebecca Edwards Jones, the beautiful "Indian Queen" and second wife of General Allen Jones.

Despite the fact that Edwards was born into old English landholding families of considerable distinction, his early life and legal training is uncertain although various circumstances point to his having spent some time in England. His first wife was Martha Williamson, but nothing is known of her except that she died early. Edwards himself first appeared in the public records of the Province of North Carolina (probably in midsummer of 1765 although the entry is undated) when he came before the governor's council to take an oath of allegiance to King George III as well as an oath of secrecy—necessary because he was succeeding Mrs. Tryon's English cousin, Fountain Elwin, as private secretary to Governor Tryon.

According to items preserved in the *Colonial and State Records of North Carolina*, Edwards's new position was a grueling one. Not only did he copy scores of requisitions, letters, proclamations, writs of election, and militia commissions, but he also served as bookkeeper, messenger, and diplomatic attaché as well as making a steady succession of arduous journeys on horseback to the backcountry. On Tuesday, 12 Aug. 1766, he appeared before the Inferior Court of Pleas and Quarter Sessions in Hillsborough and qualified as an attorney, possibly replacing the deceased Crown prosecutor, Daniel Weldon. This was the beginning of Edwards's five-year connection with Hillsborough and the backcountry, a connection that was part and parcel of his secretaryship. In May 1767, then listed as a captain in the provincial militia and as aide-de-camp to the governor, he accompanied Tryon on the extravagant Cherokee boundary expedition to western North Carolina to run the "Hunting Line." From 17 to 21 Sept. 1767, he accompanied Tryon, Edmund Fanning, and Henry Eustice McCulloh on a visit to Bethabara.

In late April 1768, after a meeting of the council, Tryon hurriedly dispatched Edwards on a swift journey to Hillsborough to bring to the backcountry settlers a special proclamation warning against "unlawful assemblages." Edwards addressed and dispersed an angry, potentially dangerous crowd of backwoodsmen, but Tryon more or less repudiated his secretary's speech, saying that Edwards had exceeded the authority delegated to him. On 6 July the governor and his entourage arrived in the backcountry to recruit militiamen in Rowan County for what is sometimes called the "First Campaign" against the Regulators. Edwards, however, apparently remained in Hillsborough and on 29 August purchased two town lots (Numbers 96 and 77) on West Tryon Street for 40 shillings, perhaps to encourage the town's first expansion program. He promptly built the sixteen-by-twenty-foot "mansion house" required to "save" a lot as well as a small law office (neither is now standing). He also bought a modest farm "on the branches of Buckwater Creek" northeast of Hillsborough and somewhat later bought two additional town lots (Numbers 97 and 78) to create a neat four-acre estate next to the Town Burial Ground. It may have been during this long three-month stay (until 2 October) among the people of the Carolina backcountry that Edwards had his sympathies actively roused in their favor.

Evidently he was back in Hillsborough again on 15 Aug. 1770, just before the September riots, for he bought his third lot on that date. According to Judge Richard Henderson, "Mr. Edwards' [House] did not escape" having its windows broken during the riots.

On 6 Feb. 1771 Edwards began to dispose of his Orange County property by selling his Buckwater Creek farmland to Samuel Cleniay (Clenny) for £230 Proc. Since both Governor Tryon and his secretary had known of Tryon's impending removal to the Province of New York well before the Battle of Alamance on 16 May 1771, the sale was undoubtedly part of Edwards's severance from his secretaryship. His Hillsborough house, office, and four lots were also sold on 21 Mar. 1772 to Francis Nash for £360 Proc. Although Edwards was listed officially as one of Tryon's four aides-de-camp for the Alamance campaign, both Edwards and William Palmer resigned on 14 May 1771, two days before the battle, to be replaced by Thomas Clark and Willie Jones. Tryon had chosen Edmund Fanning as his new private secretary and, so far as is known, did not invite Edwards to accompany him northward.

The new royal governor, Josiah Martin, had first intended to appoint Colonel John Frohock as deputy auditor of the province, but on Frohock's illness and death he selected Isaac Edwards in his stead. On 28 Nov. 1771, the Moravians had observed, "Mr. Edwards . . . is at present all powerful with the new Governor"; on 23 May 1772 he took the oath of his new office, which Martin later described as "one of the genteelest and most lucrative places in this Province."

Soon after Josiah Martin assumed office, Edwards married as his second wife Mary Cornell, daughter of the wealthy Royalist merchant Samuel Cornell, a member of the governor's council under both Tryon and Martin. In a deed of 18 July 1772, recorded in Craven County 15 Dec. 1772, Samuel Cornell for five shillings sterling and "more particularly in consideration of love and goodwill" conveyed to his son-in-law Lot 105 in New Bern (on the west side of Front or Water Street, now East Front Street) and the "messuage" (house) thereon, "formerly occupied by His Excellency William Tryon." This was apparently the home embellished by the "Chinese Fence" with its "neet, light Airy & elegant look" so carefully described by Edwards to Colonel John Williams in a letter from New Bern dated 20 July 1773. In the same letter he indicated unmistakably his altered political stance: "The Mother Country has not of late discovered any great desire to promote the wish of her children . . . & if I judge aright her children in this our dear Country have too sacred a regard for what they esteem their undoubted Birthright, tamely to surrender it to the Command of any Tribunal under Heaven."

Within months Governor Martin was complaining angrily in letters to the Earl of Dartmouth (then secretary of state for the colonies) that Samuel Cornell, hitherto a staunch Royalist, had become "influenced to . . . delinquent behaviour" by his son-in-law's ideas. Edwards vigorously promoted the First Provincial Congress of 25–27 Aug. 1774 and maneuvered so that it was held in New Bern. As one of the two representatives of the borough of New Bern, he boldly spoke out with passion and force for the patriot cause. "No more fiery exponent of American rights could be found among the seventy-one delegates than Isaac Edwards," wrote Alonzo T. Dill. "[He] alone went so far as to urge condemnation of Martin's attempt to prevent the meeting." Martin reported to Dartmouth that Edwards had been "the most zealous and forward in promoting the indecent Cabals that have been formed here" and finally recommended Edwards's removal from office.

Although Edwards had been elected a representative to the Second Provincial Congress held at New Bern on 3 Apr. 1775, he died in January some three months before it convened, "having persued to the last the same undutiful conduct," according to Martin. His grave site in New Bern is unknown, but he may have been buried in the old Christ Churchyard.

Edwards was survived by his wife, Mary Cornell, and their two daughters, all of whom removed to New York with Samuel Cornell. A deed of 1798, filed in Craven County, records that "Mary, relict of Isaac Edwards," was on 10 Nov. 1798 living in New York City as were her two daughters, Susannah Edwards (later Mrs. William Wallace) and Rebecca Edwards Ogden (wife of David A. Ogden of that city). The deed further records that Edwards had died intestate and that his daughters were then selling some of his local property to James Reed Emery.

The dramatic conversion of Edwards from Royalist to patriot, though gradual and complex, appears to have been absolute. It was made a major, compelling theme of Inglis Fletcher's historical novel, *Wind in the Forest* (1958).

A small profile picture of Edwards is displayed in the Secretary's Office in the east wing of the restored Tryon Palace at New Bern, together with his ingenious eighteenth-century English watch of silver, made with the twelve letters ISAAC EDWARDS on the face instead of numerals to mark the hours.

SEE: Gertrude S. Carraway, "Members of the First Provincial Congress," *DAR Magazine* 107 (August-September 1973); Walter Clark, ed., *State Records of North Carolina*, vol. 22 (1907); Deeds, Minutes of the Inferior Court of Pleas and Quarter Sessions, 1752–66, of Orange County (Orange County Courthouse, Hillsborough); Alonzo T. Dill, *Governor Tryon and His Palace* (1955); Adelaide L. Fries, ed., *Records of the Moravians*, vols. 1 (1922), 2 (1925); Marshall D. Haywood, *Governor William Tryon and His Administration in the Province of North Carolina, 1765–1771* (1903); Cadwallader Jones, *A Genealogical History. . .* (1900); William L. Saunders, ed., *Colonial Records of North Carolina*, vols. 7–10 (1890); John Williams Papers (North Carolina State Archives, Raleigh).

MARY CLAIRE ENGSTROM

**Edwards, Ward Blowers** *(21 June 1885–5 Sept. 1935)*, educator and college administrator, was born in Troupsburg, Steuben County, N.Y., the son of Charles Perry and Mary Livonia Blowers Edwards. He was educated in the public schools in New York and Colorado, where his family moved in Edwards's early childhood. He entered upon a career in teaching and educational administration after receiving an A.B. degree from Wake Forest College in 1912, serving successively as principal of Grifton High School (1912–15), principal of Jackson High School (1915–18), and superintendent of Weldon City Schools (1918–24). Meanwhile, he had been awarded an M.A. degree by Columbia University in 1920.

In 1924 Edwards was appointed professor of German and Latin and dean of Chowan College. A major portion of the administrative duties of the college was left to Edwards during the last months of the tenure of President C. P. Weaver (1923–25) and throughout the presidency of W. R. Burrell—the former being in ill health and the latter having major responsibilities as pastor of the Murfreesboro Baptist Church and as professor of Bible at the college. Recognizing his administrative talents, the board of trustees elected Edwards to succeed Burrell as president of Chowan College, effective 1 July 1926, a position he retained until his death.

An overriding concern throughout the decade of Edwards's administration was that of maintaining the educational standard recently attained by Chowan College. The institution had been recognized by the North Carolina Department of Education as a standard four-year college in 1925. Edwards aimed to increase its educational prestige through the attainment of accreditation by the Southern Association of Colleges and Schools. The maintenance of the former standard alone depended upon a guaranteed annual income of $50,000, with at least one-third of that amount having to come from sources other than student fees. Edwards advocated a policy that had been envisioned by his predecessors: the vigorous pursuit of an effort to raise an endowment of at least $500,000. The proceeds from such an endowment—together with other anticipated nonstudent revenues—would guarantee the annual operation of the college as a standard senior college for purposes of teacher certification by the North Carolina Department of Education. It would also ensure the college's eligibility for membership in the Southern Association of Colleges and Schools. It was largely through Edwards's efforts that an initial "challenge" gift of $25,000 toward his endowment goal was secured from the Benjamin N. Duke Trust. Within a year the friends of the college, under the tireless leadership of Edwards, had met the terms of the Duke challenge by pledging an additional $50,000 toward general endowment. By mid-1927 Edwards reported an endowment total of over $100,000 on hand, in cash, securities, or pledges.

After 1929, however, it became apparent that other measures would have to be employed to meet the annual operating costs of the college in order to maintain a standard rating. Anticipated nonstudent revenues had failed to materialize. Indebtedness increased as the college borrowed funds against operating deficits. The meager endowment funds were gradually depleted in the effort to make payments on loans, or to serve as collateral for the purpose of securing loans. The Baptist State Convention ceased its financial support of Chowan altogether after 1931.

In the face of these adversities, Edwards proposed and pursued several measures that were designed to maintain the educational standards of the college. An abortive attempt was made in 1930 to coordinate the curricular offerings of Chowan College with those of Wake Forest. As envisioned, the arrangement would have eliminated some of Chowan's financial burden; more importantly, it would have aligned Chowan's degree programs with an institution already accredited by the Southern Association. In 1931 males were admitted as full-time students to the previously all-female college, a course clearly designed to produce additional revenue. In the same year, efforts were projected to engage one hundred friends of the college who would provide scholarships of $100 each to meet operating costs for the following year. By May 1932, however, Edwards had to report that the college owed over $40,000 to its creditors, including back pay due the faculty and staff. The problem of meeting financial obligations to Chowan's creditors remained a pressing concern throughout the last years of Edwards's administration, despite various schemes to reduce operating costs and to obtain additional revenue from alumnae and friends of the institution.

Edwards was a Democrat, a Mason, and a Baptist. He married Cinderella Stanley of Northampton County on 26 July 1916. They had no children.

Originally interred in the Cedarwood Cemetery at Weldon, Edwards's remains were later moved to Riverside Cemetery, Murfreesboro, to be buried beside his wife who died in 1942. A portrait commissioned by the Chowan College Alumnae Association, and painted by Francis Speight, was presented to the college in 1936.

SEE: Baptist State Convention of North Carolina, *Annual* (1935); Edgar V. McKnight and Oscar Creech, *A History of Chowan College* (1964); Minutes of the Board of Trustees, Chowan College, 1924–35 (Library, Chowan College, Murfreesboro).

R. HARGUS TAYLOR

**Edwards, Weldon Nathaniel** *(25 Jan. 1788–18 Dec. 1873)*, planter, state senator, and congressman, was born near Gaston in Northampton County, son of Priscilla Williamson and Benjamin Edwards. He attended Warrenton Academy, read law, and in 1810 began to practice in Warrenton. Here he became an associate of his kinsman, Nathaniel Macon, and a powerful group of Roanoke area politicians sometimes called the Warren Junto. He represented Warren in the House of Commons of the General Assembly in 1814 and 1815.

Edwards was elected to fill Macon's seat in the U.S. House of Representatives in 1815, when Macon resigned to become a U.S. senator. He was reelected to five succeeding terms, but declined to be a candidate again in 1827; in that year he supported Daniel Turner, son of the former governor and U.S. senator, as his replacement. While in Washington Edwards lived at Alfred Dowson's Rooming House on Capitol Hill with H. G. Burton, Thomas H. Hall, Nathaniel Macon, and John Randolph, all representatives of the Roanoke area in Congress. At different times he served on the Judiciary, Roads and Canals, Elections, Public Expenditures, and Revolutionary Pensions committees. He was chairman of the latter two committees. He followed the members of his group in supporting the presidential candidacy of William H. Crawford in 1824, voting for Crawford in the House vote of 9 Feb. 1825. When the House made John Quincy Adams president, he joined the opposition. An advocate of strict construction of the federal constitution, he consistently voted against protective tariffs, internal improvements, and other extensions of federal power.

After leaving Congress, Edwards never lost interest in politics; however, his consuming passion was Poplar Mount, his plantation near Ridgeway, about twelve miles from Warrenton. Here he experimented with scientific agriculture, giving up the cultivation of cotton and concentrating on growing food crops and tobacco as well as breeding improved stock and game chickens. He often entertained important politicians passing through Warren County, including President James Buchanan when he visited the state in 1859.

Ten times between 1833 and 1852 Edwards was elected to represent Warren in the state senate, serving as president during his last two terms. In 1835, Edwards and Macon represented Warren in the state constitutional convention. Edwards opposed religious qualifications for office, direct election of governor, and submitting the constitutional changes to a vote of the people. In 1836, he was a member of the Central Committee of the North Carolina Democratic party supporting Van Buren and Richard M. Johnson. When the Whigs dominated the state, Edwards was a leader of the Democrats. He was often suggested as a candidate for governor but never ran. He was a delegate to the national convention of his party more than once, and in 1848 was chairman of the state convention.

By 1852, Edwards was beginning to sour on the direction democracy was taking in the nation as the South lost the leadership of the Democratic party. He was a steadfast supporter of southern rights and felt the times to be increasingly out of joint. With the election of Lincoln in 1860, he became a leader of the forces for secession. In March 1861, as president of a Southern Rights Convention in Goldsboro, he called for North Carolina to leave the Union. Two months later he was elected over William A. Graham of Orange to be presiding officer of his state's secession convention. This group was to hold four sessions before its final adjournment in May 1862. Edwards was frequently at odds with Governor Zebulon Baird Vance on the conduct of the war but defeat finally brought them together. On 6 Feb. 1868 he attended the Constitutional Union Party Convention, which saw many of North Carolina's old Democrats and Whigs unite in the face of the trials of Reconstruction. During the latter part of 1862, after the secession convention adjourned the final time, Edwards wrote his *Memoir of Nathaniel Macon of North Carolina*. It was a memoir of better days.

Notwithstanding the disastrous defeat that the end of the war represented for the ideals of Edwards, his last years were spent in relative comfort. He was almost eighty-six when he died; he was buried in the private cemetery at Poplar Mount. In June 1823 Edwards married Lucy Norfleet, of Halifax, who survived him.

SEE: Samuel A. Ashe, ed., *Biographical History of North Carolina*, vol. 1 (1905); *Biog. Dir. Am. Cong.* (1971); Weldon N. Edwards Papers (Manuscript Department, Library, Duke University, Durham, and North Carolina State Archives, Raleigh); P. M. Goldman and J. S. Young, *The United States Congressional Directory* (1973); J. G. deR. Hamilton, *Party Politics in North Carolina, 1835–1860* (1916), and ed., *The Papers of Thomas Ruffin*, 4 vols. (1918–20); W. S. Hoffmann, *Andrew Jackson and North Carolina Politics* (1971); Daniel M. McFarland, "Rip Van Winkle: Political Evolution in North Carolina, 1815–1835" (Ph.D. diss., University of Pennsylvania, 1954); C. C. Norton, *The Democratic Party in Ante-Bellum North Carolina, 1835–1861* (1930); J. C. Sitterson, *The Secession Movement in North Carolina* (1939).

DANIEL M. MCFARLAND

**Eelbeck, Montfort** *(d. 1790)*, county official and planter, for thirty-five years held civil office in Edgecombe and Halifax counties, appointed in turn by governor and council, Provincial Congress, and state senate and house. He was perennially a justice of the peace from his earliest known appointment to that office in 1754. From 1770 through 1772 he was sheriff of Halifax County. He also held the posts of "Receiver of Impost," Edgecombe County (1752); commissioner for repair of the Halifax County jail (1773); judge of the Court of Oyer and Terminer (appointed 1777); and entry taker for Halifax County (resigned 1785).

Eelbeck married Mary Rogers, one of the two daughters of Emanuel Rogers of Bertie Precinct who died in 1729. In 1742, Montfort and Mary Rogers Eelbeck and John and Elizabeth Rogers Hubbard joined in partitioning the more than 6,000 acres that the sisters inherited. Of Mary's part, the Eelbecks retained 1,730 acres, which were the nucleus of the estate of over 4,000 acres—largely on Quankey Creek—bequeathed in Montfort's will. Although he rarely sold land except to purchase other suitable tracts to consolidate his holdings, in the three years before his death he sold three tracts totaling 1,100 acres to three friends and neighbors, John Kinchen, William R. Davie, and Willie Jones, who was one of the executors of his will.

Montfort and Mary Eelbeck reared nine children. Their sons were Henry (m. Jane Lane), Montfort, Jr. (m. Susannah Elbank), and John (wife's name unknown). Their daughters were Ann (m. Richard Howson), Elizabeth (m. James Shine), Penelope (m. David Day), Anna Maria (m. Dr. Mungo Ponton), another daughter (m. Thomas Frohock), and Dorothea Miriam (unmarried).

In his will Eelbeck stated that he considered "an entertainment at a funeral a gross piece of nonsense," but specified that "on the occasion" of his own a sermon was to be preached in the town of Halifax by a minister of the Church of England.

SEE: Deeds, Wills, and Minutes of the Court of Pleas and Quarter Sessions, 1784–87, of Halifax County (North Carolina State Archives, Raleigh); J. Bryan Grimes, ed., *Abstracts of North Carolina Wills* (1910); William L. Saunders, ed., *Colonial Records of North Carolina*, vol. 5 (1887).

RUTH L. BARRETT

**Efird, Ireneus Polycarp** *(6 Jan. 1834–11 Dec. 1902)*, farmer, schoolmaster, and textile manufacturer, was born in Montgomery County. A descendant of pioneer Jacob Efird who came to North Carolina from Pennsylvania abut 1783, he was the son of Solomon and Eliza Furr Efird. A firm believer in education, he erected a log school building near his home in Stanly County and for many years taught the children of the community. He also operated a gristmill and a cotton gin and served fourteen years as a county commissioner of Stanly County. In 1896 he, his son, John Solomon, and J. W. Cannon erected at Albemarle the Efird Manufacturing Company, the first textile plant in Stanly County. This firm was merged with the American Yarn Company in 1952.

Efird, who married Mary Catherine Treece on 13 Apr. 1856, was the father of twelve children: John Solomon Melanchthon, James William Franklin, Paul Joshua Cornelius, Eliza Lavinia Emarelda, Joseph Ireneus Luther, Judah Ida Rosanah, Daniel Ephraim, Adam Alfred, Flora Belzora, Margaret Melinda, Arthur Lee, and Killian Polycarp.

He was a leading member of St. Martin's Lutheran Church in Stanly County and was buried in St. Martin's Cemetery.

SEE: O. O. Efird, *The History and Genealogy of the Efird Family* (1964).

FRANK P. CAUBLE

**Efird, John Solomon Melanchthon** *(27 Jan. 1857–19 Jan. 1927)*, textile executive, was born on a farm near Albemarle. A son of Ireneus and Mary Catherine Treece Efird, he was christened John Solomon Melanchthon but later dropped Melanchthon from his name. Educated chiefly by his father, he operated a gristmill, a store, and a sawmill at Efird's Mills in Stanly County. From 1896 until his death he managed the Efird Manufacturing Company, a textile plant in Albemarle. He also was a director of two banks and several other North Carolina cotton mills. In 1907 and 1915 he served as a state senator. At the time of his death, he was a trustee of Lenoir-Rhyne College at Hickory and of Jackson Training School at Concord.

Efird made generous donations to Mount Pleasant Collegiate Institute and Mont Amoena Seminary, Lutheran schools at Mount Pleasant, and gave a new building to St. Martin's Lutheran Church in Stanly County. The nurses' home at the Stanly County Hospital is named in his honor, and Efird Hall at the Lutheridge Assembly Grounds, Arden, is a memorial to Mr. and Mrs. John S. Efird.

On 14 Aug. 1879 Efird married Sophronia Isabella Foreman; they were the parents of eight children: William Titus, Robert Lee, Columbus Polycarp, Clara Florence, Walter Guy, Jasper Jerome, Bessie May, and a daughter who died in infancy. He married Bertha Estelle Snuggs, his second wife, on 27 June 1900; they had one adopted child, Minnie Estelle.

SEE: O. O. Efird, *The History and Genealogy of the Efird Family* (1964); Raleigh *News and Observer*, 18 July 1947.

FRANK P. CAUBLE

**Efird, Joseph Bivens** *(13 May 1883–11 Jan. 1966)*, department store executive, was born in Anson County, near Wadesboro. A descendant of early German settlers, he was a son of John Emory and Anna Maria Turner Efird. After attending Wingate Junior College, he began his mercantile career at Charlotte in 1902 and eventually established more than fifty Efird department stores in the Carolinas and Virginia. There were seven Efird brothers, Hugh Martin, Samuel Morton, Edmund Lilly, John Ray, Joseph Bivens, Paul Haywood, and Jasper Wilson. All of them except Samuel Morton participated in the management and operation of the Efird stores. J. B. Efird, who always maintained his office at Charlotte, served as president and directing manager of the Efird stores until they were sold to the Belk Department Stores in 1956. He was a pioneer in the operation of one-price cash stores and in providing insurance and pension benefits for his employees.

Efird was a member of the board of trustees of Queens College, Wingate Junior College, the North Carolina Baptist Hospital, and the Charlotte YMCA and YWCA. An active member of the Baptist church, he donated the site for the Myers Park Baptist Church in Charlotte.

On 8 May 1917 Efird married Margaret Elizabeth Withers. They had three children: Elizabeth Withers, Joseph Bivens, Jr., and Hugh Martin II. He was buried in the Elmwood Cemetery, Charlotte.

SEE: *Charlotte Observer*, 21 Oct. 1923, 26 July 1936, 15 Jan. 1966; O. O. Efird, *The History and Genealogy of the Efird Family* (1964); Raleigh *News and Observer*, 22 Sept. 1956, 13 Jan. 1966; *Who's Who in Commerce and Industry* (1959).

FRANK P. CAUBLE

**Efird, Oscar Ogburn** *(12 Jan. 1892–13 May 1974)*, lawyer, jurist, teacher, and genealogist, was born in Winston, the son of Francis Bruner and Minnie Victoria Ogburn Efird and the grandson of the Reverend Adam Efird, a Lutheran minister in South Carolina. He attended the public schools in Winston, and received an A.B. from Roanoke College (1912), an A.M. from Princeton University (1913), an LL.B. from Harvard Law School (1919), and an honorary LL.D. from Roanoke College (1971). During World War I he served for a short time in the U.S. Army, attended a summer session at The University of North Carolina, and in August 1918 was licensed to practice law in North Carolina.

From 1919 to 1921, Efird was a professor of law at The University of North Carolina where he introduced the casebook system of teaching law. He then returned to Winston-Salem to engage in private practice and established a new index of the records and conveyances in the office of the Register of Deeds of Forsyth County. He served as assistant judge of the municipal court in Winston-Salem from 1926 to 1928, and was judge of the Forsyth County Court for fourteen years. Although he received more than 180,000 votes, he was an unsuccessful candidate in the 1948 Democratic primary for the office of associate justice of the North Carolina Supreme Court.

From 1953 to 1964, Efird compiled a history and genealogy of the Efird family which was published in 1964. His wife assisted him in gathering data for this book and some of her paintings are reproduced in it.

He married Frances Kathrina Susan Koiner on 9 Sept. 1920. There were no children. He was a lifelong member of the Lutheran church, and was buried in the Salem Cemetery, Winston-Salem.

SEE: O. O. Efird, *The History and Genealogy of the Efird Family* (1964); *Winston-Salem Journal*, 14 May 1974; Winston-Salem *Journal-Sentinel*, 26 July 1964; Winston-Salem *Twin City Sentinel*, 31 May 1971, 13 May 1974.

FRANK P. CAUBLE

**Ehringhaus, John Christoph Blucher** *(5 Feb. 1882–31 July 1949)*, legislator, solicitor of the First Judicial District, and governor of North Carolina during the early New Deal, was born in Elizabeth City, the son of Erskine and Catherine Colville Matthews Ehringhaus. His father was a leading merchant in Elizabeth City and later head of the bookkeeping department of First and Citizens National Bank. His mother died when he was ten years old. On both his mother's and his father's sides, the family dated back to important leaders in the Revolutionary War, though his Ehringhaus ancestors emigrated in 1812 from Germany to Elizabeth City where they became involved in banking.

Ehringhaus attended schools in Elizabeth City and was graduated from Atlantic Collegiate Institute of that city in 1898. At age sixteen he enrolled in The University of North Carolina, where he obtained a bachelor's degree with Phi Beta Kappa honors in three years. He remained at the university to study for a law degree, which he received in 1903. Admitted to the bar in the same year, he returned to practice in Elizabeth City. In 1905, he won election to the North Carolina House of Representatives as a Democrat from his native Pasquotank County. He continued to serve for two terms, leaving the house in 1908. While in the legislature, he was coauthor of the bill creating East Carolina Teacher's Training School, which later became East Carolina University. He also supported legislation creating a high school system for the state. Both bills presaged his great interest in education, an enduring concern when he later became governor.

In 1910, Ehringhaus was elected solicitor for the First Judicial District, which included the counties of Currituck, Camden, Pasquotank, Perquimans, Chowan, Gates, Tyrell, Dare, Hyde, Beaufort, and Washington. Reelected twice, Erhinghaus served in this capacity until 1922. Meanwhile, on 4 Jan. 1912 he had married Matilda Bradford Haughton, the daughter of Thomas Benbury and Susan Lamb Haughton. His wife's father had been an Episcopal minister and chaplain in the Confederate Army. The couple had three children: John C. B. III and twins, Haughton and Matilda.

For the remainder of the twenties Ehringhaus busied himself with his flourishing law practice and with civic duties, including the Masons, Odd Fellows, and Elks; and with work for the Democratic party. In 1925, he was active in obtaining a toll bridge to link his native Albemarle area more closely to the rest of the state and to reduce the area's dependence on Virginia, its natural neighbor. He campaigned for Al Smith's candidacy for president in 1928 and for O. Max Gardner, who was elected governor of North Carolina in that year.

In 1932, as the state experienced increasing economic difficulty, Ehringhaus began a campaign for governor with the support of Gardner, an association that led him to be identified with the "Gardner Machine." With A. J. Maxwell eliminated in the first gubernatorial primary, Ehringhaus then won a heated runoff against Richard T. Fountain. In the fall, he defeated Republican Clifford Frazier by the largest majority accorded a Democratic nominee up to that time.

As governor, Ehringhaus was noted for his support of economy in government, of creating a state sales tax, and of the state assuming financial responsibility for the public school system. His stern insistence on economy in government led to an early cut of the budget by nearly one-third. He inherited a deficit of $15 million in the state treasury but left office with a surplus of $5 million because of his successful battle for a three-percent sales tax in the 1933 session of the legislature. The sales tax provided the necessary funds for the state government to assume the financing of the public school system; Ehringhaus guaranteed a public school education on an eight-month basis for all children in the state. The state's assumption of educational expenses allowed local governments to reduce property taxes and to have sufficient funds to support local government debts. Ehringhaus had inherited a state in which bonds were selling at 60 to 75 percent of face value; he shortly restored the full credit of the state so that bonds could be issued at the lowest rate ever (3.76 percent), thus saving the state hundreds of thousands of dollars in interest. Greatly criticized for his monetary policies, he was so unpopular when he left office that he probably could not have been elected to another position.

Aside from the economy, however, Ehringhaus helped to maintain the educational system at a time when other states had to close schools or pay teachers in temporary scrip. No schools had to close in North Carolina, nor did teachers lose their pay. Moreover, Ehringhaus established a rental system for state textbooks and inaugurated busing for students within one mile of rural schools. He brought reorganization to the prison system, combining it with the highway department and making it self-supporting through the work of prisoners on the highways. He inaugurated a modern parole system and improved the facilities at Central Prison. He also had the highway department purchase the lime deposits in the state in order to provide essential lime to farmers at lower prices. He supported the Rural Electrification Association and saw North Carolina build 4,000 miles of the first 6,000 miles of REA lines built in the nation.

Efforts of the tobacco farmers to raise prices for their crops created repeated crises for the governor. In 1933, he closed all tobacco warehouses until a price system could be worked out under federal statutes. In 1935, he resisted pressure for a special session of the legislature to pass a state compact law for tobacco.

His resistance to a special session of the legislature in 1935 and 1936 was primarily motivated by his fear that the General Assembly would repeal the carefully nurtured sales tax. Also a factor was his long feud with the Social Security Administration to gain acceptance for a state unemployment insurance plan, which did not technically comply with federal statutes. Finally, faced with the certainty that state unemployment taxes would be lost to the federal government, and assured of the election of his successor Clyde Hoey, he called the legislature into session in the waning days of his administration.

Thus, Ehringhaus emerged from his term dependent on perspective to vindicate his efforts. Although in 1937 he briefly served as assistant attorney general of the United States to prosecute some special cases, he soon settled into private practice without seeking other elective offices. The Ehringhauses bought a house in Raleigh where with his son, J. C. B. Ehringhaus, he maintained a law practice until his death. In 1946, he moved from his home to a suite in the Sir Walter Hotel. He died there of heart failure three weeks after suffering an acute attack of rheumatic fever. His funeral was held at the Episcopal Church of the Good Shepherd, Raleigh, attended by overflow crowds. Like the relative simplicity of his life, his funeral bore no special trappings. He was buried in the Episcopal cemetery, Elizabeth City.

Ehringhaus had been anxious to promote the publication of his official papers. Although prepared in 1940, they were not published until 1950 after his death. The Ehringhaus papers are held in the North Carolina State Archives in Raleigh; his correspondence with other prominent people of his time appears in related collections in the archives and other North Carolina manuscript collections. Although many portraits of him can be found throughout the state, a special portrait was hung in the legislative building in 1960.

SEE: *Asheville Citizen*, 2 Aug. 1949; Earley W. Bridges, *Masonic Governors of North Carolina* (1937); *Charlotte Observer*, 1–3 Aug. 1949; John L. Cheney, Jr., ed., *North Carolina Government, 1585–1974* (1975); David L. Corbitt, ed., *Addresses, Letters, and Papers of John Christoph Blucher Ehringhaus, Governor of North Carolina, 1933–1937* (1950); Beth G. Crabtree, *North Carolina Governors* (1958); Daniel L. Grant, *Alumni History of the University of North Carolina* (1924); *Greensboro Daily News*, 1 Aug. 1950; Thomas S. Morgan, "A 'folly . . . manifest to everyone': The Movement to Enact Unemployment Insurance Legislation in North Carolina, 1935–1936," *North Carolina Historical Review* 52 (1975), and "A Step Toward Altruism" (Ph.D. diss., University of North Carolina, 1969); *North Carolina Biography*, vol. 4 (1919); Elmer Puryear, *Democratic Party Dissension in North Carolina, 1928–1936* (1962); Raleigh *News and Observer*, 21 May 1933, 6 July, 28 Nov. 1934, 7 Jan. 1937, 19 Nov. 1939, 1–3, 20 Aug. 1949, 8 Feb. 1957; Gary Trawick and Paul Wyche, *One Hundred Years, One Hundred Men* (1971).

THOMAS S. MORGAN

**Elder, Alfonso** *(6 Feb. 1898–7 Aug. 1974)*, college president, was the son of Lucy Lillian Phinizy and Thomas J. Elder, of Sandersville, Ga., who were also the parents of Blanche and Charles Elder. Alfonso received his early education at the Thomas J. Elder High and Industrial School, where his father was principal from 1889 to 1942. At the age of twenty-three, he was graduated magna cum laude from Atlanta University and began teaching at Bennett College, a black female college in Greensboro, N.C. During the academic year 1922–23, he taught mathematics at the Elizabeth City State Teachers' College, an all-black, four-year teacher education institution in Elizabeth City. In 1924 he earned an M.A. degree from Teacher's College, Columbia University, and in 1938 an Ed.D. degree from Columbia. He also studied at the University of Chicago during the summers of 1930 and 1931 and at the University of Cambridge, England.

From 1924 to 1943, Elder served as dean of the College of Arts and Sciences at the North Carolina College for Negroes, Durham, where he had been appointed professor of education earlier in 1924. In 1943, he left the college to accept a temporary position as chairman of the Graduate Department of Education at Atlanta University. He remained there four years, eventually becoming dean of the Graduate School of Education. Returning to Durham, he was inaugurated as the second president of the North Carolina College on 4 June 1949. On 29 Aug. 1931 he had married Louise Holmes; they had no children.

Active in numerous professional and civic organizations, Elder helped found the Durham chapter of the all-black Alpha Phi Alpha fraternity. He was a member of the National Association for the Advancement of Colored People and of the first Mayor's Committee on Human Relations in Durham. In addition, he was treasurer of the North Carolina Teachers Association (1941–43); a member of the board of directors of the Durham County Tuberculosis and Health Association, of the Mutual Building and Loan Association, of the Lincoln Hospital, of the Resource Education Commission, and of Family Services, Inc.; a member of the board of trustees of Hammock's Beach Corporation for Teachers; and chairman of the Committee of the National Clinic on Teacher Education (1947). He was a registered Democrat.

Elder retired as president of North Carolina College on 30 June 1963, after having been honored many times for his service by the faculty, staff, and student body. At his retirement he was named president emeritus of the college. Eight years later he suffered a fatal heart attack. An Episcopalian, his funeral service was conducted by the rector of St. Titus Episcopal Church; he was buried in the Beechwood Cemetery, Durham.

SEE: *Durham Morning Herald*, 11 Sept. 1972; *Durham Sun*, 28 July 1972, 8 Aug. 1974; General Assembly, *Session Laws of North Carolina*, 1975; *New York Times*, 4 June 1949; Raleigh *Carolina Times*, 24 Jan. 1947; *Who's Who in Colored America*, 1927, 1933, 1937, 1940; *Who's Who in the South and Southwest*, 1950.

G. W. REID

**Eliot, John G. ("Ghost")** *(24 Feb. 1800–13 Nov. 1881)*, teacher, was the son of George Eliot of Ellerslie on Lower Little River, Cumberland County. The father was born in Dumfriesshire, Scotland, in 1747, educated at the University of Edinburgh, and came to America as a young man. He had four sons, Henry, Alexander, George, and John, all of whom attended The University of North Carolina. John, who acquired the nickname "Ghost" as a student in Chapel Hill, was a member of the class of 1820 but was away for a time and received his degree in 1822. He accepted the nickname and was known for the remainder of his life as Ghost Eliot, even using it in signing his name. He was very tall and thin with a disproportionately large head and short cropped hair. In later life he came to be regarded as an eccentric man but was described as the "oracle of the neighborhood."

He taught at various academies including one in Wilmington that had formerly been Innes Academy and Spring Vale Academy in Sampson County. He also was a schoolmaster in Duplin, Pitt, Scotland, and Wayne counties and often served as a private tutor in prominent families. Eliot was long remembered for his excellence in Latin, geometry, algebra, and surveying. He was also an effective teacher of chemistry, geology, mineralogy, and the classics. He returned to Chapel Hill in 1847, when his old classmate, President James K. Polk, attended commencement; it was said that Polk and Eliot were overheard on that occasion conversing in Greek. The good influence of Eliot as a teacher has been widely recorded in family correspondence, newspaper stories, and reminiscences.

Eliot never married, although a former pupil recalled that he once mentioned the death of a young lady to whom he had been engaged. In this connection he taught the student Robert Burns's song, "Highland Mary," and he wept when she sang it. Eliot died while visiting in the home of Dr. W. L. Best at Johnson Mill, Pitt County, and was buried in a community cemetery near Grifton.

SEE: Kemp P. Battle, *History of the University of North Carolina*, vol. 1 (1907); William E. Cox, *Our Family Genealogy* (1938) and *Southern Sidelights: A Record of Personal Experiences* (1942); Edward M. Deems, ed., *Autobiography of Charles Force Deems* (1897); John G. Duncan, *Pitt County Potpourri* (1966); Dunn *State's Voice*, 15 Jan. 1933; John G. Eliot file (Alumni Office, University of North Carolina, Chapel Hill); John G. Eliot Papers, William Harris Garland Papers, DeRosset Papers, and Eliot Family Papers (Southern Historical Collection, University of North Carolina, Chapel Hill); *Goldsboro Messenger*, 21 Nov. 1881; Daniel L. Grant, *Alumni History of the University of North Carolina* (1924); Henry T. King, *Sketches of Pitt County* (1911); *Kinston Journal*, 4 Mar. 1880, 24 Nov. 1881; M. C. S. Noble, *History of the Public Schools of North Carolina* (1930); John A. Oates, *The Story of Fayetteville and the Upper Cape Fear* (1950); Raleigh *News and Observer*, 4 Nov. 1918; James Sprunt, *Chronicles of the Cape Fear River, 1660–1916* (1916).

WILLIAM S. POWELL

**Ellenwood, Henry Small** *(16 June 1790–3 Apr. 1833)*, teacher, author, poet, and newspaper editor, was born in Newburyport, Mass., the eldest son of Elisha Small, a mariner who died in the West Indies in 1806, leaving a widow and two young sons. Just before her husband's death, Mrs. Small moved to Boston and worked as a domestic in the family of Chief Justice Theophilus Parsons. At the age of sixteen Henry Small was apprenticed to Joseph T. Buckingham, printer for the largest bookselling establishment in New England and later editor of the *Boston Courier*. In the course of his association with Buckingham, or perhaps self-taught, he acquired the elements of a classical education and developed a propensity for rhyming. He also began to contribute anonymous paragraphs and epigrams to local newspapers which were highly praised. Buckingham later commented that "His perception was so rapid, that, without seeming to study, he usually mastered the contents of every book that came in his way in a surprisingly short time. . . . He had a fund of varied intelligence, and possessed an extensive knowledge of history, the sciences, and politics, and, even when a boy, was a skillful disputant on almost every point of theological controversy."

In 1811, when he was twenty-one, Henry Small legally changed his surname to Ellenwood and in the same year began to work for Samuel Etheridge, a printer in Charlestown, Mass. After two or three years he returned to his birthplace and purchased the *Newburyport Herald*, but due to a misunderstanding between him and the original owner he soon relinquished the paper and for a short time became a schoolmaster. In the spring of 1816 he opened a school in Boston for boys and girls and operated it with considerable success. Abandoning the classroom for personal reasons, he briefly operated a shop selling stationery and schoolbooks before moving to New York where he undertook the management of a school in Brooklyn. There he became acquainted with the rector of the Episcopal church and, as Ellenwood expressed it, "fell in love with the Liturgy of the Church." He became an Episcopalian and considered studying for Holy Orders. For the rest of his life devotion to the church was his only constant sentiment.

From New York, where he had remained about two years, Ellenwood returned to Boston for another stint at teaching. Here it was said he "trifled with his talent" and was not diligent in his employment. About 1820, after some three years, he relinquished his position and took a packet for North Carolina, where he joined a settlement of New England tradesmen who around 1810 had established a shipbuilding business on the Tar River near Pactolus, Pitt County. The settlement, known as Yankee Hall, included a school of which Ellenwood was principal for a year. After a period of time spent in "the Depths of a wilderness," he was employed in the spring of 1825 to head an academy in Greenville. He was still in the area as late as 1827 but in 1829 was in Raleigh. Afterward he moved to Hillsborough where he probably taught school for a time. Early in 1833 he moved to Wilmington and became editor of the *Wilmington Advertiser*.

Ellenwood was a man of unusual gifts and keenly observant of his environment. A polished writer, he made regular contributions to newspapers, particularly the *Raleigh Register* but also to the *Newbern Centinel* and the *American Recorder*. He wrote a series of sketches about North Carolina published in the *Boston Courier* describing the state's politics, physical geography, wildlife, people, religion, social customs, agriculture, schools, and other features. He was also a poet of note. He is particularly remembered for "The Marriage of the Sun and the Moon," a poem inspired by an annular eclipse of the sun and the moon in February 1831 and widely circulated throughout the country. A number of his poems were published in the *New-England Magazine* of June 1833; one appears in Mary Bayard Clarke's *Wood-Notes*. While residing in Hillsborough, Ellenwood, under the pseudonym of Dr. Barnabus Bolus, launched an attack on quack doctors. In 1832 he delivered an address on "Elocution" before the North Carolina Institute of Education at Chapel Hill.

Generous by nature, Ellenwood was warm in his friendships and delighted in intellectual companionship. As a native New Englander he held strong anti-Jackson views in politics. Reportedly in his youth he was "disqualified by a disease in the knee—a sort of scrofulous affection—which afflicted him severely for three or four years, and which was not entirely cured before the age of twenty-five." A bachelor, he died suddenly from a paralytic stroke and was buried in Wilmington.

SEE: "Authors and Books," *International Monthly Magazine* 4 (December 1851); Mary Bayard Clarke, *Wood-Notes*, vol. 1 (1853); D. W. Jordan Papers (Manuscript Department, Library, Duke University, Durham); *Newburyport Herald*, 16, 26 Apr. 1833; *New-England Magazine* 4 (June 1833); *Raleigh Register*, 31 Mar. 1831; James Sprunt, *Chronicles of the Lower Cape Fear River* (1916); St. James Episcopal Church records, Wilmington; Wilmington's *People's Press*, 3 Apr. 1833.

PERCIVAL PERRY

**Eller, Adolphus Hill** *(9 Apr. 1861–7 Dec. 1941)*, lawyer, banker, and political leader, was born in New Hope community, Wilkes County, the son of James E. and Mary Ann Carlton Eller. He was prepared for college at the Moravian Falls Academy and was graduated from The University of North Carolina with honors in 1885. At Chapel Hill he was president of the Dialectic Society, editor of the *University Magazine*, and winner of the debaters' medal. After teaching briefly at the State Normal School in Boone, he read law at Folk's Law School at Cilley near Lenoir and was admitted to the bar in 1886. He practiced law until 1914, when he became trust officer and vice-president of Wachovia Bank and Trust Co. He managed the gubernatorial campaign of Robert B. Glenn in 1904, served in the North Carolina Senate from 1905 to 1907, was secretary and treasurer of the North Carolina Railroad from 1908 to 1912, and served as a trustee of The University of North Carolina for twenty-seven years following his first appointment to that post in 1906. In 1908 Eller helped organize and was president of the Standard Building and Loan Association; he also was one of the founders of the North Carolina State Baptist Hospital in Winston-Salem and furthered the development of the Winston-Salem Teachers College, of which he was a trustee and secretary for a number of years. He retired from his position with Wachovia Bank and Trust Co. shortly before his death.

Eller married Laura Winifred Newland in 1896 and they were the parents of two sons, John DeWalde and A. H., Jr., and of a daughter, Mary, who died young. He was a Baptist and was buried in the Salem cemetery.

SEE: Daniel L. Grant, *Alumni History of the University of North Carolina* (1924); University of North Carolina *Alumni Review*, January 1942, and records in the Alumni Office, Chapel Hill; Winston-Salem *Journal-Sentinel*, 24 Apr. 1938, 8 Dec. 1941.

WILLIAM S. POWELL

**Ellington, Douglas D.** *(26 June 1886–27 Aug. 1960)*, architect, was born in Clayton, the eldest of three sons of Jesse and Sallie Williamson Ellington. His father was from Clayton and his mother from Suffolk, Va. Educated at Randolph-Macon College in Virginia, Douglas demonstrated a talent for the arts and continued his training in architecture at Drexel Institute and the University of Pennsylvania in Philadelphia. In 1913 he was accepted to the renowned Ecole des Beaux Arts in Paris where he won two distinctive awards, the Paris Prize and the Prix de Rougevin. He was the first southerner to win the Paris Prize and the only American at the time to win the latter. Ellington remained in Europe until the United States entered the war in 1917. Returning home, he enlisted in the navy and as a chief petty officer was assigned to the newly established camouflage department.

After the war, Ellington resumed his architectural work. His early employment was in the offices of George B. Post and Sons, New York; Joseph H. Freelander, New York; and E. B. Lee, Pittsburgh. Until 1920 he held the post of professor of architecture at Carnegie Institute of Technology in Pittsburgh. Additionally, he taught at Drexel Institute for two years and at Columbia University for one year. In 1920 he set up his own architectural office with his brother, Kenneth, as business manager, in Pittsburgh. His commissions there included the Gates Building, Steel's Restaurant, Nixon's Restaurant, and the architectural design for the approaches to the steel bridges across the Allegheny and Monongahela rivers.

In 1926, Ellington was invited to design the First Baptist Church in Asheville, N.C. The structure, octagonal in plan and surmounted by a colorful tile dome, is notable for its highly individual decorative detail as well as for its engineering. At the end of the same year, he was commissioned by the city of Asheville to design a new city hall. The design was soon expanded to include a twin facility of city and county offices joined by a central bus depot. Once again, the architect's individual perception of color, proportion, and engineering resulted in a building of unusual drama and dignity with strong geometric forms softened by muted tones, "selected so as to embrace a transition in color paralleling the natural clay-pink shades of the local Asheville soil," he said. Because it was disputed that one architect should be commissioned to do both the city and county buildings, the original plan of engaging Ellington only for the city hall proceeded. Thus, the uniform concept was destroyed and a county building in the classical style was constructed instead. Still, the city hall retains its distinction as one of the fine examples of civic architecture of the 1920s.

In 1929 Ellington designed the Lee Edwards High School between Asheville and Biltmore. It is a fortress-like stone structure of three wings radiating from a low rotunda. The plan was designed to be expanded in the future to include a junior college, each educational center occupying its own eminence and connected by a bridge. Like the earlier commission, only half of the design was realized. Again, color and geometry predominate in the use of rough cut Balfour Pink granite from Salisbury, N.C., and earth tones in the detailing. The concept was so dramatic that the architect was honored by Teachers College, Columbia University, for "the best and most beautiful school building of its classification in this country."

A fourth commission in Asheville was the S & W Cafeteria facing Pritchard Park, also designed in 1929. Continuing in the previous vein with exotic and geometric color and decoration, the building is considered to be one of the finest Art Deco structures in North Carolina.

Again in 1929, Ellington entered an international competition for the design of the Christopher Columbus Lighthouse Memorial in Santo Domingo and was one of three American architects considered for the award. His submittal won first place but the memorial was never constructed. While in the Virgin Islands, however, he painted a series of watercolors. These were selected to be shown as the United States' entry in the Intercolonial Exhibition in Paris, 1930–31.

During the 1930s, the architect became directly involved in the creation of a model community. Named Greenbelt, the community was developed north of Washington in Maryland and received praise from Senator Robert A. Taft as well as from General Francisco Franco of Spain. The model was chosen by Franco as the guide for similar projects in Spain. The design is still considered an important concept in community planning.

In 1937 Ellington and his family moved to Charleston, S.C., where he began restoration of the old Dock Street Theater. Only the exterior fabric remained from the early structure, and the architect created an unusually elegant and classical theater/restaurant complex within the tightly controlled space. The family continued to visit Asheville, centering their activities around the architect's home in Chunn's Cove. This remarkable house, which evolved without a plan and incorporated pieces of broken tile, glass, and cast-off architectural ornament in the design, was selected by *House Beautiful* magazine as one of the fifty most artistic and interesting dwellings in North America.

In addition to these projects, Ellington designed Biltmore Hospital, the Merrimon Avenue fire station, and the Park Avenue School auditorium—all in Asheville; several distinctive homes in Wilmington; Kappa Sigma and Kappa Alpha fraternity houses in Chapel Hill; numerous private residences and churches in Pennsylvania, Virginia, South Carolina, and Mississippi; and St. Andrews Presbyterian Church, Charlotte.

Ellington was a member of many professional organizations, including the American Institute of Architects, the Beaux Arts Institute of Design, the Society of Beaux Arts Architects, the Society for Preservation of Old Dwellings of Charleston, the Carolina Art Association, the Charleston Art Commission, the Philadelphia Water-Color Club and Sketch Club, the Associated Artists of Pittsburgh, the Artists' Guild of Charleston, and the South Carolina Historical Society. He died at his home in Chunn's Cove after a short illness.

SEE: *Asheville Citizen*, 28 Aug. 1960; *North Carolina Architect* 11 (December 1964); *Southern Architect* 6 (October 1960).

EDWARD F. TURBERG

**Ellington, Kenneth Raynor** *(25 Dec. 1888–2 Sept. 1962)*, partner in architectural firm, was born in Clayton, the son of Jesse and Sallie Williamson Ellington. In 1914 he received the LL.B. degree from The University of North Carolina where he was a member of Gorgon's Head, an honorary society. After serving in the Navy Air Corps during World War I, he joined the architectural office of his brother Douglas in Asheville and participated in the work of the firm. (*See* **Ellington, Douglas D.**) A Baptist, he married Margaret Roberts in 1922 and they were the parents of a son, Eric Edward.

SEE: Alumni records, University of North Carolina, Chapel Hill; Douglas D. Ellington, "Architecture of the City Building," *Architectural Record* 64 (August 1928); Daniel L. Grant, *Alumni History of the University of North Carolina* (1924).

GEORGE MYERS STEPHENS

**Elliott, Aaron Marshall** *(24 Jan. 1844–9 Nov. 1910)*, philologist, was the son of Aaron Elliott and Rhoda Mendenhall Elliott. He was born near Elizabeth City, Pasquotank County, and lived there until 1847, when his family moved to Deep River Community in Guilford County. Elliott's early education was no better than that of the average country boy, as he worked on his father's farm and attended various rural schools for a few months. However, in 1860, when he went to live with his uncle, Dr. Nereus Mendenhall, in Florence, N.C., he began studying with the definite view of later entering Haverford College in Pennsylvania. In February 1861, Mendenhall obtained a teaching position at New Garden Boarding School (which later became Guilford College). Elliott also went to New Garden and studied for the remainder of that school year as well as the following year.

At the outbreak of the Civil War, Elliott failed to secure exemption from the army. Opposed to the bearing of arms, he went north to attend Haverford College. He entered the college in 1862 as a sophomore but had to repeat the year because he could not keep up with his class. After graduating in 1866, he returned to North Carolina and taught at New Garden Boarding School for one year. He then entered Harvard on 13 Sept. 1867 as a senior and was graduated third in his class on 15 July 1868.

Elliott spent the next eight years in Europe, first as a tutor and then as a student. In Paris he tutored the sons of a Mr. Parker of Boston until the outbreak of the Franco-Prussian war, when his charges returned to the United States. Elliott remained in Paris but escaped to Italy after the Germans invaded the city. In Italy, he came under the influence of Professor Angelo De Gubernatis, a Sanskrit scholar of some note. At this point, Elliott turned his attention to Oriental languages, making them his chief concern for the following six years. He studied at various universities in Europe: the Collège de France and the Ecole des Hautes Etudes from 1868 to 1871, the Instituto degli Studii Superiori in Florence from 1871 to 1872, and the University of Madrid in 1873. Later in 1873, after escaping from Spain during the Carlist Revolution, he entered the University of Munich and spent time at the universities of Tübingen and Vienna. While in Germany he decided to become a professor of comparative philology. He returned to America in 1876.

Elliott proved to be a scholar around which a language department could be built at Johns Hopkins University. He joined the faculty on 5 June 1876 as an assistant professor of Romance languages. Although he first intended to devote himself to the Eastern tongues at Hopkins, he quickly shifted his concentration to the Romance field and to organizing the department of Romance languages, which was in a discouraging state. At the beginning of his professional career Elliott also did much pioneer work in organizing the scientific study of modern languages and literature. In 1883 he was instrumental in establishing the Modern Language Association and for nine years was its secretary. He edited the association's publications for twenty-five years, even after becoming its president in 1894. In 1886 he founded the *Modern Language Notes*, the first technical journal in this field. Because Johns Hopkins would not finance the journal, Elliott printed it in a shed on his property for seventeen years. The Johns Hopkins Press took over its management in 1903, when it became too large for private hands. It became the property of the university at Elliott's death.

The authorities at Johns Hopkins were slow to recognize Elliott's contributions. In 1880 B. L. Gildersleeve declared his junior colleague to be "as much a riddle to me now as he was four years ago." By 1884, however, the uncertainty about him had largely dissipated and he was promoted, first to associate professor and, in 1892, to professor. After his first promotion, Elliott received a letter from the president of Johns Hopkins asking for better things from his department. That year Elliott created the Romance Seminary, which became a seedbed of Romance scholars for American universities. He seemed to know instantly of impending vacancies in his field and was always ready with a candidate from his department, whether a beginner or an experienced teacher. If the latter was required, Elliott recommended one of his older men and moved a graduate of the current year into the job thus vacated.

Elliott was prized both for his talents and for his never-failing cheerfulness. He was a member of a number of clubs and organizations, including the American Philological Association, the National Educational Association, and the North Carolina Society of Baltimore. He received a Ph.D. from Princeton in 1877 and an LL.D. from Wake Forest College in 1891. He was an official delegate to the Paris Exposition in 1900 and was awarded the Cross of the Legion of Honor by the French government in 1907.

Although Elliott's training as a scholar was excellent, it was as a teacher that he rendered his greatest service to education. He never ceased to be actively interested in the welfare of his students, and his altruism was reflected in all of his dealings. Even those who knew him only by correspondence quickly came to feel that his interest in them and their work was personal and lasting. As a token of appreciation, several of his friends published a two-volume memorial shortly after his death entitled *Studies in Honor of A. Marshall Elliott*.

He was married on 14 June 1905 to Lily Tyson Manly, daughter of James E. Tyson of Ellicott City, Md.

SEE: "A. Marshall Elliott," *Modern Language Notes* 25 (1910); *DAB*, vol. 6 (1937); John C. French, *A History of the University Founded by Johns Hopkins* (1946); Hugh Hawkins, *Pioneer: A History of Johns Hopkins University, 1874–1889* (1960); George C. Keidel, *The Early Life of Professor Elliott* (1917); *Who Was Who in America*, vol. 1 (1943).

JUANITA ANN SHEPPARD

**Elliott, Gilbert** *(10 Dec. 1843–9 May 1895)*, Confederate officer and builder of the Confederate ram, *Albemarle*, lawyer, and law directory publisher, was born in Elizabeth City, the third child of Gilbert Elliott (20 May 1813–20 May 1851), a businessman in Elizabeth City, and his wife, Sarah Ann Grice. She came from a family of shipbuilders who had established Elizabeth City. Gilbert had two brothers, Charles Grice and Warren Grice, and two sisters, Mary Burgess who died in infancy and Susan Elizabeth. While a very young lad he was employed in the law office of Colonel William F. Martin of Elizabeth City, who owned a shipyard at Deep Creek, Va. Undoubtedly exposure to the shipyard activity, combined with his mother's shipbuilding heritage, stimulated Gilbert's interest, which would later be recognized by Confederate naval authorities.

At seventeen Elliott joined the Seventeenth North Carolina Regiment as first lieutenant and adjutant. After a heroic defense of Fort Hatteras under Colonel Martin, the regiment surrendered on 27 Aug. 1861. Later Elliott was detached for special naval service, for which he was commended by the Confederate Naval Command. In the spring of 1863 he was assigned the task of building an ironclad ram. Collaborating with a friend, Peter Evans Smith, the son of planter William Ruffin Smith of Halifax County, he selected a construction site in a cornfield on the Smith farm at Edwards Ferry along the Roanoke River just north of present-day Scotland Neck. Friends and neighbors in the immediate neighborhood donated tools, a sawmill, a blacksmith shop, and their full cooperation in the building of the ship. Plans and specifications had been prepared by John L. Porter, chief constructor of the Confederate Navy, using experience gained in converting the frigate *Merrimac* into the ironclad *Virginia* at the Gosport Navy Yard.

The *Albemarle* was 152 feet long between perpendiculars. Her extreme beam was 45 feet and her depth from gun deck to keel was 9 feet; when launched she drew 6½ feet of water. After being fitted with iron plates and completed, her draught was about 8 feet. Over the 4-inch thick planking were fastened two courses of iron plating extending from the knuckle to 4 feet below the deck. The plates, 7 inches wide and 2 inches thick, were rolled at the Tredegar Iron Works in Richmond. Lieutenant Elliott had scavenged scrap iron and railroad rails to ensure the required quantity of plates. Two steam engines of 200 horsepower each with 20-inch cylinders drove two propeller shafts that were geared together. Armament consisted of two rifled Brooke guns mounted on pivot carriages, each gun firing through one of three portholes from within each end of the armored shield. The prow for ramming was built of oak, running 18 feet astern on center keelson, solidly bolted and covered on the outside with iron plating 2 inches thick. It tapered to a 4-inch wide edge at the bow.

Final fitting of the *Albemarle* was accomplished at Halifax, upriver from the building site. On 18 Apr. 1864, about one year after the keel had been laid, her skipper, Captain James W. Cooke, a seasoned seaman, floated her stern first down the Roanoke River toward Plymouth. Elliott was on board as a volunteer aide to Captain Cooke. When confronted with submerged torpedoes and sunken debris, Elliott and Pilot John Luck took soundings from a small boat and determined that the *Albemarle* could safely drift over the obstacles. The Union Navy had placed the charges in hopes of preventing the ram from entering the waters adjacent to Plymouth. Immediately she was engaged in battle with the *Miami* and *Southfield*. Captain Cooke dispatched the *Southfield* by ramming while the *Miami* escaped being sunk. These and succeeding engagements supported Confederate General R. F. Hoke's Division in the attack and recapture of Plymouth. During the night of 27 Oct. 1864, while moored to her wharf at recaptured Plymouth, the *Albemarle* was sunk by a charge placed by Lieutenant W. B. Cushing of the Union Navy.

On 13 Apr. 1865, Gilbert Elliott married Lucy Ann

Hill, a great-granddaughter of Whitmel Hill who served in the Continental Congress from 1778 to 1781. A son, Gilbert III, was born in Scotland Neck on 5 Jan. 1866. In 1867 Elliott and his family moved to Norfolk, Va., where he joined his younger brother Warren in the practice of law. Three daughters were born in Norfolk: Nannie Hill, Elizabeth Grice, and Rebecca Norfleetin.

In 1878 Elliott moved to St. Louis where he tried to establish his law practice. Because of his wide knowledge of and acquaintance with lawyers throughout the United States, he began to publish a law directory which was favorably received. Later, after his son had completed his legal studies, he sent young Gilbert to New York City to open a law firm. Shortly thereafter, he joined his son in New York. He selected Staten Island for his residence but lived only a brief time, dying at age fifty-one. Both he and his wife were buried in Greenwood Cemetery, Brooklyn, N.Y.

SEE: Elizabeth City *Daily Advance*, 26 Oct. 1963; Gilbert Elliott, "The Ram *Albemarle*, Her Construction and Service" (North Carolina State Archives, Raleigh); Elliott family papers (in possession of John Page Elliott, Charlottesville, Va., and Robert G. Elliott, Daytona Beach, Fla.); Raleigh *News and Observer*, 27 Feb. 1927, 17 June 1928; Scotland Neck *Commonwealth*, 16 Feb. 1922.

ROBERT G. ELLIOTT

**Elliott, Harriet Wiseman** *(10 July 1884–7 Aug. 1947)*, teacher, administrator, and political leader, was born in Carbondale, Ill., the daughter of Allan Curtis and Elizabeth Ann White Elliott. Her father was a merchant in Carbondale and later in Herrin. Her grandfather, James Elliott, was killed fighting for the Union during the Civil War. Early in her life she developed an interest in politics, for her relatives were active Democrats in a Republican area. Harriet Elliott began her education at the Practice School at the State Normal School in Carbondale but was later sent to Park College Academy at Parkville, Mo., so that she could receive a better education. She returned to Carbondale where she taught first grade for two years to earn money to attend Hanover College in Indiana, from which she was graduated in 1910 with a B.A. in history.

After teaching for two years in Hanover, Miss Elliott attended Columbia University where she met Dr. Anna Howard Shaw, who stimulated her interest in political science and in woman suffrage. Receiving her M.A. in 1913, she went to the State Normal and Industrial College (now The University of North Carolina at Greensboro) as an instructor in history. In 1921 she became a professor and in 1935 dean of women. As professor of history and political science, she worked with Walter Clinton Jackson to establish a Department of Social Sciences. As dean of women, she helped the students organize the student government association and established and supervised the counseling service in the residence halls. In 1941 she was awarded the honorary degree of doctor of laws by Hanover College.

Miss Elliott's interest in politics was recognized by her selection as delegate-at-large to the Democratic National conventions in 1932 and 1936. In 1935 James Farley appointed her director of study groups for the women's division of the National Democratic Committee. She was granted a leave from the college at Greensboro to organize study groups throughout the nation. In 1936 she led a movement at the national convention to have women appointed as alternates to the platform committee and was one of the first women selected for this position.

State and national women's organizations found a staunch advocate in Miss Elliott. She served on the boards of the Federation of Women's Clubs and the League of Women Voters. She was chairman of the National Committee on Legislative Programs of the American Association of University Women from 1937 to 1943, and with Mrs. Franklin Roosevelt she presided over the Washington Conference on Unemployment of Young Women in 1937. On the state level, she served on the advisory commission of the State Emergency Relief Administration (1933–35) and on the state committee of the Conference of Southern Governors (1940). She was also president of the North Carolina Social Service Conference (1939–40).

Three presidents appointed Miss Elliott to national committees. Under Woodrow Wilson, she served on the Women's National Defense Council during World War I. Herbert Hoover appointed her to the White House Conference on Children in 1928, and Franklin Roosevelt asked her to be consumer adviser on the National Defense Advisory Commission in 1940. The latter position was changed to deputy director of the Office of Price Administration in 1941. In 1942 she was a member of the Advisory Committee on Women's Naval Auxiliary, which organized the WAVES. The same year she became head of the women's division of the Treasury's War Bond Program and made speeches in forty-six states. In 1945 she was adviser to the United Nations Educational Conference in London.

Miss Elliott died in Carbondale and was buried in Woodlawn Cemetery.

SEE: Elisabeth A. Bowles, *A Good Beginning* (1967); Cordelia Camp, ed., *Some Pioneer Women Educators of North Carolina* (1955); Harriet W. Elliott Papers (Archives, Library, University of North Carolina, Greensboro); Virginia T. Lathrop, "Harriet Elliott," University of North Carolina at Greensboro *Alumni News* 55 (July 1967).

ELISABETH ANN BOWLES

**Elliott, James Carson** *(12 July 1845–17 June 1936)*, Confederate soldier, teacher, writer, and civic leader, was born in Cleveland County, the eldest son of William Martin (1813–69) and Barbara Rudisill Carson (1820–1909) Elliott. Descended from pioneer stock in Virginia and North Carolina, with ancestors who had fought in the American Revolution, his father was a farmer, a small slaveholder, and an ardent Whig. At the outbreak of the Civil War, young Elliott organized and served in the local home guards until his eighteenth birthday, when, on 17 Aug. 1863, he joined Company F, Fifty-sixth Regiment, North Carolina troops, a Cleveland County company. Nine first cousins and his mother's brother also served in the Confederate Army, three of whom survived. His own Confederate service was in many respects the pivotal point in his life.

As recounted in his reminiscences, *The Southern Soldier Boy: A Thousand Shots for the Confederacy* (1907), Elliott's initial duties included guarding prisoners of war and hunting deserters in the state. The regiment received its baptism of fire in the Eastern Carolina campaign of 1864 against New Bern and in the recapture of Plymouth (April 1864). Ordered to Petersburg, Va., in May 1864, Elliott survived sickness, a wound, and the last hard winter of the Confederacy, only to be captured in the abortive Confederate assault on Fort Stedman (March 1865), which sealed the doom of the Confederacy. He was imprisoned at Point Lookout, Md., until 12 June 1865, when he took the oath and was released.

Reaching Charlotte by train, he walked the sixty miles to his home, arriving there on 20 June.

Possessed of a modest formal education, augmented by his participation in a prewar "literary society," Elliott attempted to eke out a living as an itinerant teacher in North Carolina, Kentucky, and eventually as far away as Illinois before returning to his native state. On 5 Dec. 1872 he married Biddy Gettys (1853–97) at her home in Rutherford County. They settled in Cleveland County, raising a family of nine: Lizzie Lee (m. David Anderson Beam), Barbara Eugenia, Lottie Cline, Leona Nora (m. Rufus Alexander Bingham), George Alexander, William Martin (m. Elizabeth Noller), James Carson, Jr., Henry Bedford, and Plato Jefferson (m. Eugenia Lollar).

In December 1880 Elliott purchased from Henry Summitt the first town lot sold in Cherryville, where he built a combination store-house and moved his family the following March. In May 1881, the year Cherryville was incorporated, Elliott was elected its first mayor. There he taught school and served for eight years as justice of the peace until February 1890, when he returned permanently to Cleveland.

Throughout his adult life Elliott was a prolific and articulate writer for newspapers of the area, including the *Shelby Aurora, Shelby Star, Charlotte Observer, Rutherford Sun,* and *Forest City Courier.* His subjects were government, politics, history, local and family matters, philosophy, or whatever attracted his wide-ranging interests. Optimistic by nature and driven by a strong sense of integrity and personal worth, he preached the betterment of America's youth and the challenge of the future. His writings, which continued until shortly before his death at ninety-one, were "alive with ideas and were as vital and contemporary as if written by a much younger man, . . . always voicing a constructive and progressive policy. He gave suggestions backed by long years of experience and cool judgment and for the most part he was always right." Illustrating his vision is a statement in *The Southern Soldier Boy* in which he foresaw (in 1907) eventual war with Japan.

A lifelong Democrat and a Methodist, Elliott "hewed his success out of a wilderness of difficulties and then studied and reasoned his way to a position of respect and honor in the hearts of thousands." "One of [Cleveland County's] best citizens and friends" and her oldest Confederate veteran when he died, he was buried in the Elliott cemetery at Polkville.

SEE: *Cleveland Times,* 30 Nov. 1965; James Carson Elliott, *The Southern Soldier Boy: A Thousand Shots for the Confederacy* (1907); Family scrapbook, newspaper clippings, Elliott's wartime correspondence (in possession of Mrs. Plato Elliott, Lawndale); *Shelby Star,* 26 Sept. 1974.

DAVID WINFRED GADDY

## Elliott, John G. ("Ghost"). *See* Eliot, John G. ("Ghost")

**Elliott, Philip Lovin, Sr.** *(22 Sept. 1891–14 Apr. 1961),* minister, educator, and college president, was born of Scottish and English ancestry in Wayside, Swain County, a former community in the Smoky Mountains now under the waters of Fontana Lake. His father, Isaac Bartley Elliott, a Confederate soldier and later farmer and merchant, fought in the Battle of Atlanta. At the age of eighteen, filled with a consuming desire for an education, Philip Elliott walked the twenty miles from Wayside to Robbinsville where he enrolled in a small Presbyterian mountain academy. In 1912 he went to Mars Hill, then a high school, to complete his preparation for college. While a student there, he was ordained to the Christian ministry. The young Reverend Mr. Elliott began his ministry by riding horseback once a month across Bald Mountain down into Flag Pond, Tenn., to preach to a small mountain Baptist congregation. From Mars Hill, he went to Wake Forest College in 1915 where he was graduated in 1919 as an outstanding student in English literature and journalism.

For forty years Elliott devoted himself to the work of his denomination, to teaching, and to college administration. His first teaching assignment was in a small green valley at Proctor where, at the time, the Ritter Lumber Company had a sawmill village. There in a one-room schoolhouse, made of rough boards, he taught a four-month subscription school at a salary of forty dollars a month. Following graduation from Wake Forest College, he went to Bakersville to take charge of Mitchell Collegiate Institute, one of a number of Baptist boarding schools at that time supported by the Southern Baptist Home Mission Board. Here, virtually under the shadow of Roan Mountain, he was principal, dean, business manager, and teacher in a school for three hundred boys and girls, many of whom were too poor to pay even the modest fees of the struggling mountain school. The next three years he gave to his ministry—as missionary pastor to Graham County (1920), as enlistment secretary of the North Carolina Baptist State Convention for all of western North Carolina (1921), and as pastor of the Cullowhee Baptist Church (1922). Nevertheless, in 1923 his strong commitment to Christian education led him to accept an appointment as dean and head of the English department at Mars Hill College.

The years between 1923 and 1930 were full ones for Professor Elliott. After receiving a master's degree in 1925 from The University of North Carolina, he was made vice-president of Mars Hill College. Two years later, taking a leave for more graduate study, he followed the eminent Renaissance scholar, Dr. Edwin A. Greenlaw, to Johns Hopkins University, where he worked from 1927 to 1928 with Professor Greenlaw and others on the Johns Hopkins *Variorum Edition of the Works of Edmund Spenser.* In 1930, he resigned his post at Mars Hill to become head of the English department at Western Carolina Teachers College (now Western Carolina University), a position he held for thirteen years.

It was, however, at Gardner-Webb College that he was to make his most enduring and significant contributions in higher education. Governor O. Max Gardner, on one occasion, called Boiling Springs Junior College a school that "refused to die." In 1942 two significant things occurred in the life of that institution: Governor Gardner began to devote his energies, time, and wealth to guiding and strengthening the school; and its name was changed to Gardner-Webb College. In July 1943, Elliott left Western Carolina Teachers College and went to Gardner-Webb as its president, bringing with him a community service concept of education that was destined to make it unusual among small liberal arts colleges. Under his direction Gardner-Webb became a member college of the North Carolina Baptist Convention, and the building of the modern campus was pushed forward. In his tenth report to the board of trustees in 1953, President Elliott reviewed the college's progress during the first decade of his administration.

Total assets had increased sixfold, the operating fund had increased twelvefold, the endowment had increased thirtyfold, and the college was now fully accredited. Progress continued to characterize his administration until his death seven years later. However, Elliott did not regard the physical and financial growth of the college to be the most significant aspect of his presidency. Rather, he considered his crowning achievement to be the assembling at Gardner-Webb of a faculty that understood the needs of youth and was devoted to the serious business of teaching without which all else would be meaningless. In recognition of his educational leadership and achievement, he was awarded an honorary Ed.D. degree by Carson-Newman College in 1951 and the LL.D. degree by Wake Forest University in 1959.

On 27 Aug. 1918 Elliott married Etta Maurine Carringer of Robbinsville. Four children were born to the union: Ruth Eleanor, Diane Jayne, Philip Lovin, Jr., and Rachel Elizabeth. Elliott died of a heart attack in his office on the Gardner-Webb campus.

SEE: Francis B. Dedmond, *Lengthened Shadows: A History of Gardner-Webb College, 1907–1956* (1957); *Who's Who in America*, 1956–57; *Who's Who in American Education*, 1951–52; *Who's Who in the South and Southwest*, 1950, 1952.

FRANCIS B. DEDMOND

**Ellis, John Willis** *(23 Nov. 1820–7 July 1861)*, legislator, superior court judge, and governor, son of Anderson and Judith Bailey Ellis, was born in the section of eastern Rowan County that later became part of Davidson County. He grew up on the plantation that his father had inherited from Ellis's grandfather, Willis, in 1806. Young Ellis attended Randolph Macon College and was graduated from The University of North Carolina on 3 June 1841. He spent the following year studying law under Richmond Mumford Pearson at Mocksville. This was the forerunner of Pearson's famous law school begun in 1847 at his home, Richmond Hill, in Yadkin County. Ellis commenced the practice of law in Salisbury in July 1842. On 1 Aug. 1844, a few months short of his twenty-fourth birthday, he was elected a member of the North Carolina House of Commons as a Democrat from a predominantly Whig county.

Shortly after the election, on 25 Aug. 1844, Ellis was married in Philadelphia to Mary White, the daughter of Philo and Nancy White formerly of Salisbury. White was editor of the Salisbury *Western Carolinian* (1820–30) and the Raleigh *North Carolina Standard* (1834–36) and a member of the diplomatic corps (1849–58). Ellis and his wife were married only a few weeks when she died of an unknown malady, possibly typhoid fever, on 19 Oct. 1844 upon their return to North Carolina.

As soon as he took his seat in the House of Commons on 18 Nov. 1844, Ellis began to champion internal improvements, a concern throughout his political career. He was again elected a member of the General Assembly in 1846 and 1848. A few days into the 1848 session he was chosen by Dorothea L. Dix to present a memorial to the house urging the construction of an asylum for the protection and care of the insane in North Carolina. As chairman of the Joint Select Committee to study this proposal, Ellis on 8 Dec. 1848 favorably reported out a bill to provide for the establishment of a state hospital for the insane. The bill became law on 21 December. On 16 Dec. 1848 Ellis, who a few weeks earlier had celebrated his twenty-eighth birthday, was elected a judge of the Superior Court of North Carolina by the General Assembly. During his tenure in the legislature and on the bench one of his most influential political mentors was William W. Holden, the powerful editor of *The North Carolina Standard*. As early as January 1852 Holden was urging Ellis to run for the U.S. Senate and the following year he tried to persuade him to run for governor, but Ellis declined both offers. Six years later the two men would oppose each other for their party's nomination for governor.

The Democratic convention, which convened in Charlotte on 14 Apr. 1858, nominated Ellis for governor the following day. After serving almost ten years on the bench, he resigned on 29 April. He was elected governor on 5 Aug. 1858. Six days later the widower of fourteen years married Mary McKinley Daves, daughter of John P. Daves, in New Bern. On 1 Jan. 1859 Ellis was inaugurated governor. In his address he acknowledged that animosity existed toward the Northern view of slavery, but he voiced the overriding feeling in the state at that time when he said, "Grievous as are these causes of discontent, we are not prepared for the acknowledgement that we cannot enjoy all our constitutional rights in the Union." He continued to counsel moderation with firmness in dealing with the central government.

During his first administration Ellis was vitally interested in internal improvements, especially in the completion of the navigation works on the Cape Fear and Deep rivers from Fayetteville to the coal fields in Chatham County. He also continued a progressive program of improving plank roads, navigation, turnpike roads, and the state's educational system. Another high point during his first term was the visit of President James Buchanan to Chapel Hill to deliver the commencement address at the university on 1 June 1859. Ellis escorted the president on his many stops en route to Chapel Hill. The dominant theme of the president's remarks at every stop was the preservation of the Union and the Constitution. Shortly after Buchanan's departure, the governor's wife gave birth on 8 June to a daughter, Mary Daves. A second daughter, Jean Graham, was born on 9 Oct. 1860.

Ellis was reelected governor for a second term on 2 Aug. 1860 by a smaller majority than he had received in 1858. There is some speculation that he lost votes because of his strong advocacy for states rights at a time when most North Carolinians supported the central government. His message to the General Assembly on 20 Nov. 1860 was not a call for secession, but a plea for the "prevention . . . of civil war and preservation of peace." However, he did recommend that North Carolina consult with other Southern states on the question of secession and then let the people express their opinion in a convention. He also recommended reorganization of the militia.

On 1 Jan. 1861 Ellis was formally installed as governor for a second term, taking the oath before the judges of the state supreme court, there not being a quorum of the General Assembly in Raleigh on that day. On 29 January, at the governor's bidding, the Assembly passed a convention bill; a few days earlier it had sent a delegation to the peace conference in Washington, which Ellis had little confidence would succeed. The following day Ellis urged the members of the Southern Convention meeting in Montgomery, Ala.—to which the Assembly had also sent a delegation—not to delay their business by waiting for the Virginia delegates to arrive because "Va. N. Ca. and other border slave states will much sooner join an organized government than secede without such government." The majority of North Carolinians did not seem to agree with their governor's strong views because on 28 February they defeated the call for a convention. On 13 Apr. 1861 Fort Sumter fell to South Carolina troops. This act of aggression against the central government caused President Lincoln to call for 75,000 troops to coerce the seceded states. When requested on 15 April to furnish two regiments for this undertaking, Ellis replied by telegram the same day that Lincoln would "get no troops from North Carolina."

Ellis immediately ordered state troops to seize the federal forts in North Carolina as well as the federal arsenal at Fayetteville. On 17 April he telegraphed Confederate President Jefferson Davis that he was "in possession of Forts, Arsenals, etc. come as soon as you choose. We are ready to join you to a man. Strike the blow quickly and Washington will be ours." Called into session by Ellis on 1 May, the General Assembly immediately passed a convention bill and authorized Ellis to send troops to Virginia at once to help defend that state. The convention called in Raleigh on 20 May 1861 unanimously adopted an ordinance of secession. Whereupon Ellis promptly telegraphed President Davis the news.

In delicate health for some time, Ellis was compelled during the latter part of June to journey to Red Sulphur Springs, Va., in an attempt to regain his strength. A few days later he died at the age of forty-one. He was buried in the family cemetery in Davidson County; sometime later he was reinterred in the Old English Cemetery, Salisbury.

SEE: Noble J. Tolbert, ed., *The Papers of John Willis Ellis*, 2 vols. (1964).

NOBLE J. TOLBERT

**Ellis, Richard** *(fl. 1765–1790)*, Revolutionary War patriot and shipowner, was a native of Ireland living in New Bern prior to 1765. On 16 May of that year he was one of the forty residents requesting Governor William Tryon to seek an annual salary from the Society for the Propagation of the Gospel in Foreign Parts for schoolmaster Thomas Thomlinson. A shipowner and shipper, Ellis ordered harpoons and dories from Boston in 1768 for his sloop *Sally*, the first vessel in the town to be so equipped, in his unsuccessful attempt to start a whaling industry. During late 1771 he was among those petitioning for a charter to start a Masonic lodge in New Bern. On 9 Jan. 1772, the day before the date of the charter, he was one of eight men attending the first meeting of St. John's Lodge. The following December he was elected its senior warden. After the Revolutionary War when the lodge was reorganized, he was unanimously chosen its Worshipful Master on 16 Mar. 1787. At the organizational session of the Grand Lodge of North Carolina in December 1787 at Tarboro, he received one of the nine votes cast for Grand Master and two for Deputy Grand Master. He was elected its first Senior Grand Warden.

Ellis was among those who insisted that the First Provincial Congress be held in New Bern, and he was a New Bern representative to the Third Provincial Congress at Hillsborough in August 1775. At the provincial council meeting in Johnston County in December 1775, he was appointed a commissioner for Port Brunswick and as such was one of several entrusted with purchasing, arming, and outfitting vessels to guard the main ports of North Carolina. In June 1775 he had been instrumental in arranging a meeting between Governor Richard Caswell and French representatives en route to Philadelphia. A letter to Caswell of 9 Feb. 1778 indicates that Ellis was well informed about English affairs. He was in charge of outfitting the *Pennsylvania Farmer* in October 1776 and the *Caswell* in June 1778. Ellis, it was said, "has been accustomed to the sea from his youth, & consequently pretty well acquainted with maritime affairs." He was one of the men commissioned to seize and sell the personal estate of Josiah Martin in December 1776. His privateers, with those of John Wright Stanley also of New Bern, were instrumental in keeping the ports open along North Carolina's Outer Banks during the Revolution as about the only lifelines of water shipments of supplies to General Washington.

On 4 July 1778 Richard Cogdell wrote to Governor Caswell: "In celebration of this day great numbers of Guns have been fired, at Stanley's wharf and Mr. Ellis' ship, three different firings from each from early morning, midday and evening, and Liquor given to the populace. Stanley and Ellis seemed to vie with each other, in a contest who should do the most honor to the day, but Mr. Ellis had the most artillery." This is believed to have been the first observance of the Fourth of July as Independence Day in North Carolina, following only those in Boston and Philadelphia.

The 1790 census of North Carolina records Ellis as living alone in his household but owning six slaves. After his death his New Bern home went to a nephew, George Ellis, who in 1800 and 1801 represented New Bern in the North Carolina House of Commons. George Ellis was also active in the local Masonic lodge until his accidental death on 6 Sept. 1808 in a gunpowder explosion while "blowing up a House to stop the ravages of a Fire." His wife was Amaryllis Sitgreaves, sister of Judge John Sitgreaves; their daughter, Arete S., was a religious worker and a teacher at Moses Griffin's school, one of the first free trade schools for orphan girls. Twin stained glass windows in Christ Episcopal Church, New Bern, memorialize Arete Ellis.

SEE: Gertrude S. Carraway, *Years of Light* (1944); John L. Cheney, Jr., ed., *North Carolina Government, 1585–1974* (1975); Walter Clark, ed., *State Records of North Carolina*, vols. 11–14 (1895–96), 23–24 (1904–5); Ellis family records (in possession of Gertrude S. Carraway); William S. Powell, ed., *The Correspondence of William Tryon and Other Selected Papers*, 2 vols. (1980–81); William L. Saunders, ed., *Colonial Records of North Carolina*, vols. 7–10 (1890).

GERTRUDE S. CARRAWAY

**Ellison, Stewart** *(8 Mar. 1832–24 Oct. 1899)*, building contractor and one of the first three black men elected as Wake County legislator and Raleigh city commissioner, was born in Beaufort County, a slave on the estate of Abner P. Neal. At age thirteen he began a seven-year apprenticeship in carpentry under Marrs Newton, a black mechanic in Washington, N.C. Later he obtained some education through night school and independent reading.

During 1852–54 Ellison was employed in Raleigh in the construction of several Fayetteville Street buildings following a widely destructive December 1851 fire; he also worked on the first buildings at Dorothea Dix Hospital for the Insane. Except for the period 1855–62, when he was again in Washington, Raleigh was his home for the rest of his life. After the Civil War he was a grocer and commission merchant. Reverting again in

1867 to the building trade, he became, according to a contemporary, Charles N. Hunter, "probably the most extensive colored contractor in the state," with a reputation for superior workmanship in the "many elegant residences in and around Raleigh and in other sections of the State." He also built schoolhouses, hospitals, and offices for the Bureau of Refugees, Freedmen, and Abandoned Lands.

In the North Carolina Freedmen's Convention in Raleigh, 29 Sept.–3 Oct. 1865, Ellison played a leading role as a vice-president. He was assistant grand marshal and a featured speaker for Raleigh's Emancipation Day observance on 1 Jan. 1870. A year earlier, on 4 Jan. 1869, he had been one of the first three Negroes elected to Raleigh's Board of Commissioners (Governor Holden having appointed the two blacks who served briefly in 1868). His first committee assignment was as one of three commissioners to make plans for a new city hall and market house to replace the 1840 structure destroyed by fire a few weeks earlier. For the entire decade, January 1869–May 1879, he was reelected annually to Raleigh's governing board, during which time city charter revisions changed elections from January to May in 1871 and substituted seventeen aldermen in five wards for nine commissioners in three beginning in 1875. Ellison's constituents thereafter formed the southeastern Second Ward. In his eleventh campaign, that of 1879, he was defeated for the city post, but blacks continued to be elected to the board through the remainder of the century.

During this decade he served as Wake County Republican representative in six General Assembly sessions, those of 1870, 1871, 1872, 1873, 1879, and 1880. He declined his party's nomination in 1876. During his last term (1879–80) he was a member of the committees on Education; Deaf, Dumb, and Blind; and Public Buildings. J. S. Tomlinson, who compiled short biographies of members of that legislature, termed him "far above the average of his race as to intelligence," and stated that he took "practical views of most subjects of general importance." Ellison's defeat in the 1880 election by fewer than twenty votes caused "universal dissatisfaction among the colored voters," according to Negro legislator and editor James H. Harris, who charged that white Republican betrayal was "ominous of future evil to the unity of the Republican party" in Wake.

Also during the 1870s Ellison served three terms as a director of the state penitentiary. At the end of the first year, March 1874–March 1875, he was nominated for another term by Governor Curtis Brogden on 10 March, but the senate refused to confirm him. Two months later the governor appointed him to fill a vacancy, and he served from 26 May 1875 to 15 Feb. 1877.

Following the close of his legislative and municipal board careers, Ellison was business manager of the *North Carolina Republican* edited by James H. Harris. He was active in the 1880 antiexodus movement to encourage blacks not to migrate out of the state and was a founder of the North Carolina Industrial Association, which sponsored separate Negro fairs beginning in 1879. He was Grand Master of the Prince Hall Grand Lodge of Masons during 1886–90.

Ellison continued to be listed as a carpenter in Raleigh city directories from 1875–76 through 1899–1900, residing until 1886 at 517 South Person Street. In the late 1880s he served as county jailer and in the 1890s was janitor in the United States Courthouse and Post Office in Raleigh, living then in Raleigh's Southside at 24 Hayti Alley. He died of heart failure, apparently in comparative poverty, probably in Raleigh. His widow's name recurs in city directories as a domestic or laundress from 1901 until 1913–14 at their Hayti Alley address. He was buried at Mount Hope Cemetery, Raleigh.

Ellison's first wife was Mary Davis of Beaufort County, by whom he had three daughters. On 7 June 1866 he was married, second, to Narcissa Lucas in Raleigh by the Reverend G. W. Brodie, pastor of St. Paul's A. M. E. Church, of which he was an early member. His eldest daughter, Sophia E., married, also at St. Paul's, John W. Lee, Jr., on 12 Nov. 1880. A second daughter was Mary J. Ellison; and a third, Bettie, was the first wife of Spanish-American War Colonel James H. Young. A great-grandson (through the third daughter Bettie), James Young Carter (b. 20 Apr. 1915), was an instructor in law at North Carolina College, Durham, before moving to Illinois where he was a member of the Illinois state legislature (1955–73) and commissioner of the Public Vehicle License Commission, City of Chicago (1960). Carter's only daughter, Christine Maudette Carter, was one of the first black officers employed in the bond department of the First National Bank of the City of Chicago.

SEE: Board of the Penitentiary, Minutes, 1869–80 (North Carolina State Archives, Raleigh); *Branson's North Carolina Business Directory, 1877–1878*; James Young Carter to Elizabeth D. Reid, letter, 18 Feb. 1975; John L. Cheney, Jr., ed., *North Carolina Government, 1585–1974* (1975); General Assembly, *Laws of North Carolina*, 1879; Governor's Papers, Brogden (North Carolina State Archives, Raleigh); "History of [St. Paul's A. M. E.] Church," Raleigh, 1915 (Unsigned manuscript in church office); Charles N. Hunter Papers (Manuscript Department, Library, Duke University, Durham); Frenise A. Logan, *The Negro in North Carolina, 1876–1894* (1964); Marriage bonds of Wake County (North Carolina State Archives, Raleigh); Raleigh city directories, 1875–1913; Raleigh newspapers: *Banner-Enterprise*, 31 May 1883, *Daily Examiner*, 19 Feb. 1894, *Daily News*, 7 May 1878, 6 May 1879, *Daily Sentinel*, 20, 30 Sept. 1865, 5, 30 Jan. 1869, 15 Mar. 1870, 2 May 1871, 7, 11 May 1872, 6 May 1873, 5 May 1874, 1 May 1875, *Farmer and Mechanic*, 18 Nov. 1880, *Hale's Weekly*, 20 Jan. 1880, *News and Observer*, 4 Nov. 1880, 24, 25 Oct. 1899; *North Carolina Republican*, 12 Nov. 1880, *North Carolina Standard*, 5, 11 Jan. 1869, 1, 3 Jan. 1870, *Observer*, 8 May 1877; *The Masonic Journal* 10 (Fall 1970); John S. Tomlinson, *Tar-Heel Sketch Book, 1879*.

ELIZABETH DAVIS REID

**Elmsley, Alexander** *([27?] Jan. 1730–29 Jan. 1797)*, assemblyman, attorney, colonial agent, and business representative, was born probably in Aberdeenshire, Scotland, but was in North Carolina by 1762 when he was borough representative from Halifax in the April session of the Assembly. He represented New Bern in the November 1762 session as well as in the sessions of February 1764, May 1765, November 1766, and December 1767–January 1768. In the Assembly he was active in having New Bern named the provincial capital and was copatron of the appropriations act for Tryon Palace there. He served frequently on committees to draw up answers to the governor's speeches and to draft addresses to the king, and he was active in preparing legislation concerning the courts, the regulation of duties of sheriffs, provisions for the established clergy and vestries, prison repair, military preparedness, the care of orphans, and the distribution of intestate estates. He was often named to deliver bills from the Assembly to the Council.

In a private connection Elmsley was employed by Samuel Johnston of Edenton, Henry Laurens of South Carolina, and others to transact business affairs with merchants and financial institutions in England. Business records as well as correspondence that passed between Johnston and Elmsley, preserved in the Hayes Collection papers, demonstrate the skill and care with which both men conducted their business. The letters, however, also contain evidence of genuine friendship between the two families. While in North Carolina Elmsley was often in Edenton serving as an attorney for Crown interests, and young John Elmsley (who was just six when he was taken to England) later recalled many pleasant incidents that occurred there. Alexander Elmsley also transacted legal business in Halifax, New Bern, and Wilmington and undoubtedly elsewhere in the province. In letters to Johnston he mentioned interests in South Carolina as well as "my West India Adventure." In November 1772 he related that he had purchased some property in the West Indies. He was deeply interested in relations between the colonies and the mother country and often commented on events in America and in London. His remarks frequently were slanted in favor of the colonies, and he made several suggestions to Johnston as to how differences might be adjusted. Elmsley visited France and his observations on the French Revolution are harsh and critical; he had no love for the people of France.

Elmsley and his family had left North Carolina for England by the summer of 1768 and settled in London where he continued to serve as business representative for planters. In time he also became one of the official agents of the province of North Carolina. Thomas Barker had been designated North Carolina's agent in London in 1761, but in 1774 both Barker and Elmsley were named special agents to represent North Carolina in the court and attachment controversy before the board of trade. In June 1775 they achieved an exemption of the province from the Trade Restraining Act that had been passed two months earlier by Parliament. It was to Elmsley that the Assembly sent assorted petitions and addresses to the king; Elmsley put these documents into more acceptable form than when they arrived and explained much about protocol to the North Carolinians. He seems to have been sincerely concerned for the welfare of North Carolina and to have represented its interests fairly and honestly. He did his utmost to keep leaders in the colony fully informed about acts of Parliament and went to great lengths to explain them to the committee of correspondence. In a final prewar letter to Samuel Johnston on 24 May 1776, Elmsley assured him of his lasting friendship no matter what political convictions might interrupt them. There was no further communication between them until 11 Dec. 1783 when their correspondence was renewed in news-filled letters. Accounts on both sides, long in abeyance, were settled promptly. Thereafter as long as Elmsley lived they continued to exchange friendly and affectionate letters filled with personal, family news on many occasions. Elmsley asked for information about and commented on conditions in the new state of North Carolina and was especially interested in the reaction to the new federal constitution. He expressed the good wishes of the people of England for North Carolina and observed that many there were thinking of moving to America. Johnston, on the other hand, once sent his congratulations on the recovery of King George from illness.

In his correspondence with North Carolina acquaintances, Elmsley referred to his wife as "my Rib" and often mentioned her health and activities. They were the parents of four children: John (1762–1805), born in Halifax, who became a judge in Canada; Alexander, about whom nothing further is known except that he was in Canada in 1800; a daughter who died of hydrophobia in 1771 and whose loss deeply affected her father; and Peter (1773–1825), classical scholar on Sophocles and Euripides, Camden professor of ancient history at Oxford, and Anglican clergyman. In 1793 Alexander Elmsley wrote his friend Samuel Johnston that he had considered returning to North Carolina or Virginia and buying between two and three thousand acres of land on which one of his sons would settle. "I have now three boys to provide for," he wrote; "one of them shall take one of your girls off your hands, if she cannot dispose of herself better." After Elmsley's death his widow lived for a time with her son, Peter, but was in Canada with John for a visit in the early summer of 1801. After the American Revolution Mrs. Elmsley was in frequent contact with Mr. and Mrs. Robert Palmer, formerly of Bath, and with members of the Rutherfurd and Schaw families, formerly of New Hanover County, all of whom were then in England. Nor was Mrs. Elmsley forgotten in North Carolina. In addition to the frequent passing of messages between her and the women of Samuel Johnston's family, Mrs. Mary Conway of New Bern willed silk and linen apparel to Mrs. Elmsley.

Elmsley died at his home in London after a brief period of declining health and was buried in the churchyard of St. Marylebone of which he was a member. In addition to his wife and three sons, he was survived by a brother, Peter, noted London bookseller, who took over the financial business for various North Carolinians and other Americans that remained to be handled. Peter, in fact, had been a financial representative for some of them for several years. This brother had no children, and Alexander's son, Peter, inherited his extensive estate.

SEE: John L. Cheney, Jr., ed., *North Carolina Government, 1584–1974* (1975); *Gentlemen's Magazine* 95 (April 1825); J. Bryan Grimes, *Abstract of North Carolina Wills* (1910); Hayes Collection (Southern Historical Collection, Library, University of North Carolina, Chapel Hill); Ella Lonn, *Colonial Agents of the Southern Colonies* (1945); William S. Powell, ed., *Correspondence of William Tryon*, 2 vols. (1980–81); William L. Saunders, ed., *Colonial Records of North Carolina*, vols. 6–9 (1888–90); St. Marylebone burial fee book (P89/MRY1/443), Greater London Record Office; H. Braughn Taylor, "The Foreign Attachment Law and the Coming of the Revolution in North Carolina," *North Carolina Historical Review* 52 (January 1975).

WILLIAM S. POWELL

**Elmsley, John** *(1762–1805)*, chief justice of Canada, was born in Halifax, the son of Alexander Elmsley and his wife. He moved to England with his parents in the summer of 1768 and was graduated from Oriel College, Oxford, in 1786. Called to the English bar at the Middle Temple in 1790, he was named chief justice of Upper Canada (now southern Ontario) six years later. Also in 1796 he became a member of the Legislative Council of the province and speaker in 1799. He became chief justice of Lower Canada (now Quebec province) in 1802. His appointment to these posts came through the patronage of William Henry Cavendish Bentinck, Duke of

Portland, a family friend. In Canada Elmsley acquired property in York (afterwards named Toronto) and was active in promoting its growth and development. Government House there was erected on property owned by him. He married Mary Hallowell of Boston, Mass., sister of Admiral Sir Benjamin Hallowell Carew (1760–1834). They were the parents of three children: John, Ann Gee, and Mary Bond. The son, John (1801–63), became a captain in the Royal Navy and a member of the executive council of Upper Canada.

After settling in Canada Justice Elmsley wrote to old friends in North Carolina mentioning events of his childhood and suggesting that they visit him. He recalled with pleasure life in Edenton when he was a child. His father once expressed the hope that one of his sons, presumably John, might marry the daughter of one of their North Carolina friends. Alexander Elmsley once considered purchasing several thousand acres in North Carolina in expectation that one of his sons would settle there.

Elmsley died suddenly as he was preparing to return to England and was buried in the cemetery at Dorchester. A number of his descendants now live in Canada, Michigan, Connecticut, Illinois, and elsewhere.

SEE: Francis-J. Audet, *Les Juges en Chef de la Province de Québec* (1927); Hayes Collection (Southern Historical Collection, Library, University of North Carolina, Chapel Hill); Le R. P. L. Le Jeune, *Dictionnaire Général de Biographie . . . du Canada* (1931); David B. Read, *The Lives of the Judges of Upper Canada and Ontario* (1888); W. Stewart Wallace, ed., *The Macmillan Dictionary of Canadian Biography* (1978).

WILLIAM S. POWELL

**Elwin, Fountain** *(1736–January 1833)*, private secretary to Governor William Tryon and later an attorney, was born at Booton in the north central part of the county of Norfolk, England, where his family had owned various estates for generations. A marriage in 1621 between an Elwin and a daughter of the Fountain family accounts for his unusual first name. Margaret Wake Tryon, wife of Governor Tryon and the daughter of Elizabeth Elwin Wake, was Fountain Elwin's first cousin. In 1764 he accompanied the Tryons to North Carolina where he served as the governor's private secretary until 1767, when he returned to England. In 1808 Elwin was admitted to Grays Inn.

He married Ann Maria Gibson and in 1779 the first of their children was born. They were the parents of three sons and three daughters, all of whom survived childhood, which was remarkable in those days. In 1808 he traveled from Enfield, where he was living, to Yoxford, Suffolk, to visit his cousin Margaret Tryon and while there he helped her make a will. He was one of the numerous beneficiaries of her estate, she having no surviving children. Elwin died at the age of ninety-six and was buried at Dulwich. A miniature portrait of him as a young man and a pencil sketch of him as an old man are in the possession of the Nash family in England, descendants of his daughter Rebecca. His family was related to that of John Rolfe, and the well-known portrait of Pocahontas descended in his family until it was sold in America; the portrait is now in the National Portrait Gallery, Washington, D.C.

SEE: Elwin family papers (in possession of D. E. Fountain Stokes, Thompson, Norfolk, England); William S. Powell, ed., *The Correspondence of William Tryon and Other Selected Papers*, vol. 1 (1980 [portrait]).

D. E. FOUNTAIN STOKES

**Emerson, Isaac Edward** *(24 July 1859–23 Jan. 1931)*, chemist, manufacturer, sportsman, and philanthropist, was born in Orange County, the son of Robert J. Emerson, a farmer, and his wife, Cornelia Lewis Hudson of Wake County. Because of the early death of his mother, Isaac and his brother, John W., moved into the home of their uncle and aunt, Mr. and Mrs. A. J. McDade, in the town of Chapel Hill. Emerson entered The University of North Carolina in 1876 and was graduated with a degree in chemistry in 1879. While a student, he was employed as an assistant in A. B. Roberson's drugstore on the corner of Franklin and Columbia streets. Shortly after graduating, Emerson married the former Mrs. Emily Askew Dunn, daughter of Colonel W. F. Askew of Raleigh. Mrs. Dunn was divorced from a previous marriage. In 1881 the Emersons moved to Baltimore, Md. There Emerson earned the fortune for which he was later known. From 1884 to 1889, he established several drugstores and at some time during this period developed the formula that he later patented as Bromo-Seltzer, a widely known headache remedy. To promote the remedy, he founded the Emerson Drug Company in 1891.

The commercial success of Bromo-Seltzer was due in large measure to Emerson's foresight in recognizing the growing importance of advertising. His product was advertised in many countries and in many languages, often by unusual devices. As his wealth increased, he turned from business activities to sports and social pursuits. He purchased several yachts including the *Susquehanna*, the *Margaret*, and the *Queen Anne*. These were used for hunting expeditions, social entertainment, and extensive world travel.

In 1894 Emerson organized the Maryland Naval Reserves, which he commanded from 1894 to 1901. During the Spanish-American War, he personally financed an entire naval squadron, was commissioned a lieutenant in the U.S. Navy, and was made assistant to the chief of the Auxiliary Naval Force. The Maryland Reserves elected him captain in 1900, and he was subsequently known as "Captain Emerson" or "Captain Ike."

Emerson's interest in sports resulted in the gift to The University of North Carolina of Emerson Stadium, the university's first athletic stadium. Donated in 1914, the structure served as the university's official stadium from 1916 until 1927, when Kenan Stadium was built. After many years' service for many sports, the stadium was demolished in 1971.

In 1911 Emerson was remarried to Anne Preston McCormack of Irvington, N.Y., having previously divorced his first wife. During his later years he lived at Brooklandwood, a handsome estate in the Green Spring Valley outside Baltimore, where he operated a model dairy and developed a herd of government-tested cattle. The original part of this home was built by John Carroll of Carrollton. Emerson died at Brooklandwood. He was survived by his second wife, two stepdaughters (Mrs. W. W. Keith and Mrs. James McVickar), and his only daughter, Mrs. Charles Amory.

Two oil portraits of Emerson hang in buildings on the campus of The University of North Carolina, Chapel Hill. One belongs to the Dialectic Literary Society of which Emerson was a member while a student at the university; the other is in Beard Hall, the School of Pharmacy.

SEE: *Chapel Hill Weekly*, 13 Jan. 1950, 2 July 1959; *Durham Morning Herald*, 7 Nov. 1954; Isaac Edward Emerson (typescript, North Carolina Collection, University of North Carolina, Chapel Hill [character sketch, obituary]); Daniel L. Grant, *Alumni History of the University of North Carolina* (1924).

GEORGE T. BLACKBURN II

**Emmons, Ebenezer** *(16 May 1799–1 Oct. 1863)*, geologist, educator, and physician, was born in Middlefield, a village in western Massachusetts, of English ancestry. The single son of five siblings, his parents were farmer Ebenezer and Mary Mack Emmons. The Reverend Dr. Nathaniel Emmons, an uncle, was a preacher of some note. At an early age, Emmons's interest in natural science became apparent. He received most of his training for college from the Reverend Moses Hallock, a teacher in nearby Plainfield. In 1814 he enrolled at Williams College in Williamstown, Mass., where he further developed his interest in natural science under Amos Eaton, who introduced geology into the curriculum at Williams, and Chester Dewey, who initiated the teaching of chemistry there. Emmons was graduated in 1818 and the same year married Maria Cone of Williamstown.

In 1824 Emmons continued his studies in geology at the new Rensselaer (Polytechnic) Institute, where Eaton had become senior professor. Also that year he assisted Dewey in producing a geological map of Berkshire County, Mass. Emmons was graduated from the institute and published his *Manual of Mineralogy and Geology*, a handbook for students, in 1826.

Emmons pursued a vigorous tripartite career for over a decade. Apparently between his days at Williams and Rensselaer, he had studied medicine at the Berkshire Medical College and become a practising physician in Chester, Mass. Nevertheless, he continued to pursue his work in academic science. In 1828 he returned to Williams College as lecturer in chemistry while continuing an extensive medical practice. Two years later he accepted an appointment as junior professor at Rensselaer, a post he would hold for nine years. Meanwhile, he began to enlarge the cabinet of mineralogical and geological specimens at Williams and gave lectures at the Medical School of Castleton. His position at Williams was expanded in 1833 to a professorship of natural science, which he would retain until 1859. In 1838 he was named professor of chemistry in the Albany Medical College and moved to Albany; his association with that school, later in obstetrics, lasted until 1852. During that period he remained on the faculty of Williams College and traveled annually to Williamstown for his classes.

In 1836, Emmons became one of the four head geologists of the new geological survey for the state of New York. His territory included the northeastern counties, and he acquainted the public with the Adirondack region and named its principal mountains. He also named, described, and classified the Potsdam sandstone and other rocks. Of the latter, Emmons caused a great furor among geologists when he discovered and proposed the presence of a system of stratified rocks, which he named the Taconic system, beneath the Potsdam. The controversy would not subside for decades, and Emmons reportedly became embittered by the ostracism and ridicule of other geologists who refused, at times contemptuously, to accept the Taconic theories. The state published his geological report in 1842, and he took charge of the collections of the geological survey. He subsequently investigated the agricultural resources of New York. The work resulted in five volumes (1846–54) dealing with topography, climate, agricultural geology, the Taconic system, soils, grains, vegetable products, fruits, and harmful insects in New York.

In the meantime the legislature of North Carolina in 1851 revived the state geological survey, defunct since 1827. In January 1852 Emmons became its chief, a position he would fill until his death. Indefatigable, Emmons himself did much of the field, office, and laboratory work. He guided most of the efforts toward development of mining, minerals, and agriculture yet undertook very little work west of the Blue Ridge. The state in 1852 published his *Report of Professor Emmons on His Geological Survey of North Carolina*, which dealt chiefly with the agriculture and geology of the eastern counties and the coal fields by the Deep River. Emmons's *Geological Report of the Midland [Piedmont] Counties of North Carolina*, which appeared in 1856, contained a discussion of the geology of the area, a view of the coal fields, and wide-ranging comments on deposits of gold, silver, copper, lead, zinc, and manganese. Two years later he produced a lengthy volume on agriculture of the eastern counties centering around soils, fertilizers, marls, and fossils found in the marls. In 1860 he prepared shorter studies on the principles and practice of agriculture in the state as well as analyses of soil from swamp lands. Under his direction, botanist Moses Ashley Curtis wrote two volumes on descriptive botany of the state, and agriculturalist Edmund Ruffin prepared a description of the agriculture and geology of lower North Carolina. During these busy years, Emmons also found time to publish a major book on *American Geology* and, in 1860, a brief text and manual on the subject. In addition, he served as private consultant to individuals involved in mining metals in the state.

The Civil War shattered Emmons's life and much of his work. Loyal to the Union, he was caught in the South. Anxiety and separation from friends probably fostered the ill health that eventually confined him to his home in Brunswick County, where he died in 1863. He was buried in the City Cemetery, Raleigh, but his remains later were moved to Albany, N.Y. During the war much of the work of Emmons and his assistants was lost, including personal papers (after his death), cabinets of minerals and fossils, manuscript geological maps, and written manuscripts sufficient for several volumes. The conflict interrupted the regular work of the geological survey, and his successor's task was to look after the manufacture of certain war products.

A persevering and enthusiastic worker and teacher, Emmons reportedly was an able man with a kindly yet distant disposition. A religious man, he had served as a deacon in Williamstown. His portrait is preserved in books by Stuckey and Youmans cited below. Emmons had a son, Ebenezer, Jr., and two daughters, Amanda (Conklin) and Mary (Watson).

SEE: *DAB*, vol. 1 (1928); Deeds and estate records of Brunswick County (North Carolina State Archives, Raleigh); Calvin Durfee, *A History of Williams College* (1860), and *Williams Biographical Annals* (1871); Jules Marcou, "Biographical Notice of Ebenezer Emmons," *American Geologist* 7 (1891); and "Ebenezer Emmons," *Science* 5 (1885); John M. Nickles, *Geologic Literature on North America, 1785–1918*, 2 vols. (1923–24); Jasper L. Stuckey, *North Carolina: Its Geology and Mineral Resources* (1965); U.S. Department of the Interior, *Geological Sur-*

*vey*, Bulletin 746 (1923); William J. Youmans, *Pioneers of Science in America* (1896).

R. F. KNAPP

**Empie, Adam** *(5 Sept. 1785–6 Nov. 1860)*, clergyman and educator, was born in Schenectady, N.Y., the son of John Empie, of Dutch descent. Empie was educated at Union College, Schenectady. Ordained in the Protestant Episcopal church, he began his ministry in 1809 as assistant rector of St. George's Church in Hempstead, Long Island. In November 1811 the Reverend Mr. Empie went to St. James Parish in Wilmington, N.C., where his energy and enthusiasm greatly enlarged the church.

In the spring of 1814, Empie left Wilmington to become chaplain and professor of geography, history, and ethics at the U.S. Military Academy at West Point. He returned to St. James Parish in 1816 or 1817. Under his direction the church again grew, services expanded, and the side galleries had to be opened to accommodate the parishioners. While serving in Wilmington, Empie was active in trying to organize the Episcopal church in North Carolina.

Empie again left Wilmington in 1827 to assume the presidency of the College of William and Mary in Williamsburg, Va. During his administration, which lasted until 1836, the college grew and prospered. Then, after a brief stint as principal of the Episcopal diocesan school in Raleigh, Empie moved to Richmond, Va., in 1837. In Richmond his congregation soon built a church and named it St. James in honor of Empie's former Wilmington parish. In 1853, he resigned because of poor health and returned to Wilmington to live with one of his sons. He died in Wilmington and was buried in Oakdale Cemetery.

On 24 Mar. 1814 Empie married Ann Eliza Wright, daughter of Judge Joshua Wright of Wilmington. She died in Richmond in 1842. They had five children: John Joshua, Anna Catharina, Adam, Charles Wright, and Ann Smith. Empie was the author of several books and pamphlets on religious subjects.

SEE: Caroline D. Flanner and Leora Hiatt McEachern, *St. James Church, Wilmington, N.C., 1729–1974* (1974); *The National Cyclopaedia of American Biography*, vol. 3 (1893); John H. Wheeler, *Reminiscences and Memoirs of North Carolina and Eminent North Carolinians* (1884).

ALICE R. COTTEN

**Emry, Thomas Leyburn** *(18 Dec. 1842–8 Sept. 1910)*, industrial organizer and promoter, is remembered for his role in discovering the advantages of what is now the city of Roanoke Rapids as a manufacturing site. A prosperous merchant and farmer of Weldon, he realized the value of harnessing the power of the Roanoke River to increase the prospects of industrialization and persuaded a group of northern and Virginia investors to provide capital of $200,000 for the construction of a dam (known as the "bulkhead") and canal between the old Roanoke Navigation Company and the river.

Born in Petersburg, Va., Emry was orphaned at the age of six. In 1859 he moved to Halifax, N.C., where he worked as a tinner for more than a year and joined the Halifax Light Infantry. Following the secession of South Carolina in December 1860, Emry, then only eighteen, went there and volunteered his services in the war effort. Attached to the Sixth Regiment of the South Carolina Volunteers, he was present at the bombardment of Fort Sumter on 12 Apr. 1861. In July he and his regiment were ordered to Virginia, reaching the battlefield of Bull Run on the afternoon of 22 July. At his request, Emry was later transferred to the Halifax Light Infantry. He served in the Seven Days' Battle around Richmond, and his gallantry at Malvern Hill elicited the commendation of Colonel B. O. Wade. As a result of wounds received in the latter battle, "Major Emry"—as he was later known—was forced to retire from active service in the Confederate Army.

After the war, Emry returned to Halifax and engaged in the mercantile business. In 1869, he moved to nearby Weldon where he took an active part in the industrial development of the town. For nearly twenty years he served as mayor of Weldon and for over fifteen years he was president of the Roanoke and Tar River Agricultural Society. In 1886 he was elected to the Halifax County Board of Commissioners; two years later he was elected to the state senate as a Democrat.

Turning his attention to development of the water power of the Roanoke River, Emry purchased a large tract of land near Great Falls (now Roanoke Rapids), about five miles west of Weldon. In 1892 he succeeded in gaining the interest of several capitalists in the possibility of utilizing the more than 50,000-horsepower river for industrial development. This resulted in the formation of the Great Falls Waterpower Manufacturing and Improvement Company (later the Roanoke Rapids Power Company), which by 1894 owned about 2,285 acres of land, of which some 774 acres—the largest tract—belonged to Emry. In April 1891 he had already assembled a crew of one hundred laborers, including convicts, to build the canal. The job was completed in early 1893.

In December 1893 John Armstrong Chaloner, a scion of the wealthy Astor family, visited Great Falls and negotiated with Emry's company to build the first industrial building in the area. The bricks for this factory were hauled by barge from Emry's brickyard up the Roanoke Navigation Canal. The United Industrial Company, a knitting mill, turned out cotton yarn; due to financial losses, it closed around 1901. But other factories followed. The Roanoke Mills Company began operations in 1897 with more than 12,000 spindles and 320 looms and employed two hundred workers. Within five years, it was producing more than seven million yards of cloth annually; later it became one of the largest producers of fancy flannels in the United States. The Rosemary Manufacturing Company, which was organized in 1900 and started production the next year, became the largest maker of cotton damask in the world. The Patterson Mill Company, which produced chambray, flannel, and gingham, was founded in 1909 and began operations in 1910, the year of Emry's death.

Emry and his wife, Emma Jane Spiers (20 May 1847–3 July 1913) were buried in the Weldon Cemetery. They had one child, Charles Ransom Emry.

SEE: W. C. Allen, *History of Halifax County* (1918); D. H. Hill, ed., *Confederate Military History*, vol. 4 (1899); *The Roanoke Rapids Herald*, 23 Mar. 1969.

RALPH HARDEE RIVES

**Engelhard, Joseph Adolphus** *(27 Sept. 1832–15 Feb. 1879)*, soldier and editor, was born at Monticello, Miss., the only son of Edward and Sarah Benson Engelhard. He attended the local schools of his birthplace, a preparatory school in New Albany, Ind., The University of North Carolina, where he was graduated in 1854, and

Harvard Law School, completing his preparation for the law under Judge W. H. Battle in Chapel Hill and Judge Daniel G. Fowle in Raleigh. Two Chapel Hill classmates—R. H. Battle, Jr., and William L. Saunders—were his lifelong friends. The latter also became his brother-in-law on 26 Sept. 1855 when Engelhard married Margaret Eliza Cotten, daughter of John W. Cotten of Raleigh, and Saunders married her sister Florida Cotten. The Engelhards were the parents of two sons and two daughters.

In 1857 Engelhard began a law practice in Tarboro. In May 1861 he left his growing practice to serve as captain and quartermaster of the Thirty-third Regiment, commanded by Colonel L. O'B. Branch who later fell in battle at Sharpsburg. Rising to the rank of major, Engelhard was made adjutant general and transferred to General W. D. Pender's brigade, replacing Captain Samuel Ashe who had been taken prisoner. From May 1863 until the close of hostilities he was division adjutant, first under General Pender, then—after Pender fell at Gettysburg on 2 July 1863—under General C. M. Wilcox. Assuming command of the right flank of his division after the loss and wounding of many officers, Major Engelhard had his horse shot from under him as he reached the opposing lines. At the request of General Robert E. Lee, Engelhard later prepared the official report of the performance of Pender's division during the three-day Battle of Gettysburg.

When the war was over, President Andrew Johnson restored North Carolina to the Union in the summer of 1865 and set up a provisional government. The following November a legislature was elected. A strong Democrat all his life, Engelhard was selected as secretary of the senate; he was reelected to this post in 1866.

Meanwhile in December 1865 death claimed James Fulton, longtime editor of the *Wilmington Journal*, founded by Alfred Lanier Price. In March 1866 Engelhard acquired a substantial interest in the newspaper, which then had a statewide circulation. For ten years his editorial policies and business management enhanced the appeal and influence of the *Journal* far beyond Wilmington. In 1872, at Engelhard's instigation, the North Carolina Press Association was organized by journalists in the state who met in Charlotte.

The *Journal*'s editor became the voice of the Cape Fear region in protest of the acts of Reconstruction. In 1870, Engelhard championed the candidacy of Colonel A. M. Waddell in his bid for Congress. He also espoused the Democratic organization of the northern states as "the hope of the South," and so brought white southerners by droves into the Democratic party in North Carolina. In 1872, he was a delegate from the Cape Fear region to the Democratic National Convention in Baltimore. When the Negro populace came to dominate county governments in eastern North Carolina, Engelhard called for a state convention in 1875 to revise the Constitution as it related to local governments. Thereafter the unreasonable issues of Reconstruction were considerably mitigated.

By a majority of approximately 18,000 votes Engelhard was elected secretary of state for North Carolina in 1876. Less than three years later, he died in Raleigh after a brief illness. His funeral was held at Christ Episcopal Church and burial was in Oakwood Cemetery. He was succeeded in office by his Chapel Hill classmate and brother-in-law, Colonel William L. Saunders, after John Manning declined the appointment.

SEE: Joseph A. Engelhard Papers and related materials (Manuscript Department, Library, Duke University, Durham); Raleigh *Observer*, 16 Feb. 1879; *Representative Men of the South* (1880); *Wilmington Morning Star*, 18 Feb. 1879; *Wilmington Review*, 15, 17 Feb. 1879; *Wilmington Sun*, 18 Feb. 1879.

D. F. GRANT

**Erskine, Emma Payne** *(10 May 1853–4 Mar. 1924)*, writer, painter, and civic leader, was born in Racine, Wis., the daughter of Alfred and Olive Child Payne. Her father, a native of England, was a portraitist and taught at the Art Institute of Chicago. Through her mother, she was a tenth-generation American. Emma was educated at home. On 8 Apr. 1873, she married Charles Edwin Erskine, a musician and gardener. Their children were Alfred, Harold, Ralph, Violet (Mrs. Macdermid Parish-Watson), Malcolm, and Susan (Mrs. Carroll Pickens Rogers). The Erskines first went to Tryon, N.C., in 1885 with their three small sons and fell in love with the region; in 1895 they moved permanently to Lynncote, their home built of native stone designed by the architect of Biltmore Village. They participated wholeheartedly in community affairs, and Lynncote became a center of civic and artistic activity. He was interested in providing schools and churches. She was energetic in building up the Lanier Library, meanwhile clearing and donating the land for Tryon's golf club. She painted dozens of landscapes and "portraits of old ex-slaves still living in the vicinity." Of her seven books, three are works of fiction set in the North Carolina mountains: *When the Gates Lift Up Their Heads* (1901); *The Mountain Girl* (1912); and her best known, *A Girl of the Blue Ridge* (1915). The last two went through many reprintings. *Iona, a Lay of Ancient Greece* (1888) and *The Harper & the King's Horse* (1905) are books of poems. The other novels are *The Eye of Dread* (1913) and *Joyful Heatherby* (1913).

Charles Erskine died in July 1908. Nine years later Emma married Cecil Corwin in August 1917. In her later years she was president of the Holly Hills Co., a real estate concern engaged in designing and building homes on land she owned. She was an Episcopalian and a Republican. She was buried in Racine. Her son Ralph married Barbara Peattie, daughter of her close friend, the Tryon writer Elia W. Peattie. An oil portrait of Emma Erskine, painted by her father, is a family possession.

SEE: *Asheville Citizen*, 8 Mar. 1924; Sadie S. Patton, *Sketches of Polk County History* (1950); Mrs. C. P. Rogers to Richard Walser, letter, 29 Mar. 1974; *Who's Who in America*, 1920–21.

RICHARD WALSER

**Ervin, John Witherspoon** *(27 Mar. 1823–15 Apr. 1902)*, teacher and writer, who was called Witherspoon Ervin, was born at Cheraw, S.C. His parents were Colonel James Robert Ervin, of Cheraw, a lawyer and legislator, who was a leader of the opposition to John C. Calhoun's Doctrine of Nullification in the Convention of 1832, and his first wife, Elizabeth Powe. His paternal grandparents were Colonel John Ervin, of Pee Dee, S.C., who commanded the Britton's Neck Regiment of General Francis Marion's brigade during the American Revolution, and his first wife, Jane Witherspoon; his maternal grandparents were General Erasmus Powe, of Cheraw, who commanded the Ninth Brigade of South Carolina militia during the War of 1812, and his wife, Esther Ellerbe.

After attending South Carolina College (now the University of South Carolina) as a sophomore and junior (1841–42), Ervin began teaching in the Brewington community on Black River in Clarendon County, S.C. On 21 Nov. 1844 he married Laura Catherine Nelson, daughter of Captain Jared John Nelson, of the Brewington community, who served in the War of 1812, and his wife, Susan McGill Conyers. They were the parents of nine children: Lawrence Nelson, a farmer of Indiantown, S.C.; Erasmus Ellerbe, a Presbyterian minister; John Conyers, a farmer of Fountain City, Tenn.; Donald McQueen, a merchant of Indiantown, S.C.; Susan Elizabeth, wife of James Ervin Kennedy of Manning, S.C.; Samuel James, a lawyer of Morganton, N.C.; Louise Nelson, wife of William Cowan Ervin of Darlington, S.C.; Annie Davis, wife of James Leslie Michie of Darlington; and Henry Flinn, who died in infancy.

In 1849 Ervin moved his family to Sumter, S.C., where he served as principal of the academy and for a time edited the *Black River Watchman*, a regional newspaper. In 1857, the family moved to the new village of Manning, S.C., where Ervin conducted the Clarendon Grammar School and edited Clarendon County's first newspaper, the *Clarendon Banner.* While at Manning, he joined the Masonic order, served as a ruling elder in the Presbyterian church, and was a member of the Democratic party.

During the Civil War Ervin served as collector of the Confederate War tax and member of the home guards in Clarendon County. His sons, Lawrence Nelson, Erasmus Ellerbe, and John Conyers, saw active service with the army. His brother, James Robert Ervin, a soldier of the Confederacy, was killed on 28 July 1864 in a skirmish on the Darbytown Road near Richmond, Va. Three of his wife's brothers also served in the Confederate Army. As a member of the home guards, Ervin participated in the engagement against General Edward W. Potter's vandalizing Federal raiders at Dingle's Mill on 18 Apr. 1865. It was one of the last encounters of the Civil War.

In 1874 all of the Ervin family, except Lawrence Nelson and Erasmus Ellerbe, moved to Morganton, N.C., where Witherspoon Ervin taught school for a time. Except for a brief period about 1884, when he resided in Wilkesboro and was principal of schools at Wilkesboro and Trap Hill, he made his home in Morganton for the remainder of his life.

While teaching in Sumter, Witherspoon Ervin was inspired by his wife to enter a contest for a $100 prize for the best original story by a South Carolinian. He won the contest over sixty competitors with a story entitled "A Shot in Time." During ensuing years he supplemented his income by writing verse and fiction, which was published in the *Baltimore Home Journal, Columbia Banner, Darlington Family Friend, Sumter Watchman, Yorkville Enquirer*, and other newspapers and periodicals. He wrote a number of short or medium-length stories, most written while he was living in South Carolina. Some, however, such as "The Fiddler of Linville Cove, A Legend of Western North Carolina," published in *Fetter's Southern Magazine* in 1892, were written in Morganton.

Laura Catherine Ervin predeceased her husband, dying at Morganton on 29 July 1887.

SEE: Elsie C. Edmonds, *John Chapman, of Spotsylvania County, Virginia, and Thomas Powe, of Cheraw, South Carolina, and Related Families* (1971); Anne K. Gregorie, "John Witherspoon Ervin," *South Carolina Historical and Genealogical Magazine* 46 (1945); Virginia K. G. Orvin, *History of Clarendon County, 1700 to 1961* (1961); Edward W. Phifer, Jr., *Burke: The History of a North Carolina County* (1977); Emily B. Reynolds and Joan R. Faunt, *Biographical Directory of the Senate of the State of South Carolina, 1776–1964* (1964).

SAM J. ERVIN, JR.

**Ervin, Joseph Wilson** *(3 Mar. 1901–25 Dec. 1945)*, congressman, was born in Morganton of Scotch-Irish, English, Welsh, and French Huguenot ancestry. His father, Samuel James Ervin, practiced law in Morganton and the surrounding area for sixty-five years; his mother was Laura Theresa Powe. Ervin received his early education in private and public schools at Morganton. After graduating from the Morganton High School in 1916, he entered The University of North Carolina where he joined the Dialectic Literary Society and the Alpha Tau Omega social fraternity, participated actively in campus politics, and served as managing editor of the *Yackety Yack*, the annual student publication. Having lost a year's study through illness, he was awarded his A.B. degree by the university in 1921; he then entered its law school, where he was a student from 1921 to 1923 and became a member of Phi Delta Phi legal fraternity. He was admitted to the North Carolina bar in August 1922. Upon leaving the university he practiced law in Gastonia until the spring of 1925, when he moved to Charlotte where he made his home the rest of his life.

Active in Democratic party affairs, Ervin served briefly as prosecuting attorney in Charlotte City Court and formed a partnership for the general practice of law with another Burke County native, Guy Thomas Carswell. Carswell's talents as a trial lawyer and Ervin's thorough legal scholarship soon made Carswell and Ervin a well known and successful law firm in Mecklenburg County. Ervin held memberships in the Lions Club, the Knights of Pythias, the Masonic order, the Society of Mayflower Descendants in the State of North Carolina, and the Myers Park Presbyterian Church.

Ervin won the Democratic nomination for Congress over two other contestants in the primary of 27 May 1944, then defeated his Republican opponent by a vote of 50,605 to 26,757 in the general election in November 1944. He represented the Tenth Congressional District in the Seventy-ninth Congress from 3 Jan. 1945 until his death at the end of the year. As a member of the House, he advocated the admission of Alaska to statehood, the conservation of the nation's natural resources, and the establishment of a national academy to train Americans for diplomatic service; he opposed legislation designed to confer upon the federal government control of the hiring practices of private employers. He died in Washington, D.C., and was buried in Forest Hills Cemetery, Morganton.

On 10 Sept. 1930, at Richmond, Va., Ervin married Susan Graham Erwin, daughter of Joseph Ernest Erwin and his wife, Susan Clark, of Morganton, and granddaughter of Chief Justice Walter Clark of the North Carolina Supreme Court. She survived him and contracted a second marriage with W. Harold Williamson.

SEE: *Biog. Dir. Am. Cong.* (1961); John L. Cheney, Jr., ed., *North Carolina Government, 1585–1974* (1975); *Congressional Directory*, 79th Cong., 1st sess.; Seventy-ninth U.S. Congress, *Joseph Wilson Ervin, Memorial Addresses* (1948 [portrait]); *Who's Who in America*, 1946–47.

SAM J. ERVIN, JR.

**Ervin, Samuel James, Jr.** *(27 Sept. 1896–23 Apr. 1985)*, lawyer, jurist, legislator, congressman, and United States senator, was descended from a family of Scotch-Irish Presbyterians who had migrated from Ulster to the coast of South Carolina in 1732. The family originally settled in Williamsburg County.

John Witherspoon Ervin (27 Mar. 1823–15 Apr. 1902), Senator Ervin's grandfather, became a teacher in Clarendon County, S.C., upon his graduation from South Carolina College in the early 1840s. He married Laura Catherine Nelson in 1844, and they eventually had six sons and three daughters. The family lived in Sumter and Manning where John Ervin became the first editor of Clarendon County's earliest newspaper, *The Clarendon Banner*. Ervin stayed in Manning until 1874, when he accepted an opportunity to teach in Morganton, N.C. Financially torn and emotionally embittered by the Confederate defeat in the Civil War, Ervin wrote poetry and fiction for various newspapers and periodicals until his death in 1902.

John Ervin's fifth son, Samuel James Ervin (21 June 1855–13 July 1944), was born in Sumter and reared in Manning. He attended Manning Academy, a school conducted by his father. After the family moved to Morganton, the young man served as deputy postmaster for the community between 1875 and 1880. He studied law in his spare time and passed the North Carolina bar examination in 1879. Ervin was extremely thorough in his study of the law and from modest beginnings became one of the most prominent lawyers of his time in western North Carolina. Though denied the privilege of a college education, Ervin possessed several of the qualities that would characterize his son's career: a devout respect for the Constitution coupled with a detestation of governmental tyranny; a devotion to civil liberties coupled with a sincere belief in the individual's responsibility for his own welfare; and a mastery of the King James version of the Bible coupled with a hatred for religious and other forms of intolerance.

Samuel Ervin married his second cousin, Laura Theresa Powe (25 June 1865–14 June 1956), on 6 Oct. 1886 in Morganton. She was a native of Salisbury and had moved with her parents to Burke County in 1869. Educated in private schools in Charlotte and Morganton, she changed her affiliation from the Episcopal church of her parents to the Presbyterian church of her new husband upon their marriage. She became president of the Burke County chapter of the American Red Cross during the First World War.

Samuel James Ervin, Jr., the fifth of ten children, was born in Morganton in 1896. He attended public schools in Morganton and developed a love for history and reading. After graduation from high school in 1913 he attended The University of North Carolina from 1913 through 1917.

While at the university, Ervin studied under several teachers who had a lasting impact on him. He studied poetry and literature under John Manning Booker, Daniel Huger Bacot, and Edwin A. Greenlaw. He developed a capacity for the study of history under J. G. deRoulhac Hamilton. He gained insight into the areas of philosophy and ethics under Henry Horace Williams; constitutional law under Lucius Polk McGehee; and Latin under Wilbur Hugh Royster. Ervin was an excellent student who served as class historian during his junior and senior years. He won historical prizes offered by the Colonial Dames for the best essays on colonial North Carolina, and two of his articles were published by the History Department in the *James Sprunt Historical Publications*. Ervin also became assistant editor of the *University Magazine*; a member of the Dialectic Literary Society; vice-president of his senior class; a commencement marshal; and permanent president of the class of 1917. He was also elected to membership in Sigma Upsilon because of his literary ability, and to Phi Delta Phi because of his knowledge of law.

Ervin volunteered for the armed forces in May 1917, a month prior to graduation. He underwent officer training at Fort Oglethorpe, Ga., and in September sailed for France, where he spent eighteen months serving in Company I, 28th Infantry Regiment, First Division of the American Expeditionary Forces. Ervin received the Silver Star for gallantry in action in May 1918 at Cantigny. He was wounded there but received a more serious wound in July after being hit by a shell fragment while leading an advance party in an attack on a German machine gun post at Soissons, during the Aisle-Marne offensive. For his heroism in this battle, Ervin was awarded the Distinguished Service Cross. In addition, he received the Purple Heart and the French Fourragere for his service during the war.

Returning to the United States in April 1919, he immediately took a refresher course in law at The University of North Carolina that summer, was admitted to the North Carolina bar in August, and subsequently enrolled at Harvard Law School. While at Harvard, Ervin developed a deep respect for the law. He especially admired Roscoe Pound's emphasis on individual liberties and the arguments that Zechariah Chafee, Jr., made in defense of such libertarian principles as an individual's freedom of speech. Ervin was graduated from Harvard with the Bachelor of Law degree in 1922 and returned to Morganton to practice with his father.

Prior to his graduation from law school, Ervin received news from home that he had been nominated as Burke County's Democratic Party candidate for the state legislature. Although he had not actively sought political office, Ervin accepted the nomination, won the election, and went to Raleigh in January 1923 as a legislator. During his months in the North Carolina General Assembly, Ervin spent the time he had back home studying and practicing law in a room adjoining his father's small office building directly across from the courthouse in Morganton. Ervin returned to the state legislature for two other terms, in 1925 and 1931.

On 18 June 1924, Ervin married Margaret Bruce Bell of Concord, whom he had met in Morganton in 1916. Margaret, who received her Bachelor of Arts degree from Converse College in 1919, taught at Concord High School before their marriage in 1924. In 1926, the couple had a son, Samuel James Ervin III, who would eventually follow his father in the study and practice of law. The Ervins also had two daughters: Leslie, born in 1930; and Laura Powe, born in 1934.

During the 1925 session of the state legislature, Ervin made his first strong speech in favor of civil liberties. With the General Assembly on the verge of passing a bill to prohibit the teaching of evolution in the North Carolina public school system, Ervin took the floor and dismantled the arguments of those who supported the bill (which eventually was defeated). Remarking that it would "gratify the monkeys to know that they are absolved from all responsibility for the conduct of the human race," Ervin employed the subtle, home-spun humor and legal acuity that would characterize his later career as a United States senator.

While in the state legislature, Ervin served on the Judiciary Committee; he supported changes in judicial procedure, higher spending for education, and legislation to allow juries to recommend mercy in capital cases and to care for the employment needs of the deaf. Ervin preferred, however, to stay out of the political limelight during the early years of his legal career, devoting his energies toward building a successful law practice in Morganton.

Between the mid-1930s and his appointment to the United States Senate in 1954, Ervin accepted several judicial appointments. He served as a judge in the Burke County Criminal Court between 1935 and 1937 and was appointed to the North Carolina Superior Court by Governor Clyde R. Hoey in 1937. After suffering from a bleeding ulcer, Ervin resigned from the Superior Court in 1943 to resume his practice of law in Morganton.

Shortly thereafter, Ervin was again appointed to fill a political office. His brother, Joseph W. Ervin, was a member of the United States House of Representatives from the Tenth Congressional District of North Carolina. Joseph, who had from childhood suffered from a painful bone disease, committed suicide in 1945, and his brother was called upon as a compromise candidate who could break a political deadlock in his home district by filling the vacant seat. Ervin served in the House in 1946, for the sole purpose of completing his brother's term. He refused renomination and returned to his law practice later that year. Ervin was then appointed by Governor Gregg Cherry as an associate justice of the North Carolina Supreme Court in 1948, and served in that capacity for six years. During that time, Ervin wrote several notable decisions and probably would have become chief justice had circumstances not again intervened.

North Carolina Senator Clyde Hoey died in office on 12 May 1954, and Governor William B. Umstead was left with the task of choosing a successor. One of the leading contenders for the seat, Irving Carlyle of Winston-Salem, hurt his own political fortunes by encouraging a stance of compliance with the *Brown v. Board of Education* decision by the United States Supreme Court. Again, Sam Ervin was summoned as a compromise candidate to fill a vacant seat, this time in the United States Senate. Ervin was sworn into office on 11 June 1954 by Vice-President Richard M. Nixon and began his twenty-year tenure as a United States senator from North Carolina.

One of Ervin's first committee assignments as a senator was one several of his peers were hesitant to accept. The Select Committee to Study Censure Charges against Senator Joseph McCarthy was convened in 1954, at a time when McCarthy was browbeating witnesses and finding alleged Communists in all areas of American life. In response to the censure investigation, McCarthy charged that the Communist party had "extended its tentacles" to certain members of the Senate itself, including Arthur Watkins, chairman of the Select Committee; Lyndon Johnson, Senate minority leader; and Sam Ervin. It was at this point that Ervin rose in a special session of the Senate and made a pivotal speech against McCarthy that helped bring about the overwhelming vote to censure the Senator from Wisconsin.

Another challenging committee assignment for Ervin was his 1957 appointment to the Select Committee on Improper Activities in Labor or Management, more widely known as the Rackets Committee. Between 1957 and 1959, Ervin worked closely with Massachusetts Senator John F. Kennedy and his brother Robert, the Committee's chief counsel. After the labor hearings, during which Ervin questioned and dented the credibility of union leaders like Teamster President Jimmy Hoffa, Ervin and Kennedy jointly sponsored major labor reform legislation designed to combat corruption in unions and to protect the rights of rank-and-file members.

During the first decade of Ervin's career in the Senate, he steadfastly opposed civil rights legislation for black Americans. He disagreed with the 1954 school desegregation decision by the Supreme Court and fought against the 1957 and 1960 civil rights bills. Ervin's hardest fight, however, was against the civil rights bill sent to Congress by President Kennedy in 1963, which granted sweeping powers to the federal government in an effort to eliminate obstruction of black voting, to desegregate all public facilities and public schools, to end employment discrimination, and to strengthen the United States Civil Rights Commission.

As a member of the Senate Judiciary Committee, Ervin was in a unique position to oppose the efforts of the Kennedy administration. Along with other southern senators like John Stennis of Mississippi and Strom Thurmond of South Carolina, Ervin repeatedly came into conflict with the administration, and especially with Attorney General Robert Kennedy. The basis of Ervin's opposition to civil rights legislation was his understanding of the limits the Constitution was designed to place on the power of the federal government. A champion of civil liberties for whites and blacks throughout his career, Ervin believed that the Civil Rights Act (finally passed in June 1964) both posed a severe threat to individual liberties and increased the likelihood of government tyranny. The tide of events made Ervin's fight against civil rights one of few that he lost in the Senate.

During virtually his entire senate career, Ervin served on the Judiciary Committee, and this was perhaps his most important committee assignment. Ervin became chairman of three subcommittees of the Judiciary Committee—Constitutional Rights, Separation of Powers, and Revision and Codification of the Laws. It was in the capacity of a powerful member of the Judiciary Committee that Ervin not only obstructed civil rights legislation but also sponsored and advocated several pieces of legislation in support of civil liberties.

Ervin's major legislative accomplishments in the area of civil liberties came after his appointment in 1961 as chairman of the Constitutional Rights Subcommittee. Ervin sponsored the Criminal Justice Act of 1964, which provided legal counsel for indigent defendants in criminal cases. The Bail Reform Act of 1966 offered the chance for defendants who could not afford bail to be released from custody pending trial. In addition to these measures, Ervin opposed the Nixon administration's efforts to pass the District of Columbia Crime Bill of 1969. While liberal congressmen hedged because of the Administration's appeal for "law and order," Ervin sharply attacked provisions such as the preventive detention of suspects and a "no-knock" clause that would allow police to enter suspects' homes without knocking. Ironically, liberals who had attacked Ervin for his stand against civil rights now praised him for his defense of the rights of suspected criminals.

In 1964, Ervin sponsored the District of Columbia Hospitalization of the Mentally Ill Act, which served as a model law that other states quickly copied. This legislation encouraged voluntary hospitalization, tried to remove the stigma attached to mental illness, and asserted a "bill of rights" for the mentally ill, including the right to treatment and to periodic review. Ervin's advocacy of such legislation stemmed in great measure from painful visits he had made to observe the operations of the North Carolina state psychiatric facility at Morganton.

Ervin also sponsored the Military Justice Act of 1968, which protected the rights of servicemen in military courts of justice, and became an advocate of the constitutional rights of American Indians. He had introduced legislation in 1966 that would guarantee the same rights to reservation Indians which white Americans enjoyed and for which black Americans had been struggling. When it was apparent that his "Indian Bill of Rights" was being allowed to die in committee, Ervin attached his bill as an amendment to the Fair Housing Bill. Taunting Senate liberals by noting the inconsistency that "anybody supporting a bill to secure constitutional rights to black people would be opposed to giving constitutional rights to red people," Ervin won Senate approval for his amendment and saw it become law.

Ervin fought against a number of threats he perceived to civil liberties during the latter part of his Senate career. He opposed the Voluntary School Prayer Amendment introduced by Senator Everett Dirkson in 1966, on the grounds that the civil liberties of students and teachers in the public schools would be violated if prayer were allowed in the classroom. Every year from 1966 into the early 1970s, Ervin introduced legislation to protect the privacy of federal employees, who were required to supply personal information and take lie detector tests in order to secure work with the federal government.

Several of Ervin's civil liberties battles were waged against the Nixon administration. For example, when President Nixon issued an executive order to grant the long-dormant Subversive Activities Control Board vast new powers and funding, Ervin helped defeat the effort by attacking it as a violation of an individual's free expression of ideas under the First Amendment. In the early 1970s, Ervin not only was instrumental in defending the press's freedom to conceal its sources; he also worked to expose the military's practice of surveillance of civilians considered dangerous by the government, especially those people who exercised their right to demonstrate peacefully against the War in Vietnam.

Although Ervin was willing to protect the civil liberties of those opposing American involvement in Vietnam, he supported the war effort. Ervin's primary regret regarding Vietnam, in fact, was that America did not demonstrate a stronger commitment to win the war. Ervin was a member of the Senate Armed Services Committee, as well as chairman of that committee's Subcommittee on the Status of Forces Treaty. Throughout his senate career, Ervin supported heavy military spending, the development of a strong nuclear deterrent, and the draft.

Ervin was also a member of the Government Operations Committee and was chairman of the committee during his last two years in the senate. He supported most traditional senate procedures such as unlimited debate, seniority, and denial of public financial disclosure. At the same time, Senator Ervin opposed a variety of executive practices such as the impoundment of appropriated funds and the plea of executive privilege before investigative committees.

The latter weapon was used against the Senate to an unprecedented extent during the Nixon administration. Sam Ervin will perhaps be best remembered for chairing, from 1973 until 1974, the Senate's Select Committee on Presidential Campaign Activities, which became known popularly as the Watergate Committee. After five burglars broke into the Democratic National Committee headquarters in June 1972, the White House began a campaign to cover up both the break-in itself and the ensuing destruction of evidence and intimidation of witnesses, most of which was financed with campaign funds from the Committee to Re-Elect the President.

Ervin worked to sort out the legal and constitutional complexities surrounding the activities of the Nixon administration, and did so with a degree of the humor and home-spun story-telling that had characterized his speeches during his previous senate career. Ervin had been assigned to chair the committee because he was a senator without presidential aspirations who was most respected by both his Democratic and Republican colleagues. Ervin accepted the chairmanship out of both a sense of duty and the belief that Watergate posed the most serious challenge ever to the United States Constitution.

The Watergate affair ended with the demise of President Nixon and with the preservation of the Constitution that Sam Ervin so cherished. Ervin made the decision not to run for reelection in late 1973, and he left the Senate at the close of the 93rd Congress in 1974. Ervin retired to his home in Morganton, where he became actively engaged in writing, practicing law, doing historical research, traveling, and giving lectures. He died in a hospital in Winston-Salem after a brief illness and was buried in Morganton.

SEE: Herb Altman, ed., *Quotations from Chairman Sam: The Wit and Wisdom of Senator Sam Ervin* (1973); David Leon Chandler, *The Natural Superiority of Southern Politicians: A Revisionist History* (1977); Paul R. Clancy, *Just a Country Lawyer: A Biography of Senator Sam Ervin* (1974); Albert Coates, "Sam Ervin," in "Three North Carolinians Who Have Stood Up to Be Counted for the Bill of Rights," prepared for delivery to the North Carolina Democratic Club in Washington, D.C., 18 Oct. 1973; Dick Dabney, *A Good Man: The Life of Sam J. Ervin* (1976); Samuel Dash, *Chief Counsel: Inside the Ervin Committee—The Untold Story of Watergate* (1976); Sam J. Ervin, Jr., *Humor of a Country Lawyer* (1983), *Preserving the Constitution: The Autobiography of Senator Sam J. Ervin, Jr.* (1984), *The Whole Truth: The Watergate Conspiracy* (1980); Samuel James Ervin, Jr., Papers (Southern Historical Collection, University of North Carolina, Chapel Hill); Marshall Frady, "Sam Ervin, Saving the Republic, and Show Business," in *Southerners: A Journalist's Odyssey* (1980); Stephen Klitzman, *Sam J. Ervin, Jr.: Democratic Senator from North Carolina*, in Ralph Nader and Robert Fellmeth, eds., *Ralph Nader Congress Project: Citizens Look at Congress* (1972); "Remarks by the Honorable Samuel J. Ervin, Jr., *The Bookmark* 45 (1975); Thad Stem, Jr., and Alan Butler, *Senator Sam Ervin's Best Stories* (1973); Clifford Kenneth Van Sickle, "The Oral Communication of Senator Sam J. Ervin, Jr., in the Watergate Hearings: A Study in Consistency" (Ph.D. diss., Michigan State University, 1976).

MITCHELL F. DUCEY

**Ervin, William Carson** *(16 Dec. 1859–16 July 1943)*, lawyer, newspaper editor, and financier, was born in Marion. Nicknamed "Buddie" by his family and called "Will" in later years, Ervin was the son of James S. Ervin, a Methodist minister, and Anna Matilda Carson Ervin. His paternal great-grandmother was Martha Marion, daughter of Francis Marion. Ervin attended Finley High School in Lenoir before reading law for two years with Judge Clinton A. Cilly of Lenoir. In 1879 he entered The University of North Carolina law school where he studied with Professor Kemp P. Battle and received his degree in 1880. During the June 1880 term of the state supreme court, at the age of twenty, he was admitted to the North Carolina bar. However, his interests soon changed when he became involved in the newspaper business the following year. He edited the *Lenoir Topic* from 1881 to 1884, the *Morganton Mountaineer* from 1884 to 1886, and, later, the *Morganton Herald* from 1889 to 1895 when he ended his newspaper career.

In 1889 Ervin and Isaac T. Avery formed one of the earliest law partnerships in Burke County. Their successful Morganton firm specialized in corporation law until 1926 when it was dissolved by mutual consent. Afterwards Ervin practiced alone until 1929, when he and J. E. Butler formed a partnership that lasted until Ervin's death.

Displaying a dislike for trial work, Ervin concentrated on business law, especially the drafting of legal documents. He provided much of the legal guidance for the industrial development of Burke County. A noted financier, he served as president of Morganton Building and Loan for thirty-seven years. He was on the board of directors of many Burke County banks, utilities, and mining companies. In 1899 he was an incorporator of the Burke County Telephone Company, and in 1916 he was an officer of the Morganton Chamber of Commerce. Ervin was also instrumental in establishing the Waldensian settlement in Valdese.

An active Democrat, Ervin served as mayor of Lenoir from 1887 to 1889 and as mayor of Morganton from 1911 to 1913. Even though he refused other offices, he remained active in state and local politics. He was chairman of the Burke County Democratic Executive Committee for six years as well as a member of the state Democratic Executive Committee. As a delegate to the Democratic National conventions at Baltimore in 1912 and St. Louis in 1916, Ervin helped nominate Woodrow Wilson as the Democratic presidential candidate.

Ervin's main outside interest was local western North Carolina history. He was a member of the North Carolina History Club, the Hobby Club, and the Masons. He also enjoyed singing with his wife. Ervin was a longtime member of the First Presbyterian Church in Morganton where he taught a men's Bible class for many years.

On 9 Mar. 1887 Ervin married Kate Lee Sheetz, the daughter of a Presbyterian minister. They raised two children to maturity: Morton Sheetz, who married Lillian Cowart of St. Petersburg, Fla., and Julia Reid Ervin Coburn. Ervin was buried in Morganton.

SEE: William Carson Ervin Papers (Southern Historical Collection, University of North Carolina, Chapel Hill); Daniel L. Grant, *Alumni History of the University of North Carolina* (1924); North Carolina Bar Association, *Reports*, vols. 1–46 (1899–1944); *North Carolina Biography*, vol. 3 (1928); Edward W. Phifer, Jr., *Burke: The History of a North Carolina County* (1977); *Prominent People of North Carolina* (1906); A. D. Smith, *Western North Carolina, Historical and Biographical* (1890); *Who's Who in the South*, 1927.

KAREN S. HOOD

**Erwin, Alexander** *(6 June 1750–ca. October 1829)*, Revolutionary soldier, public official, and legislator, was born in Bucks County, Pa., of Scotch-Irish ancestry. His parents, Nathaniel and Leah Julian Erwin, moved to Rowan (now Burke) County, N.C., shortly before the American Revolution and established their home at Cherryfields on the east side of Upper Creek. During the Revolution Erwin saw much guerrilla service with the Whig forces. As a lieutenant in Captain David Vance's company, he fought against the loyalist militia under Major Patrick Ferguson in the crucial Battle of Kings Mountain on 7 Oct. 1780. He subsequently attained the rank of colonel in the Burke County militia.

After the Revolution Erwin entertained an undying hatred for those who had been Tories. A tradition still survives in Burke County that ex-Tories were allowed to come to Morganton, the county seat, only during court week, and that it was Erwin's habit to make public proclamation on each day of court week for all Tories to leave town before sunset. It is suggested that his proclamation was always obeyed. Erwin's hatred of Tories had its origin in an experience of his first wife, Sarah Robinson Erwin, during the Revolution while he was absent from home with the Whig forces. Having been severely wounded in the service of his country, Samuel Alexander, a neighbor and friend, came to Erwin's home for shelter and care. Sarah Erwin put him in an outhouse near the dwelling, hoping to conceal him from the Tories until his wounds healed. A marauding band of Tories came to the Erwin dwelling in quest of Whigs and searched it over Sarah's protests. After plundering the house, the Tories approached the outhouse where Samuel Alexander lay helpless. Sarah placed herself at the outhouse door and denied them admittance. Thrusting her aside, they entered the structure and discovered the wounded Whig. As one of the men was in the act of striking Alexander with his sword, Sarah Erwin threw herself between the Tory and Alexander with her right arm over the injured man's head. From the descending blade she received a dreadful wound that maimed her for life.

Upon the organization of Burke County in June 1777, Erwin became the first clerk of the County Court of Pleas and Quarter Sessions. He held this office until 1793, when he resigned and was succeeded by his son, James Erwin, who acted as clerk until 1833. James Erwin, in turn, was followed in this post by his son, Joseph J. Erwin, who served until 1845. Altogether these men held the clerkship for a continuous period of sixty-eight years.

In the legislature of 1781 Alexander Erwin's name was placed in nomination for the office of delegate to the Continental Congress, but he failed to win election. He was again prominently mentioned as a candidate for this post in 1784. The General Assembly of 1781 named him one of the three district auditors for the counties of Burke, Lincoln, Rutherford, Sullivan, Washington, and Wilkes, vesting in these auditors "full power and authority finally to settle and adjust all claims against the state for militia pay and for articles which are or may be purchased for the use of the state." Upon the creation of Morgan District in 1782, Erwin was appointed one of the three auditors for the new district. He also became one of the original trustees of Morgan Academy, which was chartered in 1783 as the first institution of learning in Burke County. When Morganton was incorporated in 1784, Erwin was one of the commissioners of "the said Town of Morgan" who were directed to build "a courthouse and a prison in the same for the District of Morgan." Acting under this legislative authority, the commissioners laid out the town of Morganton. In addition, Colonel Erwin was a member of the North Carolina House of Commons from Burke County in 1793–97 and 1804. He ended his public service as a justice of the Burke County Court of Pleas and Quarter Sessions. He was a member of the Quaker Meadows Presbyterian

Church and the Masonic order, in which he was secretary of Rising Sun Lodge No. 38 at Morganton.

Erwin was married twice. In 1770 he married Sarah Robinson (1750–85), a daughter of James and Catherine Robinson of South Carolina. They were the parents of Catherine, who married her first cousin, John Erwin; Mary ("Polly"), who married John McKamie Wilson, a Presbyterian minister; James, who married Margaret Phifer; Margaret ("Peggy"), who married Hugh Tate; Hannah, who married Major Zebulon Baird; and Joseph, who died unmarried. Major Zebulon Baird and his wife, Hannah Erwin, were the parents of Myra Margaret Baird, who married David Vance, Jr., and became the mother of two famous sons, Zebulon Baird Vance, war governor and U.S. senator, and Robert Brank Vance, Confederate general and U.S. congressman.

On 21 Jan. 1786, Erwin married Margaret Crawford Patton, the widow of Joseph Patton, a Revolutionary comrade who fell at Kings Mountain. They were the parents of Sophia, who married William Alexander; Cynthia, who married Dr. Stephen Fox; Sarah Myra, who married Freeland Henson; Abdial Hiempsel, John McKamie Wilson, and Milton Pinckney, all of whom died unmarried; Ulysses Stanhope, who married Eliza G. Tate; and Harriet Dorcas, who married Lewis Dinkins. Lewis Dinkins and his wife, Harriet Dorcas Erwin, where the grandparents of Charles Betts Galloway, a Methodist bishop of Mississippi.

Erwin and his first wife, Sarah Robinson, were buried in adjoining graves in the old Quaker Meadows Cemetery.

SEE: Samuel A. Ashe, ed., *Biographical History of North Carolina*, vols. 3 (1906), 7 (1908); Alphonso C. Avery, *History of the Presbyterian Churches at Quaker Meadows and Morganton* (1913); John L. Cheney, Jr., ed., *North Carolina Government, 1585–1974* (1975); Walter Clark, ed., *State Records of North Carolina*, vols. 17 (1899), 22 (1907), 24 (1905); Clement Dowd, *Life of Zebulon B. Vance* (1897); John Hugh McDowell, *History of the McDowells, Erwins, Irwins, and Connections, Being a Compilation from Various Sources* (1918); *North Carolina Biography*, vol. 5 (1941); Edward W. Phifer, Jr., *Burke: The History of a North Carolina County* (1977); Frederick A. Verkus, ed., *Abridged Compendium of American Genealogy*, vol. 2 (1925).

SAM J. ERVIN, JR.

**Erwin, Clyde Atkinson** *(8 Feb. 1897–19 July 1952)*, educator, was born in Atlanta, Ga., the son of Sylvanus and Mamie Putnam Erwin. He attended school in Charlotte and Waco, N.C., and was a student at The University of North Carolina in 1915–16 and subsequent summer schools. He held honorary doctorates from Catawba College and North Carolina State College. After a brief period as a classroom teacher, he became principal of various schools in the western Piedmont section of the state and from 1925 to 1934 was superintendent of the Rutherford County schools. He gained statewide prominence as president of the North Carolina Education Association when he campaigned for a state-supported school system and adequate support in the 1933 General Assembly.

In 1934 Erwin was appointed by Governor J. C. B. Ehringhaus to succeed the late Arch T. Allen as state superintendent of public instruction. Erwin was one of the youngest men to hold a major state office. He served eighteen years in the position, winning reelection easily each time he was a candidate. While head of the state's school system, he took the lead in raising the minimum school term from eight to nine months, adding a twelfth grade to the high schools, and reducing the teacher load; expenditures grew from $19 million in 1934–35 to $103 million at the time of his death.

Erwin was a member of and officer in numerous regional and national educational organizations and served on advisory committees and as consultant to state and national officials. The day before his death he returned home from Chicago where he served as a consultant on the education plank in the Democratic party's 1952 platform. He also served on the boards of trustees for East Carolina Teachers College, the Greater University of North Carolina, North Carolina College at Durham, Agricultural and Technical College at Greensboro, and Elizabeth City State Teachers College. Erwin was active in Boy Scout work and was especially vigorous in encouraging cooperation between scouting and public schools. In 1950 he was state chairman of the National Conference of Christians and Jews, and in the same year he was chairman of the U.S. delegation to the International Conference on Public Education in Geneva, Switzerland. An active member of the Methodist church, he had a lengthy record as an adult Sunday school teacher in Rutherfordton and in Raleigh.

Erwin married Evelyn Miller of Waco, and they were the parents of two children: Frances Elizabeth (Mrs. George Withers) and Clyde A., Jr. He was buried at Capernium near Waco.

SEE: *Asheville Citizen-Times*, 20 July 1952; *Charlotte Observer*, 28 Mar. 1932; *New York Times*, 20 July 1952; *North Carolina Manual* (1951), for a list of his many offices and professional positions; Raleigh *News and Observer*, 23 Oct. 1934, 28 May 1935, 10 Aug. 1940, 20, 21 July 1952.

ROBERT O. CONWAY

**Erwin, Jesse Harper** *(3 Mar. 1864–7 Aug. 1962)*, textile executive, was born at the family estate, Bellevue, near Morganton, of Scotch-Irish ancestry. His father, Joseph J. Erwin, described as a "model of the old-time Southern gentleman," was a graduate of Washington College (Washington and Lee University) and served as vestryman of Grace Episcopal Church in Morganton, clerk of the superior court, member of the state legislature for several terms, and member of the staff of Governor W. A. Graham. His mother, Elvira Holt Erwin, was the daughter of Dr. William Raney Holt of Lexington who served as the president of the first North Carolina State Fair.

Erwin was the ninth of eleven children and grew up at Bellevue within view of Grandfather Mountain. He received his education in private and public schools before entering Catawba College in Newton. At the age of nineteen he moved to what was then Company Shops (Burlington) where he worked for approximately a year in a general store before joining his brother-in-law, Lawrence S. Holt, Sr., in the management of Aurora Cotton Mills. Later he became secretary-treasurer of the E. M. Holt Plaid Mills in Burlington.

With fifteen years of experience in textiles, Erwin moved to Durham to accept the position of secretary-treasurer of the Durham Cotton Manufacturing Company, the first textile mill in Durham, founded by Julian S. Carr in 1884 and acquired by Benjamin N. Duke in 1899. He also became associated with Pearl Cotton Mills as secretary-treasurer. Both of these companies were involved in the manufacture of ginghams and a variety of other cotton goods. Erwin was a member of the board of directors of the Durham and Southern Railway, Oxford Cotton Mills, Peoples Bank located in East Durham, and Erwin Mills, which was managed by and named for his brother, William A. Erwin. He was influential in the organization of Randolph Mills, Inc., of Franklinville, where he served as chairman of the board of directors for a number of years until his death.

On Governor Charles B. Aycock's staff from 1901 to 1905, Erwin served as an aide-de-camp with the rank of colonel. He particularly enjoyed accompanying Governor Aycock to the South Carolina Interstate and West Indian Exposition, in Charleston, where President Theodore Roosevelt reviewed the North Carolina troops after the exposition opened on 1 Dec. 1901. In Durham Erwin was a charter member of the Durham Kiwanis Club and served on the board of directors of the Durham Young Men's Christian Association.

A lifelong member of the Episcopal church, Erwin served a number of terms as a member of the vestry of St. Philip's Episcopal Church and later in the same capacity at St. Joseph's Episcopal Church, a church built as a memorial to his parents near Erwin Cotton Mills (afterward a part of Burlington Industries, Inc.) in Durham. On 5 Nov. 1895 he was married in St. Luke's Episcopal Church, Atlanta, to Eleanor Drane Hayes of Americus, Ga. The wedding was held in Atlanta while the Cotton States and International Exposition was in progress. Their children included Mary Erwin Michie, Eleanor Erwin Griswold, Josephine Erwin MacManus, Jesse Harper, Jr., and Eugene.

Erwin's home, Sunnyside, was located near Erwin Mills. He was buried in Maplewood Cemetery, Durham.

SEE: Samuel A. Ashe, ed., *Biographical History of North Carolina*, vols. 3 (1906), 7 (1908); W. K. Boyd, *The Story of Durham, City of the New South* (1925); *Durham Morning Herald*, 29 Apr. 1945, 8, 9 Aug. 1962; *Durham Sun*, 28 Oct. 1949, 8 Aug. 1962; J. Harper Erwin, *Alexander Erwin and His Descendants, 1750–1946* (1946), and "St. Philip's Episcopal Church," *The Parish Pantry* (1959); John Hugh McDowell, *History of the McDowells, Erwins, Irwins, and Connections, Being a Compilation from Various Sources* (1918); *North Carolina Biography*, vol. 3 (1928).

B. W. C. ROBERTS

**Erwin, William Allen** *(15 July 1856–28 Feb. 1932)*, textile manufacturer, was born in Burke County near Morganton. His father, Joseph J. Erwin, served Burke County as clerk of the superior court and as a member of the legislature. His mother, Elvira J. Holt, was a daughter of William R. Holt of Lexington, a physician, a graduate of The University of North Carolina, and a founder of the state agricultural society. E. M. Holt, his great-uncle, was a leading pioneer in the textile industry in North Carolina.

Erwin attended local elementary schools and Finley High School in Lenoir, then studied at the University of Kentucky. After two years family misfortune forced him to leave the university and enter business in order to help his parents. He began his business career in 1874 as a salesman in the general store of Holt, Gant, and Holt at Company Shops (now Burlington). In 1877 he joined the North Carolina Railroad as bookkeeper. Then, in 1878, he started his own mercantile business in Company Shops. He left it in 1882 to become secretary-treasurer and general manager of the E. M. Holt Plaid Mills under L. Banks Holt and Lawrence E. Holt. Erwin remained there until 1892, when he moved to Durham and joined Benjamin N. Duke to build the Erwin Mills.

The Erwin-Duke partnership flourished. In their first mill, in Durham, they began by producing tobacco bag cloth, then expanded to manufacture other textile products. By 1895–96, Erwin Mills was Durham's largest mill and one of the largest in North Carolina, employing a thousand workers and running 25,000 spindles and 1,000 looms. In 1900, Erwin succeeded Duke as president of the company and remained in the post until 1931. Eventually, Erwin Mills opened another mill in Durham, two mills at Erwin (formerly Duke), and one at Cooleemee. By 1932 Durham had incorporated the 5,000 residents of West Durham, site of the mills, into Durham; Erwin had 4,000 residents and Cooleemee, 2,500. At one time, William Erwin had more spindles under his management than any other textile executive. He also served as president of Pearl Mills in Durham, Oxford Mills in Oxford, Alpine Cotton mills in Morganton, Erwin Yarn, Incorporated, in Philadelphia, and the Bank of Harnett in Erwin.

At an early date Erwin became involved in welfare work at the mills he managed. He supported churches, schools, parks, and community centers, in several cases paying for construction of the facilities. As early as 1895, he became an advocate of reducing the workday from twelve to eleven hours and of prohibiting anyone under age twelve from working in factories.

An active Episcopal layman, Erwin served variously as a Sunday school superintendent, men's Bible class teacher, delegate to several general conventions of the North Carolina diocese, and member of the board of trustees of St. Mary's School, Raleigh. He also was chairman of the committee that bought the building site for St. Mary's. He gave the money to build St. Joseph's Episcopal Church, Durham, in his parents' memory, and to construct a new sanctuary for the Chapel of the Cross Episcopal Church, Chapel Hill, in memory of his maternal grandfather, William R. Holt. During the administration of Governor Robert Glenn (1905–9), his civic activities included service as a member of the state hospital commission that enlarged the facilities of the state mental hospitals. During World War I, he was district food administrator, chairman of the county Council for Defense, and chairman of the United War Work drive for seven North Carolina counties. He was also president of the American Cotton Manufacturers Association (1912–13).

On 2 Oct. 1889 Erwin married Sadie L. Smedes, daughter of Dr. Aldert Smedes, founder of St. Mary's School. They had six children, three of whom survived Erwin: Mrs. Hamilton O. Jones, Mrs. Jack Glenn, and Mrs. Hargrove Bellamy. His only son, William A., Jr., died in 1931. Erwin died in Durham and was buried in Oakwood Cemetery, Raleigh.

SEE: Samuel A. Ashe, ed., *Biographical History of North Carolina*, vol. 3 (1906); Robert F. Durden, *The Dukes of Durham, 1865–1929* (1975); *Durham Morning Herald*, 29 Feb. 1932; *Greensboro Daily News*, 29 Feb. 1932; Archibald Henderson Papers (Southern Historical Collection, University of North Carolina, Chapel Hill); Edward W. Phifer, "Slavery in Microcosm: Burke County, North Carolina," *Journal of Southern History* 28 (1962); Raleigh *News and Observer*, 29 Feb. 1932; Marjorie W. Young, ed., *Textile Leaders of the South* (1963).

TOM E. TERRILL

**Etheridge, Henry Emerson** *(28 Sept. 1819–21 Oct. 1902)*, congressman and clerk of the U.S. House of Representatives, was born in Currituck, the son of Thomas and Elizabeth Harvey Etheridge. In 1831 he moved with his family to West Tennessee, settling near the middle fork of the Obion River in Weakley County, where he received a common school education, read law, and was admitted to the bar in 1840. Beginning his practice at Dresden, Tenn., he was soon active in Whig politics and served in the state house of representatives from Weakley County from 1845 to 1847. Possessing the ability to absorb and recall at will large quantities of information as well as a gift for political satire, Etheridge became one of the most noted orators in the state. In 1852, he was elected as a Whig to the U.S. House of Representatives. Reelected as a candidate of the American, or Know-Nothing, party in 1854, he lost his bid for a third consecutive term in 1856. Two years later, again carrying the banner of the American party, he was successful and served in the strife-filled congressional session of 1859–61.

While in Congress, Etheridge was forced to make agonizing choices between sectional and national allegiances as the country moved closer to civil war. He strongly opposed the Kansas-Nebraska Act of 1854 with its repeal of the Missouri Compromise restriction on slavery. He saw this as a misguided Democratic proposal that might rekindle emotions North and South on the slavery issue. Condemning the measure as one that would add no new slave states to the nation but would dangerously heighten sectional tensions, he joined a small group of seven Southern Whigs who voted against the measure. Although he supported the institution of slavery, Etheridge opposed the calls of some in the late 1850s for a reopening of the African slave trade. He characterized it as an inhuman traffic repugnant to all civilized and Christian people. Concerned about growing sectional bitterness, in 1857 on the floor of the House he denounced Northern and Southern extremists and declared that dismemberment of the nation would endanger or destroy slavery and the liberty of all Americans. There was a remedy for every sectional complaint and grievance through the ballot box within the Union, he said. In 1860, Etheridge backed fellow Tennessean John Bell for president on the Constitutional Union ticket. The following January he tried unsuccessfully to have the House consider a compromise proposal, similar to that of Senator John J. Crittenden of Kentucky, designed to placate both sections on the slavery question.

The war years were tumultuous ones for Etheridge. Returning home in the spring of 1861, he joined other Tennessee Unionists in an effort to defeat the movement for secession in the state. On one occasion when he attempted to make a Union speech in Paris, Tenn., secessionist supporters broke up the meeting, and one Unionist was killed in the disorder that followed. When Tennessee joined the Confederacy, he fled to Washington. His dedication to the Union earned him election to the post of clerk of the House of Representatives in July 1861. After Tennessee came under military control, Etheridge became a political supporter of military Governor Andrew Johnson. President Abraham Lincoln's decision to make emancipation of slaves a war aim alienated Etheridge from the Republican party. Angry at what he considered a Republican betrayal of Southern Unionists, he cooperated in an unsuccessful plot in December 1863 to give control of the Thirty-eighth Congress to a coalition of Democrats and border state Unionists. The plan involved his use of his position as clerk to invalidate the credentials of a number of Republican congressmen. As a result of this, he was defeated in his bid for reelection as clerk, and he became an ardent opponent of the Republican administration.

In the Reconstruction era immediately following the war, Etheridge emerged as a leader among Conservative Unionists in Tennessee opposed to the Radical Republican administration of Governor William G. Brownlow. While running for Congress from his home district in 1865, he denounced the state government so stridently that he was arrested by federal army troops and tried before a military commission on charges of encouraging sedition and insurrection. He was held until after the election and then was acquitted on both counts. Two years later, Etheridge was the Conservative Union party candidate for governor. He and Governor Brownlow engaged in an aggressive and acrimonious campaign marred by incidents of violence and voter intimidation. Unable to attract the ballots of newly enfranchised blacks and lacking the votes of ex-Confederates who backed him but were disfranchised, Etheridge lost the election. Defeat was followed by victory, however, for in 1868 he was elected to a two-year term in the state senate representing Henry, Obion, and Weakley counties. Unhappy with the policies of the resurgent Democratic party, which absorbed the Conservative organization following Reconstruction, Etheridge returned to the Republican party in 1876 and campaigned actively for presidential nominee Rutherford B. Hayes. The Republican state convention selected him to run for governor in 1878, but he declined the nomination. From 1891 through 1894 he served as surveyor of customs in Memphis.

In addition to his political activities, Etheridge was also a dedicated supporter of the temperance movement. In 1870 the state legislature authorized the creation of a new county called Etheridge, named for this prominent politician, but it was never organized. He married Fannie M. Bell of Dresden in 1849 and they had two children, Emma and John Bell. Congressman Etheridge died in Dresden and was buried in Mt. Vernon Cemetery, Sharon, Tenn.

SEE: T. B. Alexander, *Political Reconstruction in Tennessee* (1950); H. Belz, "The Etheridge Conspiracy of 1863: A Projected Conservative Coup," *Journal of Southern History* 36 (1970); *Biog. Dir. Am. Cong.* (1971); *Biographical Directory of the Tennessee General Assembly, Weakley County* (1973); J. G. Blaine, *Twenty Years in Congress* (1884); Cleveland (Tenn.) *Weekly Herald*, 27 Oct. 1876; *Congressional Globe*, Thirty-third, Thirty-fourth, and Thirty-fifth Congresses; Mrs. Roy J. Dennis, Nashville, and Mrs. Ruth D. Smith, Sharon, Tenn., for Etheridge family information; Archelaus M. Hughes Diary (Tennessee State Library and Archives, Nashville); Memphis *Commercial Appeal*, 22 Oct. 1902; Memphis *Evening Scimitar*, 22 Oct. 1902; Nashville *Daily American*, 12 Sept. 1876; J. W. Patton, *Unionism and Reconstruction in Tennessee* (1934).

ROBERT B. JONES

**Etheridge, Robert Bruce** *(31 July 1878–19 Oct. 1964)*, legislator, government official, political leader, educator, and banker, was born at Mother Vineyard near Manteo on Roanoke Island. His father, Van Buren Etheridge, served for more than thirty years in the U.S. Lifesaving Service, most of the time as "Keeper" (noncommissioned officer in charge) of the Nags Head Station. His father and his mother, Matilda Tillett Etheridge, encouraged him to continue his education after he completed the limited academic courses then available in the public elementary and secondary schools of Dare County, so they shipped him off by boat to Elizabeth City, where he completed the equivalent of a high school education in the Atlantic Collegiate Institute. In 1895 he enrolled in Trinity College at Durham and in 1899 was graduated with a bachelor of arts degree.

In July 1899, one month after his graduation from Trinity College at age twenty-one, Etheridge was elected superintendent of Dare County schools, a position he held until 1907, when he resigned to become cashier of Dare County's first financial institution, the Bank of Manteo, of which he was an organizer. Never content to be involved in a single occupation, and concerned throughout his life with the peculiar problems resulting from the geographic isolation of his native Outer Banks, he offered himself as a candidate of the Democratic party and was elected to serve as the Dare County representative in the 1903 session of the state house of representatives. This was the beginning of service in the General Assembly spanning more than half a century. He was reelected to the house for the 1905 session, and then represented the Second District in the state senate in 1907, the only time he sought election to the upper chamber. Subsequently he represented Dare County in the house of representatives in 1929, 1931, and 1933, and again in 1951, 1953, 1955, 1957, and 1959.

Known affectionally by the home folks in Dare County as "Uncle Bruce," Etheridge was widely recognized elsewhere in the state as "The Duke of Dare," an appellation reputedly given him by a fellow legislator as much a result of his stately demeanor as for his championing of causes affecting his native coastal county. Active throughout his adult life in the Democratic party, he served for twenty-four years (1928–52) both as chairman of the Dare County Democratic Executive Committee and as a member of the State Democratic Executive Committee. He was clerk of superior court for Dare County from 1906 to 1910 and postmaster for Manteo from 1914 to 1922.

In 1933 Governor J. C. B. Ehringhaus appointed Etheridge director of the Department of Conservation and Development. He served until May 1949, by far the longest period of service for any of the directors of that department from the time of its formation in 1925 until it became part of the Department of Natural and Economic Resources when the state government was reorganized in 1971.

His active business life was centered around banking—specifically his position as cashier of the Bank of Manteo, 1907–33, which throughout that period was the only banking institution in Dare County. For a number of years he was also a partner, with the late Theodore S. Meekins, in an insurance and realty business in Manteo. He served on the New York World's Fair Commission; was ex officio chairman of the Cape Hatteras National Seashore Commission; and was a founder of the Roanoke Island Historical Association, producer of the Lost Colony drama at Fort Raleigh. He was a member of the Junior Order, Woodmen of America; Red Men; and Kappa Sigma, his college fraternity. His membership in Wanchese Masonic Lodge 552 covered a period of fifty-two years, including twelve years as treasurer. A lifelong Baptist, he was a member of the Manteo Baptist Church.

On 22 Apr. 1908, while serving as superintendent of Dare County schools, Etheridge married a teacher in the Manteo School, Elizabeth Webb, daughter of John and Francis Webb of Edenton. They had two children, a son, Webb, who died in 1942 while serving in the Merchant Marine, and a daughter, Matilda Etheridge Inge.

Etheridge died in Elizabeth City and was buried in Manteo. Sixteen days later his wife died and was buried beside him.

SEE: *Asheville Citizen*, 26 Jan. 1951; John L. Cheney, Jr., ed., *North Carolina Government, 1585–1974* (1975); Carl Goerch, *Characters . . . Always Characters* (1945); Raleigh *News and Observer*, 30 Apr. 1953, 1 May 1955, 1 Aug. 1958, 20 Oct. 1964; *Trinity Alumni Register* (1916).

DAVID STICK

**Ettwein, John (Johann)** *(29 June 1721–2 Jan. 1802)*, Moravian leader, was born at Freudenstadt in Würtemburg, Germany, the son of Matthias Ettwein (1694–ca. 1755), a local cobbler, and Elizabeth Margaretha Vogler Ettwein (d. 1735), who were descended from French Huguenot and persecuted Austrian Protestant stock, respectively. As the oldest son, young Johann at a very early age was dedicated by his parents to the work of the church, and so they put him through the local Latin school in spite of their poor financial situation. Here he developed a passion for religion, holding the ambition of becoming a martyr. He first came under the influence of the Moravian church at the age of thirteen when missionaries of that sect came into the area to preach in place of the local clergymen, all of whom had recently died in an epidemic that also took the life of his mother. By 1739, he had been converted to the Moravian faith and had begun taking religious instruction at Marienborn, the home of Moravian leader Count Nicholas von Zinzendorf and at that time the center of the Moravian community. Moving up in the church organization, he was selected in 1747 to travel in a missionary party with the Countess Zinzendorf throughout northern Europe and in England.

In 1749, Ettwein was given his first important commission in the church when he was appointed leader of adult programs at the church at Herrnhut; he left the position after six months, however, feeling that he was incapable of handling the heavy responsibility. By the end of the year he was commissioned to a post in London. While in that city he became interested in the Moravian attempts to move into North America. Emigrating there in 1754, he was first placed in charge of the Christian education of children in Bethlehem, Pa. Impressed by the work that had been done in Christianizing the Indians, he soon began missionary trips throughout many of the American colonies.

He was sent in 1758 to Wachovia, the Moravian settlement in North Carolina, as a temporary substitute for its minister Christian Sidel, but the arrangement turned out to be permanent when Sidel died the following year. Here Ettwein began preaching to the Indians again, often letting himself be captured by more hostile Indians so he could minister to them. In this area he also traveled widely, especially among the many German-speaking people of the backcountry of the Carolinas and Georgia. In 1763, he was given responsibility for all Moravian work in North Carolina, and in this capacity was one of the men in charge of selecting and surveying a site for the new settlement that was to be called Salem. In early 1766, he was named as special envoy on religious matters to Governor William Tryon and was North Carolina's delegate to the Moravian Provincial Synod in Pennsylvania. Shortly afterwards he was called to return to Pennsylvania as a special assistant to Bishop Nathaniel Sidel. Over the next two years he visited Wachovia on his travels; thereafter, his work in the church and the Revolutionary War kept him from returning to the area. During this period in Bethlehem came what he felt was his crowning achievement in his attempts to Christianize the Indians when he managed to arrange for the resettlement in the Tuscarawas Valley, Ohio, of the converted Indians of central Pennsylvania.

Because of his warm welcome in England, and because of the special considerations the Moravians were given as an episcopal church by the British colonial government, Ettwein always had a special fondness for the British. As a result, when the American Revolution began he was a strong supporter of the loyalist cause, even to the point of "thanking God in the public services on the occasion of the news of a British victory." For his outspoken activities he was arrested in Northampton County, Pa., and was imprisoned for a while at Easton. After concluding that the war was a political matter in which the church should not involve itself, he was released and became a special envoy of the church to the new American government. He negotiated with the Continental Congress when the Moravians refused to serve in the Continental Army for religious reasons, winning special consideration for members of his church. He also pleaded the Moravian case on the Pennsylvania Test Acts of 1777 before that state legislature, winning an exemption from the test oath for all Moravians. In addition, in 1776–77 he acted as chaplain at the Continental Army hospital in Bethlehem.

During the war much of the Moravian missionary work had been disrupted or destroyed. At times restrictions on the missionaries had been tight for fear that some were British spies, and the Indians of the Tuscarawas Valley had been massacred by militiamen. On 25 June 1784, Ettwein was consecrated as bishop of all Moravians in North America, succeeding Nathaniel Sidel, and in that capacity assumed the burden of rebuilding the work of the church. He managed to get Congress and the Pennsylvania legislature to set aside land for the Indians whom the Moravians were Christianizing, and in 1787 he revived and personally led the Society of the Brethren for the Propagation of the Gospel among the Heathens. As bishop his extensive travels continued; he even returned to Germany in 1788–89 for the General Synod of the governing board at Herrnhut, which had become the headquarters of the church. He led the North American branch of the church until 1801, when he had to step down because of failing health.

In 1746 Ettwein married Johannetta Maria Kymbel (26 Sept. 1725–8 Sept. 1789), who traveled and worked closely with him throughout his career. They had six children: Anna Benigna (1749–1834), Christian (1752–98), Anna Johanna (died in infancy), John (1758–77), Jacob (1760–98), and Maria Magdelena (1765–1803). His personal life was marred by tragedy. He had to leave his infant daughter behind when he was moved to London and did not see her again until she was forty years old. He grieved at the early deaths of two sons, of whom John had hoped to follow his father into the ministry. Probably the most devastating of all, however, was his son Jacob's expulsion from the church for marrying a woman who ridiculed Moravian teachings. He died in Bethlehem, Pa., where he was buried beside his comrade Nathaniel Sidel.

SEE: *DAB*, vol. 3 (1959); J. deSchweinitz and J. T. Hamilton, eds., *Transactions of the Moravian Historical Society*, vols. 2 (1886), 6 (1900); Adelaide L. Fries, ed., *Records of the Moravians*, vol. 1 (1922); Kenneth G. Hamilton, *John Ettwein and the Moravian Church in the Revolutionary Period* (1940), and ed., *The Papers of John Ettwein* (1940).

MARTIN REIDINGER

**Evans, Charles Napoleon Bonaparte** *(18 Oct. 1812–10 Mar. 1883)*, editor and civic leader, was born in Norfolk County, Va., the son of James E. and Jane Shirley Evans. He left home at an early age after his father's death, and learned the printing business by working in Virginia and South Carolina as a journeyman and then as a printer's assistant to two North Carolina publishers, Philo White of Raleigh and Dennis Heartt of Hillsborough.

Because of a kinship with the widow of William Swaim, Evans became editor of the *Greensborough Patriot* in 1835 and the following year purchased the newspaper. He published the *Patriot* until 1839 in partnership with, first, Alfred E. Hanner; second, E. S. Zeverly; and third, John D. Clancy. The latter was Evans's father-in-law, as the publisher married Elizabeth Clancy in 1836. Though apparently successful in this endeavor, Evans disposed of the Greensboro paper and moved to Milton, N.C., in 1840. He purchased a printing plant from a former publisher, Nathaniel J. Palmer, and in the year of his arrival in the Caswell County town launched the *Milton Chronicle*, which he published until his death.

Evans was gifted with a literary style and fluency superior to the average North Carolina editor of his day, and his paper was soon widely read. Under the motto, "Willing to Praise—Not Afraid to Blame," the editor staunchly defended his preference for the Whigs in politics, but nevertheless promised, "*Our press shall be a free and independent press*—a channel admissable of political communications from opponents as well as from friends." Adherence to this policy was one of the reasons for the success of the *Chronicle*, as the editor promoted the interests of the town and county while championing a strict interpretation of the Constitution, limiting the power of the federal government, and opposing the growing sectionalism in the United States. With the demise of the Whigs, Evans became a loyal Democrat, unhesitatingly both praising the policies of his party and criticizing its errors. Throughout the antebellum period, the editor discouraged the trend toward secession; once the Confederacy was formed, however, he became one of its most loyal supporters. During Reconstruction, he caustically assailed both the carpetbaggers and the Ku Klux Klan, narrowly escaping physical injury because of his condemnation of the latter movement. When political affairs became normal again, he devoted his editorial talents to promoting internal improvement and commercial development of the resources of Milton and Caswell County.

Thomas Clancy Evans became a partner with his father in the publication of the *Chronicle* in 1861, but shortly afterward left the paper to serve in the Confederate Army for several years as a captain of the "Milton Blues." With his enrollment in military service, young Evans continued the tradition of his family, which had furnished a captain in the War of 1812 and a soldier in the American Revolution. After the war, he returned to his post in the *Chronicle* office.

The greatest literary asset of the elder Evans was his ability to intersperse humor cleverly among his compositions for the paper. The most outstanding achievement in this respect was his creation of a fictitious character named "Jesse Holmes, the Fool Killer." This reformer supposedly wrote letters periodically to the editor who published them in the paper. Through this means Evans was able to express his views subtly but pungently on many current events of local or statewide interest. The popularity of the mythical Holmes grew to such an extent that he has become a significant unit in North Carolina folklore. A cousin of Evans, William Sydney Porter, entitled one of his short stories "The Fool Killer," and many other authors have used the fictitious character in their literary creations. Unfortunately only five of these letters exist in the sixty-five known surviving issues of the *Milton Chronicle.*

Beginning in 1866, Evans edited a newspaper in Danville, Va., for two years, after which he and his son purchased the *Hillsborough Recorder*, in Hillsborough, N.C. The Evans family eventually sold this paper and published only the *Chronicle.*

In 1882, Evans was elected to the North Carolina Senate to represent the Twentieth District. While the legislature was in session he died of bronchial pneumonia. Eloquent eulogies were delivered in both houses of the Assembly, which also voted to pay the funeral expenses. As no account of the services has survived, the burial place is unknown, and no information has been found indicating whether Evans was a member of any religious denomination. No photograph of the editor has been identified, but he was described in his later years by a contemporary as a tall man with a shock of snow white hair, a kindly but resolute facial expression, and a quiet, dignified demeanor.

The *Chronicle* ceased publication shortly after the death of its founder; Captain Evans, the only one of seven children to survive his father, engaged in another line of business and left numerous descendants who became prominent in the civic and commercial life of North Carolina and Virginia.

SEE: Ethel Stephens Arnett, *William Swaim, Fighting Editor* (1963); Jay R. Hubbell, "Charles Napoleon Bonaparte Evans, Creator of Jesse Holmes, the Fool-Killer," *South Atlantic Quarterly* 36 (1937); *Milton Chronicle*, scattered issues, 1840–83; Durward T. Stokes, "Charles Napoleon Bonaparte Evans and the *Milton Chronicle,*" *North Carolina Historical Review* 46 (1969), and "Five Letters from Jesse Holmes, the Fool Killer, to the Editor of the Milton Chronicle," *North Carolina Historical Review* 50 (1973).

DURWARD T. STOKES

**Evans, George** *(ca. 1745–ca. 1784)*, Revolutionary patriot, was born in Bath, Beaufort County, the son of Richard and Mary Lillington Evans. In 1758 he moved with his brother Richard to what is now Pitt County, and in 1773 he represented Pitt in the colonial assembly. He early became active in the Revolutionary cause and was a member of the standing committee of Pitt in 1774. Later he was a member of the committee to assist the vestry of St. Michael's Parish in collecting for the benefit of the sufferers in Boston. From the beginning he was a member of the Safety Committee of Pitt and later was made chairman. In 1775 he was appointed first major of the Pitt militia. Although a delegate to the Congress at Hillsborough in August 1775, he declined to serve, saying that "circumstances would not permit his attendance." In November 1776, he was a delegate to the Congress in Halifax that drew up the state constitution. He later declined to serve as lieutenant colonel. As his last public service, he represented Pitt County in the House of Commons in 1782.

Evans married Anne Hines, the daughter of Peter and Elizabeth Edmunds Hines of the Old Sparta section of Edgecombe County. His will was destroyed when the early Pitt County wills were burned, but deeds on record in Edgecombe show that his wife's brothers Henry and Peter Hines were his executors and all property was devised to his son Peter and an unborn child. The unborn child was Susanna Evans, who died unmarried in Edgecombe County in 1808. His widow married Benjamin Spruill of Tyrrell County who died in 1791. By her second husband the widow Evans had two daughters and a son, George Evans Spruill (A.B. Yale, 1814), who was a member of the legislature from Halifax County in 1826 and 1828.

SEE: Walter Clark, ed., *State Records of North Carolina*, vols. 14, 16, 17, 19, 23 (1896, 1899, 1901, 1904); Deeds and wills of the counties of Beaufort and Edgecombe, deeds of Pitt County (North Carolina State Archives, Raleigh); Fitzhugh Lee Morris, comp., *Lineage Book of the North Carolina Society S. A. R.* (1951); William L. Saunders, ed., *Colonial Records of North Carolina*, vols. 9, 10 (1890).

CLAIBORNE T. SMITH, JR.

**Evans, Henry** *(ca. 1760–17 Sept. 1810)*, popular black preacher, was credited with being "the father of the Methodist Church, white and black, in Fayetteville, and the best preacher of his time in that quarter," according to Bishop William Capers, who, as a youthful probationer in the ministry, was appointed to Fayetteville a few months before Evans's death. Evans was the son of free Negroes from Virginia, a shoemaker by trade, and a licensed Methodist preacher. En route to Charleston, S.C., about 1780, he stopped in Fayetteville. Dismayed by the depravity of the slave populace, he decided to stay and preach. When town authorities forbade such "agitation," he was obliged to go into the surrounding sandhills to hold services, changing from place to place to escape mob violence. In time, however, white masters began to recognize an improvement in the manners and morals of his listeners, and eventually the leaders of the Fayetteville community allowed him to preach in town.

Sometime before 1800, a rough building was put up to house Evans's congregation. Soon white visitors filled the seats reserved for them and began to preempt the Negroes' space, and after a few years sheds had to be built onto the sides to accommodate the crowds. Indeed, Capers records, Evans "was so *remarkable*, as to have become the greatest curiosity of the town; insomuch that distinguished visitors hardly felt that they might pass a Sunday in Fayetteville without hearing him preach."

Evans's church was visited on several occasions by Bishop Francis Asbury, who, in his *Journal* (14 Jan. 1805), called it the "African meeting house." It was built on the site of the present-day Evans Metropolitan A.M.E. Zion Church. Evans lived in a room at the back of the chancel and continued to stay there after ill health forced him, about 1806, to turn the care of his congregation over to preachers appointed by Asbury. In a unique will, dated 9 Dec. 1809, he bequeathed the part of the building and lot used for church purposes to the Methodist Episcopal church, but provided that his residence and the rest of the lot were to go to the church only at the death of his widow.

Capers, in his brief acquaintance with Evans, noted that he was unusually "conversant with Scripture," that his conversation was "instructive as to the things of

God," and that he seemed "deeply impressed with the responsibility of his position." Capers recorded a moving account of Evans's last words to the congregation and his funeral:

"On the Sunday before his death . . . the little door between his humble shed and the chancel where I stood was opened, and the dying man entered for a last farewell to his people. He was almost too feeble to stand at all, but supporting himself by the railing of the chancel, he said, 'I have come to say my last word to you. It is this: None but Christ. Three times I have had my life in jeopardy for preaching the gospel to you. Three times I have broken the ice on the edge of the water and swum across the Cape Fear [River] to preach the gospel to you. And now, if in my last hour I could trust to that, or to any thing else but Christ crucified, for my salvation, all should be lost, and my soul perish for ever.' A noble testimony! Worthy, not of Evans only, but St. Paul. His funeral at the church was attended by a greater concourse of persons than had been seen on any funeral occasion before. The whole community appeared to mourn his death, and the universal feeling seemed to be that in honoring the memory of Henry Evans we were paying a tribute to virtue and religion. He was buried under the chancel of the church of which he had been in so remarkable a manner the founder."

SEE: William K. Anderson, ed., *Methodism* (1947); Elmer E. Clark, ed., *Journal and Letters of Francis Asbury* (1958); C. Franklin Grill, *Methodism in the Upper Cape Fear Valley* (1966); Nolan B. Harmon, ed., *Encyclopedia of World Methodism*, vol. 1 (1974); Elizabeth Lamb, *Historical Sketch of Hay Street Methodist Episcopal Church, South* (1914); John A. Oates, *The Story of Fayetteville* (1950); Raleigh *Minerva*, 27 Sept. 1810; William M. Wightmen, *Life of William Capers* (1859).

RALPH HARDEE RIVES

**Evans, Peter** *(12 Dec. 1781–25 Dec. 1852)*, planter and businessman, was born in Pitt County of English ancestry. His father was Major George Evans, a member of the colonial Assembly from Pitt County, a delegate to the Provincial Congress at Halifax in 1776 that formed the constitution and bill of rights of North Carolina, and a member of the General Assembly of North Carolina in 1782. His mother was the former Ann Hines, daughter of Peter Hines of Pitt County. In 1800, Peter Evans settled in Edgecombe County on a plantation called Piney Prospect near Old Sparta. Here he lived until about 1830, when he sold his old house and established a new residence on the Deep River in what was then Chatham (now Lee) County. This 2,700-acre-plantation, which was previously known as La Grange, Evans named Egypt because people going there to get corn associated it with the biblical land of Egypt. Considered a very wealthy man, Evans owned more than a hundred slaves and lived after the fashion of typical southern planters of romance and tradition. Around 1847, his health began to decline and he moved to Scotland Neck where he built a small house called Piney Prospect after his Edgecombe home. He died of cancer of the throat on Christmas Day at his daughter Susan's home, Kelvin Grove, near Scotland Neck.

In his will Evans directed that his Egypt lands be examined for coal. This was done and by 1855 the Deep River coal fields were being mined. With the coming of the Civil War, a railroad was built from these coal fields to Fayetteville. The coal was soft and inferior, therefore avoided by the blockade runners as its excessive amounts of smoke enhanced detection by the enemy. The noted blockade runner *The Advance* was finally sighted and captured because she had been reduced to burning Egypt coal.

Evans's father died when he was two, and with few resources and little education Evans had a remarkably successful business career. He was a pioneer in the great agricultural revival that made Edgecombe County noted throughout the South. He and his brother-in-law, Joel Battle, established the cotton mill at Rocky Mount. He later had interests in mills, canals, and iron foundries in other parts of the state. His son, Peter G. Evans, married Eliza Morehead, the daughter of Governor John Motley Morehead, and together father and son supported the establishment of the railroad from Greensboro to Morehead City. This was to provide North Carolina with an outlet to the sea and was a great impetus to the development of the state.

Evans married Ann Johnston (1789–1866), the daughter of Amos and Dorcas Williams Johnston of Edgecombe County. He was buried in the Evans cemetery, Greenville, and his wife in Trinity Churchyard, Scotland Neck. There were four daughters of the marriage: Eliza (m. Dr. Isaac Hall of Scotland Neck), Mary Ann (m. Dr. Samuel Southerland of Warren County), Susan (m. William Ruffin Smith of Kelvin Grove, near Scotland Neck), and Adelaide (m. James Norfleet Smith of Magnolia Hall, near Scotland Neck). His two sons were George N. (m. Hettie Rowland) and Peter G. (m. Elizabeth Morehead). Young Peter was colonel of the North Carolina Sixty-third Regiment and a cavalry officer in General J. E. B. Stuart's Brigade. He was killed near Upperville, Va., on 21 June 1863.

SEE: William C. Allen, *History of Halifax County* (1918); Samuel A. Ashe, *History of North Carolina*, vol. 2 (1925); Wade H. Hadley and others, eds., *Chatham County, 1771–1971* (1976); John W. Moore, *History of North Carolina*, 2 vols. (1880); Records of Halifax County (North Carolina State Archives, Raleigh); William L. Saunders, ed., *Colonial Records of North Carolina*, vols. 4, 9, 10 (1886, 1890).

ELIZABETH W. MANNING

**Evans, Richard** *(ca. 1735–ca. 1774)*, planter, legislator, and town founder, was born in Bath, Beaufort County, the son of Richard Evans, "Mariner," and Mary Lillington Evans. In 1758 Evans and his brother, George, sold their property in Bath and bought several tracts of land on the Tar River in the part of Beaufort that became Pitt County in 1760. Richard was a captain in the Pitt County militia in 1764 and represented Pitt in the colonial Assembly in 1769. In 1771, the Assembly passed an act authorizing him to lay out a town on his one hundred acres on the south side of Tar River in the county of Pitt. For the town, called Martinborough, commissioners were also appointed in the act. In addition to Richard Evans, Wyriot Ormond, Charles Forbes, Henry Ellis, and George Evans were named. Richard Evans died before the Assembly passed a special act in 1774 confirming the lot holders in their titles. The act also moved the courthouse of Pitt County to Martinborough. In 1787, the name of Martinborough was changed to Greenville.

Evans was buried in the Evans family cemetery on Evans Street in Greenville. His will has been lost, but from deeds and other sources he appears to have had sons Benjamin, Richard, Michael Coutanche, and

George and daughters whose names are not known. The name of his wife is not known. In 1769 Evans had acquired from his first cousins, James and Lillington Lockhart, the fine plantation known as Scotch Hall in Bertie County. His son Michael resided there and left a will in Bertie in 1796. On Michael's death Scotch Hall was sold to the Jacocks family, which has owned it since that time. Among the prominent descendants of Richard Evans were Colonel Fred Olds, of the Hall of History in Raleigh, whose mother was Pauline Evans; and Dr. Augustus Coutanche Evans, who was a special agent for the Confederate government in Europe.

SEE: Walter Clark, ed., *State Records of North Carolina*, vols. 23 (1904), 24 (1905); Deeds and wills of the counties of Beaufort and Bertie, deeds of Pitt County (North Carolina State Archives, Raleigh); William L. Saunders, ed., *Colonial Records of North Carolina*, vol. 4 (1886); Tombstone inscriptions, Evans cemetery (Greenville).

CLAIBORNE T. SMITH, JR.

**Everard, Sir Richard** *(24 June 1683–17 Feb. 1733)*, governor, was born at Langleys, Much Waltham (now Great Waltham), Essex, England, the son of Sir Hugh Everard and his wife, Mary Browne, daughter of John Browne, M.D., of Salisbury, Wiltshire. Richard, who succeeded to the baronetcy at the death of his father in January 1706, became a captain in Queen Anne's army. He may have been present with Admiral Sir George Rooke's force that attacked Gibraltar in 1704, and he remained in garrison there for eighteen months. Upon returning to England he resigned his commission. This was about the time he succeeded his father and sold the family property at Langleys to pay debts; he then purchased property at Broomfield Green. In St. Alphage Church, London, on 13 June 1706, he married Susannah Kidder, daughter of the Right Reverend Richard Kidder, bishop of Bath and Wells.

A descendant of the Duke of Clarence, brother of Edward IV and Richard III, Everard's great-grandmother was a first cousin of Oliver Cromwell and the granddaughter of Winifred Pole Barrington, niece of Reginald, Cardinal Pole. His great-grandfather, Sir Richard, was created a baronet in 1628 by Charles I. During the Civil War the family served the Parliamentary cause and received special favors through Cromwell. Nevertheless, they protected church property and resumed local positions of leadership after the Restoration.

Complaints from the Council in North Carolina against Governor George Burrington, delivered to the Lords Proprietors by Chief Justice Christopher Gale, were responsible for Burrington's removal from office in January 1725. At the meeting of the Proprietors when this action was taken a letter was read from Sir Richard seeking appointment as his successor. It was promptly consented to and a formal appointment made on 7 April. This was approved by the Crown, and Everard was required to post a bond to enforce the acts of trade. He was soon granted two thousand acres of land in the colony, and in May 1726, after she had joined her husband in North Carolina, Lady Susannah Everard was granted three thousand acres. Burrington received a notice of his dismissal on 17 July when Everard appeared in Edenton before the Council and took the oath of office.

Everard was the last Proprietary governor of the colony. After the purchase of Carolina by the Crown in 1729, he remained in office until 25 Feb. 1731 when Burrington succeeded him as the first royal governor of the province. Between the time of his dismissal and July 1726 when he returned to England, Burrington remained in North Carolina where he was the cause of considerable political unrest as well as responsible for several physical attacks on Everard and other leaders with whom he disagreed. It was a time of distress for many people, and factions developed that contributed to unstable conditions throughout most of Everard's administration.

In spite of the opposition, however, Everard attempted to maintain peace and to abide by his Instructions. He worked with local leaders insofar as possible and was concerned for the welfare of the colony. For example, because of poor port facilities most of North Carolina's exports were shipped through Virginia, but officials there began to charge excessive fees for this service or to prohibit it entirely. Everard attempted to persuade the Board of Trade to declare a port on the Nansemond River in Virginia free to Carolinians for shipping tobacco. He further demonstrated genuine concern in maintaining peace between Indians in North Carolina and those in Virginia. Two new counties, New Hanover and Tyrrell, were created during his term of office.

It was apparent from the time of his appointment that the Crown was intent on purchasing the Proprietary rights in Carolina, and it fell to Everard's lot to cooperate with Virginia in running the boundary between the two colonies. As commissioners for that purpose, in 1728 he designated Christopher Gale, John Lovick, and William Little, each of whom had friends in England in common with Everard and who up to that point had been strong supporters of the governor. He also named Edward Moseley to the commission. The line was fairly run and North Carolina retained land long in dispute with Virginia.

Knowing from the beginning that North Carolina was likely to become a royal colony, the governor seems to have worked diligently to improve conditions in North Carolina while at the same time attempting to please officials at home. Perhaps he hoped for future royal favor. He strictly obeyed his instructions that the granting of land cease. This was a reversal of the practice recently followed by Burrington in violation of directions from home. He had continued to permit land to be taken up, particularly in the Cape Fear region, an area rapidly developing and with the prospect of a good seaport. It may have been Everard's action in this respect that displeased "popular" leaders in the colony and turned some of Everard's oldest supporters against him. By mid-year 1728 it became clear that Burrington, in England, was again in favor and that upon sale of the colony to the Crown he was likely to return to office. After all, one of the charges against Burrington had been that he was suspected of working with South Carolinians who favored a shift from Proprietary to royal control for North Carolina as had already occurred in the southern province. With this about to become a reality, Everard realized that his days in office were limited, and he changed his policies. Land sales were resumed and much land was taken up through the use of "blank patents," documents signed by the proper officials but with the quantity and location of the land filled in by the new "owner" and inadequately recorded as a means of avoiding the payment of quitrents. Everard also approved the issuance of £40,000 in paper currency, something for which the Assembly rewarded him with a gift of £500.

Although Burrington was named the new governor of North Carolina when it became a royal colony in

January 1730, he did not arrive until February 1731. Shortly afterwards the Everards left for England by way of Virginia.

Sir Richard and his wife were the parents of four children: Richard (ca. 1709–42), who succeeded to the baronetcy but died a widower without children; Hugh (d. 1745), who then succeeded to the baronetcy but died childless at which time the baronetcy became extinct; Susannah, who married David Meade in Virginia in 1731 and from whom descended many prominent families in Virginia and North Carolina; and Anne, who married George Lathbury in England. Susannah Meade bought a house in Halifax, N.C., where she lived after the death of her husband. Sir Richard died at his home in Red Lion Street, London, and was buried in Great Waltham. He was a member of the lodge of Freemasons at Ross Tavern Without Temple Bar in London.

SEE: Robert J. Cain, ed., *North Carolina Higher-Court Minutes, 1724–1730* (1981); *Calendar of State Papers, Colonial Series, America and West Indies*, vols. 34–39 (1938–39); George E. Cokayne, ed., *Complete Baronetage*, vol. 2 (1902); A. Roger Ekirch, *"Poor Carolina" Politics and Society in Colonial North Carolina, 1729–1776* (1981); *Gentleman's Magazine*, February 1733; Lawrence Lee, *The Lower Cape Fear in Colonial Days* (1965); Henry J. Peet, ed., *Chaumiere Papers, Containing Matters of Interest to the Descendants of David Meade* (1883); William L. Saunders, ed., *Colonial Records of North Carolina*, vols. 2–5 (1886–87); Louis B. Wright, ed., *The Prose Works of William Byrd of Westover* (1966).

WILLIAM S. POWELL

**Everett, Reuben Oscar** *(20 Oct. 1879–27 Apr. 1971)*, attorney and civic and cultural leader, was born at Hamilton, Martin County, the son of Justus and Elizabeth Purvis Everett. Shortly afterwards he moved with his family to their plantation home, Swamplawn, near Palmyra, where his father was a large planter. After completing his early education at Vine Hill Academy in Scotland Neck, Everett attended The University of North Carolina where he held various class offices and was graduated in 1903. He studied law in the first class at Trinity College while he taught at Durham High School. Later he continued the study of law and other subjects at the summer schools of Columbia University and Harvard University.

Immediately after obtaining his law license in 1905, Everett began practicing in Durham. He was the first Durham city attorney and the first prosecuting attorney in Durham Recorder's Court (1921–33). He also was the first attorney (1906) for and later secretary of the Durham Merchants Association, which he helped form. In 1926, he became an early member of the American Law Institute and later was a life member. He was admitted to practice law before the United States Supreme Court, U.S. Court of Military Appeals, federal district courts, and North Carolina state courts. By then he was president of the Durham Bar Association; a senior member of the North Carolina Bar Association and American Bar Association, with which he was affiliated from 1913 until his death; and a member of the judicial district bar. His law partners included former Governor W. W. Kitchin and former Attorney General James S. Manning.

On 24 June 1926 Everett married Kathrine Robinson, of Fayetteville, who was then one of the few women attorneys in North Carolina. Their only child, Robinson Oscar Everett, was born on 18 Mar. 1928; he subsequently was associated with his parents in the practice of law under the name of Everett, Everett & Everett. The senior Everett was devoted to his profession and never retired from it, actually dying in his office at the age of ninety-two.

Everett and three of his brothers, Justus, Benjamin B., and Alphonso, served in the North Carolina General Assembly. R. O. Everett served five terms in the state house of representatives between 1921 and 1933. His public service also included membership on the board of trustees of The University of North Carolina for twenty years. He served as chairman of the Durham County Board of Elections for a decade (when he initiated the use of voting machines there), of the Durham-Orange Historical Commission for many years, and of the Bennett Place Memorial Commission from 1923 until his death. Everett was a commissioner for North Carolina, a representative of the American Cotton Association to the World Cotton Conference in Europe (1921), and president of the North Carolina State Fair. He also was one of the state's delegates to the Democratic National conventions at San Francisco, Calif. (1920), and Houston, Tex. (1928). At the latter he made a nominating speech for Cordell Hull, who later became secretary of state in Franklin D. Roosevelt's administration.

Long active in the civic and religious affairs of the community, Everett, an Episcopalian, was a member of St. Phillips Episcopal Church in Durham, the Knights of Phythias, the North Carolina Literary and Historical Association, the North Carolina Society of County and Local Historians, and the English Speaking Union. As chairman of the Bennett Place Memorial Commission, he headed the restoration of the Bennett Place in 1965. In addition, as chairman of the George Washington Statue Commission, he was instrumental in placing the present statue in the capitol rotunda in Raleigh, an event that received national publicity. Earlier he traveled to Italy to examine the model for the statue of George Washington made by Antonio Canova in 1820. The original was destroyed by a fire in the North Carolina capitol in 1831.

Everett was chief marshal for the North Carolina State Fair, and a street in West Raleigh and a street in Durham were named in his honor. A suggestion by him is credited with leading to the establishment of the Sir Walter Cabinet in North Carolina, a society for wives of legislators and chief state administrators. He was active in marking and preserving points of historical interest in North Carolina. Widely known by persons in all walks of life, he participated in many projects for the good of his community, state, and nation. He assisted in forming the Legal Aid Society in North Carolina, and for his work in bettering race relations he received a special award from the Durham Committee on Negro Affairs.

He was buried in Cross Creek Cemetery, Fayetteville.

SEE: William C. Dula, *Durham and Her People* (1951); *Durham Morning Herald*, 22 Oct. 1966, 28 Apr. 1971; *North Carolina Biography*, vol. 4 (1941); *North Carolina Manual* (1921, 1923, 1925, 1927, 1933); Raleigh *News and Observer*, 7 Sept. 1915, 29 Apr. 1971.

WILLIAM A. CREECH

**Everett, Sallie Baker** *(26 Feb. 1888–29 Apr. 1975)*, farm and political leader, was born in the Halifax County town of Palmyra to LaFayette John and Pattie Norman Spruill Baker. Following education at Halifax

County public schools, she attended Louisburg College from 1900 to 1904 and Meredith College from 1905 to 1909. On 25 Feb. 1914, she married Benjamin Bryan Everett, a four-term representative in the North Carolina General Assembly, member of the North Carolina Prison Board, trustee of State College and of the consolidated University of North Carolina, and president of the North Carolina Crop Improvement Association. It was not until she had raised and educated her five children (three daughters and two sons) that Mrs. Everett decided to become active in political, farming, and women's organizations in addition to being a partner with her husband in extensive farming and merchandising in the area.

The Democratic party was a main beneficiary of her efforts. Nationally, she served on the executive committee of the Democratic National Committee from 1950 through 1960; for much of that time she also was a member of the advisory council. In addition, she represented North Carolina as a national committeewoman from 1952 through 1960. For the North Carolina Democratic Executive Committee she served as vice-chairman for seven years (1942–48, 1950). In 1952, she was chairman of the women's campaign for Governor William B. Umstead.

Farm concerns were another major part of her service to the state. From 1942 through 1952 she was chairman of the women's division of the North Carolina Farm Bureau and while serving in this capacity lobbied extensively on behalf of state and national legislation to improve rural education, libraries, consumer education, health, and hospitals. She also was a director of the Agricultural Foundation of North Carolina State College and of the North Carolina Farm Bureau. In recognition of her efforts on behalf of farming interests, she was named the *Progressive Farmer* magazine's Woman of the Year (1946) and received the North Carolina Farm Bureau's Distinguished Service Award (1947).

Active in other state and local groups, Mrs. Everett was a member of the North Carolina Federation of Women's Clubs, serving as both president of her local club and chairman of various committees for the state club. She belonged to the North Carolina State Art Society, the Roanoke Island Historical Association, the State Literary and Historical Association, and the state United War Fund.

A dedicated churchwoman, she was a lifelong Episcopalian and was buried in the cemetery of Trinity Church, Scotland Neck.

SEE: Sallie Baker Everett Papers (Manuscript Collection, East Carolina University, Greenville); William S. Powell, ed., *North Carolina Lives* (1962); *Progressive Farmer*, January 1947; Cameron P. West, *A Democrat and Proud of It* (1959).

WILLIAM R. PITTMAN

**Ewart, Hamilton Glover** *(23 Oct. 1849–28 Apr. 1918)*, attorney, congressman, and judge, was born in Columbia, S.C., the son of James Beckett and Mary A. McMahon Ewart. He was valedictorian of his graduating class at the University of South Carolina in 1872, when he received the degree of bachelor of laws. In 1875 he opened a law office in Hendersonville, N.C., and in 1878 and 1879 was elected to one-year terms as mayor of the town. Under U.S. Chief Justice Morrison R. Waite he was appointed register of bankruptcy for the Eighth Congressional District, a post he filled from 1874 until it was abolished in 1880. Several of his opinions were published in the *National Bankruptcy Reporter*. Originally a Democrat, Ewart is reported to have become a Republican in 1872 because he could not support Horace Greeley in the presidential race, preferring Ulysses S. Grant. In 1876 he was a delegate to the Republican National Convention at Cincinnati and on the state electoral ticket in the Rutherford B. Hayes campaign. On several occasions Ewart declined to be nominated for the General Assembly, but in 1886 he accepted the nomination for Congress by the Republican convention in his district. Although he was defeated, his opponent won by a much smaller majority than Democrats had enjoyed in previous elections.

In 1886, Ewart was nominated for the North Carolina House of Representatives and won by a large majority; he served during the 1887 session when he was chairman of the Committee on Corporations and a member of the Committee on Judiciary. At that time he introduced the bill to establish a Railroad Commission. Subsequently he was elected as a Republican to the United States Congress and served from December 1889 until March 1891; he was defeated for reelection in 1890 and for election in 1904. In Congress he was a member of the Committee on Claims, the Committee on the Merchant Marine, and the Committee on Private Land Claims. He also played a prominent role in the investigation of the Civil Service Commission. He spoke strongly in opposition to the federal election bill and stressed that if passed it was likely to renew animosity between North and South; he also favored federal aid to education and urged the repeal of internal revenue laws. Following his service in Congress Ewart was elected to the General Assembly of the state and served during the 1895 session but resigned immediately upon its adjournment; he served again in 1911.

In 1898, President William McKinley appointed Ewart judge of the United States District Court for the Western District of North Carolina; however, despite the fact that he was nominated on three different occasions, he was never confirmed. Nevertheless, he took his seat on the bench and served from 16 July 1898 to 4 Mar. 1899 and from 14 Apr. 1899 to 7 June 1900. Finally his nomination was withdrawn. After leaving Congress Ewart was charged with attempting to sell government publications that had been delivered to him for free distribution among his constituents. In 1916, Ewart moved from Hendersonville to Chicago where he continued to practice law. He died in Chicago and was buried in Oakdale Cemetery, Hendersonville.

Ewart owned extensive farming interests around Hendersonville and was a member of the Farmers' Alliance. In 1874 he married Sarah Cordelia Ripley, daughter of his stepfather, Colonel Valentine Ripley. They were the parents of seven children: Mary D., Eliza Adger, Hamilton Gustavus, Sarah Cordelia, Valentine, James Beckett, and Matthew Quay.

SEE: John P. Arthur, *Western North Carolina, A History* (1914); Samuel A. Ashe, ed., *Cyclopedia of Eminent and Representative Men of the Carolinas* (1892); *Bio. Dir. Am. Cong.* (1961); Crockette W. Hewlett, *The United States Judges of North Carolina* (1978); *Legislative Biographical Sketch Book, Session 1887* (1887); *North Carolina Manual* (1911); *Ought Hon. H. G. Ewart to be Confirmed as Judge of the United States District Court for the Western District of North Carolina?* [1898?] (Pamphlet in the North Carolina Collection, University of North Carolina, Chapel Hill); Sadie S. Patton, *The Story of Henderson County* (1947).

WILLIAM S. POWELL

**Exum, Benjamin** *(ca. 1725–89)*, Revolutionary patriot and legislator, was born in Isle of Wight County, Va., the son of John and Elizabeth Exum. In 1750 he moved with his father to Edgecombe County, N.C., but later settled in Dobbs County. His land fell in the new county of Wayne when it was formed in 1779 from the western portion of Dobbs.

With the outbreak of the American Revolution, Exum was one of the most active patriots in Dobbs County. On 18 Oct. 1775, he was certified as a lieutenant of the Second Company of Minutemen. On 6 May 1776 he was on a committee to extract sulphur for ammunition in Dobbs County, and he represented the county at the Provincial Congress at Halifax in November 1776. In 1777, he was a member of the state senate. The Benjamin Exum of Dobbs who was clerk of the House of Commons for the same session was probably the son of the senator. Again a member of the senate in 1778 and 1779, the elder Exum was also treasurer of the New Bern District in the latter year.

Early in 1780, after he was made colonel of the Wayne militia, Exum and his regiment were ordered to join General Horatio Gates in South Carolina. Here, in the following August, the regiment took part in the disastrous Battle of Camden and suffered heavy losses. In 1781, Colonel Exum was listed as commander of the Second Regiment of North Carolina militia.

Exum was again elected treasurer of the New Bern District in 1784. Subsequently, he and some of his associates in office became involved in financial difficulties. A committee was appointed by the House of Commons to investigate, but no action was taken and the matter was dropped.

On 21 Feb. 1780, he and his wife Martha, whose surname is unknown, deeded to Hugh Shaw a tract of land on the north side of the Neuse River lying partly in Wake and partly in Johnston counties. In 1788, he deeded his Wayne lands to his sons William and Mathew. Exum died shortly afterwards as his name does not appear in the census of 1790. Benjamin and Martha Exum were the parents of three sons, Benjamin, William, and Mathew, and two daughters, Martha and Tabitha. Tabitha married Benjamin Smith of Wayne County.

SEE: John B. Boddie, *Seventeenth Century Isle of Wight County, Virginia* (1938); John L. Cheney, Jr., *North Carolina Government, 1585–1974* (1975); Walter Clark, ed., *State Records of North Carolina*, vols. 14–16 (1896–99).

CLAIBORNE T. SMITH, JR.

**Faduma, Orishatukeh** *(1855–25 Jan. 1946)*, teacher and minister, was born in Guyana, South America (formerly British Guiana), to John and Omolofi Faduma, freed African slaves from Yorubaland (now in southwestern Nigeria, West Africa). The inhabitants of this region, the Yoruba, constitute one of the largest ethnic groups in the country. British antislavery policies provided for the settlement in Sierra Leone of Africans taken from British and other slavers whose countries had reciprocal right of search and equipment treaties with Britain. Sierra Leone, a British colony, had been established in West Africa in 1787 for the settlement of such recaptives. In this way, Faduma and his parents were settled in Freetown, the seat of administration in the colony.

Apparently like many other children, Faduma was baptized a Christian upon arrival in Sierra Leone. In keeping with the missionary attitudes then of regarding African names as "heathenish," he was given the name of William James Davies, by which he was known until 1887 when he changed it to Orishatukeh Faduma. Also like the children of other captives, he attended school in one of the leading Christian establishments in the colony, the Methodist Boys High School. Upon graduation from the school, where he must have excelled, he continued his education at the Wesleyan (now Queens) College, Taunton, England, from 1882 to 1883. He then attended London University, where in 1885 he became the first Sierra Leonean to obtain the intermediate bachelor of arts degree.

After completing his studies in England, Faduma returned to Sierra Leone where he probably taught school for a time. It is definite that between 1885 and 1891 he was senior master at the Methodist Boys High School, a position he would not have obtained without prior teaching experience. In 1891 he came to the United States for additional education, one of the few Africans to do so. Receiving a scholarship of $400 to study the philosophy of religion, he continued his postgraduate work at Yale Divinity School (1894–95) where he was awarded a B.D. in 1895. Afterward he remained in the United States.

Sometime between 1891 and 1895 Faduma became affiliated with the American Missionary Association, whose major focus was the evangelization of Afro-Americans and Africans. During this period he also became more closely associated with the African Methodist Episcopal church and most likely was ordained a minister. From 1895 to 1914, he was principal and pastor-in-charge of Peabody Academy, Troy, N.C., which was established in 1880 for the education of blacks—mostly as teachers to work in the rural areas of North Carolina under the sponsorship of the American Missionary Association. In the early 1900s the academy had four teachers, excluding the principal, two of whom were Henrietta Faduma, Faduma's wife, and Ada Smitherman, a resident of Troy.

Returning to Sierra Leone, Faduma was principal of the United Methodist Collegiate School from 1916 to 1918. Between 1918 and 1923, he served as inspector of schools in the colony, as well as instructor and officer-in-charge of the Model School. Somewhat equivalent to the American junior high school, the Model School prepared pupils for entry into the job market provided they failed to continue their education through the high school level.

In 1924 he returned to the United States and continued teaching in North Carolina until 1939. He served as assistant principal and instructor in Latin, ancient and modern history, and English literature at Lincoln Academy, Kings Mountain. Both Peabody Academy and Lincoln Academy afterwards closed. Upon his retirement, Faduma took up another assignment at the Virginia Theological Seminary and College, Lynchburg.

Faduma's life was not confined to teaching, however. He was very much a public man influenced by the contemporary trends of politics, religion, culture, race, and social relations not only in Sierra Leone, but also in Africa at large and the United States. Thus, soon after his return from England in 1887 he joined with other public-spirited members of the Freetown community in Sierra Leone—such as Dr. Edward Blyden and A. E. Tobuku-Metzger—to form what was known as the Dress Reform Society. The aim of the society was to foster the wearing of African robes, which were more suited to the climate in Sierra Leone and reflected the African cultural heritage, rather than the "Victorian" coat and tie imposed on the westernized settlers or Creoles.

It was at this time that Faduma, who had previously been known as William Davies, changed his name. He adopted Orishatukeh, derived from the Yoruban deity Orisha, and Faduma, his father's name. Many other Creoles also either dropped their baptismal English names for African ones or appended African names to the ones they already had. This cultural movement was part of the Creole response to British racial and cultural paternalism, as well as an attempt to return to their African roots in the hope of finding security in the dilemmas resulting from straddling both the African and European worlds. Much later, Professor Faduma, as he was commonly called, continued to display his political awareness and breadth of vision. In 1923, he was a delegate to the second meeting of the National Congress of British West Africa held in Freetown. The formation of the congress was the earliest effort by West African nationalists from the middle class to create a movement to pressure the British government for political concessions.

In the United States, Faduma also was active publicly. In 1892, he was a member of the Advisory Council in African Ethnology at the World's Exposition in Chicago. Two years later he was Yale's delegate to the Inter-Seminary Missionary Alliance at Rochester, N.Y., and contributed a paper entitled "Industrial Missions in Africa." In 1895 he delivered two papers on Yoruban religion and missionary work in Africa at a missionary congress on Africa, which was held simultaneously with the Cotton States Exposition in Atlanta. It was at the exposition that Booker T. Washington made his important "Atlanta Compromise" speech and established himself as the spokesman for Afro-Americans in the United States. Other important black leaders attending the congress were Bishop Henry McNeil Turner, Dr. Alexander Crummell, and T. Thomas Fortune.

Faduma was a member of the American Negro Academy, based in Washington, D.C., which had been established by Afro-American intellectuals as a forum to express their views on important issues affecting blacks. He was the only African to address the academy, where he spoke in 1904 on "The Defects of the Negro Church." He is also said to have addressed the North Carolina Teachers Association on "The Value of Education in Civic Life" in June 1915.

In September 1895 Faduma married Henrietta Adams, a teacher at Peabody Academy. They had two children: Jowo (b. 1902), who was given a Yoruban name; and Dubois (b. 1922), who was presumably named after W. E. B. Dubois, the great Afro-American leader and Pan-Africanist.

There can be no doubt that Faduma enjoyed public speaking. On several occasions he went on lecture tours in both the United States and Sierra Leone. Apparently because of these and other activities he was awarded an honorary doctorate of philosophy by Livingstone College in Salisbury, N.C.

Faduma seems to have been a prolific writer as well as a poet. Among his published works were "A Ballad on Egbaland," in *AME Church Review* (July 1888); "In Memoriam, The Centenary of Sierra Leone," in *AME Church Review* (October 1889); "Thoughts for the Times, or the New Theology," in *AME Church Review* (October 1890); "Africa or the Dark Continent," in *AME Church Review* (July 1892); "Religious Beliefs of the Yoruba People in West Africa" and "Success and Drawbacks of Missionary Work in Africa by an Eye-Witness," in *Africa and the American Negro*, J. W. E. Bowen, ed. (1896); "Africa the Unknown," in *Mission Herald* (November-December 1939); "An African Background: My Pagan Origin and Inheritance," in *Mission Herald* (September-October 1940); and "The Defects of the Negro Church," *Occasional Paper No. 8* (1904).

The speeches, writings, and activities of Orishatukeh Faduma reveal that during his long life he was endowed with a keen wit, tremendous energy, and a passion for involvement in political and social issues. His prime avocation undoubtedly was education, and it may be assumed he was successful at it judging by the number of significant and responsible teaching positions he held. He was also a devoted Christian minister. It appears that as he grew older, however, he became more aware of the contradictions regarding race and contempt for black and African values within the Christian ministry. This consciousness led him to greater flexibility. As he once observed, "No foreign missionary introduces God to the African. What he does is to interpret God to him. I owe much in my foundation to my pagan inheritance of qualities which are needed and exalted in Christianity. For these things, I thank God. Of what can I boast?" Again he observed, "The aim and purpose of Christian missions is not to Anglicize, Americanize, or Germanize the world, but to Christianize it."

Professor Faduma's experiences in America at the height of "Jim Crowism" particularly sharpened his consciousness of race. Although he must have developed emotional mechanisms of accommodation to racial segregation, he inveighed against the system and sought to elevate the black man—not only in his work but also by his thoughts and writings. He was nevertheless a temperate man not given to bitter fulminations, but caustic wit. Consider, for example, his reminiscence of a "racial" episode in the United States. "I was once asked in a public lecture whether my father was a white man anywhere, the gentleman who questioned me said. 'What am I?' 'A pink man' I replied. As if to clarify his question, he said 'I mean whether you have white blood in you.' 'White blood?' said I. 'All Bloods I have seen are red, not white. I have seen men of different colors, but not different-color bloods.' "

Faduma also emerges as one of the earliest African nationalists and Pan-African patriots. From his earliest days as a founding member of the Dress Reform Society in Freetown, Sierra Leone, and his membership in the National Congress of British West Africa to his relentless devotion to the education and elevation of Afro-Americans, especially in North Carolina and Virginia, his pride and faith in the potential of his African heritage remain outstanding. Further research into the life and times of Faduma may yet reveal the many dimensions of his life and establish him as an important figure in African and Afro-American history.

SEE: Charles Alexander, *One Hundred Distinguished Leaders* (1899); Edward W. Blyden, *Pan-Negro Patriot, 1832–1912* (1967); William H. Ferris, *The African Abroad, or His Evolution in Western Civilization, Tracing His Development under Caucasion Milieu* (1913); Christopher Fyfe, *A History of Sierra Leone* (1968); *Who's Who in Colored America* (1940).

GUSTAV H. K. DEVENEAUX

**Faircloth, William Turner** *(8 Jan. 1829–29 Dec. 1900)*, lawyer, Confederate officer, legislator, and judge, was born at the family farm on Otter Creek in Edgecombe County, the son of William and Susan Edwards Faircloth. He was the oldest of five children including S. E., Bennett, Mary, and Martha. At twenty-one, Faircloth enrolled at Wake Forest College and taught school during the vacations. After graduating at the head of his class in June 1854, he attended Richmond M. Pearson's law school at Richmond Hill in Yadkin County. He was licensed to practice on 1 Jan. 1856 and moved to Snow Hill, Greene County, where he served as county solicitor until May 1856. He then moved to Goldsboro, Wayne County, and practiced law until June 1861.

Although a Whig and Unionist, Faircloth aligned himself with North Carolina when the crisis at Fort Sumter precipitated the state's secession. Appointed first lieutenant on 16 May 1861, he helped organize the Rip Van Winkle Company in Wayne County and had his rank confirmed by election on 16 July. The company was accepted into state service at Camp Mason in Wayne County as Company C of the Second Regiment, North Carolina Infantry, on 21 Aug. 1861; it was transferred to the Second Corps, Army of the Potomac, on 23 September. After being stationed at Middleton in Hyde County and Garysburg in Northampton County, the regiment went to Virginia in November or December 1861 and drilled at Camp Potomac. Faircloth was promoted to captain and assistant quartermaster on 14 Mar. 1862; he served in that capacity and rank throughout the Civil War. In May 1862 the Second Regiment was moved to Camp Wyatt in New Hanover County, N.C., to help defend Fort Fisher from the expedition of Ambrose E. Burnside. When Robert E. Lee was named commander of the Army of Northern Virginia on 1 June, the Second Regiment was made part of the Second Corps and joined Lee's forces in time for the Seven Days' Battle, which began on 25 June at Oak Grove, Va.

Except for a convalescent period at Goldsboro in August 1862 and at Chimborazo Hospital in Richmond, Va., Captain Faircloth remained with the Army of Northern Virginia throughout the war. The Second Regiment, North Carolina Infantry, participated in the major battles of South Mountain, Antietam, Fredericksburg, Chancellorsville, Gettsyburg, Spottsylvania, Winchester, and the siege of Petersburg. Upon his surrender at Appomattox Court House on 9 Apr. 1865, Faircloth was paroled. He then returned to Goldsboro and resumed his law practice.

After obtaining a pardon, Faircloth was elected as a Wayne County delegate to the state constitutional convention, which met from 2–20 Oct. 1865 and from 24 May to 25 June 1866. While voting with the majority in the repudiation of secession and the approval of the new constitution, he did not identify himself with either the Republican or Democratic party. Faircloth was also a member of the state legislature from 27 Nov. 1865 to 12 Mar. 1866. The legislature elected him solicitor of the Third Judicial District, a position he held until July 1868, when the Republican administration of William W. Holden took office.

Faircloth returned to his law practice and on 10 Jan. 1869 married Eveline Eliza Wooten (13 Nov. 1833–8 Nov. 1904), a daughter of Council and Eliza Wooten of Mosely Hall (now LaGrange) in Lenoir County. They had no children.

Faircloth did not reenter politics until 1874. In that year he applied for an appointment to a vacant associate judgeship of the North Carolina Supreme Court and was told to identify himself more closely with the Republican party. He campaigned for Republican candidates in the 1874 elections and in 1875 was elected as a delegate to the state constitutional convention that met at Raleigh from 6 Sept. to 11 Oct. 1875. In November he was appointed associate justice of the North Carolina Supreme Court by Governor Curtis H. Brogden and held court until the term expired in the fall of 1878. He was the Republican nominee for lieutenant governor in 1884 and canvassed the state from Cherokee to Currituck in an unsuccessful bid. Four years later he was the Republican nominee for associate justice of the state supreme court and again lost the election.

In the election of 1894 Populists in North Carolina fused their ticket with the Republican party. Without his knowledge or approval, Populists nominated Faircloth for chief justice of the North Carolina Supreme Court, and, almost simultaneously, a conference of Republican leaders asked him to run for the same post on the Republican ticket. Having accepted one party's nomination, he accepted the other's and was elected to an eight-year term.

In addition to his legal practice and political activity, Faircloth was a businessman and an active supporter of the Baptist church and higher education in North Carolina. He was a major stockholder and onetime director of the Bank of Wayne in Goldsboro and was on the directing boards of the Wilmington and Weldon and the Atlantic and North Carolina railroads. Other major investments included one-third ownership of Goldsboro's Hotel Gregory, stock in the Goldsboro Furniture Factory, and real estate in Goldsboro and in Wayne County.

A member of the First Missionary Baptist Church in Goldsboro, Faircloth served on the board of trustees of Wake Forest College (1891–1900), the Baptist Orphanage at Thomasville (1889–95), and Meredith College (1891–1900). He was also an attorney for the Baptist Orphanage (1885–1900). Buildings constructed partly from his legacy at the orphanage and at Meredith College now bear his name. His law library was given to Wake Forest's law school. He served North Carolina as a trustee for the state insane asylum and for The University of North Carolina (1874–1895). In 1895, The University of North Carolina conferred upon him the honorary degree of doctor of laws.

Faircloth was regarded by fellow members of the bar and associates on the bench as a thoroughly knowledgeable, conservative, commonsense man of the law. After five years as chief justice, his health deteriorated, and shortly after the 1900 session he died of a stroke in his Goldsboro home. He was buried in Fairview Cemetery in LaGrange.

SEE: Samuel A. Ashe, ed., *Cyclopedia of Eminent and Representative Men of the Carolinas of the Nineteenth Century*, vol. 2 (1892), and "William Turner Faircloth" (C. L. Van Noppen Papers, Manuscript Department, Library, Duke University, Durham); Walter Clark, ed., *Histories of the Several Regiments and Battalions from North Carolina in the Great War 1861–65* (1901), and "History of the Superior and Supreme Courts of North Carolina," *The North Carolina Booklet* 18 (1918); Compiled Service Records of Confederate Soldiers Who Served in Organizations from North Carolina (National Archives, Washington, D.C.); Frank A. Daniels, *History of Wayne County* (1914); Jerome Dowd, *Sketches of Prominent Living North Carolinians* (1888); Arthur E. Fink, "Changing Philosophies and Practices in North Carolina Orphanages," *North Carolina Historical Review* 48 (1971); J. M. Hallowell, *War-Time Reminiscences and Other Selections* (1939); J. G. deR. Hamilton, *Reconstruction in North Carolina* (1914); Mary L. Johnson, *A History of Meredith College* (1956); R. C. Lawrence, "Chief Justice Faircloth," *The State* 14 (10 Aug. 1946); Louis H. Manarin, *North Carolina Troops, 1861–1865: A Roster* (1971); North Carolina Baptist State Convention, *Annual Report* 3 (1901);

*North Carolina Biography*, vol. 3 (1919), vol. 2 (1929); George W. Paschal, *History of Wake Forest College*, vol. 3 (1943); Raleigh *News and Observer*, 26 July 1959, 5 Nov. 1968; Bernard W. Spillman, *The Mills Home: A History of the Baptist Orphanage Movement in North Carolina* (1932); Joseph F. Steelman, "Republican Party Strategists and the Issue of Fusion with Populists in North Carolina," *North Carolina Historical Review* 47 (1970); Ruth S. Williams and Margaret G. Griffin, *Marriages of Early Edgecombe County, North Carolina, 1733–1868* (1958) and *Tombstone and Census Records of Early Edgecombe* (1959), Wills of Wayne County (North Carolina State Archives, Raleigh).

PAUL E. KUHL

**Faison, John Miller** *(17 Apr. 1862–21 Apr. 1915)*, physician and congressman, was born on a plantation near Faison, the son of Henry W. and Martha Hicks Faison, the paternal grandson of Isham and Sallie Thomson Faison, and the maternal grandson of Dr. James H. and Sara Elizabeth Miller Hicks. He was educated in private schools and at Davidson College where he was graduated with a B.S. degree in 1883. He then attended the Medical College of the University of Virginia and did his internship at the Polyclinic Hospital in New York, receiving his M.D. degree in 1885.

In 1887 Faison married his cousin, Eliza Faison DeVane, a daughter of Colonel William S. (C.S.A.) and Laura Murphy DeVane. They had seven children: Louise Murphy, who died young; Laura Murphy, Henry W., and William DeVane, veterinarian, who all died unmarried; Isham Rowland, who married Louise Oates; John M., who married Esther Ramsdell; and Martha Hicks, who taught school for a number of years.

Dr. Faison built a house in Faison and had a large medical practice in the community. He was a member of the board of directors of the State Hospital in Goldsboro. For several years he was editor and publisher of a local newspaper, the *Faison Journal*.

In politics, he was a Democrat and gained a reputation as a public speaker and debater. He was active in the Red Shirt Campaign of 1898, and advocated the prohibition of alcoholic beverages. In 1910 he was elected to the United States Congress from the Third District of North Carolina and served from 4 Mar. 1911 to 3 Mar. 1915. In the House he worked hard for the Underwood-Simmons Tariff Act of 1913 and for the Glass-Owen Federal Reserve Act; he also supported the Clayton Antitrust Act and the Federal Trade Commission Act.

Faison was a lifelong member of the Faison Presbyterian Church. He was buried in the Faison Cemetery in Faison.

SEE: *Biog. Dir. Am. Cong.* (1961); Clinton *The Sampsonian*, 4 Mar. 1971; Faison family records (in possession of Martha H. Faison, Faison, N.C.); *U.S. Congressional Directory* (1915).

CLAUDE H. MOORF

**Faison, Samson Lane** *(29 Nov. 1860–17 Oct. 1940)*, brigadier general, U.S. Army, was born in Faison, Duplin County. His father, Elias James Faison, was of French Huguenot and Dutch stock and his mother, Elizabeth Maria Lane, was of English ancestry. His father fought in the Civil War and his great-grandfather, Henry Faison (1744–88), fought in the American Revolution under Colonel James Kenan and Captain M. J. Kenan, both of Duplin County. His maternal grandfather, Samson Lane, for whom he was named, was a friend of President Andrew Jackson.

As a youth, Faison attended private schools in the Faison area, notably Faison Academy. In 1878, he received an appointment to the U.S. Military Academy at West Point from his congressman, Colonel A. M. Waddell. Upon graduation on 13 June 1883, Second Lieutenant Faison was assigned to the First Infantry, which was attempting to subdue Apache uprisings in the Arizona Territory. Faison was constantly in the field and ably performed his duty, earning the approval of General George Crook. The young lieutenant was one of the few officers present at the surrender of Geronimo, chief of the Chiricahuas, in May 1885. For his services, he was commended in General Orders 41, Headquarters of the Army, 1891, for "bearing uncomplainingly the almost incredible fatigues and privations as well as the dangers" incident to the operation.

The First Infantry was rewarded with a station in the San Francisco area, Department of California, from 1886 to 1890. During this period, Faison served a brief tour at Fort McDermitt, Nev. Promoted to first lieutenant on 24 Feb. 1891, he attended the Army's Torpedo School at Willett's Point, New York Harbor, graduating in October 1891. In December he was assigned recruiting duty in Oregon and in March 1892 was transferred to the Department of California. During August and September 1894 he inspected the National Guard at Carson City, Nev., and in October 1895 returned to recruiting duties in Lynchburg, Va., where he served until October 1896. From 1896 to 1899, he was senior instructor in the Department of Infantry Tactics at West Point.

Following promotion to captain on 1 July 1898, Faison was determined to take part in the suppression of the Philippine Insurrection. At his request, he was relieved of his duties at West Point early in 1899 and sailed with the Thirteenth Infantry in April. Arriving in Manila on 29 May, he immediately went into the field and saw action at Guadeloupe Ridge, Cavite Veijo, and San Francisco de Malabon. In November 1899 he was included in General Lloyd Wheaton's Expeditionary Brigade, which proceeded by sea and disembarked under fire to capture San Fabian on the Lingayen Gulf. This strategic move forced the evacuation of Dagupan, the terminus of the only railroad, and opened direct communication with Manila; it was followed by a skirmish to Rabon River and later by the repulse of a strong night attack by insurgents upon the town of San Jacinto. During this tour, Captain Faison served as adjutant general of different units. Perhaps his most valuable duty was to restore order in the wake of the insurrection and reestablish civil government. He also realized an early ambition—pursuit of the legal profession—when he was frequently employed by the division commander, General Arthur MacArthur (father of General Douglas MacArthur), who was governor general of the Philippines, as judge advocate of military commissions and as judge of the provost court, the first American so appointed.

The regiment sailed for home in the fall of 1902 and was stationed on Angel Island in the San Francisco area. Although not qualified by seniority, Faison was assigned command of Fort Mason, headquarters of the commanding general of the Department of California, in recognition of his accomplishments and reliability. After three years, he was transferred on 5 Oct. 1905 to the office of quartermaster general in Washington, D.C. Following his promotion to major on 30 June 1906, he was—at his request—relieved of duty in Washington and assigned to the Twenty-fourth Infantry. He then returned to the Philippines, where he commanded Camp Downs on Leyte Island. In February 1908 he came back to the United States via Suez and was stationed at Madison Barracks, N.Y. In 1910, he received the coveted honor of attending the Army War College as a student. There he so distinguished himself that, upon graduation in 1911, he was retained as an instructor and assistant director.

On 27 Sept. 1911 Faison was promoted to lieutenant colonel and assigned to the Fifth Infantry at Plattsburg Barracks, N.Y., where he arrived in time to command the extensive maneuver exercises of 1912. Two years later he was ordered to Panama for duty in the Canal Zone. Following his promotion to colonel on 2 Oct. 1915, he took command of the Twenty-fifth Infantry, stationed at Schofield Barracks in Honolulu, Territory of Hawaii, in January 1916. With the entry of the United States into World War I, Colonel Faison was transferred in July 1917 to the command of the Forty-second Infantry at Fort Douglas, Utah. On 30 Aug. 1917 he was promoted to brigadier general, National Army, and given command of the Sixtieth Infantry Brigade (comprised of North Carolina troops) of the Thirtieth ("Old Hickory") Division at Camp Sevier (Greenville), S.C. As senior brigade commander, General Faison was in command of the division from January to May 1918 when, training completed, it was ordered to France, via England, arriving at Calais on 8 June 1918. The division was attached to a British corps and served mostly in Belgium, where it saw action in Canal Sector (defensive) from 16 July to 30 August in Ypres-Lys (offensive) from 31 August to 2 September, when the division was transferred to France and took part in the Somme offensive until 20 Oct. 1918. While in France, Faison was acting major general until General Lewis took command. General Faison and the Sixtieth Infantry Brigade were conspicuous in leading the attack on Germany's supposedly impenetrable Hindenburg Line at Bellicourt, France, on 29 Sept. 1918, and were the first Americans to break through, resulting in victory for the Allied forces.

After the armistice, the division moved to the Le Mans and remained there until March 1919, when it embarked for the United States. Arriving in April, the division took station for demobilization at Camp Jackson, S.C., which was commanded by General Faison. He reverted to his permanent grade of colonel on 15 July 1919, and served in the office of the adjutant general in Washington, D.C. He subsequently commanded the Forty-third Infantry at Camp Lee, Va., and the Twenty-second Infantry at Fort Jay, Governor's Island, N.Y. While at Fort Jay, he was promoted to brigadier general, Regular Army, on 14 June 1922. After more than forty years of service, he retired on 1 Dec. 1922 because of severe arthritis. He settled in Baltimore, Md., in order to be near Johns Hopkins Hospital.

Faison had four brothers: Dr. Isaac Wellington, a graduate of Harvard Medical School, who was an internist, a specialist in children's diseases, and a founder of the Presbyterian Hospital in Charlotte; Henry J., planter; Isham Francis, planter, merchant, and produce broker; and Isaac Lane, planter and produce broker. (Faison, N.C., was one of the world's leading produce markets.) The general had two sisters: Mary Jane, who married Christopher Dudley Pierce, a New York grain broker; and Virginia Maria, who married Dr. William Broadhurst Pritchard, a prominent early psychiatrist in New York City.

On 19 Dec. 1906 Faison married Eleanor Kerfoot Sowers, the daughter of Dr. Zachariah T. Sowers, a physician of Washington, D.C. They had one daughter, Eleanor Sowers, a graduate of Smith College and an active force in the Women's City Club of New York City. Their only son, Samson Lane, Jr., attended Williams College, Harvard, and Princeton. He taught at Yale before returning to Williams College where he was a professor of art history, chairman of the art department, and director of the art museum. From 1942 to 1946 he served in the U.S. Navy, attaining the rank of lieutenant-commander. Assigned to the Office of Strategic Services, where he investigated art looting by the Nazis, he was instrumental in obtaining the return of over one million dollars worth of art to the governments of France and The Netherlands. For the latter service he was named a Chevalier of the French Legion of Honor.

General Faison was a Presbyterian and a member of the Army-Navy Club. In May 1929 he joined American Legion Post No. 1 in Raleigh; his wish, he said, was to become a member of the first post of his native state. He was the author of *Strategy and Tactics,* which for many years was used by the army as a training manual. He also wrote accounts of the surrender of Geronimo and of the breaking of the Hindenburg Line. He was decorated with the American Distinguished Service Medal and the French Croix de Guerre with Palms, and was an officer of the French Legion of Honor.

Faison died at the age of seventy-nine at his home in Baltimore. He was buried with military honors in Arlington National Cemetery.

SEE: Baltimore *Sun*, 18 Oct. 1940; G. W. Cullum, *Biographical Register of the Officers and Graduates of the U.S. Military Academy at West Point* (1901); Duplin County—Dorothy Wightman Library, Kenansville, for information on Faison's life and military career; Duplin County Historical Collection (James Sprunt Technical Institute, Kenansville); Extract from "Seventy-second Annual Report of the Association of Graduates of the United States Military Academy, West Point, N.Y., June 10, 1941" (North Carolina Collection, University of North Carolina, Chapel Hill); Information supplied by S. Lane Faison, Jr. (Williams College, Mass.), and by Jane Faison, Frances Faison Johnson, and Dr. Virginius Faison Williams (Faison, N.C.); United States Army History Research Collection (Army War College, Carlisle, Pa.); "What's Going on in North Carolina," *The State Magazine* 5 (9 Oct. 1937).

CHARLES M. INGRAM

**Falkener, Sarah DeRippe** *(1755–24 Feb. 1819)*, pioneer in female education and organizer of the Falkener Seminary for Young Ladies of which she was preceptress, was born in London, England, where she married William Falkener about 1775. By 1787 Sarah, William, and their young son had come to America and by 1790 were living in Warrenton, N.C.

In January 1801 Mrs. Falkener, as "Lady Principal," opened the Falkener Seminary, the first boarding school for young ladies in that section of the country. The many notices appearing in the Raleigh, Halifax, and Petersburg (Va.) newspapers were all in the name of Sarah Falkener until 1811, when her husband's name accompanied hers—even though he was active in the undertaking from the start. Besides instruction in decorum and etiquette, Mrs. Falkener taught her pupils the art of needlework including sample making and dressmaking.

Mrs. Falkener's school was a success from the beginning, and by 1805 an instructor at several European seminaries was engaged to teach French, music, and dancing. The dancing lessons were given in the front room of the nearby Warrenton Eagle Tavern, owned by Marmaduke Johnson. His daughter, who married the Falkeners' only son in 1807, was probably one of the day students in the school. In connection with the teaching of vocal and instrumental music, Ellen Mordecai wrote in her history of Warrenton that, before the arrival of a "spinnett," the piano keys were marked in chalk on a table so that the pupils could practice the scales to a violin accompaniment by the teacher. By 1808 considerable additions had been made to the school buildings to accommodate additional pupils, and five persons besides the music teacher were employed in their tuition. According to the 1810 census, there were thirty-one young girls listed in the Falkener household; these, in addition to the day pupils, appear to have comprised the student body.

Except in 1811 and 1812, and possibly 1814, Sarah Falkener's female seminary was operated through 1815 and may have functioned until her death. She died in Warrenton, where she had lived for almost thirty years, and it appears that she was buried in the Johnson family burying ground.

SEE: Charles L. Coon, *North Carolina Schools and Academies, 1790–1840* (1915); Halifax *North Carolina Journal*, 16 Dec. 1805; Ellen Mordecai, "Fading Scenes Recalled, or By Gone Days of Hastings, by Esther Whitlock" (Southern Historical Collection, University of North Carolina, Chapel Hill); *Raleigh Register*, 12 Jan. 1801, 14 Jan., 8 Apr. 1805, 23 May, 2 June 1808, 30 Dec. 1814, 26 Mar., 10 Dec. 1819; U.S. Census, 1810, Warren County.

MARY HINTON DUKE KERR

**Falkener, William** *(1751–6 Dec. 1819)*, merchant, justice of the county court, teacher, and pioneer in female education, was born in London, England, where members of his family operated a tea warehouse in Newgate Street. Before emigrating to America he married Sarah DeRippe, who later organized a seminary for young ladies in Warrenton, N.C. Family tradition that the vessel on which he sailed for America with his wife and young son was wrecked at sea may be substantiated by the Warrenton history written in 1845 by Ellen Mordecai, who probably had been one of his pupils. She told how Falkener frequently described his joy in escaping from the dangers of the ocean and how, on their safe arrival, he knelt to kiss the beach in gratitude and penciled the date on a scrap of paper from his portfolio.

Falkener was residing in Philadelphia, Pa., in 1787, when he first bought land in Franklin County, N.C. It appears that by 1790 he was in Warrenton, living in a house rented from General Thomas Person until buying his first town lots and houses in 1793. In 1792 he witnessed the will of James Milles, one of the original trustees of the Warrenton Academy for boys. Milles's son taught "a few scholars and them chiefly English", one of whom may have been Falkener's son.

Falkener's general interest in education is evidenced by the fact that he was a trustee of the Warrenton Academy and secretary to the board of trustees by 1792. Until 1805, when the steward's house for the academy was built, the students had to board in homes in the town. The 1800 census shows that twenty-six young boys were in Falkener's household; the five young men besides his own son living with him may have been instructors in the academy. In addition, he assisted his wife in the management of the Falkener Seminary for Young Ladies from the time it was opened in 1801; and the 1810 census lists thirty-one girls in his household in Warrenton. One of the most elegant pensmen of his day, Falkener instructed the pupils in penmanship, reading, spelling, and English literature, utilizing his large and valuable collection of books. He also made their copybooks and taught them lessons on fortitude and English customs and history.

Falkener's merchandizing operations were on a large scale from the start; in the course of his business he dealt with merchants in Philadelphia and Petersburg and imported merchandise from Europe. He also served as justice of the Warren County Court of Pleas and Quarter Sessions (at least from 1795 to 1806) and at times acted as a handwriting expert in proving signatures on legal documents. From 1798, when he assigned all of his property to his son and only child, William Augustus Keppel Falkener, the two worked together in most of their many undertakings; both were closely associated with Marmaduke Johnson, whose daughter the younger Falkener married in 1807. Some of their operations were transacted as Falkener & Co. and as Johnson, Falkener & Co. Falkener's store was located next to the Warrenton Eagle Tavern, owned by Marmaduke Johnson, on Main Street, a block from his wife's Seminary for Young Ladies. The younger Falkener was entry taker for Warren County in 1801, proprietor of the Warrenton Race Course and the Warrenton Eagle Tavern in 1810 and 1811 (both of which he bought from his father-in-law and sold to his brother-in-law), county trustee in 1813, and, at the time of his death in 1819, clerk of Warren County Court and district collector of U.S. Revenue.

The elder Falkener died in Warrenton of dropsy, having survived his wife by only ten months, his son (who died a month after his mother), and his daughter-in-law (who died within a month after writing her will three days after her husband's death and the day after the death of her father). Ellen Mordecai tells of refreshments being served to the company assembly for Falkener's funeral consisting of small blocks of cake enveloped in white paper sealed with black wax and wine and brandy in decanters, each with a weeper of black crepe tied around its neck.

It appears that Falkener was buried next to his wife in the Johnson family burying ground, located just south of Warrenton and east of Highway 401, which has a number of unmarked graves. Many of his descendants were buried in the Plummer cemetery in Warrenton as both of the Falkener grandchildren married children of Kemp Plummer, a descendant being Kemp Plummer Battle, president of The University of North Carolina.

SEE: Deeds and Wills of Warren County and Deeds of Franklin County (North Carolina State Archives, Raleigh); Halifax *North Carolina Journal*, 31 Oct. 1792; Ellen Mordecai, "Fading Scenes Recalled, or By Gone Days of Hastings, by Esther Whitlock" (Southern Historical Collection, University of North Carolina, Chapel Hill); *Raleigh Register*, 10 June 1805, 18 Oct. 1810, 10, 17 Dec. 1819; U.S. Census, 1790–1810, Warren County.

MARY HINTON DUKE KERR

**Fanning, David** *(1755–14 March 1825)*, loyalist partisan leader in the American Revolution, was born in the settlement of Beech Swamp, Amelia County, Va., the son of David Fanning who drowned in the Deep River in North Carolina before his son was born. Before the death of the elder Fanning the family had moved to that part of Johnston County, N.C., that is now Wake County. By 1764 young Fanning and his older sister, Elizabeth, were orphaned and bound to guardians. Needham Bryan, Jr., a county justice, became David's guardian, and the boy was apprenticed to Thomas Leech, who may have been a loom mechanic. Although Fanning was reported to be working as a loom builder in Chatham County during the Revolution, he said nothing of his early years other than the statement that he was "farmer bred." Although he later attempted to recover his father's Virginia property of 1,100 acres, he never secured his inheritance. Eli W. Caruthers repeated several traditions about Fanning's sojourn with the John O'Deniell (O'Daniel) family in Orange County. It was here that the young Fanning was cured of the disease scald head, which left him bald, and that he gained a wide reputation as a tamer of horses. In 1773 he journeyed to western South Carolina and settled with Joseph Kellet on Raeburn's Creek, a tributary of the Reedy River. In addition to farming, Fanning may have traded with both the Cherokee and the Catawba Indians.

Upcountry South Carolina did not readily follow the lead of Charleston in the revolutionary movement; the region in 1775 was primarily loyal to the Crown, and the militia of the district was commanded by Colonel Thomas Fletchall, a loyalist. At this time David Fanning was a sergeant in Captain James Lindley's company, which was mustered on 15 May and found to be solidly loyalist. During the summer, Whig delegates traveled through the upcountry to convince the inhabitants to support the rebellion, but they met with little success. Finally hostilities began and, with North Carolina's support, the South Carolina Whigs defeated the Loyalists in the "Snow Campaign" of December 1775. During the loyalist rising, Fanning was involved in the capture of a quantity of Whig gunpowder being sent to the Cherokees and in the capture of Ninety-Six by the loyalists. On 22 December at the Battle of the Big Cane Brake, where most of the loyalists were taken prisoner, Fanning escaped and fled to the Cherokees. His capture a month later was the first of fourteen captures over the next three years. He was allowed to return home when news was received of an amnesty for loyalists.

In June 1776 the Whigs became alarmed over rumors of an impending Indian attack. Uncertain about the position of the former loyalists, the Whigs arrested many of them, including David Fanning. In the confusion following the Indian raid of 1 July, Fanning escaped and led a company of loyalists to the Cherokees. He participated in an unsuccessful Indian attack on a Whig fort, and then he went to North Carolina for nine months. There was no haven for him there. After being imprisoned and rescued three times, he returned home to Raeburn's Creek settlement by 10 March 1777.

For the next eighteen months, until August 1779, Fanning was either commanding loyalist units in the field, hiding in the forest from Whig pursuit, or imprisoned by the Whigs. He was confined in the Ninety-Six jail several times, twice in chains, and each time he escaped. He was only brought to trial for treason, in November 1777, and he was acquitted. In the loyalist rising that began in March 1778, he commanded a company that ranged on the Georgia border, taking Whig prisoners and supplies. During his escapes he was wounded once and vigorously pursued. The Whigs offered a reward of $300 in currency for him in 1779. After being nearly killed and seeing his supporters banished from the state, he agreed to a conditional pardon from Governor John Rutledge in August 1779.

Fanning returned home and soon agreed to serve in the Whig militia, possibly as a frontier scout. Not until the British victory at Charleston in May 1870 did he return to the loyalist cause. When the British began to gain control of the state, he took to the field with William Cunningham, recruiting loyalist militia and reducing the few Whig strongholds left in the upcountry.

For several months Fanning scouted on the Indian border. Following the defeat of Major Patrick Ferguson's loyalists at Kings Mountain in October 1780, the Whigs began to regain control of the upcountry region. Consequently, Fanning left South Carolina and went to the Deep River settlement in Chatham County, N.C., where he lived for several months, quietly seeking followers in anticipation of a British invasion of the state.

Fanning revealed his intentions to raise a loyalist force in February 1781, when Lord Cornwallis and his British army occupied Hillsborough. Both before and after the Battle of Guilford Court House on 15 Mar. 1781, Fanning actively recruited loyalists, skirmished with the Whig militia, and scouted for Cornwallis. After the British retreated to Wilmington, he established a fortified base at Cox's Mill on the Deep River in Randolph County. From this camp his company began to range through the surrounding counties, frequently sparring with the Whigs and capturing their supplies. Dissension among the loyalists led him to request and receive a commission from Major James H. Craig, commander of the British garrison in Wilmington. On 5 July 1781, Fanning was appointed colonel of the Loyal Militia of Randolph and Chatham counties. He promptly called a general muster of the loyalist militia on 12 July and recommissioned officers for twenty-two companies in the counties of Randolph, Chatham, Orange, Cumberland, and Anson.

For the next year Fanning's loyalist militia dominated central North Carolina. His own courage and resourcefulness were unsurpassed. Samuel A. Ashe remarked in an earlier biographical sketch that he was "one of the boldest men, most fertile in expedients, and quick in execution, that ever lived in North Carolina." Riding usually with no more than a few dozen men, Fanning caught and paroled numerous Whig prisoners, captured and destroyed supplies, and fought thirty-six skirmishes and battles. At times several hundred Whig militia were assigned the fruitless task of stopping him, but they were frustrated in every attempt to capture or defeat him. Unfortunately, the partisan struggle was a bitter civil war, bringing death and destruction to both Whig and loyalist families in the region. Both sides executed prisoners, destroyed the homes and property of their opponents, and violated truces, but only the loyalists were condemned for their actions.

In July, shortly after reorganizing the Loyal Militia, Fanning led a raid on the seat of Chatham County to stop the court-martial and probable execution of loyalists. In the process he took fifty-three prisoners, including most of the court officials and militia officers, as well as several members of the General Assembly. In August he ravaged the Cape Fear valley on a trip to Wilmington for ammunition and supplies. While returning to Chatham County, he joined Colonel Hector McNeil of Bladen County who was being pursued by a superior Whig force commanded by Colonel Thomas Wade. On 1 September near McPhaul's Mill on Drowning Creek, Fanning assaulted and routed the Whigs.

Upon his arrival at Cox's Mill, Fanning issued a call for the loyalist militia to muster. His fame brought a number of new recruits, and he soon found himself at the head of 950 men. He was reinforced by contingents of 200 men under Colonel Archibald McDugald of Cumberland County and 70 men with Colonel McNeil. In command of this sizable force, Fanning undertook his most daring exploit of the war, the capture of the temporary state capital, Hillsborough. With complete surprise, the loyalists entered the capital on the foggy morning of 12 September. After brief skirmishing, primarily by Governor Thomas Burke and his aides, loyalists were released from the jail and some 200 Whig prisoners were gathered. Among the prisoners were the governor, his council, many Continental officers and soldiers, and members of the General Assembly. In an effort to rescue the governor, the Whig commander, General John Butler, rallied the militia and intercepted Fanning on 13 September on the banks of Cane Creek near Lindley's Mill. The ensuing battle, one of the largest of the war in North Carolina, lasted four hours and cost nearly 250 killed, wounded, and captured of the forces engaged. Carelessness of the loyalist advance guard, resulting in the death of Colonel McNeil, nearly brought defeat, but Fanning flanked the Whigs, attacked them in the rear, and caused Butler's outnumbered but stubborn militia to retreat. Severely wounded in the left arm, Fanning was left with loyalists in the area, and Colonel McDugald delivered the prisoners to the British at Wilmington.

After his recovery, Fanning again took to the field, but he now faced overwhelming Whig numbers. The evacuation of Wilmington by the British in November 1781 removed his source of supplies and arms; accordingly, in January 1782 he began negotiations for a pardon through General Butler. Over the next five months several truces were arranged and violated by both sides. A crescendo of violence, murder, and destruction broke over the central counties in these early months of 1782. In late April, Fanning married Sarah Carr and thereafter sought to leave the state. Finally in May, he and his bride reached a truce area in South Carolina and then made it to Charleston. In an Act of Pardon and Oblivion passed in North Carolina in May 1783, David Fanning was one of three men specifically exempted.

In September 1782 the Fannings left Charleston for Saint Augustine, Fla., where they remained until September 1784, when they embarked for Canada. David Fanning lived the rest of his life in the provinces of New Brunswick and Nova Scotia. He settled at Long Reach, King's County, New Brunswick, eventually acquiring land and two mills. He represented King's County in the Provincial Assembly from 1791 until 27 Jan. 1801, when he was expelled. A few months earlier he had been convicted of the rape of Sarah London and sentenced to death. Protesting that he had been falsely accused, he appealed his conviction and was pardoned by the provincial governor. Ordered to leave the province, Fanning moved to Annapolis County, Nova Scotia. In Nova Scotia he undertook shipbuilding and was the part owner of two merchant vessels. His last home was in Digby where he died and was buried at Holy Trinity Church. He had one daughter, Ferebee, and two sons, Ross Currie Carr (1791–1871) and David William (1793–1810). A master of partisan warfare, Fanning was truly, in the words of Samuel A. Ashe, "one of the most extraordinary men evolved by the Revolutionary War." Surrounded through most of his life by conflict and controversy, much of it generated by himself, he finally found peace in his last years in Nova Scotia.

SEE: Archives, New Brunswick Museum, St. John, and Public Archives of Nova Scotia, Halifax, for holdings concerning Fanning's life in Canada; Samuel A. Ashe, ed., *Biographical History of North Carolina*, vol. 3 (1906); Lindley S. Butler, ed., *The Narrative of Col. David Fanning* (1981); E. W. Caruthers, *Revolutionary Incidents* (1854); Walter Clark, ed., *State Records of North Carolina*, vols. 15, 16, 18, 19, 22 (1898–1907); R. O. DeMond, *The Loyalists in North Carolina During the Revolution* (1940); J. Hannay, *History of New Brunswick*, vol. 2 (1909); W. H. Hoyt, ed., *The Papers of Archibald D. Murphey*, vol. 2 (1914); J. B. O. Landrum, *Colonial and Revolutionary History of Upper South Carolina* (1847); A. I. Newlin, *The Battle of Lindley's Mill* (1975); J. H. Wheeler, ed., *The Narrative of Col. David Fanning* (1861).

LINDLEY S. BUTLER

**Fanning, Edmund** *(24 Apr. 1737–28 Feb. 1818)*, North Carolina loyalist, lawyer and land speculator, colonial official, private secretary to Governor William Tryon in New York, lieutenant governor of Nova Scotia and of Prince Edward Island, and British army general, was born in Suffolk County, Long Island, N.Y., the fifth son of the ten children of British army captain James Fanning of Riverhead, Long Island, and Hannah Smith of Smithtown. He was the grandson of Thomas Fanning of Groton, Conn., and the great-grandson of Edmund Fanning of Kilkenny, Ireland, who had migrated to Pequot (New London), Conn., in 1653, and his wife Catherine Hayes, daughter of Hugh Hayes, Earl of Connaught. The boy Edmund was sent in his ninth year to a grammar school on Long Island and in 1753 to Yale College, New Haven, where he was graduated in 1757 with a B.A. degree, winning sixth highest honors and a Berkeley Scholarship. He immediately proceeded to Harvard College, Cambridge, Mass., where he subsequently earned an M.A. degree. He is also thought to have studied law for a period at King's College (now Columbia University), N.Y., which later awarded him an M.A.

As early as 1760 Fanning settled in Childsburgh (Hillsborough), N.C., a location selected possibly because his eldest brother, the Reverend William Fanning, an Episcopal clergyman, was already established in Williamsburg, Va. A somewhat later Virginia connection was his nephew, the eminent Richmond lawyer, John Wickham (1763–1839), son of Fanning's sister Hannah ("Nancy") and Major John Wickham of Connecticut. Still another prestigious Virginia kinsman was the distinguished Williamsburg lawyer, Henry Tazewell.

In a "Statement Prepared by Gen. Edmund Fanning" but finished by one of his daughters, he asserted that "in the year 1760 I was elected a trustee and Commissioner of the incorporated Town of Hillsborough, N. Carolina, and one of the two representatives of the County of Orange." From local records it appears that Fanning was elected a town commissioner in 1760 to replace one Daniel Cane (or Kain) and continued in the post for nearly eleven years until his departure from the province in 1771. The Inferior Court Minutes of Tuesday, 19 May 1761, recorded his appointment as "Prosecutor for the Crown," the first preserved official mention of him in the county. Thereafter, valuable appointments and opportunities came swiftly.

Fanning early formed two brief business partnerships. One, with the Virginians Thomas Hart and James Thackston, was called Fanning & Co.; the other, with Francis Nash and John Dowell, was listed as Dowell & Co. In 1762 and again in 1766–68, Fanning sat with Thomas Lloyd of Orange as the two representatives of the county of Orange in the colonial assemblies at New Bern. The "Dear Ned" letters written by land speculator and Selwyn agent H. E. McCulloh to Fanning make it clear that McCulloh had planned to buy Borough status for £10 "as a gift to Hillsborough" to ensure Fanning's continued seat in the Assembly. The borough charter, dated 9 July 1770, was very likely purchased by Governor William Tryon, however; and Fanning, defeated in the regular election, served as the first borough representative for Hillsborough during 1770–71.

He was also appointed on Tuesday, 3 May 1763, as the second public register of Orange County, a key position that he held until October 1768. In 1765 he was appointed judge of the superior court for the Salisbury District. In 1763 he had been given a commission in the Orange Country militia, and in 1767 he was elevated to the rank of colonel for special service in connection with running the Cherokee boundary line. He was also appointed one of a seventeen-member board to establish Queen's College (known in the Revolutionary period as "Liberty Hall") in Charlotte. Fanning was promptly elected president of the fledgling "college," which, his autobiographical memoir states, conferred upon him the M.A. The college is said to have been disallowed in London because of its preponderance of Presbyterian trustees.

From the outset, Fanning had steadily acquired lots in Hillsborough (prompting a waggish correspondent to address his letter to "Fanningsburg") as well as various tracts in Orange, Anson, and Rowan counties. The will of William Churton, probated 5 Jan. 1768, bequeathed him not only Churton's home lots in Hillsborough but also an immensely valuable 1,100-acre tract south and east of the town. Within little more than a decade, Fanning in various ways acquired at least twenty-nine town lots in Hillsborough, Charlotte, Cross Creek (Fayetteville), New Bern, and Salisbury and some 10,485 acres of land in Orange, Anson, and Rowan counties.

Extreme discontent in the western counties over high fees for registration services as well as over taxes imposed and the sheriffs' high-handed and oppressive collections of them led finally to the widespread, violent disturbance now generally known as the "War of the Regulation." Although the attorney general of the province in London and John Morgan of the Inner Temple ruled that Fanning's registration charges had not been exorbitant (6 shillings for Deed 13 as opposed to the usual charge of 2 shillings 8 pence), the London legal opinion had little weight with Carolina backwoodsmen. Much of the general unrest was animated by the settlers' intense hatred of Fanning himself and by their profound distrust of his intimate friendship with royal Governor Tryon.

In April 1768 a few shots were fired through the roof of Fanning's house by disgruntled Regulators, but in the riots of September 1770 his house was cut from its sills and leveled to its foundations, "every article of furniture destroyed," and his papers and wearing apparel "carried into the street by armfulls and destroyed." Somehow his law office on the opposite side of West King Street was left undamaged. At the same time, the Regulators, armed with wooden cudgels and cowskin whips, overran a session of superior court and physically maltreated various members of the "Courthouse Ring," including Fanning. Subsequently, Fanning requested a corps of militia to suppress the Regulators, and at the ensuing Battle of Alamance on 16 May 1771 he commanded the left wing (some 200 men) of the front line of the provincial forces, successfully led by Governor Tryon.

Shortly afterward he followed Tryon to New York as his private secretary, serving also as surrogate of the city of New York. In 1774 he was appointed surveyor-general of the province of New York by Lord North "in consequence of my losses, sufferings, and services during the insurrection in North Carolina," as his memoir states. The same year, on 6 July, he was awarded a D.C.L. degree by Oxford University, possibly at the recommendation of Lord North, as was another prominent American loyalist, Thomas Hutchinson of Massachusetts, on 4 July 1776. On his final departure from North Carolina Fanning had designated his friend, the Scottish merchant William Johnston, as his "Agent" in charge of his considerable estate. Although Fanning's properties were officially eligible for confiscation after 1779, Johnston did a masterful, sleight-of-hand job of evasion until his death on 3 May 1785, when that portion of the estate still in Fanning's name came into the hands of Johnston's executors. Eleven of Fanning's town lots and a single tract of 300 acres were sold at auction at the confiscation sale on 25 Aug. 1786. The remainder of his large estate had been quietly disposed of long before. For at least thirty years Fanning tried, with the reluctant aid of Tazewell, Wickham, and others, to lay hand on some portion of his vanished North Carolina holdings. In the end, the Loyalist Claims Commission granted him only £3,098.3 on a claim of £17,396.1.

In New York Fanning in 1776 raised and commanded a corps known as the Associated Refugees of the King's American Regiment of Foot, serving as its colonel throughout the Revolutionary War in which he was twice wounded. On the dissolution of his regiment, he was in December 1782 made a colonel in the regular British army; on 24 Feb. 1783, he was appointed councillor and lieutenant governor of Nova Scotia, then a haven for refugee loyalists.

On 30 Nov. 1785, at Point Pleasant, near Halifax, Nova Scotia, the forty-eight-year-old Fanning married Phoebe Maria Burns, a twenty-year-old refugee. They had four children: Louisa Augusta (b. ca. 1787), Frederick Augustus (1789–1812), Maria S. Matilda (b. 1791), and Margaret William Tryon (b. 1801). On 26 July 1786 Fanning was appointed lieutenant governor of Prince Edward Island, a post that he held for nineteen years until his resignation in July 1805 at age sixty-eight. The people of Prince Edward Island, however, had early preferred charges of tyranny against him, but these were investigated and dismissed by the British Privy Council in 1792. Surviving letters indicate that as late as 1814 Fanning was still preparing to answer questions of an investigative board.

Fanning was promoted to major general in the British army on 12 Oct. 1793, to lieutenant general on 26 June 1799, and to general on 25 April 1808. Although he had set up an establishment at No. 57 Margaret Street, Conduit Square, when he visited London in 1806 after his retirement, he apparently did not remove there permanently until 1813. After a period of intermittent "infirmity and low health," he died at his home in Upper Seymour Street at the age of eighty-one, survived by his wife and daughters. Of special interest is the extremely laudatory obituary published in the May 1818 issue of the *Gentleman's Magazine*.

Fanning's reputation, like Tryon's, has been undergoing a gradual process of reassessment at the hands of research historians, and some of the more extreme Regulator accusations have long since been proved untrue. There can be scant doubt, however, that Fanning's arrogance toward his inferiors and his tendency toward cruelty, felt by nearly every small landowner in the county of Orange, inflamed the Carolina backcountry people beyond endurance—far more than did his six shilling fees, his landed estates, and his political maneuvering.

A likeness engraved by Goddard is reproduced in the *American Portrait Gallery*, and a similar small picture is preserved in the Preston Davie Collection, Southern Historical Collection, University of North Carolina Library. A family monument at Riverhead, Long Island, lists items in the Fanning genealogy. The subject of this biography is not to be confused with the famous nephew, Captain Edmund Fanning (1796–1841), the explorer and navigator known as "the Pathfinder of the Pacific," for whom the Fanning Islands were named.

SEE: Walter Alves Papers and the Preston Davie Collection (Southern Historical Collection, University of North Carolina, Chapel Hill); Deed books, 2–20, and Minutes of Inferior Court of Pleas and Quarter Sessions, 1752–66, of Orange County (Orange County Courthouse, Hillsborough); Fanning-McCulloh Papers (North Carolina State Archives, Raleigh); Marshall D. Haywood, *Governor William Tryon and His Administration in the Province of North Carolina, 1765–1771* (1903), and "The Story of Queen's College or Liberty Hall in the Province of North Carolina," *North Carolina Booklet* 11 (January 1912); A. D. Jones, "General Edmund Fanning," *American Portrait Gallery* (1869 [portrait]); "Obituaries," *Gentleman's Magazine* 88 (May 1818); William S. Powell, ed., *The Correspondence of William Tryon and Other Selected Papers*, 2 vols. (1980 [portrait]); William L. Saunders, ed., *Colonial Records of North Carolina*, vols. 7-9 (1890); Edmund J. Wood, "Edmund Fanning," *University Magazine* 16 (February 1899).

MARY CLAIRE ENGSTROM

**Fanning, William** *(26 Oct. 1728–1782)*, clergyman of the established church, was born at Riverhead, Long Island, N.Y., the son of Captain James and Hannah Smith Fanning. On 10 Mar. 1754 he was ordained priest by the Bishop of Gloucester in England, and seventeen days later he left for America at the direction of the Bishop of London. By 1758 the Reverend Mr. Fanning had assumed his duties as the first rector of St. George's Parish, Northampton County. This parish had been established by the North Carolina Assembly in that year by a division of Northwest Parish. On 3 Jan. 1759 Joseph Thomas sold "The Revd. Doct. William Fanning of the parish of St. George" 350 acres on the Roanoke River. Among the witnesses to the deed was William's younger brother Edmund, later to play a stormy role in the history of the colony.

Unlike the majority of the colonial clergy in North Carolina, Fanning was not a missionary under sponsorship of the Society for the Propagation of the Gospel in Foreign Parts. His stay in Northampton was a short one for on 4 Mar. 1761, as "William Fanning, present minister of the parish of Tilletson" in Albermarle County, Va., he sold his North Carolina lands. On 3 Oct. 1765, however, he again purchased land in Northampton on the Meherrin River near the Virginia border. This bears out a tradition mentioned by Bishop William Meade that Fanning had become rector of Meherrin Parish in what is now Greensville, the Virginia county just above Northampton.

In 1772 Fanning married Mary Gray, the widow of Littleton Tazewell and the daughter of Joseph Gray, of "the White House," a prominent citizen of Southampton County, Va. During the American Revolution he was in Greensville County, Va., as from there he wrote Thomas Jefferson asking for a passport for his relative John Wickham, a loyalist, who was a prisoner of the patriots and wanted to leave the country. Jefferson replied that Wickham must be considered an enemy and prisoner of war. He added that the Virginia government was "thoroughly satisfied of the decided principles of Whigism which has distinguished the Character of the revered Mr. Fanning that they shall think this young Gentleman perfectly safe under his Care." Jefferson was to hear of Wickham again many years later. As a brilliant Richmond lawyer, Wickham was chief defense attorney for Aaron Burr at his trial for treason in 1807.

Fanning died at the residence of his sister-in-law, Mrs. John Flood Edmunds, in Brunswick County, Va. The only record of issue was a daughter who married the John Wickham mentioned above. A son of this marriage, William Fanning Wickham, resided at Hickory Hill, Hanover County, Va. During the Civil War, General Robert E. Lee's son, "Rooney," was captured by the Federals while recuperating from war wounds at the Wickham home.

SEE: George M. Brydon, *The Established Church in Virginia and the Revolution* (1930); R. A. Lancaster, *Historic Virginia Homes and Churches* (1915); Henry W. Lewis, *Northampton Parishes* (1951); *Virginia, A Guide to the Old Dominion* (1940); John H. Wheeler, *Historical Sketches of North Carolina* (1851).

CLAIBORNE T. SMITH, JR.

**Faris, William** *(ca. 1705–3 Jan. 1757?)*, colonial leader and merchant, was born probably in Virginia and settled in the Wilmington, N.C., area in the early 1730s. He conducted business in that town in the partnership of Faris and Lindsay, which operated on Market Street. In 1739 he was named justice of the peace for New Hanover County and commissioner for the town of Wilmington, serving in the former post until shortly before his death and in the latter until 1750. He was elected as Wilmington's first borough representative to the Assembly, taking his seat in the second session of the fourth assembly in July 1740. That fall he was named commissary general for the troops then being raised in North Carolina for the War of Jenkins' Ear. Remaining in the Assembly until September 1745, he served on several committees; in the last two of these years he had an influential role in the Committee on Public Accounts.

On leaving the legislature Faris was named commissioner of roads, bridges, cuts, and waterways for the eastern portion of New Hanover County, and in 1751 was appointed church commissioner for the entire county. A bachelor, he died in Wilmington, leaving much of his estate to complete the building of St. James's Church in that town.

SEE: John Cheney, *North Carolina Government 1663–1974* (1974); Mae Blake Graves, *Land Grants of New Hanover County* (1980); Ida Brooks Kellam and Elizabeth F. McKoy, *St. James Church, Wilmington, North Carolina, Records*, vol. 1 (1965); Donald R. Lennon and Ida Brooks Kellam, *The Wilmington Town Book 1743–1778* (1973); Elizabeth F. McKoy, *Early New Hanover County Records* (1973); William L. Saunders, ed., *Colonial Records of North Carolina* (1886); Alexander M. Walker, ed., *New Hanover County Court Minutes 1738–1769* (1958).

MARTIN REIDINGER

**Farmer, Foy Elisabeth Johnson** *(6 Oct. 1887–29 May 1971)*, teacher and missionary, was born in Riverton, Scotland County, which was her father's birthplace. She was the second child and the eldest daughter of Livingston Johnson, a longtime leader among North Carolina Baptists, and Mary Frances Memory Johnson of Whiteville. She was educated in the public schools of Greensboro and Cary and in the Baptist Female University (now Meredith College), where she received an A.B. degree in 1907. For a year following her graduation, she taught every subject in all four years of a Wake County high school, with a classmate teaching the seven elementary grades. From 1908 to 1911, she taught in the preparatory department of Meredith College.

On 7 June 1911 she married Calder T. Willingham, a Southern Baptist missionary, and went with him in August to Kokura, Japan, where she did evangelistic work and taught classes in cooking, English, and the Bible. Willingham died in 1918, when the two were beginning their furlough in this country; in 1920 she returned alone to Japan. As the sole replacement of a missionary couple, she had charge of the book store and the program of evangelism in the city of Shimoneseki. In 1921 illness due to overwork forced her permanent return to the United States. The following year she married James S. Farmer, the business manager and later editor of the *Biblical Recorder*, who died in 1938. The Farmers had two children: Fannie Memory (Mrs. Thornton W. Mitchell) and James S., Jr.

Soon after her return from Japan, Mrs. Farmer was elected a member-at-large of the executive board of the Woman's Missionary Union of the North Carolina Baptist State Convention, a responsibility that marked the beginning of a long and vital association with that organization. Miriam Robinson, its executive secretary, wrote of her in 1972: "The stamp of Foy Johnson Farmer is seen on every page of WMU history in North Carolina from the early 1920's through May, 1971." She was for three years mission study chairman, for three years prayer chairman, and for five years vice-president of that organization. These offices preceded her seven years' presidency from 1942 to 1945 and from 1946 to 1950. In 1945, she served as interim executive secretary. During these years she was also a vice-president of the Woman's Missionary Union of the Southern Baptist Convention.

From 1954 to 1960 Mrs. Farmer served on the Foreign Mission Board of the Southern Baptist Convention and from 1943 to 1963 she was a member of the board of directors of the University of Shanghai. Her deep interest in missions is evidenced not only by her active work in organizations, but also by her personal contact with missionaries. Unknown even to her immediate family for many years she kept prayer diaries, little volumes in which she recorded causes and people for whom she prayed as well as thanksgiving for answered prayers. Again and again the names of missionaries throughout the world appear, often with some special need for prayer of which she had learned from her correspondence with home and foreign missionaries. Many of them she came to know personally as guests in her home. It was sometimes said that her home was really a missionary hostel.

Her larger interests did not blind her to needs at home. She was often president of the missionary society and almost continuously teacher of a Sunday school class first in a country church and then in the two Raleigh churches she joined after her return from Japan. She was a trustee of Shaw University (1946–53) and of Meredith College (1933–63), in each case serving on the executive committee of the board. She was also active in the Meredith Alumnae Association and in the Raleigh branch of the American Association of University Women.

Mrs. Farmer was the author of seven books: *At the Gate of Asia, Publishing Glad Tidings, Mrs. Maynard's House, Sallie Bailey Jones, Hitherto, The King's Way,* and *Sacrifice and Song*.

Her funeral service was held in Pullen Memorial Baptist Church, Raleigh and she was buried in Oakwood Cemetery. Her portrait hangs in the classroom of the Jones-Farmer Bible Class in the First Baptist Church of Raleigh.

SEE: Author's correspondence with the Foreign Mission Board of the Southern Baptist Convention; William S. Powell, ed., *North Carolina Lives* (1962); John S. Ramond, *Among Southern Baptists*, vol. 1 (1936).

MARY LYNCH JOHNSON

**Farragut, George Anthony Magin** *(29 Sept. 1755–4 June 1817)*, pioneer, soldier, sailor, and father of Admiral David Glasgow Farragut (1801–70), was born under the British flag in Ciudadella, Minorca, the son of Anthony and Juana Mesquida Farragut. His Spanish surname seems to have been pronounced "Farragood." Having received some schooling at Barcelona, Spain, he took to the sea at the age of ten. According to Farragut's own account, written some forty-four years later, he was a fireship crew member during the Russian naval victory over the Turks at Chesma in July 1770.

Arriving in the western hemisphere in 1773, Farragut plied the Caribbean Sea and the Gulf of Mexico where he learned of the outbreak of the American Revolution. At the beginning of 1776 he proceeded to Charleston, S.C., to offer his services, first as an officer on a privateering vessel, then as a lieutenant in the state navy of South Carolina. Farragut fought the British both at sea and ashore. As a galley officer he was present at the fall of Savannah, Ga., in December 1778 and at the unsuccessful Franco-American attempt to recover that port the next year. When in early 1780 the British mounted a threat to Charleston, S.C., he went ashore with the rest of Commodore Abraham Whipple's Continental and state squadron. During the siege of Charleston he commanded a battery, and he became a prisoner upon General Benjamin Lincoln's capitulation of the city on 12 May. Following his exchange at Philadelphia, Farragut returned to the South, served as a volunteer in the American victory of January 1781 at Cowpens, S.C., where he reportedly saved the life of Colonel William Washington, and then obtained a commission—initially as a captain and later as a major—from Governor Abner Nash to serve with North Carolina state troops. Briefly with artillery and afterward with cavalry, Farragut fought through the final stages of the war in the lower South.

With hostilities at a close, Farragut returned to the sea. By 1790 he had arrived in the Southwest Territory, which in 1796 would become the state of Tennessee. There, both by purchase and by compensation for his wartime services to North Carolina, he obtained title to acreage in Knox County. For about seventeen years he enjoyed some prominence in the affairs of Tennessee: he served as muster-master of the territory's militia forces, participated in General John Sevier's 1793 campaign in northern Georgia against the Cherokee and Creek Indians, and apparently performed services, both official and personal, for his old friend William Blount, the territorial governor. Neither Farragut's hispanic background—he seems to have struggled in vain to master idiomatic English—nor his association with Blount (of Blount-conspiracy notoriety), prevented his 1807 appointment, through the intercession of his friend Governor William C. C. Claiborne of Louisiana, as a U.S. Navy sailing master.

Farragut's last years were spent in and around New Orleans, an area congenial to him because of his Latin origins. He commanded (1810–13) the gunboat *Alligator* on Lake Borgne, helped as Claiborne's personal representative to facilitate the absorption of portions of Spanish West Florida into the Orleans territory, and served as parish magistrate for Pascagoula. Prematurely aged after an adventurous life filled with exposure, hardship, and pain—a disabled arm dated back to the Revolution—Farragut was dismissed without prejudice from the navy in 1814. Even so he served during the 1814–15 New Orleans campaign as a volunteer reporter of British activities between Pass Christian and Pascagoula. He died at his Point Plaquet, Miss., plantation.

In 1795 Farragut married Elizabeth Shine (1765–1808) of Kinston, Dobbs County (her birthplace is now in Lenoir County), N.C. Two of the couple's five children became naval officers. One of them, the future admiral, James Glasgow Farragut (named in honor of his father's friend in North Carolina, James Glasgow), took the name "David" in honor of his foster-father, David Porter. Porter was a naval officer who, after the death of Mrs. Farragut, adopted the youth in appreciation of George Farragut's deathbed kindness to Porter's father. Of restless, even fiery, temperament, George Farragut was considered a reckless man by some contemporaries; in his mature years he once piloted a pirogue from New Orleans to Havana, Cuba. His boldness and daring were inherited in full by his illustrious son.

SEE: Marshall D. Haywood, "Major George Farragut," *The Gulf States Magazine* 2 (September 1903); Charles Lee Lewis, *David Glasgow Farragut: Admiral in the Making* (1941); Samuel Cole Williams, "George Farragut," *East Tennessee Historical Society's Publications* 1 (1929).

RICHARD G. STONE, JR.

**Fels, Joseph** *(16 Dec. 1853–22 Feb. 1914)*, soap manufacturer and reformer, was born in Halifax County, Va., the second son and fourth of seven children and the first American-born child of Lazarus and Susanna Frieberg Fels, German-Jewish immigrants who came to the United States in 1848. Following in the path of other German immigrants from Palatinate who had settled in Virginia and North Carolina, the Fels family made their home in Halifax.

In 1855, shortly after Joseph's birth, the family moved to Yanceyville, N.C., where Lazarus Fels established the leading general store and ensured his family's well-being through thoughtful investments in real estate and speculation in agricultural produce. Evidently determined to make Yanceyville his home, he became an American citizen in 1855. Six years later he was appointed postmaster of Yanceyville in the Confederate States of America. Little is known of the early life of Joseph Fels, who grew up in this community; family traditions tell only of his dislike of formal schooling. When his father, ruined by the Civil War, decided to move his family to Baltimore, Joseph Fels's contact with the South ended.

In Baltimore Lazarus Fels sought a livelihood through the manufacture and selling of soap. He apparently had begun making soap while still in Yanceyville. Though soapmaking was later the basis of the family fortune, the early years were difficult. In 1870, when the family soap-making business failed, Joseph Fels became a commission salesman for a coffee company and began to play an active role in the family's business affairs. In 1876 he established Fels and Company of Philadelphia, which, under his direction, grew and prospered. Still, until 1893 Fels and Company was only one of many small soap companies competing for a share of the market. That year Joseph bought part interest in an experimental laundry soap using a naphtha solvent. Only a year later he bought out his partner; Fels-Naphtha soon dominated the American market and eventually achieved worldwide sales. After 1893 Fels began to turn his attention to other interests.

In addition to business success, Fels searched for a philosophy that would give his life purpose and meaning. He was particularly interested in the economic, social, and political problems that accompanied industrialization. The Ethical Culture movement, with its emphasis on "deed not creed" and its concern with social problems, appealed to Fels's humanitarian instincts. In 1889 he joined the Philadelphia chapter. There he met Horace Traubel, the leader of a coterie that surrounded Walt Whitman in his final days. Their vision of Whitman as the prophet of a future social justice and universal brotherhood made a lasting impression on Fels. Traubel also introduced Fels to Henry George's *Progress and Poverty* (1879). George held that the rise in land values was attributable to changing social conditions and to community endeavor, not to any effort of the landowner. Therefore he proposed a single tax on this unearned income. The single tax, he argued, would end poverty, provide enough revenue to abolish all other taxes, and ensure a future of equality, justice, and brotherhood. George's vision of the future gave his program a religious dimension. Thus, for Fels and other supporters of the single tax, it was not only a reform proposal but also the basis of their faith in the possibility of a better world.

The depression of 1893 occurred at the same time as Fels-Naphtha's financial triumph. For Fels, this conjunction may have made George's concern with the paradox of poverty accompanying progress distressingly concrete. As a result, Fels helped finance the movement to put Philadelphia's unemployed to work cultivating vacant lots. This project appealed to Fels's desire not only to help the poor, but also to eliminate the causes of poverty. He always claimed that he was a reformer not a philanthropist, and that his purpose was to promote change, not offer charity. In an effort to test Henry George's single tax doctrine, Fels supported the experimental single tax colony at Fairhope, Ala.

In 1901, when he went to England to establish a distributing branch of his business, Fels made friends with English humanitarians and reformers. In England, as in Philadelphia, he supported efforts to give the unemployed land to work. It seemed to him that the limited success of these ventures corroborated George's ideas, and he increasingly devoted his energies and fortune to campaigning for the single tax. Thus, much to the chagrin of some Englishmen, Fels, an American, influenced English politics in that he could claim some credit for the inclusion of the land tax feature in the British budget of 1909.

Supporting worldwide efforts to promote George's ideas, Fels traveled in Europe and throughout the United States and Canada to speak on behalf of the single tax. Through the Joseph Fels Fund, he also contributed large sums from his personal fortune to the cause. As one part of its effort to enact single tax legislation in the United States, the fund supported progressive campaigns to promote the direct initiative and the referendum.

The single tax was not the only reform issue that interested Fels. Penal and educational reform, the woman suffrage movement, and Zionism all received his backing. Nevertheless, the single tax was central to his view of current problems and the possibility of progress. Therefore, he was determined that any Zionist state be based on single tax principles.

Fels's reformist sympathies and his hostility to Czarist Russia with its landed aristocracy and virulent anti-Semitism, involved him in a key episode in pre-Revolutionary Russian politics. When the Russian Social Democratic Labor party desperately needed funds at its fifth congress in London in 1907, Fels lent it money. At the time this was only a minor incident in Fels's affairs; in light of the Russian Revolution of 1917, however, his involvement in the 1907 congress seems to be one of the most significant events in his career.

Only in the last decade of his life did Fels become a prominent public figure. Although during this period his forceful speeches, messianic fervor, and personal fortune made him a formidable advocate of the single tax, the movement virtually disappeared after his death. In time Fels's accomplishments would seem problematical. Louis F. Post, another single-tax advocate, thought that "as long as the world remembers the names of Henry George and Tom L. Johnson, it will link them with Joseph Fels." Thus Fels's claim to lasting fame is linked to the assessments later generations would make of the accomplishments and dreams of his generation of reformers.

On the eve of a planned lecture trip through the South, Fels was stricken with pneumonia and died. He was buried in Mount Sinai Cemetery, Philadelphia. His wife, Mary, who shared his views, subsequently wrote sympathetic accounts of his life and work.

SEE: Chicago *The Public*, 27 Feb. 1914; *DAB*, vol. 3 (1930); Arthur P. Dudden, "Joseph Fels of Philadelphia and London," *Pennsylvania Magazine of History and Biography* 79 (1955), *Joseph Fels and the Single Tax Movement* (1971), "The Single-Tax Zionism of Joseph Fels," *American Jewish Historical Quarterly* 46 (1957) and with Theodore H. Von Laue, "The RSDLP and Joseph Fels: A Study in Intercultural Contact," *American Historical Review* 61 (1955); Mary Fels, *Joseph Fels: His Life-Work* (1916) and *The Life of Joseph Fels* (1940); F. W. Garrison, "Joseph Fels, Single Taxer," *Single Tax Review* 14 (1914); Frederic C. Howe, "Personals," *Survey* 32 (1914); Elwood Lawrence, *Henry George in the British Isles* (1957); William S. Powell, *When the Past Refused to Die, A History of Caswell County* (1977); Lincoln Steffens, *Autobiography of Lincoln Steffens* (1931); Israel Zangwill, "Joseph Fels," *Fortnightly Review* 107 (1920).

JERROLD HIRSCH

**Fenner, Richard** *(d. ca. 1766)*, lawyer, was born in Dublin, Ireland, probably the son of William Fenner and the grandson of Richard Fenner, both lawyers, and the descendant of a Richard Fenner who had received forfeited estates and interests in Ireland in 1688. In 1757 Fenner was in New Bern, N.C., serving as deputy clerk of council, deputy secretary, and deputy register of the Court of Chancery under Governor Arthur Dobbs. He was appointed in 1760 to the commission of the peace for Carteret County, where he had bought land in 1758. He served the town of New Bern as recorder, was appointed a commissioner to oversee the completion of a courthouse for Craven County (1759), was one of seven trustees of a school to be built for New Bern (1764), and signed a petition to the lieutenant governor for a salary for the teacher. He also represented clients before the Craven County court.

Fenner married, before his emigration to America and probably as his second wife, Ann Coddington, of another Anglo-Irish family of record in County Dublin from the early years of the seventeenth century. In 1768 his widow was living in New Bern on Hancock Street on Lot 89, which he had bought in 1759. Ann Fenner's will, probated in March 1777, was witnessed by James Reed, the first regular rector of Christ Episcopal Church. Her heirs were her three sons, William, Robert, and Richard, all of whom served as officers in the Second Regiment, North Carolina Continental Line, during the Revolutionary War.

SEE: Sir Bernard Burke, *Landed Gentry of Ireland* (1958); Walter Clark, ed., *Colonial Records of North Carolina*, vols. 5–7 (1887, 1888, 1890); Deeds and wills of the counties of Carteret and Craven, Minutes of the Craven County court (North Carolina State Archives, Raleigh); John O'Hart, *The Irish and Anglo-Irish Landed Gentry* (1884); William L. Saunders, ed., *State Records of North Carolina*, vol. 25 (1906); Sir Arthur Vicars, *Index to the Prerogative Wills of Ireland, 1536–1810* (1897).

RUTH L. BARRETT

**Fenner, Richard** *(1758–12 May 1828)*, physician, was born in New Bern to Richard and Ann Coddington Fenner. He was commissioned ensign in the Second Regiment, North Carolina Continental Line, in January 1779, was promoted to lieutenant while a prisoner of war at Charleston, and served until the end of the war when he settled in Halifax with his older brother, Robert. In Halifax he studied medicine with a young Scot, Dr. Mungo Ponton, who later married Montford Eelbeck's youngest daughter. In 1788 Fenner married Ann McKinnie Geddy, daughter of John and Patience McKinnie Geddy. About 1792 both he and his father-in-law moved from Halifax to Franklin County, where Fenner practiced medicine for twenty-five years. In 1799 he was elected first president of the North Carolina Medical Society. In 1817 he went to Raleigh and lived there about five years.

In 1823, Fenner emigrated with his family, including his daughter Ann's husband, Thomas Henderson, to Madison County, Tenn., where Fenner bought land near Jackson, the county seat. He died and was buried at Cotton Grove. His widow and various of their children lived on the plantation until she died in 1852 at eighty-five, outliving seven of her ten children. Those children were Margaret, who died in infancy; Ann (m. Thomas Henderson); Richard H. (m. Sarah M. Outerbridge); Mary (m. John M. Johnson)· William K.; Eliza Geddy (m. James Vaul); Martha Matilda (m. Lewis Coorpender); Erasmus Darwin (m. Annie America Collier); John McKinnie (m. Miriam Williams); and Juliana (m. David McKnight). Four of Dr. Fenner's seven sons and three of his grandsons became physicians and two of his daughters married doctors.

SEE: Deeds and wills of Halifax County (North Carolina State Archives, Raleigh); Francis B. Heitman, *Historical Register of Officers of the Continental Army* (1941); Dorothy

Long, *Medicine in North Carolina*, vol. 1 (1972); Deeds and wills of Madison County, Tenn. (County Courthouse, Jackson); Mid-West Tennessee Genealogical Society, *Family Findings* (July 1972 [Jackson-Madison Sesquicentennial Issue]); *Raleigh Register*, 3 June 1828.

RUTH L. BARRETT

**Fenner, Robert** *(ca. 1755–October 1816)*, army officer, county official, and planter, was the son of Richard and Ann Coddington Fenner of New Bern. In 1771 he was a member of the Craven County Militia and an ensign in the campaign against the Regulators. In 1772 he was paid £15 (proclamation money) for making 3,400 abstracts of patents for the secretary of state. His Revolutionary War service began with his commission as lieutenant in the Second Regiment, North Carolina Continental Line, in 1776 and lasted throughout the war. He was commissioned captain in May 1777 and was brevetted major in 1783. He also was paymaster of the Second Regiment from 1776 to 1783, and for a time he was a prisoner of war at Charleston. After the war he was agent for the late North Carolina Line in the settlement of army accounts with the United States, and was the first treasurer of the North Carolina Society of the Cincinnati (1783–91).

In 1783 Fenner settled in the town of Halifax and lived there until his death. He became clerk and master of equity for Halifax District in 1788 and, according to existing records, was serving in 1810; he probably continued in the office until his death. He was justice of the peace and magistrate of the lower court from 1796 at least until 1802, was regularly appointed to take the list of taxables and taxable property for District 9, and served Halifax as police magistrate. He supported education, in 1801 joining with William R. Davie and John Sitgreaves in advertising for a teacher, and in 1807 with Richard Long, Thomas Hall, and Willie William Jones in organizing and sponsoring a school in Halifax. Fenner became a member of the Methodist Episcopal church and gave land for the site of a meeting house. He acquired lots in the town of Halifax, where he had his residence, and land in Halifax and Northampton counties. His holdings in the middle district of Tennessee amounted to 10,000 acres.

Fenner married Mary Howson (1765–1831), a granddaughter of Montford Eelbeck. Children of record were a daughter, Mary, who married Dr. John Marrast, and three sons. Robert Jr., a captain in the Eighteenth Infantry (1814–15), married Lucy Maclin Saunders of Brunswick County, Va., migrated to Alabama, and in 1847 died of dysentery in the War with Mexico. Dixie C. married Ann Harwell and died in Halifax County in 1834. The third son, John Howson, who lived in Halifax County until his death in 1871, became a planter on an extensive scale. He married Rebecca Eaton and, through his son, William Eaton Fenner, left descendants in North Carolina.

SEE: Betty G. C. Cartwright and Lillian J. Gardiner, *North Carolina Land Grants in Tennessee, 1778–1791* (1959); Walter Clark, ed., *State Records of North Carolina*, vols. 11 (1895), 13 (1896), 16 (1899), 18 (1900), 21 (1903), 22 (1907), 25 (1906); Curtis C. Davis, *Revolution's Godchild* (1976); Deeds, Wills, and Minutes of the Court of Pleas and Quarter Sessions of Halifax County (North Carolina State Archives, Raleigh); Halifax *North Carolina Journal*, scattered issues, 1792–1810; Francis B. Heitman, *Historical Register of Officers of the Continental Army* (1914); William L. Saunders, ed., *Colonial Records of North Carolina*, vols. 8–10 (1890).

RUTH L. BARRETT

**Ferebee, Dennis Dozier** *(9 Nov. 1815–27 Apr. 1884)*, Confederate officer and political leader, was born in Currituck County but in 1834 moved to Camden County to make his permanent residence in South Mills. His grandfather, William Ferebee, represented Currituck in colonial assemblies and his father, Samuel Ferebee, was a man of considerable local prestige. His mother, Peggy Dauge Ferebee, was a descendant of the French Huguenot immigrant, Peter Dauge. (The name Dauge was later changed to Dozier). Dennis Dozier was the fourteenth child of Samuel and Peggy Ferebee. After he was graduated from The University of North Carolina in 1839, he studied law with Judge William Gaston of New Bern but practiced only briefly. In 1842 he married Sarah McPherson, the daughter of a wealthy planter, Willie McPherson; she inherited a substantial share of her father's vast estate, which Ferebee returned to South Mills to manage. Three years later he was elected to the House of Commons; he was reelected in 1848, 1856, 1858, and 1860.

Ferebee opposed secession as unconstitutional, maintaining that the Constitution of the United States "is not a league of confederacy but a government founded on the adoption of the people" and "no state authority has power to dissolve these relations." He lost his point, of course, and, like the majority of his fellow citizens, wholeheartedly cast his lot with the Confederacy and joined the Southern army. He was the first commander of the Fifty-ninth Regiment of North Carolina troops (Fourth Cavalry), which was organized at Garysburg in the summer of 1862. On 8 May 1863 orders came for Colonel Ferebee to report to General Robert E. Lee for duty. His regiment fought with distinction and valor from North Carolina to Gettysburg.

After the downfall of the Confederacy, Ferebee became an active state figure. He was elected to the North Carolina Convention of 1865, where he took a prominent part in the debates. In the General Assembly that followed the convention, he was defeated by Thomas Settle for speaker of the senate. He was later appointed by Governor Jonathan Worth to work with W. A. Graham and Judge William H. Battle as a committee to investigate the circumstances of the university, which was closed from 1871 to 1875 because of political control and lack of support from the public. After submitting the committee's report Ferebee returned to his home and family in Camden County.

In his diary his son Nelson wrote, "When we returned home to South Mills in November 1865, everything was in a bad way. My father was in debt and had no capital to start again. My mother cooked and I did the out-door work. My father was trying to get his affairs in shape to farm during the coming year." He succeeded and he did farm not only the coming year, but also for many years afterward. He died at his home in Camden County and was buried in the nearby family graveyard. A portrait of Colonel D. D. Ferebee in his Confederate uniform is owned by his great-great-granddaughter, Mrs. Basil M. Duncan of Columbus, Ohio.

His only son, Nelson McPherson Ferebee, attended The University of North Carolina in 1867–68. After the university was closed, he went to Baltimore and later was graduated from the medical department of the University of Maryland. He practiced medicine one year in South Mills. On 12 Sept. 1872, he received an appointment as assistant surgeon in the U.S. Navy. In 1902 he was made medical director, the highest rank he could obtain. Dr. Ferebee married Martha Thweat Gregory of Granville County. They had two sons and three daughters. Among his grandchildren is Nelson Ferebee Taylor, who in 1972 became chancellor of The University of North Carolina at Chapel Hill.

SEE: Samuel A. Ashe, ed., *Biographical History of North Carolina*, vol. 4 (1905); Ferebee-Gregory-McPherson Papers (Southern Historical Collection, University of North Carolina, Chapel Hill); J. G. deR. Hamilton, *Reconstruction in North Carolina* (1914); Jesse F. Pugh, *Three Hundred Years Along the Pasquotank* (1957).

MARY FEREBEE HOWARD

**Ferebee, Percy Bell** *(29 May 1891–30 Dec. 1970)*, banker and developer, was born in Elizabeth City, the son of James B. and Alice Bell Ferebee. Upon graduation from North Carolina State College in 1913 he became an engineer for the U.S. Forest Service; however, he soon became interested in public financing and bought a bank, which he served as president for forty years. After his bank was sold to Wachovia Bank and Trust Company, he continued as chairman of its local advisory board. Residing in Andrews, he was publisher and editor of the *Andrews Sun* between 1915 and 1918, and served as mayor of the town for a number of years. From 1929 until his death he was president and treasurer of the Nantahala Talc and Limestone Company; president of Ferebee and Company; dealer in municipal bonds, from 1918 until his death; and president of the Andrews Development Corporation.

During his long career, Ferebee was active in public affairs statewide. He served in the North Carolina General Assembly (1957–59) and was chairman of the Western North Carolina Regional Planning Commission, which he helped to organize. He also served on the North Carolina National Park, Parkway, and Forest Development Commission and was president for five terms of the Western North Carolina Association of Communities, which launched the outdoor drama, *Unto These Hills*, through the Cherokee Historical Association of which he also was an officer. Ferebee was a member of the board of trustees of The University of North Carolina, of the State Highway and Public Works Commission, of the board of the North Carolina Department of Conservation and Development, and of the North Carolina Battleship Commission. He was sometime treasurer of the North Carolina Bankers Association, a trustee of the John C. Campbell Folk School, and benefactor of the District Memorial Hospital of Southwestern North Carolina. He donated a 6,000-acre tract in scenic Nantahala Gorge to the U.S. Forest Service.

In 1920 Ferebee married Florence Flood of Watkins Glen, N.Y., and they were the parents of a son, James B. Ferebee II. He was buried in Valleytown Cemetery near Andrews.

SEE: *Asheville Citizen*, 31 Dec. 1970; John B. Cheney, Jr., *North Carolina Government, 1518–1974* (1975); *Who's Who in the South and Southwest* (1967).

GEORGE MYERS STEPHENS

**Fergus, John** *(October 1741–May 1802)*, surgeon in the French and Indian War and the American Revolution, became a leader in Wilmington and New Hanover County as justice of the peace and commissioner for examining veterans' claims. He was the son of James Fergus, described as a "chirurgion," who before 1737 lived in the town of Brunswick and in 1745 was a large landowner and seller of real estate. James owned land on the Cape Fear River, part of which passed to his son, John, and came to be known as Belle Meade. This is now the property of the Wilmington Historical Association.

According to Griffith John McRee, a descendant, John Fergus studied medicine in Edinburgh, Scotland. McRee once showed David L. Swain a commission from Governor Arthur Dobbs to John Fergus as surgeon of a company of foot commanded by John Paine, Esq., dated 20 Jan. 1758, just a few months after Fergus's sixteenth birthday. Fergus was later a surgeon of the First Battalion of Fort Dobbs, for in November 1760 he was allowed a claim of £15 for medicines for the garrison of the fort. In the House journal of October 1784 a petition asked that Dr. John Fergus, a surgeon in the Indian War of 1761 under the command of the late Colonel Hugh Waddell, be permitted to enter land in the district of Wilmington left vacant and in the quantity allowed by an earlier proclamation of the king. The petition was approved on 16 Nov. 1784.

Fergus was appointed surgeon for the First Battalion of North Carolina troops in May 1776 but resigned in April 1777. While he was medical officer at Wilmington in July 1777, he tried to help young John James Ward get an appointment as surgeon and mate to work with him. Dr. Ward wrote to Governor Caswell asking for the job, but apparently the governor turned him down because he soon left the temporary service of assistant to Fergus.

Fergus was first made a justice of the peace in December 1788 and continued to serve in the New Hanover County Court until the end of his life. Critical of "unruly" justices in New Hanover County who had forced others to give them the oath so they could sit on the bench, he took his grievance to the state senate at its 1786 meeting in Fayetteville. Another instance of his sense of fair play was evident earlier in his career when he signed a memorial, along with thirty-two merchants and traders of Wilmington, questioning the propriety of the Confiscation Act. Although it pointed out that the justice of the legislature would be called into question, the memorial was rejected in May 1780. Sometime during this period Fergus served as trustee for building a jail and a school in Wilmington.

The 1790 census for New Hanover County lists John Furgus [sic] as head of a family consisting of five free white males over the age of sixteen, two free white females, and thirty-three slaves.

Fergus died at the Sound below Wilmington at the age of sixty-one. His obituary in the Raleigh *North Carolina Minerva* appeared on Monday, 17 May 1802. His will, signed in 1799, listed as heirs his daughter, Ann McRee, and son-in-law, Captain Griffith John McRee; John Fergus, Jr.; Margaret Bruff, wife of James Bruff, of Maryland and a Revolutionary War prisoner in 1781; and Jane Wheaton. John Fergus, Jr., who also served in the American Revolution, was justice of the peace in Wilmington in 1795, studied law, and became state attorney for New Hanover County. In 1806 he was the commandant of the port of Wilmington. John Fergus II was one of the original subscribers to the first American medical journal, the New York *Medical Repository* (1799).

The James Fergus listed in Fergus's will was probably the eldest son of John Fergus II. James served eighty-four months in the Continental Army and was later a justice of the peace in Wilmington. When George Washington visited Wilmington on his southern tour in 1791, a select group of citizens presented an address to the president in April. One of the several signers was "J. Fergus," who, according to one historian, was James Fergus, "son of Dr. John Fergus." This statement should read, "James Fergus II, eldest son of John Fergus II." The address may be the basis for the apocryphal story that Dr. John Fergus was visited by George Washington when he was in Wilmington.

Fergus was the grandfather of James Fergus McRee of Wilmington, the distinguished physician and botanist, and the ancestor of Griffith John McRee, the historian.

SEE: Walter Clark, ed., *State Records of North Carolina*, vols. 11, 13, 15, 16, 18, 19, 22–24 (1895–1907); Court Minutes, 1738–1800, and Records of Inferior Court of Pleas and Quarter Sessions, June Term, 1767, of New Hanover County (North Carolina State Archives, Raleigh); Archibald Henderson, *Washington's Southern Tour, 1791* (1923); R. Don Higginbotham, *The Papers of James Iredell*, 2 vols. (1976); Dorothy Long, ed., *Medicine in North Carolina*, vol. 1 (1972); Lois S. Neal, comp., *Abstracts of Vital Records from Raleigh, North Carolina, Newspapers*, 1799–1819 (1979); Fred A. Olds, comp., *An Abstract of North Carolina Wills* (1925); Philadelphia *General Advertiser and Political, Commercial, and Literary Journal*, 4 June 1791; William L. Saunders, ed., *Colonial Records of North Carolina*, vol. 11 (1890).

VERNON O. STUMPF

**Ferguson, Garland Sevier, Jr.** *(30 May 1878–13 Apr. 1963)*, chairman of the Federal Trade Commission, was born in Waynesville, the son of Garland S. and Sarah Frances Norwood Ferguson. He entered The University of North Carolina in September 1894 but withdrew the following April to attend the U.S. Naval Academy. He left the academy before graduating, however, and subsequently entered The University of North Carolina law school from which he was graduated in 1900. In 1939 the university awarded him an honorary LL.D. degree.

Admitted to the bar in 1900, Ferguson established a practice with his father in Waynesville. After his father's elevation to the bench two years later, he moved to Greensboro to practice law in association with W. P. Bynum and others before moving to Washington, D.C., in 1908. From 1908 to 1918 Ferguson served as a referee in bankruptcy in the United States District Court, Western District of North Carolina; from 1903 to 1918 he was also special counsel to the Southern Railway in Greensboro. In 1918, during World War I, he became assistant to the general counsel of the Newport News Shipbuilding and Dry Dock Company, headquartered in Washington, and held the position until 1921. From 1921 to 1927 he practiced in Greensboro.

In 1927 Ferguson was named to the Federal Trade Commission by President Calvin Coolidge. He remained on the commission until 1947, serving under presidents Coolidge, Hoover, Roosevelt, and Truman; during much of this time he was chairman. Between 1921 and 1949 he served on a number of federal committees and related posts, including the National Emergency Council (1934) and the Temporary National Economic Committee (1938–41) of which he was chairman in 1939. He also was the chairman of a committee appointed by the secretary of the army in 1948 to conduct hearings in Frankfurt, Germany, and elsewhere, to review the decartelization and deconcentration program in Germany. Upon his retirement in 1949, Ferguson was praised by President Truman for "his immense contributions in protecting the public interest."

Ferguson married Margaret Merrimon in 1907, and they were the parents of three children: Margaret Merrimon, Sarah Norwood, and Garland S., III. He was a member of the Methodist church; he died in Washington after a lengthy illness.

SEE: Alumni files, University of North Carolina, Chapel Hill; Daniel L. Grant, *Alumni History of the University of North Carolina* (1924); *North Carolina Biography*, vol. 3 (1928 [portrait]); *Who's Who in America* (1940); *Who's Who in the South* (1927); *Who's Who in the South and Southwest* (1950).

JUANITA ANN SHEPPARD

**Ferguson, Harley Bascum** *(14 Aug. 1875–29 Aug. 1968)*, U.S. Army general and engineer, was born in Waynesville, the oldest son of William Burder and Laura Adelaide Reeves Ferguson. He was graduated from the U.S. Military Academy, West Point, N.Y., in 1897. Commissioned a second lieutenant, he served with the Corps of Engineers during the Santiago Campaign in Cuba in 1898 and in the Philippines in 1899. He was promoted to first lieutenant in 1900.

In 1900–1901, Ferguson served as chief engineer of the China Relief Expedition (Boxer Rebellion) at Pietsang, Yangtsun, and Peking. In addition to his other activities, he reported to the state and war departments on the foreign engineering troops sent to China by the British, French, German, Italian, Japanese, and Russian governments. He was promoted to captain in 1904, while serving as instructor of engineering at the U.S. Military Academy. After a brief tenure as district engineer with the U.S. Army Corps of Engineers in Montgomery, Ala., he became executive officer in charge of raising the U.S.S. *Maine* in Havana, Cuba, from 1910 to 1912. His excellent work in analyzing the remains of the *Maine* to discover the facts of her sinking earned him a promotion to major in 1911. From 1913 to 1916, he was district engineer, Milwaukee, Wis., in charge of navigation and flood control on the Fox River and on the Illinois and Michigan Canal. For the balance of his military career, Ferguson's engineering work focused primarily on the use and control of rivers for navigation in the eastern United States.

In preparation for European Service, Ferguson was promoted to lieutenant colonel at New London, Conn. in 1917. The same year he was elevated to colonel while en route to France as the commanding officer of the 105th Engineers, 30th Division, American Expeditionary Force. In 1918 he was promoted to brigadier general and appointed chief engineer of the Second Army. The following year he went to Newport News, Va., as commanding officer of the Port of Debarkation. He spent 1920 in Pittsburgh, Pa., as district engineer but 1921 found him drawn to Washington, D.C., as director of industrial mobilization in the office of the assistant secretary of war, Dwight F. Davis. Ferguson served in the latter position until 1928 as well as directing the Army Industrial College from 1924 to 1928.

In 1928, Ferguson returned to the field as an engineer for the use and control of waterways. He served as division engineer, Gulf Division, New Orleans (1928); Ohio River Division, Cincinnati (1928–30); and South Atlantic Division, Norfolk, Va. (1930–32). From 1932 until his retirement as major general in 1939, he was division engineer, Lower Mississippi River Division, Vicksburg, Miss., and president of the Mississippi River Commission. His latter work was invaluable to flood control and navigation along the lower Mississippi River. Ferguson was also a member of several special engineering boards including River and Harbors (1930–32), St. Lawrence Waterway (1930–31), Muscle Shoals (1930–32), Delaware River (1932), Lexington Dam, Mouth of the Columbia River, and Mouth of the Mississippi River (1933–39).

On 3 Jan. 1907 Ferguson married Mary Virginia McCormack of St. Paul, Minn. and they were the parents of three children: Adele, Virginia, and Harley Bascum, Jr. For many years after his retirement, Ferguson lived in Vicksburg, Miss., and retained an office there. He died and was buried in Lafayette, La.

SEE: Data file, H. B. Ferguson (Office of Alumni Affairs, U.S. Military Academy, West Point); H. B. Ferguson Papers (Southern Historical Collection, University of North Carolina, Chapel Hill).

CLAUDE H. SNOW, JR.

**Ferguson, Robert** *(fl. 1785–93)*, printer, operated a printing press next to the courthouse in Hillsborough from 1785 to 1792. There he printed the *North Carolina Gazette* in 1785 and 1786 and perhaps even longer, as well as the journal of the Constitutional Convention of 1788. In the latter year and at other times he may also have printed for the state. On the 1790 Hillsborough tax list he is recorded as owning two town lots, a 150-acre farm, and one slave. In 1791, Governor William Blount of the Southwest Territory engaged the services of Ferguson and George Roulstone, editor of the *Fayetteville Gazette*, to establish a printing press beyond the mountains. Some time that year they began printing the *Knoxville* (Tenn.) *Gazette* in Rogersville. Ferguson and Roulstone moved to the new town of Knoxville about seven months after it had been established. Ferguson retired with the issue of 4 May 1793, and no further record of his life has been found.

SEE: George F. Bentley, "Printers and Printing in the Southwest Territory, 1790–1796," *Tennessee Historical Quarterly* 8 (1949); Clarence S. Brigham, *History and Bibliography of American Newspapers, 1690–1820*, vol. 2 (1947); *Fayetteville Gazette*, 21 Feb. 1791, 9 Oct. 1792; William H. Masterson, "William Blount and the Establishment of the Southwest Territory, 1790–1791," *East Tennessee Historical Society's Publications* 23 (1951); *North Carolina Gazette*, scattered issues, 1785–86; *State Gazette of North Carolina*, 4, 1 Feb. 1791; Samuel C. Williams, "George Roulstone: Father of the Tennessee Press," *East Tennessee Historical Society's Publications* 17 (1945).

MARK F. MILLER

**Fernándes (Fernando), Simon or Simão** *(ca. 1538–1600?)*, Anglo-Portuguese seaman and master pilot who guided the English colonial movement to the shores of North America, was born about 1538 in Alcuna, Terciera, Azores, the son of Gaspar Fernándes. As a young man, he appears to have been trained as a navigator in Portugal and later sailed with Spanish voyages to the New World, perhaps including one or more of the expeditions to explore the eastern coast of America north of Florida between 1561 and 1573. He may have been the Domingo Fernández who was pilot on the Spanish expedition of 1566, which was seeking the Baya de Santa Maria (Chesapeake Bay) and apparently discovered what is now the Currituck peninsula in North Carolina.

About 1573 Fernándes went to England, residing first in Plymouth and later in London. He married an English girl and became an English subject. He was a Protestant, who described himself as a "merchant of London"; elsewhere, however, he was described as a "pirate," "a thorough-paced scoundrel," and "one of the best pilots in the country."

Fernándes was first recorded in English service in 1574, when he sailed as pilot of the *Elephant*, commanded by the notorious pirate John Challice and owned in part by the queen's cousin, Henry Knollys. The next year, he bought a small bark of his own and joined with Challice in marauding Latin shipping in the Atlantic. As a result of protests from the Portuguese ambassador, he was arrested for piracy and sent to London for trial. Perhaps due to the lack of evidence, but more likely through influence in high places, he was acquitted and released in 1577. Soon afterward he entered the service of Sir Francis Walsingham, the queen's secretary of state, who was a leading proponent of transoceanic expansion of England. This, together with his acknowledged skill as a pilot, doubtless led to Fernándes's employment in the first venture of Sir Humphrey Gilbert under his royal patent to exploit North America for the Crown. In late autumn 1578, he sailed with the expedition as master of the *Falcon*, an old ship of Henry VIII's navy that had been sold by the Crown to London merchants in 1575. On this voyage, he became acquainted with Gilbert's younger half-brother, Walter Raleigh, who, though it was his first ocean voyage, sailed as captain of the *Falcon*. After this venture, Fernándes continued in the service of Gilbert. In 1580 he sailed from Dartmouth in Gilbert's eight-ton "frigot," the *Squirrel*, "upon a voyage of discovery." With a crew of about ten men, he "came to and from said coasts [North America] within three months." In 1582–83 he was employed as pilot of the four-hundred-ton galleon, the *Leicester*, the admiral ship of a large venture under Sir Edward Fenton that was intended to find a route to the East Indies by way of the South Atlantic.

In 1584, Fernándes's talents were again turned toward North America. Serving as pilot and master of the principal ship, he carried Philip Amadas and Arthur Barlowe on an expedition for Walter Raleigh; during this voyage the explorers scouted the coast of what is now North Carolina and Virginia, took possession of it for England, and gathered information for English colonization of the area. The following year, when the first colony sailed for America, Fernándes was pilot and master of the royal ship *Tiger*, admiral ship of Sir Richard Grenville, "general" of the venture. In 1587, the second colony (the "Lost Colony") sailed. On this expedition he was master of the principal ship, the *Lion*, pilot major, and, apparently, the sea commander of the venture. However, disregarding instructions from Raleigh, he deposited the colony on Roanoke Island instead of taking it to Chesapeake Bay.

In late 1587, when Fernándes returned from Virginia, England was mobilizing to meet the threat of the Spanish Armada. He joined the fleet and in 1588 served against the Armada as an officer (boatswain) on the royal ship *Triumph*, the largest vessel in the English fleet. He was last recorded at sea in 1590 when, as master of the royal ship *Foresight*, he sailed in a naval expedition under Sir John Hawkins and Sir Martin Frobisher to intercept shipping between Spain and its overseas colonies. After this voyage, he lapsed into obscurity; though perhaps he returned to Portugal and was the "Simon Fernandez, a pilot of Lisbon" whom Richard Hakluyt met in London in March 1604.

The coarse language and piratical delights of Fernándes disgusted some of his more pious associates; but his skill and knowledge were such that even John White, artist and governor of the Lost Colony, who abhorred him, followed his advice during the 1587 voyage. In early times, an entrance opposite Roanoke Island in the vicinity of modern Oregon Inlet was called "Port Fernando," which may indicate that Fernándes discovered Roanoke Island and the North Carolina mainland.

SEE: Elizabeth S. Donno, ed., *An Elizabethan in 1582, The Diary of Richard Madox, Fellow of All Souls* (1976); David B. Quinn, *England and the Discovery of America* (1974), ed., *The Roanoke Voyages* (1955), and ed., *Voyages and Colonizing Enterprises of Sir Humphrey Gilbert* (1940); E. G. R. Taylor, ed., *The Troublesome Voyage of Captain Edward Fenton, 1582–83* (1959); L. A. Vigneras, "A Spanish Discovery of North Carolina in 1566," *North Carolina Historical Review* 46 (1969).

THOMAS M. GLASGOW

**Ferrand, Stephen Lee** *(18 Nov. 1787–15 Nov. 1830)*, physician and civic leader of Rowan County, was born in Swansboro, the son of Guillaume (William) Ferrand. The elder Ferrand, who was born in France in 1755 of Huguenot descent, first appeared in Carteret County about 1785; there he bought a large farm on Pettivers (Pettifords) Creek and promptly anglicized the spelling of his given name. Stephen Lee Ferrand's mother was Mary Williams Backhouse Ferrand, widow of John Backhouse and daughter of Colonel John Pugh Williams of Fort Barnwell, Craven County. Named for his uncle by marriage, Colonel Stephen Lee of the White Oak River community, young Ferrand lived with his parents in Swansboro until he moved to New Bern in order to receive further education from the rector of Christ Church. In 1802, at age fifteen, he entered Princeton University as a sophomore and was graduated in 1805. He subsequently entered Columbia Medical College and was graduated in 1808, the same year that his younger brother, William Pugh Ferrand, was graduated from The University of North Carolina.

From Columbia Medical College, Ferrand went to Salisbury where he began a medical practice and became a member of Saint Luke's Episcopal Church. In 1817 he was elected to represent Salisbury, a borough town, in the state legislature.

In 1819 he married Margaret Gillespie Steele, daughter of John Steele; she died on 24 May 1824. Dr. Ferrand was still residing in Salisbury at the time of his death. He left two daughters: Ann Nessfield Steele Ferrand (m. John B. Lord) and Mary Steele Ferrand (m. Archibald Henderson). Through the latter daughter, Ferrand was the grandfather of John Steele Henderson and the great-grandfather of Dr. Archibald Henderson, a mathematician.

SEE: *Carteret County News-Times*, 27 May, 3 June 1960; *Greensboro Daily News*, 12 May 1935; Archibald Henderson Papers (Southern Historical Collection, University of North Carolina, Chapel Hill); Laura Macmillan, comp., *The North Carolina Portrait Index, 1700–1860* (1963 [portraits]).

TUCKER REED LITTLETON

**Ferrand, William Pugh, Sr.** *(24 Apr. 1789–28 Oct. 1874)*, merchant, exporter-importer, naval stores manufacturer and dealer, public official, postmaster, and large landowner, was born in Swansboro. He was the second son of Guillaume (William) Ferrand, who was born in France in 1755 of Huguenot descent and first appeared in Carteret County about 1785; he bought a large farm on Pettivers (Pettifords) Creek and promptly anglicized the spelling of his given name. William Pugh Ferrand's mother was Mary Williams Backhouse Ferrand, the widow of John Backhouse and the daughter of Colonel John Pugh Williams of Fort Barnwell, Craven County. Like his elder brother, Stephen Lee Ferrand, William lived with his parents in Swansboro until it was time for him to receive college preparatory instruction in New Bern. From there he went to The University of North Carolina and received the A.B. degree in 1808.

After his graduation, Ferrand seems to have returned to New Bern for a few years, acquiring land in Craven County in 1810 and 1813 by deeds that indicate the grantee was "of New Bern." By 1816, however, he was back in Onslow County, for in that year he was named one of the managers (incorporators) of a company formed to improve the navigation of the New River.

On 21 Jan. 1817 Ferrand married Leah Yates Cobb of Jones County whose grandfather, Daniel Yates, had represented Onslow County in the North Carolina House of Commons, the state senate, and the North Carolina conventions of 1788 and 1789. In the year of his marriage, Ferrand was appointed by the county to take the list of taxables for the Swansboro District and to receive the district's congressional votes. On 9 Sept. 1817 he was named the fifth postmaster of Swansboro, a position he retained until 7 Dec. 1836.

In January 1819 Ferrand bought from Captain Otway Burns lot number six in the town of Swansboro where he evidently located a store, for in May of that year he was licensed to retail spirituous liquors at his store in Swansboro. This store was burned on 14 Apr. 1838, and in late 1838 and early 1839 Swansboro's "Old Brick Store" was built to replace the earlier one. Despite heavy losses from the fire, Ferrand continued to expand his mercantile enterprises, becoming one of the county's wealthiest merchants, with stores, warehouses, and taverns at both Swansboro and Onslow Court House (later Jacksonville). He also owned several sailing vessels, a watermill at what is now Hubert, N.C., and a windmill and turpentine distillery at Swansboro.

In 1821 Ferrand was again appointed to take the congressional votes for the Swansboro District. In 1823 he was made a commissioner for the town of Swansboro and in 1824 was named one of the incorporators and trustees of the Swansboro Academy. In 1826 he successfully ran for the Onslow County seat in the North Carolina House of Commons. When Dr. Elisha Mitchell visited Swansboro in 1827, he remarked in his diary that William P. Ferrand was "the principal man of the place."

Long identified with the Democratic Party in Onslow County, Ferrand was elected on the Van Buren ticket to represent the New Bern District in the electoral college in 1836. On 22 Dec. 1840, he was appointed to a second term as postmaster of Swansboro; he remained in the position until 31 Oct. 1845, bringing his total years as postmaster to slightly less than a quarter of a century. In addition, he appears to have become increasingly involved in local port activities. He was appointed the wreck master for the Port of Swansboro in 1838 and again in 1845. There is also record of his appointment as one of the commissioners of navigation for the port of Swansboro in 1842, 1843, and 1845.

Returning to politics after his wife's death on 1 Apr. 1843, Ferrand was elected a state senator from Onslow County in 1846. His career was terminated by his death in Swansboro at the age of fifty-eight. He and his wife were buried in the Ferrand family cemetery on Pettivers

Creek, Carteret County, across the White Oak River from the town of his birth. Their children were William Pugh, Jr., who was born in Swansboro on 20 Aug. 1819, attended The University of North Carolina (1835–36), and was last heard from while residing at Richmond, Va.; Stephen Lee, who was named for his uncle in Salisbury and died in 1826 at the age of five; and Eugene, who studied at The University of North Carolina (1849–51) and died in 1859. At the death of his brother in 1830, William Pugh Ferrand, Sr., became the guardian of Stephen's two daughters.

SEE: *Carteret County News-Times*, 27 May, 3, 17 June, 1, 29 July 1960; Daniel L. Grant, *Alumni History of the University of North Carolina* (1924); Archibald Henderson Papers (Southern Historical Collection, University of North Carolina, Chapel Hill).

TUCKER REED LITTLETON

**Ferrell, John Atkinson** *(14 Dec. 1880–17 Feb. 1965)*, health director, was born in Clinton, the son of James Alexander and Cornelia Murphy Ferrell. After attending the local schools he entered The University of North Carolina where he was graduated with a B.S. degree in 1902. He then taught in the Sampson County schools, eventually becoming county superintendent. Ferrell reentered the university to study medicine but maintained his school superintendency by commuting by horse and buggy between Chapel Hill and Sampson County. On receiving his M.D. degree in 1907, he began to practice in Kenansville and for a short time was superintendent of the Duplin County Health Department. Thereafter public health became his lifework.

In 1910 Dr. Ferrell was appointed assistant secretary of the State Board of Health in charge of the campaign against hookworm disease inaugurated by the Rockefeller Sanitary Commission. His work in the control of hookworm and typhoid set an example in the public health field for the control of many other communicable diseases. In 1913 he was granted a doctor of public health degree from the Johns Hopkins University. Based on his accomplishments in his native state, he was named director of the Rockefeller Foundation's public health activities in the United States and in that capacity supervised the development of state and county health departments throughout the country. Later his responsibilities were extended to include Canada and Mexico. On his retirement in 1944, Ferrell held the post of regional director of the International Health Department of the Rockefeller Foundation. After leaving the Rockefeller Foundation, he was medical director of the John and Mary R. Markle Foundation for two years. He retired in 1946.

Ferrell's retirement was short-lived for in the same year he agreed to become temporary executive secretary of the State Medical Care Commission. Expecting to remain only a few months until a permanent secretary could be found, he held the position for ten years. During that period he directed the use of federal funds from the Hill-Burton Act for the construction of 127 hospitals and other medical facilities throughout North Carolina. In doing so, he established a pattern for the ideal use of such funds in hospital planning and health center construction.

During his distinguished career, Ferrell received many honors including the chairmanship of the National Malaria Commission (1924), the presidency of the American Public Health Commission (1933), and the chairmanship of the latter's executive board (1935–39). In 1940 he was awarded an LL.D. degree by his alma mater, The University of North Carolina. The university later gave him a distinguished alumnus award. Ferrell contributed numerous articles to public health journals.

On 28 Jan. 1909 he married Lucile Devereux Withers of Charlotte. They were the parents of a son, John A. Ferrell, Jr., of Kenansville, and a daughter, Bettie Devereux Ferrell. Ferrell was buried in Elmwood Cemetery, Charlotte.

SEE: *American Men of Science* (1960); *Charlotte Observer*, 21 Feb. 1965; Daniel L. Grant, *Alumni History of the University of North Carolina* (1924); Raleigh *News and Observer*, 29 Sept. 1946; *Who's Who in America*, 1950.

CLAIBORNE T. SMITH, JR.

**Fessenden, Reginald Aubrey** *(6 Oct. 1866–22 July 1932)*, physicist and inventor, was born in East Bolton, Quebec, Canada, the son of the Reverend Elisha Joseph and Clementina Trenholme Fessenden. When Fessenden was nine, the family moved to Niagara Falls, Ontario, where he attended De Veaux Military College; he later continued his studies at Trinity College School, Port Hope, Ontario, and Bishop's College and Bishop's College School, Lennoxville, Quebec. Following two years in his first position as principal of Whitney Institute, Bermuda, he moved to New York as a tester for the Edison Machine Company. Shortly after his twentieth birthday he became one of Edison's assistants at the Llewellyn Park Laboratory. When the Edison companies encountered financial difficulties, Fessenden was laid off and subsequently was employed by the United States Company, the eastern branch of Westinghouse Company. Then after a brief period with the Stanley Company, he was named professor of electrical engineering at Purdue University. A year later he received a similar appointment at Western University of Pennsylvania (University of Pittsburgh), where he taught for seven years.

In 1900, the United States Weather Bureau proposed that Fessenden develop a system to transmit the bureau's weather forecasts. After initial experiments at Cobb Island, Md., during which intelligible speech was transmitted by electromagnetic waves between two masts fifty feet high and one mile apart, the work was moved in December 1900 to Roanoke Island, N.C., with subsidiary stations at Hatteras and Cape Henry weather stations. From headquarters at Manteo, between January 1901 and August 1902, Fessenden developed a system of transmitting sound waves over water between the three stations by means of a liquid barreter of his own invention.

After disagreement with the chief of the Weather Bureau over patent rights, he left the bureau in August 1902 and in November helped create the National Electric Signaling Company to which he transferred all of his patents. From its station at Brant Rock, Mass., the company transmitted voice signals over long distances in 1906. During the same year, Fessenden transmitted two-way trans-Atlantic telegraphy between Brant Rock and Machrihanish, Scotland. On Christmas Eve 1906, he made a memorable broadcast consisting of a short speech and a violin solo. In 1911, he and his associates split over the establishment of a Canadian subsidiary, and the inventor filed suit for breech of contract, forcing the National Electric Signaling Company into receivership.

During World War I, Fessenden's invention of an oscillator led to his association with the Submarine Signal

Company. One of his last inventions of a total of nearly 500 was the fathometer, a sonic depth finder for ships. In 1921, he filed suit against the Radio Corporation of America on the grounds that he was prevented from selling devices based on his own patents. The suit was settled in 1928, and Fessenden bought a home in Bermuda.

In his later years, Fessenden began research on the beginning of history—the predeluge civilization. In 1923 he published six chapters of *The Deluged Civilization of the Caucasus Isthmus*, which was followed by a seventh chapter in 1927. In 1933, his son Reginald compiled additional notes and published four more chapters and several articles. The principal thrust of the book was to tabulate all myths of predeluge history in relation to a major catastrophe—the deluge.

Fessenden died in Bermuda. He was survived by his widow, Helen M. Fessenden, and a son, Reginald Kenneth Fessenden. Photographs of the inventor are in the photographic collection of the North Carolina State Archives, Raleigh.

SEE: Gleason L. Archer, *History of Radio to 1926* (n.d.); *DAB*, vol. 3 (1959); Helen M. Fessenden, *Fessenden, Builder of Tomorrows* (1940); Reginald A. Fessenden Papers (North Carolina State Archives, Raleigh); Ormond Raby, "Reginald A. Fessenden, Canada's Great Radio Pioneer," *Electron* 4 (July 1967).

THORNTON W. MITCHELL

**Fetter, Manuel** *(29 July 1809–27 Jan. 1889)*, teacher, was born in Lancaster, Pa., the son of Frederick Fetter, a cabinetmaker of German descent, and his wife, Anna Yarrell Fetter. Baptized Emmanuel Yarrell Fetter in the Old Moravian Church in Lancaster on 12 Aug. 1809, in adulthood he abbreviated his name to Manuel. While the Reverend William Augustus Muhlenburg, the Episcopal clergyman and educator, was rector of St. James Church, Lancaster (1820–26), he noted young Fetter's ability and took charge of his education. On leaving Lancaster, the Reverend Mr. Muhlenburg went to Long Island, N.Y., where he founded St. Paul's College and the Flushing Institute. (The latter was used as a model for the short-lived Episcopal School for Boys in Raleigh.) Fetter attended the Flushing Institute, where he was well trained in the classics, Hebrew, French, and German. He then studied at Columbia College (now Columbia University) and received the A.B. and A.M. degrees before returning to Flushing Institute for a short time as professor of ancient languages. In December 1837 he was elected to the chair of ancient languages at The University of North Carolina, succeeding the Reverend Dr. William Hooper. In the autumn of 1838, when the department was divided, Fetter became professor of Greek language and literature. He remained in that position until the university was reorganized in 1868.

Fetter was one of the original members of the Church of the Atonement (later the Chapel of the Cross) when the parish was organized in the village of Chapel Hill in 1842. In 1868 he was riding in a carriage with David Swain, then president of the university, when an accident occurred from which Swain eventually died. When in Chapel Hill, Professor Fetter lived in what came to be known as the Hooper-Kyser house on Franklin Street.

After leaving the university in 1868, Fetter taught at various classical schools in the state, particularly in Henderson and Goldsboro. However, he had been a university professor too long to be effective and found the work uncongenial. He died in Jackson, N.C., at the home of his son Charles, who was then teaching school there, and was buried beside his wife in the village cemetery in Chapel Hill.

Kemp P. Battle, who knew Fetter well, described him as an accurate scholar and a Christian gentleman. Nevertheless, he felt the professor overemphasized grammar and gave his students little idea of the beauty of Greek literature. A former student, Peter Mitchell Wilson, said there was no preposition hidden from him and he could repeat from memory, in the original Greek, St. Paul's sermon on Mars Hill. Fetter, who had unusually large feet, was sensitive to ridicule, and when he first came to Chapel Hill he had difficulty adjusting to southern ways. Eventually, however, he gained the respect and admiration of his students who referred to him as "Old Fet." A tintype of Fetter—that of a handsome man in the prime of his life—appears in published sources.

While in New York, Fetter married Sarah Cox (1816–1 Mar. 1867), who was described by a Chapel Hill contemporary as a lady of great vivacity and kindness of heart. They were the parents of four sons, Frederick Augustus, Charles, Henry, and William Muhlenburg, and three daughters, Susan, Catherine, and Martha. All four sons were graduated from The University of North Carolina and served in the Confederate Army. Frederick and Charles both became teachers and late in life were ordained to the priesthood of the Episcopal church on the same day in 1895 by the Right Reverend Joseph B. Cheshire.

SEE: Kemp P. Battle, *History of the University of North Carolina*, vol. 1 (1907); Moravian Church Records (Lancaster County Historical Society, Lancaster, Pa.), for information on the Fetter family; *North Carolina University Magazine* 9 (March 1860 [portrait]); U.S. Census, 1860, Orange County (microfilm, North Carolina Collection, University of North Carolina, Chapel Hill); Peter M. Wilson, *Southern Exposure* (1927).

CLAIBORNE T. SMITH, JR.

**Few, James** *(1746–17 May 1771)*, Regulator, was born in Maryland, the son of William Few, Sr., and Mary Wheeler Few. He was the brother of William Few, Jr., who became a U.S. senator and judge. In 1758 the family moved to North Carolina and settled near Hillsborough. James Few married, probably in 1769, Mary Howard, and also settled near Hillsborough where he was a farmer and carpenter. The couple had twin children, William and Sally, born 9 Feb. 1771.

Few's role in the Regulator disturbances is not clear. In 1768 his father had signed a bond for two leading Regulators, William Butler and Herman Husband. On the other hand, James Few's brothers William and Benjamin seem not to have been seriously involved. James Few was indicted in the May term of court in 1771 in New Bern for participation in the Regulator riot of the previous September. Because he had never been arrested, he was technically an outlaw at the time of the Battle of Alamance on 16 May 1771. After the battle, in which Governor William Tryon's forces defeated the poorly organized Regulators, Few was hanged on or near the field of battle. Six other Regulators were hanged later after a military trial. The reason for Few's immediate hanging seems to be that he was the one "outlaw" taken during the battle, although several other theories have come down as local traditions. One of these is that Few was a religious fanatic, at least partially insane, who fought with such fury on the battlefield that the governor's troops demanded his life when he was captured. Another is that he was an enemy of Edmund Fanning, a government official in Hillsborough, who insisted that he be executed. Whatever the cause, Few's hanging seems to have been an unnecessary assumption of power on the governor's part, and even his apologists do not condone it.

Following the Battle of Alamance, William Few, Sr., moved his family to Georgia, taking with him the twin children of James and Mary Few. James's son William became prominent in Georgia and was the great-grandfather of William Preston Few, twentieth century president of Duke University.

SEE: E. W. Caruthers, *A Sketch of the Life and Character of the Rev. David Caldwell* (1842); Marshall D. Haywood, *Governor William Tryon and His Administration of the Province of North Carolina* (1903); William S. Powell, ed., *The Correspondence of William Tryon and Other Selected Papers*, vol. 2 (1980), and with James K. Huhta and Thomas J. Farnham, eds., *The Regulators of North Carolina, A Documentary History, 1759–1776* (1971); Arthur D. Vinton, "The First American Anarchist," *Magazine of American History* 16 (1886); *Virginia Gazette*, 7 Nov. 1771.

ELMER D. JOHNSON

**Few, William, Jr.** *(8 June 1748–16 June 1828)*, member of the Continental Congress and of the constitutional convention, U.S. senator, and judge, was born near Baltimore, Md., the son of William Few, Sr., and Mary Wheeler Few. In 1758, the family moved to North Carolina where the elder Few purchased a 640-acre farm on the banks of the Eno River near Hillsborough; he also operated a gristmill and tavern in cooperation with his brother, James. Young William studied briefly with itinerant schoolmasters and had some schooling in law, but educated himself largely through reading on his own. In 1767 his father bought another farm about seven miles from Hillsborough, and William at age nineteen took over its management.

As the Regulator disturbances developed in Orange County during 1768–71, William Few, Sr., sympathized with the movement and became involved at least to the extent of giving bond for two of the leaders, William Butler and Herman Husband, to assure their appearance for trial. It was probably because of this, and because of the Regulator activities of his son James, that the Few farm was destroyed by Governor William Tryon's forces after the Battle of Alamance on 16 May 1771. The following winter, the Few family moved to Georgia, settling in St. Paul's Parish near Wrightsboro. William Few, Jr., remained behind in North Carolina to take care of the family's properties but moved to Georgia sometime between 1773 and the summer of 1776.

Once in Georgia, Few advanced rapidly in the political hierarchy and took a prominent role in the colony's move toward independence. In 1776 he was a member of the convention to form a constitution for Georgia as well as a member of the first assembly, which elected him to the state council in 1777. Subsequently he served as surveyor general, commissioner of confiscated estates, and senior justice of Richmond County, returning to the assembly in 1779 and 1780. In 1780 he was elected to the Continental Congress, where he served several terms, and in 1787 he represented Georgia in the constitutional convention in Philadelphia. From 1789 to 1793 he was a U.S. senator from Georgia, and after that served as federal judge of the state's Second Judicial District.

In addition to his political activities during the American Revolution, Few served as an officer in the Georgia militia. With his brother, Benjamin, he led Georgia troops in skirmishes with the Tories in South Carolina and Georgia in 1779–80. He acquired a plantation in Columbia County, Ga., as well as other tracts of land in Jackson County. One of the latter he later sold to the state of Georgia for the use of the proposed state university. He was also one of the first trustees of the University of Georgia.

In 1799, due to ill health, and also possibly due to disillusionment with the institution of slavery, Few moved to New York City, the home of his wife Catherine Nicholson, whom he had married while a member of the U.S. Senate. They became the parents of three daughters. In New York, Few carved out a new career for himself as a member of the state legislature, alderman in New York City, commissioner of loans for the state, and inspector of state prisons. In private life he was a bank director and president, as well as a "gentleman farmer." He died at the home of his son-in-law, Albert Chrystie, in Fishkill, N.Y.

SEE: E. M. Coulter, *The Toombs Oak and Other Chapters of Georgia History* (1966); *DAB*, vol. 3 (1959); William Few, "Autobiography of Col. William Few of Georgia, from the Original Manuscript in the Possession of William Few Chrystie," *Magazine of American History* 7 (1881); Charles C. Jones, Jr., *Biographical Sketches of the Delegates from Georgia to the Continental Congress* (1891); Marion Letcher, "William Few, Jr." in *Men of Mark in Georgia*, ed., W. J. Northen, vol. 1 (1906 [portrait]).

ELMER D. JOHNSON

**Few, William Preston** *(29 Dec. 1867–16 Oct. 1940)*, the first dean (1902–10) and the fifth president (1910–24) of Trinity College, was the first president of Duke University (1924–40). His English ancestor, Richard Few, was in Pennsylvania in 1682; his great-great-grandfather, William Few, Sr., left Maryland to settle in Orange County, N.C., near Hillsborough. William's son, James, became involved in the Regulator movement and, though not a principal leader, was captured by the forces of Governor William Tryon and hanged on 17 May 1771 after the Battle of Alamance. James left infant twins, William and Sarah. William moved to upper Greenville County, S.C., at an early age, married Sarah Ferguson, and became the father of sixteen children, one of whom was Benjamin Franklin Few (1830–1923). Benjamin, who was graduated from the South Carolina Medical College and served as an assistant surgeon in the Confederate Army, married Rachel Kendrick (1840–1922), a cousin, in 1863; they had two girls and three boys. After the war, he returned to Greenville County and settled in a rural community called Sandy Flat, where William Preston Few was born.

"Willie" was, he said later, "an invalid boy." Thus he received his early education from his mother and did not attend school regularly until he was about thirteen. He was baptized into the Methodist church on 27 Sept. 1871, and religion never ceased to be a formative influence in his life. Few finished high school in Greer, S.C., then attended Wofford College in nearby Spartanburg where he was graduated in 1889. Despite some illness he had an excellent record in a course of study that included physics, trigonometry, Latin, Greek, and Old English. In addition, he was one of the founders of *The*

*Journal,* the Wofford literary monthly, as well as a member of the Chi Phi social fraternity and the Preston Literary Society. He also learned to play tennis.

Few's teaching career began at St. John's Academy in Darlington, S.C. The next year he was invited to teach in the Wofford College preparatory school. Two years later he entered the graduate school of Harvard University where he received the master of arts (1893) and doctor of philosophy (1896) degrees—both in modern languages. At Harvard, as at Wofford and St. John's, he was plagued by ill health; he later wrote that "until about 1924 I had bad health all my life." He welcomed the opportunity to return to a softer climate when he received an invitation from President John C. Kilgo, whom he had known in South Carolina, to teach for one year at Trinity College. Recently the college had been moved from Randolph County, N.C., to Durham, a rising city of the New South with a population of about 8,000. Few's appointment became permanent when at the end of the year Kilgo reported to the trustees that both the college and the town recognized him "as a man of superior ability." Few, who took an active part in college affairs, soon was "Manager of Athletics" as well as professor of English. In 1902 he became the first dean of Trinity, "invested with all the authority of the President in his absence."

A significant event early in Few's deanship was the so-called Bassett affair. John Spencer Bassett was a member of the faculty and editor of the *South Atlantic Quarterly,* recently established at Trinity. In an article appearing in the magazine he discussed the growing antipathy toward the Negro race, deplored recent restrictive legislation, predicted that blacks would continue to struggle toward equality, and referred to Booker T. Washington, the Negro leader and educator, as "the greatest man, save General Lee, born in the South in a hundred years." The press of the state raised an intemperate outcry. The issue was academic freedom and whether the trustees would sacrifice Bassett to those who were making him an excuse to get at Kilgo, the Dukes, and Trinity—all somehow related to such odious things as the Tobacco Trust, the Republican party, and a trend in education opposed to native institutions. The upshot was that when the trustees met in December 1903 Kilgo presented them with an eloquent plea in behalf of free speech. The trustees declined Bassett's proffered resignation and brought in a report asserting the principle of academic freedom. This report had been prepared in advance by Dean Few with the assistance of William Garrott Brown, a journalist and intimate friend of Few, who happened to be visiting him at the time. The episode put Trinity in a good light in the view of educators and foundations, and it illustrates Few's willingness to take a firm stand while avoiding an open confrontation.

Kilgo resigned as president of Trinity after he was elected bishop in the Methodist Episcopal Church, South, and on 6 June 1910 Few was chosen to succeed him as of 1 July. There is no doubt that Benjamin N. Duke and Kilgo were the prime movers in the appointment. The student newspaper acclaimed Few's election, as it had his deanship, and the elaborate inauguration ceremony on 9 Nov. 1910 was attended by distinguished educators. In his well-received address, the new president indicated that he would continue on the path marked by his predecessor, and that the greatness of the college would depend not on size but on "the quality of the men who teach and the quality of the men who learn."

On 17 Aug. 1911, in Martinsville, Va., President Few married Mary Reamey Thomas in a ceremony performed by Bishop Kilgo. Miss Thomas was a graduate of Trinity and a former pupil of Few; by chance they had renewed their acquaintance in 1908 on the ship Few took to Scotland for a summer in the Shakespeare country and in France. The couple had five sons: William, Lynne Starling, Kendrick Sheffield, Randolph Reamey, and Yancy Preston. A devoted family man, Few considered the loss of Preston at age sixteen a great tragedy.

From the beginning Few had cast his lot with Trinity. Though inclined to keep a low profile as far as political pronouncements and public issues were concerned, he worked quietly and persistently to raise the standard of excellence in education while continuing to teach and even tutor some students privately. For nearly ten years (1909–19) he was coeditor of the *South Atlantic Quarterly* and a frequent contributor. He also was a member of the committee of the Board of Overseers, which visited Harvard's Graduate School of Arts and Sciences in 1911. In 1913 he was president of the North Carolina Literary and Historical Association, and in 1918 he became a trustee of the Negro Rural School Fund, which was supported by the Anna T. Jeanes Foundation. Since 1897 he had been a delegate to many meetings of the Southern Association of Colleges and Secondary Schools, and in 1932 he was elected its president.

Benjamin N. Duke, who had favored Few's election as president, continued to support him, and there developed a bond of affection between the two men. Other friends of Few who were associated with the Dukes, especially Clinton W. Toms, a Trinity trustee, were encouraged to keep the needs of Trinity before James B. Duke; undoubtedly the latter's appraisal of Few was a factor in Trinity's future. Although the Dukes made frequent and generous gifts to Trinity, Few was anxious to enlist their financial support on a more permanent basis. In 1916 James B. Duke "spoke definitely," in Few's words, "concerning his purpose to give away during his lifetime a large part of his fortune." However, World War I intervened and it was not until February 1919 that Few proposed to Duke a plan for the creation of a Duke Foundation to be interlinked with Trinity through a self-perpetuating board. Duke, Few suggested, could become a member of the executive committee of the college (Benjamin N. Duke had been a trustee since 1889, and his son Angier B., a graduate of Trinity, since 1913), could "manage the property" of the foundation, and could "determine the allotments to be made each year." James B. Duke became a trustee of Trinity College in 1918, attended the commencement of 1919, and seemed to Few "happier than I have seen him in a long time." Soon Few wrote Benjamin N. Duke, "I am sure that we are now on the eve of developments beyond our dreams."

Early in 1921 Few began to work on a plan for the establishment in Durham of a hospital and clinical medical school as a joint enterprise of Trinity, The University of North Carolina, and possibly Wake Forest and Davidson colleges. Few enlisted significant support, some from outside foundations and some from James B. Duke, but skeptics influenced public opinion against the project, and in the end Few's plan failed. Few, who had foreseen this possibility, later wrote that the undertaking "served two good purposes—it kept the road open for a first-rate School of Medicine later on, and it put Mr. James B. Duke on his mettle."

Discussions between Few and Duke continued until a plan of organization took shape in 1921. The idea of a university, rather than Trinity alone, emerged; Few "suggested that the new institution be called Duke University." In the spring of 1924 James B. Duke authorized the purchase of land near the campus. This was not easy, and it came to seem, wrote Few, "as if we had a difficult task before us." On an afternoon walk Few "accidently rediscovered a beautiful woodland tract to the west of the campus." More than 5,796 acres of this land was acquired, some in small parcels, without any public knowledge of the identity of the purchaser. Then it was learned that a local stone, near Hillsborough, was "easily available, durable, beautiful, and in every way fitted for our building requirements."

In December 1924 James B. Duke established the Duke Endowment, which provided financial assistance for educational institutions, hospitals, and agencies of the Methodist church in the two Carolinas. Twenty percent of the income from the initial endowment of $40 million was to be accumulated until an additional $40 million was available. By his will Duke provided further support for the Duke Medical School, hospital, and other purposes, eventually giving the university a total of some $19 million apart from the annual income from the endowment. The fact is, however, that this was not enough to do all that Duke had envisioned, and some hard priority decisions had to be made. One of the problems Few never mastered was how to keep the public from being misinformed by the press on this apparently endless wealth.

James B. Duke died in 1925 and thus did not play a further direct part in the metamorphosis of a small college, with professional training restricted to law and engineering, into a university equipped with a hospital, medical school, divinity school, college of engineering, school of forestry, graduate school, and a coordinate women's college. If there were those who thought Few not equal to the task of working successfully with this complex problem, they soon found that he had a toughness, a resilience, a shrewdness, and a latent capacity to be firm and resolute. But his tendency was to be cooperative and conciliatory and to expect tolerance and reason to prevail. Long before his death the university had taken much the form he had envisioned. That he was for progress and futuristic is seen in his attitude toward academic freedom, the education of women, and the unification of the Methodist church, as well as in his lively distrust of the demagogue.

Few was a modest man, even to the point of shyness at times, but he had a quiet charm especially noticed in small gatherings. Although he had to do a good deal of public speaking, he was never a platform orator. The words of a longtime friend give an accurate summation: "He was as kind and tenderhearted as a woman. But to imagine him without will or backbone would be to err grossly." He died at Duke Hospital and was buried in the crypt of Duke Chapel.

SEE: Robert F. Durden, *The Dukes of Durham, 1865–1929* (1975); Few, Duke, and Trinity College Papers (University Archives, Library, Duke University, Durham); James F. Gifford, Jr., *The Evolution of a Medical Center; A History of Medicine at Duke University to 1941* (1972); Earl W. Porter, *Trinity and Duke, 1892–1924* (1964); Raleigh *News and Observer*, 17, 18, 19 Oct. 1980; Hersey Everett E. Spence, *"I Remember," Recollections and Reminiscences of Alma Mater* (1954); Robert H. Woody, ed., *Papers and Addresses of William Preston Few* (1951).

ROBERT H. WOODY

**Field, Ada Martitia** *(30 Oct. 1887–30 May 1972),* teacher and researcher in nutrition, was born near Climax, N.C., the daughter of Christopher and Louise Emily Wilson Field. Because of a heart defect she was forced to live a circumscribed life, yet it was filled with activity. She was graduated from Guilford College with a B.S. in chemistry in 1898 and attended Bryn Mawr for three years. From 1908 to 1909 she was employed as an instructor in chemistry at Washington University, Seattle, which awarded her an M.A. degree in science in 1909. Returning to North Carolina, she was professor of chemistry at Guilford College from 1910 to 1912. Because of her deep interest in nutrition, she accepted an invitation to be a lecturer on nutrition at Woman's College of New York from 1913 to 1914, at the same time serving as an instructor at Teachers College, Columbia University. From 1914 to 1925 she was assistant and associate professor of home economics at George Peabody College, Nashville, Tenn. These, she said, were the happiest years of her life and the ones that produced her most fruitful teaching. Afterwards she returned to Columbia University for the doctorate in organic chemistry, which she received in 1928 at the age of fifty-one. From 1929 to 1931 she was a lecturer at the University of California.

In 1931 she retired from teaching to do private research in nutrition. Having built a flour mill near Guilford College, she succeeded in discovering how to mill wheat and preserve the heart bud so that flour could be stored indefinitely. Her product was a true whole wheat flour called "Good Wheat," a name registered by her and manufactured and marketed by the Lexington Roller Mills, Inc., in Kentucky.

Ada Field was a devoted teacher, a disciplined scientist, a researcher and humanitarian, and a believer in peace through education. She was a sincere worker for peace through the Society of Friends (Quakers) of which she was a member. She died in Greensboro.

SEE: *Greensboro Daily News*, 1 June 1972; Memorial to Ada Field (Quaker Collection, Library, Guilford College, Greensboro); Raleigh *News and Observer*, 18 May 1941.

B. RUSSELL BRANSON

**Finch, Josiah John** *(3 Feb. 1814–21 Jan. 1850),* clergyman and educator, was born in Franklin County, the fourth child and oldest son of Caswell and Temperance Bridges Finch. According to his son's biographer, Caswell Finch spent forty years of his life as a teacher who "stood without rival" in the region in which he lived. Young Josiah manifested an early interest in books and learning, and gained the rudiments of an English education from his parents. He experienced a religious conversion at the age of seventeen, joining the Maple Springs Baptist Church; he was ordained to the ministry one year later. Sensing his need for further education if he was to be an effective minister, Finch spent two sessions at the Louisburg Male Academy, then under the care of John D. Bobbitt, and attended the Raleigh Academy during the better part of 1834. His formal education was completed with studies at Wake Forest College in 1836–37.

Upon his ordination by the Maple Springs Baptist Church, Finch became pastor of his home congregation (1832–34). Later he served the Baptist churches in Edenton (1835–37), New Bern (1838–44), and Raleigh (1845–48). Upon their removal to Raleigh, Finch's wife began the operation of Sedgwick Female Academy. Within two years the school attained such rank and prominence that Finch was obliged to devote a considerable amount of his time and energies to its work. The combined duties of both school and church soon took a heavy toll upon his delicate health, and he decided, reluctantly, to relinquish his pastoral duties with the congregation in Raleigh, while maintaining his interest in Sedgwick Academy. His death—from consumption—occurred some eighteen months later.

Finch's published writings included a booklet entitled *Conditions of Discipleship*, published in New Bern in 1842, and occasional articles for the *Biblical Recorder*, a journal of the Baptist denomination in North Carolina. A collection of his sermons was published in 1853 by his brother, Gilbert Mortier Lafayette Finch. Of this collection, George Washington Paschal noted: "The sermons are on a wide variety of topics and show clearness of conception and good analytic powers."

Warmly attached to the Baptist State Convention and its objectives, Finch was a "special agent" for Wake Forest College in 1844. He also served the convention as recording secretary (1842–43, 1845–46), corresponding secretary (1845–47), and member of its board of managers for most of the years after 1836. An indication of the esteem in which Finch was held by his colleagues can be seen in the very warm and glowing tribute paid to his memory by the convention's "Committee on Special Changes" (Obituaries) at the 1850 session of that body.

On 13 Feb. 1838 Finch married Mary Louise Wills. They had two sons and two daughters: William H., Martha E. (m. W. T. Hodge), Mary Wills (m. W. I. Royster), and Alonzo.

SEE: Baptist State Convention of North Carolina, *Proceedings*, 1850; Gilbert M. L. Finch, *The Sermons of the Rev. Josiah J. Finch, with a Memoir of his Life* (1853); George W. Paschal, *History of Wake Forest College*, vol. 1 (1935); Ruby F. Thompson, *Finch Families of Dixie* (1972).

R. HARGUS TAYLOR

**Finch, Thomas Austin, Sr.** *(7 Apr. 1890–11 Jan. 1943)*, nationally known industrialist, was born in Trinity Township, Randolph County, the son of Thomas Jefferson and Hannah Louise Brown Finch. His brothers were Gray, Alfred Brown, Charles, Doak, and George Davis Finch. His mother, who was graduated from Greensboro College in 1885, was the daughter of Dempsey and Eliza Ann Laughlin Brown and the granddaughter of John Brown, a builder of Brown's Schoolhouse on his plantation near Trinity in Randolph County. This school was the beginning of Trinity College, which became Duke University some years after its removal to Durham. At the age of fifteen, Thomas Austin Finch was graduated from Trinity High School where he was awarded a scholarship to Trinity College. In college he made a well-nigh perfect record, becoming a member of the "9019" Honor Society, and was asked to teach there upon graduation in 1909. Instead, he accepted the challenge of a new venture in the Piedmont area, the small factory called Thomasville Chair Company, owned by his father and uncle, where he had spent two vacations working at every kind of job in the making of chairs. Thereafter his life was intertwined with the record of the growth and expansion of this industry.

Finch began his career during the first decade of furniture manufacturing in Thomasville. This period witnessed the construction of many factories, some of which were soon offered for sale. Within five years three of them were bought by the Thomasville Chair Company. Finch was secretary and treasurer of this large company, which was becoming known for its capable management, efficiency of operation, and consideration of employees. In the 1920s changing conditions and customs necessitated a complete reorganization of production. Each factory was equipped with new machinery to streamline production of suites of furniture for a room; two more factories were added to complete the manufacturing of furniture for an entire house. Under Finch's guiding genius the various factories were consolidated into an enormous, unified operation known all over the nation. Upon the death of his father in 1929, he became president of the company and continued to direct its course during and after the dark of the depression.

Throughout this period of growth from one small factory to a large, complex corporation, the employees of Thomasville Chair Company highly respected Finch for his signal executive ability; they also regarded him more as their leader than as an employer. They knew that he expected from them full devotion to their work but that he asked no more from them than from himself. In 1939, upon completing thirty years of service, he was presented a valuable collection of books with one volume containing the signatures of nearly 1,700 employees of the company. Engraved in the front of this book was a tribute to his dynamic leadership, rare vision, personal sacrifice, and tremendous investment of time and energy in guiding the company through the years, some of which were very difficult and precarious for furniture manufacturing.

Finch served in a number of other important business capacities. From 1934 to 1943 he was president of the First National Bank of Thomasville, of which he had previously been a director. He was a director of the Wachovia Bank & Trust Company, of the Security Life & Trust Company of Winston-Salem, of the Carolina Bank & Trust Company of Denton, and of the Thomasville Realty & Trust Company; one of the first directors of the Home Building & Loan Association; vice-president of the High Point, Thomasville & Denton Railway; a member and president of the Southern Furniture Manufacturers Association; and member and chairman of the board of governors of the American Furniture Mart of Chicago.

He also worked for the betterment of the city of Thomasville and the state of North Carolina. At various times he filled the following posts: mayor of Thomasville (1923–25); member of the Thomasville School Board; chairman of the board of trustees of the City Memorial Hospital; chairman of the board of stewards of Main Street Methodist Church; and first president of the Thomasville Rotary Club. On the state level he served on the North Carolina Transportation Council, the North Carolina Employment Council, and the State Board of Vocational Education. In addition, he was a director of Winston-Salem Teachers College and of the Methodist Children's Home.

During the depression years the outstanding ability of Thomas Austin Finch was in demand on a national level. From time to time he was called to Washington by President Franklin D. Roosevelt for consultation on critical issues relating to the nation's economy. He served with distinction on the Industrial Advisory Board of the National Recovery Administration and the Business Advisory Council of the U.S. Department of Commerce. At the time of his death he had been serving the government in an advisory capacity on the furniture panel of the War Production Board. He was a lifelong Democrat.

On 6 Nov. 1919 Finch married Ernestine Lambeth, the daughter of John Walter, Sr., and Daisy Hunt Sumner Lambeth, and a graduate of Thomasville High School and Greensboro College. They became the parents of one son, Thomas Austin, Jr., born 12 Aug. 1922. After graduating from Woodberry Forest Preparatory School and Princeton University and serving three years as an officer in the U.S. Navy during World War II, the younger Finch returned home and became vice-president of the Thomasville Chair Company. In 1974 he became president of the Thomasville Furniture Industries, Inc., which in 1968 had merged with Armstrong Cork Company, a world enterprise of which he was named a senior vice-president. He married Meredith Clark Slane (daughter of Willis H. and Meredith Clark Slane, and a graduate of Salem Academy and Sweet Briar College) and had five children: Thomas Austin III, John Lambeth, David Slane, Sumner Slane, and Meredith Kempton Finch.

After the death of the senior Finch, his widow and son set up the Thomas Austin Finch Foundation for religious, charitable, and educational purposes. Funds from this foundation were used to construct the Austin Finch Chapel of Memorial United Methodist Church, the Thomasville Public Library, and rooms in the Community General Hospital. In his memory the Thomasville Furniture Industries, Inc., established a large scholarship fund for qualifying children of its employees.

Thomas Austin Finch, Sr., was buried in the Thomasville City Cemetery.

SEE: Nora Campbell Chaffin, *Trinity College, 1839–1892: The Beginnings of Duke University* (1950); *Chicago Market Daily*, 12 Jan. 1943; *High Point Enterprise*, 5 July 1939, 11 Jan. 1943; Mary G. Matthews and M. Jewell Sink, *Pathfinders, Past and Present, A History of Davidson County, North Carolina* (1972); and *Wheels of Faith and Courage, A History of Thomasville, North Carolina* (1952); *North Carolina Biography*, vol. 3 (1956); Jessie Owen Shaw, *The Johnsons and Their Kin of Randolph* (1955).

M. JEWELL SINK

**Finch, Thomas Jefferson** *(1 Dec. 1861–20 July 1929)*, pioneer furniture manufacturer, banker, and farmer, was descended from English settlers who came first to Virginia and then to Person County, N.C. Succeeding generations moved to Randolph County. He was born in the Pleasant Hill section of Tabernacle Township in Randolph County, about ten miles south of Thomasville, the son of Alfred Benjamin (son of Pettis and Frances Ranchor Pope Finch), and Lucy Andrews Finch who also had six other children. Thomas Jefferson was the oldest of three sons to reach maturity; all were successful farmers and together owned a general store. Thomas Jefferson, who worked in the store and on the farm in early life, learned the value of industry and thrift.

Young Finch received his education in the country school near his home and later at Trinity College, then in Randolph County. Between Trinity and Thomasville his uncle and aunt, Thomas Austin and Rebecca Dorsett Finch, a childless couple, resided on a large farm. At their insistence nineteen-year-old Thomas Jefferson went to live with them and look after their affairs. When they died he inherited their estate, including the farm, Wheatmore, which became his home for the remainder of his life. A few months after their death, he married Hannah Louise Brown, daughter of Dempsey and Eliza Ann Laughlin Brown and granddaughter of John and Jane Clark Brown. In 1837–38 John Brown and his kinsmen had built on his plantation in Randolph County Brown's Schoolhouse for the schooling of their own and neighbor's children. This school was the beginning of Trinity College (later Duke University). Hannah's father, Dempsey Brown, in later years donated land for Hopewell Methodist Church and its cemeteries for Negroes and whites. Hannah Brown Finch was an 1885 graduate of Greensboro College.

Thomas J. and Hannah Brown Finch were the parents of six sons: Thomas Austin; Brown, who was killed in a railroad wreck in 1925; Gray and Charles, who died in their youth; Doak; and George Davis. When the younger sons reached school age, Finch built and opened a schoolhouse at Wheatmore for his own, the farm employees', and a few of his neighbors' children; the schoolteacher lived at the "Big House." Wheatmore also had a post office, which was operated by Mrs. Finch in the absence of her husband.

After Finch had added four hundred acres to his original tract and had developed the farm until it was a model for the county, he turned his attention to politics. A lifelong Democrat, he was elected county commissioner in 1892, and remained in office for several years. Later, he served two terms as sheriff of Randolph, a county normally Republican. He was for some time a county school board member and took much interest in public issues of the day. During World War I President Woodrow Wilson appointed him to the state exemption board, which consisted of three members from across the state. For a time he served on the state agricultural board and in his later years was a director of the North Carolina Railroad. In 1924 he was a delegate to the Democratic National Convention in New York.

Finch first became interested in Thomasville in 1897, when he and his nephew, C. L. Harris, opened a general store there. Two years later he joined Jesse F. Hayden in organizing a telephone company and in purchasing the High Point Telephone Company. The same year he was one of the incorporators of the Bank of Thomasville, and in 1907 he became a director and vice-president of the First National Bank. In 1917 he was named president of the First National Bank, a position he held through the war years and the recession immediately thereafter. He was one of the first directors of the Peoples Building and Loan Association (1909), an organizer and first president of the Carolina Bank & Trust Company of Denton (1924), president of the Thomasville Realty & Trust Company, and a director of the High Point, Thomasville & Denton Railroad.

His greatest contribution to Thomasville and the Piedmont area, however, was his pioneering in furniture manufacturing. About the turn of the century he and his brother, Charles F., went into the lumbering business, buying timber and sawing it into lumber, which they sold for building material and furniture making. This led to their purchase in 1907 of the Thomasville Chair Company, then consisting of only one small factory. They bought another factory in 1909 and two more a few years later. Thomas Austin, the oldest son of Thomas Jefferson Finch, joined the business in 1909 and another son, Brown, in 1914. By purchasing the interest of Charles F. Finch in 1925, Thomas Jefferson Finch and members of his family became the owners of the company and incorporated it; the same year his sons Doak and George also joined in its operation. Thomas Jefferson Finch remained at the head of this large family enterprise for the remainder of his life. In twenty-two years the company grew from one small factory to one of the largest plants in the Piedmont area with capital stock of $1.5 million and close to a thousand employees. Along with a few other leaders, he had recognized the potential of furniture manufacturing in the South and had begun developing Piedmont North Carolina into an industrial region.

Finch was a member of the Masonic Lodge, of the local Rotary Club, and of many other civic organizations. His interest in the building of Memorial Hospital in Thomasville led him to contribute a large sum—matching the Duke Foundation grant—to ensure its construction. He was a member of Hopewell Methodist Church, where he was a steward for many years. He was interred in the family mausoleum in Hopewell Cemetery.

SEE: Nora Campbell Chaffin, *Trinity College, 1839–1892: The Beginnings of Duke University* (1950); Mary G. Matthews and M. Jewell Sink, *Pathfinders, Past and Present: A History of Davidson County, North Carolina* (1972), and *Wheels of Faith and Courage, A History of Thomasville, North Carolina* (1952); Jessie Owen Shaw, *The Johnsons and Their Kin of Randolph* (1955); Thomasville *News and Times*, 25 July 1929.

M. JEWELL SINK

**Finckley, Thomas** *(d. ca. 1695)*, council member, was in the North Carolina colony, then called Albemarle, by March 1675/76 and owned a plantation on Finckley's Point in Perquimans Precinct. In November 1681 he was a member of the council of the colony and ex officio justice of the General Court. Whether he held office at other times is not shown in the few surviving records of the period.

Finckley left Albemarle between September 1683 and the following February. He may have moved to Princess Anne County, Va., where a Thomas Finckley died about 1695. Another Thomas Finckley of the same county, who died about 1722, may have been his son. Otherwise, nothing is known of his private life.

SEE: Council minutes, wills, and inventories, 1677–1701 (North Carolina State Archives, Raleigh); Charles F. McIntosh, comp., *Abstract of Lower Norfolk and Norfolk County Wills, 1637–1710* (1914); Mattie Erma E. Parker, ed., *Colonial Records of North Carolina, Higher-Court Records, 1670–1696*, vol. 2 (1968); Clayton Torrence, comp., *Virginia Wills and Administrations, 1632–1800* (1972).

MATTIE ERMA E. PARKER

**Finger, Sidney Michael** *(24 May 1837–26 Dec. 1896)*, educator, state assemblyman, merchant, and manufacturer, was born in Lincoln County, the son of Daniel (1806–88) and Sallie Finger (1813–57). He was the great-grandson of Peter Finger (ca. 1730–ca. 1793), who emigrated from Germany by way of Pennsylvania to settle on Leeper's Creek near Sherrill's Ford, Lincoln County, before the American Revolution. Daniel Finger was one of the founders and elders of St. Matthews German Reformed Church, Lincoln County, and gave land adjoining the church lot for the building of a common school. It was at a St. Matthews Church camp meeting that the idea for establishing a college to train ministers originated. In 1851 the church founded Catawba College at Newton, Catawba County.

Until he was eighteen, Sidney Michael Finger followed in his father's occupations as a farmer and tanner, attending the four-month school near his home. He entered Catawba College in 1855. During vacation months he taught school, and during half of his four years at Catawba he served as a tutor. In 1859 he was accepted in the junior class at Bowdoin College, Maine, where he received a B.A. degree in May 1861. For a short time he taught school in Bishopville, S.C., before returning home to join the Confederate Army. On 22 Mar. 1862 he enlisted in Lincoln County and subsequently joined Company I, Eleventh Regiment, North Carolina Troops, as a first corporal. By the end of the war he had achieved the rank of major and was responsible for tax in kind for the state of North Carolina. He was paroled at Charlotte on 3 May 1865; thereafter he was generally addressed as Major Finger. His three brothers were casualties of the war.

During the Civil War Catawba College lost its endowment and but for the efforts of the Reverend Jacob C. Clapp would have closed entirely. Following his release from the army, Finger took up residence in Newton and with the Reverend Mr. Clapp conducted the Catawba English and Classical High School, serving as associate principal and teacher. On 22 Dec 1866 Finger married Sarah Hoyle Rhyne (24 Feb. 1839–17 May 1903), daughter of Daniel Rhyne (1795–1875) and Louisa McGee Rhyne (b. 1801) of Gaston County. He and his wife were active members of Grace Reformed Church in Newton. In 1871, Finger took an A.M. degree at Bowdoin. Three years later, with the arrival of a competent staff at Catawba and because of ill health, he retired from the school.

In 1872 Finger entered politics as mayor of Newton. Somewhat unexpectedly, he was nominated by the Democratic party and elected to represent Catawba County in the 1874–75 General Assembly. At that session he served on the education committee and was chairman of the house branch of the joint committee on enrolled bills. In the following election he was returned to the legislature as a senator representing the Thirty-seventh District, comprised of Catawba and Lincoln counties. In the 1875–76 General Assembly Finger was appointed to the committee on claims and to the senate branch of the joint select committee on state debt; he was also chairman of the committee on education. It was at this legislative session, held during the closing days of Reconstruction, that the public school law was consolidated and updated and the rudiments of a postwar common school system established. Finger again returned to Raleigh as a senator representing his district in the General Assembly of 1881. He served as chairman of the committee on the state debt and as a member of three other committees—education, finance, and internal improvements. Once again, the school law was rewritten; significantly, the law of 1881 provided the foundation for North Carolina's modern public school system.

In the fall of 1882 Governor Thomas J. Jarvis appointed Finger to the first board of directors of the Western Insane Asylum at Morganton; that board, which assumed responsibility from the building committee, prepared the hospital to receive patients in April 1883. During his second year on the board, Finger was its president.

In 1884, Finger was elected superintendent of public instruction on the Democratic ticket and served for two terms (1 Jan. 1885–31 Dec. 1892). One of the first tasks he set for himself was to review textbooks recommended for use in the schools. Upon finding that none of the school readers included mention of the South, he rejected them. Before accepting new readers he examined the page proofs not only to assure adequate coverage of the subject but also to see that the South was treated justly. Throughout his administration Finger worked assiduously to professionalize teaching by establishing high standards for the training of teachers in subject matter as well as in pedagogical methods and school management. In his biennial reports to the governor he recommended, among other things, compulsory school attendance, federal aid to education, vocational training, the establishment of at least one library in each school district, and a restriction on the employment of children in factories. He successfully pressured the General Assembly to authorize increased local taxes to finance the four-month school term promised in the state constitution; however, he was unable to persuade the legislators to make a direct appropriation in support of the school system. In addition to his duties as supervisor of public schools for whites and Negroes throughout the state, he served as secretary of the Board of Education and was state administrator of the Peabody Fund. Upon Finger's recommendation, the General Assembly of 1889 abolished the ineffectual normal school system and appropriated funding for teacher institutes to be held for one week in each county. Superintendent Finger was charged with the management of these ninety-two institutes. He, with the advice of the Board of Education, assembled an excellent roster of educators to travel across North Carolina making available abbreviated normal school curriculums to teachers and to the interested general public.

At the Democratic state convention in 1893, Finger was nominated for another term as superintendent of public instruction, but his name was removed as a candidate in order to place a Baptist on the ticket. He returned to Newton, where he continued to be active in local and state politics and looked after his longtime investments in a general store and in flour and cotton mills. In 1894 he published a textbook entitled *Civil Government in North Carolina and the United States: A School Manual and History*. Although a self-described conservative and—like many contemporaries—paternalistic toward the Negro, Finger believed that qualified blacks should have an opportunity to advance professionally and economically. With W. M. Kendrick, he edited Edward Augustus Johnson's *A School History (Fourth Grade Reader) of the Negro Race* (1894) and recommended its use in the Negro schools of North Carolina.

The achievement in which Finger took most pride was the establishment of the North Carolina State Normal and Industrial School at Greensboro. In 1886 he, along with A. M. Alderman and C. D. McIver, was appointed by the State Teachers Assembly to propagandize the need for a normal school for women. These three men wrote the legislation enacted by the General Assembly in 1891 authorizing the selection of a site and the building of such an institution, and they saw that the law was expeditiously implemented. After the school opened in 1893 Finger served on the board of directors, attending business meetings and commencements with much pleasure. He also was a trustee of The University of North Carolina from 1893 until his death.

Finger and his wife had no children. Both were buried at Eastview Cemetery, Newton, beside Finger's father, Daniel.

SEE: Samuel A. Ashe, ed., *Cyclopedia of Eminent and Representative Men of the Carolinas of the Nineteenth Century* (1892); Edward A. Johnson, *A School History of the Negro Race in America* (1969); A. R. Keppel, et al., *A College of Our Own: A Brief History of Catawba College, 1856–1951* (1951); Jacob C. Leonard, *History of Catawba College* (1927); Newton *Enterprise*, scattered issues, 1879–97; Alfred Nixon, *The Finger Family of Lincoln County with a Brief Sketch of Saint Matthews Church* (1903); M. C. S. Noble, *A History of Public Schools in North Carolina* (1930); North Carolina General Assembly, *Journals*, 1874–96, and *Public Laws*, 1874–96; Banks J. Peeler, *A Story of the Southern Synod of the Evangelical and Reformed Church* (1968).

MARIE D. MOORE

**Finley, James Bradley** *(1 July 1781–6 Sept. 1856)*, minister, was born in North Carolina (place unknown), the son of Robert W. and Rebecca Bradley Finley. Robert Finley was a Presbyterian minister turned Methodist, and three of his sons became Methodist ministers. He was teaching a Latin school at Rocky River (Anson County?) soon after the American Revolution, and it may have been there that his son James was born. The elder Finley was licensed by the Orange Presbytery on 9 Oct. 1783, but he was not then ordained. While James was a young lad, his parents moved to Virginia and then to Kentucky; in 1796 they settled in Ohio near Chillicothe.

James Finley studied medicine but decided he had little aptitude for it. On 3 Mar. 1801, he married Hannah Strane and they went into the backcountry of Highland County, Ohio, where they lived for several years as backwoods farmers, with Finley supplying the meat for their table from regular hunting expeditions. In August following his marriage, he attended the Methodist camp meeting at Cane Ridge, Ky., and experienced conversion. He later felt a powerful call to preach the Gospel, which he ignored and fought against for seven years before finally entering on trial in 1809 the Western Conference of the Methodist Episcopal Church. In Ohio he served large pioneer circuits and after 1816 was appointed time after time as presiding elder of frontier districts. From 1821 to 1827 he served as a missionary among the Wyandott Indians and wrote at length pleading the cause of these native Americans. Later he served for three years as chaplain of the Ohio penitentiary.

In 1844, Finley was a delegate to the General Conference of the Methodist Episcopal Church where he was the author of the resolution calling for the deposition of Bishop James O. Andrew. The adoption of this resolution led finally to the great division of the church, and Finley was named one of the commissioners to act with a like body from the southern church to define the equity the South might have in the denomination's publication revenues should the annual conferences adopt the plan of separation.

Among the books written by Finley were *Autobiography . . . or Pioneer Life in the West*, *Wyandott Mission*, *Sketches of Western Methodism*, *Life Among the Indians*, and *Memorials of Prison Life*, all of which contain invaluable information about frontier life.

Finley died at Eaton, Ohio, and was buried in a rural cemetery at the outskirts of that village.

SEE: Cincinnati Conference, Methodist Episcopal Church, *Minutes*, 1857; Nolan B. Harmon, ed., *Encyclopedia of World Methodism* (1974); W. P. Strickland, ed., *Autobiography of Rev. James B. Finley; or, Pioneer Life in the West* (1853).

LOUISE L. QUEEN

**Finley, Robert Corpening** *(7 Nov. 1905–24 Mar. 1976)*, musician, attorney, and judge, was born in Marion, the son of Robert Sylvester, a pharmacist, and

Willie Corpening Finley. He and his brother, Frank A. ("Buzz"), were reared in Asheville and attended Asheville High School. Finley began his undergraduate studies at the University of Florida but completed his bachelor of arts degree in English at Duke University in 1930. Then turning his talents to music, he formed a jazz band that he advertised as "Not the Best Band in the World, but a Good Band." After filling engagements up and down the Atlantic Coast, he joined Hal Kemp's orchestra. During the 1930s Finley returned to Duke and in 1934 earned the bachelor of law degree; he then entered private practice in Chattanooga, Tenn. After further study at Georgetown University, he was awarded the LL.M. degree in 1936.

Returning to his native state, Finley worked for the North Carolina prison system as a probation officer. He also served for a time as an attorney for the Federal Alcohol Control Administration of the U.S. Department of Justice. Later he served as chief enforcement attorney and then director of food enforcement for the U.S. Office of Price Administration. In 1940, he moved to the state of Washington and became assistant attorney general; when World War II began, he went to work for the Office of Price Administration in that state. As a prosecutor, he dealt with all infringements on the jurisdiction of the state OPA and soon expanded his jurisdiction to cover federal cases as well.

In 1951, Finley was elected to the Washington State Supreme Court where he was one of the founders of the Bench-Bar-Press Committee to work for a more cooperative, responsible relationship among the judicial institutions and a better public understanding of the judicial system. He remained on the supreme court for twenty-five years and served two terms as chief justice. At his death, the courts housed in the Washington Temple of Justice established the Robert C. Finley Memorial to provide scholarships for law students receiving special training in the area of administrative law, which had been Finley's major interest and field of study.

On 4 Dec. 1937 Finley married Werdner Phillips, daughter of Andrew Johan and Mary Gaddy Phillips of Olympia, Wash. For a time they made their home in Asheville, N.C., where their first child, Patricia, was born. They were also the parents of two other children, Mary Ellen and Robert Andrew. Finley was a member of the Methodist Church.

SEE: *Alumni Directory Duke University School of Law* (1961); *Asheville Citizen*, 26 Mar. 1976; *Asheville Times*, 18 Sept. 1950; Duke University alumni records, Durham; Olympia, Wash., *News Tribune*, 25 Mar. 1976; Raleigh *News and Observer*, 19 Apr. 1967; *Seattle Times*, 13 June 1971.

F. CRAIG WILLIS

**Fish, Sewall Lawrence.** *See* **Fremont, Sewall Lawrence.**

**Fisher, Charles** *(20 Oct. 1789–7 May 1849)*, congressman and speaker of the House of Commons was born near Salisbury, the son of Frederick Fisher, who moved to Rowan from Shenandoah County, Va., before the American Revolution and served in the militia during that war. The son was educated by tutors, among whom were John Robinson of Cabarrus County and William McPheeters of Raleigh. He studied law but never practiced that profession. Fisher began his public career when elected to the state senate from Rowan County in 1818. At the end of that year, however, he defeated a Dr. W. Jones in a special election to fill the seat vacated by Congressman George Mumford of the Salisbury District upon his death. Two years later he won reelection by defeating John Long. He declined to be a candidate for a third term. In Congress he served on the public buildings, manufactures, elections, and public lands committees. During his brief tenure in Washington he became a strong supporter of John C. Calhoun.

Returning to North Carolina, Fisher was elected to represent the borough of Salisbury in the House of Commons. During the next fifteen years he was returned to the house seven times by Salisbury and four times by Rowan County, and in the sessions of 1830 and 1831 he was speaker of the house. In the legislature Fisher supported western interests. In 1821 he introduced resolutions calling for a constitutional convention that might shift more power to the western part of the state. In 1823 he was a leader in a constitutional reform convention held in Raleigh. By 1829 he was supported by western legislators as their candidate for U.S. senator, but Bedford Brown obtained the post. When the constitutional convention finally met in 1835, Fisher represented Rowan County.

Fisher was ardent in whatever cause he undertook and was usually loved or hated. As early as 1822 he supported the presidential aspirations of Calhoun. In December 1823 he attempted to block the Roanoke forces and their campaign to elevate W. H. Crawford to the presidency. In the House of Commons he introduced the Fisher Resolutions denouncing the nomination of presidents by caucus, but the resolutions failed to pass. In 1828 he supported a Jackson-Calhoun coalition against Adams, but when Calhoun later broke with Jackson, Fisher followed his leader in opposing Jackson's administration. Fisher was a delegate to the Philadelphia antitariff convention of 1831, a leader of the Barbour forces in 1832, and an open supporter of nullification by 1833. Nullification was such an explosive issue in Rowan County that David Caldwell challenged Fisher to a duel, which fortunately never occurred.

By 1834 Fisher was willing to become a Whig if the Whigs would support Calhoun, but the Whigs were reluctant to oblige and Fisher eventually joined the southern wing of the Democrats. In 1838 he returned to the hustings, again campaigning under the Democratic banner, and defeated Dr. Pleasant Henderson in a bitter congressional contest by fewer than two hundred votes. Once more he took his place on the elections and public lands committees on which he had served long ago. He was not a candidate to succeed himself in 1840, but in 1844 he was persuaded to run again against Daniel M. Barringer. He was defeated by fewer than fifty votes, the first time he had ever lost a popular election. Although he was approached in 1846 as a possible Democratic gubernatorial candidate, he declined to run.

Charles Fisher married Christine Beard, daughter of Lewis Beard and granddaughter of John Lewis Beard. She died in 1848. The following year the old congressman died while on a business trip and was buried in Hillsboro, Miss., survived by two daughters and a son. The son, Charles F. Fisher, served a term in the state senate from Rowan County and died in the Battle of First Manassas fighting for the states' rights his father had so fervently championed.

SEE: *Biog. Dir. Am. Cong.* (1971); John L. Cheney, Jr., ed., *North Carolina Government, 1585–1974* (1975); Charles Fisher Papers (Southern Historical Collection,

University of North Carolina, Chapel Hill); W. S. Hoffmann, *Andrew Jackson and North Carolina Politics* (1971); Daniel M. McFarland, "Rip Van Winkle: Political Evolution in North Carolina, 1815–1835" (Ph.D. diss., University of Pennsylvania, 1954); Albert R. Newsome, *The Presidential Election of 1824 in North Carolina* (1939).

DANIEL M. MCFARLAND

**Fisher, Charles Frederick** *(26 Dec. 1816–21 July 1861),* president of the North Carolina Railroad, politician, and soldier, was born in Salisbury, the only son of Charles and Christine Beard Fisher. His grandfather, Frederick Fisher, migrated to western North Carolina from Shenandoah County, Va., and was a militia officer during the American Revolution. His mother was the daughter of Lewis Beard and Susan Dunn, whose father, John Dunn, was a lawyer and ardent Tory; her father was the son of John Lewis Beard, a pioneer settler of Salisbury. While Charles Frederick Fisher was still an infant his father, aged twenty-nine in 1818, began his twenty-eight-year political career.

In the fall of 1835 young Fisher entered Yale, but, whether from homesickness or youth's characteristic impatience to "succeed," he did not complete his freshman year. He returned to Salisbury and concurrently became a farmer, a miner, and a journalist. For many years he was copublisher of the *Western Carolinian*, an opportunity that he seized evidently for the emulation and development of his father's political qualities. He worked faithfully for the Democratic party, then on the ascendancy in the state, but not until 1854 was he elected to public office as state senator from Rowan County.

The following year, even though by experience he was not qualified, he was elected president of the North Carolina Railroad, succeeding John M. Morehead. Three years later, while still holding this office, he was the contractor for the extension of the road to Morganton. His election as head of the road was totally unexpected and his management caused so much criticism that Jonathan Worth organized and headed an investigative committee. When Fisher forcefully protested the committee's report, Chairman Worth found his rebuttal "insolent and insulting." However, the report was not the unanimous opinion of the committee. One member refused to sign because "it is greatly wanting in thoroughness, completeness and impartiality."

Though Jonathan Worth personally continued to attack Fisher in the press and in public speeches, in July 1859 Fisher was again elected president of the railroad by an all but unanimous vote, including that of the largest Whig stockholders. This election was Fisher's vindication and the controversy aroused by Worth subsided. It was during this period that Fisher and S. L. Fremont, chief engineer and superintendent of the Wilmington and Weldon road in Eastern North Carolina, became close friends.

When hostilities began between North and South, Fisher immediately volunteered for Confederate service. Elected colonel of the sixth North Carolina Regiment, he was killed in the Battle of First Manassas while serving under General Thomas Lanier Clingman. The following month S. L. Fremont, then a colonel in the North Carolina state militia, assumed command of coastal defenses and planned the fortification at Federal Point on the Cape Fear River, which he named Fort Fisher in honor of his fallen friend.

Fisher married Elizabeth Ruth Caldwell, the daughter of David F. Caldwell (1790–1867) and Fanny Alexander Caldwell, the daughter of William Lee Alexander. Of this marriage there were three children who were reared by their aunt, Christine Fisher, after the death of their father. Their daughter, Frances, under the pen name Christian Reid, was the author of *The Land of the Sky*, a story of mountainous western North Carolina, and other novels. Though the Fishers were Lutheran, Christine Fisher became a Roman Catholic in 1860, much to the distress of "wealthy and influential relatives" who warned her: "we hope your self-respect, your interest in the moral and religious welfare of the orphans and your love for your brother's name will deter you from impressing on their tender minds a creed professed only by a few low and ignorant foreigners."

SEE: *Documents: Executive and Legislative Session 1858–59* nos. 71 and 74 (1859); J. G. deR. Hamilton, ed., *Correspondence of Jonathan Worth*, 2 vols. (1909); J. J. O'Connell, *Catholicity in the Carolinas and Georgia* (1879); Jethro Rumple, *History of Rowan County* (1881); John H. Wheeler, *Reminiscences and Memoirs of North Carolina and Eminent North Carolinians* (1884).

D. F. GRANT

**Fisher, Edward Carrington** *(16 Nov. 1809–12 Jan. 1890),* physician and hospital administrator, was a native of Richmond, Va., and one of ten children born to Ann Ambler and George Fisher. His aunt, Mary Willis Ambler, was the wife of Chief Justice John Marshall. From 1824 to 1828 he attended Hampden-Sydney College and was graduated with the A.B. and M.D. degrees. He also studied medicine at the University of Maryland in 1831. Fisher practiced in Richmond and Staunton, Va., until 1849, when he was appointed assistant physician to the superintendent of the Western Lunatic Asylum in Staunton. The superintendent of the asylum, Dr. Francis T. Stribling, was the adviser to the legislative commission establishing the North Carolina Asylum for the Insane in Raleigh, and Virginia officials charged that he had hired Fisher for "the admitted purpose of qualifying him to fill an office in a similar institution in a neighboring state." An investigating committee of the Virginia asylum's trustees found no reason for censure of Fisher's appointment, and he served for eighteen months.

On 1 Oct. 1853, upon Stribling's recommendation, Fisher was appointed superintendent of construction and medical superintendent of the North Carolina Asylum for the Insane at a yearly salary of $1,200. He succeeded Dr. Edmund Strudwick, of Hillsborough, who had served as interim superintendent in overseeing the construction of the hospital. The hospital, designed by the noted New York architect Alexander Jackson Davis, was among the most modern in the nation and was equipped with its own gas lighting and steam heating plants. During its construction, Fisher traveled as far as Boston to compare and inspect other hospitals. To obtain additional insights on the details of constructing, equipping, and staffing the hospital, he visited and frequently corresponded with Dorothea Dix, the country's leading proponent for the improved care of the mentally ill and the original instigator for the North Carolina asylum.

Upon his arrival in 1853, Fisher found the hospital in a financially unstable condition. It was due to his efforts that an $80,000 bond was raised to complete and furnish the asylum, and that legislation was enacted providing the asylum with a steady income from county land and poll taxes. The hospital admitted its first patient under Fisher in February 1856; by the outbreak of the Civil War there were 195 patients. In recognition of his work at the hospital, Fisher was elected to membership in the North Carolina Medical Society in 1857.

During the Civil War the asylum continued to operate under Fisher's guidance, although it faced many "difficulties and embarrassments" because Raleigh merchants refused to honor state-issued money. Upon the federal occupation of Raleigh the asylum suffered a serious loss in the destruction of the wall that enclosed the asylum grounds, forcing the patients to be kept indoors. Fisher, however, applied to Union Major General John M. Schofield, who repaired the damage and—along with General Jacob D. Cox and General Thomas H. Ruger—kept the asylum supplied with provisions.

In April 1865, Fisher's contract as superintendent was renewed for seven years by the provisional state government. But the Reconstruction legislature of 1868 declared Fisher's office vacant, and he "resigned" to be replaced by Dr. Eugene Grissom. Returning to Virginia, Fisher became an assistant physician at the Western Lunatic Asylum in Staunton in 1871. He served at this institution until his death, except for the period from 1881 to 1884 when Virginia Reconstruction politics caused his removal. At the time of his death, Fisher was assistant superintendent of the asylum.

Fisher and his wife, Lavinia Page Fisher, had six children: George, Charles, Eliza, Ann, John Page, and Edward Carrington. Fisher was a Democrat and an Episcopalian. He died in Staunton, but his funeral service was held at St. James Episcopal Church in Richmond where he was buried in Hollywood Cemetery.

SEE: George D. Fisher, *Descendants of Jacquelin Ambler* (1890); *General Catalog of the Officers and Students of Hampden-Sydney College, 1776–1906* (n.d.); House Bill No. 31, North Carolina Legislative Documents, 1858–59 (North Carolina Collection, University of North Carolina, Chapel Hill); Margaret C. McCullock, "Founding the North Carolina Asylum for the Insane," *North Carolina Historical Review* 13 (1936); "Report of the Superintendent of the Insane Asylum," North Carolina Constitutional Convention Documents, 1865–66 (North Carolina Collection, University of North Carolina, Chapel Hill); *Staunton* (Va.) *Vindicator*, 19 Jan. 1890; *Virginia Medical Monthly* 16 (1890); Stephen B. Weeks Scrapbook, vol. 2 (North Carolina Collection, University of North Carolina, Chapel Hill); Western Lunatic Asylum, *Annual Reports* (1850, 1873, 1884, 1889), and *Report of the Investigating Committee* (1851); *William and Mary College Quarterly* 15 (1906); Richard D. Wills, Medical Librarian, Western State Hospital, Staunton, Va., correspondence with author, May-June 1978.

J. MARSHALL BULLOCK

**Fisher, Frances Christine.** *See* **Tiernan, Frances Christine Fisher.**

**Fitch, William Edwards** *(20 May 1867–12 Sept. 1949)*, physician and author, was born in Burlington, the son of William James Fitch, a farmer, and Mary Elizabeth King Fitch. He was a descendant of Thomas Fitch, who came to America in 1637 and settled in Norwalk, Conn. Fitch received his secondary education in the Burlington public schools, went on to earn the M.D. degree from the College of Physicians and Surgeons of Baltimore in 1891, and did postgraduate work at the New York University Medical College. He then returned to North Carolina, where he established successive practices in Graham, Burlington, and Durham. On 5 Oct. 1892, in Salisbury, he married Minnie Crump; they had three children: Lucille, Elizabeth, and William Edward.

In 1897 Fitch moved to Savannah, Ga., where he continued to practice until 1904, when he moved to New York City to remain until 1916. Fitch was a specialist in metabolic diseases, medical hydrology, and dietotherapy. From 1907 to 1909 he lectured on the principles of surgery at Fordham University, and from 1907 to 1916 he was the attending gynecologist at the outpatient clinic of Presbyterian Hospital in New York City, the attending physician at Vanderbilt Clinic, and an assistant in surgical clinics at St. Luke's Hospital.

Fitch served with the military in different capacities during the Spanish-American War and World War I. In the former, he was acting assistant surgeon of the U.S. Public Health Service and served in the Marine Health Service (1898). On 3 July 1912 he became first lieutenant of the Medical Reserve Corps, U.S. Army, rising to captain on 16 July 1917 and to major on 25 Sept. 1917. After serving as commanding officer of the base hospitals at Fort Terry, Fort Totten, and Fort Schuyler, N.Y., Fitch became chief nutritionist and director of mess at the base hospital at Camp Jackson, S.C. Later he was an adviser to the surgeon's office at Camp Jackson. He was honorably discharged on 3 Dec. 1918.

In 1931, Fitch became medical director and consultant medical hydrologist at the Fort Lick (Ind.) Springs resort. From 1932 to 1935, he served in a similar capacity at the Crazy Hotel and Spa in Mineral Wells, Tex.

Deeply involved in medical publishing, Fitch was editor of *Gaillard's Southern Medicine* from 1900 to 1909 and editor of *Pediatrics* from 1908 to 1917. During the period 1918–19, he was coeditor and publisher of the *American Journal of Electrotherapeutics and Radiology*. He also wrote extensively about the state and local history of North Carolina. Among his books and papers are *The Battle of Alamance, Some Neglected History of North Carolina, Some Things North Carolina Did and Did First in Establishing American Independence, The First Founders of America, The Origin, Rise and Fall of the State of Franklin, Fitch's Medical Pocket Formulary, Dietotherapy, Great American Spas*, and *Diseases of Metabolism*.

Fitch was president of the Alamance Battleground Commission and a member of the Society of Cincinnati, the Society of Foreign Wars, the Society of Colonial Wars, the Society of the Sons of the American Revolution, the Medical Society of Greater New York, and the American, Virginia, and Indiana state medical associations.

He was a Democrat and an Episcopalian. During his later years he returned to Burlington and remained there until 1948, when he moved to Coral Gables, Fla., to live with a daughter until his death. Fitch was buried in the cemetery of the Episcopal Church of the Holy Comforter, Burlington.

SEE: *Nat. Cyc. Am. Biog.*, vol. 38 (1953); *Who Was Who in America*, vol. 2 (1950).

JAMES D. GILLESPIE

**FitzGerald, Frederick** *(1825–31 Aug. 1866)*, Episcopal clergyman and Confederate chaplain, was born in London but came to North Carolina at an early age and was reared in the family of Josiah Collins at Scuppernong. FitzGerald became a candidate for holy orders in 1847 during the episcopate of the Right Reverend Levi S. Ives, bishop of North Carolina. He attended Berkeley Divinity School, then studied in Middletown, Conn. After further preparation for the ministry at Valle Crucis, N.C., he was ordained to the diaconate by Bishop Ives at St. Paul's Church, Edenton, on 29 Apr. 1851. Immediately, he was sent to Northampton County to take charge of the Church of the Saviour at Jackson. While there he lived with the planter Henry K. Burgwyn at his estate, Thornbury, and tutored the Burgwyn children. When Bishop Ives defected to the Roman Catholic church in 1852, there was no bishop in the diocese to ordain FitzGerald to the priesthood. Consequently, at the request of the standing committee, the Right Reverend John Williams, assistant bishop of Connecticut, ordained him in Christ Church, Philadelphia, on 4 Sept. 1853. During this period, the young clergyman served congregations at Jackson, Halifax, and Occoneechee Neck. The latter group consisted of some of Burgwyn's slaves who met in a chapel at Thornbury. FitzGerald also held services periodically at Murfreesboro and Woodville. It seems to have been his practice to write a history of his parish, and in some cases these survive in manuscript in the front of the parish register.

In 1855 FitzGerald was called to become rector of the Episcopal congregation at Goldsboro, where he was largely responsible for the construction of St. Stephen's Church. Two years later he was recalled to the Church of the Saviour. He felt, however, that he could not leave St. Stephen's and remained in Goldsboro although he gave the Jackson congregation two Sundays a month for about a year. At the same time he also served St. Mary's Church, Kinston. In 1859 FitzGerald was awarded the master of arts degree honoria causa by Trinity College, Hartford, Conn., in recognition of his outstanding contributions to the growth of the Episcopal church in North Carolina.

In 1860 FitzGerald removed to Raleigh. The census of that year lists his household as consisting of his wife Mary, age twenty-four, a native of Connecticut, daughters Elizabeth and Mary, three and one, respectively, and mulatto domestic Louise Steward, twenty-eight, together with Edward and Lady, four and two, apparently her children. In Raleigh he served in the dual capacity of assistant to Dr. Aldert Smedes at St. Mary's School and editor of the newly established *Church Intelligencer*, one of the three church papers published in the Confederacy at the opening of the Civil War. The first issue appeared on 14 Mar. 1860 under the editorship of FitzGerald. On 6 June he resigned both positions to become a chaplain in the Confederate Army. With the rank of major, he served with the Twelfth North Carolina Regiment and at hospitals in and near Raleigh. A chaplain from Maine, captured during the war and imprisoned in Richmond, was once charged with violating his parole; he cited FitzGerald as a reference on his behalf.

After the war FitzGerald observed that he had "neither occupation or revenue." Consequently, he accepted a call to become rector of Trinity Church, Hoboken, N.J., in November 1865. Less than a year later he was called to the Church of the Advent in Nashville, Tenn. While preparing to accept the post, he was stricken with a fatal heart attack in late August. His funeral was held at Trinity Church, Hoboken, and he was buried in Cedar Hill Cemetery, Hartford, Conn. He was survived by his widow, the former Mary Louisa Jarvis, daughter of the Reverend William J. Jarvis of Hartford. A son, Frederick, was born after his father's death.

SEE: Alumni records, Trinity College, Hartford, Conn.; *Church Intelligencer*, 13, 27 Sept. 1866; *Church Review*, October 1866; Henry W. Lewis, *Northampton Parishes* (1951); Lawrence F. London, "Literature of the Church in the Confederate States," *Historical Magazine of the Protestant Episcopal Church* 17 (1948); *Official Records of the Rebellion*, ser. 2, vol. 2 (1897); Records in the files of the Confederate Roster Project (North Carolina State Archives, Raleigh).

JAMES ELLIOT MOORE

**Fitzgerald, Oscar Penn** *(24 Aug. 1829–5 Aug. 1911)*, Methodist clergyman, editor, educator, and author, was born in Caswell County near Ruffin, the son of Richard and Martha Jones Hooper Fitzgerald. He attended local schools until he was thirteen and then went to Lynchburg, Va., to work for the *Lynchburg Republican* for six years. When his father enlisted for the Mexican War, Oscar returned home and taught in a country school in Rockingham County to help support his mother. After his father's return he worked in newspaper offices in Richmond, Va., Columbia, S.C., and Macon, Ga.

In 1853, Fitzgerald entered the ministry of the Methodist Episcopal Church, South, by way of the Georgia Conference and was stationed at Andrews Chapel in Savannah. In 1854, he married Sarah Banks of Georgia and soon afterward they left for California on a missionary assignment. There he became editor of the *Pacific Methodist Advocate* and the *Christian Spectator*. From 1867 to 1871 he served as state superintendent of education in California; in this position, to which he was elected by popular vote, he was instrumental in the establishment of an institution that has since become the University of California at Berkeley. During this period he offered himself for the Democratic nomination for the U.S. Senate.

In 1878, he went to Nashville, Tenn., headquarters of the Methodist Publishing House, to become editor of the *Nashville Christian Advocate*, the official organ of the southern church. With 25,000 subscribers it had the widest circulation of any newspaper. After twelve years in the post, he and Atticus Greene Haygood (1839–96) were elected bishops of the Methodist Episcopal Church, South. Fitzgerald served from Maryland to California.

He was the author of twenty books. His excellent command of the English language and keen sense of humor, much of it aimed at himself, make his *California Sketches*—first published in 1878 and reprinted many times—lively reading. He produced book-length biographies of Dr. Thomas O. Summers, John B. McFerrin, Judge Augustus B. Longstreet, and others. In politics he demonstrated a "stanch and outspoken allegiance to the Confederacy." His final years were spent on the campus of Vanderbilt University, and he died at Monteagle, Tenn. Because of his "wit, geniality, and sweet Christian spirit," Fitzgerald came to be known as the "St. John of Methodism." For many years one of his sons was a professor at Duke University.

SEE: Edwin A. Alderman and others, eds., *Library of Southern Literature*, vol. 4 (1907); Emory S. Bucke, *The History of American Methodism*, vol. 3 (1964); Elmer T. Clark, *Methodism in Western North Carolina* (1966); Oscar Penn Fitzgerald, *Sunset Views* (1901); Albea Godbold, ed., *Methodist History* (1968); Harold W. Mann, *Atticus Greene Haygood: Methodist Bishop, Editor and Educator* (1965); *New York Times*, 6 Aug. 1911.

GRADY L. E. CARROLL

**Fitzgerald, Robert George** *(24 Oct. 1840–4 Aug. 1919)*, soldier, farmer, educator, and businessman, was born to Thomas Charles Fitzgerald (ca. 1808–79) and Sarah Ann Burton Fitzgerald (ca. 1818–ca. 1889) in New Castle County, Del. Robert earned his freedom at age twenty-four after living in Chester County, Penn., and attending Ashmun Institute (1858), which became Lincoln University. Before that he had studied at the Philadelphia Institute for Colored Youth. In 1861, Fitzgerald served with Union quartermaster troops as a contract laborer driving a four-horse and six-mule team. The following year he was wounded and discharged. Subsequently, he enlisted in the Union navy and served on the bark *William G. Anderson*, which patrolled from the Gulf of Mexico to the lower Mississippi River. On 15 June 1864 he enlisted in the Fifth Massachusetts Cavalry, Company F, where he served until the end of the war.

Concerned with the plight of the southern black, Fitzgerald went south to establish Freedmen Bureau schools in Goldsboro and Hillsborough, N.C. On 8 Aug. 1869 he married Cornelia Smith, mulatto niece of Mary Ruffin Smith, a benefactress of The University of North Carolina. Subsequently, he erected the largest brick structure in Durham, and joined with his brother, Richard B. Fitzgerald, in establishing the first Negro bank (which became the Farmers and Mechanics Bank) and Coleman Manufacturing Company, a cotton mill owned and operated by Negroes. He also participated in the founding of a Negro insurance company. In 1884, the Fitzgerald brick factory produced over two million bricks, and three Fitzgerald brothers participated in major construction projects in the Durham-Chapel Hill area until Robert's war wounds restricted his activities.

Fitzgerald gradually lost his eyesight and retired to the family home in the Maplewood Cemetery section of Durham. After his death, his six children moved to various sections of America where they contributed to science and literature.

SEE: Fitzgerald Family Diary (Southern Historical Collection, University of North Carolina, Chapel Hill); Pauli Murray, *Proud Shoes* (1956).

MARVIN KRIEGER

**Flake, Nancy** *(13 Apr. 1917–15 Dec. 1968)*, radio entertainer with the Columbia Broadcasting System and WABC in New York City and a vocalist with the big bands of Charlie Barnett, Al Kavelin, and Frank Dailey, was the central figure in *Flake v. News Co.*, a case heard by the North Carolina Supreme Court in the fall term of 1937 that established recognition of the tort of invasion of privacy in the state.

Nancy was the daughter of W. F. Flake and his wife, the former Elsie Myrtle Baker. She was educated in the Winston-Salem public schools before preparing for a career as a radio entertainer, beginning with singing lessons at about age thirteen. She first studied music in Winston-Salem, sang on the local radio station, and later went with her mother to New York City where she was coached by Eleanor McClelland for about three years. In New York Nancy also studied sight singing under Miss Johnnie Hereford. Her first big band engagement was with Al Kavelin's orchestra at the Hotel Lexington in New York City. She next appeared as a vocalist with the orchestra of Frank Dailey at the Meadowbrook Club in Cedar Grove, N.J. For a year she toured with Dailey's band in Pennsylvania, New York, Delaware, and North Carolina where they played in Winston-Salem, Sedgefield, Laurinburg, and Durham. During this period she recorded four songs for the Victor Recording Company. She then left Dailey's employ and joined Charlie Barnett's organization at Glenn Island Casino.

Publicity photographs made of Nancy Flake for the use of the Columbia Broadcasting Company appeared in various magazines featuring radio entertainers. One magazine, *Popular Songs*, published a picture of her in a bathing suit and described her as "Nifty Nancy Flake in this fetching attire, proves that singers who have what it takes can be equally alluring flirting with the high seas or the high C's." One of the bathing suit publicity photographs taken by CBS appeared in the *Greensboro Daily News* on 11 Mar. 1936 to advertise a burlesque-type show touring in Greensboro and Winston-Salem. Miss Flake was not identified by her own name but as "Mademoiselle Sally Payne, exotic Red Haired Venus in the touring stage production of Folies de Paree." This advertisement was used to sell Melts Bakery goods, particularly bread, which the advertisement suggested would help one achieve a "Sylphe-like Figure."

When Nancy's sister, Ruth, saw the advertisement, she called her mother. Early that afternoon Mrs. W. F. Flake went to the law firm of Slawter and Wall in Winston-Salem and discussed with John D. Slawter the possibility of a lawsuit. Nancy subsequently received a copy of the *Greensboro Daily News* that had been mailed to her in New York by her mother. In the meantime Mrs. Flake received many telephone calls from friends about Nancy's picture in the advertisement associating her with the tawdry burlesque show.

In Forsyth superior court Nancy testified that she "was hurt more than . . . embarrassed" by the advertisement "and naturally I wrote my mother and explained it to her." Because Nancy was nineteen years old and still a minor, her mother filed a suit entitled *Nancy Flake, by Her Next Friend, Mrs. W. F. Flake v. The Greensboro News Company, North Carolina Theatres, Inc., L. Melts, Trading and Doing Business Under the Style and Firm Name of "Melts Bakery," Anton Scibilia and Nick Boila, Trading and Doing Business Under the Style and Firm Name of "Folies De Paree."*

On 12 Apr. 1937, special judge Frank S. Hill began the trial by jury in Forsyth superior court. Scibilia and Boila could not be found according to the sheriff, Joe S. Phipps, of Guilford County. The other defendants were summoned to appear before Judge Hill. On the all-male jury were Robert Brown, Robert Lee, Charlie T. Ketner, C. R. Whitaker, E. J. James, L. S. Lewis, W. A. Angel, K. D. Mayberry, V. C. Atwood, J. K. Barbee, B. B. Vaughn, and M. A. Nifong. The attorneys for the defendants were Frank P. Hobgood, R. D. Douglas, Sr., Kenneth M. Brim, and John I. Ingle. The attorneys for the plaintiff were John D. Slawter, Roy L. Deal, a Mr. Parrish, and a Mr. Wall.

Despite the fact that on 3 Apr. 1936 the Greensboro News Company had published a retraction described as an "Error in Publication of Portrait in Advertisement," the jury found that the defendants had exposed the plaintiff to ridicule and contempt. Damages of $6,500 were granted to Nancy Flake.

On 17 Apr. 1937 the defendants filed appeals to the North Carolina Supreme Court where the case was heard in the fall term, 1937. The court recognized that the plaintiff's second cause of action was based on the right of privacy. It raised questions, which have since been considered by other U.S. courts, such as free speech and press, libel and slander, distinction between private life and public office, and how these issues can violate the right of privacy of a group or an individual. Although the supreme court ordered a new trial, a final judgment was signed by Mr. Slawter and Colonel Hobgood that Nancy Flake should receive one dollar for damages and the cost of the court action.

The tort of the invasion of privacy was first discussed in an article by Samuel D. Warren and Louis D. Brandeis published in the *Harvard Law Review* in December 1890. Since then interest in the subject has grown and many cases have been based on it. In North Carolina one other case on the invasion of privacy has cited the Flake case. In *Phillip Barr v. Southern Bell Telephone and Telegraph Company*, which was heard by the North Carolina Court of Appeals in the fall term of 1971, a picture of someone else was printed over the plaintiff's name. The court found that the plaintiff's right of privacy had been invaded by his employer and that he would be entitled to nominal damages.

Nancy Flake married B. M. Purtill and by him had two sons.

SEE: William M. Beaney, "The Right to Privacy and American Law," *Law and Contemporary Problems* 31 (Spring 1966); *Biographical Directory of Guilford Bar Association* (1939); Ruth Cash, conversations with the author, 4, 8 Sept. 1981; Consent Final Judgment 99–216 Between Nancy Flake et al. and the Greensboro News Company et al., signed by W. Church, Assistant Clerk, Superior Court of Forsyth County, N.C., 1 Nov. 1938 (Superior Court Civil File No. 11021); E. L. Godkin, "The Rights of the Citizen to His Own Reputation," *Scribner's Magazine*, July 1980; *Greensboro Daily News*, 11 Mar. (photograph), 3 Apr. 1936; Harry Kalven, Jr., "Privacy in Tort Law—Were Warren and Brandeis Wrong?" *Law and Contemporary Problems* 31 (Spring 1966); *Martindale-Hubbell Law Directory*, vols. 3 (1973), 5 (1981); *North Carolina Court of Appeals Reports*, Partin and White, 13; *North Carolina Reports in the Supreme Court*, Fall Term, 1937, vol. 212 (1973); North Carolina Supreme Court Cases No. 744, Fall 1937, *Flake v. Greensboro News* (212 N.C. 780) (North Carolina State Archives, Raleigh); William L. Prosser, *Law of Torts* (1971) and with John W. Wade and Victor E. Schwartz, *Tort Cases and Materials* (1976); Samuel D. Warren and Louis D. Brandeis, "The Right to Privacy," *Harvard Law Review* 4 (December 1890).

VERNON O. STUMPF

**Flanagan, Edward Gaskill** *(3 Dec. 1875–17 June 1942)*, businessman and politician, was born in Greenville, the son of John Flanagan and Mary Wise Gaskill. After completing his education at the Greenville Academy, he went to Texas where for two years he worked on a ranch near San Antonio. He returned to Greenville to head the John Flanagan Buggy Company established by his father. The company successfully made the transition to the automobile age by becoming Greenville's Ford dealership and in 1934 sold more Ford automobiles than any other dealer. Flanagan was also president of the Twin County Motor Company, the Ford dealer in Rocky Mount. As the John Flanagan Buggy Company also made and sold coffins, Flanagan studied embalming in Georgia and became a funeral director. He served as president of the North Carolina Funeral Directors and Embalmers Association from 1909 to 1910 and helped both to create the State Board of Embalmers and to institute the examining and licensing of undertakers and embalmers. He was the first to take the test and to be licensed.

From 1915 until his death Flanagan was president of the Guarantee Bank and Trust Company in Greenville (now merged with Wachovia) and a director of the Wachovia Bank and Trust Company. He was the founder and first president of Carolina Sales Corporation of Greenville as well as a director of the Occidental Life Insurance Company and of the Reconstruction Finance Corporation of Charlotte. He served on the Greenville City School Board (1915–42) and was a charter member of the board of trustees for East Carolina Teachers College (now East Carolina University), serving as vice-chairman of the board and as chairman of the building committee. Flanagan Building was named in his honor.

A Democrat, Flanagan served four terms (1927–29 and 1931–33) in the North Carolina House of Representatives and one term (1937) in the North Carolina Senate. There he supported the growth of East Carolina, the improvement of highways, the reform of prisons, and the expansion of institutions for the tubercular. He was an opponent of slot machines and the law forbidding them bears his name. A delegate to the Democratic national conventions of 1928, 1932, and 1936, Flanagan, who was a Baptist, actively supported Al Smith in 1928.

On 18 Oct. 1899 he married Rosa Mildred Hooker. They had six children: E. Graham, Rosamond (Mrs. Tyrus Wagner), John, Charles, William, and Gertrude. The latter two died in infancy. Flanagan was buried in Cherry Hill Cemetery, Greenville. Portraits of him are in the possession of Mrs. E. Graham Flanagan, Sr., and Mrs. Tyrus Wagner, both of Greenville.

SEE: "From Buggies to Autos," *State Magazine* 13 (18 Aug. 1945); *Greenville Daily Reflector*, 18 Oct. 1899; *Greenville News Leader*, 18 June 1942; R. C. Lawrence, "Colonel Ed," *State Magazine* 11 (15 Apr. 1944); Wade H. Lucas, "Legislative Personalities: No. 34, E. G. Flanagan," *State Magazine* 2 (2 June 1934); *North Carolina Biography*, vol. 5 (1941).

JOHN D. NEVILLE

**Flanagan, John** *(6 Feb. 1829–10 July 1902)*, manufacturer, was born in Pitt County, the son of Thomas Flanagan (d. 1831) and Sophia Turnage (d. 1829). After completing his apprenticeship at the Nelson Carriage Factory in Greenville, Flanagan worked in Washington where on 5 Dec. 1855 he married Mary Wise Gaskill (24 Aug. 1841–24 Apr. 1926), daughter of John Stanley Gaskill (1817–48) and Mary Ann Liverman (1818–81). In 1856 he moved to Hamilton where he set up his own business. Six years later he enlisted in the Seventeenth North Carolina Regiment in which he served until the end of the war. His business having been destroyed in General J. G. Foster's raid, Flanagan in 1868 moved to Greenville where he established the John Flanagan Buggy Company. By 1896 the company produced an average of one vehicle per day; it also manufactured and sold coffins.

Active in local affairs, Flanagan served terms as Greenville town commissioner and Pitt County commissioner, tax collector, and treasurer. Elected mayor of Greenville, he declined the honor because he did not have time to devote to the post. He was the father of eleven children: John Gaskill, Florence (Mrs. George Dancey), Sophia (Mrs. Edward H. Shelburn), John William, Laura, Charles, Roy Chetwynd, Edward Gaskill, Blanche (Mrs. James F. Davenport), Anna Doris (Mrs. Benjamin E. Patrick), and Lela. A Baptist, Flanagan was buried in Cherry Hill Cemetery, Greenville. A charcoal portrait of him is in the possession of the family.

SEE: *Greenville Daily Reflector*, 5, 29 June 1896, 11, 12 July 1902.

JOHN D. NEVILLE

**Flannagan, Eric Goodyear** *(18 July 1892–15 Apr. 1970)*, architect and engineer, was born in Albemarle County, Va., of Irish, Dutch, and English ancestry. His father was Broadus Flannagan, son of Benjamin Collins and Ann Virginia Timberlake Flannagan; his mother was Lottie Goodyear Flannagan, daughter of George C. and Elizabeth Van Antwerp Briscoe Flannagan. Young Eric grew up in Lynchburg and Charlottesville, and at age fifteen entered the Miller Manual Training School in Albemarle County where he became proficient in mechanical drawing. His father died in 1910 leaving him without family support; needing additional credits for graduation, he became a part-time teacher of drawing for two years. He was graduated in 1912 as president of his class and subsequently served two years as head teacher in the school's Mechanical Drawing Department.

Flannagan's summer work experiences in 1912 and 1913 as one of two hundred draftsmen at the American Locomotive Works, Schenectady, N.Y., and as a maker of Patent Office drawings for a Washington, D.C., patent attorney led to his employment as resident engineer with the West Virginia Pulp and Paper Company (Westvaco Corporation) in Covington, Va. Remaining with the firm eight years, he later became superintendent of construction and head of the engineering department and at times had as many as four engineers and a thousand construction workers working under him. In 1922 he moved with his wife and young family to Henderson, N.C., to set up his own business as a consulting engineer. In 1926 he established an architectural and engineering firm, having by this time obtained licenses to practice in both fields in Virginia as well as in North Carolina after additional private study through the International Correspondence School.

An active member and officeholder in the North Carolina chapter of the American Institute of Architects, Flannagan had been one of the leaders of the parent organization who worked for the national charter. In 1951 he was appointed a member of the State Board of Architectural Examination and Registration by Governor W. Kerr Scott; he served until 1956 and as vice-president from 1955 to 1956. During his years of practice, his office was recommended by the Department of Architectural Engineering at North Carolina State College as one that would provide the experience necessary to obtain a license and registration certificate to practice in the state.

For the most part Flannagan's architectural commissions consisted of institutional buildings in the health and education fields, although he also designed churches and commercial and residential buildings. For the periods stated he was the architect for all or most of the construction at North Carolina Sanatorium, McCain (1925–50); Caswell Training School, Kinston (1938–51); and East Carolina College, Greenville (1938–64), where his structures included the Flanagan Building (named for Edward G. Flanagan, chairman of the college trustees), Joyner Library, and dormitories totaling 2,064 beds (Slay, Umstead, Jones, Scott, and Aycock). He was also the architect for buildings at Asheboro, including Asheboro High School, Randolph Hospital, Acme-McCrary Recreation Building; hospitals at Sanford, Concord, Lenoir, Graham, Siler City, Dunn, Oxford, Burlington, Roanoke Rapids, and Henderson; school buildings in ten counties—Halifax, Northampton, Lee, Granville, Edgecombe, Pitt, Craven, Martin, Randolph, and Vance, where the Henderson High School built in 1934 received statewide attention; three dozen residences in the eastern part of the state; and churches in Williamston, Hamilton, Oxford, and Henderson. Two distinctive stone structures in Henderson are the Gothic-style First Methodist Church and the colonial-style Stonewall Apartments. In 1965 Flannagan retired from full-time practice and served until his death as a consultant to the architect-engineer partnership of his two sons.

Flannagan was a Mason, Rotarian (past president), and member of the Henderson Chamber of Commerce. At the Holy Innocents Episcopal Church he served as a vestry member, church school superintendent, and men's Bible class president. On 26 June 1915 he married Beryl Morris, and they were the parents of three children: Eric, Jr., Stephen, and Effie Louise (Mrs. Robert Dortch Baskervill). His wife died in 1968, and on 5 Sept. 1969 he married Clara Hamlett Robertson, the widow of one of his Miller School contemporaries. He was buried in Elmwood Cemetery, Henderson, Vance County.

SEE: Documents and letters of Eric G. Flannagan, Sr. (on file in the office of Eric G. Flannagan and Sons, Architects-Engineers, Henderson); *Henderson Daily Dispatch*, 16 Apr. 1970.

CLARA H. FLANNAGAN

**Fletcher, (Minna) Inglis** *(20 Oct. 1879–30 May 1969)*, novelist, was born in Alton, Ill., of English ancestry, the daughter of Maurice William and Flora Deane Chapman Clark. Her great-grandfather was Joseph Chapman of Tyrell County, N.C. From public schools in Edwardsville, Ill., she attended the School of Fine Arts of Washington University in St. Louis, Mo., intending to become a sculptor. After her marriage to John George Fletcher, a mining engineer from Colorado, she went with him to sparsely settled areas in Alaska, the state of Washington, and California, where, during one five-year period when he was "experting mines" in the Shasta country, she moved twenty-one times in five years. His often sudden departures explain the title of her autobiography; the wife of an engineer was left behind to "pay, pack, and follow." The Fletchers' first "permanent" homes were in Spokane, Wash., where they spent about eight years, and then in San Francisco where they lived for thirteen years (1925–38).

In San Francisco Mrs. Fletcher operated a lecture bureau, presenting such celebrities as the writers John Erskine and Will Durant and the explorers Lowell Thomas and Vilhjalmur Stefansson, the last of whom she had known in Spokane. One of her first attempts at serious writing was a novel about the freeholder in Alaska, but she destroyed the manuscript when the publisher returned it for revision. She then contemplated a book on witchcraft and resolved to go to Africa for first-hand investigation. At the invitation of Rodney Wood, a Nyasaland game warden whom she had met in Spokane, Mrs. Fletcher set forth in 1928 on a seven-month trip to British Central Africa. During her stay, Wood organized a *ulendo* (hunting expedition) for her into the primitive bush country. Back in San Francisco, she put aside the poems and notes written in Africa and allotted herself three years to complete a novel. *The White Leopard*

(1931), a Junior Literary Guild selection for older boys, was based on the adventurous life of Rodney Wood. This was followed by *Red Jasmine* (1932), an adult novel with autobiographical overtones set in a colonial African town similar to Blantyre.

At this point, while on a casual genealogical search for her Tyrell County forebears, she came upon some tantalizing passages in the *Colonial Records of North Carolina*. A North Carolina story, she decided, would be her next effort. More reading among the old wills, inventories, and court records sidetracked her first plan for a novel on Lord Cornwallis. After two trips to North Carolina in 1934 and 1937, four long-hand drafts, and six years of helpful advice and cooperation from her scholarly editor D. Laurance Chambers of Bobbs-Merrill, she published *Raleigh's Eden* (1940), a brightly panoramic historical novel of heroic North Carolinians from 1765 to 1782, centering on the plantation families of the Albemarle as they faced head-on the events of revolution. Famous names from history mingled among the fictional characters. This first publication of a novel since Thomas Wolfe's *Look Homeward, Angel* eleven years earlier produced much excitement among readers in the state, who alternately praised Mrs. Fletcher for finally awarding North Carolina what they considered its significant, rightful role in the American Revolution and condemned her for "errors" in history. To placate the latter, she participated in a public meeting and countered each accusation with documentary quotations.

The writing of *Raleigh's Eden* was completed at Balboa Beach, Calif., where the Fletchers had moved after leaving San Francisco. A lengthy stay at the Joseph Hewes Hotel in Edenton was spent proofreading. Rarely thereafter was Inglis Fletcher not employed in planning and writing the next book of her twelve-volume Carolina Series about early North Carolina. Her schedule was one year of research and one year of writing. During 1941–42 she and her husband, at the invitation of Mrs. George Wood of Greenfield in Chowan County, lived at an abandoned fishery on Albemarle Sound. In 1943, when Fletcher was with the wartime shipyards in Wilmington, they rented Clarendon, a river house on historic land on the lower Cape Fear, where she determinedly pursued her research and writing. In December 1944 the Fletchers purchased Bandon, a plantation mansion on the Chowan River thirteen miles northwest of Edenton. The house, which was badly in need of repairs, dated from 1800. Among the many smaller buildings on the grounds was a schoolhouse from an earlier period.

During the next decades the Fletchers were proud and active Tar Heels, participating in the annual Valentine's Day hunt at Nags Head and serving on the Governor's Highway Safety Committee. In 1949 Inglis Fletcher was awarded a Litt.D. degree by the Womans College of The University of North Carolina. She promoted interest in establishing the Elizabethan Gardens on Roanoke Island, and she was named to the Tryon Palace Commission and the Richard Caswell Memorial Commission. In 1964 she was one of the first citizens to receive the prestigious North Carolina Award. Her citation read that because of her "no longer can it be said that our colonial and Revolutionary heroes are unknown; for, within the pages of her books, they have found a new life and a new grandeur." During these years, she and her husband were certain to be present at almost every meeting of a literary or historical group in the state.

The death of John Fletcher on 25 June 1960, and the burning of Bandon on 6 Oct. 1963, altered the pattern of Inglis Fletcher's life. From time to time she lived with her sister, Jean (Mrs. Lloyd Chenoweth), in Perquimans County; with her son, John Stuart Fletcher, a graduate of Annapolis and retired commander of the U.S. Navy, in Charleston, S.C.; and with her grandson, J. S. Fletcher, in Chapel Hill and Greenville.

The Carolina Series, with one title or another translated into seven languages, and with millions of hardbound and paperback copies sold in the United States, had a common theme. According to the author, they attempted to show—over a period of two hundred years—the joint struggle of the common man and the gentle born to establish sound government in a wilderness. The time span is from 1585 to the ratification of the Constitution in 1789. *Raleigh's Eden*, which focused on the causes and events of the Revolution, was followed by *Men of Albemarle*, (1942), on the evolution of law and order in the colony during the Queen Anne period (1710–12); *Lusty Wind for Carolina* (1944), on the expansion of trade and the elimination of pirates from the coastal waters (1718–25); *Toil of the Brave* (1946), on the critical contests of the Revolution and the climactic battle of Kings Mountain (1778–80); *Roanoke Hundred* (1948), on Sir Walter Raleigh's first unsuccessful attempt to plant an English colony in the New World (1585–86); *Bennett's Welcome* (1950), on the migration of permanent settlers to North Carolina down from the James River settlements (1651–52); *Queen's Gift* (1952), on the struggle for constitutional liberties following the Revolutionary War (1783–89); *The Scotswoman* (1955), on the Whig patriots' fight with the Scottish loyalists under Flora Macdonald (1774–76); *The Wind in the Forest* (1957), on defining individual liberty as symbolized by the confrontation between Governor William Tryon and the backwoods Regulators (1770–71); *Cormorant's Brood* (1959), on the formation of responsible government in the Albemarle (1725–31); *Wicked Lady* (1962), on the last years of the war along the Albemarle (1781–82); and *Rogue's Harbor* (1964), on the initial protest of settlers against the irresponsible agents of British officials (1677–89). Within the accepted traditions of historical fiction, these twelve novels aptly blended intricate plots and love stories with actual personages and events of the past. Some of Mrs. Fletcher's favorite characters appeared from book to book, and a leading figure in *Toil of the Brave* was the grandfather of a heroine in *Raleigh's Eden*. In the best sense, the books were "popular" historical novels.

Mrs. Fletcher was a Democrat and an Episcopalian. In 1964 she donated her oil portrait by the North Carolina artist William C. Fields to Fletcher Hall at East Carolina University on the occasion of the dedication of a new woman's dormitory named for her. She died in Edenton. She and her husband were buried in the National Cemetery, Wilmington.

SEE: Inglis Fletcher, *Pay, Pack, and Follow: The Story of My Life* (1959); Inglis Fletcher Papers (Manuscript Collection, Library, East Carolina University, Greenville); Harrison G. Platt, *Inglis Fletcher of Bandon, Chronicler of North Carolina* (1946); Richard Walser, *Inglis Fletcher of Bandon Plantation* (1952); *Who's Who in America*, 1952–53.

RICHARD WALSER

**Flowers, Robert Lee** *(6 Nov. 1870–24 Aug. 1951)*, educator and university administrator, was born at York Collegiate Institute in Alexander County, the son of George Washington and Sarah Jane Haynes Flowers. His father, a onetime instructor at the institute, entered the mercantile business in nearby Taylorsville, where the family moved in 1883. Robert, the eldest of nine children, was graduated from Taylorsville Male Academy in 1887. He then received a congressional appointment to the U.S. Naval Academy at Annapolis, Md., completing the requirements for his commission in 1891. However, young Flowers declined a naval career and instead accepted an appointment as instructor in mathematics and electrical engineering at Trinity College, then located in Randolph County but already constructing a new campus in Durham. Indeed, one of Flowers's first responsibilities at the college, in the summer of 1891, was to wire the new buildings in Durham for electricity.

Flowers was one of only four faculty members who moved with the college from Randolph County to Durham early in the fall of 1892. There, as "professor of pure and applied mathematics," he quickly established a reputation as an effective and kindly instructor in the often mystifying science of numbers. He built a handsome home on the Trinity campus that housed a succession of younger brothers and other boarders until his marriage; it is still used for campus activities. After John C. Kilgo, a strong-willed churchman, became president of Trinity in 1894, Flowers assumed the role of mediator, softening the frequent confrontations among the administration, an independent-minded faculty, and spirited students. Although not a prolific scholar, he contributed to the intellectual climate of the college. He served as an editor of the *Christian Educator* (1896–98) and as a founding officer of the South Atlantic Publishing Company, sponsor of the lively and sometimes controversial *South Atlantic Quarterly* (1902).

After Kilgo left Trinity in 1910, there were changes in the college's administration. William Preston Few became president and Flowers was appointed "Secretary to the Corporation." The latter's duties included managing the institution's official correspondence and records and acting as liaison with the board of trustees. Gradually these administrative chores took more of Flowers's time, although he remained a nominal member of the mathematics department until 1934.

In 1923 Flowers, who as secretary had also overseen the business administration of the college, was named to the post of treasurer as well. This responsibility assumed great importance as tobacco millionaire and power tycoon James B. Duke neared completion of his great plan to establish a charitable trust for the benefit of the people of the Carolinas. In the fall of 1924, Flowers worked personally with Duke and his advisers, ironing out the details that would create the Duke Endowment and transform Trinity College into Duke University. Flowers had already been busily preparing for the public announcement of the Duke benefaction in December 1924. He quietly conducted a campaign whereby Trinity College obtained options on large tracts of land on the western edge of Durham. This property became the site of the university's new main campus and formed the core of a preserve soon to be known as the Duke Forest. When the new university was organized in 1925, Flowers was named vice-president in the business division. Flowers, President Few, and William H. Wannamaker, vice-president in the educational division, became the "triumvirate" that led the once obscure institution to international renown.

His warm manner, good sense, and devotion to duty made Flowers an attractive and reliable member of governing boards. In 1926, following the death of James B. Duke, Flowers was elected to succeed the philanthropist as a trustee of the Duke Endowment; the next year he was named to the board of trustees of Duke University. These positions, combined with his vice-presidency, allowed him to make significant contributions to the development of the university. Certainly no single man at Duke was more beloved and appreciated for his loyalty and kindness than "Professor Bobby" Flowers.

When President Few died suddenly in October 1940, Flowers, as senior vice-president, was immediately named acting president of the university. In January 1941, when the full board of trustees met to consider a replacement for Few, it elected Flowers to the post by acclaim. Despite his then considerable age of seventy, Flowers was in good health, alert, and active, and a successful, if not lengthy, incumbency was anticipated. However, the American involvement in World War II and the ensuing commitment of the university to national defense for the next five years robbed Flowers's presidency of its opportunity for independent development. By the time the school resumed its traditional program, Flowers was gradually taking a less active role in the administration of the university. Early in 1948 he announced his imminent retirement upon the selection of a new president. In November of that year, as A. Hollis Edens assumed the leadership position at Duke, Flowers was named to the newly created post of chancellor, an advisory position of lifetime tenure. At the time of his death, he had served Trinity College and Duke University for over sixty years.

Flowers's educational and civic interests were by no means restricted to Duke University. He served on the board of trustees of the North Carolina College for Negroes (now North Carolina Central University) in Durham for many years (1923–51, chairman from 1926), of Greensboro College, of the Methodist Orphanage (Raleigh), of the Masonic Orphanage (Oxford), and of Lincoln Hospital (Durham). He was an active Rotarian and a director of the Durham Chamber of Commerce and the Durham YMCA. Flowers was an influential layman in the Methodist church, serving on the board of education and as a delegate to the general conference. He also was a director of the Durham and Southern Railway and of the Fidelity Bank of Durham. In 1946, President Harry S Truman appointed him to the board of visitors of the U.S. Naval Academy. Flowers took all of these responsibilities seriously, attending meetings whenever possible and never merely lending his name to a good cause. In addition, he belonged to numerous honorary and fraternal organizations, including Phi Beta Kappa, the North Carolina Academy of Science, and Alpha Tau Omega. He received honorary degrees from Trinity College (A.M., 1904), Davidson College (LL.D., 1927), and The University of North Carolina (LL.D., 1942).

On 21 June 1905 Flowers married Lily Virginia Parrish (d. 1948), daughter of Durham financier and merchant Edward J. Parrish. They had two daughters, Virginia and Sybil Parrish. Flowers died from arteriosclerosis and was buried in Durham's Maplewood Cemetery. A portrait hangs in the Robert L. Flowers Student Activities Building at Duke University.

SEE: Biographical file and Robert Lee Flowers Papers (Manuscript Department, Duke University, Durham); *Durham Morning Herald*, 2 June 1941, 28 Nov. 1948, 25 Aug. 1951; *Nat. Cyc. Am. Biog.*, vol. G (1946); *Who's Who in America*, 1950–51.

MARK C. STAUTER

**Flowers, William Washington** *(5 Nov. 1874–1 May 1941),* business executive, was born at York Collegiate Institute near Taylorsville, the third of eight sons and two daughters of Colonel George Washington Flowers and Sarah Jane Haynes Flowers. At the age of sixteen he entered Trinity College, then located in Randolph County, where he became an outstanding scholar, athlete, and campus leader. After graduation in 1894 he began teaching in the public school system of Durham, the new location of Trinity College since 1892. From 1897 to 1899 he was superintendent of schools in Durham. Meanwhile, he had received the M.A. degree from Trinity (1896) and undertaken advanced study in Germany and at Harvard. In 1899 Flowers became an instructor in German at Trinity College and after only one year was named adjunct professor of French and German. With a leave of absence for the academic year 1900–1901, he entered Harvard in the fall. Ill health soon forced him to leave, however.

After returning to Durham in 1900, Flowers was employed by the American Tobacco Company. His health was restored, and by 1906 he was general manager of the former Blackwell tobacco factory in Durham. After the dissolution of the American Tobacco Company in 1911, he was transferred the following year to the Liggett and Myers Tobacco Company. At Liggett and Myers he was successively promoted to director in charge of operations (1913), vice-president (1919), and chairman of the board of directors (1936). Between 1933 and 1935 he also served the federal government as a member, and later chairman, of the code committee for the tobacco industry.

Flowers's continuing interest in Trinity College and Duke University, of which his brother Robert Lee was president from 1941 to 1948, was demonstrated by his services as trustee from 1925 until his death. Furthermore, he was a generous patron of the Duke Library, where, in conjunction with other members of his family, he established the George Washington Flowers Memorial Collection in honor of his father, a longtime trustee of Trinity College. It was due largely, however, to his own gifts and an endowment fund created by his will that the Flowers Collection became, and remains, the most important single collection in the Duke Library and one of the most notable collections on the South. Will Flowers was genuinely interested in books, read widely, and was a charter member of the Trinity College Historical Society. It is appropriate, therefore, that an ever-expanding library collection exists as a monument to him as well as to his father.

A handsome, quiet, soft-spoken man, Flowers gained wide respect for his gentlemanly qualities as well as for his sound judgment and close application to business. He was a member of several social clubs and the Methodist church, which was among the beneficiaries of his generous spirit. Although he lived in New York for many years, he kept close ties with his family in Durham. He never married and spent most of his last two years in the home of his sister, Estelle, and her husband, Judge Marshall T. Spears of Durham. He was buried in the Flowers mausoleum in Maplewood Cemetery, Durham.

SEE: *Durham Morning Herald,* 2 May 1941; *Durham Sun,* 2 May 1941; Flowers family papers (in possession of Mrs. Marshall T. Spears, Durham); New York *Herald Tribune,* 2 May 1941; *New York Times,* 2 May 1941; Various records and scattered publications of Trinity College and Duke University, 1899–1941; Robert H. Woody, "William Washington Flowers, 1874–1941," *Library Notes* 1 (1941).

MATTIE U. RUSSELL

**Floyd, Dolphin Ward** *(1807–6 Mar. 1836),* defender of the Alamo, was born in North Carolina. As a young man, he migrated to Texas and settled in the town of Gonzales. He was a private in the Texas army and, like many men in Gonzales, was active in the Texas independence movement. On 23 Feb. 1836, the Committee of Safety of Gonzales comandeered his horse for military use. Six days later, he joined thirty-one other men from Gonzales who were going to the relief of the Alamo in San Antonio de Béxar. They slipped into the Alamo on the night of 1–2 Mar. 1836. Floyd perished when the Alamo fell five days later. In 1876, Floyd County, Tex., was named in his honor.

SEE: *Houston Telegraph and Texas Register,* 24 Mar. 1836; Lon Tinkle, *The Alamo* (1958); W. P. Webb, ed., *The Handbook of Texas,* vol. 1 (1952); Amelia W. Williams, "A Critical Study of the Alamo and the Personnel of Its Defenders," *Southwestern Historical Quarterly* 37 (1933–34).

R. H. DETRICK

**Foard, Frederick Theophilus, Jr.** *(30 Mar. 1889–7 Aug. 1966),* physician and U.S. Public Health director, was born in the Vale section of Bandy Township, Catawba County, the fourth child of Dr. Frederick Theophilus (1855–1933) and Mary Frances Hudson (1853–1914) Foard. After receiving his secondary education at Oak Ridge Military School in Oak Ridge, he attended The University of North Carolina in 1910 and 1911 as a premedical student. In 1916 he was graduated from the University of Maryland School of Medicine, where he had served as a resident clinical assistant at the university's hospital in Baltimore from July 1914 to June 1916.

Following a six-month medical internship at the U.S. Marine Hospital, Chelsea, Mass., he practiced with his father in Catawba County for several months before accepting a position with the U.S. Public Health Service in February 1917. His first assignment was to field duty with the Rural Sanitation Demonstrations section in Hill County, Tex., where he worked in the control of typhoid fever. Remaining with this section throughout World War I, he was assigned to duty on Extra Cantonment Zone Sanitation at Camp Dodge, Des Moines, Iowa; Camp Wheeler, Macon, Ga.; Camp MacArthur, Waco, Tex.; and the Fifth Naval District, which included the city of Portsmouth and Norfolk County, Va.

At the end of the war, Foard became director of Public Health Service field activities in the Fifth Naval District where he remained until July 1919. In that capacity he was instrumental in forming a full-time county health department for Norfolk County, Va., to include the city of Portsmouth. Reassigned as a member of the staff of the U.S. Marine Hospital in Boston from 1 July 1919 to August 1920, he was again placed on field duty and sent to Montana, where he established and assisted in operating the Cascade County and City of Great Falls Health Department. It became the first full-time county health department in the northern Rocky Mountain states. During the two years he was there, Foard worked closely with state health officials in continuing to develop full-time local health services.

From January 1923 to June 1927 he was an assistant to the U.S. Public Health Officer for the San Joaquin Local

Health District, Stockton, Calif. During this time he also acted as a field representative in the development of full-time local health departments in the California counties of San Diego, Imperial Santa Barbara, Monterey, Orange, and San Louis Obispo. In June 1927 he was assigned to the Mississippi State Department of Health in connection with flood sanitation work and the promotion of full-time local health service in the Mississippi Delta counties. After eight months, he was sent to West Virginia to serve for a short period with the state Department of Health in Charleston, but in August 1928 he was reassigned to California as a representative of the U.S. Public Health Service in the development of local health service in the eleven Rocky Mountain and Pacific Coast states, Hawaii, and Alaska. In his next post, from August 1933 to September 1935, Foard was assistant to the state health officer of West Virginia where he had charge of the organization and administration of the WPA sanitation program to improve the sanitary conditions in mining villages and rural areas throughout the state.

In September 1935 Foard returned to his former assignment in the western states with headquarters in San Francisco. Through his efforts and those of Dr. Platt W. Covington, both of whom worked as a team for periods between 1923 and 1933, the groundwork had been laid for the rapid expansion of state and local health services throughout the west that began after the Social Security Act was passed in 1936. The increased federal grant-in-aid funds provided under the act enabled Foard to play an important role in initiating statewide public health surveys in the western states over the next ten years. These health surveys were instrumental in developing full-time state departments of health in Arizona, Idaho and Nevada and in reorganizing state departments of health in Colorado, Washington, and Wyoming. His work also helped bring about state legislation to provide for the organization of county and district health services in New Mexico and Utah.

On 27 June 1936, Foard was commissioned as a surgeon (captain) in the U.S. Public Health Service; he retired on 1 Nov. 1952 with the rank of medical director (colonel).

When war with Japan was declared, he was placed in charge of the Federal Civil Defense Medical and Health Program for the Rocky Mountain and Pacific Coast states with headquarters in San Francisco, where he served until the end of World War II. He was then appointed regional medical director of the U.S. Public Health Service Region VIII in Denver, Colo. He remained in this position until 1947, at which time he was temporarily assigned to the States Relations Division of the Public Health Service in Washington, D.C.

During his years with the Public Health Service, Foard recognized the acute need of the western states for better trained public health personnel in all fields of health service. To this end he advocated and was instrumental in the formation of the School of Public Health at the University of California at Berkeley.

In November 1947 he became regional medical director of Public Health Service activities to organize health services in Puerto Rico and the Virgin Islands. On 3 Apr. 1948, Foard was injured in a gas explosion that demolished his office at San Juan, P.R., and took the life of his wife. After his recovery he was assigned to the Bureau of Indian Affairs, Department of the Interior, as director of medical services for the United States and Alaska. His service in the western states had made him thoroughly familiar with the inadequacy of the health and hospital care being provided reservation Indians by the federal government. In an attempt to rectify the situation, he obtained increased funds for the employment of urgently needed professional personnel to staff the seventy-four hospitals being operated exclusively for American Indians. He also initiated the training of Indian boys as sanitarians to serve on reservations where they could speak the tribal language of the people. However, his most significant achievement during this period was his untiring effort to secure the transfer of all hospital and health services from the Bureau of Indian Affairs to the U.S. Public Health Service. To bring the plight of American Indians to the attention of those in a position to endorse his proposal, Foard wrote numerous medical papers on their health care needs. Among them were "The Health of the American Indians" (*American Journal of Public Health*, November 1949), "The Federal Government and American Indians' Health" (*Journal of the American Medical Association*, February 1950), "Health Services for the North American Indians" (*Medical Woman's Journal*, November 1950), and "The Tuberculosis Problem Among Indians" (Forty-eighth Annual Meeting of the National Tuberculosis Association, 1952). The transfer finally became law on 1 July 1955—over two years after his retirement from the Public Health Service in 1952.

Upon retirement, Foard returned to his native state where he accepted a post with the North Carolina State Board of Health as director of the Epidemiology Division. He retired from that position in January 1965 at the age of seventy-five, but remained a consultant to the Board of Health until his death.

Foard received the Distinguished Service Medal and Citation from the Department of the Interior, presented by the secretary for his pioneering "in the development of local health units in the Western States" and his "effort to arouse interest in Indian health problems" (1952); the Carl V. Reynolds Award for Outstanding Contributions to Public Health from the North Carolina Public Health Association (1959); the Sedgwick Award from the American Public Health Association, for his distinguished pioneer service in the public health field (1960); and the honorary degree of doctor of laws from The University of North Carolina, "In recognition of his contributions to public health" as a "devoted servant of the public" (1962).

He was a fellow of the American Public Health Association and of the American College of Preventive Medicine, a lifetime service member of the American Medical Association, an honorary life member and president of the Northern California Public Health Association, an honorary life member of the Western Branch of the American Public Health Association and of the Idaho Public Health Association, a diplomate of the American Board of Preventive Medicine, and a member of the North Carolina Medical Society and of the California Medical Association.

Foard was first married on 6 Aug. 1929 to Helena Wilhelmine Krause (1882–1948). They had no children. On 25 July 1958 he married Elsie Fredericka Dochterman. He was a Democrat, Lutheran, Mason, and Shriner.

SEE: *Charlotte Observer*, 6 Apr. 1948; Dr. Fred T. Foard Papers (North Carolina Public Health Library, Raleigh); Foard Family Papers (in possession of John H. Foard, Kannapolis); *Hickory Daily Record*, 6 Jan. 1965; North Carolina State Board of Health, *The Health Bulletin* 81

(July 1966 [portrait]) and "In Memoriam" (August 1966 [portrait]); *The Newsletter of the N.C. State Board of Health,* 29 July 1963.

JOHN HANBY FOARD, JR.

**Foard, John Frederick** *(12 Apr. 1827–11 May 1909),* physician, author, and planter, was born in Rowan (now Davie County), the son of Eunice Doomas Bradshaw and Frederick Foard. Orphaned at the age of three, he was reared at Concord in the home of his oldest brother, Major Robert Wyatte Foard, and his wife, Maria Partee Foard. According to his *History of the Foard-Bradshaw Families,* published in 1905, he attended Jefferson Medical College. Although he practiced medicine in Salisbury in 1860 and in Olin following the Civil War, after 1850 medicine was secondary to his farming, business, religious, and social interests.

Beginning in 1846, Foard acquired over a dozen tracts of land in western Rowan County on Witherow's Creek, Third Creek, Second Creek, and elsewhere and carried on considerable farming operations either himself or in partnership with his older brother, Osborne Giles Foard. The two brothers were instrumental in the formation of a county agricultural society and actively supported agricultural improvements. Perhaps their most successful venture was the construction and operation of Rowan Mills, a steam flour mill near the site of the present town of Cleveland. The two also were partners in the construction of the Western North Carolina Railroad and the Salisbury and Taylorsville plank road through western Rowan. In July 1858, as part of the apparent dissolution of their partnership, Osborne sold his interest in the plank road to his brother and Foard, in turn, sold Osborne his half interest in Rowan Mills as well as other property. A strong advocate of temperance, Foard was worthy grand patriarch of the Sons of Temperance in North Carolina in 1859–60.

Foard, a Methodist, supported that denomination as well as the New Institute (renamed Olin in 1857), a center for Methodism in the antebellum period under the leadership of Baxter Clegg and Brantley York. In 1855 Foard and his brother Osborne loaned the New Institute Association Society $10,000 for the construction and outfitting of a school. A few years after it opened, however, the three-story brick school was on the verge of collapse, owing in part to conflicts within the leadership of the North Carolina Conference. During the war years it was revived through the efforts of Charles Force Deems, who convinced Foard and his brother to provide an endowment. Because of the war, however, the school served only young boys and girls and never became the college that Deems and others proposed. The disillusioned Deems abandoned the project after the war and left North Carolina. A school continued to operate there for a time under James Southgate until the Foards sold the property. The building was pulled down in 1883.

After the war Foard settled at Olin where he was operating a mercantile establishment in 1867. That year he acquired the Powder Springs property northwest of Olin but did not develop the resort, which he renamed Eupeptic Springs, until 1873 when he mortgaged it to Wilfred Turner for $3,000 to raise funds for the construction of a hotel and other resort facilities. Through Foard's efforts, a post office was established at the springs in 1875. The resort apparently was unsuccessful for Foard was unable to repay the loan, and in 1881 Turner acquired the property at a commissioner's sale. As late as 1896 a resort was operated there by J. A. White. About 1895 Foard moved to Statesville where he resided until his death.

While at Eupeptic Springs, he wrote and published *North America and Africa, Their Past, Present and Future,* a sixty-seven-page pamphlet printed in 1875 in Salisbury by J. J. Brunner. In the pamphlet Foard advocated the colonization of the Negro in Africa, a subject that concerned him until he died. It was reprinted in 1877 in Raleigh by J. Nichols. A third edition, printed in 1904 in Statesville by Brady, carried an advertisement for *The Advocate of Missions,* a monthly magazine to be published by Foard.

On 25 Mar. 1847 Foard married Laura Catherine McConnaughey, the daughter of Ann Elizabeth Partee and George C. McConnaughey, and the niece, through marriage, of his brother Robert Wyatte Foard. She died in Statesville on 22 Dec. 1903. The couple had at least five children, three of whom survived Foard: Kate Partee (m. Stark Perry Graham), Ira Coke, and George McConnaughey. Foard also died in Statesville and was buried in Oakwood Cemetery.

SEE: James S. Brawley, *The Rowan Story* (1953); Iredell County Deed Books X, Z, 1, 3–5, 7, 9 (North Carolina State Archives, Raleigh); Homer Keever, *Iredell-Piedmont County* (1976); Rowan County Deed Books, 38–43, 48, 84 (North Carolina State Archives, Raleigh); Salisbury *Carolina Watchman,* scattered issues; J. Edward Smoot, *Marshal Ney Before and After Execution* (1929); Statesville *The Landmark,* 14 May 1909 and scattered issues.

DAVYD FOARD HOOD

**Foard, John Hanby** *(28 Sept. 1901–19 Jun. 1977),* textile executive, manufacturer, museum director, and Civil War historian, was born in Wilmington, the fourth child of Charles Deems (1863–1951) and Florence Hanby (1875–1932) Foard. He was a grandson of Osborne Giles Foard. Young Foard attended the Cape Fear Academy in Wilmington and Horner Military Institute. During the years he was growing up in and around Wilmington, he spent a great deal of time at Wrightsville Sound where his grandfather, John Hazard Hanby (1841–1910), owned a summer resort hotel called Atlantic View. Here, he gained a love of the sea, and later he became a member of the Carolina Yacht Club at Wrightsville Beach. In the early 1920s he participated in speedboat racing and, along with Julius T. Herbst, a marine engineer and inventor, raced some of the first hydroplane boats in the country.

About 1919 Foard went to work for the Atlantic Coast Line Railroad; eventually he was a traveling freight agent working out of Atlanta, Ga. During the depression of the 1930s, he was sent to Washington, D.C., to represent the Coast Line when executives of the nation's railroads gathered to standardize freight rates. Around 1939, he accepted a position with Ragean Ring Company in Atlanta as a salesman of textile spinning rings for use in the manufacturing of yarn and moved his residence to Newton to be near the center of the regional textile industry.

Recognizing the need for a stronger and longer lasting spinning ring, he patented a process for producing one around 1954; shortly afterward he entered into a partnership with Albert Kluttz, Kluttz Machine and Foundry Company of Gastonia. As president of Kluttz Rings, Inc., he produced a product that virtually cornered the spinning ring market. In 1954–55, he was chairman of the Associate Members Division of the Southern Textile Association.

With the coming Civil War centennial, Foard began in 1960 to research and produce a miniature replica of the Model 1857 12-pound Napoleon Gun-Howitzer as a gift for his customers. The cannons received so much publicity that in 1961 he formed Centennial Guns, a division of Kluttz, to manufacture serial numbered cannons for sale as collector's items. For his contributions in preserving military history, he was elected a member of the Company of Military Historians. On 6 Apr. 1962, the commanding general of Fort Sill, Okla., conferred upon Foard a Certificate of Membership in the Ancient Order of Artillerists in recognition of his keen interest in preserving the history of artillery. During this period, he became interested in seeing the battleship U.S.S. *North Carolina* brought to Wilmington. For his contribution to the project, which was accomplished in October 1961, he was made an honorary admiral of the North Carolina Navy.

In 1962, Foard sold his interests in Kluttz Rings and Centennial Guns and formed the John H. Foard Company, a textile consulting and machinery sales firm. At this time he represented Perfect Circle Corporation as a textile consultant.

As a boy, Foard delighted in hearing tales from his grandfather Hanby, a Confederate veteran, and others, about the Civil War, blockade-runners, and Fort Fisher. These tales remained with him and stirred a lifelong interest in the study of Civil War history. As he approached retirement, he began to seek a way to present the importance of Wilmington as a seaport receiving vital supplies for the Confederacy through blockade-running and the protection of Fort Fisher. In 1964, he persuaded a group of businessmen to form a corporation for the purpose of building a museum in the Wilmington area. The result was the Blockade Runner Museum, Inc., at Carolina Beach. In 1965 he moved his residence from Newton to Carolina Beach, and after several years of intense research and construction he opened the museum to the public on 4 July 1967. Foard was the director and secretary-treasurer of the corporation. His efforts were rewarded on 1 Dec. 1967, when the museum received an Award of Merit from the American Association for State and Local History "for its outstanding contribution to local history."

Through the years Foard continued to believe in the value of preserving local and national history for future generations. In January 1974 he found that the historically important "Sugar Loaf" historical site was being destroyed by vandals, so he launched a one-man campaign to have it protected. By bringing the matter to the attention of the public, he was able to convince federal officials to turn over the site, which adjoined the Masonboro State Park, to state officials for its preservation.

While living at Carolina Beach, Foard also became active in community affairs. He was responsible for getting the Richmond Glove Company, of Richmond, Ind., to locate a plant in the town in 1965; in June 1967 it became a part of the Carolina Glove Company. As a committee member of the Greater Wilmington Chamber of Commerce, he enthusiastically supported tourism for the area. In 1976, he worked through the local Lions Club to obtain some kind of medical facility in the Carolina Beach area. Subsequently he was appointed to a committee to determine the feasibility of opening and operating a clinic to be staffed by a special type registered nurse and to be periodically visited by physicians. Through his efforts, the facility, which was a new concept in medical care (there was only one other in the state), opened on 16 May 1977.

Foard was an associate member of the Southern Textile Association and a member of the American Textile Manufacturers Institute, the North Carolina Textile Manufacturers Association, the Company of Military Historians, and the American Ordnance Association. He was a Democrat, Methodist (later Presbyterian), and Lion. On 17 Apr. 1943 he married Kathryn Augusta Sandusky (b. 1911). Their children were John Hanby, Jr. (b. 1944) and William Sandusky (b. 1945). Foard died unexpectedly in his sleep in his home at Carolina Beach and was buried in the Eastview Cemetery, Newton.

SEE: R. O. Ackerman, "Scale Models for Artillery Buffs," *Shooting Times* (December 1962); *Carolina Beach Beach-O-Gram*, 23 June 1977 (portrait), 30 Aug. 1979; *Charlotte Observer*, 21 June 1977; Foard family papers (in possession of John H. Foard, Jr., Kannapolis); *Gastonia Gazette*, 26 Aug. 1962 (portrait); *Greensboro Daily News*, 29 Apr. 1962; Harry Haden, *Rah! Rah! Carolina* (1966); *Hickory Daily Record*, 30 June 1961; Frank A. Montgomery, Jr., "They Thumbed Their Noses At the Yankees," *State Magazine* 35 (15 July 1967); Newton *Observer-News-Enterprise*, 20 Mar. 1961, 6 Apr. 1962, 4 June 1965, 20 June 1977; "Reminders of the Blockade Runners," *Southern Living* 9 (April 1974 [portrait]); *Wilmington Gazette*, 1977, No. 2 (portrait); *Wilmington Morning Star*, 24 Jan., 12 Feb. 1971, 20 June 1977; *Wilmington Star-News*, 2 Dec., 3 Dec. 1967 (portrait), 27 Jan. 1974, 12 Apr. 1975, 2 Sept. 1979.

JOHN HANBY FOARD, JR.

**Foard, Osborne Giles** *(5 Feb. 1820–13 Oct. 1882)*, planter, state legislator, contractor, local official, and religious lay leader, was born in the fork of the Yadkin and South Yadkin rivers in what is now southern Davie County, the second of three children of Frederick (1783–1831) and Eunice Doomas Bradshaw (1792–1830) Foard. Having been orphaned in 1831, he went with his two brothers to live with his uncle, John Foard (1790–1866), at South River. He received his formal education in 1832, and possibly 1833/34, near Mocksville from the mysterious schoolmaster, Peter Stuart Ney. Shortly afterward, he went to Salisbury where he worked as a clerk in a general merchandise store owned by his older brother, Robert Wyatte Foard (1811–76).

On 15 Dec. 1838, with his brother Robert, Foard purchased from Thomas Gilchrist Polk, brother of President James Knox Polk, 1,268 acres of land in western Rowan County near present-day Cleveland. Here he soon built a Greek Revival plantation home, later known as Rowan Mills, and eventually purchased his brother's interest in the land. In order to care for his household, slaves, and surrounding community, Foard secured the medical services of Dr. Matthew A. Locke, paid him a regular salary, and provided him with living quarters and an office on the plantation. Later, he brought his ailing schoolmaster friend, Ney, to live on the property. While there, Ney instructed the children of the Third Creek community. Shortly before his death in 1846, Ney claimed that he was really Michael Ney, marshal of the empire under Napoleon Bonaparte of France. Foard administered Ney's meager estate and erected a tombstone at his grave in the Third Creek Presbyterian Church cemetery.

Before 1856, Foard and his brother John built a five-story steam flour mill on Osborne's plantation and became the largest flour producers in the county. According to the 1860 census, this mill—known as Rowan Mills—produced 5,000 barrels of flour, which was more than three times that of the nearest competitor for that year. In 1856, the nearby community of Cowansville (now Cleveland) had its name changed to Rowan Mills with Foard as the postmaster. Foard was one of the first tobacco growers of the region, and he was instrumental in forming a county agricultural society. In 1851, with his brother, Dr. John Frederick Foard (1827–1909), he formed a corporation to build the Salisbury and Taylorsville plank road, a toll road from Salisbury to Third Creek. The venture proved to be unsuccessful due to unforeseen costs of construction and upkeep. Foard also was one of the original backers in the movement to construct the North Carolina Railroad from Goldsboro to Charlotte and the Western North Carolina Railroad from Salisbury to Asheville. He supported both of these projects politically and financially, and contracted to build portions of the railroads at a profit.

In 1861, he moved his household to Olin in Iredell County and lived there until after the Civil War, when he returned to his plantation at Rowan Mills. Olin had become a center for the formation of a Methodist college, and Foard loaned the project a large sum that he never fully recovered after it failed.

In 1871, Foard was residing in Newton where he served a term as mayor from 1873 to 1875. In 1878, he was appointed to serve an unexpired term as justice of the peace for Newton Township; he was reappointed in 1881 and served until his death. Twice elected as Rowan County's representative to the legislature, he served in 1850 as a member of the Whig party and in 1866 as a Democrat.

Foard had joined the Methodist church in 1837 and, together with his brother John and Elkana D. Austin, formed and built Ebenezer Methodist Church. He also organized, built, and maintained a Methodist camp meeting ground on his plantation and was a leader and supporter of the Sons of Temperance movement.

He was married three times, first, on 22 Nov. 1838 to Lucile L. Ellis (1818–45), sister of Governor John Willis Ellis. They had three children, but none lived past the age of two. His second marriage was on 15 Jan. 1846 to Ann Foster Cowan (1821–54). To this union were born four children: Robert Osborne, Ann Elizabeth, Mary Alice, and Hubbard Milton. His third marriage was to Elizabeth Ann Allison (1831–97) on 11 Oct. 1854, and they had nine children: Dr. Frederick Theophilus, Lelia Doomas, Orston Bradshaw, John Fletcher, Lucy Lee, Charles Deems, Minnie Bosanquet, Lillian Allison, and Ella Giles.

Foard died from complications of pneumonia and was buried in the Eastview Cemetery, Newton.

SEE: James S. Brawley, *The Rowan Story, 1753–1953* (1953); Census schedules, 1850 and 1860, and deeds and marriage bonds of Rowan County (County Clerk's Office, Salisbury); *Charlotte Observer*, 28 Aug. 1932; John L. Cheney, Jr., ed., *North Carolina Government, 1585–1974* (1975); John K. Fleming, *History of the Third Creek Presbyterian Church* (1967); Foard family papers (in possession of John H. Foard, Kannapolis); John F. Foard, *History of the Foard-Bradshaw Families* (1905); J. G. deR. Hamilton, ed., *The Correspondence of Jonathan Worth*, vol. 1 (1909); *Hickory Daily Record*, 8 Mar. 1966; Homer M. Keever, *Iredell-Piedmont County* (1976); McCubbins Papers (Rowan County Library, Salisbury); *Newton Observer and News-Enterprise*, 29 Nov. 1954; Orders and decrees of Catawba County (County Clerk's Office, Newton); Charles J. Preslar, Jr., *A History of Catawba County* (1954); Salisbury *Carolina Watchman*, 30 Jan. 1846, 12 Oct. 1854; *Salisbury Post*, 31 Aug. 1975, 6 July 1980; Salisbury *Western Carolinian*, 19 Nov. 1838; J. Edward Smoot, *Marshall Ney Before and After Execution* (1929); Statesville *Express*, 4 May 1860; *Statesville Record and Landmark*, 5 May 1960; George V. Taylor, *Scholarship and Legend* (1960); John H. Wheeler, *Historical Sketches of North Carolina* (1851).

JOHN HANBY FOARD, JR.

**Folger, Alonzo Dillard** *(9 July 1888–30 Apr. 1941)*, attorney, judge, and U.S. representative, was born in Dobson, the son of Thomas W. and Ada Robertson Folger. After attending the public schools, he entered The University of North Carolina where he received an A.B. degree in 1912 and an LL.B in 1914. In the latter year he passed the bar examination and returned to Surry County where he began to practice law in partnership with his brother, John H. Folger, in Mount Airy. On 13 Oct. 1919 he married Gertrude Reece of Dobson, and they later had two sons, Alonzo Dillard, Jr., and Jack.

Although he soon had a flourishing law practice and eventually acquired an interest in the Surry County Loan and Trust Company, one of the county's leading banks, politics proved to have a stronger attraction for young Folger than the law or banking. Possessed of a genius for political organization, he assumed the post of chairman of the Surry County Democratic party and with the assistance of his brother John revived a moribund party. He not only gave Surry a two-party system, but also in the process he created a political machine that by the 1920s could deliver sizable blocs of votes in party primaries to candidates it favored.

The heyday of the Folger organization was in the 1930s after the effects of the Great Depression loosened the Republican leanings of Surry countians, and the Democrats won overwhelming control of all local offices. In 1936, Folger served as state campaign manager for Lieutenant Governor A. H. ("Sandy") Graham in his bid for the Democratic gubernatorial nomination. Although Graham lost, Folger in June 1936 was elected Democratic national committeeman, largely due to the supporters of Clyde R. Hoey, who hoped to win Graham votes for their candidate in the second primary. On 4 November of the same year, Governor J. C. B. Ehringhaus appointed Folger a special judge of the superior court, but he served only slightly more than two months because of his desire to remain national committeeman; he resigned on 10 Jan. 1937.

In 1938, Folger won election to the U.S. House of Representatives from the Fifth Congressional District. Appointed to the Committee on Banking and Currency—an unusual honor for a freshman congressman—he generally gave strong support to the proposals of Franklin D. Roosevelt. Reelected in 1940, Folger was just beginning to establish himself as one of the leading members of the House when, while on his way to deliver a commencement speech, he suffered a heart attack, wrecked his automobile, and died the same day in Mount Airy. He was buried in the Dobson Cemetery.

SEE: *Biog. Dir. Am. Cong.* (1971); David L. Corbitt, ed., *Addresses, Letters and Papers of Clyde Roark Hoey, Governor of North Carolina, 1937–1941* (1944), and *Addresses, Letters and Papers of John Christoph Blucher Ehringhaus, Governor of North Carolina, 1933–1937* (1950); *Nat. Cyc. Am. Biog.*, vol. 42 (1958); Elmer L. Puryear, *Democratic Party Dissension in North Carolina, 1928–1936* (1962); Seventy-Seventh U.S. Congress, *Alonzo Dillard Folger*, Memorial Addresses (1942); Seventy-sixth, Seventy-seventh U.S.

Congresses, *Congressional Record* (1939, 1941); *Who's Who in America*, 1940–41.

RALPH J. CHRISTIAN

**Folger, John Hamlin** *(18 Dec. 1880–19 July 1963),* attorney, state legislator, and U.S. representative, was born in Rockford, the son of Thomas W. and Ada Robertson Folger. Shortly after being graduated from high school in 1898, he entered Guilford College, later transferring to The University of North Carolina law school. In 1901 he was admitted to the bar and for four years practiced in Dobson. Meanwhile, he had married Maude Douglas on 5 Nov. 1899. They eventually had four children: Fred, Nell, Henry, and Frances.

In 1905 Folger moved to Mount Airy where he was to make his home the rest of his life. In addition to practicing law, he came to play an increasing role in Democratic politics and in 1908 was elected to a four-year term as mayor of Mount Airy. After forming a law partnership with his younger brother Alonzo in 1914, Folger's political involvement increased. While Alonzo Folger served as Surry Democratic chairman, John Folger ably assisted him in the task of reviving the weak county party, giving Surry a viable two-party system for the first time in decades and in the process creating a political machine that could deliver sizable blocs of votes to favored candidates in party primaries.

In 1926 Folger won election to the state house of representatives and in 1930 to the senate. In the legislature, education was one of his primary interests. As chairman of the senate committee on education in 1931, Folger helped push the bill for a six-month school term to final passage. From 1927 to 1935 he was a member of the state Board of Equalization and from 1933 to 1937 and 1939 to 1941 he served on the state school commission. A Franklin D. Roosevelt supporter, Folger was a delegate to the 1932 Democratic National Convention and in 1940 led a successful fight at the state convention to elect delegates to the national gathering who favored drafting Roosevelt for a third term.

On 14 June 1941, Folger won a special election in the Fifth Congressional District to fill the unexpired term of his deceased brother Alonzo. Reelected to the Seventy-eighth, Seventy-ninth, and Eightieth congresses, he established a record of strong support for presidents Franklin D. Roosevelt and Harry S Truman. In 1941 he supported such preparedness policies as extension of the peacetime draft and repeal of the neutrality acts, declaring in a speech on 12 Nov. that Adolf Hitler had to be stopped.

In the area of domestic policy Folger proved to be perhaps the most liberal member of the North Carolina delegation and one of the most liberal Southern Democrats. In 1942 and 1944 he supported measures to make it easier for soldiers to vote. An advocate of organized labor, he was one of few southerners to oppose passage of the Smith-Connally Act in 1943 and the Taft-Hartley Act in 1947. In 1946, Folger was instrumental in the passage of the bill establishing the school lunch program after Negro congressman Adam Clayton Powell offered an amendment that would have cut off funding for segregated school systems. Folger countered with an amendment to ensure that Negro schools would get their fair share of money for the program. Powell accepted it, and the bill passed.

During his last term in Congress, Folger became increasingly critical of the direction of American foreign policy, especially the hard line approach to the Soviet Union. In several speeches he expressed fear of a rebuilt Germany and criticized the growing fashion of extreme anticommunism. To Folger communism and fascism were equally bad, and he feared that U.S. support for repressive right-wing dictatorships would hasten the spread of communism. As a result, he opposed the Truman Doctrine for Greece and Turkey in 1947 and efforts to revive the peacetime draft. He did support the 1948 Marshall Plan, however, because he believed it might help restore democratic life.

In his early campaigns for reelection, Folger faced relatively weak opposition in both primary and general elections. In 1946, however, he was challenged by wealthy industrialist Thurmond Chatham in a contest billed as a showdown between the New Deal and more conservative factions of the North Carolina Democratic party. Chatham attacked him as a lackey of the CIO and ran slightly ahead of him in the first primary. Although Folger won the second primary handily, Chatham's determination to run again in 1948 was probably an important factor in his decision to step down. After he left Congress in 1949, Folger returned to Mount Airy where he practiced law until his retirement in 1959. He died in a nursing home in Clemmons and was buried in Oakdale Cemetery, Mount Airy.

SEE: *Biog. Dir. Am. Cong.* (1971); Ralph J. Christian, "The Folger-Chatham Congressional Primary of 1946," *North Carolina Historical Review* 53 (1976); David L. Corbitt, ed., *Addresses, Letters and Papers of Clyde Roark Hoey, Governor of North Carolina, 1937–1941* (1944), *Addresses, Letters and Papers of John Christoph Blucher Ehringhaus, Governor of North Carolina, 1933–1937* (1950), *Papers and Letters of Angus Wilton McLean, Governor of North Carolina, 1925–1929* (1931), and *Papers and Letters of Governor O. Max Gardner, 1929–1933* (1937); Elmer L. Puryear, *Democratic Party Dissension in North Carolina, 1928–1936* (1962); Seventy-seventh-Eightieth U.S. Congresses, *Congressional Record* (1941–49); *Who's Who in America*, 1946–47.

RALPH J. CHRISTIAN

**Folk, George Nathaniel** *(8 Feb. 1831–14 May 1896),* lawyer and president of his own law schools, was born in Isle of Wight County, Va., the son of William and Annie Folk. He was educated at the College of William and Mary and at the age of twenty moved to North Carolina where he spent the next year in Charlotte studying law. He was admitted to the bar in 1851. Moving to Boone, Folk practiced law and in 1856 and 1860 was elected as a Whig to represent Watauga County in the House of Commons. In 1861 he moved to Asheville, only to return to Boone with the outbreak of the Civil War. Although originally a Union man, Folk voted for secession and was one of first to volunteer for Confederate service. He was also the first to enlist volunteers in Watauga County. In the Confederate Army, Folk quickly attained the ranks of captain, lieutenant colonel, and colonel in the Sixty-fifth Regiment, North Carolina Troops (Sixth Regiment, North Carolina Cavalry). He was wounded at the battles of Chicamauga and Pea Vine Church and in East Tennessee. From 22 June 1864 to 15 Dec. 1864, he was a prisoner of Union forces but was later exchanged and paroled at Charleston Harbor, S.C., on 15 Dec. 1864.

After the war Folk returned to Boone, but in 1866 moved to Lenoir and opened a law school in the Jones house. Most of his students were Confederate veterans. He soon purchased Cherry Hill on North Main Street in Lenoir where he continued teaching law during the winter until 1882. From 1867 to 1895 he also operated law schools in Boone and Blowing Rock in the summer. Folk's report to the U.S. commissioner of education in 1889 concerning his law school in Boone lists one resident professor and nine students. This number compares favorably with the twenty-two students enrolled in law at The University of North Carolina during the same period. There were 600 volumes in Folk's library, the annual charge for tuition was $75 per person, and receipts from these fees came to $675. In 1889 the total income from the law school was $3,000. In 1882, Folk purchased Riverside in Caldwell County and moved his law school there. Among his students were Edmund Jones, William Horton Bower, E. B. Cline, Henry Starbuck, and Frank Osborne.

An active and patriotic citizen of the Lenior community, Folk exerted considerable political influence after Reconstruction. He served on the vestry of St. James Episcopal Church and was influential in the formation of the Masonic Lodge, serving as junior warden in 1866. In 1876, Folk became a senator for Caldwell County in the General Assembly where he was chairman of the Judiciary Committee. In 1882 he was nominated and ran for state supreme court judge as a liberal Democrat but lost. He returned to Lenoir in 1894 and spent the last two years of his life at Hillside Cottage on North Main Street.

In 1853 Folk married Elizabeth A. Council, the daughter of Jordan Council, Jr., who kept the only store and post office in the Watauga section. In 1850 the Council Store community became the town of Boone; the same year Council donated the land for the first courthouse in Boone. The Folks had four children: Henry Clay, Sally Virginia, John Woodfin, and George Blackwell, but only the latter survived infancy.

Folk was buried in Bellavue Cemetery, Lenoir. His widow died in 1912.

SEE: George N. Folk, *Speech on the Convention Question* (1861); Louis A. Manarin, ed., *North Carolina Troops, 1861–1865, A Roster*, vol. 2 (1968); John Nichols, *Directory of the General Assembly of North Carolina* (1860); R. A. Shotwell and Natt Atkinson, *Legislative Record (1877).*

KIMBERLY P. BARGER
RICHARD D. HOWE

**Fontaine, Peter** *(1691–1757?)*, Church of England priest, rector of Westover Parish, Va., chaplain for the Dividing Line Commission of Virginia and North Carolina and missionary in North Carolina, was born at Taunton, England, the son of the Reverend James Fontaine. He was descended from John de la Fontaine (1500–1563), of the province of Maine near the border of Normandy, France, who was martyred in France in 1563.

Young Fontaine emigrated to Virginia in 1716 and was rector of Westover Parish in Charles County for nearly forty years. Governor Alexander Spotswood of Virginia mentioned him to the bishop of London in a letter dated 13 June 1717. In 1728, Fontaine accompanied the Dividing Line Commission of Virginia and North Carolina as a chaplain. During the boundary survey, he preached to many citizens and baptized a number of children on both sides of the line.

On 22 March 1714 Fontaine married Elizabeth Fourreau, and they became the parents of two children: Mary Ann (m. Isaac Winston) and Peter (m. Elizabeth Winston), who in January 1774 was a trustee for a relief fund for clergymen's widows in Virginia. Fontaine later married Elizabeth Wade in Virginia. They had a son, Thomas, and a daughter whose name is unknown. A brother of Peter, the Reverend Francis Fontaine (1697–1749), was in Virginia in May 1721. He held the York Hampton Parish in May 1724 but in 1729 became a professor of Oriental languages at the College of William and Mary. Francis was married twice. His first wife was M. Glanmission by whom he had John and Francis, who settled near New Bern, N.C.; his second wife has not been identified.

Authorities disagree on the year of Peter Fontaine's death. Some believe it was 1757, whereas Kennedy argues for 1755.

SEE: William K. Boyd, ed., *William Byrd's History of the Dividing Line Betwixt Virginia and North Carolina* (1929); R. A. Brock, ed., *Collections of the Virginia Historical Society*, vol. 2 (1885); Mary S. Kennedy, *Seldens of Virginia and Allied Families*, vols. 1–2 (1911); William L. Saunders, ed., *Colonial Records of North Carolina*, vols. 2–3 (1886); *Virginia Gazette*, scattered issues, 1716–57.

VERNON O. STUMPF

**Foote, Eli** *(30 Oct. 1747–9 Sept. 1792)*, merchant, was born in Colchester, Conn. the son of Daniel and Margaret Parsons Foote. Educated for the practice of law, Foote was the only Tory in a large family of Whigs during the American Revolution. His wife, Roxana, was the daughter of General Andrew Ward, a renowned patriot. Bereft of influence and the opportunity for professional advancement at the close of the war, Eli sought a livelihood for himself, his wife, and their six children in maritime commerce at Guilford, Conn. Failing in an enterprise involving the building of a ship for seagoing trade, he became a partner of his brother, Justin Foote, on a trading voyage to North Carolina in 1789. The pair took up winter quarters at Murfreesboro, a village that had been incorporated and laid out only in the preceding year. Owners of a schooner, the Foote brothers began to develop a three-cornered trade involving North Carolina farm produce and naval stores exchanged for New England and West Indian goods. Eli established residence at Winton, on the Chowan River ten miles below Murfreesboro, which is located on the Meherrin River, an arm of the Chowan.

Between 1789 and 1792 the Footes sponsored several trading voyages to Martinique, St. Croix, St. Martin's, and St. Eustatius. Their Murfreesboro warehouse was packed with articles of commerce when, on the night of 17 Apr. 1791, they became victims of Murfreesboro's first crime of record. Thieves broke into the warehouse and made off with chintz, linen, silk, and other goods. Most of the stolen merchandise was recovered the next day, but the responsibility of prosecuting the thieves fell to Eli, who found it necessary to remain in North Carolina during the following summer to testify against them. In August 1792 he contracted yellow fever, dying in delirium at Winton. His gravestone, which still stands at Winton, lists the date of his death as August 1791 and his age as fifty-five (he was actually forty-four). The reason for the errors is that his gravestone was not erected until 1822 by order of the will of General Joseph F. Dickinson, in whose family cemetery Foote had been buried. Justin Foote, in company with John P. Foote, Eli's son, continued in seasonal commerce in the Albemarle Sound area for more than a quarter of a century after Eli's death.

The ten children who survived the death of Eli Foote

included his daughter Roxana who, in 1799, married the Reverend Lyman Beecher and became the mother of Harriet Beecher Stowe. It may have been the family's acquaintance with the Albemarle region that led Mrs. Stowe to use it as the locale for one of her novels, *Dred: A Tale of the Dismal Swamp* (1856).

SEE: Nathaniel Goodwin, *The Foote Family; Or, the Descendents of Nathaniel Foote. . . .* (1849); T. C. Parramore, "The Merchants Foote," *North Carolina Historical Review* 46 (1969); Will of Joseph F. Dickerson and Deed books of Hertford County (North Carolina State Archives, Raleigh).

T. C. PARRAMORE

**Foote, Percy Wright** *(13 Aug. 1879–23 June 1961)*, naval officer, was born at Roaring River, Wilkes County, the son of Confederate Major James Henry Foote (writer, educator, and a founder of Wake Forest College) and Susan Hunt Foote. He was a descendant of Major Francis Wright and Ann Washington Wright, daughter of Colonel John Washington who was the grandfather of General George Washington. His Revolutionary War ancestor was Captain John Wright of the Continental Army's Fourth North Carolina Regiment.

Foote grew up in the brick mansion on the old family plantation. In an insatiable desire for a good education he spent hours in his father's library. He was soon attracted to the Naval Academy from which he was graduated in 1901. As an ensign he saw action in 1905 with troops landed from the *Baltimore* to protect American interests in Shanghai. In 1906, his highly effective method of fire control resulted in the *Baltimore* winning the cruiser trophy with a record never before equaled. The Navy Department commended him for the thoroughness and intelligence of his work with his men. His sharp practical insight into every task and his knack of evoking intense loyalty and zealous devotion to duty from his men remained a mark of the man thereafter.

When lieutenant, Foote was a chief engineer of the battleship *Louisiana* from 1909 to 1912. Though lacking engineering skills he acquitted himself so well that he was chosen for the highly technical duties of inspector of engineering materials at General Electric's plant in Schenectady, N.Y., during the period 1912–15. Enthused with the potentials of electricity, he presented in 1913 to acting navy secretary Franklin D. Roosevelt his study, "Turbine Electric Propulsion of a Battleship Compared with Other Means." His recognized authority and keen perceptions were influential in the Navy's adoption of this concept in 1914, an important milestone in naval history.

After becoming lieutenant commander, Foote was given the choice assignment of gunnery officer of the battleship *Nevada*, the Navy's most powerful vessel when launched on 2 Mar. 1916. He is best known for his heroic command of the troop transport *President Lincoln*. Returning from its fifth voyage with seven hundred aboard, including wounded, it was torpedoed on 31 May 1918 and sank in 18 minutes. But because of his superb emergency procedures and drills (later adopted for the entire Troop Transport Service) only twenty-six perished. Though together a scarce eight months, the crew was so disciplined and devoted to its rescue and fighting duties that the ship's guns were blasting almost to final submersion. He received a special commendation from navy secretary Josephus Daniels; the Silver Star Medal for gallantry in action; and the Distinguished Service Medal. The Navy Department memorialized this epic with a painting, which the survivors' USS *President Lincoln* Club depicted in a handsome bronze plaque in memory of those who lost their lives. Both are now in possession of the curator of the Department of the Navy. A vivid description is preserved in Commander Foote's "Narrative of the *President Lincoln*."

For his gallant conduct Secretary Josephus Daniels chose him as aide during 1918 to 1921, and found him "efficient in the highest degree." During this time, King Albert of Belgium visited the United States and personally bestowed on Foote the Belgian Order of the Crown medal.

There followed many sea assignments during which Foote commanded almost every type of naval vessel; wrote his third useful study, "Engineering—Its Value to the Captain" (1923); became captain (1 Jan. 1924); was graduated from the Naval War College (1929); and served twice at Washington's Naval Gun Factory, first as inspector and later as senior inspector. There, using his vast sea experience and technical knowledge, he designed a number of important ordnance changes, some remaining useful during World War II and beyond. In 1933, while commanding the battleship *Arkansas* and the training squadron of the fleet's scouting force, he was cited by the fleet commander, Admiral R. H. Leigh, for relief work in the Long Beach, Cal., earthquake disaster. This was the twenty-seventh citation on his record.

Foote's last three years in the navy were spent ashore at the Philadelphia Navy Yard as chief of staff of the Fourth Naval District. He was promoted to rear admiral and retired on 30 June 1936. He continued living in the Philadelphia area. Soon Pennsylvania Governor George H. Earle tapped him to be police commissioner to combat the mounting traffic death toll. In an outstanding two-year record, Foote reduced it over 40 percent and received the Pennsylvania Meritorious Service Medal.

He returned to North Carolina, making his home in Chapel Hill. In May 1942, he was recalled to active duty as senior inspector of the newly created Eighth Naval District coving Arkansas, Oklahoma, Louisiana, and Texas. With his usual energy and understanding, he soon had this cotton-oil-cattle country so highly geared to the war effort that, from January 1943 to May 1944, it averaged shipments of $50 million monthly, excluding shipbuilding.

At the war's end, with forty years of distinguished public service behind him, Foote again retired, this time living in Charlotte. He died there and was buried at Arlington National Cemetery, Washington, D.C.

On 1 Oct. 1910 Foote married Genevieve Clary of Great Falls, Mont. She died on 27 July 1969. Surviving were a son, Colonel Thomas Clary Foote, USA; a daughter Diana, wife of Brigadier General James F. Lawrence, USMC; and several grandchildren. A portrait is in possession of his son. He was a Democrat, Episcopalian, and Mason and a member of the Army and Navy Club, the New York Yacht Club, and the Sons of the American Revolution.

SEE: Bureau of Naval Personnel, Department of the Navy, Washington, D.C., for service and other records; *Charlotte Observer*, 1 Dec. 1946, 24 June 1961; *Greensboro Daily News*, 24 Feb. 1929; *Houston Chronicle*, 30 May 1944; *Journal of the American Society of Naval Engineers* 27 (1915); *Lucky Bag*, 1910, and *Shipmates*, August 1961 (Archives, U.S. Naval Academy, Annapolis); *New York Times*, 24 June 1961; Raleigh *News and Observer*, 28 June 1936, 29 May, 5 July 1940, 10 May 1942, 24 June 1961;

U.S. House of Representatives, *Congressional Hearings*, no. 435, 1935, for H.R. 7092 and Captain Foote's promotion to rear admiral; U.S. Naval Institute, *Proceedings* 48 (1922) and 49 (1923); *Who's Who in the South and Southwest* (1950); *Who Was Who in America*, vol. 4 (1968).

ELTON FOOTE HALL SAMOUCE

**Foote, William Henry** *(20 Dec. 1794–22 Nov. 1869)*, Presbyterian clergyman and historian, the son of Stephen and Hannah Waterman Foote, was born at Colchester, Conn. He was graduated from Yale in 1816 with an A.B. degree, devoted slightly more than two years to teaching, and spent one year at Princeton Seminary (1818–19). After his licensure on 20 Oct. 1819, he preached at various points in Virginia. Several months before Winchester Presbytery ordained him to the full work of the ministry of 7 Sept. 1822, he settled at Woodstock, Va., where he served a congregation, along with that of Stoverstown (Strasburg), until 1824. His next charge was that of the Mt. Bethel, Hampshire County, Va., (now West Virginia), Church, which in 1833 was divided into five formally organized congregations. Foote retained a portion of this field, residing at Romney until 1838. For the next seven years he was a regional representative for the cause of foreign missions in the Old School Presbyterian Church. From 1845 until his death he served churches at Romney, Springfield, and Patterson's Creek (1845–60), except for "three years, six months, and four days" of "protracted exile" in lower Virginia during the Civil War. While a refugee, he supplied vacant churches, served as hospital chaplain, and for a short time was an agent for Hampden-Sydney College which in 1847 awarded him a D.D. degree. In addition to his pastoral work, he conducted academies at Woodstock and Romney.

Foote was neither a native nor at any time a resident of North Carolina. However, while an agent, or traveling secretary, for the Central Board of Foreign Missions of the Presbyterian church (1838–45), he visited many North Carolina counties where he not only promoted the missionary enterprise, but also collected considerable material of a historical nature. His *Sketches of North Carolina, Historical and Biographical*, written at the request of the Presbyterian Synod of the state, and published in 1846, permanently linked his name with North Carolina. A reprint of the *Sketches* appeared in 1912 and a second in 1965. The volume has consistently demonstrated its value for reference, both in the religious and secular spheres. The author's incorporation into the text of a number of earlier documents, some of which have since disappeared, substantially enhances its usefulness. Notable among the items included but now missing is the original of Hugh McAden's journal of his tour of North Carolina made during 1755–56. Foote also was the author of *Sketches of Virginia, Historical and Biographical* (1850); of a similar work bearing the same title with the addition of *Second Series* (1855); and of *The Huguenots, or Reformed French Church*, published in the year after his death.

Foote's first wife was Eliza Wilson Glass, daughter of the Reverend Joseph Glass of Frederick County, Va., whom he married on 21 Feb. 1822. Two daughters, Ann Waterman and Eliza Wilson, were born of this union. After the death of Mrs. Eliza Foote (21 Apr. 1835), he married Arabella Gilliam of Petersburg, Va., on 31 Oct. 1838; they had one child, Mary Arabella. Foote died at Romney and was buried in the nearby Indian Mound Cemetery.

SEE: *DAB*, vol. 3 (1959); William Henry Foote Journal and Papers and MS Minutes of Winchester Presbytery (Library, Union Theological Seminary, Richmond).

THOMAS H. SPENCE, JR.

**Forbes, William** *(d. ca. September 1751)*, colonial official, immigrated to North Carolina from Scotland early in the 1730s. Settled in the Lower Cape Fear region, he soon gained the notice of Governor George Burrington, who placed him on the royal council briefly in 1733 to fill the vacancy of a recently deceased member. With over 1,400 acres of land in Bladen County, Forbes became a prosperous man. In 1734 he was made a justice of the peace for Bladen, and in 1736 he assumed the same office in New Hanover County. He was liked by fellow Scot Gabriel Johnston, the new governor, who named him assistant baron of the exchequer court in 1735. In May Johnston also nominated him to the Privy Council; although confirmed by the council six months later, Forbes for some unexplained reason did not take his seat until January 1741. However, he did serve in the lower house of assembly from Bladen in 1736 and 1739 and was made county sheriff in the latter year. Late in 1743 he was appointed as one of the surveyors for the Granville grant and performed that service the following year. At some point in the early 1740s Forbes apparently purchased a home in or near Brunswick. He was named to the vestry of St. Philip's Parish in 1741 and to the committee to prepare the defense of Brunswick against the Spaniards in 1747.

Forbes's service on the council was marked by uneven attendance and a lack of controversy except for an argument with James Murray over seniority in October 1749, an argument that Murray won. Afterwards Forbes dropped out of politics, disabled by "sickness and old age" as Governor Johnston reported. When he dictated his will in New Hanover in September 1751, Forbes mentioned no family and left his whole estate, including six slaves, to two friends in the county.

SEE: William S. Price, " 'Men of Good Estates': Wealth Among North Carolina's Royal Councillors," *North Carolina Historical Review* 49 (1972); William L. Saunders, ed., *Colonial Records of North Carolina*, vols. 3 and 4 (1886); Wills of New Hanover County (North Carolina State Archives, Raleigh).

WILLIAM S. PRICE

**Forbus, Wiley Davis** *(14 Mar. 1894–3 Mar. 1976)*, pathologist and medical educator, was born in Zeiglerville, Miss., the son of William Peyton and George Ellen Davis Forbus. After completing his secondary education in 1912 in local schools of Laurel, Miss., he entered Washington and Lee University, Lexington, Va., from which he was graduated with honors in 1916. During his senior year he was assistant in chemistry. Subsequently he taught general sciences at St. Albans, National Cathedral School for Boys, Washington, D.C., and in 1918 was an artillery observer in the U.S. Army Air Service. Following his first year of military service he taught at Friends' School, also in Washington.

In 1919 Forbus enrolled in the School of Medicine of the Johns Hopkins University, Baltimore, Md., and was graduated in 1923 with the M.D. degree. The same year he accepted a commission as first lieutenant in the U.S. Air Service Reserve, an appointment he held for ten years. Upon graduation he was invited to remain at

Johns Hopkins, where for seven years he served successively as assistant instructor and associate in pathology and as assistant resident and associate pathologist. In 1928 he was guest assistant at the Pathologisches Institut de Ludwig Maximilians Universität, Munich, Germany.

In 1930, when Duke University established a medical school, Forbus joined several of his colleagues from Johns Hopkins in forming the faculty and program of the new institution. Afterward he became professor and chairman of the department of pathology and chief pathologist to the Duke Hospital, the teaching adjunct of the Duke University School of Medicine. There he spent the rest of his career and became recognized as one of the world's great men of science and an international leader in pathology. In 1953 and 1954 he was acting dean of the medical school. When he officially retired in 1961, he was given life tenure as professor and chairman emeritus of the department of pathology.

Forbus was always in demand as a lecturer and a consultant for both military and civilian medical services and education. In that capacity he served many hospitals throughout the nation, including the Walter Reed Army Hospital in Washington, D.C. On military assignment, he was a consultant to the secretary of war on infectious diseases (1941–46), to the Armed Forces Institute of Pathology (1941), and to the Division of Biology and Medicine (medicolegal) of the Atomic Energy Commission (1952). For the Veterans Administration, he was branch section chief in pathology (1948) as well as a consultant.

Several major appointments sent him to other nations as a consultant. He was a member of the Foreign Operations Administration Mission to China (1953), external examiner in pathology at the British Colonial University Medical School in Hong Kong (1953), consultant to the surgeon general of the U.S. Army for the Far East Command (1953) and in Europe (1958), a visiting consultant to the Atomic Bomb Casualty Commission in Japan (1953, 1956), adviser on medical education at Keio University, Tokyo, under the auspices of the Rockefeller Foundation (1956), and visiting consultant on medical education in the Far East (1956) under the auspices of the China Medical Board. He was chief of party, University of California–Airlangga University (Indonesia) Affiliation in Medical Education (1961–62).

Earlier he had served as chairman of the joint committee of the North Carolina Medical Society and the North Carolina Pathological Society on medicolegal affairs, and was author of the first North Carolina medical examiner law enacted in 1955. A proponent of forensic medicine, Forbus led a long campaign in North Carolina to upgrade the coroner system. Through his efforts legislation was passed establishing the state's medical examiner program. He was also medicolegal educator and consultant to the Duke University School of Medicine. Its library has the "Forbus Collection—Pathology in Lantern Slides," which includes indexes and catalogues he collected through the years and collated in 1964 and 1973.

Forbus was a continuous member of the Durham-Orange Medical Society, the North Carolina Medical Society, the North Carolina Pathological Society, and the American Medical Association. In the North Carolina Medical Society he was chairman of the section on pathology and a member of the committees on the coroner system and North Carolina medical history. He also belonged to the American Association for the Advancement of Science; American Association of Pathologists and Bacteriologists (president, 1947); Pathology Study Section, Division of Research Grants and Fellowships, National Institutes of Health (1946–48); and National Board of Medical Examiners (1935–47). He was a consultant to the Committee on Clinical Fellowships of the American Cancer Society.

A tireless student and a prolific writer in his field, Forbus contributed more than sixty scholarly articles and reviews to professional journals and collections of essays. One of his most noted works was "Reaction to Injury, Pathology for Students of Disease," a 797-page study published in 1943. He prepared over twenty series of scholarly lectures—some published, others in typescript—located in half a dozen libraries including those at Duke University and The University of North Carolina at Chapel Hill. Many of the lecture series he delivered in other countries were published in those countries. He served on the editorial board of the North Carolina Medical Society's *Medicine in North Carolina, Essays in the History of North Carolina Medicine*, to which he also contributed, and was associate editor of the national *Archives of Pathology* (1945–61).

During his undergraduate years at Washington and Lee University he was elected to Phi Beta Kappa (scholastic), Sigma Xi (scientific), and Phi Gamma Delta (social) fraternities. In 1956 the same university awarded him the honorary degree of doctor of science. He was also tapped for membership in Alpha Omega Alpha, the honorary medical fraternity. From the American Association of Pathologists and Bacteriologists he received the prestigious Gold Headed Cane, "the highest recognition from his peers." Duke University established the Wiley D. Forbus Educational Center for Pathology and, at the time of his death, created the Wiley D. Forbus Memorial Fund at the Duke Medical Center.

On 25 Sept. 1926 Forbus married Elizabeth Knox Burger, the daughter of Louis John and Elizabeth Rogers Terry Burger of Baltimore, Md. They had three daughters: Georg'Ellen Davis (Mrs. Wilmer Conrad Betts), Elizabeth Terry (Mrs. Henry Adams), and Martha Caroline (Mrs. Henry Suski).

Forbus died in the Duke Hospital from a terminal illness diagnosed in 1971, although he had been active until a month before his death. His ashes were deposited behind a bronze plaque in the Memorial Wall in the foyer of the Duke University School of Medicine.

SEE: Curriculum vitae (School of Medicine, Duke University, Durham); Data Sheet, Wiley Davis Forbus (Office of Information, Duke University, Durham); *Durham Herald*, 4 Mar. 1976; Raleigh *News and Observer*, 4 Mar. 1976.

C. SYLVESTER GREEN

**Forey, Martin Rudolph** *(24 Dec. 1817–13 June 1881)*, clergyman and educator, was born in Troy, N.Y. In 1840 he matriculated in the preparatory department of Madison University (now Colgate) upon recommendation of the Tabernacle Baptist Church in New York City. After two years of preparatory study, he spent two additional years in the collegiate department before moving to South Carolina in 1844. There he was principal of Barnwell Academy, Barnwell District, from 1844 to 1845 and a teacher in the Charleston Female Seminary from 1845 to 1847. While in Charleston he served for a time as an assistant to the pastor of Wentworth Street Church.

By October 1847, Forey was in New Bern, N.C., and

serving as pastor of the Baptist Church. He was ordained by that church to the full work of the ministry on 30 Jan. 1848, and continued to serve as pastor until January 1849. On 20 May 1849 the trustees of Chowan Female Institute, Murfreesboro, appointed him to succeed Archibald McDowell as principal, a position he held until August 1854. During his first two years in Murfreesboro he also was pastor of the Murfreesboro Baptist Church.

Forey's administration witnessed two events of special significance for the life of the institute. First, he helped to devise and execute a plan to permit the expansion of its already crowded physical facilities while ensuring financial solvency. The plan called for the incorporation of a joint stock company, with shares of stock in the institute to be sold at $25 each and to provide 6 percent interest to the shareholders. A spacious new building was to be erected upon the subscription of the first $4,000 in the company. Within six months of the announcement of this plan, the friends of Chowan had subscribed over $10,000. Second—and as a direct consequence of the initial success of this financial scheme—the "Columns Building" was constructed on a 28-acre site that had been obtained for this purpose. By November 1852 the four-story building was ready for occupancy. Constructed at a cost of $15,725, the "Columns Building" remains a central landmark on the present campus of Chowan College.

However, the initial financial success did not continue. Even before the new structure had been completed, Forey had to report that the financial affairs of the board were "somewhat embarrassed in consequence of the recent reverses of the agricultural portion of the community, from whom our subscriptions were chiefly obtained." Financial arrangements became a bone of contention between Forey and the board of trustees, and between Forey and the Murfreesboro Baptist Church. It is also probable that Forey felt that the board was interfering unduly with his management of the academic affairs of the institute. At any rate, he made it known that he was resigning his position in order to open a new female seminary in Hampton, Va.

During his later years, Forey served as principal of the Chesapeake Female College (1854–57); as a missionary of the Baptist Missionary Convention of New York, located in Delhi, N.Y. (1859–60); as pastor of the Baptist Church in Oswego, N.Y. (1860–63); and as a general agent for the Chicago Baptist Theological Seminary (1863–67). He was a leading spirit in the formation of a "Baptist College Colony," which in 1870 established Judson University and the town of Judsonia, in White County, Ark.

Forey's published works included *Female Education, Premature Church Membership* and *The Bible in Advance of Science.*

In October 1852 Forey maried Elizabeth DeLancey of Hamilton, N.Y. He was buried in Unadilla, N.Y.

SEE: *Biblical Recorder*, 11 Mar. 1848, 10 Mar. 1849, 5 Nov. 1852; *First Half Century of Madison University* (1872); *Historical Catalogue of Colgate University*, vol. 1 (1937); Edgar V. McKnight and Oscar Creech, *A History of Chowan College* (1964); Minutes of the Board of Trustees of Chowan College, 1849–54 (Chowan College, Murfreesboro).

R. HARGUS TAYLOR

**Forman, Joshua** *(6 Sept. 1777–4 Aug. 1848)*, jurist, builder, and promoter, was born in Pleasant Valley, Dutchess County, N.Y., the son of Joseph and Hannah Ward Forman, both natives of New Jersey. He first came into prominence for his development in 1819 of the site that became the city of Syracuse, N.Y., and capped an energetic and successful business career with the development—beginning in 1829—of a large tract of land in Rutherford County, N.C.

After attending public and private schools in his native county, Forman entered Union College, Schenectady, N.Y., from which he was graduated with honors in 1798. For the next two years he read law in Poughkeepsie and New York City; in the latter, he studied in the office of Samuel Miles Hopkins, a nationally known jurist of his day. In 1800, Forman was admitted to the New York State bar and settled in Onondaga Hollow, N.Y., where he practiced for nineteen years. One biographer of Forman wrote: "Since land titles at that time were in a state of almost hopeless confusion, and litigation was consequently brisk, lawyers could prosper in apparently insignificant hamlets."

In 1806 Forman was elected to the house of representatives of the state of New York. Serving one term, he distinguished himself with the advocacy of building a canal to connect the Hudson River and Lake Erie. This eventually was the Erie Canal, a vital transportation link in the commercial development of upper New York State. Forman himself was a prime mover in that development. In 1807 he built the first gristmill on the Oswego River, and a year later he established the Plaster Company at Camillus, N.Y. A highly respected and popular lawyer, he was appointed judge of the Onondaga County Common Pleas Court in 1813 and served on the bench with distinction for ten years.

In 1818 he moved from the village of Onondaga Hollow to the present site of the city of Syracuse. There he had purchased a large tract of land, which included a major portion of the present city that he had platted in 1818. He subsequently sold city lots and secured the passage of legislation to lower the level of Lake Onondaga. That resulted in the control through drainage of unhealthy, swampy areas as well as making usable a vast acreage formerly covered by the lake. He had an equal interest in the establishment of many local institutions, including schools, churches, public buildings, and profitable commercial properties. For all of these efforts Forman was hailed as "the Founder of Syracuse." To his earlier business concerns he added the manufacture of salt, and he is credited with the innovative production of solar salt. All together, he laid both the material and cultural foundations of the city.

It is reported that "due to his investments his affairs become involved." This is given as an explanation for his unexpected removal in 1826 to New Brunswick, N.J., where he began the operation of a very rich copper mine. During the next three years he formulated the banking concept of "mutual guarantee of indebtedness," which encouraged Martin Van Buren, recently elected governor of New York, to call upon the legislature to pass the Safety Fund Act (1829). Many historians have credited Van Buren's astute interest in financial management to the early influence of Joshua Forman.

Forman was restless and ambitious. The same year he saw his Safety Fund Act become law, he purchased an enormous tract, estimated at several hundred thousand acres, in Rutherford County, N.C. He then moved to the town of Rutherfordton, where he spent the rest of his life. Although it has been suggested that he had associates in the North Carolina land deal, the record indicates he alone handled the development on a proprietary basis, devoting his full time to the sale of parcels of land, exercising influential control over its use, and planning and working for the improvement of the town and area. That was much the plan he had followed in the development of Syracuse.

In 1800 Forman married Margaret Alexander of Glasgow, Scotland, the daughter of Boyd Alexander, a member of Parliament. They had one daughter. Margaret Alexander Forman died about 1828, just before Forman moved to North Carolina. About 1831 he married Sarah Garrett of Warm Springs, Tenn. There is no record of issue.

Forman suffered a disabling stroke about 1844 but lived four years. He died at his home in Rutherfordton and was buried in the Oakwood Cemetery, Syracuse, N.Y., one of the city's public facilities for which he had originally been responsible.

SEE: *DAB*, vol. 6 (1930); Clarence Griffin, *History of Old Tryon and Rutherford Counties, North Carolina, 1730–1936* (1937); *Nat. Cyc. Am. Biog.*, vol. 6 (1896); John H. Wheeler, *Historical Sketches of North Carolina* (1851); *Who Was Who in America* (1963).

C. SYLVESTER GREEN

**Forney, Daniel Munroe** *(May 1784–15 Oct. 1847)*, planter, public official, congressman, and army officer, was born in Lincoln County, the son of Peter and Nancy Abernathy Forney. He was educated in local schools before attending The University of North Carolina in 1804 as a member of the junior class. An officer in the local militia, he was commissioned a major in the regular army during the War of 1812. Initially he was assigned recruiting duties and then served with the Second Regiment of Artillery. Although agricultural pursuits occupied him much of his life, he also was a public servant. He was a member of the U.S. House of Representatives for most of two terms beginning in 1815 and ending on 6 Oct. 1818, when he resigned. His letter of resignation to Govenor John Branch gave no reason why he was stepping down. In 1820 he was appointed by President James Monroe as a member of a commission to treat with the Creek Indians. Between 1823 and 1827 he served four terms in the North Carolina Senate, and in 1829 was elected by the General Assembly to the first of two successive terms on the Council of State.

Forney married Harriett Brevard, daughter of Alexander Brevard, and they were the parents of several children. While his father was a member of Congress, Forney reportedly became acquainted with the Washington architect, Benjamin Henry Latrobe, designer of the national capitol, who apparently prepared the plans for a home, Ingleside, built by Forney on his plantation. Ingleside still stands. Mrs. Forney is said to have prevailed upon her husband to move in 1834 to Lowndes County, Ala., where she believed the family would flourish even more as planters. After a little over a dozen years in his new home, Forney died of what was described as a "chronic disease." He was buried in the family cemetery on his plantation.

SEE: *Biog. Dir. Am. Cong.* (1971); John L. Cheney, Jr., *North Carolina Government, 1585–1974* (1975); Daniel L. Grant, *Alumni History of the University of North Carolina (1924)*; Sarah M. Lemmon, *Frustrated Patriots, North Carolina and the War of 1812* (1973); Undated newspaper clipping (North Carolina Collection, Library, University of North Carolina, Chapel Hill).

LOUISE C. SMITH

**Forney, John Horace** *(12 Aug. 1829–13 Sept. 1902)*, soldier, Confederate officer, civil engineer, and planter, was born in Lincoln County. His father was Jacob Forney and his grandfather was Peter Forney, who served in the partisan corps during the American Revolution and afterward in the North Carolina House of Commons (1794–96), state senate (1801–2), and Congress (1813–15). His mother was Sabina Swope Hoke, the daughter of Daniel Hoke, also of Lincoln County. Of his brothers, George Hoke became a lieutenant colonel in command of the First Confederate Battalion and was killed at the Battle of the Wilderness in May 1864; and William Henry rose to the rank of brigadier general in command of a brigade of Alabama troops in General Robert E. Lee's Army of Northern Virginia.

In 1835, the Forney family left North Carolina and settled in Calhoun, (then Benton) County, Ala. After completing his preparatory course, young Forney was appointed to the U.S. Military Academy at West Point in 1848 and was graduated in 1852 with the rank of brevet second lieutenant in the Seventh United States Infantry. Subsequently he served in garrison in Kentucky and on the frontier in the Indian Territory. In 1855, he was on the staff of General Charles F. Smith during an exploring expedition to Pembina, and in 1858 he commanded the pioneer corps on General Albert S. Johnston's expedition to Salt Lake. In 1860, while an instructor of tactics at West Point, he was commissioned first lieutenant of the Tenth United States Infantry; however, foreseeing the approaching sectional conflict between North and South, he resigned and offered his services to Governor Andrew B. Moore of Alabama on 23 Jan. 1861. Commissioned a colonel of artillery in the Alabama state troops, Forney commanded at Pensacola, Fla., until 16 March when he was promoted to captain in the regular Confederate Army and assigned to the staff of General Braxton Bragg.

Upon the formation of the Tenth Alabama Regiment in Montgomery in May 1861, Forney was elected its colonel and commissioned on 4 June. His brother, Captain William Henry Forney, commanded a company in the same regiment. The Tenth Alabama soon was sent to Virginia, where it became part of General Kirby Smith's brigade after the Battle of First Manassas. Colonel Forney commanded this brigade for three months. In the Battle of Dranesville on 20 Dec. 1861, Forney, again in command of the Tenth Alabama, led his men in battle for the first time. During a gallant charge in the fighting both he and his brother William Henry were seriously wounded. On 14 Mar. 1862, Forney was promoted to brigadier general, to rank from 10 March (confirmed 13 March), and on 27 Oct. 1862 he received the rank of major general, to rank from the same date (confirmed 22 Apr. 1863). The reason for such a rapid promotion has never been explained in the records. Afterwards General Forney was assigned to the Department of South Alabama and West Florida, with headquarters in Mobile.

During the campaign for Vicksburg in the summer of 1863, he led a division of Alabama, Louisiana, Mississippi, and Texas troops comprising two brigades under brigadier generals Louis Hebert and John C. Moore. This division took part in the siege of the city and became part of Lieutenant General John C. Pemberton's army. Forney's men held the center of Pemberton's line of defensive trenches and earthworks and successfully repulsed Union forces in the attacks on 19 and 22 May 1863. After the fall of Vicksburg, Forney was paroled and during July 1863 commanded a parole camp at Enterprise, Miss. For a time he appears to have been a supernumerary officer without a command, but from July 1864 until the end of the war he commanded a division of troops in the District of Texas under General John B. Magruder in the Department of the Trans-Mississippi. He was paroled in Galveston, Tex., on 20 June 1865.

After the war Forney returned to Alabama and engaged in farming and planting in Calhoun and Marengo counties. He also took up civil engineering. He died and was buried at Jacksonville, Ala. Forney married Septima Sexta Middleton Rutledge, a daughter of Colonel Henry A. Rutledge of Talladega, Ala., and a granddaughter of Edward Rutledge of the celebrated South Carolina family of that name.

SEE: S. A. Cunningham, "Maj. Gen. John H. Forney," and W. W. Draper, "How Forney Saved the Day at Manassas," *Confederate Veteran* 15 (November 1907); C. A. Evans, *Confederate Military History*, vol. 8 (1899); T. M. Owen, *History of Alabama and Dictionary of Alabama Biography*, vol. 3 (1907); Ezra Warner, *Generals in Grey* (1959); *Who Was Who in America*, vol. 1 (1943); Marcus J. Wright, *General Officers of the Confederate Army* (1911).

PAUL BRANCH

**Forney, Peter** *(21 Apr. 1756–1 Feb. 1834)*, planter, Revolutionary War officer, iron manufacturer, legislator, and congressman, was born in Anson (now Lincoln) County. His father, Jacob Forney, was a French Huguenot from Alsace and his mother, Maria Bergner Forney, was Swiss. About 1754, shortly after their arrival and marriage at Philadelphia, the Forneys moved to North Carolina where Jacob became known as an intrepid Indian fighter. As a member of the Tryon County Committee of Safety, he signed the resolutions adopted there in August 1775. In January 1781 British General Charles Cornwallis used Forney's house for headquarters. British troops also stripped the plantations of Peter Forney and his frugal, industrious father of food and valuables.

Peter Forney and his brothers, Jacob and Abram, all saw military service during the American Revolution. Peter volunteered for many expeditions against the Cherokee, against Tories, and against British troops in the Carolinas and elsewhere on the frontier. In 1780, he was promoted to the rank of captain in the North Carolina Rangers and attached himself to General Griffith Rutherford's army of North Carolina troops. They arrived at Ramsour's Mill (20 June 1780) after the battle was over, although Abram Forney distinguished himself there and at the Battle of Kings Mountain (7 Oct. 1780).

When Cornwallis left his father's plantation, Peter Forney commanded a company of militia under General William Lee Davidson that attempted unsuccessfully to prevent the British from crossing the Catawba River. After Davidson was killed at Cowan's Ford on 1 Feb. 1781, Forney and many of the militia fled to Adam Torrence's tavern where they engaged in a brief skirmish with Colonel Banastre Tarleton. Forney then retreated east of the Yadkin River, where he remained about six weeks cooperating with patriot troops in the area. Later that year he commanded a company of dragoons that marched to Wilmington, and, it is said, helped persuade the British to evacuate the town. The British thought Forney's force was larger than it was. After the war, he was commissioned a general in the North Carolina militia.

In 1783, Forney married Nancy Abernathy. In 1787, he and Abram Forney began building an ironworks in eastern Lincoln County, where they produced wrought iron the following year. In 1789, the legislature granted the iron deposit east of Lincolnton known as the Big Ore Bank to the Forneys and two others, whose interest Peter Forney later purchased. In 1791, Forney sold interests to Alexander Brevard, Joseph Graham, and John Davidson. This company built Vesuvius Furnace. Forney also built a large forge near his home, Mount Welcome. After a few years he sold his interest in the partnership to the others and in 1809 built Madison Furnace on Leepers Creek, which produced cast iron. Both Vesuvius Furnace and Madison Furnace manufactured cannonballs used in the War of 1812. Forney's son-in-law, Dr. William Johnston, and Johnston's sons operated the Mount Welcome forge until 1860.

Forney served in the lower house of the North Carolina legislature, (1794–96), in the state senate (1801–2), and on the Council of State (1811). He was named a presidential elector five times. In 1804, he supported Thomas Jefferson and George Clinton, in 1808 Clinton and James Madison, in 1816 James Monroe and Daniel Tompkins, and in 1824 and 1828 Andrew Jackson and John C. Calhoun. In 1813, Forney was elected to the United States Congress. In the House he usually voted with the Republicans against measures the Federalists favored. He supported Madison's administration on questions relating to the conduct of the war and on the embargo on exports, and he voted to levy taxes to pay for the war. Existing records indicate that, although he almost always attended, he rarely spoke on the floor of the House and served on few committees. His Federalist colleague from North Carolina, Joseph Pearson, sarcastically commented that Forney "does not often favor the House with his remarks, although he sometimes addresses circulars to his constituents." Pearson was unhappy because Forney supported Felix Grundy of Tennessee in his attempt to expand the constitutional definition of treason to include refusing to support the government or trying to dissuade others from supporting it. Pearson charged that it was Forney who had interpreted the ideas of the Presbyterian minister and Revolutionary leader, John Witherspoon, so as to support this concept of "moral treason."

Forney declined to run for reelection in 1815 or to accept public office thereafter. His son David Munroe, succeeded him in Congress but resigned his seat in 1818. In the 1830s David Forney and his brother Jacob moved to Alabama, where Jacob's son, William Henry, was a congressman from 1875 to 1893.

Peter Forney has been described as hospitable, generous, charitable, honest, candid, and unaffected. According to the epitaph on his tombstone in a private burial ground in Lincoln County, he always acted on "Republican principles." He and his wife were the parents of David Monroe, Jacob, Moses (died young), James M., Joseph (died young), Mary or Polly (Mrs. Christian Reinhardt, Jr.), Eliza (first Mrs. Henry Y. Webb and then Mrs. John Meek), Susan (Mrs. Bartlett Shipp), Lavinia (Mrs. John Fulenwider), Caroline (Mrs. Ransom G. Hunley), Sophia (Mrs. Cyrus L. Hunter), and Nancy (Mrs. William Johnston).

SEE: *Biog. Dir. Am. Cong.*, (1961); L. F. Crawford, *Forney Forever*, and *William Webb Crawford, Dean of Birmingham Bankers* (1967); C. W. Griffin, *History of Old Tryon and Rutherford Counties* (1937); C. L. Hunter, *Sketches of Western North Carolina* (1877); *Raleigh Register*, 18 Nov. 1800, 19 Sept., 17 Nov. 1801, 15 Nov. 1802, 21 May 1813, 25 Aug. 1815; W. L. Sherrill, *Annals of Lincoln County* (1937); Thirteenth U.S. Congress, *Annals of Congress*

(1813); J. H. Wheeler, *Historical Sketches of North Carolina* (1851).

LAURA PAGE FRECH

**Forney, William Henry** *(9 Nov. 1823–16 Jan. 1894),* lawyer, congressman, and Confederate soldier, was born in Lincolnton, the son of Jacob and Sabina Swope Hoke Forney and the grandson of General Peter and Nancy Abernathy Forney. Peter Forney, a native of Lincoln County, led a partisan corps in the American Revolution; he also was a member of the North Carolina House of Commons (1794–96), a state senator (1801–2), a congressman (1813–15), and an elector during the presidential campaigns of Jefferson, Madison, Monroe, and Jackson. William's granduncle, Daniel Hoke Forney, also represented North Carolina in Congress. Of William's brothers, John Horace became a major general in the Confederate army; George Hoke became lieutenant colonel of the First Confederate Battalion and was killed at the Battle of the Wilderness in 1864; and Daniel P. became major of the Second Alabama Regiment.

In 1835, the Forney family left North Carolina and settled in Calhoun (then Benton) County, Ala. Here young William grew to manhood, being six feet tall with a stout frame. He entered the University of Alabama at Tuscaloosa and pursued classical studies. After he was graduated in 1844 with an A.B. degree, he studied law in the office of his older brother Daniel in Jacksonville, Ala. At the outbreak of the Mexican War, William enlisted for a year in Colonel John R. Coffee's First Alabama Volunteers and served as a lieutenant during the siege of Vera Cruz. At the end of his enlistment period he returned to Jacksonville and resumed the study of law under T. A. Walker. Admitted to the bar in 1848, Forney formed a partnership with James B. Martin of Talladega and practiced until 1859, when he represented Calhoun County in the state legislature.

At the outbreak of the Civil War, Forney entered Confederate service as captain of a company of the Tenth Alabama Regiment, organized on 4 June 1861. On 3 July the regiment was sent to Virginia where on 20 December, while doing detached duty, it participated in a sharp engagement at Dranesville. In this encounter, Captain Forney was severely wounded in the leg and unable to resume command for some two months. The day after the engagement, however, he received a commission as major of the regiment. On 16 Mar. 1862, he was promoted to lieutenant colonel. The regiment then serving in Wilcox's Alabama Brigade, Longstreet's division, Forney participated in the fighting around Yorktown. In the rearguard action at Williamsburg he was severely wounded in the right shoulder. Taken to William and Mary College, which was being used as an improvised hospital, he was captured by Union soldiers and held prisoner for four months.

On returning to his regiment he discovered that his brother-in-law, Colonel John J. Woodward, who commanded the regiment, had died and that he had succeeded him as colonel. In this capacity, Forney led the Tenth Alabama at Fredericksburg, Chancellorsville, and Salem Church where he was slightly wounded in the leg. Again leading the regiment at Gettysburg, he received flesh wounds in the arm and chest. Soon his right arm—the one injured at Williamsburg a year earlier—was shattered and he collapsed in shock. While lying prostrate on the field, a shell blew away one-third of his ankle bone. In this dire condition he fell into enemy hands and was imprisoned for thirteen months in Fort Delaware, Baltimore, Md. He was then selected as one of fifty Confederate officers to be sent to Morris Island near Charleston, S.C., and exposed to the fire of Confederate batteries as a retaliatory measure. Afterwards he was sent to Port Royal, S.C., for the same purpose; however, the retaliation differences were finally worked out and Forney was exchanged. Hobbling on crutches, he returned to Lee's army to join his regiment in the siege of Petersburg. He soon found himself in command of the old Alabama brigade in which his regiment served. The brigade contained the Eighth, Ninth, Tenth, Eleventh, and Fourteenth Alabama regiments. On 23 Feb. 1865, he was promoted to brigadier general to rank from 15 February (confirmed 23 February). Forney led the brigade at Hatcher's Run and, in the retreat to Appomattox, in the battles of High Bridge and Farmville. At Appomattox, he surrendered the 952 officers and men of his brigade, one of the largest left in Lee's army, and was paroled.

Returning to Jacksonville after the war, Forney resumed his law practice broken in body, having been wounded thirteen times in battle, but undaunted in spirit. In 1865 he served in the state senate, but under the shackles of Reconstruction he was denied his seat. After the carpetbaggers were overthrown in the state, Forney was elected on the Democratic ticket to serve in the Forty-fourth Congress. Beginning on 4 Mar. 1875, he served and was reelected to eight succeeding congresses ending on 3 Mar. 1893. He was not a candidate for reelection in 1892. Forney was also appointed a member of the Gettysburg Battlefield Commission by President Grover Cleveland and served until his death. He died in Jacksonville and was buried there in the city cemetery.

On 4 Oct. 1854 Forney married Mary Eliza Woodward, the daughter of E. L. Woodward, a prosperous merchant of Calhoun County. They had two sons and three daughters.

SEE: Willis Brewer, *Alabama: Her History, Resources, War Record, and Public Men* (1872); *DAB*, vol. 3 (1959); John W. DuBose, *Notable Men of Alabama*, vol. 2 (1904); Albert B. Moore, *History of Alabama and Her People* (1927); North Carolina Board of Agriculture, *Handbook of the State of North Carolina* (1883); Thomas M. Owen, *History of Alabama and Dictionary of Alabama Biography* (1915); Benjamin F. Riley, *Makers and Romance of Alabama History* (1915); Ezra Warner, *Generals in Gray* (1959); Marcus J. Wright, *General Officers of the Confederacy* (1911).

PAUL BRANCH

**Forster, Anthony** *(11 Jan. 1785–18 Jan. 1820),* Unitarian clergyman, was born in Brunswick County but beyond that little is known of his early life. His father is referred to as "a respectable farmer," which would place him in the yeoman class, and died when Forster was quite young, leaving the lad under the guardianship of a friend. One account mentions General Benjamin Smith as Forster's guardian, and this is logical because Smith was a wealthy planter of Brunswick County—in the 1790 census he is listed as holder of 221 slaves. We are led to believe that there were other children in the family, but, as with the parents, no names are given. Forster's obituary notice, appearing in the *Raleigh Register* for 21 Jan. 1820, states that a brother and two sisters were among his survivors.

At the age of twelve Forster was sent to the preparatory school of The University of North Carolina and remained there, or in the university, for five years. His name appears twice in the list of students standing examinations in June 1800; the records report that he "acquitted himself as superior" in reading and spelling, and for the Latin class he is listed as one of those who was examined and passed. What other courses, or how many, Forster was enrolled for we do not know. There is no note in either the minutes of the trustees or of the faculty to indicate that he received a bachelor of arts degree from the university in 1815 as is sometimes reported.

Between 1800 and 1804 the record of Forster's activities remains blank. Presumably, he attended the preparatory school or the university until 1802, though this is not substantiated. At whatever time he may have left Chapel Hill it appears that upon the advice of friends he began to study law, only to become disenchanted and join the army in March 1804. He was granted an ensign's commission, immediately sent to join troops on Georgia's western frontier, and within a short time promoted to the rank of lieutenant.

By October 1806 Forster had tired of army life and resigned his commission, yet remained at the fort as a civilian employee in the government's trading post. From this employment Forster returned to the study of law, reading under the tutelage of a Milledgeville, Ga., attorney. During his residence in Milledgeville he suffered a lengthy and serious bout with fever, and this seems to mark the beginning of the ill health that was to claim his life while still a young man.

When sufficiently able to travel Forster returned to North Carolina for a visit with friends, and from there he had planned a trip to Ballston Springs, N.Y., in hope of regaining more strength. But the northward journey ended in King and Queen County, Va., when he had a severe attack of rheumatism that caused a change of plans and a return to North Carolina.

Again in North Carolina, and with his health slightly restored, Forster was offered employment as private secretary to General Benjamin Smith, the governor-elect. This was in December 1810 and the appointment brought Forster to Raleigh. How long he held the position, we do not know; biographical accounts say, "for only a short period" and that "he did not continue long in the situation." At some point, however, his thoughts turned toward the ministry, and, realizing the need for further study, he accepted the position of assistant teacher in the Raleigh Academy, a school operated under the direction of the Reverend Dr. William McPheeters, pastor of the Presbyterian Church. His free time was spent studying theology, with Dr. McPheeters as his teacher.

Early in 1813, Forster appeared before Orange Presbytery at its meeting in Raleigh and was licensed to preach. For the next few months he served without pay as a missionary in parts of South Carolina and Georgia, and at the end of the year was called by the congregation of the Independent Church at Wappetaw, S.C. But this pastorate was short-lived, for in the summer of 1814 he supplied the pulpit of Charleston's First Presbyterian Church, and in the fall he became minister for the Independent Church on John's Island.

Forster's next pastoral relationship was with the Independent Church of Charleston, familiarly known as the Circular Church. His call to this charge was as interim pastor, substituting for the ailing and elderly senior minister, Dr. William Hollinshead. This congregation offers an interesting sidelight on church and denominational history in view of its custom, which was followed for more than thirty years, of having two ministers conduct services for two bodies of worshipers, one at the Circular Church on Meeting Street and the other at the church on Archdale Street. At the time the invitation was extended to Forster, the Reverend Benjamin M. Palmer, uncle of the better-known Presbyterian clergyman of the same name, had been with the church for a year as Dr. Hollinshead's associate.

Forster assumed his duties with the Circular Club in 1815 and filled the appointment to the entire satisfaction of members of the two groups; apparently he possessed a warm and pleasing personality and was blessed with a keen mind and the talents of an effective pulpit orator. Unfortunately another siege of illness soon overtook him, with his lungs seriously affected, and he was forced to take several months' rest. It was apparently at this time, during the year 1815–16, that his thoughts and studies led him away from Calvinism, for by the spring of 1816 he was to advise Harmony Presbytery of his wish to withdraw from membership in that body. He could no longer accept in good faith the doctrine of the Trinity, but instead had become Unitarian in his belief. The Reverend Dr. Hollinshead died in February 1817, and this of course raised the question as to his successor. Though members of the congregation respected Forster, all of them were by no means prepared to accept his Unitarianism. The result was a separation of the two groups. Forster became minister for the Archdale Street congregation, and the name Second Independent Church of Charleston was adopted. This was the congregation later to be served for so long by the distinguished Unitarian clergyman, the Reverend Samuel Gilman.

Ill health, which by this time had developed into tuberculosis, cut short Anthony Forster's career. In 1817 and again in 1818 it was necessary for him to have a period of rest, and his last sermon was preached on 7 Mar. 1819. With his wife and children he returned to Raleigh where he died early in the following year.

On 28 Dec. 1813 Forster had married Altona Holstein Gales, daughter of Joseph Gales, editor of the *Raleigh Register* and a leader among the South's Unitarians. The religious convictions of his father-in-law led Forster to read widely in Unitarian literature in efforts at rebuttal, but instead he was brought to a rejection of Calvinism. The change in theological views, however, did not deprive Forster of old friendships; his funeral service was conducted by Dr. McPheeters under whom he had studied theology. Interment was in Raleigh's City Cemetery. He was survived by his wife and a young son, Thomas Gales Forster, and daughter, Annie.

Forster's career was marked by changes that indicate a certain lack of self-assurance and firmness of purpose; in fact, only in the last years of his life did he seem to find himself, and then to die as a relatively young man. But it is in a larger sense that Forster's life assumes significance. In him we have examples of religious tolerance and of the intellectual approach to religion during the first decades of the nineteenth century that have too frequently been overlooked in studies of the antebellum South. The congregation that he nurtured merely as an independent church later became Unitarian in its affiliation and, under Gilman's leadership, made a major contribution to Charleston's religious and cultural life.

SEE: Raymond Adams, *The Charleston Unitarianism Gilman Began With* (n.d.); Earl Wallace Cory, "The Unitarians and Universalists of the Southeastern United States During the Nineteenth Century" (Ph.D. diss., University of Georgia, 1970); George N. Edwards, *History of the Independent or Congregational Church of Charles-*

*ton, South Carolina* (1947); Anthony Forster, *Sermons, Chiefly of a Practical Nature* (1821 [portrait]); "Gales Reminiscences," by Winifred and Joseph Gales (Southern Historical Collection, University of North Carolina at Chapel Hill); "Minutes of the Board of Trustees and Student Records and Faculty Reports of The University of North Carolina" (1800–1815); *Raleigh Register*, 21 Jan. 1820; William B. Sprague, ed., *Annals of the American Unitarian Pulpit* (1865); William Ware, ed., *American Unitarian Biography*, vol. 2 (1851).

J. ISAAC COPELAND

**Forsyth, Benjamin** *(early 1760s–28 June 1814)*, officer in the Rifle Corps during the War of 1812, was born probably in Virginia, although some accounts give Stokes County, N.C. Family tradition says that his parents were James and Elizabeth Forsyth, that his father died while the boy was still young, and that his mother remarried. Benjamin received some education, as evidenced by his letters, and he also possessed property, for beginning in 1794 he bought land in Stokes County and by 1810 owned 3,000 acres and seven slaves. In 1797 he married Bethemia Ladd, by whom he had six children: Elizabeth Bostic (1798), Sally Almond (1800), Effie Jones (1803), Bethemia Harding (1805), James N. (1808), and Mary L. (1811). Forsyth served in 1807 and 1808 as a representative in the General Assembly from Stokes County.

Commissioned a second lieutenant in the Sixth United States Infantry on 24 Apr. 1800, Forsyth served two months after which he was honorably discharged. Eight years later, when the United States went on a war footing following constant friction with both Great Britain and France during the Napoleonic Wars, he was commissioned a captain in the Rifle Regiment and thereafter served in the army until he was killed in action, being promoted to major on 20 Jan. 1813 and breveted lieutenant-colonel on 6 Feb. 1813. The Rifle Regiment (later the Rifle Corps) was the elite branch of the service. In 1809 their uniforms consisted of green coats "faced and turned up" with brown and yellow, green pantaloons, fringed white vests, and leather caps high in front with "U.S.R.R." in large yellow characters and finished off with "tall nodding black plumes."

In August 1812 the Rifle Regiment arrived on the Canadian front where it engaged in guerrilla tactics, brief encounters, and scouting, and where it also spearheaded larger operations combining land and water movements. Forsyth led his troops in attacks on Gananoque (1812) and Elizabethtown (1813); in combined operations against York (1813) and Fort George (1813); at the Battle of Chrysler's Island (1813); and in his final campaign around Odell Town (1814). The most noted of his hit-and-run operations was the night raid across the frozen St. Lawrence River on Elizabethtown. At about 10:00 P.M. on 6 Feb. 1813, Forsyth led a band of volunteers on a twelve-mile march up the American side of the river, across the ice, and back down the Canadian side to surprise the sleeping British garrison. The Americans liberated a group of their own prisoners, captured 52 British and 134 stand of arms, and returned home safely by 8:00 A.M. North Carolinians were bursting with pride over the exploit, following as it did on the heels of such dismal news as Hull's surrender at Detroit. A typical toast was offered to "Major Forsyth and his gallant band of North Carolinians; May their Eagles, as heretofore, always summon them to victory and to glory."

Forsyth led the landing party in the capture of York on 26 Apr. 1813; and again on 25 May 1813 he led the initial attack on Fort George. "Distinguished marks of respect" were received by the riflemen for their valor. He was with Colonel Alexander Macomb during the miserable march through snow, sleet, and rain to Chrysler's Island where he was slightly wounded in the American defeat. Following a grim winter at French Mill, Forsyth was again in the forefront of the American army as it attacked LaColle Mill and attempted to capture Odell Town. Because he could not bring himself to follow orders by retreating into an ambuscade, he was killed. Brigadier General George Izard reported, "The Indiscretion of poor Forsyth prevented the entire success of the [ambush]—he has paid for it with his life." He became legendary to his men and his North Carolina compatriots because of his dazzling excursions and flashy achievements. Yet he was reprimanded by his superior officers upon occasion for the very same qualities, although in a final evaluation Dearborn regarded him as "an excellent officer, and, under suitable circumstances, would be of important service."

At the close of the war the Forsyth family moved to Tennessee, never to return. A resolution of appreciation was adopted in December 1817 by the General Assembly offering to educate his son and authorizing the presentation of a sword to him. When James N. Forsyth was fifteen years old, he was sent to the Academy at Hillsborough at state expense and then to The University of North Carolina. James left the university, joined the navy as a midshipman, and died when his ship was lost at sea in 1829. The county of Forsyth was erected by the legislature in 1849 and so named in honor of the military hero of the War of 1812.

SEE: Samuel A. Ashe, ed., *Biographical History of North Carolina*, vol. 5 (1906); Adelaide Fries and others, *Forsyth: A County on the March* (1949); Francis Heitman, *Historical Register and Dictionary of the United States Army*, vol. 1 (1916); S. M. Lemmon, *Frustrated Patriots: North Carolina and the War of 1812* (1973); *Raleigh Minerva*, 15 July 1814.

SARAH MCCULLOH LEMMON

**Fortsen (Fortson), Mary** *(d. 1664 or 1665)*, was the first woman who is known to have owned North Carolina land. By patent dated 25 Sept. 1663, issued by Sir William Berkeley, governor of Virginia and Proprietor of Carolina, she was granted 2,000 acres of land on the west side of Pasquotank River. The land adjoined tracts granted to John Battle and Thomas Keele on the same date. The reasons for issuance of the grant to Mary instead of her husband, Frederick, are not known. Presumably, there were legal technicalities involving the twenty headrights on which the grant was based, for ordinarily such a grant was not made to a married woman.

Mary Fortsen also was exceptional in that she made a will that she signed herself, evidence that she was literate. In her day a married woman had no legal right to dispose of her property by will unless her husband consented, and few wives made wills. Mary's will appears to have been made primarily to enable her husband, in the event of her death, to give clear title to 900 acres of her land, for which a sale was being negotiated when she became ill. The will also gave her husband greater flexibility in handling the remaining land than he would have been allowed otherwise under the common law. The will, dated 20 Jan. 1663/64, is the oldest North Carolina document of its kind now on record. It was proved on 15 Nov. 1665 before the governor and council of the North Carolina colony, which was then called Albemarle. It empowered Frederick to give bills of sale for the land involved in the pending transaction and confirmed his right under the common law to a life estate in the remaining 1,100 acres. Under the will, as under common law, that land was to go to the Fortsens' son, Theophilus, at Frederick's death. The will provided, however, that Frederick, if he saw fit, was to have power to sell the portion retained and invest the proceeds in cattle for the benefit of the child. It further provided that the land or cattle should be equally divided between Theophilus and an unborn child that Mary then carried, if that child should live.

It is not certain that Mary and her family ever lived in North Carolina. They appear to have been residing in Virginia at the time of the grant. The original will of Mary Fortsen is in the North Carolina State Archives, Raleigh.

SEE: John Bennett Boddie, *Seventeenth Century Isle of Wight County, Virginia* (1938); J. Bryan Grimes, ed., *North Carolina Wills and Inventories* (1912); Nell Marion Nugent, comp., *Cavaliers and Pioneers* (1934); William S. Powell, ed., *Ye Countie of Albemarle in Carolina* (1958).

MATTIE ERMA E. PARKER

**Fortune, Roma Coxey** *(9 Feb. 1879–27 Oct. 1942)*, Episcopal priest, son of John L. and Mary Coxey Fortune, was born in Black Mountain. Having lost his hearing at age eight after a severe case of scarlet fever, he received his education at the North Carolina School for the Deaf in Morganton. In 1906, he and his family moved to Durham to join other deaf persons who had gone there seeking employment in the textile and tobacco industries. Fortune worked first for the Durham Hosiery Mill and later for the American Tobacco Company.

Because of the large number of deaf persons living in Durham, the Reverend Oliver J. Whildin, Episcopal missionary to the deaf in the southern states, went there in early 1906 to begin a mission for the deaf. Working with the Reverend Sidney S. Bost, rector of St. Philip's Church, Whildin organized and taught a group of deaf persons who displayed an interest in the Episcopal church. After several weeks of instruction, he presented to the bishop for confirmation a class of seventeen deaf people who were confirmed on 20 May 1906. One of the members of the class was Roma C. Fortune. From that time on Fortune took an increasingly active part in the development of his church's work among the deaf.

Following Whildin's commencement of the mission in Durham, the Reverend Mr. Bost organized a Bible class for the deaf and held services for them at St. Philip's Church each Sunday afternoon. Fortune assisted him by interpreting the services in the sign language. The extent to which members of the congregation participated in the liturgy of the Episcopal church appealed to the deaf. They made all the responses, read the psalter, and sang the chants and hymns in the sign language. As the deaf congregation grew, Fortune relieved Bost by teaching the Sunday school and by being licensed as a lay reader. After working for several years as a layman, he decided to study for the ministry. Both he and Bost felt that the deaf needed one of their own to serve them. Fortune read theology under Bost's direction and on 13 Feb. 1917 was admitted as a candidate for holy orders. On 5 May 1918 Fortune was ordained to the diaconate by Bishop Joseph B. Cheshire in St. Philip's Church. The bishop placed him in charge of the deaf work in Durham under Bost's guidance and authorized him to extend his work to other parts of the diocese. He was also permitted to hold services in the two neighboring dioceses if they requested his assistance.

At the end of his first two years in the ministry, Fortune reported that he had visited ten places in the diocese and delivered 144 sermons and addresses. In 1924, he regularly officiated in fourteen stations in the state; he preached to "over a thousand people, and ministered to them in other ways." In eight of the stations he organized Bible and Sunday school classes with "about 200 members of various denominations attending," the majority of them Episcopalians. However, Fortune welcomed the deaf of other communions as well as those not affiliated with any church. During the years he was caring for his widely scattered mission posts, he continued his theological studies under Bost. On 27 Jan. 1929 he was ordained a priest by Bishop Cheshire in St. Philip's Church, becoming the first deaf Episcopal priest in the southern states. The ordination service was interpreted to the deaf people in the congregation by James R. Fortune, a son of the candidate.

From the time the Episcopal church began working for the deaf, services and Sunday schools were held in established churches for the hearing on Sunday afternoons or evenings. The plan worked well in most places, but in Durham the deaf congregation had grown large enough to justify a church building of its own. Fortune felt that they had imposed long enough on the goodwill and cooperation of the rector and members of St. Philip's parish. In May 1926 he addressed the annual meeting of the Episcopal Church Women on the need for a separate church building for the deaf of Durham. The church women responded to his appeal with a pledge of $3,000 toward a building. With the additional assistance of other Episcopalians throughout the diocese, a neat brick structure seating two hundred persons was completed five years later. It was consecrated on 17 May 1931 and given the name Ephphatha, the Aramaic word meaning "be opened," used by Christ when he healed a deaf mute. This church was the first in the South and the fourth in the nation to be built for the use of the deaf. Fortune became priest in charge of the mission as well as having responsibility for all the deaf work in the diocese.

Three years after the consecration of Ephphatha, the deaf congregation of Burlington acquired a church building of their own, St. Athanasius. It was an unused church building belonging to the Church of the Holy Comforter, whose vestry remodeled it and presented it to the deaf of Burlington. Under Fortune's care the deaf work in Burlington had grown steadily since the beginning of his ministry. When St. Athanasius was reconsecrated in 1934, the deaf congregation of Burlington was ready for a church of its own.

From the beginning of his ministry to deaf people, Fortune did not limit his efforts to their spiritual needs but tirelessly assisted them in their everyday social and economic life. He made them feel free to call on him for advice and help with personal and community problems. In this way he inspired and won the affection of his congregations. In a tribute to him Bishop Edwin A. Penick remarked: "Considering the handicap under which he labored, Mr. Fortune's ministry was not only dramatic and appealing, but far reaching in its extent and substantial in results. We honor him as one of the outstanding pioneers of the Church. . . . We never heard the sound of his voice, but we never failed to catch the muted sweetness of his personality."

On 17 Oct. 1900 Fortune married Elsie Carter, of Kinston, a classmate at the North Carolina School for the Deaf. They had seven children: Robina (Mrs. R. E. Register), Maude Addie (Mrs. A. L. Thompson), Robert F., Sidney C., Roma C., Jr., James R., and Edward L.

He was buried in Maplewood Cemetery, Durham.

SEE: *Carolina Churchman*, April 1912, August 1916, August 1917, October 1919, June 1926, December 1928, February 1929, January, December 1930, June/July 1931, November 1942; *Durham Sun*, 2 Sept. 1938; Family information supplied by the Reverend James R. Fortune, Littleton, N.C.; *Journals of the Diocese of North Carolina*, 1906–43; Raleigh *News and Observer*, 28 Oct. 1942; Winston-Salem *Twin City Sentinel*, 22 Nov. 1930.

LAWRENCE F. LONDON

**Foster, Charles** *(18 Feb. 1830–14 Mar. 1882)*, lawyer, editor, and politician, was the son of Cony and Caroline Brown Foster of Orono, Maine. After graduating from Bowdoin with first honors in 1855, he read law under Israel Washburn, later governor of Maine, and was admitted to the bar in 1856. Owing perhaps to a condition of intermittent deafness, Foster declined to practice law and instead pursued a career in journalism. Having campaigned actively for Buchanan in the 1856 election, he became editor in 1857 of a Democratic, Southern rights newspaper at Norfolk, Va., the *Southern Statesman*. Later that year he became assistant editor of a larger paper, the Norfolk *Day Book*. He was a delegate to the Democratic state convention at Petersburg in 1858 and published some essays and poetry in the *Southern Literary Messenger*, *Knickerbocker Magazine*, and other periodicals.

At the end of 1859, Foster purchased *The Citizen*, a small Democratic weekly at Murfreesboro, N.C., and moved there to become the new editor. Active from the first in First District politics, he was elected an alternate to the Democratic National Convention at Charleston in 1860 and represented North Carolina at the Baltimore convention later in the year. Still vociferously the champion of Southern rights, he supported the nomination of John C. Breckinridge as the Democratic candidate. Earlier in the year, he married Susan A. Carter of Murfreesboro.

In October 1860, Foster sold his newspaper and applied for a position in the Post Office Department from the outgoing Buchanan administration. He also announced as a candidate to the state convention of February 1861, which was to consider the question of North Carolina's secession from the Union. In his campaign, and in articles published in W. W. Holden's Raleigh *Standard*, Foster now came forward as a strong Union man, appealing against secession. He withdrew from the race when W. N. H. Smith, another Union man, announced for the convention, and left Murfreesboro in February to accept a clerkship in the Post Office Department, Washington, D.C. On a visit to his family in Murfreesboro in May, he was suspected by some in the community to be a spy for Lincoln and was forced to flee the town, leaving his wife and infant daughter behind. He returned to Washington and began to seek a seat in Congress to represent the Unionists of North Carolina.

After an abortive bid to take a seat in the special session of July 1861, Foster contrived a series of letters, postmarked from various North Carolina towns, representing that Unionism was rife throughout the state. The letters also publicized a "Unionist election" in North Carolina in August for the purpose of sending representatives to Congress. Having mysteriously absented himself from Washington in July and August, Foster reappeared in September bearing credentials attesting to his election to Congress by the Unionists. It was subsequently determined that he had probably been in hiding in Lexington, Ky., during these months and that the views represented in his series of letters carried in the *New York Tribune* and other papers were largely false or highly exaggerated. Although further efforts to gain a congressional seat by holding elections in 1861 and 1862 at reoccupied Hatteras Island and elsewhere on the North Carolina coast were futile, it was not until 1863 that he finally abandoned hope for the office. His ambition was evidently nourished by the practice of the Lincoln administration of awarding seats to representatives elected from reoccupied portions of Virginia, Louisiana, and other Confederate states in the early part of the war. Military governor John Stanly and his allies succeeded in effecting the thorough discrediting of Foster during the winter of 1862–63.

In the meantime, Foster had found employment as a recruiting agent for the Union Army in eastern North Carolina. He recruited most of the First North Carolina Union Regiment and won a guarantee that he could take command of a second regiment if he could raise it. This he accomplished in 1863 and was commissioned lieutenant colonel of the Second North Carolina Union Volunteers, a position he held until banished from the army and, temporarily, from North Carolina by order of General Benjamin F. Butler in 1864. Butler's actions were taken on the grounds of Foster's inefficiency as an officer and because of complaints to Washington by Unionists close to Governor Stanly.

Having established a law practice on the North Carolina coast in the closing months of the war, Foster returned to Murfreesboro in the spring of 1865 and remained there until 1878. During these years he was an active but not particularly successful Republican political figure, a merchant, and an erstwhile correspondent for the *New York Herald* and various papers in North Carolina and Virginia. In 1878, pleading the ill health of his wife as the reason, Foster moved with his family to Philadelphia and became an editorial writer for the Philadelphia *Record*. He died there four years later. Foster was an active layman in the Episcopal Church.

SEE: Norman D. Brown, "A Union Election in Civil War North Carolina," *North Carolina Historical Review* 43 (1966); Charles Foster's diary for 1865 (Southern Historical Collection, University of North Carolina, Chapel Hill); Murfreesboro *Citizen*, scattered issues, 1859–60; Philadelphia *Record*, 15 Mar. 1882; Raleigh *North Carolina Standard*, 3 Jan. 1861.

T. C. PARRAMORE

**Foster (Forster), Diana Harris** *(b. ca. 1644)*, innkeeper, was one of the first businesswomen in North Carolina. She came to the colony, then called Albemarle, with her first husband, Thomas Harris, about 1665. In a deposition made in 1676, she gave her age as thirty-two. Diana and Thomas Harris lived in Perquimans Precinct, where Thomas held 600 acres of land granted him by patent and additional land that he bought. In 1665 Thomas was clerk of the Albemarle Council, and he later became public register, or secretary, of the colony. In the early 1670s he operated an inn, referred to in contemporary records as "the house of Thomas Harris." He died in October 1677, leaving a substantial estate in cattle and hogs and other property in addition to his land. He bequeathed his estate to Diana and his two sons, Thomas and John, provided Thomas, who had left the colony, should return within five years. Young Thomas appears not to have returned.

By March 1679/80 Diana had remarried. Her second husband, William Foster, was a widower with two children, Francis and Elizabeth. He was a justice of the county court of Albemarle in 1684. Like Harris, he lived in Perquimans Precinct and operated an inn. The county court met at "the house of William Foster" in 1686 and apparently the following year. Foster died in October 1687, leaving his estate to Diana and his two children.

After Foster's death Diana operated the inn, first in partnership with her son, John Harris, and then as sole proprietor after his death in 1693. The fact that the inn went to Harris and his mother, instead of Foster's children, indicates that the property was inherited from Thomas Harris rather than Foster. If so, the establishment known in the 1680s as the house of William Foster was no doubt the one known earlier as the house of Thomas Harris. During the partnership between Diana and her son, the inn was called the house of John Harris. After his death it was called the house of Diana Foster. Although Harris participated in the business to a degree, Diana seems to have been in charge during the partnership as well as afterward. Her chief assistant was one Thomas Hassold, whom she employed to keep books and perform other services. The county court continued to meet regularly at the inn from 1691 to 1693. Its successor, the General Court, met at the same place.

By the time the General Court was organized in September 1694, the inn had yet another name, for Diana had married again. In May or June 1694 she wed Thomas White, and thereafter the inn was known by his name.

Diana's marriage to White proved unfortunate for her and the inn. White, who was fourteen years younger than Diana, was heavily in debt. He took over the financial affairs of the inn and immediately initiated numerous lawsuits to collect outstanding accounts. His own creditors and those of the inn reciprocated in kind. Within a short time there were nearly fifty suits in the General Court involving White and Diana or White individually. The amounts collected by White apparently were not sufficient to pay his debts, for he sold much of his wife's property to satisfy his creditors. White's handling of the business and other aspects of his conduct caused the marriage to collapse. Within a year after their wedding, Diana sued White for separate maintenance, alleging that he had sold most of her household goods and furniture, had ejected her from her home, and had left her "destitute of a Convenient Lodginge and all other necessaryes."

The inn continued to operate for some months after Diana's complaint to the court, but it was either closed or sold about the end of February 1695/96. No reference to it appears in extant records after 26 February, when the General Court, which had held its winter term there, adjourned. It is likely that Thomas White was stricken with his last illness while the court was sitting. By 8 Apr. 1696 his will had been probated, and creditors had begun to file suit against his estate. Despite his assiduous collection of accounts and his sales of Diana's property, White left debts that far exceeded his assets.

Diana was allowed to have certain goods and furniture from White's estate, but she was left with meager resources. There is no evidence that she resumed business as innkeeper, although she appears to have taken a lodger or two. Her situation was alleviated in 1697, at least to a degree, by a bequest from Richard Bentley, who apparently was related to her.

On 17 Feb. 1703/4 Diana married her fourth husband, Thomas Mercer. The couple went to court the following year in an effort to obtain a tract of land that had belonged to Thomas Harris and had escheated, but the courts ruled against them. Mercer died on 21 Nov. 1706. The date of Diana's death is not known.

John Harris appears to have been Diana's only child. Although Thomas Harris named two sons in his will, it was stated by the son-in-law of John Harris that John was Diana's only son by Harris. If that is correct, Harris's other son, Thomas, was born of an earlier marriage. Diana had no children by her later husbands.

John Harris was married twice. In 1687 or 1688 he married Elizabeth Waller, widow of Thomas Waller and daughter of George and Ann Durant. Elizabeth died shortly after the marriage, and Harris remarried. His second wife, Susanah, gave birth to a daughter, Sarah, on 20 Sept. 1689. John Harris died between May and November 1693. His only surviving child, Sarah, married Nathaniel Nicholson.

SEE: J. Bryan Grimes, ed., *Abstract of North Carolina Wills* (1910); J. R. B. Hathaway, ed., *North Carolina Historical and Genealogical Register*, 3 vols. (1900–1903); North Carolina State Archives, Raleigh: Albemarle Book of Warrants and Surveys, 1681–1706; Births, Marriages, and Flesh marks, 1659–1739, and Precinct Court Minutes, 1688–93, of Perquimans County; Council Minutes, Wills, Inventories, 1677–1701; Will of William Foster; Mattie Erma E. Parker, ed., *Colonial Records of North Carolina, Higher-Court Records, 1670–1696*, vol. 2 (1968), and *1697–1701*, vol. 3 (1971); William S. Price, Jr., ed., *Colonial Records of North Carolina, Higher Court-Records, 1702–1708*, vol. 4 (1974); William L. Saunders, ed., *Colonial Records of North Carolina*, vol. 1 (1886); Ellen G. Winslow, *History of Perquimans County* (1931).

MATTIE ERMA E. PARKER

**Foster, Francis** *(d. after 1735)*, colonial Council member, was the son of William and Margaret Foster of Accomack, Va. The earliest record of Foster in North Carolina occurs in January 1689, when one Anthony Dawson successfully brought suit against him in the Perquimans Precinct court to recover a carpenter's adz. Foster served as a justice on the Perquimans Precinct court from January to October 1700 and again in 1702 and 1703. He is recorded as being a member of the Council from 1705 until 1710, but it was not until 10 Aug. 1714 that he presented to the Council his appointment as deputy for Lord Proprietor John Dawson. Foster served on the Council or upper house of the Assembly as Dawson's deputy from 1714 until 1725. When Dawson died in 1724, leaving his proprietorship entangled in legal affairs, the other Lords Proprietors appointed Foster to the Council where he served until 1731. While on the Council, he was involved in such issues as the "Six Confirmed Laws," which codified all statutes prior to 1715 not deemed obsolete; legislation in 1715 for establishing the Anglican church in the colony; and the proceedings concerning the running of the dividing line between North Carolina and Virginia in 1728.

Perquimans Precinct court records reveal that in January 1697 Foster proved headrights for William Foster, Frances Foster, Jane Swetman, and a Negro woman, but the relation between them and Foster is not known. On 14 Aug. 1694 Foster married Mrs. Hannah Gosby, widow of John Gosby. In 1699 Thomas Hallon, an orphan, was bound to Foster and his wife until he came of age. Foster was an Anglican, being appointed a vestryman in Perquimans Parish in 1715. The last reference to Foster was made in June 1735, when he was listed as being in arrears of his quitrent from September 1729 to March 1732 on 186 acres in Perquimans Precinct.

SEE: John L. Cheney, Jr., ed., *North Carolina Government, 1585–1974* (1975); Walter Clark, ed., *State Records of North Carolina*, vols. 22–23 (1907, 1904); J. Bryan Grimes, ed., *Abstract of North Carolina Wills* (1910); J. R. B. Hathaway, ed., *North Carolina Historical and Genealogical Register*, vol. 3 (1903); Mattie Erma E. Parker, ed., *Colonial Records of North Carolina, Higher-Court Records, 1697–1701*, vol. 3 (1971); William S. Price, Jr., ed., *Colonial Records of North Carolina, Higher-Court Records, 1702–1708*, vol. 4 (1974), and *1709–1723*, vol. 5 (1977); William L. Saunders, ed., *Colonial Records of North Carolina*, vols. 1–3 (1886); Mrs. Watson Winslow, *History of Perquimans County* (1931).

J. MARSHALL BULLOCK

**Foster (Forster), Richard** *(b. ca. 1622)*, Council member and a leader in Culpeper's Rebellion, settled in the North Carolina colony, then called Albemarle, before 7 Sept. 1669. He may have been the Captain Richard Foster who lived in Lower Norfolk County, Va., in the 1640s and 1650s and served as member of the House of Burgesses in 1655–56. However, there were other Richard Fosters in Virginia and elsewhere who might have moved to Albemarle.

Foster first appears in North Carolina records as a member of the Albemarle Council on 7 Sept. 1669, when Samuel Stephens was governor. He remained on the Council under Governor Peter Carteret, serving at least through April 1672. In the early 1670s he also was lieutenant colonel of the Albemarle militia.

In the fall of 1676, Sir George Carteret, a Proprietor, commissioned Foster to serve on the Albemarle Council as his deputy. When the commission reached Albemarle in the summer of 1677, Foster at first rejected it, for acceptance would require him to serve under Thomas Miller, whose pretensions to the governorship Foster and others deemed invalid. Later Foster accepted the commission and served several months in Miller's government, but in the fall he joined those planning Miller's overthrow and took a leading part in the uprising called Culpeper's Rebellion. During the revolt, Foster performed the valuable service of restraining the colonists from actions that would have been treasonable and guiding them in procedures that had a show of legality. He was made a member of the "rebel" Council, which governed the colony from December 1677, when Miller was imprisoned, until the fall of 1679, when the Proprietors established a legitimate government under John Harvey. Foster, like several other participants in the uprising, was named to Harvey's Council. After Harvey's death he served under John Jenkins at least through November 1681. He was again a Council member in May and November 1684 when Seth Sothel was governor. His tenure under Sothel probably was longer than is indicated by the few surviving records of Sothel's administration.

Little is known of Foster's private life. About 1682 he made a deposition in which he gave his age as "sixty yeares and upwards." He appears to have lived in Currituck Precinct. His name disappears from North Carolina records about the middle of the 1680s, but there is no record of his death.

SEE: Noel Currer-Briggs, ed., *Virginia Settlers and English Adventurers* (1970); J. R. B. Hathaway, ed., *North Carolina Historical and Genealogical Register*, 3 vols. (1900–1903); William Waller Hening, ed., *Virginia Statutes at Large* (1823); John C. Hotten, ed., *Our Early Emigrant Ancestors* (1962); Edward W. James, ed., *Lower Norfolk County, Virginia, Antiquary*, vol. 1, pt. 1 (1895); North Carolina State Archives, Raleigh: Albemarle Book of Warrants and Surveys, 1681–1706; Timothy Biggs, A Narrative of the Transactions Past in the County of Albemarle in Carolina since Mr. Tho. Miller his Arrivall there (January 1678 [photocopy, autograph MS]); Council Minutes, Wills, Inventories, 1677–1701; Nell M. Nugent, ed., *Cavaliers and Pioneers* (1934); Mattie Erma E. Parker, ed., *Colonial Records of North Carolina, Higher-Court Records, 1670–1696*, vol. 2 (1968), and "Legal Aspects of 'Culpeper's Rebellion,'" *North Carolina Historical Review* 45 (1968); William S. Powell, ed., *Ye Countie of Albemarle in Carolina* (1958); Hugh F. Rankin, *Upheaval in Albemarle* (1962); William L. Saunders, ed., *Colonial Records of North Carolina*, vol. 1 (1886); William G. and Mary S. Stanard, comps., *The Colonial Virginia Register* (1902); Clayton Torrence, comp., *Virginia Wills and Administrations, 1632–1800* (1972).

MATTIE ERMA E. PARKER

**Fountain, Richard Tillman** *(15 Feb. 1885–21 Feb. 1945)*, lawyer, legislator, lieutenant governor, and gubernatorial candidate, was born at Cedar Lane near Tarboro, the son of Almon Leonidas and Sarah Louisa Eagles Fountain. After attending Edgecombe County schools and Tarboro Male Academy, he entered The University of North Carolina where he received a law degree in 1907. During the same year he began to practice law in Rocky Mount. From 1911 to 1918 he served as the first judge of the Rocky Mount municipal court, and from 1919 to 1927 he represented Edgecombe County in the North Carolina House of Representatives. During the 1927 session of the General Assembly he served as speaker of the house. The following year he was elected lieutenant governor of North Carolina and served from 1929 to 1932.

In 1932 Fountain sought the Democratic nomination for governor, running against J. C. B. Ehringhaus of Elizabeth City and Allen Jay Maxwell of Raleigh. Fountain ran as an anti-administration liberal and a champion of the common man. He strongly opposed the centralization policies of the O. Max Gardner administration and the "machine politics" of his major opponent. After a first primary defeat of less than 50,000 votes, Fountain demanded a runoff. Campaigning virtually without funds or political organization, he lost the second primary by only 13,000 votes (182,055 for Ehringhaus to 168,971 for Fountain).

In 1936 and again in 1942 Fountain unsuccessfully challenged the incumbent, Josiah W. Bailey, for the Democratic nomination for U.S. senator. Once more operating on a very limited budget, Fountain polled 184,000 votes in 1936.

In addition to his law practice, Fountain owned and edited the Rocky Mount *Herald* newspaper (1934–42), served as director of the Home Building and Loan Association of Rocky Mount, director of the First National Bank of Rocky Mount, member of the board of trustees of The University of North Carolina, chairman of the State Board of Equalization, and member of the Great Smoky Mountain National Park Commission. He also served as president of the Rocky Mount Bar Association, vice-president of the North Carolina Bar Association (1922–23), member of the American Bar Association, member of the Rocky Mount School Board (1917–35) and its chairman for seven years, and charter member and president of the Rocky Mount Civitan Club. In the legislature he was the author of the bill that created the East Carolina Industrial Training School for Boys in Rocky Mount. He served as chairman of the board of trustees of that institution, which subsequently became known as the Richard T. Fountain School.

In 1918 Fountain married Susan Rankin of Gastonia. They had four children: Susan Rankin (Mrs. Thomas G. Thurston), Anne Sloan (Mrs. Thomas G. Dill), Margaret Eagles (Mrs. John H. Paylor, Jr.), and Richard T., Jr.

SEE: Richard Tillman Fountain Papers (Manuscript Collection, East Carolina University, Greenville); Martha H. Tharrington, "Richard Tillman Fountain and the Gubernatorial Primary of 1932 in North Carolina" (Master's thesis, East Carolina University, 1974).

DONALD R. LENNON

**Foust, Julius Isaac** *(23 Nov. 1865–15 Feb. 1946)*, teacher, school superintendent, and college president, was born in Graham, the son of Thomas Carby and Mary Robbins Foust. As a boy he worked on his father's farm and attended Graham Academy and later Graham Normal School (now Elon College). From 1885 to 1887 he was a student at The University of North Carolina after which he taught at Caldwell Institute in Orange County. He returned to the university in 1888 and received a Ph.B. degree in 1890. The following year he was principal of the Graded School for White Children in Goldsboro. He then was appointed superintendent of schools in Wilson, where he married Sallie Price and later had two children, Henry P. Foust and Mary Foust Armstrong; for the latter a residence hall is named at The University of North Carolina at Greensboro. From 1894 to 1902 he was superintendent of schools in Goldsboro and conducted teacher institutes.

In 1902, Foust went to the State Normal and Industrial School for Girls (now The University of North Carolina at Greensboro) as principal of the practice school and head of the department of pedagogy, a position vacated by P. P. Claxton. The following year he was made dean of the faculty, and upon the sudden death of Charles Duncan McIver he became acting president. In 1907, he was appointed president.

When Foust began his presidency, it was as head of a small normal school of 461 students. With improvements in curriculum and faculty it was accredited by the Southern Association of Schools and Colleges, and in 1919 its name was changed to North Carolina College for Women. Although teacher education was always important, the school placed heavy emphasis on the liberal arts. In 1931, when it became the Woman's College of the University of North Carolina, Foust was named a vice-president of the university and head of the Woman's College. Phi Beta Kappa recognized the standards of the college by establishing a chapter there in 1934, the year Foust retired. At that time there were 1,800 students.

Foust was noted for his ability to win financial support for the college. In 1906, the value of the physical plant was estimated to be $490,000; in 1930, it was appraised at $6,709,087. Over thirty buildings were erected during that period. To obtain additional property that came up for sale when the legislature was not in session, Foust persuaded the Alumnae Association to sign a $60,000 mortgage when there was less than $400 in the treasury. Subsequently the legislature purchased the property for the Curry Building.

At a time when there was much controversy about the teaching of Darwinism, Foust supported academic freedom. In 1925 Dr. Albert Keister was accused of making an atheistic statement in a discussion following an extension class in Charlotte. Letters of protest came from church groups, parent-teacher organizations, alumnae, and other citizens. In his replies Foust defended the right of the individual to his own religious beliefs, and Keister remained at the college.

Foust was a life member of the North Carolina Education Association (now part of the North Carolina Association of Educators) and was named to the North Carolina Education Hall of Fame in 1957. He was president of the North Carolina Association of City School Superintendents (1902), of the North Carolina Teachers Assembly (now the North Carolina Association of Educators) (1904), and of the North Carolina Association of Colleges (1912). He also served for a time as chairman of the board of trustees of Agricultural and Technical College (now A & T State University).

In 1932, after the death of his first wife, Foust married Clora McNeill of North Wilkesboro. He died in Lakeland, Fla., where he spent his winters after retirement, and was buried in Green Hill Cemetery, Greensboro.

SEE: Julius I. Foust Papers (Archives, University of North Carolina at Greensboro); Daniel L. Grant, *Alumni History of the University of North Carolina* (1924); *North Carolina Biography*, vols. 6 (1919), 3 (1928 [portrait]), and 4 (1941); *Who Was Who in America*, vol. 2 (1950); *Who's Who in the South*, 1927.

ELISABETH BOWLES

**Fowle, Daniel Gould** *(3 Mar. 1831–8 Apr. 1891)*, lawyer, state legislator, judge, and governor, was a descendant of George Fowle, who emigrated from England to Concord, Mass., in 1638. Daniel G. Fowle was born in Washington, N.C., the fourth of ten children of Samuel Richardson Fowle, who had moved to Washington from Massachusetts in 1815, and Martha Barney Marsh Fowle. As a boy, young Fowle enjoyed the water sports of swimming, sailing, and fishing on the Pamlico River but was a studious sort as well. At fourteen, he entered the school of William J. Bingham in Orange County. He later attended Princeton where he was a member of the literary society and a junior orator. He was graduated in 1851, and went on to study law under Judge Richmond M. Pearson. After being admitted to the bar in 1853, he settled in Raleigh and practiced law.

From the onset of the dispute between North and South, Fowle opposed secession. Nevertheless, at the beginning of the Civil War he volunteered as a private in the Confederate Army. He became a member of the

Raleigh Rifles Company and soon afterwards a second lieutenant. He was appointed major of the commissary branch of the state military department but resigned the post in order to help raise the Thirty-first Regiment. Captured on Roanoke Island by General Ambrose Burnside, he was for a short time a prisoner of war. In October 1862, Fowle was elected to serve in the state legislature from Wake County. When this session adjourned, he was appointed adjutant general of North Carolina. He was promoted to the rank of major general by Governor Zebulon B. Vance but resigned in 1863.

In 1864, Fowle was reelected to serve in the state legislature. The following year Governor W. W. Holden appointed him judge of the superior court. Although the North Carolina legislature of 1865–66 elected him to this office for life, he stepped down instead of being forced to carry out the orders of the military commander of North Carolina and South Carolina during Reconstruction. After being defeated as a Democratic candidate for the convention of 1867, he was named chairman of the North Carolina Democratic Committee of 1868. Because of his hard work during the election, he was considered for the position of attorney general of the United Sates. In 1880, Fowle entered the North Carolina governor's race but was defeated by Thomas Jordan Jarvis. Four years later he was defeated by W. R. Cox in a bid for the Democratic nomination for the United States Congress. However, members of the 1884–85 Democratic legislature petitioned President Grover Cleveland to appoint him solicitor general.

In 1888, Fowle was nominated for governor by the so-called "Liberal Democrats" and won the election. When inaugurated on 17 Jan. 1889, it was raining and the ceremonies had to be held in Stronarch's Warehouse. Fowle was the first governor to live in the present governor's mansion. Upon taking office, he and his family moved into the then unfinished Executive Mansion in Raleigh. The governor brought his own furniture with him, filing a careful list with the state treasurer's office in order to keep a record of who owned what. Soon after assuming his duties as chief executive, he held a reception for legislators and other government officials. With this first social function in the mansion, a tradition was set for future governors to entertain returning and newly elected legislators. As governor, Fowle created and presided over a railroad commission that would protect the railroad interests as well as the people of the state against any abuse of power; recommended a tax levy in areas which found it difficult to comply with the four-month minimum school year; and advocated the establishment of a university as well as some form of higher education for women, devoting a portion of the 1891 address to the General Assembly to the matter.

Fowle was married in 1856 to Ellen Brent Pearson, the daughter of Judge Richmond M. Pearson under whom Fowle had studied law. She died in 1862 leaving two daughters, Margaret and Martha. In 1867, he married Mary E. Haywood, the daughter of Dr. Fabius and Mary Helen Haywood of Raleigh. Four children were born to them: Helen, Mary, Daniel G., Jr., and Fabius Haywood who was killed in a hunting accident as a boy. Governor Fowle was a Presbyterian. He died in office and was buried in Oakwood Cemetery, Raleigh. His portrait hangs in the grand entrance hall of the Executive Mansion.

SEE: Beth G. Crabtree, *North Carolina Governors, 1585–1958* (1958); Jerome Dowd, *Sketches of Prominent Living North Carolinians* (1888); Fowle Papers, Martha Matilda Fowle Wiswell Diary of a Civil War Era, and Wiswell Papers (North Carolina History Room, Brown Library, Washington, N.C.); Ursula F. Loy and Pauline M. Worthy, *Washington and the Pamlico* (1976); C. L. Van Noppen Papers (Manuscript Department, Library, Duke University); *Washington Daily News*, 30 Oct. 1953.

JULIA JONES HICKS

**Fowler, Charles Lewis** *(17 Nov. 1877–12 Feb. 1974)*, minister and educator, was born on a farm near Monroe, the son of Thomas Lafayette and Alice Riggins Fowler. Educated at Weddington Academy, Union County, at Furman University (A.B., 1904), and at the Newton Theological Seminary, Newton, Mass., Fowler entered the ministry of the Baptist church and served four years (1907–11) as pastor of the First Baptist Church, Clinton, S.C. In 1911, he gave up preaching to become president of tiny Lexington College, Mo. Three years later he became "co-president" of Cox College, Atlanta, a women's institution. While president, he undertook a wholesale renovation of the curriculum. Fowler left Cox in 1917 to found his own college, Lanier University, in Atlanta.

At the time, Atlanta was in the midst of a college building boom. In less than a decade Agnes Scott Institute had achieved collegiate status, Emory College had left the small town of Oxford, Ga., and moved to Atlanta to become a university, and Oglethorpe University had been revivified and located there. Fowler planned to capitalize on this enthusiasm, hoping that Lanier would receive substantial support from the community. In an attempt to show that his college filled a definite need, he promoted it as the state's first coeducational Baptist institution. Prominent Atlanta businessmen joined in the successful attempt to win a charter for Lanier, while numerous prominent Georgians participated in its opening ceremonies in the autumn of 1917. One hundred and forty students enrolled initially, a respectable number when compared to the enrollments of Atlanta's other white colleges. Fowler undertook successful public relations campaigns, regularly announced major financial gifts to the institution, and conducted a capital campaign intended to raise money to build a campus near Emory University in the fashionable Druid Hills area of the city.

When the Georgia Baptist Association rebuffed efforts to include Lanier in its system of higher education, Fowler began to shift the emphasis of the college from a religious to a more secular orientation. Now Lanier would be known as an "All-Southern" college, a term that Fowler had unsuccessfully sought to attach to Cox College. The projected campus would also reflect this orientation, with each building constructed as a replica of some famous southern edifice. The main building, which stood at the entrance to the campus, was a copy of Robert E. Lee's Arlington Hall.

In addition, Lanier's curriculum began to take on an "All-Southern" cast as a number of courses were added to glorify the southern heritage. Prominent among these was a course in Civil War and Reconstruction history to be taught by the institution's special lecturer in southern history, "Colonel W. J. Simmons, A.B., L.L.D. and Ph.D." Simmons, of course, was Imperial Wizard of the rejuvenated Ku Klux Klan. Soon there were other suggestions of Klan involvement when Klan sympathizers were appointed to the board of trustees and it was rumored that Fowler himself had become a Klansman.

The school fell on hard times, however, and it began to appear that it had few real assets. Although there were announcements of new gifts to the institution, the financial structure of Lanier began to collapse in 1920. By the spring of 1921, faculty members threatened to sue for back pay, the college could not meet its other debts, and Fowler began to explore the possibility that the Klan might come to the rescue. The Klan agreed to assume the college's debts if new trustees were elected, the institution became nonsectarian, and Colonel Simmons was named president. College officials consented and Lanier University officially and publicly became the property of the Klan. Simmons declared that Lanier would be a "One Hundred Per Cent University," whose primary task would be to save white civilization from "submergence" by nonwhites.

Despite considerable ballyhooing by the Klan, the college was doomed. Atlantans were not ready to support such an institution and apparently the Klan's membership was not impressed with announced plans to build a "Hall of the Invisibles" where the teaching of "Klan-Kraft" would be conducted. Within a year, the college was in federal bankruptcy court. Soon it disappeared altogether from the Atlanta scene, the only visible reminder being the replica of Arlington Hall, which was still standing in 1981.

When the Klan assumed control of Lanier, Fowler became an organizer for the hooded order. During the Democratic National Convention of 1924 he campaigned vociferously against Alfred E. Smith, relying on anti-Catholic arguments. The author of *The Ku Klux Klan: Its Origin, Meaning and Scope of Operation* (1922), Fowler organized for the Klan in New Jersey and New York, work that brought him under the scrutiny of the police in both states.

During the mid-1920s, Fowler remained in New York where he apparently founded the *American Standard,* a newspaper, and radio station WHAP. He returned to Atlanta later in the decade and became a salesman for a time before moving to St. Petersburg, Fla., where he resumed his religious work. In St. Petersburg, Fowler became president of a religious publishing house and pastor of the Kingdom Message Association. By 1949, he may have revised some of his earlier views as he apparently contemplated publishing a book to be entitled "The Jew Our Brother." In the early 1960s, he expanded his activities to include anticommunism and was involved in construction of a Temple of American Freedom "to stimulate the white race in freedom." He reported to his alma mater, Furman University, that he was then serving as executive secretary of the Anti-Communist Foundation and president of the Maranatha Bible Seminary.

Fowler was married twice, first to Nancy C. Hunter of Simpsonville, S.C., and second to Ann Hatch. Five children were born of the first marriage: Lewis Hunter, Hallett Judson, Clarence Dixon, Archie Clifford, and John Calhoun. There were no children born of the second union.

SEE: Thomas G. Dyer, "The Klan on Campus: C. Lewis Fowler and Lanier University," *South Atlantic Quarterly* (Autumn 1978); C. Lewis Fowler File (Alumni Office, Furman University, Greenville, S.C.); B. J. W. Graham, ed., *Baptist Biography* 1 (1917); Lanier University Catalogue (Special Collections Division, University of Georgia Library, Athens).

THOMAS G. DYER

**Fowler, John Edgar** *(8 Sept. 1865–4 July 1930),* congressman, was born on his family farm in Honeycutts Township, Sampson County, the son of Miles Beatty and Mary Victoria Herring Fowler. He was a direct descendant of John Fowler (1747–1844), a soldier of the American Revolution, and of Richard Herring of Sampson County who operated a gun shop for the patriots during the Revolution. Young John Fowler was educated in the common schools in his home community and later in Salem Academy in Salemburg. After attending Wake Forest College for two years, he taught school near Salemburg for a year. He studied law at The University of North Carolina from 1892 to 1894, was admitted to the bar in 1894, and began to practice in Clinton.

Fowler was first a Democrat, but in 1894 he joined the Populist party and was elected in the same year to the North Carolina Senate. He advocated the regulation of railroads, the increased support of public education, the establishment of agricultural and normal colleges, and the reform of the election laws. In the legislature he served on the judiciary, privileges and elections, insane asylums, and banking and finance committees. He was the author of a bill passed on 5 Feb. 1895 that fixed the legal rate of interest at six percent.

In 1896, Fowler was elected as a Populist to the U.S. House of Representatives from his home district and served from 4 Mar. 1897 to 3 Mar. 1899. In Congress he supported legislation in keeping with the Populist and Republican platforms as well as the Spanish-American War. In the election of 1898, he was defeated in his bid for another term in the House.

After the collapse of the Populist party in North Carolina, Fowler aligned himself with the Republican party. He represented Sampson County in the lower house of the legislature in 1905, after which he returned to his law practice in Clinton. Though a loyal Republican, he endorsed Alfred E. Smith for president in 1928.

Fowler never married. A Baptist and a Mason, he was buried in the Clinton Town Cemetery.

SEE: *Biog. Dir. Am. Cong.* (1971); John A. Oates, *The Story of Fayetteville and the Upper Cape Fear* (1950); *Sampson Observer,* 6 July 1930.

CLAUDE HUNTER MOORE

**Fox, Michael Leonard** *(12 Jan. 1825–22 July 1888),* physician, teacher, Lutheran minister, legislator, and farmer, was born in Liberty Township, Randolph County, the eldest son of Christian and Charity Moser Fox. After reading medicine with a local doctor, he attended Jefferson Medical College, Philadelphia, in 1852. He then returned to the Sandy Creek community where he practiced medicine and, to a lesser extent, engaged in farming and other activities. In 1867 he became a Lutheran minister and for the remainder of his life served three churches: Melanchthon, near his home; Coble, in Guilford County; and Mt. Pleasant, in Alamance County.

In 1853 he had married Sarah Lutterloh, the daughter of Lewis and Julianna Rives Lutterloh of Chatham County. They had six sons and three daughters: William Alexander, Lewis Michael, Dennis Luther, Thomas Israel, Junius Claudius, Charles, Julia, Sarah, and Cora. Charles and Julia died in infancy. The first four sons became physicians and practiced in Randolph County. From 1883 to 1885 the family lived in Conover so that the younger children could receive parochial schooling at the Concordia Lutheran Academy. While there, Fox continued his medical practice and served several nearby churches.

Fox was a pioneer in methods of medical treatment.

He also laid the foundation for the careers of several young men, including two of his four sons, by preparing them for entry to medical school. A little house on his farm served as a classroom and was known as the "school." Perhaps his greatest achievement as physician was to save the life of his son Dennis, whose feet were almost severed by a large mower on the farm in 1873 when the boy was six years old. The left ankle was cut through both bones and the right one through the tibia. Fox placed the feet in their proper position and successfully restored their usefulness. As a result, Dennis was able to walk most of his life. Although the left foot finally was amputated when he was sixty-three, he practiced medicine until he was eighty.

From 1876 to 1877, Fox served in the North Carolina General Assembly but discovered that he had no desire for a life of politics. An early private conservationist, he provided his farm with ponds for water storage and fishing. He arranged the ponds on three levels so that fish traps could be set where water from the top ponds flowed to the lower ones.

Fox and his family, including the four physician sons, were buried in the cemetery of Melanchthon Church, near Liberty, where he had been a pastor for twenty-one years.

SEE: John L. Cheney, Jr., ed., *North Carolina Government, 1585–1974* (1975); Michael Leonard Fox Papers and related items (Archives, North Carolina Synod, Lutheran Church of America, Salisbury); Jacob L. Morgan and others, *History of the Lutheran Church in North Carolina, 1803–1953* (1953); *North Carolina Biography*, vol. 4 (1941).

CHARLESANNA L. FOX

**Foy, James** *(1772–14 Mar. 1823)*, planter and defendant in a landmark legal case, was perhaps the son of the Major James Foy who died in Onslow County on 11 Dec. 1822 at the age of eighty-five. Major Foy's wife had died twelve days earlier. One James Foye represented New Hanover County in the state House of Commons in 1803 and 1804, but whether he was one of these is unknown. James, the planter, was married first to a Miss Montford of Onslow County and second to Henrietta Rhodes (1775–1840), daughter of Lieutenant Colonel Henry Rhodes, a delegate to the Provincial Congress from Onslow County in 1776. His children, apparently all by his second wife, were Henry R., Elizabeth (m. Alfred Shepard), Fanny, Hiram W., William G., and Joseph M. All were left extensive property by their father. Joseph M., the son, built Poplar Grove plantation house at Scotts Hill, Pender County, in 1850; the house is now open to the public.

The General Assembly in 1789 granted escheats to The University of North Carolina as a source of support; in 1794 unsold confiscated Tory lands were also assigned to the university. In 1800, the legislature repealed the laws granting such property and the trustees of the university brought suit to recover some land escheated prior to the 1800 act. This case, *University v. Foy*, eventually reached the court of appeal in Raleigh where a very significant decision was rendered in favor of the university. The General Assembly, the court held, could not deny support to the university, which had been created by the people of North Carolina in a constitutional convention—a body superior to the Assembly.

Foy was involved in this case as the recent owner of property claimed by the university.

SEE: John L. Cheney, Jr., ed., *North Carolina Government, 1585–1974* (1975); Edgar W. Knight, "North Carolina's 'Dartmouth College Case,'" *Journal of Higher Education* 19 (March 1948); Hugh T. Lefler and Albert R. Newsome, *North Carolina, The History of a Southern State* (1973); Elizabeth Moore Collection (North Carolina State Archives, Raleigh); New Hanover County Estate Records and Wills (North Carolina State Archives, Raleigh); *North Carolina Reports* 5:58 (June 1805); *North Carolina Star*, 21 Mar. 1823; Blackwell P. Robinson, *The History of Escheats* (1955?).

WILLIAM S. POWELL

**Francisco, Peter** *(ca. 1760–16 Jan. 1831)*, "giant" and Revolutionary War hero, was brought to America as a small child. He was landed at City Point (later Hopewell), Va., from a ship, presumably Spanish or Portuguese, in 1765, and was subsequently indentured to Judge Anthony Winston, of Buckingham County, an uncle of Patrick Henry. Francisco grew up on the Winston plantation, Hunting Towers, and early showed signs of his future physical size and strength. At about the age of sixteen, he was reported to be over six feet in height and over two hundred pounds in weight. Although a favorite of Judge Winston (some accounts say he was legally adopted), he apparently received very little if any education.

In 1776, he enlisted as a private in the Tenth Virginia Regiment of Continental Troops, and joined Washington's army in the north. He fought at Brandywine, Germantown, and Monmouth, and took part in the storming of Stony Point in 1778 when he was severely wounded. He attracted the attention of General Washington, who ordered that an especially large sword be made for Francisco, who by this time was becoming known as the "Virginia Giant" because of his large size and extraordinary strength. After his three-year enlistment was up in 1779, he returned to Virginia briefly but soon reenlisted. This time he joined the forces of General Horatio Gates, who was on his way to South Carolina and the disastrous Battle of Camden. At Camden, Francisco distinguished himself by killing several British soldiers, and by single-handedly moving a cannon from one part of the battlefield to another.

Francisco's North Carolina connections largely relate to the Battle of Guilford Court House in March 1781. His courage and prowess there were later honored when a monument was erected to him on the battlefield. The inscription on the monument notes that it marks the site where "Peter Francisco, a giant of incredible strength, killed eleven British soldiers with his own broad sword, and although badly wounded by bayonet, made his escape."

After the Revolution, Francisco opened a tavern and general store in Buckingham County, Va. He became a celebrated figure due to his great strength and his Revolutionary War record. Many stories were told of his strength and courage, and visitors often traveled for many miles to see him. In 1811, he was again a hero, this time at a theater fire in Richmond, when he carried several people to safety from the burning building. In 1825, he was in the party that honored General Lafayette on his visit to Richmond, and in the same year he was appointed sergeant at arms in the Virginia legislature. He held this post until his death in Richmond. His funeral was attended by the governor of Virginia and many other prominent Virginians. He was buried in Shockoe Cemetery, Richmond.

Francisco married three times. His first wife was

Susannah Anderson, who died in 1790, leaving one son. His second wife was Catherine Brooke, whom he married in 1794; she died in 1821, leaving two sons and two daughters. In 1823, he married a widow, Mrs. Mary Beverly Grymes West, who survived him. His five children were James Anderson, Benjamin, Peter, Susan (Mrs. Edward Pescud), and Catherine (Mrs. Dandridge Spotswood). Among Francisco's North Carolina descendants are families bearing the names of Pescud, Strudwick, Nash, Withers, Albertson, and Gatling. The Virginia Historical Society in Richmond has Francisco's sword, and the North Carolina Museum of History in Raleigh has a razor case presented to him by General Nathanael Greene.

SEE: Fred J. Cook, *What Manner of Men* (1959); J. R. V. Daniel, "The Giant of Virginia," *Virginia Cavalcade* 1 (1951); Nannie F. Porter and Catherine Albertson, *The Romantic Record of Peter Francisco* (1929); Alma Power-Waters, *Virginia Giant, The Story of Peter Francisco* (1957); Lyon G. Tyler, ed., *Encyclopedia of Virginia Biography*, vol. 2 (1915), and "Peter Francisco, American Soldier," *William and Mary Quarterly* 13 (1905).

E. D. JOHNSON

**Franck, John Martin** *(ca. 1680–May 1745)*, a leader among the Palatine and Swiss colonists who founded New Bern in 1710, member of the colonial Assembly, county official, merchant, planter, and educator, is said in family tradition to have been born in the vicinity of Heidelberg in what was then the Upper Palatinate of the Rhine, the son of a prominent schoolmaster. The tradition says that on the journey to North Carolina he was married aboard ship to Civilla (variously spelled), a daughter of Jacob Mueller, another of the Palatine colonists in the first of the two von Graffenried expeditions sent from England to settle the Neuse River country in North Carolina. The earliest extant written family history note is by General David Blackshear, Franck's grandson, who was born at New Germany on the Trent River on 31 Jan. 1764. General Blackshear's note reports the year of arrival as 1735 but mentions no family traditions relating to nativity, parentage, marriage, kindred, and so forth of his immigrant ancestor. Intensive research has not disclosed his parentage or the place of his birth. No writings of his have been found other than a few formal legal documents bearing only the slightest hints of possible past associations. His first home plantation, established on a large grant on the Trent River about seven miles upstream from the present town of Trenton, he named New Germany. This thread of fact has helped inspire much legend and romance.

Research identifies Franck first as a young European who came from Canada to Virginia to serve as an assistant and interpreter for Francis Louis Michels, who was employed by the Canton of Berne and encouraged by other Swiss and English groups and individuals "to find out a Tract of land in the English America, where that Republick might settle some of their People." Michels conducted investigations in Virginia and neighboring areas of Pennsylvania, Maryland, and coastal Carolina from 1701 to 10 Jan. 1709. Franck seems to have been the "very ingenious French Gentleman" with whom John Lawson, the historian, says he frequently conversed in company with "my ingenious Friend, Mr. Francis Louis Mitchell, of Berne, Switzerland." It seems that Michels was the person whom Lawson notes he met accidentally in London in 1700 and whose exciting conversation turned Lawson's thoughts from going to Rome to going to Carolina, a place described by this much traveled chance acquaintance as "the best Country I could go to." In any event, Michels was at his work in Virginia by 1701. He and Lawson met for long visits at intervals during the years that followed until they sailed for England together in mid-January 1710, having agreed and arranged with supportive friends to seek the diversion of the next expeditions of Palatine and Swiss colonists from the previously proposed Potomac River destination to the Neuse River. Franck probably accompanied them to England on this mission. He is believed to have been one of the persons appointed as overseers on board ship during the trip from Gravesend near London to the James River in Virginia, and from Williamsburg to the confluence of the Neuse and Trent where the refugees from Palatine camps around London arrived in late May 1710. Nearly half of the approximately six hundred who sailed are reported to have died on the journey.

The journals of Baron Christoph von Graffenried and of John Lawson rarely mention names of subordinates or persons other than individuals regarded as ranking above the yeoman class. Franck is not named in any of von Graffenried's three versions of his journal or in Lawson's writings. The records of Archdale (later Craven) Precinct for the period prior to October 1711 were lost when the Tuscaroras burned the precinct court building and much of the town of New Bern in the first onslaught of the Tuscarora Indian War (22 Sept. 1711–24 Mar. 1713). The name of Martin Franck does appear on a series of Craven Precinct lists running from 1712 to 1719. Each year is represented by one or more of the following: a poll tax list, a land tax list, or a list of tithables. Franck also appears on a list of Tuscarora Indian War claims paid residents of Craven Precinct (including deceased persons). The extant list reports payments only in 1714 and makes reference to two earlier lists not now in the records. In 1713, Franck sold his lot in the town of New Bern, evidently in preparation for moving to his new plantation home on Mill Creek in the New Germany tract.

Numerous petty lawsuits brought against him or by him in the courts of several precincts in North Carolina, and in a number of county and precinct courts in Virginia, disclose the nature and extent of his activities in trying to get food and other necessities for the colonists of the Neuse and Trent rivers during the starving time after the Tuscarora massacre of late September 1711. The massacre, which killed or decimated many families of the colonists, was followed by widespread depredations until the Indians were brought under siege in their own forts in the spring of 1712. The documentary evidence shows that Franck had the confidence of and credit with merchants and planters in old Albemarle County precincts and parts of Virginia. His boats gathered principally salt meats and grain and other necessities on promise to pay in such forest-derived commodities as bayberry wax, animal pelts, and cooperage and wood products. The quantities he committed himself to pay indicate organized cooperation of the other surviving settlers. Baron von Graffenried is reported to have abandoned the New Bern colony some weeks after the outbreak of hostilities and also to have departed from North Carolina in the summer of 1712. The records of precinct courts in the Albemarle and neighboring Virginia disclose no known items of commercial activity by the baron or his representatives during the starving time or thereafter. His activity on behalf of himself can be noted in his journals and in the North Carolina chancery court records.

By May 1711, Franck seems to have become aware of what he perceived to be a dangerous unreliability on the part of the baron, the North Carolina Provincial Council, and possibly Governor Pollock and John Lawson. The promise of grants of land to the Palatine and Swiss colonists (to be exempt from quitrents for ten years) grew less and less likely of fulfillment. In May 1711, Franck visited the Indian tribes holding rights under the Tuscarora nation's council to lands between the Neuse and Trent rivers. He bought from the Indians acres of land in that area and, with their cooperation, surveyed it and filed his claim with the provincial government. His objective was to make available modest tracts of this land to the cheated Palatine and Swiss colonists at low cost and on easy terms. The deed records of Craven show that his objective was attained in a significant degree over a period of several years. In 1730, title to the tract was contested by persons prominent in the provincial government. A resurvey proved that the area in Franck's 1711 claim approximated 16,000 acres, rather than 10,000. A compromise settlement left Franck and his purchasers with about 6,800 acres. Again, he had gone far toward performing for the Palatine and Swiss colonists the promises left abandoned by von Graffenried and others. This fidelity also led him to start a school on Rocky Run near his plantation home on Mill Creek. The school continued for many decades and closed at last with the consolidation of Jones County elementary schools after 1950.

Franck was elected by the Craven freeholders to the North Carolina General Assembly of 1715 and of 1727. He served as a justice of the county court for many years and for some years as treasurer of the county. He early established a gristmill (when there were only two others in North Carolina). He also served on the vestry of the parish and in other positions of public trust.

Franck was married first late in 1711 or early in 1712 to Susannah, the war-widowed relict of Enoch Ward the elder, of Craven Precinct. Susannah died about 1720; she was survived by her husband and at least five of his children who lived to be grown. In August 1722, Gasper Timberman (alias Timmerman), another Palatine, died survived by his young wife Civilla and an infant daughter, Mary. Timberman's widow married Franck in 1723 and had by him at least six children to reach adulthood. The names of Franck's children who are of record in adulthood are William (b. ca. 1713, living in 1761 in Rowan County), Susannah (b. ca. 1714), Mary (b. ca. 1716), Jacob (b. ca. 1717, d. 1793 in Cabarrus County), Elizabeth (b. ca. 1719), David (b. ca. 1724), Edward (b. ca. 1725), Catherine (b. ca. 1728), Anna Civilla (b. ca. 1729), John Martin, Jr. (b. ca. 1730), and Barbara (b. ca. 1732). The last two appear as minors under guardianship after their father's death. Barbara married Captain Daniel Shine and is the Barbara Shine who entertained President George Washington at Shine's Inn on his southern tour. Her nephew, General David Blackshear, reports that she died in 1814 at age ninety-five. The records prove she was much younger in 1814 and married late in life a second husband named Jacov (?) Johnston. On 7 Nov. 1814 she made a deed to her son, James Shine.

Late in life Franck moved to his White Rock plantation on the north side of Trent River. He made this plantation a showplace of progressive agriculture and entertained hospitably both as private host and as proprietor of the White Rock Tavern. He died there and was probably buried in that vicinity. His wife Civilla survived him and married as her third husband another aging Palatine of considerable distinction, Jacob Sheets. The fact that she had at least one child by this husband is some evidence that she was born after 1700. She was living and active as late as 1758. Civilla most likely was the daughter of John Wixdell (alias Waxdale) whose will was probated in Craven in 1739.

SEE: "A Memoir of General David Blackshear," *Georgia Bench and Bar*, vol. 1 (1858); North Carolina State Archives, Raleigh: Craven County Deeds; Governor's Office (C.O. 110), Lovit Hines Collection, Notes and Papers of Sybil and Delia Hyatt; William S. Price, ed., *North Carolina Higher-Court Minutes, 1709–1723* (1977); William L. Saunders, *Colonial Records of North Carolina*, vols. 2–4 (1886); Vincent H. Todd, ed., *Christoph von Graffenried's Account of the Founding of New Bern* (1920); *Virginia Magazine of History and Biography* 24 (1916), 29 (1921).

CHARLES R. HOLLOMAN

**Franklin, Jesse** *(24 Mar. 1760–31 Aug. 1823)*, Revolutionary War soldier, representative, U.S. senator, and governor, was born in Orange County, Va., the son of Bernard and Mary Cleveland Franklin. A brother, Meshack, also served in Congress and in the North Carolina General Assembly. The Franklins moved to the Mitchell River area of Surry County on the eve of the American Revolution. Enlisting in the regiment of his maternal uncle, Colonel Benjamin Cleveland, Jesse was present at the battles of Kings Mountain and Guilford Court House. He ended his military career with the rank of major. Settling in Wilkes County after the Revolution, he represented that county in the House of Commons from 1784 to 1787 and from 1790 to 1792. In December 1789 the Assembly appointed him a councillor of state. In 1792 he moved to Surry, which he represented in the House of Commons in 1793 and 1794. He then served one term in the U.S. House of Representatives from March 1795 to March 1797. Surry returned him to the legislature in Raleigh in 1797 and 1798.

The 1798 General Assembly sent Franklin to the U.S. Senate, electing him over Alexander Martin and Benjamin Smith. As president pro tempore from March 1804 to January 1805, he presided during the period of the impeachment trials of federal judges John Pickering and Samuel Chase and the Burr-Hamilton duel. Near the end of 1804 the General Assembly selected Montford Stokes to replace him in Congress. Stokes, however, refused the Senate seat. Back home for the moment, Franklin was again sent by Surry County to the state senate in 1805. In late 1806, he was returned to the U.S. Senate where he served until replaced by David Stone in March 1813. In the assemblies of 1814 and 1815 Franklin was again a nominee for his old senate seat in Washington, but was defeated by Francis Locke in 1814 and by Nathaniel Macon the next year. Between 1805 and 1817 he served as trustee of The University of North Carolina.

Franklin, David Meriwether, and Andrew Jackson were appointed commissioners to treat with the Cherokee and Chickasaw Indians in 1816. The same year Franklin was a Republican elector in the presidential election; he also was elected by the Assembly to serve the first of four successive terms as a councillor of state. Finally, in 1820 the Assembly honored him once again, this time by electing him governor over Gabriel Holmes. Franklin was now sixty years old, weighed over two hundred pounds, and was in poor health. Twelve months later he declined another term, and Holmes succeeded him.

Franklin married Meckey Perkins, daughter of Hardy Perkins of Rockbridge County, Va. They had three sons and five daughters. The old governor died at home in Surry County after nine months' confinement with edema or dropsy. Like Macon, he had never allowed a portrait of himself to be painted. He was buried at Guilford Court House National Military Park, Greensboro.

SEE: J. T. Alderman, "Governor Jesse Franklin," *The North Carolina Booklet* 6 (January 1907); Samuel A. Ashe, ed., *Biographical History of North Carolina*, vol. 4 (1906); *Biog. Dir. Am. Cong.* (1971); John L. Cheney, Jr., ed., *North Carolina Government, 1585–1974* (1975); *DAB*, vol. 6 (1931); W. R. Edmonds, "Sketch of Jesse Franklin," *The University Magazine* 28 (1911); D. H. Gilpatrick, *Jeffersonian Democracy in North Carolina, 1789–1816* (1931); Raleigh *Register*, 3 Oct. 1823.

DANIEL M. MCFARLAND

**Franklin, Meshack** *(1772–18 Dec. 1839)*, congressman and legislator, was born in Orange County, Va., the son of Bernard and Mary Cleveland Franklin. In 1778 his parents sent their eldest son, Jesse, to North Carolina to find a suitable place for a new family home. Jesse selected a location near the headwaters of the Mitchell River where Meshack grew to maturity, the fifth of eight children. He received little formal education but apparently overcame this handicap, for as an adult he wrote with considerable facility.

Like his brother Jesse, Meshack became interested in politics as a young man. In 1800 and 1801 he served as a representative in the North Carolina legislature, and from 1807 to 1815 he represented the state in the U.S. House of Representatives. In Congress Franklin spoke rarely. A Democratic-Republican, he espoused a political philosophy much like that of Nathaniel Macon, who sat with him in the North Carolina delegation in the House. He believed strongly in popular government and wrote vigorously in support of the popular election of the president. In 1828–29 and 1838, he served in the state senate, and in 1825–28, 1832–33, and 1835, he was a councillor of state. Neither as a state nor as a federal official were his accomplishments great.

Franklin married Mildred Edwards, and the couple had eleven children who reached maturity: sons Gideon, Columbus, Jesse, and Hardy; and daughters Anne, Sarah, Mary, Martha, Mildred, Frances, and Meeky. A prosperous farmer, he left a substantial estate at the time of his death.

SEE: *Biog. Dir. Am. Cong.* (1950); Walter Clark MSS and Superior Court Records of Surry County (North Carolina State Archives, Raleigh); W. R. Edmonds, "Sketch of Jesse Franklin," *The University Magazine* 28 (1911); Meshack Franklin, *To the Freemen of the 13th Congressional District of the State of North-Carolina* (1825); William Lenoir, *To the Citizens of the 12th Elective District, in the State of North-Carolina* (1806).

THOMAS J. FARNHAM

**Frazer, William Henry** *(16 Sept. 1873–19 June 1953)*, clergyman and educator, was born in Lafayette, Ala., the son of John Alexander and Nancy Emiline Abernathy Frazer. He was a direct descendant of John Frazer, a native Scot, who settled in Richmond County, N.C., in 1747. After attending local schools at Lafayette, Frazer entered Southwestern Presbyterian University, Clarksville, Tenn., in 1893 and was graduated with a bachelor of arts degree four years later. He spent the next two years at Union Theological Seminary, Richmond, Va., where he earned the bachelor of divinity degree. Later he was the recipient of three honorary degrees: doctor of divinity, Presbyterian College of South Carolina (1909); doctor of literature, Davidson College (1929); and doctor of laws, Southwestern University of Memphis (1937).

Ordained to the Presbyterian ministry in 1899, Frazer served successively as pastor of the Georgia Avenue Presbyterian Church, Atlanta (1899–1901); the Tatnall Square Presbyterian Church, Macon, Ga. (1901–6); and the First Presbyterian Church, Anderson, S.C. (1906–17). While in Anderson, his interest in youth produced the innovative Frazer Fitting School for Boys, an academy-type institution that emphasized the classics and current literature to prepare males of high school age for college and university. He served as headmaster of the school until 1917. That summer he accepted the presidency of Belhaven College, Jackson, Miss., a coeducational institution established in 1894 under Presbyterian auspices. His four years of successful leadership there attracted the attention of church leaders, including the trustees of Queens College, Charlotte, N.C., who in 1921 offered him the presidency of that Presbyterian school. Frazer accepted the appointment. In 1930 Chicora College, Columbia, S.C., was merged with Queens to become Queens-Chicora College.

Frazer may have been the only college president in the history of American education who served eleven years before his formal inauguration—a ceremony hallowed by most institutions and their leaders. He insisted he not be inducted until he had accomplished several projects at Queens College. The first of these was its accreditation by the appropriate regional agencies. He found the college deficient in twenty-one brackets, which were not attained until the fall of 1932. He also wanted to add at least $400,000 to the college's endowment. A third objective was to effect the merger between Queens and Chicora College, then a struggling church school, with the blessing and support of Chicora's alumna and Presbyterian churches in South Carolina. When these goals were met, his inauguration was included as part of the commencement program in late May 1933. During his presidency, Queens-Chicora was fully accredited by the Southern Association of Colleges and Secondary Schools, enrollment doubled, and gifts to the college totaled more than $600,000—one-third for buildings and two-thirds for endowment. In addition, Frazer was a popular lecturer and civic club and commencement speaker.

Throughout his career in educational administration, Frazer was in great demand as a supply and interim preacher in churches of all denominations. After his retirement in 1939 from the presidency of Queens-Chicora College (later to be known again as Queens College) at age sixty-six, he served eight years as pastor of the Presbyterian Church of Pineville, N.C., before "retiring" again in 1947. For the next six years, he was stated supply at several Presbyterian churches in Alabama and Florida.

An avid reader, Frazer owned a large private library and in his middle years devoted much of his free time to writing. Among his published works were *Bible Notes for Bible Students* (1924), *The Possumist and other Stories* (1924), *Fireside Musings of Uncle Rastus and Aunt Randy* (1925), and *Challenging Mantles* (1926). During the years after 1906, he often contributed articles to various denominational journals and periodicals and wrote frequently on problems of race and society. Typical were his series on "The Afro-American—His Past, Present and Future" and "The Social Separation of the Races." His observations were tolerant and prophetic.

In fraternal circles, Frazer was an active leader in Masonry completing the Scottish Rite and the York Rite. He was also a Shriner and a member of the Knights of Pythias. In both of these organizations he held high local and state offices; at one time he was grand chaplain of the grand chapter, and of the grand council of Masons in South Carolina. While he lived at Jackson, Miss., he continued his membership in Kiwanis International and was for one term governor of the Kiwanis district that included the entire states of Louisiana and Mississippi. In his heyday he was one of Kiwanis International's most popular speakers and committeemen.

On 29 Oct. 1899, at Lafayette, Ala., Frazer married his childhood sweetheart, Sarah Winnie Jones, daughter of James Thomas Jones and his wife of Lafayette. They had three children: Winnie Love, William Henry, Jr. (who died in his youth), and Emily (Mrs. James B. Kuykendall, Jr.).

While vacationing in Charlotte, N.C., Frazer was the victim of an automobile accident and died a few days later. Burial followed in Lafayette, Ala., where his wife had been interred several years before. Both of his daughters survived him.

SEE: *Asheville Citizen*, 20 June 1953; *Charlotte Observer*, 2 July 1922, 7 Dec. 1933; *Leaders in Education* (1948); *Nat. Cyc. Am. Biog.*, vol. E (1938); *Who's Who in the South and Southwest* (1950); *Who Was Who in America*, vol. 3 (1950).

C. SYLVESTER GREEN

**Freeman, Edmund B.** *(8 Sept. 1795–30 June 1868)*, longtime clerk of the North Carolina Supreme Court, was born in Sandwich, Mass. He was the son of the Reverend Jonathan Otis Freeman, a Presbyterian clergyman and educator of note who taught in several North Carolina communities; a nephew of the Right Reverend George Washington Freeman, who served as a rector of Christ Church in Raleigh and later as missionary bishop of Arkansas and the Southwest; and the grandson of Brigadier General Nathaniel Freeman of the Massachusetts militia in the Revolutionary War.

In 1805, Freeman moved with his father to North Carolina, where he received his basic education. He studied law and was licensed to practice, but it appears that he never engaged actively in the profession. In October 1829 he and others bought the *Halifax Minerva*, the title of which was changed to the *Roanoke Advocate* with the issue of 4 Mar. 1830. Freeman, for a time in partnership with John Campbell and later alone, published the paper until January 1834, when he sold it and moved to Raleigh. Soon afterward he became a deputy clerk of the North Carolina Supreme Court.

From 1831 until his defeat in 1842, Freeman served as clerk assistant of the House of Commons. On 5 June 1835, he was elected "Principal Secretary," or clerk, of the Constitutional Convention of 1835.

On 13 July 1843, after the death of Clerk John L. Henderson, Freeman was named to the vacancy by the justices of the supreme court. The *Raleigh Register* of 18 July noted that "A better appointment could not have been made." Freeman served until his death.

On 5 Dec. 1843, he took his seat on the Board of Commissioners of Raleigh, filling the unexpired term of Middle Ward Commissioner Alexander J. Lawrence, who had resigned. Freeman himself resigned on 30 May 1845; the next year, however, he was a candidate for the same office but was defeated in the city election held on 19 January.

A review of deeds, tax lists, and his will reveals that Freeman owned a moderate amount of property, including real estate in Raleigh, land outside the town, and slaves, of which he owned as many as sixteen in 1848, 1849, and 1850. A scrutiny of deeds shows that he was capable of shrewdness and on several occasions realized sizable profits from his transactions. Though he lost a considerable amount during the Civil War, his Raleigh lot and house and its furnishings were valued at about $4,000 when he died; he also left shares of stocks and other personal property.

Freeman married twice. On 27 Oct. 1822, a marriage bond was given for his marriage to Mary McKinney Stith of Halifax (d. 25 Jan. 1835); they had one daughter, Emily, who married Hampden S. Smith. His second wife, whom he married on 14 Nov. 1837, was Mrs. Elizabeth Ellis Williams Foreman of Pitt County (d. 11 Nov. 1848), widow of William Foreman. They had no children. Freeman was survived by his daughter and several grandchildren.

The supreme court clerk was a member of Christ Episcopal Church in Raleigh, where he served as junior warden. He was also a member of the Masonic Order, where he held the office of junior grand warden.

The Constitution of 1868, which abolished the distinction between courts of law and courts of equity, was to become effective 1 July 1868. Freeman's death on the last day the courts operated under the old system was a coincidence that caused considerable comment. Chief Justice Richmond M. Pearson said:

"His attachment to the Old Court was so strong that on several occasions he said to the Judges: 'I cannot outlive the Court, or work in any other traces!'

"That the Court should have *died* on the same day with its Clerk, is a co-incidence that is remarkable, and to theorists may form a topic for discussion."

Freeman had died after an illness of only three or four days. The *Daily Sentinel* of 3 July 1868 referred to his efficiency and the high regard with which he had been held. Records of the supreme court, however, show that he was capable of using his office at times to impede matters.

A poem was written in memory of Freeman by Mary Bayard Clarke in which she referred to the unusual circumstances surrounding his death and to his long and faithful service. The poem was recorded in the minute docket of the North Carolina Supreme Court for 1 July 1868.

Funeral services were held at Christ Church, and Masonic rites were conducted at the grave, presumably in Raleigh's City Cemetery. A portrait of Freeman hangs in the office of the clerk of the supreme court, Raleigh.

SEE: *Centennial Ceremonies Held in Christ Church Parish, Raleigh, North Carolina, A. D. 1921*; Constitutional Convention, *Journal*, 1835; Deed books, wills, and inventories, tax lists, and settlements of estates of Wake County (North Carolina State Archives, Raleigh); *Halifax Minerva*, 29 Oct., 5 Nov. 1829; Halifax *Roanoke Advocate*, 4 Mar. 1830; Marshall D. Haywood, "The Officers of the Court, 1819–1919," *Centennial Celebration of the Su-*

*preme Court of North Carolina, 1819–1919* (1919); House of Commons, *Journals*, 1831–42; Daniel M. McFarland, "North Carolina Newspapers, Editors, and Journalistic Politics, 1815–1835," *North Carolina Historical Review* 30 (1953); Printed reports and original records of the North Carolina Supreme Court, 1834–68 (North Carolina State Archives, Raleigh); Raleigh *Daily Sentinel*, 1–3 July 1868; *Raleigh Register*, 8 Dec. 1843, 3 June 1845, 23 Jan. 1846; John H. Wheeler, *Reminiscences and Memoirs of North Carolina and Eminent North Carolinians* (1884).

MEMORY F. MITCHELL

**Freeman, George Washington** *(13 June 1789–29 Apr. 1858)*, clergyman, was born in Sandwich, Mass., to the Reverend Nathaniel Freeman (1741–1843), a Congregationalist minister, and his first wife, Tryphosa Colton, of Killingly, Conn. George was their twelfth and youngest child, although Nathaniel had eight more children by a second wife. His early manhood was spent in secular occupations, but he later came to North Carolina to pursue his calling as a teacher and to study for the ministry of the Protestant Episcopal church.

In 1820, before taking on full-time church responsibilities, Freeman became principal of the Warrenton Male Academy, where he stayed until 1823. During that time, he was a delegate to the 1822 diocesan convention at Emmanuel Episcopal Church in Warrenton. When he resigned as principal of the academy, he went to Raleigh where he conducted a school that had just opened.

In Raleigh Freeman often served as lay reader in Christ Episcopal Church (established 1821) in the absence of Bishop John Stark Ravenscroft. He was ordained deacon in that church on 8 Oct. 1826 and priest in Christ Church, New Bern, on 20 May 1827 by Bishop Ravenscroft. For two years he served as a missionary in the diocese of North Carolina. On 31 Aug. 1829, he was elected rector of Christ Church, Raleigh, a position he held until 1840. While he was rector, the church acquired a new organ in 1833, much to the horror of some of his old-fashioned parishioners. The next year, two new side galleries were erected, increasing the church's seating capacity.

Freeman was deeply interested in the spiritual welfare of both slaves and masters. He did not favor emancipation because he had observed the condition of freed blacks and decided that their lot was worse. His message was one of mutual consideration and forbearance for both slaves and masters. On 27 Nov. 1836 he delivered two discourses on the rights and duties of slaveholders. The first discourse traced the biblical basis for slavery. In the second message, he instructed slaveholders on how to treat their slaves based on the passages in the New Testament dealing with slaves and masters. Because masters are the guardians of their slaves, he said, they should bring up their slaves as Christians, instruct them in Christian doctrines, and set good Christian examples for them to follow. The North Carolina General Assembly was meeting at the time of the discourses, and four members—large slaveholders themselves—succeeded in getting the two sermons published.

On the issue of "worldly pleasures," Freeman's Puritan views, still ingrained from his New England days, clashed with those of his congregation, a conflict that eventually led to his resignation. He discouraged dancing, whist games, the theater, circuses, and parties. He also preached against the fashions of the day, including satin, lace, ribbons, and feathers. Apparently his congregation had begun to see no harm in these activities, much to the displeasure and disappointment of its rector.

On 18 June 1840, Freeman wrote a letter of resignation to the vestry and included a separate letter of explanation. When he had first come as pastor, he wrote, church members would not even consider taking part in such amusements. "Since that period, however," he said, "a change has come over the congregation, a new spirit has arisen, and the Pastor and his flock are no longer of one mind." According to one member of the vestry, the congregation did not want Freeman to leave; although it disagreed with certain of his views, it valued him as a preacher. The vestry reluctantly accepted his resignation.

After delivering a "valedictory sermon," a loving and encouraging farewell at Christ Church, Freeman went to Columbia, Tenn., and a year later to Swedesborough, N.J. He then accepted a call to become rector of Immanuel Church in Newcastle, Del. Soon afterward, he was elected missionary bishop of Arkansas and the Indian Territory. He received the degree of D.D. from The University of North Carolina in 1839. On 26 Oct. 1844, he was consecrated in St. Peter's Church in Philadelphia. He died in Little Rock, Ark.

Freeman's wife was Anne Yates Gholson (d. 1855), daughter of Colonel William Yates of Virginia and widow of William Gholson. They were the parents of three sons: George Russell (b. 1819 in Raleigh), Andrew Field (b. 1822 in Warrenton), and Charles Edward (b. 1826 in New Bern).

SEE: M. N. Amis, *Historical Raleigh* (1913); *Appleton's Cyclopedia of American Biography*, vol. 2 (1887); Kemp P. Battle, *The Early History of Raleigh* (1893); Frederick Freeman, *Freeman Genealogy* (1875); George W. Freeman, *Letter of Resignation from Christ Church*, (1840), *Two Discourses: The Rights and Duties of Slaveholders* (1836), and *A Valedictory Sermon delivered in Christ Church* (1841); Lizzie Wilson Montgomery, *Sketches of Old Warrenton* (1924); Nell Joslin Styron, *Christ Church: 150 Years at the Heart of Raleigh* (1970).

MOLLY MANNING

**Freeman, Ralf** *(fl. 1807–31)*, Baptist minister, was born a slave in Anson County; his parents are not known. He belonged to John Culpeper, a Baptist minister and pastor of the Rocky River Baptist Church, Anson County. Most of the information concerning this early black pastor comes from George W. Purefoy's history of the Sandy Creek Baptist Association. Freeman was probably baptized by the Rocky River Baptist Church, of which he became a member. Within a short time, when it was discovered that he had the ability to preach, he was licensed by the church. Soon afterward he was ordained and began to preach in the counties of Moore, Randolph, and Davidson.

In 1801, John Culpeper was elected a member of the North Carolina House of Commons from Anson County. In 1806, he won election to the U.S. House of Representatives from the Seventh District, serving in 1807–9, 1813–17, 1819–21, 1823–25, and 1827–29. When he rode off to Washington, he left the church and congregation of Rocky River in the hands of his servant Ralf, who then began his own years of service to the church. In imitation of John Culpeper, his preaching was forceful, his faith firm, and he handled his master's flock with unusual ability. He officiated at sacraments and burials, made pastoral calls, and attended to numerous church duties. He was also frequently called upon to preach at the annual meetings of the Pee Dee Baptist Association and was held in high regard by all who knew him.

Freeman served as a delegate from Rocky River to the Sandy Creek Baptist Association in the period 1807–10. In 1809, he was listed as "Elder Ralf (a colored minister)." In 1811, he was a delegate from the Sandy Creek Baptist Association to the Raleigh Baptist Association. At this session he was listed as "Elder Ralf Freeman." Before then he had been listed as "Ralf" with no surname. Thus he evidently received his freedom sometime during 1810–11. He continued to represent the church as a delegate through 1814. He also preached the Sunday sermon at the Sandy Creek Association in 1809 and 1814. Purefoy says that he was a good reader and was well read in the Scriptures.

The earliest minutes of Rocky River Baptist Church are for 5 Apr. 1828, when Ralf Freeman was in attendance and led the church in prayer. He was also listed in the black male section of the church roll for 1828. In May 1828 he assisted in the establishment of the Brown Creek Baptist Church. That fall he was elected as a delegate to the Pee Dee Baptist Association. In May 1830 he helped organize the Kendalls Baptist Church, and in July of the same year he was appointed to attend to the constitution of the arm of the Fork of Little River at Suggs Creek.

Purefoy described Freeman as being of common size, "perfectly black," with a smiling countenance, especially when conducting religious services. One writer recorded that "he would have no money for preaching; he only wanted food and clothing." At the session of the Pee Dee Baptist Association held with the church at Elizabeth, a preacher from Charleston, S.C., recommended that Freeman give the Sunday sermon. He had heard of Ralf and had come to hear him preach. Freeman did preach on "The Temptation of Christ." In the middle of the sermon he read the passage, "All these things will I give thee"; then, smiling at the congregation, he said, "Poor devil, he didn't have a foot of land in the world."

Freeman became a close friend of Elder Joseph Magee, a Baptist minister. They preached and traveled together, and both agreed that the survivor would preach at the other's funeral. Magee moved to Tennessee and died first. At his death he bequeathed to Freeman his riding horse, overcoat, Bible, and fifty dollars in cash; he also requested that Freeman preach at his funeral. In company with a white brother, Freeman rode to Tennessee to carry out the wish of his friend. At the conclusion of his sermon the congregation contributed fifty dollars to his support.

The career of this gifted individual was darkened near its end in the aftermath of the Nat Turner insurrection in Southampton County, Va., in 1831, when restrictions on slaves and free blacks were tightened. They were forbidden to preach or exhort in public or in any way officiate as preacher or teacher at prayer meetings or meetings for worship where slaves of different masters were collected.

The last record of Freeman is in 1831. According to one writer it is probable that Freeman died in the fellowship of the Primitive or Antimission Baptists, but this was more by accident than by choice. When the arm of Rocky River at Bethlehem (near Ansonville) became a regular church in March 1831, Freeman moved his membership there. The church later became Primitive and soon afterward extinct. Freeman was buried in the church cemetery by his white friends and a small stone was placed at the head of his grave. In 1907, this was replaced by a more substantial memorial marker.

Freeman's wife was probably named Genny, (as listed in the 1828 church roll). Their daughter, Judy, married Abraham McRae. Abraham and Judy had a daughter, Sarah Jane, who became the wife of Allen Ratliff and the mother of William Martin Ratliff.

SEE: E. M. Brooks, *History of Rocky River Baptist Church* (1928); Ralf Freeman biography folder (Baptist Historical Collection, Wake Forest University, Winston-Salem); George W. Purefoy, *A History of the Sandy Creek Baptist Association from its Organization in A.D. 1758, to A.D. 1858* (1859).

JOHN R. WOODARD

**Fremont (née Fish), Sewall Lawrence** *(30 Aug. 1816–1 May 1886)*, army officer, chief engineer, and superintendent of the Wilmington and Weldon Railroad, was born in Bellows Falls, Vt. (in the year of "no summer"), the third child and second son of Salmon and Tizrah Dutton Fish. He was named for his ancestors Samuel Sewall, the American jurist, and James ("Don't give up the ship!") Lawrence. When he was a child his parents moved to Charleston, Sullivan County, N.H. Appointed from Charleston to the U.S. Military Academy, West Point, N.Y., he was graduated seventeenth in a class of fifty-two on 1 July 1841 and commissioned a second lieutenant in the Third Artillery.

He served in the Florida War (1841–42) and in garrison at Fort Johnston, N.C. (1842–45). During this time (1843) he changed his name to Fremont, and persuaded his father and family to do likewise. He was ordered to the military occupation of Texas (1845–46), and in the War with Mexico he took command of Major David Ringgold's battery when Ringgold was killed in action at Palo Alto on 8 May 1846. After the Battle of Resaca-de-la-Palma (11 May 1846), Fremont was promoted in rank and ordered to Fort Moultrie, S.C. That fall he became assistant professor of geography, history, and ethics at West Point. Advanced to captain on 3 Mar. 1847, he was placed on quartermaster duty in Washington, D.C., but was mustering North Carolina volunteers at Fort Johnston by the end of 1847. While quartermaster in the Third Artillery, he survived the wreck of the USAT *San Francisco* on Christmas Eve of 1853 while she was on her maiden voyage to San Francisco; this wreck was memorialized by John G. Whittier in "Three Bells." Fremont resigned from the army on 4 Apr. 1854.

As an assistant engineer of the United States, he was then assigned to the improvement of the Cape Fear and Savannah rivers. He assumed full management of the Wilmington and Weldon Railroad on 8 Dec. 1854. On 25 Feb. 1861, Governor John W. Ellis appointed him colonel of the North Carolina militia as chief of artillery and engineer. Later he held the same rank in the Confederate States Army. On 31 Aug. 1861, after the fall of Hatteras, he assumed full command of the coastal defenses from the New River south to the state line. He planned the fortification at Federal Point, which he named Fort Fisher in honor of his close friend Charles Frederick Fisher, of Salisbury, who was killed in the Battle of First Manasses. Subsequently, to his consternation, Colonel William Lamb deviated from his original design for the fort while Fremont was attending to the movement of troops and supplies. General Robert E. Lee commended the Wilmington and Weldon Railroad as the "lifeline of the Confederacy." Through a Northern friend in Massachusetts Fremont brought into Wilmington from Nassau, through the Union blockade, rails and other needed hardware made in Northern steel mills to keep the road in efficient running order.

After the fall of Fort Fisher, Fremont was arrested on 3 Apr. 1865 by his West Point classmate W. T. Sherman, who offered "a pass to Nassau or a foreign port, but if he remains in our lines he is simply tolerated and must keep close indoors." By an act of the North Carolina legislature on 1 Apr. 1869, the name of the then small town of Nahunta, north of Goldsboro, was changed to Fremont in recognition of his service to the Confederacy.

At the end of December 1871, he resigned from the Wilmington and Weldon to assume the same position with the Wilmington, Charlotte and Rutherford Railroad, which was subsequently reorganized as the Carolina Central. In 1876, he acquired Clarendon Plantation on the Lower Cape Fear River. Though now a rice planter he continued his professional work, serving as architect for the North Carolina Asylum for Colored Insane at Goldsboro (1878) and as city surveyor for the city of Wilmington (1880–83). In 1886 he was the U.S. architect at Memphis, Tenn., where he died in May.

On 6 Apr. 1848, Fremont married Mary Elizabeth Langdon, the only daughter of Richard Langdon, a merchant, and Mary Eliza Everitt Langdon, daughter of Dr. Ruben Everitt and sister of Dr. Sterling Bird Everitt, all of Smithville (now Southport). The ceremony took place in the Langdon home where Mary was born, located in Smithville directly opposite Fort Johnston. She was the great-granddaughter of the Reverend Dr. Samuel Langdon, of Hampton Falls, N.H., pastor of the Old North Church, Boston (1747–74), president of Harvard (1774–80), and cartographer of the present Canada-United States boundary. Her grandfather, Samuel's son Paul, was founder and first principal of Fryeburg Academy, Maine, which is still extant.

Fremont and his wife had six children. The first three, Ellen Mae, Richard Langdon, and Mary Lawrence, with their mother also survived the wreck of the *San Francisco*, but the girls died in childhood and Richard died at twenty-three. The younger children were Sewall Lawrence, Jr. (1854–1908); Mary Elizabeth (1856–1931), who married John Dancy Battle; and Francis Murray (1858–1900), who married Henrietta Brown Addison. All six children and their parents were buried in Oakdale Cemetery, Wilmington.

Fremont was an Episcopalian and a charter member and senior warden of St. John's Church when it was formed from the congregation of St. James' Church, Wilmington. At the time of his death, he was a trustee of the Episcopal Diocese of East Carolina. A political conservative, he was a strong Union man and cherished the old army but was also a firm believer in states rights. He was a stern disciplinarian, "a thorough soldier at heart, . . . his rigid principles of integrity were dreaded by those . . . whose influence was sufficient to remove him from positions where he was a stumbling block . . . to their money-making notions."

SEE: Abstract log of the ship *San Francisco*, 1853–54 (Records of the Weather Bureau, Library of Congress, Washington, D.C.); Atlantic Coast Line Railroad, *Annual Reports*, 1854–71; G. W. Cullum, *Biographical Register of the Officers and Graduates of the U.S. Military Academy at West Point* (1868); Howard D. Dozier, *History of the Atlantic Coast Line Railroad* (1920); Dorothy Fremont Grant Collection (North Carolina State Archives, Raleigh); *New England Historical and Genealogical Register* 30 (1876); *New York Herald*, 15 Jan. 1854; James Sprunt, *Chronicles of the Cape Fear River, 1660–1916* (1916); War Records Branch, National Archives Records Service, Washington, D.C., for information on Fremont's military career; *Wilmington Evening Journal*, 8 Dec. 1854; Wilmington *The Morning Star*, 8 May 1886.

DOROTHY FREMONT GRANT

**French, John Robert** *(16 Jan. 1818–2 Oct. 1890)*, journalist, bureaucrat, politician, and congressman, was born in Gilmanton, Belknap County, N.H. After receiving an education in Gilmanton and Concord, he worked in the office of the *Herald of Freedom* where he learned the printer's trade in preparation for a career as publisher and editor. For five years he was associated with the *New Hampshire Statesman* at Concord. He then edited the *Eastern Journal* at Biddeford, Maine, for two years before settling in Lake County, Ohio, in 1854. There he was successively editor of the *Telegraph*, the *Press*, and the *Cleveland Morning Leader*. A partisan Republican, French was twice a member of the Ohio House of Representatives (1858 and 1859). When Salmon P. Chase, Ohio's Republican leader, became Abraham Lincoln's secretary of the treasury, he appointed French to a position in the Treasury Department. French remained in treasury service throughout the Civil War. In 1864 Lincoln appointed him a member of the Board of Direct-Tax Commissioners for North Carolina.

At the close of the war, French settled in Edenton and became a leader in the organization and direction of the North Carolina Republican party. He represented Chowan County in the Constitutional Convention of 1868. After North Carolina had complied with the requirements of the congressional reconstruction acts, he was elected as a Republican to represent the First District in the Fortieth Congress, where he served from 6 July 1868 to 3 Mar. 1869. He was a member of the Committee on Expenditures in the War Department, introduced one resolution of a private nature, and on 9 Feb. 1869 delivered one recorded speech. This speech, entitled "Equal Suffrage and the Material Development of the Country," was a highly partisan, dramatic appeal for black suffrage nationwide. In support of the proposed Fifteenth Amendment, French contended that emancipation had cleansed the American soul and that the valiant service of the black soldier was a natural prelude to equal political rights. His humanitarian and political instincts led him to contend: "History, sir, will compel us to say that it was the black skin that could always be trusted; it was the black man who never betrayed; where ever you found a negro there was a soul loyal to the Union and true to our country's flag." Having established the black man's loyalty, French turned to recent political restructuring in the South. He concluded: "In the light, then, of experience does not the trial of black voting in the South warrant its extension to all the States? Where in all the history of the world has there been better voting than by the colored men of the rebel states during these last eighteen months? And does not the nation owe it to these faithful friends and their white Union allies in the South that she lift the ban from colored voting and make it universal throughout the Republic?" These sentiments, though hardly representative of southern opinion, do suggest the methods by which Republican ascendency in the former Confederate states was achieved.

In the regular election in 1868 the Republican organization bypassed French and nominated C. L. Cobb as its candidate for Congress in North Carolina's First District. French bolted and ran in his own interest but was defeated. He quit North Carolina. At the expiration of his term in the Fortieth Congress, he was elected sergeant at arms of the U.S. Senate and served from 22 Mar. 1869 to 24 Mar. 1879. In July 1880 he was appointed secretary of the Ute Commission. Later he moved to the West and eventually settled in Idaho, where he was editor of the *Boise City Sun* until his death. Following a funeral in the Methodist church, French was buried in the Boise City Cemetery, far from eastern North Carolina where the political circumstances of the moment had elevated him far beyond the level to which he might otherwise have risen.

French was married in 1846; his wife, whose maiden name probably was Kimball, died in Edenton. He was survived by a son, E. R. French, of Omaha, Nebr.

SEE: *Biog. Dir. Am. Cong.* (1961); Boise City *Idaho Daily Statesman*, 3, 4, 9 Oct. 1890; Fortieth U.S. Congress, *Congressional Globe* (1868–69); J. G. deR. Hamilton, *Reconstruction in North Carolina* (1914); *Raleigh Daily Sentinel*, 8 Jan. 1868.

MAX R. WILLIAMS

**Frerichs, William Charles Anthony** *(2 Mar. 1829–16 Mar. 1905)*, painter of landscapes, portraits, and genre works and professor of art and languages, was born in Ghent, Netherlands, the son of Willem Daniel and Helen Eugenia Crommelinck Frerichs. At a very early age he studied art in The Hague; he later studied medicine at the University of Leyden and then returned to the study of art at Brussels Academy where he completed his formal education with a "Grand Tour." During his formative years in The Hague, Frerichs worked under two important masters, Andreas Schelfhout (1787–1870) and Bartholomeus J. van Hove (1790–1880), forerunners of the late nineteenth century flowering of Dutch art known as "The Hague School." The beauty of billowing clouds broad-shadowed on the flat Dutch landscape, the lingering, lucid northern light, the shifting dune valleys near Scheveningen Beach, the complicated play of light on water—all these visual images were part of Frerichs's artistic heritage. The Hague at mid-century was the "Paris of Holland."

Frerichs's father pursued a double career of army officer and newspaper editor. This implies a home atmosphere of adventure and change, which must have contributed to young William's decision to make his way to America. With a passport dated 4 July 1850, he sailed to New York and remained there until 1854, when he set his sights on North Carolina. That year he accepted a position as professor of arts and languages at Greensboro Female College (now Greensboro College).

Frerichs painted twenty-four paintings of a single stream with each painting showing a different waterfall on that stream. The excitement of cascading water and the beauty of the haze lingering over a Blue Ridge terrain were incorporated into a visual index already rich with the memories of ocean spray and the rhythmic crest and fall of waves in the Atlantic. On the Piedmont Plateau, an ancient, isolated range, the Sauratown Mountains thrust skyward within forty miles of Greensboro, providing gorgeous views of the Blue Ridge range spreading southward from Virginia to South Carolina. These mountains were documented many times by Frerichs's paintings; life around the popular spa, Piedmont Springs, was also depicted in his works. Frerichs was the first artist of consequence to travel to the Cherokee country. Here he painted the vast western country of North Carolina for the first time. Some of his scenes remain the only documentary record of certain landmarks such as "The Falls of the Tamahaka," which is now flooded by Fontana Lake.

As Frerichs worked his way into seemingly inaccessible territory, unexpected problems arose. Indians stole his studies from nature, his painting materials, even his easel. He had a great deal of difficulty recovering them. His problems increased in 1863, when his entire collection was destroyed by a fire that consumed Greensboro College. Discouraged by the Civil War and the loss of his studio, he decided to take up farming and moved east to Williston on the Scuppernong River. The trip was over 400 miles, for it was necessary to skirt around Federal and Confederate troops that were blocking the regular route. After a short time, Frerichs and his family abandoned their property on the coast and went to New York. For most of the remainder of his life, he worked in Tottenville, Staten Island, N.Y. Although he made several painting trips to New England, he always painted in the style he developed in North Carolina.

On 1 Jan. 1854 Frerichs married Mrs. Clara Butler of New York City. Her father, Peregrine Branwaite, came from England in 1842. Clara was a friend of Charles F. Deems, the Methodist minister who was president of Greensboro College. Deems returned to New York about the same time as Frerichs and with the help of a group of fifteen persons, including Commodore Cornelius Vanderbilt, founded the "Church of the Strangers," the first nondenominational church in the United States. Frerichs had three children, William D., Lena, and Charles. Clara Frerichs died on 18 Sept. 1874 at age fifty and was buried in the churchyard of Bethel Methodist Church, Tottenville, Staten Island. Frerichs was married again in 1880 to Miss E. Whalen of New York City and they had two sons, Eugene and Alexander. Frerichs died at the age of seventy-six. Funeral services were conducted from the South Baptist Church and burial was in the cemetery of Bethel Methodist Church, Tottenville.

Frerichs's works can be found in private and public collections throughout the country, including the North Carolina Museum of Art and the Museum of Santa Barbara, Calif., as well as in Salem, Ore.; Baltimore, Md.; Newark, N.J.; New Jersey State; and Staten Island, N.Y. The first retrospective exhibition of the work of William C. A. Frerichs was held at the North Carolina Museum of Art, 15 Sept.–20 Oct. 1974.

SEE: *Dictionary of Artists in America, 1564–1860* (1957); Mantle Fielding, *Dictionary of American Painters, Sculptors and Engravers* (1960); Hildegard J. Safford, "William C. A. Frerichs, Artist, 1829–1905," *The Staten Island Historian* 31 (October–December 1970); Ben F. Williams, *William C. A. Frerichs, 1829–1905, A Retrospective Exhibition* (1974).

BENJAMIN F. WILLIAMS

**Friar, Daniel Boone** *(4 Apr. 1800–January 1858)*, pioneer Texas settler, was born probably in Bertie County, the son of Willice Friar or Fryer and his wife, Sarah. In 1828 young Friar and his bride of about a year, Annie Graeme Friar, went to Texas as part of Stephen F. Austin's second colony, settling at Washington-on-the-Brazos. Friar in 1835 was authorized to employ and command twenty-five rangers to patrol between the Brazos and Colorado rivers with headquarters in the Indian village that became Waco. He was also captain of a company of volunteers at the Battle of San Jacinto on 21

Apr. 1836. He then moved to south Texas, where his home and store were made the temporary county seat of the newly formed DeWitt County in 1842. Friar and his wife were the parents of nine children. A Presbyterian, he is said to have organized the first Masonic lodge in the county. He died at his home on Coleto Creek at the small farming community of Yorktown in southern Texas.

SEE: Bertie County wills (North Carolina State Archives, Raleigh); Walter P. Webb, ed., *Handbook of Texas* (1952).

WILLIAM S. POWELL

**Fries, Adelaide Lisetta** *(12 Nov. 1871–29 Nov. 1949)*, archivist, historian, author, and genealogist, was born in Salem. Her father, John William Fries, was an industrialist, inventor, church leader, and student who encouraged his daughter in her scholarly pursuits. Through her mother, Agnes Sophia deSchweinitz, Miss Fries was descended from four bishops of the Moravian Church (Unitas Fratrum): Count Nicholas von Zinzendorf (1700–1760), who played an important role in the renewal of the ancient church; his son-in-law, Johannes von Watteville (1718–88); John Gottlieb Herman (1789–1854); and her grandfather, Emil Adolphus deSchweinitz (1816–79). Her great-grandfather, Ludwig David von Schweinitz (Lewis David deSchweinitz, 1780–1834), was a botanist of international renown. In 1888 Miss Fries was graduated from Salem College, where she received an A.B. degree in 1890 and an M.A. in 1916.

Reared in a devout Moravian family, she became actively interested in her church's history while in her teens. When she questioned her father about Cornwallis's visit to the area, he urged her to go to her primary sources, the church diaries, and find the answers for herself. She objected, reminding her father that the diaries were not only in German but also handwritten in old German script. According to Miss Fries's account, he said, "Well, Adelaide, you'll never learn to read it any younger," and, smiling, left her. Thus challenged, she began her mastery of Moravian church history and of the old German script in which it was, often carelessly, written.

In 1899 John W. Fries was a delegate from the southern province to the worldwide synod of the Moravian church held every ten years in Herrnhut, Germany, and he took his daughter Adelaide with him. It was an exhilarating experience for her to examine for herself the earliest records of her ancient church. She returned to Herrnhut in 1909 to spend a few weeks studying these old manuscripts in the Moravian archives and visiting friends with whom she corresponded for the rest of her life. Her father, who had first interested her in such scholarly work, remained her mentor and inspiration. The dedication of the *Records of the Moravians* (1920) reads: "To my Father[,] my comrade in the silent places of historical research." From her mother she learned the art of fine sewing, which she greatly enjoyed as well as gardening, a lifelong hobby.

But her work with the church records claimed most of her time. One day when "a prominent citizen" of Salem suggested to her that it might be wise to find a room in which to keep the various old papers she was working with, she enthusiastically agreed and thus began, without any official authority, to gather and store the many old Moravian manuscript records scattered throughout the province. It was due chiefly to Miss Fries's persistence in ferreting out these valuable papers and diaries that most of them have not been lost or destroyed. The single room gave way to a shedlike building, which provided more space but worried her constantly because of the fire hazard. At length in 1942 she happily supervised the moving of the archives into the present fireproof building on the corner of South Main and Bank streets, only a block from Home Moravian Church and Salem Square.

On 26 Sept. 1911 Miss Fries was officially appointed archivist of the Moravian Church, Southern Province, a position she held for the rest of her life, almost forty years. As archivist she carried on a voluminous correspondence with people from many foreign countries as well as from all the states in this country. Whereas most of the letters contained questions regarding the records and history of the church, many writers asked help in tracing their family back to certain Moravian ancestors. "Memoirs" (brief biographies of Moravian church members read at their funeral services and then filed in the archives) together with the church diaries and other records proved a valuable source of information for Miss Fries in her role of genealogist. She enjoyed this work and became a member of the National Genealogical Society, the New England Genealogical Society, and the Institute of American Genealogy.

Her own memoir speaks of her passion for accuracy, her deep interest in her church and in history, and her abundant sense of humor. An entry in her personal diary notes: "There were four visitors at the archives today—two students engaged in research, one caller investigating a family tree, and a visitor who did not know when it was time to leave." Although a certain dignity and reserve might have discouraged some from seeking her help, those who did approach her were warmed by her friendliness and her sincere desire to aid in any project if it were possible for her to do so. She gave freely of her time to anyone asking it, whether it was a student doing research in the archives or someone requesting that she address a club group. Her friend Dr. Douglas L. Rights remarked that as a speaker she was "noted for her good sense, adaptability, felicity of expression, and inspiration, combined always with the voice of authority." She once admitted that she did not know how to say "No" to her church or her community.

Part of her popularity as a speaker and author resulted from her ability to make the past come alive for her audiences—whether composed of small children, with whom she had a fine rapport, or adults. Her success was no doubt due to the fact that she tried to put herself—and her audiences—back into the period, place, and thoughts of the people of whom she was speaking or writing. In a letter to a friend she wrote: "It has always seemed to me that one of the most difficult and most necessary things in historical work is to catch the point of view of the people who took part in any action. Their standpoint, and theirs alone, determines their relation to that action." This ability was certainly evident in *The Road to Salem* (1944), the longest and best known of the books of which she was sole author and for which she received the Mayflower Cup. Other books include *The Moravians in Georgia, 1737–1740* (1905), *Some Moravian Heroes* (1936), *Distinctive Customs and Practices of the Moravian Church* (1949), and, with J. Kenneth Pfohl, *The Moravian Church Yesterday and Today* (1926). Miss Fries was the author of a number of pamphlets concerning the history or customs of the Moravian Church and of North Carolina, and she contributed a number of articles to historical periodicals. She also was well known as an editor. An example is

*Forsyth, a County on the March,* which received a silver cup as the best county history written in 1949. As an editor, her most important work was the seven-volume *The Records of the Moravians in North Carolina* (1922–47). Volume 8 was in process of completion at the time of her death. Miss Fries not only selected the material to be included, but also translated it from the handwritten old German script, a monumental task.

Her important contributions were officially recognized by the honorary degree of doctor of letters awarded her first in June 1932 by Moravian College, Bethlehem, Pa., "for excellence in the fields of history, literature, and genealogy"; in May 1945 by Wake Forest College; and in June 1945 by The University of North Carolina. In Chapel Hill she proudly wore the cap and gown her father had used when he received the same degree nineteen years earlier.

She was an active member of many organizations. She was a charter member (1895) and on the board of directors of the Wachovia Historical Society; she helped organize the North Carolina Federation of Women's Clubs and served as president from 1913 to 1915. She was also president of the State Literary and Historical Association (1923); a member of the board of the *North Carolina Historical Review* (1928–49); president of the Historical Society of North Carolina (1947); and a member of the American Association for State and Local History, of the North Carolina Folklore Society, and of the North Carolina Society for the Preservation of Antiquities. For many years she was president of the Women's Missionary Society of the Home Moravian Church. Her love for her alma mater kept her active in the Salem College Alumnae Association as president for many years and then as chairman of the scholarship committee.

Miss Fries was engaged in her usual activities until a few hours before her death. She was buried in the Moravian graveyard, "God's Acre," in Winston-Salem.

SEE: Geraldine B. Eggleston, "Dr. Adelaide L. Fries" (Masters thesis, University of North Carolina, 1964); *Greensboro Daily News*, 11 May 1947; "Memoir of Sister Adelaide Lisetta Fries" (Archives, Southern Province, Moravian Church in America, Winston-Salem); Paul Murray, "Thirty Years of the New History," *North Carolina Historical Review* 32 (1955); *North Carolina Authors: A Selective Handbook* (1952); *North Carolina Biography*, vol. 5 (1928); D. L. Rights, "Dr. Adelaide Lisetta Fries," *North Carolina Historical Review* 29 (1952); Gary Trawick and Paul Wyche, *One Hundred Years, One Hundred Men* (1971); *Who's Who in America*, 1934–35.

ANNA WITHERS BAIR

**Fries, Francis Henry** *(1 Feb. 1855–5 June 1931)*, manufacturer, banker, and railroader, was born in Salem, the son of Francis Levin and Lisetta Maria Vogler Fries. His mother was the granddaughter of the silversmith, John Vogler, a prominent figure in early Salem; his father was active in community affairs and politics, serving in the General Assembly in 1858–59. Young Fries attended the Salem Boys School and then was graduated from Davidson College in 1874. His career resembled that of his father, who founded the first successful textile mill in Salem. The Fries Manufacturing Company was built in 1839, became the F and H Fries Manufacturing Company in 1846, and was operated until 1928. It produced the famous "Salem Jeans." Fries, like his brothers, became a partner in the firm at age twenty-one; he was superintendent until 1887. In 1881 he built Arista Mills, the first mill in North Carolina to have electric lights. Shortly afterward, he started the Indera Mills.

In 1887, at the urging of R. J. Reynolds and others, Fries assumed the task of building a 122-mile railroad to cross the mountains and connect Winston and Salem to Roanoke. Completed in 1891 at a cost of $2 million, the Roanoke and Southern Railway, which Fries served at times as president and general manager, became part of the Norfolk and Western rail system in 1892. Plans to build another line from Winston and Salem to Wadesboro in order to connect with the Atlantic Coastline Railroad were postponed because of the depression of the 1890s. Later, in 1909–10, Fries helped his brother, Henry Elias Fries, then president of the Winston-Salem Southbound Railroad, complete the line to Wadesboro. The purpose of these rail lines was to prevent Winston and Salem from being commercially isolated.

In 1893, Fries went into banking as president of the first trust company in North Carolina, the Wachovia Loan and Trust Company, organized in 1891 by his uncle Henry, his brother John, and others. In 1911, this company joined with the Wachovia National Bank to become the Wachovia Bank and Trust Company, which became one of the largest in the South. Fries remained president until his death.

He also stayed heavily involved in the textile industry. In addition to his responsibilities at Arista Mills and Indera Mills, he founded Mayo Mills and the town of Mayodan in 1896, the Avalon Mills near Mayodan in 1899, and the Washington Mills at Fries, Va., in 1901. In 1923, these last three mills were consolidated as the Washington Mills at Fries, Va. Fries was president of the mills he organized as well as vice-president and director of the Oakdale Mills in Jamestown, president of the Brown and Williamson Tobacco Company, and a director of several other companies.

A Democrat, Fries limited his political participation to serving on the staff of Governor Alfred M. Scales (1885–89), acquiring the title "Colonel," which he used thereafter as a convenient way to distinguish his name from that of his father. In 1904, he was elected president of the North Carolina Bankers Association, and he headed the trust section of the American Bankers Association. During World War I, he was a director of War Savings in North Carolina. Active in the Moravian church and his community, Fries was a Sunday school superintendent for twenty-five years and a trustee of Salem Academy and College. He initiated the Winston-Salem Foundation, which in 1970 had assets of $25 million.

On 23 Nov. 1881 he married Letitia Walker Patterson, granddaughter of Governor John Motley Morehead and daughter of a leading North Carolina textile family; she died in 1884. Their only child, Louis Morehead, died in 1882. Fries's second wife, whom he married on 19 Aug. 1886, was Pauline deSchweinitz, daughter of a bishop of the Moravian church. Their only child, Rosa Eleanor, married Richard Furman Willingham. After his death in Winston-Salem, Fries was buried in Salem Cemetery.

SEE: Francis L. Fries Papers (Southern Historical Collection, University of North Carolina, Chapel Hill); Gilbert T. Stephenson, *The Life and Story of a Trust Man: Being That of Francis Henry Fries. . . .* (1930); Gary Trawick and Paul Wyche, *One Hundred Years, One Hundred Men* (1971); *Who Was Who in America*, vol. 1 (1943); *Who's Who in the South* (1927); Winston-Salem *Journal and Sentinel*, 11 Oct. 1970; Margery W. Young, *Textile Leaders of the South* (1963).

TOM E. TERRILL

**Fries, Francis (Franz) Levin** *(17 Oct. 1812–1 Aug. 1863)*, cotton manufacturer, was born in Salem, the son of John (Johann) Christian William (Wilhelm) Fries, who had been born in Barby, Germany, 22 Nov. 1775. William was trained as a cabinetmaker and in 1809 arrived in Salem, where he worked in the Single Brothers cabinet shop in which he was master from 1811 to 1815, when he opened a shop of his own. However, after about 1820 he did very little cabinetwork himself but turned to farming and other business, culminating in textile manufacturing. On 11 Oct. 1811 William married Johanna Elisabeth Nissen, daughter of Tycho Nissen, a wainwright and cabinetmaker. They had three children: Francis Levin; Carolina Amanda (16 June 1817–14 Feb. 1881), who married Edward Belo, also a cabinetmaker and the son of a cabinetmaker; and Henry William (Heinrich Wilhelm) (5 Mar. 1825–4 Nov. 1902).

Francis Levin was baptized in the Moravian church the day after his birth. On 12 May 1818, when he was five and a half, he entered the school for little boys. He did so well that his parents wanted him to continue his formal education rather than be apprenticed to a trade. On 28 Sept. 1827 he was accepted in the "Paedagogium," Nazareth Hall, in Nazareth, Pa., to study theology. He completed school and arrived home on 23 June 1830 "for a visit," with prospects of returning in October to teach at Nazareth Hall. But in September, when a vacancy occurred in the Salem Boys School and Francis was preferred to another candidate with more experience, he remained in Salem and taught until 1 July 1835, when he resigned to go north for "a years visit" to learn about manufacturing. Returning on 30 Apr. 1836, he supervised the building of the Salem [cotton] Manufacturing Company's plant, of which he became an officer.

On 24 Mar. 1838, Fries married Lisetta Maria Vogler (3 Mar. 1820–23 Oct. 1903), the daughter of John Vogler, a prosperous Salem silversmith. They had four daughters and three sons: Carolina Louisa (8 Oct. 1839), Mary Elisabeth (31 Aug. 1844), John William (7 Nov. 1846), Emma Christina (25 June 1852), Francis Henry (1 Feb. 1855), Henry Elias (22 Sept. 1857), and Louisa Sarah (8 Dec. 1859).

Fries was highly respected in Salem, especially for his business ability, though like his father with whom he became associated in business, he had a mind of his own. Capable citizens in Salem were called upon to perform a variety of gratis civic duties. Fries and his father both provided many of these services. Almost as soon as he started working at the cotton mill, Francis was elected a member of the *Aufseher Collegium*, the supervisory committee in charge of business in Salem; at times he also kept its minutes. He was continually reelected for two-year terms. In April 1838 and again in February 1845 both he and his father resigned because of differences of opinion on the Negro question in Salem. Each time, however, Francis was soon reelected. He also was an officer in the Salem (municipal) Fire Company in 1845. In 1849 the county in which Salem was situated was split and a court established adjacent to Salem; in 1851 the new town was incorporated as Winston. Fries was made chairman of the county court, and in succeeding years he was elected one of the seven commissioners of the town of Winston. In 1858–59 he represented Forsyth County in the state legislature.

Like his father, Fries found business more to his liking. It was probably due to him that he and his father in October 1839 decided to build a wool spinning mill run by steam power. Wool carding operations began in 1840; shortly afterward, dyeing and fulling and spinning and weaving processes were undertaken. In 1846 Fries's brother Henry joined the firm, which then went by the name of F and H Fries. Two years later they added a cotton mill, which ran until 1880 when it was converted to the enlarged woolen mill.

In addition to the textile enterprises Fries designed and built a house for the minister, probably the bank building for Salem, a gunpowder storage building (with Edward Belo), and a brick kiln. In 1847 he rented the Schober paper mill.

Although the Salemites always had a few slaves, mainly as domestic servants, they frowned on slavery. With their growing manufacturing enterprises, the Frieses found slaves a good investment, but as a consequence they acquired more slaves than the town fathers approved. In 1847 they had seven white and sixteen black (slaves and free) people working in the factory and in their homes. The number increased until the Civil War. They treated their slaves very well and Francis, who called his factory help "my boys," frequently gave them time off for rest while he continued working. Sometimes he shut down the factory while he and the crew went skating, or to the circus, or rabbit hunting: "Myself and the boys went skating till noon," he once wrote in his diary.

He died of "bronchites" after a long and lingering illness. A portrait of Fries and his wife, painted in 1839 by Gustavus Grunewald, is own by Old Salem, Inc.

SEE: Diary and Memoir of Francis Levin Fries, Minutes of the *Aufseher Collegium*, and Minutes of the Elders Conference (Archives, Southern Province, Moravian Church in America, Winston-Salem); Adelaide L. Fries and others, eds., *Records of the Moravians*, vols. 7–11 (1947–69).

FRANK P. ALBRIGHT

**Fries, Henry Elias** *(22 Sept. 1857–3 Mar. 1949)*, industrialist, third son of Francis Levin and Lisetta Maria Vogler Fries, was born in Salem and began his education at Salem Boys School. At age seventeen he enrolled at Davidson College, but failing eyesight forced his departure after three years without receiving a degree. He then became manager of Wachovia Mills, a subsidiary of F and H Fries Manufacturing Company, which produced flour. In 1881, he married Rosa Mickey of Salem; they had one daughter.

An active promoter and organizer, Fries was secretary of the State Industrial Exposition held in Raleigh in 1884 and in the following year organized the Southside Cotton Mill in Winston, of which he became president. In 1887, he filled one term as Forsyth County representative to the North Carolina General Assembly and was for years a Democratic party national committeeman. He also served as mayor of Salem for three terms; as a member of the Forsyth County Board of Education, which undertook the building of new schoolhouses for the entire system; and as trustee of Slater Industrial and Normal School (later Winston-Salem State University). He was instrumental in establishing the North Carolina College of Agriculture and Mechanic Arts as one of its three-man organizational committee and was a member of the board of trustees for ten years.

In 1897, Fries pioneered in electrical development when he founded the Fries Manufacturing and Power Company, which built a hydroelectric dam on the Yadkin River to supply the mills of Winston-Salem with electricity, the first long-distance transmission established in North Carolina. By the time this project was sold in 1913, Fries was operating an electric streetcar system and supplying homes as well as factories with electricity. As a member of the town board of Salem, he was credited with being one of the primary advocates of the consolidation of Winston and Salem. He helped organize the Winston-Salem Chamber of Commerce and a Red Cross chapter, and he served many years in the Rotary Club, becoming its president in 1935.

Because there was no rail link from Winston or Salem to the south, Fries joined with his brother Francis in 1909 to form the Winston-Salem Southbound Railway creating a link from Winston-Salem to Wadesboro. Henry Fries served as the railroad's president until his death. He also headed the Forsyth Manufacturing Company and Arista Mills.

Besides his involvement with the beginnings of what is now North Carolina State University, Fries served on the State Board of Agriculture, in which he was known for pioneering in guernsey cattle breeding, and on the State Geological Board.

Fries never ceased to be an enthusiastic promoter and worker. He died at his desk in the Reynolds Building of a coronary thrombosis at age ninety-two and was buried in the Salem Cemetery. Probably more than any one person, Fries paved the way for the modern industrial center of Winston-Salem.

SEE: Death Certificates of Forsyth County (Forsyth County Courthouse, Winston-Salem); Henry E. Fries Papers (Manuscript Department, Library, Duke University, Durham); *North Carolina Biography*, vol. 5 (1919); North Carolina General Assembly, *Legislative Sketchbook* (1887); Winston-Salem *Journal and Sentinel*, 4 Mar. 1949, 11 Oct. 1970.

ROGER N. KIRKMAN

**Fries, John William** *(7 Nov. 1846–21 Nov. 1927)*, industrialist, inventor, student, and church leader, was born in Salem, the oldest son of Francis Levin and Lisetta Maria Vogler Fries. In 1840 Francis L. Fries had opened a textile factory in Salem, which became known as the F and H Fries Woolen Mill in 1846 when he took in his younger brother, Henry, as partner. John Fries's education at Salem Boys School ended at the age of fourteen when he went to work full time in his father's mill. This early experience with machinery and metals proved valuable, for in later years he became known as an inventor of cotton mill machines and processes for dyeing yarns and cloth. Francis L. Fries died in 1863, leaving to his young son John the burden of taking his place in the family business. Nevertheless, John Fries always found time for reading and studying. At twenty he entered The University of North Carolina where he continued his formal education for a year and a half; he then returned to Salem to become a partner with his uncle Henry in the family mill. On 25 Oct. 1870, he married Agnes Sophia deSchweinitz by whom he had two children: Adelaide Lisetta and Mary Eleanor, who married William A. Blair.

Adding civic duties to his full schedule, Fries served several terms as Salem town commissioner and magistrate. A Democrat, he became a member of the County Board of Commissioners where he worked for better roads, and for six years he served as judge of the county court. Because he was for "sound money," that is, gold instead of silver, Fries voted for McKinley instead of Bryan in the presidential election of 1896. The same year, at a meeting in Indianapolis, he was elected a member of the executive committee of a national group of commercial organizations concerned with the means of perpetuating the gold standard. In 1897, President McKinley appointed him a member of the Monetary Commission meeting in Washington, D.C., to make a "thorough and exhaustive study of America's financial system and its need." Fries also contributed several magazine articles on sound money questions. In June 1926 he went to Chapel Hill to receive the honorary LL.D. degree from his alma mater, which he had served for forty years as a member of the board of trustees.

The son of devout Moravian parents, Fries became a communicant member of the Home Moravian Church in Salem on 20 Mar. 1864. For thirty years he was a member of the church's board of trustees, serving as chairman from 1897 to 1909. On 14 Dec. 1899 he was chosen by the synod as a member of the Provincial Elders Conference, the governing board between triennial synods, of the Southern Province of the Moravian Church; he was reelected at each of the succeeding synods. He was chosen delegate to represent the Southern Province at two of the general synods (meeting every ten years) held in Herrnhut, Saxony, in 1899 and 1909 and served on the finance committee. For thirty years he was a member of the board of trustees of Salem College and Academy.

Fries also was president of the F and H Fries Company, Arista Mills Company, Peoples' National Bank, Salem Cemetery Company, and the Chamber of Commerce; a director of the North Carolina Midland Railroad, Wachovia Bank and Trust Company, and Fries Manufacturing and Power Company; and a member of the Society of Chemical Industry and of the Academy of Social Science. After a lingering illness, he died at his home in Winston-Salem and was buried in the Salem Moravian graveyard.

SEE: Samuel A. Ashe, ed., *Biographical History of North Carolina*, vol. 3 (1906); Adelaide L. Fries, *Forsyth, A County on the March* (1949); "Memoir of John William Fries" (Archives, Southern Province, Moravian Church in America, Winston-Salem); *Who's Who in America* 1899–1900; Winston-Salem *Twin City Sentinel*, 22 Nov. 1927.

ANNA WITHERS BAIR

**Frohock, John** *(d. [after 2 Jul.] 1772)*, colonial official and land speculator, was living in southeastern Bucks County, Pa., before 1725, the son of John Frohock, Sr., who apparently was a Quaker. The family may have come to America from Cambridgeshire, England, as there were several graduates of Cambridge University of that name from the county. The younger Frohock was for a time an associate of his uncle, Hugh Parker, a wealthy merchant of Prince Georges (later Frederick) County, Md., and active in the trading ventures of the newly organized Ohio Company. After the death of the elder Frohock in 1748 and Parker's death in 1751, the families moved to east-central North Carolina and John Frohock soon acquired land in Northampton, Edgecombe, Halifax, and Granville counties, as well as in Virginia. He became associated with several prominent families already there, notably the McCullohs. By 1753 Frohock was living in the new county of Rowan on the frontier of North Carolina. He served as justice of the peace as well as commissioner for the county and for the town of Salisbury. Within ten years he probably was the wealthiest and most influential man in that part of the province. Waightstill Avery referred to Frohock's plantation and house as "the most elegant and large within one hundred miles." He represented the county in the Assembly during each session from 1760 through 1768, beginning with the second one called by Governor Arthur Dobbs and lasting through Governor Tryon's first when he was succeeded by a Regulator.

Frohock was witness to countless wills and deeds in Anson, Mecklenburg, and Rowan counties as well as elsewhere from 1753 until as late as March 1772. Among his early activities in the province was service as surveyor for Henry E. McCulloh, the agent of George Selwyn who owned a very large tract of land in Mecklenburg County. Sent to survey the land in 1765, Frohock and his associates were soundly beaten by squatters. He had been one of the commissioners charged with the creation of Mecklenburg County in 1762 and the county seat, Charlotte, in 1766. He also served on the committees named by the Assembly to build the courthouse and prison in Anson County and the jail in Salisbury. Frohock became clerk of court in Rowan County in 1756 and in 1769 Chief Justice Martin Howard named him clerk of the superior court for the District of Salisbury. In 1767 Governor Tryon named him a member of a small group of commissioners to run a boundary line setting off the Cherokee Indians in the western part of the province. For £150 Frohock once sold an office to which he had been appointed. The Reverend Theodorus Swaine Drage of St. Luke's Parish, Rowan County, reported to Governor Tryon that he was disappointed with the cooperation he received from Frohock. Nevertheless, he was a close friend of many important people in the province, including, of course, the governor. In 1767 Frohock and one of his brothers accompanied Governor and Mrs. Tryon on a visit to the Moravian town of Bethabara.

As a public official Frohock was in a position to be suspected of and perhaps even guilty of extortion and corruption. The Regulators regarded him, along with Edmund Fanning and others, as their enemy. Although Frohock was an officer of the Rowan County militia, rising from captain to colonel, he was eventually excused by Tryon from an active role in the conflict that developed, perhaps because he would have been a special target sought out by many Regulators. After the defeat of the Regulators at the Battle of Alamance in the spring of 1771, William Hooper, as deputy attorney general, drew up a bill of indictment for extortion against Frohock, but the grand jury rejected it for lack of adequate evidence. Nevertheless, Frohock and his two brothers, Thomas and William, also public officials, were forced to disgorge exorbitant fees taken from some of the Regulators. A Regulator leader, James Hunter, and a delegation of his associates had precipitated this action in an appeal to Hooper.

Frohock was ill from pleurisy in the spring of 1764, and in June 1767, while in the Cherokee country, he was seriously injured when a creek bank caved in and his horse fell on him. Whether because of this it is not known, but his will was drawn up in the early fall of 1768. He continued active as clerk of court through May 1772 although he died before the end of the year. In Hillsborough on 2 July the merchant William Johnston gave Frohock a cordial letter of introduction to Richard Bennehan. An extensive landowner with property in various parts of North Carolina, including a number of grist and sawmills, he was never married and willed his property and possessions, including thirty-eight slaves, to his two brothers, to an aunt, Mrs. Mary McManus of Halifax County, and to Mary McCulloh, daughter of Alexander. One slave, Absalom, Frohock's body servant, was to be educated for a year then given his freedom. Perhaps because of the extent of his property holdings, the will was not admitted to probate until 10 Apr. 1801.

SEE: John L. Cheney, Jr., ed., *North Carolina Government, 1585–1974* (1975); Walter Clark, ed., *State Records of North Carolina*, vols. 22 (1907), 23 (1904); Adelaide L. Fries, ed., *Records of the Moravians*, vols. 1 (1922), 2 (1925); Jo White Linn, *Abstracts of Wills and Estate Records of Rowan County, North Carolina, 1753–1805* (1980); William S. Powell, ed., *Correspondence of William Tryon and Other Selected Papers*, vols. 1 (1980), 2 (1981); William S. Powell and others, eds., *The Regulators in North Carolina* (1971); Robert W. Ramsey, *Carolina Cradle, Settlement of the Northwest Carolina Frontier, 1747–1762* (1964); Jethro Rumple, *A History of Rowan County* (1881); *Virginia Gazette*, 15 Aug. 1771, 3 Oct. 1777.

VERNON O. STUMPF

**Frontis, Stephen** *(18 July 1792–12 Apr. 1867)*, Presbyterian minister, was born in Cognac, France, the son of John Baptist Jehoiachin and Etiennette Borel Frontis who were married on 7 Apr. 1786 at Port au Prince, Santo Domingo. His father was a Roman Catholic and had all his children baptized as Catholics. His mother was born of Protestant parents in Geneva, Switzerland, where Stephen spent sixteen years of his childhood and youth. Initially, the Frontises had lived in Port au Prince, where John Frontis acquired a moderate fortune as a tailor and merchant-trader. After the revolution forced them to leave in April 1792, they settled in Cognac, France. In April 1793 John Frontis left his wife and children in France to establish a business as merchant-trader in Philadelphia and Jamaica; he did not see his family again until 1800. Mrs. Frontis and their three children lived in Cognac for a year in straitened circumstances, then moved to Geneva, Switzerland, to be near her relatives. While living there, Stephen was trained as a cabinetmaker and took special training in drawing and writing. During his youth he was under the influence of his Protestant relatives and joined the Church of Geneva.

In 1810 young Frontis left Switzerland to avoid conscription in Napoleon's army and joined his father in Philadelphia. There he worked as a journeyman cabinetmaker and endured a brief and unsatisfactory experience as a clerk. His friend Joseph Conrad, who later became a ruling elder in the Presbyterian church in Lexington, N.C., invited him to hear the Reverend James K. Burch, and in 1813 he joined the Presbyterian church. In 1817 Burch was offered a post as head of an academy in Oxford, N.C., and he asked Frontis to go with him to teach French and Latin. The Oxford connection lasted only a short time, so Stephen Frontis went to Raleigh where the Reverend Dr. William McPheeters engaged him to teach French in the female academy. In October 1820 he entered the Theological Seminary in Princeton, N.J., where he was graduated with honors in the class of 1823. He was ordained by the Orange Presbytery in November 1823.

For five years Frontis did missionary work in Maryland, Michigan, Pennsylvania, and Delaware. He then became stated supply and pastor of Bethany Presbyterian Church in Iredell County. While serving in that capacity, he was chosen as one of the commissioners to select a site for Davidson College, where he later taught.

On 2 Feb. 1830, at Lincolnton, N.C., Frontis married

Martha Dews, who had come from the Guernsey Islands with her parents in 1817. In April 1836 he became stated supply of the Presbyterian church in Salisbury and was ordained on 12 Sept. 1839, remaining as pastor until 1846. During the nine years he was with the Salisbury church, forty-four people were received into membership including two of his sisters, Jeanne Marie Euphrosine Frontis and Elizabeth Frontis, who were received by certificate of transfer from their church in Geneva, Switzerland. Frontis also taught French in the Salisbury Female Academy.

In Salisbury, he purchased from Maxwell Chambers a frame house where he lived while serving as stated supply to Thyatira and Franklin churches during the period 1846–49. Martha Dews Frontis died on 10 July 1849 and was buried in the Lutheran cemetery in Salisbury beside their two small children, Martha Dews and Thomas Dews Frontis.

From 1849 to 1856 Frontis served Center Grove Church in Iredell County. He purchased a farm near Prospect Presbyterian Church in Rowan County, and on 20 June 1854 he married Rachael Beaty in Iredell County, intending to retire from church work in favor of farming. This plan was not carried out, however, because in 1856 he became an acting professor at Davidson College where he taught until his death. He was buried in the Prospect Presbyterian Church cemetery beside his daughter, Mary Long. He was survived by his second wife, two sons, Stephen, Jr., and David Beaty Frontis, and by two daughters, Catherine Chambers and Elizabeth Euphrosine Frontis, as well as a sister, Jeanne Marie Euphrosine Frontis.

SEE: Stephen Frontis, "Memoirs of My Life" (Southern Historical Collection, University of North Carolina, Chapel Hill); Kannapolis *Daily Independent*, 7 Oct. 1962; Raleigh *Daily Sentinel*, 18 Apr. 1867; Eugene C. Scott, *Ministerial Directory of the Presbyterian Church in the United States* (1942); *Semi-Centennial catalogue of Davidson College . . . 1837–1887* (1891).

EDITH M. CLARK

**Fulenwider, John** *(ca. 1756–4 Sept. 1826)*, iron manufacturer, was born in Switzerland and as a young boy came to America with his father and family, who settled in Rowan County. During the American Revolution, he was a Whig and, as a member of the Rowan County militia, fought at Ramsour's Mill and Kings Mountain. After the war he moved to Lincoln County, where he soon entered the iron manufacturing business. Fulenwider was one of the first in the area to make pig iron from iron ore. From iron extracted from the rich deposits of mid-Lincoln County, he produced such items as wagon tires, plows, horseshoes, chain iron, nails, and farm tools; during the War of 1812 he made cannon balls for the American army. His most important foundry was located at High Shoals on property that he had purchased earlier from Martin Phifer, Sr. He also operated several forges in Lincoln County.

As a result of his industry and resourcefulness, Fulenwider became a prosperous citizen and acquired a considerable amount of property. At his death at least 20,000 acres of land as well as a good deal of capital were distributed to his heirs. He married Elizabeth Ellis, an aunt of Governor John W. Ellis. They had eight children: John, Jr. (m. Lavinia Forney, daughter of Peter Forney), Henry (m. Ann Ramsour, daughter of David Ramsour), William (m. Martha Hayes, daughter of John Hayes), Jacob (m. Mary Hoyle, daughter of Andrew Hoyle), Sarah (m. George Phifer, son of Martin Phifer, Jr.), Esther (m. John Phifer, another son of Martin Phifer, Jr.), Elizabeth (m. Alfred Burton, son of Colonel Robert Burton), and Mary (m. Robert H. Burton, another son of the colonel).

Fulenwider died at the age of seventy and was buried at High Shoals, N.C.

SEE: Deeds and Wills of Lincoln County (North Carolina State Archives, Raleigh); William L. Sherrill, *The Annals of Lincoln County* (1937).

EMMETT R. WHITE

**Fuller, Bartholomew** *(24 Sept. 1829–28 Nov. 1882)*, lawyer, magazine editor, government employee, and civic leader, was the second of three children born to Thomas and Catherine Eleanor Raboteau Fuller in Fayetteville, where Thomas Fuller, a native of Franklin County, operated an extensive mercantile business until his premature death at the age of thirty-two. Widowed at twenty-five, Catherine Fuller went to her husband's former home in Louisburg to raise her children. She saw her daughter married and her two sons practicing law together in Fayetteville before she was remarried on 21 Dec. 1851 to the Reverend Simeon Colton, a Connecticut-born Presbyterian minister and educator of note who moved to North Carolina in 1832.

Of English and French descent, Fuller's paternal ancestors were living in Virginia before 1667; but by 1730 many had migrated to North Carolina. His great-grandfather, Captain Jones Fuller, served with the Granville County militia during the Revolutionary War before becoming a wealthy landowner in Franklin County, near Louisburg. A first cousin, Edwin Wiley Fuller, was a writer of distinction whose first novel, *The Sea Gift*, written when the author was only eighteen, received wide acclaim after the Civil War. Bartholomew's maternal forebears were Huguenots who in 1658, after the Edict of Nantes, moved to England from Rochelle, France, to escape religious persecution. His great-grandfather, Charles Cornelius Raboteau, emigrated to Pennsylvania in 1754 and became schoolmaster at the Trappe Schoolhouse in New Providence. His grandparents, John Samuel and Susannah Raboteau, were residents of Philadelphia before moving to North Carolina and settling in Raleigh, where his mother was born.

Fuller received his early education in Fayetteville and then entered The University of North Carolina, where he became a member of the Dialectic Society and a serious student. After graduating with first honors in 1851, he studied medicine for a time before turning to the law as a profession. His training in the latter field was under the tutelage of Warren Winslow of Fayetteville, representative from that district in the United States Congress and later governor of North Carolina for a short period. Fuller established his first practice with his brother, Thomas Charles, who became a colonel in the Confederate Army, a member of the Confederate Congress in 1864, and, after the Civil War, a judge of the North Carolina Court of Appeals.

Raised in the Presbyterian faith, Fuller was an active layman, a ruling elder, and clerk of the session in the First Presbyterian Church of Fayetteville. He was also coeditor of the Fayetteville *Presbyterian*, a weekly publication he established in 1858 with the Reverend George McNeill. Described as a man of great power and fluency of speech, Fuller frequently held services at the church in the absence of the pastor "to the great edification of the congregation."

After some years as a practicing attorney in Fayetteville, Fuller was appointed fifth auditor of the U.S. Treasury in Washington, D.C.; but he resigned at the outbreak of the Civil War, obtained a position with the Confederate post office in Richmond, and worked there until the war ended. In 1865, he resumed his law practice in Fayetteville until 1881 when he moved with his family to Durham, where he became legal adviser and personal secretary to Julian S. Carr, president of Blackwell's Durham Tobacco Company, manufacturers of the world-famous Bull Durham brand of smoking tobacco. Fuller immediately entered into the life of the fast-growing town of Durham as a tireless champion of the proposed public school system and became one of the three members of the first board of education when, after considerable controversy, the system was finally established. One of the first schools to be built in Durham was named for him; Fuller School later was used as administrative offices for the Durham County school system.

Another of Fuller's efforts toward public improvement was as one of the organizers of the Lyceum, a group dedicated to the promotion of culture, a quality many felt was sadly lacking and desperately needed to balance the almost single-minded pursuit of money that occupied most of Durham's citizens. In addition to considering matters related to social and public improvement, members wrote essays, read them at meetings, and engaged in debating. Many of the state's best public speakers polished their skills in the Lyceum, where Fuller served as presiding officer from its inception until his death. He was also a charter member of the Commonwealth Club, designed to promote industrial development and a forerunner of the chamber of commerce.

On 23 Dec. 1853, Fuller married Wilhelmina Haldane Bell, Scottish-born daughter of William Bell, architect and builder of the U.S. arsenal in Fayetteville, and Margaret Robinson Bell, of Edinburgh. Their seven children were Agnes (1854), Thomas Blount (1857), Kate Shepherd (1860), Margaret Hall (1863), Marion Sanford (1869), Eleanor Robinson (1871), and Ralph Bell (1873). Fuller and his wife were buried in Maplewood Cemetery, Durham.

SEE: W. K. Boyd, *The Story of Durham* (1925); Bartholomew Fuller Papers (Southern Historical Collection, University of North Carolina, Chapel Hill); Theodore A. Fuller, *Early Southern Fullers* (1967); Hiram V. Paul, *History of the Town of Durham* (1884).

CAROLYN F. RANEY
MENA F. WEBB

**Fuller, Blind Boy.** *See* **Allen, Fulton.**

**Fuller, Edwin Wiley** *(30 Nov. 1847–22 Apr. 1876)*, poet and novelist, was born in Louisburg, Franklin County, the son of Jones Fuller, a cotton broker and merchant, and of Anna Long Thomas, a lady of culture, religion, and gentility, who provided a home atmosphere that nurtured his literary bent. She was the great-granddaughter of William Richmond, who was the brother-in-law of Sir Peyton Skipwith of Prestwould, near Boydton, Va. Her grandfather was Colonel Gabriel Long, of Halifax, whose residence, Quankee, had more than a state reputation. Colonel Nicholas Long, her great-grandfather, had been a Continental officer from North Carolina during the American Revolution.

Contemporary records describe Edwin Wiley Fuller as a man short in stature; with "eagle eye" and "gentile, winsome manners," he was respected for the strength of his character. He completed his secondary education at Louisburg Male Academy during the Civil War and entered The University of North Carolina as a freshman in the fall of 1864. After two years' study in Chapel Hill, he returned home and helped his father with his business for a year. In October 1867 he and his roommate and first cousin, George Gillett Thomas of Wilmington, enrolled in the University of Virginia, Charlottesville, from which Fuller received diplomas in the schools of English literature and moral philosophy in 1868.

Interested since childhood in literary pursuits, Fuller joined Delta Psi fraternity and was chosen as its anniversary orator his freshman year. In 1866, he was one of the sophomore declaimers at commencement. Although he wrote some verse before entering the university, his first published items were the poems "The Village on the Tar" and "Requiescam", which appeared in the *University Magazine* at Chapel Hill. After a year's lapse his publications resumed with the printing of a number of items—poems, "The Angel in the Cloud," "An Elegy, Written on the Rotunda Steps," and a short story, "The Cat and the Corpse"—in the *University of Virginia Magazine*, 1868 spring issue.

Poe, Tennyson, and Dickens were Fuller's favorite writers. Some of his early poems were parodies—"The Village on the Tar" apes Caroline Norton's famous "Bingen on the Rhine," and his "Lines Written on an Analytical Geometry" is patterned after Poe's "The Raven." Another poem, "Requiescam," and his single published short story, "The Cat and the Corpse," are after the manner of Poe. At Charlottesville in 1867–68 Fuller and his roommate often made forays into the Ragged Mountains, about which Poe had written, and they taught briefly at a rural school.

In a letter written in the spring of 1867, while he was at home working in his father's store, Fuller expressed dissatisfaction with the idea of a merchant's career. He said he wanted to be a lawyer. Because of his father's failing health, however, he returned to Louisburg in the summer of 1868 after graduating from college. In a letter of 12 Mar. 1870 Fuller told a friend that he had for a time desired to enter the ministry, but, after "wrestling with the great cross" of leaving his father to conduct the business alone, he had decided against it. On 17 July 1870 Fuller's father died, leaving the young man in charge of the business, which was renamed E. W. Fuller's.

By January 1871 he had completed the manuscript of his first book, a lengthy revision of his didactic poem, *The Angel in the Cloud*; it was published that summer by the transplanted Tar Heel firm of E. J. Hale & Son in New York City. The book, which received favorable notice in such newspapers as the *New York Times* and the *St. Louis Advocate*, remains his best-tailored literary production. An 1892 reviewer for *The Wake Forest Student*, a North Carolina college magazine, said, the poem "rises to almost Miltonic grandeur," and an 1876 obituary notice in *The Evening Review*, Wilmington, N.C., opined that, had he lived, Fuller might have become "the Milton of America." *The Angel in the Cloud* was reprinted with a new author's preface in 1872. In 1878 a third edition was brought forth, enlarged to contain a twenty-five-page biographical sketch, and a number of Fuller's minor poems. The book was reprinted again in 1881 and, by the author's family, in 1907.

Fuller's novel, *Sea-Gift*, published by Hale in 1873, did not achieve its greatest popularity until after his death. Its frank treatment of sensitive aspects of southern life offended many North Carolinians who had been "inspired to rapture" by his religious poetry. It was to be a writer of prose, however, rather than of poetry, that Fuller aspired. He was sensitive to criticisms that his novel's manuscript was, in some respects, crudely done, and he planned to make revisions but did not live to do so. *Sea-Gift* is, in some respects, autobiographical. It describes the youth of one John Smith, his career at The University of North Carolina, and his participation in the Civil War. The novel is interesting for a number of reasons. It was the first novel set, in part, in the town of Chapel Hill. Second, it contains a tall-tale telling contest including a definition of the tall-tale presented over thirty years before Mark Twain's essay was published on the same subject. Third, the plot incorporates the university's "Dromgoole Myth" concerning a famous duel fought near Piney Prospect in Chapel Hill. The book became known as "The Freshman's Bible" in the latter nineteenth century and its influence probably had a bearing on the formation of the Order of the Gimghoul at The University of North Carolina and the construction there of Gimghoul Castle. Finally, elements of the *Sea-Gift* plot involving, first, a long train ride to enter college, and second, the burning of a plantation house by Yankee soldiers, may have influenced Thomas Wolfe and Margaret Mitchell in the writing of their later novels, *Look Homeward, Angel*, and *Gone With The Wind*, respectively.

Fuller was interested in local politics and believed in participating. He was elected, first, a town commissioner, next, mayor of Louisburg, and, finally, a Franklin County commissioner.

On 26 Sept. 1871, he married Mary Elisabeth Malone, daughter of Dr. Ellis Malone of Louisburg. Their first child, Ethel Stuart, who died in December 1874 at the age of sixteen months, inspired several poems of mourning such as "The Last Look" and "Out in the Rain," which were widely reprinted in newspapers in several states. Another daughter, Edwin Sumner, was born only five weeks before the author's death; she married Asa Parham of Henderson. The author's only sister, Anna Richmond Fuller, married Dr. James Ellis Malone, brother of Fuller's wife, in 1878.

Ill with consumption for many months before his death, Fuller composed verses entitled "Lines, Written After Having a Hemorrhage From the Lungs," which he instructed his wife to unseal and read only after either his recovery or his death. He died after dramatically dictating in his last moments a poem for the Ladies Memorial Association of Wilmington, which was sung at Confederate memorial services at Oakdale Cemetery by a choir of two thousand persons on 10 May 1876.

Fuller died in Louisburg and was buried in the Green Hill House Cemetery. He was a Democrat and a Methodist. A photographic portrait and many of his letters belong to the Fuller-Thomas Collection in the manuscript department of Duke University Library, Durham. A limited edition of *Sea-Gift* was reprinted in 1940.

SEE: E. A. Alderman, J. C. Harris, and C. W. Kent, eds., *The Library of Southern Literature*, vol. 4 (1909); Samuel A. Ashe, ed., *Biographical History of North Carolina*, vol. 7 (1908); R. L. Flowers, "Edwin W. Fuller," *Trinity Archive* 9 (1896); Greensboro *Daily News*, 15 Aug. 1940; Louisburg *Franklin Courier*, 9 June 1876; Ted Malone, "Edwin W. Fuller and the Tall Tale," *North Carolina Folklore* 20 (1972); *New York Times*, 31 Aug. 1871; *North Carolina Biography*, vol. 2 (1941); Raleigh *News and Observer*, 13 July 1887; Rufus Weaver, "Southern Literary Portraits—Edwin W. Fuller," *Wake Forest Student* 11 (1892).

E. T. MALONE, JR.

**Fuller, Robert Thomas** *(b. ca. 1824)*, attorney, circuit judge, and planter, was born at Leasburg, Caswell County. He was graduated from The University of North Carolina in 1844 and studied law. Beginning about 1850 he was a practicing attorney in Arkansas for more than forty years. Fuller settled at Princeton, Ark., in Dallas County and never relocated. His interests included Whig politics and his 2,300-acre plantation with twenty-three slaves. When Arkansas's first Secession Convention met on 4 Mar. 1861, the day of Abraham Lincoln's inauguration, Fuller was among the delegates who opposed secession. On 6 May 1861, however, after Fort Sumter, he joined those in the second convention who voted for secession and thereafter gave his firm support to the Confederacy. After the war he served as a state circuit court judge.

Fuller married Agnes B. Smith, the daughter of Dr. W. F. Smith, a physician. They had six children: J. W., Robert C., Alex J., Samuel G., Agnes, and Thomas F.

SEE: *Biographical and Historical Memoirs of Southern Arkansas* (1890); Daniel L. Grant, *Alumni History of the University of North Carolina* (1924); Jonathan Kennon Smith, *The Romance of Tulip Ridge* (1966); Ralph Wooster, "The Arkansas Secession Convention," *Arkansas Historical Quarterly* 13 (1954).

RICHARD L. NISWONGER

**Fuller, Thomas Blount** *(28 July 1857–8 Jan. 1927)*, manufacturer, civic leader, and Presbyterian layman, was born in Fayetteville of English, French, and Scottish ancestry. He was the son of Bartholomew Fuller, an attorney, and Wilhelmina Haldane Bell Fuller, daughter of architect William Bell, of Scotland, who, after emigrating to America in 1834, assisted in the construction of the U.S. arsenal in Charleston, S.C., and designed and built the U.S. arsenal in Fayetteville.

Fuller's formal education began and ended in the Fayetteville schools, as he was prevented from entering his father's alma mater, The University of North Carolina, by its closing in 1871 for five years because of adverse conditions in the state after the Civil War. He was, however, a prolific reader who, as a child, often had to be physically restrained from reading and ordered outdoors to play, so he was in large measure self-educated.

His early business ventures are unknown, but, after moving to Durham in 1881, he became associated with Julian S. Carr, pioneer tobacco and textile magnate. In 1894 he was made the first manager of the Golden Belt Manufacturing Company, organized by Carr and John Smith, of Durham, to make cloth bags for tobacco, a procedure done by hand until that time. Fuller later became president of the company, which began to manufacture hosiery as well as tobacco bags, and which still later engaged primarily in gravure printing, a process especially suited to the printing of labels for tobacco products and bottled beverages.

As a prosperous businessman, Fuller was able to gratify his humanitarian instincts. One of his initial projects was the Associated Charities of Durham, which he organized with the help of a Methodist minister, the Reverend W. L. Cunninggim, after a severe blizzard in 1899 left many people destitute. Financed first by personal contributions and later by appropriations from the city council, the organization evolved into a Board of Charities and Welfare chiefly through Fuller's efforts, and eventually became affiliated with the North Carolina Department of Public Welfare. Fuller was also concerned with sanitary conditions and the prevention of contagious diseases. After a smallpox epidemic in 1909, when a board of health was organized, he was made one of its five members.

Because of his intense love for books and reading, Fuller was an enthusiastic supporter of a movement to start a public library in Durham and became, with Julian S. Carr and Mrs. Eugene Morehead, one of the earliest and heaviest contributors to that cause. On 1 Feb. 1898, the first library in North Carolina available to the public without payment of dues or fees opened in Durham; it was also the first in the state to receive municipal support, and by 1911 had outgrown its first quarters. It is on record that, faced with the need for a new building, "the Trustees, through the persistent efforts of Thomas B. Fuller, secured from the Carnegie Corporation an appropriation of $32,000 toward a new plant to cost $40,000, with the proviso that $4,000 be appropriated annually toward maintenance by the local government." As had been the case with Associated Charities, the Durham Public Library came into being and was expanded largely because of Fuller's enthusiastic and unflagging support.

In addition to his civic ventures, Fuller gave a great deal of time and financial assistance to the First Presbyterian Church. In 1892, his concern for employees of the Golden Belt Manufacturing Company who wanted and needed Christian education led him to establish a Sunday school in the eastern section of Durham known as Edgemont, where the company was located, and to serve as its superintendent. Eventually the school became Edgemont Chapel, a mission of First Presbyterian, and Fuller transferred his membership there in order to give it full support. When the congregation became large and affluent enough to construct a larger building, it was named the Fuller Memorial Presbyterian Church in his honor.

Probably because his father's death at fifty-two left Fuller solely responsible for his mother, four sisters, and one eight-year-old brother, he never married. When his health declined in 1926, he went to Battle Creek, Mich., in search of a cure. He died there early in the following year and was buried in Durham at Maplewood Cemetery.

SEE: W. K. Boyd, *The Story of Durham* (1925); John B. Flowers III, *Bull Durham and Beyond* (1976); Bartholomew Fuller Papers (Southern Historical Collection, University of North Carolina, Chapel Hill); Theodore A. Fuller, *Early Southern Fullers* (1967).

CAROLYN F. RANEY
MENA F. WEBB

**Fuller, Thomas Charles** *(27 Feb. 1832–20 Oct. 1901),* Confederate congressman and federal judge, was born in Fayetteville, the son of Catherine Raboteau and Thomas Fuller. His grandparents were living in North Carolina before the American Revolution. His father, a prosperous merchant, died young and the mother took her three children to the Fuller family home in Franklin County. Thomas prepared for college in Louisburg under John B. Bobbitt, then entered The University of North Carolina in 1849. He left after three years, however, and went to work for a Fayetteville merchant. When the job proved distasteful, he began studying law in 1855 under Richmond M. Pearson at Richmond Hill. The next year Fuller was admitted to the bar and began practicing in Fayetteville. On 5 Nov. 1857, he married Caroline Douglas Whitehead of Fayetteville.

In politics Fuller was a Union Whig. In the election of 1860 he supported the Bell-Everett ticket and afterward opposed secession as both unwarranted and unwise. But after President Abraham Lincoln's call for troops, he enlisted as a private in the Lafayette Light Infantry, which became Company F of the First North Carolina Regiment. He spent his six-month enlistment term on the Virginia Peninsular, participating in the battle at Bethel on 10 June. After his discharge he helped raise a battery of light artillery and was elected its first lieutenant. "Starr's Battery" was attached to the Tenth Regiment and served from January to September 1862 at Fort Fisher. It was then transferred to Kinston, where on 17 December it fought in the Battle of Neuse River Bridge. In the summer of 1863, Fuller resigned his commission to campaign for a seat in the Confederate House of Representatives. His opponents were secession Democrats, and he won an easy victory on the tide of discontent sweeping North Carolina.

Fuller was a reticent congressman, possibly because he was the youngest member and the poorest, the census of 1860 showing him to have no property. But his voting record indicated grim resistance to encroachments on state or individual rights. At every chance he voted to undo controls already in effect and to retract emergency powers previously delegated to the executive. The few suggestions that Fuller made aimed to correct inequities in the tax and habeas corpus laws. He was an early peace advocate and by 1865 was privately working for separate state negotiations on the best terms obtainable.

Although elected to the United States Congress in 1865, Fuller was not seated. When nominated again in 1868 he was defeated, and in 1872 he failed to win as a Democratic elector. Meanwhile, he was developing one of the state's most prominent law practices. He was counsel for defendants in the Ku Klux Klan cases, and when Chief Justice Pearson feared impeachment in 1870, he asked Fuller to defend him. In 1873 Fuller moved to Raleigh and formed a partnership with Samuel A. Ashe and Augustus H. Merrimon. Fuller made his chief reputation in criminal cases, though he never took any involving capital crimes. His erudition, careful preparation, and skilled cross-examination made him one of the best trial lawyers in the state.

In 1891 President Benjamin Harrison appointed Fuller associate justice of the U.S. Court of Private Land Claims, which ruled on titles based on Mexican grants in the territory acquired from Mexico, at a salary of $5,000 a year. He maintained a residence in Raleigh, but spent considerable time in Santa Fé and Denver. Fuller held the federal judgeship until his death in Raleigh after a long and debilitating illness. He was buried in Oakwood Cemetery.

Fuller was a member of the Presbyterian church. Of his eleven children, six reached adulthood: Mrs. W. E. Borden, Mrs. E. M. Braxton, Mrs. J. F. Hill; and Frank L., Jones, and Williamson W. Fuller.

SEE: Samuel A. Ashe, ed., *Biographical History of North Carolina*, vol. 1 (1905 [portrait]); Walter Clark, ed., *Histories of the Several Regiments and Battalions from North Carolina in the Great War, 1861–1865*, vols. 1, 4 (1901); Confederate Congress, *Journal*, vol. 7 (1905); *DAB*, vol. 5 (1937); Thomas Charles Fuller Papers (Southern Historical Collection, University of North Carolina, Chapel

Hill); Raleigh *News and Observer*, 22 Oct. 1901; Raleigh *North Carolina Standard* scattered issues, 1863–65.

W. BUCK YEARNS

**Fuller, Thomas Oscar** *(25 Oct. 1867–21 June 1942)*, state senator, Baptist minister, and educator, was born at Franklinton, the son of J. Henderson Fuller, a house carpenter and wheelwright. Though born into slavery, the elder Fuller taught himself to read; during Reconstruction he was a delegate to Republican conventions and a magistrate, as well as a deacon in the Baptist church. Young Fuller's mother was "Mary Elizabeth."

In 1882, Fuller attended the normal school at Franklinton; its principal, the Reverend Moses A. Hopkins, was later appointed minister to Liberia by Grover Cleveland. Fuller entered Shaw University in 1885, worked his way through college and was graduated with a B.A. degree in 1890. He was soon ordained by the Wake County Baptist Association. His first pastorate was the Belton Creek church at Oxford, held in a log cabin schoolhouse, at a salary of $50 a year. Fuller also taught at a public school in Granville County for $30 a month. In 1892, he returned to Franklinton to form and run a "colored graded" school, subsequently known as the Girls Training School. Two years later he became principal of the Shiloh Institute at Warrenton.

Politically this section of the state was strongly "colored Republican," for many blacks held office in the party hierarchy. When in 1898 Charles A. Cooke, a white Republican representing the Eleventh District (Warren and Vance counties), had to relinquish his nomination for the senate, it was offered to Fuller, who accepted with hesitation but won the election without difficulty. The reasons for the misgivings he had entertained soon surfaced, primarily due to inflammatory cries of white supremacy and Negro domination. Nevertheless, though the only black in the senate, Fuller achieved several objectives. He was largely responsible for getting the circuit court to hold hearings every four months instead of every six, thus easing the confinement terms of arrested persons and reducing the docket. He persuaded the senate not to reduce the number of Negro normal schools from seven to four. He also supported publication of sketches of North Carolina regiments in the Civil War, but contended that credit should be given to "those who stayed home and raised cotton and corn."

In 1899, the Democratic party pushed its constitutional amendment to disfranchise the Negro. In debate, Senator Fuller took the floor and in an impassioned speech argued against the proposal, stating among other things that Negro domination was unlikely with 210,000 white to 125,000 black votes. According to the press, "He was one of the most fluent speakers of the convention. He swept the audience away on wings of oratory." Nevertheless, the amendment, including the Grandfather Clause, passed 42 to 6.

In November 1900, Fuller accepted a call to the First Baptist Church at 217 Beale Street in Memphis, Tenn. There he found a splinter group with only $100 in assets and a rented hall. A born organizer and persuader, he soon increased the size of the congregation and embarked on a building program. (In later years a second church was erected on St. Paul's Avenue and still later, in 1941, a new church was built at Lauderdale and Polk streets.)

In 1902, Fuller was appointed principal of Howe Institute, which subsequently merged with Roger Williams College, where he held classes in theology for local pastors. Howe was a training school to give young blacks—soon men and women—manual skills as well as exposure to academic and cultural subjects, including Latin and Greek. With Fuller's drive and with active support from northern Baptists, the building was enlarged, growing fivefold in value in the next ten years.

In 1906, Fuller received a doctor of philosophy degree from the Agriculture and Mechanical College of Normal, Ala. Shaw University awarded him an M.A. in 1908 and a doctor of divinity degree in 1910. He gave the invocation at a ceremony when President Theodore Roosevelt visited Memphis in conjunction with the Philippine governor, Luke Wright, a former Confederate soldier and native of the city. Hopes that Roosevelt might name Fuller as minister to Liberia were not fulfilled, somewhat to Fuller's relief.

He was married four times: to Lucy G. Lewis of Franklinton; to Laura Faulkner, mother of Thomas and Erskin; to a woman named Rosa; and to Dixie Williams. Thomas Fuller, Jr., was the only one of his children to reach adulthood.

Fuller died in Memphis and was buried at New Park Cemetery. Notables from the city, county, and state as well as leading Baptists attended the funeral. One Baptist leader remarked that Dr. Fuller had fulfilled the four requirements for distinction needed by a man. He had left a son, built a house, planted a tree, and written a book. He was the author of *Flashes and Gems* (1920); *Pictorial History of the American Negro* (1933); *History of Negro Baptists in Tennessee* (1936); *Bridging the Racial Chasm* (1937); *Story of Church Life Among Negroes* (1938); and *Notes on Parliamentary Law* (1940).

SEE: Thomas O. Fuller, *Twenty Years in Public Life* (1910); Fuller's correspondence with family members and others (North Carolina Collection, University of North Carolina, Chapel Hill); William Hartshorn, *An Era of Progress and Promise* (1910); *National Baptist Publishing House* (1910); *National Baptist Voice* 24 (15 July 1942 [portrait]); Raleigh *News and Observer*, 30 Nov. 1941.

JOHN MACFIE

**Fuller, Williamson Whitehead** *(28 Aug. 1858–23 Aug. 1934)*, lawyer and general counsel for the American Tobacco Company, was born in Fayetteville of Scottish ancestry, the eldest son of Thomas C. and Caroline Whitehead Fuller. In 1891 his father, a law partner of Judge Augustus H. Merrimon and Captain Samuel A. Ashe, was appointed associate justice of the U.S. Court of Private Land Claims by President Benjamin Harrison. Young Will Fuller received his education at the Little River Academy near Fayetteville, the Horner and Graves Academy in Hillsborough, the University of Virginia at Charlottesville, and the Dick and Dillard Law School in Greensboro. In 1880 he was admitted to the bar and began to practice in Raleigh, joining his father's firm, Merrimon and Fuller, which in 1879 had succeeded the firm of Merrimon, Fuller, and Ashe.

In 1881 Fuller wrote the bill for the creation of Durham County, which was introduced in the General Assembly of that year. The bill failed to pass and a motion to reconsider it was tabled, a move that usually meant certain death to any bill, but Fuller came up with a solution to the problem. Observing that there is no limitation on a legislature examining its own creation, he said that if the legislature makes a mistake or finds new light on a subject, justice requires that it reconsider the previous action. Although his premise engendered strong opposition, it also had considerable support, including that of Lieutenant Governor James L. Robinson, president of the senate. A move to reconsider the vote passed, and two days later, after a stiff fight, the bill to establish Durham County passed its third reading and became law.

Shortly afterwards, Fuller moved to Durham and went into partnership with W. S. Roulhac. After Roulhac's death he practiced alone until 1889, when he formed a partnership with his brother, Frank Lanneau Fuller, which continued until 1895. It was during this time that Will Fuller gained the reputation of being one of the most able lawyers, with one of the most lucrative practices, in the state. Rather than specializing, he covered the whole field of the law, and it was said that he could assume any personality that would best serve his cause in a trial: terse and homely, urbane and gracious, scholarly and philosophical, or practical and persuasive. These talents did not escape the shrewd eye of James Buchanan Duke, and in 1890 W. Duke Sons and Company retained Fuller as its legal counsel in Durham. It was in that capacity that he assisted in the organization of the American Tobacco Company. As the head of the new company, Duke frequently called on Fuller to advise him and his associates, and in 1895 he asked the young lawyer, then just thirty-seven, to move to New York and become American's chief legal counsel. From that time until his retirement in 1912, Fuller's services were almost exclusively linked to the giant tobacco trust.

After his retirement Fuller devoted himself to his family and to farming and country life at his home, Haymount, in Briar Cliff Manor, N.Y. His wife, whom he married in 1880, was the former Annie Staples of Greensboro. They had six children: Thomas Staples, Janet Douglas, Margaret Hereford, Caroline Whitehead, Annie Norman, and Dorothy. At various times he was a trustee of the endowment fund of the University of Virginia, president of the New York Southern Society, president of the North Carolina Society in New York, and president of the University of Virginia Alumni Society in New York. A cousin of Edwin Wiley Fuller, the poet and novelist, Will Fuller was the author of a book of poems and essays called *By-Paths* (1926). He also wrote a sketch of James B. Duke that appeared in Samuel A. Ashe's *Biographical History of North Carolina*. A staunch Presbyterian, Fuller gave considerable sums of money to the First Presbyterian Church in Fayetteville and the Old Bluff Church, near Fayetteville, for the restoration of their buildings.

After an illness of some months, he died and was buried in the Sleepy Hollow Cemetery at Briar Cliff Manor, N.Y. Portraits of Will Fuller and his father hang in the Supreme Court Buildings in Raleigh.

SEE: W. K. Boyd, *The Story of Durham* (1925); *Durham Recorder*, 16 Apr. 1900; W. W. Fuller Papers (Manuscript Department, Library, Duke University, Durham).

MENA F. WEBB

**Fulton, David Bryant** *(1863?–14 Nov. 1941)*, black polemicist and author, was born in Fayetteville to Benjamin and Lavinia Robinson Fulton. His early childhood was spent in the Fayetteville area, but he grew up in Wilmington where he attended the Williston School and later the Gregory Institute. In the spring of 1887 he left Wilmington for New York, joining the Pullman Palace Car Company as a porter in 1888. He and his wife, Virginia Moore Fulton, settled in Brooklyn, where he later worked for Sears, Roebuck, the Brooklyn YMCA, and a large music publishing house. In 1895 Fulton founded the Society of Sons of North Carolina, a social and benevolent organization in Brooklyn. He was a member of the Prince Hall Masonic Lodge No. 38 of Brooklyn and an active Presbyterian churchman after his second marriage in 1917 to Katie Gummer, also of Wilmington. He died and was buried in Brooklyn, N.Y.

Fulton's earliest writing was done for the Wilmington *Record*, a black-owned newspaper whose editor solicited Fulton's observations on the condition and activities of black people whom he encountered during his travels as a porter. In 1892 these observations were published in a forty-five-page pamphlet entitled *Recollections of a Sleeping Car Porter*, in which Fulton used his pen name "Jack Thorne" for the first time. His second book, a novel called *Hanover, or the Persecution of the Lowly* (1900), focused directly on violent racial conflict in the South of his day. Part exposé, part tract, and part fiction, *Hanover*, according to its author, was designed to provide "a truthful statement of the causes" that led up to the bloody "Wilmington Massacre" of 10 and 11 Nov. 1898.

Between 1903 and 1906, Fulton gained prominence in Brooklyn for his letters and articles, which were published in a number of New York newspapers. Bits of verse, autobiographical sketches, and a number of "Pullman Porter Stories" testify to the varied purposes to which Fulton turned his pen at this time. However, as he said in an introduction to a collection of his newspaper contributions, the bulk of his writing consisted of "answering traducers and endeavoring to ward off the blows aimed at my people by the enemy." Most of the pieces in *Eagle Clippings* (1907) show Fulton as a controversialist in matters of social and racial concern.

After 1907 he divided his literary attention between the writing of poetry, essays, and short stories. Most of his short stories never found a publisher. Two occasional poems that he was commissioned to write were more popular. One, a celebration of the life and achievements of Abraham Lincoln, he read to a large gathering in Brooklyn on the centennial anniversary of Lincoln's birth. This *Poem to Abraham Lincoln* was published in 1909 and contains a picture of Fulton.

In 1912 the Negro Society for Historical Research published his *A Plea for Social Justice for the Negro Woman*, an eleven-page pamphlet printed in Yonkers, N.Y., by the Lincoln Press Association. In July 1923 he presented "Mother of Mine; Ode to the Negro Woman" to the annual convention of New York Colored Women's Clubs. A third poem, "The Cooner Man," published in 1913, relates in dialect verse Fulton's memories of local Christmas traditions and customs in Wilmington.

An essay on "Race Unification; How It May Be Accomplished," which appeared in a British periodical in 1913, constitutes Fulton's most direct statement on his most characteristic subject. The future welfare of black people, he maintained, does not rest on amalgamation with or reliance upon whites but rather on a knowledge of "race history," "race achievement," and "race literature" as a stimulus to "race pride" and advancement. Fulton's polemical writings, his poetry, and his fiction reflect his personal dedication to the establishment of a "race literature" in the United States. Nevertheless, the preponderance of North Carolina scenes, history, and customs in his writing requires that he be recognized also as a North Carolina author.

SEE: Fulton's own autobiographical works; Margaret F. Paterson, "Suspended Animation: Race Relations in the

Literature of Charles Waddell Chesnutt, David Bryant Fulton, and James Ephriam McGirt" (M.A. thesis, University of North Carolina, 1972); Wilmington *Cape Fear Journal*, 10 Feb. 1934 [picture].

WILLIAM L. ANDREWS

**Fulton, Hamilton** *(d. 1834)*, civil engineer, was born in Great Britain into a Scottish family presumably connected with the engineering family of that name in Glasgow. He studied under John Rennie (1761–1821), the Scottish engineer noted for his work in London, before working under Thomas Telford (1757–1834), the builder of Ellesmere Canal (1793), Caledonian Canal (1802–22), and Gotha Canal (between the Baltic and North seas, 1808–10). Under these masters Fulton gained experience in computing specifications for and designing canals, locks, and bridges; in draining marshes and fens; and in constructing turnpike roads. His employment at Malta and Bermuda by the British Board of Admiralty gave him experience in constructing harbor jetties and breakwaters and taught him something of hydrography.

While living in Charles Street, London, in 1819, Fulton made the acquaintance of Peter Browne, of North Carolina, who was then in England looking for a principal engineer for the state. Browne persuaded Fulton to undertake the supervision of projected internal improvements, and in the early summer of 1819 Fulton moved with his family to North Carolina. He was accompanied by his friend and fellow pupil under Rennie, Robert H. B. Brazier, who had been engaged by Browne as assistant engineer. Fulton and Brazier arrived in Raleigh in July 1819 and signed contracts with the state on 19 July.

The two engineers set about their business immediately. Fulton examined the principal coastal inlets, the sounds, and the primary rivers of the state with an eye to practical improvements to navigation, whereas Brazier was responsible for making surveys and delineating them in plats and maps. During 1820, Fulton fully investigated a method of overcoming the difficulty of navigating vessels through Roanoke Marshes in the passage between Albemarle and Pamlico sounds (a feat requiring a good wind blowing almost due north). To rectify this deficiency so as to improve coastal navigation in those waters, it was proposed to reopen Roanoke Inlet, which had been closed since 1795. Fulton's report on the subject is marked by a clear understanding of the nature of the contemplated task and conveys to the reader a ready appreciation of Fulton's skill. He offered specific proposals for employing natural and mechanical forces to keep the inlet open once it was reestablished as a viable passage for vessels; he understood the necessity for preserving the marshes; and he was careful to avoid any deleterious effect that the projected work could have on vegetation. Though the reopening of Roanoke Inlet, like so many other of the state's projects, failed of realization, Fulton's report and specifications remained the basis for state planning for the next twenty years.

Neither Fulton nor Brazier was satisfied with the operation of the internal improvements program of North Carolina. Political machinations involving internal improvements, a depressed economy that prevented execution of sound projects, the willingness of the Board of Internal Improvements and the legislature to sacrifice quality in a search for inexpensive engineering work, and the illusionary expectations of the general public that demanded immediate results from the improvements programs hindered the effectiveness of the two engineers. At the end of his first year in North Carolina, Fulton gave notice of his resignation as principal engineer effective 18 Jan. 1821. He was prevailed upon to remain with the state's program, however, and continue his work. In April 1821 Fulton designed the Roanoke Canal Aqueduct. Originally conceived as two eliptical arches with 30-foot spans, the design was eventually altered to a single eliptical arch with a 30-foot span built into a 110-foot-long aqueduct spanning Chockoyotte Creek in Halifax County. Constructed of dressed stone, the Roanoke Canal Aqueduct is Fulton's best known work in North Carolina; it still stands in remarkably good condition despite a century of neglect. This visible and impressive testimony to Fulton's skill and art has been entered on the National Register of Historic Places. Unfortunately, his equally impressive bridge of eight eliptical stone arches over Dan River, begun in 1825 at Milton, Caswell County, has not survived.

During his work on Roanoke Canal, Fulton had occasion to consult with Thomas Moore, the Virginia engineer from whom he appears to have gained a favorable impression of Virginia's program of internal improvements. In any event, when that state's office of principal engineer fell vacant through Moore's death, Fulton applied to Virginia's Board of Public Works for appointment to the position in 1822. He was unsuccessful, and for the next three years he remained principal engineer to the state of North Carolina.

During 1822 and 1823 Fulton continued to supervise practically every major navigation and transportation scheme in the state, both of a public and private nature. He drew up specifications for dams and locks for the Neuse River Navigation Company, continued to supervise execution of his plans for the Roanoke Navigation Company, renewed efforts to perfect the locks and canals of the Clubfoot and Harlowe Creek Canal, and planned the establishment of the Brown and White Marsh (Columbus County) Drainage Company. Much of Fulton's effort was expended to correct the ill-judged and ruinous proceedings of the Cape Fear Navigation Company. The company had contracted piecemeal work at diverse, scattered locations, and had departed the bed of the river. As a result no section from which revenues could be drawn had been completed, and the company was nearly bankrupted by the expenses incurred in erecting an artificial watercourse that offered no advantage over cheaper improvements of the natural flow of the river. As with navigation companies, so with turnpikes. Fulton examined, reported on, and made recommendations relating to the Wilkesboro-Tennessee Turnpike, the Swannanoa Gap Road, and the Cherokee Road. He proposed a new network of state roads in Buncombe County, outlined plans for a turnpike that would carry produce from the Roanoke River estuary to Pamlico Sound, and prepared elaborate specifications for a turnpike from Fayetteville to the Virginia Line. In this connection it may be worthwhile to note Fulton's advice to the board in 1823 in which he advocated that a system of state roads, county roads, and private roads be classified, financed, and maintained in the manner now current in the state.

By 1824 the failure of many of the private stock companies had convinced the Board of Internal Improvements of the necessity of concentrating on one important project at a time. Consequently, during 1824 and 1825 Fulton was directed by the board to devote his efforts to the improvement of Cape Fear River. In 1823 he had designed embankments and jetties, and in 1824 he oversaw their construction. In addition, he engaged a steam engine to reduce the flats that effectively blocked the estuary of the river, and secured machinery for removing the logs and sunken trees that spoiled the navigational potential of the river between Fayetteville and Wilmington.

But Fulton was not destined to complete his ideas for improving Cape Fear River. The state legislature, frightened by the failure of many of the private navigation companies, and exercised by popular dissatisfaction with the course of internal improvements in North Carolina, proceeded to take measures that Fulton considered inimical to his professional interests. Not only did it completely reorganize the Board of Internal Improvements during its 1824 session, but it also directed that the principal engineer be hired out to other states on a part-time basis. In January 1826 Fulton resigned his office.

The state of Georgia, which had attempted to engage Fulton under a part-time arrangement in 1822, now negotiated with him for full employment. As a result, Fulton sold his real and personal property in Raleigh on 16 Mar. 1826, and shortly afterward moved to Georgia. The situation in Georgia was not dissimilar to that in North Carolina, and Fulton discovered that he had been engaged by a discredited board. By the end of 1826 he found himself in Milledgeville, a private, rather than a public, engineer. At the close of 1828 he returned to London where, until his death, he worked and taught engineering to his son Hamilton Henry Fulton (1813–86), subsequently a well-known London engineer.

Fulton's wife Sarah, a native Londoner, was a handsome, red-haired woman who was admired for her superior mind and praised for her graceful mien and open and unaffected manners. When in 1822 it was feared that Fulton would leave North Carolina, David Lowry Swain wrote to a correspondent that Mrs. Fulton "is worth $1000 per annum to Raleigh, & the society of the place would suffer an irreparable loss by her removal." Fulton was described by Swain as blunt but of very friendly disposition and "one of the most scientifical men in the county." In addition to their son Hamilton Henry, the Fultons had two daughters, Emily M. and Julia Jane, the latter of whom was born in Raleigh in October 1823. Fulton and his family were Anglicans who communicated with Christ Church, Raleigh, during his years in North Carolina.

Fulton's surviving writings are to be found in the annual reports of the North Carolina Board of Internal Improvements from 1820 to 1825, except for his *Report of Sundry Surveys, Made By Hamilton Fulton, Esqr., State Engineer Agreeably to Certain Instructions from Judge Murphey . . . and Submitted to the General Assembly at their Session in 1819*, which in 1819 was separately published in Raleigh as a seventy-page pamphlet. Delineation of his surveys of Croatan and Roanoke sounds with the embankments and inlet (1820), the stage road from Fayetteville to the Virginia line (1822), and the road from Salem to Fayetteville (1823) survive in the drawings of Robert H. B. Brazier. No maps and drawings from the hand of Fulton are known to have survived, though it is assumed that some may still exist among family papers in Great Britain.

SEE: James H. Craig, ed., *The Arts and Crafts in North Carolina, 1699–1840* (1965); Governor's Office Records—Internal Improvements, Map Collection, Records of Christ Church (Raleigh), and Tax Records of Wake County, 1821–25 (North Carolina State Archives, Raleigh); W. H. Hoyt, ed., *The Papers of Archibald DeBow Murphey*, vols. 1, 2 (1914); North Carolina Board of Internal Improvements, *Records*, 1820–25; Swain Correspondence, 15 June, 13 July, 24 Nov. 1822 (Elizabeth D. Reid, MS. History of Wake County, North Carolina Collection, University of North Carolina, Chapel Hill); Records of the Board of Public Works—Papers of Road Engineers and Assistants, 1825–82 (Virginia State Archives, Richmond).

GEORGE STEVENSON

**Furches, David Moffatt** *(21 Apr. 1832–8 June 1908)*, lawyer, jurist, and chief justice of the North Carolina Supreme Court, was born in Davie County, the son of Stephen Lewis Furches, a justice of the peace and farmer, and Polly Howell Furches of Rowan County. The Furches family was originally from Delaware. Young Furches attended the Union Academy in Davie County before studying law for two years under Richmond Pearson, the noted chief justice of the North Carolina Supreme Court. Admitted to the bar in 1857, Furches began his law practice as solicitor for Davie County in Mocksville, where he remained until 1866 when he moved to Statesville in Iredell County. When the Civil War broke out, Furches joined the Confederate Army for a short time, even though as a county solicitor, he was exempt from military service. However, his three brothers and four brothers-in-law served, and, as Furches put it, he "concluded to stay out."

A sturdy Whig before the war, Furches served as a Davie County delegate to the Constitutional Convention that met in Raleigh in October 1865. Following the guidelines announced by President Andrew Johnson, that convention adopted ordinances abolishing slavery, abrogating the secession act, and repudiating the Confederate debt. During Reconstruction, Furches's Whiggery and Unionism led him into the Republican party. As a Republican, he waged a number of futile campaigns for office. In 1872 he was defeated in a bid for Congress, but in 1875 he was appointed judge of the superior court in Iredell County and served for three years. In 1880 he made another unsuccessful run for Congress. When the North Carolina Republican party nominated him for associate justice of the state supreme court in 1888, he was again defeated.

Disillusioned and disheartened by an unending string of defeats since Reconstruction, the Republican party in North Carolina had become badly factionalized by the 1890s. One wing of the party, resenting Negro aspirations for local party leadership and fearing the Democratic use of the race issue, opposed a statewide ticket and leaned toward cooperation with the newly established Populist party. The Old Guard, however, continued to insist on a full slate of candidates and objected bitterly to any association with the Populists. In 1892 Furches was the Republican candidate for governor, although the lily-white faction of the party had threatened to support the Populists. When he lost the election, Furches charged that the "true theory of Republican defeat in North Carolina was fraud." According to him, the Democratic registrars had prevented many blacks from voting. Furches's claims notwithstanding, there is considerable evidence that many Republicans defected to the Populist cause.

In 1894 Furches, whom Josephus Daniels once termed a Republican of the "old order," again supported efforts for a full Republican slate and opposed cooperation, or "Fusion" as it was known, with the Populists. Demanding a straight Republican ticket,

Furches argued that the Republican party could not be transferred like cattle from one field to another. But the Populists shrewdly nominated a nonpartisan judicial ticket that included Furches, the Republicans accepted the coalition ticket, and the Fusionists swept into office. As a result, Furches became an associate justice on the state supreme court.

Furches's career on the North Carolina Supreme Court was marked by the same acrimony and controversy that characterized the politics of the period. His elevation to the chief justiceship was not without its share of intrigue. In December 1900 Chief Justice William T. Faircloth died a mere two weeks before the inauguration of Democrat Charles B. Aycock as governor. Republican Governor Daniel L. Russell came under intense pressure from various interest groups to resign his office and accept appointment to the chief justiceship from the lieutenant governor who would succeed him. Corporate titans such as Alexander B. Andrews, vice-president of the Southern Railway Company, and Benjamin N. Duke, the Durham tobacco magnate, urged Russell to pursue that course. Many Democrats such as Robert Furman, editor of the Raleigh *Morning Post*, and Robert B. Glenn, future governor, applauded the idea because it was widely believed that Russell supported the recently adopted suffrage amendment disfranchising North Carolina blacks. Russell, however, resisted the pressures and in a surprising move appointed Furches chief justice. The governor and the supreme court justice had been feuding since the 1892 election when Russell, a leading Fusionist, had refused to support Furches's candidacy for governor.

Furches barely had assumed the chief justiceship when he was impeached by the Democratic-controlled General Assembly of 1901. Political passions had been inflamed dangerously by the Democratic white supremacy campaigns of 1898 and 1900 that overturned Fusionist rule. Eager to regain control of the state courts, zealous Democrats in the legislature, urged on by Josephus Daniels's "tocsin-sounding" Raleigh *News and Observer*, plotted the impeachment and conviction of Republican justices David Furches and Robert M. Douglas. Conservative Democrats like Henry G. Connor and Thomas J. Jarvis, the former governor and senator, were appalled. Jarvis wrote Connor: "It will be a great mistake in our party to put these Judges on trial. It is hard to conceive of a worse political error." Jarvis did not believe that Furches and Douglas had acted "corruptly," although they may have made legal mistakes. Some Democrats, Jarvis confided, insisted on impeachment "to save the Constitutional Amendment." Connor, agreeing with Jarvis, led the fight against impeachment in the General Assembly.

The crux of the impeachment articles against Furches and Douglas related to the state supreme court's ruling that the holder of a public office had a property right in that office. So long as the duties of that office continued, the officeholder could not be deprived of his property during his term of office. Furches and Douglas were charged with violating the state constitution by issuing a mandamus against the state auditor and state treasurer in 1900 to compel payment of the salary of Theophilus White, a shell fish commissioner and a Fusionist, whose office had been abolished by the 1899 legislature. The duties of the office had been vested in a seven-member commission.

The precedent for office as property had been set in *Hoke v. Henderson* (1833). In 1897 the supreme court had upheld that precedent in the state hospital cases—notably *Wood v. Bellamy* and *Lusk v. Sawyer*—the effect of which was to continue in office Democrats and to prevent Fusionists from assuming control of state institutions. The court, though dominated by three Republicans and one Populist, had voted unanimously in those cases. In later cases arising in 1899, however, justices Walter Clark, the Progressive Democrat, and Walter Montgomery, the Populist, had rejected the *Hoke v. Henderson* precedent even though the Republican majority, consisting of Faircloth, Furches, and Douglas, continued to uphold it. Thus, the supreme court ruled in *White v. Hill* and *White v. the Auditor* that the office of shell fish commissioner had not been abolished by the 1899 legislature because the same duties still resided with the new commission. According to the Republican majority on the court, White was entitled to serve the last two years of his term and receive proper compensation as stipulated by the mandamus. Justice Clark lodged a vigorous protest and warned that any state officials executing the mandamus might be subject to impeachment as the court had not voted unanimously for the measure.

Despite the objections of Henry Connor, the house passed the articles of impeachment and a senate trial, lasting seventeen days, commenced. The key to the prosecution's case was whether the mandamus that ordered the payment of White's salary came within the constitution's definition of a "claim against the State." The senate, refusing to convict the justices, acquitted them of all charges. Fabius H. Busbee, a counsel for the respondents in the senate trial, declared afterwards that "the impeachment was political prosecution and instituted to prevent apprehended dangers, rather than to punish past offenses." Connor, who was elected to the supreme court in 1902, had the privilege of writing the opinion in the case of *Mial v. Ellington* (1903), which overruled the precedent of *Hoke v. Henderson*.

Furches's term expired in 1903, and he returned to Statesville to practice law in the firm of Furches, Coble, and Nicholson. Although he was married twice—to Eliza Bingham and Lula Corpening—he had no children. Furches was a member of the Episcopal church.

SEE: "Address of William P. Bynum, Jr., Presenting a Portrait of the Late Chief Justice David M. Furches to the Supreme Court of North Carolina, May 11, 1909" (North Carolina Collection, University of North Carolina, Chapel Hill); Samuel A. Ashe, ed., *Biographical History of North Carolina*, vol. 1 (1905); Aubrey L. Brooks, *Walter Clark: Fighting Judge* (1944); Henry G. Connor Papers, Allen Jay Maxwell Papers, and Thomas Settle Papers, MSS No. 2 (Southern Historical Collection, University of North Carolina, Chapel Hill); Josephus Daniels, *Editor in Politics* (1941); Benjamin Newton Duke Papers (Manuscript Department, Library, Duke University, Durham); Robert F. Durden, *Reconstruction Bonds and Twentieth-Century Politics: South Dakota v. North Carolina* (1962); Helen G. Edmonds, *The Negro and Fusion Politics in North Carolina, 1894–1901* (1951); Theron P. Jones, "The Gubernatorial Election of 1892 in North Carolina" (M.A. thesis, University of North Carolina, 1949); Joseph F. Steelman, "Republican Party Strategists and the Issue of Fusion with Populists in North Carolina, 1893–1894," *North Carolina Historical Review* 47 (1970), and "Vicissitudes of Republican Party Politics: The Campaign of 1892 in North Carolina," *North Carolina Historical Review* 43 (1966).

JEFFREY J. CROW

**Furman, Robert McKnight** (*21 Sept. 1846–12 May 1904*), editor and state official, was born in Louisburg to William H. and Rebecca Furman. Despite the fact that his father was a tailor of modest means, Robert attended the Louisburg Academy and the Norfolk Military Academy. When the Civil War began, he was the youngest man in his company to enlist but was discharged after a few months for reasons of health. He reenlisted in 1864 and was appointed second lieutenant in Company H, Seventy-first North Carolina Regiment, where he served under General Joseph E. Johnston until the end of the war.

In 1866, Furman took charge of the Louisburg *Eagle* and managed it for one year before establishing the Henderson *Index* and, in 1869, the Norfolk *Courier*. In 1870, he moved to Raleigh and worked on the *Sentinel* for over a year. Moving to Asheville in 1872, he bought the *Citizen*, at that time a vigorous Democratic weekly, which he operated until 1876, when Jordan Stone joined him as coowner and proprietor.

Furman's first venture into politics occurred in 1872, when on four successive ballots in the Democratic convention he received the next highest vote for the office of secretary of state. In 1876, the state senate elected him its clerk, a position he held until 1892 when he was elected state auditor. In 1880 and 1892, he was a delegate to the Democratic National Convention. In 1896, the Fusionists took over the state administration and Furman was relegated to private life. Two years later he returned to Raleigh and became editor of the *Morning Post*, which he managed until his death in Beaufort.

Furman's contemporaries described him as a man of "fine personal appearance, [and] affable manner." On 18 June 1873, he married Mollie Mathewson of Tarboro.

SEE: John P. Arthur, *Western North Carolina, A History* (1914); Asheville *Citizen and the Times*, 28 Jan. 1939; Walter Clark, ed., *Histories of the Several Regiments and Battalions from North Carolina in the Great War, 1861–'65*, vol. 4 (1901); R. A. Shotwell and Matt Atkinson, *Legislative Record, 1877*; J. S. Tomlinson, *Assembly Sketch Book, Session 1883*; W. F. Tomlinson, *State Officers and General Assembly of North Carolina, 1893*; U.S. Census, 1850–1910 (microfilm edition).

W. BUCK YEARNS

**Gaddy, Charles Winfred** (*25 Oct. 1880–4 May 1941*), textile pioneer, churchman, and civic leader, was born in Anson County, the second son in a family of eight. His father, George Washington Gaddy (1853–1912), was a tenant farmer who had lost his own father in Confederate service in 1862. His mother, Sara Lou Cinda Morgan (1861–99), was descended from the Redfearn and Morgan families. His forebears were solidly English, and his great-great-grandfather, Thomas Gaddy (1753–1817), was a soldier in the American Revolution.

At an early age, Fred Gaddy, as he was familiarly known, assumed much of the burden of supporting the large family. By the time he was nineteen, when his mother died, he had already experienced a variety of work throughout Anson County, cooking in a contractor's camp, digging wells and foundations, and clerking in a company store at Steele's Mills. During those formative years he acquired the characteristics by which he was known in later life: his strong, robust, six-foot-plus frame; his respect for hard, honest work and its rewards; his religious upbringing in a staunchly Baptist household with high moral standards; and his thirst for learning, having been deprived of a formal education after the fourth grade. He helped to nurse his mother through a succession of illnesses, as measles led to pleurisy and then tuberculosis, which brought on her death at thirty-eight. He assumed the debt of her medical and burial expenses, which he finally paid off three years later, along with the balance on a farm account. His assumption of those obligations made a marked impression, both on creditors and neighbors, who saw the promise of a bright future from such a man.

After his mother's death, Gaddy went to the town of Albemarle, in neighboring Stanly County, where he was hired as a sweeper in the Wiscassett Mills, working a fourteen-hour day. Sensing a potential for knit goods in the growth of the textile industry, the young sweeper learned to knit on the few, rather primitive machines then available. That was the beginning of what came to be the knitting department of the Wiscassett Mills Company. Gaddy became a fixer, overseer, superintendent, and finally general manager, as the company, under his leadership and direction, became "one of the finest hosiery mills in the country." A trade journal, *The Southern Knitter*, pointed out in May 1941 that "He started the hosiery industry in Albemarle, and from a humble position climbed to the top. He was recognized as an authority in the industry, and his advice and counsel were sought continuously by other textile leaders. He was quick to anticipate changes in the industry, and as the styles changed from cotton hosiery to silk, he was in the forefront in bringing about changes in the knitting department of Wiscassett Mills Company. His mill was one of the first, if not the first, to install central station air conditioning in the knitting department, which was characteristic of his vision and progressiveness in manufacturing. Practically all the knitting machines in the mill are of recent manufacture and latest design. Mr. Gaddy was primarily a manufacturer, and no matter whether it was seamless or full fashioned goods, his product was always of such quality as to find favor with buyers."

Hailed as "dean of the knitting industry," Gaddy served a term as director of the Southern Hosiery Manufacturing Association and in 1934 was appointed a member of the Hosiery Code Committee under President Franklin D. Roosevelt's National Recovery Administration, a national recognition of his standing in the industry. He was one of the first southerners to place an order for full-fashioned hosiery machinery, and he engaged in the manufacture of such stockings when the process was almost unknown in the South. He was one of the first to operate a seamless hosiery mill, and his career spanned the change from cotton to silk, and with the advent of synthetics, to Dupont nylon.

Throughout his life he identified with the common man. His concern for his workers became legendary when the plight of the southern mill worker was a subject of national comment. An empathy born of his own experience led him to stress education and frugality. He preached these virtues through a company newspaper, *The Windemere Watchman*, which he edited as a newsletter and community organ for "his people"; he also ran a lending library for their benefit. The mill village was considered a model, and he encouraged the workers to save their earnings and buy their own homes. His employees gained him the reputation of running a first-class training school for the industry. The mill itself, part of the Cannon chain, was kept spotlessly clean and bright to create a healthy work environment. Thus, in the labor union unrest that swept the Carolinas, his workers remained loyal to his management.

Lacking a formal education, Gaddy became a dedicated reader and through books educated himself. Poetry was a favorite form of literature, and a scrapbook shows not only his taste in its clippings but also examples of his own writing. Kipling, Dickens, O. Henry, Stoddard's lectures, encyclopedias, and other works made up his library. He was especially fond of books about Lincoln (in whom he may have seen a kindred spirit), and his collection of the writings of Mark Twain tells something of his own hearty (and sometimes mischievous) sense of humor; but his self-education embraced a wide range of technical and professional matter as well. Through his reading and through long practice he acquired a writing style with a wit, conciseness, and forcefulness that his contemporaries admired.

On 29 Apr. 1903, Gaddy married Mary Frances Bacon (1884–1966), a daughter of Joseph Daniel and Dora Ellen Lindley Bacon. Educated at Woman's College in Greensboro and a devout Christian who devoted much of her life to the work of the church missionary society, she complemented his personality with a gentle disposition and a talent for home management that matched his at the mill. Two sons, Joseph Winfred (1904–68) and Robert Herring (1905–55), followed their father into the textile business, and a daughter, Ellen Geraldine (b. 1913), married a textile executive.

Gaddy was a Baptist and a member of the board of deacons at the First Baptist Church in Albemarle, where he served as assistant superintendent of the Sunday school. He maintained a strong interest in the Baptist Children's Home in Thomasville and left a substantial bequest to that institution. A lifelong Democrat, he served his community as a member of the board of aldermen and the library board. He fought for construction of a dam and the first city water works, and both the city hall and the county library used from the forties through the sixties were built during his tenure. He was a Mason, a member of the wildlife club, and a charter member of the local chapter of the Lions Club, the second in the state.

After an illness of several weeks, Gaddy died at his home in Albemarle.

SEE: *Encyclopedia of American Biography* (1942); Nathan Mobley, "A Man from the Ranks and His Method of Handling Labor," *Blue Ridge Magazine* 1 (April 1920); *The Stanly News and Press* clippings and other materials (in possession of Mrs. Geraldine Gaddy Holbert, Albemarle).

DAVID WINFRED GADDY

**Gaines, Francis Pendleton** *(21 Apr. 1892–31 Dec. 1963)*, president of Wake Forest College and Washington and Lee University, was born in Due West, S.C., the son of William Arnold and Emma Brookhardt Gaines. Before Francis was a year old, his father, a Baptist minister, moved the family to Virginia—first to Lebanon and then to Wytheville. Young Gaines was graduated from Fork Union Academy in 1909 and received the A.B. degree from Richmond College in 1912. After serving one year as principal of the public school at Green Bay, Va., he entered a graduate program at the University of Chicago, where he received the A.M. degree in 1914. During the next thirteen years Gaines combined graduate study at Columbia University (Ph.D., 1924) with teaching English at Mississippi Agricultural and Mechanical College (1914–23) and Furman University (1923–27). For several summers during this period he taught at Richmond, the University of Virginia, and Columbia. He also served for a time as literary editor of the Greenville (S.C.) *Piedmont*.

By 1927, when Wake Forest College was searching for a president, Gaines had become known in educational circles as an engaging teacher and gifted speaker. On 25 June of that year the Wake Forest board of trustees unanimously elected him president of the college. He accepted without ever having seen the campus or having been seen by the faculty.

George Washington Paschal stated in his *History of Wake Forst College* that, even though Gaines was little known to the general public, his "enthusiastic spirit and helpful disposition . . . soon won him favor." In his inaugural address he emphasized three points: "1. Wake Forest must be a small college; 2. It must be a cultural college; 3. It must be a Christian college." There were no recorded complaints against the last two points. The first, however, was regarded by many as counter to the purposes of the founders, the traditions of the institution, and the policies of all former presidents. Gaines subsequently proposed that the college adopt "a definite policy of limitation and selection of students," but the board declined to adopt the plan. Most Wake Forest officials favored admitting those who "met the terms of admission generally in force in the educational institutions of the State." Even so, during Gaines's administration the enrollment decreased from 742 to 617, with the number of entering freshmen dropping from 230 to 178. The size of the student body was the only major issue on which the president and other Wake Forest officials failed to agree.

The single factor that contributed most to Gaines's career was his oratorical skill. Professor Paschal, who knew him well, said he was "a ready speaker on many subjects—religion, education, literature, athletics, college affairs, dedications of buildings and stadiums, and was heard gladly whatever his subject, and his services were in constant requisition." In the 1940s he received approximately four hundred invitations a year to speak at functions throughout the country. In a typical year he made forty major addresses in twenty states. The *New York Times* (2 Jan. 1964) noted that "Dr. Gaines was one of the South's most respected orators, known for precision and felicity of expression."

In 1930, Gaines resigned his position at Wake Forest in order to accept the presidency of Washington and Lee University, where he remained until his retirement in 1959. After he retired the trustees named him chancellor. As president of Washington and Lee, Gaines remained committed to the concept of a small university with high standards. Under his leadership, for example, Washington and Lee was the first university or college for men in the South to require specific College Entrance Examination Board scores for admission. During his administration the financial assets of the institution increased fivefold, and many improvements were made in educational programs as well as in the physical plant.

Although President Gaines's favorite pursuit was teaching comparative literature, his activities extended far beyond the Lexington campus. Among the off-campus positions he held after 1930 were director, Woodrow Wilson Birthplace Foundation; director, George C. Marshall Foundation; president, Cooperative Education Association of Virginia (1932–33); chairman, Federal Emergency Relief Administration for Virginia (1933–34); trustee, Carnegie Endowment for International Peace; trustee (1932–34), and member, Board of Visitors (1935–36), U.S. Naval Academy; president, Southern University Conference (1939–40); chairman, State War Finance Committee of Virginia (1941–46); chairman, Virginia State Planning Board (1942–48); president, Association of American Colleges (1944–45); chairman, Virginia Association for Independent Colleges (1953–55); and chairman, general awards jury, Freedom Foundation (1956).

In 1946, he was decorated by Great Britain with the King's Medal for Services. The same year the Virginia State Chamber of Commerce presented him its Distinguished Service Scroll for "cumulative services to Virginia and the nation." The wide recognition he received was further reflected in the variety and number of his honorary degrees: Litt.D., Duke (1928, his first) and Columbia; L.H.D., Rollins; LL.D., Baylor, Chattanooga, Furman, Hampden-Sydney, Mercer, North Carolina, Richmond, Wake Forest, Washington and Lee (1963, his last), Waynesburg, and William Jewel; and D.C.L., University of the South.

Gaines was the author of *The Southern Plantation* (1924), *Lee—The Final Achievement* (1933), and *Southern Oratory* (1947). He was also a contributor to the *Library of Southern Literature*, the *Dictionary of American Biography*, and other publications. He was a member of the Modern Language Association, the Society of the Cincinnati, Phi Gamma Delta, Phi Beta Kappa, and Omicron Delta Kappa. He was a Democrat and a Baptist. His hobby was collecting walking canes, of which he had about two hundred.

On 15 Mar. 1917, Gaines married Sadie du Vergne Robert, daughter of Joseph Clarke Robert, then dean of Mississippi Agricultural and Mechanical College. They had three sons: F. Pendleton, Jr., Edwin M., and W. Robert.

Gaines died at his home in Lexington, Va., and was buried in Stonewall Jackson Cemetery. There are portraits at Wake Forest and Washington and Lee universities.

SEE: *Nat. Cyc. Am. Biog.*, vol. D. (1934); *New York Times*, 2 Jan. 1964; George W. Paschal, *History of Wake Forest College*, vol. 3 (1943); *Richmond Times-Dispatch*, 1, 3 Jan. 1964; *Who's Who in America*, 1958–59.

HENRY S. STROUPE

**Gaither, Basil** *(d. August 1803)*, Rowan County senator, was born in Anne Arundel County, Md., the son of Edward and Eleanor White Gaither, both Maryland natives. He was directly descended from John Gater, a German immigrant to Jamestown, Va., in 1621, who upon settling in Maryland became the first of a distinctive line of Gaithers in that colony. Basil was the brother of Burgess Gaither, who also became a prominent politician. After spending their childhood in Maryland, the two brothers moved in 1781 to a portion of North Carolina that is now Iredell County. Burgess remained in Iredell whereas Basil settled in Rowan County.

Basil Gaither was first involved in colonial affairs when he was commissioned into the Maryland militia on 30 Aug. 1777. He rose to the rank of first lieutenant in Captain Bristow's Revolutionary Company. After his arrival in North Carolina, he served as senator from Rowan County every term from 1788 to 1802 with the exception of 1798. In that capacity he played a major role in the controversial political issue of county creation in the late 1780s. In 1788, he and other Federalists helped pass a bill to create Iredell County. He was then appointed to a commission responsible for running the dividing line separating newly formed Iredell County from Rowan County. From 3 Mar. 1798 to 28 June 1799 he served on a committee investigating the infamous land warrant issue involving James Glasgow, North Carolina's secretary of state. The investigation concerned fraudulent warrants issued to persons who neither appeared in Revolutionary muster rolls nor were lawfully entitled to land by voucher. Gaither aided in uncovering this practice as well as exposing related forged powers of attorney. As a result of the investigation, the General Assembly passed an act in 1799 authorizing judges of the supreme court to meet in Raleigh for purposes of land grant; it also empowered the government to commission judges to investigate James Glasgow.

In the late 1780s Gaither was among the conservative leaders of the state who supported ratification of the Constitution. Although not a seasoned politician, he exemplified a rising class of men who by natural leadership ability and education were worthy of the confidence of the masses. Gaither denounced the professional, educated politician as unaware of the needs of the common man. His esteem in Rowan County was demonstrated in his long and continuous service in the General Assembly.

Due to his age and failing health, Gaither retired from public life in 1802 and died in the following year. He was survived by his wife Margaret Watkins, also a Maryland native, and seven children who all remained in North Carolina.

SEE: Samuel A. Ashe, ed., *Biographical History of North Carolina*, vols. 2 (1905), 8 (1917); James S. Brawley, *The Rowan Story* (1953); Homer Keever, *History of Iredell County* (1976); *North Carolina Journal* , 4 Sept. 1793, 3 Sept. 1794, 7 Sept. 1795; *North Carolina Minerva*, 10 Oct. 1803, *Raleigh Minerva*, 15 Dec. 1798, 26 Nov. 1799; *Raleigh Register*, 10 Oct. 1803; H. M. Wagstaff, *The Papers of John Steele*, 2 vols. (1924).

KENT GAITHER

**Gaither, Burgess Sidney** *(16 Mar. 1807–23 Feb. 1892)*, lawyer, solicitor, speaker of the North Carolina Senate, member of the Confederate States Congress, and superintendent of the U.S. Mint at Charlotte, was born on Rocky Creek in the Tabor Church community near Turnersburg in Iredell County. He was the eighth son of Burgess and Amelia Martin Gaither. His father represented Iredell in the House of Commons each year from 1796 through 1801. The Gaithers descended from a distinguished Maryland family that traced its ancestry to Jamestown, Va. Young Burgess was educated at Dr. James Hall's school at Bethany Church in Iredell and, after moving to Morganton about 1829, at Morganton Academy. For a brief period in 1830 he studied at the University of Georgia. Before that he studied law under his older brother, Alfred Moore Gaither, and after his brother's death under Judge David F. Caldwell of Salisbury. He was admitted to the bar in 1829.

From the outset of his career Gaither impressed his peers with his legal ability. Appointed clerk of the superior court of Burke County in 1830 by Judge Willie P. Mangum, he served until 1837. At age twenty-eight he was elected to represent Burke in the Constitutional Convention of 1835, which convened in Raleigh on 4–11 July. He was the last surviving member of that convention. In 1840–41 he represented Burke County in the state senate.

A staunch Whig party leader, Colonel Gaither, as he was generally called, was a delegate to the Whig National Convention of 1839 in Harrisburg, Pa. Rewarded for his party loyalty, he was appointed superintendent of the U.S. Mint in Charlotte by President John Tyler in 1841; resigning from the state senate on 31 August to accept that post, he served until 1843. He was reelected senator from Burke in 1844 and served that year as speaker. Continuing in public office, he was from 1844 to 1852 solicitor of the geographically large Seventh Judicial District, which extended from Burke and Cleveland counties to the Tennessee border; travel and court sessions provided a good political base in western North Carolina. In 1851 and 1853 he sought a seat in the United States Congress but failed to defeat the Democratic nominee, Thomas L. Clingman. He served in the House of Commons in 1852 and in the state senate in 1860–61.

As the divisive issues leading to the Civil War were incubating in 1860, Gaither supported the Consolidated Union party; however, when Abraham Lincoln called for troops on 15 Apr. 1861, he changed his position and sided with the Confederacy. Earlier that year, on 12 February, he had written William A. Graham that he strongly opposed secession but could "see no hope for anything else but a civil war of interminable extent."

Having made the change to a Secessionist Gaither was elected to the first Confederate States Congress from the Ninth District and qualified on 18 Feb. 1862, representing Alexander, Alleghany, Ashe, Burke, Caldwell, Davie, Iredell, Surry, Wilkes, and Yadkin counties. Easily reelected two years later to the Second Confederate Congress, he qualified on 2 May 1864 and served to the end of the Confederacy in 1865. As a delegate, he was chairman of the committee to investigate the Roanoke Island disaster. Supporting the Confederacy's central government when its jurisdiction was clear, Gaither vigorously opposed any effort to encroach on the rights of states and individuals. He led the defense in March 1863, when the loyalty of North Carolina was impugned in legislative debate in Richmond. He was the lone member of the North Carolina delegation who favored arming the slaves.

After the war Gaither resumed the practice of law in Morganton. As a Conservative party advocate and later as a Democrat, he strongly opposed Radical Reconstruction. Although Governor Jonathan Worth and others sought a presidential pardon for Gaither, W. W. Holden refused to approve it. Nominated in 1868 for the U.S. House of Representatives by the Conservative party, he was defeated by Alexander H. Jones of Asheville. During the campaign he spoke out strongly against the 1868 Constitutional Convention.

Gaither married twice. His first wife was Elizabeth Sharpe Erwin, of Morganton, whom he married on 30 July 1830 and who died 30 May 1839. The children by his first marriage were two sons, William and Alfred Haywood, and a daughter, Delia Emma, who married Dr. R. T. Pearson of Morganton. Later he married Sarah F. Corpening by whom he had a son, Burgess Sidney, Jr. A member of the Presbyterian church and a leader in the Sons of Temperance, he continued to practice law in Morganton until his death. He was buried in the old Presbyterian Church cemetery in Morganton. When the cemetery was altered to enlarge the church, his gravestone was lost and his grave is not marked.

SEE: Samuel A. Ashe, ed., *Biographical History of North Carolina*, vol. 2 (1905); *Catalogue of the Trustees, Officers, Alumni, and Matriculates of the University of Georgia, 1785–1906* (1906); Walter Clark, ed., *Histories of the Several Regiments and Battalions from North Carolina, in the Great War, 1861–'65*, vol. 5 (1901); John L. Cheney, Jr., ed., *North Carolina Government, 1585–1974* (1975); J. G. deR. Hamilton and M. Williams, eds., *Papers of William A. Graham*, 6 vols. (1957–76); Frontis W. Johnston, ed., *Zebulon B. Vance Papers*, vol. 1 (1963); Henry T. Shanks, ed., *Papers of Willie P. Mangum*, 5 vols. (1950–56); Joshua D. Warfield, *The Founders of Anne Arundel and Howard Counties, Maryland* (1905); Ezra J. Warner and W. Buck Yearns, *Biographical Register of the Confederate Congress* (1975).

T. HARRY GATTON

**Gaither, Ephraim Lash** *(30 Apr. 1850–10 Feb. 1943)*, lawyer and businessman, was born in Mocksville, the son of Ephraim and Sarah Hall Johnston Gaither. He was a descendant of John Gaither, who came from England and settled at Jamestown, Va., in 1621. Subsequent descendants lived in Anne Arundel County, Md. The first of the line to move to North Carolina were Burgess Gaither, who settled in what is now Iredell County, and his brother, Basil, who settled in the part of Rowan County that later became Davie County.

Gaither bore his father's name and that of Israel G. Lash, a close friend of his father. He had three brothers and three sisters. His early education was provided by private schools in Mocksville; among his teachers were Mrs. Andy Brown, Mary Jane Clement, Robert Knox, Pinkney Turner, and, principally, Jacob Eaton, whom Gaither credited with preparing him for college. An incident of his early days was the Battle of Lisha Creek. When he was a lad of fifteen, he joined a hurriedly assembled patrol of "old men and boys" and helped repulse a group of "Bushwhackers" later identified as a part of General Stoneman's Federal soldiers headed for Salisbury. That happened in April 1865, a short time after General Lee's surrender ending the Civil War.

After three years at Davidson College, Gaither's education was interrupted by illness in 1871. He returned in the fall of 1872 and was graduated the following year with the degree of bachelor of arts with honors. In September 1873 he enrolled in the private law school at Richmond Hill, in Yadkin County, taught by Chief Justice Richmond M. Pearson. After two years of study, he was admitted to the bar in June 1875, appearing before the supreme court with Chief Justice Pearson presiding. In 1876 he was the commencement orator of the Philanthropic Society at Davidson College.

Gaither practiced law independently in Mocksville for five years before forming a partnership with his father-in-law, John Marshall Clement, in 1881. The firm of Clement and Gaither was dissolved upon the death of Clement in 1886. Throughout his long career, spanning nearly sixty-five years, Gaither built a statewide reputation as a meticulous student of the law who prided himself on hard work and diligent preparation for the many cases he represented in court. Early in his practice, as counsel for several Confederate soldiers and former slaves, he was frequently commended by presiding judges for his handling of the cases. He never sought public office beyond a short term before 1890 as solicitor of the Davie County court, although one time he was recommended for a judicial appointment that went to another. In 1900, Democratic leaders in Davie County proposed him as a candidate for the North Carolina House of Representatives but his health would not permit him to accept. In the business community, however, he was a longime president of the Bank of Davie and a director of the Wachovia Bank and Trust Company, Winston-Salem.

Gaither was a member of the American Bar Association and the North Carolina Bar Association, of which he was president for a term. During World War I he was chairman of the Davie County Board of Defense, and throughout his active years he served on numerous community boards. Like his parents, who had been active in the local Presbyterian church, Gaither became a church leader locally, serving in the presbytery and the general assembly of the church.

On 1 Dec. 1880, he married Florence Adelaide Clement, the daughter of John Marshall and Mary J. Hayden Clement and a graduate of Salem College, her mother's alma mater. The Gaithers had four daughters: Adelaide Marshall (Mrs. Rufus B. Sanford), Sarah Hall, Jane Hayden (Mrs. David Murray), and Dorothy Sophie (Mrs. Edwin Cecil Morris). All four daughters also were graduated from Salem College.

Gaither died at his home in Mocksville and was buried in the Clement cemetery.

SEE: *Alumni Catalogue of Davidson College* (1924); Samuel A. Ashe, ed., *Biographical History of North Carolina*, vol. 8 (1917); *Mocksville Enterprise*, 17 Nov. 1938, 12 Feb. 1943; *North Carolina Biography*, vol. 4 (1919 [portrait]), and vol. 4 (1928 [portrait]).

C. SYLVESTER GREEN

**Gaither, Nathan** *(1788–12 Aug. 1862)*, physician and congressman, was born in the northern part of Rowan County that later became Davie County near the present site of the county seat, Mocksville. He was the youngest son of Nicholas and Margaret Watkins Gaither. The Gaither family had come to North Carolina from Maryland when others had gone to Kentucky. Young Gaither is described as having "received a fair English education at Bardstown College" in Kentucky. He then studied medicine in Philadelphia, where he was one of eighteen students who volunteered to receive the new smallpox innoculation as an experiment. During the War of 1812 he was a surgeon to a regiment of Kentucky volunteers and afterward settled in Columbia, Ky., to practice medicine. Elected to the Kentucky House of Representatives, he served two terms between 1815 and 1818. In 1828 he was a presidential elector on the successful Democratic ticket of Andrew Jackson and John C. Calhoun. In the same election Gaither was himself a candidate for Congress and won a seat in the House of Representatives. He served in the Twenty-first and Twenty-second congresses between 1829 and 1833 but was defeated in his bid for a third term. In 1849 he was a delegate to the Kentucky constitutional convention and from 1855 to 1857 he again served in the state legislature. Between service in the General Assembly and in Congress, Gaither continued his medical practice.

In 1817 he married Martha Morrison of Madison County, Ky., and they became the parents of Edgar B., W. N., George B., Margaret, Kate, and Mattie. Edgar was a graduate of the U.S. Military Academy, and he and George served in the Mexican War. A grandson served in the Confederate Army. Dying in the midst of the Civil War, Nathan Gaither's last remarks to his longtime medical partner were "I have outlived the liberties of my country and it is time for me to die."

SEE: *Bio. Dir. Am. Cong.* (1961); *Filson Club History Quarterly* 30 (1956); *History Quarterly of the Filson Club* 3 (1928–29); W. H. Perrin and others, *Kentucky, A History of the State* (1887); *Who Was Who in America*, vol. H (1963).

C. SYLVESTER GREEN

**Gale, Christopher** *(ca. 1679–1735)*, colonial chief justice of North Carolina, was born in York to a family that hailed from the neighborhood of Scruton, North Riding, Yorkshire, England. He was the oldest of the four sons of the Reverend Miles Gale and Margaret Stone, his wife. Three of their sons settled and died in North Carolina. Both the Gale and the Stone families were respectable gentry, the former having furnished lord mayors of York in the sixteenth and early seventeenth centuries. Gale's grandfather, Christopher Stone, was chancellor, and his first cousin once removed, the celebrated antiquarian, Thomas Gale, was the "good dean" of the archiepiscopal cathedral of York. Gale's sense of the dignity owing to his family appears to have colored his life, to have lent him a certain imperiousness, and to have affected his relationships with his peers. His thirty-five-year career may be said to have been characterized by conflicts and struggles of increasing intensity and bitterness with nearly every governor of North Carolina from shortly after Gale's arrival in the colony until his death.

Gale was presumably educated at St. Peter's School in York. He subsequently read law as an articled clerk under an unnamed Lancashire attorney. Almost immediately upon achieving his majority, he emigrated to North Carolina to seek his fortune as a trader. In order to be in the center of the Indian trade in North Carolina, Gale settled in the newly developing country south of Albemarle Sound, Bath County. His marriage in January 1702 to Sarah Laker Harvey, daughter of councillor Benjamin Laker and widow of Governor Thomas Harvey, increased Gale's working capital. By 1703 his coastal trade extended through Virginia into New England, and his Indian trade was expanded into a copartnery that was to extend as far west as the Catawba and Cherokee nations. These promising beginnings brought Gale political office under Governor Robert Daniel who was developing the Bath County area. In 1703 Gale was commissioned by Daniel as one of the justices of the supreme court of law in the colony, the General Court, and on 4 Apr. 1704 he was concurrently commissioned as attorney general for the colony. The following year saw the removal from office of Governor Daniel, who had provoked the ire of the Quakers because of his attempt to establish the Church of England in the colony and because of his licentiousness (he had abandoned his wife in Charleston in favor of his mistress and mother of his children, Martha Wainwright). He also had aroused the opposition of some of the Albemarle County leaders because of his development of Bath County.

Economic, social, and political differences between the two counties resulted in a struggle that eventually broke out into an armed conflict called Cary's Rebellion. One faction in the struggle was led by Thomas Cary and the other by William Glover, both of whom claimed the right to govern the colony. Gale's role in Cary's Rebellion is shadowy. Neither Glover nor Cary seems to have been willing to rely upon him altogether. Initially, however, Glover appears to have put his trust in Gale who was allowed to continue in his office as attorney general. Similarly, Glover commissioned Gale major of the Bath County militia in 1706 and went with him on an armed expedition against the Pamticough Indians that autumn. Although Glover bestowed on Gale the presidency of the General Court (that is, the chief justiceship) at the time he originally assumed the executive office in July 1706, Glover vacated the commission in April 1708 and gave the office to John Blount. As part of the Glover-Cary compromise of the following month, the commission was vacated once more, and Edward Moseley was created president of the court. Gale was kept off the bench for the next four years by Cary, Glover, and their successor, Governor Edward Hyde.

In fact, Gale was almost without office until the first administration of Thomas Pollock (September 1712–May 1714). Although Gale had secured for himself a commission as receiver general directly from the Lords Proprietors while in London in 1709, he appears neither to have qualified nor to have served in that office. Finally, after the Tuscarora Indian massacre of 22 Sept. 1711, Hyde trusted Gale sufficiently to send him to Charles Town as an envoy to secure military assistance from South Carolina. Gale's mission was a success, but his return to North Carolina was delayed for a few months on account of his capture by the French who held him briefly as a prisoner of war on Martinique. Taking in Charles Town again on his return from Martinique to North Carolina, Gale persuaded Lady Eliza Blake to grant him a commission naming him deputy in North Carolina to her minor son Joseph, one of the Lords Proprietors of Carolina. By July 1712 Gale was home again, and he was rewarded with a commission from Hyde that restored him to the presidency of the General Court, replacing Nathaniel Chevin who had been the first president of the court to be styled "chief justice" in the records (see the July 1711 minutes).

With this restoration, Gale's star appeared once more to be ascendant. Under authority of the deputation from Lady Blake, he took his seat on the executive council in Pollock's first administration on 12 Sept. 1712 (Hyde having died four days earlier). When Governor Charles Eden arrived and assumed the government from President Pollock on 28 May 1714, he continued Gale in his offices and entrusted him as well with the colonelcy of the Bath County militia. Despite this fair beginning, Gale was soon engaged with Eden in a bitter political quarrel. Gale was eager to strengthen the General Court and his position on it, whereas Eden was eager to strengthen the position of the governor and to increase his power. So long as the two desires remained compatible, there was no struggle between the two men.

Gale had served on the General Court from October 1703 until April 1708 and had returned to the bench in July 1712. Of those seven years, he had sat four years as president, or chief justice, of the court. During all that time it had been the practice for the governor to name six or more men in the commission of the peace erecting the court. The rule of the commission was that the first man named was the president of the court, the next two were his associate justices, and the remainder were assistant justices. The president and the two associates were justices of the quorum, without the presence of one of whom no court could be held even if every assistant justice was present. Gale sought to have this system altered. He advised that the chief justice be commissioned as such directly by the Lords Proprietors, that he alone be a justice of the quorum, and that the chief justice enjoy the prerogatives usually belonging to that officer. The commissioning of associate justices he believed should be discontinued altogether, and he felt that no more than two assistant justices should be appointed by the governor. These measures, clearly, would put the chief justice completely in control of the court and would, ideally, free the court from danger of political intrusion by the chief executive. Governor Eden looked for some such arrangement for himself, for he hoped to persuade the Lords Proprietors to authorize him to hold an executive council consisting of himself and two councillors only, rather than the usual four.

It is unclear to what extent Eden understood the full measure of Gale's ambition. In his first commission to Gale on 2 July 1714, Eden designated Gale under the style "chief justice" but appointed eight associate justices (and no assistants). Two months later, on 15 September, Eden wrote to the Lords Proprietors recommending the direct commissioning of the chief justice by their board, and requesting authority to hold an executive council consisting only of himself and two councillors. In their response of 26 Mar. 1715, the Proprietors refused Eden's request concerning the executive council but agreed to commission Gale separately. Eden appears to have felt betrayed. When Gale presented his new commission from the Proprietors and sought to qualify before the executive council on 21 Jan. 1716, Governor Eden attempted to block publication of the new commission until instructions should arrive from the Proprietary Board in London, but was overruled by the councillors. Eden, in the absence of clarifying instructions, then insisted upon the retention of ten additional justices to share the bench with Gale and issued a commission of the peace to that effect. The groundwork for a rupture was thereby completed. The rupture took place during a meeting of the executive council seven months later. On Friday, 3 Aug. 1716, while the council was in session a blowup appears to have occurred during the course of which Gale walked out of the meeting. The source of the trouble was probably the journal of the lower house of the 1715 General Assembly, which was discussed by the council on the following day in Gale's absence. The journal was found to include a set of resolves condemning certain actions of Eden's administration and appointing a committee of Bath County men to represent grievances against the governor to the Lords Proprietors. The council ruled that the resolves had never formed a part of the journal of the lower house, but had been clandestinely inserted in order to foment rebellion against Eden's government. Although Gale continued to preside as chief justice through the spring of 1717, he never attended another of Governor Eden's executive councils.

In March 1717 Gale put his affairs in order and granted a full power of attorney to his wife and four of their friends. About mid-June he set sail for England in order to appeal in person to the Lords Proprietors. It was believed in the colony at the time that Gale was in concert with Edward Moseley and the Bath County faction to remove Eden from the governorship. If so, the minutes of the Proprietary Board do not reflect it. Neither is there evidence connecting Gale with Moseley's subsequent attempt to implicate Eden in the career of the pirate Edward Teach ("Blackbeard"). Gale did appear before the Proprietary Board on 19 Feb. 1718, but he seems to have been there only on behalf of firmly establishing his concept of the office of chief justice in the minds of the Lords so as to secure it from attack in the colony. In this he was theoretically successful. The minutes of that meeting leave no doubt as to the Proprietors' concurrence in Gale's theories. The chief justice was to be supreme, not to be first among equals; he was to have no associates and only two assistants, neither of whom could act without him, though he could hold a court in their absence; the records of the General

Court were to be in custody of the chief justice; and he was to have power to name his own clerk of court. By way of soothing Governor Eden, the Lords agreed to create him a Landgrave of Carolina.

Surprisingly, Gale did not return at once in triumph to North Carolina. Instead, he became distracted by Woodes Rogers and the projected expedition against the pirates in the Bahamas. Rogers offered Gale a commission as chief justice of the Bahamas (subsequently approved by royal warrant on 31 Jan. 1719) which Gale accepted; presumably he sailed for New Providence in company with Governor Rogers in July 1718. In October of that year Rogers appointed Gale to the Bahamian executive council, and, according to the contemporary Oldmixon, Gale served as register to the colony as well. How much actual service Gale saw in these offices is unclear, for he spent a good deal of his time in Charles Town. It was from there that he wrote an account to Colonel Thomas Pitts on 4 Nov. 1718 of the pirates then bottling up the Charles Town harbor. A year later he was in Charles Town again, at which time (October 1719), he wrote the account of the Spanish plan to invade South Carolina that was used by the anti-Proprietary faction in that colony to consolidate public opinion against the Lords. Gale's November 1719 letters to James Craggs, secretary of state for the Southern Department (who had come to trust Gale implicitly in Bahamian affairs), gave assurances of South Carolina's loyalty to the Crown and conveyed the colony's wishes to be taken under the direct protection of the king. These actions on the part of Gale very probably aided the South Carolinians in their successful revolt against the Lords Proprietors.

It was presumably at this time that Gale sat in his Bahamian judicials for his pastel portrait by Henrietta Johnston, widow of the bishop of London's late commissary in Charleston. From here he went home to his family in North Carolina for a visit that lasted from the 1719 Christmas holidays until midsummer 1720. On 23 Feb. 1720 he wrote an account of the South Carolina revolution at the request of Governor Eden and his executive council. Gale executed another power of attorney on 1 June 1720, this time empowering his brother Edmond, his wife Sarah, and his son Miles to act for him, and acknowledged it before Eden on 10 June.

By this time the Bahamian adventure was clearly coming to an end. In the early days of the experiment, Gale had entertained the notion of removing his family, stock, and capital from North Carolina and beginning anew in the Bahamas. The Indian wars of 1711–15 had destroyed the Tuscarora nation on whom a successful Indian trade had depended, and with the loss of that trade there was little to tempt Gale to remain in Bath County. In fact, it is clear from his dispatches that Woodes Rogers had expected a large number of Carolinians to settle in the Bahamas. Upon reflection, Gale did not make such a move. He determined instead to remove from Bath to Albemarle County. On 21 Mar. 1721 the Lords Proprietors issued a new commission to Gale as chief justice of North Carolina, and Crown officials vacated his Bahamian commission on 19 Aug. 1721. Shortly thereafter, Gale was in his new residence at Edenton (of which town he was made one of the commissioners in 1722). He was almost immediately involved in a matter that led to a course of events that haunted the remainder of his life and touched him both in name and fame.

The Christmas holiday of 1721 was Governor Eden's last one. Fatally ill, he had house guests to help him keep the season. Henry Clayton, Gale's son-in-law, was one. William Badham, Gale's old clerk of the General Court, and his wife Mary were included. John Lovick, secretary of the province, was the principal guest. Christopher Gale may have been no more than a calling guest. The house guests arrived on Christmas Eve. On Christmas Day the subject of Governor Eden's last will and testament was discussed. On St. Stephen's Day, John Lovick wrote the governor's will, which was then signed by Eden and witnessed by the house guests, Clayton and Mr. and Mrs. Badham. The only relative named in the will was Eden's niece, Margaret Pugh, who was to receive £500 sterling. Four friends were left smaller bequests (one of them subsequently revoked by codicil). The residuary legatee was John Lovick. The will mentioned neither Governor Eden's stepchildren, Penelope Galland Maule and John Galland (both of whom lived in the colony) nor any relative in England other than the niece. Eden died on 26 Mar. 1722. The will was proved before Gale on either 2 April (Lovick's endorsement date on the record copy of the will) or 9 April (Badham's note in the General Court minutes), and Lovick immediately put himself in possession of the estate.

With the death of Eden, Gale reentered the government. On 27 Mar. 1722 he assumed the office of chief justice by virtue of his 1721 commission. Three days later he presented that old 1712 deputation from Lady Blake and was seated on the council on the strength of it despite the fact that at least three of the councillors had been present when that deputation had been vacated in favor of Frederick Jones more than five years earlier. Gale was able to regularize his position on the council very shortly, however, for on 14 June 1722 he presented a deputation from another of the Lords Proprietors, James Bertie. From this point Gale's career went along almost without untoward incident through the presidencies of Thomas Pollock and William Reed. It was not until the autumn of 1723 that he felt the earth give slightly under his feet. There was every indication that Governor Eden's heirs-at-law were going to make an issue of the will and the circumstances under which it was written. On 21 Nov. 1723 Lovick petitioned the council to permit the testimonies of Clayton, Gale, and the Badhams to be made a part of the council record, which was accordingly allowed. After that, it was a matter of waiting for the heirs-at-law to make their move against the will and its principal legatee.

When George Burrington qualified as governor of North Carolina on 15 Jan. 1724, gossip about the circumstances of the Eden will may already have been current in the colony. Gale later testified that Burrington's enmity toward him dated from the new governor's first month in the colony. Perhaps this was so, but the contrary is suggested by the records. Burrington's temperament was not that of a man who would willingly surround himself with known enemies, let alone put into their hands the complete administration of justice in the colony he governed. One of Burrington's first acts was to make Gale's son-in-law, Henry Clayton, the provincial provost marshal. The other son-in-law, William Little, was created attorney general by Burrington on 2 Apr. 1724, the same day he accepted Gale on his council. A week later the governor commissioned Gale's brother Edmond as one of the two assistant justices of the General Court. Gale's old clerk, William Badham, had been restored to his office in the court by Gale two years previously. It is hard to believe that Burrington was envenomed against Gale at this time.

The rage broke out a few months later. Toward the end of July 1724 Burrington received a petition asking him to grant redress in his capacity as ordinary of the colony. The petition was from Eden's niece, Margaret Pugh, and Ann and Roderick Lloyd. They denounced the will said to be Eden's as a fraud and alleged that Lovick had obtained it illegally. On 31 July, Burrington carried the petition to a meeting of the council that was attended by both Lovick and Gale. The governor explained that the council would proceed in the matter as a Court of Ordinary. An order-in-council was issued requiring the recordation of the London petition and power in the records of the General Court. (The court was then in session.) It must have been an exhilarating occasion. To have proceeded in the matter would have meant an examination and scrutiny of Lovick, Clayton, the Badhams, and possibly Gale himself.

Gale refused to give his clerk Badham the order necessary for the recordation required by the order-in-council. Burrington exploded in rage and suspected the very worst of the entire lot. In his anger he threatened to ruin Mr. and Mrs. Badham and declared that he would have Lovick and Gale in irons. In fact, he announced his intention to crop Gale's ears and slit his nose like a common felon. In his initial burst of fury, Burrington had entered the General Court and denounced Gale on the bench as a rogue and a villain. The outraged Burrington did not cool off until he discovered during a nighttime attack on Gale's house in August that Gale had left Edenton.

Gale had not only left Edenton, but he had also left the colony. Burrington and the council declared Gale's offices vacant on 24 Oct. 1724 and filled his seat on the council as well as the office of chief justice. Gale's son-in-law Henry Clayton was dismissed as provost marshal, his brother Edmund was turned off the General Court, and after the October term Badham was replaced as clerk of the court by Samuel Swann. On 29 Oct. 1724 Lovick, through his attorney William Little, made an answer to the petition of Eden's English heirs in which he denied all their allegations. In response to the replication of the heirs, the council admitted itself powerless to oblige Lovick to give security for the Eden estate, valued by the petitioners at £8,000 sterling. Here the matter was to rest for half a year.

In leaving the colony, Gale had gone posthaste to London armed with depositions against Burrington from allies on the council. That Gale had a powerful friend and protector on the Proprietary Board is obvious, but the identity of this person is unknown. Gale easily effected the removal of Burrington by the Lords Proprietors. In the summer of 1725, almost a year after the crisis over the Eden will had erupted, Gale arrived back in Edenton, leading the newly appointed governor of North Carolina, Sir Richard Everard, who was promptly characterized by Burrington as a noodle.

The peremptory removal of Burrington ended any real threat from Eden's English heirs. The heirs petitioned the Court of Chancery for relief in April 1725, Burrington presiding; their bill was thrown out in July 1725, Sir Richard presiding, when the death of one of the plaintiffs was falsely suggested. The bishop of St. Asaph joined the cause of the heirs-at-law and appealed directly to the Lords Proprietors in March 1726. The Proprietors took no action other than to assure the bishop that they had received an account of the proceedings relating to Eden's will and that he could have a copy of the account upon application to their secretary. Stalemated by the Proprietary Board, the bishop introduced the bill of complaint once more in the Court of Chancery in July 1726, Sir Richard still presiding, and the bill was again thrown out on the grounds that the power of attorney from the heirs to Robert Lloyd and Edmond Porter had not been sufficiently proved. No more was heard from the English heirs after this. The two stepchildren in the colony did not make an issue of the will. Eden's stepdaughter, Penelope Galland Maule, was widowed early in 1726 and Lovick very quickly married her. After the marriage Penelope and Lovick gave Eden's stepson, John Galland, the ferry slip near the plantation of Mount Gallant, and Gale's son-in-law, William Little, "for love and affection" gave Galland the ferryboat that went with it. Even with this, Lovick never felt perfectly secure in the estate left by Eden. His dying instructions to his wife were never to pay a penny from the Eden estate to the heirs in England, and to ensure her compliance he made Christopher Gale, Edmund Gale, and William Little executors of Governor Eden's will upon his own demise.

In a letter to Lord Carteret (who was very probably Gale's powerful friend and protector), Burrington traced his difficulties and the upheaval in the colony directly back to the matter of the Eden will. Certainly, the Eden will was not the *cause* of the ideological and political difference in the province, but there can be little doubt that the controversy over it influenced political alignments and precipitated a quarrel that permanently marked Gale's career and reputation.

There had been political divisions and struggles in the colony before now, but none of them equaled the fight that arose upon the removal of Burrington and the substitution of Sir Richard Everard as governor. Gale resumed his seat as chief justice, Little was restored as attorney general, and Gale gave back to Badham his old office as clerk of the General Court. For a time the coalition of Everard, Lovick, Gale, and Little ruled the colony. The General Court became first a political tool in the hands of Gale and his faction, then an object of contempt in the province. Similarly, the Court of Vice-Admiralty in the hands of Edmond Porter (who had been one of the attorneys for Eden's heirs-at-law) became a tool of political opposition against Gale's faction. The responsibility for the jurisdictional fight that broke out between the two courts must be shared in large part by Gale. Waiving all considerations of the deleterious effects on impartial justice that were bound to arise from such a contest, he was foolish to have undertaken the political risk of pitting the Proprietary common law court against the Crown maritime court. The Court of Vice-Admiralty was bound to win such a struggle, and it did. Governor Everard fell out with Gale in the summer of 1728 after the governor was presented by the grand jury for assaulting one of Gale's friends, and Lovick was presented for assaulting Sir Richard. From that time Everard issued writs of nolle prosequi against criminal indictments brought for political purposes in the General Court and began to take the side of Edmond Porter and the Court of Vice-Admiralty. Thus the maritime court gained the upper hand. Porter's use of the Vice-Admiralty Court as a political weapon was far more unscrupulous and less subtle than Gale's similar use of the General Court. Porter aimed for nothing less than the destruction of the General Court. The province was treated to the spectacle of first the attorney general, then the chief justice, briefly in jail at Edenton by order of the judge of the Court of Vice-Admiralty.

In 1729 the sale of North Carolina and South Carolina to the Crown by the Lords Proprietors was completed. Upon the sale, many held that Gale's commission from the Lords as chief justice was no longer in effect. Gale continued to style himself chief justice through December 1730 and to hold terms of the General Court through April 1730, but less and less business was effectively handled there. By the time the newly appointed George Burrington took up the reins of government as North Carolina's first royal governor early in 1731, the General Court had been wrecked and the former chief justice had left the colony.

When Gale made his last visit to England in 1731, it was very much doubted that he would ever return to North Carolina. The fears proved to be groundless. The voyage was a business and pleasure trip, not a flight. Part of Gale's visit was spent with his kinsmen. Otherwise he attended to business on behalf of the colony. In July he attended a meeting of the Board of Trade and presented a memorial intended to assist tobacco planters in Albemarle County. In November he attended the meeting of the Privy Council at which recent charges against Governor Burrington were aired. Then Gale quietly moved behind the scenes to come to Burrington's assistance despite their old troubles. While in the capital, Gale discussed conditions in the colony with the bishop of London, and he addressed the Society for the Propagation of the Gospel on the need to send missionaries to North Carolina. It is doubtful that he much busied himself on his own account. For some years he had been one of the collectors of His Majesty's Customs in North Carolina, first at Port Beaufort (1722–23), then at Port Currituck (1723–25), and after July 1725 at Port Roanoke. When Gale returned to North Carolina in the spring of 1732, he returned in the same office he held when he left—collector of Port Roanoke. He remained collector of this port for the rest of his life; he never sat again as chief justice.

Whatever his role in the matter of Eden's will, regardless of whether the will was fraudulent or not, and despite the result of the chain of events that was set off by the threat of an inquiry into the circumstances under which the will had been written, Gale's contribution to North Carolina was enormous. The unfortunate politicization of the administration of justice during the last four years of his chief justiceship wrecked the General Court, but did not destroy it. His basic conception of the court and the role of the chief justice in it was a valid one, and his lifework was to realize the concept. Though it continued to be debated beyond his death, Gale's theory proved finally to be the model upon which the court was based throughout the colonial period. Clearly imperious and perhaps occasionally inequitable in his orders, Gale was careful to hold himself within the bounds of the law in his administration of the court. We may assume that he was as legally scrupulous in his other offices. When William Byrd of Westover charges that Gale, as one of the commissioners to determine the North Carolina-Virginia boundary in 1729, abused his appointment by attempting to enrich himself by landgrabbing, we can conclude that Byrd is speaking out of animosity rather than from fact. We may also rest assured that the abuse of blank land patents bearing his signature with others of the council during the years 1729 and 1730 took place without his knowledge or consent.

Brought up as he was in the shadow of York Minster, Gale was an active Anglican who sought to establish and nourish the established church in North Carolina. His first wife, Sarah Laker Harvey, and mother of his children Miles, Penelope, and Elizabeth, died about 1730. He then married Sarah Isabella Ismay, widow of his friend John Ismay, about 1733. In his will, written in 1734, Gale gave back to his widow the property that she had brought into the marriage; otherwise everything he owned was left to his children, granddaughter, and nephews. One bequest bears quotation: "To All my friends I leave my hearty prayers & Good wishes, To my Enemys forgiveness & prayers for their Repentance for the many ill offices done me." The Henrietta Johnston pastel portrait of Gale is owned by the Museum of Early Southern Decorative Arts, Winston-Salem.

SEE: Great Britain, P.R.O., *Calendar of State Papers, Colonial Series, America and West Indies*, vols. for 1700–35; North Carolina State Archives, Raleigh, for Albemarle County Records, Bertie County Deed Book 3, British Records Collection, Colonial Court Records, Little-Mordecai Papers, and Secretary of State Wills; William S. Price and Robert J. Cain, eds., *Colonial Records of North Carolina (Second Series)*, vols. 4–7 (1974–83); William L. Saunders, ed., *Colonial Records of North Carolina*, vols. 1–3 (1886).

GEORGE STEVENSON

**Gale, Edmund** *(d. December 1738)*, provincial official, was the son of Miles (1647–1721) and Margaret Stone Gale. His father, an Anglican clergyman, was rector of Keighley in Yorkshire, England; his mother was a daughter of the chancellor of York. The third of four sons, Edmund spent most of his life in the shadow of his eldest brother, Christopher.

Edmund first appears in North Carolina in 1715. By January of the following year he was serving in the Assembly. He was again elected to the lower house in November 1723. Unquestionably Gale benefited from a name made prominent by his brother. During the early part of his life in the colony, he lived in Pasquotank Precinct and was named to the vestry of Southwest Parish there in 1715. In 1734, he purchased a house in Edenton where he spent the rest of his life. As he grew older, Gale attained increasingly more significant political positions. He was treasurer of Pasquotank in 1720. In April 1722 he became a justice of the General Court and served for four years. Elevated to Governor Richard Everard's council in the summer of 1725, Gale remained a member for three years. In this position and because of his kinship with Christopher, he gained the enmity of George Burrington. Robert Forster, the clerk of the council in the late Proprietary period, said in 1730 that he had heard Burrington promise revenge on certain councillors who had caused him trouble in 1725—Edmund Gale being one of those named. Yet when Burrington arrived in the colony to assume his duties as royal governor in February 1731, he and the younger Gale developed a growing friendship. One of the things that drew Burrington to Edmund was his opposition to Edmund Porter, the unpopular vice-admiralty court judge. Gale and John Lovick had led a group that violently disrupted Porter's court in January 1731. Burrington wished to remove Porter from the royal council and, through a questionable emergency appointment, elevated Gale to the council on 26 July 1731. Despite his difficulties with every other councillor seated in 1731, Burrington retained Gale until his own removal as governor in November 1734. Gale's tenure on the council ended at the same time.

Gale succeeded Edmund Porter as vice-admiralty court judge in January 1732, and he served as naval officer for the port of Roanoke the following year. When Gale died in 1738, he left a widow, Mary, and two sons, Roger and Edmund. His will listed eleven slaves, and his whole estate was valued in excess of £8,000.

SEE: William S. Price, Jr., "'Men of Good Estates': Wealth Among North Carolina's Royal Councillors," *North Carolina Historical Review* 49 (1972); William L. Saunders, ed., *Colonial Records of North Carolina*, vols. 1, 2 (1886); Colonial Council Records and Secretary of State Papers (North Carolina State Archives, Raleigh).

WILLIAM S. PRICE, JR.

**Gales, Joseph** *(4 Feb. 1761–24 Aug. 1841)*, journalist and reformer, was born in Eckington, England, the eldest son of Thomas Gales, a local artisan and schoolmaster. Trained in the printing trade by J. Tomlinson, a printer and bookbinder of nearby Newark, Gales in 1784 established himself as a printer, stationer, and auctioneer in Sheffield, an important manufacturing town in northern England. On 4 May 1784, he married Winifred Marshall, a young writer and native of Newark. The couple soon became active in the constitutional reform movement then beginning in England and centered in Sheffield. On 8 June 1787, Gales issued the first number of the Sheffield *Register*, a weekly newspaper that quickly rose to prominence among those interested in political and labor reform. This was supplemented on 3 Apr. 1792 by another weekly, *The Patriot*, printed by Gales but edited by Matthew C. Brown, which was devoted to printing extracts from the works of the leading reformers of the time—such men as Thomas Paine, Joseph Priestley, Henry Redhead Yorke, and James Mackintosh, all acquaintances of Joseph Gales. Following the outbreak of the French Revolution in 1789 Gales devoted considerable space in the *Register* to reporting its progress.

In 1791, he helped launch the Sheffield Society for Constitutional Information, an organization dedicated to "the enlightenment of the people" in their need for political and labor reform, serving several times as chairman. When war broke out between France and Great Britain in 1793, those engaged in reform activities came under the surveillance of government authorities. The habeas corpus act was suspended, a committee in the House of Commons launched a heresy hunt for those suspected of treason, and a number of reformers were arrested. Thomas Hardy, secretary of the London Corresponding Society, an important cog in the reform movement, was arrested in May 1794. Found among his papers were letters incriminating Gales. Word reached Sheffield that warrants had been issued for his arrest, and Gales went into hiding. When it became apparent that he could no longer remain safely in England, he fled to Hamburg, a free city and important trading port of northen Europe.

Left behind in Sheffield, Winifred Gales carried on the business, ably assisted by James Montgomery, the poet, who had joined Gales in 1792 as an assistant. Two of Gales's creditors took out bankruptcy proceedings against the firm, but Montgomery got himself appointed as agent of the creditors. When the printing office and the *Register* were put up for sale, a local citizen made an offer of £300 on condition that Montgomery would remain as editor. It was accepted. The bookshop passed into the hands of Gales's three maiden sisters, who continued to operate it for many years. Montgomery changed the name of the *Register* to the *Iris*; but determined not to suffer Gales's fate, he ceased to champion the cause of reform openly. With affairs in order, Winifred Gales and her four children—Joseph, Jr., Sarah, Thomas, and Winifred—accompanied by a young orphan apprentice, left Sheffield in July 1794 to join her husband, who had located in Altona, the principal city of the Duchy of Holstein, then under the Protectorate of Denmark. Hamburg was a mile distant.

As soon as his family arrived, Gales made plans to leave for America and he secured passage on a ship leaving on 17 September for Philadelphia. Once on board, delays in getting underway and the apprehensions of his wife caused Gales to reconsider. The family returned to Altona and obtained an apartment; on 17 Nov. 1794 Winifred Gales gave birth to a daughter who, in honor of their temporary home, was named Altona. While his wife recovered, Gales learned French and German, practiced shorthand taught him by a visitor to Sheffield several years earlier, and made friends among the many refugees gathered in Hamburg. He also met Joel Barlow, the American diplomat and poet.

In March 1795 Gales received a letter from friends in Sheffield expressing the hope that he might return. This hope was dashed on further inquiry by Gales. To soften the blow his friends sent a sum of money and the assurance that they would cover the cost of type and printing supplies to be sent to America if Gales would order them from London. With Joel Barlow's help, passage was obtained on a ship bound for Philadelphia. The young apprentice chose to return to England. On 31 May 1795, Joseph and Winifred Gales and their five children took leave of Altona. Two months later, on 30 July, the family arrived in Philadelphia. Gales found employment—first as a typographer, then as a reporter—with Claypool and Dunlop, publishers of the *American Daily Advertiser*. His verbatim accounts (taken in shorthand) of speeches delivered in the U.S. Senate established his reputation as a reporter while affording him a chance to meet some of the nation's leading politicians.

The printing materials promised from London arrived in the spring of 1796. Gales left the *Daily Advertiser*, purchased the semiweekly *Independent Gazetteer* from the widow of its founder, Eleazer Oswald, and on 16 Sept. 1796 issued the first number of *Gales' Independent Gazetteer*. Though his prospectus promised an impartial reporting of the news, it at once became apparent that the *Gazetteer* sympathized with the partisan views of the Jeffersonian Republicans. The paper and its publisher prospered and once again the Gales family was comfortably situated. But on 12 Sept. 1797 Gales announced the sale of his *Gazetteer* to Samuel Harrison Smith, who was then publishing a daily newspaper in Philadelphia, *The New World*.

Gales's reasons for selling his newspaper are not clear. Undoubtedly the annual outbreak in Philadelphia of yellow fever played a part; in the fall of 1797 Mrs. Gales was stricken when the family delayed leaving the city because of the pressure of business. Though she recovered it was a frightening experience. Also, Gales complained of difficulty in collecting subscription debts. Although the Alien and Sedition laws were not passed until the summer of 1798, sentiment in favor of such action certainly was apparent before that time and would have been known by the editor of a newspaper. Gales as an immigrant newspaper editor, sympathetic to France, and clearly on the side of Jefferson in the contest between Federalists and Republicans, was again courting official disfavor. Whatever the reason, he continued his printing business, doing work for a number of congressmen.

Early in 1798, Gales was approached by certain members of the North Carolina delegation to Congress about locating in Raleigh. Nathaniel Macon, in particular, recognized in Gales the type of editor needed by Republicans in North Carolina. With the crucial election of 1800 approaching and the party in need of a forceful editor to promote the Jefferson cause, Macon and his friends urged Gales to move to Raleigh, the state's new capital, and begin a newspaper. As an inducement he was promised the state printing contract. Pleased with the idea, Gales made a trip to Raleigh. What he saw and heard convinced him, for he engaged a house and returned to Philadelphia for his family.

There were now seven children, two daughters having been born since the family arrived in Philadelphia. On 20 Aug 1799, they embarked on a schooner bound for Norfolk, Va., Soon after leaving Philadelphia the youngest daughter died and was buried at sea. At Norfolk a carriage was hired for the overland trip to Raleigh. The family arrived on 4 Sept. 1799. Their furniture, supplies, and printing materials followed shortly thereafter. Types were sorted, the press erected, and on 22 Oct. 1799 the first number of the *Raleigh Register, and North-Carolina Weekly Advertiser* appeared.

The *Raleigh Register*, published by Gales until his retirement in 1833, became one of the major newspapers in the state. It was the leading political voice in North Carolina, first for the Republicans and, after 1824, for the National Republicans of Adams and Clay. In 1800 he was awarded the state printing contract, a position he held for ten consecutive years. To indicate his official status, Gales changed the title of his paper to *Raleigh Register, and North Carolina State Gazette*. In 1811, when he withdrew from the contest to choose a state printer, he again altered the title, this time to *Raleigh Register, and North Carolina Gazette*.

As a rival for political dominance in the newspaper field of Raleigh, Gales first encountered the Federalist paper of Abraham Hodge and his nephew William Boylan, who had begun publishing the *North-Carolina Minerva* in Raleigh five months before Gales issued the *Register*. Boylan, who was the active partner in the Raleigh paper, was especially hostile to Gales. From the beginning he attacked the *Register* editor in the columns of the *Minerva*, calling attention to Gales's foreign birth, criticizing his flight from England, and questioning his character. Gales, a temperate editor in such matters, ignored the attacks. But in 1804 a series of charges, coinciding with an unexplained fire that badly damaged his printing plant, provoked a response from Gales. The climax came with the exchange of abusive handbills, which so infuriated Boylan that he severely beat Gales with a cane when he encountered him on the steps of the capitol. Gales sued Boylan for assault and won. He donated the money, less legal fees, to the Raleigh Academy.

When beginning the *Register* in 1799, Gales was assisted by Richard Davison, a printer who had worked with him on the Sheffield *Register*. He, too, had found it convenient to immigrate to America. Davison left the *Register* in 1802 to edit the *North-Carolina Messenger*, a Republican paper established in Warrenton. After that Joseph Gales, Jr., who had been expelled from The University of North Carolina in 1801, joined his father to learn the printing trade along with Francis Lumsden, another apprentice, who in 1836 was the cofounder of the New Orleans *Picayune*.

In January 1809 Gales took on as a partner William Winston Seaton, a native Virginian, who came to Raleigh first in 1806 to aid William Boylan in publishing the *North-Carolina Minerva*. The next year Seaton acquired the *North Carolina Journal* at Halifax, transferring the allegiance of that paper from Federalist to Republican. While in Raleigh Seaton met and fell in love with Sarah Gales, oldest daughter of the *Register* editor. It was thus no problem for Seaton to give up the *Journal* at Halifax for a position as coeditor of the *Register*. He and Sarah Gales were married in Raleigh in April 1809.

Before this Gales had concluded that Joseph, Jr., needed more experience in the art of printing than he could gain in Raleigh. Therefore, in 1806 he sent the young man to Philadelphia to work under William Young Birch, a printer and friend of the elder Gales. The next year Samuel Harrison Smith, who had bought Gales's Philadelphia paper in 1797 and later moved to Washington, D.C., to begin the *National Intelligencer* in 1800, advertised the paper for sale. Gales was interested. He proposed to Smith that he accept Joseph, Jr., as a partner, with the understanding that if he proved capable he would assume sole control of the paper. Smith agreed and until the summer of 1810 young Gales worked as an assistant to the *Intelligencer* editor. During the 1807–8 session of Congress, Joseph Gales himself went up from Raleigh to help in reporting the debates. On 31 Aug. 1810 Joseph Gales, Jr., became editor of the *National Intelligencer*. Then in 1812, Seaton left the Raleigh *Register* to join his brother-in-law as coeditor of the *Intelligencer*.

Gales ran the *Raleigh Register* alone until 1821, when he brought his youngest son Weston into the firm as a partner. Weston, born in Raleigh in 1802, had been expelled from Yale; like his older brother Joseph, he had found college life uncongenial. On 18 Nov. 1823 the two Galeses began publishing the *Register* as a semiweekly, the first to appear in North Carolina. Gales had issued the *Register* semiweekly during the session of the General Assembly in 1804, but on a temporary basis only. However, the twice-weekly schedule proved unsatisfactory because North Carolina's population was too sparse to support it. Therefore on 11 Nov. 1831 the *Register* reverted to weekly publication.

A semiweekly publication was but one of the many innovations made by Joseph Gales in newspaper publishing in North Carolina. Not the least was the verbatim accounts of speeches delivered in the halls of Congress and the chambers of the state capitol. Many a famous speech was saved from oblivion by the shorthand reporting of Gales. He taught the art to his sons Joseph, Jr., and Weston, his son-in-law William W. Seaton, and a number of apprentices. E. J. Hale, longtime editor of the Fayetteville *Observer*, learned his trade as a printer and reporter from Joseph Gales.

But Gales did more. He used the columns of the *Register* to promote improvement and reform within Raleigh and North Carolina. Before the *Register* was a month old, Gales advocated a medical society for the state as a means of combating "the fatal and criminal practices of Quacks and Empyrics." The "bloodthirsty and lawless" custom of dueling he opposed as "repugnant to religion, justice & mercy." Education also enlisted Gales's interest, as it had when he edited the Sheffield *Register*. Not only did he champion the cause of schools in his paper, but also in 1801 he was one of the incorporators of the Raleigh Academy, which opened in 1804. Libraries, too, were high on Gales's list of needs for society. He declared on one occasion that a public library would go further "to improve the condition of society than any other means that could be devised."

By 1815, Joseph Gales had become one of Raleigh's leading citizens. He served as director of the State Bank, as secretary of nearly every civic and benevolent society in Raleigh, as commissioner and treasurer of the town, and, from 1819 until his retirement in 1833, as mayor. His home was the center of social activity, made attractive by his reputation and, as one visitor said, by the "hospitality of his brilliant wife and accomplished daughters." A contemporary described Gales as "a man of few words," but his wife as "a great conversationalist."

In June 1819 a branch of the American Colonization Society was organized in Raleigh and Gales became its secretary. Later, after his retirement and move to Washington in 1834, he became treasurer of the national organization, a position he held until 1839. Though Gales favored the emancipation of slaves he did not openly attack the institution, believing that to do so was unwise. "It will be of no use," he wrote an acquaintance, "to attack the people's prejudices directly in the face." The end of slavery, he felt, must be brought about by gradual means. Indeed, in the columns of the *Register* he opposed any restriction on slavery such as that intended by the Talmadge Amendment on the admission of Missouri to statehood in 1820. If slavery was to be abolished, he contended, the proper agency to do so was the state, not the federal government.

When the state capitol burned in 1831, there was some agitation to relocate North Carolina's capital, a disturbing move to the people of Raleigh. Joseph Gales, as mayor, hit upon the idea of building a railroad—a new innovation in transportation—from a stone quarry nearby to the site of the ruined capitol. His argument was that a railroad would afford a facility for obtaining cheap, durable building stone and thus influence the legislators to rebuild in Raleigh. Gales suggested the idea to other interested citizens, a company was formed, and in 1832, when the legislature met, everything was in readiness "to treat the members of the legislature with a ride on a Railroad." Though just a mile and a quarter in length, with power provided by horse, this railroad had much effect in developing support for a more extensive undertaking, a cause of great interest to Gales. Since 1823, when elected secretary of the Internal Improvements Board, he had been active in promoting better transportation facilities for North Carolina.

Gales regarded religion as "the key-stone which locks and cements, and beautifies the grand arch of society." Before leaving Sheffield both he and Winifred Gales were active in the Sunday school movement, an interest they continued after settling in Raleigh. Joseph served as superintendent of the Sunday school conducted in the Presbyterian church. While in Sheffield, the Galeses had formed an attachment for the Unitarian faith, becoming acquainted with Joseph Priestley, the English chemist and religious reformer. After coming to America, Gales published the writings of Priestley, also a refugee in Philadelphia, in his *Gazetteer*. With Priestley, Joseph and Winifred Gales organized the first Unitarian Society in Philadelphia, and Joseph became the first lay reader. As editor of the *Raleigh Register* Gales aided the Unitarian cause in North Carolina, publishing extracts from the *Unitarian Miscellany*, edited by Jared Sparks, a man with whom both Joseph and Winifred enjoyed a loyal friendship.

Not only did Joseph Gales edit an influential newspaper; he also managed a thriving printing establishment, conducted a bookstore, and operated a paper mill begun in 1808. In 1804, he published a romantic novel on English life, *Matilda Berkley, or Family Anecdotes*, written by his wife. This was but one of the many books produced by the Gales press. By far the greater number were state documents, but many volumes were of poetry, religion, and other topics. In 1819, Gales published George W. Jefferys's *Farmer's Own Book*. In 1828, Joseph Caldwell, president of The University of North Carolina, had Gales publish his *Numbers of Carlton*, a series of essays advocating railroads as a superior means of transportation over canals and turnpikes. This was followed in 1832 by his *Letters on Popular Education*, also published by Gales.

In 1833, Gales decided to turn the *Register* and other business over to Weston and retire to Washington, D.C. Both he and Winifred were beginning to tire of their active life. They were now in their seventies and wished to spend some of the time remaining to them with their children in the nation's capital. Obligations to the family in Raleigh were no longer demanding. Two daughters had died leaving young children whom the grandparents had reared. Weston had matured into a capable editor and responsible leader in Raleigh. The people of Raleigh, of course, were reluctant to see them go. Before their departure they were given a public dinner presided over by Governor David L. Swain.

Shortly after arriving in Washington, Gales began editing a "History of the Proceedings and Debates of the Early Sessions of Congress," the first part of the *Annals of Congress*, a publishing project long entertained by Gales and Seaton of the *National Intelligencer*. Two volumes were completed by Gales and published in 1834 when the work was suspended. In the late spring of 1839 Winifred Gales died and was buried in Washington. Joseph Gales returned to Raleigh. In January 1840 he was again elected mayor of Raleigh, an honor repeated the next year. But he did not live out the second term. He died at the age of eighty and was buried in the City Cemetery. Thomas Loring, editor of the Raleigh *Standard*, summed up the sentiments of the people of Raleigh when he wrote in his paper of 1 Sept. 1841, "when such a man dies, his loss is felt by all around him."

SEE: W. H. G. Armytage, "The Editorial Experiences of Joseph Gales, 1786–1794," *North Carolina Historical Review* 28 (1951); Willis G. Briggs, "Joseph Gales, Editor of Raleigh's First Newspaper," *North Carolina Booklet* 7 (1907); Clement Eaton, "Winifred and Joseph Gales, Liberals in the Old South," *Journal of Southern History* 10 (1944); Robert N. Elliott, Jr., *The Raleigh Register, 1799–1863* (1955); Joseph and Winifred Gales, Reminiscences (Southern Historical Collection, University of North Carolina, Chapel Hill); Gales Papers (North Carolina State Archives, Raleigh); W. W. Holden, *Address on the History of Journalism in North Carolina* (1881); William S. Powell, ed., "The Diary of Joseph Gales, 1794–1795," *North Carolina Historical Review* 26 (1949); Mary L. Thornton, "Public Printing in North Carolina, 1749–1815," *North Carolina Historical Review* 21 (1944); P. G. Wallis, "A Further Note on Joseph Gales of Newark, Sheffield, and Raleigh," *North Carolina Historical Review* 30 (1953).

ROBERT N. ELLIOTT

**Gales, Joseph, Jr.** *(10 Apr. 1786–21 July 1860)*, editor and publisher, was born in Eckington, England, the eldest son of Joseph and Winifred Marshall Gales. He began school in Sheffield, England, where his father had established himself as a printer and newspaper publisher. From his mother, a classics scholar and novelist, he learned to read Latin fluently and to appreciate literature. In 1795, the family fled England for America, victims of the political unrest afflicting England during the French Revolution. Settled in Philadelphia, young Joseph resumed his education. In 1799 the family moved to Raleigh, when the elder Gales accepted an offer to publish a Jeffersonian newspaper in the new capital city of North Carolina.

The senior Gales had hoped that his son would receive a strong academic education in addition to training as a printer. With that end in mind, he enrolled Joseph in The University of North Carolina in the fall of 1800. But because of an altercation involving one of the literary societies on the campus, young Gales was expelled the next year. He returned to Raleigh and entered newspaper work with his father. There he improved his shorthand skill and knowledge of printing. In 1806, his father sent him to Philadelphia to work with William Young Birch, a printer and close friend of the elder Gales. Upon completion of this training Joseph received a diploma from the Typographical Society of Philadelphia.

In 1807 Samuel Harrison Smith offered to sell the *National Intelligencer*, the first newspaper established in Washington, D.C. The chance to gain control of the "Court Paper" of the Jeffersonian Republicans appealed to the elder Joseph Gales, who had known Smith while living in Philadelphia. He wrote Smith and asked if he would accept his son Joseph as a partner, with the understanding that if the young man proved able he would assume full ownership. Young Gales was only twenty-one, and his father felt he needed more experience before undertaking the task of editing and publishing a newspaper on his own. Smith hesitated, for he wished to retire altogether from newspaper work; but as he received no better offer he accepted. In the summer of 1807 Joseph Gales, Jr., joined the staff of the *National Intelligencer*. Three years later, in August 1810, he assumed full control.

Gales was a short man, five feet two inches in height. He had a large head, with a broad face and thick black hair. His complexion was dark, his face dominated by black, piercing eyes. Harrison Gray Otis, the Massachusetts Federalist, wrote his wife that Gales "has very much the face & manner of a Malay." His employer's wife, Margaret Bayard Smith, in whose home he lived during his first years with the *Intelligencer*, thought the young man to be a "country bumpkin" and attempted to "soften" his manners. But another early acquaintance described him as "affable and easy," gracious, and exceedingly polite.

The *National Intelligencer* was one of the more important newspapers published in the United States, a reputation it enjoyed during its more than fifty years of existence. Under Smith's direction it had become the semiofficial voice of the presidency, a function it continued to serve through the administration of James Monroe. By the nation's newspapers, the *Intelligencer* was regarded as the basic source for news of the national government. When young Gales assumed control, the paper was issued as a triweekly.

In October 1812, Gales was joined in publishing the *Intelligencer* by his brother-in-law, William Winston Seaton. Seaton, a Virginian, had married Sarah Gales, the oldest daughter of Joseph Gales, Sr., in April 1809. Three months before that, in January, he had become associated with the elder Gales as coeditor of the *Raleigh Register*. The addition of Seaton to the staff of the *Intelligencer* lightened the work of Gales. On several occasions before this he had called on his father to help him report the affairs of Congress. Now these brothers-in-law divided the labor; in reporting the debates in Congress, performed exclusively by the two until 1820, Gales covered the Senate and Seaton the House. Then on 1 Jan. 1813 they began a daily edition, continuing to publish the triweekly for national circulation. During the War of 1812 the *Intelligencer's* office was sacked by the British in their raid on Washington, the only private establishment so treated. Gales's support of the war was given as the reason by Admiral Sir George Cockburn, the British commander. During this time the editors were on duty with the American forces defending Washington.

Gales married Sarah Juliana Maria Lee, the daughter of Theodorick Lee and niece of "Light Horse Harry" Lee, on 14 Dec. 1812 in Winchester, Va. They had no children but adopted a niece of Mrs. Gales named Juliana. Before he married Gales had selected a spot for a country home some two miles from the center of Washington. But until commercial development drove them out, the couple lived on Ninth Street not far from the *Intelligencer* office at Seventh and D streets, N.W. Eckington, the name Gales chose for his country estate, became the center for lavish entertaining as well as a refuge for the editor. Both the Gales and Seaton families were among the social elite of Washington. Numbered among Gales's close friends were Henry Clay, Daniel Webster, and Nicholas Biddle.

In its early years the *Intelligencer* supported the Jeffersonian Republicans. But with the disarray into which that party fell in 1824, Gales turned first to John Quincy Adams, and then, with the opening of the Jacksonian period, to Henry Clay and the Whig party. With the rise of the slavery controversy and the drift toward disunion, Gales tried to follow a neutral course. For nearly his whole career he argued for a policy of moderation regarding the slavery issue, urging the Northern states to leave the solution up to slaveholders and the Southern states. But toward nullification and secession, from the Hartford Convention on, Gales was implacably opposed. This stand in the 1850s threatened the very life of the *Intelligencer*, for a majority of the paper's subscribers lived in the South.

Gales was usually given credit for the "sound conservatism" of the *Intelligencer's* editorials. Daniel Webster wrote that Gales "knows more about the history of this government than all the political writers of the day put together." It was Webster's opinion that the editorials printed in the *Intelligencer* and widely reprinted by newspapers in all sections of the nation helped win support for the Webster-Ashburton Treaty in 1842. James Polk believed Gales's refusal editorially to oppose ratification of the treaty with Mexico was an important factor in securing acceptance of that treaty in 1848.

Beginning in 1825, Gales and Seaton began the *Register of Debates in Congress*, an annual record of congressional proceedings. To many people this series, which continued through 1837, was the most valuable publishing contribution made by the two editors of the *Intelligencer*. Of equal importance, however, were the *American State Papers*, the first volume issued in 1832, a collection of the major documents dealing with foreign relations, Indian affairs, and other matters. This thirty-eight-volume series has been termed by one historian "the high-water mark of historical publication . . . up to the period of the Civil War." Another publishing venture of note undertaken by Gales and Seaton was the *Annals of Congress*. The first two volumes, published in 1832, were edited by Joseph Gales, Sr., who had retired as editor of the *Raleigh Register* and moved to Washington. Publication was resumed in 1849. It was completed in 1856, totaling forty-four volumes.

These publishing activities of Gales and Seaton were heavily subsidized by Congress, a testament to the political friendships enjoyed by the editors. Indeed, it was this patronage that enabled the *Intelligencer* to remain in business while operating as an opposition newspaper. Yet the paper was never a financial success. Neither Gales nor Seaton was a good enough financier to build up the business side of the *Intelligencer*. During the Jacksonian period the editors were heavily indebted to the United States Bank, an institution they warmly supported along with the American System of Henry Clay.

Both Gales and Seaton were active in the affairs of Washington, Seaton more so than Gales. From 1827 to 1830 Gales served as mayor of the city. He was also active in the American Colonization Society and a member of the first Unitarian church organized in the nation's capital. Though Gales no longer reported the debates in the Senate, Webster asked him to report his debate with Hayne in 1830.

Physically, Joseph Gales, Jr., was never a strong man. In fact, it was an extended illness suffered in 1812 that led to the decision by Gales and his father to invite Seaton to become a partner in publishing the *Intelligencer*. There were further bouts with sickness, and by the early 1850s Gales was badly crippled. Nevertheless, he lived to be seventy-four. His funeral, held at his home Eckington, was a state occasion. President Buchanan and his cabinet attended as a body, along with other dignitaries. Schools and stores were closed. He was buried in the Congressional Cemetery. Seaton survived him by six years and the *Intelligencer* by nine.

SEE: William E. Ames, *A History of the National Intelligencer* (1972); Clarence C. Carter, "The United States and Documentary Historical Publication," *Mississippi Valley Historical Review* 25 (1938); Robert N. Elliott, Jr., *The Raleigh Register, 1799–1863* (1955); Joseph and Winifred Gales, Reminiscences (Southern Historical Collection, University of North Carolina, Chapel Hill); Frederick Hudson, *Journalism in the United States from 1690 to 1872* (1873); Frank L. Mott, *American Journalism* (1940); Josephine Seaton, *William Winston Seaton of the "National Intelligencer"* (1871).

ROBERT N. ELLIOTT

**Gales, Seaton,** *(17 May 1828–29 Nov. 1878),* editor, was born in Raleigh, the son of Weston R. and Love Freeman Gales. Graduated with honors from The University of North Carolina in 1848, Seaton became editor of the *Raleigh Register* on the sudden death of his father in July of that year, thus becoming the third generation Gales to edit that newspaper. Two years later he married Mary A. Cameron, daughter of Dr. Thomas N. Cameron of Fayetteville. They had seven children, four sons and three daughters.

Seaton Gales was the first college trained editor in North Carolina journalism. Under his direction the *Register* was enlarged and telegraph service introduced. On 19 Nov. 1850, a daily edition was begun—the first daily newspaper to be published in North Carolina. However, this effort proved unsuccessful and was discontinued on 29 Jan. 1851. In 1852 and 1853, Gales completely refitted the *Register* office and purchased a cylinder power press. These expenditures, combined with a decline in circulation, strained the financial resources of the paper. In December 1856 the *Register* was sold at public auction to John W. Syme of Petersburg, Va.

Until 1861, Gales was associated with the North Carolina Bank. With the outbreak of the Civil War he was appointed adjutant of the Fourth Regiment of North Carolina Volunteers. Promoted to major, he served in northern Virginia. Gales was captured at the Battle of Fisher's Hill on 19 Oct. 1864 and imprisoned at Johnson's Island, a federal prison near Sandusky, Ohio. After the war, in 1866, he became associate editor of the Raleigh *Sentinel*. Three years later he gave this up and became secretary of the North Carolina Home Insurance Company of Raleigh. Gales was highly regarded throughout the state as a public speaker. He died suddenly at the age of fifty in Washington, D.C., where he was serving as superintendent of the document room of the House of Representatives.

SEE: Robert N. Elliott, Jr., *The Raleigh Register, 1799–1863* (1955); Gales Papers (North Carolina State Archives, Raleigh); *A Tribute . . . to Major Seaton Gales* (North Carolina Collection, University of North Carolina, Chapel Hill).

ROBERT N. ELLIOTT

**Gales, Weston Raleigh,** *(28 Apr. 1802–23 July 1848),* editor, was born in Raleigh, the youngest son of Joseph and Winifred Marshall Gales. He spent his youth in Raleigh where he attended the Raleigh Academy. In 1820, to escape Raleigh's "young men of loose habits," of which he was apparently fond, he was sent by his parents to a private school in Connecticut to prepare for Yale College, and, as his mother wrote, "to acquire steady habits." This was to no avail, for, though he entered Yale in the fall of 1820, he was expelled the following January for engaging in a fistfight with another student. Returning to Raleigh, Weston was taken into business with his father, who had published the *Raleigh Register* and operated a printing establishment and bookshop since 1799. Here he was trained in the printing trade. In late 1821, Weston became a partner; the *Register* of 7 December bore the new firm name Gales & Son. He assumed full charge in 1833, when his father retired and moved to Washington, D.C.

On 21 Apr. 1825, Gales married Love S. Freeman. She died on 24 Jan. 1842 after a long illness. On 8 Jan. 1844, he married Mary Spies of New York City. Four years later, when returning from a vacation at Old Point Comfort, Va., Gales collapsed and died in Petersburg, Va. He was succeeded as editor of the *Register* by his son Seaton, who had just graduated from The University of North Carolina.

Weston Gales was conscious of the service that a newspaper owes to the community. He believed that to a great extent "the language of the newspaper was the public conversation of the country." Especially was he opposed to the publicity given crime. In his view if less notoriety were given news of this kind and if public executions and punishments were abolished, the crime rate would be greatly reduced. In 1843, Weston Gales was chosen mayor of Raleigh, a post his father had held for many years. Two years later he was elected to represent Wake County in the state legislature. His death was a shock to the people of Raleigh. He was buried in the City Cemetery.

SEE: Robert N. Elliott, Jr., *The Raleigh Register, 1799–1863* (1955); Joseph and Winifred Gales, Reminiscences (Southern Historical Collection, University of North Carolina, Chapel Hill); Gales Papers (North Carolina State Archives, Raleigh); *Tribute to Weston R. Gales* (North Carolina Collection, University of North Carolina, Chapel Hill).

ROBERT N. ELLIOTT

**Gales, Winifred Marshall,** *(1761–26 June 1839),* writer, was born in Newark, England, the youngest daughter of John Marshall, scion of a family of distinction though not wealthy. She was educated in the classics, and at an early age demonstrated a literary talent, writing stories and poems. When she was seventeen, she published *Lady Julia Seaton,* a romantic novel. On 4 May 1784 Winifred married Joseph Gales, a printer, the son of a village schoolmaster in nearby Eckington. The young couple located in Sheffield, where, in 1787, Joseph began publishing the Sheffield *Register,* a newspaper which became the voice in that area for the liberal movements then stirring England. Though from a staunch Tory family, Winifred joined her husband in his agitation for political and religious reform.

In 1794, Joseph Gales was forced to flee England because of his reform activities. He went to the free city of Hamburg, leaving Winifred to look after the business of running a bookshop and publishing the *Register.* When it became apparent that her husband would not be allowed to return, she sold the shop and the newspaper, and, with her four children, joined Joseph. They took up residence in nearby Altona. After a year the family, now enlarged by a daughter born in Altona, embarked for America, arriving in Philadelphia on 30 July 1795.

The Galeses adapted easily to Philadelphia. The older children were enrolled in school; in 1796 Joseph began a newspaper, *Gales' Independent Gazetteer,* which he sold the next year; and Winifred renewed friendships with other refugees from England, among them Dr. Joseph Priestley, the religious reformer and scientist. Both Winifred and Joseph took an active part in organizing the Unitarian Society of Philadelphia.

In the summer of 1799, in response to an offer from Nathaniel Macon of North Carolina, Joseph Gales left an established business in Philadelphia to locate in Raleigh. There, on 22 Oct. 1799, he began the *Raleigh Register,* a newspaper established to promote the cause of Jeffersonian Republicanism in North Carolina. Winifred made the change without complaint. There were five children: a daughter born in Philadelphia died en route to Raleigh; a sixth, a son and the last child, was born in Raleigh in 1802. Within a short time, Winifred Gales had established a home noted for good conversation and generous hospitality, and had actively entered the life of the new capital city. In 1804, she wrote, and her husband published, *Matilda Berkley or Family Anecdotes,* the first novel published in North Carolina that was written by a resident of the state.

Winifred and Joseph Gales were leaders in establishing Unitarianism in Raleigh and the South. Both were friends of Jared Sparks, who visited in their home. Winifred's correspondence with Sparks casts much light on religious conditions in the South. By 1831, however, the tolerance and liberalism that the Gales exemplified was becoming difficult to maintain amidst the growing orthodoxy of North Carolina. In 1833, they left Raleigh to reside in Washington, D.C., where their eldest son, Joseph Gales, Jr., edited the *National Intelligencer.* There Winifred Gales died at the age of seventy-eight. She was buried in the Congressional Cemetery.

SEE: Clement Eaton, "Winifred and Joseph Gales, Liberals in the Old South," *Journal of Southern History* 10 (1944); Joseph and Winifred Gales, Reminiscences (Southern Historical Collection, University of North Carolina, Chapel Hill); Gales Papers (North Carolina State Archives, Raleigh); Roger P. Marshall, "A Mythical Mayflower Competition," *North Carolina Historical Review* 27 (1950); *North Carolina Authors: A Selective Handbook* (1952); Josephine Seaton, *William Winston Seaton of the "National Intelligencer"* (1871).

ROBERT N. ELLIOTT

**Gallaway, James** *(d. 1798),* merchant and state legislator, was born probably in Scotland and moved to North Carolina before the American Revolution. His uncle, Charles Gallaway, was by 1765 living in the section of Rowan County that is now Rockingham County. Charles, a merchant, formed a partnership with Constantine Perkins of Pittsylvania County, Va., called Charles Gallaway and Company. On 1 Sept. 1778, James became a partner in this mercantile company. The Gallaways had widespread commercial interests across Piedmont North Carolina and southern Virginia. They became large landowners, accumulating thousands of acres in the Dan River Valley in present Rockingham County and some land in Virginia. Although not as active in public affairs as his nephew James, Charles Gallaway was appointed to the Committee of Safety for the Salisbury District on 9 Sept. 1775. He attended the first state convention for ratification of the federal Constitution at Hillsborough in 1788, as well as the second in Fayetteville the following year, and served a term in the state senate in 1791.

James Gallaway was active in the General Assembly from 1783 until 1789. Representing Guilford County, he served two terms in the House of Commons (1783 and April 1784) and two terms in the state senate (October 1784 and 1785). When Guilford County was divided on 29 Dec. 1785, creating from the northern half the county of Rockingham, Gallaway became the new county's first senator and was reelected for four terms (1786–89). A very industrious senator, he served in various sessions on committees on public taxes, finance, propositions and grievances, and Indian affairs, as well as on a number of special and joint committees dealing with petitions and specific issues. His progressive outlook is demonstrated by his legislative support for bills liberalizing criminal punishment, permitting limited emancipation of slaves, reforming fiscal policy, encouraging education, and sponsoring internal improvements. In 1784 he was named a trustee for the improvement of navigation on the Dan and Roanoke rivers. Gallaway introduced the bill for the Dismal Swamp Canal Company and was appointed a member of the Virginia-North Carolina joint commission on the canal that met in Fayetteville in December 1786. The canal company was chartered in 1790.

As a strong Anti-Federalist and influential senator, Gallaway had a key role in opposing the ratification of the federal Constitution and any measure that strengthened the federal government at the expense of the states. In the April 1784 session of the House of Commons, he signed a protest against ceding the state's western lands to the national government. When ratification of the Constitution became the central issue of the November 1787 General Assembly, he supported an unsuccessful senate resolution opposing the proposed convention.

Gallaway was elected to Rockingham County's Anti-Federalist delegation to the Hillsborough convention that opened on 21 July 1788. Although Willie Jones was the Anti-Federalist leader, Gallaway seconded the various motions made by Jones, and on the third day of the convention he moved that the convention become a committee of the whole to debate the Constitution. In the ensuing debate Gallaway was one of the chief opponents of the Constitution, and the Anti-Federalist majority succeeded in preventing ratification at Hillsborough. In the Fayetteville convention of November 1789, however, the Federalists dominated. The defeat of Willie Jones left Gallaway as the leading spokesman of the Anti-Federalists. He was appointed to the convention rules committee, and on the second day he successfully maneuvered to prevent immediate ratification, ensuring another lengthy debate on the Constitution. Although it was finally ratified, Gallaway secured five additional amendments to be proposed to Congress.

After 1789 Gallaway did not return to public office, but continued his careers as a partner in Charles Gallaway and Company and as a planter. In 1790, he was recorded as having twelve slaves. Gallaway married Elizabeth Spraggins of Halifax County, Va., and they had two sons, one of whom was named James E.

SEE: Accounts, Court Minutes, and Deeds of Pittsylvania County, Va. (Courthouse, Chatham); John L. Cheney, Jr., ed., *North Carolina Government, 1585–1974* (1975); Walter Clark, ed., *State Records of North Carolina*, vols. 18-21 (1900–1905); Deeds of Guilford County (Courthouse, Greensboro); Deeds of Rockingham County (Courthouse, Wentworth); Marriage Bonds of Halifax County, Va. (Courthouse, Halifax); Minutes, North Carolina Court of Equity, 1822 (North Carolina State Archives, Raleigh); U.S. Census, 1790, Rockingham County.

LINDLEY S. BUTLER

**Gallaway, John Marion** *(13 Dec. 1835–21 July 1909)*, Confederate officer and tobacco planter, was the son of Thomas Spraggins and Lucinda Chalmers Gallaway of Rockingham County. Before the American Revolution the Gallaway family settled in the Dan River Valley and became one of the great planter families of the region, owning thousands of acres of land in both Virginia and North Carolina. John M. Gallaway received his early education from a local academy; he then entered The University of North Carolina and was graduated in 1854 with second honors. After teaching school in Wentworth and Lexington for several years, he received the A.M. degree from the university in 1858. By 1860 he had decided upon a career in business and agriculture, taking first a position in a commission firm in Richmond, Va. The next year he was in the Yazoo River Valley, Miss., seeking a plantation site.

When the Civil War began, Gallaway returned to his home state and on 7 Oct. 1861 enlisted as a private in a company commanded by Captain Peter G. Evans in the Third North Carolina Cavalry (Forty-first North Carolina Regiment). Immediately after his discharge on 10 May 1862, he began raising a company of partisan rangers in Rockingham County. Gallaway was appointed captain on 1 Aug. 1862. His company, the "Rockingham Rangers," was mustered in at Kinston as a unit of the Fifth North Carolina Cavalry (Sixty-third North Carolina Regiment), commanded by Colonel Peter Evans. By November the company joined the regiment at Garysburg and participated in the capture of Plymouth, where Gallaway was severely wounded in a cavalry charge that broke the ranks of the Union defenders. After recovering from his injury, he returned to the regiment, which was ordered to join the Army of Northern Virginia in May 1863. Through the summer the regiment was engaged constantly in scouting, raids, and skirmishes. The regiment wintered in North Carolina, and by April 1864 it had returned to service in Virginia. In two skirmishes in the spring of 1864, at Ground Squirrel Church and Blacks and Whites, Gallaway had a key role in leading charges and in reconnaissance. He was seriously wounded again on 21 August but returned to duty by October and was promoted to major. During the Battle of Five Forks, the regiment's last major action in March 1865, Gallaway had another wound treated at Petersburg. He became the ranking officer of the regiment in the first week of April, but the war ended too soon for his command to be confirmed.

After the war Gallaway went to Gallaway, Fayette County, Tenn., to manage a family-owned, 3,000-acre tract of timber. There he opened a sawmill and soon had a prosperous crosstie and lumber business. In January 1873 he married Mary Haviland Lawson (1841–1917) of Leaksville, N.C., and they had four children. All of the children died young except a son, John Marion, Jr., born on 3 Mar. 1880. Gallaway was elected to the lower house of the Tennessee legislature in 1875.

Upon the death of his father in 1879, he returned to Rockingham County to settle the estate and manage his inheritance. The Gallaways lived at the family seat, Mon-Vue, near Leaksville until 1882, when they moved to Madison. With the same energy and ability that he had exhibited in the lumber business, Gallaway became a tobacco planter and eventually had some 15,000 acres under cultivation by three hundred tenant farmers. By the turn of the century he was known as the "biggest grower of flu-cured tobacco in the world." In 1885, he was elected to one term in the North Carolina General Assembly as a representative. Although he quickly earned the sobriquet "watchdog of the treasury," he firmly supported a crucial appropriation for The University of North Carolina. In the same year he was named a trustee of the university and continued on the board until 1893.

Active in local politics, Gallaway served as a county commissioner from 1885 to 1898, as chairman of the county commissioners from 1885 to 1889 and as mayor of Madison for sixteen years. In 1899, he was a founder and became the first president of the Bank of Madison. He died in Madison and was buried at the family cemetery on the Mon-Vue plantation.

SEE: Samuel A. Ashe, ed., *Biographical History of North Carolina*, vol. 6 (1905 [photograph]); Kemp P. Battle, *History of the University of North Carolina*, vol. 1 (1907); Walter Clark, ed., *Histories of the Several Regiments and Battalions from North Carolina in the Great War, 1861–'65*, vol. 3 (1901 [photograph]); Gallaway Cemetery, Mon-Vue Plantation, Leaksville, for tombstone inscriptions; Daniel L. Grant, *Alumni History of the University of North Carolina* (1924); *Madison Messenger*, 7 April 1932; Louis A. Manarin, ed., *North Carolina Troops, 1861–1865, A Roster: Cavalry*, vol. 2 (1968); Nannie M. Tilley, *The Bright-Tobacco Industry, 1860–1929* (1948).

LINDLEY S. BUTLER

**Galloway, Abraham H.**, *(d. 1 Sept. 1870)*, legislator and civil rights advocate, was born in Brunswick County. His mother was a slave and his father an unidentified member of the wealthy Galloway family of the Cape Fear region. He spent his early life as a slave of his father, but in 1857 he escaped to freedom in Ohio, where he later became involved in the abolitionist movement. He returned to North Carolina in 1862 or 1863 as a spy in the secret service of the Union Army under General Benjamin F. Butler. In 1864, Galloway was a delegate to the National Convention of Colored

Citizens of the United States, in Syracuse, N.Y., which established the National Equal Rights League to secure political and civil rights for Negroes. He returned to his native state as an agent of that organization. Because of his effectiveness as an orator and his determined crusade for Negro rights, Galloway became a principal spokesman for his race with a widespread personal following. He was instrumental in organizing a statewide Freedmen's Convention, which met at Raleigh in September and October 1865. At the convention Galloway, with James H. Harris, drew up a series of resolutions calling for, among other things, education and equal protection under the law for the freedman.

For a time Galloway resided in New Bern, but by 1867 he had moved to Wilmington, where he began a short-lived but eventful political career. In that year he helped organize the Republican party in North Carolina. When the state constitutional convention met in Raleigh in January 1868, Galloway was a delegate from New Hanover County. He was a leader of the Negro delegates as well as an important member of the convention's Radical majority. In addition to his continued and successful advocacy of civil rights for Negroes, he proposed an amendment granting suffrage to women. Soon afterward he was a delegate to the Republican state convention.

In April 1868 Galloway was elected state senator from New Hanover County. His brief legislative career was again characterized by concern for the advancement of his race as well as securing political and civil rights for women. Among other things, he advocated the ten-hour workday, a ban on segregation by businesses requiring state or municipal licenses, and legislation to suppress Ku Klux Klan terrorist activities. In 1868 he was a Republican presidential elector and in August 1870 he was reelected to the senate. In the latter year he escaped an attempt on his life, only to die a few months later from jaundice and bilious fever.

In physical appearance, Galloway was said to resemble an Indian. He had a fair complexion; long, black curly hair; and a medium but sturdy build. He was a member of St. Paul's Episcopal Church in Wilmington and a Mason. A wife and two children survived him.

SEE: Sidney Andrews, *The South Since the War* (1866); Elizabeth Balanoff, "Negro Legislators in the North Carolina General Assembly, July, 1868–February, 1872," *North Carolina Historical Review* 49 (1972); Leonard Bernstein, "The Participation of Negro Delegates in the Constitutional Convention of 1868 in North Carolina," *Journal of Negro History* 34 (1949); John R. Dennett, *The South As It Is: 1865–1866* (1965); W. McKee Evans, *Ballots and Fence Rails* (1966); J. G. deR. Hamilton, *Reconstruction in North Carolina* (1914); *New York Times*, 17 Sept. 1865; Raleigh *Weekly Standard*, 7 Sept. 1870; Jack B. Scroggs, "Carpetbagger Influence in the Reconstruction of the South Atlantic States, 1865–1876" (Ph.D. diss., University of North Carolina, Chapel Hill, 1953); *Wilmington Herald*, 1 Sept. 1870; Wilmington *Journal*, 30 July 1869; Wilmington *Morning Star*, 1 Sept. 1870.

WILLIAM R. TITCHENER

**Gano, John** *(22 July 1727–10 Aug. 1804)*, Baptist clergyman, was born at Hopewell, N.J., the third of six children of Daniel and Saran Britton Gano. His great-grandfather, a French Protestant, came to New Rochelle, N.Y., soon after the Edict of Nantes was revoked in 1685. After an illness at age six that almost cost him his life, young Gano grew up on his family's farm with intentions of becoming a farmer. He showed an early interest in religion, however, often questioning his Presbyterian father and his Baptist mother and grandmother on religious matters. Although he first inclined to Presbyterianism, his reservations concerning infant baptism and his talks with Baptist ministers channeled him into the Baptist faith. Eager for knowledge, Gano learned what he could from ministers and sat in on classes at Princeton. Illness prevented him from enrolling formally at the college, but he continued private study and was ordained as a Baptist minister in May 1754.

Gano made three missionary journeys south, one in 1754 (actually before his ordination), another in 1756, and a third in 1758, when he became minister to a congregation in the "Jersey settlement" in Rowan County. Though a small man, Gano was athletic, healthy, and energetic and made many converts to the Baptist faith. He returned to New Jersey in 1760 because of Indian trouble in North Carolina. In 1762, he became minister of the newly organized First Baptist Church in New York City, where he remained for twenty-six years except for a brief absence when he served as chaplain in the American Revolution. According to family tradition, he became a close friend of George Washington and baptized the general near Valley Forge.

Always a friend to educational institutions, Gano helped found Rhode Island College (Brown University) and served as a regent of the University of the State of New York and as a trustee of King's College (Columbia). In 1788, he left New York and went to Kentucky to preach. Though he was injured in a fall from a horse in 1798 and shortly afterward suffered a stroke, he continued preaching until his death in Frankfort.

Gano was married twice. He and his first wife, Sarah Stites, had at least eleven children: John Stites, who died before 1768; Daniel (b. 1758); Peggy (b. 1760); Stephen (b. 1762), who became a prominent Baptist clergyman; Sarah (b. 1764); John Stites (b. 1768); a daughter (1768–ca. 1771); Isaac Eaton (b. 1770); Richard Montgomery; Suzannah (b. 1777); and William. Shortly after their move to Kentucky in 1788, Sarah Stites Gano died. While on a preaching journey into North Carolina, Gano met and married the daughter of Colonel Jonathan Hunt; she was the widow of Captain Thomas Bryant.

SEE: *DAB*, vol. 4 (1960); John Gano, *Biographical Memoirs* (1806); *Nat. Cyc. Am. Biog.*, vol. 10 (1900).

ALICE R. COTTEN

**Gans, Joachim** *(fl. 1581–89)*, mineral expert with the Ralph Lane colony on Roanoke Island, 1585–86, and first American Jewish colonist, was born in Prague, Bohemia, possibly the son of or otherwise related to David Gans (1541–1613), Prague chronicler, mathematician, geographer, and astronomer. He appears as Ganz, Gannes, or Gaunse and sometimes his first name is given as Dougham or Doughan; he is also referred to as Master Jochims and Master Yougham. Gans went to England in 1581 to introduce an improved method that he had invented for smelting copper and was employed at the Mines Royal near Keswick, Cumberland. Accompanied by George Nedham, German-speaking shareholder in the mines and agent of Sir Francis Walsingham, Gans shortened the time required to refine copper and reduced the cost of production. Afterwards he also worked at Neath near Swansea in south Wales. It undoubtedly was because of his success in these operations that Ganz was selected as the "mineral man" to accompany the Lane colony. Thomas Harriot, the scientist on the expedition, reported that the mineral man found both iron and copper. After returning to England with the colony in 1586, Gans lived at one time in the Blackfriars section of London. In 1589 he was arrested in the port city of Bristol as an infidel. During a preliminary hearing he admitted that he was a circumcised Jew who did not believe in the Christian religion, upon which he was taken to London for trial. However, probably because he was known to such important persons as Sir Walter Raleigh and Secretary of State Walsingham, no trial seems to have taken place. There is no record of his burial in the Jewish cemetery of Prague, so it is unlikely that he returned there. The register of St. Andrew's Church, Plymouth, under date of 13 Oct. 1589 notes the marriage of one John Geynes and Alce, whose surname is not recorded; whether Geynes is a form of Gans is, of course, not known.

SEE: Israel Abrahams, "Joachim Gaunse: A Mining Incident in the Reign of Queen Elizabeth," The Jewish Historical Society of England *Transactions, 1899–1901*, 4 (1903); W. B. Collingwood, *Elizabethan Keswick* (1912); M. C. S. Cruwys, *The Register of Baptisms, Marriages, and Burials of the Parish of St. Andrew's, Plymouth* (1954); Maxwell B. Donald, *Elizabethan Copper* (1955); *Encyclopaedia Judaica*, vol. 7 (1971); Thomas Harriot, *A Brief and true report of the new found land of Virginia* (1588); David B. Quinn, *The Roanoke Voyages, 1584–1590*, 2 vols. (1955).

GARY C. GRASSL

**Garber, Paul Neff** *(27 July 1899–18 Dec. 1972)*, clergyman and educator, was born at New Market, Va., the son of Samuel and Ida Neff Garber. He was raised in the Church of the Brethren and educated at Bridgewater College, Bridgewater, Va. (A.B., 1919), Crozier Theological Seminary, and the University of Pennsylvania (M.A., 1921; Ph.D., 1923). After teaching for a year at Brown University, he joined the department of history of Duke University in 1924. Two years later, he was ordained to the ministry of the Methodist Episcopal Church, South, and became a member of the original faculty of Duke Divinity School. In 1928 he was professor of church history and in 1941 dean of the Divinity School. In the 1920s Duke University established a summer school at Lake Junaluska, which was held annually for about fifteen years with Dr. B. G. Childs of the university faculty as first dean and Garber his successor. In 1939, Garber was a delegate to the Uniting Conference in Kansas City. He never held a pastoral appointment.

In 1944, at the Southeastern Jurisdictional Conference at Atlanta, Garber was elected to the episcopacy, the first clergyman with an earned doctorate to be chosen for this post by the jurisdiction. Initially he was assigned to the Geneva area, which included Methodist work in North Africa, Switzerland, Belgium, Spain, Yugoslavia, Hungary, Austria, Bulgaria, Poland, Czechoslovakia, and the Madeira Islands. In 1951 he succeeded William Walter Peele (1881–1959), a native of Gibson, N.C., as bishop of the Richmond area, which included the Virginia and North Carolina annual conferences (fifty-six easternmost counties), one of the largest episcopal areas. As his final post, he was assigned in 1964 to the newly created Raleigh area of the Methodist church with his office in Raleigh. When he retired from the episcopacy in 1968, he was succeeded in the Raleigh area by Bishop William Ragsdale Cannon, a native of Georgia. Garber was instrumental in founding the No-Silent-Pulpit program, the Ten Dollar Club for church extension, North Carolina Wesleyan College at Rocky Mount (1956), and Methodist College at Fayetteville (1956). Garber Chapel in the North Carolina Conference was named in his honor. After his retirement, he resided in Geneva.

Garber was the author of *That Fighting Spirit of Methodism* (1928), *The Romance of American Methodism* (1931), *John Carlisle Kilgo: President of Trinity College, 1894–1910* (1937), *The Methodists Are One People, The Methodist Meeting House* (1941), and *The Methodists of Continental Europe* (1949). He was a contributor to *Methodist Magazine* (founded in 1962) and a member of the editorial board that supervised preparation of *The History of American Methodism* (1964) in three volumes, the first general history of American Methodism in several decades. In 1963 he was a member of the executive committee of the American Association of Methodist Historical Societies, and in April 1966 he was chairman of the General Bicentennial Committee of the Bicentennial Celebration of American Methodism in Baltimore and the originator of its theme: "Forever Beginning." Before retiring he was president of the council of bishops. Garber delivered a series of lectures at Gammon Theological Seminary, Emory University, Southwestern University, and Randolph-Macon College. He received honorary doctorates from Bridgewater College, Randolph-Macon College, Simpson College, Duke University, Emory University, and Washington and Lee University.

He was married twice: in 1927 to Orina Winifred Kidd and later to Nina Fontana of Geneva; no children were born to either union. Funeral services were held in the Cremation Chapel in Geneva, and a memorial service was held at Edenton Street United Methodist Church, Raleigh. His ashes were buried in the family plot in Oak Lawn Cemetery, Bridgewater, Va. Garber's library is at Randolph-Macon College and his papers are at the Methodist Building, 1307 Glenwood Avenue, Raleigh. A portrait hangs in the Methodist Building.

SEE: Elmore Brown, *Paul Neff Garber: A Bishop of Destiny* (1978); Elmer T. Clark, *Junaluska Jubilee* (1963), and *Methodism in Western North Carolina* (1956); C. Franklin Grill, *Methodism in the Upper Cape Fear Valley* (1966); Joseph Mitchell, *Episcopal Elections in the Southeastern Jurisdiction of the United Methodist Church* (1971); Raleigh *News and Observer*, 18 Dec. 1972; *Raleigh Times*, 18 Dec. 1972; W. W. Sweet and Umphrey Lee, *A Short History of Methodism* (1956).

GRADY L. E. CARROLL

**Gardner, Fay Webb** *(7 Sept. 1885–16 Jan. 1969)*, businesswoman, civic leader, and wife of North Carolina governor Oliver Max Gardner, was born in Shelby, the younger of two daughters of James L. and Kansas Andrews Webb. Her family had long been prominent in the Shelby area. Her paternal great-grandfather, the Reverend James Milton Webb, was the first pastor of the First Baptist Church of Shelby. Her father, a superior court judge, was active in local politics, as was her uncle, E. Yates Webb, who was a U.S. congressman and federal judge. After attending public schools in Shelby, she went to Lucy Cobb School for Girls in Athens, Ga., from which she was graduated in 1905. She spent two years traveling in Europe before her marriage in 1907 to Oliver Max Gardner of Shelby.

Much of Mrs. Gardner's activity during the next forty years was defined by her husband's career as Shelby lawyer and businessman, state legislator, lieutenant governor, governor, Washington lawyer, and assistant secretary of the Treasury. "Miss Fay," as she was known to the North Carolina public as well as to her friends and acquaintances, became well known for her hospitality, her graciousness, and her attractiveness of dress and demeanor. Indefatigable in her efforts to promote civic and cultural improvements, she was active in the Red Cross, the Civic League, the Garden Club, the League of Women Voters, the Saint Cecilia Music Club, the North Carolina Symphony Society, the Twentieth Century Literary Club, and numerous other organizations. In addition, she was a member of the United Daughters of the Confederacy, the Daughters of the American Revolution, and the Colonial Dames of America.

Mrs. Gardner also displayed executive abilities in less conventional roles. She owned and managed business properties, was an executive of Cleveland Cloth Mills of Shelby, and was director of Gardner Land Company. In 1942, she and her husband took up the challenge of revitalizing the near-bankrupt Boiling Springs Junior College, a small, church-related institution nine miles from Shelby. During the following years, they gave unstintingly of both time and money to achieve financial and academic viability for the institution, whose grateful board of trustees renamed it Gardner-Webb College in honor of Mrs. Gardner's family as well as that of the former governor. Mrs. Gardner served as trustee of the college and as president of the Gardner Foundation, which was instrumental in preserving the school.

Her allegiance and devotion to the Democratic party, nurtured during her childhood, were manifested both before and after her husband's death. In addition to her campaigning activities, she served on the state and national democratic committees and was twice elected a delegate to the Democratic National Convention. She helped to arrange several important Washington politico-social events including President Harry S Truman's birthday dinner in 1954 and John Kennedy's inaugural ball in 1961. In 1949, she was chosen chairman of the women's committee for the Jefferson-Jackson Day dinner in Washington, D.C.

The Gardners had four children: Margaret Love Gardner Burgess (b. 1908), James (1910–46), Ralph (b. 1912), and Oliver Max, Jr. (1922–61).

Mrs. Gardner's personal diaries and scrapbooks, which are at Gardner-Webb College, are an important source of information on the governorship of Oliver Max Gardner as well as on other facets of their life together. In addition to her scrapbooks about the governor's term in office, her papers include genealogical data, a governor's mansion diary for the years 1929–33, and a European travel diary of 1927.

She was buried in Sunset Cemetery, Shelby.

SEE: *Charlotte Observer*, 17 Jan. 1969; *Greensboro Daily News*, 7 Sept. 1930; Joseph L. Morrison, *Governor O. Max Gardner* (1971); Raleigh *News and Observer*, 17 Jan. 1969; *Who's Who in the South and Southwest*, 1967–69 and 1969–70.

ERIKA S. FAIRCHILD

**Gardner, Monroe Evans** *(3 Oct. 1895–29 Jan. 1975)*, educator, scientist, and administrator, was born in Blacksburg, Va., the son of Charles Wesley and Flora Evans Gardner. He was educated at Blacksburg High School and Virginia Polytechnic Institute, where he received a B.S. degree in horticulture in 1918. He served in the U.S. Army Air Corps in 1917. From 1919 to 1922 he was assistant horticulturist with the Virginia Agriculture Experiment Station; from 1922 to 1925 he was instructor in and then associate professor of horticulture at Clemson College, S.C.; and from 1925 to 1927 he was principal and teacher of agriculture in Consolidated High School, Charlotte Courthouse, Va.

The remainder of Gardner's career was spent at North Carolina State College as assistant horticulturist, North Carolina Agriculture Experiment Station (1927–30); acting head (1930) and head (1931–56), Department of Horticulture; and professor of horticulture (1956–65). For nineteen years he was chairman of the faculty buildings and grounds committee. He was also a member of the building committee; an elected member of the first advisory committee to then dean of administration, John W. Harrelson; a member of the first Consolidated University Advisory Council, representing North Carolina State College; and a member of the board of directors of the college's YMCA for fifteen years and chairman for twelve years. He was adviser to the Agriculture Club and the Horticulture Club as well as junior and senior adviser to the Agriculture Council.

Gardner organized the North Carolina Association of Nurserymen in 1936, the North Carolina Apple Growers Association in 1947, and the North Carolina Commercial Flower Growers Association in 1954. In 1937, he initiated the movement that resulted in the first direct appropriation for agricultural research ever made by the North Carolina General Assembly. He won the L. M. Ware Distinguished Teaching Award in 1961 and became a Fellow of the American Society for Horticultural Science in 1967. He belonged to Phi Kappa Phi (1963), Alpha Zeta, Pi Alpha Xi, and the Farm Fraternity. The M. E. Gardner Arboretum was named for him in 1972. In addition to numerous articles for trade journals, he wrote a weekly newspaper column, "Garden Time," for sixteen years and was editor of "Challenging Careers in Horticultural Science." He stated: "There is nothing glamorous about teaching as far as professional recognition is concerned, but there are deep and lasting satisfactions."

Gardner married Margaret W. Coleman of Danville, Va., who died in 1973; the couple had two sons: Charles Evans and Monroe Evans, Jr. He was buried in Montlawn Cemetery, Raleigh.

SEE: Monroe Evans Gardner, Jr., correspondence and telephone interview, March–April 1975, Raleigh; Monroe Evans Gardner Papers (Library, North Carolina State University, Raleigh); Raleigh *News and Observer*, 28 June 1965, 6 Feb. 1972, 30 Jan. 1975; Marguerite E. Schumann, *Strolling at State* (1973).

GRADY L. E. CARROLL

**Gardner, Oliver Maxwell (O. Max)** *(22 Mar. 1882–6 Feb. 1947)*, attorney and governor, was born in Shelby. His father, Dr. Oliver Perry Gardner, had two children by his first wife and ten by his second, Margaret Young. Max was the youngest of the twelve children. The father, a farmer, served as a Whig and Anti-Secessionist in the state legislature, fought in the Civil War, and then, having lost his property as a result of the war, made his livelihood in the hard life of a country medical doctor. Max's mother died in 1892 and his father seven years later, and he was brought up by his older sisters.

After attending local schools in Cleveland County, he entered North Carolina College of Agriculture and Mechanic Arts and received the bachelor of science degree in 1903. While in college he excelled in debating and athletics; he was captain of the football team and president of his class. Two years after his graduation he taught chemistry—his major in college—there while reading law in Raleigh with Richard J. Battle. Afterward he entered the law school of The University of North Carolina where he again played football. In 1931, the university gave him an honorary LL.D. Gardner passed the bar examinations in 1906, coached football that fall at Hampden-Sydney College, and then began to practice law in Shelby. On 6 Nov. 1907, he married Fay Webb, the daughter of James L. Webb, judge of the local superior court and the brother of Congressman E. Yates Webb. In the meantime, Gardner's sister, Bess, had married Clyde R. Hoey, local newspaper owner and lawyer, later governor and U.S. senator. These marriages created what came to be known as the "Shelby dynasty," sometimes called the Gardner machine, which succeeded the F. M. Simmons organization as the leading center of political power in the state. The Gardners had four children: Margaret Love (1908), James Webb (1910), Ralph Webb (1912), and O. Max, Jr. (1922).

Gardner became active in local politics in 1907. In the following year he supported the victorious campaign for prohibition, which he described as hopefully "the last great battle against the drink evil in our state." He was elected to the North Carolina Senate in 1910 and again in 1915, when he supported a statewide primary law; a year later he was elected lieutenant governor. In spite of his youth, Gardner became a leading candidate for governor in 1920. The Democratic primary was a three-cornered race between Gardner, Robert N. Page, and Cameron Morrison. Morrison had the advantage of being a longtime political friend of Senator F. M. Simmons. Gardner, however, hoped to rally the young men to his cause in an attempt, as he put it, to "smash the old boys." He did succeed in forcing Morrison into a runoff, but Morrison won easily in the second primary. Nevertheless, Gardner emerged from the campaign with an enhanced reputation, although he decided not to challenge Simmons's friend, Angus W. McLean, for governor in 1924, perhaps in accord with the tradition that governors should alternate between the eastern and western portions of the state. In any case, there seems to have been a tacit agreement with Simmons that Simmons would not oppose Gardner in 1928. In the meantime, while keeping his political irons in the fire, Gardner devoted himself to his family, teaching the men's Bible class at the First Baptist Church, practicing law, buying land, raising cotton, experimenting with rural electrification, and building up what was to become a multimillion dollar rayon mill, Cleveland Cloth Mills, at Shelby.

In 1928, although Gardner was nominated for governor without opposition, the party was divided over the nomination of Alfred E. Smith for president. Gardner disliked Smith's stand on prohibition, but, concluding that Smith as president could not repeal the Eighteenth Amendment, supported him with consummate caution in order not to jeopardize the state ticket. Gardner defeated his Republican opponent, but Smith, whom Simmons opposed, did not carry the state. In 1930, Josiah Bailey, with Gardner's support, defeated the seventy-six-year-old Simmons in the Democratic primary for U.S. senator. Now Gardner was clearly the leading political power in the state.

He began his term as governor hoping to promote "reorganization, retrenchment and consolidation." Despite the unforeseen complications of the depression, he carried forward a constructive program. He succeeded in pushing through an Australian ballot bill and a workman's compensation act. He achieved greater centralization in administration by making more officers appointive rather than elective, creating a permanent tax commission, shuffling and reorganizing state agencies, and consolidating The University of North Carolina, North Carolina State College, and the North Carolina College for Women. He gained state responsibility for maintaining roads and the public school system. Faced from the beginning with a perhaps unprecedented financial crisis, he cut state salaries, raised the gasoline tax, and, after a bitter fight, helped persuade the legislature to increase corporation taxes and impose a modest ad valorem tax on property. In an equally bitter fight, he succeeded in defeating the imposition of a sales tax. Throughout this critical period, his personal reputation was an important factor in maintaining the state's credit and in securing short-term loans to pay state employees.

As governor, he was compelled to deal with serious labor unrest. In 1929, it hit the textile towns of Gastonia and Marion. In Gastonia Communist labor organizers were involved. In both cases, violence erupted, people were killed, and local justice was found wanting. Gardner's actions during these crises, however, won national praise. He called out the National Guard and attempted to see that justice was done in the courts. He expressed a lack of sympathy for communism, but insisted that Communists had the right of protection under the law. He attacked doctrinaire employers, criticized long hours in textile plants, and stated that "we cannot build a prosperous citizenship on low wages."

In the presidential campaign of 1932, Garner supported Franklin D. Roosevelt, with whom he had become acquainted as a fellow governor, and during the 1930s North Carolina had considerable influence on the national government. In 1933, Gardner opened a law firm in Washington and was admitted to practice before the Supreme Court. A specialist in tax matters, he soon became an effective lobbyist for numerous organizations such as the Cotton Textile Institute, the Rayon Producers Group, and Coca-Cola. Generally he supported the New Deal and approved its legislation regarding hours, wages, working conditions, and collective bargaining. Roosevelt frequently called upon him for advice and for help in writing speeches, and Gardner occasionally carried out semiofficial chores such as negotiating the government's air mail contract. However, he opposed the plan for reconstituting the Supreme Court and was so disturbed by Roosevelt's attempts to defeat senators Walter George, Ellison D. Smith, and Millard Tydings in the primaries of 1938 that he quietly helped organize Senator George's campaign to retain his senatorial seat.

During the war years, Gardner's principal official contribution was as chairman of a twelve-member advisory board to the Office of War Mobilization and Reconversion. In this capacity he occasionally came into conflict with the office's director, James Byrnes. Under Gardner's leadership, the advisory board insisted upon the authority of the War Man Power Commission, rather than Selective Service, to supervise assigning draft-age men to civilian employment, urged Congress to work out an "equitable tax program," and in the summer of 1945 supported the continuation of the Office of Price Administration. In February 1946, President Harry S Truman appointed Gardner undersecretary of the Treasury. His post on the advisory board had been unsalaried, and he had accepted it with the understanding that he might continue his law practice. Now he resigned from the law firm and renounced any claim to "fees for legal services rendered" before assuming his responsibilities as undersecretary. He continued as chairman of the advisory board until the summer of 1947. Gardner was passed over when Vinson left the Treasury to become chief justice of the Supreme Court, and inexperienced John Snyder was appointed secretary. But Gardner remained loyally at his post. He worked hard to reorganize the Bureau of Internal Revenue and the Bureau of Customs, and developed a joint accounting system that was to coordinate the Treasury, the Budget Bureau, and the General Accounting Office.

On 3 Dec. 1946, Truman appointed Gardner ambassador to the Court of Saint James, perhaps because of his part in negotiating a British loan and his attempts to improve trade relationships with that country. Gardner's health had not been good for years. He had given up the thought of a senatorial campaign against Robert R. Reynolds in 1943, largely because of low blood pressure, gall bladder trouble, and chest pains. On 19 Oct. 1946 he suffered a heart attack, but rested only over the weekend. At 3:00 A.M. on 6 Feb. 1947, the morning that the Gardners were to sail for England, he was awakened by extreme chest pains, and at 8:25 A.M. he died of a coronary thrombosis. The funeral service was at the First Baptist Church, Shelby, and the burial in Sunset Cemetery.

Gardner was a handsome man, six feet two inches tall with broad shoulders and ruddy complexion; a fascinating storyteller; and fond of good food and drink. Although tactful and pragmatic, he was ready to stand on principle and to defend his position brilliantly and loudly. He established himself as North Carolina's most influential politician by an ability to make and retain friends, by shrewd appointments and an effective centralization program while governor, and by his strength and probity of character. He was a successful lawyer and businessman (he sold his principal mill in Shelby for more than $3 million in 1946); yet he fought for improved labor conditions, scientific agriculture, the elimination of tenant farming, and more equitable race relations. While in Washington, he was a popular and influential personality moving easily in the company of businessmen and bureaucrats, newspapermen, congressmen, and presidents. Withal he had the virtue of modesty, which made him uncomfortable, for example, when his favorite philanthropy, Boiling Springs Junior College, was renamed Gardner-Webb College.

SEE: David L. Corbitt, ed., *The Public Papers and Letters of Oliver Max Gardner, Governor of North Carolina, 1929–1933* (1937); O. Max Gardner, "One State Cleans House," *Saturday Evening Post* 204 (1 Jan. 1932); Joseph L. Morrison, *Governor O. Max Gardner* (1971); Papers of Josiah Bailey, Clyde Hoey, and F. M. Simmons (Manuscript Department, Library, Duke University, Durham); Elmer L. Puryear, *Democratic Party Dissension in North Carolina, 1928–1936* (1962); Records, Advisory Board of the Office of War Mobilization and Reconversion (National Archives, Washington, D.C.); Richard L. Watson, Jr., "Furnifold M. Simmons: 'Jehovah of the Tar Heels?' " *North Carolina Historical Review* 44 (1967); Edwin Yates Webb Papers (Southern Historical Collection, University of North Carolina, Chapel Hill).

RICHARD L. WATSON, JR.

**Garibaldi, Angelo** *(26 Jan. 1815–23 Oct. 1892)*, steamboat captain and shipbuilder, was born in Italy of unknown parentage. He is said to have come to Baltimore as a boy with an uncle. On the death of this relative, young Garibaldi was reared by one Maitland in that city. By 1849, he had settled in Plymouth, Washington County, N.C., and entered into a business relationship with James Cathcart Johnston of Hayes plantation in Chowan County. Johnston carefully preserved his business correspondence with Garibaldi. These letters and the personal papers of Angelo Garibaldi give an indication of his activities for the decade preceding the Civil War. With headquarters in Plymouth, he was in charge of the extensive shipping carried on in several steamboats and schooners owned by Johnston. In this capacity he made frequent trips to Norfolk, Charleston, and northern ports. Apparently familiar with steam navigation before coming to North Carolina, Garibaldi was sent north by Johnston in 1854 to purchase a steamboat. In that year Garibaldi supervised the construction of such a ship by Pusey and Company of Wilmington, Del. Johnston later acquired a second steamboat, the *Caledonia*, built by John Williams and Company of Baltimore and named after Johnston's vast Halifax County plantation. Garibaldi was part owner of this ship and for much of the time was her captain. The maintenance and repair of the *Caledonia* and other steamboats owned by Johnston, including one named the *Chieftan*, were under his direct supervision.

In 1855 Garibaldi wrote Johnston regarding the construction of a stone warehouse and wharfs in the town of Plymouth. By the eve of the Civil War he had undertaken the construction of a vessel for Johnston in Plymouth. When the town was taken by Federal forces, the boat was destroyed on the stocks. With the occupation of the coast of North Carolina, Johnston's shipping activities came to an end. One boat was seized at port in Baltimore when the war broke out, and at least one vessel was taken over by the Confederates. During the war, Garibaldi wrote Johnston that he had learned that the schooner *Howland*, one of the latter's ships, had died an honorable death in the defense of her country.

In a short time Garibaldi accumulated a respectable fortune. He may have had assets before moving to North Carolina. In the census of 1850, as "Angelo Garibaldi, mariner," he was living in Plymouth with real property valued at $900. In 1860 he was listed in the census as living on income with real property of $8,000 and personal property of $20,000. The larger amount no doubt represents in large part Garibaldi's share in the Johnston steamboats.

On 18 Jan. 1852 William B. Hathaway, overseer for Johnston on his Caledonia plantation, resigned his position and wrote his employer that he had hired Henry J. Futrell to take his place at a salary of $100 a year. Although Hathaway and Johnston had not gotten on well, Futrell soon enjoyed Johnston's confidence and was eventually one of the men who inherited his large landed estate. In the course of plying the Roanoke between Caledonia and Plymouth, Garibaldi and Futrell became friends, and after the Federal occupation of Plymouth Garibaldi refugeed in Halifax County. Futrell's wife, Caroline, was the daughter of Henry Hancock of Halifax County. Her sister Nancy married one Gay and was left a widow with an only child, Indiana Virginia. The daughter Ivy, so called from her initials, married a young farmer, Alexander Lewis, from the Crowells section of Halifax County who died very shortly after their marriage. In 1866 the young widow, in her twenties, married the fifty-three-year old Garibaldi who thus became connected with Futrell by marriage. In his 1863 will, which was probated in 1867,

Johnston devised his holdings in Northampton and Halifax counties to Futrell. Shortly before his death, however, Johnston orally before witnesses deeded 900 acres of the Caledonia tract in Halifax County to Garibaldi. To gain title to this land and for other debts owed him by Johnston's estate, Garibaldi brought suit against Futrell. The suit appears to have been friendly, for, when Futrell died during the litigation, Garibaldi was named executor of his estate and guardian of his children.

Garibaldi eventually settled on a farm near Crowells that his wife seems to have inherited from her first husband. Here he operated a gristmill, gin, and general store and acted as a cotton broker. He was moderately successful for the times but hardly on the scale of his success in Plymouth before the war. During this period he acquired a tract of land in Rutherford County in the North Carolina mountains. Although he was referred to as "Captain" until the end of his life, there is no indication that he piloted steamboats on the Roanoke after he moved to Halifax County. They continued to operate on the river for several decades after his death. He and his wife, who survived him for many years, had no children. He was buried under an elaborate monument in Old Trinity Cemetery in Scotland Neck. Garibaldi was described as having a strong, robust constitution and as one who enjoyed the affection and esteem of his neighbors.

SEE: Wills, Deeds, and Marriage Bonds (North Carolina State Archives, Raleigh); Hayes Collection (Southern Historical Collection, University of North Carolina, Chapel Hill); Stuart Hall Smith and Claiborne T. Smith, Jr., *History of Trinity Parish* (1955); George Stevenson, Summary of Personal Papers of Angelo Garibaldi in possession of a descendant of Mrs. Garibaldi (North Carolina State Archives, Raleigh); U.S. Census, 1850, 1860, Washington County (North Carolina State Archives, Raleigh); Weldon, *Roanoke News*, 27 Oct. 1892.

CLAIBORNE T. SMITH, JR.

**Garinger, Elmer Henry** *(13 July 1891–21 Aug. 1982)*, educator, school administrator, and state legislator, was born in Mount Vernon, Mo., the oldest of four children of John A. and Julia Catherine Moore Garinger. His father was a farmer whose grandfather had moved to Missouri from Greensboro, N.C., in 1845. Upon his graduation from the University of Missouri in 1916, Elmer Garinger planned a business career. But, refusing a fellowship in economics at Cornell University, he became instead a teacher and high school principal in Mount Vernon. During World War I he was a sergeant in the Tenth Division Medical Corps, U.S. Army. In 1921 he earned the M.A. degree at Teachers College, Columbia University. That fall he went to Charlotte, N.C., to be principal of Alexander Graham High School and to help set up a new senior high school as well as the first junior high school in North Carolina, Alexander Graham. He then became principal of the new Central High School when it opened in 1923.

Garinger quickly built a reputation as a leader and innovator. The results of a statewide testing program he developed in the early 1920s helped persuade the North Carolina legislature to add the twelfth grade to the state curriculum. In his dissertation, *The Administration of Discipline in the High School*, published by Columbia University in 1936, the year he received the Ph.D. degree, Garinger concluded that the best way to prevent misbehavior was to keep students busy. Accordingly, he developed a varied curriculum and activities, encouraged team teaching, and established a guidance program. He also was instrumental in getting libraries in the schools.

In 1945 Garinger became associate superintendent of the Charlotte schools and in 1949, superintendent. When the Charlotte and Mecklenburg County schools were consolidated in 1960, he was named superintendent of the new system. Under his leadership, many new programs were developed, such as industrial education, language laboratories, advanced placement courses, the teaching of foreign languages in the elementary schools, and the use of social workers. In 1946, Garinger initiated the first pupil accident insurance plan in the United States. It was because of his contacts at Columbia that the Ford Foundation offered the Charlotte schools a grant to introduce television in the classroom. Garinger used the money to bring educational television to schools throughout North Carolina as well as in Charlotte. His interest in innovations in school architecture led him to recommend in 1926 that the Charlotte school board hire his former adviser at Columbia, Dr. N. L. Engelhardt, as a consultant. Engelhardt's firm brought to Charlotte many new ideas in school planning.

In 1945, when existing colleges did not have room for the veterans returning from World War II, the state supervisor of high schools asked Garinger to assist in developing a community college system. Garinger persuaded the Charlotte school board to allow evening classes to be held at Central High School under the supervision of the extension division of The University of North Carolina. The resulting Charlotte College Center became a community junior college in 1949.

Immediately after retiring as superintendent in 1962, Garinger was elected to the North Carolina House of Representatives. He led the Democratic ticket in Mecklenburg County in 1962 and 1964. In the legislature, Garinger worked for larger appropriations for higher education. He was dubbed a "liberal" because he advocated reapportioning the legislature to conform to population changes, opposed the 1963 law banning "known Communists" from speaking on state-owned campuses, and criticized secret hearings held by the Joint Appropriations Subcommittee in 1965. He sought but did not receive the Democratic nomination to the North Carolina Senate in 1966.

One of Garinger's two aims was achieved when Charlotte College became a branch of The University of North Carolina in 1965. A portrait of Garinger hangs in the building named for him on that campus. His second goal, improved retirement benefits for state employees, was achieved with passage of the bill he drew up to reform the state retirement program. In 1976 he was a member of the legislative committee of the North Carolina Retired Governmental Employees Association, Inc. In May 1963 Garinger was appointed to the board of the newly established Governor's School for Gifted High School Students at Winston-Salem. He served as chairman from 1966 to 1973, when he retired from the board.

In addition to his dissertation, Garinger's publications include two chapters in N. William Newson and R. Emerson Langfitt, eds., *Administrative Practices in Large High Schools* (1940), and several articles and papers. Between 1921 and 1967 he was visiting professor of education at George Peabody College, the universities of North Carolina and Missouri, Clark University, Appalachian State University, and Queens College. In 1957 he was a member of the American Assembly and participated in an institute at Harvard on teaching about communism. Garinger was a director of the National Education Association, of the North Carolina Education Association, and of several other professional associations. The American Association of School Administrators, the Charlotte branches of the Association for Childhood Education, and the Charlotte Rotary Club all gave him distinguished service awards in 1962. He was a fellow of the American Association for the Advancement of Science and a member of Phi Delta Kappa and Omicron Delta Kappa. He received the City of Charlotte Citizenship Award in 1962 for his service as a director of the Charlotte Rehabilitation Hospital and the Charlotte-Mecklenburg Public Library, as secretary of the Mecklenburg Community College System, and as a member of the Juvenile Court Advisory Committee.

In 1963 Garinger was elected a director of the Bank of Charlotte. He became a vice-president in 1969 and worked for a year on ways to develop new business. His wife, the former Katherine Thomas, who had also taught in Mount Vernon, died in 1968. The couple had no children. He died in Charlotte where funeral services were held at Myers Park United Methodist Church.

SEE: Jaques Cattell and E. E. Ross, eds., *Leaders in Education* (1948); *Charlotte News*, 29 June 1963, 26 May 1965; *Charlotte Observer*, 7 Sept. 1959, 20 Feb., 27 Apr., 5 June 1962, 8 Feb., 20 Feb., 12 Mar., 29 June, 1 July 1963, 31 Mar., 3 June 1965; 11 Jan., 10 Mar. 1966, 21 Mar 1968, 20 Apr. 1969, 13 Jan. 1973, 20 July 1975; *Dictionary of International Biography* (1970); H. P. Harding, "History of the Charlotte City Schools" ([typescript] Curriculum Library, Charlotte-Mecklenburg Education Center); Raleigh *News and Observer*, 23 Aug. 1982; Transcript of taped interview with Garinger by LeGette Blythe (Oral History Collection, University of North Carolina, Charlotte); *Who's Who in American Education* (1942); *Who's Who in Methodism* (1952); *Who's Who in the South and Southwest* (1954, 1959).

LAURA PAGE FRECH

**Garrett, Paul** *(3 Nov. 1863–18 Mar. 1940)*, wine producer, was born in Edgecombe County, the son of Dr. Francis Marion Garrett, a Confederate surgeon, and Della Elizabeth Williams Garrett. His twin brother, Phillip, died at the age of six months. Paul was educated in a small local school and for a brief time attended the Bingham School at Mebane. At age fourteen he began a seven-year apprenticeship under his uncle, Charles Garrett, as an "agriculturist" and in the wine business. In 1865 Charles and his brother, Dr. F. M. Garrett, purchased Sidney Weller's commercial winery, Medoc Vineyard, in Halifax County. Here Paul learned the business, doing almost everything that was necessary in its operation. He then became the buyer of grapes around the state and elsewhere as well as a salesman. After the death of Charles Garrett the business passed into other hands, but Paul continued as a commission salesman under a contract. His sales were so great and his commission so large that the new owners wanted to break the contract. When they refused to ship wine to fill his orders, young Garrett established his own winery at Littleton and afterwards near Weldon, operating under the name Garrett & Company.

As a salesman Garrett had ranged as far away as Arkansas and Texas, and he built upon contacts already made. He rapidly developed a national trade, distributing wine made largely from the native scuppernong but blended with grapes from New York and California. Soon after the opening of the twentieth century he had wineries and vineyards at many places in the state including Aberdeen, Plymouth, and Roanoke Island. Anticipating prohibition in North Carolina, he moved a portion of his operation to Virginia and a few years later to New York. He established vineyards and wineries at several places in the Finger Lakes District as well as in southern California. By the time of national prohibition in 1919 Garrett was a billionaire but he had no idea of retiring. Although not all of his ventures were profitable, he undertook several new projects. For a number of years he had marketed both red and white wines under the trade name of "Virginia Dare," and used Confederate battle flags in his trademark. He now distributed a dealcoholized Virginia Dare "wine" to which consumers might add their own alcohol. He also added a cola-type grape flavored drink to his list of products. His most nearly successful undertaking, however, was the production and marketing of a superb grape syrup, under the name Vine-Glo, with which purchasers could make their own wine. The dry forces concluded that this was taking matters a bit too far and the production of Vine-Glo was prohibited. During this period Garrett continued to make and distribute wine for sacramental purposes, one of the few legal uses permitted. An Episcopalian, he generously gave wine for the use of the church. With the repeal of prohibition, he was ready to tap the market and soon the Virginia Dare brand was available in every wet state. He pioneered the singing commercial for wines: "Say it again . . . Virginia Dare."

Garrett did much to publicize the use of wine and its history. He spoke and wrote on the subject and contributed an especially significant article to the *New York Times* of 8 Dec. 1935. Often referred to as "dean of American wine-makers," he was widely known around the country.

As a young man in North Carolina, Garrett married Sadie Walton Harrison, a neighbor, but she died soon afterwards of influenza. About this time he moved to Weldon and there he married Evelyn Edwards. Three of their four sons died very young and the fourth, Charles, died at the age of sixteen. Three daughters, Evelyn Garrett, Mrs. Howard Paulson, and Mrs. Douglas B. Weed, survived him. He was buried at the Episcopal chapel at Bluff Point, N.Y., overlooking Keuka Lake, which he built as a memorial to his son, Charles.

SEE: Leon D. Adams, *The Wines of America* (1973); Paul Garrett Reminiscences (Duke University Library, Durham); Clarence Gohdes, Durham, correspondence with the author; *New York Times*, 4 Nov. 1935, 8 Dec. 1935, 20 Mar. 1940; Raleigh *News and Observer*, 21 Mar. 1940.

WILLIAM S. POWELL

**Garrett, Thomas Miles** *(13 June 1830–12 May 1864)*, attorney and Confederate officer, was one of three children of Jesse Garrett and his wife, Cynthia Rayner. His father died relatively young and his mother married Wiley Hayes, by whom she had two children. Garrett was reared near Colerain in Bertie County and prepared for college by John Kimberly at Buckhorn Academy, Como, in neighboring Hertford County. In 1848, Garrett entered The University of North Carolina where he soon made a name for himself. He joined the Philanthropic Society the same year and eventually finished second in scholarship and deportment. From June 1849 to November 1850 Garrett kept an interesting diary, which is now in the Southern Historical Collection at Chapel Hill. He was graduated with the A.B. degree in 1851.

Afterwards, Garrett became an attorney and established a practice at Murfreesboro. In 1854, he was involved in a highly controversial case. A Hertford County committee for the Know-Nothing party sued one of its members for $10,000 after he became disenchanted with the organization and printed a violent denunciation of it in the *Murfreesboro Gazette*. Garrett was one of four attorneys engaged to represent the defendant. The political committee lost the case and Garrett's client was awarded a token payment of a few dollars.

Early in the Civil War Garrett enlisted in the Confederate Army and on 16 May 1861 was appointed captain of Company F, which became part of the Fifth Regiment of North Carolina State Troops. He soon ran into trouble, for on 23 December he was arrested and accused of submitting false reports of those absent without leave. At the same time, it was charged that he had established headquarters in a house intended for the regimental commander and then had disregarded orders from his superior to vacate the residence. Garrett was detained until 7 Mar. 1862 and not formally cleared of charges until 9 December. However, he had rejoined his company in time to take part in the Battle of Williamsburg on 5 May 1862, when he was wounded in the arm and captured by the Union forces. He was treated first at Fort Monroe, Va., and later transferred to Fort Delaware, Del. After his release in August, he returned home to recuperate until September. He next saw action in the Battle of Sharpsburg on 17 Sept. 1862, when he was slightly wounded in the foot.

Garrett, who had been active in Whig politics, was elected to the state senate from Bertie County while a prisoner of war. However, finding that the demands of a legislative seat conflicted with his duties as an officer, he resigned in a letter to Governor Zebulon B. Vance on 20 Oct. 1862. Upon his return to duty, he became embroiled in a dispute with Captain Peter J. Sinclair, his rival for the post of colonel of the Fifth Regiment. Earlier, Garrett had been passed over for promotion to major. In a letter of 1 Sept. 1862 to Governor Vance, he complained that he was being discriminated against because of his former Whig affiliations. The officers of the regiment clearly favored Garrett. Consequently, Vance appointed Garrett commander and Sinclair resigned.

Governor Vance's choice was vindicated as Garrett proved to be an excellent commander. He was wounded in the leg at Chancellorsville on 2 May 1863 and did not rejoin the regiment until late July or early August. Colonel Garrett was cited for bravery and recommended for promotion to brigadier general by General Robert E. Rodes, but no action was taken. Again Garrett was ignored when General Alfred Iverson was relieved of his command after mismanagement of his brigade at Gettysburg. Instead, Colonel Robert D. Johnston of the Twenty-third North Carolina Regiment was made brigadier general. This state of affairs prompted Governor Vance to charge in a letter of 9 Mar. 1864 to President Jefferson Davis that, because of their pro-Union stand at the opening of the war, Garrett and other deserving men were being passed over in favor of avowed Secessionists. Davis denied that he had been influenced by political considerations in promoting officers.

Garrett's history of discrimination doubtlessly caused him to remark on the eve of the Battle of Spotsylvania Court House that he would "come out of the fight a brigadier-general or a dead colonel." He was killed in battle on 12 May at the "Mule Shoe" during the Battle of Spotsylvania. The next day, Garrett's commander received a dispatch from Richmond promoting him to brigadier general. Nevertheless, he had died a colonel. He was unmarried.

SEE: Walter Clark, ed., *History of the Several Regiments and Battalions from North Carolina in the Great War, 1861–'65*, vols. 1, 2, and 5 (1901); Daniel L. Grant, *Alumni History of the University of North Carolina* (1924); John W. Moore, *History of North Carolina from the Earliest Discoveries to the Present Time* (1880).

JAMES ELLIOTT MOORE

**Garrison, Sidney Clarence** *(17 Oct. 1887–18 Jan. 1945)*, psychologist, graduate dean, and college president, was born in Lincolnton, the son of Rufus J. and Susie Elizabeth Mooney Garrison. After attending Salem School in Lincolnton and South Fork Institute in Marion, he enrolled in Wake Forest College. He was graduated with a bachelor of arts degree in 1911 and received a master of arts in 1913.

Garrison's earliest professional experience was gained in the public schools. From 1911 to 1913 he taught in Crouse, a small town in Lincoln County, and then became the county superintendent of education, a position he filled until 1914. At some point in his studies or teaching, Garrison became interested in educational psychology, and this undoubtedly led him to George Peabody College for Teachers in Tennessee. The decision was a logical one. Under its new and vigorous president, Bruce R. Payne, Peabody moved from its campus in South Nashville to a site in the western part of the city directly across from Vanderbilt University, where it developed a teacher training program that was rapidly gaining recognition in the fields of education and psychology. An additional attraction was the availability of certain courses offered by the Vanderbilt University Medical School, an opportunity of which Garrison took advantage. In 1916 he was awarded the master of arts degree by Peabody College, then continued his studies until they were interrupted by military service during World War I.

In the army Garrison rose to the rank of captain. For a time he was assigned to Washington's Walter Reed Hospital as personnel adjutant; he later worked with a psychological unit in developing the Alpha Intelligence Test. After the war he returned to Peabody to complete his work for a Ph.D. in psychology, which was conferred in 1919. The same year he was appointed to the institution's faculty. Garrison would remain with Peabody until his death. In 1933 he was named dean of the Graduate School, a position he held until 1936, when he was appointed acting president after President Payne's death. The following year the board of trustees elected him the fifth president of the college.

Though Garrison did not publish extensively, he was a sound scholar and respected by his fellow psychologists. His best-known books were *Psychology of Elementary School Subjects* (1929) and *Fundamentals of Psychology in Secondary Education* (1936), both with his brother, Karl C. Garrison, as coauthor. He also was a contributor to various scholarly journals.

His years as a college president were marked by closer cooperation between Peabody and Vanderbilt and the beginning of what is now referred to as a university center. The development of a cooperative library program involving Peabody, Vanderbilt, and Scarritt College and the construction of the Joint University Library received his full support. On his own campus Garrison was able to expand several departments, notably music, home economics, and business education; at the time of his death he was deeply involved in planning for the school's postwar years.

Garrison was a tall, red-headed man who walked erectly and with a vigorous stride. In spite of the strain of a presidency that spanned a period of financial depression followed by war, he found time for community service in Nashville. He was active in the Nashville Area Council of the Boy Scouts of America, a member of the Chamber of Commerce, a Rotarian, a member of the board of the Nashville Trust Company and of the Guaranty Trust Company, an officer in the First Baptist Church, and a member of the Baptist Sunday School Board. The educational world also made claims upon his services, and in turn honored him. He was a member of the Tennessee State Board of Education and a trustee of several colleges, among them Meharry Medical College. He received honorary degrees from Wake Forest and Southwestern-at-Memphis, and he was a fellow of the American Association for the Advancement of Science.

Garrison died suddenly of a heart attack. He was survived by his wife, Sara Elizabeth McMurry Garrison, whom he had married in 1919, and their five children, S. C., Jr., Lucy Fuqua Garrison Crabb, William Louis, Frank McMurry, and Rufus James. Funeral services were held in the Social-Religious Building on the Peabody College campus and burial was in Mount Olivet Cemetery, Nashville.

SEE: *Nashville Banner*, 18, 19 Jan. 1945; *Nashville Tennessean*, 19 Jan. 1945; *New York Times*, 19 Jan. 1945; *The Peabody Reflector and Alumni News*, June 1936, January 1945; *Who's Who in America*, 1944–45.

J. ISAAC COPELAND

**Garrott, Isham Warren** *(1816–17 June 1863)*, lawyer and Confederate soldier, was born in Wake County, the son of Isham Garrott, one of eleven sons of Thomas Garrott, and Mary Sims Garrott. The family lived for a time in Anson County, but then young Garrott apparently returned to Wake County from which he attended The University of North Carolina during the years 1837–40. After studying law there, he was admitted to the bar. Garrott's parents were not wealthy so he had to make his own way in the world. He moved first to Greenville, Ala., and in the following year to Marion, Perry County, where he formed a law partnership with James Phelan, who was afterward a Confederate senator from Mississippi. Garrott soon became interested in public affairs and in 1845–49 represented Perry County in the Alabama legislature. Later he practiced law with Judge William M. Brooks. In the presidential election of 1860, Garrott served as a Breckinridge elector. When Alabama joined the Confederacy in 1861, he was sent as a commissioner to his native state by Governor Andrew B. Moore to seek the cooperation of the North Carolina General Assembly in the movement for secession. Upon returning to Alabama, Garrott, with the assistance of E. W. Pettus, raised the Twentieth Alabama Regiment, which was organized at Montgomery on 16 Sept. 1861 with Garrott as its colonel.

The Twentieth Alabama saw service in the Civil War first as part of General J. M. Wither's army in the defense of Mobile, Ala., where it spent the fall and winter of 1861. In February 1862, the regiment was sent to Knoxville, Tenn., to join General E. Kirby Smith's army in the Department of Eastern Tennessee. During the great Kentucky campaign in the fall of 1862, Garrott and his men served in General Edward D. Tracy's brigade of Smith's army. That December Tracy's brigade accompanied the division of General Carter L. Stevenson to Mississippi to reinforce General John C. Pemberton's army at Vicksburg against Union forces under General Ulysses S. Grant. Here Garrott and his regiment passed the winter. When Grant began his famous campaign to envelop the rear of Vicksburg at the end of April 1863, Tracy's brigade was ordered to reinforce General John S. Bowen's command at Port Gibson, Miss., which was contesting Grant's advance. After a grueling forty-four-mile forced march from Vicksburg, the brigade joined Bowen's division and took part in the Battle of Port Gibson on 1 May. In this first engagement of the Twentieth Alabama Regiment, Garrott showed great skill in directing his men under fire. Tracy's brigade, which formed the right flank of Bowen's line, came under heavy attack from overwhelming Union forces and General Tracy was killed early in the fighting. As senior colonel, Garrott assumed command of the brigade and served with distinction for the rest of the engagement. The Union forces outnumbered Bowen's command about three to one and at nightfall the general was forced to retire from the field. During the day's fighting, the Twentieth Alabama had suffered dire losses—a total of 272 men killed, wounded, and missing. Garrott later returned to lead the regiment when General Stephen D. Lee assumed command of Tracy's brigade.

On 16 May 1863, Garrott and his men took part in the Battle of Champion Hill, east of Vicksburg, where the colonel again proved to be a skilled and efficient commander in battle. He then led his men in the siege of Vicksburg, which began two days later. During the siege, Garrott frequently appeared along his lines and at his outposts to speak with and encourage his men. On 17 June he made such a visit to one of his outposts. Seeing an opportunity to take a shot at the enemy, he asked to borrow the rifle of one of his men. As Garrott was taking aim, he was shot through the heart by a Union sharpshooter. Unfortunately, though he had been promoted to brigadier general on 29 May (to rank from 28 May), his commission, which had been forwarded from Richmond, failed to reach him before his untimely death cut short a promising military career. Beloved by his men, Garrott was buried at Vicksburg. He has been described as persistent and energetic, and an untiring worker.

Garrott was a Whig and a Baptist. He married Margaret Matilda Fletcher, daughter of Dr. and Mrs. Emiline Moore Fletcher. They had seven children: William Burrell, Mary Sims, Sims Burrell, Emma (died young), John Fletcher (m. Floria Bute), Thomas Ritchie (m. Nannie Collier and later Alice Rushing), and Julia (died in childhood).

SEE: W. Brewer, *Alabama: Her History, Resources, War Record and Public Men* (1872); Clement A. Evans, *Confederate Military History*, vol. 8 (1899); Daniel L. Grant, *Alumni History of the University of North Carolina* (1924); Thomas M. Owen, *History of Alabama and Dictionary of Alabama Biography*, vol. 3 (1921); *War of the Rebellion: The Official Records of the Union and Confederate Armies*, vols. 1, 2, and 4 (1880–1882); Ezra Warner, *Generals in Gray* (1959); Marcus J. Wright, *General Officers of the Confederate Army* (1911).

PAUL BRANCH

**Garvey, Patrick** *(d. 1810)*, merchant and physician, first came to public notice in Philadelphia in 1780. In the course of a heated and extended controversy involving charges against Dr. William Shippen, director general of the Army Medical Service, for his so-called misuse of funds, Garvey emerged as one of Shippen's critics. As an accountant employed by Dr. Andrew Craigie, apothecary general of the Continental Army, Garvey declared that he had been urged by Shippen to alter the books to cover certain neglects by the director general. During the controversy, Garvey was jailed briefly on suspicion of illegally trading with the British Army. By 1782 he had been released.

In 1783 Garvey, who supported himself as a merchant but claimed to be a physician, moved to Winton, N.C. Here he was publicly active for several years as a merchant, physician, and promoter of various enterprises. He gained some further notoriety in 1786, when he composed and circulated a satirical manuscript lampooning various prominent figures in eastern North Carolina. Described by an acquaintance as a "bold, loquacious Irishman," Garvey became an ardent Federalist in the struggle over adoption of the new federal Constitution in 1787 and 1788. In the spring of 1788, as the election for the North Carolina constitutional convention approached, Garvey became embroiled in the contest in Hertford County and in a confrontation with anti-Federalist leader, the Reverend Lemuel Burkitt. Chased by anti-Federalists from a church where Burkitt was delivering a harangue against the new constitution, Garvey and Elkanah Watson, another dedicated Federalist, drew a cartoon of Burkitt and posted it at the courthouse door in Winton on the morning of the election. The incident touched off a riot, but Burkitt was elected and that summer cast his vote with the anti-Federalist majority.

In 1789, Garvey moved to the newly created village of Murfreesboro, also in Hertford County, and became a partner in a rum and whiskey distillery. He was an active Mason, a justice of the peace, and a leading citizen of Murfreesboro until his removal to Jonesborough, Camden County, around 1799. There he was postmaster for some time before his death.

SEE: T. C. Parramore, "Doctor Patrick Garvey," *North Carolina Medical Journal* 29 (1968).

T. C. PARRAMORE

**Gary, Emily Gregory Gilliam** *(12 Dec. 1867–11 Oct. 1962)*, moving force behind the development and preservation of historic buildings and sites in colonial Halifax, N.C., was the daughter of George and Marie Antoinette Mullen Gilliam and a native of Hertford, Perquimans County. "Miss Emily," as she was affectionately known in her later years, moved to Halifax when she was five. A school teacher for nineteen years, she was active in the work of St. Mark's Episcopal Church in Halifax, the Halifax Home Demonstration Club, the United Daughters of the Confederacy, the Halifax Garden Club, and the Parent-Teacher Association. She was granted life membership in the National PTA Congress. In 1901 she married Frederick Sterling Marshall Gary, who served for forty years as clerk of the court in Halifax.

Mrs. Gary early realized that many of the historic buildings in Halifax, dating from the period when the town was one of North Carolina's cultural centers, were being sadly neglected and allowed to fall into ruin. She felt that the state and nation should devote greater emphasis to the significance of the Halifax Resolves, adopted 12 Apr. 1776, the first action by any of the colonies calling for independence from Great Britain. Tirelessly devoting her energies to the preservation of the rich history of Halifax, she sought financial aid from the Ford Foundation and the Firestone family in hopes that they would adopt Halifax as the Rockefeller Foundation had done with colonial Williamsburg in nearby Virginia. In the mid-1950s, Mrs. Gary gained the enthusiastic support of the Halifax County Board of Commissioners in purchasing the old gaol in Halifax, which at the time was scheduled to be sold and possibly demolished. Later, assisted by Mrs. R. L. Applewhite and other ladies in Halifax, she served as a volunteer hostess on Sunday afternoons at the Halifax Museum established at the gaol.

Largely through Mrs. Gary's efforts, the Halifax Historical Restoration Association was established and for many years she served as its efficient and dedicated secretary. She was also instrumental in having the old clerk of court's office building converted into the Halifax County library. Her own residence, formerly the Eagle Tavern, was eventually moved to the Halifax historic site area for restoration.

After her death at age ninety-five, Mrs. Gary was buried in the local Episcopal cemetery.

SEE: William S. Powell, ed., *North Carolina Lives* (1962); Raleigh *News and Observer*, 12 Oct. 1962; Records of the Halifax Historical Restoration Association (Halifax); *Roanoke Rapids Herald*, 11 May 1958.

RALPH HARDEE RIVES

**Garzia, John** *(ca. 1700–29 Nov. 1744)*, Anglican clergyman, is thought to have been a native of Spain. Some time before 1723 he was in charge of a Roman Catholic parish, presumably in England. By that year he had become an Anglican and was referred to as a protégé of one Dean Norcourt. By order of the bishop of London, the Reverend Mr. Garzia received the King's Bounty for transportation to the Bahamas on 9 Aug. 1723. Soon afterward, at Gravesend, he boarded the *Hanover*, a ship under charter to Mrs. George Phenney, wife of the governor of the Bahama Islands. However, Garzia left the ship at Cork after being charged with the theft of a chalice from a Roman Catholic church where he had formerly officiated. When he disembarked, he also took a box of books the bishop of London had donated for a library at Harbor Island in the Bahamas.

Garzia seems to have resolved his difficulties in Cork, for a few months later—on 8 Apr. 1724—he again received the King's Bounty, this time for Virginia. After Garzia's arrival in that colony, Commissary James Blair wrote the bishop of London from Williamsburg on 17 July 1724 that Garzia had been sent to Lower Norfolk and that he, Blair, feared that his imperfect English might antagonize some. Garzia did not remain long in Lower Norfolk, as he served North Farnham Parish in Richmond County on the Rappahannock from 1725 to 1732. He then moved to North Carolina. Commissary Blair and Governor William Gooch both gave him a certificate of good character, dated 17 Mar. 1733, when he left Virginia. The available records in Virginia reveal little of his life there. Some years later, he petitioned the Society for the Propagation of the Gospel to pay him the allowance promised for instructing Negroes in Virginia according to directions from the Reverend Thomas Bray.

On arriving in North Carolina in 1733, Garzia became

rector of St. Thomas Parish, Beaufort County. The following year, construction was begun on the parish church in the town of Bath. This building, St. Thomas Church, is the oldest standing church in North Carolina and one of the oldest in the United States. On 8 May 1735 the rector wrote the bishop of London asking him to secure a gift of Bibles and church furnishings. Earlier, when the colonial Assembly met in Bath on 11 Feb. 1735, Garzia was voted £20 for performing divine service and preaching a sermon before the governor, council, and Assembly on the previous Sunday.

In the beginning, Garzia was engaged by the vestry of St. Thomas Church, which later had difficulty paying his salary. On 10 Oct. 1734, the vestry petitioned the Society for the Propagation of the Gospel in London that Garzia, who was then serving as its rector, be appointed a missionary of the society. At this time the organization maintained only two missionaries in the province. On the death of the Reverend John Boyd in 1739, Garzia was appointed missionary for that part of North Carolina north and east of the Neuse River. Apparently, fifteen years in North America had not improved the clergyman's command of the English language, for the Reverend George Whitefield, one of the founders of Methodism, on meeting Garzia in Bath in 1739 commented that he could scarcely be understood.

Garzia died from a fall from a horse while visiting the sick, leaving a widow, Mary, and three small children. On 9 July 1748 the Reverend Clement Hall, another society missionary, reported to London that "the widow Garzia" was in low circumstances because creditors had sold all her land and houses. The society accordingly awarded her a small pension. Still in the possession of St. Thomas Church is a silver chalice, 9⅜ inches high, which is thought to date from 1700. It is inscribed, "D. D. Johannes Garzia, Ecclesiae Aglicanae Presbyter," and may have some bearing on the chalice that figured earlier in Garzia's career.

SEE: Marshall D. Haywood, *The Lives of the Bishops of North Carolina* (1910); E. Alfred Jones, *The Old Silver of American Churches* (1913); William W. Manross, *Fulham Papers in the Lambeth Palace Library* (1965), and *S. P. G. Papers in the Lambeth Palace Library* (1974); William L. Saunders, ed., *Colonial Records of North Carolina*, vol. 4 (1890).

CLAIBORNE T. SMITH, JR.

**Gaston, Alexander** *(ca. 1735–20 Aug. 1781)*, patriot, was the fifth son of William Gaston of County Antrim, Ireland. The Gastons were Huguenots, having fled from France to Scotland in the seventeenth century and thence to northern Ireland. Two of the sons of William of Clough Water, County Antrim, were educated at Glasgow University; Alexander was preceded there by his brother Hugh, who became a distinguished Presbyterian clergyman. According to early sources, Alexander studied medicine at the University of Edinburgh, but his name does not appear in the catalogues from that institution and his university training was doubtless completed at Glasgow. He joined the British navy as a ship's surgeon and was present with the fleet in 1762, when Havana was taken by the British in the Seven Years War. An epidemic of dysentery broke out in the fleet and Dr. Gaston was stricken while attending the sick. His health was so seriously undermined that he determined to seek the salubrious air of America for recovery. By May 1764 he had settled in New Bern, the largest town in the colony of North Carolina, and soon became a leading citizen, purchasing 2,000 acres of land in the Trent River area two miles from the town.

In May 1775 he married Margaret Sharpe, a native of Cumberland County, England, who was visiting her two brothers in New Bern where they were engaged in the mercantile business. Margaret was a devout Roman Catholic and had been educated in a convent in Calais, France. It is possible that her husband had become an Episcopalian, though reared a Presbyterian, because in 1765 he signed a petition asking that the academy in New Bern be encouraged to promote the education of youth "and imprint on their tender minds the principles of the Christian religion agreeable to the establishment of the Church of England."

From the beginning of the Revolutionary War, Gaston espoused the cause of American liberty. On 23 June 1775 he was one of the band of patriots, including Richard Cogdell and Abner Nash, who seized six pieces of artillery in front of the Governor's Palace in New Bern soon after the flight of Josiah Martin, the last of the royal governors of the province. On 9 August he was appointed a member of the Committee of Safety for the District of New Bern by the Provincial Congress at Hillsborough. He was later captain of a company of volunteers who operated against the forces of Sir Henry Clinton when that officer threatened Wilmington. Gaston was also distinguished for his services in civil affairs. In December 1776 he was elected a justice of the court of pleas and quarter sessions for Craven County, and in May 1777 he was elevated to judge of the Court of Oyer and Terminer for the District of New Bern.

His wife, a woman of great dignity, superior education, and decided loyalties, was as ardent a patriot as he. A chapter is devoted to her contributions in Elizabeth F. Ellet's *The Women of the American Revolution* (vol. 2, 1852). Three children were born to the Gastons in New Bern. The oldest, a son, died in infancy. The younger son, William Joseph, became North Carolina's eminent jurist. Their daughter, Jane, became the second wife of John Louis Taylor, chief justice of the supreme court of North Carolina.

Naturally, Gaston was much hated by the local Tories, of which there seemed to have been a considerable number in and around New Bern. In August 1781 a raid was made on New Bern by Major James H. Craig, commandant at Wilmington, with his force of regulars and Tories. The martyrdom of Gaston as a result of this raid is nowhere better told than in the words of his son, Judge William Gaston. "The circumstances of his death," he wrote, "I have so often heard from my weeping mother that I can never forget them. An ineffectual attempt to check the march of Major Craig's detachment from Wilmington had been made, and no idea was entertained of further resistence to its entry into New Bern. Dr. Gaston was one of those who were peculiarly obnoxious to the Tories, and it was deemed advisable for all such to keep out of the way of their ferocity. He had retired to his plantation on the South side of Trent, but misled by some information respecting the movements of the detachment, he returned to town on Saturday, and stayed with his family until after breakfast on the next day. Rumors of the approach of the Tories, joined with the entreaties of Mrs. Gaston induced him then to revisit his plantation. He had quitted his house (which stood on the spot where the Bank of New Bern now stands) but a short time, when the mounted men, who consisted entirely of Tories, under the command of Captain Cox, and formed the advance of the detachment, galloped into town, and proceeded directly to the wharves. Mrs. Gaston, fearful that her husband might not have crossed the ferry, and unable to endure the agonies of suspense, rushed down the street to the Old County Wharf, and found them actually firing at him. He was in the ferry boat, at a very short distance from the shore, and alone, the boy who had been rowing the boat having jumped overboard. She threw herself between him and the assailants, and on her knees, with all a woman's eloquence, implored them to spare the life of her husband. The captain of the savage band answered these cries by damning him for a 'rebel' and his followers as 'blunderers,' called for a rifle, levelled it over her shoulder, and stretched him a corpse."

Margaret Gaston, who was only twenty-six years old at the time, never ceased to mourn her husband's death and wore black for the thirty remaining years of her life. She has been described as a lady of calm, gray eyes, beautiful features, and stately carriage. It was said that she never permitted her shoulders to touch the back of a chair. Although sometimes pressed for ready money, she apparently operated the plantation with considerable success. The census of 1790 lists her as the owner of thirty slaves, a considerable estate for that time. Her piety, kindness to the sick and destitute, and faithfulness to the church in which she had been reared made her an outstanding figure of her community until her death on 17 Dec. 1811 in New Bern.

There are descendants of Alexander Gaston through the female lines, but the last of his name, a great-grandson, Captain Hugh Jones Gaston, was killed in the Confederate Army in the Battle of Sharpsburg in 1862.

SEE: Samuel A. Ashe, ed., *Biographical History of North Carolina*, vol. 7 (1908); Walter Clark, ed., *State Records of North Carolina*, vols. 11-14, 16, 18, 22-24 (1895–1907); Chalmers G. Davidson, *Gaston of Chester* (1956); William Gaston, "Account of the Death of Dr. Alexander Gaston," *Publications of the Southern History Association* 9 (1905); William L. Saunders, ed., *Colonial Records of North Carolina*, vols. 7-10 (1890).

CHALMERS G. DAVIDSON

**Gaston, William Joseph** *(19 Sept. 1778–23 Jan. 1844)*, lawyer, legislator, congressman, and jurist, was born in New Bern. His father, Alexander Gaston of Huguenot ancestry, was a native of Ireland, trained in medicine, and served as a surgeon in the British navy before settling in Craven County prior to May 1764. His Roman Catholic mother, Margaret Sharpe, went to New Bern from England nine years later. In May 1775, she married Dr. Gaston, who became an ardent patriot with the advent of the American Revolution. He was killed by a party of Tories in August 1781, leaving a widow and two children, William and Jane. Thereafter, the pious and intelligent Mrs. Gaston proceeded to mold her son's character and to instill in him a lasting devotion to the Roman Catholic church. This upbringing in time made Gaston worthy to be called "the greatest lay Catholic in America."

Gaston's formal education began in 1791. After a five-month visit in Philadelphia, he arrived in the autumn of that year in Georgetown on the Potomac River to enroll as the first student at Georgetown College, a recently founded Roman Catholic institution of higher learning. Ill-health, however, compelled him to leave in the spring of 1793. Back in his native town, Gaston regained his strength and spent the next year as a student at New Bern Academy, where he gave the valedictory in July 1794. After another sojourn in Philadelphia, he was admitted in November to the junior class of the College of New Jersey at Princeton, from which he was graduated at age eighteen at the head of his class. Gaston then returned to New Bern to study law under François-Xavier Martin, an eminent attorney. He developed such legal competence that he was admitted to the bar in September 1798. He immediately took over part of the law practice of his brother-in-law, John Louis Taylor, who had been selected a superior court judge. Although Gaston excelled in land cases, he also emerged as a superlative criminal lawyer. A number of students prepared for the bar under his direction.

Politics soon attracted Gaston's attention, and he proved to be an energetic Federalist leader. In 1800 he was elected to the state senate, where he served on several committees and was chairman of three others. He was sent to the House of Commons in 1807, 1808, and 1809. In 1808 he was chosen both speaker of the house and a presidential elector. He ran unsuccessfully for the U.S. House of Representatives in 1810, but again won a seat in the state senate in 1812. The next year he went to Washington as a member of the House in the Thirteenth Congress. He gained experience on several relatively minor committees before working on the important Ways and Means Committee; he was reelected to the Fourteenth Congress. As a congressman Gaston gained a national reputation for the eloquence of his speeches, especially those supporting the Bank of the United States and opposing the Loan Bill, by which President James Madison was to be entrusted with $25 million for the conquest of Canada. He denounced generally the War of 1812 as "forbidden by our interests, and abhorrent from our honour." His speech in reply to Henry Clay's "defense of the previous question" was a particularly noteworthy piece of parliamentary oratory. In January 1815 he presented a petition asking for authority for Georgetown College to award academic degrees. A congressional charter for the school resulted. In 1817, he voluntarily retired from Congress and resumed the practice of law. Daniel Webster, one of many national figures known by Gaston, described him as the greatest man of the War Congress.

Craven County sent Gaston to the state senate in 1818 and 1819. At both sessions he served as chairman of the Judiciary Committee; he was also chairman of the joint legislative committee that in 1818 framed the act creating the North Carolina Supreme Court. Although Gaston never reentered national politics after leaving Congress, President John Quincy Adams considered naming him secretary of war in 1826 because of his faithful support of the administration. In a circular prepared by Gaston for the Committee of Correspondence and Vigilance of New Bern, he announced that the president's wisdom and honesty entitled him to a second term. In his keynote address to the anti-Jackson convention in Raleigh in December 1827, he once more urged that Adams be reelected. Gaston was returned to the House of Commons in 1827 to fill the vacancy for New Bern occasioned by John Stanly's resignation. The next year he was elected to the lower house for a full term and was returned to that body in 1829 and 1831. Besides serving on the judiciary committee during these years, Gaston was chairman of the finance committee, a position that coincided with his interest in banking. In 1828, he was appointed president of the Bank of New Bern and while in the house was able to cooperate with conservative financial groups in an effort to maintain sound banking policies for North Carolina.

He also took a lively interest in internal improvements for the state. In 1827, he was elected the first president of the Agricultural Society of Craven County. The same year he was a delegate to a convention in Washington, N.C., for the purpose of deciding on ways to improve navigation at Ocracoke Inlet; he then tried to help put the measures agreed upon into effect. In July 1833 he attended an internal improvements convention in Raleigh, serving as chairman of the committee to prepare an address to the state and to lay the convention's proceedings before the state legislature. The address, which was his own handiwork, stressed the need for colleges, railroads, hospitals, and asylums for the handicapped. As a member of the House of Commons, Gaston had the satisfaction of introducing the bill to charter the North Carolina Central Railroad.

Gaston's career as a public servant entered a new phase in November 1833, when the House of Commons elected him to the North Carolina Supreme Court. Although Article 32 of the state constitution denied the right to hold state office to anyone who did not believe in "the Truth of the Protestant Religion," Gaston and the politicos concluded that a Roman Catholic was not disbarred by the provision. More than thirty years earlier, former governor Samuel Johnston had given him a written opinion expressing approbation when Gaston first became a member of the state legislature. His most famous decision on the bench came in 1834 with the case of *State v. Negro Will*. Gaston ruled that a slave had the right to defend himself against an unlawful attempt of a master, or an agent of a master, to kill him. In the significant case of *State v. William Manuel* in 1838, he held that a manumitted slave was a citizen of the state and thus entitled to the guarantees of the constitution. This opinion was cited as "sound law" in 1857 by Benjamin R. Curtis of the United States Supreme Court in his dissent in the Dred Scott case. The better for the justices to render decisions, Gaston purchased a library for the state supreme court while on a trip to New York City in 1835. When Chief Justice John Marshall died that year, there was speculation that Gaston would succeed him on the United States Supreme Court, a possibility championed by various state newspapers.

Elected by Craven County as its representative to the Constitutional Convention of 1835, Gaston spoke out in favor of continued suffrage for free blacks, federal representation as the basis for representation in the House of Commons, and biennial meetings of the state legislature. However, it was to the fight against Article 32 of the state constitution that he gave most of his considerable oratorical skills, delivering a two-day address against religious tests for public office. In the end, the attempt to expunge all religious qualifications from the constitution failed, but the word "Christian" was substituted for "Protestant." Gaston served on the committee appointed at the convention to draft the proposed amendments to be submitted to the voters of North Carolina.

A deeply religious man, Gaston was also an active Roman Catholic. When Bishop John England visited New Bern from Charleston, S.C., in May 1821, he celebrated in the parlor of the Gaston house his first recorded mass in North Carolina. The bishop designated Gaston one of five Catholics to conduct services every Sunday in the improvised chapel; at the same time a treasury, to which Gaston contributed $700, was established to receive funds for a church building. Appointed a church warden in February 1824, on another visit by England, Gaston suggested a few amendments to the constitution for the Catholic church in North Carolina which the bishop published in New Bern. Plans for a wooden church were finally presented at a meeting in Gaston's law office in October 1839, and he pledged an additional $500 toward the amount needed to construct the edifice. A contract was drawn up between Gaston and the builder the next year. Work on the church was completed in 1841, thus making St. Paul's Church the oldest Roman Catholic church in North Carolina.

Gaston, who owned slaves and a plantation in Craven County, purchased a townhouse in New Bern in April 1818. Built about 1767 by James Coor, this fine Georgian structure is one of the few relatively untouched pre-Revolutionary frame buildings in North Carolina. It is particularly distinguished by its Chinese Chippendale balustrades on the double porches. The Gaston house, placed on the National Register of Historic Places in 1972, has been restored by the Justice Gaston House Restoration Association. Gaston's restored law office stands one block from his house in New Bern.

During the sessions of the supreme court in Raleigh, Gaston stayed at the home of Mrs. James F. Taylor. At his office nearby, in 1840 he wrote the words for "The Old North State," the music for which he apparently adopted from a melody sung by a group of Swiss bellringers who had visited the capital. A bronze tablet at the site of the office commemorates the writing of what has been since 1927 the official state song of North Carolina. It was played in public for the first time at the Whig state convention in Raleigh in October 1840. Gaston, himself now a Whig, took no direct part in the presidential campaign of that year, but to the Whigs in control of the state legislature he became the leading choice for the U.S. Senate. He declined the offer as he likewise turned down the next year the post of attorney general in the cabinet of President William Henry Harrison. His name had often been presented by newspaper editors to the country as a vice-presidential prospect.

The honors bestowed upon Gaston in his lifetime reflect the esteem in which he was held throughout the United States. In 1817 the American Philosophical Society elected him a member, and two years later the American Antiquarian Society made him counselor for his state. In 1819 the University of Pennsylvania conferred on him the honorary degree of doctor of laws, a degree similarly awarded him later by Harvard College and Columbia College. He was a member of the American Academy of Languages and Belles Lettres and an officer of the Cliosophic Society and of the Literary Society of the College of New Jersey. In 1835, the Philodemics Society of Georgetown College made him an honorary member, as did the Phi Beta Kappa Society of Yale College. Over the next few years he was elected to honorary membership by the literary societies of the University of Alabama, Rutgers College, the University of Georgia, St. Mary's College of Baltimore, Caldwell Institute, and Davidson College. He also belonged to the Erodelphian Society of Miami University, the Franklin Society of Randolph-Macon College, the Philo Society of Jefferson College in Cannonsburg, Pa., and the Euzelian Society of Wake Forest College. Gaston served as a director of the state institution for the instruction of the deaf and dumb, a trustee of the Griffin Free School in New Bern, and a trustee of The University of North Carolina from 1802 until his death.

With his recognized speaking ability, Gaston was invariably called upon to deliver commencement addresses by colleges and universities far and wide. One of his most outstanding orations he gave in June 1832 at The University of North Carolina, where he entreated his audience to uphold the Constitution and to preserve the Union. He condemned the institution of slavery and insisted upon its abolition, although at the time of his death he owned over 200 slaves. He stated his antinullification position so emphatically that his address went through five printings, one of which carried a preface written by his friend Chief Justice John Marshall. In 1830, 1834, and 1835, the College of New Jersey asked Gaston to give the commencement address, as did Wake Forest College and The University of North Carolina in 1834. Many times he was requested to send copies of his different speeches to editors collecting oratory masterpieces for publication.

Gaston made out his will in December 1843, citing among his legatees his surviving daughters, grandchildren, and St. Paul's Church. The next month he suddenly became ill while hearing a case in Raleigh and died in his office several hours later. His last words were said to have been: "We must believe there is a God—All wise and All mighty." He was buried temporarily in Raleigh; his remains were later moved for interment in Cedar Grove Cemetery, New Bern. There Gaston was laid to rest near his parents in a grave marked by a fine marble tombstone.

Gaston was married three times: on 4 Sept. 1803, to Susan Hay; on 6 Oct. 1805, to Hannah McClure; and on 3 Sept. 1816, to Eliza Ann Worthington. By his second wife, he had one son and two daughters and by his third, two daughters.

Several portraits of Gaston exist. Early in his public career he was asked for a portrait to be hung in the National Gallery in Washington. Portraits are also owned by his descendents and by the Philanthropic Society of The University of North Carolina, which possesses a fine oil on canvas. A portrait of Gaston was given to the state supreme court in 1893; another has hung in his law office in New Bern since 1954. A marble bust of Gaston is located in the Philanthropic Society Hall in Chapel Hill. One of the most interesting likenesses of Gaston is a small watercolor on ivory executed by James Peale in 1796. Gaston stood six feet tall, with blue eyes and dark hair. As he grew old, he became somewhat stout, his complexion got florid, and his hair turned gray. His face, according to a friend, continued to express "the benignity of soul which animated his life."

A treasure trove of material is located in the William Gaston Papers in the Southern Historical Collection at The University of North Carolina, Chapel Hill. This valuable collection consists of much of Gaston's personal, business, and political correspondence over the years from 1791 to 1844. The William Gaston Papers in the North Carolina State Archives, Raleigh, contain a much smaller number of items. Gaston County and Gastonia are both named in honor of this remarkable man.

SEE: R. D. W. Connor, *William Gaston: A Southern Federalist of the Old School and His Yankee Friends, 1778–1844* (1934); Deed and Will Books of Craven County (Office of the Clerk of Court, County Courthouse, New Bern); W. H. Dillingham, "Biographical Notice of Judge Gaston," read 15 Mar. 1844 (Library, American Philosophical Society, Philadelphia); *Fayetteville Observer*, 9 Jan. 1975; Calvin Jarrett, "Judge William Gaston: Catholic Crusader," *Liberty* 63 (May–June 1968); Raleigh *News and Observer*, 6 Nov. 1960; Records, St. Paul's Church (St. Paul's Rectory, New Bern); J. H. Schauinger, *William Gaston, Carolinian* (1949).

CHARLES H. BOWMAN, JR.

**Gatlin, Alfred Moore** *(b. 20 Apr. 1790)*, lawyer and congressman, was born in Edenton, one of six children of James and Mary Gatlin of Craven County. Alfred's older brother James, Jr., was the father of Radford Gatlin, eponym of Gatlinburg, Tenn. The will of James Gatlin, probated in 1801, directed that his property be rented, sold or otherwise completely "appropriated to the use of raising and educating my son Alfred." A guardian was appointed by the Craven County Court in 1804 to oversee Alfred's education. He pursued classical studies in New Bern before entering The University of North Carolina, where he received an A.B. in 1808 and an M.A. in 1812. Deeds settling a family estate in June 1810 reveal that Gatlin was then living in New Bern. A Chowan County marriage bond of January 1813 shows him to have been bondsman at the Edenton wedding of Thomas S. Singleton and Harriet H. Skinner. Gatlin may have studied law in Edenton, although after he was admitted to the bar in 1823 he is said to have commenced practice in Camden County.

Concurrent with the birth of his legal career in 1823, Gatlin was elected to the Eighteenth Congress. A Democrat, he represented the First Congessional District which then included Hertford, Gates, Chowan, Perquimans, Pasquotank, Camden, and Currituck counties. Gatlin defeated incumbent Lemuel Sawyer, a native and resident of Camden County. It is thought that this campaign inspired the minor plot in Sawyer's play *Blackbeard* (1824), which describes the defeat of an honest candidate (Sawyer) by an unscrupulous opponent. Sawyer subsequently staged a successful comeback, frustrating Gatlin's own bid for reelection. This seems to have ended Gatlin's political career, although he may have served as a colonel in the local militia.

Gatlin's later life is obscure. He acquired over 400 acres of land in Camden County just south of the county seat of Jonesborough (now Camden). About 1830 he built the substantial sidehall plan house that still stands on the property. In 1835 Gatlin sold all his real estate to Meriam Grandy, a Camden County businesswoman, and emigrated to Florida. The scanty records available do not reveal the details of his marriage, which must have taken place during his Camden residency. In 1840, Gatlin's household in Tallahassee included one boy age 10-15, two girls under 5, one girl 5-10, one girl 15-20, and three women 20-30, as well as five slaves. Gatlin either died or left Florida before 1850. However, North Carolina natives James Gatlin (age 20) and Louisa Gatlin (age 16) are probably his older children. Louisa may be the daughter of Alfred Gatlin who is said to have married into the Dubose family in Florida.

SEE: Architectural Inventory Files of Camden County (North Carolina State Archives, Raleigh); *Biog. Dir. Am. Cong.* (1950); John L. Cheney, Jr., ed., *North Carolina Government, 1585–1974* (1975); Daniel L. Grant, *Alumni History of the University of North Carolina* (1924); J. R. B. Hathaway, ed., *North Carolina Historical and Genealogical Register*. 3 vols. (1900–1903); Eva L. McDuffie, ed., *The Gatlin Family in America* (n.d.); Jesse Forbes Pugh, *Three Hundred Years Along the Pasquotank: A Biographical History of Camden County* (1957); U.S. Census, 1840, 1850, Leon County, Fla.

JAMES D. EVERHART, JR.

**Gatlin, Richard Caswell** *(18 Jan. 1809–8 Sept. 1896)*, soldier, Confederate officer, and farmer, was born at Kinston, Lenoir County. His father was John S. Gatlin, the son of John Gatlin who was one of the early settlers of Kinston; his mother was Susannah Caswell, the youngest child of Governor Richard Caswell. Gatlin's brother, John Slade Gatlin, became an assistant surgeon in the U.S. Army and was killed by the Seminole Indians in the Dade's Defeat massacre in Florida in December 1835. Young Gatlin attended The University of North Carolina in 1824–25 before his appointment to the U.S. Military Academy at West Point on 1 July 1832; he was graduated on 31 May 1834 with the rank of second lieutenant in the Seventh United States Infantry. He was assigned to frontier duty in the Indian Territory and on 31 Aug. 1836 was commissioned first lieutenant.

After serving in the Seminole War in Florida from 1839 to 1842, Gatlin was stationed in Louisiana until 1845. On 30 September of that year he was made a captain and joined the occupation army in Texas. He participated in the War with Mexico and in the defense of Fort Brown in May 1846. At the storming of the Mexican works in the Battle of Monterey he was wounded, for which he received the brevet of major for gallant and meritorious service on 23 Sept. 1846. In 1847, Gatlin declined the commission of colonel of the First North Carolina Volunteers. Thereafter he successively served in Missouri and Louisiana; took part in another Seminole War (1849–50); saw frontier duty in Kansas, the Indian Territory, Arkansas, and Dakota; accompanied General Albert S. Johnston's expedition to Salt Lake; and was stationed at Fort Craig, N.M. (1860). In February 1861, he was promoted to major in the Fifth United States Infantry.

While on a visit to Fort Smith, Ark., he was captured by Arkansas State forces on 23 Apr. 1861 when the state was on the verge of secession. After his parole, he resigned his commission in the U.S. Army and offered his services to North Carolina. He was first made adjutant general of the state, with the rank of major general of militia; later he received the rank of colonel of infantry in the regular Confederate Army and was given command of the Southern Department, in charge of coastal defense, with headquarters at Wilmington. On 15 Aug. 1861 he was appointed brigadier general, to rank from 8 July (confirmed 16 August). Placed in charge of the Department of North Carolina, he was assigned the almost hopeless task of building the state's coastal defenses. Gatlin found little to work with, as gunboats, artillery, equipment, labor, and especially troops were not available to defend the Outer Banks, its ports, and its hundreds of miles of inland sounds and rivers. Inevitably, the Union Army—in its initial attack against the coast—easily overpowered the weak defenses of Hatteras Inlet in late August 1861. Gatlin then attempted to strengthen the defenses of Roanoke Island and New Bern, making numerous appeals to Confederate authorities in Richmond for reinforcements. However, because of the demands for troops and supplies in other parts of the Confederacy, his requests were ignored. Consequently, his men could not resist the powerful Union forces of General Ambrose Burnside when they arrived on the coast in late January and early February 1862. Roanoke was captured on 8 February and New Bern fell on 14 March.

Gatlin, of course, received all manner of public criticism and blame for the reverses. He was scorned for not being with his men on the field of battle, although at the time of the fall of New Bern he was seriously ill at his headquarters in Goldsboro. He was even falsely accused of being intoxicated on the day of the battle. Perhaps Gatlin was too old for the monumental task assigned him, but in reality there simply had not been enough troops, equipment, and supplies to defend the coast. On 19 March, five days after the fall of New Bern, he was relieved of his command, ostensibly for health reasons. On 8 Sept. 1862, he resigned his commission because of his advanced age and served as adjutant and inspector general of North Carolina.

After the war Gatlin moved to Arkansas where he engaged in farming in Sebastian County until 1881, when he moved again to Fort Smith. He died at Mount Nebo, Yell County, Ark., at the age of eighty-seven, and was buried in the National Cemetery at Fort Smith. Gatlin's first wife, Scioto, died on 3 Jan. 1852, apparently from complications during childbirth. His second wife was Mary Ann Gibson. Both were buried with him in the National Cemetery, as were a son, Alfred Sandford Gatlin, and a daughter, Susan Caswell Gatlin Corley.

SEE: John G. Barrett, *The Civil War in North Carolina* (1963); C. A. Evans, *Confederate Military History*, vol. 4 (1899); Daniel L. Grant, *Alumni History of the University of North Carolina* (1924); F. B. Heitman, *Historical Register and Dictionary of the United States Army*, vol. 1 (1903); D. H. Hill, *Bethel to Sharpsburg*, vol. 1 (1926); T. C. Johnson and C. R. Holloman, *The Story of Kinston and Lenoir County* (1954); Ezra Warner, *Generals in Gray* (1959); Marcus J. Wright, *General Officers of the Confederate Army* (1911).

PAUL BRANCH

**Gatling, James Henry** *(15 July 1816–3 Sept. 1879)*, inventor, farmer, businessman, and wine maker, was born in Maney's Neck Township, Hertford County, the son of Jordan Gatling, an inventor and farmer, and Mary Barnes Gatling. He and his brothers William, Thomas, and Richard were educated at Buckhorn Academy in Maney's Neck Township. Gatling grew up in a very inventive and tinkering family. His father was a self-taught blacksmith and carpenter who taught his sons the same trades as well as the principles of sound business management. Richard Jordan Gatling, brother of James Henry, received international recognition for his invention of numerous farm implements and his most famous device, the Gatling gun.

James Henry Gatling spent much of his life trying to solve the mysteries of manned flight. Throughout his childhood and into early manhood he was known to have devoted many hours to building model "aeroplanes." Before the Civil War he became seriously involved in an attempt to construct a "flying machine." He received a severe setback in 1865, when a band of "Buffaloes" or robbers raided his plantation and stole over $1,700 that he had saved for the project. Nevertheless, Gatling was determined to build and fly an airplane. Approximately seven years later he nearly accomplished his objective. The machine was launched from the roof of his cotton gin but crashed into a nearby tree on its maiden flight. Having suffered a broken leg in the crash, Gatling did not rebuild his flying machine. He died a violent death when he was murdered near his hogpen. Gatling never married and spent all of his life on the family plantation in Maney's Neck Township where he was buried.

SEE: F. Roy Johnson, *The Gatling Gun and Flying Machine of Richard and Henry Gatling* (1979), and with T. C. Parramore, *The Roanoke-Chowan Story* (1962); J. R. Parker, ed., *The Ahoskie Era of Hertford County* (1939); T. C. Parramore, "The North Carolina Background of Richard Jordan Gatling," *North Carolina Historical Review* 41 (1964);

*A Preliminary Document of the Characteristics of the Murfreesboro Adaptive Restoration and Community Development Program and the Severe Cultural and Educational Deprivation of the Roanoke-Chowan Region of North Carolina* (1977); E. Frank Stephenson, *Renaissance in Carolina*, 2 vols. (1971, 1973); B. B. Winborne, *State and Colonial Political History of Hertford County, North Carolina* (1906).

E. FRANK STEPHENSON

**Gatling, Richard Jordan,** *(12 Sept. 1818–26 Feb. 1903),* inventor of the machine gun and numerous other devices, was born in the Maney's Neck section of Hertford County. His father was Jordan Gatling, a slaveholder who owned an almost completely self-sufficient plantation containing more than a thousand acres; his mother was Mary Barnes Gatling. Richard Jordan had three brothers, Thomas B., James Henry, and William J., and two sisters, Mary Ann and Martha. The entire family is remembered for its exceptional intellect. Jordan Gatling was himself an inventor and in 1835 patented machines for planting and for thinning cotton. James Henry, an older brother of Richard Jordan, was greatly interested in heavier-than-air flight by man and in the 1870s constructed a crude hand-powered aircraft with which he experimented unsuccessfully; he also invented and patented devices for chopping cotton stalks and for converting pine into lightwood. It was in this climate of intellectual curiosity that Richard Jordan Gatling spent his boyhood. He had brief formal education at Buckhorn, a local common school. He then became a schoolmaster but gave up teaching to open a country store near the town of Winton. During this period Gatling's inventive genius first found expression. Having observed an experimental steamboat trial while on a visit to Norfolk, Va., in 1841, he conceived the principle of the screw propeller as a substitute for the slow and cumbersome paddle-type wheels then in use. At first his father refused him permission to go to Washington to patent the principle, but relented seven months later. When Gatling arrived in Washington, he learned that the celebrated Scandinavian-American inventor, John Ericsson, had patented the identical invention only a few days before.

Three years later Gatling obtained his first patent. It was for a rice-seed planter. He then left North Carolina and moved to St. Louis to manufacture and market his planter. There, converting his machine to a wheat-planter, he amassed a fortune in the midwestern wheat fields. During the winter of 1845, Gatling contracted smallpox while on a business trip by riverboat. For two weeks, when the steamer was ice-locked, he was unable to obtain medical attention. Upon recovering from this near-fatal illness, he decided to study medicine simply to be able to care for himself and his family. Accordingly, Gatling attended both Indiana Medical College and Ohio Medical College, receiving a diploma as a physician in 1850. At this time he moved to Indianapolis, where he practiced medicine only briefly. Returning to his creative interests, he invented and patented a hemp-breaking machine and later invented a steam-plow.

The outbreak of the Civil War stimulated Gatling to produce the greatest invention of his career and one that revolutionized warfare. This was the machine battery gun that became known the world over as the "Gatling gun."

One of the most interesting aspects of the life of Gatling is his own conception of the meaning of the terrible weapon that he had created. When he invented his famed gun he acted not as a merchant of violence but as a humanitarian who wished to reduce the number of men required to fight wars and thereby reduce the incidence of death. At the beginning of the Civil War, Gatling frequently visited the trains bringing in dead and wounded troops from the battlefields and army camps. From his examinations, he learned that only three out of eighteen died from their bullet wounds; the remainder died from fever, pneumonia, and other illnesses contracted in camp. The loss of life due to illness impressed Gatling with the idea that, if a weapon could be devised to shoot more bullets, fewer men would be required to fight wars and, therefore, fewer and smaller concentrations of men would be necessary. This, he contended, would cut down the rate of death by both illness and combat. He also hoped that the terror created by such a weapon would tend to discourage war altogether.

Although Gatling's humanitarian theories have proved fallacious, the essentially humanitarian conception of his invention was accepted in many respectable quarters, particularly in England where the Gatling gun was early adopted. A British newspaper of the period commented: "The general use of the formidable weapon will tend to diminish the barbarity and actual carnage of warfare, as its known relentless certainty of execution will help to prevent wars and thereby aid in keeping the peace of Christendom." The first gun was tested and patented in 1862. Although crude, it had a firing capacity of more than 200 rounds a minute. There is some evidence that this early model was used by Union forces on the James River near Richmond on 6 May 1864, but the actual facts have never been ascertained. Gatling worked diligently to refine his invention, and in 1865 an improved model was patented. Twelve guns of this model were subsequently manufactured and submitted to the U.S. Army for tests. In 1866, the Gatling gun was officially adopted by the War Department.

The gun consisted of a group of ten rifle barrels grouped around a central shaft that was revolved by gear action and a hand crank. Bullets were automatically fed into the barrels, the hammers of which revolved continuously as the hand crank was turned. A later model was capable of firing 1,200 shots a minute and, before selling his patent rights to the Colt Fire Arms Co., Gatling experimented with a model that stepped up firing to 3,000 shots a minute. The Gatling gun was eventually adopted by every European power except Belgium. It was used with particularly telling effect by the British in the Boer War and by the American armies in Cuba.

In 1854 Gatling married Jemima Sanders, the daughter of Dr. John H. Sanders of Indianapolis. The couple had four children: Mary S. (b. 1855), Ida (b. 1858), Richard Henry (b. 1870), and Robert B. (b. 1872). Gatling became a member of the Methodist church during his boyhood in North Carolina. In Indiana in 1864 he was reported to have been a member of the Order of American Knights, an organization regarded as treasonable by the federal government. He died in New York City at age eighty-four. He and his wife were buried in a family plot in Crown Hill Cemetery, Indianapolis, Ind.

SEE: C. H. Foster, "The Modern Vulcan," *Potter's American Monthly* 12 (May 1873); F. Roy Johnson, *The Gatling Gun and Flying Machine of Richard and Henry Gatling* (1979); T. C. Parramore, "The North Carolina Background of Richard Jordan Gatling," *North Carolina Historical Review* 41 (1964); Raleigh *News and Observer*, 14

Apr. 1952; Philip V. Stern, "Doctor Gatling and His Gun," *American Heritage* 8 (October 1957); *War of the Rebellion: A Compilation of the Official Records*, Ser. II, vol. 7 (1899); Benjamin B. Winborne, *Colonial and State Political History of Hertford County* (1906).

JOHN RICHARD JORDAN, JR.

**Gattis, Samuel Mallett** *(7 Mar 1863–16 Apr. 1931)*, attorney and public official, was born in Orange County about two and a half miles north of Chapel Hill, the son of Samuel Gattis, a well-to-do farmer, and his wife Nancy. His great-grandfather, John Gattis, who arrived in North Carolina from Pennsylvania in the mid-eighteenth century, was the first of the family to settle in the state. Both John and his son Alexander fought in the American Revolution and were respected members of the community; Alexander was one of the founders of the Orange Methodist Church and a justice of the peace for Orange County.

After attending public schools, young Samuel went to Chapel Hill and for two years attended a college preparatory school conducted by a Reverend Mr. Heitman. In 1880 he entered the freshman class at The University of North Carolina. Although his time was limited because of the financial necessity that he work, he was graduated with a bachelor of philosophy degree in June 1884. For the next three years he was employed as a school principal, first at Wentworth Academy, Johnston County, and then at Hertford Academy, Perquimans County, before he decided to study law. In 1887 he entered the university law school where his preparation under the direction of John Manning enabled him to be licensed by the North Carolina Supreme Court in the February term of 1888. Gattis immediately set up a practice in Hillsborough. The following December Judge Gilmer appointed him clerk of the Orange County superior court to fill the vacancy left by the resignation of Dr. Pride Jones. Gattis was elected to the office in 1889 and served until 1894.

About the same time that his legal career began, a long political career was also blossoming. In 1888, he was elected chairman of the Orange County Democratic executive committee as well as a delegate to the Democratic National Convention in Kansas City. He would hold the latter post again in 1924, when the convention met in New York City.

Gattis resumed the practice of law after leaving the superior court clerkship in 1894. Four years later he was elected to the General Assembly where he represented Orange County in the sessions of 1899, 1901, and 1903; in the latter year he was speaker of the house. In the legislature Gattis rendered untiring service as chairman of the Committee on Cities and Towns and of the committee investigating the management of North Carolina's prisons, as well as a member of the committees on education, printing, judiciary, elections, and penitentiary. Afterward, he returned to his practice in Hillsborough. Apparently because of his ability at the bar, he was elected solicitor of the Ninth Judicial District in 1909 where he remained until the lines were changed in 1913. He then held the same office in the Tenth Judicial District for ten years—serving with distinction as solicitor for a total of fourteen years. In 1923 he once more took up his private law practice.

Although unquestionably his chief interests, Gattis did not confine himself solely to politics and law. As a former teacher and supporter of public education, he was a member and chairman of the executive committee of the Normal and Industrial College in Greensboro and a trustee (1907–11) of The University of North Carolina, his alma mater. He also was a charter member and a director of the Bank of Orange. A Mason, he was a member of Eagle Lodge in Hillsborough and served as Grand Marshall, Grand Senior Deacon, Grand Junior Warden, and Grand Senior Warden (1908–9) of the Grand Lodge of North Carolina. He was affiliated with the Methodist Episcopal Church, South, and a member of the Hillsborough Methodist Church where for many years he was a steward.

On 3 Dec. 1890 Gattis married Margaret Williams Parish of Hillsborough, and they were the parents of one child, Samuel Mallett, Jr. Gattis died at his home in Hillsborough and was buried in the town cemetery.

SEE: Daniel L. Grant, *Alumni History of the University of North Carolina* (1924); *Greensboro Daily News*, 22 June 1924, 17 Apr. 1931; *Who's Who in the South*, 1927.

LUCIUS MCGHEE CHESHIRE, JR.

**Gault, Francis Beers** *(26 Nov. 1875–7 Oct. 1946)*, lumberman, was born in St. Peter, Minn., the oldest child of Zuriel Samuel and Mary Lincoln Lampman Gault. He was a descendant of the Woolseys of Long Island, thought to be the oldest family of English origin in New York State; of Philip Pinckney of Eastchester; of the Burr, Sturges, Ogden, and Beers families of Fairfield, Conn.; and of Major Simon Willard, the Reverend Thomas Carter, and the Otis, Joslin, Wilder, and Lincoln families of Massachusetts. Gault attended Gustavus Adolphus College and during spare time and in the summers worked with engineering location crews in central South Dakota and in the Black Hills. At the age of twenty he became acting city engineer of St. Peter. In 1907 he moved to Columbus County, N.C., where he joined his granduncle, Charles O. Beers, in shingle and lumber manufacturing and became an ardent North Carolina booster and lifelong proponent of the state's people, traditions, products, and multifaceted progressiveness.

For more than two decades Gault was president and general manager of the North Carolina Lumber Company, maintaining salesmen in Baltimore, Md., Trenton, N.J., and Philadelphia, Pa. Though himself caught in serious financial straits during the Great Depression of the 1930s, he was able to look after his several hundred employees, both white and black, during the more than two years that his mills were shut down. For many years he was a director of the Peoples Savings Bank and Trust Co., Wilmington, and of the Southern Pine Association. He was also a member of the National Hardwood Lumber Association. In his last years after retirement he served as chairman of the Columbus County school board. A member of St. James's Episcopal Church, Wilmington, he also was a 32° Mason and a member of various social clubs.

In 1909 Gault married Susie Bell LaMotte of Wilmington, and they were the parents of four children: Charles Beers, Mrs. Miriam Ashe Holt, Mary Lampman, and Francis Alexander. After his death of heart failure, he was buried in Oakdale Cemetery, Wilmington. The site of his home at Lake Waccamaw is now the Boys Home of North Carolina.

SEE: Gault family papers (in possession of Charles B. Gault, Chapel Hill); Whiteville *News Reporter*, 7, 10 Oct. 1946.

CHARLES B. GAULT

**Gause, Lucien Coatsworth** *(25 Dec. 1836–5 Nov. 1880)*, Arkansas congressman, was born in Brunswick County, not far from Wilmington. While he was still a youth, his family moved to Lauderdale County, Tenn. Prepared for college by a private tutor, Gause was graduated from the University of Virginia at Charlottesville and then enrolled at Cumberland University in Lebanon, Tenn., to study law. Upon completing his studies there, he was admitted to the bar and began to practice at Jacksonport, Ark., in 1859. During the Civil War, he joined the Confederate Army as a lieutenant and was eventually promoted to the rank of colonel. After the war, he returned to his law practice in Jacksonport.

Gause entered politics in 1866, when he was elected to the Arkansas House of Representatives. Later, he was a member of the commission sent to Washington in an unsuccessful attempt to contest the election of Asa Hodges to the Forty-third Congress. Gause himself ran as a candidate on the Democratic ticket in 1874 and was elected to the Forty-fourth Congress. He served two terms but was not a candidate for renomination in 1878. Returning to Arkansas, he continued to practice law and died in Jacksonport. He was buried in a private cemetery nearby.

SEE: *Biog. Dir. Am. Cong.* (1961); *New York Times*, 7 Nov. 1880.

JAMES ELLIOTT MOORE

**Gautier, Thomas Nicholas Boudet** *(1764–5 Sept. 1848)*, naval officer, was born in Bristol, England, served in the Royal Navy as a midshipman, and came to America some time before 1800. From 1808 until his death at age eighty-four, he was a citizen of Wilmington, N.C.

From 1800 to 1814 Gautier made a career in the U.S. Navy, serving as commander of the North Carolina naval defenses during the War of 1812. Commissioned as a lieutenant in 1800, he was assigned to the *Chesapeake* in 1801 but because of ill health applied for a discharge. In 1807 he again entered the service, this time at the lower rank of sailing master, and was assigned to assist in the construction of gunboats at Wilmington. At that time the parsimony of the national government was notorious, and Gautier struggled constantly to obtain money, materials, and labor to do the job, often spending from his own pocket. When three gunboats were finally assembled, the same problems arose with obtaining crews. After three years, gunboats and crews were ready in 1811. Reported Gautier, "Sans an article of military equipment, sans money, sans officers or men, I have done as much . . . as in some places would have been done having everything at hand."

As war approached, his duties included laying buoys to protect the Wilmington bar, maintaining the embargo, and checking all ports from Swansboro to Elizabeth City. Constantly he was directed by the secretary of the navy to distribute his tiny flotilla so as to guard many miles of coast and ease citizens' fears of British invasion. To his utter dismay, in March 1813 he was ordered to call in all the gunboats and lay them up. Wrote Gautier, "I then shall sit down in sullen retirement and view the Boats in the mud and to reflect on the situation of my state not a single armed vessel allotted for her defence."

The British rudely awakened the navy by capturing Ocracoke and threatening New Bern in July 1813. Gautier was named acting lieutenant (30 Aug. 1813) and the gunboats came out of the "mud." Based at Smith's Anchorage below Wilmington, he took charge with a firm hand, especially at Beaufort where there was trouble with disaffection and smugglers. Supplies arrived from Norfolk to Elizabeth City, from which port the gunboats convoyed them to Wilmington. Five of these, plus a barge and a felucca that Gautier had converted into a schooner, constituted his fleet. He coped with hurricanes, with desertions to higher-paying privateers, with explosions, and with rumors of British invasions. In the end he resigned on 25 Nov. 1814.

Gautier had a firm sense of an officer's duty and position, undoubtedly instilled in him by the Royal Navy. To a merchant he wrote, "I have worn a sword for 30 years and am not to be taught at this period what is allowed for, or what the Service requires." He reprimanded a subordinate for engaging in "idle conversation with the men," and accused one Captain Creighton of presuming to interfere with Gautier's naval arrangements during an absence. The sight of a sea fencible from "the backwoods" "dashing around" in a navy uniform offended him. His somewhat feisty manner irritated many persons. James Taylor wrote to Secretary of the Navy William Jones bringing "charges" against Gautier. Others accused him of enlisting prisoners and even slaves, which he denied. An officer who was put in irons for allowing or conniving at the desertion of four sailors spread the word that Gautier was an ogre. Undoubtedly such charges, added to his heavy duties, encouraged his resignation.

After the war he appears to have been an unfortunate businessman. His first wife, Anna Bella, was a woman of wealth who, upon her death around 1823, left her houses, lots, and slaves to be managed by executors and the income paid to her husband. Because he was in "the decline of life" and was in debt from "misfortune in mercantile transactions," she wished him to have a sufficiency with which to live. The "declining" Gautier not only lived for twenty-five years more, but remarried immediately a woman half his age. They appear to have had two daughters and one son, and to have enjoyed Anna Bella's estate and eighteen slaves. There were no heirs by his first wife.

Upon his death, "Capt." Gautier was praised as "one of our oldest citizens [who] has filled many offices of trust with honor to himself, and dies universally respected." To pay honor to his memory, ships in port flew their ensigns at half-mast for a day. A member of the Episcopal church, he was buried in the cemetery of St. James's Church, Wilmington.

SEE: Census and Wills of New Hanover County (North Carolina State Archives, Raleigh); Records of the U.S. Navy (National Archives, Washington, D.C.), Tombstone, St. James's Episcopal Cemetery (Wilmington); *Wilmington Journal*, 8 Sept. 1848.

SARAH MCCULLOH LEMMON

**Gay, James** *(20 Mar 1744–4 Feb. 1819)*, farmer, soldier, and poet, was born in Ulster, Ireland, of Devon forebears. In lieu of a formal education, he avidly read history and the Scottish poems of Allan Ramsay. At age sixteen he was apprenticed to a carpenter at Bangor; three years later he plied his trade in Scotland where his family had moved. In 1765, Gay immigrated to Pennsylvania. He married Margaret Mitchel in 1768, and became the father of a son. In 1771, seeking land, he settled in the Oak Forest community on Fourth Creek in Rowan (later Iredell) County, N.C. During the

American Revolution he served in the patriot forces. A highly moral man, he donated the site for a church (subsequently called Gay's Chapel) in 1788. At the turn of the century, he owned more than 1,500 acres in Iredell County.

Gay's first poem, written in 1805 at the age of sixty-one, was delivered at a Fourth of July celebration in Statesville. Annually thereafter, he prepared patriotic verses for the occasion. His *Collection* (1810), supported by 71 subscribers pledged to purchase 235 copies, contained his Fourth of July toasts, a number of poems expressing his Federalist bias, and a nine-page "poetic sketch of his life," some of it in Scottish dialect. Gay's *Collection* is the first substantial book of poetry written by a resident North Carolinian. He had two sons and two daughters, and to each of his sons he gave a farm and half his books and pamphlets. His wife died in 1796.

SEE: James Gay, *A Collection of Various Pieces of Poetry, Chiefly Patriotic, Published at the Earnest Request of a Number of Good Citizens for the Improvement of Patriotic Minds* (1810); William H. Gay, *A Story of the Gay Family* (1920); *Statesville Record & Landmark*, 7 Apr. 1962.

RICHARD WALSER

**Geddy, John** *(1748–1799)*, silversmith and patriot, was born in Williamsburg, Va., the son of James and Anne Geddy. His brother, James, was a prominent silversmith whose restored shop on Duke of Gloucester Street is one of the exhibition buildings in Colonial Williamsburg. Ann Geddy, a younger sister of James and John, was the wife of the Reverend Henry John Burges, whose father, the Reverend Thomas Burges, was the last Church of England clergyman in Halifax County, N.C. She died in 1771.

John Geddy settled in the town of Halifax in 1768 at the time of his marriage to Patience McKinnie of Halifax County. From Halifax, he advertised in the *Virginia Gazette* in 1773 that he had for sale a large assortment of silver and goldsmiths' work and was able to repair clocks and watches and to do engraving of all sorts. In August 1774, he was elected to represent the borough of Halifax in the Assembly in the place of Joseph Montfort; the same year he was a member of the Provincial Congress at New Bern. He again represented his county in the Provincial Congress at Hillsborough in 1775. Geddy was appointed first major of the Halifax County militia in 1776 and promoted to lieutenant colonel two years later. In 1779 he resigned his commission to become captain of a volunteer company of horse. After the war, he was a member of the House of Commons from Halifax in 1783 and sheriff of the county in 1785 and 1786. About 1790 he moved to Cool Harbor, near Louisburg in Franklin County. In 1797 he advertised in the *North Carolina Journal* that he would be in Raleigh to repair clocks and watches when the Assembly convened. He died in Franklin County two years later.

Geddy's wife, Patience, was the daughter of John and Mary McKinnie. Her sister Mary was the wife of Colonel Nicholas Long. Another sister, Martha, married Dr. Charles Pasteur, a physician during the American Revolution; he represented the town of Halifax in the House of Commons in 1785. Patience and John Geddy had five daughters: Betsy, who never married; Sally, who married William Hill, the secretary of state of North Carolina for many years; Martha, who married John Marshall of Raleigh; Mary, who married William Gilmour of Halifax, and Anne, who married Dr. Richard Fenner of Franklin County. Mrs. Geddy died in 1814.

SEE: Archives, Museum of Early Southern Decorative Arts (Winston-Salem), for information on John Geddy; Walter Clark, ed., *State Records of North Carolina*, vols. 12 (1895), 13 (1896), 19 (1901), 21 (1903); George B. Cutten, *The Silversmiths of Virginia from 1694–1850* (1952); Deeds and Wills of Halifax County (County Courthouse, Halifax); William L. Saunders, ed., *Colonial Records of North Carolina*, vols. 9, 10 (1890); Williamsburg *Virginia Gazette*, 29 July 1773.

CLAIBORNE T. SMITH, JR.

**Gentry, Meredith Poindexter** *(15 Sept. 1809–2 Nov. 1866)*, Tennessee congressman, was born in Rockingham County, N.C., the youngest of eleven children of Watson Gentry, a prosperous farmer and Revolutionary War veteran, and Theodosia Poindexter Gentry. When he was four, his parents moved near College Grove, Williamson County, Tenn., a migration coinciding with that of other Gentrys who settled in the mid-state area. Essentially self-educated, Gentry read widely. Encouraged by his father to study law, he showed no taste for the profession but displayed an aptitude for oratory and politics. He reportedly delivered his first public speech before he was twenty-one. In 1835 he became a Whig representative in the legislature, serving two terms. Here he stood strongly against a Bank of Tennessee, asserting that the prerogatives conferred might sometime redound to the public injury—a stance that foreshadowed his opposition to a powerful presidency.

So valuable were Gentry's kith and kin, so formidable his "speechifying," and so Whiggish the local temper, that his constituencies gave him six nonconsecutive terms in Congress between 1839 and 1853. Pleading family affairs and yearning to return home, he declined candidacy in 1843. The following year he lost both his wife, Emily Saunders (granddaughter of Colonel John Donelson of Davidson County), whom he had married in 1837, and his father. He returned to Washington in 1845; during this decade he was also a gubernatorial possibility.

In the House Gentry soon became prominent, and eventually, as a friend of John Adams and Henry Clay and an intimate of Daniel Webster, Zachary Taylor, and Millard Fillmore, important in party councils. Fundamentally he may be seen as a constitutionalist, albeit something of a latitudinarian; Southern states-righter, though never an "ultra"; and partisan, exorcising the demons of loco focoism. He inveighed against extension of executive power via general appropriation, patronage, and veto, yet he advocated assumption of state debts and declared that authority for internal improvements was "from its very nature inherent in the Government." Defending the planter class, he insisted that slavery, with ameliorations, should be retained, yet he urged that abolitionist petitions be considered. In a speech that became a campaign document, he justified log-cabin and hard-ciderism as depriving the democracy of its most successful weapon, the appeal to popular prejudices. He anathematized the "traitor" John Tyler, who recruited a "party not unlike 'a gang' during the Revolution . . . who fought for neither side" but "sold beef to both armies." He poured hot shot into James Polk's 1846 message, charging that the Mexican War was waged for conquest and that "a usurping President was more dangerous . . . than a hundred Mexican armies." At the decade's end Gentry ardently supported

Zachary Taylor and, despite reservations, endorsed the Compromise of 1850.

The Tennessean was nearing his zenith. Notwithstanding Whig restiveness at home, he polled 5,766 votes against token opposition in 1849; two years later, he had no opponent. He worked closely with Taylor, who offered him the postmaster generalship, and with Fillmore. Meanwhile, in November 1846 he had married Caledonia Brown, daughter of Dr. Thomas and Eliza Brown of Columbia, Maury County—"a tall girl" of twenty-four, "beautiful and accomplished, and a small fortune of $15,000."

Yet Gentry was inevitably drawn into the acrimonious debates that accompanied the Mexican Cession. Increasingly he shared the South's apprehensions about the future. Despising John C. Calhoun's Southern Rights movement, he nonetheless distrusted his own party's antislavery wing. During a Whig caucus in December 1849, Southern rebels offered a resolution designed to head off "Wilmotism"; rebuffed, Gentry and others walked out. In the ensuing contest for the House speakership, he was the bolters' candidate.

But the schismatic had not "effectually prostrated himself." Indeed, he had abundant fellowship, for thousands of Tennessee Whigs left the party, most embracing Know-Nothingism. He became their gubernatorial candidate in 1855, chosen not by state convention but by general acclaim. In Governor Andrew Johnson, who would subsequently call him "a Fourth of July orator," he faced a redoubtable foe. During a hot, dusty summer they shared time without personal rancor, addressing such issues as Know-Nothingism, which Johnson attacked and Gentry defended; a temperance law, which the governor unequivocally opposed whereas Gentry preferred limited liquor sales; the plebeian's "unorthodox" democracy and the patrician's apostasy. In the end Gentry lost by 2,157 votes, carrying both east and west, but lagging by nearly 5,000 in rural middle Tennessee counties.

Again he returned to the farm in a sequestered valley in Bedford County. By 1860 his estate, valued at $120,000 encompassed 900 acres, with fifty slaves, horses and mules, cattle, sheep, and swine. He produced wheat, corn, potatoes, butter, and wool. Hillside, his home, built earlier in the decade, was handsomely furnished, with a library of several hundred volumes. Although retirement had its compensations, Gentry still liked an audience. On occasional Sunday afternoons, he "would stand on the front balcony," friends and neighbors ensconced on the lawn, and "inform them of current events and the latest political news."

For one who cherished the old flag, disunion and war were depressing news. The South seceded, and Tennessee eventually followed suit; ironically, William Seward had recommended Gentry for the Lincoln cabinet. Why go South? Subsequently he was quoted as saying that he neither believed in the right of secession nor considered it a panacea: "but a d——d old worm-eaten, rickety stern-wheel boat . . . came along"; and when, despite his pleadings, friends, neighbors, and kinsmen rushed pellmell aboard, "I shouted to them hold on! . . . we'll all go to Hell together." First he went to Richmond. As a representative in the first regular Confederate Congress, he had little stomach for debate, made one desultory speech, attended only one session, and did not seek reelection. Yet in 1863–64 he sold his estate, books and "One fine Gold Watch" included, investing in Confederate securities. Peace found him destitute, dependent upon his eldest daughter who had married a wealthy ironmonger thirty-four years her senior. He died soon afterward and was buried in Mt. Olivet Cemetery near Nashville. This magnificent orator, adroit in debate, scathing in satire, master of the *mot juste*, was fiercely independent, a partisan unfettered by strictest ties of loyalty. Therein lies an irony: impelled by conviction and caught by circumstance, he seceded—first from party, then from country. So near to eminence, Gentry is a study in "what might have been."

SEE: Bedford County Historical Society, *Doors to the Past: Homes of Shelbyville and Bedford County* (1969); Hubert B. Bentley, "Andrew Johnson, Governor of Tennessee, 1853–57" (Ph.D. diss., University of Tennessee, 1972); Virginia M. Bowman, *Historic Williamson County, Old Homes and Sites* (1971); Campbell Family Papers (Manuscript Department, Library, Duke University, Durham); Robert L. Caruthers Papers (Southern Historical Collection, University of North Carolina, Chapel Hill); *Congressional Globe*, 26th-27th, 29th-32nd Congs. (1839–53); Deeds of Bedford County, Tenn. (County Courthouse, Shelbyville); Susie Gentry, *Sketches from the Life of Meredith P. Gentry* (1899); Knoxville *Whig*, scattered issues, 1850–56; Nashville *Republican Banner*, scattered issues, 1837–61; T. A. R. Nelson Papers (McClung Collection, Lawson-McGhee Library, Knoxville); Alexander H. Stephens, *A Comprehensive and Popular History of the United States* (1884); Oliver P. Temple, *Notable Men of Tennessee from 1833 to 1875* (1912), and Papers (Library, University of Tennessee, Knoxville); U.S. Census, 1860, Bedford County, Tenn.; C. Van West, "The Evolution of a Whig Stronghold: Rutherford County, Tennessee, 1834–1845" (Seminar paper, University of Tennessee, 1978); Wills and Inventories of Williamson County, Tenn. (County Courthouse, Franklin); Yeatman-Polk Collection (Tennessee State Library and Archives, Nashville).

RALPH W. HASKINS

**George, Marcus** *(ca. 1760/65?–7 Oct. 1810)*, educator and classical scholar, was born in Ireland. He obtained his U.S. citizenship in Warren County August Court in 1802. His first known appearance in North Carolina was in 1788 at the time of the constitutional convention at Hillsborough, where he was in search of employment as a teacher. The Warrenton Academy had been created by legislative act in 1786, and five of the twenty trustees named in the act who were delegates to the Hillsborough convention engaged the young Irishman as principal to organize and conduct the school.

The male academy was well attended from the start and many students came from other communities as well as from Warren County. Many were sons of the leading citizens of eastern North Carolina and of the bordering counties of Virginia. Thomas Ruffin (later chief justice of North Carolina), who was sent to the Warrenton Academy from his home in Essex County, Va., was so well instructed by George that he entered the junior class at Nassau Hall (now Princeton University) in 1803. The scholastic achievements of George's students who furthered their education at The University of North Carolina so impressed President Joseph Caldwell that an unsuccessful effort was made in 1805 to induce George to accept the chair of ancient languages at Chapel Hill.

Despite the numerous references to him as the Reverend Mr. George, no evidence of his church affiliation has been found. His reputed previous experience on the stage, however, contributed to the success of theatrical performances to raise money for buildings and equipment for the school during his twenty years as principal of the Warrenton Academy. As early as 1793 he instigated the performance of a comedy and farce, followed by a ball the next night. The institution flourished and a new building was authorized in 1800 to replace the unpretentious building that had been completed in 1792; George conducted the subscription and directed the activities to finance the undertaking. This "Red Academy," so called because of the dark red paint used on the exterior of the building, continued to be used as a school building, with some alterations and additions, for over a hundred years until a high school was built on the site in 1923.

Until 1805 students at Warrenton Academy lived in homes in the town, but that year a steward's house was built at the academy for the accommodation of the students with board and lodging under the immediate supervision of the principal. Various activities were offered to supplement the money raised by contributions. Among them was a theatrical performance by the gentlemen of the town on the evening of the first day of the Warrenton spring races in June 1805. Jacob Mordecai was steward at the academy in 1807, the year of George's marriage to Mary F. Campbell. One of Mordecai's daughters later wrote that George's marriage, late in life, was an unhappy one and that his wife was an artful widow who induced him to move from Warrenton to Petersburg, Va. Apparently they had no children.

Not long before leaving Warrenton in 1809, George built a new dwelling house across Main Street from the Warrenton Academy on town lots totaling two acres that he had bought in 1802. After moving to Petersburg, he sold his house to Jacob Mordecai. In Petersburg he was principal of an academy when he died "after a short but severe indisposition."

SEE: Kemp P. Battle, *History of the University of North Carolina*, vol. 1 (1907); Walter Clark, ed., *State Records of North Carolina*, vol. 24 (1905); Charles L. Coon, *North Carolina Schools and Academies, 1790–1840* (1915); Court Minutes, Deeds and Marriage Bonds of Warren County (North Carolina State Archives, Raleigh); Halifax *North Carolina Journal*, 31 Oct. 1792, 15 Jan. 1794, 1 Jan. 1798, 7 Jan. 1799, 22 Apr., 6 May, 11 Nov. 1805, 8 Dec. 1806; Joseph G. deR. Hamilton, ed., *The Papers of Thomas Ruffin*, vol. 1 (1918); Sarah Lemmon, ed., *The Pettigrew Papers*, vol. 1 (1971); Elizabeth W. Montgomery, *Sketches of Old Warrenton* (1924); Mordecai Family Papers (Southern Historical Collection, University of North Carolina, Chapel Hill); *Raleigh Register*, 8 Apr., 9 Sept. 1800, 12 Jan. 1801, 19 Jan. 1802, 10 June 1805, 24 Nov. 1806, 18 Oct. 1810; University Papers (Southern Historical Collection, University of North Carolina, Chapel Hill).

M. H. D. KERR

**Gerrard, Charles** *(ca. 1750–6 Oct. 1797)*, Revolutionary patriot and philanthropist, was born in Beaufort County. Little is known of his antecedents. His mother, Dinah, was married a second time—to one Sirmon—and was living as late as 1797. Gerrard was mentioned as a brother in the will of Forbes Gerrard, probated in Beaufort County in 1786. During the American Revolution, Charles Gerrard was a lieutenant of the Fifth Regiment of the Continental line of which Edward Buncombe was colonel. After the war the rank of lieutenant entitled him to a grant of 2,560 acres, which he located at the junction of Yellow Creek and the Cumberland River not far below the present city of Nashville, Tenn. He seems to have lived on this land for some years, for in 1789 he represented Davidson County in the constitutional convention of North Carolina. A year later Davidson was included in the newly organized "Territory South of the River Ohio."

At an undetermined date Gerrard returned to North Carolina and settled in the town of Tarboro, where he went into business with Edward Hall, a prominent merchant. Gerrard had a contract with the U.S. postmaster general for carrying the mail between Louisburg, Nash Court House, and Tarboro once a week in each direction for which he was paid $46.67 quarterly. Late in life he married, in Tarboro, Elizabeth Hill, the daughter of James Hill. They had no children. His widow married Henry Hunter in 1805 and had a son, Charles Gerrard Hunter, who moved to Louisiana and married a cousin, Rosalie Barrow.

Gerrard died at the residence of General William Arrington in Nash County. His obituary in the *North Carolina Journal* described him as a brave and persevering soldier who "as a citizen, husband, father, friend, and neighbor was justly admired by all who knew him." The obituary further reported that he had been afflicted with dropsy (congestive heart failure) for three years before his death, and in the last year of his life had been tapped nineteen times, the quantity of water taken from him amounting to 55 gallons, 3 quarts, and 1½ pints.

Gerrard's will, dated 2 Mar. 1797, was probated in Edgecombe County in August 1798. In addition to providing for his wife and other relatives, he bequeathed his sword and $25 for a ring of rememberance to his friend and executor, Thomas Blount of Tarboro; his pistols to General William Brickell, another friend; and his land in his native county of Beaufort for the benefit of the poor. The bulk of his estate, 13,000 acres of land in the state of Tennessee, was left to The University of North Carolina. This legacy stipulated that the 2,560 acres granted him for service in the army never be sold and that the remainder of the acreage be held for at least seven years. The university gradually sold off these holdings but for thirty-five years honored Gerrard's request for the 2,560 acres. In 1833, attorneys William Gaston and Edmund Badger gave the opinion that the trustees had the right to sell the service tract of land. Acting through Colonel William Polk as attorney, the university sold the 2,560 acres for $6,400. Of this sum, $2,000 was applied toward the new chapel then under construction in Chapel Hill. According to President Kemp P. Battle, it was resolved that, to show gratitude for the liberality of the donor and to perpetuate his memory, the building would be known as Gerrard Hall.

SEE: Kemp. P. Battle, *History of the University of North Carolina*, vol. 1 (1907); Deeds and Wills of the Counties of Beaufort and Edgecombe (North Carolina State Archives, Raleigh); *North Carolina Journal*, 16 Oct. 1797.

CLAIBORNE T. SMITH, JR.

**Gheen, James** *(fl. 1778–96)*, cabinetmaker, may have moved to Rowan County from Chester County, Pa., in the late 1770s. The Rowan County tax list for 1778 shows that he resided in "Capt. Craige's District." Nothing of Gheen's parentage is presently known. It is believed that he was married and had several children when he arrived in Rowan County. The 1790 census lists James Gheen, Jr., and James Gheen, Sr., in the county with families composed of four and ten persons, respectively. In addition, Thomas Gheen is listed with a family of four. None of them held slaves.

Two land transactions for Gheen are recorded in Deed Book 14 of Rowan County, 1778–92. In 1780 he purchased 270 acres on the north side of the Yadkin River, and in 1792 he bought 500 acres on Second Creek. Like other cabinetmakers in the Piedmont area, Gheen probably supplemented his income by farming. Although he acquired two acres and four lots in the town of Salisbury, he did not establish a shop there. His will, written in 1796, bequeathed the land on Second Creek and the house, shop, and shop tools to his youngest son, Joseph.

Thirteen pieces of furniture have been attributed to Gheen. One piece—a combination desk and bookcase—was made in 1794 for the Reverend Samuel E. McCorkle, pastor of Thyatira Presbyterian Church and a founder of The University of North Carolina. A signed and dated bill of sale for the piece survives. The other pieces are nine desks-and-bookcases, two chests of drawers, and a desk. All of the items are similar in design vocabulary and distinctive construction techniques. In addition to his cabinetmaking business, Gheen was a constable for his district in 1782–83.

The name of his wife is not known, but there were at least seven children. The date of his death and place of burial are also unknown.

SEE: Archives, Museum of Early Southern Decorative Arts (Winston-Salem), for information on James Gheen; Carolyn Weekly, "James Gheen, Piedmont North Carolina Cabinetmaker," *Antiques Magazine* 103 (May 1973).

WHALEY W. BATSON

**Gibbon, John** *(20 Apr. 1827–6 Feb. 1896)*, career soldier, was born near Holmesburg (now within Philadelphia), Pa., the son of Dr. John Heysham and Catherine Lardner Gibbon. The family soon moved to Charlotte, N.C., where John obtained an appointment to the U.S. Military Academy. He was graduated twentieth in the thirty-eight-member class of 1847. Commissioned into the artillery too late for active fighting in Mexico, he spent the next fourteen years in a succession of routine peacetime assignments highlighted by five years at West Point teaching artillery tactics. He was promoted to captain in 1859.

A staunch Unionist in the secession crisis, Gibbon had predicted that North Caroina would secede "quietly." Three of his brothers joined the Confederacy and a sister waited until the summer of 1864 to pass northward through the lines. The outbreak of the Civil War found Gibbon stationed in the Utah Territory. Shortly after his arrival in Washington, D.C., late in the summer of 1861, he obtained command of the artillery of General Irvin McDowell's division, Army of the Potomac. Unlike many regulars, Gibbon flourished in the difficult task of whipping raw volunteers into trained soldiers. Ironically, his advancement to brigadier general (volunteers) was delayed until May 1862, because there were no North Carolina congressmen available to press his case. He subsequently led the Black Hat Brigade (First Corps) in the battles of Groveton, Second Bull Run, and Antietam with such distinction that the unit was renamed the "Iron Brigade" and he was elevated in November 1862 to head a First Corps division. Although pleased with the promotion, Gibbon was angered when his superior, General Joseph Hooker, nominated the politically potent but militarily unfit Solomon J. Meredith to succeed him as commander of the Iron Brigade. Gibbon's own politics were conservative Unionist; he respected General George B. McClellan and was personally close to General George G. Meade.

In the First Corps' attack on the Confederate right wing at Fredericksburg, Gibbon was wounded and had to give up his division. He took charge of another in the Second Corps when he returned to duty. The unit participated in the successful assault on Marye's Heights in the Chancellorsville campaign of May 1863. Twice during the Gettysburg campaign of June and July he assumed temporary command of the Second Corps. Because he enjoyed the esteem of General Meade, the army commander, he was included as a voting member of a corps commanders' council after the second day of heavy fighting at Gettysburg. The next day, both Gibbon and his superior, General Winfield S. Hancock, were severely wounded in the Second Corps's successful repulse of the Pickett-Pettigrew-Trimble charge.

Gibbon spent most of the fall and winter of 1863–64 recuperating in the successive command of conscript depots in Cleveland and Philadelphia. He managed to be present for Abraham Lincoln's dedicatory address at the Gettysburg National Cemetery and to defend both verbally and in print his friend and commander, General Meade, who labored under heavy Republican criticism for his alleged failure to follow up the victory at Gettysburg. Even after Meade's death, Gibbon continued defending his reputation by collecting testimony from fellow officers.

Although an experienced divisional commander and despite the fact that Meade had him in mind to succeed General John Sedgwick as commander of the Sixth Corps, Gibbon was made a major general only in June 1864 and only after Lieutenant General Ulysses S. Grant—in command of all federal armies since the preceding March—recommended him. Gibbon had been too proud to beg promotion from Secretary of War Edwin M. Stanton.

Gibbon's division sustained losses of 47 percent in the desperate May–June 1864 fighting from the Rapidan to the James; at one time or another it had nine different brigade and forty regimental commanders. By July and the early phases of the siege of Petersburg, the unit was badly worn down and Gibbon's relations with General Hancock, formerly cordial, had become acrimonious. On 25 August the command suffered a humiliating setback at Reams' Station, an engagement it would have won easily in its prime. Gibbon felt obliged to divest three regiments of their battle standards. But neither Reams' Station nor the quarrel with Hancock deprived him of Meade's and Grant's confidence; he was soon given temporary command of the Eighteenth Corps, Army of the James. Returning reluctantly to his old assignment and still sensitive about Reams' Station, Gibbon protested the appointment of General Andrew A. Humphreys to replace Hancock in the Second Corps as a slight to himself. But he was soon assuaged when in January 1865 he took permanent command of the Twenty-fourth Corps, which contained most of the newly reorganized Army of the James's white troops. The corps was conspicuous in the Appomattox campaign, and Gibbon was recognized by being named to head a three-general commission to oversee the formal capitulation of the Confederate Army of Northern Virginia.

During the half-year immediately following the close of the fighting, he commanded the Nottoway, Va., occupation district. However, the termination of wartime generals' commissions in early 1866 plummeted him back to captain. Fortunately, when the regular army was reorganized later that year he was given the colonelcy of the Thirty-sixth Infantry. In 1869, he took over the Seventh Infantry, which participated seven years later in General Alfred H. Terry's Little Bighorn campaign against the Sioux. Gibbon's troops were the first to reach the scene of the Custer massacre about two days after it had happened. The next year, on 9-10 Aug. 1877, the Seventh Infantry intercepted and surprised Chief Joseph and the Nez Percé at Big Hole Basin, Mont., when that tribe was trying to fight its way northeast from the Idaho Territory to sanctuary in Canada. After a very hard fight in which Gibbon was wounded, the Indians withdrew when General Oliver O. Howard approached from the west.

Promoted to brigadier general (regular) in 1885 and given command of the Department of the Columbia, Gibbon and his troops from Fort Vancouver, Wash., restored order in Seattle when the town was wracked by anti-Chinese turmoil. Retiring from the army in 1891, he spent his last years in Baltimore, Md., the home of his wife, Frances North Moale, whom he had married in 1855. His fellow Civil War veterans honored him with the command of the Loyal Legion.

Over a long, active career Gibbon did a surprisingly large amount of writing including *The Artillerist's Manual* (1860). His war memoirs, fair-minded, straightforward, and often vividly descriptive, are among the best of the genre. They show him to have been a loyal, diligent subordinate, little given to speculation about grand strategy. Although he did not regret his adherence to the Union, his postwar relationships with Confederate friends from the old army, such as his classmate Henry Heth, were cordial.

SEE: George W. Cullum, *Biographical Register of the Officers and Graduates of the U.S. Military Academy at West Point*, 3 vols. (1891); *DAB*, vol 4 (1960); John Gibbon, *Gibbon on the Sioux Campaign of 1876* (1877), Official Report on Big Hole (National Archives, Washington, D.C.), *Personal Recollections of the Civil War* (1928), and "The Battle of the Big Hole," *Harper's Weekly* 39 (28 Dec. 1895).

RICHARD G. STONE, JR.

**Gibbons, James** *(23 July 1834–24 Mar. 1921)*, Roman Catholic prelate, was born in Baltimore, Md., the son of recent Irish immigrants, Thomas and Bridget Walsh Gibbons. In 1837 financial reverses forced the family to return to Ireland where young Gibbons received his early education. Returning to the United States in 1853, the family settled in New Orleans. Two years later James Gibbons entered a seminary in Baltimore, and he was ordained at the end of June 1861. During the Civil War he served as pastor of a church in Baltimore as well as chaplain at nearby forts and military prisons. Although a Unionist in sympathy, he showed little or no outward sign of his feelings; he had a brother who was a Confederate soldier. In 1865 he became secretary to the archbishop in Baltimore and remained in that position until 1868, when he was consecrated bishop. At age thirty-four, he was the youngest Roman Catholic bishop.

In that capacity Gibbons was assigned to serve the newly created diocese of North Carolina, which previously had been within the jurisdiction of a bishop resident in Charleston, S.C. There were few Roman Catholics in his new diocese but the young bishop, who arrived in Wilmington in October 1868 to make his home, undertook a tour of the state. He afterwards traveled frequently to serve small, scattered congregations. He was warmly welcomed and often preached to large congregations in Protestant churches as well as in courthouses and other public buildings. Bishop Gibbons's pleasing personality, his friendly manner, and his open mind earned him many friends. As new converts were made and his church grew, he came to be recognized as a spiritual leader of great force. His ability to work with people of various faiths was significant in his future and the reputation he gained in North Carolina had much to do with the course of his life. In 1872 he became bishop of Richmond, and in the spring of 1877 he was named archbishop coadjutor of Baltimore. In October, at the age of forty-three, Gibbons became the archbishop and in 1886 he was made a cardinal. In Washington, D.C., which lay within his jurisdiction, Gibbons founded the Catholic University of America. He was also the author of several books, a supporter of organized labor, and a defender of the principle of separation of church and state. He counted among his friends many presidents of the United States, justices, and other public officials who often sought his advice. Gibbons was praised for his role in eliminating prejudice and in breaking down many barriers between men. He died in Baltimore and was buried in the crypt of Baltimore Cathedral.

SEE: *DAB*, vol. 7 (1931); John T. Ellis, *Life of James Cardinal Gibbons* (1952); Louis T. Garaventa, "Bishop James Gibbons and the Growth of the Roman Catholic Church in North Carolina, 1868–1872" (M.A. thesis, University of North Carolina, 1973); *New York Times*, 25 Mar. 1921; Raleigh *News and Observer*, 5 May 1912; Allen S. Will, *Life of Cardinal Gibbons*, 2 vols. (1922); Day Allen Willey, "Cardinal Gibbons Forty Years Ago, The Work of a Zealous Young Bishop in North Carolina," *Putnam's Monthly* 4 (August 1908).

WILLIAM S. POWELL

**Gibbs (Gibbes, Gibs), John** *(fl. 1682–95)*, acting governor, presumably was the John Gibbs of Norwich, England, whom the Proprietors of Carolina named to the nobility of their province, with the rank of cacique, on 9 Oct. 1682. The appointment provided a plausible basis for him to claim the governorship of North Carolina and to exercise its powers for several months some years later. Gibbs was a kinsman of Christopher Monck, Duke of Albemarle, the Proprietor who nominated him to the nobility. His family, which had roots in Devonshire, had long been active in American colonization, both as promoters and settlers. Among its members were prominent colonists in Virginia, Barbados, and South Carolina, several of whom were named John but appear not to have been the John Gibbs associated with North Carolina.

In November 1682 and again the following March, the Proprietors directed South Carolina officials to grant Gibbs extensive tracts of land upon his application, but he appears not to have taken up land in that colony. By 1690, however, he held several tracts in North Carolina and at least 3,400 acres in Virginia. When in North Carolina he apparently lived on a plantation in Pasquotank Precinct. His Virginia home was in Lower Norfolk County in the Currituck area.

Gibbs bought his Pasquotank plantation on 16 Nov. 1689. He arrived in North Carolina at some earlier date, for he was identified in the deed as "Governor" of the colony. He probably assumed the governorship soon after the banishment of Governor Seth Sothel, which seems to have occurred in September or October 1689. It is not known whether Gibbs was in the colony when Sothel was ousted or whether he came from his Virginia plantation or elsewhere upon news of Sothel's banishment.

One of the few surviving records of Gibbs's career is a copy of an act of assembly headed, "An act of Sembly made in the year 1689 Capt. John Gibbs being then Governor." The act, intended for "the better Establishing of unity and tranquillity," prohibited use of "opprobrious language" against any person concerned in "the late transactions of the County." The council members named in the manuscript were Thomas Jarvis, William Wilkison, Richard Sanderson, Thomas Miller, and John Hunt. The speaker was John Nixon, and the burgesses were Henderson Walker, John Lewis, John Wingate, Thomas Pollock, and John Philpott. Participation in his government by these prominent leaders indicates that Gibbs's claim was generally considered valid by the colonists. Little more is known of his administration, which ended in effect the following spring when Philip Ludwell took office as governor under a commission from the Proprietors.

Extant documents do not state the grounds on which Gibbs claimed the governorship, but they make it clear that he believed himself legally entitled to the office under the Fundamental Constitutions of Carolina. It also is evident that knowledgeable men of his day thought his claim had merit. Even Philip Ludwell appears to have been uneasy about his own right to the office, despite his commission from the Proprietors. The governor of Virginia likewise indicated doubt as to the validity of Ludwell's appointment.

The Fundamental Constitutions did contain provisions that appear to have been good ground for Gibbs's claim. Both of the versions adopted in 1682 restricted the office of governor, or "palatine's deputy," to Proprietors, heirs apparent of Proprietors, landgraves, and caciques, giving precedence to those ranks in the order named, with preference to the eldest member, and requiring personal presence in the colony for qualification as governor. So far as extant records show, there were no Proprietors, heirs apparent of Proprietors, or landgraves in North Carolina after the departure of Sothel (a Proprietor), and Gibbs was the only cacique then in the colony. Under the apparent meaning of the constitutions, therefore, it seems that Gibbs would have become interim governor automatically, as he was the only person then in the colony who was in one of the categories of persons designated to act as governor when a vacancy developed. Moreover, the pertinent provisions also appear to mean that the Proprietors, in formally filling the vacancy, had no choice but to commission Gibbs unless some other person in one of the specified categories were to come to the colony in the interim.

Although Gibbs seems to have had a strong claim as a cacique, he appears to have contended that he was a Proprietor and to have claimed the governorship in that capacity. The Fundamental Constitutions provided plausible support even for that claim, for under their provisions concerning the descent of proprietorships by inheritance, Gibbs probably would have inherited the proprietorship of his kinsman, Christopher Monck, who died childless in 1688. Those provisions specified that in the absence of male heirs the proprietorship was to go to "that Landgrave or Cacique of Carolina . . . descended of the next Heir Female." Inasmuch as Gibbs apparently was the only relative of Monck, who was a member of the Carolina nobility, he probably thought that this and related provisions of the constitutions made him heir to Monck's proprietorship. Inheritance of Monck's proprietorship, however, was not determined by the Fundamental Constitutions of Carolina but, like the rest of Monck's estate, by the laws of England. After lengthy litigation in England, another kinsman, John Grenville, Earl of Bath, was designated heir at law.

Whatever rights Gibbs had under the "Fundamentals," they were ignored by the Proprietors, who never considered the constitutions fully in effect or binding upon themselves. In December 1689 they appointed Philip Ludwell of Virginia to be governor of North Carolina. Although Ludwell in no way met the specifications set forth in the constitutions, he took office and set up his government the following spring, probably in May.

Gibbs did not relinquish the governorship quietly. On 2 June 1690 he issued a "declaration" denouncing Ludwell as "Rascal, imposter and usurper" and offering to fight with swords, "as long as my Eyelidds shall wagg," anyone who undertook to justify Ludwell's assumption of the office. He commanded the colonists to "consult the Fundamentals" and render him "due obedience," forbidding them to assume any office by virtue of a commission from Ludwell and proclaiming his determination not to permit himself to be wronged by "the Lords Proprietors, or Country."

Gibbs did not content himself with words. On 6 July 1690, assisted by a group of armed men, he broke up the Pasquotank Precinct court, which was sitting under commission from Ludwell. He seized two of the magistrates and took them to his Virginia plantation, where he held them prisoners. As Ludwell was in Virginia at the time, the deputy governor, Thomas Jarvis, sent the militia to rescue the magistrates. The attempt was unsuccessful, for the forces could not follow Gibbs into Virginia. Jarvis then wrote to the Virginia governor, requesting assistance in releasing the prisoners. He also wrote to Ludwell, informing him of the episode and the actions taken. Ludwell likewise wrote to the Virginia governor, who effected the release of the North Carolina justices and advised both Ludwell and Gibbs to refer their dispute over the governorship to the Proprietors.

Subsequently, both Gibbs and Ludwell went to London and laid the matter before the Proprietors, who upheld their appointment of Ludwell. They also suspended the Fundamental Constitutions, removing whatever basis the "Fundamentals" afforded for Gibbs's claim.

Although Gibbs desisted from efforts to assert his claim by force, he did not abandon belief in his right to the governorship. In late June 1695 the Proprietors wrote Ludwell that there was "no force" to Gibb's claim, which Gibbs had recently reasserted in a letter to Ludwell.

If Gibbs returned to North Carolina after his seizure of the Pasquotank justices, it was only briefly. By February 1690/91 he had appointed an attorney, Edward Mayo, to handle his affairs in the colony. Mayo sold a portion of Gibbs's land, the remainder of which eventually escheated and was granted to other colonists.

Gibbs's wife apparently was named Mary. He had a son, John, Jr., and a daughter, Mary, who became the wife of Martin Bladen (1680–1746), a member of Parliament and of the Board of Trade. In surveying the dividing line between North Carolina and Virginia in 1728,

William Byrd noted that "the neck of land included betwixt North River and Northwest River, with the adjacent marsh, belonged formerly to Governor Gibbs but since his decease to Colonel Bladen." Nothing is known of Gibbs's later life. He may have spent his latter years in Princess Anne County, Va., where a Captain John Gibbs held 3,100 acres of land in 1704.

SEE: Colonial Court Records (North Carolina State Archives, Raleigh); Mattie Erma E. Parker, ed., *Colonial Records of North Carolina, Higher-Court Records, 1670–1696*, vol. 2 (1968), *1697–1701*, vol. 3 (1971), and *North Carolina Charters and Constitutions, 1578–1698* (1963); William S. Powell, *The Proprietors of Carolina* (1963); William S. Price, Jr., ed., *Colonial Records of North Carolina, Higher-Court Records, 1702–1708*, vol. 4 (1974); W. Noel Sainsbury and others, eds., *Calendar of State Papers, Colonial Series, America and West Indies*, vols. 9-14 (1860–1903); William L. Saunders, ed., *Colonial Records of North Carolina*, vol. 1 (1886); "Virginia Quit Rent Rolls, Princess Anne County, Rent Roll 1704," *Virginia Magazine of History and Biography* 30 (1922); Louis B. Wright, ed., *The Prose Works of William Byrd of Westover* (1966).

MATTIE ERMA E. PARKER

**Gilbert, Katherine Everett** *(29 July 1886–28 Apr. 1952)*, educator and philosopher, was born in Newport, R.I., the daughter of Thomas Jefferson and Sue Morrison Everett. After attending local schools in Newport, she taught for a year in an ungraded school at Mount Hope, Conn. In the fall of 1904 she entered Brown University, where she was graduated with a bachelor of arts degree in 1908 and a master of arts in 1910. During the master's program, she was an assistant in philosophy to Dean Alexander Meiklejohn and Professor Walter G. Everett. Continuing her graduate studies at Cornell University, she was a scholar and fellow in the Sage School of Philosophy and received a doctor of philosophy degree in 1912. On 1 Aug. 1913 she married Allan H. Gilbert. Two years later she became the assistant of Professor James E. Creighton, editor of the *Philosophical Review* at Cornell.

When her husband became associated with Duke University, Durham, Mrs. Gilbert accepted a post as Kenan Research Fellow in Philosophy at The University of North Carolina, Chapel Hill, where she worked from 1922 to 1929, the last year as acting professor of philosophy. In 1930 she was appointed professor of philosophy at Duke, and in 1942 she was named head of its newly established Department of Aesthetics, Art, and Music. Mrs. Gilbert was the first woman to become a full professor and, until the time of her death, the only woman to hold the chairmanship of a liberal arts department at Duke University, where she also was instrumental in inaugurating the Chamber Arts Society.

Early in her career, she joined the American Philosophical Society; later she was a member of the program committee, served a term as vice-president of the eastern division, and subsequently was elected president—one of the three women up to that time to hold the office. Other memberships included the International Spinoza Society, the Southern Philosophical and Psychological Association, the American Society for Aesthetics (president, 1947–48), and the American Association of University Women (member, National Committee on Standards, 1942–46). In 1938 she organized a program on the education of women for Duke's Centennial. The previous year she had served as a representative of the U.S. State Department to students of philosophy in Italy.

Mrs. Gilbert was a meticulous and prolific writer. Many of her articles appeared in the *American Philosophical Journal*; she also reviewed numerous books for that and other journals and magazines. As a research student, she was continually accumulating information on subjects in her field that had received scant attention from others. Consequently, her works were highly creative. Principal among her published books are *Maurice Blondel's Philosophy of Action* (1924); *Studies in Recent Aesthetics* (1927); with Helmut Kuhn, *A History of Aesthetics* (1939); and *Aesthetic Studies: Architecture and Poetry* (1952). She was a contributor to *Philosophical Essays: Studies in Honor of James Edward Creighton* (1917). In 1942 she was awarded the honorary doctor of letters degree by Brown University.

Her husband, a distinguished English and Renaissance scholar, taught at Duke University for thirty-six years. They had two sons: Everett Eddy, a chemist and investigative scientist; and Creighton Eddy, an international authority on art history and education.

Mrs. Gilbert died in Durham at the age of sixty-six. The Gilbert-Addoms dormitory on the East Campus of Duke University was named in honor of her and a contemporary.

SEE: *Durham Morning Herald*, 29 Apr. 1952; Office of Information, Duke University, Durham, for information on Katherine Gilbert; Raleigh *News and Observer*, 29 Apr. 1952.

C. SYLVESTER GREEN

**Gilbert, William** *(1735–90)*, legislator and Revolutionary War figure, was born in Ireland and as an infant was brought to Massachusetts by his parents. In Pennsylvania, about 1760, he married Sarah McCandless against her parents' wishes and moved to western North Carolina. Beginning in 1769, he purchased land and cattle until he became the largest taxpayer and property holder in Tryon (now Rutherford) County. Gilbert paid the passage of a number of Irish laborers whom he employed in his farming endeavors. His home and farms became known as Gilbert Town.

Active in local politics, Gilbert served as juror, justice of the peace, and member of the court of pleas and quarter sessions from 1770 to 1775. In 1775, he and twenty-five other Whigs signed the "Association Oath" as members of the Tryon Committee of Public Safety. During the American Revolution he acted as a commissary for the militia in the Tryon area. In 1779 he represented Tryon County in the General Assembly, where he presented local bills and was concerned with the improvement of river navigation and Indian affairs. Later that year, after a six-month inquiry, he was expelled from the Assembly for "intentionally defrauding the publick." Rutherford County (created out of Tryon in 1779) immediately reelected him in 1780 and again in 1782 and 1783.

Gilbert Town was the highwater mark of Lieutenant Colonel Patrick Ferguson's northward advance in September 1780. Ferguson kept his troops there because of Gilbert's reputation as a "warm Whig." Mrs. Gilbert also had used the home as an arms storage point for the Whigs. Controversy raged when wounded British Major James Dunlap, whom Ferguson left behind in the Gilbert home, was murdered by a group of avenging Whigs. After the Battle of Kings Mountain, Tory prisoners were executed at Gilbert Town. From 1775 to 1783, Gilbert continued to serve as justice of the peace, tax assessor and collector, and member and chairman of the Rutherford Court of Pleas and Quarter Sessions. His home, which also doubled as a tavern, was used as the county seat during this period.

In 1784, charges were again brought against Gilbert and the General Assembly, finding him guilty of forgery, removed him as justice of the peace in Rutherford. He sold his property to his son-in-law, North Carolina legislator Major James Holland, and moved to Charleston, S.C. There he lost a great deal of his property, and several of his children died in epidemics. Returning to Rutherford, he remained embattled in countless law suits over real estate and in personal disputes. After his death, this fiery Irishman's 5,000-acre tract in Tennessee and his land in North Carolina were snarled in litigation until 1806. Surviving him were his wife and three children, John, Alexander McCandless, and Sarah Gilbert Holland. Mrs. Gilbert died at Major Holland's home in Maury County, Tenn., on 22 Dec. 1822.

SEE: Walter Clark, ed., *State Records of North Carolina*, vols. 12, 13, 16, 17, 19, 21 (1895–1903); S. S. L. Cochrane, "Memorabilia" (Tennessee Archives, Nashville); Clarence W. Griffin, *Old Tryon and Rutherford Counties* (1937); Nashville *American*, 11 Oct. 1896; H. H. Newton, *Rutherford County, North Carolina, Abstracts* (1974); North Carolina Land Grants in Tennessee (Tennessee Archives, Nashville); William L. Saunders, ed., *Colonial Records of North Carolina*, vols. 9, 10 (1890); Wisconsin State Historical Society, *Calendar of the Tennessee and King's Mountain Papers of the Draper Collection of Manuscripts* (1929).

N. C. HUGHES, JR.

**Gilchrist, Peter Spence** *(10 Aug. 1861–31 Dec. 1947)*, chemical engineer and specialist in sulfuric acid and fertilizer plants, was born in Manchester, England. His father, John Gilchrist, a Scotsman, was a chemical engineer and manager of the Manchester Alum Works; his mother, Jessie Stuart Howie Gilchrist of Dundee, was closely related to Peter Spence, who owned the Manchester Alum Works. Spence had initiated radical alterations in the manufacture of alum in 1845 and held numerous chemical patents. Young Gilchrist attended Chalmers Presbyterian Day School and, for three years, the venerable Manchester Grammar School where he excelled in mechanical drawing. He was apprenticed at age sixteen to Wren & Hopkins, an engineering firm, and also continued to develop his skill in drawing, both at night school and at home. In a British Empire competition, with entries from all over the world, he was awarded the Queen's Medal; his prize-winning engineering drawing was displayed in Kensington Museum.

Gilchrist made his first visit to the United States in 1882, when he was sent by his father and Peter Spence to install a pyrites furnace for the W. G. Crenshaw Sulphur Mines Company in Richmond, Va. On returning to England soon after his twenty-first birthday, he was retained by an engineering firm to supervise the construction of Spence burners. Soon afterward he became superintendent of the North Dean Chemical Works, Yorkshire, where he gained experience in the manufacture of sulfuric acid; then, for several years, he was superintendent of the Spence-owned Goole Alum Works, also in Yorkshire.

In 1888, he crossed the Atlantic again to Point Orient on Long Island, N.Y., where for three years he was superintendent of a company that produced sulfuric acid and fertilizers and operated a fleet of menhaden fishing boats. In January 1892, Gilchrist married Ethel Gertrude Porter in Goole and brought her to the United States.

For the next six years he worked as a chemical engineer in Baltimore, Md., and in Charleston, Darlington, and Blacksburg, S.C., the latter place being the site of a gold mine that he operated for a British syndicate. During these years, which included some reverses, his consulting work took him to cities in the Midwest, East, and South; on his travels he also sold the Small Herreshoff Furnace for General Chemical Company of New York and white quartz (used as packing in acid towers) for Fred Oliver of Charlotte, N.C.

In January 1898 Gilchrist settled in Charlotte, where he was to live the rest of his life. From his North Carolina base, he built plants in a large area of the United States and abroad. His specialty was designing, erecting, putting into operation, and improving plants for the production of sulfuric acid and fertilizers. Some of the great phosphate mining operations in Florida were created under his direction. For years he personally handled and carefully recorded much of the detail of his innovative work. Always he was an indefatigable student of technical literature. During the years 1905–10, Gilchrist also had an interest in the Southern Card, Clothing, and Reed Company, manufacturers, and served as its president. He became a director of the Union National Bank of Charlotte when it was established in 1908.

In December 1914 he was one of the organizers of Chemical Construction Company, with headquarters at Charlotte. His associates were Ingenuin Hechenbleikner from Innsbruck, Austria, who had come to the United States as a consultant for James B. Duke; Thomas C. Oliver, a mining engineer, who managed the New York office; and A. Mangum Webb of Charlotte. Gilchrist was president of this instantly successful company of engineers. In the ensuing years it handled contracts for many types of chemical plants and industrial chemical processes in the United States and in more than twelve foreign countries. To ensure the capital needed to maintain worldwide operations, James B. Duke lent his credit with the proviso that he hold 51 percent of the stock. Gilchrist was concurrently vice-president of Oliver Quartz Company, a supplier of massive quartz and acid-proof cement, of Hood Brick Company, which made acid-proof brick and spiral rings; and of Charlotte Chemical Laboratories, research and manufacturing chemists.

Early in World War I, Chemical Construction Company built the Gilchrist Plant at Queens Ferry, Wales, the largest sulfuric acid plant in the British Isles. In the United States, the company was involved in the production of essential war materials, the rapid buildup of chemical plants, and the construction of nitric acid and ammonium nitrate plants for the government installations at Muscle Shoals and Sheffield, Ala., and Cincinnati and Toledo, Ohio. The Chemical Construction Company was sold in 1929, before the market crash, to American Cyanamid Company. When the office moved to New York in 1933, Gilchrist, who remained in Charlotte, was retained as consultant. During the 1930s he often traveled in Europe and Latin America, accompanied by members of his family, to investigate chemical possibilities for the company. In his seventies he was actively engaged in the Charlotte Chemical Laboratories and also continued a private practice as consulting engineer.

By 1943 the number of sulfuric acid plants that he had built during his career was reckoned at 66; he also had built 62 fertilizer plants and made additions to 55 others. His son estimated that Gilchrist's engineering files contained between 5,000 and 6,000 drawings that he and his draftsmen had made. He was a member of the American Society of Chemical Engineers and the Society of Chemical Industry in England.

For more than forty years Gilchrist participated actively in the life of the community. He was a charter member of the Westminster Presbyterian Church (later merged with Covenant Presbyterian Church), served as an elder, and several times was commissioner to the denomination's General Assembly. He was on the local school board and the board of Queen's College, Charlotte; a trustee of the Presbyterian Foundation; president of the Blue Ridge Association; and a director and president (1923–35) of the Charlotte YMCA.

Throughout his life in his adopted country, Gilchrist kept in close touch with his homeland, going back to visit and having Gilchrist and Porter relatives come over for extended visits in his household. Though he counted it a privilege to live in America, he did not become a U.S. citizen until 1926, and even then he regretted having to relinquish his English citizenship in the process.

Small of stature, Gilchrist was referred to affectionately by his colleagues in the industry as the "Big Little Chief." He is remembered in Charlotte as a lively, attractive, and sympathetic person, whose handsome, ruddy-pink face reflected frankly his reactions and emotions. Conservative in personal habits and manner of living, he contributed quietly to many philanthropies and took particular pleasure in helping young men who were seeking a college education. It was, finally, his upright and unselfish character rather than his extraordinary career that became the focal point of the tributes paid to him both before and after his death. He died in the house where he had lived for half a century and was buried in Elmwood Cemetery, Charlotte. His children were John W. Stuart, Cecil Waltham, Edith Muriel (m. Herman P. Hamilton), and Peter Spence, Jr. A portrait painted by Peggy Parsley is owned by Peter S. Gilchrist, Jr.

SEE: *Charlotte Observer*, 27 Mar. 1920, 1 Jan. 1948; Peter Spence Gilchrist Business Papers (Southern Historical Collection, University of North Carolina, Chapel Hill); Peter Spence Gilchrist, Jr., *My Father, Peter Spence Gilchrist* (1943); A. M. Webb, "Peter Spence Gilchrist," *Industrial Engineering and Chemistry* 25 (September 1933).

ANNA BROOKE ALLAN

**Gilchrist, Thomas** *(ca. 1735–89)*, merchant, was the subject of an unusual episode in the Revolutionary annals of North Carolina. Married to Martha Jones, sister of the Halifax Whig leaders Willie and Allen Jones, Gilchrist for a time was under suspicion of treason. He was a native of Scotland, and there is some indication that he came from Galloway in the southwestern section of that country. With his brother, John, Thomas Gilchrist settled in Virginia and established a mercantile business in the town of Suffolk. While there he was active in the affairs of the Upper Parish in Nansemond County. He served as a vestryman and church warden, and in 1768 was directed to employ an attorney to prosecute one Lunan on behalf of the parish. The attorney engaged was Thomas Jefferson, and this is thought to have been the young lawyer's first case.

In 1773 Gilchrist went on a business trip to Scotland, leaving his affairs in the hands of his brother John, who was living in Norfolk. During his absence, John Gilchrist committed suicide and one John Campbell became administrator of the estate. The American Revolution broke out before the estate could be settled, and Thomas Gilchrist, who on his return to America had settled in Halifax, N.C., was unable to secure his property. Campbell, an ardent Tory, left Norfolk when it was evacuated by Lord Dunmore and eventually went to Bermuda. According to the petition of Martha Jones Gilchrist to the Assembly of North Carolina, dated 1 Aug. 1778, her husband was loyal to the American cause but had to feign adherence to the king in order to obtain his property from John Campbell. Hence Thomas Gilchrist had left North Carolina without taking the required loyalty oath to the new state and followed Campbell to Bermuda. Successful in his mission, he immediately sailed to Savannah where he took the oath of allegiance to the state of Georgia. A short time later he did the same in South Carolina. Mrs. Gilchrist succeeded in obtaining permission for her husband to return to Halifax and his reputation was cleared. Though Willie Jones was considered a political radical during the Revolution, his opposition to the Assembly's act of 1779 confiscating the estates of certain loyalists may have been influenced by the difficulties of his brother-in-law.

After the Revolution, Gilchrist moved to Tarboro, which was growing more rapidly than Halifax, where he was a town commissioner in 1785. His will, dated 6 Aug. 1789, was probated in Edgecombe County in the fall of that year. It referred to his share in Richard Henderson's land company and named his brothers-in-law, Willie and Allen Jones, executors. Following his death, his widow moved back to Halifax where she died, leaving a will probated in 1800. Thomas and Martha Gilchrist were the parents of two daughters, Elizabeth and Grizelda, and a son, Allen. Elizabeth married Thomas Hogg, and Grizelda was the first wife of the Revolutionary hero, Colonel William Polk. Allen Gilchrist represented the borough of Halifax in the House of Commons in 1805. After his marriage in 1806 to Dolly Lane, the daughter of Joel Lane of Raleigh, he moved to Wake County, which he represented in the House of Commons in 1808. Afterward he and his wife left the state.

SEE: Walter Clark, ed., *State Records of North Carolina*, vol. 13, (1907); Deeds and Wills of Edgecombe County (County Courthouse, Tarboro); Deeds and Wills of Halifax County (County Courthouse, Halifax); Wilmer Hall, *The Vestry Book of the Upper Parish* (1954); Thomas Jefferson, *Reports of Cases Determined in the General Court of Virginia from 1730 to 1740 and from 1768 to 1772* (1829).

CLAIBORNE T. SMITH, JR.

**Gill, Edwin Maurice** *(20 July 1899–16 July 1978)*, lawyer and public official, was born in Laurinburg, the son of Thomas Jeffries and Mamie North Gill. After attending local schools, he entered Trinity College in 1922 but left in 1924 after passing the bar examination. He established his practice in Laurinburg, and was elected to represent Scotland County in the General Assembly in 1929 and 1931. In the legislature he was a member of the subcommittees that drafted the state's local government act and the bill authorizing the state to take over the construction and maintenance of county roads. He also supported legislation for the Australian ballot, workmen's compensation, university consolidation, and benefits for the blind.

On 1 July 1931, after the General Assembly adjourned, Gill became private secretary to Governor O. Max Gardner and remained in that post during Gardner's administration. Afterward he compiled the governor's letters and papers for publication. In 1933 Governor J. C. B. Ehringhaus appointed Gill to head the newly created North Carolina Paroles Commission, a position he filled until 1942. Organizing the office and adopting procedures for the commission, he created a model agency that was widely copied throughout the nation and commented upon favorably by federal officials. Between 1942 and 1949 Gill served as commissioner of revenue by appointment of Governor J. Melville Broughton; at the end of that period he joined a law firm in Washington, D.C., founded by former Governor Gardner. President Harry S Truman named him collector of internal revenue in North Carolina in 1950. He left the post in 1953 when he was appointed state treasurer by Governor William B. Umstead. Thereafter Gill was elected to this office until he retired in 1976. Under his direction, the state attained the highest possible credit rating. It was he who coined the phrase, "In North Carolina, we have made a habit of good government." Gill himself was often referred to as "Mr. Integrity."

In addition to his public offices, Gill was also a member of and an officer in various organizations including the State Banking Commission, Local Government Commission, Tax Review Board, Sinking Fund Commission, Capital Planning Commission, Southeastern State Probation and Parole Association, American Prison Association, and National Tax Association.

As a young man Gill studied for a year at the New York School of Fine and Applied Arts. In later years his hobby was painting and he took a deep interest in the North Carolina Museum of Art, serving as an active and effectual member of the board of trustees and a director of the State Art Society. He was also interested in music and was considered a "respectable" pianist and organist. An indefatigable reader, he was an avid but generous book collector. Many libraries in the state benefited from his gifts.

Gill was a Methodist and taught Sunday school at the Edenton Street Methodist Church in Raleigh. He was also a Democrat. Both Duke University and Campbell College awarded him honorary degrees. He never married. Burial took place in Hillside Cemetery, Laurinburg.

SEE: Ola Maie Foushee, *Art in North Carolina* (1972); *Greensboro Daily News*, 17 July 1978; *North Carolina Manual* (1975); Raleigh *News and Observer*, 7 May 1950, 17 July 1978.

WILLIAM S. POWELL

**Gillespie, James** *(1747–11 Jan. 1805)*, legislator and congressman, was born in County Monaghan, Ireland, the oldest of three sons of David Gillespie. James received a classical education in Dublin, and, while still a young man, emigrated with his Scottish Presbyterian family to New Bern. Before the American Revolution he bought a plantation (later called Golden Grove) one mile east of Kenansville in Duplin County.

With the outbreak of war, Gillespie received a captain's commission in the First Battalion of North Carolina Volunteers in November 1776. Although he performed assigned military duties and even suffered the burning of his home by Tories, his most significant contributions to the state in the war years were his political and administrative activities. In 1776, he served as a member of the North Carolina Provincial Congress at Halifax that drew up the state constitution, and two years later he was appointed a commissioner to consolidate the towns of Campbellton and Cross Creek (later named Fayetteville). In 1779, Gillespie won election to the North Carolina House of Commons, participating in its deliberations in 1779–80 and 1782–84.

After the war his political involvement increased. He served in the state senate in 1784–86, 1789, and 1792. In 1785, he received appointments as a trustee to establish an academy in Duplin County, as secretary to the governor, and as a member of the state council, to which he was reappointed in 1789. Gillespie attended the constitutional conventions of 1788 and 1789, voting with the anti-Federalists against ratifications on both occasions; however, he later won election to the U.S. House of Representatives, serving during the years 1793–99 and 1803–5 as a Federalist from the Sixth Congressional District.

At the time of the 1790 census Gillespie owned over 2,000 acres of land and thirty slaves. In addition to his wife, Dorcus Mumford Gillespie of Onslow County, his household consisted of seven children: Catherine, David, Lucy, Joseph, Elizabeth, Jane, and Mildred. His son David (1774–1829) attended The University of North Carolina in 1795, served as a major in the War of 1812, and represented Bladen County in the House of Commons; he also was a member of the council.

Gillespie died in Washington and was buried in Presbyterian Cemetery in Georgetown, D.C.; in 1891 his remains were moved to the Congressional Cemetery in Washington.

SEE: *Biog. Dir. Am. Cong.* (1950); John L. Cheney, Jr., ed., *North Carolina Government, 1585–1974* (1975); Walter Clark, ed., *State Records of North Carolina*, vols. 12-22 (1895–1907); Gillespie-Wright Papers (Southern Historical Collection, University of North Carolina, Chapel Hill).

RICHARD A. SCHRADER

**Gilmer, Jeremy Francis** *(23 Feb. 1818–1 Dec. 1883)*, military engineer, Confederate major general, and industrialist, was a native of Guilford County, the son of Robert and Anne Forbes Gilmer, both of whom were of Scotch-Irish stock. His father was a Revolutionary soldier, farmer, and wheelwright; his older brother was Congressman John A. Gilmer. Jeremy attended the U.S. Military Academy at West Point, where in 1839 he was graduated fourth in a class of thirty-one and commissioned a second lieutenant of engineers.

Gilmer's experiences as a career officer were varied and his success uniform. He was successively assistant professor of engineering at West Point (1839–40), assistant engineer in building Fort Schuyler at New York harbor (1840–44), assistant engineer at Washington, D.C. (1844–46), and chief engineer of the Army of the West during the Mexican War (1846–48). Subsequently he was assigned to duty in Georgia where he superintended the improvement of the Savannah River and the construction of Fort Jackson and Fort Pulaski. He was promoted to first lieutenant in 1845 and to captain in 1853. Afterward he was engaged for five years throughout the South in fortification work and in the improvement of rivers.

In 1858 Captain Gilmer was transferred to the West Coast, where he superintended construction of defenses at the entrance of San Francisco Bay. When word of the firing on Fort Sumter reached California, the local military society, of which Gilmer was a member, was of divided sentiment. Gilmer refused to take the prescribed oath of allegiance to the United States and was relieved of duty. He resigned his commission on 29 June 1861 and planned to return to the South. An attack of rheumatic fever delayed his departure until August, when he sailed with his wife and young son. Warned by fellow officers that possible arrest awaited him in Federal territory, Gilmer left his family and made his way to Georgia via the Ohio Valley and St. Louis, reaching Savannah on 1 Oct. 1861. He was prepared to begin a new career in the Confederate Army.

Gilmer was commissioned major of engineers and posted to the Army of Tennessee as chief engineer on the staff of General Albert Sidney Johnston. Reporting to Johnston at Bowling Green, Ky., on 15 Oct. 1861, he was promptly ordered to supervise defensive preparations at Nashville, Clarksville, Fort Donelson on the Cumberland River, and Fort Henry on the Tennessee. Because forts Henry and Donelson were lost in February 1862 and Nashville rendered untenable, Gilmer's role in fortifying these crucial Confederate positions is controversial among historians. James Lynn Nichols (*Confederate Engineers*) contends that Gilmer's plans were well conceived, and that blame for failure to complete all fortifications before Grant's attack lay elsewhere. Thomas Lawrence Connelly (*Army of the Heartland, The Army of Tennessee, 1861–1862*) characterizes Gilmer as gullible for expecting civilian aid and dilatory in preparing fortifications. Gilmer himself believed that the losses of forts Henry and Donelson had resulted from too few men and guns. On 6-7 Apr. 1862 he was severely wounded at Shiloh, where Albert S. Johnston was killed. On 1 July Gilmer was notified of his promotion to lieutenant colonel (to date from 16 Mar. 1861) and ordered to join Lee's Army of Northern Virginia. He hoped for field service; but Lee, aware of his Shiloh wound and his old rheumatic ailments, placed him in charge of defense construction at Richmond and Petersburg. Gilmer soon was behind a Richmond desk. Promoted to colonel in October 1862, he became chief of the Confederate Engineer Bureau, a post he would hold, despite extended absences from Richmond, until the war ended.

Gilmer proved to be an effective administrator and was especially influential with President Jefferson Davis and Secretary of War James A. Seddon. He was instrumental in organizing engineer companies and regiments and urged that they accompany all field armies. He insisted that all engineer activity, both technical and administrative, be regulated by the engineer chain of command and sought to institute this principle in all Confederate armies and departments. In the summer of 1863 Gilmer secured the publication of General Order #90 as a supplement to the pertinent sections of *Army Regulations*. It outlined the responsibilities and duties of Confederate engineers, who were to engage in reconnaissance, to prepare maps, to locate all defensive positions, to supervise fortification construction, and to plan and execute mining operations as well as river and channel obstructions. These were ambitious aspirations for an engineer bureau that was always confronted by shortages of men and money.

In August 1863 Gilmer was promoted from colonel to major general of engineers. Concerned about Federal activity around Charleston, Secretary Seddon sent Gilmer south to inspect Atlantic defenses. He was placed second in command to Beauregard for the Department of South Carolina, Georgia, and Florida. In this capacity he was involved in improving the defenses of Charleston and Atlanta. Ordered in December 1863 to command at Savannah and later to inspect Confederate defenses of Mobile Bay, Gilmer yearned to return to Richmond so that he might manage bureau affairs more efficiently. Despite distance and poor communication he had, with the assistance of an acting chief, maintained effective control of the engineer bureau. Finally, in June 1864 Gilmer returned to Richmond where he remained. He accompanied the Davis party in the flight from Richmond at the end of the war, having served the Confederacy ably and loyally. He has been described as the outstanding military engineer in Confederate service.

On 18 Dec. 1850, Gilmer married Georgian Louisa Frederika Alexander (1824–95), daughter of Adam Leopold Alexander and his first wife, Sarah Hillhouse Gilbert. After the Civil War, Gilmer settled in Georgia and was for eighteen years (1865–83) president and engineer of the Savannah Gas Light Company. For many years he was also a director of the Central Railroad and Banking Company of Georgia. He was a trustee of the Independent Presbyterian Church. Gilmer was survived by his wife and two children. He was buried in the family vault in Laurel Grove Cemetery, Savannah.

SEE: *Appleton's Cyclopaedia of American Biography*, vol. 2 (1887); Mark M. Boatner, *Civil War Dictionary* (1959); Thomas L. Connelly, *Army of the Heartland* (1967); Jeremy F. Gilmer Papers (Southern Historical Collection, University of North Carolina, Chapel Hill); James L. Nichols, *Confederate Engineers* (1957); Ezra J. Warner, *Generals in Gray* (1959).

MAX R. WILLIAMS

**Gilmer, John Adams** *(4 Nov. 1805–14 May 1868)*, state senator and U.S. and Confederate States congressman, was born near Alamance Church in Guilford County. He was the oldest of the twelve children of Robert and Anne Forbes Gilmer, both of whom were of Scotch-Irish descent, their families having come from Ireland to North Carolina by way of Pennsylvania. His father, a farmer and wheelwright, and both of his grandfathers had fought in the Revolutionary War. As a boy, Gilmer worked on his father's farm in the summer and attended an old-field school in the winter. At seventeen he began to teach in the neighborhood, and at nineteen he entered Eli W. Caruthers's academy in Greensboro. After studying there for two years, he taught for three years in a grammar school in Laurens County, S.C. Returning to North Carolina in 1829, he read law in the office of Archibald D. Murphey and in 1832 was admitted to the bar. He soon built up a large and profitable practice, which enabled him to accumulate slaves and other property. During the same period he rose to local prominence, serving as chairman of the Greensboro town board and as solicitor of Guilford County. A zealous defender of slavery, he led in prosecuting two

Wesleyan Methodist preachers for the dissemination of abolitionist propaganda and in rousing mobs that drove them from the state (1850–51). The 1860 census gave his occupation as both the law and agriculture and credited him with owning fifty-three slaves and an estate worth $112,000, more than six times as much as the average for the county.

Elected to the state senate as a Whig in 1846, Gilmer was reelected four times and served until 1856. Soon after entering the senate he gained a statewide reputation for eloquence when he spoke in favor of establishing an asylum for the insane. He also was one of the foremost advocates of the improvements program launched by the legislature in its 1848–49 session. In particular, he championed the North Carolina Railroad, helped to have it routed in an arc so it would pass through Greensboro, and raised money from private investors to supplement the state's subscription. While in the legislature, he resisted efforts to eliminate the freehold qualification for voters. The requirement was necessary, he argued, for preventing the undue taxation of land.

When the national Whig party disintegrated, Gilmer along with Zebulon Vance and other prominent North Carolina Whigs joined the American or Know-Nothing party. In 1856 he ran as the Know-Nothing candidate for governor, proposing the establishment of a partially state-owned bank and upholding his party's antiforeigner and anti-Catholic principles as the grounds upon which "honest men" might unite and save the country from sectional fanatics. He lost the election to the Democratic incumbent, Governor Thomas Bragg, by the fairly decisive margin of more than 12,000 votes.

In 1857 and again in 1859, Gilmer won election to Congress as the representative of the Fifth District. In the House he distinguished himself as a friend of the Union and a foe of both Northern and Southern extremists. He opposed the Buchanan administration's scheme for bringing about the admission of Kansas as a slave state under the Lecompton constitution. During the struggle over the House speakership in 1859–60, he tried to prevent the slavery issue from being raised. He was himself the speakership candidate of the "South Americans," the Know-Nothings of the South, who held the balance of power in the House, but he received no more than 36 votes. Despite his slave ownership and his proslavery record he was viewed by many Southern Democrats as little better than an abolitionist because of his moderate stand. After the House was organized, he was appointed chairman of the Committee on Elections.

In the crisis of 1860–61 Gilmer tried his best to head off secession and war. Because the Secessionists made much of Abraham Lincoln's supposed abolitionism, he wrote to Lincoln (10 Dec. 1860) and asked him to make a public statement clarifying his views on slavery. This the president-elect declined to do, but, impressed by his standing as a Southern Unionist, he invited Gilmer to visit him in Springfield, Ill. His object, he explained to William H. Seward, was "if, on full understanding of my position, he would accept a place in the cabinet, to give it to him." A further goal of Lincoln was to attract Southern support for his administration and counteract secessionism in the South. While sympathetic, Gilmer felt that a visit to Springfield "would not be useful" without a prior meeting of minds. On Seward's urging, Gilmer reconsidered Lincoln's invitation, but he finally turned it down. At about the same time, on 26 Jan. 1861, he pled for sectional compromise in one of the most moving speeches of his career. He sent thousands of copies of this speech to North Carolina to help defeat the proposal for a secession convention in the February referendum.

After Lincoln's inauguration Gilmer continued to correspond with Seward, now secretary of state, and was influential in the shaping of Seward's conciliatory policy. He urged that the administration remove the federal garrisons from the seceded states so as to avoid a clash of arms, which he feared would precipitate secession in the upper South. Seward gave the impression that the government would withdraw its troops from Fort Sumter. When, instead, Lincoln sent his Sumter expedition, Gilmer was "deeply distressed" at the "madness" that now prevailed. On the day the fort was fired upon (12 Apr. 1861), he was taking the Union side in a public debate in the Stokes County courthouse. Six days later, in the Guilford County courthouse, he stood with other Greensboro leaders in calling upon the local militia company, the Guilford Grays, to defend the state against any and all invaders. When the North Carolina secession convention finally met the following month, he attended as a delegate and joined in the unanimous vote for a secession ordinance.

During the last year of the Civil War, Gilmer was a representative in the Confederate Congress, serving as a member of the Ways and Means Committee and as chairman of the Committee on Elections. He generally opposed extreme measures for the conduct of the war. In February 1865 he offered a peace and reconstruction plan according to which the Union and the Confederacy would keep their separate identities but would send representatives to an overall "American diet." In March, after William T. Sherman's army had entered North Carolina, Gilmer recommended that peace talks be undertaken with General Sherman. After the war he endorsed President Johnson's reconstruction program, and in 1866 he attended the Philadelphia National Union convention as a delegate.

Gilmer was a tall, sturdily built, commanding figure, with an open and friendly manner and an engaging sense of humor. On 3 Jan. 1832 he had married Juliana Paisley, the daughter of a leading Presbyterian minister and the granddaughter of a Revolutionary War officer. Their son, John Alexander (22 Apr. 1838–17 Mar. 1892), rose to the rank of lieutenant-colonel in the Confederate army and served from 1879 to 1891 as a superior court judge. Of the elder Gilmer, John H. Wheeler, a contemporary, wrote: "The melancholy effects of the unhappy intestine war preyed heavily on his spirits, naturally elastic, and on his robust constitution, and so brought his life to a premature close." He died in Greensboro and was buried in the cemetery of the First Presbyterian Church, of which he had long been a member.

SEE: Thomas B. Alexander and Richard E. Beringer, *Anatomy of the Confederate Congress* (1972); Bettie D. Caldwell, comp., *Founders and Builders of Greensboro* (1925 [portrait]); *DAB*, vol. 4 (1960); Frontis W. Johnston, *Papers of Zebulon Baird Vance*, vol. 1 (1963); *North Carolina Biography* vol. 1 (1941); W. J. Peale, *Lives of Distinguished North Carolinians* (1898); Sallie W. Stockard, *History of Guilford County* (1902); John H. Wheeler, *Reminiscences and Memoirs of North Carolina and Eminent North Carolinians* (1884).

RICHARD N. CURRENT

**Gilmer, Robert D.** *(2 May 1858–1 Nov. 1924)*, lawyer and politician, was born in Mount Airy, the son of Samuel L. Gilmer, a merchant and native of Guilford County, and Matilda C. Moore Gilmer, the granddaughter of Jesse Franklin, governor of North Carolina in 1820–21. In 1879 Robert entered Emory and Henry College, Va., where he studied for two years before attending Dick and Dillard's Law School in Greensboro. He returned home and practiced law in Mount Airy from 1882 until he moved to Waynesville in 1885. In 1884 he married Love Brannon and later had two children, Joseph and Josephine. In 1886, he was chairman of the Haywood County executive committee of the Twelfth Judicial District. He then served two terms in the North Carolina House of Representatives in 1890 and 1892. In the legislature, where he was chairman of the Committee on Education and a member of numerous other committees, Gilmer introduced a bill to establish the Normal and Industrial College at Greensboro. For a number of years he was a member of the college's board of trustees. In 1894, he was chairman of the Democratic Congressional Committee of the Ninth District, and in 1896 he was a presidential elector. Afterwards he served with distinction as state attorney general in 1898 and 1904.

Gilmer, a member of the Methodist church, died after retiring to his home in Waynesville. Burial was in Greenwood Cemetery. He was the author of *The Trial of the Sparrow for Killing Cock Robin* (1889).

SEE: W. C. Allen, *Annals of Haywood County* (1935), and *Centennial of Haywood County* (1908); *Greensboro Daily News*, 2 Nov. 1924, 27 Dec. 1953; Oliver H. Orr, Jr., *Charles Brantley Aycock* (1961); C. B. Poland, *20th Century Statesmen: North Carolina's Political Leaders, 1900–1901* (1900); *Prominent People of North Carolina* (1906); W. F. Tomlinson, *Biography of the State Officers and the Members of the General Assembly* (1893 [portrait]).

CHARLES S. POWELL

**Gilmer, William Franklin ("Dixie")** *(7 June 1901–9 June 1954)*, congressman, was born at Mount Airy, the son of W. F. and Emma Elizabeth Prather Gilmer. The family soon moved to Oklahoma, where young Gilmer attended the public schools of Oklahoma City. From 1911 to 1919 he was a page in the U.S. House of Representatives during the speakership of Champ Clark. Gilmer was graduated from the law school of the University of Oklahoma at Norman in 1923. The same year he was admitted to the bar and began practicing in Oklahoma. In 1925 he was elected to the state legislature.

In 1929 Gilmer moved to Tulsa, where he was assistant county attorney from 1931 to 1933. He then became county attorney, remaining in the post until his resignation in 1946. That year saw his unsuccessful bid for the Democratic gubernatorial nomination. Two years later, however, he was elected congressman from the First Oklahoma District; he served in the Eighty-first Congress from 3 Jan. 1949 to 3 Jan. 1951. Gilmer failed to retain his seat in the election of 1950. Returning to Oklahoma, he became commissioner of police and highway patrol in the Oklahoma Department of Public Safety, Oklahoma City, and served until his death.

Gilmer married Ellen McClure on 19 May 1928. He was a Presbyterian and a Masonic Shriner.

SEE: *Biog. Dir. Am. Cong.* (1961); *Who's Who in the South and Southwest*, 1954.

PHILLIP W. EVANS

**Gilmore, Walter Murchison** *(10 Jan. 1869–19 Dec. 1946)*, clergyman and Baptist publicist, was born on a farm in Lee County, three miles from the town of Sanford, the son of David Chandler and Margaret Frances Murchison Gilmore. He attended the Jonesboro public schools, Mount Vernon Springs Academy in Chatham County, and Sanford High School, from which he was graduated in 1886. After one year as an assistant teacher at Sanford High School, he entered Wake Forest College in 1887; four years later he was graduated with the bachelor of arts degree. In 1891 he became a high school principal. He also served for seven months as pastor of the Cool Springs Baptist Church, near Jonesboro, which he had joined in November 1882. He had been licensed to preach by the same church in August 1887 at age eighteen. At the request of the Cool Springs church, he was ordained a Baptist minister on 1 Oct. 1892 at Bethlehem Baptist Church, Moore County. The examining and ordaining presbytery was appointed by the Sandy Creek Baptist Association.

Gilmore enrolled at the Southern Baptist Theological Seminary, Louisville, Ky., in October 1892 and was graduated with a bachelor of theology degree in May 1894. From the seminary he went to Brunswick, Ga., as pastor of the First Baptist Church (1895–1904). He then served in Baptist pastorates at Marshallville, Eastman, and Atlanta, Ga., between 1904 and 1911; and at Louisburg and Sanford, N.C., between 1911 and 1923.

Early in 1923, he became secretary of stewardship and missions of the North Carolina Baptist State Convention, with headquarters in Raleigh, where he had held leadership positions for more than twelve years. He was assistant recording secretary (1914–15), and then recording secretary, a post he held from 1916 to 1929. During those years he also became a publicist for the convention and Baptist work in general. He wrote many articles for the *Biblical Recorder*, served as reporter for press services and newspapers covering various convention sessions, and wrote and edited countless tracts, pamphlets, and promotional brochures on convention activities.

During his pastorates in Georgia, Gilmore was clerk of the Piedmont and New Ebenezer Baptist associations. His comprehension of denominational organization was vast and his capacity to interpret the denomination's plans and programs was early recognized and utilized. In every community where he served as pastor, he had been active in civic affairs both as a trustee of numerous educational institutions and as a member of multiple committees and boards of the denomination. In 1918–19 he served as publicity director for the North Carolina Baptist Million-Dollar Campaign to support Baptist schools and colleges in the state. In late 1919 this campaign was merged with the Southern Baptist Seventy-Five-Million-Dollar Campaign "to provide greatly increased support for all Baptist missionary, educational and benevolent work in the states and the Southern Baptist Convention, and set a new pattern for Baptist cooperation." It accomplished both of those goals, and a large portion of the success in North Carolina, which received $5.5 million from the effort, is credited to Gilmore's effective use of every media available to publicize the campaign.

As a result of his outstanding work for the North Carolina Baptist State Convention, he was called to

Nashville, Tenn., in 1930 to become director of publicity, and later treasurer of the executive committee, of the Southern Baptist Convention headquarters' operation. For the next fourteen years he developed an innovative program of denominational publicity as editor of *The Baptist Program*, director of the Baptist Bulletin Service, and press representative for the convention. He dispensed news to the Baptist and secular press of the several states and developed a completely new type of publicity service that provided advance copies of all addresses and reports, as well as day-to-day coverage of the annual meetings of the convention. He was an indefatigable worker until his death at the age of seventy-seven. He was the author of *Seven Marks of a Good Steward* (n.d.).

On 4 Nov. 1903 Gilmore married Mary Estelle Taylor, the daughter of John W. and Laura China Taylor of Dunn. They had one son, Walter Sledge Gilmore (b. 6 Aug. 1907), himself a graduate of Wake Forest College and the Southern Baptist Theological Seminary.

SEE: *Encyclopedia of Southern Baptists*, vol. 1 (1953); *History of the Cool Springs Baptist Church, 1848–1973* (n.d.); North Carolina Baptist Historical Collection (Wake Forest University, Winston-Salem) and Southern Baptist Historical Collection (Dargan-Carver Library, Nashville, Tenn.), for information on Gilmore; J. S. Ramond, ed., *Among Southern Baptists* (1936); T. J. Taylor, *A History of the Tar River Baptist Association, 1830–1921* (n.d.).

C. SYLVESTER GREEN

**Glasgow, James** *(ca. 1735–17 Nov. 1819)*, Revolutionary patriot and secretary of state of North Carolina, was born in Maryland, the son of the Reverend James Patrick, native of Scotland but rector of All Hallows Parish, Snow Hill, Md., and Martha Jones Glasgow, daughter of Thomas and Mary Wilson Jones of Cecil County, Md. After receiving his formal education at parish schools and at the College of William and Mary, he became an accounting and corresponding clerk for an import-export house in Suffolk, Va. Its clients included Colonel Abraham Sheppard and his son Benjamin, merchant-planters of Dobbs County, N.C. Glasgow became a visitor at Contentnea, Colonel Sheppard's plantation, and in time married the colonel's daughter. Afterwards Benjamin Sheppard became a widower with three small daughters by his first wife and he married Martha Jones Glasgow, sister of James. Both marriages produced large families.

By 1763, Glasgow was studying law at Kinston, N.C., under David Gordon, a former barrister in the Court of King's Bench at Westminster. Glasgow was admitted to the bar in Johnston County on 17 July 1764, with license to practice in the inferior courts. He next became a planter. His father-in-law had recently bought the plantation of Dr. James Adair on the northeast side of Great Contentnea at Sheppard's Bridge. On 10 Oct. 1765, the colonel made a deed of gift "to my daughter Pherebe and her husband James Glasgow, Esq., . . . a tract of land, . . . being the part of Fairfields Plantation where the Houses and Improvements are and where the said Glasgows now live." This remained Glasgow's home until he built a new one in 1790 on a 3,000-acre plantation in the north fork of Nahunta Swamp at its mouth on Great Contentnea Creek.

In 1765 Glasgow, with Timothy Lee and others, established Lee's Chapel (Anglican) east of Fairfields on a branch of Sandy Run. In 1768, he joined the Masonic order at "the First Lodge in Pitt County" (chartered ca. 1766 by the Grand Lodge of Massachusetts). His first political office was county coroner of Dobbs, in 1771. By 1769, however, he was attending sessions of the General Assembly and serving as an assistant. This provided opportunities to establish and maintain friendships with men who would be leaders in the impending American Revolution and in the state. Meantime, he and his Sheppard in-laws were active in the northern Dobbs militia; they stood firmly against a popular sentiment there in favor of the Regulators. In the peaceful interlude that followed the Battle of Alamance, he rose to the rank of major as adjutant of the Dobbs County militia. He was reappointed by the Revolutionary Provincial Congress of August–September 1775. Military accounts show that he spent most of the period from October 1775 to February 1776 conducting 22-day training exercises for the ten companies of Dobbs militia and 10-day intensive training exercises at New Bern for all minutemen companies of the New Bern District.

On 12 Feb. 1776, military elements in the New Bern District marched on an expedition against Tory insurgents moving upon the Lower Cape Fear to support a British fleet expected there. On this expedition and in the ensuing Battle of Moore's Creek Bridge, Glasgow served as major in the Dobbs regiment. In 1777, when Colonel Abraham Sheppard was given command of the Tenth Regiment in the North Carolina Continental Line, Glasgow succeeded him as colonel of the Dobbs militia. In this capacity he received and befriended George Farragut, a Spaniard who had become an officer in the South Carolina Navy and managed to escape from British captors at Charleston. Through Glasgow's recommendation, Farragut was commissioned captain of an independent company of light horse.

During the Revolutionary era, Glasgow was involved in the provincial congresses in North Carolina—usually serving as an officer rather than as a delegate. In the Provincial Congress at Hillsborough in August-September 1775, however, he was a delegate from Dobbs County. This congress had seized the governmental apparatus of the province and the powers of government, as the royal governor had fled to a British warship in May 1775. On 9 September, the Hillsborough congress elected Glasgow a member of the Committee of Safety for the New Bern District.

In December 1776, the Provincial Congress at Halifax adopted a constitution for the state; it also chose state officers to serve until election of a General Assembly the following March. On 20 December the congress elected Glasgow secretary of state, and the Assembly of 1777 reelected him and established the term of that office as three years. Other state offices, including that of governor, had terms of one year. This distinction remained and became to some a source of invidious resentment. Successive assemblies reelected Glasgow until he resigned under fire in December 1799 to defend himself against charges of knowingly and willfully committing fraud in his administration of the military land grant program.

The General Assembly of 1783 adopted legislation reserving a large area of its western lands (now in Tennessee) to be granted to Continental veterans (or to heirs of those who had died). The legislation directed the secretary of state to issue to each qualified applicant a warrant of survey for the quantity of reserved western lands due the applicant. The warrant was addressed to the state surveyor of military lands, who was required by the act to maintain a land office and certain records at Nashville. This land office became known as the "Armstrong Office" because the Assembly appointed

General John Armstrong to head it and, when he died, his brother Colonel Martin Armstrong. Each warrant of survey eventually found its way to the Armstrong Office where the surveyor recorded the entry, executed the warrant, and returned it with the survey report and plat to the office of the secretary of state. The latter was required by law to make out a military land grant form to be authenticated by the governor, countersigned by the secretary of state, and recorded in a land grant registry book in the secretary's office. The original grant and a copy of the survey and plat were then delivered to the applicant.

This administrative structure was defective in many respects, but two aspects of the system were of dire consequence for Secretary Glasgow, even if he had been scrupulously honest: first, the general assembly appointed all officers, including those whom the secretary of state had a theoretical responsibility to supervise and direct; and second, any warrant issued was transferable by endorsement, assignment, or other appropriate writing. It could be transferred repeatedly. Hundreds of them became, in effect, monetized. This greatly increased the likelihood of forgeries, counterfeiting, theft, and other fraudulent activities. The reading public and the General Assembly were well aware of this risk. The incubus of the earlier "Fraud Trials at Warrenton" in the 1780s sprang from a similar act of assembly involving certificates given by the state in partial settlement of Revolutionary War accounts. That experience spilled a taint upon the burgeoning military land grant program. That Glasgow continued to serve at his peril from the time of the Warrenton trials is seen from the fact that the allegations brought against him by the commission in 1799 are based largely on transactions that occurred from 1785 to 1789. The two indictments upon which the petit jury found him guilty were, however, of later date, and it appears that knowledge of wrongdoing was imputed from the fact that in those cases two of his sons-in-law were involved in alleged forgeries on warrants. Both had married daughters of Glasgow while serving as state officials in the military land grant program, and both had become employees by legislative appointment. One of them, Lieutenant Colonel Willoughby Williams, was a gentleman of otherwise unblemished integrity who had served in the Continental line as regimental commissary officer, as deputy secretary of state, as a member of the House of Commons, and as deputy clerk of the county court in Dobbs and later as clerk of the county court in Glasgow County. The other son-in-law, Colonel Stockley Donelson, brother-in-law and confidant to rising political star Andrew Jackson, was certainly the most active, charming, accommodating, cunning, and indefatigable practitioner of fraud and deceit to be found in the state service. He was hardly twenty-one years old when appointed by the General Assembly in October 1783 (through the influence of Blount family members) as a field surveyor under the Armstrong Office. Within ten years he had accumulated more than 200,000 acres of western and eastern lands of North Carolina (including the area that became Tennessee). In April 1797 he procured, by what later was perceived to be fraud and deceit, a marriage with Elizabeth Glasgow Martin, a very wealthy widowed daughter of Secretary Glasgow and the mother of two small sons by her deceased husband, John Martin, a merchant of Snow Hill, Md., and Snow Hill, N.C. James Glasgow became Donelson's adversary at the time he was trustee for his daughter's prenuptial deed of marriage agreement. Donelson cultivated a friendship with Andrew Jackson, who came to Nashville in 1788 at age twenty-one as state prosecuting attorney for the western district. Jackson met and fell in love with Mrs. Rachel Donelson Robards, Donelson's sister who by then was separated from her husband. It was known that her husband had petitioned the Virginia legislature for a divorce. Jackson seems never to have suspected Donelson as being the source of the misinformation that the Virginia legislature had granted the divorce, a hoax that beguiled Jackson and Rachel to marry at Natchez in August 1791, some two years before she became divorced.

Both Andrew Jackson and Stockley Donelson played roles in the disaster that befell James Glasgow's public life in the period from December 1797 to June 1800, during which Glasgow's character suffered an almost total eclipse and degradation.

On 6 Dec. 1797, the year he was elected to the U.S. Senate by the Tennessee legislature, Andrew Jackson told North Carolina Senator Alexander Martin an astonishing tale about frauds in the military land grant program of North Carolina. The story, Jackson said, had been related to him by John Love of Virginia who said he eavesdropped in his room at a lodging house in Nashville while the landlord, William Tyrell, and his nephew, William Tyrrell Lewis, systematically intoxicated some former officers of the North Carolina Continental line so they would sign fraudulent certificates of Continental military service to be used in procuring land warrants from the office of the secretary of state. At Senator Martin's request, Jackson put his statement in a signed and dated writing for Martin to send to the governor of North Carolina, promising also to get Love before a federal judge to make oath concerning what he had witnessed. Love's oath was never forthcoming. Although he was not clearly identified or officially contacted, the hearsay submitted by Jackson was readily believed by Governor Samuel Ashe and by many members of the General Assembly. It seems to have been a case of everyone being shocked but no one surprised. Ashe placed the onus immediately upon Secretary Glasgow, declaring in biblical paraphrase, "An Angel hath fallen!" That same day (18 Dec. 1797) he reported the matter to the General Assembly, then in session, noting: "From the continued buzzing of these flies about the office, my suspicions have long been awake." Jackson's tale from Love had activated Ashe, and he dutifully managed to activate the Assembly. Both houses rejected a proposed resolution to remove Glasgow from office, although they adopted measures suspending the military land grant business in most respects. A legislative Committee of Inquiry was formed; and, on its report and recommendation, a special commission or board was created and directed to make a thorough investigation, determine who was involved in frauds, if any one, and collect evidence reflecting the particulars relating to any offender.

The special commission found the record books in the Armstrong Office were in such worn and dilacerated condition that transporting them the great distance to Raleigh, over the rough routes and by the rude vehicles available, involved risk of even greater disaster. The problem was resolved by sending to Nashville special agents who made exact copies of all records, proofread and certified their accuracy, and delivered them to the investigation commission. The commission was equally careful and resourceful in recording its findings and in preparing its recommendations. The evidence of any overt wrongdoing by Secretary Glasgow was found to be weak and scarce. The commission specifically declined to suggest whether impeachment proceedings ought to be instituted against him, and it found no grounds for prosecuting him for a felony. Rather, it recommended that he be charged with a misdemeanor—dereliction or neglect of duty as a public officer—in twelve cases. These cases were summarized in the commission's report which, after some debate as to whether the report should be kept secret, the General Assembly voted overwhelmingly to make public. The editor of the *Raleigh Register* permitted Glasgow to publish each of these together with his answer to the charge. The court before which he would be tried on a misdemeanor would ordinarily have been the county court, but the Assembly enacted legislation requiring trial before a court comprised of superior court judges *en banc*. In this court defense lawyers were not allowed to address the court orally with argument, present witnesses for the defense, or question state witnesses. Adversary proceedings had not become standard practice in criminal courts of those times, at least not in North Carolina. The allegations made against Glasgow by the commission were considered by a grand jury drawn from several counties specified in the legislation. A number of the allegations were dismissed. Indictments were brought on about five cases. A petit jury gave the verdicts on the basis of the state's evidence only. Glasgow was found guilty in two cases and fined £1,000 on each.

The course of his fortune from decade to decade during approximately forty years in North Carolina can be indicated approximately. When he came to North Carolina he owned neither land nor slaves. He married Pherebe Sheppard about 1762. In 1769 he owned three slaves and about 250 acres of land in Dobbs County. Sixty Dobbs planters owned more slaves and thirty owned as many. By 1780, however, the Dobbs County tax assessment roll valued Glasgow's taxable estate in lands and slaves in the county at £26,150, a figure nearly equaled by six other Dobbs taxpayers but exceeded by only two. In 1790, his comparative wealth-status indicators among Dobbs County planters had changed little since the 1780 report. He was third largest in slaves owned, but at least six Dobbs planters owned more land in the county. In March 1800, he owned twenty-two slaves. Eight Greene County planters owned more. His son James, then married with a family, also owned twenty-two slaves. Glasgow's home plantation at Nahunta still consisted of nearly 3,000 acres.

Within a few months after his trial, Glasgow left North Carolina with a wagon train of his kindred and friends, bound for a new home in Tennessee. The popular fable that he had accumulated vast land holdings there does not find a factual basis in the records. On the way, his son-in-law Willoughby Williams died suddenly while the train was encamped at Dandridge, Tenn. A few months later Glasgow and his widowed and unmarried daughters were living at a home on the Emory River in Roane County. By 1810, however, he was settled on a plantation about seven miles from Nashville on the old Nolensville Road in the direction of Murfreesboro. He was residing there at the time of his death, six days after he had written his last will and testament and had it witnessed by family members—children and grandchildren. He was eighty-five years old.

Ten of Glasgow's children are known to have lived to adulthood. Two daughters were wives of justices of the supreme court of Tennessee, and one married a Tennessee governor. His children were Elizabeth (b. ca. 1763), Patrick (b. ca. 1765), Nancy Ann ("Annie," b. 22 Apr. 1770), Phereby Sheppard ("Freddy," b. ca. 1775), James (b. ca. 1776), John (b. ca. 1791), Susan (b. ca. 1793), Maria Anderson, Clarinda Jones, and Mary. Census evidence indicates the last three were born after 1800. If so, they certainly had to be children by a second wife, as his first wife was born about 1744. He had no wife to survive him, but the three last-named children were living with him at his death and are among those named as children in his will. His son James and his grandson James Glasgow Martin were named executors. His grave has not been located, and no picture of him has been found.

SEE: Samuel A. Ashe, ed., *Biographical History of North Carolina*, vol. 7 (1908); John Spencer Bassett, ed., *Correspondence of Andrew Jackson*, vol. 1 (1926); Kemp P. Battle, "The Trial of James Glasgow," *North Carolina Booklet* 3 (May 1903); Walter Clark, ed., *State Records of North Carolina*, vols. 11-25 (1895–1906); Davidson County, Tenn., Wills and Inventories, vol. 7, 1816–21 (Courthouse, Nashville); Andrew Jackson Papers (North Carolina State Archives, Raleigh); North Carolina Court of Conference Minutes, book 7, and North Carolina Secretary of State documents, nos. 743-756 (North Carolina State Archives, Raleigh); W. J. Peele, *Lives of Distinguished North Carolinians* (1898); *Raleigh Register*, 31 Dec. 1799, 17, 24 June, 29 July, 12 Aug. 1800, 25 Feb. 1820; William L. Saunders, ed., *Colonial Records of North Carolina*, vols. 9-10 (1890); *State v. Glasgow* Papers (North Carolina State Archives, Raleigh); *State v. Glasgow*, 1 *N.C. Reports* 264 (Spring Term 1800); Superior Court Records, New Bern District (North Carolina State Archives, Raleigh).

CHARLES R. HOLLOMAN

**Glasson, William Henry** *(26 July 1874–11 Nov. 1946)* economist, first dean of the Duke University Graduate School, author, and editor, was born in Troy, N.Y. A first-generation American whose parents had emigrated from England shortly before his birth, he was the son of John Glasson, a native of Cornwall, and Agnes Allen Pleming Glasson, the daughter of a master tailor in Probus. He received the Ph.B. degree from Cornell University in 1896, the Ph.D. from Columbia University in 1900, and the LL.D. from Duke University in 1939.

Glasson began his professional career as a fellow in political economy and finance at Cornell (1896–97), Harrison Fellow of Economics, University of Pennsylvania (1897–98); and fellow in administration, Columbia University (1898–99). From 1899 to 1902 he was head of the history and civics department in the George School, Newtown, Pa. He became professor of political economy and social science at Trinity College in 1902; was appointed chairman of the faculty committee on graduate instruction in September 1916, when the college had only six graduate students; and was named the first dean of the graduate school of arts and sciences at Duke University in 1926, in which capacity he served until 1938. By that time 249 graduate students were enrolled. Glasson continued to teach at Duke until 1940. He was also professor of economics during the summer session at Cornell University in 1907, acting professor of economics and politics at Cornell in 1910–11, nonresident lecturer at Johns Hopkins University during the spring of 1913, and professor of economics at the University of Virginia during the summer quarter of 1928.

In addition to his teaching and administrative responsibilities, he was coeditor of the *South Atlantic Quarterly* with Edwin Mims (1905–9); and both joint editor with President William P. Few, of Trinity College, and managing editor of the *Quarterly* (1909–19). He also served as advisory editor of the *National Municipal Review* (1912–22). From 1940 to 1945 he was a director of the South Atlantic Publishing Company. An authority on the U.S. pension system, Glasson was the author of *History of Military Pension Legislation in the United States* (1900) and *Federal Military Pensions in the United States* (1918), as well as a contributor to *The South in the Building of the Nation* (1910) and the *Cyclopaedia of American Government* (1913). Many of his articles appeared in the *South Atlantic Quarterly* (1905–19), *Annals of the American Academy of Political and Social Science, National Municipal Review, Review of Reviews, Survey*, the publications of the American Economics Association and of the North Carolina Literary and Historical Association, and other economic and historical periodicals. He contributed poetry to various newspapers and magazines, and in 1945 was a feature writer for the Cornell *Countryman*.

His influence extended far beyond university campuses and scholarly publications. When he gave up the deanship of the graduate school in 1938, A. A. Wilkinson, director of the Duke University News Service, wrote: "It is entirely no coincidence that Dean Glasson's years of activity have paralleled development in the educational, economic, and social life of the South: he has had a definite part in those phases of life that have come within the range of his participation." His academic and other achievements were often so closely interwoven that they cannot be easily separated.

Glasson's first experience in helping to mold public opinion came with his involvement in the famous Bassett case, which centered national attention on Trinity College and, in particular, John Spencer Bassett, who was being excoriated by much of the southern press for an opinion he had stated in the *South Atlantic Quarterly* of October 1903. The affair was concluded when Trinity College took a strong, unequivocal stand on academic freedom. Glasson served on the committee that wrote the memorable document on the subject which was duly signed by the faculty and accepted by the college trustees on 1 Dec. 1903.

As early as 1909 he was an advocate of the Australian ballot in North Carolina elections. Also in 1909, he was appointed by President William H. Taft to serve as the supervisor of the U.S. Census of 1910 for the Fifth District of North Carolina. He resigned after a few months, however, because of the political opposition of John Motley Morehead, Republican congressman from the district. (His objection was that Glasson had not been born and reared in the state.) During 1913–18 Glasson was a collaborator in the division of economics and history of the Carnegie Endowment for International Peace. Soon after World War I Mayor John M. Manning appointed him a member of the Durham City Housing Commission; from 1919 to 1923 he was on the City Board of Education. For many years he was a director of the Home Building and Loan Association and of the Morris Plan Industrial Bank. Because of his early interest in medical insurance, he became one of the first directors and vice-president of the Hospital Care Association of North Carolina (1933–35). In the summer of 1934 he visited Germany on the Carl Schurz goodwill tour, visiting a number of cities including those in the Saar district. He was appointed by Governor J. C. B. Ehringhaus to serve as a member of the North Carolina State Commission for the Study of Plans for Unemployment Compensation or Insurance (1934–35).

Glasson was a Methodist and a Republican. He was a member of Phi Beta Kappa (charter member and president of the Trinity chapter when it was installed on 29 Mar. 1920, and secretary for the South Atlantic District 1925–37); Kappa Delta Pi; American Economics Association (member of the executive committee, 1916–18); Conference of Deans of Southern Graduate Schools, 1927–37 (an organizer of the conference and, in 1929, president); and Quill and Dagger, Cornell University.

On 12 July 1905, he married Mary Beeler Park, a native of Speedwell, Ky., and a 1902 graduate of Cornell. They were the parents of four children: Lucy (Mrs. Harold Wheeler), Mary (Mrs. Thomas Preston Brinn), Marjorie (Mrs. Norman Ross), and John, M.D. While returning from a meeting in Raleigh on 9 Dec. 1934, he was seriously injured in an automobile accident. After years of invalidism, he died at his home in Durham and was buried in Maplewood Cemetery. His papers and a portrait by Irene Price are in the William R. Perkins Library, Duke University.

SEE: *Durham Morning Herald*, 12 Nov. 1946; William H. Glasson File, Duke University News Service (Durham); *Greensboro News*, 28 Aug. 1938; *Raleigh Christian Advocate*, 17 Apr. 1913; *Who Was Who in America*, vol. 2 (1950).

ESTHER EVANS

**Glenn, Edwin Forbis** *(10 Jan. 1857–5 Aug. 1926)*, major general, U.S. Army, was born in Greensboro, the son of Dr. Robert Washington Glenn, a surgeon during the Civil War, and Julia Gilmer Glenn. After attending Lenoir School for Boys in Caldwell County and Dr. Simmons Preparatory School at Sing Sing, N.Y., he received an appointment from North Carolina to the U.S. Military Academy, West Point, from which he was graduated in 1877. At the academy, his swarthy complexion won him the nickname of "Mohawk." He placed in the infantry, which thereafter became the center of his professional interests.

As second lieutenant in the Twenty-fifth Infantry, young Glenn served in Texas, Dakota, Minnesota, and Montana. In 1888, he was appointed professor of military science and tactics and assistant professor of mathematics at the University of Minnesota. While there, he studied law and received an LL.B. in 1890. Admitted to the bar in Minnesota, he took a leave of absence from the army to practice in St. Paul with the firm of Stephens, O'Brien, and Glenn. He became an authority on international law and later published *Glenn's Internationl Law* (1895) and, under War Department orders, *Rules of Land Warfare* (1914).

Returning to the army, Glenn saw duty with the Minnesota National Guard and then was assigned as quartermaster and commissary officer at Fort Missoula, Mont. In the spring of 1894, he was detailed to the judge advocate general's department, serving in the Department of Dakota and later in the Department of Columbia at Vancouver Barracks. In early 1898, he was given command of an exploring and relief expedition to Alaska that ended the following November. He subsequently commanded another expedition to Cook's Inlet and other points in Alaska that was concluded in January 1900. These explorations were recognized by the National Geographic Society, of which he became a member. Moreover, the highway linking Anchorage and the Alcan was named the Glenn Highway.

Glenn's next assignment (he was then a captain) was as acting judge advocate, Department of the Visayas, in the Philippine Islands. On his promotion to major in 1901, he became judge advocate of the Fifth Brigade and was put in charge of the Military Information Division of the Philippines. In 1903, he returned to the United States where he served until July 1908, when he was sent again to the Philippines. Afterward he was assigned to the Twenty-third Infantry on the Mexican border and at Fort Benjamin Harrison, Ind.

In 1913, Glenn entered the War College as a student. At the same time he became president of the Infantry Association and in that capacity secured the same rate of pay for the officers of the infantry as for the mounted branches of the service. He was next detailed as chief of staff of the Eastern Department until July 1916, when he assumed command of the Eighteenth Infantry. He was serving with this regiment on the Mexican border when the United States entered World War I. From there he was sent to take charge of the First Officer's Training Camp at Fort Benjamin Harrison, Ind.

Promoted to the rank of brigadier general, Regular Army, in May 1917 and to major general, National Army, in August, Glenn was given the command of the Eighty-third Division at Camp Sherman, Chillicothe, Ohio. In June 1918, he took his division to France, where it was divided. Part of the division was used for training cadres at Le Mans, Sarthe, France. The establishment of this Replacement Depot, Training, and Embarcation Center was one of the outstanding achievements of Glenn's career. For this work, the French government made him a commander of the Legion of Honor. He commanded the Eighty-third Division until his return to the United States in June 1919 and reassignment to Camp Sherman, Ohio. After forty-six years of active service, he retired the following December at the age of sixty-two.

Glenn was a member of the Army-Navy clubs of New York and Washington, D.C. and of the Cosmos Club in Washington. He received honorary degrees from Union and Kenyon colleges, Ohio, and from DePauw and Vermont universities. Following retirement, he participated in the presidential campaign of General Leonard Wood and contributed to civic projects in his native state of North Carolina, including state drainage reclamation and the development of trade and commerce through a combined system of land and water transportation. While visiting a daughter in Mentor, Ohio, he became seriously ill and died two weeks later. He was buried in Arlington Cemetery.

In 1886 Glenn married Louise Smythe of St. Paul, Minn. They had four children: Mrs. H. T. Matters (Margaret) of Boston; Mrs. James A. Garfield (Edwina) of West Palm Beach, Fla.; Mrs. O. R. Cole (Louise) of southern California; and Mrs. H. R. Tyler (Elizabeth) of Waterville, N.Y.

SEE: Association of the Graduates of the U.S. Military Academy, *59th Annual Report* (1877); George W. Cullum, *Biographical Register of the Officers and Graduates of the U.S. Military Academy at West Point* (1920); *Greensboro Daily News*, 6, 7 Aug. 1926; Greensboro *Daily Record*, 18 July 1916; A. E. Potts, *Seventy Years of Military Training at the University of Minnesota, 1869–1939* (1939); Mary Roberts Rinehart, *My Story* (1931); *Who Was Who in America*, vol. 1 (1942).

K. S. MELVIN

**Glenn, Robert Brodnax** *(11 Aug. 1854–16 May 1920)*, attorney, state political leader, and governor, was the son of Chalmers L. and Annie S. Dodge Glenn of Rockingham County. Chalmers Glenn, a tobacco planter and lawyer, became a captain in the Thirteenth North Carolina Regiment in the Civil War and was killed at the Battle of South Mountain, Md., in 1862.

In 1871, Glenn entered Davidson College. After studying there for three years, he took a law preparatory course at the University of Virginia for one year. He then enrolled in Judge Richmond Pearson's law school in Richmond Hill, N.C., and in 1877 was admitted to the bar in Rockingham County. He soon moved to Stokes County where he practiced for eight years. In 1885, he went into law practice in Winston with William B. Glenn and later with Clement Manly and W. M. Hendren. A successful lawyer, Glenn was the attorney for the Western Union Telegraph Company and for Southern Railway. His political career began with election to the state legislature from Stokes County in 1880. In 1886 he was state solicitor, and in 1884 and 1892 he was a Democratic presidential elector. President Grover Cleveland appointed him U.S. attorney for the Western District of North Carolina from 1893 to 1897. In the election of 1898, Glenn was one of the chief speakers for the Democrats' white supremacy campaign to regain control of the state legislature. The following year he served as state senator from Forsyth County.

In 1904, Glenn's political career culminated with his election as governor. During his term of office (1905–9) the state debt was satisfactorily settled, education and public health services were expanded, low passenger rates on railroads were maintained against strong opposition, and in May 1908 North Carolinians voted for prohibition after ardent support of the measure by Governor Glenn, the "prohibition governor."

After his term as governor, Glenn did not hold another state political office. Known as a fine orator, he lectured for the Board of Home Missions of the Presbyterian Church and for the Lyceum Bureau, as well as on Chatauqua platforms. In 1915 President Wilson appointed him to the International Boundary Commission, which dealt with matters between the United States and Canada. He died in Winnipeg, Canada, while attending a session of the commission and was buried in Winston-Salem.

Glenn married Nina Deaderick of Knoxville, Tenn., on 8 Jan. 1878. They had two children, Chalmers L. and Rebecca (Mrs. D. E. Hoffman). Glenn was a Presbyterian, a Democrat, a Mason, and an officer of the North Carolina National Guard (1890–93). The Museum of History in Raleigh has a portrait painted by Henry Rood, Jr.

SEE: Margaret L. Chapman, "The Administration of Governor Robert B. Glenn" (M.A. thesis, University of North Carolina, 1956); *Nat. Cyc. Am. Biog.*, vol. 19 (1926); *Who Was Who in America*, vol. 1 (1942).

ALICE R. COTTEN

**Gloster, Thomas Benn** *(1763–1819). See* **Brehon, James Gloster.**

**Glover, William** *(d. before October 1712)*, acting governor, councillor, and judge, moved to the Albemarle region of North Carolina prior to 1690 from Henrico County, Va., where he was a justice in 1688. He owned land there on the north side of the James River which he sold in 1701. His origins otherwise are unknown, but his letters indicate that he was well educated. He made his home at Little River, long the center of government in Albemarle County, and was clerk of the

Council as early as November 1690 and as late as 1698. By 1695 he was clerk of court for Perquimans Precinct, a position he also held at times in Pasquotank Precinct until 1698. He also was a clerk in the office of the secretary of the colony in 1694–95. Commissioned a judge of the general court by Governor Robert Daniel in 1704, he was retained in that post the following year by Thomas Cary when he succeeded Daniel.

From 1700 until 1712 Glover was a member of the Council and as president was acting governor from 1706 to 1708. He therefore was a participant in the early stages of the so-called Cary Rebellion. During this time a struggle for supremacy was underway between many longtime residents of the Albemarle who, for the most part, were Anglicans (and were sometimes called Tories) against dissenters. The latter were primarily Quakers who had some Baptist assistance as well as support from residents of the newly settled, but politically isolated, Bath County south of Albemarle Sound. These people were sometimes called Whigs. Thomas Cary, a friend of the Proprietary governor of Carolina, resident in Charles Town, was sent to the northern part of Carolina as deputy governor for that region in 1705 as authorized by the Proprietors. In the political struggle, Cary's opponents sent John Porter to London to seek support from the Proprietors. At Porter's departure in 1706 Cary returned to Charles Town to attend to personal business, but while there he ran for and was seated in the assembly. In North Carolina, William Glover served as governor because he was president of the Council. Upon Porter's return in October 1707 with instructions that Cary should be removed and authorizing the Council to elect a chief executive, the Council agreed that Glover was satisfactory and retained him. Cary, however, returned and took a seat on the Council. When Glover upset his Quaker supporters by requiring them, in contravention of their religious tenets, to swear an oath of office, Cary made common cause with them to remove Glover and establish himself as governor in October 1708. Glover withdrew for the time being into Virginia.

Glover owned many large tracts of land in different sections of the colony including Albemarle and Bath counties and along the Neuse River as well as in Virginia, some of which he acquired in that colony as late as 1703. As an attorney he was involved in a large number of legal cases such as the settlement of estates and various suits at law. He also was frequently the consignee of Robert Quary, judge of the Pennsylvania vice-admiralty court, and of the New Pennsylvania Company. Described as one of the four wealthiest men in the colony, he was a devout Anglican and, of course, a representative of the Tory or ruling faction in dispute with the Quakers and others.

Although documentation is lacking, William Glover surely was the man of this surname, not otherwise identified, who married Mary Davis in Virginia; land that Glover sold there adjoined that of one John Davis. If this is correct, they were the parents of Thomas (b. 1685), Charlesworth (b. 1688), and Joseph (b. 1691). In September 1696 Glover proved his rights to 300 acres of land in North Carolina for importing himself, Mary, Charlesworth, and Joseph Glover, and Elizabeth and William Davis. The elder Glover was survived by his second wife, Catherine, whom he married before March 1707, and a daughter, Elizabeth. The daughter became the ward of Edward Moseley. Catherine married Tobias Knight before 4 Feb. 1713, and at his death in 1719 she and her daughter, Elizabeth Glover, were his sole heirs. Catherine later married Joshua Porter at some time before 1721, but she appears to have predeceased him.

The approximate date of Glover's death suggests that he may have been a victim of the Tuscarora Indian uprising or of the yellow fever epidemic of which another victim was Governor Edward Hyde, Cary's successor.

SEE: John L. Cheney, Jr., ed., *North Carolina Government, 1585–1979* (1981); J. Bryan Grimes, comp., *North Carolina Wills and Inventories* (1912); J. R. B. Hathaway, ed., *North Carolina Historical and Genealogical Register*, vols. 1 (1900), 3 (1903); Margaret M. Hofmann, ed., *Province of North Carolina, 1663–1729, Abstracts of Land Patents* (1979); William P. Palmer, ed., *Calendar of Virginia State Papers*, vol. 1 (1875); Mattie Erma E. Parker, ed., *North Carolina Higher-Court Records, 1670–1696* (1968), and *North Carolina Higher-Court Records 1670–1701* (1971); William S. Price, Jr., ed., *North Carolina Higher-Court Records, 1702–1708* (1974), and *North Carolina Higher-Court Records, 1709–1723* ([1977]); Worth S. Ray, comp., *Ray's Index and Digest to Hathaway's North Carolina Historical and Genealogical Register* (1956); William L. Saunders, ed., *Colonial Records of North Carolina*, vols. 1, 2, 4 (1886).

WILLIAM S. POWELL

**Godbey, Allen Howard** *(21 Nov. 1864–8 May 1948)*, minister and educator, was born in Pettis County, Mo., the son of William Clinton and Caroline Smith Godbey. At the age of fourteen he suffered a severe attack of brain fever, which lasted three or four weeks. Godbey received his early education at home, and in 1883 was graduated by Morrisville (Mo.) College, where he was a brilliant student. Afterward he taught at Morrisville for three years and then moved to St. Louis to become assistant editor of the *Southwestern Methodist*. During this period he was the author of several books.

In 1895, Godbey joined the Southwest Missouri Conference of the Methodist Episcopal Church, South, and served as a pastor for four years. Later he was transferred to the St. Louis Conference and served city pastorates for eight years. However, he was best known for his proficiency in Semitics and his work as an educator. After serving as principal of the academy at Central College from 1899 to 1902, he went to the University of Chicago as a fellow in Semitics; he was awarded the Ph.D. in 1905. From 1906 to 1909 Godbey was president of Morrisville College.

In 1926, when the Divinity School of Duke University was established, Godbey accepted the chair of professor of Old Testament and continued in that position until his retirement in 1932. Over the years he became well known as an archaeologist and historian; he also maintained a strong interest in the affairs of his church, attending numerous conferences and religious gatherings. He was a member of the American Oriental Society, the Society of Biblical Literature, and a number of other learned societies that promoted biblical and archaeological research. Among his writings were *Code of Hammurabi* (with R. F. Harper), *The Lost Tribes, A Myth*, *New Light on the Old Testament*, and several other volumes. Despite his brilliance, Godbey was somewhat eccentric, and there was speculation that his erratic behavior at times was the result of the brain fever he had suffered as a lad. On 16 June 1892 he married Emma L. Moreland, and they had one daughter, Elizabeth Beulah (Mrs. Glenn W. Johnson).

While attending the 1948 meeting of the General Conference of the Methodist Church in Boston, Godbey was struck by a truck as he crossed the street on the way to his hotel after the evening session on 7 May. He died a few hours later. Following funeral services in Durham, he was buried beside his wife in New Bethlehem Cemetery, St. Louis.

SEE: Clarence H. Brannon, *Allen H. Godbey, A Biography* (1949); Nolan B. Harmon, ed., *The Encyclopedia of World Methodism* (1974); The Methodist Church, *Minutes of the St. Louis Conference* (1948).

LOUISE L. QUEEN

**Godfrey, Francis** *(d. October or November 1675),* Council member, was in the North Carolina colony, then called Albemarle, by 21 Apr. 1669. At that time he was a member of the Albemarle Council, an office that he held at least through 1670. In the latter year he was Proprietor's deputy for Sir Peter Colleton. He may have been the Francis Godfrey who was graduated from Peterhouse, Cambridge University, in 1629. His business connections and other circumstances suggest that he may have come to Albemarle from Barbados. There is no firm evidence, however, on any aspect of Godfrey's life before he settled in Albemarle.

Godfrey lived in Perquimans Precinct, where he owned at least 1,400 acres of land. He operated a public house or inn, at which the Council met and held court in 1673. He also conducted a mercantile business, serving as factor for a Barbados merchant, John Swinsted. He and his wife, Joane, had three children who lived to adulthood: Frances, William, and John. At his death, Godfrey left a substantial estate in addition to his land. His will, dated 20 Oct. 1675, was probated on 5 November.

His widow, Joane, married William Therill in December 1676. She died the following February, leaving Godfrey's estate, of which she was executrix, unsettled because of disorders then afflicting the colony. In March 1680/81, when settled government had been restored, Godfrey's will was again probated and Therill was appointed administrator.

Frances Godfrey, the only daughter of Francis and Joane, married Thomas Hawkins. The couple had two children: John (b. 18 Feb. 1671/72) and Mary (b. 13 Jan. 1674/75). Both Frances and her husband died before October 1675. Their children were made the wards of William Therill after the death of their grandmother, Joane.

William Godfrey, the elder son of Francis and Joane, was born about 1658. He was married twice and had five children: two daughters, Frances and Mary, and three sons, John, Francis, and Thomas. Two of his children, John and Frances, may have been born to his first wife, Jane, who is named as their mother in some records although in others his second wife, Sarah, is named as their mother.

John Godfrey, the younger son of Francis and Joane, was born on 17 Aug. 1665. He married Elizabeth Bagster, widow of Nathaniel Bagster, on 19 Feb. 1685/86. John and Elizabeth had only one child, Elizabeth, who died when she was about thirteen. John Godfrey died on 29 Oct. 1697. His widow married John Hecklefield.

SEE: J. Bryan Grimes, ed., *Abstracts of North Carolina Wills* (1910); J. R. B. Hathaway, ed., *North Caroilna Historical and Genealogical Register*, 3 vols. (1900–1903); Mattie Erma E. Parker, ed., *Colonial Records of North Carolina, Higher-Court Records, 1670–1696*, vol. 2 (1968), and *1697–1701*, vol. 3 (1971); William S. Powell, ed., *Ye Countie of Albemarle in Carolina* (1958); William S. Price, Jr., ed., *Colonial Records of North Carolina, Higher-Court Records, 1702–1708*, vol. 4 (1974); William L. Saunders, ed., *Colonial Records of North Carolina*, vol. 1 (1886); Unpublished sources, North Carolina State Archives, Raleigh: Albemarle Book of Warrants and Surveys, 1681–1706; Council Minutes, Wills, Inventories, 1677–1701; Perquimans Births, Marriages, Deaths, and Flesh Marks, 1659–1739; Perquimans Precinct Court Minutes, 1688–93, 1698–1706; Will of Francis Godfrey.

MATTIE ERMA E. PARKER

**Godfrey, Thomas, Jr.** *(4 Dec. 1736–3 Aug. 1763),* mercantile agent, poet, and dramatist, was born in Philadelphia. His father was the inventor of the quadrant and one of the original members of the American Philosophical Society organized by Benjamin Franklin. Educated at home and at the Philadelphia Academy, young Godfrey was intimately associated with a group of students who became painters and poets. He was first attracted to painting, but early switched to poetry, which engaged him for the rest of his short life. In 1758, he was an ensign during the campaign against Fort Duquesne. In the spring of 1759, he sailed to Wilmington as factor for a commission merchant. There he was accepted into a society of "politeness, and ease, and enjoyment," and quickly made friends of those who were interested in books and music.

After a few months in Wilmington, Godfrey retreated to the vacation home of Colonel Caleb Grainger at the nearby summer colony on Masonborough Sound and successfully completed the writing of *The Prince of Parthia*, a play begun in Philadelphia. At Masonborough Sound he enjoyed the acquaintance of such enlightened men as Cornelius Harnett, Alexander Lillington, and Archibald Maclaine. So pleasant were his sojourns there that, in 1760, he twice was fined for defaulting on his citizen's duty to work the streets and wharves of Wilmington. Among the poems written at this time was "Piece upon Masonborough," a pastoral paean to his favorite summer quarters. After three years in Wilmington, Godfrey returned to Philadelphia on the death of his employer, but sailed back in the early summer of 1763. He died at age twenty-six of a fever contracted on a short riding trip, and was buried in the churchyard of St. James Episcopal Church in the heart of Wilmington. Although his tombstone disappeared during the nineteenth century, the exact spot of the grave is known.

During his lifetime, a number of his poems were printed in America and England, and *The Court of Fancy* (1762), a tribute to Chaucer and Alexander Pope, was published in Philadelphia. Godfrey's fame, however, rests almost entirely on *The Prince of Parthia*, a tragedy of ancient times written in blank verse. Its plot of villainies and murders was original with Godfrey. Performed by the American Company in Philadelphia on 24 Apr. 1767, it was the first play written by an American to be staged by professionals. In 1962, a truncated version was performed by the Wilmington College Theater, and the following year the full play was produced at the Parkway Playhouse in Burnsville. A portrait of Godfrey by his friend Benjamin West has been lost.

SEE: *DAB*, vol. 7 (1931); Thomas Godfrey, *The Prince of Parthia*, ed. Archibald Henderson (1917); *Juvenile Poems on Various Subjects, with the Prince of Parthia, a Tragedy, by the Late Mr. Thomas Godfrey, Junr. of Philadelphia, to Which is Prefixed Some Account of the Author and His Writings* (1765); Donald R. Lennon and Ida B. Kellam, eds., *The*

*Wilmington Town Book, 1743–1778* (1973); *North Carolina Authors* (1952); Richard Walser, ed., *North Carolina Drama* (1956).

RICHARD WALSER

**Godwin, Archibald Campbell** *(1831–19 Sept. 1864)*, miner, rancher, and Confederate soldier, was born in Nansemond County, Va., the son of Lewis and Julia Campbell Godwin. His mother was the daughter of General Archibald Campbell, who in 1837 was in charge of U.S. Public Lands of Missouri and the Northwest Territory. In the year of Godwin's birth the family moved to Portsmouth, where young Godwin was reared by his grandmother, Julia Hatton Godwin, after the death of his father. Godwin, who grew to be a well-proportioned six feet six inches tall, left home in 1849 at age nineteen to seek his fortune in the gold fields of California. For many years he was a miner and later branched out into ranching, lumber, and milling businesses. He soon amassed a considerable fortune. At one time he owned a large part of Vancouver Island but gave it up when a boundary dispute between the United States and Great Britain placed the estate inside Canada. In 1860, he came within one vote of winning the Democratic nomination for governor of California.

At the outbreak of the Civil War in 1861, Godwin turned over his property and the greater part of his fortune to two men and hurried east to his native Virginia. Offering his services to President Jefferson Davis, Godwin was commissioned a major in the regular Confederate Army and assigned as assistant provost marshall at Libby Prison in Richmond. So efficient was he in this post that President Davis sent him to North Carolina to organize and construct a prison stockade at Salisbury. With Godwin as its commandant, the prison housed Union prisoners captured in the early battles of the war as well as civil and political enemies of the Confederacy. On 6 July 1862, Godwin organized a regiment of soldiers from the men who guarded the prison. The regiment was commissioned as the Fifty-seventh North Carolina Regiment and Godwin was made its colonel on 17 July. He took his new command to Richmond, where it was attached to General Joseph R. Davis's brigade of General G. W. Smith's division defending the city.

For the rest of the summer and through the autumn of 1862, the regiment was carefully drilled and trained by Colonel Godwin. On 6 November it was sent northward to join General Robert E. Lee's army along the Rapidan River. Attached now to General E. M. Law's brigade of General John B. Hood's division, the regiment took part in the Battle of Fredericksburg on 13 Dec. 1862. In the battle Hood's division occupied the center of Lee's lines, and during the day a sizable Union force was able to gain a position in Hood's front in a railroad cut crossing a small creek. Godwin's regiment, supported by the Fifty-fourth North Carolina, was called on to dislodge the Union force. With parade ground precision, Godwin and his men advanced through a blizzard of bullets and shells and drove the Union soldiers out of the railroad cut. Having no orders to halt at any given point, they pressed on some distance beyond the railroad toward the main Union lines. When an order came from General Law to return to the railroad, Godwin had his regiment break off the action and move back—again with parade ground precision despite the fact that heavy musketry and artillery fire was being poured on the regiment. Godwin held his advanced position at the railroad until darkness ended the battle. The twenty-five minutes it had taken to dislodge the Union soldiers from the railroad cut had cost the regiment 250 of its 800 men, but it had gained Godwin a reputation as a hard fighter, as well as the compliments of both General Hood and General Lee.

In April 1863 Godwin and the regiment were assigned to Hoke's brigade in the division of General Jubal Early. The following month, in the Chancellorsville campaign, they fought again at Fredericksburg where Godwin was slightly wounded. In the Gettysburg campaign, he and his men served in the second Battle of Winchester and made up the extreme left of the final Confederate charge on the first day of the Battle of Gettysburg (1-3 July 1863). On the second day of the latter battle, Hoke's brigade, now led by Colonel Issac Avery, participated in the attack on the Union position known as Cemetery Hill. Early in the action Colonel Avery was mortally wounded and the command of the brigade fell to Godwin as senior colonel. He led the brigade for the remainder of the battle and in the retreat back to Virginia. In October Godwin's brigade took part in the Bristoe Station campaign. When Lee's army took position along the line of the Rappahannock River, Godwin's brigade and General H. T. Hays's Louisiana brigade were sent to the enemy's side of the river to occupy a series of light earthworks that blocked the enemy's approach to a bridge over the river known as Rappahannock Bridge. On 7 Nov. 1863, Union forces attacked the bridgehead in overwhelming strength. Hays's brigade soon gave way and Union soldiers poured into the works, cutting off Godwin's escape route via the bridge back to the opposite bank where the rest of the army remained. Darkness had fallen and confusion was complete. Godwin's brigade disintegrated, as most of its soldiers were either killed, wounded, captured, or lost in the darkness. With a handful of only sixty or seventy men, however, Godwin continued to resist even though Union soldiers swarmed down on all sides. Suddenly from somewhere in the ranks someone shouted that Godwin had given an order to surrender. Furious, Godwin called for the man, threatening to blow his brains out if he found him. The thought of surrender had never entered Godwin's mind; when Union soldiers finally overpowered the little group, he was captured with his weapons still in his hands. Godwin and most of his men were then hustled to a military prison in the North.

For the remainder of the winter and spring, Godwin was incarcerated at the infamous Johnson's Island prison. Meanwhile, his divison commander, General Early, had been asking that a special effort be made to have Godwin exchanged. The exchange was accomplished in the summer of 1864, and Godwin soon rejoined his brigade, now a mere 800 strong, which was serving with Early's army in the Shenandoah Valley. On 9 Aug. 1864 Godwin was promoted to brigadier general (to rank from 5 August), and on 19 September he led his brigade in what became the third Battle of Winchester. After much heavy fighting there was a lull in the battle, and Godwin rode out to inspect his lines. While speaking with Captain John Beard, who now commanded Godwin's old regiment, the Fifty-seventh North Carolina, a Union artillery shell exploded directly overhead. A fragment struck Godwin in the head, killing him instantly as he fell into the arms of Captain Beard. As a soldier and leader, Godwin was esteemed by superiors and subordinates alike. He was buried in the Stonewall Jackson Cemetery at Winchester.

SEE: Mrs. John H. Anderson, "Confederate Generals of the Old North State" ([typescript] North Carolina Collection, University of North Carolina, Chapel Hill); Walter Clark, ed., *Histories of the Several Regiments and Battalions from North Carolina in the Great War, 1861–'65* (1901); Clement A. Evans, ed., *Confederate Military History*, vol. 4 (1899); Douglas S. Freeman, *Lee's Lieutenants*, vol. 3 (1944); "Gen. Archibald C. Godwin," *Confederate Veteran* 28 (April 1920); John W. Moore, *Roster of North Carolina Troops in the War between the States* (1882); Ezra S. Warner, *Generals in Gray*, (1956); *War of the Rebellion: Official Records of Union and Confederate Armies*, vols. 1, 2 (1885); Marcus J. Wright, *General Officers of the Confederate Army* (1911).

PAUL BRANCH

**Godwin, Hannibal Lafayette** *(3 Nov. 1873–9 June 1929)*, congressman, was born on a farm near Dunn, the son of Archibald Bryant and Rebecca Eliza Reeves Godwin. He was educated in local schools, attended Trinity College, and studied law at The University of North Carolina (1895–96). Licensed to practice in 1896, he served as mayor of Dunn for the year 1897–98, in the state senate in 1903, as Democratic presidential elector in 1904, and as a member of the state Democratic executive committee in 1904–6. Between 1907 and 1921, he served seven successive terms in the U.S. House of Representatives. As a congressman Godwin demonstrated an interest in the reclamation of swamp land, river and harbor improvement, civil service reform, and Indian problems. He introduced numerous resolutions in favor of individual constituents and in support of public works in his district. As an attorney he practiced in all courts including the United States Supreme Court; he also was a farmer and dealt in real estate.

Godwin was a 32nd degree Mason, a member of the Scottish rite, and an active Methodist. In 1898 he married Mattie Block Barnes; they were the parents of Ruby, Mattie Belle (Mrs. Paul Jones), Marjorie Elizabeth (Mrs. J. O. Warren), Eloise Davis (Mrs. Murdock Dowd), Hannibal Lafayette, Jr., Hugh Archibald, and Robert Barnes. He was buried in Greenwood Cemetery, Dunn.

SEE: *Bio. Dir. Am. Cong.* (1971); *Charlotte Observer*, 10 June 1929; John L. Cheney, Jr., ed., *North Carolina Government, 1585–1974* (1975); Daniel L. Grant, *Alumni History of the University of North Carolina* (1924); *North Carolina Biography*, vol. 3 (1929); *Proceedings*, North Carolina Bar Association (1929); Raleigh *News and Observer*, 10 June 1929.

WILLIAM S. POWELL

**Godwin, Howard Gibson** *(8 Nov. 1902–25 Feb. 1976)*, lawyer and jurist, was born near Dunn in rural Harnett County, the son of Leander A. and Ella Norris Godwin. After attending the public schools of Dunn, he entered The University of North Carolina where he received a bachelor of arts degree in 1928 and a bachelor of laws in 1934. At Chapel Hill, he completed a normal six-year course in five years and worked in many student jobs to defray his college expenses. Nevertheless, he found time for numerous campus activities. He was a member of the Debating Council, played varsity football during his three undergraduate years, won the Holt Scholarship as a junior, and joined Lambda Chi Alpha (social) and Phi Delta Phi (legal) fraternities. He also was a law librarian and an editor of the *North Carolina Law Review*.

Godwin was admitted to the North Carolina bar in the late summer of 1928, and in the same year accepted an editorial position with the Edward Thompson Law Publishing Company, Northport, N.Y., where he worked for five years. However, preferring active participation in the legal profession, he returned to Dunn where he engaged in private practice from 1933 to 1938. In the latter year he was elected clerk of the superior court of Harnett County and served with distinction until 1950, when Governor W. Kerr Scott appointed him a special judge of the state superior court. The appeal of private practice and the desire to spend more time at home caused him to resign from the bench in 1953. He spent the remaining years of his life as a practicing attorney in Dunn. For seven of those years he was city attorney and for four years, prosecuting attorney of the Dunn recorder's court.

An active churchman, Godwin was a member of the First Baptist Church, Dunn, where he taught Sunday school and was a longtime member of the diaconate. He belonged to the Dunn club of Lions International, serving in many leadership posts. He was also a lifelong Democrat and a member of the Harnett County (president), North Carolina, and American Bar associations.

On 20 Feb. 1943 Godwin married Nettie Mae Motes of Appling, Ga.; they had two children: Howard Gibson, Jr. (b. 28 Apr. 1944) and Virginia Ann (b. 31 Oct. 1949). The elder Godwin became ill in 1970 and thereafter limited his activities until his death six years later. He was buried in Greenwood Cemetery, Dunn.

SEE: *Dunn Dispatch*, 25, 26 Feb. 1976; H. G. Godwin, Jr., Dunn, personal information; William S. Powell, ed., *North Carolina Lives* (1962); Raleigh *News and Observer*, 25 Feb. 1976.

C. SYLVESTER GREEN

**Goerch, Carl** *(10 June 1891–16 Sept. 1974)*, editor, author, and broadcaster, was born in Tarrytown, N.Y., the son of Augusta Boetcher and Herman Goetsch, both natives of Pomerania. He received his formal education at the public schools of Tarrytown and was graduated from Washington Irving High School. Devoting his early years to journalism, he first served on the staff of his hometown newspaper. Subsequently he was editor of the Orange, Tex., newspaper; editor of the *Daily News* of Washington, N.C. (1916–20); editor of the New Bern *Sun-Journal* (1920–22); publisher and editor of the *Wilson Mirror* (1922–25); and editor of the *Progress* in Washington, N.C. (1925–33).

In 1933, Goerch moved to Raleigh and began publishing *The State*, a magazine promoting industry, tourist attractions, and the state's natural resources. In 1951 he sold the enterprise to Bill Sharpe and Bill Wright, yet continued to contribute to its columns regularly. Eighteen years earlier, in June 1933, he had also started a series of Sunday night broadcasts entitled "Carolina Chats" on radio station WPTF in Raleigh; this series continued for twenty-eight years until 10 Sept. 1961. As a third undertaking in 1933, he joined the Durham Life Insurance Company and broadcast for them on WPTF a series of programs called "Doings of the Legislature," which were aired for fourteen regular sessions and three extra sessions. In 1937, Goerch began the "Man on the Street" program, broadcasting from the front of the Wake County courthouse every Saturday morning. In addition to radio and television work, he spoke to civic organizations and groups in nearly two hundred communities in North Carolina and in thirty-one states. He was also a pilot and for fifteen years a member of the Raleigh-Durham Airport Authority. An inveterate traveler, he visited fifty-two foreign countries.

Goerch was the author of *Down Home* (1943), *Carolina Chats* (1944), *Characters . . . Always Characters* (1945), *Pitchin' Tar* (1948), and *Just for the Fun of It* (1954), each consisting primarily of short pieces taken from articles in *The State* and radio talks, usually "full of good humor." *Ocracoke* (1956) tells the story of the remote North Carolina island he learned to love. He also wrote feature articles for national magazines and various newspapers.

In 1965, Goerch was named "Tar Heel of the Week" by the Raleigh *News and Observer*; in 1968, he was named "Distinguished Citizen of the Year" by North Carolina Civitans for "accurately informing North Carolinians of their history and progress" during his fifty-five years as a writer and speaker; in 1969, the North Carolina General Assembly commended him in a resolution for service to the state; and in 1971, the General Assembly designated him "Mr. North Carolina." For many years he served as reading clerk for the state house of representatives.

In 1916 Goerch married Sibyl Wallace, a teacher in the Orange, Tex., school system; they were the parents of two daughters; Doris (Mrs. Harry P. Horton) and Sibyl (Mrs. E. K. Powe). He was a Baptist. After his death at age eighty-three, funeral services were held at the First Baptist Church in Raleigh and burial was in Montlawn Cemetery.

SEE: Mrs. Doris Goerch Horton, Pittsboro, personal information; *North Carolina Authors: A Selective Handbook* (1952); *North Carolina Biography*, vol. 3 (1941); Raleigh *News and Observer*, 17 Sept. 1974; *Raleigh Times*, 17, 25 Sept. 1974; Gary Trawick and Paul Wyche, *One Hundred Years, One Hundred Men* (1971).

GRADY L. E. CARROLL

**Goffe, Arthur** *(d. by June 1737)*, Council member and receiver general of North Carolina, was living in the colony by 1723. On 15 January of that year, after he produced for Governor Burrington and the Council his commission and instructions from the Lords Proprietors appointing him receiver general, Burrington appointed him to the Council.

By 1725, Goffe was in the lower house of the Assembly as a representative from Bertie Precinct. He was evidently among those in the lower house who protested the dismissal of Governor Burrington that year by the Lords Proprietors and the appointment of Sir Richard Everard as his successor. In November 1725 the lower house selected Goffe, Edmund Porter, and Sir Nathaniel Duckenfield as its agents to present a true "State & Condition of this Your Province" to the Lords Proprietors, including charges of corrupt administration of Everard and a request for the restoration of Burrington; however, Goffe was the only agent to travel to England. On 19 Jan. 1726 Governor Everard informed the Council that Goffe had left for England without leave from himself and the Council and thus declared Goffe's office of receiver general vacant. Everard then appointed William Little to the position with the stipulation that, should the Lords Proprietors approve Goffe's trip, Goffe would still receive his salary. It would seem that Goffe proved an able spokesman for the lower house, as Everard was removed and replaced by Burrington.

No further mention is made of Goffe after his return from England late in 1726. He may have spent most of the remainder of his life in Edenton or on his land in Bertie Precinct; in 1724 he had bought 130 acres from William Maule for £30 Crown money and in 1725 another 320 acres from Thomas Hoskins for £60 sterling. Goffe's will, written on 29 Nov. 1725 and proved in the Craven County Court in June 1737, named James Winwright of Carteret County as friend, executor, and sole legatee of his estate. Winwright had served as an assistant to Goffe during his term as receiver general. In 1743, Winwright sold 600 acres in Craven County on the north side of the Neuse River at Orchard Creek which had been patented by Arthur Goffe "of Edenton."

Whether Goffe ever married or was survived by relatives is not known; however, it seems unlikely that he was as they were not mentioned in his will. Nevertheless, the Bertie County Court Minutes of 1724–39 mention several individuals with the surname of Goffe.

SEE: John L. Cheney, Jr., ed., *North Carolina Government, 1585–1974* (1975); County Court Minutes and Deeds of Bertie County (North Carolina State Archives, Raleigh); J. Bryan Grimes, *Abstract of North Carolina Wills* (1910); J. R. B. Hathaway, *North Carolina Historical and Genealogical Register*, 3 vols. (1900–1903); Elizabeth Moore, *Records of Craven County*, vol. 1 (1960); William L. Saunders, ed., *Colonial Records of North Carolina*, vols. 1, 2 (1886).

J. MARSHALL BULLOCK

**Gold, Daisy ("Mabel") Hendley** *(26 Oct. 1893–7 Apr. 1975)*, journalist and writer, was born in Iredell County, the daughter of Alvis Francis and Celeste Rimmer Norris Hendley. By her father's first marriage, she was a half sister of Charles, Myrtle and Alvis Eugene Hendley. Floyd F. Hendley was a full brother. Her ancestors were Scotch-Irish, French, and English. After attending local schools, she went to the North Carolina State Normal and Industrial College in Greensboro for three years but did not graduate. Her newspaper career began with the *Statesville Landmark* and continued with the *Greenville* (S.C.) *Piedmont*. In 1920, she became managing editor of the *Wilson Daily Times*. During World War I, she was invited to accept a post as foreign correspondent in Europe, but her parents dissuaded her from accepting it.

On 7 Feb. 1924, she married John Daniel Gold (1867–1954), a widower who was editor and publisher of the Wilson paper, and acquired three stepdaughters. Her own children were Celeste and John Daniel, Jr. After her marriage Mrs. Gold worked irregularly at the *Times* until 1947, taking particular pleasure in turning out feature stories on coastal and eastern North Carolina. *Tides of Life* (1932) was a book of lyric poems. At Morehead City, where she and her husband built a second home in 1935, she embarked on a novel of the North Carolina coast. *It Was Forever* (1940) tells the story of a young married woman from coastal North Carolina who is in love with a British sea captain. A Democrat and a Presbyterian, Mrs. Gold was always active in civic and church affairs. She was able to complete a second (unpublished) novel and was writing a history of Wilson County before her health failed. She died in a nursing home in Lillington and was buried in Wilson.

SEE: Mrs. Celeste Gold Broughton, interview, 11 Dec. 1975, Raleigh; Raleigh *News and Observer*, 1 Dec. 1940; *Wilson Daily Times*, 8 Apr. 1975.

RICHARD WALSER

**Gold, Pleasant Daniel** *(25 Mar. 1833–6 June 1920)*, Primitive Baptist leader and publisher, was born in Rutherford County, now Cleveland County, to Milton and Martha Fortune Gold. His grandfather, Daniel Gold, had moved to North Carolina from Virginia about 1798. Young Gold worked on his family's farm until he was about twenty years old, when he borrowed money to go to school. Soon he began studying law. He received his license in 1856 and started practicing in Shelby. About two years later Gold decided to enter the ministry. With little money and still in debt from previous schooling, he attended Furman University in Greenville, S.C., and later the Southern Baptist Theological Seminary. His formal education ended with his enlistment in the Confederate Army, where he was both chaplain and nurse until a fever ended his military career.

In 1863, while serving as a missionary Baptist pastor in Goldsboro, Gold married Julia Pipkin, the daughter of Willis Pipkin of Lenoir County. They had eleven children: Cora, Paul, John Daniel, Mary Virginia, Joseph Milton, Charles Willis, Pleasant Daniel II, Martha, William, Julia Ruth, and Elizabeth Bynum. Cora, Paul, Martha, and William all died in infancy.

In the late 1860s Gold switched from the "New School" or Missionary Baptists to the "Old School" or Primitive Baptists, joining the Kehukee association. Elder Gold (as he was then known) and Elder L. I. Bodenheimer in 1867 established *Zion's Landmark* as an organ of the Primitive Baptist church. Gold became associate editor in 1871 and editor in 1872; he held the latter post until May 1920.

As a minister in the Primitive Baptist church, Gold served pastorates in Wilson, Falls of the Tar, Rocky Mount, Tarboro, and Durham and was a leading figure of the Primitive Baptist religion in North Carolina for half a century. In addition to his pastoral duties, he founded the P. D. Gold Publishing Company in Wilson, wrote extensively for *Zion's Landmark*, and published *A Treatise on the Book of Joshua*.

Gold's first wife died in 1913. He later married Eugenia Burton, of Winston-Salem, who died in 1940. There were no children from the second marriage. Gold was buried in Maplewood Cemetery, Wilson.

SEE: Samuel A. Ashe, ed., *Biographical History of North Carolina*, vol. 3 (1905); Pleasant D. Gold, *Gold Generations in England and America* (1946); *North Carolina Biography*, vol. 6 (1919); R. H. Pittman, ed., *Biographical History of Primitive or Old School Baptist Ministers of the United States* (1909).

ALICE R. COTTEN

**Golden, Harry Lewis** *(6 May 1902–2 Oct. 1981)*, author, journalist, and social critic, was born Harry Goldhirsch to a Jewish family in eastern Galicia, then part of the Austro-Hungarian Empire. In 1905 his parents, Leib and Anna Klein Goldhirsch, immigrated to New York City, where they settled on the Lower East Side with other immigrant families. Here, the family name was changed to Goldhurst. Leib Goldhurst became a Hebrew teacher and later editor of the *Jewish Daily Forward*.

As a youth Golden developed an unquenchable appetite for reading; unabashedly he consumed volumes of literature, history, and social and political philosophy. After he was graduated from public grade school in 1917, he enrolled in the East Side Evening High School and received his diploma three years later. He then attended night classes for three years at City College of New York, but left about 1922 without a degree. Although Golden liked school and excelled in his studies, his education was shaped as profoundly by his participation, from about 1918 to 1923, in the Round Table Literary Club, a discussion group for teenage boys founded by his employer, Oscar Geiger. Under Geiger's influence, Golden became a frequent soapbox speaker for Henry George's single-tax movement and for the Socialist party.

Throughout his boyhood, Golden worked peddling newspapers, manufacturing straw hats, and clerking in Geiger's fur business. After leaving college, he became a stock broker. He first was employed in his sister Clara's firm, but by 1926 he was established independently as head of the firm Kable and Company. In the same year Golden married Genevieve Alice Marie Gallagher (b. 1898), an Irish Catholic schoolteacher. They had four sons, Richard (b. 1927), Harry, Jr., (b. 1927), William (b. 1929), and Peter (1938–57).

In 1929 Golden's brokerage firm declared bankruptcy, and he was jailed for mail fraud. The charge stemmed from his practice of crediting depositors for stock that his company had not bought, and for encouraging them to invest in worthless stock. Golden spent three and a half years in the Atlanta Federal Penitentiary. After his parole in 1933, he returned to New York where he worked in his brother Jacob's hotel. He had resolved, however, to enter the newspaper business. Between 1939 and 1941, he sold advertising for the New York *Daily Mirror* and the New York *Post*.

There is conflicting evidence about Golden's employment during the late 1930s. Some sources indicate that he worked for the *Charlotte Observer* and then the Hendersonville *Times-News* between 1939 and 1941 before settling permanently in Charlotte. In his autobiography *The Right Time*, however, Golden does not indicate that he lived or worked in North Carolina before 1941. Early that year he accepted an offer from the Norfolk *Times-Advocate* to work in sales and advertising. He separated from his family and legally adopted the name Golden to distance himself from his prison record. While in Norfolk he also wrote periodically for the United Mine Workers' publications. This experience, combined with his sales background, brought him an offer from the Charlotte *Labor Journal* to sell advertising and write editorials. In late 1941, after only eight months in Norfolk, he moved to Charlotte.

It was in Charlotte that Golden's reputation would emerge. While working for the *Labor Journal*, and later for the *Charlotte Observer*, he frequently was exposed to the injustices of racial segregation. Piqued by the denial of first-class citizenship to a large but silenced black minority, Golden espoused the civil rights issue, then in its infancy, as a cause worth promoting. He envisioned as his medium a personal journal in newspaper format. His vision materialized in October 1942, when he commissioned the services of the *Charlotte News* to print the first issue of his paper, which he called the *Carolina Israelite*. In 1944 Golden assumed the publishing and printing duties and began issuing the *Israelite* more regularly, usually monthly or bimonthly. In the twenty-four years of publication that followed, this sixteen-page tabloid, comprised exclusively of Golden's essays and of advertisements, acquired an international circulation of 30,000 at the peak of its popularity in the late 1950s and early 1960s. It survived an office fire in 1958 that destroyed Golden's subscription lists, an anonymous revelation later that year of his prison record, and constant criticism from the southern community.

Through the *Carolina Israelite*, Golden became an unreserved spokesman for civil rights as well as other social and political issues. He addressed subjects heretofore treated obliquely in the South, such as desegregation, unionization, and Jewish-Gentile relations. He was, as *Time* revealed in its 1 Apr. 1957 issue, a " 'member of three minorities' "—a Yankee, a liberal, and a Jew. He survived amid his critics because he made people laugh. His weapon was satire: he needled his way to notoriety when in 1956, in the wake of recent Supreme Court school desegregation decisions, he introduced his "vertical integration" plan, which promised to abolish segregation by removing seats. This solution was drawn from his observation that southerners seemed to object less to standing in public areas with blacks than to sitting down among them.

Aside from political commentary, Golden's essays were filled with anecdotes and seasoned with experiences common in the American culture. He acquired a large and loyal following among a varied audience. Publication of the *Carolina Israelite* ceased in 1968, however, because of declining subscriptions.

Golden became a best-selling author in 1958 with the publication of a collection of his essays entitled *Only in America.* In 1959 this book was adapted for presentation on Broadway by Jerome Lawrence and Robert E. Lee. Golden also wrote an informal biography of his friend Carl Sandburg (*Carl Sandburg,* 1961). Other books by Golden include *Jews in American History; Their Contribution to the United States of America* (with Martin Rywell, 1950), *Jewish Roots in the Carolinas; A Pattern of American Philo-Semitism* (1955), *For 2¢ Plain* (1959), *Enjoy, Enjoy!* (1960), *Five Boyhoods* (edited by Martin Levin, 1962), *You're Entitle'* (1962), *The Harry Golden Omnibus* (1962), *Forgotten Pioneer* (1963), *Mr. Kennedy and the Negroes* (1964), *So What Else is New?* (1964), *Ess, Ess, Mein Kindt* (1966), *The Best of Harry Golden* (1967), *The Right Time; An Autobiography* (1969), *So Long As You're Healthy* (1970), *The Israelis; Portrait of a People* (1971), *The Golden Book of Jewish Humor* (1972), *The Greatest Jewish City in the World* (1972), *Travels through Jewish America* (with Richard Goldhurst, 1973), *Our Southern Landsmen* (1974), and *Long Live Columbus* (1975). At his death he left an unpublished manuscript, "America, I Love You."

In addition, he was the author of numerous articles published frequently in *Nation, Commentary, Life,* and *Congress Weekly,* among others. He covered the Eichmann Trial for *Life* in 1961. During the early 1960s he syndicated a series of newspaper columns called "Only in America." According to information Golden provided for his entry in the 1959 edition of *Current Biography,* he also wrote "a million pamphlets and articles for the Zionists, the New Deal, the Socialists, and the Democratic Party," including " 'Jews of the South' (1950)" and " 'Tammany Hall and the Immigrant' (1948)." He frequently spoke before civic and religious groups.

Golden received several awards and commendations, including the L.H.D. from Belmont Abbey College (1962), Johnson C. Smith University (1965), and the University of North Carolina at Charlotte (1977). Named Man of the Year by Carver College (1957), by Johnson C. Smith University (1958), and by the National Federation of Temple Brotherhoods (1959), he received the National Newspaper Publishers Association's Russwurm Award (1958), the Annual Award for Distinguished Journalism from the Joint Defense Appeal of the American Jewish Committee and the Anti-Defamation League (1959), and the North Carolina Award for Literature (1979). In 1969 he was honored by the University of North Carolina at Charlotte with the establishment of a Harry Golden Lecture Series, which sponsored speeches by political liberals from 1971 through 1974. Golden was a member of the American Jewish Congress, the N.A.A.C.P., the Southern Regional Council, the Catholic Interracial Council, and B'nai B'rith. He was buried in Hebrew Cemetery, Charlotte.

SEE: *Charlotte Observer,* 3 Oct. 1981; *Contemporary Authors,* New Revision Series, vol. 2 (1981); *Current Biography* (1959); Harry Lewis Golden Papers (Atkins Library, University of North Carolina, Charlotte); Harry Lewis Golden, *The Right Time; An Autobiography* (1969); "Golden Rule," *Time,* 1 Apr. 1957; Raleigh *News and Observer,* 3 Oct. 1981; David C. Roller and Robert W. Twyman, eds., *Encyclopedia of Southern History* (1979); Elizabeth Smith, "Charlotte's Golden Harry," *Tar Heel,* January-February 1979; *Washington Post,* 3 Oct. 1981; *Who's Who in America,* vol. 1 (1980–81).

DEBORAH MCCACHERN

**Goler, William Harvey** *(1 Jan. 1846–22 Feb. 1939),* educator, church leader, and president of Livingstone College, Salisbury, was born in Halifax, Nova Scotia. Although orphaned at an early age, he was able to attend the Halifax public schools. In 1861, he became an apprentice bricklayer and plasterer. His church activity and conversion occurred six years later. By 1870, Goler had emigrated to the United States and worked as a mason in Boston. With his savings, he entered Lincoln University, in 1872, where he met Joseph Charles Price, the founder of Livingstone College, and the Reverend E. Moore, a future instructor there. Goler was graduated as valedictorian in June 1878 and entered the seminary, where he earned a B.D. degree in 1881. He married Emma U. Unthank of Greensboro and made North Carolina his home for the next fifty-eight years.

Goler began his career at Livingstone College as a librarian but shortly afterward became a professor. In April 1891, he received an honorary doctor of divinity degree from Lincoln University. He was named president of Livingstone in 1894 and served until his retirement in 1917. In 1895, he delivered the featured address at the Anti-Slavery Society in Philadelphia. The A.M.E. Zion church, in which he held various pastoral appointments, benefited from his many activities and elected positions. After his retirement, Goler served as president emeritus of Livingstone College until his death.

SEE: J. W. Hood, *One Hundred Years of the African Methodist Episcopal Church* (1895); W. H. Quick, *Negro Stars in All Ages of the World* (1898 [portrait]); *Who Was Who in America,* vol. 4 (1968).

MARVIN KRIEGER

**Goodloe, Daniel Reaves** *(28 May 1814–18 Jan. 1902),* abolitionist and journalist, was born in Louisburg, the son of Dr. James Kemp Strother Goodloe, a schoolteacher who studied medicine but never practiced it, and Mary Reaves Jones Goodloe, the daughter of a Granville County planter, Daniel Jones. Although the Goodloes were of modest means, they traced their American ancestry to George Goodloe, who received a grant of land in Middlesex County, Va., in May 1674. Goodloe's mother died at his birth, and he was raised by his father's mother, Ann Goodloe. He attended oldfield schools in Louisburg until he was seventeen, when he was apprenticed to an Oxford printer for two and a half years. He later claimed that these were the most important years of his life, when he acquired the means to style and thought through setting type. At the same time, during the furor caused by the Nat Turner Rebellion, he admitted to being prepared "to suppress imaginary combinations of insurgent negroes." In the following year, however, his lifetime course as an abolitionist was unswervingly fixed, as he read the arguments for emancipation in exchange papers from Virginia.

For a short time after his apprenticeship, he attended the Louisburg Academy of John B. Bobbitt before moving to Maury County, Tenn., to stay with his uncle, Dabney Minor Goodloe, who sent him to school in Mount Pleasant where he was influenced by William H. Blake, a Harvard graduate. In 1836 Goodloe volunteered to fight the Indians, but before the Maury County Volunteers could rendezvous at Fayetteville, Tenn., the Creeks surrendered. The volunteers then agreed to serve as mounted infantry against the Seminoles in Florida. For his six months' service Goodloe was eligible for a pension, which became his primary means of support in later years. After returning to Tennessee for a short time, he went to Oxford, N.C., in 1837, where he purchased and for a year published an unprofitable weekly paper, *The Examiner*. Afterward he studied law under Robert B. Gilliam and received approval to practice in the county and superior courts. But Goodloe was unsuited for the law, being unable either to speak or think on his feet. Although by this time he had established himself as a promising young Whig leader, he turned aside the advice of Priestly H. Mangum, who thought politics might provide him fluency of speech and public presence. Goodloe claimed his antislavery views would leave him without a tenable defense and harm the party; altruistic and honest, the rough and ready of politics would never suit him.

Unable to find his way to fortune in either North Carolina or Tennessee, which he revisited, Goodloe set out for the nation's capital, where he arrived penniless on 22 Jan. 1844. Because of Goodloe's friendships in North Carolina, Willie P. Mangum took an interest in him and obtained him a post as associate editor of *The Whig Standard*. When that campaign paper suspended publication after Clay's defeat, Goodloe sought a place in the federal bureaucracy. Meanwhile, he moved on to short-term editorial associations with *The Georgetown Advocate* and the *Christian Statesman*. Then for three years he taught school in Prince Georges, Md., in order to repay loans from his benefactor, Mangum. In 1849, he returned to North Carolina for several months but decided his best possibility for employment was in Washington, where he found a post in the Tyler administration first as a clerk in the auditor's office and later in the Navy Department.

In 1841, Goodloe had begun work on a manuscript exposing the economic shortcomings of the slave system; his first and possibly best know essay, it was published in 1846 as a twenty-seven-page pamphlet in an edition of five hundred copies under the title, *Inquiry Into the Causes Which Have Retarded the Accumulation of Wealth and Increase of Population in the Southern States; In Which the Question of Slavery is Considered in a Politico-Economical Point of View. By a Carolinian.* While he was with *The Whig Standard* in 1844, he obtained an interview with John Quincy Adams, who read the manuscript and recommended that it be published. In March 1844 it appeared in Charles King's *New York American*; it was republished in *The National Era* in 1847 and subsequently in other abolitionist newspapers. The pamphlet was later praised by John Stuart Mill, to whom Goodloe sent a copy in 1846. In 1849, Goodloe replied to the proslavery indictment of city life in Quaker Elwood Fisher's *Lecture on the North and the South* with another economic condemnation of slavery in *The South and the North*. During the heated debate over the admission of slavery into the territories engendered by passage of the Kansas-Nebraska Act, he presented additional arguments concerning the unproductivity of slavery in an 1854 pamphlet, *Is It Expedient to Introduce Slavery Into Kansas? A Tract for the Times. . . .* In 1855, he drafted a petition to the North Carolina legislature, entitled "Memorial of Citizens of North Carolina to the General Assembly Asking for Certain Reforms in the Laws relating to Slaves and Free Persons of Color," urging a law to recognize slave marriages, to prevent the disruption of slave families, and to allow free blacks and slaves to learn to read. In the midst of opposition to the Dred Scott case, he tried to show that constitutional decisions affecting popular interests should be made by the representatives of the people with a compilation of quotations from the leaders of the original Republican party of Jefferson in his *Federalism Unmasked: Or the Rights of the States, the Congress, the Executive and the People, Vindicated Against the Encroachments of the Judiciary, Prompted by the Modern Apostate Democracy. Being a Compilation from the Writings and Speeches of the Leaders of the Old Jeffersonian Party*. The fifteen-page pamphlet was reissued by the Republican National Convention in 1860 for circulation as a campaign document. In *The Southern Platform: Or Manual of Southern Sentiment on the Subject of Slavery* (1858) he made a direct appeal to the mind of Southerners by quoting the antislavery sentiments of the founding fathers from the South. The latter two compilations were typical of Goodloe's work. His prose was humdrum, even tedious, rather than impassioned, though his judiciousness was greatly admired by such newspapermen as Horace Greeley and Henry Raymond. Although his writings were relatively mild, especially in comparison to the radicalism of Hinton Rowan Helper whom he found abhorrent, they were denounced in his native state. After the appearance of *The Southern Platform*, Frank L. Wilson declared that Goodloe was a "God-forsaken soulless, honorless abortion of North Carolina—a thing . . . of fanaticism and hypocrisy."

He was released from his clerkship in the Navy Department when he allowed a letter approving *Uncle Tom's Cabin* to be published in Stowe's *Key*. Afterwards he began a regular connection with *The National Era*, a paper that had carried his works in serial form. During the summer and fall of 1853 and 1854 he relieved the ailing owner, Dr. Gamaliel Bailey, by writing the lead editorials over the signature, "G." Although his name appeared in the prospectus for 1858 as assistant editor of the abolitionist paper, by 1855 he had apparently become Bailey's assistant and the chief political writer for the *Era*. When Bailey died in 1859, he ran the paper until Bailey's widow was forced to close shop in March 1860. His editorials continued to emphasize the economic instability of the slave system. While for the most part his syntax was mild, at times he could turn harshly sarcastic; his barbs were aimed at the shortcomings of political leadership in the South as well as the stupidity of Northern politicians. His connection with the *Era* not only brought him in contact with Bailey and the paper's corresponding (honorable) editor, John Greenleaf Whittier, but also allowed him to become the ally and friend of America's leading writers of the time including Grace Greenwood, Mary Mapes Dodge, and Mrs. E. D. E. N. Southworth. He was particularly close to Harriet Beecher Stowe, who greatly admired his work and in 1853 proposed to carry copies of his essays with her to England.

When the *Era* folded, both Greeley's New York *Tribune* and Raymond's *New York Times* carried political leaders by Goodloe. As the Washington correspondent for the *New York Times* in 1860 and 1861, he became convinced that civil war between the North and the South was inevitable and that peace would be impossible as long as slavery existed. In *Emancipation and the War. Compensation Essential to Peace and Civilization. In Which It Is Made Apparent That the Resources of the Country Are Three Fold Greater Than the Emergency, Which Will Call for Little If Any Additional Taxation*, a pamphlet subsidized and published by Raymond in 1861, Goodloe recommended that the slaveholders be paid for their slaves, believing compensation would be cheaper than an extended war.

In 1861, he received his first wartime federal appointment as clerk to the Potter Commission, charged with evaluating the loyalty of government workers, and he drafted the commission's report. Because of his pamphlet on emancipation, which attracted the attention of Abraham Lincoln, he also served on the commission appointed to establish payment for slaves emancipated in the District of Columbia. Goodloe held a number of other federal appointments during the war. He was offered a federal judgeship for the court of Eastern Carolina, which he refused, and it was rumored that Lincoln considered appointing him military governor of North Carolina. From 1864 to 1865 he was the associate editor of the *Daily Morning Chronicle* in Washington as well as a correspondent for the *New York Times*. From his wartime experiences he wrote two particularly important editorials, "Downfall of the Rebellion and Conciliation" (19 June 1864) and "Industrial Prospects of the South" (24 Oct. 1865) which appeared under his name. The latter article came from his work in the Department of Agriculture and that portion of the commissioner's annual report for 1865, entitled "Resources and Industrial Condition of the South," evaluating the prospects of the South for reconstruction. Before his assassination Lincoln intended to appoint Goodloe the U.S. marshal for the District of Columbia; however, the commission was not signed before the president's death.

Perhaps from a sense of guilt but even more likely because of political pressure, Andrew Johnson offered Goodloe the federal marshalship for North Carolina. Goodloe held the post from September 1865 to May 1869. In returning to North Carolina, his design was to establish a moderate, effective, and honorable Republican party by appealing to religious groups that had once favored abolition and to former Unionists who had opposed secession. His plan was doomed from the outset. He soon found himself in opposition to the president, then to the Congress, and constantly to the state's radical Republican coalition of scalawags and carpetbaggers led by William Woods Holden. Goodloe opposed Johnson's Reconstruction policies, and in 1866 he was among the Southerners who signed the call for a convention to oppose the president's programs. Although the conservatives demanded his immediate resignation because of his attendance at the National Union Convention, he cautioned the convention to moderation and with John Botts of Virginia he earnestly opposed the Negro suffrage resolution. But with the passage of the Reconstruction acts, his moderation became the target of the radicals, and a growing frustration and political ineptness on his part left him in a powerless and divided minority.

In the summer of 1867 he and Hardie H. Helper obtained the shop of the Greensboro *Union Register* and transferred it to Raleigh, where they began issuing the *Raleigh Register* as an opposition paper to Holden's radical *North Carolina Standard*. Again in the journalistic traces, Goodloe as editor of the paper urged a moderate course of Reconstruction in the state. But he was totally alienated by the Radical Republican convention assembled in Raleigh on 4 Sept. 1867. The two opposition papers reflected the split between the two wings of the Republican party that they represented. Goodloe was particularly incensed by the referendum for the adoption of the Constitution of 1868, which he denounced as a fraud. He promptly turned over the management of the paper to Helper in order to run against Holden for governor, though he attempted to withdraw before the campaign was over; he also broke all ties with the *Register* over a disagreement with Helper regarding editorial policies. Goodloe detailed these events in his *The Marshalship in North Carolina. Being a Reply to Charges Made by Messrs. Abott, Pool, Heaton, Deweese, Dockery, Jones, Lash and Cobb, Senators and Representatives of the State*, which appeared serially in the newspapers before its publication as a pamphlet in 1869. He baldly renounced congressional Reconstruction in an 1868 pamphlet, *Letter of Daniel R. Goodloe to Honorable Charles Sumner on the Situation of Affairs in North Carolina*. He also published in 1868, "Shall Equality Supplant Liberty? Being a Review of Mr. Sumner's Bill and Speech." In March 1869 his enemies managed to have him turned out of office as U.S. marshal. In 1872, he supported Horace Greeley for the presidency and was elected secretary of the national executive committee for the Liberal Republicans at Cincinnati. Active in North Carolina during the campaign, he was one of the state's leaders who met Carl Schurz in Reidsville and escorted him to Greensboro.

After his final foray into North Carolina politics, Goodloe returned to Washington where he became a free-lance writer, a habitué of the Library of Congress, and for some time a Washington correspondent for the Raleigh *News and Observer*. In June and July 1873, he wrote a series of four letters for the Raleigh paper entitled "John Quincy Adams." In keeping with his ethic of journalistic honesty, he was one of the first writers to brave the truth about the purported Mecklenburg Declaration of Independence, publishing pieces in the *Raleigh Sentinel* (June-September 1873), in an extra of the New York *Herald* (20 May 1875) and in the *Washington National Republican* (20 May 1875) (drafts of the "Mecklenburg Declaration of Independence" are in his Papers). Between 1878 and 1880 he published three articles in the *South Atlantic*: "The Congresses Before the Constitution" (June 1878), "Finances of the Revolution" (May-June 1879), and "Emancipation in the District of Columbia" (October 1880). His "North Carolina in the Colonial Period" was published in John Hill Wheeler's *Reminiscences and Memoirs of North Carolina* (1884). His interest in liberal economics and sympathy with the small freeholders were sustained in *A History of the Demonetization of Money* (1890) and in "Western Farm Mortgages," which appeared in *The Forum* (November 1890).

In 1889, Goodloe issued *The Birth of the Republic: Compiled from the National and Colonial Histories and Historical Collections from the American Archives and from Memoirs, and from the Journals and Proceedings of the British Parliament*, a major compilation of legislative proceedings relating to the history of the United States, published by Bedford, Clarke & Co. Earlier he had offered a twelve-page prospectus, "Synopsis of Congressional Legislation for a Century. . . ." A number of his newspaper pieces came from *Birth of the Republic* including "The Previous Question," published by the *New York Times* (22 Feb. 1891). In 1883, he registered with the Copyright Office of the Library of Congress a book to be entitled "Reconstruction of the Southern States—Being a Complete History: Embracing the plans and Experiments of Presidents Lincoln and Johnson, and the actions of the People, through their Conventions and Legislatures, under them: the reconstruction measures of Congress adopted in 1864 and the debates which led to them: the South under Military Government: the Operations of the Freedmans Bureau and of the "Ku-Klux-Klan": and the restoration of the States on the basis of Universal Negro Suffrage, and restricted White Suffrage," but he was never able to publish it. Desperate for money, he sold the rights to Samuel Sullivan "Sunset" Cox, who published it in his *Three Decades of Federal Legislation. 1855 to 1885 . . .* (1885) without giving credit to Goodloe, even though the section provided by him was the only worthwhile part of the book.

Starting in 1894, while he was the Washington correspondent for the *News and Observer*, a number of his extensive feature series were carried in the Sunday papers. The first one, "Men of Half a Century, Personal Reminiscences of Washington and Public Men for the Last Fifty Years," which began in August 1894, came from his memories of antebellum and wartime Washington (the manuscripts in letters addressed "My Dear Mary" are continued in his Papers). The second set of features dealt with events and personalities from the early history of the United States under the Constitution. But the most important series, derived from Goodloe's experiences during Reconstruction, were a severe indictment of those "knaves," who "were the founders of the Republican party as we have it now in North Carolina." The features concluded with an article on "The Trent Affair" (5 Jan. 1896). They were his last substantive work. His final publications included "Purchase of Louisiana, and how it was brought about," Southern History Association *Publications* (1900), and two posthumously published works, "An Omitted Chapter in North Carolina History," *State Normal Magazine* (February 1904), and "The North Carolina and Georgia Boundary," *The North Carolina Booklet* (April 1904).

A shrewd, able journalist admired by his contemporaries, even his enemy Holden who recognized his capability as a newspaperman, Goodloe seemed incapable of managing his own affairs. Although he was a moderate abolitionist and Republican party leader with close ties to the literary abolitionists, he possessed the personal naïveté of the dogmatic and zealous reformer. Although there is no proof to the story of his intended matrimony, his biographers have felt obligated to contend with it. Supposedly, he was engaged to a Washington society belle who gave birth to a child sired by someone else without Goodloe's knowledge at the time of the marriage. The story illustrates a peculiar lack of sophistication in his makeup. It also reveals another side of his personality that made him friends of even his political enemies, because he had the marriage annulled with the full support of the bride's father, a prominent congressman. The story was known to his contemporaries and related in newspaper accounts after his death. Its acceptance, combined with his seeming disdain for material well-being and political incapacity, is as revealing of Goodloe as are his writings that successfully dealt with social and political realities.

In the spring of 1896 Goodloe returned to North Carolina and four years later suffered a paralytic stroke, which left him crippled. He died in Warrenton and was buried in Fairview Cemetery. A lifelong Unitarian, he was influenced early in life by the works of William Ellery Channing. A photograph of Goodloe by Charles Parker of Washington was published in *The Birth of the Republic*. But his personality is better revealed in a drawing by George Randall reproduced in the *North Carolina University Magazine* (December 1894). Randall's portrayal shows a man of integrity and reason as well as an idealist perplexed by the harsh reality of modern politics.

SEE: John Spencer Bassett, *Anti-Slavery Leaders of North Carolina* (1898); *DAB*, vol. 7 (1931); Douglas C. Daily, "The Elections of 1872 in North Carolina," *North Carolina Historical Review* 40 (1963); Daniel Reaves Goodloe Papers (Southern Historical Collection, University of North Carolina, Chapel Hill); Benjamin Sherwood Hedrick Papers (Manuscript Department, Library, Duke University, Durham); William Woods Holden, *Address on the History of Journalism in North Carolina* (1881); Edward Ingle, *The Negro in the District of Columbia* (1893); *Nat. Cyc. Am. Biog.*, vol. 10 (1909); Raleigh *News and Observer*, 26 Jan. 1902; Henry T. Shanks, ed., *The Papers of Willie Person Mangum* (1955); E. D. E. N. Southworth Papers (North Carolina State Archives, Raleigh); Joseph F. Steelman, "Daniel Reaves Goodloe; A Perplexed Abolitionist During Reconstruction," *East Carolina Collection Publications in History* 2 (1965); Harriet Beecher Stowe Papers (North Carolina State Archives, Raleigh); Charles Leonard Van Noppen Papers (Manuscript Department, Library, Duke University, Durham); Stephen B. Weeks, "Anti-Slavery Sentiment in the South; with Unpublished Letters from John Stuart Mill and Mrs. Stowe," *Southern History Association Publications* 2 (1898); Frank L. Wilson, *Address Delivered before the Wake County Workingmen's Association* (1860).

D. A. YANCHISIN

**Goodrich, Frances Louisa** *(15 Sept. 1856–20 Feb. 1944)*, artist, teacher, and craftsman, was born in Binghamton, N.Y., the daughter of the Reverend William Henry and Mary Prichard Goodrich. She spent her early years and was educated in Cleveland, Ohio. When she was sixteen, her father's health broke and the family went abroad from 1872 to 1874 so that he might have complete rest. For nearly a year she lived with a French family; her reading of French books, begun at that time, was maintained throughout her life. During the same period she also began the serious study of art. Returning to the United States, she attended the Yale Art School and later studied in the studio of a distinguished New York artist. Before 1890, she was exhibiting and selling pictures. Such success, however, did not completely satisfy her. Her great desire was to serve those about her in some more direct and personal way, and in the autumn of 1890 she welcomed the opportunity to join a lonely teacher at Riceville, near Asheville, N.C. After two years, she moved to Brittain's Cove where she built a cottage for herself and a teacher; soon afterwards a schoolhouse and later a church, in memory of her father, were erected.

In 1897, Miss Goodrich moved into the heart of the laurel country at Allanstand in Madison County, at that time a wild and remote area. Allanstand would remain the center of her chief activity until retirement. As the years passed, her educational work spread throughout the region until there were seven day schools under her supervision, most of them also centers for religious activity and for the improvement of agriculture. It was through the cooperation of the Home Board of the Presbyterian Church of the U.S.A. that these schools were built and funds provided to secure excellent teachers for the whole school year.

Though Miss Goodrich's various homes in the mountains were all built at her expense, she found that it gave her a more established position to receive a commission from the Presbyterian Board. During the greater part of her working years, she also was paid a small salary.

While she and the school teacher were living in Brittain's Cove, the seeds of the future Allanstand Cottage Industries were sown. A neighbor brought Miss Goodrich, as a gift, a forty-year-old coverlet, woven in the "Double Bowknot" pattern, golden brown on a cream-colored background. The brown had been dyed with chestnut oak. With the coverlet was the "draft" by which it was woven, a long strip of paper covered with figures—very mysterious to her. As Miss Goodrich wrote: "I was put to my studies." Before her lay a new world—the spinning of wool thread, vegetable dyeing, and weaving, not to mention the techniques involved, especially the weaving. She turned to her mountain neighbor women, many of whom had inherited a knowledge of hand skills from their mothers and grandmothers. With her encouragement they started weaving coverlets for the northern market.

When she reached Allanstand, Miss Goodrich found that in the country about her handweaving was going on as in olden times. There she and her neighbors recognized the potential for a real business, and it was natural to give it the name of Allanstand Cottage Industries and to make that place the center of the work. As the enterprise developed, she had the satisfaction of achieving her three original goals: to save the old craft from extinction, to give paying work to isolated women, and to bring interest into their lives through the joy of making useful and beautiful things. Many related crafts such as quilting, basketry, whittled articles, charming toys, and birdhouses found their way into the sales shop that opened in Asheville in 1908 under the name of Allanstand Cottage Industries. The business was incorporated in 1917.

In 1918, Miss Goodrich retired to live in Asheville. She is recognized as *the* pioneer in western North Carolina in reviving the traditional mountain hand skills and in adapting them to products salable in contemporary markets. In 1930, she and a group of mountain workers organized the Southern Highland Handicraft Guild. About that time she was approached by several business concerns who wished to buy the Allanstand shop. It was not for sale, but in the spring of 1931 she gave it to the infant craft guild. Also in 1931, she published *Mountain Homespun*, an account of the revival of crafts in the Southern Appalachians; it included stories of her mountain neighbors with whom she always had enjoyed friendly relations. Moreover, she had the unique characteristic of bringing out the best in her craftsmen.

From her earliest years in the Asheville area, Miss Goodrich was interested in church and civic affairs. In 1923, she became a member of the First Congregational Church. She was long active in the Business and Professional Women's Club of Asheville, and she was a member of the YWCA and the Current Literature Club. She also had strong ties with Asheville College—a merger of the Home School and the Normal and Collegiate Institute. She became active in the affairs of these two schools soon after her arrival in Asheville and frequently arranged to send students from isolated regions to them. This interest continued after the merger. In 1938, she was awarded the degree of doctor of humanities by the College of Wooster, Wooster, Ohio.

She died in Asheville and was buried in the Goodrich plot, Lakeview Cemetery, Cleveland, Ohio.

SEE: *Asheville Citizen*, 20 July 1961; *Asheville Citizen-Times*, 5 Jan. 1941, 28 Jan. 1951 (picture); Francis R. Bellamy, *The Story of White Rock* (1921?); *Christian Century*, 6 Aug. 1930; Durham *Herald-Sun*, 28 Mar. 1941 (picture); *Durham Morning Herald*, 21 Feb. 1944; *We the People* 3 (March 1946).

L. L. PITMAN

**Gordon, James Byron** *(2 Nov. 1822–18 May 1864)*, merchant, farmer, politician, and Confederate soldier, was born at Wilkesboro. His family, of Scottish descent, was founded by John George Gordon who emigrated from Scotland in 1724 and settled first in Maryland and finally in Spotsylvania County, Va. Two of the sons of John George Gordon's large family, George and Charles, later moved south and settled in Wilkes County. Charles Gordon was the great-grandfather of Major General John Brown Gordon, a Confederate general who served in the infantry of Lee's army. George Gordon fought in the Battle of Kings Mountain; his son Nathaniel represented Wilkes County in the General Assembly. Nathaniel married Sarah Lenoir Gwyn and their son was James Byron Gordon. Nathaniel Gordon died when James was about six years old.

At age ten, young James went to the school of Peter Stuart Ney at Hunting Creek in Iredell County but left after two years because of ill health; he subsequently did light chores on the family farm. At age eighteen Gordon entered Emory and Henry College, Va. Although he did not take the regular course, he remained there for two or three years before returning to Wilkesboro and entering the mercantile business. Gordon also supervised the farm he inherited from his father, and became involved in local politics, representing Wilkes County in the General Assembly in 1850. When the Civil War broke out in 1861, he enlisted as a private in the Wilkes Valley Guards on 9 May. The company was reorganized with Montford S. Stokes as captain and Gordon as first lieutenant. When it became Company B of the First North Carolina Regiment, Captain Stokes was elected colonel of the regiment and Gordon succeeded him as captain of Company B. Later, however, the First North Carolina Cavalry (Ninth North Carolina Regiment) was organized and Gordon was appointed its major. North Carolina heroes Robert Ransom and Laurence S. Baker served as colonel and lieutenant colonel, respectively.

The First North Carolina Cavalry was to become one of the finest cavalry regiments to serve in the war, with some fifty actions to its credit. After the regiment was organized, it was sent to Virginia where, on 26 Nov. 1861, it fought its first engagement at Vienna. In March 1862 the regiment was sent back to North Carolina to meet Union forces under Ambrose Burnside; it returned to Virginia in June to face McClellan's Union army, which was threatening Richmond. Meanwhile, Colonel Ransom transferred to the infantry, Laurence S. Baker became colonel of the regiment, and, on 3 Apr. 1862, succeeded Baker as lieutenant colonel. Participating in the Seven Days' battles before Richmond (26 June–2 July, 1862), the First North Carolina Cavalry served in the brigade of famous Confederate General

"Jeb" Stuart. On 29 June the regiment was ordered to make a reconnaissance of the Union line of retreat at Willis' Church, resulting in a bloody engagement with Union infantry and cavalry. The regiment continued service as part of General Wade Hampton's brigade of Stuart's cavalry, participating in the campaigns of Second Manassas, Sharpsburg, Fredericksburg, and Chancellorsville, as well as in Stuart's "Horse Raid" into Pennsylvania. Gordon commanded a detachment of the regiment that took part in Hampton's raid on Dumfries in December 1862. In these actions he was frequently complimented by Stuart for his courage and leadership. Gordon was one of many officers in Lee's army to become an outstanding military leader with no previous military experience, and he easily became one of General Stuart's favorites.

On 9 June 1863, Union cavalry attacked at Brandy Station to begin the bloodiest cavalry engagement of the war. In the battle, the First North Carolina Cavalry had a conspicuous part in driving back the enemy forces. Afterward the regiment accompanied Stuart on his controversial raid around the Union Army in the Gettysburg campaign. In the cavalry engagement in the rear of the Union army at Gettysburg on 3 July 1863, General Hampton was wounded and Colonel Baker succeeded to the command of his brigade. Lieutenant Colonel Gordon found himself temporarily in charge of the regiment and continued in this capacity during the retreat of the Confederate Army to Virginia. At Hagerstown, Md., he met and repulsed a Union attack with a fragment of the Fifth North Carolina Cavalry. Of this General Stuart was to write in his report of Gordon: "that officer exhibiting under my eye individual prowess deserving special commendation." On 11 Aug. 1863, Gordon was made colonel and assigned to the Second North Carolina Cavalry (Nineteenth North Carolina Regiment), replacing its former commander, Colonel Sol Williams, who was killed at Brandy Station. He was shortly transferred back to the First North Carolina Cavalry, however, and later commanded Hampton's old brigade in the Battle of Jack's Shop on 22 Sept. 1863.

In the meantime, Colonel Laurence S. Baker, the First North Carolina Cavalry's former commander, had been promoted to brigadier general and placed in command of a new brigade composed exclusively of the First, Second, Third, and Fifth North Carolina Cavalry regiments; however, he had been so badly wounded in action as possibly to be invalided from further field service. To succeed him the choice of both generals Lee and Stuart fell on Colonel Gordon, who was promoted to brigadier general on 28 Sept. 1863, to rank from the same date (confirmed 17 Feb. 1864), and given command of the North Carolina cavalry brigade. His first opportunity to lead his new command in battle was not long in coming, for in October he accompanied Lee's army in its pursuit of Meade's Union army from near Culpeper Court House. On 10 Oct. 1863, Gordon drove back a Federal force at Bethesaida Church. Three days later his command was part of a column under General Stuart that was cut off and surrounded by moving columns of retreating Union infantry. The following morning Stuart attempted to cut his way out of the trap, and Gordon called on the First North Carolina Cavalry to attack and hold off the Union forces while the rest of Stuart's command escaped. This was done and the whole of Stuart's force was able to get away though Gordon himself had been slightly wounded when a bullet grazed his nose, breaking the skin and causing some profuse bleeding. On 16 October, Gordon commanded in an engagement on Bull Run. In November he led the center in what was known as the "Buckland Races" and was active in the Mine Run engagements, having his horse shot out from under him at Parker's Store.

At the beginning of March 1864, he took part at Atlee's Station in turning back Kilpatrick's and Dahlgren's raid on Richmond. On 4 May 1864, there began the great Wilderness campaign as Grant's Union army moved southward for Richmond. Gordon's outposts were the first Confederate units to make contact with the Union Army as it crossed the Rapidan River. Gordon served through the Battle of the Wilderness and at the beginning of the Battle of Spotsylvania. On 9 May, Union General Sheridan began his famous drive on Richmond with some 12,000 Union cavalrymen. To check this threat, Stuart hurried ahead with two brigades to intercept Sheridan's raiders while Gordon and his own brigade were instructed to harass the rear of the raiding column and slow it down as much as possible. Gordon did admirable work to this end, though it involved almost constant riding and fighting day and night. Stuart was able to get ahead of Sheridan and confront him at Yellow Tavern, outside Richmond, on 11 May 1864. Though Stuart's command was overpowered and he himself was mortally wounded, Sheridan was forced to turn back. Just before his wounding at the height of the battle, Stuart was heard to mutter: "Would to God, Gordon were here." Gordon had been following and harassing the rear of Sheridan's column all this time and had beaten it at Ground Squirrel Church on 10 May. On the twelfth, he again confronted Sheridan at Meadow Bridges near Brook Church. Here he fought with reckless courage, remaining mounted though bullets flew about him and urging his men to hold on until infantry reinforcements came up to relieve them.

Just before his exhausted little command was relieved late in the evening, Gordon was struck by a minie ball in the arm, ranging out at the elbow. At first the wound was not thought too serious but he lived only a few days, dying in the officers' hospital in Richmond. His remains were taken back to Wilkesboro where he was buried at the Episcopal church. Gordon left no heirs to carry on his name. He was truly one of the finest soldiers North Carolina produced.

SEE: Mrs. John H. Anderson, "Confederate Generals of the Old North State" ([typescript] North Carolina Collection, University of North Carolina, Chapel Hill); Samuel A. Ashe, ed., *Biographical History of North Carolina*, vol. 8 (1917), and *Cyclopedia of Eminent and Representative Men of the Carolinas of the Nineteenth Century* (1892); Walter Clark, ed., *Histories of the Several Regiments and Battalions from North Carolina in the Great War, 1861–'65* (1901); William H. Cowles, *Memorial Address on the Life of General James B. Gordon* (1887); Clement A. Evans, ed., *Confederate Military History*, vol. 4 (1899); Douglas S. Freeman, *Lee's Lieutenants*, vol. 3 (1944); *War of the Rebellion: Official Records of Union and Confederate Armies*, vol. 2 (1885); Ezra S. Warner, *Generals in Gray* (1956); Stephen B. Weeks Scrapbooks (North Carolina Collection, University of North Carolina, Chapel Hill); John H. Wheeler, *Reminiscences and Memoirs* (1884); Marcus J. Wright, *General Officers of the Confederate Army* (1911).

PAUL BRANCH

**Gordon, Patrick Duff** *(18? Aug. 1719–[5-11?] Nov. 1773)*, attorney, was the son of John Duff (second son of

Patrick Duff of Craigston, Scotland) and his wife, Margaret Gordon of Farskane. He was the nephew of Margaret Duff, Lady Farskane. John Duff was well educated and held municipal office in Elgin, Moray, where he lived. In addition to Patrick, the Duffs were the parents of Archibald, William, John, James, and Anne (who married James Leslie of Bennebeith). All of the children were well educated. Patrick, also called Peter, was the second but oldest surviving son and was "bred to the Law at Edinburgh and entered Writer to the Signet." He would have been well employed, but he fell into a life of dissipation and pleasure, and at last into an itch for gaming. He kept company with some of the great folks at Edinburgh, and, after losing his own money, played away other people's entrusted to him until he was obliged to retire to North America. "He married a gentleman's daughter in Fife, an agreeable, pretty woman, and had a daughter," but both had been dead for many years in 1773. This wife was Grisell Balfour; their daughter was Grisell or Jean, and she inherited property from her mother in 1752. When he left for America and settled in North Carolina, Patrick Gordon Duff quietly changed his name to Patrick Gordon or Patrick Duff Gordon.

Some time before sailing from London on 14 Mar. 1757, he married, a second time, a woman named Mary who had been a domestic in his family. They became the parents of three children: Margaret Duff Gordon, who died in 1780; James Duff Gordon, born in August 1770, who left North Carolina soon after the death of his mother, and who was drowned en route to India as a midshipman on 18 May 1791; and Peter Duff Gordon, who was sent to Scotland to be educated and afterward returned to New York during the American Revolution on board a British ship. Peter eventually went to Charleston, S.C., where he died before 1808. Patrick Gordon's second wife survived him, dying in New Bern in March 1784.

Settling first in the town of Bath, Gordon was elected to represent the borough in the Assembly in 1762; he was again a candidate in 1766, but his election was contested and he was not seated. By 1767, he was living in New Bern where he held a number of important positions as well as serving as an attorney. He was interested in education and endorsed the appointment of Thomas Thomlinson to head the New Bern Academy. In New Bern he was commissary and judge of the Court of Vice-Admiralty of North Carolina. Royal governor William Tryon apparently thought highly of Gordon and called upon him for service on numerous occasions.

Gordon was the author of the lengthy and detailed account of the various agencies of government in colonial North Carolina that Governor Tryon sent to his superiors in London on 28 June 1767. Entitled "A View of the Polity of the Province of North Carolina in the Year 1767," it is a thorough explanation of the obligations and privileges of officials at all levels in the colony. The duties of each is carefully spelled out and the laws that governed them are cited. The author clearly had a thorough understanding of North Carolina law and government.

Gordon was employed as assistant counsel of the Crown in the trial of some of the Regulators at Hillsborough charged with riot in the early spring of 1771. Tryon reported that Gordon presented sixty-one indictments and that without exception they were found true.

Patrick Gordon died apparently rather unexpectedly at the age of fifty-four. His will, dated 5 Nov. 1773, was proved before Governor Josiah Martin one week later. When his estate was being settled, Mrs. Mary Grainger applied for refund of a fee that she had paid him to represent her in a pending court but he died before court was convened. Gordon died before the split brought on by the American Revolution divided people into opposing camps, but his widow lived until 1784, well after the war was over. In 1782, she entered claims against several Loyalists who had left North Carolina owing her late husband for legal services.

SEE: William Baird, *Genealogical Memoirs of the Duffs* (1869); Estate Records of Craven County (North Carolina State Archives, Raleigh); William S. Powell, ed., *The Correspondence of William Tryon and Other Selected Papers*, 2 vols. (1980, 1981); Alistair and Henrietta Tayler, *The Book of the Duffs*, vol. 1 (1914).

WILLIAM S. POWELL

**Gore, Joshua Walker** *(10 Jan. 1852–8 Apr. 1908)*, engineer, inventor, and professor, was born in Frederick County, Va. His father was Mahlon Gore (d. 1860), the son of Thomas and Sarah Walker Gore. His paternal great-grandfather was John Gore, who came from England about 1778 and settled in Loudon County, Va. His mother was Sydney Sophia Cather Gore, daughter of James Cather of Glasgow, Scotland, and Nancy Howard Cather of Belfast, Ireland. His maternal great-grandfather arrived in Frederick County shortly after the end of the American Revolution. Joshua W. Gore had two brothers, James Howard and Perry Cather.

Young Gore attended Loudon Valley Academy and in 1871 entered Richmond College, where he received certificates in mathematics and physics. In 1873 he enrolled in the University of Virginia and was graduated with a degree in civil engineering in 1875. He then spent two years at Johns Hopkins studying mathematics and physics. In 1878 he became professor of physics and chemistry at Southwestern Baptist University, Jackson, Tenn., and remained there until 1881, when he returned to the University of Virginia as assistant to C. S. Venable in mathematics. In 1882 Gore became professor of natural philosophy and engineering at The University of North Carolina. In addition to his teaching duties, he was responsible for the establishment of the electric light plant and, in part, for the heating and water plants. For many years he was university registrar and from 1884 to 1886 he served as secretary of the faculty. In 1895 he became professor of physics. He was active in the establishment of an early university press and the YMCA building, and at a convention held in Chapel Hill in 1886 he was elected permanent president of the YMCA. For a time he was secretary of the Elisha Mitchell Scientific Society and was a member of the American Association for the Advancement of Science.

Gore was dean of the School of Mining during the terms 1902–3 and 1903–4, and dean of the Department of Applied Science during the terms 1904–5 to 1907–8. While a member of the university faculty, he published five papers. He also served on the Chapel Hill board of aldermen and was president of the Bank of Chapel Hill.

During the absence of President Edwin A. Alderman from the campus Gore was acting president, and at Alderman's resignation Gore was recommended as his successor. He was also recommended for the same position at the College of Agriculture and Mechanic Arts in Raleigh, but he declined both. In Chapel Hill Gore lived in the house built originally for the president at the site now occupied by Swain Hall. On 9 Nov. 1883 he married Margaret Corinthia Williams, daughter of the Reverend J. W. M. Williams of Baltimore and Corinthia Read Williams. They had no children. He was a Democrat and an active member of the Baptist church. He died of tuberculosis at the age of fifty-nine in Baltimore, where he had gone for treatment.

SEE: Samuel A. Ashe, ed., *Biographical History of North Carolina*, vol. 5 (1906); Kemp P. Battle, *History of the University of North Carolina*, vol. 2 (1912); *Durham Recorder*, 10 Apr. 1908; Raleigh *News and Observer*, 10 Apr. 1908; L. R. Wilson, *The University of North Carolina, 1900–1930* (1957 [portrait]); *Winchester* (Va.) *Evening Star*, 3 Apr. 1957.

JOHN LEONARD RIGSBEE

**Gorham, James** *(1745–24 Dec. 1804)*, legislator and officer in the American Revolution, was born in Barnstable, Mass., the son of Captain Isaac Gorham and his wife, Mary Cobb. The Gorham family was prominent among the early settlers of Cape Cod. As the youngest son, James inherited the family homestead by the will of his father in 1751. At an undetermined date he moved to North Carolina and settled in Pitt County. Active early in the patriot cause, he was chairman of the Committee of Safety for Pitt County in 1775. He represented the county at the Provincial Congress that met at New Bern in April 1775 and, at this session, he was appointed major of militia. Gorham again represented Pitt County at the provincial congresses in Hillsborough in August 1775 and in Halifax on 12 Nov. 1776. According to the proceedings of the safety committee of Pitt County, meeting at Martinborough (Greenville) on 23 Mar. 1779, a petition was received from Major Gorham on behalf of the county "to discharge Mr. Carson from teaching dancing." This may be a reflection of the major's Puritan youth in New England. In 1779, he was elected to the House of Commons where he was placed on the Committee for Public Accounts. Gorham was again in the General Assembly for the sessions during 1781–82.

When the scene of conflict in the American Revolution shifted from North to South, Gorham soon saw active combat and began to appear in the records as a colonel. In the spring of 1781, Cornwallis marched north from Wilmington to Virginia with Lieutenant Colonel Banastre Tarleton as an advanced guard. On 6 May 1781 General Jethro Sumner informed General Nathanael Greene, commanding the southern campaign, that a party of Tarleton's horse and fifty Tories had "put to route" 400 militia under Colonel Gorham at Peacock's Bridge on Contentnea. On 27 August of the same year, Richard Caswell wrote Governor Thomas Burke that the enemy had evacuated New Bern and gone up the Neuse to Bryans Mills and almost surprised the post there under command of Colonel Gorham. The colonel advanced on the enemy, but the party of horse ordered to protect his right flank had not done so—"which was attributed to their finding some liquor and most of them got intoxicated." Gorham was forced to withdraw and conducted an orderly retreat of two miles across the Neuse.

There are few facts regarding Gorham's life with the return of peace. According to his obituary in the *Raleigh Register* of 21 Jan. 1805, he "was attacked at 2 o'clock in the morning by a quimcey [quinsy] and died within four hours. He was an old Revolutionary officer, a firm Republican, a kind parent and husband." Before leaving Massachusetts, Gorham married a widow, Mrs. Mary Baker. There is no record of children by her. In 1792, he married Mrs. Sarah Davis McClure, the daughter of James Davis, the New Bern printer. They were the parents of four children: John Churchill (b. 1793); George Franklin (b. 10 July 1794); Penelope (b. 1800), the wife of R. G. Green; and Edwin (b. 1802). Franklin Gorham represented Pitt County in the House of Commons in 1811, and John C. Gorham served in the same capacity in 1824, 1825, and 1838.

SEE: Walter Clark, ed., *State Records of North Carolina*, vols. 13 (1896), 15 (1898); Fitzhugh Lee Morris, comp., *Lineage Book of Past and Present Members of the North Carolina Sons of the American Revolution* (1951); William L. Saunders, ed., *Colonial Records of North Carolina*, vols. 9, 10 (1890); Sarah Webb and Burnham S. Colburn, "The Gorhams of North Carolina," *New England Historical and Genealogical Register* 82 (1928).

CLAIBORNE T. SMITH, JR.

**Gorman, Alexander M[axwell?]** *(1814–24 Jan. 1865)*, newspaper and journal editor and publisher, was born in Raleigh, the son of Henry, a native of Ireland, and Mary Gorman. He became a printer, working with Joseph Gales, editor and publisher of the *Raleigh Register*. Upon reaching his majority, Gorman moved to Georgia where he married Mary J., a native of that state, whose maiden name has not been discovered. Upon returning to Raleigh he became foreman of the *Register* office but in September 1848 joined J. B. Whitaker in purchasing the *Family Visitor*, a "miscellaneous and Temperance newspaper" published there. No copies of this paper are known to have survived. On 13 June 1849 a new paper, *The Spirit of the Age*, appeared in place of the *Family Visitor* as a result of reorganization. Slave labor was used to operate the press. Beginning with a small format and limited circulation, this paper was soon adopted by the Sons of Temperance as their official organ. Gorman bought a power press in August 1853, and his paper rapidly grew in both size and circulation until it became one of the largest of its kind in the South. It attained a paid circulation in excess of 5,000. In 1858 it was described as "a Weekly Family Journal; Devoted to Temperance, Literature, Education, Agriculture and the News of the Day."

On 2 Sept. 1855 Gorman's wife died, and on 4 Dec. 1855 he married Mary E. ("Mollie") Jordan of Isle of Wight County, Va., She was "editress" of the "Ladies Department" of *The Spirit of the Age* from 1859 until the fall of 1861. In March 1864 Gorman sold his paper, which continued to be edited by others until 1894. In 1858 he began publishing the *North Carolina Planter*, a monthly journal devoted to agriculture, horticulture, and the mechanic arts as a successor to William D. Cooke's *Carolina Cultivator* and Thomas J. Lemay's *Arator*. Although the *Planter* continued publication at least until May 1861, Gorman apparently was not associated with it after the appearance of the third volume, which concluded with the issue of December 1860. Widely read throughout the South, this journal presented a broad range of agricultural information and advice. Gorman also printed various pamphlets on such diverse topics as temperance and land drainage. He also did job printing and produced books, cards, and circulars. The first issue of the Raleigh *Christian Advocate* in 1856 came from his press.

The sale of *The Spirit of the Age* did not mean that Gorman was forsaking his profession. In January before its sale, he acquired the semiweekly edition of the *State*

*Journal,* another Raleigh newspaper, and converted it into the *Daily Confederate* beginning with the issue of 26 Jan. 1864. In its management he was joined by Duncan K. McRae, and they produced a newspaper that demonstrated complete devotion to the Confederate cause.

Gorman, a Methodist and a Freemason, died unexpectedly after an illness of just a few hours. His will, drawn up on the day of his death, left his possessions to his wife and four children: Maxwell Jordan, George H., Alexander Maxwell, and Florence P. Another son, Howard Littleton, had died in 1859. On 23 Mar. 1869 his widow married William P. Weatherell of Assonet, Mass.

SEE: Charlotte *Western Democrat,* 1 Feb. 1859, 23 Mar. 1869; *Hillsborough Recorder,* 8 Feb. 1865; Interview with Patsy Gorman Mitchner in George P. Rawick, ed., . . . *North Carolina [Slave] Narratives,* part 2 (1972); Guion Johnson, *Ante-Bellum North Carolina* (1937); *Raleigh Register,* 6 Nov. 1840; *Spirit of the Age,* 5 Sept. 1855, 2 Jan. 1856, and passim; U.S. Census, Wake County, 1850, 1860; R. H. Whitaker, *Whitaker's Reminiscences, Incidents and Anecdotes* (1905); Daniel J. Whitener, *Prohibition in North Carolina, 1715–1945* (1945).

WILLIAM S. POWELL

**Gorman, Mary E. ("Mollie").** *See* **Weatherell, Mary E. Jordan Gorman.**

**Gorrell, Joseph Hendren** *(25 Aug. 1868–28 Mar. 1942),* college teacher, the son of B. H. and Sara Virginia Hendren Gorrell, was born at Lexington, Va. His father was a druggist who "had moved there . . . after the war, because he was so fond of General Robert E. Lee who had just come to Lexington to head the institution which soon became Washington and Lee University." The elder Gorrell was an artillery officer under Lee for four years. Young Gorrell received his elementary and secondary education in private schools and academies in Lexington before enrolling in Washington and Lee at age sixteen. His undergraduate days were marked by numerous honors and awards including membership in Phi Beta Kappa, the University Scholarship in Greek, the New Shakespeare Society prize, the Young Scholarship prize for proficiency in moral philosophy, the Early English Society prize, and the Robinson medal for scholarship in philosophy and literature. In his senior year he was the honored Cincinnati Orator. He received the bachelor of arts degree in 1888 and the master of arts degree in 1890.

For the session 1890–91, Gorrell stayed on at Washington and Lee as an instructor in English and modern languages. During the next three years he did graduate study at the Johns Hopkins University, Baltimore, earning the doctor of philosophy degree in 1894. At Johns Hopkins he was classed as an "honorary scholar," which meant that he paid no fees to the university. His graduate major was English, with a minor in modern languages, and he chose college teaching as a career. In September 1894 he was offered, on the same day, the presidency of a small college in Louisiana and a position as acting professor of modern languages at Wake Forest College in North Carolina, the latter at one fourth the salary of the former job. Because of his Baptist heritage and his personal bent for teaching, he went to Wake Forest and taught there for forty-five years before retiring in 1939. Often teaching eighteen hours a week, Gorrell made German, French, and Spanish come alive for thousands of students. He was head of the Department of Modern Languages for forty years, and professor emeritus for the next five years. On campus, he was the epitome of friendliness and once remarked, "In every student I have a friend." Seldom called "Dr. Gorrell," except to his face, he was affectionately known as "Phinxtus," a nickname derived from his acquired enunciation in mixing several modern languages with classical Greek and his Valley-of-Virginia English. He was an avid reader, a patient teacher, a demanding scholar, and a provocative thinker who taught by leading his pupils into the world of culture through communicative design.

For twenty years, from 1894 to 1914, he was faculty editor of the *Wake Forest Student,* the college magazine. From April 1916 he served continuously as secretary-treasurer of the Denmark Loan Fund for needy students. He was for many years chairman of the buildings and grounds committee of the college. He was also architect and construction superintendent of the Alumni Building, which was completed in 1907 after three years of tedious efforts to raise money, purchase materials, and employ and direct workmen. But the building was opened "free of debt"; in appreciation, the Alumni Association gave Gorrell an engraved silver cup.

As a faithful member of the Wake Forest Baptist Church, Gorrell was Sunday school superintendent for twelve years, church clerk for fifteen years, and deacon and chairman of the finance committee, financial secretary, and treasurer for more than thirty-five years. Although not an ordained minister, he served several times as "supply pastor" at the churches at Wake Forest, Dunn, Olive Chapel, and Rolesville, and was a frequent pulpit guest in many local and state churches. In the town of Wake Forest, he served for ten years as a town commissioner and was a founder and longtime president of the Wake Forest Building and Loan Association.

Although he had ambitions to become a research student and writer, Gorrell's time was completely occupied with teaching. One biographer commented, "In his all too rare publications he shows himself a master of a correct and easy style English." One of those publications was a series of articles in the *Biblical Recorder* "dealing with the period of Jewish history lying between the close of the Old Testament and the opening of the New Testament."

On 1 June 1897, Gorrell married Fannie Taylor, of Wake Forest, the eldest daughter of the president of Wake Forest College, Dr. Charles E. Taylor. They had two children: a son, Charles Benjamin, died in 1915; a daughter, Virginia (Mrs. Andrew Clifford Hall), survived him. He died in Duke Hospital, Durham, after a brief illness and was buried "with many other Wake Forest great" in the Wake Forest Cemetery.

SEE: Alumni Files and the North Carolina Baptist Collection (Library, Wake Forest University, Winston-Salem) for information on Gorrell; *Biblical Recorder,* 14 June 1939, 8, 29 Apr. 1942; "Herr Doktor Gorrell," *Wake Forest Student* 53 (1939); Raleigh *News and Observer,* 21 May 1939.

C. SYLVESTER GREEN

**Gorrell, Ralph** *(12 May 1803–14 Aug. 1875),* lawyer, was the eldest son of David (1770–1848) and Euphemia

Stewart Gorrell (1770–1850) of Guilford County. His grandfather was Ralph Gorrell, Jr. (1735–1816), who migrated from County Donegal, Ireland, to Boston in 1750, and thence to Guilford County where he settled near and became an active member of the Alamance Presbyterian Church. Ralph, Jr., was a member of the Halifax Provincial Congresses of April and December 1776, of the North Carolina House of Commons in 1784, and of the state senate in 1777–78, 1795, and 1796. He was commissioned during the American Revolution to raise troops to keep the Indians in check. In 1808 he sold, for $98, the forty-two acres of land on which the town of Greensboro was laid out.

Like his grandfather, Ralph Gorrell developed an interest in politics. After graduation from Greensboro Academy in 1820 and The University of North Carolina in 1825, he was licensed to practice law in 1827. He ran for the House of Commons in 1832, but withdrew when he discovered that he was three acres under the constitutional property requirement of one hundred acres. He was elected to the House of Commons in 1834, 1835, and 1854. He also served Guilford County in the state senate in 1856 and 1858; there the minority party supported him for presiding officer. Like other Whig leaders of his day, Gorrell supported public education, state aid to railroads, and ad valorem taxation of slaves, and he stood firm for the Union until the advent of war led him to cast his vote for secession in the Convention of 1861. During the war the Confederate Treasury Department appointed him a depositary at Greensboro. Until the office was abolished in 1868, Gorrell served for many years as Guilford County clerk and master in equity. Appointive positions that he held were commissioner of the Fayetteville and Western Railroad and director of the North Carolina Railroad. Gorrell's political life was characterized by honesty, a rational speaking style, and a refusal to use demagoguery.

As a lawyer and a businessman, Gorrell achieved a good reputation and moderate wealth. From 1830 to 1835 he organized a business partnership with William Kerr and Calvin J. Chisholm to operate mercantile houses in Greensboro and Morganton. In 1851, he became the first president of the Greensboro Mutual Life Insurance and Trust Company. Gorrell also owned a plantation—in 1860 he listed the value of his property at $46,000, but the war impoverished him—and had a flourishing law practice. In the 1850s he drafted construction contracts for the North Carolina Railroad in addition to routine legal affairs. His most notable legal case involved the defense of the abolitionist Daniel Worth on charges of distributing incendiary literature in 1860. Although Worth was convicted in two separate trials and the convictions were upheld on appeal, Gorrell obtained for Worth reasonable bail that permitted the elderly abolitionist to escape to the North rather than serve his two one-year prison sentences. Gorrell's colleagues at the bar praised his honesty, devotion to principle, ability to keep confidences, industry, and reliability.

In his family life, Gorrell was a devoted husband and father. He married Mary Jennings Chisholm of Richmond County, but their lives were saddened by the deaths of seven of their ten children. One son, Captain Henry Clay Gorrell, died leading troops in the Civil War. Anne Eliza Gorrell, who married Joseph B. Fariss in 1869, was the only child to bear him grandchildren. Gorrell was noted for holding daily family devotions after he joined the Presbyterian church in 1843. He became the ruling elder of his church in 1849 and was regularly called upon to represent it at meetings of the presbytery, synod, and general assembly. Gorrell's spacious home was a meeting place for preachers as well as lawyers and statesmen. It was there in 1865 that General Joseph E. Johnston delivered the last message to his troops before surrendering. After Gorrell's death, the Cape Fear and Yadkin Valley Railroad Company purchased his homeplace for its general offices.

SEE: Ethel S. Arnett, *Greensboro, North Carolina* (1955); Bettie D. Caldwell, *Founders and Builders of Greensboro* (1925 [portrait]); Ralph Gorrell Papers (Southern Historical Collection, University of North Carolina, Chapel Hill); *Greensboro Daily News*, 22 Oct. 1922, 18 Oct. 1925; Greensboro *New North State*, 20 Aug. 1875; *Greensboro Patriot*, 18 Aug. 1875; William C. Rankin Papers (Southern Historical Collection, University of North Carolina, Chapel Hill); Noble J. Torbert, "Daniel Worth: Tar Heel Abolitionist," *North Carolina Historical Review* 39 (1962).

JOHN L. BELL, JR.

**Gould, Robert Simonton** *(16 Dec. 1826–30 June, 1904)*, attorney, Confederate officer, and judge, was born in Iredell County, the son of Daniel and Zilpha Simonton Gould. His father, who was a New Hampshire native and a Presbyterian minister, died when Robert was seven, after which his mother moved the family to the university town of Tuscaloosa, Ala., where she opened a boarding house.

In 1840, at age fourteen, Gould entered the University of Alabama and was graduated four years later. In 1845, he started to read law, but his studies were interrupted by his appointment to a tutorship in mathematics at the university. In 1849, he left the university faculty and, in partnership with former Mississippi Governor Joshua L. Martin, opened a law practice in Macon, Miss. The following year he moved to Centerville, Tex., and in 1853 was elected district attorney of the Thirteenth Judicial District, serving for two terms. In 1855 he married Lenna Barnes, a native of Georgia.

Gould was a member of the Texas Secession Convention of 1861. In the same year, he became judge of the Thirteenth Judicial District, but in early 1862, he resigned his judgeship and joined the Confederate Army. He served as a major in a battalion known as Gould's Battalion, and participated in the Mansfield, Pleasant Hill, and Jenkin's Ferry battles. In the latter engagement he was seriously wounded. By the war's end he had been promoted to the rank of colonel.

After the war, Gould resumed his legal practice. In 1866, he was again elected judge of the Thirteenth District, but his election was invalidated by Reconstruction military officials on the grounds that it was detrimental to a successful reconstruction. Gould spent the next three years at his farm. In 1870, he moved his law practice to Galveston. In May 1874 he was appointed associate justice of the Texas Supreme Court to fill the unexpired term of Judge Peter W. Gray, and in 1876 he was elected to a six-year term on the court. In 1881, after the resignation of Chief Justice George F. Moore, Gould was appointed to a one-year term as chief justice. In 1882, he failed to receive the Democratic party's endorsement as a candidate for a full term as chief justice; however, before his one-year appointment expired, Gould was appointed to the law faculty of the newly opened University of Texas. He served on the faculty until the spring of 1904.

During his tenure on the bench, Gould delivered a

number of important decisions. Among them were his dissenting opinion in *Ex Parte Towles* (48 Texas 413) and majority opinions in *Yancy v. Battle* (48 Texas 46), *Johnson v. Harrison* (48 Texas 257), and *Veramendi v. Hutchins* (48 Texas 531).

Gould was a member of the Free Presbyterian Church of Austin and was buried in that city.

SEE: *DAB*, vol. 7 (1928); James D. Lynch, *The Bench and Bar of Texas* (1885); *The Austin Statesman*, 1-2 July 1904; W. P. Webb, ed., *The Handbook of Texas* (1952).

ROBERT H. DETRICK

**Govan, Daniel Chevilette** *(4 July 1829–12 Mar. 1911)*, Confederate general, was born at New Bern, the son of Andrew Robison Govan, who represented the Orangeburg District of South Carolina in the United States Congress from 1822 to 1827. At an early age young Govan was taken to Somerville, Tenn., and thence to Marshall County, Miss., where his father built the plantation Snowdown near Holly Springs. Here Govan spent his childhood. He was educated at Columbia University, Columbia, S.C., graduating in 1848. In 1849 he joined a group of prospectors headed for California led by future Confederate general Ben McCulloch, for whom Govan had vast admiration and after whom he subsequently named one of his children. When California failed to meet his expectations, Govan returned to Mississippi in 1852. The following year he married Mary Otey, the daughter of Bishop James Hervey Otey, Episcopal bishop of Tennessee. In 1854, the young couple settled on newly purchased land in Phillips County, Ark., near Marianna.

When the secession crisis developed, Govan rejected the arguments of his Unionist father-in-law and raised a company for Confederate service. Elected captain of Company F, Second Arkansas Regiment, he was rapidly promoted to colonel and then to brigadier general on 29 Dec. 1863. He served conspicuously at Shiloh, Murfreesboro, Chickamauga, and Missionary Ridge. In the Atlanta campaign he was captured at the Battle of Jonesboro but was exchanged in time to take part in Hood's ill-fated Tennessee invasion. General Patrick Cleburne, who had ranked Govan as one of the four best officers in the Confederacy, was killed at the Battle of Franklin within twenty feet of Govan. However, Govan survived to surrender with General Joseph E. Johnston in North Carolina on 26 Apr. 1865.

Returning to Arkansas, Govan managed his affairs at Marianna until 1894, when he accepted an appointment as an Indian agent in Washington. He served in that capacity for four years. Buried at Snowdown, he was survived by two daughters, Mrs. P. H. McKellar of Memphis, Tenn., and Mrs. J. J. Sample of Magnolia, Miss., and one son, B. M. Govan of Marianna, Ark. Four of his brothers fought for the Confederacy and a younger brother, George H. Govan, commanded the First Mississippi Infantry in the Spanish-American War.

SEE: *Confederate Veteran* 19 (September 1911); Forrest City (Ark.) *Times*, 17 Mar. 1911; Memphis *Commercial Appeal*, 24 Dec. 1925, 16 Jan. 1926; Ezra J. Warner, *Generals in Gray* (1959).

MICHAEL B. DOUGAN

**Gove, Anna Maria** *(6 July 1867–28 Jan. 1948)*, physician, was the only child of George Sullivan and Maria Clark Gove, of an eminent New England family; she was born in Whitefield, N.H., where her father, a graduate of Dartmouth, was a physician. Anna's interest in medicine was inspired by her father. It was her own and his plan that she be well educated and that she have the best medical training available in New England. After private schooling and graduation from St. Johnsbury Academy, Vt., she took the premedical course at the Massachusetts Institute of Technology, where she was one of a small group of young women, unusual in their ability and ambition, to "master the course at the hardest school in New England." From Boston she went to New York and was graduated in 1892 from Woman's College of the New York Infirmary. The next year she spent at the New York Infant Asylum, where her "chief" said years later that she did "A 1 medical work," seemed "a born doctor," and "won the hearts of all by her tact and kindness.

In 1893, at age twenty-six, Dr. Anna M. Gove moved to Greensboro, N.C., to the newly established State Normal and Industrial School (now The University of North Carolina at Greensboro) at the beginning of its second year. There she served as resident physician, head of the department of physiology and physical culture, and teacher of physiology and hygiene. She was also a pioneer in health education and in medicine as a career for women.

When in 1892 the State Normal and Industrial School adopted a policy of employing a female resident physician, it took a daring step—especially in a state where there were only two women doctors. During her first year at the institution, Dr. Gove took the state medical examinations and was granted a license. As the third woman to receive a medical license in North Carolina, she was invited to join the Medical Society. Although the other physicians were sometimes awkward and embarrassed in the presence of the "female, lady, doctress," we have her own word for it that they were always courteous and kind. The students received her with the open-mindedness of youth, but parents were hesitant. One mother wrote Dr. Gove, "Please don't teach Mary so much about her insides. It ain't decent."

When Dr. Gove arrived at the new Greensboro school, she found it totally lacking in medical facilities. There was no dispensary, no infirmary or rooms set aside for this purpose, no nurse, no office assistant, and no hospital in the town of Greensboro. However, records of the State Normal and Industrial School reveal the steady progress achieved by Dr. Gove. In 1896 an infirmary was built and initially employed a caretaker, followed by a practical nurse and then a trained nurse. A new infirmary, completed in 1912 under her direct supervision, was the first well-equipped infirmary for women students in this part of the United States. Medical and physical examinations were begun when only two colleges, Amherst and Vassar, required them. The Greensboro institution was one of the first in the country and the first in North Carolina to add X-rays to these examinations. Under Dr. Gove's directions, a study department of health was established; with her stimulation and encouragement, the department of physical culture gradually developed into a nationally recognized department with two years of physical culture education required of all students.

In the early 1920s, Dr. Gove was instrumental in obtaining for the state three substantial appropriations from the American Social Hygiene Association, Inc. One grant of $48,929 was for the program at Samarcand Manor; a second, of $26,000, for the prevention, treatment, and control of venereal disease; and a third, of $21,600, for the State Normal and Industrial School to use in promoting the teaching of health under the school's medical service.

As a physician, Dr. Gove practiced the highest professional ethics. She was affiliated with and participated in the deliberations of numerous medical, health, and civic organizations on the local, national, and international levels. Improvements to health facilities in the college paralleled her own growth and development. Her travels included a leave of absence for graduate study in Vienna and attendance as a delegate at the International Medical Association meeting in Moscow (1896–97); summer vacations at the University of Chicago (1899) and Cornell University (1901); and leaves of absence to teach physiology at Vassar and engage in private practice in Yonkers, N.Y. (1901–3), to study in Vienna (1913–14), and for Red Cross work in Europe during World War I (1917).

Many honors came to Dr. Gove. The infirmary completed at Greensboro in 1953 bears her name. She served as national vice-president of the American Student Health Association and she was given life membership in the American Medical Association of Vienna. After her retirement in 1936, she continued to keep an office and serve in an advisory capacity. She died at age eighty-one.

SEE: Nell Craig, *Dr. Anna M. Gove* (1939); *North Carolina Medical Journal* 9 (April 1948); Records of the Alumni Association (University of North Carolina, Greensboro) for information on Dr. Gove; *Some Pioneer Women Teachers of North Carolina* (1955).

GLADYS AVERY TILLETT

**Grady, Benjamin Franklin** *(10 Oct. 1831–6 Mar. 1914)*, educator, soldier, congressman, and farmer, was born in Albertson Township, Duplin County, the oldest son of Alexander Outlaw and Anne Sloan Grady. His Grady forebears were in North Carolina by 30 June 1718, when his progenitor William Grady (or Graddy) received fifty acres on Deep Creek in Bertie County from James Rutland. The name is said to have been pronounced Graddy in Duplin County, to which William's son John moved in 1739 to land on the fork of Burncoat Creek and Northeast River. He married Mary, daughter of William Whitfield. Two of their sons, John and Alexander, fought in the Battle of Moore's Creek Bridge in 1776; John was killed and a monument placed there to his memory. After the war, Alexander and his wife Nancy Thomas lived on the Grady farm. Their son Henry married Elizabeth Outlaw, daughter of James Outlaw, on 6 Jan. 1799. They were the paternal grandparents of Benjamin Franklin Grady. His mother was the daughter of Gibson and Rachel Bryan Sloan. Through his Bryan grandmother, Benjamin was connected with William Jennings Bryan of Nebraska as well as with the North Carolina Bryans, one of whom was Colonel Needham Bryan who represented Johnston County in the provincial congresses of 1774 and 1775. The family is descended from a daughter of Lord Needham (the family name of the Earls of Kilmorey) of Ireland who married a Bryan and immigrated to America.

Grady attended public and private schools and was prepared for college by the Reverend James M. Sprunt at Grove Academy, Kenansville. He was one of the student orators at his graduation from The University of North Carolina on 4 June 1857. After earning the A.B. degree with highest honors, he returned to Grove Academy to teach. In 1859, he became professor of mathematics and natural sciences at Austin College, then located at Huntsville, Tex., where he taught until the college suspended operations at the outbreak of the Civil War.

Illness from typhoid fever prevented his enlisting until the spring of 1862, when he joined a Texas cavalry unit that became Company K in the Twenty-fifth Regiment and was soon dismounted. Throughout the war he served with the rank of orderly sergeant, twice refusing a captaincy. The entire command was captured at Arkansas Post on 11 Jan. 1863 and confined at Camp Butler, near Springfield, Ill., for about three months before being exchanged in April. Afterwards, Grady was sent to Tullahoma, Tenn., to join General Bragg's army; he served until the close of the war in Granbury's Brigade, Cleburne's Division, Hardee's Corps. Except at Nashville and Bentonville, he participated in all battles and skirmishes in which his brigade was engaged. Toward the end of the war, he once more became ill with typhoid fever and, from 19 March to 2 May 1865, was in Peace Institute, Raleigh, then being used as a hospital.

After the war, Grady returned to his home community, called Chocolate, in Duplin County, and soon resumed his life's work of teaching. He organized a school at Moseley Hall (now LaGrange) where he taught for two years. In 1868, he and Professor Murdock McLeod founded the Clinton Male Academy in Clinton, Sampson County, where he taught until 1875 when failing health forced him to abandon teaching for farming. A few years later, however, he returned to his old residence in Duplin County and for several years conducted, in his home, a private school for young men who were unable to go to college. He also founded a Sunday school at old Sutton's Branch School House where he taught music, the Bible, classical literature, and the sciences. During this period he was appointed a justice of the peace.

Grady served as a trustee of The University of North Carolina during 1874–91. In 1881 he was elected superintendent of public instruction for Duplin County, a position he held for eight years. Twice elected on the Democratic ticket to the United States Congress, he represented the Third District from 4 Mar. 1891 to 3 Mar. 1895. He then moved to Turkey in Sampson County where he and his son Henry established a school, the Turkey Academy. Around 1900, he moved to Clinton where he spent his last years studying and writing. He published pamphlets, letters, and two books dealing with the South and its struggle: *The Case of the South Against the North* (1899) and *The South's Burden* (1906). Earlier he had published *An Agricultural Catechism* (1867) as a textbook for the common schools.

Grady's first wife, Olivia Hamilton of Huntsville, Tex., died while he was a prisoner at Camp Butler, leaving one child, Franklin. His second wife, Mary Charlotte, daughter of Dr. Henry A. and Celestial Robinson Bizzell of Clinton, bore him nine children: Henry A., who became a superior court judge; Cleburne; James B.; Stephen S.; Benjamin; Louis D.; Lessie R.; Mary Eva; and Anna B. He died in Clinton and was buried in the Clinton Cemetery.

SEE: Benjamin Franklin Grady, *The Case of the South Against the North* (1899); *Bio. Dir. Am. Cong.* (1961); *Carolina and the Southern Cross*, vol. 2 (August 1914); Daniel Lindsey Grant, *Alumni History of the University of North*

*Carolina* (1924); *North Carolina Biography*, vol. 5 (1919); University of North Carolina Alumni Office Files; University of North Carolina Order of Exercises for Commencement, 4 June 1857 (1857).

KATHLEEN S. H. CHEAPE

**Grady, Henry Alexander** *(19 Sept. 1871–23 Feb. 1958)*, teacher, lawyer, and judge, was born in Clinton, the son of Benjamin Franklin and Mary Charlotte Bizzell Grady. His ancestors came to America from Ireland, and one William Grady (or Graddy) settled in Bertie County about 1718. William's son, John, moved to Duplin County and settled on the Northeast River on a tract of land that is still in the family. The history of this area of the county, known as Chocolate, and the genealogy of the Grady, Outlaw, and other families with whom they intermarried, were the topics of a lengthy poetical narrative written by Henry Alexander.

Grady was born in his maternal grandfather's house in Clinton, where his father was conducting a preparatory school. Several years later his family returned to his father's old home in Duplin County, and young Grady was reared on the farm. At age nineteen he secured a teaching certificate from the superintendent of Duplin County schools and taught for two years. In 1892 he enrolled at The University of North Carolina, where he pursued a special course in mathematics and literature. In 1894 he went to Washington, D.C., as private secretary to his father, then a member of Congress. While in Washington, he enrolled in the law school at Georgetown University for one year and was elected president of his class. In 1895, he accepted a position with the U.S. Coast and Geodetic Survey and was sent to Alaska to assist in surveying and establishing the boundary between that territory and Canadian British Columbia, and in making astronomical observations.

In early 1896, Grady returned to North Carolina for a short rest. Afterward he went to New York City, where he studied law under his half brother, Franklin. Primarily for financial, and not philosophical, reasons, he was employed by a reform club and worked in the 1896 Free Silver Campaign. Later, he was principal clerk in the New York law office of John Sprunt Hill, of Duplin County and Durham, N.C. When the Spanish-American War broke out, Grady returned to Duplin County and organized a group of volunteers, but the war was over before they could be mustered into service. In 1898, he joined with his father in establishing an academy in the small Sampson County town of Turkey, where he taught for two years. In 1900, he reentered The University of North Carolina to take a summer law course under Judge James C. McRae. In the fall he sat for the bar examination by the state supreme court, passed, and received his license to practice. Returning to Clinton, he formed a law firm with Henry E. Faison, but the venture was short-lived due to Faison's failing health. At some time between 1904 and 1906, he established a law practice with his brother-in-law, Archibald McLean Graham, and remained with the firm until 1922.

Prominent in the public affairs of his county, Grady served as a member of the North Carolina Democratic State Executive Committee for twenty years (1902–22) and of the North Carolina National Guard from 1910 to 1912. He held the rank of colonel on the staff of Governor W. W. Kitchin. In 1902, he made an unsuccessful bid for the state house of representatives, losing primarily because Democrats were in the minority in Sampson County. Two years later, however, he was elected to the state senate. About 1917 he was elected mayor of Clinton and served until 1921.

Grady was initiated into the Masonic order in 1901, and in time held a large number of offices. In 1919, he was elected Grand Master of Masons in North Carolina and was later a member of the Committee on Masonic Jurisprudence, serving for a number of years as chairman. In 1918, at the request of the Grand Master, he attended a conference in Cedar Rapids, Iowa, where he was a member of the committee that drafted the constitution for the Masonic Service Association.

In 1922, Grady was elected a judge of the superior court and took office on 1 Jan. 1923. A popular judge, he easily won reelection in 1930 but declined to seek a third term in 1938, probably due in part to the death of his wife in 1935. After his retirement, he served as emergency judge for life. In 1952 and 1953, then over eighty years old, he held more sessions of superior court than any other judge in North Carolina.

About 1923, Judge Grady was elected Grand Dragon of the Ku Klux Klan in North Carolina, an organization then promoting law and order. A moderate, he endeavored to steer the organization away from extreme actions. He supported legislation banning the wearing of masks, both as a way to keep the Klan from getting into trouble and to keep it from being blamed for the acts of others. Following a split with the national leadership, primarily because it was felt that he was too restraining an influence, he resigned as Grand Dragon in 1927.

On and off the bench, Grady was a tireless worker. His favorite pastimes included carpentry and cabinetmaking, and he enjoyed building grandfather clocks. A fiddler of no mean accomplishment, he took pleasure in entertaining his friends and guests. His love of literature remained with him all his life, and his favorite authors were Tennyson and Burns. Grady was a poet himself, penning "Chocolate," "The Land of Never Come Back" (describing death to the young son of a friend), and "Immortality." He also enjoyed history and genealogy, and was an authority on several North Carolina families. He gathered and catalogued genealogical data from every available source. His exhaustive research is nowhere more evident than in his "Charge to the Grand Jury" in Duplin County in 1933; this work is a masterpiece of family and legal history and jurisprudence.

A noted storyteller, Grady often kept listeners entranced for hours. He was much in demand as a public speaker at bar meetings and at historical and other public gatherings. His numerous speeches, spiced with anecdotes, incidents, history, and philosophy, have been described as uplifting and thought provoking. Among them were "The Two Spaights of New Bern" (7 June 1923), "The Battle of Moore's Creek" (13 Apr. 1925), the address at the first Grady-Outlaw reunion (29 Aug. 1930), the address upon the presentation of a portrait of Superior Court Judge Chatham C. Lyon to Bladen County (29 Apr. 1935), and the address upon the presentation of a portrait of Albert T. Outlaw, former register of deeds, to Duplin County, in which Grady recited his inspirational poem, "Tell Him Now" (10 Apr. 1953)—all of which are preserved in the North Carolina Collection, University of North Carolina, Chapel Hill.

Judge Grady has been described by those who knew him as having the wisdom of Solomon. He is said to have had the "common touch," with a keen understanding of human nature and of the problems and lives of those with whom he came into contact. Always helpful to those who were sincere and earnest, he was capable of ascertaining falsehood and pretense and hated a lie. In the courtroom, he knew no fear, on occasion wielding a firearm to maintain order. He demanded justice and fairness, for which he had a passion, and is said to have managed the business of the court with firmness and expedition and to have presided with dignity and discretion.

On 23 Oct. 1901, Grady married Anne Elizabeth Graham, the only daughter of Dr. Daniel McLean and Elizabeth Ann Murphey Graham of Wallace. She was the cousin of Frank Porter Graham, president of The University of North Carolina and later a U.S. senator from North Carolina and United Nations ambassador. After their marriage, the Gradys lived in Clinton and became the parents of three daughters, all of whom died, and three sons, Henry A., Jr., an attorney in Clinton and New Bern; Franklin McLean, a physician in New Bern; and Graham Montrose, a career army officer.

Grady died at the age of eighty-six. After a funeral service in the Clinton Presbyterian Church, he was buried in the Clinton Cemetery.

SEE: *Charlotte Observer*, 18 Dec. 1938; John L. Cheney, Jr., ed., *North Carolina Government, 1585–1974* (1975); Clinton *Sampson Independent*, 24 Feb. 1958; Daniel L. Grant, *Alumni History of the University of North Carolina* (1924); *Makers of America* (1916 [portrait]); *Proceedings of the Grand Lodge of North Carolina* (1919); Raleigh *News and Observer*, 23 Jan. 1938, 4 Aug. 1951, 24, 25 Feb. 1958; *Warsaw-Faison News*, 28 Jan. 1971. Copies of Grady's publications are in the North Carolina Collection, University of North Carolina Library, Chapel Hill, and the North Carolina State Library, Raleigh.

CHARLES M. INGRAM

**Grady, Paul Davis** *(5 Sept. 1890–8 July 1970)*, businessman and legislator, was born in Seven Springs, Wayne County, the son of James Calhoun and Ella Smith Outlaw Grady. He attended Tennessee Military Institute and Wake Forest College and was graduated from Washington and Lee University. Admitted to the bar in 1911, he practiced in Smithfield and in Kenly, where he made his home. He represented Johnston County in the General Assembly from 1919 until 1921 and served in the Senate in 1925, 1933, and 1935; in the latter year he was president pro tempore. On 11 Apr. 1935 he introduced a bill to make Easter Monday a legal holiday in the state and it was passed by both houses. He was an unsuccessful Democratic candidate for nomination as lieutenant governor in 1936, for utilities commissioner in 1938, and for governor in 1940. Long associated with the insurance industry, Grady was chairman of the boards of Nationwide Life Insurance Company and of Tectum International; he was also a director of National Casualty Company, Northwestern National Life Insurance Company, North American Insurance Company, and others. For long periods he served on the boards of broadcasting, manufacturing, and investment corporations. Although he continued to maintain his home in Kenly, he had offices in Columbus, Ohio, and elsewhere. He owned and operated Grady Farms in Johnston County. In 1969 President Richard M. Nixon appointed him to the advisory board on minority business enterprise.

Grady was married in 1909 to Lelia Grace Swink, and they were the parents of Eloise (Mrs. Albert S. Eskridge), Elsie (Mrs. W. F. Rainey), Paul D., Jr., James C., and Fred. A Freemason and a Presbyterian, he was buried in the Kenly cemetery.

SEE: John L. Cheney, Jr., ed., *North Carolina Government, 1585–1979* (1981); *Journal of the Senate of the General Assembly of the State of North Carolina* (1935); *North Carolina Manual* (1935); William S. Powell, ed., *North Carolina Lives* (1962); Raleigh *News and Observer*, 10 July 1970.

WILLIAM S. POWELL

**Graff, Johann Michael** *(28 Sept. 1714–29 Aug. 1782)*, Moravian minister, was born in Heyna, Saxe-Meinungen, to Nicholas and Margaretha Graff. He was raised as a Lutheran and educated by private tutors at the Gymnasium of Henneberg and at the University of Jena. While at Jena, Graff became acquainted with the Moravian Brethren and joined the Unity in 1739. Two years later, he was ordained a presbyter of the Unitas Fratrum and for the next few years he served as pastor in various European congregations. In his youth, Graff studied music, especially the clavier, and later composed a number of hymns. While serving in Herrnhut, Graff was called to Bethlehem, Penn., to take charge of the children of the town and country congregations. He and his wife reached Bethlehem on 3 Oct. 1751 and immediately began the appointed rounds with the children of the district. In 1753, the Graffs moved to Nazareth where Johann Michael became pastor and inspector of the nursery; later they were put in charge of the married people.

In June 1762 the couple moved to Wachovia in North Carolina, settling in the Moravian community of Bethabara. There Graff served as pastor and, with his wife, as curator of the married people. In 1772, the Graffs were elected members of the Aeltesten Conferenz or Board of Elders (the governing board of Wachovia concerned primarily with spiritual guidance). The next year they moved to Salem, the largest of the Moravian settlements in North Carolina, where Graff was pastor at the Home Church in Salem and associate pastor for all of Wachovia. Also in 1773, he went to Pennsylvania to be ordained a bishop in the Moravian church.

During Fredrick Marshall's absence in 1775, Graff was appointed administrator of Salem. In 1781, because of failing health, Graff relinquished his duties as congregation diarist, a position he had held for many years. He died the following year and was buried in God's Acre, Salem.

Graff married Gertrude Jacke on 3 July 1740. They had seven children, but only two daughters, Anna Johanna and Justine Gertraut, survived Graff. Photographs of portraits of both Johann Michael and Gertrude Graff are in the collection of Old Salem, Inc. The original portraits are in the Bethlehem Archives.

SEE: Salem Moravian Archives (Winston-Salem) for Aufseher Collegium Minutes; Elders Conference Minutes; Graff's personal memoir, hymns, and papers; Salem Diary; Wachovia Diary.

JAN HIESTER

**Graffenried, Christoph, baron von** *(15 Nov. 1661–November? 1743)*, founder of New Bern and a leader in early Swiss and German colonization of America, was born in his ancestral village of Worb in the Canton of

Bern, Switzerland. His father, Anton, was Lord (*Herr*) of Worb and a minor government official. Young Graffenried studied at the universities of Heidelberg and Leyden. During his travels to London, he met the Duke of Albemarle and other Lords Proprietors of Carolina. Among them he could call Sir John Colleton "my special friend." On his return to Bern, he married Regina Tscharner.

About this time he became acquainted with the explorer-adventurer Franz Ludwig Michel who persuaded him to join and invest in Georg Ritter & Company, a venture that proposed to mine American silver deposits and to settle indigent Swiss and Swiss Anabaptists in Pennsylvania or Virginia. Graffenried's influence appears to have overshadowed that of Ritter, a Bernese seal and stone engraver, and under his leadership the company broadened its plans to settle the colonists in the Province of Carolina and to include among them many of the distressed victims of the War of the Spanish Succession, the "poor Palatines" whom the English had transported from the devastated Rhineland to refugee camps on the Thames River. The Ritter company purchased from the Lords Proprietors nearly 19,000 acres of land on the Neuse and Trent rivers, including the future site of New Bern, and on the White Oak River, which Graffenried called by the Indian name of Weetock. Graffenried held, apparently as a personal investment, 5,000 of these acres. In recognition of this holding, the Lords Proprietors conferred upon Graffenried the title "Landgrave of Carolina and Baron of Bernburg" in accordance with the scheme of nobility envisioned by Locke's Fundamental Constitutions.

Graffenried embarked 650 Palatines from English ports and about 150 Swiss from Dutch ports after their voyage down the Rhine River. He joined Michel and the surveyor John Lawson in the Neuse-Trent area and soon laid out, in a cruciform plan, his *Stättli*, the little town that he called New Bern. In the town he settled most of the craftsmen he had transported. In outlying areas up the Trent, approaching the present-day site of Pollocksville, he settled the farmers among the emigrants. This was in 1710. Within a matter of months, the colony was overwhelmed by the Indian uprising led by the Iroquoian Tuscarora. Most of the Swiss were massacred, and Graffenried and Lawson were taken prisoner and held at the Indian town of Cotechney, near the modern town of Snow Hill. Lawson was executed and Michel also "died among the Indians," though the manner of their deaths is not known. In negotiations with Iroquoian tribes on Virginia's border, Lieutenant Governor Alexander Spotswood of Virginia interceded on behalf of Graffenried, with whom he had been corresponding. The Swiss leader was released unharmed, but his colony was doomed to fail. One cause was the Indian troubles, which lasted until 1718. Another was the lack of support from the badly divided Proprietary government, paralyzed at this time by internal dissensions between Quakers and Anglicans. A third cause was an outbreak of yellow fever. Graffenried fell ill, and Governor Edward Hyde, from whom he might have expected support, died during the epidemic.

Hoping to establish a new settlement in Virginia, Graffenried visited Spotswood in Williamsburg and journeyed to the falls of the Potomac. In the spring of 1713 he sailed for England, having mortgaged all the Ritter landholdings to Thomas Pollock of Chowan County. "No good star shone for me," wrote Graffenried of his disappointment at having to forsake the remnants of the colony. He returned to Switzerland in 1714 to live out the rest of his days. He was buried in the family chapel at Worb. His son, Christoph, emigrated to the New World. Landing at Charleston, S.C., the young man married Barbara Tempest Needham, of Hertfordshire, England, and their issue founded the American branch of the family, which adopted the French version of the name, De Graffenried. The family became prominent in both Virginia and Tennessee.

SEE: Thomas J. de Graffenreidt, *History of the de Graffenreid Family from 1191 A.D. to 1925* (1925); "De Graffenreidt Family," *William and Mary Quarterly* 15 (1907); Walter Havighurst, *Alexander Spotswood: Portrait of a Governor* (1967); Vincent H. Todd and Julius Goebel, eds., *Christoph von Graffenreid's Account of the Founding of New Bern* (1920).

A. T. DILL

**Graham, Alexander** *(12 Sept. 1844–2 Nov. 1934)*, father of the North Carolina graded school system, was born near Fayetteville of Scottish ancestry, the son of Archibald and Anne McLean Graham. He was a descendant of Colonel Alexander McAllister, a field officer in the Revolutionary War. Graham grew up in a large family and attended private schools in Fayetteville until he was sixteen. In 1862, he became headmaster of Richmond Academy near Spring Hill where he taught for two years. He closed the school in order to fight for the Confederacy, serving during the last year of the war in Company B, Third Regiment of North Carolina State Troops. He was captured by Sherman's army in the Battle of Bentonville and released at the end of the war.

For a short time, Graham taught in Bladen County, but his small salary was often unpaid and he was determined to further his education. To earn money for college, he drove a peddler's wagon in South Carolina. In 1866 he entered The University of North Carolina, where he became a member of Zeta Psi fraternity and the Philanthropic Literary Society; he also was captain of the baseball team. The university awarded him a bachelors degree in 1869, a masters degree in 1880, and an honorary doctor of laws in 1920. Following graduation he taught for two years in Bladen County. Afterwards in New York City he taught Greek in the Anthon School for two years and studied law at Columbia University, receiving the LL.B. degree in 1873. The same year he returned to Fayetteville and established a law practice.

During the next five years, Graham married and began to raise a family. As his children grew, he became increasingly interested in public education. Greensboro and Charlotte already had graded schools, whereas Fayetteville had only private and ungraded public schools. Graham was asked to organize a graded school in Fayetteville and to become the superintendent as well as one of the teachers. Subsequently he established a high school, integrating in the curriculum subjects that would prepare students for college. By 1888, he had become so well known that he was frequently asked by other municipalities to organize their schools into graded systems. For fifty years, in addition to his other work and at his own expense, Graham traveled throughout the state organizing graded schools.

In 1888, he began a long relationship with the Charlotte city schools—as superintendent for twenty-five years, as assistant superintendent for another fourteen years, and as superintendent emeritus until his death at age ninety. In 1892, he established in the Charlotte system the first manual training school in North Carolina.

Before his educational duties became statewide, he taught Latin, Greek, physics, geometry, astronomy, and literature. A number of graded school buildings in the state were named in his honor—among them, one in Fayetteville and one in Charlotte.

Graham held various offices in the educational field, including the presidency of the North Carolina Education Association and the trusteeship of the Agricultural and Technical College in Greensboro, He also wrote a history of Mecklenburg County and was an active member of the Second Presbyterian Church of Charlotte.

In January 1875, Graham married Catherine ("Kate") Bryan Sloan, the daughter of Dr. David Dickson Sloan of Sampson County. They had nine children: David, the oldest, who was killed at Château-Thierry in World War I; Archibald, who became a physician in Minnesota; Neill, who died early in adult life; George, who became a prominent educator in Atlanta; Mary and Hattie, who were teachers in the North Carolina public schools; Frank Porter, who became president of The University of North Carolina; and Mrs. Shipp Sanders and Mrs. Henry Shanks, who became the wives of university professors at Chapel Hill. Graham also was an uncle of Dr. Edward Kidder Graham, president of The University of North Carolina from 1915 to 1918.

Graham died at his home in Charlotte and was buried in Elmwood Cemetery.

SEE: *Chapel Hill Weekly*, 9 Nov. 1934; *Charlotte Observer*, 3 Nov. 1934; *Fayetteville Observer*, 3 Nov. 1934; Edgar W. Knight, *Alexander Graham, 1844–1934* (1936); John A. Oates, *The Story of Fayetteville and the Upper Cape Fear* (1972); Raleigh *News and Observer*, 3 Nov. 1934.

LOU ROGERS WEHLITZ

**Graham, Alexander Hawkins ("Sandy")** *(9 Aug. 1890–3 Apr. 1977)*, lawmaker, lieutenant governor, and highway administrator, was born in Hillsborough, the only child of the Confederate Army veteran Major John Washington Graham's second marriage to Maggie Forrester Bailey. A descendent of a long line of prominent public officials, Graham grew up in Hillsborough as the youngest member of a family of four boys and two girls. His father had been a state senator five times and chairman of the state tax commission; his grandfather, Governor William Alexander Graham, had served as a U.S. senator, secretary of the navy, and governor; and his great-grandfather, General Joseph Graham, fought in the Revolutionary War.

Nicknamed after an uncle, Sandy Graham attended Orange County schools, Episcopal High School in Alexandria, Va., and The University of North Carolina. While at the university, he was editor of the *Yackety Yack* yearbook, cheerleader, commencement marshal, and member of the Dialectic Society, Gorgon's Head, and Zeta Psi fraternity. He was graduated with an A.B. degree in 1912. To continue his education, Graham studied law at the university during the summer session of 1912–13 and the following year entered Harvard, where he roomed with Colonel William Joyner of Raleigh.

After finishing his education, Graham returned to Hillsborough to join his father in law practice. Within a year, he had become the attorney for Orange County and the town of Hillsborough. His practice was interrupted, however, when he joined the army as a volunteer on 13 May 1917. He attended officer's training camp at Fort Oglethorpe, Ga., was commissioned as a second lieutenant, and served overseas with the 81st ("Wildcat") Division. After arriving in France in August 1918, Graham won two promotions in three months—from second lieutenant to captain. He also was a regimental adjutant for the 324th Infantry. When discharged on 15 July 1919, he had served a total of twenty-seven months with the army.

Graham's political career began upon his return to Hillsborough. In 1919, he was named chairman of the Orange County Democratic party, a post he held until 1947. In 1921, he won a seat in the state house of representatives. As a freshman legislator, Graham began his fight for better highway systems by urging the passage of a $50 million road bond issue. He served five consecutive terms in the state house, culminating in the position of speaker in 1929. During his years in the General Assembly, Graham fought for highway maintenance and education. In 1927, he became chairman of the house finance committee. While holding this office, he was also an ex officio member of the advisory budget committee. In August 1931 Governor O. Max Gardner appointed Graham to act as speaker of the executive council in the absence of O. M. Mull.

The highest political office Graham held was the lieutenant governorship in 1933–37. During his term, he tried to keep schools open and to extend the school year to nine months. He also presided at the economic war council of the state's leading bankers in the senate chambers.

After an unsuccessful gubernatorial campaign in which Graham finished third in the first primary behind Clyde R. Hoey of Shelby and Dr. Ralph McDonald, he returned to Hillsborough to practice law. In 1944 he campaigned for Gastonia's R. Gregg Cherry for the governorship, and in 1945 the new governor appointed Graham to head the State Highway and Public Works Commission. Graham organized the state's reconstruction and repair program after the war, when over 5,000 miles of road were paved during his administration. At the completion of his term in 1949, Graham again was active as a Hillsborough lawyer in the firm of Graham and Levine.

In 1953, Governor William B. Umstead of Durham asked Graham to return to his post as highway commissioner. Graham agreed to lead the new fourteen-division, fourteen-commissioner organization. As a highway administrator, he instigated two major studies of highway operations, the Parsons Report and the Haskins-Sells study, and he crusaded for a limited access highway policy in North Carolina. When Graham left the post in 1957, the state was rated the leading state in terms of progress made on the interstate highway system. His retirement in 1957 marked the end of a career of public service that had spanned over thirty-five years.

Graham married Kathleen L. Long, sister of former lieutenant governor J. Elmer Long, on 28 Aug. 1917. They had two sons, A. H. "Sandy," Jr., and John W. Mrs. Graham died in 1975.

As an Episcopalian, Graham served on the vestry and as senior warden of St. Matthew's Episcopal Church. He was a member of the North Carolina Bar Association and active in the Hillsborough Post of the American Legion. The Hillsborough Exchange Club noted his extensive career in public service with a certificate of entry in the "Book of Golden Deeds." Graham supported The University of North Carolina throughout his career, serving as a trustee for many years. He was a member of the Rocky Mount Mills board of directors for fifty years; at the time of his death, he was chairman.

SEE: *Chapel Hill Newspaper*, 5 Apr. 1977; *Chapel Hill Weekly*, 19 Nov. 1959, 26 May 1963; *Charlotte Observer*, 29 June 1935; *Daily Tar Heel*, 2 Apr. 1932; *Durham Morning Herald*, 8 Nov. 1959, 14 Nov. 1976, 7 Apr. 1977; Daniel L. Grant, *Alumni History of the University of North Carolina* (1924); John Harden, *North Carolina Roads and Their Builders* (1966); Hillsborough *News*, 3 May 1945; Raleigh *News and Observer*, 8 Feb. 1932, 11 May 1935, 10 Mar. 1957, 5 Apr. 1977; Capus Waynick, *North Carolina Roads and Their Builders* (1952).

CATHERINE L. ROBINSON

**Graham, Augustus Washington** *(8 June 1849–12 Oct. 1936),* lawyer and jurist, was born in Hillsborough, the son of William Alexander and Susannah Sarah Washington Graham. His paternal grandfather was General Joseph Graham, a military leader, a onetime member of the North Carolina General Assembly, and a founder of The University of North Carolina. His father (b. 5 Sept. 1804), a graduate of the university, was a lawyer and legislator who subsequently served as a U.S. senator (1841–44), governor of North Carolina (1845–49), and secretary of the navy in President Millard Fillmore's administration (1850–52) before he was an unsuccessful candidate for the vice-presidency of the United States. The career of William Alexander Graham was distinguished by his advocacy of education and civic progress.

With such a background, Augustus Washington Graham began his formal education in the Nash and Kollock School at Hillsborough and later at Alexander Wilson's School in Alamance County. He was graduated from The University of North Carolina with a bachelor of arts degree in 1868. For four years he read law, first under the preceptorship of his father in Hillsborough and then under William K. Ruffin. He was admitted to the North Carolina bar in 1872. Graham practiced in Hillsborough for sixteen years, then moved to Oxford where he formed a partnership with his brother-in-law, Robert W. Winston. In 1890 Winston was elected to the superior court, and for the next five years Graham practiced independently until elected to the superior court, succeeding Judge Winston. He served only two years and refused reelection, preferring to return to private legal practice.

In 1900, he formed a partnership with William A. Devin. After Devin became a superior court judge in 1913, Graham's son, Augustus W., Jr., who received the bachelor of arts (1912) and bachelor of laws (1914) degrees from The University of North Carolina, joined him in Oxford to establish the firm of A. W. Graham and Son, Attorneys. That partnership continued until 1927, when Judge Graham suffered a stroke and retired from active practice. He lived nine more years, dying at the age of eighty-seven.

Although his law practice was always his major professional interest, Graham held many important related positions while declining others. He was secretary of the Board of Arbitration, created by the legislatures of Virginia and Maryland to determine amicably the boundaries of those states long in dispute, and served three years on the board (1873–76). In 1883, however, he turned down the secretaryship of the newly created U.S. Civil Service Commission. Later he served on the Board of Town Commissioners of Oxford (1889–92) and as chairman of the board of education of Granville County (1907–8). Under presidential appointment in 1915, Graham became the attorney for the U.S. Cotton Futures Association and for three years was its full-time president, living alternately in Washington and New York. He returned to Oxford in 1922 to concentrate on the practice he shared with his son.

Graham was also active in state politics. In 1885, he began a one-term membership in the North Carolina Senate, representing Orange, Durham, Person, and Caswell counties. Having been chairman of the Democratic Executive Committee for fourteen years while living in Hillsborough, he was a logical choice to represent Granville County in the North Carolina House of Representatives in four regular sessions and one special session. He was speaker of the house in the session of 1909. In addition, he was a delegate to the Democratic national conventions in Cincinnati (1880) and Baltimore (1912), when Woodrow Wilson was nominated.

Of all his public service, Graham was proudest of the thirty-four years he served as a trustee of The University of North Carolina, continuing the tradition of dedication established by his grandfather and father before him.

On 21 Nov. 1876 Graham married Lucy Anne Horner, whose father founded the Horner Military Academy in 1851. They had five children: Susan Washington, Augustus Washington, Jr., Sophronia Moore, Alice Robertson (Mrs. H. G. Shirley), and a child who died in infancy.

Graham and his family were members of the Oxford Baptist Church, where he held numerous positions of leadership through the years. He was buried in Elmwood Cemetery, Oxford.

SEE: Samuel A. Ashe, *Cyclopedia of Eminent and Representative Men of the Carolinas of the Nineteenth Century* (1892); John L. Cheney, Jr., ed., *North Carolina Government, 1585–1974* (1975); Daniel L. Grant, *Alumni History of the University of North Carolina* (1924); *North Carolina Biography*, vol. 4 (1928); *Oxford Public Ledger*, 12 Oct. 1936.

C. SYLVESTER GREEN

**Graham, Edward Kidder** *(11 Oct. 1876–24 Oct. 1918),* educator and university president, was born in Charlotte, the son of Archibald and Elizabeth Owen Barry Graham. He was the nephew of Alexander Graham whose son, Frank Porter Graham, became president of The University of North Carolina in 1930. Young Graham received his early education in the public schools of Charlotte, of which his uncle, Alexander, was superintendent, and at the Charlotte Military Institute. In 1894, at age eighteen, he entered the freshman class of The University of North Carolina; he received the bachelor of philosophy degree in 1898, ranking second in his class. In addition to high academic honors, he won the coveted Mangum Medal in 1898. As an undergraduate his college record was distinguished for soundness of scholarship, high ideals, and a passion for "fair play" and "square dealing"—a record that was prophetic of his later achievements.

After graduation, Graham returned to Charlotte and taught school for a year. He established close ties with other alumni and gained an intimate knowledge of the schools, churches, newspapers, and rapidly growing industries of his native city, knowledge that served him well when he assumed the administration of The University of North Carolina.

President Edwin A. Alderman, who had known Graham intimately as an undergraduate, called him back to the university as librarian in 1899. Within a year Graham became an instructor in English under his former professor, Dr. Thomas Hume. From this position he rapidly climbed the academic ladder. He remained an instructor until 1903, taking off the year of 1902–3 to study at Columbia University where he received the master of arts degree in English (1903). From 1903 to 1907 he was associate professor and spent the year 1904–5 at Columbia University in further graduate study. In 1907 he was appointed to a full professorship, and in 1909 he became head of the Department of English and dean of the College of Liberal Arts. In 1913, while President Francis P. Venable was in Europe, he served as acting president, and in 1914 he was elected president by unanimous vote of the board of trustees.

Even though it had been suggested that Graham would make an excellent U.S. senator, he chose teaching as his lifework. He turned to the classroom, the deanship, and the presidency of the university in order to strengthen the forces of education in North Carolina and through them to broaden and enrich the concepts of education and liberal citizenship. His philosophy was expressed in three convictions: first, the teachers of North Carolina would shape the state's future; second, the chief end of education was the molding of citizens who would place community development above personal material well-being; and third, the university was the state's principal instrument for achieving its high purposes.

Graham was aware of the importance of public opinion in advancing the usefulness of a public institution such as the university. In preparing it for leadership in a new era, he realized his first task was to interpret the university to its public in such a way that it would not only be understood but also would be accorded the generous support it required to carry out its mission. The process of orienting the student mind was already well under way when Graham became president. However, few university leaders have had a higher regard for good teaching. As a teacher, he insisted on hard, exacting work and inspired in his students the desire for thoroughness and personal excellence. As dean, he successfully prodded the fraternity men about their poor grades with gratifying results. Through chapel talks he aroused interest not only in problems of student life but also in the wider issues of the state and nation. As president, he began to give the students increased responsibility for participation in a larger and more meaningful college life, and for the further development of effective student government as preparation for citizenship in an increasingly enlightened state.

As a second task, Graham envisioned making the university campus statewide in its area of service. Through the extension services of the university he multiplied a thousandfold the work of one of his early teachers. He often made notes in an odd-looking blank book bound in olive green leather. It was referred to as Graham's "want book," not for himself, but for the university and through it for North Carolina and the nation. Unfortunately the book was burned in a fire that destroyed a part of the Graham residence after his death. After having laid the foundation for an extension service that would make the boundaries of the campus coextensive with those of the state, he set about developing five major fields of interest he "wanted" for the university: rural economics and sociology, rural education, the education of women, training in the dramatic arts, and instruction in commerce and industry. Whether they appeared in his "want book" will never be known. Although these objectives were not achieved during Graham's life, his vision and organizing skills made their attainment possible by his successors.

The untimely death of President Graham at age forty-two occurred during the deadly influenza epidemic. Funeral services were held at the Presbyterian Church in Chapel Hill with burial in the town cemetery adjoining the campus. His death was a tremendous shock to thousands of people. To express their admiration and loss, many attended his memorial service in December 1918. His most important addresses and articles were published and distributed the following year, and a portrait painted by Clement Strudwick was presented to the university by the class of 1920. The Graham Memorial Building, a student center, was completed and dedicated in 1931–32. Its lounge, considered one of the most beautiful in the nation at the time, provided students with surroundings whose informality and attractiveness had long had high priority in Graham's "want book" for the university, as well as a vantage point from which his portrait has looked down upon succeeding college generations.

On 25 June 1908, Graham married Susan Williams Moses in Raleigh. She died on 22 Dec. 1916. They were the parents of a son, Edward Kidder, Jr.

SEE: Kemp P. Battle, *History of the University of North Carolina*, vol. 2 (1912); E. K. Graham, *The Function of the State University*, (1915); Archibald Henderson, *The Campus of the First State University* (1949); Louis R. Wilson, *The Chronicles of the Sesquicentennial* (1947), and *The University of North Carolina, 1900-1930* (1957).

HELEN OLDHAM DENNIS

**Graham, Edward Kidder, Jr.** *(31 Jan. 1911–13 Mar. 1976)*, educator and college administrator, was born in Chapel Hill, the son of E. K. Graham, president of The University of North Carolina, and of Susan Williams Moses Graham. Frank Porter Graham was his cousin. Orphaned at the age of seven, he was raised in the family of his uncle by marriage, Louis Graves, founder and editor of the *Chapel Hill Weekly*. Graham attended the Chapel Hill public schools, the Asheville School, and Woodberry Forest School in Virginia. He received the A.B. (1933) and A.M. (1934) degrees from The University of North Carolina. For further graduate study, he went to Cornell University, which granted him a Ph.D. in medieval history in 1938. For three years (1937–40) he was assistant to the president of Cornell, and for seven years (1940–47) he was secretary to that university.

Thereafter Graham served on the faculties of numerous educational institutions. At Washington University, St. Louis, Mo., from 1947 to 1950, he was successively dean of students, assistant dean of the faculty, and dean of the faculty. In 1950 he was appointed chancellor of the Woman's College of the University of North Carolina at Greensboro, where he remained for six years. From 1956 to 1960 he was dean of the College of Liberal Arts, dean of the College of General Education, and acting dean of the Graduate School at Boston University. He left to become vice-chancellor and dean of the faculty at Denver University. In 1963, Graham was named president of the College Center of Finger Lakes, an organization consisting of seven colleges in northern New York State. Later he was dean of the faculty at Kingsborough Community College in Brooklyn, N.Y. In semiretirement, while pursuing a personal interest in creative writing, he served as consultant for Hampton (Va.) Institute and for New York State University at Albany.

Graham was a president of the Association for Higher Education, a member of the national selection committee for Fulbright awards (1953), a consultant for the Department of Health, Education, and Welfare (1953), and an adviser for the National Student Assocation (1954–56). He was a member of the American Historical Association and of the Medieval Academy of America. Graham was a Democrat and an Episcopalian.

He was married first in 1935 to Elizabeth Ann McFadyen, of Concord, N.C., by whom he had three children: Susan (b. 1938), Julia Graves (b. 1941), and Edward Kidder (b. 1945). His second wife, Elvira Prondecki, survived him when he died in Elsmere, N.Y. He was buried in the old Chapel Hill Cemetery.

SEE: *Chapel Hill Newspaper*, 16 Mar. 1976; *Chapel Hill Weekly*, 9 Aug. 1957; *Directory of American Scholars* (1957); *Durham Morning Herald*, 23 July 1950; *Greensboro Daily News*, 10 July 1950; *Greensboro Record*, 23 May 1950; *New York Times*, 11 July 1956, 31 July 1960; Raleigh *News and Observer*, 7 Sept. 1963.

ROSAMOND PUTZEL

**Graham, Frank Porter** *(14 Oct. 1886–16 Feb. 1972)*, university president, U.S. senator, and United Nations mediator, was born in Fayetteville, the son of Alexander and Katherine Bryan Sloan Graham. His father was a major founder of the public schools in Fayetteville and superintendent of the Charlotte school system for twenty-five years. Frank Graham was graduated from the Charlotte High School and received an A.B. degree (Phi Beta Kappa) from The University of North Carolina in 1909. As a student at Chapel Hill, he made many warm and lasting friends who were his staunch supporters in his later career. He also studied law at the university and received a law license although he never practiced. He pursued graduate work in history at Columbia University, from which he received the A.M. degree in 1916, the University of Chicago (winning the Amherst Memorial Fellowship), the Brookings Institution, and the London School of Economics.

After beginning his teaching career in the Raleigh High School for two years, he returned to Chapel Hill as secretary of the campus YMCA. In 1914, he was appointed an instructor in history and began those years of brilliant classroom teaching that were to influence the lives of countless undergraduates who enrolled in his courses. His academic career was interrupted by volunteer service in the U.S. Marine Corps in World War I, in which he rose from the rank of private to first lieutenant. He returned to The University of North Carolina as an assistant professor and served for a time as dean of students. He was made an associate professor in 1925, and even though his graduate study had not resulted in the doctorate, his outstanding teaching earned him the rank of professor of history in 1927.

Graham was certainly one of the university's best and most highly regarded teachers. His interest in students and the stimulating quality of his classes attracted a large and diverse following, including the gifted and serious students as well as many of those who despite limited interest in scholarship found his provocative presentation of history appealing.

In addition to his university activities, Graham's active support of a progressive program of expansion of schools, colleges, and good roads for the state during the administration of Governor Cameron Morrison influenced many of the state's leaders to think of him for a larger role. When The University of North Carolina presidency became vacant in 1930, he was named president. With the merger of the university in Chapel Hill, North Carolina State College, and the North Carolina College for Women into the Consolidated University of North Carolina in 1932, Graham became its first president, a position he held until 1949.

Graham's presidency of The University of North Carolina coincided with a critical era in the nation's history—the era of the Great Depression and World War II and its aftermath. During the 1920s the university had attained increasing stature as one of the nation's leading universities, exemplified by its election to the American Association of Universities. In the face of critically short financial support, Graham labored mightily and successfully to maintain the university's stature in the world of higher education. With so many North Carolinians unable to afford a college education, he worked tirelessly to raise scholarship funds for needy students.

In an era of intense and sometimes fierce controversy over political, social and economic policies, Graham courageously defended the essential freedoms of the university—freedom to seek, freedom to learn, freedom to believe, freedom to speak, and freedom to publish. Although on occasion he himself was subject to personal attack for supporting unpopular causes or persons, he never wavered in his belief in the young and in the future of a free, democratic society.

Graham did not limit his interests and commitments to the university and the educational world, but devoted much of his time, thought, and energies to the needs of the poor and the deprived during the depression. He was twice president of the North Carolina Conference for Social Service. He joined and took an active part in organizations promoting social change and responded to President Franklin D. Roosevelt's call to serve on federal boards and commissions, including the National Advisory Council on Social Security of which he was chairman.

During World War II, Graham gave much of his time to public service, first as a member of the National Defense Mediation Board and then of the National War Labor Board. In 1946, President Harry S Truman appointed Graham to the President's Committee on Civil Rights, which in 1947 made a historic report on the nation's racial problems and proposals for their solution. In 1947, Truman called on him to serve as the U.S. Representative, along with representatives from Australia and Belgium, on the United Nations Committee of Good Offices on the Dutch-Indonesian dispute. This committee's efforts contributed significantly to a final settlement. During those early postwar years, he also helped organize and was the first president of the Oak Ridge Institute of Nuclear Studies (1946–49).

In 1949, Graham's career took a new turn when he was appointed by Governor Kerr Scott to fill an unexpired term in the U.S. Senate. In his bid for renomination, though he was far in the lead, he failed to win a majority in the Democratic primary by a few thousand votes. He was narrowly defeated in the second primary by Willis Smith in a heatedly contested election in which the winning side used the racial issue extensively to Graham's disadvantage. Despite urging by some of his advisers, Graham refused to respond in kind. Just prior to the second primary the United States Supreme

Court rendered a decision looking toward desegregation of public education. In this context and in the type of campaign conducted by his opponents, although he had taken no public position in support of desegregation, Graham's membership on the President's Committee on Civil Rights and his widely known commitment to human rights and association with many liberal causes made him politically vulnerable and contributed substantially to his defeat.

After serving briefly as defense manpower administrator for the U.S. Department of Labor, in 1951 he was appointed United Nations representative to mediate the dispute between India and Pakistan over Kashmir. Although he devoted the remainder of his active life to this intransigent issue, with persistence and patience, he was unable to achieve a settlement. As an assistant secretary general of the United Nations, he made hundreds of speeches over the years to religious, labor, and civic groups advocating world peace and the role of the United Nations in achieving a peaceful world order.

Throughout his long, varied, and distinguished career, Graham received many awards and honors including honorary degrees from more than twenty colleges and universities, among them Amherst, Birmingham Southern, Catawba, Columbia, Davidson, Duke, Harvard, Hebrew Union, North Carolina A. and T., University of North Carolina (at Chapel Hill, Charlotte, and Greensboro), North Carolina State, Princeton, Shaw, Swarthmore, Temple, Wake Forest, William and Mary, and William Jewel. The new (1968) student union building on the Chapel Hill campus is named for Graham.

A deeply religious man, Frank Graham was active and influential in the work of the Presbyterian church. More importantly, the Christian faith was the basis of his personal philosophy and a constant guide throughout his life.

In July 1932 Graham married Marian Drane and until her death in April 1967 she was his devoted companion. They had no children. Graham died in Chapel Hill and was buried in the old Chapel Hill Cemetery. There are portraits in the Morehead Planetarium, the student union building, and the General Administration Building in Chapel Hill.

SEE: Warren Ashby, *Frank Porter Graham: A Southern Liberal* (1980); Henry Brandis, Jr., "Frank Porter Graham" ([typescript] 1972, Office, Secretary of the Faculty, University of North Carolina, Chapel Hill); *Chapel Hill Weekly*, 26 Mar. 1972; *Charlotte Observer*, 17 Feb. 1972; Clipping file, North Carolina Collection (University of North Carolina, Chapel Hill) for information on Graham; Frank P. Graham Papers (Southern Historical Collection, University of North Carolina, Chapel Hill); *New York Times*, 20 Feb. 1972; Raleigh *News and Observer*, 17 Feb. 1972; *Who Was Who in America*, vol. 5 (1973); Louis R. Wilson, *The University of North Carolina, 1900–1930* (1957).

J. CARLYLE SITTERSON

**Graham, James** *(7 Jan. 1793–25 Sept. 1851)*, congressman, lawyer, and planter, was born in Lincoln County, the fourth child and second son of Joseph (1759–1836) and Isabella Davidson Graham. His paternal grandfather, for whom he was named, immigrated from Ireland in 1714. His father was a veteran of the American Revolution, sheriff of Mecklenburg County, state senator, iron manufacturer, planter, and general during the War of 1812. A younger brother, William A. Graham (1804–75), was a U.S. senator, governor of North Carolina, secretary of the navy, Whig candidate for vice-president in 1852, and Confederate senator.

James Graham was graduated from The University of North Carolina in 1814 and read law with Thomas Ruffin of Hillsborough. In 1818, he was admitted to the bar and began to practice in Rutherfordton. He represented his county in the House of Commons in 1822–24 and again in 1828–29. In Raleigh he was identified with the supporters of William H. Crawford in 1824, but by 1828 he was in the ranks of President Adams. In the General Assembly he advocated internal improvements and revision of the state constitution.

In 1825 Graham made his first bid for a seat in Congress. The incumbent, Robert B. Vance, and another candidate, Samuel P. Carson, were both Jackson men, whereas Graham was opposed to Jackson. Carson won, with Graham second. By 1833, Carson had become an advocate of nullification and Calhoun and opposed Jackson. David Newland, a loyal Jackson man, and Graham, now a supporter of Henry Clay, vied for Carson's seat and Graham won the three-way contest. Two years later Graham defeated Newland by a margin of just seven votes. Newland contested the result, and the House of Representatives, controlled by Democrats, voted to unseat Graham. A special election was held in August 1836 and Graham was returned by a safe margin. He faced no serious opposition in 1837 or 1839 and defeated Thomas L. Clingman in 1841. By 1841 a split was developing between states' rights Whigs, who were loyal to John Tyler, and national Whigs, who backed Henry Clay as party leader. Clingman, as a states' rights Whig, captured the Whig nomination in the mountain district and forced Graham out of Congress. Two years later Graham ran as an independent Whig with Democratic support and defeated Clingman one final time by a margin of 326 votes. But political tides were changing. States' rights Whigs were fusing an alliance with Democrats to overwhelm the national Whigs. Clingman regained the mountain district seat in the Thirtieth Congress as a Democrat and held it for a decade. In Congress Graham served at different times as a member of the Indian affairs, claims, District of Columbia, naval affairs, and territories committees. His political convictions generally coincided with those of Henry Clay.

Leaving Congress in March 1847, Graham devoted his final years to managing his Earhart plantation in Rutherford County and his South Point plantation on the edge of South Carolina below Charlotte. Friends tried to persuade him to oppose Clingman again and he considered a move to the West, but an old throat affliction gradually grew worse and within a short time he died at South Point. He never married.

SEE: *Biog. Dir. Am. Cong.* (1971); P. M. Goldman and J. S. Young, *United States Congressional Directory* (1973); J. G. deR. Hamilton, *The Papers of William A. Graham*, vols. 1-4 (1957–61); H. D. Pegg, "The Whig Party in North Carolina, 1834–1861" (Ph.D. diss., University of North Carolina, 1932).

DANIEL M. MCFARLAND

**Graham, John** *(1 Aug. 1847–6 May 1921)*, educator, was born in Fayetteville, the son of Archibald and Ann McLean Graham. He inherited the red hair, fair complexion, and Presbyterian faith of his Scotch-Irish forebears. Graham claimed among his ancestors Alexander McAlister, a signer of the Halifax Resolves and patriot officer. Prepared for college by John DeBerniere Hooper and Jesse R. McLean, he chose instead to follow in the footsteps of his Revolutionary ancestor and in 1863, at the age of sixteen, enlisted in the Confederate Army.

In 1865, four months after his parole, Graham began the career that was to make him one of the outstanding educators in North Carolina. On the recommendation of Hooper, Charles M. Cook of Warrenton hired Graham to prepare his son Charles Alston for The University of North Carolina. When Cook left for Chapel Hill three years later, Graham's reputation had been established and he opened Fork Institute, which attracted students from Warren and surrounding counties. In 1877, he succeeded John E. Dugger as principal of the Warrenton Male Academy. Dugger returned from the Centennial School in Raleigh in 1880, and Graham went back to Fork Institute. After a fire at the Institute in 1890, he became principal of Ridgeway High School.

When another disastrous fire in 1897 destroyed the Ridgeway school, Dr. J. P. Macon, a former pupil, persuaded Graham to resume his former position as principal of Warrenton Male Academy. Graham changed the academy's name to Warrenton High School, purchased an additional building to serve as a dormitory and dining hall, and erected suitable outbuildings. As a result of this expansion, enrollment increased to over 100 boarders. In 1903, the school became coeducational and Graham purchased the home of William Plummer for a girls' dormitory, which he called Mordecai House after the earlier Warrenton girls school immortalized by Ellen Mordecai in *Hastings*.

Graham, who had specialized in Latin, believed in the value of the traditional studies of Latin, Greek, and mathematics as the basis of a sound education. According to one of his students, he "possessed unusual power of imparting knowledge and teaching his pupils how to study . . . he gripped the interest and attention of his classes." He had a reputation for instilling discipline as well as learning, and it was said that "a large number of bad boys were reformed under his tutelage."

Described by a contemporary as "a small man but of impressive manners, a careful dresser and sensitively handsome," Graham also won a deserved reputation for classical scholarship and educational leadership. He served one term as president of the North Carolina Teachers Assembly and held office in state and local agricultural organizations. The success of his students, including state supreme court justice Charles A. Cook, editor William Polk, actor Sidney Blackmer, and two administrators of The University of North Carolina, Frank Porter Graham and Robert B. House, attests to the effectiveness of his methods and curriculum.

On 28 Dec. 1868, Graham married Frances Gideon Daniels of Halifax County. "Miss Frankie" and three of their children, William Alexander, Amma, and Maria, worked with Graham at the school. When an attack of influenza impaired his health in 1914, Graham's son became acting principal. John Graham returned to the helm briefly when his son entered the army in 1917, but at the end of the next academic year (June 1918) he closed the doors of "the last of Warrenton's great private high schools." He died three years later and was buried in the family plot at the Episcopal church in Ridgeway.

Graham was survived by his wife and five children: William Alexander, who was to become superintendent of schools in Wilmington and Kinston; Amma, a longtime member of the Warren County Board of Education; Maria, later head of the English department at East Carolina Teachers College; Flora (Mrs. William Henry Horne); and Virginia (Mrs. Phillip G. Alston). In 1929, in recognition of his service to education, his former students presented a portrait of Graham by William Steen to the high school in Warrenton.

SEE: Charles A. Cook Papers (Southern Historical Collection, University of North Carolina, Chapel Hill); Lizzie W. Montgomery, *Sketches of Old Warrenton* (1924); Raleigh *News and Observer*, 18 Apr. 1920, 8 May 1921, 24 Nov. 1929; Warrenton *Warren Record*, 13 May 1921; Manly W. Wellman, *The County of Warren* (1959).

ELLEN BARRIER NEAL

**Graham, John Washington** *(22 July 1838–24 Mar. 1928)*, Confederate major, attorney, and politician, was born in Hillsborough, the second son of William A. and Susannah Washington Graham. The grandparents, the Joseph Grahams of Lincoln County and the John Washingtons of New Bern and Kinston, were well connected and influential in their respective sections of North Carolina. The father, William Alexander Graham (1804–75), was destined to become one of the state's most trusted political leaders. John Washington Graham attended the Caldwell Institute (where Alexander Wilson was principal), Abbott's Classical Academy in Georgetown, D.C., and The University of North Carolina. Especially capable in Latin and mathematics, he read law with William Horn Battle and Samuel Field Phillips and eventually received A.B. (1857), M.A. (Special Alumni, 1859), LL.B. (1860), and LL.D. (Honorary, 1921) degrees. He served his alma mater as tutor from 1858 to 1860 and as an active trustee from 1876 to 1928.

Graham began his legal practice in 1860, only to have this undertaking interrupted by the Civil War. He entered Confederate service in April 1861 and performed the duties of a junior staff officer until March 1862, when he returned to Orange County. There he raised Company D, Fifty-sixth North Carolina Regiment, leading his company as captain until he became regimental major in September 1863. He was seriously wounded in late March 1865, some two weeks before General Robert E. Lee's surrender at Appomattox. Shot through both legs, he eventually recovered fully. His action against Federal artillery at the Battle of Plymouth (April 1864) was especially meritorious. Noted as an officer genuinely concerned for his men, Graham was characterized as "one of the hardest fighting soldiers in the Southern army."

After the war, Graham was influential among those who "redeemed" the state from Republicanism. He became a leading Conservative, joined his illustrious father in denouncing Radical Reconstruction and black suffrage, and became a staunch opponent of Governor William W. Holden. From 1865 to 1868 he was Orange County solicitor, in a time when critical decisions regarding social and legal prerogatives were commonplace. As a delegate to the Constitutional Convention of 1868, he joined Thomas J. Jarvis, Plato Durham, and a few others in vainly stating the Conservative position to an overwhelming, hostile majority. Graham served in the state senate from 1868 to 1872 and voted for Holden's impeachment, while glorying in the denunciation of the Republican party and its programs. An unsuccessful candidate for state treasurer in 1872, he supported the call for the Constitutional Convention of 1875 and the changes made therein. Subsequently his public service included terms in the state senates of 1876, 1907–8, and 1911. In the latter two legislatures he was chairman of the railroads and judiciary committees, respectively. Also, he was trustee of the sinking fund of the North Carolina Railroad Company (1877–89) and chairman of the North Carolina Tax Commission (1886–87)—a three-man panel whose report provided the basis for the state's tax policies for several years. In financial matters he was cautious and always mindful of North Carolina's fiscal integrity and best interests. He was an unsuccessful candidate for Congress in 1886, receiving the Democratic party's nomination in his district after 153 ballots.

An eminently successful attorney and constitutional authority, he practiced his profession until his eighty-fourth year. He had a succession of partners including his father, his brother, James, and Thomas Ruffin, Jr. His practice was centered in Orange, Durham, Person, Alamance, and Caswell counties. He was an effective orator and frequently swayed juries by biblical quotations or humorous anecdotes, or both.

Graham was married twice. On 9 Oct. 1867, he married Rebecca Bennehan Cameron Anderson (1840–83), a daughter of the Paul C. Camerons and the widow of Lieutenant Robert Walker Anderson, Graham's friend and comrade-in-arms, who was killed in the Wilderness in May 1864. Their five children who lived to adulthood were Paul Cameron, Isabella Davidson, William Alexander, Joseph, and Annie Cameron Graham. In December 1887 he married Mrs. Margaret Forrester Bailey of Tallahassee, Fla. This union produced one son, Alexander Hawkins Graham (1890–1977), himself a distinguished attorney and public servant.

When John W. Graham died in his ninetieth year, he was widely lamented. An overflow crowd, including Governor Angus W. McLean and other dignitaries, attended his funeral services in St. Matthew's Episcopal Church, Hillsborough, where for fifty years he had been vestryman or warden. Called by his rector a "Christian gentleman" in the "fullest sense," Graham was buried in the peaceful parish churchyard.

SEE: Samuel A. Ashe, *Cyclopedia of Eminent and Representative Men of the Carolinas of the Nineteenth Century* (1892); Walter Clark, ed., *Histories of the Several Regiments and Battalions from North Carolina in the Great War, 1861–'65* (1901); John W. Graham, *Some Events in My Life, An Address to the North Carolina Bar Association* (1918); J. G. deR. Hamilton, *Reconstruction in North Carolina* (1914); North Carolina Bar Association, *Proceedings* 30 (1928); *North Carolina Biography*, vol. 3 (1929); Raleigh *News and Observer*, 25, 26 Mar. 1928; St. Matthew's Rector William D. Benton, *An Address Commemorative of Major John W. Graham, LL.D.* (1928).

MAX R. WILLIAMS

**Graham, Joseph** *(13 Oct. 1759–12 Nov. 1836)*, Revolutionary soldier, politician, and iron entrepreneur, was born in Chester County, Pa. James Graham, his father, was Scotch-Irish and had settled in Berks County, Pa., in 1733. His mother, Mary McConnell Barber Graham, also of Scotch-Irish descent, was James Graham's second wife. Their union produced five children; Joseph Graham was the youngest son but had two younger sisters. Widowed in 1763, Mary Barber Graham moved her family through Charleston to the Carolina backcountry, locating permanently in Mecklenburg County, N.C. Joseph Graham was educated at Charlotte's Queen's Museum (later Liberty Hall Academy), where he proved himself a good scholar of "mannerly bearing." He was in Charlotte when the patriots of that town adopted the Mecklenburg Resolves on 31 May 1775. The events of May made a lasting impression on the young scholar. Throughout his long life, Graham attested to the revolutionary intent of his Mecklenburg neighbors.

Perhaps it was the inspiration of this patriotic moment or perhaps his Scotch-Irish temperament, but whatever the motivation young Graham was an eager participant in the struggle against British tyranny. Serving periodically from 1778 to 1781 as a volunteer, Graham, aged eighteen to twenty-one years, fought in fifteen minor engagements in North Carolina and South Carolina, while rising in rank from private to major. His most memorable service was commanding the rear guard action against Tarleton's cavalry, which enabled General William R. Davie to evade Cornwallis's troops after the British capture of Charlotte. Wounded nine times, six by saber and three by lead, the bleeding and exhausted Graham was left on the field for dead; however, he survived and, after two months' recuperation, became major of a company of dragoons that engaged Tories and British regulars in the Cape Fear region. Graham demonstrated capacity as a soldier and impressed those who knew him with his youthful determination and devotion to duty.

After the American Revolution, Graham farmed near the Catawba River and held several public offices of varying importance. He was sheriff of Mecklenburg County (1784–85) and for a time served as government commissioner in land transactions. As a delegate to the 1788 Hillsborough convention to discuss the federal constitution, he voted with the majority against ratification. Later, in the Convention of 1789, he supported adoption of the Constitution. He took no part in the debates in either convention. From 1788 to 1793 Graham represented his county in the North Carolina Senate. There he manifested an interest in education—he served on the first board of trustees for The University of North Carolina—and in internal improvements.

Graham's political horizons seemed unlimited; however, his 1787 marriage to Isabella Davidson, a refined daughter of Revolutionary hero John Davidson, was destined to divert him to more remunerative endeavors. By the early 1790s Davidson, a practical blacksmith who became a wealthy planter and ironmonger, had convinced Graham and another son-in-law, Alexander Brevard, that their future lay in Lincoln County's nascent iron industry. In October 1791 Graham purchased twenty-eight acres, mostly sand and water, on the Lincoln County side of the Catawba. Soon afterwards the three kinsmen—Davidson, Brevard, and Graham—bought an interest in a productive ore bank from Peter Forney. With Forney they formed the Iron Company. Other land was obtained in 1792, and Graham built Vesuvius Furnace on Anderson Creek in east Lincoln County. A suitable residence was constructed on a nearby bluff. There Graham settled his growing family.

These early iron manufacturers were essentially planters with an outside interest, and they learned the techniques of forge and furnace through experimentation. Fortunately the demand for iron products increased apace with the growing population of the western Carolinas. In 1795, Brevard built Mount Tirzah Forge and established his family about three miles from Vesuvius. In the same year the Iron Company was dissolved, with Peter Forney retaining control of the ore bank. Graham, Davidson, and Brevard continued their partnership under the name of Joseph Graham and Company. Industry and good management increased their holdings. In 1804, when Davidson sold his interests to his sons-in-law, the company's assets were valued at $28,510. Ten years later when Brevard and Graham amicably ended their partnership, both were wealthy men. Their products were marketed throughout the region and down the Catawba into South Carolina. During the War of 1812 Graham alone sold the U.S. government 30,000 pounds of shots, shells, and cannon balls of various sizes, making delivery anywhere by wagon.

The War of 1812, which also resulted in an uprising among the Creeks, touched Graham more directly. Long interested in military affairs, he was appointed brigadier general of a brigade of North Carolina and South Carolina militiamen in 1814. Although the brigade arrived after Andrew Jackson's victory over the Creeks at Horseshoe Bend, General Graham was considered an efficient officer. Major General Thomas Pinckney, a South Carolinian who commanded the Sixth Military District, characterized him as having "conducted his Brigade with judgment and propriety" and noted "that he and the officers and men under his command have displayed much zeal, patriotism and attention to discipline." For many years after this renewed military service, Graham was major general of the Fifth Division, North Carolina Militia.

Active in public and business affairs until late in life, Graham was a councillor of state in 1814, a trustee of Lincolnton's Pleasant Retreat Academy, a justice of the peace for nearly forty years, and a ruling elder of the Unity Presbyterian Church. After 1820 he assisted Archibald D. Murphey, who hoped to prepare a state history, by writing a series of remarkably accurate accounts of military activities in western North Carolina and South Carolina. His vivid account, based on memory, of the events of May 1775 proved to be the principal authority for the disputed Mecklenburg Declaration of Independence. Although Murphey never completed his history, many of the Graham manuscripts eventually were included in the archives of North Carolina.

Eleven children were born to Isabella Davidson Graham (1762–1808) and her husband in their twenty-one years of marriage. Their offspring were Polly (1788–1801); John Davidson (1789–1847); Sophia (1791–1865), who married Dr. John Ramsay Witherspoon and settled in Hale County, Ala.; James (1793–1851), who settled in Rutherford County and was a Whig congressman; George Franklin (1794–1827), a physician of Shelby County, Tenn., who died of yellow fever; Joseph (1797–1837); Robert Montrose (1798–1821); Violet Wilson (1799–1868), the wife of Dr. Moses Winslow Alexander of Mecklenburg County; Mary (1801–64), the wife of the noted Presbyterian minister and educator Robert Hall Morrison; Alfred (1803–35); and William Alexander (1804–75), a North Carolina political leader for over forty years.

Upon his death Joseph Graham was buried at Machpelah Presbyterian Church, the burial grounds of the Brevards and Grahams located between the family plantations.

SEE: Lester J. Cappon, "Iron Making—A Forgotten Industry of North Caroilna," *North Carolina Historical Review* 9 (1932); Chalmers G. Davidson, *Major John Davidson of "Rural Hill"* (1943); *Descendants of James Graham (1714–1763) of Ireland and Pennsylvania* (1940); William A. Graham, *General Joseph Graham and His Papers on North Carolina Revolutionary History* (1904); H. G. Jones, *For History's Sake* (1966); Sarah Lemmon, *Frustrated Patriots* (1973); *Obituary of Major General Joseph Graham* (broadside, North Carolina Collection, University of North Carolina, Chapel Hill); William L. Sherrill, *Annals of Lincoln County, North Carolina* (1967); Louise I. Trenholme, *The Ratification of the Federal Constitution in North Carolina* (1932); Max R. Williams, "William A. Graham, North Carolina Whig Party Leader, 1804–1849" (Ph.D. diss., University of North Carolina, 1965).

MAX R. WILLIAMS

**Graham, Mary Owen** *(13 Oct. 1872–29 Mar. 1957),* educator and civic leader, was born in Wilmington, the daughter of Archibald and Eliza Owen Barry Graham, and the granddaughter of John Owen (1787–1841), governor of North Carolina from 1828 to 1830. Her ancestry was a blending of Scottish, Welsh, English, and French. She was a sister of Edward Kidder Graham, niece of Alexander Graham, cousin of Frank Porter Graham, and aunt of Edward Kidder Graham, Jr. She received her education in private schools, the Charlotte City Schools, Charlotte Female Institute (now Queens College) where she earned the A.B. degree in 1890, and at The University of North Carolina, University of Tennessee, and Teachers College of Columbia University.

From 1892 to 1907 Miss Graham taught in the graded school in Charlotte, often with ninety children in her primary classes; from 1908 to 1912 she was a member of the Department of Education of the North Carolina College for Women, where she trained primary teachers; and from 1912 to 1916 she was assistant superintendent of schools in Mecklenburg County, where she instituted Community Week. Because of its success the governor issued a proclamation making Community Week a statewide enterprise. From 1906 to 1914 she also taught in summer sessions in colleges and universities in North Carolina; in Fredericksburg, Va.; and in county institutes. She edited *Literature and Stories for Primary Grades* and with Ann M. Williams prepared a manual for teachers and students on teaching phonetics, which was widely used.

From 1916 to 1924 she served as president of Peace Institute (renamed Peace, a Junior College for Women in 1930), Raleigh, the first woman president of the institution. She brought to Peace Institute "the efficiency of her experience, the forcefulness of her personality, the unselfishness of her service to womanhood, and the refining grace of her personal tastes." Her objective was "the full and rounded development of the girls mentally, physically, spiritually and socially." To assist in this task student government was begun at the school. In 1942, a portrait of her by Mabel Pugh of the Art Department of Peace was presented to the college, where it hangs in the Administration Building.

Because of her achievements, "Miss Mary Owen" was sought for numerous state offices and services. She was the first woman president of the North Carolina Teachers Association (1914–15); first committeewoman from North Carolina on the National Democratic Committee (1918–27); trustee of the North Carolina School for the Blind (1916–22); member of the State Board of Examiners, of the Committee of 100 for Public Welfare, and of the YWCA's South Atlantic Committee; vice-president of the State Literary and Historical Association; speaker for the War Committee of World War I; and president of the Albemarle Presbyterial, an organization of the Presbyterian women of the church. She also was a member of the National Education Association, Federation of Women's Clubs, League of Women Voters, Bessie Dewey Book Club, Daughters of the American Revolution, United Daughters of the Confederacy, and Business and Professional Women, and an honorary member of the Altrusa Club. Miss Graham was an effective speaker before the senate and house committees of the North Carolina General Assembly. She died in the Presbyterian Home in High Point and was buried in Charlotte.

SEE: *Greensboro Daily News*, 31 Mar. 1957; *North Carolina's Capital, Raleigh* (1967); Peace College *Bulletin*, March 1972; Dr. William C. Pressly, letter to author, 26 Nov. 1974; Raleigh *News and Observer*, 31 Mar. 1957, 26 Apr. 1972, 18 Nov. 1973; Reference librarian, Jackson Library, University of North Carolina at Greensboro, letter to author (1 Jan. 1975); *Some Pioneer Women Teachers of North Carolina* (1955); University of North Carolina *Record*, 1949–50; Sidney Ann Wilson, *Personae: The History of Peace College* (1972).

GRADY L. E. CARROLL

**Graham, Robert Davidson** *(5 Dec. 1842–27 June 1905)*, lawyer, was one of the ten children and the fifth son of Susannah Sarah Washington and William Alexander Graham, governor of North Carolina, U.S. secretary of the navy, lawyer, and Whig politician. He attended the classical school conducted by Alexander Wilson at Melville in eastern Alamance County. Graham entered the freshman class of The University of North Carolina in 1859 and was one of the freshman declaimers at the commencement of 1860. He left the university to take up farming in Mecklenburg County. Upon North Carolina's secession in 1861, he joined Company D, Fifty-sixth North Carolina Regiment, of which his brother John Washington became captain in 1862, advancing to the rank of major in September 1863.

Graham succeeded David S. Ray as first lieutenant of Company D upon Ray's death in the Battle of Gum Swamp (22 May 1863) and later attained the rank of captain. He served in eastern North Carolina and in the Petersburg-Richmond area, and was especially commended for his performance during the Confederate attack on Plymouth (April 1864). Wounded seriously in the left leg during an attack on Grant's lines in March 1865, he was hospitalized near Richmond at the time of Lee's surrender on 9 April. Paroled by the Federals as soon as he was able to travel, Graham made his way back to North Carolina and resumed farming in Mecklenburg County.

In 1868, Graham was graduated with a bachelor of arts degree by The University of North Carolina; he later studied law and was admitted to the bar. In 1884 he was named secretary of the U.S. Civil Service Commission, and in 1886 he became chairman of the U.S. Board of Pension Appeals. From 1888 to 1898 he was the principal examiner of titles and contracts, U.S. General Land Office.

Each of Graham's six brothers who lived to maturity served in the Confederate armies, and each survived the war. The oldest, Joseph, became a physician in Lincoln County and later in Charlotte. Another brother, George Washington, also became a physician. Augustus Washington, James Augustus, and John Washington, like Robert Davidson, were attorneys. William Alexander, Jr., successfully combined agriculture and politics. As a Lincoln County farmer he was elected to two terms in the state senate and one in the house. From 1908 until his death in 1923, he served as North Carolina's commissioner of agriculture.

Robert Davidson Graham never married.

SEE: Samuel A. Ashe, *Cyclopedia of Eminent and Representative Men of the Carolinas of the Nineteenth Century* (1892), and *History of North Carolina*, vol. 2 (1925); Walter Clark, ed., *Histories of the Several Regiments and Battalions from North Carolina in the Great War, 1861–'65* (1901); J. G. deR. Hamilton and Max R. Williams, eds., *The Papers of William Alexander Graham*, vols. 2, 5, 6 (1959–76).

W. CONARD GASS

**Graham, William Alexander** *(5 Sept. 1804–11 Aug. 1875)*, lawyer, planter, and governor, was the eleventh child and youngest son of Joseph and Isabella Davidson Graham. He was born on Vesuvius Plantation, the family home in eastern Lincoln County. Both parents were staunch Presbyterians of Scotch-Irish ancestry; their progenitors had migrated first to western Pennsylvania before resettling in the more congenial climate of Mecklenburg County. An iron entrepreneur and sometime public servant, Joseph Graham (1759–1836) had achieved local fame as a young but dedicated Revolutionary officer. Isabella Davidson Graham (1762–1808) was the accomplished daughter of the John Davidsons whose Mecklenburg home, Rural Hill, was renowned as a seat of gracious living. John Davidson, himself a Revolutionary patriot, was a substantial farmer and practical blacksmith who, with his sons-in-law Alexander Brevard and Joseph Graham, pioneered the Catawba River valley iron industry. The Grahams and Davidsons were noted for their sagacity, frugality, diligence, and public spirit. William A. Graham embodied these familial traits.

Under the supervision of a devoted father, now a widower, young Graham enjoyed the pleasures of a rural boyhood, learned the rudiments of plantation and furnace management, and prepared for a professional career. He attended classical schools in nearby Lincolnton and Statesville before completing preparatory education in the Hillsborough Academy. In January 1821, after an examination by Professor William Hooper, he was admitted to The University of North Carolina. An active member of the Dialectic Society, Graham was an able, industrious student who shared first honors in the distinguished class of 1824.

Subsequently, as was customary for aspiring lawyers in that day, he studied with an established attorney. Graham's mentor was the eminent Thomas Ruffin, of Orange County, who later became an outstanding jurist and chief justice of the North Carolina Supreme Court. By March 1828, having received county and superior court licenses, Graham had established a practice as a member of the highly competitive Hillsborough legal community. Within a few years he became one of the more successful members of the North Carolina bar, maintaining a lucrative practice until his death. In time he owned three plantations worked by slave labor, although agriculture was never his primary interest.

It was always necessary that Graham earn a livelihood for himself and his numerous family, but clearly the law and agriculture were secondary in importance to his abiding preoccupation with public affairs. Prompted by a sense of noblesse oblige, he entered public life in the early 1830s just as new political alignments were emerging. Graham joined with other opponents of Andrew Jackson to form the Whig party. Associated with the Federal wing of that party in the state and nationally, he embraced Henry Clay's American System—supporting a national bank, a judicious tariff, federally financed internal improvements, and the distribution of excess treasury funds to the states. Despite the vicissitudes of sectional controversy and political change, he remained a conservative but ardent Unionist. However, with other Southern Unionists, he was destined to experience grave disappointments as secession, Civil War, and Reconstruction became realities.

If officeholding is any criterion, few North Carolinians have enjoyed public confidence for so long as Graham. This fact is more notable because his aristocratic bearing seems incompatible with the rise of democracy which paralleled his years in politics. He was borough representative from Hillsborough in the legislatures of 1833, 1834, and 1835; and, after the constitutional reforms of 1835, he represented Orange County as a member of the House of Commons in the 1836, 1838, and 1840 legislative sessions. He was speaker of the House of Commons in the latter two sessions. From December 1840 to March 1843, he represented North Carolina in the U.S. Senate. There he generally supported Clay in his dispute with "His Accidency," President John Tyler, but not to the extent of endangering the national Whig party. Displaced by a Democratic legislature elected in 1842, Graham ran successfully for governor in 1844, defeating Michael Hoke, a formidable western Democrat. He was easily reelected in 1846. Thus he was North Carolina's governor from January 1845 to January 1849. Much of his attention was absorbed by the Mexican War, of which he disapproved; nevertheless, Governor Graham supported the national commitment and raised and officered a politically controversial North Carolina regiment. An able administrator, his governorship was characterized by concern for humanitarian causes and internal improvements, especially railroad development.

After declining European diplomatic appointments offered by Zachary Taylor, Graham agreed to become secretary of the navy in July 1850, when Millard Fillmore formed a cabinet that supported the proposed compromise measures then before Congress. Initially his role was largely political, as he promoted passage and acceptance of the Compromise of 1850. He viewed the compromise as the final resolution of long-standing sectional controversies. To both North and South he advocated moderation, advising the North that faithful execution of the Fugitive Slave Law was essential to perpetuation of the Union. Although he knew little of naval affairs and never fully grasped the significance of contemporary technological advances, Graham was an experienced administrator. He relied heavily on knowledgeable advisers such as career officer Matthew Fontaine Maury. Secretary Graham was the moving spirit in several notable activities including a constructive program of personnel reforms, exploration of the Amazon basin, and the Perry expedition to Japan. The authoritative naval historian Samuel Eliot Morison has characterized Graham as one of the best navy secretaries in the nineteenth century.

In the summer of 1852, the Whig party nominated Winfield Scott and William A. Graham as its presidential and vice-presidential candidates, respectively. Although Graham, with most Southerners, preferred Fillmore, he sought to reassure the South that Scott was sound on the slavery question. He failed. Scott carried only four states as Democrat Franklin Pierce even outpolled the Whig ticket in North Carolina by a narrow margin. This campaign, which revealed a fatal internal division, presaged the demise of the national Whig party. Northern and Southern Whigs had diverged irrevocably because of the moral dilemma over slavery. A disappointed Graham resettled in Hillsborough and sought to provide educational and social opportunities for his maturing progeny. He served in the North Carolina Senate of 1854, but declined other requests in the 1850s that he seek office. However, he refused to abandon his Whig principles, avoiding the temptation to join many political friends in the American party. Not until 1860, in the desperate crisis of a "house dividing," did he acknowledge the futility of Whiggery. Then he united with conservative men of all sections in founding and promoting the Constitutional Union party. The hope that moderate candidates might be elected proved vain. In December 1860, James Alexander Hamilton of New York made an abortive appeal to the Pennsylvania presidential electors that they vote for Graham for president as a possible means of preserving the Republic.

After the election of Abraham Lincoln, Graham, who was sounded unofficially about a post in the new cabinet, counseled patience and conciliation. He urged North Carolinians to rely on the Constitution as a sufficient guarantor of their rights, advising that there would be time enough to seek proper remedies after an overt, illegal action by the national government. In February 1861, with the Confederacy a reality, Graham led Union men in defeating a statewide referendum to call a convention to consider disunion. However, after the firing on Fort Sumter and Lincoln's call for troops, he accepted the inevitable, declaring that "blood was thicker than water." Although he abhorred secession, he was overwhelmingly elected to represent Orange County in the Constitutional Convention of May 1861. In opposition to the original secessionists, now in the ascendancy, Graham stood unsuccessfully for the convention presidency and supported an abortive resolution upholding the right of revolution as the appropriate response to tyranny. Only when there seemed no honorable alternative did William A. Graham cast his vote for secession.

Having done his best to prevent disunion, Graham supported the Confederate cause to the extent his principles allowed. With Thomas Ruffin, he negotiated the terms by which North Carolina would enter the Confederate States of America; and he remained an active participant in the deliberations of the Convention. But the Civil War was troublesome to him and to many other Southern Unionists. On the one hand, five of his sons were Confederate officers and innumerable relatives and friends were involved militarily. (Three nieces were married to Confederate generals "Stonewall" Jackson, Daniel Harvey Hill, and Rufus Barringer.) Their commitments had to be adequately sustained by his political and economic efforts; but, on the other hand, the rights of the states and the citizenry had to be protected against the encroachments of a government at war. Herein lay the fatal flaw—how could a nation predicated on state sovereignty command the unity necessary to win the war? Graham became the champion of personal liberties, constitutional government, and states' rights. As such, he was a frequent critic of the Davis administration. He sometimes found himself in strange company. He was allied with old-line Whigs, Americans, and former southern rights Democrats—most surprisingly, perhaps, his erstwhile adversary William W. Holden.

In the spring of 1862, in order to replace Governor John W. Ellis who had died in office the previous July, Holden, indefatigable editor of the *North Carolina Standard*, encouraged Graham to run for governor and praised him in extravagant terms editorially. Graham declined, but joined Holden and many old Unionists in electing the popular Zebulon B. Vance. Subsequently, he and Holden were among Vance's most intimate advisers. Eventually the three men diverged in their views, and each came to represent a discernible segment of North Carolina opinion. While protecting the state's interests, Vance became convinced that honor required a fight to the finish. Meanwhile, by the summer of 1863, Holden was disenchanted to the extent of promoting a movement looking to separate peace initiatives by individual states. Both men sought the endorsement of Graham, who publicly affirmed confidence in Vance. Nevertheless, by 1864 Graham, now a Confederate senator and an open opponent of the Davis government, hoped earnestly for a negotiated peace based on the *status quo ante bellum*. He was a moving spirit in the fruitless Hampton Roads Conference of 3 Feb. 1865. He favored reunion over independence but balked at talk of emancipation. His conservative racial views caused him to oppose the enlistment of slaves in Confederate armies. If slavery and the accompanying social system were abolished, he believed, all was lost.

When the end was in sight, Graham left Richmond to warn Vance that the Confederacy was collapsing and to advise that North Carolina should look to its own interests. Vance demurred but authorized Graham and David L. Swain to surrender Raleigh to William T. Sherman, whose armies menaced the capital. This they did, though some North Carolinians never fully understood their motives. Years later, after both Swain and Graham were dead, Vance disparaged their realistic service to the state.

Reconstruction was particularly frustrating for Graham. He felt as though he and other former Unionists should be quickly rehabilitated politically so as to lead in the process of reunion. Instead, because of his service to the Confederacy, he was forced to apply for pardon—necessarily seeking the endorsement of William W. Holden, now provisional governor of North Carolina. His pardon application of July 1865 revealed the plight of Southerners who had worked to preserve the Union until they saw no honorable alternative. But, ironically, Holden, the erstwhile secessionist turned peacenik, was in a commanding position. Graham's pardon was delayed on the pretense that he was inopportunely critical of presidential Reconstruction. Nevertheless, he was elected to the state senate in November 1865, but declined to be seated before his pardon. In early December the legislature elected him to the U.S. Senate. He presented his credentials to that body, having been assured that admission to Congress would automatically result in the full restoration of his citizenship. But he, with others elected under the Johnson Reconstruction plan, was denied his seat. Congress had begun to assume direction of the Reconstruction process. Needless to say, the Congressional Reconstruction acts, the activities of the Union League, the organization of the Republican party, the measures adopted by the Constitutional Convention of 1868, and the election of Holden as governor galvanized Graham's opposition to imposed reunion, which he considered grossly unjust. Universal manhood suffrage for blacks, whom he deemed unprepared for full political responsibilities, was particularly galling to Graham whose own disabilities prevented him from voting and holding office. He became an outspoken advocate of the conservative position and of white supremacy. Although he never held public office after 1865 (his disabilities were not removed until 1873), William A. Graham was a leader of the redemption movement in North Carolina. Except for his role as a prosecutor in the impeachment trial that removed Holden from office in March 1871, his influence was manifest in the activities of old friends and younger men, especially his son John W. Graham, Plato Durham, and the fiery Josiah Turner, Jr. An advocate of further constitutional reform, he was elected a delegate to the Constitutional Convention of 1875, but died before it assembled.

Ironically, Graham's national reputation was more easily regained. He carried on an extensive correspondence and was evidently widely esteemed. In 1867, he was appointed to the original board of Peabody Fund Trustees and served faithfully in that capacity until his death. He was also on the arbitration commission to settle the Virginia-Maryland boundary dispute, and by 1875 he had become the principal figure in the long-delayed deliberations of that group.

On 8 June 1836, Graham married Susannah Sarah Washington (1816–90), daughter of John and Elizabeth Heritage Cobb Washington of New Bern. Their long union was felicitous and productive. The Grahams had ten children, eight of whom survived both parents. Their offspring were Joseph (1837–1907), John Washington (1838–1928), William Alexander (1839–1924), James Augustus (1841–1909), Robert Davidson (1843–1904), George Washington (1847–1923), Augustus Washington (1849–1936), Susan Washington (1851–1909), Alfred Octavius (1853–54), and Eugene Berrien (1858–63). All who survived childhood were afforded an excellent education and achieved notable careers in their own right. Four sons were attorneys, two were physicians, and one—William Alexander, Jr.—was a planter and North Carolina commissioner of agriculture. Susan Washington Graham married Judge Walter Clark.

Graham died unexpectedly at Saratoga Springs, N.Y., where he had gone to attend a meeting of the Virginia-Maryland Arbitration Commission. He was buried in the cemetery adjacent to the Hillsborough Presbyterian Church. His memory is perpetuated in the name of a small city in Alamance County and a county in western North Carolina. A marble bust of Graham adorns the capitol building in Raleigh and an oil portrait by William Garl Browne hangs in the Museum of History, Raleigh.

SEE: Edwin Rudy Andrews, " 'Poor and Unknown and Very Industrious:' A Study of W. W. Holden the Person" (M.A. thesis, Western Carolina Univeristy, 1976); *Descendants of James Graham (1714–1763) of Ireland and Pennsylvania* (1940); William A. Graham, *General Joseph Graham and His Papers on North Carolina Revolutionary History* (1904); J. G. deR. Hamilton and Max R. Williams, eds., *The Papers of William A. Graham*, vols. 1-8 (1957- [vol. 8 in preparation]); Max R. Williams, "Secretary William A. Graham, Naval Administrator, 1850–1852," *North Carolina Historical Review* 48 (1971), and "William A. Graham, North Carolina Whig Party Leader, 1804–1849" (Ph.D. diss., University of North Carolina, 1965).

MAX R. WILLIAMS

**Graham, William Alexander, Jr.** *(26 Dec. 1839–24 Dec. 1923)*, farmer and state commissioner of agriculture, was born in Hillsborough, the third of nine sons of William Alexander Graham, a governor of North Carolina and secretary of the navy, and Susannah Sarah Washington Graham, daughter of John Washington of New Bern. Through his father, William A. Graham, Jr., was related to some of the most influential families of Piedmont North Carolina: the Alexanders, Brevards, Davidsons, Morrisons, and Witherspoons. He received his early education in the various places where his father's career took the family, first in Hillsborough (Caldwell Institute), then in Raleigh and Washington, D.C. (Union Academy). He entered The University of North Carolina in 1856, but transferred in 1859 to Princeton University where he was graduated with an A.B. degree in 1860.

At the outbreak of the Civil War, Graham joined the Confederate forces as a second lieutenant in Captain Josiah Turner's cavalry unit later known as Company K, Nineteenth Regiment. From the minor skirmishes in eastern North Carolina in which he was first engaged (Gillet's Farmhouse and Brandy Station) to the Battle of Gettysburg where he was wounded, Graham displayed the dogged determination, energy, and leadership that characterized his later years as farmer and public servant. Upon his recovery, he was promoted to the rank of major (sometime earlier he had succeeded Turner as captain of the company) and was reassigned as assistant adjutant general of the North Carolina forces in Raleigh, where he spent the remainder of the war years.

On 8 June 1864 he married Julia R. Lane, daughter of John Wayles Lane of Amelia County, Va. After the war Graham, who had always intended to become a farmer, moved to the Lincoln County plantation of his grandfather, General Joseph Graham, of Revolutionary War fame, where the Grahams had first established themselves in North Carolina by land investment and iron ore production. During the difficult Reconstruction years, Graham steadily improved the resources and productivity of the plantation through hard work and shrewd management. He kept abreast of all new developments in methods and machinery, and was an active supporter of the Farmer's Alliance, serving as president in 1901, 1902, and 1905. Graham conceived and implemented the plan of the Alliance's business agency, unique in the United States, and was a trustee for its fund.

During the same period Graham's interest in politics led in 1867 to his nomination by the conservatives as a candidate to the constitutional convention. However, because of his extreme conservatism and stand against the enfranchisement of Negroes, he was defeated. Throughout his life, he maintained a belief in white supremacy along with a corresponding lack of sympathy for the plight of the Negro both in bondage and in freedom. Despite his initial defeat, he continued to pursue a political career as a conservative Democrat. In 1874 and 1878 he received the unanimous nomination for and was elected state senator from his district of Lincoln and Gaston. He also represented the district in the legislature in 1905. As might be expected, Graham served the farmers' interests and successfully introduced legislation prohibiting the traditional deduction (scale charge) for each bale of cotton, making verbal contracts legal and giving priority to labor in suits for wages against individuals and corporations. These achievements led naturally to his appointment to the Board of Agriculture in 1899. He remained in that post until 1908, when he was elected state commissioner of agriculture, a position he held until his death.

Graham is remembered best for the work he accomplished as agricultural commissioner. He first turned his attention to the causes of the economic slough in which agriculture in the state was then mired. This problem, which had never been seriously investigated or understood, preoccupied Graham for the rest of his life. The interlocking causes were poor soil, poor farming methods, poor machinery, poor crop strains and animal stock, and the consequent low production and dependence on imported foodstuff. To remedy this blight, he established laboratories and experimental stations to study and improve soil conditions and to develop new strains of seed, new varieties of crops, and new treatments for orchards and truck gardens. He imported good animal stock. Finally, he established farmers' institutes where demonstrations of improved farming methods, machinery, and home improvement helped the farmer and his family raise the performance of their varied tasks.

Within a decade Graham's work produced impressive results: the vast improvement of soil, livestock, farm machinery and methods, and overall production. His insight, resourcefulness, organizational ability, and persistence changed the course and conditions of agriculture in North Carolina.

An ardent supporter of the Baptist church, Graham served as moderator of the South Fork Baptist Association from its beginning in 1878 until 1906 and wrote a history of the association. He was a trustee of the Southern Baptist Seminary and of the North Carolina College of Agriculture and Engineering.

Interested in history, like his father and grandfather before him, he wrote various articles on the Revolutionary and Civil wars and a history of the Nineteenth Regiment and of the Adjutant General's Department for *Histories of the Several Regiments and Battalions from North Carolina in the Great War 1861–'65* (1901), edited by his brother-in-law Walter Clark. He also edited *General Joseph Graham and his Papers on North Carolina Revolutionary History* (1904), for which he wrote a biographical sketch of his grandfather and a history of iron production in Lincoln County. Equally valuable for the history they contain are many still unpublished letters from Graham to his parents in the decade 1859–69.

Graham died in Raleigh and was buried in the old Machpelah burying ground near Iron Station, Lincoln County. His second wife, Sally Hill Clark (1864–1936), whom he had married in 1914, survived him, as did eight of his eleven children, all from his first marriage to Julia Lane (1845–1909). They were Florence Lane, Susan Washington (m. Casper Walke in 1895), Evelyn Taylor (m. Slaughter W. Huff in 1892), William Alexander, Elizabeth Hill (m. James P. Parker in 1906), Mattie Lawson, Sophie Alexander, Caroline Brevard, Alice Caldwell (m. Montague Clark in 1908), Ellen Wayles (m. John Calvert in 1914), and Joseph (m. Bessie Fitzsimmons in 1915).

SEE: Alumni file, Princeton University, Princeton, N.J.; *Charlotte Observer*, 25, 26 Dec. 1923; W. A. Graham, Jr., Letters (Manuscript Department, Library, Duke University, Durham); *Greensboro Daily News*, 30 Dec. 1923; Ural N. Hoffman, "Major W. A. Graham," *Trinity College Historical Society Papers* 6 (1906); Raleigh *Extension Farm-News*, January 1924.

JEAN BRADLEY ANDERSON

**Graham, William Alexander** *(26 July 1873–3 July 1943)*, farmer leader, was born at Forest Home, Lincoln County, the son of William A. and Julia R. Lane Graham. Educated locally, he attended Horner Military Academy and was a student at The University of North Carolina in 1897–98. A farmer, member of the Grange, and president of the county farmers' alliance, he was named North Carolina commissioner of agriculture in 1923 to succeed his late father. He held that post until defeated for reelection in 1936. Graham served three terms in the state senate, the first in 1923 when he was chairman of the agriculture committee and again in 1939 and 1943. As an active Democrat he was a member of the state Democratic executive committee. In 1928, he was president of the National Association of Commissioners of Agriculture and also served on the executive committee of the Southern Association of Commissioners of Agriculture. He was active in the Baptist church, a member of the Knights of Pythias, and served as president of the North Carolina Society, Sons of the American Revolution, and as vice-president of the South Atlantic district.

Graham never married. He was buried in the cemetery of Machpelah Church near his home at Iron Station.

SEE: Alumni records, University of North Carolina, Chapel Hill; Daniel L. Grant, *Alumni History of the University of North Carolina* (1924); Raleigh *News and Observer*, 4 July 1943; *Sons of the American Revolution Magazine*, 38 (October 1943).

WILLIAM S. POWELL

**Grant, Hiram Louis** *(26 Jan. 1843–8 Mar. 1922)*, soldier, legislator, and businessman, was born in Woonsocket, R.I., the son of Lucinda C. Brown of Connecticut and John S. D. Grant, a superintendent of cotton mills. He was educated at the public schools and the academy at Woodstock.

Grant enlisted as a private in Company A, Sixth Connecticut Volunteer Infantry on 3 Sept. 1861 and gradually rose in rank to major. On 23 July 1863, he was one of twenty volunteers sent to silence the guns of Fort Wagner on Morris Island at Charleston harbor. Seriously wounded in the action, he was awarded the medal of honor by General Q. A. Gillmore on 23 Aug. 1863. After being confined for eight months to a hospital in Beaufort, N.C., Grant was reassigned to the staff of General Joseph R. Hawley of the Tenth Army Corps and served in that position during the entire Virginia campaign. Grant commanded a portion of the Union troops that made the successful assault on Fort Fisher in January 1865. Subsequently he was appointed provost marshal of Wilmington and later of Goldsboro. The white populations of these two towns greatly disliked the black troops he commanded. Grant was honorably discharged from the army on 24 Aug. 1865. During the Spanish-American War he returned to active duty for thirteen months as paymaster in the District of Columbia, Puerto Rico, and New York City.

Favorably impressed with the small town of Goldsboro, Grant settled there after the war and made it the center of his political activities. In 1868, he served as a delegate to the North Carolina Constitutional Convention. In 1869 he was appointed postmaster of Goldsboro, a position he held for seventeen years. Grant had a great interest in public education. He was a trustee of the Colored Normal School and established the first public school in Goldsboro. Having obtained the gift of an old building from the Fair Association, he moved it to his own property, rebuilt and furnished it as a schoolhouse and donated it to the city. In 1894 Grant was elected without his consent to the North Carolina Senate, and in 1896 he was reelected. As chairman of the Senate Committee on Education, he aided in the establishment of graded schools in the east. In November 1899, he was appointed clerk of the U.S. District Court for the Eastern District of North Carolina. He supervised four deputy clerks in Wilmington, New Bern, Washington, and Elizabeth City until 1913. He was once a caucus nominee for sergeant-at-arms of the U.S. Senate, but he lost by one vote.

Grant was also a leading businessman of Goldsboro. In 1874, he purchased from W. R. Lane most of the lots of the abandoned town of Waynesborough. On this property, located on a clay hill on the Neuse River, Grant established a brick manufactory which became his chief business. He was also president of H. L. Grant Realty Company and of H. L. Grant and Son, dealers in farm and city property. In 1913, he erected the six-story, fireproof Grant Office Building in Goldsboro; it is now the educational building of the First Baptist Church.

On 2 Dec. 1868 he married Elizabeth ("Lizzie") E. Greene (b. 1844), the daughter of Hannah Elliott and John J. Greene of Putnam, Conn. The following year Grant and his bride moved to Goldsboro, where they resided on William Street. They had five children: John Hiram, a Congregational minister in Elyria, Ohio; Emelyn (Mrs. Daniel Gay of Worcester, Mass.); Mabel (Mrs. J. F. Bowles of Statesville); Minnie E. (Mrs. C. E. Wilkins of Charlotte); and Louis N. of Greenwich, Conn. A graduate of Music Vale Seminary in Salem, Conn., Lizzie Greene Grant spent much of her life supporting the music program of the First Baptist Church of Goldsboro. She was also a charter member of the Women's Missionary Union organized in Goldsboro about 1891, and for many years she was vice-president of the Neuse Atlantic Baptist Association WMU. She died on 10 Jan. 1913 in Philadelphia after an operation.

Grant's community life revolved mainly around the church. Baptized in the First Baptist Church in 1874, he became an active deacon and Sunday school superintendent. He was also a member of the Grand Army of the Republic and the Loyal Legion. A liberal benefactor in his community, Grant died in Goldsboro and was buried in Willow Dale Cemetery.

SEE: Death certificate (Wayne County Register of Deeds, Goldsboro); H. L. Grant, *G.A.R. General Meade Post No. 39 Department of Virginia and North Carolina* (1908); MS census records, Wayne County, 1870, 1880 (County Courthouse, Goldsboro); North Carolina Baptist State Convention *Minutes*, 1913; *North Carolina Biography*, vol. 5 (1919); North Carolina *Senate Journal*, 1895, 1897; Charles S. Norwood to John L. Bell, Jr., letter, 26 Jan. 1976.

JOHN L. BELL, JR.

**Grant, James, III** *(12 Dec. 1812–14 Mar. 1891)*, judge, lawyer, and railroad builder, was born in Enfield, Halifax County, the second of eight children of James and Elizabeth Whitaker Grant. He entered The University of North Carolina in 1828 and was graduated in 1831. At the university he excelled in classical languages, a proficiency he maintained throughout his life. Subsequently Grant was principal and a teacher at Raleigh Academy for three years. At this time he also read law in the office of William H. Haywood, a Raleigh lawyer and U.S. senator from North Carolina in 1843–46.

Apparently motivated by a dislike of slavery, Grant left North Carolina in 1833 and established a practice in Chicago. He was always intense, and according to legend he had a fistfight over his first client. Soon afterwards Governor Joseph Duncan appointed him prosecuting attorney for Illinois' Sixth District, which included all of northern Illinois. The position required over 3,000 miles of horseback travel each year, and Grant resigned in 1836 to devote time to his legal work in Chicago. In 1838 he moved west to a farm outside what became Davenport, Iowa, where he practiced law for the rest of his life.

In 1839, he married Sarah E. Hubbard; they had one child who died young, and she died in 1842. In 1844, Grant married Ada C. Hubbard; he lost a second child, and she died in 1846. His third wife Elizabeth Brown Leonard, of Griswold, Conn., whom he married in 1848, survived him and died in 1914. They had no children.

When Grant moved from Chicago to the Iowa Territory, he took his personal law library with him. It was the largest in the territory, and after continuous additions by Grant, became the largest private law library in the west. Now owned by the Scott County Bar Association, it was in 1964 the nucleus of the most complete law library in the state except for that at the University of Iowa and possibly Drake University. Grant, who provided a room for the Iowa Supreme Court when it sat in Davenport, permitted any judge or lawyer free access to its volumes, including those working up cases against him.

In 1841 Grant was elected to the Territorial House of Representatives, and in 1844 he was a delegate to the First Constitutional Convention. Against his protest, he was appointed Iowa prosecuting attorney in 1845. Two years later he was elected a judge of the District Court of Iowa for a five-year term but did not seek reelection. In 1851, he was also elected speaker of the Iowa House of Representatives. Although Grant was a lifelong Democrat and maintained an active interest in politics, this was his last elective office. For many years, however, he was an Iowa delegate to the Democratic presidential conventions.

Grant's greatest prominence came from railroad activities. He was the first president of the Chicago and Rock Island Railroad and, after his resignation in 1852, railroad law became his specialty. According to tradition, he had more cases before the United States Supreme Court than any lawyer up to his time; when he eventually lost one, he retired.

After the Civil War, Grant extended invitations to his and his wife's southern nephews and nieces to go to Davenport for an education; seventeen of them did so. No expense was spared, and several nephews were educated in Europe, later becoming successful in their own right. One nephew, William West Grant, who became a prominent surgeon, was the first to remove an appendix surgically; he also performed the first surgical transplant of a nerve. Another, James Grant, became the first Democratic governor of Colorado (1883–85); prominent in mining and smelting, he eventually was a founder of the American Smelting and Refining Company. The elder Grant financially backed one nephew, also named James Grant, who had studied mining and metallurgy. Their venture, a smelter in Leadville, Col., established in 1877, quickly became very successful. Grant then spent some months at the Massachusetts Institute of Technology to study the field further.

About 1880 he acquired a farm near Fresno, Calif., to use as a winter home. He died there and was buried in Davenport, Iowa.

SEE: Willis B. Dowd, *James Grant, A Model American* (1909); Newell M. Grant, "James Grant" ([typescript] North Carolina Collection, University of North Carolina, Chapel Hill); W. W. Grant, *Such Is Life* (1951).

NEWELL M. GRANT

**Grant, John Gaston** *(1 Jan. 1858–21 June 1923)*, farmer and congressman, was born in Edneyville Township, rural Henderson County, the son of William C. and Elizabeth Grant. He attended local schools for a few months and afterwards was self-educated. From his early years he was engaged in farming in Henderson County, where he also worked as a blacksmith. He was a successful Republican candidate for the North Carolina House of Representatives but served only one term (1889–91), declining renomination. One year later he was elected sheriff of Henderson County and served from 1892 until 1896. He would not accept nomination for another term. Upon the termination of his duties as sheriff he was a presidential elector on the Republican ticket that put William McKinley in the White House and elected Garret A. Hobart vice-president. Grant was elected in 1908 from the Tenth North Carolina District to the United States House of Representatives and served from 1909 to 1911; he was unsuccessful in his bid for reelection. Resuming his agricultural pursuits in his native county, he was not a candidate for public office again.

Grant and his wife, Zura Edney, whom he married on 30 Mar. 1876, were the parents of four children: sons V. Echols and L. Grant, and daughters Alda and Elizabeth. He was buried in Oakdale Cemetery, Hendersonville.

SEE: *Asheville Citizen*, 22 June 1923; *Biog. Dir. Am. Cong.* (1961); *Biographical Sketches of the Members and Officers of the General Assembly of North Carolina, Session 1889* (1889); John L. Cheney, Jr., ed., *North Carolina Government, 1585–1974* (1975); *North Carolina Manual, 1911* (1911); *Who Was Who in America*, vol. 4 (1968).

C. SYLVESTER GREEN

**Graves, Calvin** *(3 Jan. 1804–11 Feb. 1877)*, legislator, lawyer, and farmer, was born in Caswell County near Yanceyville. He was a direct seventh generation descendant of Captain Thomas Graves who arrived in Virginia from London in 1608, settled on the James River, and represented Smythe's Hundred in the Virginia House of Burgesses of 1619, the first representative legislature convened in America. His grandfather, John Graves, was the first of the family to move to North Carolina, settling in Caswell County near Country Line Creek in 1770 and serving his new state in the General Assembly and the constitutional conventions of 1788 and 1789, called to consider the ratification of the Federal Constitution. His father, Azariah Graves, was general of the Sixteenth Brigade, Third Division, of the North Carolina militia during the Revolutionary War and, for seven terms, represented Caswell County in the state senate. Calvin Graves's mother was Elizabeth Williams, daughter of Colonel John Williams, also a prominent Revolutionary War leader.

After receiving his early education at Bingham Academy near Hillsborough and other schools, Graves entered The University of North Carolina in 1823 and remained one year before withdrawing to study law under his brother-in-law, Judge Thomas Settle. He remained there a year before enrolling in the law school conducted by Judge Leonard Henderson. Graves was admitted to the North Carolina bar in 1827 at age twenty-three and began to practice in 1828.

With a Jeffersonian political heritage behind him, it is not surprising that Calvin emerged as a staunch Jacksonian Democrat. He entered political life as a delegate from Caswell County to the North Carolina Constitutional Convention of 1835, held in Raleigh. In this convention he voted against any changes in the religious tests which then prevented Roman Catholics from holding public office. Graves also opposed the continued enfranchisement of the free Negroes living in the state. He supported the biennial sessions of the General Assembly and direct election of the governor by the voters for a two-year term. He also worked hard for the adoption of the proposed constitutional amendments in his home county, which were approved by a three-to-one majority.

Continuing with his law practice, Graves was first elected to the legislature as a member of the house from Caswell County in 1840, that being the first General Assembly to meet in the newly completed state capitol. He was reelected to the house and remained there through the 1844–45 session. In 1846, he was elected to the state senate where he served for two terms. As a member of the house, his leadership qualities were recognized early by his colleagues, who chose him as speaker in 1842, in only his second term. Whig control prevented his reelection as speaker during the next session. While running for the senate in 1846, he was apparently seriously considered by some members of the Democratic party leadership as a possible nominee for governor; however, he effectively removed his name from consideration as not being the "proper person" for the times. Upon his election to the senate, he was chosen as speaker pro tempore and delivered one of the more influential speeches of the session, opposing an attempt by the Whigs to engineer a mid-decade redistricting of the state for what was considered by the Democrats as political expediency. His reasoning is said to have convinced enough Whigs to change their minds so that the bill failed. In 1848, Graves was elected speaker of the senate after a week-long voting marathon caused by the successive tie votes of a deadlocked chamber. It was finally broken by a compromise that reflected the confidence in which he was held by Whigs and Democrats alike.

It was in this 1848–49 session that Calvin Graves fully revealed his qualities of statesmanship and played the part for which he is best remembered. Plagued from its very beginning by conflicting geographic features and political boundaries, North Carolina had found it difficult to reconcile the resulting economic differences—hence, the divergent political interests between the eastern and western sections of the state. With the advent of canals, and later railroads, some foresaw a means of tying the state together both economically and politically. By 1848, the Wilmington and Weldon Railroad provided the east with a north-south line to out-of-state markets, and the west wanted its own access to northern markets by the proposed Danville-Charlotte link. Some state leaders believed that the time had come to unify the state with an east-west line, the proposed North Carolina Railroad. As speaker of the senate, Calvin Graves, who served a western county through which the Danville-Charlotte link would pass, was faced with the same tie vote that had earlier blocked his election as speaker. Believing that the state's only chance for real growth and development lay in economic unity, he unhesitatingly cast his tie-breaking vote for the North Carolina Railroad, which eventually connected Raleigh, Graham, Greensboro, Salisbury, and Charlotte, with a later extension to Asheville. In voting for this act he was aware that he was ensuring the future welfare of the entire state, but at a cost of personal political oblivion. He was never again elected to political office. However, some friends apparently urged him to run for Congress in the mid-1850s, whereas others petitioned him to run for the General Assembly in 1864, but he always declined.

After the 1848–49 session adjourned, Graves joined former Governor John M. Morehead, Judge Romulus M. Saunders, and John A. Gilmer in touring the state to make a public appeal for raising the private capital required to match the state appropriated funds that would make the North Carolina Railroad a reality. As a result Governor Charles Manly, North Carolina's last Whig governor, appointed Graves a commissioner on the Board of Internal Improvements in 1849; he was reappointed to the post by Democratic Governor David S. Reid and served until 1854.

Graves also pursued other interests during these early, postlegislative years. In 1844 he was appointed a trustee of The University of North Carolina and served until 1868, when the Radical Republicans took control of the government. During the 1848–49 legislative session, he supported Dorothea Dix's plea for an insane asylum and was involved for some years thereafter in helping to ensure its establishment.

In 1837 he joined the Trinity Baptist Church near his home and throughout his life remained a staunch supporter of his church and his faith. His advice was sought by such men as Dr. Samuel Wait and Elder Thomas Meredith, who visited him often as they and others led the struggle to establish Wake Forest College and the Baptist paper, the *Biblical Recorder*. In 1844 he was elected a trustee of Wake Forest College and served until 1862. When presiding as moderator of the Beulah Baptist Association in 1857, he pledged $500 to the endowment of Wake Forest when the institution was making its first real effort in the field to create such a fund. He taught Sunday school and was very active in his home church, writing at one point that he was conducting a Sunday school class for fifty Negroes.

In the early 1850s Graves retired from his law practice and began devoting more and more of his time to managing his farms, the use of which he had been given by his father and which he inherited upon his death. By 1856, he complained that his eyes were failing him and that, after a day's work overseeing his farms, he no longer had the strength or the desire to write letters or perform his record-keeping chores. The death of his wife Elizabeth in 1858, after a two-year illness, virtually marks the end of his active participation in public affairs. Early in 1859 he remarried and continued to live quietly on his farm until his health gradually declined in the early to mid-1870s. He died at the age of seventy-three at his home, Locust Hill, about ten miles west of Yanceyville, Caswell County. His grave is located in a family graveyard about two miles southwest of his home.

Graves has been characterized as calm, stable, and deliberate in temperament, never in a hurry, very slow to anger and thorough in all endeavors. He is said to have looked with charity upon all his fellow men. His letters abound with moral counsel and religious blessings for his relatives, and with prayers for the sustenance of his friends. He was well known as a sound source of advice, political and otherwise; his letters to political leaders reflect detailed analyses of current events.

In 1830 Graves married Elizabeth Lea, daughter of John C. Lea, by whom he had four children: John Williams, a graduate of The University of North Carolina in 1854, captain in the Confederate Army, and lawyer, who died in 1872 from an illness in Salt Lake City where he was a member of the bar; George, who married and seems to have lived near his father and helped manage the farms; and two daughters, Betty and Caroline, both educated at female academies. His second wife was Mary Wilson Lea, widow of William Lea who died in 1856, and niece of his first wife. There were no children by this marriage. A portrait of Calvin Graves is published in John Livingston's *Portraits of Eminent Americans Now Living, 1853–1854*. Graves indicated that the daguerreotype for this engraving was made in New York about 1851 or 1852 especially for Livingston's book.

SEE: Samuel A. Ashe, ed., *Biographical History of North Carolina*, vol. 2 (1905); C. J. Bailey, *North Carolina Baptist Almanac for the Year 1882* (1881); Daniel Moreau Barringer Papers, Charles Iverson Graves Papers, Graves Papers, Thomas Settle Papers (Southern Historical Collection, University of North Carolina, Chapel Hill); Kemp P. Battle, *History of the University of North Carolina*, vol. 1 (1907); *Biblical Recorder*, 15, 22, 29 Apr., 6 June 1891; John L. Cheney, Jr., ed., *North Carolina Government, 1585–1974* (1975); Daniel L. Grant, *Alumni History of the University of North Carolina* (1924); Calvin Graves Papers, David S. Reid Papers (North Carolina State Archives, Raleigh); J. G. deR. Hamilton, *The Papers of Thomas Ruffin*, vol. 2 (1918); Maloy A. Huggins, *A History of the North Carolina Baptists, 1727–1932* (1957); John Livingston, *Portraits of Eminent Americans Now Living, 1853–1854* (1854); North Carolina Senate *Journal* (1848); George W. Paschal, *History of Wake Forest College*, vol. 3 (1943); *Proceedings and Debates of the Convention of North Carolina Called to Amend the Constitution of the State* (1836); M. N. Stannard, *The Story of Virginia's First Century* (1928); John H. Wheeler, *Reminiscences and Memoirs of North Carolina* (1884).

JOHN L. HUMBER

**Graves, Ernest** *(27 Mar. 1880–9 June 1953)*, army engineer, was born in Chapel Hill, the son of Ralph Henry and Julia Charlotte Hooper Graves. His father, a professor of mathematics at the University of North Carolina, died in 1889, leaving his wife with four children to raise. Julia Graves established a boardinghouse on the site of the present Carolina Inn and provided good food for many students until her children were grown and educated. In addition to Ernest, Ralph was a journalist in New York; Louis, the editor of the *Chapel Hill Weekly*; and Mary Graves Rees, a portrait painter.

The Graves and Hooper families were notable in North Carolina. William Taylor, an ancestor of Ernest's father, was the first steward of The University of North Carolina at its opening in 1795. Ernest's grandfather was graduated from the university in 1836. His father attended the university in 1867, but received his degree from the University of Virginia. In 1875, Ralph Henry Graves returned to Chapel Hill as professor of engineering at the newly reopened university. Ernest's grandfather and great-grandfather on his mother's side were both professors at the university. His great-grandfather, William Hooper, also was president of Wake Forest College in the 1840s. Hooper was buried with his mother and stepfather, Joseph Caldwell, first president of The University of North Carolina, at the foot of the Caldwell monument on the campus. An earlier ancestor, William Hooper, was one of the three signers of the Declaration of Independence for North Carolina.

Ernest Graves attended the Chapel Hill schools and studied a year at the Raleigh Male Academy. In 1896, at age sixteen, he entered The University of North Carolina where he became a member of Phi Beta Kappa and an outstanding athlete. As fullback of the football team, he scored a total of 131 points and in 1898 was a member of an undefeated, untied team. He also excelled as catcher on the baseball team, serving as captain in 1900. Graves was graduated from the university in 1900 and received an M.A. in 1901. Summer work as a surveyor in western North Carolina convinced him that his best opportunity for a career would be with the U.S. Army Corps of Engineers. He won a competitive appointment to the Military Academy at West Point, entering in July 1901. In 1905 "Pot," his nickname at the academy, was graduated second in a class of 114, though better known at West Point were his athletic achievements. After shifting from fullback to tackle on the football team, he became one of the best linemen of his times. The Army teams on which he played beat Navy teams four years straight, including a 40-5 victory in 1903. In 1904, Army achieved its first victory over the powerful Yale team. Graves, injured in that game, resigned the captaincy of the team and finished the season as coach. At the academy he also was a catcher and first baseman on the baseball team.

In 1905, Graves received the Army Athletic Association Trophy, awarded annually to the individual "who rendered the most valuable service to intercollegiate athletics during his career as a cadet." Afterwards West Point continued to call on him as a football coach. He returned in 1906, 1907, 1912–15 (head coach in 1915), and 1919–20. In 1918, during World War I, he coached at Harvard by executive order of President Theodore Roosevelt; his team beat Yale. His book, *The Line Man's Bible: A Football Textbook of Detailed Instruction* (1921), is still used by coaches.

After graduation, Graves began his engineering career with initial assignments to the Third Engineers at Fort Leavenworth and later at Fort Riley. Serving with both the Second and Third Engineers, he was posted to Cuba in 1907 in the Army of the Cuban Pacification. After a year in Washington as a student at the Engineer School at Washington Barracks (now Fort Lesley J. MacNair) he was ordered to the Philippines to build the first permanent fortifications on Corregidor, along with dwellings, store houses, a narrow gauge railroad, and a power house. From December 1911 to April 1913 Graves was engaged in river and harbor work in Dallas, Tex. Promoted to captain, he became district engineer at Vicksburg, Miss., in 1913. In February 1914, he became a company commander in the Second Engineers at Texas City. When a tidal wave hit Galveston, Tex., the following year, Graves managed to assemble his men, attach them all by rope, and lead them to safety in a warehouse.

In 1915 Graves was assigned to the Second Engineers in San Antonio, Tex; this group was charged with building and maintaining a road for truck convoys supplying General John J. Pershing on the punitive expedition against Pancho Villa in Mexico in 1916. Graves's son described his father's assignment as follows: "Supply by truck was new, as was the construction of military roads to sustain truck traffic. Pot commanded the forward company, which in the course of constructing the road marched 250 miles on half rations into the barren wilderness of Mexico, with no vehicles except a mess wagon and a tool wagon, both drawn by mules. The road was built and maintained with hand tools and a few mule drawn scrapers. Pot's axiom then, so often repeated since, was 'get the water off and the rock on.' "

Pershing included Graves on his AEF staff, which sailed to France on the *Baltic* in June 1917. As section engineer at Gievres, Bordeaux, Neufchateau, and St. Nazaire, Graves tackled major depot, camp, rail, port, and airfield construction; for this work he earned the Distinguished Service Medal and promotion to colonel (a recommended promotion to brigadier general was stopped by the armistice).

After serving with the Liquidation Committee in Coblenz, Germany, he returned to the United States. While assigned to duty in the Office of Engineers, he wrote several articles and a pamphlet entitled *Construction in War*, still one of the finest papers written on the subject. Graves commanded the Second Engineers at San Antonio, Tex., during 1920 and 1921 and coached football at West Point in the fall of 1919 and 1920. Deafness led to his retirement from the army in 1921. That fall he coached football at Princeton and for several years thereafter he was a consultant to the army.

At the urging of General Edgar Jadwin, chief of the Army Engineers, Graves returned to active duty in 1927. Following the disastrous floods of the Mississippi in the same year, he played a leading part in the preparation of a plan adopted by Congress for flood control of the lower Mississippi River—the so-called Jadwin Plan or Mississippi Flood Control Act of 1928. On 26 June 1928 he was appointed a member of the Mississippi River Commission and continued to be active in the group until his death. Among his contributions to the flood control plans were his advocacy of fuseplug levees and the utilization of natural storage areas instead of cutoffs.

In 1929, Graves was appointed to the Interoceanic Canal Board, which studied the possibility of constructing a waterway across Nicaragua. When its report was completed in 1931, he was chairman of the board.

Seven successive chiefs of engineers over a twenty-five-year period persuaded Graves to remain on active duty. In 1939, he was honored by a special act of Congress: "An act to give proper recognition to the distinguished service of Colonel Ernest Graves." Before he retired on 29 Feb. 1952 because of deteriorating health, he was the oldest officer on active duty. In May 1953 he was promoted to brigadier general on the retired list. He died the following month at Walter Reed Hospital and was buried in Arlington Cemetery.

On 8 June 1923 Graves married Lucy Birnie Horgan (12 Nov. 1881–5 Apr. 1968), a widow. Her father, Rogers Birnie, had a distinguished military career after graduating from West Point in 1872 at the top of his class. Her first marriage to Harry Horgan of the *New York Times* ended with his death in 1918; one son, R. Birnie Horgan, survived. Ernest and Lucy Graves also had one son, Ernest, Jr. (b. 6 July 1924), who, like his father, was a graduate of West Point and a general in the U.S. Army Corps of Engineers.

Among Graves's published writings are the following: "The Mental Processes of the Military and Non Military Mind as Applied to the Design of Army Wagons," "The Methods of Construction in War," "Soldiers First?" and "Through Military Channels," *The Military Engineer* 12 (1920); *Construction in War, Lessons Taught by the World War, 1917–1918*, no. 64, Occasional Papers, The Engineer School, U.S. Army; and "The Nicaraguan Canal," *The Military Engineer* 12 (1929).

SEE: *Assembly* 13 (July 1954); George W. Cullum, ed., *Biographical Register of the Officer and Graduates of the United States Military Academy at West Point* (1920); Brigadier General Harley B. Ferguson, "Flood Control of the Mississippi River" (MS, Southern Historical Collection, University of North Carolina, Chapel Hill); Graves family papers (in possession of General and Mrs. Ernest Graves, Jr., Arlington, Va.,); Louis and Mildred Graves Papers (Southern Historical Collection, University of North Carolina, Chapel Hill); Bradley Holdeen, *Pershing's Mission in Mexico* (1960); *New York Times*, 12 June 1953; Frank E. Vandiver, *Black Jack: The Life and Times of John J. Pershing* (1977); *Washington Post*, 11 June 1953.

MARTHA B. CALDWELL

**Graves, Henry Lee (Lea)** *(22 Feb. 1813–4 Nov. 1881)*, Baptist minister, college president, and teacher, was born in Yanceyville, the son of Thomas and Mary Lee Bennett Graves. He was graduated from The University of North Carolina in 1835. While at the university he was "born again" and baptized by the Reverend Dr. William Hooper. He also was a member of the Dialectic Literary Society, serving as president in November and December 1834. From August 1835 to December 1837, he was employed as a tutor by Wake Forest Institute, where he taught geometry and classical languages. He was the only native North Carolinian teaching at Wake Forest in that period. In November 1837, he was licensed to preach and ordained by the Wake Forest Baptist Church.

After leaving Wake Forest, he went to Cave Spring, Ga., where he established a manual labor school and served as principal for three years. During 1840–41 he attended Hamilton (N.Y.) Theological Seminary, as a member of the seminary class of 1842. Although he took a leave of absence in December 1841, Graves was credited with having completed the course. Returning to Georgia, he became the principal of a school in Covington. In 1845, he was a delegate from Georgia to the organizational meeting of the Southern Baptist Convention held in Augusta, Ga., in May. The following year he was elected first president of Baylor University, a Baptist institution founded in 1845 at Independence, Tex. He served as president from 4 Feb. 1847 to 13 June 1851, when he resigned because of ill health. He and his brother gave the university its first large stone building, which was called Graves Hall.

Graves returned to the active ministry in 1851 and served until 1859, when he became president of Fairfield (Tex.) Female College, a post he held until 1870. From 1871 to 1872 he was president of Baylor Female College at Independence. He then became superintendent of public schools at Brenham, Tex. He was also pastor of Baptist churches at Independence, Eagle Lake, Columbus, Schulenburg, Gonzales, and Brenham, Tex.; at various times, operated a ranch; and was part owner of drug stores in Bryan and Brenham.

In 1848 Graves was elected first president of the Texas Baptist State Convention, a position he held for sixteen years. He also was president of the Baptist Education Society from 1855 to 1858. In 1849, he was initiated into Masonic Lodge Milam No. 11 at Independence and was later raised a master mason. The author of several religious books including *What Baptists Believe, Universal Salvation*, and *Religion in the Family*, Graves held an M.A. degree from The University of North Carolina (1846) and honorary degrees of LL.D. and D.D.

On 3 Feb. 1836, at Yanceyville, he married Rebecca Williams Graves (b. 3 Oct. 1812 in Caswell County), daughter of General Azariah and Elizabeth Williams Graves, the latter his father's first cousin. They had six children: Mary Anna (m. James Isaac Kirksey), Bettie Williams (m. Theodoric G. Jones), Charles Henry, Ophelia Florine (m. William Watson Williams), Henry

Lee, and Willie Ruby (m. Thomas Jefferson White, Jr.). Mrs. Graves died on 18 Nov. 1865 in Fairfield and was buried in Fairfield Cemetery. On 9 July 1872, Graves married Mrs. Myra Crumpler, the daughter of John C. Lusk, at Brenham, Tex. He died at Brenham and was buried there.

SEE: Colgate University, *General Catalogue* (1937); Faculty minutes, 29 Oct. 1840, 2 Dec. 1841 (Colgate University Archives, Hamilton, N.Y.); Louise Graves, comp., *Graves: Twelve Generations, Some Descendants and Kin* (1977); Minutes of the Dialectic Society, vol. 29 (University Archives, Library, University of North Carolina, Chapel Hill); *Nat. Cyc. Am. Biog.*, vol. 26 (1937); George W. Paschal, *History of Wake Forest College*, vol. 1 (1935); Henry Trantham, *The Diamond Jubilee, A Record of the Seventy-Fifth Anniversary of the Founding of Baylor University, 1845–1920* (1921); *University of North Carolina at Chapel Hill Alumni Directory, Edition of 1975* (1976).

SUZANNE S. LEVY

**Graves, Jesse Dickens** *(3 May 1819–19 Sept. 1884)*, physician and artist, was born in Granville County, the son of Henry Lewis Graves and his wife, Mary Brown Dickens. He was a student at The University of North Carolina in 1837–38, but soon determined to study art in France. On 11 Feb. 1839 he sailed for Paris. His first few days there, he later recalled, almost "cured" him of a desire to study under French artists. Help came in an unusual way, however. Sitting by an open window one day, he saw a tame dove pitch on the ledge. He picked up the bird and tied a note in English around its neck explaining who he was and the difficulty he was having with the language. A knock at his door soon afterwards announced the presence of the dove's owner. A charming English woman spoke to young Graves first in French and then in English. She then taught him enough French to enable him to begin making his way around the city, and his old ambition returned. He was soon engrossed in the study of art and music. After more than seven and a half years in Paris, Graves sailed for home on 2 Sept. 1846. Among his possessions were a number of musical instruments and a large quantity of artist's supplies and equipment, to say nothing of the works he had produced during his stay. In the North Atlantic the ship encountered heavy seas, and much of his equipment was either washed overboard or thrown over purposely to lighten the ship. Some of the surviving examples of his art were damaged by water.

When the ship docked in New York, Graves, then a mature man of twenty-seven, was so distressed at his loss that he decided to remain in the city and study medicine. In due time he returned to North Carolina where his parents were then living in Moore County. Dr. Graves began to practice medicine in the Union Church community, about five miles east of Carthage, the county seat, on the Salem to Cross Creek plank road. In a few years he moved to Moffitt's Mill in adjoining Randolph County. There, on 25 Mar. 1854, he married Mary E. Foust whose cousin, Dr. Julius Foust, later was president of the State Normal and Industrial School for Girls in Greensboro (now the University of North Carolina at Greensboro). Several times during the Civil War Graves attempted to join the army, but his services at home were deemed too great for him to be accepted.

The Graves home after the war was at Kemp Mills in the southern part of Randolph County. Graves and his wife were the parents of George H. (1856), John Calvin (1858), Charles Howell (1861), Thomas S. (1863), Ralph Lewis (1865), Robert Newton (1868), and Jesse Alexander (1871). After his death at the age of sixty-five, Graves was buried in the cemetery of the Concord Methodist Church at Coleridge.

About 1930 one of Graves's sons gave The University of North Carolina a number of his father's medical books together with a large self-portrait painted when Graves was a young artist, in 1848. It now hangs in the North Carolina Collection of the university library. An oil painting of Graves's hands, which he also did as a young man, is in the possession of descendants. In the 1950s a granddaughter gave the North Carolina Collection examples of some of the stone engravings that Graves had done in Paris depicting children with whom he had made friends during his stay there.

SEE: Ashboro *Courier-Tribune*, 18 Dec. 1958; Daniel L. Grant, *Alumni History of the University of North Carolina* (1924); Graves family records (in possession of Mrs. Jessie G. Shoffner, Greensboro); Raleigh *News and Observer*, 24 Apr. 1960.

WILLIAM S. POWELL

**Graves, Louis** *(6 Aug. 1883–23 Jan. 1965)*, newspaper editor, was born in Chapel Hill, the son of Ralph Henry Graves (1851–89) and Julia Charlotte Hooper Graves (1856–1944). On both sides of the family the ties with The University of North Carolina and with the state of North Carolina were very strong. Louis's father taught at the university from 1875 until his death in 1889; his grandfather was a member of the class of 1836; and an earlier ancestor was the first steward of the university at its opening in 1795. On his mother's side, Louis's grandfather and great-grandfather were professors at the university. The great-grandfather, William Hooper, also served as president of Wake Forest College; he was buried with his mother and stepfather, Joseph Caldwell, first president of The University of North Carolina, at the foot of the Caldwell monument on the campus. An earlier William Hooper was one of the three signers of the Declaration of Independence for North Carolina.

After his father's early death, Louis's mother established a boarding house on the site of the present Carolina Inn and maintained it until her four surviving children were grown and educated. In addition to Louis, Ralph was a journalist in New York; Ernest, an army engineer; and Mary Graves Rees, a portrait painter. Louis was educated in Chapel Hill and at the Bingham School in Asheville. Entering The University of North Carolina, he became a football and tennis star, as well as a member of Zeta Psi fraternity and of Phi Beta Kappa. He was graduated in 1902, the youngest member of his class. Graves's football exploits as a halfback were impressive, and his teams lost only four games in three years. The 1900 team, on which his brother Ernest also played, beat Tennessee, and, two days later, Vanderbilt; the following day it tied the University of the South. In 1901, Graves ran the opening kickoff back 90 yards in the game with North Carolina A and M, and Carolina went on to win 30-0. In 1902, Graves, a senior, led the team in points scored: 42, of which 37 came from kicking.

After his graduation in 1903, Graves joined his brother Ralph in New York on the staff of the *New York Times* until 1906. For several years he was with Ivy Lee's public relations firm and did free-lance writing. About 1913 he became active in New York city government, joining the Mitchell-McAneny administration. He served as an assistant to the president of the Borough of Manhattan and the Board of Aldermen. In 1916, Graves was appointed a member of the Mayor's Committee on National Defense; subsequently he wrote the committee's report, entitled "The Mobilization of the National Guard, Its Economic and Military Aspect." In 1917, he became a captain in Company I, 324th Infantry, 81st Division. He served in France and with the army of occupation in Coblenz, Germany, until 1919. In unpublished memoirs, Graves wrote that the notion of returning to Chapel Hill occurred to him in the winter of 1919. He was then with the Press Section, GHQ, in Coblenz with little to do except take walks and talk to colleagues. The city government job was gone and the free-lance writing he had done did not pin him down to a New York location. Moreover, he was still a bachelor with no fixed base.

In 1921, Graves accepted a position as the first professor of journalism at The University of North Carolina and as head of the university's news bureau. On 2 Mar. 1923, however, the first issue of Graves's newspaper, the *Chapel Hill Weekly*, was published. With his newspaper established, Graves resigned from the university in 1924 to serve as editor and proprietor until 1954, when he became contributing editor.

The *Chapel Hill Weekly* became a noted example of a small-town newspaper and of personal journalism. It contributed significantly to the gracious life of Chapel Hill and, through the editorials and the "Chapel Hill Chaff" columns, Graves made important and penetrating comments on many topics. In addition, he contributed often to *Atlantic Monthly*, *Saturday Evening Post*, *American Review of Reviews*, *American Magazine*, *Century Magazine*, *New York Times Magazine*, *Harper's Weekly*, *Leslie's Weekly*, *Metropolitan*, *Ladies Home Journal*, *The New Republic*, *Harper's Monthly Magazine*, *World's Work*, and other magazines. His writings also appeared in various newspapers and in volumes of collected essays.

In June 1921, Graves married Mildred Moses. "Mim," as she was called, served as a full-time volunteer for the *Weekly* and was largely responsible for "Neighborhood Notes." The couple lived in a secluded house on the corner of Hooper and Battle lanes. The book- and paper-laden living room looked out on a delightful small garden with birds flocking around the St. Francis of Assisi, a sculpture by Arnold Borden. The brick in the wall that surrounded the house was made before 1800 in a kiln located about where Wilson Library now stands. The Hillsborough flagstones in their walk inspired the state geologist to recommend them to Duke University as building material for its initial buildings.

A favorite pastime of Louis Graves was tennis. While a student at The University of North Carolina, he won championships in both singles and doubles. He was on the AEF team in 1919, touring Europe and England, and became a lifetime member of the West Side Tennis Club in New York. In Chapel Hill he played frequently as one of a regular foursome.

In the spring after his death at age eighty-two, Graves was buried in the old Chapel Hill Cemetery.

SEE: *Chapel Hill Weekly*, 27 Jan., 10 Feb. 1965; Papers of Eugene Cunningham Branson, Lenoir Chambers, Oscar J. Coffin, Frank Porter Graham, Louis and Mildred Graves, James King Hall, John J. Parker, and Henry M. Wagstaff (Southern Historical Collection, University of North Carolina, Chapel Hill); University of North Carolina *Alumni Review* 41 (April 1953), *Carolina Magazine* 66 (November 1936), and *New Carolina Magazine* 51 (March 1921).

MARTHA B. CALDWELL

**Graves, Ralph Henry** *(9 Mar. 1817–10 May 1876)*, educator, was born in Granville County, the second son of Henry Lewis and Mary Brown Dickens Graves. His mother was the granddaughter of Colonel Robert Dickens, a soldier in the Revolutionary War. Members of the Graves family migrated to North Carolina from Virginia; the family homestead, Belmont, was located near the Virginia line in the Nut Bush and Shiloh Church area. Henry Lewis Graves was a founder and trustee of the Shiloh Classical School, Granville County, where his son Ralph Henry received much of his preparatory education under the instruction of Robert Tinnin, who was hired in January 1827. Ralph's grandfather, Elijah Graves, had opened the Pleasant Grove Academy in 1812 near Bullock's store in Pleasant Grove. Thus, when Ralph Henry Graves was awarded the A.B. degree from The University of North Carolina in 1836 and began to tutor mathematics students in 1837, he was following a family line of educators. He received an M.A. degree from the university in 1839 and continued tutoring until 1843.

Graves began his teaching career at the Caldwell Institute, Guilford County, as early as 1844. In the same year he helped organize the Alumni Association of The University of North Carolina and became the treasurer and librarian. In 1845 he moved with the Caldwell Institute to the old Hillsborough Academy site, remaining there until it closed in 1850. The Hillsborough Academy reopened in 1852, and Graves became its principal the following year. In 1854 he served on the academy examining committee, which was appointed by the school board to hold examinations for teachers three times a year; those who passed were granted certificates to teach for one year.

Just before the Civil War, Graves purchased Belmont, the family homestead, where he opened a boys' school and taught until 1866. That year he moved to Williamsboro in what is now Vance County. In 1869, he moved again—to Graham in Alamance County. Two years later he became affiliated with James H. Horner in an academy at Oxford. In 1874, the Horner-Graves school was moved to the old Hillsborough Military Academy site (founded in 1859 by Charles C. Tew) at the urging of P. C. Cameron, who purchased the buildings in 1872. The Horner-Graves partnership was dissolved in 1875, but Graves continued to run the school until his death.

Politically Graves was a Whig. He was said to have been an avid supporter of both Henry Clay and Willie Person Mangum.

In 1849 Graves was married in Orange County to Emma Taylor, the daughter of John and Tempe Benton Taylor of Hillsborough. Emma's father was clerk of the superior court from 1800 to 1845. When he died in 1849, she inherited his house on lot 18 on the corner of King Street; it had been deeded to him in 1800 by her maternal grandfather, Samuel Benton of Oxford. In the 1880s the house became a part of the Occoneechee Hotel complex. Ralph and Emma Graves reared two children. Their son, Ralph, Jr. (b. 1 Apr 1851), was also a graduate of The University of North Carolina where he became a professor of engineering and related subjects, teaching from 1875 until his death in 1889. Their daughter, Emma, was the first wife of Edwin A. Alderman, a president of the university. Ralph, Jr.'s son, Ralph Henry Graves III, was the city editor (1915–17) and Sunday editor (1917–23) of the *New York Times*. In 1923 he joined the syndicate of Doubleday, Doran and Company as editor, remaining in that position until he became editor of his own syndicate in 1936.

Ralph Henry and Emma Taylor Graves were buried in the Taylor-Graves plot near the central walkway in the old town cemetery, Hillsborough.

SEE: Allen Alexander and Pauline O. Lloyd, *History of the Town of Hillsborough, 1754–1966* (1966); Ruth Blackwelder, *The Age of Orange* (1961); Charles L. Coon, *North Carolina Schools and Academies, 1790–1840* (1915); Josephus Daniels, *Tar Heel Editor* (1939); Daniel L. Grant, *Alumni History of the University of North Carolina* (1924); Frank Nash, "Ralph Henry Graves, Sr." (Manuscript Department, Library, Duke University, Durham); Henry T. Shanks, *The Papers of Willie Person Mangum*, vol. 4 (1954); Ruth H. Shields, *Abstracts of Wills Recorded in Orange County, N.C., 1752–1800* and *1800–1850* (1957–58); *Who Was Who In America*, vol. 1 (1950); G. T. Winston, "In Memoriam: A Sketch of the Life and Character of Professor R. H. Graves," *University of North Carolina Magazine* 9 (1899).

MILDRED MARTIN CROW

**Graves, Ralph Henry, III** *(11 July 1878–1 Dec. 1939)*, newspaper editor, was the son of Ralph Henry and Julia Charlotte Hooper Graves. On his father's side, an ancestor, William Taylor, was the first steward of The University of North Carolina at its opening in 1795. Ralph's grandfather, the first Ralph Henry (1817–76), was graduated from the university in 1836 and became a teacher at preparatory schools. He was at the Caldwell Institute in Hillsborough when his son, Ralph, Jr., was born in 1851. The second Ralph Henry attended the university in 1867, but received a B.S. degree in civil and mechanical engineering from the University of Virginia in 1871. After teaching for a few years at what is now Virginia Polytechnic Institute and State University, he joined (1875) the faculty of the newly reopened University of North Carolina as professor of mathematics.

Graves's mother was the daughter of John deBerniere Hooper, professor of Greek at the university. William Hooper, her grandfather, taught ancient languages at the university and was later president of Wake Forest College in the 1840s. About 1800 Hooper's mother married Joseph Caldwell, first president of The University of North Carolina. Caldwell, his wife, and stepson were buried at the foot of the Caldwell monument on the campus of the university. Two generations earlier, another William Hooper was one of the three signers of the Declaration of Independence for North Carolina.

Julia Hooper Graves was born in Warren County, lived in Fayetteville and Wilson, and moved with her parents to Chapel Hill in 1875. There she met and, on 20 June 1877, married Ralph Henry Graves, Jr. The couple had five children, but a baby son died soon after his father in 1889. The widow established a popular boarding house where the Carolina Inn now stands and maintained it until her four children were grown and educated. In addition to Ralph, newspaper editor and the subject of this biography, Ernest was a military engineer; Louis, a newspaper editor; and Mary Graves Rees, a portrait painter.

Ralph Henry Graves III received an A.B. degree, magna cum laude, from The University of North Carolina in 1897 and a master's degree the following year. He spent two years as a librarian at the university before leaving North Carolina in 1899 to begin a career in journalism in New York. In the early years he worked as a reporter for both the *New York Times* and the *New York Evening Post*; from 1899 to 1904 he was a reporter for the *Times*; from 1904 to 1906, assistant city editor for the *Post*; from 1906 to 1907, assistant city editor for the *Times*; and from 1907 to 1912, city editor for the *Post*. In 1912 he returned to the *Times* as pictorial news editor, and in 1915 he became city editor. In 1917 he was appointed Sunday editor, a position he held until 1923. Between September 1918 and January 1919 Graves took a leave of absence from the *Times* to be Washington editor of the *Red Cross Magazine*. In 1923, he joined the syndicate of Doubleday, Doran and Company in Garden City, N.Y. He established his own syndicate in 1936 to market news features and fiction. Graves also served as managing editor of *World's Work* (1924–25) and of *Personality Magazine* (1927–28). On several occasions he taught feature writing in the school of journalism at Columbia University.

Graves was a resourceful reporter. Very early in his career, he took a chartered tugboat close to a major fire that cost several hundred lives and destroyed a North German Lloyd steamer and the firm's piers in the Hudson River, scooping other reporters who remained on shore. His coverage of the Titanic disaster and the Charles Evans Hughes investigation of insurance scandals added to his reputation. The *Times* assigned him to direct the coverage of the national political conventions in presidential election years, when Graves apparently established much of the current journalistic procedures for convention coverage.

On a European trip in the 1920s, he signed a contract with Mme. Ferdinand Foch to publish her husband's memoirs and quickly sold the serial rights to the Hearst newspapers. On another trip he secured for the *Times* the memoirs of the German Kaiser, Wilhelm II. Graves also syndicated the memoirs of Marshall Joffre and Theodore Roosevelt's aide, Archie Butt. He served as agent for General Hugh Johnson, and he syndicated the early volumes of Ray Stannard Baker's biography of Woodrow Wilson.

In these later years Graves found time to do some writing on his own. In 1934, he wrote a book entitled *The Triumph of an Idea: The Story of Henry Ford*. Under the pseudonym George Grey, he also published *Ten Days: A Crisis in American History*.

Graves died suddenly in New York and was buried in the old Chapel Hill Cemetery. He was survived by his wife, Frances ("Faye") Morgan Griffin (1877–1965), formerly of York, S.C., and Charlotte, N.C., whom he had married on 20 Jan. 1906 in New York. They had no children. Graves was a member of the Zeta Psi fraternity and the Century Club, the Coffee House and the Players in New York.

SEE: *Carolina Magazine* 53 (February 1923); *Chapel Hill Weekly*, 8 Dec. 1939; Louis and Mildred Graves Papers (Southern Historical Collection, University of North Carolina, Chapel Hill); Graves family papers (in possession of General and Mrs. Ernest Graves, Arlington, Va.); *New York Times*, 3 Dec. 1939; *University of North Carolina Magazine* 9 (1889).

MARTHA B. CALDWELL

**Gray, Bowman** *(1 May 1874–7 July 1935)*, tobacco executive, was born in Winston, the son of James Alexander and Aurelia Bowman Gray. He attended local schools and was enrolled in The University of North Carolina for the year 1890–91. Withdrawing, he became a clerk in the Wachovia National Bank of which his father was cashier and one of the founders. He joined the R. J. Reynolds Tobacco Company as a salesman in 1895 and covered the state of Georgia where he was remarkably successful. After two years he was promoted to eastern sales manager and stationed in Baltimore, Md., where his two sons were born. Further promotion came in 1912, when he was made vice-president and director of the company with offices in Winston. In 1924 he became president, succeeding William Neal Reynolds, and in 1931 he became chairman of the board, the post he held at the time of his death.

Much credit has been ascribed to Gray for the rise of the Reynolds company from fourth to first place in size among tobacco manufacturing plants. Gray, a Methodist, donated the property on which Centenary Methodist Church was built in Winston-Salem. He also contributed generously to orphanages and hospitals. At the time of his death, Gray's holdings in the Reynolds company alone were valued at $12 million. A benevolent fund that he created made possible the establishment of the Bowman Gray School of Medicine of Wake Forest College in Winston-Salem.

In Baltimore on 1 Oct. 1902, he married Nathalie Fontaine Lyons, daughter of Hyman Hart and Ann Elizabeth Maffit Lyons of Asheville. They were the parents of two sons, Bowman, Jr., and Gordon. Gray died of a heart attack on a cruise ship off the coast of Norway and was buried at sea off North Cape above the Arctic Circle.

SEE: Jo White Linn, *The Gray Family and Allied Lines* (1976); *National Cyclopaedia of American Biography*, vol. 31 (1944); *North Carolina Biography*, vol. 5 (1941); Raleigh *News and Observer*, 8, 9 July 1935; Nannie M. Tilley, *The R. J. Reynolds Tobacco Company* (1985); University of North Carolina Archives (Library, University of North Carolina, Chapel Hill); *We the People of North Carolina* 8 (March 1951); *Winston-Salem Journal*, 8, 9 July 1935; Winston-Salem *Journal and Sentinel*, 6 Aug. 1939.

WILLIAM S. POWELL

**Gray, Bowman, Jr.** *(15 Jan. 1907–11 Apr. 1969)*, tobacco executive, was born in Baltimore, Md., the son of Bowman and Nathalie Fontaine Lyons Gray. He attended the Reynolda School in Winston-Salem, Woodberry Forest School in Virginia, and was graduated from The University of North Carolina in 1929. The following year young Gray became a salesman with the R. J. Reynolds Tobacco Company, in Winston-Salem, of which his father was president. Advancing through the ranks, he was assistant sales manager in 1939 and vice-president in 1949. In 1952 he was appointed sales manager and three years later, executive vice-president. Gray was president of the company from 1957 until 1959, when he became chairman of the board and chief executive officer. Stepping down as chief executive officer in 1967, he remained chairman of the board until his death.

Under Gray's leadership the Reynolds company expanded its sales, produced a number of new brands of tobacco products, and introduced filter-tipped cigarettes. During this time a Reynolds manufacture, Camel cigarettes, was reported to have been the nation's largest selling cigarette. His encouragement of research led to the establishment of a Product Development Center in 1959; the firm also contributed to cancer research. Diversification became a policy of the company under Gray's direction and transportation, food products, and packaging firms were acquired. In one of the most extensive such actions taken by a southern industry, R. J. Reynolds in 1961–62 totally integrated all of its employees. Also during Gray's administration, the company expanded employee benefits in the areas of health care, retirement, education, profit sharing, and other areas.

During World War II Gray was an officer in the naval reserve and on active duty in Norfolk and elsewhere. He developed plans and procedures for the navy's intelligence service and was considered to be the founder of operational intelligence, the branch that analyzed information about enemy operations. He not only taught this plan in an intelligence school in New York, but also implemented it in various naval stations. At Cape Henry, Va., he set up a system to direct ships through protective minefields sown off Hampton Roads, Va., and Cape Hatteras, N.C.

Gray's benefactions were numerous, particularly for orphanages and schools and for research. He aided fund-raising and philanthropic projects and played an active role in community chest and YMCA drives. He also served as a member and an officer of assorted boards, institutes, and businesses.

On 28 Nov. 1936 he married Elizabeth Palmer Christian of Richmond, Va., and they became the parents of five sons: Bowman, Frank Christian, Robert Daniel, Lyons, and Peyton Randolph. Gray died at his home, Brookberry Farm, in Winston-Salem and was buried in Salem Cemetery.

SEE: Alumni Records (University of North Carolina, Chapel Hill); Minutes of the Board of Directors, R. J. Reynolds Tobacco Co., (Winston-Salem); *National Cyclopaedia of American Biography*, vol. 54 (1973); Raleigh *News and Observer*, 16 Aug. 1959, 13 Apr. 1969; *RJR InterCom* (news release), 11 Apr. 1969; *Winston-Salem Journal*, 12 Apr. 1969; Winston-Salem *Twin City Sentinel*, 11 Apr. 1969.

NANNIE M. TILLEY

**Gray, George Alexander** *(28 Sept. 1851–8 Feb. 1912)*, cotton manufacturer of Gastonia, was one of a group of self-educated, self-trained engineers in the South who brought technical proficiency to cotton manufacturing. He was born in Crab Orchard Township, Mecklenburg County, the youngest of nine children of George Alexander Gray and his wife, Mary Wallace, daughter of Robert Wallace, whose parents had emigrated from Ireland. His paternal grandparents were Ransom Gray, of Mecklenburg, a soldier in the American Revolution, and Narcissa Alexander, daughter of Colonel George Alexander who moved to North Carolina from Pennsylvania before 1769. George Alexander Gray, Sr., gave up farming in 1853 and moved his family to the nearby Rock Island cotton factory. Before 29 June 1859, when he died suddenly of apoplexy, the family had settled near the Stowesville factory. The older children went to work but George, who was only eight, became his mother's companion and "special pet." She called him "Pluck" because of his self-confidence.

In 1861, at the age of nine, Gray entered the factory briefly before it closed with the outbreak of the Civil War. Mrs. Gray moved her family to Caleb John Lineberger's cotton factory at what was called "Pinhook" on the South Fork of the Catawba River. Here at the Woodlawn Mill (generally known as "Pinhook"), George worked as a sweeper boy; he was paid ten cents for a twelve- to fourteen-hour day. During his convalescence from an accident at the mill in which his arm was broken in three places, he attended school. He later wrote "I sought to master the 'Blueback' and my other books entirely within one year, for somehow or other I felt that that year's schooling would be my last."

Returning to the mill, he worked diligently to master the machinery. He assumed more and more responsibility and in time became assistant superintendent. At age nineteen he became acting superintendent of the Woodlawn Mill—at a wage of fifty cents per day. In 1878, Gray temporarily left "Pinhook" to start the first cotton mill in Charlotte when Oates Bros. & Co. engaged him to equip and operate the Charlotte Cotton Mills. Four years later, he was employed by Colonel R. Y. McAden to start a mill at McAdenville where Gray personally supervised the installation of the first system of electric lights to be used by any mill in the South.

By working in several mills and factories as a superintendent and adviser, Gray had saved enough money to open his own mill in 1888. With the assistance of Captain R. C. G. Love, Captain J. D. Moore, and John H. Craig, he organized the Gastonia Cotton Manufacturing Company, one of the first plants operated by steam in the state and the first mill constructed in Gastonia. He recognized in Gastonia, then a small village of barely three hundred people, a source of cheap fuel, abundant labor, raw material, and good transportation—factors that would make it an important center of cotton manufacturing.

Subsequently Gray was associated with the founding of nine of eleven cotton mills in Gastonia. In 1894, he built the Trenton Cotton Mills with the help of George W. Ragan and R. C. Pegram and, in 1897, the Avon Mill with John F. Love. The latter was the first mill in Gastonia to run on fine yarns and sheeting. Gray remained president of this prosperous mill until 1905. In 1899, he founded the Ozark Mill; in 1900, the Loray Mill (later called Firestone Textiles), which was the largest cotton mill under one roof in the state; and, in 1905, the Gray Manufacturing Co. of which Gray served as president, treasurer, and principal stockholder. The Clara, Holland, and Flint mills were founded in 1907. Gray was president of most of these companies. During his lifetime only two other mills were built in Gastonia without his assistance. He also helped organize the Wylie Mill at Chester, S.C.; the Scottdale at Atlanta, Ga.; and the Mandeville at Carrollton, Ga.

Gray installed the latest steam engines in each successive mill. In 1905, he operated the first electrically driven mill in the Carolina Piedmont. As soon as he was able to utilize hydroelectric power from Great Falls, he abandoned his steam-driven generator.

Noted for his upright, straightforward dealing, Gray followed a routine characterized by self-discipline and industry. From childhood on, he arose at five o'clock and started work by six. He was energetic—forming judgments and taking actions quickly, wasting little time on superfluous words. Gray enjoyed a keen sense of humor and read Shakespeare, Burns, and Moore for relaxation. He abstained from drinking and smoking while respecting the opinions of others. A devoted member of the Methodist Church in Gastonia, he made a large donation to the new church building in 1900.

Gray died in Gastonia, survived by his wife, Jennie Withers Gray, daughter of Jerry R. Withers, and eight of their ten children.

SEE: Samuel A. Ashe, ed., *Biographical History of North Carolina*, vol. 7 (1908 [photograph]); *DAB*, vol. 7 (1931); *North Carolina Biography*, vols. 6 (1919), 4 (1929); James R. Young, *Textile Leaders of the South* (1963).

ELLEN R. STRONG

**Gray, Gordon** *(30 May 1909–25 Nov. 1982)*, public servant, newspaper publisher, radio and television station owner, and university president, was born in Baltimore, Md., the second son of Bowman and Nathalie Fontaine Lyons Gray. In 1912 the Gray family moved to Winston-Salem, N.C., where Gray's father was associated with the R. J. Reynolds Tobacco Company. Later both Gray's father and his older brother, Bowman Gray, Jr., served as chairman of the board of the Reynolds company. One of the most important influences in Gray's life was the presence in the Gray household of Alice S. Gray, a cousin of his father. "Polly" Gray helped raise the two young Gray boys, and she imbued in Gordon a strong sense of the responsibility to serve society's needs, which, she felt, was a concomitant of the wealth and privilege to which he had been born.

Gray was educated in Winston-Salem schools, Woodberry Forest School, and The University of North Carolina, where he was graduated first in his class and president of Phi Beta Kappa in 1930. After obtaining a law degree from Yale University in 1933, he practiced with the firm of Carter, Ledyard and Milburn in New York until 1935. He then returned to Winston-Salem and began a two-year association with the law firm of Manly, Hendren and Womble. In May 1937, as president and publisher of the Piedmont Publishing Company, Gray purchased the *Winston-Salem Journal* and the *Twin City Sentinel*. At the same time he bought WSJS, a local radio station.

During this early period of his career, Gray was also active in civic and political organizations. In 1936 he was awarded the Jaycee Distinguished Service Award. He served as president of the Winston-Salem Chamber of Commerce and, in 1938, of the North Carolina Young Democratic Clubs.

Gray served three terms as a state senator, representing Forsyth County in the 1939, 1941, and 1947 legislative sessions. In 1942 he joined the U.S. Army as a private, having declined a commission. He rose through the ranks and ultimately became a captain. His military service included an assignment with General Omar Bradley's Twelfth Army Group in Europe. After his discharge from the army in 1945, Gray returned to Winston-Salem and resumed his career as newspaper publisher and owner of radio stations.

In 1947 Gray was appointed assistant secretary of the army, and shortly thereafter he became an undersecretary. When President Harry S Truman named him secretary of the army in 1949, he became the first secretary who had ever served in the army as a private. He resigned his appointment in the spring of 1950 to accept the presidency of The University of North Carolina. While secretary, Gray represented the army in its negotiations with the President's Committee on Equality and Opportunity in the armed forces. That committee recommended the integration of the races in the armed forces of the United States. In the period between his resignation as secretary of the army and his installation as president of The University of North Carolina on 12 Oct. 1950, Gray served as special assistant to the president on foreign economic policy. The Gray Report, which resulted from this work, recommended continued U.S. aid to Western Europe and increased aid to underdeveloped countries.

When Gray was president, The University of North Carolina consisted of The University of North Carolina in Chapel Hill, North Carolina State College in Raleigh, and the Woman's College of The University of North Carolina in Greensboro. Gray reorganized the administrative structure of the university, instituted a Consolidated University Development Program, and was active in formulating athletic policies that raised the standards for participation in intercollegiate athletics. He is credited with being one of the founders of the Atlantic Coast Conference. During his presidency, the Health Affairs Division of the Chapel Hill campus expanded rapidly and the four-year medical, dental, and nursing schools were opened. Gray also helped the university acquire licenses to operate an FM radio station and a statewide educational television network—both on the Chapel Hill campus. Moreover, for the first time black students were admitted to the university, initially into the graduate and professional schools but soon as undergraduates. While at Chapel Hill Gray served as chairman of the National Committee on Financing Hospital Care (1951), member of the board of trustees of the National Committee for Economic Development (1952), and chairman of the Ford Foundation Board on Overseas Training and Research (1952).

In 1951 President Truman appointed Gray director of the Psychological Strategy Board, whose mission was to coordinate the activities of governmental agencies in nonmilitary aspects of the cold war. In 1954 Gray was chairman of the Personnel Security Board to Review the Case of J. Robert Oppenheimer. Gray voted with the majority (in a 2 to 1 vote), which, while affirming belief in Oppenheimer's loyalty, nevertheless denied him the security clearance necessary to serve as a consultant to the Atomic Energy Commission.

In 1955 Gray resigned as president of The University of North Carolina to accept the position of assistant secretary of defense for international security affairs. The following year President Dwight David Eisenhower appointed him director of the Office of Defense Mobilization. From 1958 to 1961, Gray was a special assistant to President Eisenhower on national security affairs.

Upon the election of John F. Kennedy as president in 1960, Gray resigned his governmental position and returned to the Piedmont Publishing Company, where he served as chairman until 1969. From 1969 until 1975 he was chairman of the Triangle Broadcasting Company, and from 1975 until his death he was chairman of Summit Communications, Inc., which owned and operated a number of television stations as well as cable television franchises. Among his other business affiliations, he was a director of R. J. Reynolds Industries, Media General, Inc., and the American Security Trust Company. At the time of his death he was also president of Kensington Orchids, Washington, D.C.

One of Gray's abiding interests was in historic preservation. From 1962 to 1973, he was chairman of the board of trustees of the National Trust for Historic Preservation. Under his leadership that organization grew from 4,000 members in 1962 to 42,000 members in 1973. As president of the National Trust and as a member of the Advisory Council on Historic Preservation (1967–73), Gray frequently testified at congressional hearings to obtain governmental support for historic preservation and the National Park Service.

Gray was a member of the Foreign Intelligence Advisory Board from 1961 until 1977, when the board was dissolved by President Jimmy Carter. He was a trustee of the Brookings Institution and of the Corcoran Gallery of Art, and in 1961 he was chairman of the board of the Research Triangle Foundation in North Carolina.

In 1957 and again in 1961 President Eisenhower awarded Gray the Medal of Freedom, the highest award given to a civilian. In 1971 Gray received the Sylvanus Thayer Award, which is presented by the graduates of the U.S. Military Academy to the citizen whose service to the United States best exemplifies "Duty, Honor and Country." Other awards included the Conservation Service Award from the Department of the Interior (1973), the Medal for Historic Preservation from the Garden Clubs of America (1974), and the Distinguished Alumnus Award (1975) and University Award (1982) from The University of North Carolina.

Gray was a soft-spoken, shy, and serious man, with a quiet sense of humor he revealed only to those close to him. An indefatigable worker, he had a strong dedication to the various causes he espoused. Gray was devoted to his family, with whom he spent most of his leisure time. On 11 June 1938 he married Jane Henderson Boyden Craige. They had four sons, Gordon, Jr., Burton Craige, Clayland Boyden, and Bernard, before her death in 1953. He married Nancy McQuire Beebe on 12 June 1956 and enjoyed his role as stepfather to her three daughters, Cameron, Schuyler, and Alexandra.

Gray was a lifelong member of the Episcopal church and a member of the Democratic party. When he died, funeral services were held at Christ Episcopal Church, Washington, D.C., and St. Paul's Episcopal Church, Winston-Salem. He was buried in Salem Cemetery. A portrait of Gray hangs in the General Administration Building of The University of North Carolina at Chapel Hill.

SEE: *Alumni Review*, University of North Carolina (October 1950); *Durham Morning Herald*, 7 Oct. 1950; Gordon Gray Papers (Manuscript Department) and Presidents' Papers (University Archives) (Library, University of North Carolina, Chapel Hill); Jo White Linn, *The Gray Family and Allied Lines* (1976); Elizabeth D. Mulloy, *History of the National Trust for Historic Preservation* (1976); *New York Times*, 13 Apr. 1955; *Popular Government* (March 1950); Raleigh *News and Observer*, 27 Nov. 1982; *Washington Post*, 27 Nov. 1982; *Who's Who in America*, vol. 1 (1980–81).

FRANCES A. WEAVER

**Gray, James Alexander** *(21 Aug. 1889–29 Oct. 1952)*, business executive, civic leader, and philanthropist, was born in Salem, the son of James Alexander and Aurelia Bowman Gray. The youngest of four children who grew to maturity, he had a brother, Bowman, and two sisters, Mamie G. Galloway and Bess G. Plumly. Bowman (1874–1935) was president and later chairman of the board of the R. J. Reynolds Tobacco Company; in 1932 he built the home in Winston-Salem known as Graylyn, and the Bowman Gray School of Medicine was named for him. His sons, Bowman, Jr., and Gordon, later distinguished themselves in the business and civic affairs of the state and nation.

James Gray attended West End public school in Winston and in 1908 was graduated from The University of North Carolina, where he was football manager and known by his classmates as "Manager Gray." He returned to the university for the 1908 fall season as graduate football manager. Afterwards he began his business career as a clerk at the Wachovia National Bank. In 1911, he became assistant treasurer of its successor organization, the Wachovia Bank and Trust Company. He was made treasurer in 1915 and elected vice-president and a director in 1918; he served continuously as a director until his death. During this period

Gray was president of the North Carolina Bankers Association (1918–19) and a member of the executive council of the American Bankers Association (1920–21).

On 18 Apr. 1918, he married Pauline Lisette Bahnson (1891–1955) of Winston-Salem. They had three sons, James, Jr., Bahnson, and Howard, and then three daughters, Christine (Mrs. John Gallaher), Pauline (Mrs. Norwood Robinson), and Aurelia (Mrs. John Eller, Jr.).

As a young man Gray assumed positions of leadership in the community and state, serving on the board of directors of the YMCA, as a member of the City Hospital Commission (1914), and as chairman of the Forsyth County Highway Board (1915–16). From 1917 to 1920 he served in the North Carolina Senate for two terms. As chairman of its finance committee during both terms, he introduced the bill creating the Advisory Budget Commission and was cointroducer of the bill amending the state constitution to provide for a state income tax.

On 1 Jan. 1920 Gray joined the R.J. Reynolds Tobacco Company as a vice-president and a director. In 1934, he was elected president and served in that position for twelve years, longer than any other person except R. J. Reynolds himself. From 1946 to 1949 he was chairman of the executive committee, and from 1949 until his death he was chairman of the board of directors.

In August 1939 Gray, his brother's widow, Nathalie, and his nephews, Bowman, Jr., and Gordon, offered the $600,000 discretionary charitable bequest of his late brother to Wake Forest College for the establishment of a four-year medical school in Winston-Salem. The Bowman Gray School of Medicine opened in the fall of 1941. Partly as a result of this action, a decision was made in 1946 to move the remainder of Wake Forest College to Winston-Salem, which was accomplished in the fall of 1956.

Influenced by the fact that his brother had not lived to see the fruits of his benevolence, James Gray felt strongly that he should undertake charitable giving during his lifetime. Thus, on 1 Jan. 1947, he established an endowment fund then worth approximately $1,700,000 for the benefit of eleven North Carolina colleges and universities as follows: Wake Forest College (Bowman Gray School of Medicine), $900,000; The University of North Carolina at Chapel Hill (Chair of Bible), $250,000; Salem Academy and College, $150,000; Winston-Salem Teachers College (Chair of Bible), $100,000; Greensboro College, High Point College, Brevard College, and Louisburg College, $50,000 each; and Davidson College and Saint Mary's Junior College, $25,000 each. Included among other gifts made during his lifetime were a dormitory at the Methodist Children's Home, a gymnasium at Salem Academy and College, a building at the Salem Home for elderly women, a dormitory at the Memorial Industrial School, the land for the YWCA building, parks and playgrounds in black neighborhoods (all in Winston-Salem), an infirmary at Greensboro College, and a children's hospital in Alleghany County. He was also a generous contributor to many Methodist causes and churches, including the church in Chapel Hill that he attended as a student.

Additionally, Gray was a member of the original Good Health Committee appointed by Governor J. Melville Broughton. The work of this committee led to a statewide hospital program under the North Carolina Medical Care Commission, expansion of The University of North Carolina Medical School into a four-year institution, and construction of the North Carolina Memorial Hospital at Chapel Hill. Gray was a trustee of The University of North Carolina for forty consecutive years and chairman of the finance committee of the board of trustees for twenty years. He was the first chairman of the University's Development Council. He received honorary degrees from The University of North Carolina (1941) and Duke University (1952).

Despite his many accomplishments, Gray was a modest, unassuming man. At his death, he was still living in the house at 138 North Cherry Street where he was born. A lifelong member of Centenary Methodist Church, he rarely missed a Sunday service and served on the board of stewards for over thirty years. The following preamble to his will is noteworthy: "I desire to . . . give thanks for the goodness of God who has blessed me far beyond my merit; for the constant devotion of my wife; the steadfast loyalty of my family; the rich fellowship of my friends; . . . the strength for daily toil; the joy of living; the beauty of the world; the inexpressible reward of striving, even in a most imperfect way, to follow Christ; and the glorious certainty of life eternal and abundant—these comprise my real possessions."

Gray died from a heart attack in Winston-Salem at age sixty-three and was buried in Salem Cemetery. Inscribed on his headstone are these concluding words from the funeral sermon preached by Dr. Mark Depp: "God's church he loved; God's truth he cherished; God's will he sought; God's servant he was; with God he is."

SEE: Coy C. Carpenter, *The Story of Medicine at Wake Forest University* (1970); *Fortune* 42 (July 1950); James A. Gray family records (in possession of Thomas A. Gray, Winston-Salem); Jo White Linn, *The Gray Family and Allied Lines* (1976); *North Carolina Christian Advocate* 97 (20 Nov. 1952); *State Magazine* 7 (16 Sept. 1939); Nannie M. Tilley, *The R. J. Reynolds Tobacco Company* (1985); Trustees, University of North Carolina, *In Memoriam: James Alexander Gray* (1953); *The Wachovia*, January 1953; *The Wake Forest Magazine* 6 (December 1959); *Winston-Salem Journal* and *Twin City Sentinel*, scattered issues, 1 Jan. 1947–1 Nov. 1952.

JAMES A. GRAY, JR.

**Gray, Julius Alexander** *(6 Sept. 1833–14 Apr. 1891),* banker and railroad president, was the son of Alexander (1768–1864) and Sarah Harper Gray. His paternal grandfather, Robert Gray, lived first in New Castle, N.J., later in Orange County, Va., (where Alexander was born), and finally in Randolph County, N.C. Robert Gray, who had a good education for that day, was a noted raconteur and social leader. He served in the North Carolina Senate in 1798–99, 1804–7, 1812, 1823–24, and 1826–29. In 1812, the state appointed Gray a general in the state militia, but he did not serve on active duty. Julius A. Gray's mother was the daughter of Jeduthan Harper, a resident of Randolph County, a colonel during the American Revolution, and a relative of Robert Goodloe Harper of Maryland.

Gray's early years were carefree; he never was exposed to systematic labor, and he enjoyed good health and a strong body. After attending Caldwell Institute near Greensboro, he studied with the Reverend Jesse Rankin in Lexington. He then entered Davidson College as a sophomore in 1850 and was graduated in 1853.

From 1855 to 1869 Gray served a business apprenticeship that adequately prepared him for more responsible positions. In 1855, he became teller and bookkeeper of the Greensboro branch of the Bank of Cape Fear. The president of the bank was Jesse H. Lindsay, Gray's brother-in-law and a brother of Mrs. John Motley Morehead. In 1858, Gray moved to Virginia where he was cashier of the Bank of Danville. In the fall of 1860 he resigned this position to improve his poor health by spending a winter in Florida. Upon his return to North Carolina in the spring of 1861, his father-in-law, John Motley Morehead, appointed him manager of his cotton mills at Leaksville. Later he received a post in the Confederate Treasury Department, where he served through the Civil War. For three years after the war, Gray was administrator of the estates of his father, his only brother Robert (a lieutenant colonel in the Second Regiment of North Carolina Troops), and two brothers-in-law, all of whom had died during the war. Gray's entrepreneurial experience was broadened in this period by helping in the business ventures of his father-in-law.

The second phase of Gray's business career, when he resumed banking and related enterprises, extended from 1869 to 1879. In 1869 he purchased the building used by the Bank of Cape Fear and, with Jesse H. Lindsay and Eugene Morehead, reorganized it into the Bank of Greensboro. Lindsay was president of the bank and Gray was cashier. In 1876 this bank was reorganized as the National Bank of Greensboro, and in 1887 Gray became president. Because of Gray's strong support of Zebulon Vance for governor in the election of 1876, Vance appointed him a director of the North Carolina Railroad. In this position Gray learned the fundamentals of railroading, which prepared him for his crowning achievement.

On 3 Apr. 1879 the board of directors of the newly chartered Cape Fear and Yadkin Valley Railroad Company elected Julius A. Gray president. A momentous task lay ahead of him. Originally chartered in 1852 as the Western Railroad, the CF & YVRR had only forty-two miles of track from Fayetteville toward the coal fields of Chatham and Moore counties, and it was heavily indebted. Moreover, the state of North Carolina had come into possession of 77 percent of the stock, and the railroad was involved in complicated litigation. Gray's first task was to purchase the state-owned stock and to settle the debt. He formed a company to buy the state-owned stock and borrowed money from New York banks and the state of North Carolina to make the company solvent. He then helped to charter the North State Improvement Company, of which he was vice-president and general manager, to complete the construction. By the time of his death in 1891, the company was operating in the black and had expanded its main line from Wilmington through Fayetteville and Greensboro as far as Mount Airy. Because of this remarkable achievement and Gray's other activities, Greensboro regarded him as the keystone of its prosperity.

In the 1880s Gray was also involved in ancillary business activities. In 1887, he helped to found the North Carolina Steel and Iron Company, which constructed blast furnaces in Greensboro in the hope of using native coal, iron ore, and limestone to make the city a steel center. The venture failed when the local iron ore proved to have too much titanium and was difficult to smelt. Gray was also president of the Greensboro Chamber of Commerce (1887), a director of the Central Land Company, and president of the Mount Airy Granite Company.

In addition to his business affairs, Gray found time for community activities. He was a town commissioner in 1870. In 1882, he helped found the Guilford Battle Ground Company to preserve the site of the Battle of Guilford Court House. When the Greensboro Female College was sold for debt, Gray helped organize a company to purchase the institution's property and equipment so that it might resume operation. On 4 Dec. 1881 he joined the First Presbyterian Church of Greensboro.

After the death of John Motley Morehead, Gray's family life centered around the Morehead home, Blandwood, which became his residence. In 1858, Gray had married Emma Victoria Morehead, the daughter of John Motley and Ann Eliza Lindsay Morehead. The children who survived him were Annie (Mrs. J. W. Fry), Robert Percy, Jessie (Mrs. E. E. Richardson), Mary (Mrs. J. Allison Hodges), Eugenia (Mrs. George C. Heck), and Morehead. Gray was buried in Green Hill Cemetery, Greensboro.

SEE: Ethel S. Arnett, *Greensboro, North Carolina* (1955); Samuel A. Ashe, ed., *Biographical History of North Carolina*, vol. 5 (1906 [portrait]); Roland B. Eytsler, "A History of the Cape Fear and Yadkin Valley Railway" (M.A. thesis, University of North Carolina, 1924), and "The Cape Fear and Yadkin Valley Railway," *North Carolina Historical Review* 2 (1925); Edmund W. Jones Papers, William T. Sutherlin Papers, and Zebulon B. Vance Papers (Southern Historical Collection, University of North Carolina, Chapel Hill); James H. Myrover, *In Memoriam. Julius A. Gray* (copy in Southern Historical Collection, University of North Carolina, Chapel Hill).

JOHN L. BELL, JR.

**Green, Charles Sylvester** *(23 Sept. 1900–10 Jan. 1980)*, clergyman, newspaper editor, college president, and executive, was born in Greensburg, Ky., the son of Thomas Madison and Rosealthea Buck Green. The family moved to the Leaksville-Spray area of North Carolina in 1914. Green was graduated from Wake Forest College in 1922 and received the master of arts (1924) and bachelor of divinity (1930) degrees from Duke University and the master of theology degree from Union Theological Seminary, Richmond, Va., in 1954. He also received honorary doctoral degrees from Washington and Lee and from the University of South Carolina. He taught and was assistant principal in Durham from 1922 until 1926 but in 1925 also began serving Watts Street Baptist Church, Durham, of which he became pastor in 1926. Leaving Durham in 1932, he became pastor of a church in Richmond, where he served until September 1936, when he became president of Coker College, Hartsville, S.C. In 1943 he was chaplain to the South Carolina Defense Force until he resigned his position at Coker at the end of 1943 and became editor of the *Durham Morning Herald*. Between 1950 and 1955 he was executive vice-president of the newly created Medical Foundation of North Carolina, an agency formed to assist in the development of the medical school and North Carolina Memorial Hospital at The University of North Carolina. In 1955 he became vice-president in charge of alumni activities and public relations at Wake Forest College and in 1958 took a similar position at William Jewell College in Missouri. Returning to North Carolina in 1960, he became executive director of the Pitt County Development Commission; living in Greenville, he retired in 1971 but continued to work as a free-lance writer.

Green was married on 8 June 1926 to Mary Morris of Durham and they became the parents of two children, Nancy Rose and Charles Morris. He died in Statesville where he had moved in 1978 to be near his son.

SEE: *Durham Morning Herald*, 18 Dec. 1949, 26 Dec. 1954, 11 Jan. 1980; C. Sylvester Green, *Greens form Westmoreland County, Virginia* (1975); Raleigh *News and Observer*, 17 Dec. 1943, 18 Dec. 1949; Winston-Salem *Journal and Sentinel*, 25 May 1958; *Who's Who in the South and Southeast* (1950).

WILLIAM S. POWELL

**Green, Farnifold** *(30 May 1674–1714)*, planter, colonial militia officer, commissary, and Indian fighter, was born in St. Stephen's Parish, Northumberland, Va., the son of Timothy and Anne Farnifold (Farneffold, Farnifould, Furnsfield, etc.) Green. Anne Farnifold Green was the daughter of John Farnifold, an Anglican minister who served on the first Board of Visitors at William and Mary College, and the granddaughter of Sir Thomas Farnifold, MP, of Steyning, Sussex, England. Farnifold Green married Hannah Consolvo Smithwick (ca. 1675–ca. 1730), a widow and the daughter of Laurence and Sarah Consolvo of Princess Anne County, Va.

In 1697 Farnifold and Hannah Green moved to North Carolina, where he obtained land on Indian Creek in Perquimans Precinct. Around 1707 the Lords Proprietors granted Green 1,700 acres on the north side of the Neuse River between two creeks, Farnifold Green's Creek and Broad (now Smith's) Creek. This plantation where he settled, called Green's Neck, is near present-day Oriental, now in Pamlico County but from 1693 to 1722 known as Bath County. Here as a planter Green was involved in a number of land transactions and held the rank of captain in the Bath militia.

Soon after the Tuscarora massacre of 22 Sept. 1711, Captain Green wrote to Governor Alexander Spottswood of Virginia that the Indians "have killed about 100 people and have taken prisoners about 20 or 30" and that "we are forced to keep garrisons and watch and guard, day and night." Together with many of his neighbors, he also sent another letter to Governor Spottswood about this time saying "we must likewise perish with our brethren . . . [unless you] send to our relief some considerable force of men, arms and ammunition." This letter closes with the assurance that Captain Green and his fellow colonists "are ready to the utmost of our ability to assist the army if your Excellency pleases to send them."

Naturally the fear of another massacre stirred morbid thoughts among the North Carolinians, and on 26 Oct. 1711 Green prepared a will whose preamble represents this dark outlook. It states that he is "seriously considering the frailty and uncertain state of life at all times, especially in the dreadful times of Almighty God's visitation by sword and fire under which we tremble." His fears at this time would presage his own violent death a few years later.

As a part of the mobilization efforts to counter the renewed Indian attacks in the summer and fall of 1712, Governor Thomas Pollock appointed Green as "Commissary to impress and supply the army with anything that is to be had in Bath County." Yet even in their desperate plight at this time, the Bath County residents were beginning to relax their vigil and to attend to daily affairs, as evidenced by Green's sale to Martin Frank of 250 acres at Nottingham's Neck on 21 Dec. 1712.

Soon, however, the "visitation" came that Green had dreaded. According to a family legend, it came on a Sunday while his son and namesake, Farnifold II, had taken his mother and other members of the family to church, thus sparing them from violent death. In a surprise attack, the Indians murdered Captain Green, one of his sons, a white servant, and two Negroes. They also shot another of Green's sons through the shoulder before he escaped. And they destroyed the plantation house and plundered the stock of cattle and hogs. The attack may have been in reprisal for Green's key role as a military officer and government official throughout the Tuscarora War.

Green's will mentions his sons Thomas, John, Farnifold II (m. Sarah Graves), and James, one of whom died with him in 1714; daughters Jane and Elizabeth (m. Daniel Shine); brother Titus Green; "daughter-in-law" (stepdaughter) Ann Smithwick; and wife Hannah, who eventually married Richard Graves, a surveyor of Craven Precinct.

SEE: Blanche Humphrey Abee , *Colonists of Carolina in the Lineage of Hon. W. D. Humphrey* (1938); Beverley Fleet, *Virginia Colonial Abstracts*, vol. 3 (1938); J. Bryan Grimes, ed., *North Carolina Wills and Inventories* (1912); Elizabeth Moore, "Historical Gleanings" (North Carolina Department of Archives and History, Raleigh); Plaque, Sir Christopher Wren Building, The College of William and Mary; William L. Saunders, ed., *Colonial Records of North Carolina*, vols. 1 (1886), 2 (1886), and 5 (1887); Frederick Lewis Weiss, *The Colonial Clergy of Virginia, North Carolina, and South Carolina* (1955).

W. KEATS SPARROW

**Green, Fletcher Melvin** *(12 July 1895–27 Feb. 1978)*, educator and distinguished historian of the South, was born near Gainesville, Ga., the son of Robert Chambers and Mary Mahala Haynes Green. He received his early education in Murraysville, a small community in Hall County adjacent to Gainesville, and he began his college studies at Emory-at-Oxford. After serving in World War I with the American Expeditionary Force in France, he completed his studies at Emory University, receiving the bachelor of philosophy degree in 1920, with membership in Phi Beta Kappa. He was awarded the master of arts degree (1922) and the Ph.D. (1927) by The University of North Carolina.

Green's first teaching position was at Lindsey-Wilson Preparatory School in Columbia, Ky., in 1920–21. The following year he was a graduate fellow in history at The University of North Carolina, and remained there as an instructor in 1922–23. He taught at Sparks College in 1923–1924 and was an assistant professor at Vanderbilt University in 1924–25. After the year at Vanderbilt and study at the University of Chicago, Green returned to The University of North Carolina, where for two years he was a graduate student and fellow in the Institute for Research in Social Science. Upon completing the doctorate he was offered an assistant professorship in the department of history and in 1930 was promoted to associate professor. In 1933, he accepted a professorship at Emory University and remained there until the fall of 1936, when he returned to The University of North Carolina. Green taught at the university until his retirement in 1968; he was named to a Kenan professorship in 1946 and was chairman of the Department of History from 1953 to 1960.

During the academic year 1944–45, Green was a visiting professor at Harvard University, and in the spring semester of 1967 he was a research fellow at the Huntington Library. He spent the year 1968–69 at Oxford University as Harmsworth Professor of American History. For various summer sessions Green was a visiting professor at the College of William and Mary, University of Tennessee, Duke, Missouri, Columbia, Stanford, and Northwestern. He delivered the Walter Lynwood Fleming Lectures at Louisiana State University in 1949, the J. P. Young Lectures at Memphis State University in 1964, the Eugenia Dorothy Blount Lamar Lectures at Mercer University in 1968, and the inaugural Rembert W. Patrick Lecture at Guilford College in 1970. In 1962, he was one of the lecturers for the Institute of Southern Culture at Longwood College. Emory University (1957) and Washington and Lee University (1960) awarded him the honorary doctor of literature; Oxford University, the honorary master of arts (1969); and The University of North Carolina, the doctor of laws (1975).

Green's career as a graduate student and teacher was touched by three of the South's noted historians—Joseph Grégoire de Roulhac Hamilton, Walter Lynwood Fleming, and William E. Dodd. It was Hamilton who directed his graduate program at The University of North Carolina, and who was held in particular esteem and regarded with genuine affection by Green. Green was associated with Fleming at Vanderbilt University, and the study at Chicago had found him in the classes of William E. Dodd.

Historical societies and associations honored Green with numerous offices and sought the benefit of his advice and leadership. He was a charter member of the Southern Historical Association, its secretary-treasurer for four years, and a member of its executive council and of the editorial board of its *Journal of Southern History*. In 1945, he was the association's president. In 1953, Green was president of the Historical Society of North Carolina; and in 1955, of the North Carolina Literary and Historical Association. He was a member of the executive council (1946–49) and president (1960–61) of the Mississippi Valley Historical Association—now the Organization of American Historians. He also served for a term on the board of editors of the *Mississippi Valley Historical Review*. From 1955 to 1974, he was a member of the executive board of the North Carolina Department of Archives and History.

Green was the author of *Constitutional Development in the South Atlantic States, Democracy in the Old South and Other Essays*, and *The Role of the Yankee in the Old South*. His edited works included Henry Kyd Douglas, *I Rode With Stonewall; Essays in Southern History Presented to Joseph Grégoire de Roulhac Hamilton; The Lides Go South . . . and West: The Record of a Planter Migration in 1835*; John Blackford, *Ferry Hill Plantation Journal, January 4, 1838–January 15, 1839*; William Watson Davis, *The Civil War and Reconstruction in Florida*; Susan Dabney Smedes, *Memorials of a Southern Planter*; and Thomas Prentice Kettell, *Southern Wealth and Northern Profits*. He was one of the coeditors for volume one of *Travels in the New South*. A group of Green's former students prepared the *Festschrift, Writing Southern History: Essays in Honor of Fletcher M. Green*, which was published in 1965 under the editorship of Arthur S. Link and Rembert W. Patrick. This volume contains a bibliography of his writings prior to that date, and its length may have surprised some who had thought of Green solely in the role of teacher. The writings are sound, scholarly contributions covering topics in both the Old South and the New, and are particularly noteworthy for the wide range of interests they display.

Green was regarded by many as the dean of Southern historians, not only by virtue of his scholarship, but even more because of his accomplishments as a teacher and director of graduate students. He was an able lecturer whose best-known courses, "The Old South" and "The South Since Reconstruction," were always popular. More than 100 students completed their doctorate under his direction, and the number of master's students ran to considerably more than 150. In his review of *Writing Southern History*, William C. Binkley wrote: "As the director of a graduate seminar in history at the University of North Carolina for the past thirty years, Fletcher M. Green has probably had a more far-reaching influence on the writing of Southern history than has any other man of his generation." Certainly few teachers better understood the mood of their students. Green knew when to apply pressure and how much, and he had the ability to draw from a student his best performance—at times even better than the student thought himself capable of. Though demanding as a teacher and a person who was rarely deceived, Green could be charitable in his judgments. A close friendship existed between him and his students.

A man of many interests, Fletcher Green was an active churchman, the author of a centennial history of the local Methodist church, and for a number of years the teacher of a Sunday School class. Throughout life he retained his love for the outdoors and his interest in sports. As a young man he had played baseball and coached football and basketball; later he was an ardent fisherman and golfer. During all his years as a member of The University of North Carolina faculty and afterward in retirement, he was a faithful follower of the university's athletic teams.

Green married Mary Frances Black, a gracious lady and hostess who shared her husband's interest in his students. There were four children—two sons, Fletcher M., II, and Robert Ramsey, and two daughters, Mary Carolyn Green Dow and Elizabeth Haynes Green Fuller. After several months of declining health, Green died suddenly. Funeral services were conducted at the University United Methodist Church, with burial at Chapel Hill Memorial Cemetery.

SEE: *Chapel Hill Newspaper*, 28 Feb. and 2 Mar. 1978; *Durham Morning Herald*, 1 Mar. 1978; Fletcher M. Green, *Democracy in the Old South* (1969 [portrait]); Arthur S. Link and Rembert W. Patrick, eds., *Writing Southern History* (1965); Wendell H. Stephenson, *Southern History in the Making* (1964); *Who's Who in America, 1976–1977*.

J. ISAAC COPELAND

**Green, James, Jr.** *(ca. 1737–April 1784)*, colonial and Revolutionary leader, was born in Craven County, the son of James Green (ca. 1705–88), a justice of Craven County in 1754. The elder Green was the son of Captain Farnifold Green (1674–1714), one of the first settlers in the New Bern area, and one of the people killed in the disturbances with the Tuscarora Indians in the early eighteenth century.

James Green, Jr., first appears in public office in 1769 as clerk of the Assembly, serving in that post until the end of the session. On 18 Oct. 1775 he was named clerk of the Provincial Council; although also assistant clerk of the Provincial Congress, he was a delegate to neither. He rose to be clerk of the Provincial Congress for the fourth and fifth sessions, held at Halifax in April and December 1776, which adopted the Halifax Resolves and the first state constitution, respectively. In the capacity of clerk, Green served until 1780 on a committee to settle the financial accounts of the state with the United States. On 24 Dec. 1780 the Assembly appointed him treasurer of the Continental Loan Office, a post he held until his death.

After several unsuccessful bids for the Assembly seat

from the borough of New Bern, Green was finally elected in 1780. That summer he was appointed commissary general for the troops being raised in North Carolina, but was removed in August for not fulfilling his duties. He resigned his Assembly seat in 1781, when he was appointed admiralty judge pro tempore of Beaufort County until the regular judge, William Tisdale, was cleared of charges of bribery and corruption, which he soon was. In the early 1790s many discrepancies were found in the books of the loan office from Green's tenure, but because he was already dead no investigation was undertaken.

He married Margaret ("Peggy") Cogdell on 10 Oct. 1777. They had at least one child, a son, Bryan. Green died in New Bern and was buried in the yard of Christ Church, New Bern, of which he was a member.

SEE: Blanche Humphrey Abee, *Colonists of North Carolina in the Lineage of Hon. W. D. Humphrey* (1938); Annie Walker Burns, *North Carolina Genealogical Records* (1943); Gertrude S. Carraway, *Crown of Life* (1940); John L. Cheney, Jr., ed., *North Carolina Government, 1585–1974* (1975); *Colonial Records of North Carolina* vols. 8-10, 22 (1890–1907).

MARTIN REIDINGER

**Green, James Henderson** *(21 June 1881–23 May 1955)*, Methodist holiness evangelist, radio preacher, and educator, was born in a one-room log cabin in Ashe County near Elk Cross Roads (now Todd). Of Dutch descent and the eldest of nine children, he was the son of James Tippicanoe Green, a Civil War veteran, and his wife, Mary Jane Cook. His early years were spent with his family on the farm, where he "learned physical culture at the end of a hoe handle." Green felt that God had blessed him with the "spirit of venture"; in his later evangelistic peregrinations, he preached some 15,000 sermons during fifty years of holiness evangelism and education in North Carolina.

Converted through the revival influence of Methodist circuit rider preachers L. P. Brogle and A. J. Burrus in 1898, Green experienced a dramatic call to prepare for his life's work and left home to attend Ashe Academy in Solitude (now Ashland), N.C. After graduation, he taught in several rural public schools in the area until 1905. He operated a private high school, Camp Academy, in Buncombe County, for two years and supplemented his salary with sawmilling and farming. Although Green often spoke of the broadening influences of these experiences in his education, in 1901 he became disenchanted with teaching and received a "call" to the ministry. He was admitted on trial at the Methodist conference under Bishop A. W. Wilson in Greensboro in 1905 and met conference education requirements by correspondence courses from Vanderbilt University. He began his first pastorate with only two sermons, but eventually cultivated a homegrown homiletic style that made him a widely-known pulpiteer and holiness evangelist throughout the South. Green employed various "measures" in his revivalism to create "religious excitement" or arouse attention. He prayed for people by name and exposed sin publicly. Well endowed with idiosyncracies, on one occasion, after being introduced as speaker, he crawled on his hands and knees across the platform several times before delivering the message.

Between 1905 and 1926 Green served nine pastorates, most of them rural charges, including the legendary Rock Springs Camp Meeting circuit near Gastonia. In 1916, after his pastorate at Rock Springs, during which his evangelistic appetite was whetted with nearly a year of continuous revival meetings, he was appointed a general conference evangelist in the Western North Carolina Conference of the Methodist church. For the next forty years his interest and energies were consumed with evangelistic passion. Unsuited for the sedentary pastorate, in 1933 Green reflected that "evangelism was the ministry for which I was best suited." He conducted outstanding revival campaigns in small towns including Thomasville, Jamestown, Kannapolis, and Hiddenite. He was well known for his work in camp meetings and founded three such revival institutions, including Camp Free in Connelly Springs, Sunny South Camp in Greensboro, and with Henry Clay Morrison of Asbury College, Avon Park Camp Meeting in Florida; the latter was the first major national camp meeting "below the frost line." The Newlyn Street Methodist Church and the Jim Green Memorial Church in Greensboro are other Green institutional offspring.

Green "began his course in the holiness movement" during a pastorate at Clyde, N.C., between 1906 and 1910. "Scriptural holiness had recently invaded" the town of Clyde, but there was bitter opposition by both Baptists and Methodists in the community. Nevertheless, Green, recalling his "Christian Baptism" into "scriptural holiness" in an "eventful experience" in 1904, publicly recognized the holiness people in a community-wide evangelistic campaign. Increasingly bothered by the "baneful effects of the new methods and programs" sponsored by his church leaders, he felt that the Methodist church was drifting away from genuine revivals and toward a gradual apostasy from deep spirituality. According to him, the university-trained leadership did not believe in experiential religion or in the inspiration of the Scriptures. He believed that the church needed to recover "the original ways of Methodism," and this association with "holiness churches" early in his pastoral experiences influenced his career in the American holiness movement. Green's feeling that "modernism" was invading the Methodist church eventually led to secession from his parent church in 1926. Anguished by the decision, he described his leaving as "the saddest hour of my ministerial career. It almost killed me."

Afterwards he served as General Evangelist in the Nazarene Church from 1926 to 1930 and as pastor of the Lighthouse Mission, an independent rescue mission, in St. Louis, Mo., from 1929 to 1931. In 1938, with Helen Vincent Washburn and Kenneth Temple, Green organized an interdenominational evangelistic association. Ostensibly begun as a "chain of tabernacles" to provide preaching points for holiness propagation, the People's Christian Movement was actually an institutional consummation of Green's nearly forty years of personal tent and tabernacle revivalism throughout North Carolina. However, the movement became a full-fledged denomination when it assumed the name of People's Methodist church in 1942. At the time of its merger with the Evangelical Methodist church in 1962, the PMC consisted of 1,000 members in twenty-five churches scattered throughout North Carolina, Virginia, and Georgia. Ultimately, Green lamented secession from his ecclesiastical parent and after fomenting independent holiness institutionalism in North Carolina for over fifty years, he concluded his denominational odyssey and returned to the Methodist fold just six months before his death.

Affectionately known as "Brother Green," he left his mark all over the state and in many parts of the South through the various educational and ecclesiastical progeny of his "holiness revivalism." His most enduring influences may be seen in the two institutions, Avon Park Camp Meeting and John Wesley College. Avon Park, located in western Florida, is a winter mecca for Wesleyan leaders and followers and is one of the major holiness camp meetings in America today. On 25 Jan. 1932, Green reopened the recently defunct Greensboro Bible and Literary School, an institutional victim of the depression in the spring of 1931, as People's Bible School. The institution had been established in 1903 by Winfred R. Cox, another North Carolina holiness pioneer in the wake of a southern "tidal wave of pentecostal evangelism" by Seth Cook Rees, to train ministers, missionaries, and evangelists in the perfectionist faith. In 1959, the name was changed to John Wesley College. Later, as North Carolina's oldest undergraduate theological institution, it advertised itself as "independent, interdenominational, evangelical." It served a wide spectrum of religious denominations, while retaining its Wesleyan-Arminian theological emphasis. Green was president of the college for twenty years until ill health forced him to resign in 1952. In 1932, he began *The People's Herald*, afterward the *Crusader*, as an official literary organ of the college. This holiness periodical attained a circulation of about 4,000.

Green married Minnie May Grogan of Ashe County. He died of a stroke, survived by three sons, James C., John Kilgo, and Philip L., and by two daughters, Mrs. Max Kimmins and Mrs. W. P. Armstrong. Green and his wife were buried in Guilford Memorial Park, Greensboro.

SEE: Elmer T. Clark, *The Small Sects in America* (1965); Evangelical Methodist Church, *Minutes*, 1970; Jim Green Diaries (Library, John Wesley College, Greensboro); *Greensboro Daily News*, 24 May 1955; John Wesley College, *People's Herald* and *College Crusader*, October 1933, March 1953, August 1955, July 1968, September 1972; C. E. Jones, *Guide to the Holiness Movement in America* (1974); Frank S. Meade, *Handbook of Denominations* (1964); *The Voice of Evangelical Methodism*, 3 July 1962.

STEVE WOOD

**Green, John** *(20 May 1807–31 Aug. 1887)*, attorney, judge, farmer, and Indiana official, was born in what became Yancey County, probably in that portion that was then Rutherford County. His parents were James and Catherine Blankinship Green; the Blankinship family was fairly numerous in Rutherford County at the time of the 1810 census. When he was three the Greens moved to Jefferson County, Indiana Territory, and in 1828 young Green entered Hanover Academy, predecessor of Hanover College, where he remained for five years. While in school he intended to prepare for the Presbyterian ministry, but upon leaving he settled on a farm until 1839, when he began to study law with Wilberforce Lyle in Madison, Ind. An injury in a buggy accident that left him crippled for life delayed his studies, but he was licensed in 1842 and established his practice in Madison. He was soon permitted to practice in federal as well as state courts and enjoyed a wide clientele.

From his early thirties Green held a series of public offices in the community and state: militia officer, justice of the peace, school system trustee, state senator, and district judge. He also was active in the construction of two railroads, the Lafayette, Muncie and Bloomington and the Indianapolis, Peru and Chicago lines. From 1848 until his death Green lived on the outskirts of the town of Tipton. He was a Whig while that political party was active and then he became a Republican. He was married first to Mrs. Mary Blankenship Marshall by whom he had five children; after her death he married Catherine A. Humerickhouse (d. 1875), and thirdly, Mrs. Caroline Cottingham Passwater.

SEE: *A Biographical Directory of the Indiana General Assembly* (1980); *A Biographical History of Eminent and Self-Made Men of the State of Indiana* (1880); Charles Blanchard, ed., *Counties of Howard and Tipton, Indiana* (1883).

WILLIAM S. POWELL

**Green, John Patterson** *(2 Apr. 1845–1 Sept. 1940)*, Afro-American attorney, legislator, and author, was born in New Bern, the only son of John Rice Green, a tailor, and Temperance Durden Green, a seamstress after her husband's death in 1850. Though never a slave, young Green grew up in relative poverty after 1850, working at odd jobs in both New Bern and Cleveland, Ohio, where Mrs. Green and her three children moved in the summer of 1857. While employed in a variety of trades, Green attended grammar school and high school, completing his secondary education at age twenty-four. In the year of his graduation, he wrote and published at his own expense *Essays on Miscellaneous Subjects*, "By a Self-Educated Colored Youth," a thirty-eight page collection of five high school compositions of a didactic and hortatory nature. In 1869, he began to study law, and on 20 Sept. 1870 he passed the South Carolina bar.

Green lived in Bennettsville, S.C., from 1870 to 1872 before deciding to return to Cleveland. A practicing lawyer and active Republican campaign orator in the South, he established a similar record in Cleveland, although there he soon directed his energies toward attaining local political office. In 1873 he won his first election—as justice of the peace in Cleveland, a post he held for nine years. In 1881, the Republican party nominated him to serve in the lower house of the Ohio General Assembly. Green's successful campaign and moderate legislative record led to his reelection in 1889. Encouraged by the possibility of becoming the first black man to sit in the Ohio Senate, Green ran for and won the senatorship of Cleveland and Cuyahoga counties in 1891. His single term in the senate marked the pinnacle and conclusion of his political career.

Both during and after his stint in politics, Green maintained a successful criminal law practice in Cleveland. He was also a ready worker for the Republican party and a frequent delegate to its national conventions. In 1872, he represented the First District of South Carolina as an alternate delegate to the Republican National Convention. He attended the 1882 and 1896 conventions as an alternate delegate at large from Ohio. In recognition of his work as a traveling speaker in the presidential campaign of 1896, William McKinley appointed him U.S. postage stamp agent, a position never before held by an Afro-American. During his tenure in Washington, Green formally joined the Episcopal church, the denomination in which he had been raised as a child. In 1905 he returned to Cleveland and once again resumed his legal career at age sixty-one. Continuing his law practice until his accidental death in 1940, Green remained a respected figure in Cleveland, as evidenced by the designation of 4 Apr. 1937 as "John P. Green Day" by the mayor and city council.

In addition to his public career, Green was involved in several private literary pursuits. Eleven years after publishing his youthful essays, he brought out a volume that he had used in his political efforts on behalf of James A. Garfield's presidential campaign. Dedicated to "those unswerving Republicans" engaged in the reconstruction of the South, Green's *Recollections of the Inhabitants, Localities, Superstitions and Ku Klux Klan Outrages of the Carolinas* (1880) displays a progressive Republican attitude toward the problems of the South during that turbulent period. The book is less a political tract, however, than a miscellany of local color of the Carolinas as gleaned from the memory of "a 'Carpet-Bagger' who was born and lived there," Green's self-descriptive phrase on the title page. In his autobiography, *Fact Stranger than Fiction* (1920), he reviewed the first seventy-five years of his life in an anecdotal and episodic narrative, which is partly personal history, partly a travel book, partly a record of judicial and legislative proceedings, and partly a catalogue of Green's friends and famous acquaintances.

Upon graduation from high school, Green married Annie Walker who died in 1911. Some time afterward he married a widow, Mrs. Lottie Mitchell Richardson, with whom he spent his later years.

SEE: *Cleveland News*, 2 Sept. 1940; Cleveland *Plain Dealer*, 2 Sept. 1940; Green's own books cited above and the John P. Green Papers (Western Reserve Historical Society, Cleveland, Ohio).

WILLIAM L. ANDREWS

**Green, John Ruffin** *(23 Mar. 1832–25 July 1869)*, tobacco manufacturer, whose pioneering efforts in the production of bright-leaf smoking tobacco helped lay the economic foundation of the city of Durham, was the second of seven children of Mager A. and Ann Brooks Green of Person County. Around 1856 Green bought a farm in Orange County about five miles from Durham Station on the North Carolina Railroad. After his house burned, he purchased a farm west of what is now Morris Street in Durham and moved there. No stranger to the production and marketing of tobacco, about 1862 he bought from Robert F. Morris the first tobacco factory operated in Durham Station. It was located where the American Tobacco Company plant now stands.

Green recognized the growing trend toward switching from chewing to smoking tobacco, especially among students at the nearby University of North Carolina. To cater to this changing taste he developed a high-grade smoking tobacco, which was produced by hand from the bright, mild leaf grown in the surrounding region that came to be known as the Golden Belt. His product did become popular with the university students. During the Civil War he often received orders from former students as well as from others in the Confederate Army. At the end of the war his well-stocked factory was too great a temptation to the armies of generals Joseph E. Johnston and William T. Sherman. While the troops were milling around in the Durham area during the generals' surrender negotiations, they ransacked Green's factory. However, what appeared at the time to be a disaster soon proved to have been a blessing. After the soldiers returned to their homes, Green began to receive orders from widespread sections of the country. He decided it would be well to associate his tobacco with its town of origin and one with which so many soldiers had become acquainted. Consequently, he renamed his product "Durham Smoking Tobacco" and adopted the Durham Bull as his trademark, a symbol that his successors made known around the world.

On 23 Mar. 1856, Green married Mary Frances Chandler, daughter of Joel and Elizabeth C. Walker Chandler of Granville County. They had five children: John Morgan, James Randolph, Ida Frances, Lucius, and Viola. Green's death at age thirty-seven was attributed to tuberculosis. He was buried in Maplewood Cemetery, Durham.

SEE: Hiram V. Paul, *History of the Town of Durham, North Carolina* (1884); Records in the possession of Walter S. Lockhart, Jr., Durham; Nannie M. Tilley, *The Bright-Tobacco Industry, 1860–1929* (1948).

MATTIE U. RUSSELL

**Green, Paul Eliot** *(17 Mar. 1894–4 May 1981)*, dramatist, author, and teacher, was born in Harnett County, the son of William Archibald and Betty Lorine Byrd Green. He grew up on his father's farm engaging in the labors and pleasures of rural life. For a time he played professional baseball for a team in Lillington and was widely acclaimed as a pitcher because he was ambidextrous. Music also was an important part of his life. His mother bought an organ and taught her children to play. Green taught himself to play the violin and later composed music for his plays. After graduation from nearby Buies Creek Academy in 1914, he worked to earn money for college and entered The University of North Carolina in 1916. As a freshman he wrote poems that were published in *The Carolina Magazine*, and he was the author of the play produced by the seniors at commencement.

In April 1917, before finishing his first year at the university, Green enlisted in the army for service in World War I. Before leaving for France he published at his own expense a thin volume of poems, *Trifles of Thought by P.E.G.*, because he was not certain that he would return from the war to pursue the literary career of which he dreamed. Young Green rose rapidly through the ranks from private to corporal, sergeant, and sergeant-major with the 105th Engineers, 30th Division; afterwards he was commissioned second lieutenant with the Chief of Engineers in Paris. During a year's service at the front in Belgium and France, he participated in several months of heavy combat in the trenches. This experience had a lasting effect on him, though he was always reluctant to speak about it. He returned to the university in 1919 and was graduated with a major in philosophy in 1921. Green studied under Frederick H. Koch, a newly arrived member of the faculty, who had organized the Carolina Playmakers in 1918. The new professor encouraged Green and others to write "folk plays" based on local subjects and their own experiences. Plays by his students, including many by Paul Green, were produced. One of the students, Elizabeth Lay, daughter of the Reverend George Lay, rector of St. Mary's College in Raleigh, married Green in 1922. After a year of graduate study in philosophy under Professor Horace Williams in Chapel Hill, Green went to Cornell University for further graduate work and in 1923 became an assistant professor of philosophy at The University of North Carolina. He remained in that department until 1939, when he became a professor of dramatic art. In 1944, he resigned to devote full time to writing.

Throughout his twenty-one years as a professor, Green wrote plays as well as short stories, novels, and poetry. Although many were produced by the Carolina Playmakers in Chapel Hill, some were produced in Washington, D.C., New York, and elsewhere. In 1927 he was awarded the Pulitzer Price for *In Abraham's Bosom*, produced at the Garrick Theater in New York. His other Broadway plays included *The House of Connelly*, *Roll Sweet Chariot*, *Johnny Johnson*, and *Native Son*.

For many years Paul and Elizabeth Green collaborated with others in the production of "The Literary Lantern," a newspaper column of book reviews and book news. Green also was editor of *The Reviewer*, a literary journal, and contributed to newspapers, particularly the Raleigh *News and Observer*. Travel for educational purposes occupied some of his time. In the summer of 1926 he was at the MacDowell Colony in New Hampshire, and, while on leave of absence as a Guggenheim Fellow in 1928 and 1929, he studied the theatre in Germany and England. In 1951 he lectured in Japan and elsewhere in the Orient.

After seeing the motion picture, *The Birth of a Nation*, in 1915, Green anticipated the development of this medium as a true art form. He welcomed the opportunity in 1932 to go to Hollywood, Calif., under contract to Warner Brothers to write scripts for motion pictures. For various lengths of time and for different companies, including Metro-Goldwyn-Mayer, he wrote scripts in Hollywood for films in which George Arliss, Lionel Barrymore, Bette Davis, Clark Gable, Greer Garson, Will Rogers, and others appeared. Although well paid for his work, he was rarely satisfied with the artistic quality of the final product. He often declined to accept particular assignments and finally after 1964 ended the association.

Long interested in a new form of drama, Green was inspired by some plays he saw in Germany. As early as 1928, he wrote Professor Koch of his hope to use the theme of the "Lost Colony" of Roanoke Island in a dramatic production. This was realized in 1937, when *The Lost Colony*, a "symphonic drama" as he termed it, was produced in an outdoor theatre on Roanoke Island, site of the 1587 colony. Employing spoken word, song, music, dance, pantomime, and light, it was a notable success and except for the years of World War II has been produced by the Roanoke Island Historical Association each summer since. This was merely the first of such works by Green and others; historical dramas, presented at or near the site of the actual events depicted, have appeared all around the United States. Green himself was the author of fifteen plays written to be performed outdoors in North Carolina, Florida, Virginia, Kentucky, Texas, and elsewhere.

Green's contributions were widely recognized. In addition to the early Pulitzer Prize and the Guggenheim Fellowship, he received the Belasco Little Theatre Tournament trophy in 1925. Other honors included the National Theatre Conference plaque, the American Theater Association citation for distinguished service, the Frank P. Graham Award, the Morrison Award, the North Carolina Award, and the Sir Walter Raleigh cup. In 1979 the General Assembly named him North Carolina's dramatist laureate. He received honorary doctorates from The University of North Carolina, Davidson College, Campbell College, the North Carolina School of the Arts, and four out-of-state colleges and universities.

He was a member of the National Institute of Arts and Letters and of the executive committee of the U.S. National Commission for UNESCO (1950–52). In 1951, he was a delegate to the UNESCO conference in Paris.

From his youth, when he demonstrated sympathy and compassion for the poor, blacks, and others whom he saw around him in his rural community, Paul Green acted and spoke in support of the basic rights of all humanity. A gentle, kindly man, he knew when, where, and how to direct attention to the wrongs he witnessed and to seek redress. Civil rights, poverty, and political oppression were all causes of concern to him, and he lent support to them in person, in print, and financially. He spoke out against and wrote plays dealing with war, lynching, chain gangs, prejudice, and superstition. Even though at times his stand was unpopular in many quarters, his ideals were understood and there was little or no personal criticism of him. It was known that Green was "haunted by the ideal of perfection" and that he believed "in the uniqueness of man as responsible to his neighbor and to God."

Paul and Elizabeth Green were the parents of Paul Eliot, Nancy Byrd, Betsy McAllister, and Janet McNeill. He was buried in the old Chapel Hill Cemetery near the Paul Green Theatre on the university campus.

SEE: Agatha B. Adams, *Paul Green of Chapel Hill* (1951); *Chapel Hill Newspaper*, 30 June, 1, 2, 5 July 1976, 5, 6, 10 May 1981; Barrett H. Clark, *Paul Green* (1928); Vincent S. Kenny, *Paul Green* (1971); Walter S. Lazenby, *Paul Green* (1970); *McGraw-Hill Encyclopedia of World Drama*, vol. 2 (1972), for a list of his plays (a copy in the North Carolina Collection, University of North Carolina Library, Chapel Hill, has been updated with typed additions); *New York Times*, 6, 10 May 1981; *Pembroke Magazine* 10 (1978); Raleigh *News and Observer*, 2 Apr. 1950, 5, 6 May 1981; *Who's Who in America* (1980).

WILLIAM S. POWELL

**Green, Philip Palmer** *(23 July 1891–27 Sept. 1972)*, army medical corps officer and pathologist, was born in Davidson County, the second of six children of Robert S. and Nettie Lopp Green. His education began in a one-teacher public school, after which he completed the eighth grade in the new Thomasville graded school, attended for one year a private class taught by H. W. Rinehart, formerly president of Thomasville Female College, and met college entrance requirements at Liberty Piedmont Institute. He received B.S.(1912) and M.S. (1913) degrees from Wake Forest College, where he was a laboratory assistant in chemistry (two years) and anatomy (one year), graduating with honors in premedical courses. In September 1912, he entered Washington University Medical School, St. Louis, Mo.; he was graduated with an M.D. degree in 1914. After serving a two-year internship in St. Louis Children's Hospital, he was an assistant to Dr. Ernest Sachs, head of the neurology department at Washington University and a pioneer in brain surgery.

When the United States declared war with Germany in April 1917, Green joined the St. Louis hospital unit that reached France on 1 June. He first served in a British hospital at Rouen. Later that year he was accepted in the U.S. Army Medical Corps and was stationed at general headquarters in Chaumont. In July 1918, at his request, he was assigned frontline service with the Forty-second (Rainbow) Division near Reims. Seriously wounded by shrapnel from a bursting shell, he was sent back to U.S. hospitals in October 1918. After twenty months of treatment and surgery, he was sufficiently recovered to resume active duty.

Green made research his specialty and was certified in both bacteriology and pathology. He was recognized in the fore of medical corps pathologists. Between the two world wars he was stationed in a number of large service hospitals in this country and for one three-year term at Schofield in Hawaii. In 1940, he was sent for a second stay in Hawaii—this time at Tripler General Hospital, Honolulu. On Pearl Harbor day and afterward, he treated the many wounded in the attack. It is recorded that not one of those wounded died of infection. A year later he was appointed commanding officer of North Sector General Hospital at Schofield Barracks, the largest infantry hospital in the Pacific. There he provided skilled supervision until the end of the war. After his return to the United States, he was stationed at Fort Hamilton, N.Y.; Fort Lewis near Tacoma, Wash.; and, finally, at Fort Bragg, N.C. From his enlistment rank of first lieutenant in 1917, he had advanced to full colonel in World War II.

After his retirement in 1952, Green was a pathologist at Moore Memorial Hospital in Southern Pines, N.C., for eighteen years. During that period he saw the hospital doubled in capacity and staff. For two terms he served as chief of staff. As chief pathologist he elicited large gifts of equipment that provided especially up-to-date means of diagnosis leading to cures.

Just before going overseas, Green married Juliette Loving on 5 May 1917 in Richmond, Va. They had three children: Philip P., Jr. (B.S., Princeton, 1943; LL.B., Harvard, 1948), an associate director of the Institute of Government, University of North Carolina at Chapel Hill; Robert B. (B.S., Princeton, 1944; M.S., Massachusetts Institute of Technology, 1949; D.S., 1951); and Jean Green Rodenbough (A.B., Randolph-Macon Woman's College, 1955). Juliette Loving Green died on 30 Apr. 1964.

During his long life Green enjoyed hobbies, especially photography, in which he won awards; fishing, in all the waters near his many places of residence; and crafts, of which building superior walnut gunstocks occupied his later years. His reading was so extensive that he could speak with authority on almost any subject. He was a Mason and, at Southern Pines, an active member of the Rotary Club. Colonel Green and his wife were buried in the Thomasville City Cemetery.

SEE: *Greensboro Daily News*, 28 Sept. 1972; William S. Powell, ed., *North Carolina Lives* (1962); Records of Moore Memorial Hospital (Southern Pines); Records of the U.S. Army Medical Corps (National Archives, Washington, D.C.); *Wake Forest Alumni Directory* (1961).

MARY G. MATTHEWS

**Green, Roger** *(fl. 1653)*, Anglican clergyman in Virginia and grantee of land in North Carolina, may have been the one of this name from Norfolk, England, who matriculated at St. Catharine's College, Cambridge, at the Easter term in 1631 and was graduated with a B.A. in 1635. He received the M.A. degree in 1638 and was ordained in Norwich on 9 March 1639. In 1653, the Virginia Assembly acted favorably upon a petition from Roger Green, "clarke," when he sought a grant of 10,000 acres of land for himself and a hundred inhabitants of Nansemond County who would settle on the Moratuck or Roanoke River on the west side of the Chowan River. Green was to have 1,000 acres for himself in addition to the larger grant. His people were to select a secure site for their settlement and be prepared to defend it. The location would be chosen by Green but would be "next to those persons who have had a former grant." The Assembly added that its action was taken "in reward of his charge [expense], hazard and trouble of first discoverie, and encouragement of others for seating those southern parts of Virginia."

There is no evidence that Green settled on his land. He appears to have been more interested in seeing a system of towns established in Virginia in contrast to the scattered haphazard farms and plantations of that colony. It is apparent that he was in Virginia in 1656, as he recorded that on 27 March of that year "in my hearing" some members of the new Assembly expressed regret at the repeal of an act to establish central market places in each county. Five years later he was in London to deliver to the bishop of London a statement "to show the unhappy State of the Church in Virginia" and to enter a plea for towns as the solution to several evils that he saw in the colony. His report was printed in 1662 in a pamphlet entitled *Virginia's Cure: or An Advisive Narrative Concerning Virginia*. In this work he referred to the colony of Virginia as being bound "on the North by the great River Patomak, on the South by the River Chawan . . . and [it] contains aboove half as much Land as England."

SEE: Lindley S. Butler, "The Early Settlement of Carolina, Virginia's Southern Frontier," *Virginia Magazine of History and Biography* 79 (1971); Nell M. Nugent, *Cavaliers and Pioneers* (1934); William S. Powell, *Ye Countie of Albemarle in Carolina* (1958); John Venn, *Alumni Cantabrigienses*, vol. 2 (1922).

WILLIAM S. POWELL

**Green, Thomas Alexander** *(25 June 1846–17 July 1932)*, leading private banker and supporter of public school education in the postbellum years, was born in New Bern, the son of Thomas Green, a shipmaster, and Annie M. Curtis Green. He was the grandson of Captain Joseph Green, a Continental line commissary officer. Young Green was apprenticed to a carpenter and later paid out of his earnings for his own private schooling. In 1868, he entered the grocery business and married Harriett Howard Meadows of New Bern. He helped to found the New Bern Cotton Exchange in 1879. At this period he was interested in shipping and in the cottonseed oil business. In 1885 he joined Claude E. Foy, Clement Manley, and the later U.S. Senator F. M. Simmons in the banking house Green, Foy & Company; Green remained an officer in the successor banks of subsequent years. Three years before, with his election to the board of the New Bern Academy, he began a lifelong interest (for most of these years as chairman of the academy) in support of public school development.

In 1882, Green joined the Methodist church, which he served in many capacities. About this time he became a member and master of St. John's Lodge No. 3, A.F. & A.M., of which he would be master many times. He also was elected to the board of the Oxford Orphanage, a position he held until his death. He served a brief term on the New Bern board of aldermen and was the first captain of the old Atlantic Steam Fire Engine Company. From 1891 to 1893 he served as one of the early presidents of the North Carolina Firemen's Association. He and Mrs. Green, whose daughter Clara Maria married a New Bern mayor, A. T. Dill, were among the first patrons of the New Bern Library Association. Green continued most of his public duties until his last illness. He died in New Bern at age eighty-five and was buried at Cedar Grove Cemetery.

SEE: Samuel A. Ashe, *Cyclopedia of Eminent and Representative Men of the Carolinas of the Nineteenth Century*

(1892); Information on Green in the Minutes of St. John's Lodge No. 3, A.F. & A. M., and in the records of the New Bern Public Schools, Methodist Church, and Oxford Orphanage; Oxford *Orphan's Friend and Masonic Journal* 57 (1 Aug. 1932); Raleigh *News and Observer*, 18 July 1932.

A. T. DILL

**Green, Thomas Jefferson** *(14 Feb. 1802–12 Dec. 1863)*, planter, legislator, soldier, and author, was born near Ridgeway, Warren County, the son of Solomon and Frances ("Fanny") Hawkins Green. His father was a lifelong resident of Warren County, which he represented in both houses of the legislature and in the second (ratifying) constitutional convention (1789). Both of his grandfathers, Captain William Green and Colonel John Hawkins, as well as his great-grandfather, Colonel Philemon Hawkins, were officers in the American Revolution. Green was a student at The University of North Carolina in 1819–20. His appointment to the U.S. Military Academy in 1822 is not surprising as the then U.S. Senator Nathaniel Macon was his great-uncle; however, he was not graduated from the academy.

After representing Warren County in the House of Commons in 1826, Green moved to Florida, then a territory, where he was listed in the earliest tax roll for Leon (now Wakulla) County in 1829. By 1831 he was justice of the peace, and in 1834 he represented Leon County in the territorial legislature. In the account of his marriage in a Nashville, Tenn., newspaper in 1830, he is called "Major Thomas J. Green of Tallahassee, Florida," which suggests that he held a commission in the territorial militia. He was married in Davidson County, Tenn., on 8 Jan. 1830, to Sarah Angeline Wharton, daughter of Jesse Wharton, a U.S. senator and congressman. Their only child, Wharton Jackson Green, was born near St. Mark's in Leon County, Fla., on 28 Feb. 1831.

Green left Florida soon after the death of his wife on 11 Mar. 1835. After leaving his young son in Tennessee with the family of his maternal uncle, Joseph Wharton, he traveled to the then Republic of Texas. There he organized the Texas Land Company and, along with Dr. Branch T. Archer and the Whartons, purchased and laid out the now extinct town of Velasco at the mouth of the Brazos River. Soon after his arrival in 1836, he was commissioned brigadier general in the Texas army and returned to the United States to recruit men and collect money and ammunition for the cause of the Texas revolution against Mexico. He took his private fund of ammunition to Houston in the early part of 1836, when immigrants to Texas were raised from North Carolina, South Carolina, Mississippi, Georgia, Virginia, Louisiana, Kentucky, and perhaps other southern states. On 3 Oct. 1836, General Green represented Bexar County in the house of representatives of the first congress of the Republic of Texas. The following year he was elected to the senate of the second congress, but his seat was declared vacant twenty-five days after the session opened.

When a counter invasion to Mexican attacks was opposed by Sam Houston, Green was among the 304 men under General Alexander Somervell who remained in Mexico and thus precipitated the ill-fated Battle of Mier on 25 and 26 Dec. 1842. As commander of the Mier Expedition, Green surrendered to General Pedre Ampudia; he was held at Perote prison from which he, with fifteen others, escaped in the spring of 1843 after spending six months digging through a wall of volcanic rock eight feet thick. Returning to Velasco, Tex., he was elected in June 1843 to represent Brazoria County in the eighth Texas congress, where he introduced the bill that established the Rio Grande as the boundary line between Texas and Mexico. Green was one of the original organizers of the Texas Railroad, Navigation and Banking Company, the first chartered railroad in Texas, and was an early advocate of a railroad to the Pacific. Before leaving Texas he became a noted breeder of racing stock. During the pending negotiations for the annexation of Texas, Green was offered the post of confidential agent in the matter by President James K. Polk's administration, but he declined the position on the ground that he was then a citizen of the other contracting power.

In 1845, Green spent some time in New York in connection with his book, *The Texian Expedition Against Mier*, published that year by Harpers. There, on 24 Oct. 1846 in Grace Church, he married his second wife, Adeline Burr, the widow of John S. Ellery of Roxbury, Mass. She survived him, but the only child of their union died as an infant.

Four years after the annexation of Texas, Green went to California where, in the first election in November 1849, he was elected state senator from Sacramento County—having worked there for a short while in the mines. In this first California legislature he sponsored the bill for the establishment of the state university at Berkeley. On 11 Apr. 1850, the legislature elected him major general of the First Division of the California militia. Soon afterwards he was sent with an adequate force to suppress Indian disturbances in the interior. The mission succeeded. Later Green founded the town of Oro (which has since vanished) on land purchased from John Augustus Sutter in Sutter County, Calif.; he also helped lay out the town of Vallejo, the first county seat of Placer County.

Returning to North Carolina in 1857 to live in Warren County, Green engaged the famous Montmorenci plantation before purchasing Esmeralda, a 900-acre plantation on the south side of Shocco Creek, from Dr. Alexander B. Hawkins. At Esmeralda, his home for the rest of his life, Green farmed, bred blooded racehorses, and extended lavish hospitality to his friends and relations.

Green was a lifelong Jefferson-Jackson Democrat, bearing the name of the first and bestowing the name of the latter, his friend and mentor, on his only child. He was a delegate from North Carolina to the 1860 convention in Charleston. Green wanted to enlist in the Confederate Army but was prevented from doing so by the chronic affliction of gout. His will, written on 24 May 1862 "at home, near Shocco Springs," contains this characteristic item: "If this terrific and unholy war continues, it is my purpose to go into the service and should my son Wharton survive me, that he make such disposition of my body as he may prefer, with this exception, that he will not permit my wife to send it to Yankeydom." According to the biographical account of his son, Green's death at Esmeralda was caused by heartbreak over the reverses of the Confederacy. He was buried in his garden while his son, Colonel Wharton Jackson Green, was a prisoner of war at Johnson's Island, Ohio. In 1905, his remains were moved from the plantation to Fairview Cemetery, Warrenton.

SEE: *California Blue Book* (1907); Daniel L. Grant, *Alumni History of the University of North Carolina* (1924); Thomas Jefferson Green Papers (Southern Historical Collection,

University of North Carolina, Chapel Hill); Wharton J. Green, *Recollections and Reflections* (1906); *Nat. Cyc. Am. Biog.*, vol. 11 (1901); W. P. Webb, *The Handbook of Texas* (1952).

M. H. D. KERR

**Green, Wharton Jackson** *(28 Feb. 1831–6 Aug. 1910),* lawyer, soldier, planter, politician, congressman, and author, was born near St. Marks, Leon (now Wakulla) County, Fla., the only child of General Thomas Jefferson Green of Warren County and Sarah Angeline Wharton, daughter of U.S. senator and congressman Jesse Wharton of Nashville, Tenn. His maternal grandmother, Mary Phillips, had migrated to Tennessee from Edgecombe County with her parents. Young Green was named for his father's old and honored friend Andrew Jackson, his mother's maiden name being added later. After her death when he was four years old, he lived for ten years in the family of his maternal uncle, Joseph Wharton, on his plantation in Middle Tennessee where Green's education was started in a neighborhood school. When he was about fourteen, he spent a few months at the home of his eighty-year-old paternal grandmother near Ridgeway, Warren County, and studied Spanish under his father's old prisonmate, Captain Dan Henrie. He then accompanied his father as far as Washington, D.C., in 1845 on General Green's way to New York in connection with the publication of his book about the Mier Expedition. After introducing him to his many friends in Washington (including President James K. Polk), the general left his young son at the old United States Hotel to share a room with Dr. Branch T. Archer, "the father of the Texas revolution." Later Green was placed under the supervision of Jefferson Davis at a boarding house where a number of members of Congress lived, including John C. Calhoun.

In 1846, he entered Georgetown College as a boarding student. From 1847 to 1848 he attended the classical and English academy in Raleigh, N.C., operated by J. M. Lovejoy; and in 1849, Stephen M. Weld's select preparatory school near Boston, Mass. Green's appointment to the U.S. Military Academy at West Point was approved simultaneously with the admission of California as a state (September 1850), at which time his father's address was given as Sacramento. After three years at West Point, where the alumni records list him as Jackson Wharton Green, he studied law at the University of Virginia (where he was a member of the Jefferson Literary Society) and at the newly established Cumberland University at Lebanon, Tenn. On admission to the bar in 1854, he began practicing in Washington, D.C.; he was admitted to practice in the United States Supreme Court, and became a junior partner with the law firm of Robert J. Walker (former secretary of the Treasury) and Louis Janin.

After Green's marriage—at Montmorenci, Warren County, on 4 May 1858—to Esther Sergeant Ellery, the only child of his stepmother, he and his bride spent over a year traveling in Europe and Africa. Upon their return, they went to their country place in Jamaica Plain near Boston where their oldest child, Sarah Wharton, was born on 19 July 1859. When they settled at Esmeralda, their North Carolina home, with their one-month-old baby, Green engaged in agricultural pursuits and bred racehorses. Sarah Wharton Green later married Pembroke Jones and, secondly, Henry Walters, both of Wilmington. Their second daughter, Caroline Adeline, never married and their youngest daughter, Mable Ellery, married George Blow Elliott, also of Wilmington. Their only son died in infancy.

At the outbreak of the war, Green enlisted in the Warren Guards, Company F, Twelfth Regiment, North Carolina Troops, C.S.A. (Second Regiment, North Carolina Volunteers), which was one of the first three companies to report to the camp of organization in Raleigh. In two months he was appointed colonel in General Henry A. Wise's legion and raised and equipped a regiment. On 8 Feb. 1862, he was captured on Roanoke Island and paroled at Elizabeth City the same day. He later served as a volunteer aide on the staff of General Junius Daniels and as lieutenant colonel of the Second Battalion of North Carolina Infantry. Green was wounded at Washington, N.C., and again at Gettysburg where he was captured and detained at Johnson's Island, Ohio, until within a week of the surrender.

Returning to Esmeralda, Green renewed his interest in agriculture and became involved in politics. He was the first president of the Society of Confederate Soldiers and Sailors in North Carolina, and was a delegate to the Democratic National conventions in 1868, 1872, 1876, and 1888. In 1879, he bought the 469 acres of Tokay Vineyard near Fayetteville and moved there the next year, becoming deeply interested in viticulture. His wife did not live long in their new home, dying on 15 June 1883. The same year he was elected to represent the old Third North Carolina district in the Forty-eighth Congress. During that session two of his daughters lived with him at the hotel in Washington. On his reelection to the Forty-ninth Congress, Green rented a house in Washington where his oldest daughter, then Mrs. Pembroke Jones, kept house for her father and sisters. On 29 Oct. 1888, the year after completing his two terms in Congress, he married, at Tokay, Mrs. Adeline Currier Davis, widow of Judge David Davis and first cousin of his previous wife. There were no children by this marriage. Thereafter Green devoted his energies to the cultivation of his vineyard and to literary pursuits. During this time he published his *Recollections and Reflections*. He died at Tokay Vineyard and was buried in Cross Creek Cemetery, Fayetteville.

SEE: *Appleton's Cyclopedia of American Biography*, vol. 2 (1888); Samuel A. Ashe, *Cyclopedia of Eminent and Representative Men of the Carolinas of the Nineteenth Century* (1892); *Biog. Dir. Am. Cong.* (1949); W. W. Clayton, *History of Davidson County, Tennessee* (1880); Deeds, Marriage Bonds, and Wills of Warren County (North Carolina State Archives, Raleigh); Jerome Dowd, *Sketches of Prominent Living North Carolinians* (1888); Wharton J. Green, *Recollections and Reflections* (1906); Weymouth T. Jordan and Louis Manarin, eds., *North Carolina Troops, 1861–1865: A Roster*, vols. 3, 5 (1971–77); *Lamb's Biographical Dictionary of the United States*, vol. 3 (1900); John H. Oates, *The Story of Fayetteville and the Upper Cape Fear* (1972); John H. Wheeler, *Reminiscences and Memoirs of North Carolina* (1884); *Who Was Who in America*, vol. 1 (1942); Wills of Davidson County, Tenn. (County Courthouse, Nashville).

M. H. D. KERR

**Green, William Mercer** *(2 May 1798–13 Feb. 1887),* first Protestant Episcopal bishop of Mississippi, was born in Wilmington. His father was Lieutenant William Green, a patriot of the American Revolution, whose early death placed responsibility for his son's care upon his widow, Mary Bradley Green. His grandfather, Dr.

Samuel Green, formerly of Liverpool, had left specific directions regarding the education of his progeny. With these ideas his Quaker mother was in complete accord. Her mother had been the former Elizabeth Sharpless, a birthright Quaker; her father, Richard Bradley, also a Friend, had come from Kendal, England. Young William Green was graduated from The University of North Carolina in 1818, yielding in honors only to his classmate and friend, James Knox Polk.

Greatly influenced by an account of Bishop George Berkeley's life, he turned to the study of theology. He valued the precepts of bishops John Henry Hobart and John Stark Ravenscroft, always calling himself "a Prayer Book churchman." On 29 Apr. 1821 Green received deacon's orders from Bishop Richard Channing Moore in Christ Church, Raleigh, and on 20 Apr. 1823 he was ordained a priest by Bishop Moore in St. James's Church, Wilmington. In the latter year he nominated the Diocese of North Carolina's first bishop, John Stark Ravenscroft. Green served first in St. John's Parish, Williamsborough, and then as rector of Emmanuel Church in Warrenton. In 1825 he went to St. Matthew's in Hillsborough, where he also directed the work of the Hillsborough Female Seminary. Two years later he returned to his alma mater as chaplain and professor of belles lettres. Dissatisfied that students had to attend college chapel services regardless of their denominational preference, he was determined to provide a place for Episcopalians to worship. His arduous labors resulted in his founding the Chapel of the Cross in Chapel Hill. Its completion was achieved on the eve of his being called to Mississippi as the state's first Protestant Episcopal bishop. There he was consecrated on 24 Feb. 1850 in St. Andrew's Church, Jackson. His responsibility included not only the care of the whole diocese but also, for two years, pastoral duties in Trinity Parish, Natchez. By his thirtieth year of active service in the diocese, the number of parishes had increased from ten to fifty-one; forty-one new churches had been built and the training of clergy fostered regardless of race. An assistant was not elected until the thirty-third year of his episcopate.

Green worked zealously to promote the establishment of training schools for clergy and was one of the founders of an institution, at Sewanee, Tenn., which he named the "University of the South." After becoming chancellor of that university in 1866, he built on its domain a residence that he called "Kendal" for his grandfather's home. Here he enjoyed the visits of his close friend and parishioner, Jefferson Davis. In North Carolina Green and his family had known the ravages of war, pestilence, and fire, which all fell to their lot again in Mississippi. After the tragic death of his son, the Reverend Duncan Cameron Green, during Greenville's yellow fever epidemic in 1878, the poet Longfellow wrote "The Chamber Over the Gate" and sent it with a letter of condolence to Bishop Green whom he had met.

In addition to his pastoral and diocesan work, Green was the author of *Memoir of Bishop Ravenscroft* (1830) and *Memoir of the Rt. Rev. James Hervey Otey* (1885). He received the D.D. degree from the University of Pennsylvania in 1845 and the LL.D. degree from The University of North Carolina in 1881.

On 22 Dec. 1818, he married Sally Williams Sneed of Williamsborough, N.C. Widowed in 1832, he married Charlotte Isabella Fleming of Pittsboro on 18 Dec. 1835. Of his thirteen children, several followed the clerical, medical, or professional vocations of their forefathers. After his death at his Sewanee home, Green was buried in Greenwood Cemetery, Jackson, Miss. He was succeeded by Hugh Miller Thompson, who had become his assistant in 1883. A portrait of Bishop Green was painted by Helen Frances Colburn of Washington City.

SEE: *Appleton's Cyclopaedia of American Biography*, vol. 2 (1888); Board of Trustees, University of the South, *Proceedings, 1868–1887* (1887); Gilbert Cope, *Genealogy of the Sharples Family* (1887); George R. Fairbanks, *History of the University of the South at Sewanee, Tennessee* (1905); Archibald Henderson, *The Campus of the First State University* (1949); *Historical Magazine of the Protestant Episcopal Church* 51 (March 1972); *Journal of Mississippi History* 4 (April 1942), 8 (April 1946), 8 (July 1946), 12 (January 1950); Mississippi Historical Records Survey Project, *Inventory of the Church Archives of Mississippi, Protestant Episcopal Church* (1940); *Nat. Cyc. Am. Biog.*, vol. 9 (1899); William S. Perry, *The Episcopate in America* (1895); *Sketches of Church History in North Carolina* (1892); James Sprunt, *Chronicles of the Cape Fear River, 1660–1916* (1916); University of North Carolina *University Magazine* 7 (1887); *Who Was Who in America*, 1607–1896 (1963).

RACHEL BROWN DE ROSSET

**Greene, George Washington** *(29 June 1852–17 Dec. 1911)*, Baptist minister, teacher, and missionary to China, was born at Globe. The names of his parents are unknown. In 1865 he was baptized in the Lower Creek Baptist Church, Caldwell County by the Reverend John B. Powell, and the following year he was licensed by the church. After attending the local schools, he entered Wake Forest College in 1866 at age fourteen and was graduated with a B.A. degree in 1870. He then entered the Southern Baptist Theological Seminary, Greenville, S.C. (now at Louisville, Ky.), where he remained until 1871. Greene returned to the Watauga County area of North Carolina for a short time before serving as a state missionary in the Tarboro area. He was examined and ordained to the ministry on 2 and 3 Dec. 1871 by a presbytery called by the Wake Forest Baptist Church consisting of W. T. Brooks and Charles E. Taylor. Greene reentered the seminary at Greenville, S.C., where he was graduated in 1875. A classmate later remembered that Greene was one of the best linguists that he had ever seen. He was "at home" in Hebrew, Greek, and Latin, and while a student was always off "on Sundays preaching and teaching in obscure and destitute regions."

After graduation, Greene began his lifelong work for the Baptist denomination as Sunday school secretary of the North Carolina Baptist State Convention (1875); he later served the convention as recording secretary (1878, 1885–89). He was pastor of the Hickory Baptist Church from 1876 to 1877, when he became principal of the Moravian Falls Academy, Wilkes County, a school sponsored by the Baptist churches in Ashe, Alleghany, and Caldwell counties and at Brier Creek. While there he was responsible for educating some of the leading citizens of the area, writing *Bingham's Elementary English Grammar* (1881), and founding the Moravian Falls Baptist Church (1886). In 1890, Greene was called to Wake Forest College as professor of Latin. According to Dr. G. W. Paschal, "he was an able linguist and a master of a good English style, but he remained at the College too short a time to establish the character, good or bad of his instruction."

From time to time Greene had a strong interest in

missionary work. Finally yielding to the call, he applied to the Southern Baptist Convention's Foreign Mission Board which, on 8 June 1891, appointed him to Canton, China. After a train trip across the United States, he sailed on 26 Sept. 1891 from San Francisco on the Steamship *China* with his wife and children. A letter from Greene in November told of their safe arrival after a sixteen-day passage.

Greene spent his first year in China studying the language, preaching in English, and conducting prayer meetings and Bible schools. As a preacher, he had a message that comforted and strengthened the hearts of all classes; he also was responsible for the expansion and relocation of the cramped and unsanitary mission in Canton. As a writer, Greene realized very quickly that the Christians must have suitable literature. Most of his books were written for the preachers with whom he worked. Greene wrote the first church history in China. He also found time to compose lengthy letters to the various Baptist associations and to the *Biblical Recorder* in North Carolina. Several articles dealing with the Chinese language appeared in the *Wake Forest Student Magazine*. Greene was the author of books on Christian ethics and many small tracts and pamphlets. At his death he was within four chapters of translating *The Southern Baptist Convention Manual for Sunday School Workers* into Chinese. In addition, he was one of the first to see the need for a publication society and was active in the work of the China Baptist Publication Society. Nevertheless, Greene was—by nature and by preparation—at his best as a teacher. He was sent to China for this purpose and felt that this was his chosen work. There he worked hard to establish a model seminary for the Chinese and constantly endeavored to upgrade the curriculum. A leader among the native preachers, he was the first to suggest that the Chinese preachers were not helpers or assistants to the American missionaries but were their equals, "co-workers with their Master and ours."

Returning to North Carolina on furlough in 1910, Greene enrolled his children in Mars Hill College and for six weeks taught a course on "The Uplift of China" at Ridgecrest (Bluemont Assembly). Afterward, he went back to China to continue teaching and educating the Chinese. He was taken suddenly ill while dining with his family. A physician was summoned but it was too late. Greene had died from apoplexy.

Greene's first wife, Dora Mauldin of Greenville, S.C., died on 22 Oct. 1890 and was buried at Wake Forest. She left three children: Anna (Mrs. S. R. Moore), born 1878; Pansy (Mrs. P. H. Anderson), born 1884; and Felix Bailey, born 1888. On 17 June 1891, Greene married Valleria A. Page in Morrisville. They were the parents of George William, Valleria (Mrs. M. T. Rankin), and Mary Katherine who died as an infant. Greene's widow continued to serve in China, and George William and Valleria also received appointments as missionaries.

SEE: Biographical folders for George Washington Greene, 1852–1911, and George William Greene, 1894–1960 (Baptist Historical Collection, Wake Forest University, Winston-Salem); George Lasher, ed., *Baptist Ministerial Directory* (1899); George W. Paschal, *History of Wake Forest College*, vol. 2 (1943); Raleigh *Biblical Recorder*, 13 Dec. 1871, 29 Oct. 1890, 24 June 1891, 7 Sept. 1898, 12 Feb., 6 Mar. 1912; Richmond *Foreign Mission Journal*, July 1891, June 1892, March 1893; John R. Sampey, *Southern Baptist Theological Seminary, 1859–89* (1890); *Wake Forest Student* 32 (March 1913 [photograph]).

JOHN R. WOODARD

**Greenlaw, Edwin Almiron** *(6 Apr. 1874–10 Sept. 1931)*, Renaissance scholar and educator, was born in Flora, Ill., the first of seven children of Thomas Brewer and Emma Julia Leverich Greenlaw. His father was founder and president of Orchard City College, a normal training school at Flora; superintendent of public schools for Clay County; and founder of a newspaper, the *Clay County Record* which became the *Southern Illinois Journal-Record*. His grandfather, John Brewer Greenlaw, was a Methodist minister who married Sarah Wilder Lowell. Edwin Greenlaw was the great-grandson of William and Hannah Hersey Greenlaw and the great-great-grandson of William Greenlaw, a native of Edinburgh, Scotland, who with his father William, Sr., and five brothers, emigrated to Mount Desert Island, Maine, in 1765. They later moved to Saint Andrews, New Brunswick, where William married Catherine McNason.

Although Edwin Greenlaw had only three years of formal public school, he received an excellent education from his teacher-parents. At age twelve he entered Chester (Ill.) High School to become its top student and graduate at fourteen. After a year of postgraduate work there, he taught telegraphy, shorthand, literature, and business courses at Orchard City College until he was nineteen. He entered Illinois College in 1893, but left the next year to serve as president of Orchard City College for two years. In February 1896 he entered Northwestern University, where he received an A.B. in history in 1897 and a master's degree in history—one of the first awarded by Northwestern—in 1898. In the latter year he was elected to Phi Beta Kappa. Greenlaw taught pedagogics and English at Northwestern and English and methods of teaching at Northwestern Academy from 1897 through 1905, taking a year's leave of absence in 1901 to begin work on a doctorate at Harvard. When he returned to Northwestern in 1902, Harvard awarded him an unsolicited M.A. in English. In 1903, he became head of the English department at Northwestern Academy and continued his doctoral studies at the University of Chicago. Harvard accepted that work and awarded him a Ph.D. in English in June 1904.

In 1905, Greenlaw became head of the English department at Adelphi College, Brooklyn, N.Y., where he published his first book, *Selections From Chaucer*, and continued to grow in reputation. From 1905 until the end of his life he labored to make Edmund Spenser's writing understood by the ages.

After twenty-one years of teaching, eight of them at Adelphi, he went to The University of North Carolina in the fall of 1913 at age thirty-nine. There he "did more for the (English) Department than any other person has done, and as much for the University as any other one person in this century." In June 1914, he was appointed chairman of the English department and began immediately to collect experts and specialists (expanding the faculty from eight in 1914 to thirty-seven in 1925) and to organize the department, which had classes and offices scattered throughout the campus. During the war years he instituted a vehicle, "The Range Finder," for the publication of student papers, which was a pioneer in a new type of college journalism. He also organized a graduate club. In 1915, he became managing editor of *Studies in Philology* (established in 1906), which he immediately put on a quarterly, subscription basis and expanded to include articles from leading scholars outside the university. Within three years it had tripled in size and was ranked among the leading journals in the field.

In 1916, Greenlaw instituted a program for undergraduate honors in language and literature. In connection with this program (which included independent reading, tutorial assistance, a thesis, and an oral examination), he instituted a series of one-week "seminars" given annually by visiting professors, who chose their own topics and sent reading lists in advance.

In 1918, he persuaded Frederick Henry Koch to come to The University of North Carolina where the latter established the Carolina Playmakers. That year Greenlaw became one of the first five Kenan professors and in December he became the third dean of the Graduate School, which he then reorganized. Emphasizing research, he noted that the aim of a graduate school (unlike an undergraduate institution that exists to perpetuate knowledge) is to add to the body of knowledge through guiding student research. His department had 125 graduate students in 1920 and 310 in 1925. By 1921, Greenlaw was receiving the highest salary ever paid a professor in the history of the university.

Under the direction of a committee led by Greenlaw, a Department of Comparative Literature was established in 1920. Two years later—largely through his efforts in organizing the Graduate School—the university was elected to membership in the Association of American Universities. Also largely through his support, the University Press became a reality in March 1922. That year saw the publication of the first two volumes of his *Literature and Life*, a high school literature series that revolutionized the teaching of English in American high schools. The four volumes (volumes three and four were published in 1923 and 1924, respectively) sold over a million copies before his death. His governing philosophy that "great literature is the biography of the human spirit" was eloquently illustrated in this first major anthology of literature as the study of the history of ideas.

In 1925, Greenlaw accepted the first Sir William Osler Professorship of English Literature at Johns Hopkins University. There his scholarship attracted an increasing number of students and at his death the English department had grown from one of the smallest to one of the largest departments of university study. As a member of the academic council he played an important part in directing the work of the faculty of philosophy. His individual work included contributions to the study of medieval romance, Shakespeare, and Milton. Most importantly, his long application to Spenserian problems—beginning with an exhaustive elucidation of the poet's "Mother Hubberds Tale" in terms of the political, literary, and ecclesiastical environment at Elizabeth's court—found its fullest expression in the conception and planning of a variorum edition of the poet's work, the first two volumes of which were nearly ready for publication at the time of Greenlaw's death. Planning for the work of more than 4,000 pages began in 1922. He also founded the series of "Johns Hopkins Monographs in Literary History." His own contributions were two volumes, *The Province of Literary History* (1931) and *Studies in Spenser's Historical Allegory* (1932). The first of these was hailed by Dr. Marjorie Nicolson in later years as "one of the earliest important works in the establishment of what we now think of as the history of ideas."

Greenlaw's publications number in the hundreds; his books include: *A Syllabus of English Literature* (1912), *Outline of the Literature of the English Renaissance* (1916), and *Builders of Democracy* (1918). He edited *Selections From Chaucer* (1907), *Irving's Knickerbocker History of New York* (1909), *Familiar Letters* (1915), *National Ideas in English and American Literature* (1918), *The Great Tradition* (with J. Holly Hanford, 1918), and the four-volume anthology, *Literature and Life* (1922–24). Greenlaw was editor-in-chief of *Modern Language Notes* (1926–28), a member of the Tudor and Stuart Club, and president of the Johns Hopkins Philological Association (1929–30). The honorary degrees of LL.D. and D.Lit. were confirmed on him by The University of North Carolina (1926) and Northwestern University (1927), respectively. He was a member of the Modern Language Association, American Association of University Professors, English Association of Great Britain, American Dialect Society, National Council of Teachers of English, and the National Conference on English. He served on the advisory board of the Guggenheim Foundation from its inception in February 1925 until his death.

A deeply religious man who was active in the Methodist church and an accomplished musician (piano, clarinet, and voice), Greenlaw was married at Flora, Ill., 1 Sept. 1898, to Mary Elizabeth Durland, daughter of William Robert and Laura Eugenia Dye Durland. They had three children: Dorothy Durland, Margery Keith, and Mary Edwin. He died in Chapel Hill and was buried in the old Chapel Hill Cemetery.

Greenlaw had a fertile and stimulating mind, singularly free from dry pedantry. Although he argued eloquently for the "gospel of the infinitesimally small," his true interest lay always in the larger movements of human culture, and the province of philology was expanded by him to include not only the writings of literary merit but also every reflection of the intellectual life of the Renaissance. On 4 Oct. 1970, Edwin Greenlaw Hall was dedicated at The University of North Carolina in his honor. The university noted that "This Renaissance man with seemingly boundless energy and ambitious determination sacrificed his leisure to his study and the classroom and in his years at Chapel Hill raised himself to eminence among scholars of the English Renaissance and to primacy among students of Edmund Spenser. By means of truly great teaching he carried from the study to the classroom the riches of Shakespeare, Spenser, and Bacon." Thomas Wolfe, one of his students at Chapel Hill, wrote to him on 28 June 1930: "the men who waken us and light a fire in us when we are eighteen are so rare that their image is branded into our hearts forever, . . . we remember them always with affection and loyalty." Portraits of Greenlaw hang in the seminar room at Gilman Hall at Johns Hopkins University and in Greenlaw Hall at Chapel Hill.

SEE: *Johns Hopkins Alumni Magazine* 20 (November 1931, January 1932); *Modern Language Notes* 16 (1931); *Nat. Cyc. Am. Biog.*, vol. 22 (1932); Raleigh *News and Observer*, 12 Sept. 1931; *Studies in Philology* 29 (1932).

EDWIN GREENLAW SAPP

**Greer, Isaac ("Ike") Grafield** *(4 Dec. 1881–24 Nov. 1967)*, educator and superintendent of Baptist Children's Homes, was born in the Zionville community a few miles from Boone in Watauga County, the fifth of eight children of Phillip and Mary Greer. His parents, by precept and example, instilled in him the basic traits of honesty, industry, and Christian morals, which characterized his endeavors throughout life. As a boy he worked with his parents, brothers, and sisters on their mountain farm. His healthy respect for hard work distinguished his own life, and he taught the value of work to all the children who came under his care. During his youth in Watauga County, Greer also took a lively interest in the area's folk songs and ballads, which he later collected and sang to the delight of audiences in the United States and Europe. Indeed, he became as well known for his folk singing as for his speaking and for the quaint stories he sprinkled throughout his speeches.

Greer received his elementary schooling at Zionville, attended high school in Boone, and was a student at The University of North Carolina from 1906 to 1908. While at Chapel Hill, he worked his way by waiting on tables and doing other jobs. Afterward, he did graduate work at Columbia University. From 1908 to 1910 he taught in a one-room school and served as principal at Walnut Grove High School. He then joined the history department at Appalachian State Teacher's College, where he taught from 1910 to 1932. The class of 1916, for which he was sponsor and adviser, honored him in 1966 by establishing the I. G. Greer Distinguished Professorship in History, the first such professorship created at Appalachian. Also in 1966, the college's fine arts building was named the I. G. Greer Building.

While living and teaching in Boone, he represented Watauga County in the state legislature (1925) and served on the board of aldermen. Although qualified for further political service, his interests and commitment lay elsewhere. Greer's great compassion for people led to his interest in the Baptist Children's Homes, and in 1928 he was elected by the Baptist State Convention to the Mills Home board of trustees. In 1932, when Dr. M. L. Kesler, then general manager of Mills Home Baptist Orphanage, was killed in an accident, the trustees named Greer to succeed him as superintendent of the Children's Homes, a position he held from 1 Oct. 1932 until his resignation on 16 Dec. 1947. At the time of his appointment, the country was experiencing the Great Depression and, as a result, the Children's Homes were in debt and supplies were hard to obtain. The new superintendent, who had the gift of mixing humor with pathos in his speeches, proved to be the greatest money raiser connected with Baptist institutions during that period. When he took the story of the children and their needs to groups all over the state, the people responded. In 1931, the Children's Homes had spent $23,985 more than they received that year. Through Greer's fund-raising efforts, they had a surplus of $12,430 by 1933. Moreover, under his leadership, the Homes grew and services were extended to more children. After his resignation in 1947, he became assistant vice-president of the Business Foundation of North Carolina, Inc., with offices in Chapel Hill. He resigned from that post in 1954.

For a time Greer was president of the North Carolina Conference for Social Services, which presented him an award for outstanding leadership in child care in 1959. He also was a member of the board of trustees of the Child Welfare League of America. In 1942, he received an honorary LL.D. degree from Wake Forest College.

A prominent Baptist layman, Greer served as the first president of the Allied Church League and, in 1942, as president of the Baptist State Convention. In addition, he was president of the Folklore Society and made a large contribution to the preservation of folk songs and ballads from the mountains of North Carolina. Accompanied on the dulcimer by his wife, Willie Greer, he gave more than four hundred public performances as interpreter of ballads and folk songs. Their entire collection of these songs, which has been called the most complete in existence, was presented to Appalachian State University where it is housed with other memorabilia in the Appalachian Room of the library.

In 1916 Greer married Willie Spainhour of Morganton, and they became the parents of two sons: Isaac G., Jr., and Joseph. She died in 1959. In 1963 Greer married Mrs. Hattie O'Briant, a widow, of Rocky Mount.

SEE: *Durham Morning Herald*, 7 Dec. 1947, 15 Nov. 1967; I. G. Greer Collection (Appalachian Room, Appalachian State University, Boone); Raleigh *News and Observer*, 28 May 1950, 28 Aug. 1951; *Records of the Baptist Children's Home*, Thomasville; W. C. Reed, *Love in Action, The Story of the Baptist Children's Home of North Carolina* (1973).

LOIS V. EDINGER

**Gregory, Fletcher Harrison** *(24 Nov. 1882–3 Nov. 1970)*, banker and businessman, was born at Halifax of English and Scottish ancestry. He was the son of John Tillery and Ella Clark Gregory and the grandson of Thomas Wynns Gregory, a physician, who established the family in Halifax County in the early years of the century. His father, a merchant and farmer, served with the Confederate Army throughout the Civil War; in later life he was for many years clerk of the superior court of Halifax County. Young Fletcher, like his older brother Quentin, with whom he was closely associated throughout most of his life and who survived him, attended Horner Military Academy at Oxford and then went on to The University of North Carolina. There he received the A.B. degree in 1904 and served as an assistant in the physics department during his senior year. Returning to Halifax to help with the family store and farms, he played a key role in organizing the Bank of Halifax, which opened in October 1906. The new bank was soon his main business interest, and he guided it with skill and sound judgment.

In 1920 his brother Quentin, who had been with the British-American Tobacco Company in the Far East for fifteen years, returned to Halifax and joined him in the banking business. The two brothers, with Quentin as president and Fletcher as executive vice-president, increased substantially the capital stock of the Bank of Halifax, which grew steadily during the 1920s to become one of the soundest and strongest banks in the state. It not only took the Great Depression in stride but it also gained in deposits each month during 1933 with its "banking holiday." Between 1933 and 1936 the Bank of Halifax took over the banks of Scotland Neck, Weldon, and Littleton, and a few years later established a branch at Enfield. It was then a solid and prosperous banking system serving a sizable segment of eastern North Carolina. The bank owed much of its success to the fact that the Gregory brothers knew personally most of their clientele, and were thus personal bankers in the best and fullest sense. In 1968, when Fletcher was 86 and Quentin 88, the Bank of Halifax—still strong and solid—merged with Branch Banking and Trust Company of Wilson, the oldest banking firm in the state.

Though Fletcher Gregory made his main contribution to the economic life of his region as a banker, he was a well-rounded man who contributed in many areas. He took the lead in reorganizing the textile mill at Scotland Neck as the Halifax County Hosiery Mill and served as its president for many years, and he was active at one time or another in both ginning and milling enterprises at Halifax. Outside the business field, he served as state senator in 1929, as a member of the board of trustees of The University of North Carolina for a time, and as chairman of the Board of Education of Halifax County for several years. He also was one of the founders and a lifelong member of the Roanoke River Basin Association. Above all, Gregory was a strong family man, viewing the family as the most basic institution. In 1916 he married Boyd Thorne of Airlie, and to them were born one daughter, Mrs. Agnes Carter of Roanoke Rapids, and three sons: Fletcher H., Jr., of Weldon, Samuel T. of Scotland Neck, and Thorne of Wilson, all of whom survived him. An active Episcopalian and Mason, Gregory was a superb representative of that stratum of solid and substantial citizens who believe that hard work, honesty, and thrift are cardinal virtues and who over the years have contributed so much to the growth and strength of the state and nation. He died in Parkview Hospital in Rocky Mount and was buried at Halifax. There is a portrait of him by Barringer Studios of Rocky Mount.

SEE: Raleigh *News and Observer*, 28 Oct. 1956; Records of the Bank of Halifax (Halifax); *Roanoke Rapids Daily Herald*, 5 Nov. 1970; *Scotland Neck Commonwealth*, 5 Oct. 1956, 12 Nov. 1970; University of North Carolina *Alumni Review* 59 (February 1971).

CARL H. PEGG

**Gregory, Isaac** *(ca. 1737–April 1800)*, Revolutionary officer and public official, was born in Pasquotank County, the son of William and Judith Morgan Gregory. He was a brother of Dempsey, also a Revolutionary officer and public official. As a county justice in 1765, Isaac signed an agreement not to hold court until the Stamp Act was repealed. In 1769–70 he was collector of public debts in Pasquotank County, and in 1770 and 1773 he was sheriff—altogether he was appointed to this office eight times. In the latter year he was a trustee to build St. Martin's Anglican chapel on land given by Thomas MacKnight in neighboring Currituck County. He represented Pasquotank County in the Assembly of 1775, the last to meet at the call of a royal governor, and was also a delegate to provincial congresses in 1775 and 1776, at the last of which the state constitution was written and adopted. On 6 Apr. 1775 Thomas MacKnight, a delegate from Currituck County, refused to sign the Continental Association, and Isaac Gregory was among the five delegates who withdrew in support of him. Nevertheless, Gregory himself supported the action of the Continental Congress.

Gregory was commissioned lieutenant colonel in September 1775 and promoted to colonel seven months later. He served as a member of the Safety Committee of the Edenton District and was named by the Provincial Congress to procure arms in Pasquotank County and to take charge of Tory property. The General Assembly in July 1777 named him to a committee to establish a courthouse and other public buildings for the new county of Camden in which his extensive land holdings now lay. Soon after the Assembly elected him a brigadier general on 12 May 1779, he joined General Jethro Sumner at Yadkin Ford near Salisbury. At the Battle of Camden Gregory's men "fought with desperation" but were abandoned by others and outnumbered. The general was wounded in the battle and his horse was shot from under him. Cornwallis's report erroneously recorded the death of Gregory. Although he was engaged in military action in Piedmont North Carolina and upcountry South Carolina, he corresponded with governors Richard Caswell, Thomas Burke, and Alexander Martin.

In March and April 1781, Gregory and his troops were charged with protecting northeastern North Carolina from a possible British attack from their bases in Virginia. The militia made several forays in the direction of the enemy. During an idle evening in camp, a British officer, for amusement, wrote a letter to which he signed General Gregory's name. The text of the fanciful letter contained the suggestion that American forces might be betrayed to the British. The next morning the British abandoned their camp and the fictitious letter was left behind. Found soon afterward by Americans who knew nothing of its origin, it was assumed to be authentic. This discovery created a sensation and Gregory, charged with treason, was about to be court-martialed. Hearing of Gregory's predicament, the officer who had written the letter sent the Americans a full account of his role in the affair and expressed complete confidence in the loyalty of General Gregory to his country. This, of course, ended the charges, but Gregory was forever after deeply resentful of the doubt expressed at that time as to his patriotism.

Gregory represented Camden County in the North Carolina House of Commons in 1780–81 and in the senate for ten terms between 1782 and 1795. In 1782 he was named a trustee of Smith Academy in Edenton, and in 1789 he became a trustee of the Currituck Seminary of Learning. As a delegate to the constitutional conventions of 1788 and 1789, he was active as a Federalist. In 1787 and 1788 he served as a commissioner to promote navigation on Albemarle Sound. As customs collector for the District of Camden in 1793, he seized a schooner for improperly importing goods.

Gregory's first wife may have been a daughter of Caleb Sawyer; his second wife was Sarah Lamb. His children were William, Isaac, Mary, Sarah, Penelope, and Harriett. He was buried on his plantation, Fairfax (now often called Fairfield), in Camden County. The handsome, three-story brick house, dating from the 1740s, is still standing although not in good condition.

SEE: Samuel A. Ashe, ed., *Biographical History of North Carolina*, vol. 4 (1906); Walter Clark, ed., *State Records of North Carolina*, vols. 13-15, 18-19, 22-25 (1896–1906); Pasquotank County Historical Society *Year Book*, vol. 3 (1957); Jesse F. Pugh, *Three Hundred Years Along the Pasquotank* (1957); William L. Saunders, ed., *Colonial Records of North Carolina*, vols. 8-10 (1890); J. G. Simcoe, *A History of the Operations of a Partisan Corps, Called The Queen's Rangers* (1844).

WILLIAM S. POWELL

**Gregory, Mary Lloyd** *(1768–5 Aug. 1858)*, innkeeper, was born in Edgecombe County, the daughter of Nicholas and Mary Lloyd. Nothing is known of her early life. On 30 June 1796 she gave birth to a son, Joseph, fathered by Joseph Ross, a citizen of Tarboro. On 2 Sept. 1796 Ross deeded to Mary Lot 40 in the town, evidently in some effort to provide for mother and son. The antecedents of Joseph Ross are not known. He appears in the Edgecombe records as a merchant, and for many years he was in partnership with Weeks Parker, a prominent local citizen. Ross had moved to Petersburg, Va., by 1803, and in 1811 he settled in Raleigh. Here he lived for the remainder of his life. Joseph Ross never married and apparently had no children except his son by Mary Lloyd. It is not clear why the relationship was never legalized. The will of Ross, dated 3 Aug. 1830 and probated in Wake County in 1832, devised all his estate to his son, Joseph Ross Lloyd, who was also named executor.

In 1807 Mary Lloyd married one Edmund Gregory,

who happened to be passing through Tarboro. It is not known where he came from. He had been married before and had one daughter. Prior to marrying Gregory, Mary Lloyd took the precaution of deeding the lot given her by Ross to their eleven-year-old son, Joseph. Mary's venture into matrimony was brief and unsuccessful as Gregory left almost immediately for Tennessee. The records imply that he remained there until 1814, when his wife petitioned the state legislature for divorce from bed and board, the only recourse available to her at that time. Mary Gregory's petition has been lost but it was probably based on desertion. The plea of Edmund Gregory that the divorce not be granted has survived. His motives are questionable, for his petition contained a long diatribe as to how his wife had mistreated him and unfavorable comments on her behavior in Tarboro during his long absence in Tennessee, behavior, he floridly remarked, that would not even be tolerated by a Turkish pasha. As the years went by Mary became well-to-do. Gregory must have remained a problem, because his former wife and her advisers were not satisfied that the 1814 legislative divorce protected her estate from any claim of his. On 28 June 1836, the county sheriff sold at auction the lands of Edmund Gregory in which Mary Gregory had an interest. This included all the real estate she had acquired since her marriage in 1807. At the sale, the property was bought by her son, Joseph R. Lloyd, who very shortly afterwards appointed George W. Mordecai of Wake County as trustee to hold the property for his mother.

Mary may have begun her long and successful career as innkeeper when Ross gave her the lot in 1796. Business prospered and in 1809 she purchased Lot 37 in Tarboro from Henry Cotten and the adjoining Lot 48 the following year from David Marsh. At the time of the 1836 sale her tavern was described as being at lots 37 and part of 48, with the stable on Lot 39. The first two of the above lots were located on the west side of St. George's Street, as Main Street was then called, on the original town plot of Tarboro. Mary Gregory's tavern has been referred to as the Tarboro Tavern and in newspaper notices of the time as the Tarboro Hotel. Mrs. Gregory continued to invest her profits in real estate, not only in Tarboro but also in the Conetoe Swamp section in the eastern part of Edgecombe County. Joseph Blount Cheshire, in his book *Nonnulla* (1930), related an episode concerning Mary Gregory and her Conetoe holdings. Elder John Daniel, a prominent Primitive Baptist preacher in the section, conceived the idea of draining Conetoe Swamp to render its rich land fit for cultivation. Mrs. Gregory owned the land where the swamp drained into the Tar River and operated a mill at that site. Elder Daniel presented to the lady the advantages of a constant water supply for the mill, and she became the largest subscriber to the project. When the work was finished all went well until the mill and its dam were suddenly washed away after a heavy rain. Cheshire reported that thereafter, when Elder Daniel had business in Tarboro, he took care not to pass in front of Mrs. Gregory's tavern on Main Street, wryly commenting that few cared to face her when she had a grievance. Cheshire, a native of Tarboro, knew Mary Gregory well. He described her as a picturesque character, a woman of strength and intelligence, and among the best known and most forceful of the inhabitants of Tarboro in the days of his youth.

For the times, Mary Gregory's career was remarkable. It was not easy then for a woman to succeed in business, but succeed she did; at the time of the 1850 census she was worth $25,000, then a considerable fortune. No less difficult was the rearing of her son Joseph. The life of Joseph Ross Lloyd, though disadvantaged by his having been born out of wedlock, was an amazing success story as well. Following graduation from The University of North Carolina in 1815, he became an attorney. It is likely that he read law with George Mordecai, as there was a lifelong association between the two men and Lloyd named a son for Mordecai. In 1821 Joseph Lloyd represented Edgecombe County for one term in the legislature, and in 1832 he was one of the attorneys for his alma mater. For a while Lloyd was postmaster of Tarboro, and at the time of his death in 1841 he was president of the local branch of the state bank. Mary Gregory outlived her son by many years and died at the age of ninety. She was buried under an impressive marble obelisk in Calvary Churchyard, Tarboro, near her son and his family.

SEE: Kemp P. Battle, *History of the University of North Carolina*, vol. 1 (1907); Calvary Churchyard tombstone inscriptions (Tarboro); Lois Neal, *Abstracts of Vital Records from Raleigh Newspapers*, vol. 2 (1980); North Carolina State Archives, Raleigh, for Edgecombe County Wills and Deeds, Legislative Papers, Session of 1814, and Wake County Wills.

CLAIBORNE T. SMITH, JR.

**Gregory, Thomas Laurence Baker** *(12 May 1807–18 Dec. 1859)*, portrait painter, was born in Hertford County. The name of his father is unknown, but his grandfather was very likely one Thomas Gregory who married Priscilla Baker, the sister of General Laurence Baker. His mother, Margaret Bradford, a native of Halifax County, was a descendant of the Reverend Thomas Burges. On the early death of her husband, she returned to Halifax where she married James Whitaker. Thomas L. B. Gregory was reared and resided all of his life in the Crowells Cross Roads section of Halifax County.

Nothing is known of his education and little about the artistic influences he encountered. He undoubtedly knew the work of the itinerant painter James McGibbon, who did several portraits in the town of Halifax about 1830. Young Gregory also may have been familiar with the fine portraits of his cousin, Mary Wynns Gregory, and her husband, Dr. Isaac Pipkin of Murfreesboro, which were painted by Thomas Sully in 1825. In the Scotland Neck neighborhood, near Gregory's home, lived the descendants of John Anthony, a native of Philadelphia, who owned a portrait of him painted by his first cousin, Gilbert Stuart. The work of Jacob Marling, the Raleigh portrait painter, was known in Halifax County in Gregory's formative years.

The first notice of Thomas Gregory as a portrait painter was in 1835 when he was twenty-eight. On 3 April of that year he advertised in the Tarboro *Free Press* that he would be available to do portraits in the local hotel of that town. From succeeding issues of the paper, it appears that he was so engaged in Tarboro for several months. There is no further record of him as an artist until November 1839, when John Buxton Williams of Warren County recorded in his diary that Gregory had come to do his portrait and that of his mother, Lucy Tunstall Williams. Williams also commented that Gregory had taken away an old portrait to copy. Thomas Gregory did not sign his work. Using the portraits of John Williams and his mother as a standard of comparison, it can be established that he painted two other portraits in the Williams family connection about the same time. Although he must have done several paintings when he was working in Tarboro in the spring of 1835, no portraits by him have been found there with the possible exception of the portrait of Jonas Johnston Carr of the Old Sparta section of Edgecombe. This is of interest as Carr and John B. Williams married sisters, and Gregory would thus have been provided with an entrée to the Warren County family. No paintings by Thomas Gregory have been identified in his home neighborhood in Halifax.

As a painter, Gregory was only average. He was able to capture a likeness but other details in his pictures are clumsy. Of the portraits attributed to him, the one of John B. Williams is by far the best. Gregory's chief importance lies in the fact that he was one of the early natives of the state to attempt portrait painting as a profession.

Little is known of the last two decades of the painter's life. References to him in the deeds of Halifax County reflect mounting economic difficulties. At one point, his wife sued him for the return of property guaranteed to her in a prenuptial agreement. Thomas Gregory appears in the 1850 census as a farmer in the Crowells neighborhood. In the 1859 death schedule for the census of 1860, he is listed as an artist and as having died of consumption of several months' duration.

In 1828 Gregory married Mary Frances Pittman of Halifax County. Of their several children, only one, Frederick William, married and left descendants. Thomas L. B. Gregory, his wife, and several children were buried under a handsome monument in Old Trinity Episcopal Cemetery, Scotland Neck. Photographs of his known portraits are on file in the Frick Art Reference Library, New York. They also appear, though not attributed to him, in a book of portraits and photographs published in 1961 by the Alston-Williams family society.

SEE: *Alston-Williams-Boddie-Hilliard Society*, Society and Family Book, vol. 1 (1958–61); Edward Biddle and Mantle Fielding, *The Life and Works of Thomas Sully* (1970); Halifax County Deeds and Wills (Halifax); Laura MacMillan, ed., *North Carolina Portrait Index* (1963); Tarboro *Free Press*, 4 Apr.–23 May 1835; John Buxton Williams diary (in possession of a descendant).

CLAIBORNE T. SMITH, JR.

**Grier, Samuel Andrew** *(8 Oct. 1841–18 Mar. 1932),* surgeon, physician, and Confederate soldier, was born in the Steele Creek community of Mecklenburg County, the son of Andrew Grier and his second wife, Margaret Barringer Grier. The Grier and Barringer families were prominent early settlers in the Piedmont section of North Carolina. On Grier's paternal side, his great-grandfather was one of the early settlers of the Steele Creek community. His grandfather had fought honorably in the Revolutionary War, and his grandmother was a Spratt whose ancestors were among the first to cross the Yadkin River and settle in western North Carolina. On his maternal side, his ancestors had helped to carve Cabarrus County from Mecklenburg County, and his great-grandfather and grandfather both had served in the General Assembly. Three of his mother's brothers—Daniel Moreau, Rufus Clay, and Victor Clay Barringer—were distinguished citizens of North Carolina. Daniel, the oldest, was a congressman who later served as minister to Spain under presidents Zachary Taylor and Millard Fillmore; Rufus was a Confederate general and state legislator; and Victor, also a legislator, became the U.S. representative to the International Court in Egypt in 1874. Andrew Grier died in 1850, leaving his wife Margaret to rear eleven children: their eight, her daughter by an earlier marriage, and Andrew's two children by his first wife. In 1861 Margaret's four sons and one stepson volunteered for service in the Confederate Army. Of the five, one died of swamp fever and another was killed in action at Bristoe Station, Va., in 1863.

Samuel Andrew Grier received his early education at the Melville School, conducted by Alexander Wilson. At age nineteen he went to Charlotte to study medicine under the direction of Dr. W. W. Gregory. When North Carolina seceded from the Union in 1861 and Governor John W. Ellis called for volunteers, Grier interrupted his medical studies and joined the Hornet's Nest Riflemen commanded by Captain Lewis Williams. This was the first company to leave Mecklenburg County to serve in the war, as well as one of the first in the state to prepare to defend North Carolina against Federal troops. Grier's company was sent to Fort Caswell and then to Raleigh, where in May it became part of Company B of the First North Carolina Regiment. Afterwards this regiment was sent to Richmond and then to Yorktown, which it fortified. With his regiment, Grier saw action at the Battle of Big Bethel Church in June 1861. In 1862, when his term of enlistment was over, he returned to Charlotte and joined the Mecklenburg Rangers of the First North Carolina Cavalry as first sergeant. That July he was promoted to second lieutenant, and in September to first lieutenant. He later became a captain in Company D, Fifth North Carolina Cavalry, which was commanded by his uncle, General Rufus Barringer.

During the war young Grier was wounded three times and on one occasion had his horse shot from under him. At Upperville, Va., in June 1863, he was wounded in the arm so severely that the battlefield surgeon was preparing to amputate the arm when word came that Federal troops were approaching. By the time the Confederate wounded were evacuated, Grier's arm had begun to heal so the amputation did not occur. When he recovered, Grier rejoined his unit, but he missed the Battle of Gettysburg because of his injury. In August 1864 he was wounded again, this time in the foot. His third wound was received at Bellfield, Va., on 3 Dec. 1864, when he was shot in the side. On 4 Apr. 1865, he was captured outside Richmond and imprisoned in the Old Capitol prison in Washington. He was still there on the night Lincoln was assassinated. Grier was later moved with other Confederate prisoners to Johnson's Island on Lake Erie and remained there until his release in June 1865. Though he had fought diligently for the South, he accepted defeat and worked just as earnestly to make the reunion of the two sections a smooth one. Over the years Grier retained his affiliation with Confederate veterans' organizations. He was surgeon general on General W. H. Smith's staff, North Carolina Confederate Veterans, and an active member of the Cabarrus Camp of Confederate Veterans. He was the last survivor of the Battle of Bethel and of the Hornet's Nest Riflemen.

Returning to his home at Steele Creek after the war, Grier spent several years helping his mother run the farm and then resumed his study of medicine at Jefferson Medical College in Pennsylvania. Beginning in 1876, his career as a country doctor spanned a period of fifty-five years; for most of that time he practiced in the communities of Rocky River and Harrisburg in Cabarrus County. When the United States entered World War I, he offered his services to his country. Turned down because of his age, he was told that he could be of greater assistance by continuing to minister to the people he had served faithfully for so many years. During his long period of service as a practicing physician, Grier's name had become a household word to the people of his community. He was on call day and night, and he never refused to respond when needed. Many times he received no pay; when he was paid, it was often in goods rather than money. A reception to honor him on his ninetieth birthday was given at Harrisburg by some of his former patients, friends, and neighbors. On this occasion he was showered with congratulatory messages and tributes of appreciation.

An interesting event occurred during Grier's medical career. In 1896, a patient of his, a child named Ellen Harris, swallowed a thimble that lodged in her windpipe. Fortunately the thimble was the type that had an opening at both ends. Grier was aware that the previous year Wilhelm Roentgen had discovered the X-Ray in Germany, and that Henry L. Smith, professor of physics at Davidson College, was conducting some experiments with it. When Grier informed Smith of his patient's predicament, Smith traveled the thirty miles to Rocky River, bringing his crude apparatus with him. Using the X-Ray Smith was able to locate the thimble and marked its location by painting the child's skin with black ink in the vicinity where the thimble had lodged. The girl was then taken to Charlotte, where the thimble was removed after more than two hours of surgery. Ellen Harris recovered and the story of her operation, made possible by a discovery less than a year old, was publicized throughout the world. This was one of the first times the X-Ray was used in America.

On 25 Nov. 1868 Grier married Mary Jane Gilmer, the daughter of Dr. James F. Gilmer of Cabarrus County. She, too, was a remarkable person. An 1867 honor graduate of the Charlotte Female Institute (later Queens College), she was the ideal wife for one such as Grier. Until her death in 1907 she worked faithfully by his side aiding him in his work, serving her church and community, and raising their children with the same ideals that both parents possessed. The children were Elva and Gilmer, both of whom died in childhood; Claudia, who, with her husband J. Mercer Blain, was a Presbyterian missionary to China for forty years; Samuel Andrew, Jr., who served in the Spanish American War; Elizabeth (Butt); Margaret (Hall); Mary Gilmer (Bost); Evelyn (Richmond); Thomas, a captain in World War I; and Anna B. (Parrish). Grier died at Harrisburg six months before his ninety-first birthday.

SEE: *Charlotte Observer*, 19, 20 Mar. 1932, 27 Sept. 1953; Walter Clark, ed., *Histories of the Several Regiments and Battalions from North Carolina*, vols. 1, 3 (1901); *Concord Tribune*, 9 Oct. 1930, 19, 21 Mar. 1932; Family Bible and family papers, including war record of Grier prepared by himself (in possession of the author); *North Carolina Biography*, vol. 6 (1919); Tombstones, Harrisburg cemetery, Harrisburg, Lutheran graveyard, Concord, St. John's Lutheran Churchyard, Cabarrus County, and Steele Creek Presbyterian Churchyard, Charlotte.

MARY RICHMOND KEATING

**Griffin, Charles** *(ca. 1679–ca. 1720)*, first known schoolteacher in North Carolina, Brafferton Professor at Virginia's College of William and Mary, and a pioneer in the education of the southern Indian, was born probably in England. He migrated to North Carolina from the West Indies about 1705. At some time before immigrating to the colony, he received a reasonably good education although there is no evidence that this included university training.

While a devout Anglican, Griffin settled in the strongly Quaker precinct of Pasquotank and opened a school there for boys and girls. This is the first known school in the history of the colony. Despite the Anglican religious training Griffin gave all of his students, the Quakers sent their children to his school, which was an immediate and unqualified success. Griffin became lay reader for the ministerless Anglicans in Pasquotank Precinct and soon had "an orderly congregation" through "his decent behaviour" and "unblemished life" and "by apt discourses from house to house according to the capacities of an ignorant people."

In April 1708, two Anglican missionaries of the Society for the Propagation of the Gospel arrived in the colony. One of the ministers, William Gordon, assumed responsibility for the two parishes in Chowan and Perquimans precincts while the other, James Adams, took upon himself the care of the parishes in Pasquotank and Currituck. The difficulties of life and service on the frontier proved too much for Gordon, who returned to England after less than six months at his post. Before leaving, he persuaded Griffin, whose services as a lay reader were no longer needed in Pasquotank, to move to St. Paul's Parish in Chowan Precinct where he served as clerk of the vestry and lay reader at a salary of £20 per annum. In addition, Griffin organized a new school in Chowan while James Adams assumed charge of his old school in Pasquotank. At first all went well, but in October 1709 James Adams wrote the SPG officials that Griffin "has fallen into the sin of fornication, and joined with the Quakers' interest." This last phrase probably means that Griffin had joined the political faction in the strife torn colony led by Governor Thomas Cary, who drew much support from the Quaker element in the population. This political factionalism would break into open warfare in the spring of 1711, only to be followed by Indian massacre and war that fall.

Perhaps as a result of the charges against him or to escape the difficulties besetting the colony, Griffin moved to Virginia. By 1714, he had become involved in the plan of Governor Alexander Spotswood to protect the Indian frontier and to better regulate the Indian trade. Spotswood's plan called for consolidating friendly tributary tribes on frontier reservations where a fort would be erected and garrisoned. A minister and schoolmaster would also be located there to Christianize and civilize the Indians. In early 1715, Griffin was employed by Governor Spotswood at a salary of £50 per annum to teach the children of the Saponi Indians and other Siouan tribes at Fort Christanna on the Meherrin River. Here, in "a very handsome schoolhouse," he taught about seventy Indian children to read and write from the Bible and the Anglican Book of Common Prayer. He proved to be an outstanding success as a teacher and gained the total affection of the Indians, who on one occasion sought to make him their king. Unmarried, Griffin whiled away his time writing his observations on the benefits of a solitary life.

The act providing for the fort and its garrison was ultimately disallowed in England by an order in council, and Griffin was forced to abandon his school at Fort Christanna early in the summer of 1718. Griffin, however, had not completed his work with the Indians. He was almost immediately named master of the Indian school at the College of William and Mary. This school was maintained through funds provided by the will of the eminent English scientist, Robert Boyle, and the position of Indian master was known as the Brafferton Professorship because the Boyle funds came from the revenue of Brafferton Manor in Yorkshire. A commodious, two-story brick building housed the master and his Indian pupils on the college campus. It is here, surrounded by his Indian charges, that Griffin drops from view. His fate is unknown, but it seems likely that he had died by 1720.

SEE: William K. Boyd, ed., *William Byrd's Histories of the Dividing Line Betwixt Virginia and North Carolina* (1929); Robert A. Brock, ed., *The Official Letters of Alexander Spotswood*, 2 vols. (1887); Cecil Headlam, ed., *Calendar of State Papers, Colonial Series, America and West Indies*, vol. 29 (1930); Hugh Jones, *The Present State of Virginia* (1865); Ann Maury, *Memoirs of a Hugenot Family* (1853); Bishop William Meade, *Old Churches, Ministers and Families of Virginia*, 2 vols. (1857); Herbert R. Paschal, "Charles Griffin: Schoolmaster to the Southern Frontier," *Essays in Southern Biography, East Carolina College Publications in History* 2 (1965); William L. Saunders, ed., *Colonial Records of North Carolina*, vol. 1 (1886).

HERBERT R. PASCHAL

**Griffin, Clarence Wilbur** *(22 Mar. 1904–10 Jan. 1958)*, newspaper editor and historian, was born in Spindale, Rutherford County, the son of Lewis W. and Naomi Johnson Greene Griffin. After graduation from Spindale High in 1923, he studied for a year at North Carolina State College of Agriculture and Engineering. He then was employed as an engineer by the North Carolina State Highway Commission from 1924 to 1925.

In 1925, at age twenty-one, Griffin's interest in community affairs prompted him to seek the editorship of the *Forest City Courier*, Rutherford County's most influential newspaper. Under his guidance from 1925 until his death, this paper, renamed the *Forest City Courier-Spindale Sun* (Rutherford County Publishing Co., Inc.), became an expanding and powerful business enterprise. Beginning in 1942, Griffin was editor, general manager, and secretary-treasurer. During this time, he was also influential in such statewide press organizations as the North Carolina Press Association (historian, 1939–58) and the Western North Carolina Weekly Newspaper Association (president, secretary).

From 1933 to 1935 Griffin served a brief stint in the North Carolina General Assembly, winning election to that office by the largest vote ever given a legislator in Rutherford County. He also was an officer of the county Democratic executive committee.

Perhaps Griffin's greatest contributions came from his work as Rutherford County historian, a position he held from 1927 until his death. Almost every historical association in the county owes some of its success to his tireless efforts to promote public interest in local and state history. In addition, he served as president of the Western North Carolina Historical Association (1955–56), as vice-president of the North Carolina Society of County Historians and of the North Carolina State Literary and Historical Association (1929), and as a member of the North Carolina Historical Commission (1937–58), the North Carolina Archaeological Society, and the British Society of Genealogists. An author of some note, Griffin wrote several historical treatises including *The Bechtlers and Bechtler Coinage* (1929), *Colonel John Walker and Family* (1930), *Descendants of Chisholm Griffin* (1931), *Public Officials of Rutherford County, 1779–1935* (1935), *History of Old Tryon and Rutherford Counties, 1730–1936* (1938), *Western North Carolina Sketches* (1939), *The Story of Our State* (1942), *Essays of North Carolina History* (1951), and *History of Rutherford County, 1937–1951*, as well as many historical pamphlets. He also was managing editor of the *Historical and Genealogical Record* and president of the Rutherford Writers Club.

His zeal for public service in his native county and state were reflected in the numerous civic organizations in which he participated, among them the Great Smoky Mountains National Park Museum Commission, National Youth Administration (advisory council), Rutherford County Radio Company (secretary, 1948–58), Chamber of Commerce (board of directors), Rutherford County Library (trustee and director, 1939–58), Rutherford County Red Cross (chairman), Advisory Council for Emergency Education in Rutherford County, Rutherford County Club (president, secretary, treasurer), Cleveland-Rutherford Executives Club, Forest City First Methodist Church (board of stewards), Rutherford County Epworth League Union (secretary-treasurer), Forest City Kiwanis (president, secretary; Citizenship Achievement Cup, 1937), Society of Griffin Kindred (secretary-treasurer, historian), Rutherford County Piedmont Council Boy Scouts (vice-president, 1929; deputy scout commissioner, 1924–28), Order of American Pioneers, Order of the First Crusade, Society of the War of 1812, Sons of Confederate Veterans, Rutherford County Confederate Pension Board, and Sons of the American Revolution (governor, North Carolina).

In 1927 Griffin married Thelma Elizabeth Clay. They had a son, Donald Clay, and the family lived in Forest City.

Griffin poured his energy into his work until, at age fifty-four, he suffered a fatal heart attack in his office at the *Forest City Courier*. He was buried in Cool Springs Cemetery, Rutherford County.

SEE: John L. Cheney, Jr., ed., *North Carolina Government, 1585–1974* (1975); Leonard E. Johnson and Lloyd M. Smith, *Men of Achievement in the Carolinas* (1952 [portrait]); *North Carolina Biography*, vol. 3 (1956); *Who's Who in the South and Southwest*, 1956.

MARK DIXON LACKEY

**Griffin, Hardy** *(ca. 1735–December 1794)*, legislator and officer in the American Revolution, was the son of John Griffin, an early settler on Swift Creek in what is now Nash County. He was evidently the oldest son, as he was listed first in his father's will of 1761 and was appointed guardian for the younger children. In an undated petition, Hardy Griffin requested permission from the county court to build a water gristmill over Swift Creek "at or near his dwelling house." In 1778, he was a justice of the peace for the new county of Nash.

During the American Revolution, Griffin was an officer in the Nash militia. In a letter to Governor Thomas Burke dated 13 July 1781, General William Caswell referred to a Major Griffin in connection with enlistees from Nash County. Later that year, on 21 August, John Ramsey, writing from Deep River, commended Griffin for holding his post while another officer retreated, observing that "Major Griffin has behaved with much propriety." There is no information about Griffin's later military service other than the fact that he was colonel of the Nash militia in 1787.

With the formation of Nash County, Griffin was elected to the House of Commons in 1778 and served until 1781, when he was elected to the senate. Except for the year 1788, Griffin remained in the senate until his death. He also represented Nash County at the Constitutional Convention at Hillsborough in 1788 and at Fayetteville in 1789.

Griffin married a woman named Mary. He died intestate but, according to available records, he and his wife were the parents of six children: Archibald; Guilford; Elizabeth, the wife of Dempsey Braswell; Millerey, the wife of Mathew Drake, Jr.; Quinny, the wife of Francis Drake; and a daughter who married Benjamin Mason. Archibald Griffin, the oldest son, was born before 1770. Like his father before him, he was a justice of the peace in Nash and a member of the county militia. He also represented Nash County in the North Carolina Senate in 1797 and in the House of Commons in 1803–4 and 1806–7. Archibald married Lucy Arrington, the daughter of Arthur Arrington, a prominent early citizen of Nash. She had died by 1799, when her husband married Charity Smith, the daughter of Benjamin Smith. In 1813 Archibald Griffin sold his property in Nash County and moved to Laurens, Ga.

SEE: John L. Cheney, Jr., ed., *North Carolina Government, 1585–1979* (1981); Walter Clark, ed., *State Records of North Carolina*, vols. 12, 13, 16-22 (1895–1907); Deeds and Wills of Edgecombe and Nash counties (North Carolina State Archives, Raleigh); Griffin family records extracted by Joseph W. Watson, Rocky Mount, N.C.; Joseph W. Watson, ed., *Abstract of Early Records of Nash County, North Carolina, 1777–1859* (1963).

CLAIBORNE T. SMITH, JR.

**Griffin, Moses** *(ca. 1753–14 Mar. 1816)*, founder of Griffin's Free School at New Bern, one of the first trade schools for poor girls, if not the first, was a native and lifelong resident of Craven County. His father, Solomon Griffin, a Craven County farmer and landowner, bequeathed property to his daughter, Alie (Aley), and three sons: Solomon, Jesse, and Moses. At an early age Moses Griffin aided royal Governor William Tryon and colonial militiamen during the War of the Regulation and was wounded in the Battle of Alamance. With only a little formal education, he worked diligently at his mercantile and real estate businesses, lived alone quietly and frugally, and invested well his profits. A bachelor, he had few personal friends and seldom mingled with his neighbors, although he had frequent contacts with attorneys and bankers.

In addition to extensive properties in New Bern, Griffin owned a plantation, as evidenced by a notice on the front page of the *North Carolina Gazette* on 2 Jan. 1796: "All persons are forwarned from trespassing on my plantation called the BLUEROCK on Trent River, about five miles from Newbern, as they will otherwise be prosecuted to the utmost rigor of the law. Moses Griffin."

Known as an eccentric miser, Griffin is reported to have become fatally ill from eating too many shad when the fish were plentiful and cheap. He was buried in Cedar Grove Cemetery, New Bern. The tombstone erected there later referred to him simply as "Founder of Griffin's Free School."

His lengthy will, signed on 13 Sept. 1807 and probated in June 1816, left a small bequest to a minor nephew. Five Negro slaves were designated for freedom under specific conditions of time, their wages, and "the law." Named as executors, trustees, and managers of his estate were five prominent New Bernians: Edward Graham, William Gaston, John Devereux, Francis Hawks, and John Oliver. They were directed to invest all of his "ready money" in bank shares or to lend it out at interest; and to rent, not sell, his houses and lots "to the best advantage." As soon as funds might be sufficient from the income of his principal, they were to purchase two acres of land "in some convenient and healthy place" near New Bern and build there a 1½-story brick building, 30 feet long and 20 feet wide, with a large space on the first floor suitable for a schoolroom; the "plain" remainder of the structure was to be made "fit for the accomodation of indigent scholars, which house shall be called Griffin's Free School." When enough money became available afterward from his estate, "a proper schoolmaster shall be employed for the purpose of teaching and educating . . . Orphan Children or the children of such other poor and indigent persons as are unable to accomplish it with their own means and who in the judgement of my trustees are best entitled to the benefit of this Donacion." Besides being housed and taught, the pupils were to be maintained and clothed. At age fourteen they were to be assigned as apprentices "to trades or other suitable occupations."

Griffin's numerous relatives brought suit between 1818 and 1820 to break his will and void its trust fund, claiming they should get the money as "heirs at law and next of kin." Chief Justice John Louis Taylor, a former New Bernian, officially praised the trust as "purely benevolent" and dismissed the case.

The school was incorporated in 1833, and two years later land for its building was purchased on George Street across from and slightly to the northwest of Cedar Grove Cemetery. In 1838, John Devereux was reported as the sole "surviving executor and trustee of the late Moses Griffin." His son, Thomas Pollock Devereux, and the latter's son, John Devereux II, then "executors of the will of Moses Griffin," bought four adjoining lots on 21 July 1840. Plans then began to go forward for the construction of the schoolhouse. Because various trades were open to poor boys, the trustees decided to educate poor girls, especially orphans. Selected as headmistress was Arete (pronounced Areta) Sitgreaves Ellis, the daughter of George Ellis, New Bern's representative in the 1800 and 1801 House of Commons, and of Amaryllis Sitgreaves Ellis, sister of Judge John Sitgreaves.

Strict rules and regulations were drafted for the care and training of twenty girls. Lists of the pupils for some of the years through 1859 are extant. Not only were they housed, clothed, and fed, but also they were given medical treatment. Among the bills was one dated 1 Oct. 1847 from Dr. Peter Barton Custis (1823–63), who charged four dollars for extracting the teeth of eight children. Besides classes in the three R's, the girls were taught sewing, knitting, spinning, weaving, cooking, milking, housework, and gardening. Every afternoon, weather permitting, Miss Arete, accompanied by her St. Bernard dog, took the girls on walks through the woods to study and collect wildflowers. On Sunday she led them, all dressed alike in their uniforms of blue and white during summers and blue and gray during winters, in a dignified procession about a mile through town to attend services at Christ Episcopal Church. Many of them she sponsored for baptism, and all of them she instructed in the Bible, religion, and morality. During occasional social events "curtsey cotillions" and grab-bag prizes were featured.

A photograph of Miss Arete hangs in the Vestry Room of Christ Church, and in its sanctuary are large twin stained-glass windows memorializing this "devout religious worker and home missionary." The Reverend

William Nassau Hawks, grandson of John Hawks, supervising architect of the original Tryon Palace, who later became rector of the church, was for some time a teacher at the Griffin school. Indeed, the school was so closely associated with Christ Church that it was considered practically a church institution.

During the Civil War the school had to be closed, and the pupils were placed in local homes. Some attended classes in the parochial school held in the remaining west wing of Tryon Palace, and others later studied in a schoolroom in the rear of All Saints Chapel. After the war Thomas and John Devereux continued to serve as trustees; however, on 25 Mar. 1868 they asked that other persons be appointed to represent "Griffin's Friends." When Thomas died in 1868, John again appealed to the court to be relieved of responsibility for "the public charity." From then until 1908, other trustees were named from time to time. The last trustee was William Hollister Oliver, whose daughter, Mary Taylor Oliver, had succeeded Miss Arete Ellis as "Chairman" for the Griffin school.

With the Griffin school inactive, its property on George Street was sold to become the site for a knitting factory and Stewart's Sanatorium. Game, fish, and oyster fairs were also held on the grounds. The school building was shown on a map of New Bern about 1881, but it was burned in 1922. For some years, the income from the Griffin estate had been divided between the parochial school and the New Bern Academy. Later the entire amount went to the academy.

A final accounting was held on 6 May 1908. As recommended by District Solicitor Charles L. Abernethy, Sr., approved by the superior court and signed by Judge William R. Allen, the Griffin trustees were discharged and the assets in the Griffin school fund, amounting to approximately $4,500, were transferred to the New Bern Graded Schools, which in 1899 had succeeded the New Bern Academy.

In memory and appreciation of Moses Griffin, the "new" high school building, which was built in 1904 and enlarged in 1907 and again in 1930, was officially named the Moses Griffin Building in 1909. It is still standing but is no longer used for school purposes. Plans are being considered by its new owner, the Historic New Bern Foundation, Inc., for its eventual restoration. When a colonial front was added in 1930, a large marble plaque was taken down. It is still stored inside the building. Its inscription reads: "In Memorandum. Moses Griffin died 1816. In Grateful Remembrance of his Generous Provision for the Education of the Children of New Bern, N.C. Hunc Semper Meminisse Juvabit. 1904–09." Translated literally, the epitaph means: "The Man Should Always Be Kept Fresh in Our Remembrance."

SEE: Gertrude S. Carraway, *Crown of Life* (1940), and *Years of Light*, vol. 2 (1974); Christ Church Parish Register (New Bern); Deeds and Wills of Craven County (County Courthouse, New Bern); New Bern *Historical Celebration, 1764–1939*; Henderson L. Thomas, "Public Education in Craven County" (M.A. thesis, University of North Carolina, 1925); Tombstone inscriptions, Cedar Grove Cemetery (New Bern); John D. Whitford, "Historical Notes" (typescript, Craven County Public Library, New Bern).

GERTRUDE S. CARRAWAY

**Griggs, Lillian Baker** *(8 Jan. 1876–11 Apr. 1955)*, librarian, was born in Anderson, S.C., the daughter of William F. and Cora Wilhite Baker. From 1892 to 1895 she attended Agnes Scott College. She married Dr. Alfred Flournoy Griggs on 21 Apr. 1897, and they had one son, Alfred, Jr. After her husband's death in 1908, Mrs. Griggs enrolled in the library school of the Carnegie Library in Atlanta (later affiliated with Emory University) and received a certificate in librarianship in the spring of 1911.

Mrs. Griggs, a pioneer professionally trained public librarian, began work as librarian of the Durham Public Library on 1 July 1911. Not satisfied with just organizing the library and serving the people of Durham, she persuaded the county commissioners to fund the service to rural residents that she already had been providing informally; thus, Durham became the first North Carolina town to have a contract for library service to the rural area. Her innovations also included organizing a branch library in the mill district, developing a high school library, helping to start a library for the Negroes of Durham, and circulating small collections in the county schools.

Active in numerous professional organizations, Mrs. Griggs served as chairman of the public library section (1913), treasurer (1913–16), and president (1917–18, 1933–34) of the North Carolina Library Association. Through her work on the council of the American Library Association and its committees and as president of the League of Library Commissions (1929–30), she also contributed to national library organizations. In 1918, she took a leave of absence from the Durham library to join the War Service Activities of the American Library Association, serving first on the Gulf Coast and in 1919 with the army of occupation in Coblenz, Germany. Before her war service Mrs. Griggs had obtained Carnegie funds to build a new building for the Durham library. After its completion in 1921, she renewed her push for better rural service by persuading the Kiwanis Club to provide money for a bookmobile, the first in North Carolina.

As director of the North Carolina Library Commission in Raleigh from 1924 to 1930, Mrs. Griggs worked vigorously to extend county libraries throughout the state. She prepared the groundwork for the Citizen's Library Movement in North Carolina, which began at the 1927 North Carolina Library Association conference and was promoted by Frank Porter Graham and Louis Round Wilson. Through her work on the Rosenwald Advisory Committee Mrs. Griggs had an even wider influence on the planning for library development in the South.

In 1930, when she accepted the position of librarian of the newly created Woman's College of Duke University, Mrs. Griggs turned from a public to an academic library career. In addition to building an excellent undergraduate collection for the use of the women at Duke, she developed the students' interests in extracurricular reading and the arts through a unique browsing room and art exhibitions in the library. While at Duke Mrs. Griggs continued to be active in a broader sphere, serving on a committee with Susan Grey Akers to plan library science curricula in the consolidated University of North Carolina, working with Robert Downs on a state planning committee for libraries, and contributing through activities in the North Carolina Library Association and as president of the Southeastern Library Association in 1933–34. Mrs. Griggs retired from Duke in 1949 and died six years later.

SEE: Evelyn Harrison, "Lillian Baker Griggs," Duke University *Library Notes* 31 (1955); Manuscript Department, Library, Duke University (Durham), and Southern Historical Collection, University of North Carolina (Chapel Hill), for Griggs's papers and correspondence; *North Carolina Library Bulletin*, scattered issues, 1909–32.

BETTY YOUNG

**Grimes, Bryan** *(2 Nov. 1828–14 Aug. 1880)*, Confederate general and planter, was born on a large plantation in Pitt County, approximately eight miles west of the town of Washington. The plantation had been named Grimesland by Bryan's grandfather, and the family name is still maintained by a small town that developed near the birthplace of young Grimes. His father was Bryan Grimes, Sr., a career planter described as one of the "most upright, honest, and enterprising farmers in Pitt County"; although he did not enter public life, he was a follower of Henry Clay who thoroughly detested Jacksonian democracy. His mother was Nancy Grist, the daughter of General Richard Grist of Washington County, Ga.

Young Grimes spent his childhood on the Grimesland plantation. His mother died when he was only four months old; thus any female influence on his early training came from either his older sister, Susan, or his stepmother, Lucy Olivia Blount Grimes, whom his father later married. After attending a school in Nash County and an academy in Washington, N.C., he became a pupil of William James Bingham, at his noted school in Hillsborough. In June 1844, at age fifteen, Grimes entered The University of North Carolina. Although not among the scholastic leaders of his class, he was an active member of the Philanthropic Society. Among his classmates were Victor Clay Barringer, Oliver Hart Dockery, Seaton Gales, James Johnston Iredell, and Willie Person Mangum, Jr., all of whom became prominent in the state. Grimes was graduated in June 1848. A year later his father gave him the Grimesland plantation with approximately one hundred slaves to cultivate it. From then until 1860 he managed his large estate, achieving the rewards of a successful agriculturist. Travel abroad in 1860 added to his reputation as a distinguished southern planter.

Upon his return from Europe, Grimes found himself in the midst of great political excitement over the election of Abraham Lincoln to the presidency. With the bombardment of Fort Sumter and Lincoln's subsequent call for troops, the people of North Carolina called for a convention; on 13 May 1861, Grimes was elected without opposition to fill a seat. He took his stand with the ultra-Secessionists at the state convention, where he was active in promoting support for the army then being raised. On 20 May 1861, the members of the convention passed the Ordinance of Secession. Bryan Grimes was proud to be one of the signers on that memorable May morning. In fact, he kept and treasured the pen he used to sign the ordinance. After the first session of the convention, he resigned his seat to accept the appointment of major in the Fourth Regiment of North Carolina State Troops. Although Governor John W. Ellis offered him two other appointments of higher rank, Grimes refused both, stating that he preferred a subordinate position until he could gain needed experience.

From May 1861 until the end of the Civil War, Grimes fought gallantly for the Confederate cause. During the first year of the war he participated in the Battle of First Manassas, the Peninsula campaign, and the Battle of Seven Pines, where he and the "Fighting Fourth" received their "baptism of fire." Grimes had become the official commander of the Fourth North Carolina Regiment after First Manassas. The Seven Days' Battle in the Richmond area followed Seven Pines. Grimes, now a colonel, displayed great courage during the engagement, especially in the fighting in and around Mechanicsville. Because of an injury caused by a severe kick from a horse, he was not present at the slaughter at Antietam (Sharpsburg, Md.). He returned to active duty for the Battle of Fredericksburg, in December 1862, where he was temporarily assigned to command a brigade in General Daniel Harvey Hill's division. Chancellorsville was the scene of battle in May 1863. Once again, Colonel Grimes and his fellow North Carolinians fought gallantly. In a letter to Governor Zebulon Baird Vance, General Robert E. Lee referred to the regimental commanders as "among the best of their respective grades in the army."

Grimes and his regiment were the first to enter the town of Gettysburg on 1 July 1863. The North Carolinians drove the enemy through the town to the heights beyond; on 3 July, however, when the heaviest fighting took place, they were held in reserve. During the retreat from Pennsylvania, Grimes was placed in the rear guard to assist in protecting the withdrawing army. For the remainder of 1863 he had no further military encounters. In August of that year he presided over a meeting of North Carolina troops held in opposition to the peace movement that was developing in the state. The strong Confederate sentiment he expressed while leading this delegation further widened the gap that had recently come between Grimes and William Woods Holden, editor of the *North Carolina Standard* and one of the Unionist leaders in the state.

During the final year of the war, Grimes's continual display of courage and leadership, especially in the Wilderness campaign, led to his appointment as a permanent brigade commander and to his promotion to brigadier general. Grimes and his men were in the thickest of the fighting in the Shenandoah Valley Campaign in the fall of 1864. Afterwards, he was placed in command of General Stephen D. Ramseur's division, Ramseur having met his death in the valley fighting at Cedar Creek. Grimes remained a division commander in the Second Corps of Lee's army until the end of the war. In February 1865 he became a major general, the last officer of the Army of Northern Virginia to be promoted to that rank. Grimes and his men occupied the trenches in and around Petersburg in March 1865, participated in the defensive fighting there late in the month, and served as rear guard of the retreat from Petersburg, which began on 2 April. Upon reaching the area around Appomattox Court House, Grimes succeeded in driving the enemy from the Lynchburg Road, thus opening up a route of escape from General Ulysses S. Grant's encircling army. Orders from General Lee to fall back ended this final achievement of Grimes's division.

Upon hearing of the forthcoming surrender, Grimes thought of joining General Joseph Johnston, who was then in North Carolina, but the pungent words of General John B. Gordon changed his mind. Gordon informed Grimes that to escape while a flag of truce was pending would not only discredit him but also General Lee. Consequently, Grimes relinquished any intentions to escape surrender. Later on the afternoon of 9 April after the surrender had been publicized, he rode over to his old regiment, the North Carolina Fourth, and shook hands with each member. These men had followed Grimes through four years of suffering and toil, and he praised each of them for a job well done. As he approached one ragged, barefooted member of the regiment, the soldier grasped his hand tightly and said: "Goodbye, General; God bless you; we will go home; make three more crops and then try them again." With this, the Civil War came to an end for General Bryan Grimes.

Soon after the surrender terms were completed, he returned to North Carolina. Following a brief residence in Raleigh, he and his wife set out for Grimesland, arriving in January 1867. There he worked hard to restore the plantation to its former economic position. The years that followed were happy ones for General and Mrs. Grimes. While they raised their large family, Grimes became one of the most successful planters in the state. He contributed a portion of his earnings ($250) to The University of North Carolina, of which he was appointed a trustee in 1877. By 1880, he was considered one of North Carolina's most respected sons.

On the afternoon of 14 Aug. 1880, General Grimes was returning to Grimesland in his buggy from "Little Washington," as it was then called, where he had been to attend the Beaufort County political convention and to take care of some business. His only companion was twelve-year-old Bryan Satterthwaite, the son of a neighbor. While they were crossing Bear Creek, approximately four miles from Grimesland, the gun of a concealed assassin was discharged, killing Grimes instantly. Young Satterthwaite drove to the nearest neighbor and received assistance in taking the dead man home. A few days later funeral services were held at Grimes's residence. After burial services at the Episcopal church, he was interred in the family burying grounds about three hundred yards from his residence.

The alleged cause of the assassination was to prevent Grimes from testifying in court about some criminal matter. One William Parker, described by the Raleigh *News and Observer* as a "sorry kind of a fellow with no particular occupation, and with a reputed bad character," was arrested on suspicion of murder. The jury found him not guilty, however, and Parker was set free.

Except as a subject of conversation, the Grimes case lay dormant for the next seven years. What happened to Parker during this period is not known. At any rate, he was back in Washington on a Saturday night in early November 1888, when he got drunk and boasted that he had killed General Grimes. He was immediately picked up on a charge of drunkenness and placed in the Washington jail. Early the next morning, between ten and fifteen masked men entered the jail, took Parker out, and strung him up on the drawbridge across the Pamlico River. A coroner's jury assembled and returned a verdict of "death by hanging at the hands of parties unknown." Charges were never filed, and no serious effort was made to solve the new murder. The people had gained revenge by killing William Parker, but the hanging of the lowly assassin could never compensate for the loss of Bryan Grimes.

Grimes was married twice. On 9 Apr. 1851 he married Elizabeth Hilliard Davis, who died on 7 Nov. 1857. They were the parents of Bryan, who died in infancy, Bettie, Nancy, and Bryan. On 15 Sept. 1863 he married Charlotte Emily Bryan and they were the parents of Bryan, who died in infancy, Alston, John Bryan, Charlotte Bryan, Mary Bryan, Susan Penelope, William Demsie, George Frederick, Junius Daniel, and Theodora Bryan.

SEE: Samuel A. Ashe, ed., *Biographical History of North Carolina*, vol. 6 (1907 [portrait]); Bryan Grimes Papers (Southern Historical Collection, University of North Carolina, Chapel Hill); D. H. Hill, *North Carolina in the War between the States, Bethel to Sharpsburg*, 2 vols. (1926); Raleigh *North Carolina Standard* and *Raleigh Register*, scattered issues, 1861–65; *The War of the Rebellion: Official Records of the Union and Confederate Armies*, vols. 11, 19, 21, 25, 27, 29, 36, 42, 43, 46 (1891–95).

JAMES D. DANIELS

**Grimes, Jesse** *(6 Feb. 1781?–15 Mar. 1866)*, political and military leader in the Republic of Texas, was born in Duplin County, the son of Sampson and Bethsheba Winder Grimes. He evidently had little formal education. In January 1813 Grimes was appointed justice of the peace by the state legislature, and in the same year he married Martha Smith. Their children were Robert Henry, Harriet Elizabeth, Alfred Calvin, Rufus, Lucinda, Jacob, Mary Jane, and twins William Ward and Martha Ann; Lucinda, Mary Jane, and William Ward died in childhood. In 1817 Grimes moved his family to Washington County, Ala., where in 1817 he was appointed justice of the peace. His wife died in 1824, shortly after giving birth to twins. Grimes remarried a widow, Rosanna Ward Britton, in Alabama. Their children were Gordon, Harvey, Leonard, Helen, Emily, and Nancy; Gordon and Leonard died in childhood. The entire family moved to Texas, arriving at its eastern border in December 1826. They finally settled at Grimes Prairie in present-day Grimes County (in 1827 a part of Washington County; in 1836 a part of Montgomery County).

Grimes's participation in public life in Texas began with his election in 1829 as first lieutenant of the First Company, Battalion of Austin. The following year he was appointed *sindico procurador* of the precinct of Viesca, Department of Bexar. In 1831, he was appointed *regidor* of the Ayuntamiento of San Felipe de Austin. As relations between the centralist government in Mexico City and the Anglo-American and Hispanic populations in outlying departments deteriorated, Grimes emerged on the side of those favoring separation. In 1835, he served as delegate from Washington Municipality to the Consultation at San Felipe and continued as a member of the General Council of the Provisional Government of Texas. In that capacity he signed the Texas declaration of independence and its first constitution, both on 17 Mar. 1836. His duties expanded when he was appointed judge of his home district, Washington County, in 1836. After his son, Alfred Calvin, fell at the Alamo, Grimes enrolled a company of volunteers for the Texas Army. At the end of the war, he was seated as a member of the senate representing Washington County at the first congress of the Texas Republic. When Montgomery County was formed out of Washington, Grimes sat as its judge. From 1841 to 1843 he served in the Texas House of Representatives for Montgomery County. He returned to the senate in 1844, continuing to serve after Texas was admitted to the Union (Grimes being one of the floor leaders for annexation) until 1853; he was the senator from Grimes County, formed in 1846 and named for him. Grimes was reelected to the state senate in 1855 and continued in office until 1861.

When Sam Houston ran for governor of Texas in 1857, Grimes was nominated for lieutenant governor on Houston's independent ticket, though supported by the Know-Nothings. However, Houston was defeated because of his record in the U.S. Senate as an abolitionist sympathizer. In 1861 Grimes retired from public life, his last actions being in opposition to secession.

Late in life Grimes reflected on his career, commenting particularly on his activity as a judge: "Nobody wanted to be judged. The Texans were like the Israelites when they had no king. Every man done what seemed good in his own eyes. . . . Politically I have ever claimed to be a Democrat but it has been alleged that I am rather of the old fogey order."

The year of Grimes's birth is given as 1788 on his tombstone, but as he was mentioned in the will of his grandfather, Hugh Grimes, written in Duplin County, N.C., on 2 Apr. 1781, that date is erroneous.

Grimes was buried in the John McGintry Cemetery near Navasota, which was eventually abandoned. His remains and those of his second wife were removed to the State Cemetery in Austin.

SEE: Eric L. Blair, *Early History of Grimes County* (1930); John Salmon Ford, *Rip Ford's Texas* (1963); Z. T. Fulmore, *The History and Geography of Texas as Told in County Names* (1915); John H. Jenkins, ed., *Papers of the Texas Revolution: 1835–1836*, 10 vols. (1973); Louis W. Kemp, *The Signers of the Texas Declaration of Independence* (1959); Sister Paul of the Cross McGrath, *Political Nativism in Texas: 1825–1860* (1930).

ROGER N. KIRKMAN

**Grimes, John Bryan** *(3 June 1868–11 Jan. 1923)*, secretary of state of North Carolina, agricultural and cultural leader, historian, and public speaker, was born in Pitt County, the son of Bryan Grimes, a major general in the Army of Northern Virginia, and Charlotte Emily Bryan Grimes. His maternal grandfather was John Herritage Bryan, a well-known lawyer and member of Congress. Grimes was also a descendant of John Porter, speaker of the Colonial Assembly, and Colonel John Blount, a member of the governor's council in the colonial period. At Grimesland, the family estate in Pitt County, J. Bryan Grimes was taught by private tutors until age twelve when he entered the Raleigh Male Academy. From there he went to Trinity School, Chocowinity, and Lynch's School, High Point, before attending The University of North Carolina from 1882 to 1884. At Bryant & Stratton Business College in Baltimore he became better equipped to help manage the family's large land holdings in Pitt County.

In 1900 Grimes ran for secretary of state on the Democratic ticket and won at the youthful age of thirty-two. This was his first elective office, although he had been chairman of the executive committee of the Democratic party in his township since he was twenty-one, had served as aide-de-camp to Governor Elias Carr, and had been urged to run for Congress in 1898 but declined. As secretary of state from 1901 to 1923, Grimes classified and catalogued thousands of historical documents, maps, wills, papers, laws, grants, and other papers that had collected for many years in the secretary's office and made them available for use by the public. With land holdings in Pitt, Beaufort, and Wake counties, Grimes never lost his interest in agriculture and its development in the state. He was a member of the State Board of Agriculture (1899–1900); conservative member of the Farmers' Alliance in North Carolina, which he tried to keep out of politics; member of the North Carolina Agricultural Society and of its executive committee; and member of the Farmers Educational and Cooperative Union and of the State Grange. He was one of the organizers of the Tobacco Growers Association of North Carolina. Later, as president of that organization, he was an avowed opponent of the Tobacco Trust.

Grimes's interest in history evinced itself not only in his private collection of rare books on North Carolina but also in his membership in various societies including the North Carolina Historical Commission (for some years, chairman), the North Carolina Society of the Sons of the American Revolution (board of managers, later president), and the American Historical Association. He was also instrumental in the formation of the State Literary and Historical Association and a member of its executive committee, as well as influential in the development of the state's Hall of History. For several years he awarded the Mary Octavia Grimes Memorial, a gold medal, for the best essay by a student in Pitt County on a subject related to the section around that county.

As secretary of state, Grimes was an ex officio member of the Board of Education. He served on the board of trustees of The University of North Carolina and on the board's executive committee. Other memberships included the executive committee of the North Carolina Council of Defense, Scottish Society of America (president, 1918–19), Masons, Knights of Pythias, and Junior Order of United American Mechanics. He was a Democrat and an Episcopalian.

Grimes made many speeches in the fields of agriculture and history—some at the dedication of public monuments. He was the author of numerous pamphlets and broadsides. His *Agricultural Resources and Opportunities of the South* (1905?) was an interesting promotional tract, while two volumes that he prepared from records in his custody as secretary of state, *Abstract of North Carolina Wills* (1910) and *North Carolina Wills and Inventories* (1912), have been of great use to historians and genealogists. His illustrated monograph, *History of The Great Seal of the State of North Carolina*, went through many editions after its first publication in 1893. As secretary of state he was also responsible for the reprinting of *The Natural History of North Carolina* by John Brickell, for which he prepared an introductory note.

In 1894, Grimes married Mary Octavia Laughinghouse, the daughter of Captain J. J. Laughinghouse of Pitt County and the granddaughter of Dr. Charles J. O'Hagan. They had one daughter, Helen Elise. Mrs. Grimes died in 1899. In 1904, Grimes married her sister, Elizabeth Forrest Laughinghouse, who bore him three sons: J. Bryan, Jr., Charles O'Hagan, and Alston. Grimes was buried in Oakwood Cemetery, Raleigh.

SEE: John L. Cheney, Jr., ed., *North Carolina Government, 1585–1974* (1975); Adolph O. Goodwin, *Who's Who in Raleigh* (1916); Daniel L. Grant, *Alumni History of the University of North Carolina* (1924); *North Carolina Biography*, vol. 6 (1919); C. Beauregard Poland, *Twentieth Century Statesmen, North Carolina Political Leaders, 1900–1901* (1900); Raleigh *News and Observer*, 14 Jan. 1923; Raleigh *North Carolinian*, 26 Apr. 1900; *Who Was Who in America*, vol. 1 (1943).

MAUD THOMAS SMITH

**Grimsley, George Adonijah** *(31 July 1862–28 Mar. 1935)*, educator and insurance executive, the son of William Pope and Susan Dixon Grimsley, was born and raised on a large plantation in Greene County. At first, his parents employed a graduate of West Point to give him basic educational instruction. When he was old enough, they sent him to Bingham Military Academy, which was reputed to be one of the best in the South. From Bingham he entered Peabody Normal College in Nashville, Tenn. This institution was noted for its special training of teachers, who were greatly needed in the South after the Civil War. With a bachelor of arts degree, Grimsley returned to North Carolina and organized the graded public schools of Tarboro. Elected as the first superintendent, he made such a distinguished record that his name soon became well known all over North Carolina.

After serving for eight years in Tarboro, Grimsley was appointed superintendent of public schools in Greensboro in 1890 at the age of twenty-eight. At that time there were only two schools in Greensboro; both were controlled by a school committee that was appointed by the mayor. This committee also recommended all the officers and teachers whose names were submitted to a board of aldermen for final selection. Grimsley soon learned that this procedure had not been satisfactory, and he proposed the creation of a Greensboro school board. His plan was adopted in 1893 and has been in operation ever since.

Grimsley was a man who built for both the present and the future. Public libraries throughout the state are the result of his innovative ideas. According to his autobiographical account, he believed that one of the greatest factors in the education of a child was his training to think for himself, both orally and in writing. Moreover, boys and girls were not educated in schools, but were merely exposed to the way of getting an education. He contended that training pupils "to think and to give expression to their thoughts, and at the same time giving them a taste of the best literature, would equip them to continue their education after leaving school, and to get more out of life." Grimsley further reasoned that if one thinks there must be stimulus for thought. In learning how to think, he maintained, there is no better inspiration than that provided by a careful reading and interpretation of man's accomplishments in literature and in life. This theory led to practical applications in the classroom. He encouraged teachers to assign home reading, to open classroom discussion, and then to have the students write essays at school in order to see how well they had learned their lessons. Every Friday afternoon in each classroom the pupils were required to recite or debate the subjects they had studied.

This method of teaching in the Greensboro public schools attracted attention, and before long Superintendent Grimsley was employed to instruct prospective teachers at regular sessions and in the summer schools of The University of North Carolina. He found that wider reading required a larger selection of books, and therefore a good library was essential. From his first years with the Greensboro public schools, Grimsley worked to build up a good school library. Of this experience he wrote: "The money for the purchase of books for the school library was raised by school entertainments and by contributions from pupils and parents. Every grade had a library day once a week. Many of them denied themselves candy and gum and contributed their pin money to the library."

Success in the use of a school library led Grimsley to another thought: "the climax of the public school system should be a splendid public library—the university of all the people—maintained by public funds just as public schools." This idea was heartily supported by his community, and the Century Club, a literary organization of Greensboro to which Grimsley belonged, made plans for establishing public libraries across the state. State Senator Alfred Moore Scales, president of the club, agreed to introduce in the legislature a bill for the provision of public libraries.

In a basement room of the Normal and Industrial College (now the University of North Carolina at Greensboro) in 1897, Grimsley, Philander P. Claxton, and Annie Petty, the first trained librarian in North Carolina, backed by the Centurians, drafted a bill providing that any city or incorporated town with over a thousand inhabitants might establish a public library and maintain it by public taxation as a part of the school system. Grimsley, in his autobiographical sketch, wrote that he secured the passage of what became known as the "Scales Library Act." It was thus named because Senator Scales was responsible for getting the bill before the legislature; there is no doubt, however, that Grimsley was the prime mover of the project.

Under the Library Act, the Greensboro Public Library was opened in 1902. As chairman of the State Library Association, Grimsley led the local movement to obtain the first public library in North Carolina. At his suggestion, the books that he and the students had so assiduously collected for the public school libraries were moved to the City Hall. There, on the third floor, three rooms were turned into the general public library's first home. With 1,490 books, 32 periodicals, and 3 daily newspapers, the Greensboro Public Library began to serve the reading public.

Grimsley's next pioneering move was to open a public high school in his community. From the time the first permanent public graded schools were opened in Greensboro (also the first in North Carolina) in 1875, some courses at the high school level were offered. As early as 1888 the graded schools prepared students for college entrance, but no separate schools had been provided. Grimsley decided to do something about this situation, and in 1899 he opened one of the first public high schools in the state. Dr. W. H. Payne, chancellor of Grimsley's alma mater, was so impressed with the work of this former student that the honorary degree of master of arts was conferred on Grimsley in June 1899. The chancellor wrote: "If you were a son you could hardly stand higher in my regard."

Superintendent Grimsley had worked for twelve years with the Greensboro schools when he decided to serve North Carolina in another capacity—through the provision of life insurance. He reasoned that such insurance would not only be a personal financial protection to the family, but also its funds would be available for loans to buy homes and farms and to promote industrial expansion. He firmly believed that this field could offer social and economic growth so badly needed in the South.

In 1902, Grimsley withdrew from school work to become one of the foremost insurance leaders in the city, state, and nation. In 1901, he had proved himself an expert organizer when he launched the Security Life and Annuity Company of Greensboro and became its secretary. This was the first life insurance company established in North Carolina after the Civil War. In view of its success, Grimsley was invited to Raleigh in 1907 to help organize the Jefferson Standard Life Insurance Company. In 1912, this firm—keeping its name—merged with Grimsley's Security Life and Annuity Company and the Greensboro Life Insurance Company, each of which had more insurance in force than did Jefferson Standard. After operating in Raleigh for one year after the merger, the Jefferson Standard Life Insurance Company was moved to Greensboro and Grimsley became its president. He served in that capacity during its formative years from 1913 to 1919, adopting the motto, "Be conservative with a move on!"

In 1920 Grimsley joined with Collins C. Taylor in organizing the Security Life and Trust Company. With

Grimsley as president, the company began operations in Greensboro; during its first ninety-eight days $1,176,000 of new business was written. This amount is believed to have been a record production for a new company up to that time. The prosperous firm attracted the attention of leading businessmen of Winston-Salem, who in 1924 persuaded the officials of Security Life and Trust Company to establish headquarters in their city. Grimsley remained president until his retirement in 1932; at that time he was named chairman of the board, a position he held for the remainder of his life.

In its twenty-fifth year of operation, the Security Life and Trust Company was ranked among the top fifty-five (out of more than four hundred) life insurance companies in America by Alfred M. Best and Company of New York, a recognized authority in the field. Best stated: "the Company [Security Life and Trust] has been most ably managed in the interest of its policy-owners and the results achieved are well above the average for the business. In our opinion it has more than ample margins for contingencies."

On 30 July 1890, Grimsley married Cynthia Tull of Kinston, and they became the parents of William Tull and Harry B. During the last two years of his life, Grimsley suffered from pernicious anemia; he died at his home in Winston-Salem and was buried in Green Hill Cemetery, Greensboro.

SEE: Clipping file, Greensboro Public Library (Greensboro) for information on Grimsley; *Greensboro Daily News*, 20 June 1962; *Greensboro Daily Record*, 21 Oct. 1925; George Grimsley papers (in possession of William Brocton Lyon, Jr., Greensboro); *North Carolina Biography*, vol. 6 (1919); Raleigh *News and Observer*, 30 Mar. 1935.

ETHEL STEPHENS ARNETT

**Grissom, Eugene** *(8 May 1831–27 July 1902)*, physician and psychiatrist, was born near Wilton in Granville County, one of seventeen children of Wiley Hawes and Mary Bobbitt Grissom. His grandfather had changed the family name from Gresham to Grissom. Eugene attended Graham High School and taught for a brief time at age sixteen. In 1852 he was appointed deputy clerk of Granville County, and in 1853 he was elected clerk of the superior court. For a while he read law, but in 1855 he began studying medicine at the University of Pennsylvania where he received an M.D. degree in 1858. He also earned diplomas from the Philadelphia School of Anatomy and the Parrish School of Practical Pharmacy. He then returned to North Carolina to practice.

When the Civil War began, Grissom declined an appointment as surgeon and obtained the captaincy of Company D of the Thirtieth North Carolina Regiment. He was wounded just before the opening of the Seven Days' Battle around Richmond, and while convalescing in Richmond he was elected to the House of Commons. Reelected in 1864, Grissom was a member of the military committee for both terms, and one of his proposals resulted in the law appropriating one million dollars for the relief of indigent families of soldiers. Between sessions he served as army surgeon with the rank of major. In 1865, Grissom was a member of the constitutional convention ordered by President Andrew Johnson and served on the committee that drafted the repeal of the secession ordinance.

For the next three years Grissom practiced medicine. In 1868, he was appointed superintendent of the North Carolina insane asylum at Raleigh. While serving in that capacity he introduced new methods of treating the mentally ill, worked to improve the care and general health of his patients, and increased the physical facilities of the institution. When she visited the asylum in 1877, Dorothea Dix complimented Grissom enthusiastically for "promoting the comfort of the insane and applying all the means at your command for their restoration." Chiefly through his efforts the General Assembly appropriated money for a western asylum for whites at Morganton and one for blacks at Goldsboro. In his spare time he served as a member of the State Board of Agriculture, as surgeon-general of the state guard (1882–88), and as a trustee of The University of North Carolina (1879–90).

In June 1889 Grissom was tried for "gross immorality in connection with certain female attendants," "mismanagement" and "cruelty" to his patients, and "misappropriating the property" of the asylum. The trial lasted four weeks and created the greatest excitement. Former Governor Thomas J. Jarvis was chief counsel for the defense, and eventually Grissom was found innocent on all charges. He resigned a month after the trial and moved his practice to Denver and Colorado Springs, Colo. He died at age seventy-one on a visit to Washington, D.C.

Dr. Grissom's work with the insane won him national recognition. He contributed numerous articles—generally on mental illness—to medical journals in North Carolina and some to the *New England Medical Monthly* and the *American Medical Journal*. His more important articles were republished in pamphlet form, among them *Mania Transitoria*, *Mechanical Protection for the Violent Insane*, *The Semeiology of Insanity*, and *Deafmutism*. In 1882, Grissom was elected first vice-president of the American Medical Association; during his long membership in that group he was chairman at one time or another of most of its committees. In 1887, he was president of the Association of Superintendents of American Insane Asylums (now the American Psychiatric Association). He also served as president of the Raleigh Academy of Medicine.

Dr. Grissom was a Methodist, an active Mason (attaining the 33rd degree in 1884), and a Republican. On 10 Jan. 1866 he married Mary Ann Bryan, daughter of Michael Bryan, a North Carolina planter. They had five children: Robert Gilliam, Eugene, Mary Theodora, Adelaide, and Lillian.

SEE: Jerome Dowd, *Sketches of Prominent Living North Carolinians* (1888); *Journal of the Convention of the State of North Carolina* (1865); *Journal of the House of Commons of North Carolina*, 1862–64; R. C. Lawrence, "Eugene Grissom," *State Magazine* 11 (13 Nov. 1943); *Nat. Cyc. Am. Biog.*, vol. 22 (1932 [portrait]); Raleigh *News and Observer*, 29 July 1902; "Report of the . . . Superintendent of the Insane Asylum of North Carolina," *Public Documents of the General Assembly of North Carolina*, 1877–89; *Speech of Hon. Chas. M. Cooke, Delivered at the Dr. Grissom Trial, For the Defense, Thursday, July 18, 1889*; Stephen B. Weeks Scrapbooks (North Carolina Collection, University of North Carolina, Chapel Hill).

BUCK YEARNS

**Grissom, Robert Gilliam** *(26 Jan. 1867–25 Oct. 1955)*, businessman and tax collector, was born at Grissom, Granville County, the son of Dr. Eugene and Mary A. Bryan Grissom. His father was a Civil War veteran and an active Republican. After preparatory schooling, young Grissom entered The University of North Carolina and was graduated with a bachelor of science degree in 1887. The following year he worked as a state chemist in North Carolina and became a registered pharmacist. From 1889 to 1890 he did graduate work at the University of Pennsylvania, and in 1891 he was a deputy collector of Internal Revenue for the state of Colorado. Turning to the business world, he engaged in woolen manufacturing in 1903 and operated a flour mill in 1917.

Grissom was best known for his political activities, beginning in the 1920s when he was secretary of the state Republican executive committee. In 1922 he became the collector of Internal Revenue for the state of North Carolina and served in that agency's Greensboro office until retiring from the post in 1933. Three years later he ran against Clyde R. Hoey for governor of North Carolina. Although defeated, he polled the heaviest vote of any Republican gubernatorial candidate up to that time, receiving 140,000 votes to Hoey's 332,000. Grissom conducted his campaign on the thesis that he could cut the cost of government. He had proved that in the collector's office, where he had reduced his cost first 30 percent and later 50 percent to make it the most economical operation of any district in the United States. A news article reported of him: "He seems to have gone through these twelve years collecting several billions of dollars without making one taxpayer in North Carolina angry."

On 4 Mar. 1896 Grissom married Velma Coulter, and they were the parents of a son, Larry. He lived most of his later years at McLeansville and died at age eighty-nine in a nursing home in Greensboro, with burial in that city. He was an Episcopalian.

SEE: *Asheville Citizen*, 26 Oct. 1955; Daniel L. Grant, *Alumni History of the University of North Carolina* (1924); *Greensboro Daily News*, 17 June 1933.

C. SYLVESTER GREEN

**Grist, Allen** *(2 Jan. 1792–13 Dec. 1866)*, planter, naval stores producer, sheriff, and senator from Beaufort County, was born near Washington, N.C., the eldest son and second oldest of eight children of Reading and Elizabeth Grimes Grist. Reading Grist, a Revolutionary War soldier, served in the militia in the New Bern District and his father, John Grist, served on the Committee of Safety in Pitt County in 1775. Richard Grist, John's father, was living in Beaufort County before 1752. Allen Grist served first as deputy sheriff and later as sheriff of Beaufort County for eighteen years between 1818 and 1845, although not continuously. He also served three terms in the North Carolina Senate, from 1850 to 1852 and from 1854 to 1858, and was instrumental in getting the Bank of Washington chartered and established in 1851. Throughout his life he was affiliated with the Whig party.

Grist also owned extensive lands in Beaufort County and engaged in general farming and in the naval stores business, which since colonial times had been carried on in the Washington-New Bern area. Among the pioneers in expanding the industry south of and up the Cape Fear River in the 1840s was the firm of A. & J. R. Grist, formed in 1843 by Allen and his son James. For the next fifteen years the firm pursued the naval stores business in Brunswick, Columbus, and Bladen counties in the Cape Fear River region, making extensive use of slave labor. It operated a store and several turpentine distilleries and was involved in the Brothers Steamboat Company, which was engaged in hauling naval stores on the Cape Fear River. Declining availability of turpentine lands in North Carolina prompted the firm to remove to the Mobile Bay region of Alabama in 1858. Returns from this operation in 1860 were more than $60,000.

In 1860, Grist was listed as owning $50,000 in real estate and $92,900 in personal property, including 109 slaves, making him the largest slaveholder in Beaufort County. A. & J. R. Grist, turpentine farmers, held $44,000 in real estate and $125,750 in personal property and owned 72 slaves. In addition, as estate administrator for minor children related to his wife, Grist controlled another 48 slaves, for a total of 229. His son James R. Grist owned individually 84 slaves, giving the Grists ownership and management of 313 slaves. They leased additional slaves from other owners.

Grist appears to have had the respect of his numerous children, his relatives, and obviously of the voters from his long years in public office. He was characterized as discharging his official duties with "an energy, forbearance and fidelity which won for him ever afterwards the esteem and confidence of the people. The trust reposed in him was not betrayed, and in acknowledgement of his merits, whatever of County honors he would accept, were freely bestowed by his fellow citizens." He died at his residence near Washington at age seventy-four while still serving as chairman of the county court. The Grists were members of the Episcopal church, and he and his wife were buried in the Old Grist Cemetery near Chocowinity.

On 11 Feb. 1817 Grist married Mary Ann Williams, and they had thirteen children: James R., John W., William S., Susan E., Olivia, Mary W., Penelope and Apsley (twins), Richard, David, Margaret, Allen, and Wiley Grimes. In 1860 William Garl Browne painted oil portraits of Allen and his wife, now owned by Mrs. Clay Carter, Washington, N.C.

SEE: John L. Cheney, Jr., ed., *North Carolina Government, 1585–1974* (1975); Grist family Bible and newspaper obituary of Allen Grist (in possession of Mrs. J. D. Grimes, Jr., Washington, N.C.); Grist MSS (Manuscript Department, Library, Duke University, Durham); Ursula Loy and Pauline M. Worthy, eds., *Washington and the Pamlico* (1976); C. Wingate Reed, *Beaufort County* (1962); U.S. Census, 1860, Beaufort County.

PERCIVAL PERRY

**Grist, Franklin Richard** *(22 Sept. 1828–25 Feb. 1912)*, artist, art critic, and diplomat, was born at Egypt plantation near New Bern, the son of Richard and Elizabeth Heritage Washington Grist. His father was a merchant of Washington, N.C., and his mother, the daughter of John Washington of Kinston, was the sister of Mrs. William A. Graham and Mrs. James W. Bryan. After the death of her husband, Elizabeth married Dr. Reuben Knox in 1840. Franklin Grist was the only surviving child of her first marriage; he referred to Dr. Knox as "father" in his letters and displayed genuine affection for his stepfather.

Young Grist attended the Bingham School at Hillsborough and was graduated from Yale College in 1848 with the bachelor of arts degree. In 1848, while still a resident of New Haven, Conn., Grist, described as a "genre painter," exhibited at the National Academy of Design in New York. In the spring of 1849 he joined a U.S. Army mission under Captain Howard Stansbury going to explore and survey the Great Salt Lake area, which had been acquired by the United States the previous year in the Treaty of Guadalupe Hidalgo. Grist was engaged as an artist and to help with the mapping. The eighteen men composing the Stansbury expedition set out from Fort Leavenworth in May. Many of the handsome lithographs in Stansbury's *Exploration and Survey of the Valley of the Great Salt Lake of Utah* (Washington, 1852) were based on Grist's sketches.

Reuben Knox, who was now living with his family in St. Louis, Mo., planned a trip to California while Grist was on this expedition and, with two of his sons, a cousin, and a nephew, set out in mid-May 1850. On 1 July they picked up Franklin Grist along the way, as his work with the survey party was almost finished, and proceeded to California. During the course of his work in the West, Grist had also been to Oregon. After numerous unanticipated hardships, on 14 September the Knox party reached Sacramento where Dr. Knox expected to establish a store. He also planned to open a store in San Francisco and to engage in mining. Grist expected to work as an artist in San Francisco. The accidental drowning of Knox in the mouth of San Pablo Bay near San Francisco on 28 May 1851 ended all of these plans.

Grist returned to North Carolina with his half brothers and their relatives. Then, for about the next four years, he found employment in Washington, D.C., as a clerk in the Bureau of Construction and Repairs of the Treasury Department. He had for several years entertained the hope of studying in Italy, and in 1855 he sailed for Europe. He remained abroad for thirty-five years, traveling widely and gaining a solid reputation as an art critic. For about the first fifteen years he lived in Paris, but in 1871, following the Franco-German War, he was arrested as a suspected German spy. He was able to prove his American citizenship, however, and shortly afterward left to reside in Italy for twenty years, primarily in Florence, Rome, and Venice. During the administration of President Grover Cleveland he was named U.S. vice-counsul in Venice, serving from 1885 until 1890, when he returned to North Carolina to reside in Raleigh with his half brother, Dr. Augustus W. Knox. He died there at the age of eighty-three, unmarried.

SEE: George C. Groce and David H. Wallace, *The New-York Historical Society's Dictionary of Artists in America* (1957); Elizabeth Washington Grist Knox Papers (Southern Historical Collection, Library, University of North Carolina, Chapel Hill); Dale L. Morgan, *The Great Salt Lake* (1947); Charles W. Turner, *A Medic Fortyniner* (1974); Yale University alumni records (New Haven, Conn.).

WILLIAM S. POWELL

**Grist, James Redding** *(16 Jan. 1818–4 May 1876)*, planter and businessman, the eldest of thirteen children of Allen and Mary Ann Williams Grist, was born in Beaufort County near Washington. His forebears were in Beaufort County before 1752 and his grandfather, Reading Grist, and great-grandfather, John Grist, were patriots in the Revolutionary War. As his father was the perennial sheriff of Beaufort County and a substantial landholder, young Grist received a good education in local schools. In adult life he followed his father in farming and in the production of naval stores, staple products in Beaufort County since colonial times. Grist was a leader in the expansion of the naval stores industry south of the Cape Fear River in the 1840s. In 1843, he formed with his father the firm of A. & J. R. Grist, purchased 6,000 acres of pine land in Brunswick County, and moved there to develop a major turpentine plantation with slave labor. The firm also operated a store and a turpentine distillery.

In 1850, leaving his cousin Benjamin Grist as overseer of his Brunswick plantation, Grist moved to Wilmington from where he could better direct his expanding business interests. With the building of the Wilmington and Manchester Railroad in 1852, he sold part of his Brunswick land and purchased land along the railroad in Columbus County for a new turpentine plantation with a distillery and a shipping point, which became known as Grist's Station. With John T. Council he developed another plantation on the Wilmington, Charlotte and Rutherfordton Railroad in Bladen County, known as Council's Station. In the mid-1850s he had yet another plantation at Willis Creek on the Cape Fear River near the Bladen-Cumberland County line to which Benjamin Grist was transferred. With credit lines established through R. M. Blackwell and Company of New York, Grist was able to supply capital to other partners who owned turpentine land for development. He was also involved with the Brothers Steamboat Company, which transported naval stores and supplies on the Cape Fear River from Fayetteville to Wilmington. One of the company's vessels bore his name. With the waning of turpentine production in the Cape Fear area in the late 1850s, the firm opened an extensive turpentine plantation in 1858 in the Mobile Bay region of Alabama, with Benjamin Grist again as overseer. Production from this source in 1860 amounted to more than $60,000.

Meanwhile, in 1855, Grist had moved from Wilmington back to Washington, perhaps because of the advancing age of his father and also because he had purchased two additional plantations that would require closer supervision. Total cotton production by the Grists in 1860 was estimated to be 250 bales. In 1860, at age forty-two, Grist was listed as owning $30,000 in real estate and $76,400 in personal property, including eighty-four slaves. A. & J. R. Grist, turpentine farmers, were listed as owning $44,000 in real estate and $125,750 in personal property, with seventy-two slaves. As his wealth increased, Grist followed the planter pattern of the 1850s, building an elaborate home in Washington, Elmwood, and furnishing it with expensive furniture. Situated at the west end of Main Street facing east, with spacious lawns, it was the showplace of Washington.

During the Civil War Grist served as second lieutenant in the Washington Home Guard and attempted to carry on his business by smuggling naval stores through the blockade. In the postwar years, bereft of his fortune and his labor force, he liquidated his Mobile operation to resolve his debts, obtained new credit in 1868 through Zophar Mills, a commission merchant in New York, and resumed general farming. He purchased a cotton gin and a peanut picker and entered both cotton planting and ginning and the peanut business. His health failed, however, and he died at his home at age fifty-eight before he could recoup much of his fortune. An Episcopalian, Grist was buried in the Old Grist Cemetery near Chocowinity.

Grist was a loyal Whig throughout that party's life, but despite his father's perennial success in politics never seems to have aspired to political office. He was always the planter and businessman and his letters portray him as one who was given to close management, constant supervision, and a steady drive toward the accumulation of wealth. He seems, however, to have been a devoted husband and a loving father. On 15

Nov. 1838 he married Elizabeth Snowden Trotter Latham, and they had nine children: Mary, Samuel, Ella, Olivia, James, John, Claudia, Elizabeth, and Annie. Oil portraits of Grist and his wife were painted in 1860, probably by the same artist who painted those of his father and mother, William Garl Browne. They are currently owned by William and Elizabeth Oden of Washington, N.C.

SEE: Grist family Bible (in possession of Mrs. J. D. Grimes, Jr., Washington, N.C.); Grist MSS (Manuscript Department, Library, Duke University, Durham); Ursula Loy and Pauline M. Worthy, eds., *Washington and the Pamlico* (1976); C. Wingate Reed, *Beaufort County* (1962); U.S. Census, 1860, Beaufort County.

PERCIVAL PERRY

**Grove, Edwin Wiley** *(27 Dec. 1850–27 Jan. 1927)*, proprietary drug manufacturer and Asheville developer, was born in Whiteville, Hardeman County, Tenn., the son of James Henry and Mary Jane Harris Grove. Both of his parents were natives of Virginia; as a Confederate soldier, his father served with General Nathan B. Forrest. After attending local schools, young Grove went to Memphis, just two counties west, to study pharmacy. In 1880 he established his own pharmacy in Paris, Tenn., where he had worked earlier as a clerk in a drugstore. At Paris he developed the formula for two products that were to make him a fortune. Grove's Tasteless Chill Tonic was sold widely, particularly in the South where quinine had long been used as an antimalarial drug. Grove's formula improved the unpleasant taste of the quinine. He also developed a product that he marketed as Grove's Bromo-Quinine tablets. Shortly, it was reported, his products were bringing him a million dollars a year. Grove expanded his manufacturing facilities from those originally established at Paris to St. Louis, Mo., and to England, Australia, Brazil, and Argentina. He also planned an extensive and pioneer advertising program.

Beginning in 1897 when he built a summer home there, Grove spent a great deal of time in Asheville, N.C., as he found the climate good for his health. In 1905 he took the first step of what became a large scale development of hotel, business, and residential property on the northern edge of the town. He began with the development of Grove Park, a residential area, and in 1912–13 constructed Grove Park Inn as a resort hotel on the west slope of Sunset Mountain. Built of massive stones, with a frontage of almost 500 feet, and rising in a series of terraces, it has long been regarded as one of the finest resort hotels in the world. Grove next purchased the old Battery Park Hotel, razed it, cut down the hill on which it had stood, and erected a new Battery Park Hotel. Opposite the entrance to the new hotel he constructed a mall of shops topped by offices. Earth from the hill was used to fill a large ravine, which formed a new commercial area for the growing city. East of Asheville he developed Grovemont residential area. In and around Asheville he also established and developed other areas and businesses. His interests were not centered in just this site, however, for he owned extensive property in St. Louis, Mo., St. Petersburg, Fla., Atlanta, Ga., and elsewhere.

Grove was generous and as nearly as possible kept his benefactions secret. Contributing to charitable, educational, and religious causes, he built and endowed a high school in Paris, Tenn., and endowed a number of Presbyterian churches, of which denomination he was an active member. His first wife, whom he married in 1875, was Mary Louisa Moore of Milan, Tenn. They were the parents of two daughters, Irma and Evelyn. The latter married Fred Loring Seely who was involved in the building of the Grove Park Inn. After the death of his wife, in 1883, Grove was married in 1886 to Alice Gertrude Matthewson of Murray, Ky. Their children were Hallett Hardin, Edwin Wiley, and Helen. Grove died in Asheville and after funeral services in the city's First Presbyterian Church, of which he was a member, he was buried in the family cemetery near his place of birth.

SEE: *Asheville Citizen*, 28, 29 Jan. 1927, 8 May 1949; *National Cyclopaedia of American Biography*, vol. 21 (1931).

WILLIAM S. POWELL

**Grove, William Barry** *(15 Jan. 1764–30 Mar. 1818)*, congressman, was born in Fayetteville, the son of Richard Grove and the stepson of Colonel Robert Rowan, who married his widowed mother, Susanna. Very little is known of Grove's private life, but he did win the respect of his stepfather, who made him an executor of his will and the recipient of Hollybrook plantation. Grove studied law and was admitted to the bar, but his major business quickly became politics when, in 1784, he became the register for Fayette (Cumberland) County. As a member of the House of Commons in 1786, 1788, and 1789, he was responsible for having Fayetteville designated one of the towns in which a superior court (1788) would be held and for obtaining it borough status with an independent seat in the House of Commons (1789).

Although an unprepossessing legislator, for the most part influencing his colleagues outside of chambers, the member from Fayette district occupied a seat in every Congress from the Second to the Seventh (4 Mar. 1791–2 Mar. 1803). Therefore, it was with much glee that Nathaniel Macon boasted to Thomas Jefferson about Grove's defeat in 1802 for reelection to the Eighth Congress. Generally Grove joined the southern bloc—irrespective of party—on economic issues, but he was one of the three southern congressmen to vote in favor of the Jay Treaty. Despite his patent belief in the Federalist principle that the best should rule, apparently a great deal of his success was based on the ability to convince the members of his constituency that he best served their interests. Appointed an original member of the board of trustees of The University of North Carolina in 1789, after his political defeat he spent most of his energies in support of the university until his death.

Grove occupied the fine colonial mansion, inherited from his stepfather, on a hill at the corner of Rowan and Chatham streets in the crossroads town of Fayetteville. His gracious hospitality to the Federalist elite of the South played no small part in his political success. He was described as having brown hair sprinkled with gray and as being average in height with a dignified bearing, rather handsome but lacking a strong visage. His marriage to a daughter of Colonel William Shepperd of Hawfields made him a brother-in-law of some of North Carolina's leading Federalists including Sam Porter Ashe, Colonel Samuel Ashe, and David Hay. Moreover, Justice John Louis Taylor married a daughter of Colonel Rowan, and young William Gaston's first wife was a daughter of Rowan's son-in-law, Thomas John Hay. Grove had two sons and a daughter. He died in Fayetteville and was buried in Cross Creek Cemetery.

SEE: Samuel A. Ashe, ed., *Biographical History of North Carolina*, vol. 8 (1917); Kemp Battle, "Letters of Nathaniel Macon, John Steele and William Barry Grove, with Sketches and Notes," *James Sprunt Historical Monographs* 3 (1902); *Biog. Dir. Am. Cong.* (1961); David H. Fischer, *Revolution of American Conservatism* (1965).

D. A. YANCHISIN

**Gudger, Eugene Willis** *(10 Aug. 1866–19 Feb. 1956)*, internationally known ichthyologist, was born in Waynesville, the son of James Cassius Lowery Gudger, adjutant of the Twenty-fifth North Carolina Regiment, Confederate Army, and later a superior court judge, and of Mary Goodwin Willis Gudger. He was educated at Emory and Henry College in Virginia (A.B., 1887), the University of Nashville (M.S., 1893), and Johns Hopkins University (Ph.D., 1905), where he was an assistant in the general biological department. Before and after his doctoral studies he taught at Asheville College (1893–94), Peabody High School, Little Rock, Ark. (1895–1904), and the North Carolina College for Women at Greensboro (1905–19).

When Gudger was ten years old, Mrs. Rebecca Harding Davis, the mother of Richard Harding Davis, went to Waynesville looking for material on a series of articles about the Appalachian Mountains. There she met and was assisted by the Gudger family, and became interested in young Eugene. After returning to Philadelphia, she sent him a subscription to *Saint Nicholas Magazine* and a book, *Land and Water* by Jacob Abbot, which started his interest in natural history. Upon graduation from Johns Hopkins, he sent her an invitation to the commencement exercises and told her how she had helped him decide on his lifework.

As a young man, Gudger studied the geology of the entire Blue Ridge from the Delaware Water Gap and Big Stone Gap to the foothills of the range in Georgia. However, he soon turned to fish, becoming an authority on the breeding habits of the pipefish shark (a study begun by Aristotle before 322 B.C.) and the whale shark. When someone said the latter was dangerous, Gudger observed wryly: "About as dangerous as a cow in a pasture." In differing with one scientist he used as a source the biblical verse, "And he slew him with the jaw bone of an ass," stating triumphantly, "And I slew him with his own jaw bone."

The first time he saw the ocean was when he began working as an investigator for the U.S. Bureau of Fisheries at Beaufort, a post he held from 1902 to 1911. In 1907, he received a grant from Carnegie Institute to do research on the gaff-topsail catfish at the Carnegie Marine Laboratory in Dry Tortugus, Fla. The American Museum of Natural History in New York called on him in 1919 to edit the volumes of the *Biography of Fishes*, a work he completed in 1923 after an enormous amount of research. Some years later he was made associate curator of fishes, serving from 1934 until his retirement in 1938 with the title of honorary associate in ichthyology. During this time he was the editor for fish terms for the third edition of *Webster's International Dictionary*, published in 1935. Although named editor of the *Bashford Dean Memorial Volume*, he wrote a third of it. Gudger was the author of over three hundred articles on fish, from "Natural History of the Whale Shark" to "The Rain of Fishes."

He was a fellow of the American Association for the Advancement of Science and of the New York Zoological Society, a life member of the Museum of Natural History, and an honorary member of the Zoological Society of London. Other memberships included the Society of American Naturalists, American Society of Zoologists, American Society of Ichthyologists and Herpetologists, History of Science Society (secretary, 1907–18), Salmon and Trout Association of Great Britain, and North Carolina Academy of Science. An asterisk appeared after his name in *American Men of Science* designating him one of the thousand most outstanding scientists in the country.

A Mason and lifelong member of the Waynesville Methodist Church, Gudger enjoyed Gilbert and Sullivan operas, walking, and anything to do with mountains. He never married. In 1953 he returned to his home in Waynesville and died there three years later. At his request, the word "ichthyologist" was carved on his tombstone.

SEE: *Asheville Citizen*, 20, 21 Feb. 1956; *Asheville Citizen-Times*, 26 Apr. 1953; "Bibliography of E. W. Gudger's Contributions to the History of Ichthyology," *Isis* 42 (1951); *Elisha Mitchell Scientific Journal* 40 (1924); Scientific Papers of Eugene W. Gudger (North Carolina Collection, University of North Carolina, Chapel Hill); *Salmon and Trout Magazine*, no. 91 (June 1938 [portrait]); *Waynesville Mountaineer*, 10 Feb. 1954.

JANET QUINLAN CRITTENDEN

**Gudger, Hezekiah Alexander** *(27 May 1849–22 Sept. 1917)*, lawyer, educator, diplomat, and jurist, was born in Madison County, the son of Joseph Jackson and Sarah Emeline Barnard Gudger. He was educated in the public school system and at Weaverville College, from which he was graduated in 1869. After studying law at Bailey's Law School, Asheville, he was admitted to the bar in 1871. He married Jennie H. Smith in 1875 and they had five children: Francis, Herman, Ada, Marie, and Emma. The last was the wife of General Robert L. Eichelberger.

Gudger had a varied and distinguished career, making substantial contributions at the local, state, and national levels. He was instrumental in establishing the Buncombe County school system. Later, he served for six years as the head of the state School for the Deaf, Dumb, and Blind in Raleigh from 1877 to 1883.

Politically, he was an ardent Democrat. Elected to the state legislature from traditionally Republican Madison County, he was subsequently elected as a state senator from Buncombe County. In his later years, he switched to the Republican party over the controversial "Sound Money" question. He was well known and widely respected for his abilities as a public speaker and political campaigner.

Gudger served two terms (1891–92) as Grand Master of the Grand Lodge of Masons in North Carolina. He was also active in the Methodist church.

In 1897, he was appointed by President William McKinley as consul general in Panama, a post he held until 1907. He was typically active in Panama and instrumental in negotiating a settlement of the revolution that had rocked the country for more than three years. In 1907 he was appointed a justice of the supreme court of the Canal Zone. He was later appointed chief justice, resigning from that position in 1914, when he returned to Asheville. Gudger was active in local affairs until his death at age sixty-eight.

SEE: Samuel A. Ashe, ed., *Biographical History of North Carolina*, vol. 2 (1905 [portrait]); *Asheville Citizen*, 4 May 1951; *North Carolina Biography*, vol. 6 (1919); A. Davis

Smith, *Western North Carolina, Historical and Biographical* (1890); *Who Was Who in America*, vol. 1 (1943).

EUGENE R. COCKE

**Gudger, James Madison, Jr.** *(22 Oct. 1855–29 Feb. 1920)*, congressman, state senator, and attorney, was born in Madison County of Scotch-Irish ancestry, the youngest son of Joseph Jackson and Sarah Emeline Barnard Gudger. Gudger's great-grandparents, William and Martha Gudger, were among the earliest settlers of the Swannanoa Valley. Their son, James, Sr., was born on 22 Jan. 1782—one of the first white children born west of the Blue Ridge Mountains. He married Annie Love, daughter of Colonel Robert Love, scion of a distinguished family and an officer in the American Revolution.

Young Gudger attended Sand Hill and later Weaverville College, Weaverville, before entering Emory and Henry College, Va., where he was graduated with honors. He then studied law under Chief Justice Richmond Pearson and was admitted to the Virginia bar sometime around 1878. Gudger moved to Asheville to practice criminal law. Eventually becoming the leading attorney in Marshall, Madison County, he was, by all reports, an able, genial, and popular practitioner of the law.

Entering the political arena, Gudger was elected to the North Carolina Senate in 1900. In the legislature he served on the committees on the Judiciary, Election Law, Claims and Penal Institutions. In 1901, Governor Charles B. Aycock appointed him solicitor of the Fifteenth Judicial District in North Carolina. He served in that capacity for one year before resigning to run for a seat in the U.S. House of Representatives. Elected to Congress in 1902, Gudger served two terms and gave up his seat in 1906 to resume the practice of law. In 1910, he was reelected to Congress and again served two terms. He was an unsuccessful candidate for reelection to the Sixty-Fourth Congress in 1914. In Congress Gudger served on the Committee on Indian Affairs and the Committee on Public Buildings and Grounds; he was chairman of the Committee on Post Office Expenditures. During this period he worked assiduously to secure post offices for his congressional district, was a tireless advocate of rural free delivery, and a pioneer exponent of federal aid for public roads. As a congressman, Gudger was an effective organizer of some influence in national politics, as well as a popular representative who maintained steadfast loyalty to the Democratic party.

Gudger married Katie Yancey Hawkins of Hendersonville, and they had three children: Emmet Carlyle, winner of the French Legion of Honor and the Navy Cross in World War I; Katherine Emeline; and one other child, apparently a son who died at a young age. His brother, Judge Hezekiah Alexander Gudger, was also a state legislator, a U.S. consul general to Panama, and a justice of the supreme court of Panama. James Gudger was a member of the Masons, Knights of Pythias, and the Baptist church. He was buried in Riverside Cemetery, Asheville.

SEE: Samuel A. Ashe, *History of North Carolina*, vol. 2 (1925); *Asheville Citizen*, 25 Apr. 1920; *Biog. Dir. Am. Cong.* (1928); North Carolina Bar Association, *Proceedings* 22 (1920).

JULIAN MCIVER PLEASANTS

**Guion, Connie Myers** *(29 Aug. 1882–30 Apr. 1971)*, physician and teacher, was born at River Bend Plantation near Lincolnton. Her parents, Benjamin Simmons and Catherine Coatesworth Caldwell Guion, moved the family to Charlotte during her childhood.

Dr. Guion gained a national reputation in medicine at a time when few women even considered attempting such a career. Educated first at Kate Shipp's School in Lincolnton, she prepared for college at Northfield (Mass.) Seminary and entered Wellesley College, from which she received the A.B. degree in 1906. After earning a master's degree in biochemistry (1913) and a medical degree (1917) from Cornell University, she served an internship at Bellevue Hospital during the flu epidemic of 1918.

From 1906 to 1908, Dr. Guion taught chemistry at Vassar College, N.Y.; thereafter for four years she was chairman of the chemistry department at Sweet Briar College, Va. For a short time, she assisted her brother-in-law, a physician who operated a sanatorium near Columbia, S.C. She then began the practice of internal medicine in New York City and joined the faculty of Cornell University's Medical College. Dr. Guion was the first woman in the United States to hold the rank of professor of clinical medicine, which she attained in 1946. She was chief of Cornell's medical clinic in New York City, both before and after it became part of New York Hospital. In addition to her medical practice and teaching, she wrote numerous articles on medical topics, served as a member of the industrial council for New York State's Department of Labor, and was adviser to the National Health and Safety Council of Girl Scouts.

Dr. Guion held honorary degrees from Wellesley, the Woman's Medical College of Pennsylvania, Queens College of Charlotte, N.C., and The University of North Carolina. Cornell gave her an award of distinction. A building of the New York Hospital was named for her in 1963, as was the science building at Sweet Briar College in 1964.

Dr. Guion was a member of the Episcopal church and of the Republican party. She died in New York City at the age of eighty-eight and was buried in Charlotte.

SEE: Nardi R. Campion and Rosamond W. Stanton, *Look to This Day* (1965); Durward Howes, ed., *American Women*, vol. 3 (1939); *Who's Who of American Women*, 1968–69.

ROSAMOND PUTZEL

**Guion, Isaac** *(March 1740–24 May 1803)*, Revolutionary War surgeon, legislator, councillor of state, and merchant, the fourth in lineal descent to bear his name, was born in New Rochelle, N.Y., where his great-grandfather, Louis Guion, a French Huguenot, had settled about 1660 after fleeing from Rochelle, France, via England because of religious persecution. He first appears in the records of North Carolina as the buyer of Lot 7 in Bogue (Swansboro) on 24 May 1774, identifying himself as a merchant, "Doctor of Physics," and late of "the Island of Santa Croix in the West Indies." Thereafter he became a prominent merchant of Swansboro, with business connections in New Bern.

Entering the Revolutionary War from Swansboro, Guion was appointed surgeon to the First North Carolina Regiment on 1 Sept. 1775 and served until December of that year. Subsequently, he was appointed paymaster to the Second North Carolina Regiment. In August 1775 he was elected to represent Onslow

County in the Third Provincial Congress. On 5 July 1776 Guion was appointed commissary to the Independent Company of Militia stationed on the coast, and on 11 Dec. 1776 he was paymaster to the Ninth Battalion of North Carolina Continental troops. The following year he was transferred as paymaster to the Seventh Regiment, serving in that capacity until March 1778. One resolution of the Committee on the Treasury in Philadelphia referred to him in August 1777 as paymaster for both the Fourth and Seventh battalions of Continental troops in North Carolina.

On 3 May 1779 Guion was elected to the Council of State, and he served in the 1779–80 sessions. During this time he appears to have been importing salt and other needed supplies for the Continental Army, and he and Joseph Leech were authorized to charter vessels to transport prisoners of war out of the state. Although elected to another term in the Council of State on 21 Apr. 1780, Guion was among the patriots taken captive at Charleston, S.C., on 12 May. Near the end of the American Revolution, he appears to have moved to New Bern, though he retained business connections in Swansboro at least as late as 1796.

In January 1781 Guion was again attending sessions of the council of state, and in 1782 he was elected to represent Onslow County in the North Carolina Senate. As a senator Guion was appointed to the committee to consider and report on the governor's message and the state papers before the Assembly of 1782. He was chairman of the joint committee to examine and settle the accounts of the secretary of state, a member of the Ways and Means Committee, and a member of the Joint Committee on the State Board of Auditors. In 1785 and again in 1786 he was nominated but failed to win a seat on the Council of State.

Guion represented the borough town of New Bern in the North Carolina House of Commons in the sessions of 1789, 1790, 1793–94, and 1795. In 1789, he was also a delegate from New Bern to the North Carolina Convention, where he voted for ratification of the United States Constitution. The same year, as a member of the Assembly, he was appointed to the Committee of Propositions and Grievances, the Committee of Finance, and several lesser committees.

In 1790, Guion was granted several tracts of primarily pocosin land in Onslow County totaling more than 50,000 acres. It is not clear what he planned to do with this land, and records do not reveal any use made of the large tracts. In April 1791 he had the honor of giving the welcoming address to President George Washington on behalf of the town of New Bern and St. John's Lodge, A.F. & A.M., of which Guion was the Worshipful Master from 1788 to 1791. President Washington, a fellow Mason, visited New Bern as a part of his Southern Tour.

In the 1790 Assembly Guion again served on the Committee of Finance. Having been named one of the churchwardens for Christ Church (Episcopal), New Bern, by the Assembly of 1789, he represented New Bern at the convention of the Protestant Episcopal church, held at Tarboro in May 1794, at which a church constitution was drawn up and the Reverend Charles Pettigrew was elected first Episcopal bishop of North Carolina, though never consecrated. In 1795–96, Guion appears as a business partner in the firm of Ferrand and Guion of Swansboro. In 1800, he was one of the commissioners of navigation of the Port of New Bern.

Guion married Ferebe (Ferebee) Pugh Williams Lee, widow of Colonel Stephen Lee of the White Oak River. She was a native of Fort Barnwell, Craven County, and the sister of Governor Benjamin Williams, Rebecca Williams (m. Judge Alfred Moore), and Mary Williams (m. first John Backhouse and second William Ferrand). By her first husband, Stephen Lee, she had four children: Stephen; Mary, who married Dr. John Leigh of Tarboro, a member of the House of Commons from Edgecombe during 1790–96 and speaker of the house in 1793; Sarah, who married John Haywood, a state treasurer; and Fereby, of whom no more is known.

Isaac and Ferebe Guion had five children: Isaac Lee, an attorney who died at age thirty-nine; Ferebe Elizabeth Pugh, second wife of Francis Hawks; Ann Maria, wife of Dr. Hugh Jones; John Williams, who married first Mary Wade and second Mary Tillman; and Margaret Sarah, wife of Dr. Andrew Scott. Ferebe Guion Hawks was the mother of the Reverend Francis L. Hawks. Among the five children of Ann Guion Jones were Eliza (m. Alexander Gaston), Julia (m. Edward Stanly, son of Congressman John Stanly and grandson of John Wright Stanly), and Anne (m. Bishop Cicero Stephens Hawks). Other distinguished grandchildren included Dr. John Amos Guion and Haywood Williams Guion, who married a daughter of Governor John Owen and was president of the Wilmington, Charlotte, and Rutherford Railroad.

Isaac Guion died in New Bern and was buried in Cedar Grove Cemetery. His wife Ferebe (1746–1811) was buried beside him.

SEE: Gertrude S. Carraway, *Crown of Life* (1940); John L. Cheney, Jr., ed., *North Carolina Government, 1585–1974* (1975); Zae Hargett Gwynn, *Abstracts of the Records of Onslow County, North Carolina*, 2 vols. (1961); Minutes, St.John's Lodge, A.F. & A.M. (New Bern); Elizabeth Moore, comp., Guion Family Records (unpublished); Records, Christ Episcopal Church (New Bern); Tombstone inscriptions, Cedar Grove Cemetery (New Bern).

TUCKER REED LITTLETON
GERTRUDE S. CARRAWAY

**Gulley, Needham Yancey** *(3 June 1855–24 June 1945)*, founder and dean of the Wake Forest Law School, was born near Clayton in Johnston County, the son of N. G. Gulley, a farmer, and Jaylie Grady Gulley. After spending his early years on his father's farm, Gulley began his education at the Clayton Academy in the early 1870s. In 1874 he entered Wake Forest College, where he was graduated with an M.A. degree in 1879. As a young teacher, Gulley found his first job in nearby Raleigh at the Centennial School. He taught until July 1881. When the legislature voted to establish normal schools for the training of teachers, Gulley went to The University of North Carolina summer school to teach arithmetic and arithmetic methods to four groups daily.

After teaching for a year and a half, he returned to his native Johnston County as principal of the Smithfield public school. About this time Gulley also began his lifelong interest in the legal profession and read law under E. W. Pou. He was licensed to practice at the age of twenty-six. In 1882, he moved to Franklinton where he continued to teach and then became principal of the public school. Gulley began a law practice in 1883 and in the same year became the editor of the *Franklinton Weekly*. A successful lawyer, he was elected to the state house of representatives from Franklin County in 1885 for a single term.

In 1893, the Wake Forest College trustees made provision for the establishment of a school of law. Although the law school was advertised to begin in the fall of

1893, with N. Y. Gulley as its professor, not one student appeared during the whole academic year. Refusing to accept defeat, Gulley traveled to Wake Forest College from Franklinton once a week in a buggy pulled by a sorrell nag to give free lectures on some points of law, thereby hoping to interest enough students in the profession to start a law school the next year. Only one student appeared in the summer of 1894; however, when twelve more enrolled in the fall session, Gulley was employed as chairman of the department of law. The department continued to grow for ten years, and in 1905 he was made dean of the School of Law and another instructor was employed to assist him. Gulley set aside the old practice of asking questions, book in hand, and began teaching his students about law.

From this point Gulley's activities became more varied. He served on the Wake County board of education for many years and was chairman at the time of his death. He entered the legislative battle for improvement of the public schools and was one of its outstanding champions for over forty years. He was one of three members of the North Carolina Code Commission that revised the statutes of the state between 1903 and 1906. When national officials prepared the *Cyclopedia of Law and Procedure*, he was selected to write a chapter.

Approximately 1,700 men received instruction from Gulley during the fifty-four years he taught law; for twenty-three years everyone who studied under him passed the state bar examination. His former students included federal judges, solicitors, supreme court justices, congressmen, and senators. "I try to make what I teach so obvious that my men can't miss it," he explained on one occasion. Gerald Johnson noted that Gulley had written much of the law of North Carolina "but his important writing is the way he has written 'Justice' indelibly upon the minds of young men." Gulley retired as dean in 1935, but continued to teach until 1938, when he settled on a small farm near Wake Forest to look after his cows and horses. With Pearl Harbor, several key members of the law school were given responsible government positions in the space of three short months and replacements were hard to find. In March 1942 Gulley returned to his old post and once again began teaching civil procedure.

In 1879 he married Alice Wingate, daughter of Washington Manly Wingate, a former president of Wake Forest College. They had six children: Manly, Mary, Donald, Thomas, Isabel, and Margaret (Mrs. Augustus Bonard).

Gulley died peacefully at his home in Wake Forest after a short illness, in his ninety-first year. After funeral services in the Wake Forest Baptist Church, he was buried in the Wake Forest Cemetery. A photograph (in the Exum Beckwith Album) and an oil portrait (ca. 1894) are in the Baptist Historical Collection, Wake Forest University.

SEE: Ed Gambrell, "Dr. Needham Yancey Gulley, Foster Parent of the Law School," *Wake Forest Student* 51 (1935); Gerald Johnson, "Six Characters in Search of an Author," *Wake Forest Student* 54 (1938); David Morgan, "My Classmate's No Longer a Young Man," *Wake Forest Student* 54 (1938); Needham Yancey Gulley Biography Folder (North Carolina Baptist Historical Collection, Wake Forest University, Winston-Salem); Raleigh *News and Observer*, 9 Feb. 1930, 28 June 1936, 5 Apr., 3 June 1942, 3 June 1943, 3, 25 June 1945; *Who Was Who in America*, vol. 4 (1968).

JOHN R. WOODARD

**Gurley, Joseph** *(12 Oct. 1751–ca. 1816)*, Episcopal priest, was born in Southampton County, Va., the second child and oldest son in a family of ten children. His father, the Reverend George Gurley, was an Anglican priest stationed in Southampton County. Details of Joseph Gurley's early life are unknown. After he was ordained by Bishop William White of Pennsylvania on 25 Mar. 1788, he became assistant priest at St. Luke's Parish, Southampton County, where his father had served as rector since 1773. Gurley remained at this post until the death of his father in 1792.

The following year he appeared in nearby North Carolina. Settling at Murfreesboro, Gurley assumed the duties of rector of St. Barnabas' Parish whose boundaries were coterminous with those of Hertford County. Whatever church organization had existed in Murfreesboro in the colonial period had collapsed as a result of the American Revolution. In fact, at this time there were only ten Episcopal clergymen in the entire state. Nevertheless, Gurley took an active role in efforts to secure a bishop for North Carolina. He was one of the three ministers and three laymen who attended the abortive Tarboro convention in 1793. When North Carolina Episcopalians convened again in Tarboro on 28 May 1794, the attendance was more gratifying, and Gurley served as one of six clergymen on the Standing Committee. This convention selected the Reverend Charles Pettigrew as bishop-elect of North Carolina, although he was never consecrated.

Gurley also opened Murfreesboro's first school in 1793. An advertisement in the nearby Halifax newspaper proclaimed that the school's curriculum was evenly balanced between the classical and practical, with instruction being offered in writing, arithmetic, measuring, surveying, Latin, and Greek. Unfortunately, this educational venture does not seem to have lasted for more than a term or two.

In addition to his religious and educational interests, Gurley was active in Masonic affairs and frequently preached to lodges in the area. He was Master of Royal Edwin Lodge at Windsor and a charter member of Davie Lodge at Lewiston.

There is no record of Gurley after 1816, and it is assumed that he died around that time in Bertie County. He had married Martha Peterson and left at least two sons, John and Peterson.

SEE: G. MacLaren Brydon, "A List of Clergy of the Protestant Episcopal Church Ordained after the American Revolution, Who Served in Virginia between 1785 and 1814, and a List of Virginia Parishes and Their Rectors for the Same Period," *William and Mary Quarterly* 19 (1939); Edenton *State Gazette of North Carolina*, 2 Mar. 1793; Thomas C. Parramore, *The Ancient Maritime Village of Murfreesboro* (1969); "Some of the Genealogical Notes Collected by the Late A. E. Gurley" ([typescript] Library of Congress, 1951, made by John Miller Bradley, 4211 Overlook Rd., Birmingham, Ala.).

JAMES ELLIOTT MOORE

**Gwyn, Allen Hatchett** *(12 Nov. 1893–16 Dec. 1969)*, lawyer and judge, was born near Yanceyville, Caswell County, the son of Joseph P. and Sarah E. Hatchett Gwyn. Gwyn attended the Yanceyville graded school and received the A.B. degree from Trinity College, Durham, in 1913. After serving as a private and second lieutenant in the U.S. Army Infantry from 1917 to 1919, he entered the Trinity College law school where he was graduated in 1921. Gwyn practiced law in Reidsville from 1921 until 1938. During that time he served as city attorney (1927–38), as a Democrat from the Seventeenth Senatorial District in the state senate (1931–33), and as solicitor for the superior court of the Seventeenth Judicial District (1934–38). From 1939 until his death he was a judge of the superior court.

Judge Gwyn's work-release program was a major contribution to criminal law. His efforts to lower the high percentage of first offenders who served time in prison for twelve months or less led to effective work-release legislation. Gwyn's views and findings on the program appear in his book, *Observations on Crime and Correction: Work, Earn, and Save*, published in 1963.

At various times, Gwyn was an instructor at the National College of State Trial Judges and at the Institute of Government of The University of North Carolina. He served on the State Commission on Probation from 1961 to 1965 and was a member of the Governor's Committee on Juvenile Delinquency and Youth Crime from 1962 to 1964. In 1967–68, he served as president of the North Carolina Superior Court Judges.

Gwyn married Janie Johnston of Yanceyville on 25 Apr. 1917, and they had three children: Anne Russell, Allen, Jr., and Julius. He was a member of the Methodist church and the Masonic order. Judge Gwyn died in Greensboro and was buried in Reidlawn Cemetery, Reidsville.

SEE: John L. Cheney, Jr., ed., *North Carolina Government, 1585–1974* (1975); *Chapel Hill Weekly*, 4 Jan. 1970; Raleigh *News and Observer*, 17 Dec. 1969.

J. MARSHALL BULLOCK

**Gwynn, Walter** *(22 Feb. 1802–6 Feb. 1882)*, civil engineer and militia general, was born in Jefferson County, [West] Va., the son of Humphrey Gwynn of the Gloucester County, Va., family of that name. Appointed to the U.S. Military Academy at West Point on 10 Sept. 1818, he studied engineering under Claudius Crozet (1790–1864), an artillerist and engineer formerly under the command of Napoleon and subsequently employed by the state of Virginia as principal engineer. A distinguished graduate of the Military Academy (ranking eighth in his class), Gwynn was commissioned a second lieutenant of artillery on 1 July 1822 and was promoted to the rank of first lieutenant in 1829. In the following year, when the Petersburg and Roanoke Railroad Company was chartered, he was employed by that company as one of the engineers to locate and survey the route. In 1832 he resigned his military commission and gave himself over entirely to his career as a civil engineer, beginning with various Virginia railroad companies. By 1835 Gwynn had completed his survey of a proposed railway to run from Farmville to Cartersville, and in 1836 he published his report on the survey of the Danville, Roanoke and Junction Railroad. Concurrently, he supervised the preliminary survey for the projected route of the Danville to Evansham Railroad and served as chief engineer to the Portsmouth and Roanoke Railroad.

When the directors of the Wilmington and Raleigh Railroad Company, chartered by the North Carolina General Assembly in 1833, began seriously to consider construction of their road in 1835, Gwynn was given the office of chief engineer. Edward Bishop Dudley appears to have been the person chiefly responsible for his selection. It is probable that Gwynn's advice had an influence in the decision of the directors to alter the northern terminus from Raleigh to Weldon where connections were possible with two of the Virginia lines for which Gwynn had served as engineer, the Petersburg and Roanoke and the Portsmouth and Roanoke railroads. (In 1852 the name of the Wilmington and Raleigh Railroad was changed to the Wilmington and Weldon Railroad Company.) By August 1836 Gwynn had completed his survey of the route from Wilmington to Weldon, and on 25 Oct. 1836 Governor Edward B. Dudley lifted the first spade of earth from the proposed rail bed. On 7 Mar. 1840, the last spike was driven, completing what was then reported to be the longest track of rail in the world—161½ miles from the Cape Fear River to the Roanoke River.

Recognition of Gwynn's professional abilities came early in his career. At the February 1839 Baltimore convention of engineers, he was one of a committee of seventeen appointed to draft a constitution for an American society of engineers. Shortly thereafter, he was introduced to the Russian delegation of commissioners sent to America by Czar Nicholas I. The introduction was presumably effected by Moncure Robinson of Virginia, under whose supervision Gwynn had worked as an engineer for the Petersburg and Roanoke Railroad and who had been tendered but had refused the offer of a commission as the imperial chief engineer. The delegation then offered Gwynn the position of chief engineer of the St. Petersburg to Moscow railway at a salary of $25,000. Initially tempted by the offer, he proceeded so far as to form a corps of engineers for the undertaking, but upon learning of the severity of the Russian winter refused the commission at the last and continued his association with North Carolina and Virginia internal improvements.

During the 1840s Gwynn expended the greater part of his professional energies in connection with Virginia works, first with the Portsmouth and Roanoke Railroad, then with the James River and Kanawha Canal. As president of the former from 1842 until 1845, he assumed the role of chief opponent to Francis E. Rives in a struggle for control of the railroad bridge at Weldon. It was during this controversy that Rives removed a mile of track belonging to the Portsmouth and Roanoke Railroad, and Gwynn retaliated by restoring the track and overturning an engine and cars that Rives had borrowed from the Petersburg and Roanoke Railroad. The controversy came to an end after the Portsmouth and Roanoke was forced into bankruptcy and acquired by the Virginia Board of Public Works. Leased to the city of Portsmouth as the Seaboard and Roanoke Railroad (which acquired title to the controverted bridge in 1851), Gwynn's company eventually became the parent-stem of the Seaboard Air Line (now Seaboard Coast Line) Railroad.

Gwynn succeeded to the eleven-year tenure of Joseph Carrington Cabell as president of the James River and Kanawha Canal Company in 1846, following a series of financial disasters. During his twelve-month presidency, the Virginia legislature granted a loan of $1,300,000 to the company and Gwynn gave up the office of president in order to assume that of chief engineer. He served as chief engineer to the canal company from 1847 until 1853, during which time he completed the works from Lynchburg to Buchanan and perfected the tidewater connection by way of a series of locks and basins capable of moving vessels from the canal into the lanes of shipping in the suburb of Richmond called Rocketts, the head of navigation on the James River.

Once Gwynn had his plans and specifications

worked out for the completion of the James River and Kanawha Canal, he left the execution of them in the hands of able assistants while reserving to himself general superintendence of the work. This freed him to act concurrently as chief engineer to other works and to turn his attention once more to North Carolina. As early as 1836 Gwynn had envisioned a rail system linking North Carolina to the other southern states for their mutual commercial benefit in times of peace and for mutual defense in times of war. He had already connected the state to Virginia by way of the Wilmington and Weldon Railroad. A line chartered in 1847 to run from Wilmington to Manchester, S.C., gave him an opportunity to further realize the commercial and defense scheme he had described a decade earlier. In 1848 Gwynn accepted the office of chief engineer to the Wilmington and Manchester Railroad and held it until 1853. It was in bridging the Pee Dee River for this line that he achieved for the first time in the South the sinking of cast iron cylinders by atmospheric pressure, a technique he had seen demonstrated not long previously at West Point.

The chartering of the North Carolina Railroad in 1848 further fleshed out Gwynn's 1836 scheme of tying the southern states together, for this commenced an east to west line that could ultimately connect with western South Carolina, Georgia, and Tennessee rail systems. On 12 July 1850, he was engaged as chief engineer of the North Carolina Railroad. He began surveying the route from Goldsboro to Salisbury by way of Greensboro on 21 August, and his completed report was presented to the stockholders in May 1851. The original watercolor drawings of the survey are in the North Carolina State Archives where they are bound in five elephant folio volumes. Gwynn's relationship to the company was not altogether a happy one, a fact made apparent by the General Assembly's joint select committee (headed by Jonathan Worth) to inquire into the management of the North Carolina Railroad. The Worth report reveals that the practice of the company's committee of four directors was to settle matters without consulting the chief engineer. There was constant strife between Gwynn and the contractors who were building the road, though the chief engineer was technically empowered with final and conclusive authority to see that the contract to build the road was faithfully executed. Gwynn disapproved of the contractors' work on the eastern division of the road; it never did receive his approval.

Simultaneously with his work as chief engineer to the North Carolina Railroad, Gwynn was given the responsibility as consulting engineer for making preliminary surveys of the route of that railway's eastern and western extensions—the Atlantic and North Carolina Railroad (Goldsboro to Beaufort) and the North Carolina and Western Railroad (Salisbury to the Tennessee border). Both surveys were begun and completed in 1854, the former on 17 October and the latter on 5 December. Upon formal organization of the two new companies, the position of chief engineer was given to William Beverhout Thompson (a Virginia protégé of Gwynn's) and James C. Turner, respectively.

In 1856 Gwynn's connection with the North Carolina Railroad came to an end, and so did his career with North Carolina rail systems. It was a career that had played a leading role in every major antebellum railroad in North Carolina, except for the Raleigh and Gaston Railroad. Gwynn's work contributed largely to as much of a series of trunk lines as was available to the state during the Civil War. Had his work as chief engineer of the Rabun Gap Railroad leading from Anderson, S.C., to Knoxville, Tenn. (subsequently the Blue Ridge Railroad), been completed, and had the Western North Carolina Railroad been extended from Asheville to Ducktown, Gwynn would very nearly have seen realized his 1836 dream of a southern defense system based on interconnecting railways.

In 1857 Gwynn communicated to his daughter-in-law's father, Chief Justice Thomas Ruffin, his intention to remove with his family from Raleigh to Columbia, S.C. The opening of the Civil War, in fact, found Gwynn in Charleston where he was, at age fifty-nine, suddenly projected into the military career he thought he had abandoned a generation earlier. In March 1861 he was given the rank of major in the Provisional Army of the Confederate States of America and charged with constructing batteries at various strategic Charleston points (beyond Fort Moultrie, across the bay, on Morris Island, and on the beach at Fort Johnston). For his role in the reduction of Fort Sumter, Gwynn was subsequently praised in dispatches of Brigadier General P. G. T. Beauregard and Lieutenant Colonel R. J. Ripley. Less than two weeks after the fall of Sumter, Gwynn had toured the coast of North Carolina and returned to Virginia.

On 21 Apr. 1861, he was nominated by Governor John Letcher to the rank of major general of the Virginia Volunteers and given command of the forces defending Norfolk. When the Virginia council determined, however, that Robert E. Lee should be the only officer in the Volunteers with the rank of major general, Gwynn and his fellow officer, Joseph E. Johnston, were confirmed a rank below as brigadiers. From 21 April until the Confederate government brought the Virginia Volunteers into the regular C.S.A. Army and the defenses of Norfolk into the care of its military establishment on 23 May, Gwynn executed his command well and diligently. On 23 May he surrendered his command to Brigadier General Benjamin Huger, his commission in the Virginia Volunteers having expired with their dissolution. On 24 May Gwynn departed Norfolk for North Carolina, where he had kept up connections (and from which he had just two days earlier requested the loan of troops for the defense of Norfolk).

In Raleigh on 25 May 1861, Gwynn accepted a commission as brigadier general in the North Carolina Volunteers and assumed command of the outer coastal defenses of the state from Onslow County north to the Virginia border. He made an immediate inspection of his command. Gwynn found Fort Macon, until recently under Federal control, to be too exposed to land attack for his liking and garrisoned by too small a number of soldiers for his comfort. He urgently recommended to Governor John W. Ellis that a forward post, a string of vedettes, field batteries, and a signaling system be added. He then charged engineers under his command (formerly engineers with the state's various railroads) with constructing fortifications at Hatteras Inlet (Forts Clark and Hatteras), Oregon Inlet (Fort Oregon), and Ocracoke Inlet (Fort Ocracoke). Gwynn warned Governor Ellis that a force of 5,000 men would be needed to defend the coast. Believing that a Federal attack might be launched before the fortifications were completed, Gwynn attempted to borrow tools and slaves from Currituck County planters in early June—"Delay is dangerous," he admonished them. Activated by this sense of danger, Gwynn personally borrowed 4,000 pounds of powder from the Navy Yard at Norfolk for use of the forts, enlisted the aid of New Bern women in preparing 12,610 ball cartridges, and with his money purchased 8,000 percussion caps to be used at the fortifications. On 28 June he advised the military board at Raleigh that the privateering successes of its "mosquito navy" would force the Federal military into an offensive attack on the coast. The state's Secession Convention voted on 27 June to disband the North Carolina Volunteers effective 20 August upon expectation of their being taken into the regular Confederate establishment. Thunderstruck, Gwynn reminded Governor Henry T. Clark (Ellis having died on 7 July) that the dissolution of the Volunteers on 20 August would leave the coastal forts defenseless. When that date arrived, Gwynn found himself without a command and the northeastern coast found itself with approximately 600 defenders distributed in six fortifications strung out over 85 miles of coast. Six days later a Federal fleet of seven warships and an assault force of 880 soldiers set sail for the North Carolina coast. On 28 August Fort Clark fell and Fort Hatteras the next day. Forts Oregon and Ocracoke were abandoned during the first week of September. Fort Roanoke fell on 8 Feb. 1862, New Bern on 14 March, and Fort Macon on 25 April. Gwynn's worst fears were realized.

For the next several months the eastern rivers and their estuaries lay open to the Federal forces occupying the outer coast, and those forces seized the opportunity to terrorize the river towns and eastern railways. The North Carolina delegation to the Confederate Congress, probably under the leadership of William T. Dortch of Wayne County, began agitating for the central government to provide for the defense of North Carolina's inner coastal plain and eastern rivers. Upon their earnest solicitation Gwynn was given a commission on 9 Oct. 1862, with the rank of colonel in the regular army, and directed by the C.S.A. secretary of war to make a defensive survey of Neuse, Tar, Roanoke, and Chowan rivers. He was to obstruct the rivers and erect batteries suitable to small garrisons in sites capable of receiving and being defended by larger forces sent to succor the garrisons. Engineers for the works were to be furnished by Colonel (subsequently Major General) Jeremy F. Gilmer of the C.S.A. Corps of Engineers. Gilmer, who appears to have resented Gwynn's appointment (possibly because of the implied political intervention), carefully referred to him as "Colonel Walter Gwynn, Civil Engineer." He insisted that command of the military engineers who might be assigned to serve under Gwynn should not be placed under Gwynn's command but reserved for Gilmer's own control and direction. Relations between the two officers were cold, formal, and strained. Gilmer resisted every effort by Gwynn to augment the small garrisons with extensive defense works to be occupied by larger relief forces. On 14 October Gilmer perfected his move to cripple Gwynn's command authority by forcing upon him a junior officer with power to control the purse as a disbursement officer. Thus Gilmer succeeded in circumscribing Gwynn, countermanding his orders, and forcing revision of his work. Finally, on 18 Feb. 1863, Gilmer was able to transfer the river defense works near Goldsboro, Kinston, Tarboro, and Hamilton from Gwynn's command to that of Lieutenant Colonel W. H. Stevens. This, naturally, led to Gwynn's resignation of his commission, upon which he resumed civilian life for the duration of the war.

After the Civil War Gwynn returned briefly to North Carolina. Some of his earlier work for the state had been in the character, though not in the name, of principal state engineer for internal improvements. In April 1839, for example, Gwynn had accepted a commission from Governor Dudley to complete the drainage of the swamplands owned by the state at Pungo and Alligator lakes. In this Gwynn succeeded to the work of a friend, fellow engineer, and former West Point classmate, Charles B. Shaw of Charlottesville, Va., whom he had recommended for the job in 1837. By 1842 Gwynn had completed the reclamation of 65,000 acres from the swamplands bordering the two lakes. Simultaneously he surveyed the open grounds in Carteret County with a view to their drainage and reclamation, a work first considered in the days of Hamilton Fulton but not undertaken until 1852. Fulton's earlier examination of the possibility of reopening Roanoke Inlet, made in 1820, had also been taken into consideration by Governor Dudley who had commissioned Gwynn to make a new examination in 1840. It was with reference to this examination that the Bureau of Topographic Engineers remarked to Secretary of War Joel R. Poinsett on 28 Feb. 1840, "Any survey made under the personal superintendance of Major Walter Gwynn, would receive the confidence of this Bureau, as his intelligence and experience are well known." As had been the case in Fulton's report, Gwynn's report had not resulted in an attempt to reopen the inlet. In 1856 Gwynn had investigated the conditions of Cape Fear and Deep rivers and had reported to the General Assembly on the work of improvements in the navigation of those streams. Now, after the Civil War, Gwynn was appointed by Governor Jonathan Worth in 1867 to make a new survey of the capital and to report on the public lands in the city and on its outskirts; the first postbellum map of the city resulted from this survey. On 1 Feb. 1867, Gwynn was commissioned agent of the Literary Fund to supervise and superintend all the swamplands belonging to that agency. Gwynn's report later that year to Governor Worth was his last work for the state; it was published posthumously in 1883 in a state public document entitled *Reports on the Swamp Lands of North Carolina Belonging to the State Board of Education.*

Gwynn married Elizabeth Rush (of the Maryland family of that name) about 1829 and had by her six children: Bruce, Walter Ballard, Henry Upton, Peyton, William, and Mary. He died in Baltimore, Md. His body was returned to Richmond and buried in Hollywood Cemetery close to the crumbling remains of the James River and Kanawha Canal. Here there is more than a small touch of irony. A contemporary, writing of Gwynn's construction of the canal's tidewater connection, stated that Gwynn had "made for himself a reputation among his fellow engineers which will last for all time." Within a few years of Gwynn's death, it was as if neither the engineer nor the work had ever existed. A rather handsome portrait of Gwynn dating from the 1840s is owned by the Confederate Museum, Richmond, Va.; a photograph from much later in life was published in the fifth volume of Walter Clark's *Histories of the Several Regiments and Battalions from North Carolina.*

SEE: John G. Barrett, *The Civil War in North Carolina* (1963); Cecil K. Brown, *A State Movement in Railroad Building* (1928); Wayland F. Dunaway, "History of the James River and Kanawha Company," in *Columbia University Studies in History, Economics and Public Law* 104 (1922); North Carolina State Archives (Raleigh) for Governor's Office Records (Internal Improvements), Governor's Papers (Edward B. Dudley, John Ellis, Henry T.

Clark, and Jonathan Worth), and Supreme Court Records (Original Case Papers nos. 3863, 5646, 5647); *Official Records of the War of the Rebellion, Army*, ser. 1, vols. 2, 18, 51 pt. 2; Charles W. Turner, "Virginia Antebellum Railroad Disputes and Problems," *North Carolina Historical Review* 27 (July 1950); Virginia State Archives (Richmond) for Records of the Board of Public Works; Wilmington *The Daily Review*, 10 Feb. 1882.

GEORGE STEVENSON, JR.